D0820397

THE CAMBRIDGE HISTORY OF SOUTHEAST ASIA

VOLUME TWO

The nineteenth and twentieth centuries

THE CAMBRIDGE HISTORY OF SOUTHEAST ASIA

VOLUME TWO

The nineteenth and twentieth centuries

edited by

NICHOLAS TARLING

CAMBRIDGE
UNIVERSITY PRESS

Published by the Press Syndicate of the University of Cambridge
The Pitt Building, Trumpington Street, Cambridge CB2 1RP, UK
40 West 20th Street, New York, NY 10011–4211, USA
10 Stamford Road, Oakleigh, Melbourne 3166, Australia

Printed in Singapore by Kin Keong Printing Co.

National Library of Australia cataloguing-in-publication data

The Cambridge history of Southeast Asia.
Bibliography.
Includes index.
1. Asia, Southeastern—History.
I. Tarling, Nicholas.
959

Library of Congress cataloguing-in-publication data

The Cambridge history of Southeast Asia.
Includes bibliographical references and indexes.
Contents: v. 1. From early times to c. 1800—
v. 2. The nineteenth and twentieth centuries.
1. Asia, Southeastern—History. I. Tarling, Nicholas.
DS525.T37 1992   959   91-8808

A catalogue record for this book is available from the British Library.

ISBN 0 521 35505 2 (v. 1).
ISBN 0 521 35506 0 (v. 2).

CONTENTS

MAPS

ABBREVIATIONS

AFPFL	Anti-Fascist People's Freedom League, Burma
ASEAN	Association of South-East Asian Nations
BKI	*Bijdragen van het Koninklijk Instituut voor de Taal-, Land- en Volkenkunde*, 's-Gravenhage
BSPP	Burma Socialist Programme Party
BWS	Burmese Way to Socialism
DAP	Democratic Action Party, Malaysia
DRV	Democratic Republic of Vietnam
GCBA	General Council of Burmese Associations
ICP	Indochina Communist Party
ISDV	Indische Sociaal-Demokratische Vereeniging (Indies Social-Democratic Association)
ISEAS	Institute of Southeast Asian Studies, Singapore
JAS	*Journal of Asian Studies*, Ann Arbor
JMBRAS	*Journal of the Malay/Malaysian Branch of the Royal Asiatic Society*, Kuala Lumpur
JSEAH	*Journal of Southeast Asian History*, Singapore
JSEAS	*Journal of Southeast Asian Studies*, Singapore
JSS	*Journal of the Siam Society*, Bangkok
MAS	*Modern Asian Studies*, Cambridge, UK
MCP	Malayan Communist Party
MNLF	Moro National Liberation Front
MPAJA	Malayan People's Anti-Japanese Army
NLF	National Liberation Front, Vietnam
NPA	New People's Army, The Philippines
PAP	People's Action Party, Singapore
PAS	Partai Islam se Tanah Malaya (Pan-Malayan Islamic Party)
PKI	Partai Komunis Indonesia (Indonesian Communist Party)

PNI	Perserikatan Nasional Indonesia (Indonesian National Association)
RVN	Republic of Vietnam
SEAC	South-East Asia Command
SEATO	South-East Asia Treaty Organization
SRV	Socialist Republic of Vietnam
UMNO	United Malays National Organization

FROM c. 1800 TO THE 1930S

This part of the work deals with Southeast Asia between the late eighteenth century of the Christian era and World War II. The opening chapter, which is in a sense complementary to the closing chapter of the previous volume, describes and endeavours to account for the incorporation of most of the region within the frontiers of European empires. Subsequent chapters describe the political structures, the economic and social life, and the religions and popular culture of the region. A final chapter includes a discussion of nationalism and nationalist movements.

In the previous phase, Spanish and Dutch realms had been established in maritime Southeast Asia. By the end of the nineteenth century, only Siam (Thailand) stood outside the formal empires of external powers. Those powers sought to avoid conflict among themselves by settling the frontiers of their territories. In so doing they took more or less notice of the previous history and present condition of the lands and peoples over which they claimed authority. Yet the frontiers had a degree of rigidity unusual in Southeast Asia.

Chapter 1 describes this outcome. It also endeavours to describe the process by which it was reached, and in particular to take account of the role within it of the rulers and peoples of Southeast Asia as well as the Europeans. Within the emerging framework, there was further interaction in many fields of human endeavour. This is in a sense the subject of the subsequent chapters in this part, which also pursue lines of investigation that parallel chapters in the first volume. Chapter 5, too, deals with the emergence of nationalism within the colonial framework. The statecraft of the imperial period came under challenge.

Within the emerging framework of that period new political structures were established. This topic is the prime focus of Chapter 2. Though still necessarily relying on the collaboration of élite elements among the Southeast Asian populations, the structures set up by the outside powers were characteristically centralized and bureaucratized. By the early twentieth century the state was capable of reaching into the ordinary life of every inhabitant to a degree and with a persistence rarely known before in the region. This, indeed, applied in Siam, as well as in the territories the external powers acquired. But neither there, nor elsewhere, did centralization or bureaucratization necessarily produce uniformity: in some cases indeed what came to be seen as 'minority groups' within a realm containing a 'majority' gained a new degree of institutionalized cohesion.

None of the developments described in chapters 1 and 2 can be understood without placing them in the context of economic change. This is the subject of Chapter 3. Southeast Asia had long been affected by international commerce. In the period between 1800 and the Great Depression it had an unprecedented impact, particularly after 1850. This resulted from the development of the Industrial Revolution and the drive of Western capitalism. They contributed to the growth of state power, its centralization and bureaucratization. The relationship of governments and peoples were transformed. Migration to Southeast Asia reached new levels; so did migration within Southeast Asia. Cities expanded, often providing an extraordinarily unhealthy environment, but there was no call for substantial industry. The end in the 1930s of the long period of expansion in the world's economy exposed the narrow and dependent nature of the region's economy. The poor were hit hardest.

Intensified European penetration, political consolidation of the dominant states, and economic transformation especially mark the period from the mid-nineteenth century; it is marked also by a multitude of resistance movements, rebellions, and acts of insubordination. Those are the focus of Chapter 4. It seeks to present them in their own terms: not as the disturbances or dacoity of the apologists of colonial conquest; nor even as the precursors of more modern opposition movements. The movements are considered in terms of their thought, their perceptions of change, of community, of leadership. Religion, the other focus of the chapter, is seen as a crucial matrix for peasant interpretations of experience.

The popular movements of the later nineteenth and earlier twentieth centuries interleaved but did not coincide with more modern nationalist movements that emerged within the colonial framework. Nationalism and its alternatives are the subject of Chapter 5. There it is argued that there were alternatives to the nationalist movements that aimed to secure control of the colonial states and that were ultimately able to do so after World War II. There were those who favoured more gradual change. There were also nationalist movements among minority peoples, and there were movements, too, that sought to transcend the externally imposed frontiers of the imperial phase. Each of the colonial powers reacted in a different way. They were all to be swept aside by another external power.

CHAPTER

1

THE ESTABLISHMENT OF THE
COLONIAL RÉGIMES

From the late eighteenth century, the involvement with Europeans, with things and ideas European, deepened and affected the whole of Southeast Asia; but it varied in intensity from people to people and from place to place; it increased through time but at no constant pace; and it took differing forms. Furthermore, it was always a matter, to a greater or lesser degree, of interaction, rather than simply of Western initiative or challenge and indigenous response. Nor were Western initiatives and challenges the only ones. Others came to Southeast Asia, too, though in some sense they themselves had already been stimulated by the Western ones. Islam, for example, had increased its hold on archipelagic Southeast Asia in the preceding period of European enterprise: linked more closely with its homeland by better communications in the nineteenth century, it was deeply involved in many of the social and political changes which that region now underwent.

The capacity of Europe to affect Southeast Asia increased in this period on a number of counts. First, the industrialization of Europe enhanced its economic power and political potential, though proceeding in different countries at varying rates with varying degress of completeness. Second, the world-wide improvement of communications—the introduction of steamships, the building of railways, the construction of the Suez Canal, the development of the electric telegraph—tied world and region more closely together. Third, European states became individually more inte-grated, more able to control their people and command their resources. Fourth, although (or because) they had so much in common, the states were at odds with each other, and the rivalry overseas that had long affected the fortunes of Southeast Asia continued to do so, though in new ways. At the same time as the Western states became more powerful, they also, though to differing degrees, became more democratized. A fifth factor, this did not necessarily work against an imperialist approach: it might intensify the rivalry among states, reducing their ability to manoeuvre; it might also commit them more irrevocably to expansionist policies, turning them into missions difficult for governments to abandon. The capacity of the Europeans to influence Southeast Asia was, sixth, enhanced by the growth of their power over the great neighbouring centres of population that had so long influenced it in a number of ways, India and China. But the changes in India and China did not eliminate their influence: they gave it new forms, and the modernization of Japan was both inspiration and threat. These factors were effective in Southeast Asia at different times, in different combinations, and in different ways.

The outcome was, however, not merely the result of all or any of these factors, singly or in combination. There were other actors on the scene—from Arabia, the heartland of Islam, now in closer touch, and from the United States, an independent commercial power from the late eighteenth century, rapidly industrializing in the later nineteenth century, developing imperial aspirations at the end of it. There were, too, the peoples of Southeast Asia themselves, who interacted with the Europeans and with others in a variety of ways, fighting, resisting, accommodating, adapting, turning and being turned to account, with greater or less vision, wisdom or acumen, at the popular and élite levels. Their aims are part of the story, though less clearly defined than those of the Europeans; and indeed they faced complex changes, difficult to appraise. In most cases, the existing state structures could not cope with the pressures put upon them and existing central authorities collapsed. Their replacements were endowed with territories out of a convenience more often European than Asian, designed, in particular, to avoid dispute among Europeans. And the new authority was, in substantial part at least, extraneous.

The political map of Southeast Asia was redrawn so that the region was almost entirely fragmented among the European powers. The process of drawing the frontiers was a long one; it was not complete—even on the map, let alone on the ground—till the early twentieth century. Most of the main lines of demarcation were, however, evident by 1870, before the full effects of industrialization were felt. Only more marginal territories remained for redistribution. They were marginal more in a geographical than a political sense. For their redistribution could still prompt disputes among the imperial powers that could become more than minor; and if those disputes did not escalate, or were readily resolved, the outcome was still important for the peoples concerned as well as for the imperial powers themselves, and, ultimately, for their successors.

In the drawing of the frontiers there was something of a paradox. In Europe the concept dealt with subjects and citizens in terms of their geographical locality rather than their personal allegiance; and the state laid claim to their taxes and imposed its obligations on an impersonal basis. That contrasted with much of previous Southeast Asian practice, especially in the archipelago where, insofar as geographical frontiers existed, they might be only vaguely defined. Often more important within states, even within some of the larger ones, were personal allegiances, client–patron relations, differential connexions between court and core, court and periphery; often more important among states were overlapping hierarchies, dual loyalties. Such structures better reflected the conditions of the Southeast Asian past. But the concept that the Europeans sought to apply in Southeast Asia also contrasted with the European present. In Europe frontiers had been created over a long period of time, often as a result of struggle, and within them new loyalties had been built up. Increasingly loyalty was to the state itself, as representing the nation in whose name, it had come to be accepted, its government ruled. No such

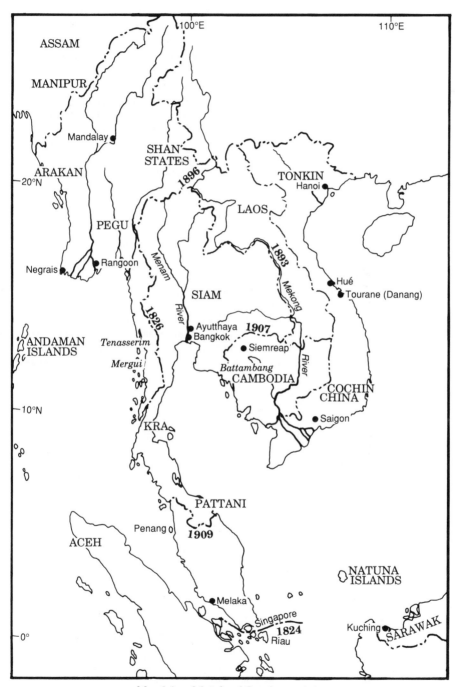

Map 1.1   Mainland Southeast Asia

ideology could apply to the colonial territories; nor was there a clear substitute for it. The colonial powers were utilizing a concept not only drawn from a system of international relations that differed but from one which they themselves were not in fact applying.

International relations in Southeast Asia came to be increasingly European. The frontiers were drawn so as to avoid disputes among the European powers. As a result, especially at the margins, they bore no firm relation to economic, social, cultural, ethnic or even geographical realities. The concept of a national frontier in Southeast Asia was applied in the general absence there of the relevant concept of nation. And it was applied with additional arbitrariness since it was designed to avoid conflict elsewhere.

The new governments, by necessity or design, often utilized or re-utilized old claims to suzerainty, old patterns of loyalty, old modes of administration, and at the same time they reshaped them. While their governments were relatively inactive, the discrepancy mattered less. And for a time they were to a greater or lesser degree 'law and order' states, 'arbitral' governments. The old central authorities might have been displaced, perhaps geographically as well as politically. But the new governments might still function in a limited way, adopting some Southeast Asian practices as well as European. Indeed they could give themselves—at least in their own eyes, and perhaps in the eyes of their subjects—a special role simply because of their limited function: they were there to reduce tensions among the 'opposite Interests and jarring Dispositions' to which, as Alexander Dalrymple said, colonies were so prone;[1] they were there to end tyranny, they sometimes rather more ambitiously claimed.

More tension would be felt when governments became more active— could old allegiances still be utilized?—and still more when they ceased to be arbitral—could the peoples then be held in the colonial framework? That question arose of course with twentieth-century moves—dictated by metropolitan politics but also by colonial change—towards indigenous participation in the central structures. Just because the pragmatic approach of the nineteenth century and the desire to avoid conflict among Europeans had made the territories often so heterogeneous, the tension was all the greater. A minority could live alongside an inactive government: it could accept alien arbitration. But could it accept majority rule?

The concept of the nation was developed in Europe to fill out the European concept of the state. It caused struggle enough there: it gave weapons to majorities and minorities, to those who would change frontiers and those who would insist on not changing them, to those who would challenge authorities and those who would uphold them. In Southeast Asia, the concept was again divisive as well as integrative. But, because the movements could initially challenge the Europeans, its divisiveness was at first often muted. Emerging nationalist movements could thus seek to play down tension, though their alien rulers might point it out

---

[1] 'Enquiry into the most advantageous Place for a Capital to the Oriental Polynesia', February 1764, Borneo Factory Records G/4/1, India Office Library.

or even play it up, so as to preserve their role. It could intensify when the Europeans withdrew and their succcessors sought to rule as nation-states these territories with frontiers which were so much the product of colonial convenience. Authority was again in question: the successor states had to be turned into nation-states.

The making of the frontiers thus assumes a primal position in an account of Southeast Asian history in the nineteenth century. Itself the product of interactions between European and Asian, it becomes, too, the framework for continuing interaction. It is also important as a factor in the history of the nationalist movements of the twentieth century and of the post-colonial states.

The nineteenth century was, more than any other, an age of migration: the economic transformations it witnessed set in motion or speeded up movements of people on an unprecedented scale. Europeans left Europe to help build up or to create new states elsewhere, in the Americas and Australasia, in Africa and, much less, in Asia. But other peoples also moved in increasing numbers as economic change picked up pace. Southeast Asia, always a recipient of Indians and Chinese, received them on a new scale, particularly in the territories which the British came to control. There was also migration, again not entirely novel, within Southeast Asia, within the frontiers that were being established and across them. For a colonial authority, again, these movements posed few problems and offered economic and political advantages. But in the twentieth century, those movements would make it more difficult to establish a participatory political system, or even an accepted central authority ruling on a national basis.

THE ROLE OF THE BRITISH

If there was varied interaction between Southeast Asia and Europe, the Europeans were also divided. Rivalry was a factor in their expansion, for the most part spurring them on. But the process of frontier-building and its outcome were also affected by the shifting distribution of power among the Europeans, the result in a sense of the differing impact on them of common factors. For much of the nineteenth century, Britain was the predominant state in Europe and thus in the world. The French presented a challenge in the eighteenth century, but they were defeated at sea in 1805 and on land in 1815. Politically secure in Europe, Britain also took the lead in the Industrial Revolution. That gave it yet greater strength, but also shaped the application of its power. Overseas its interests became substantially commercial and economic rather than territorial and political. It saw its dominion in India, begun in the earlier phase, as essential but exceptional. Elsewhere, a combination of strategic positions and economic and political influence should suffice to protect its interests. In Southeast Asia Britain sought security and stability; it did not necessarily seek to rule, though its power might be felt in other ways.

The nineteenth-century patterns of interaction in Southeast Asia were

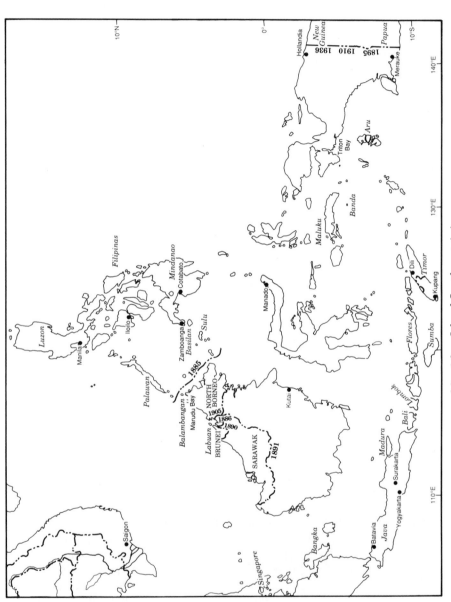

Map 1.2 Island Southeast Asia

naturally much affected by the influence and interests of the British, particularly during the period of their predominance. That predominance they did not use to eliminate their European rivals, but rather to constrain them. The Netherlands and Spain were now minor states in Europe; they were left with substantial holdings in Southeast Asia, with claims that the British were unlikely to challenge, with the option of implementing them in their own time provided they did not undermine Britain's interests. Even France, the eighteenth-century rival, was not obstructed in its Vietnam venture. In earlier centuries, European rivalry had rarely worked to the advantage of Asian states: it spurred the Europeans on, while the chance of playing the Europeans off against one another was often a chimera. But the new pattern of intra-European relations was perhaps still less advantageous. The fact that minor European powers could rely on Britain's restraint might indeed mean that they could refrain from enforcing their claims or establishing de facto occupation in other than immediately essential areas. But the autonomy which indigenous rulers might thus enjoy was somewhat illusory: they had no real chance of playing Britain off against the minor powers, and their status as independent actors on an international stage was diminished by this kind of semi-condominium. The British set the agenda for lesser European powers, and for the indigenous states also. Siam (Thailand) alone retained real independence at the end of the period: it had seen that it was no longer a matter of playing off one alien power against another, but of coming to terms with the British, and it was able to do so. Directly or indirectly, Britain's influence and interest were often decisive in determining the frontiers of the new Southeast Asian states, in locating the central authorities within those frontiers, even in shaping the policies those authorities pursued.

The challenges to the patterns thus established that emerged towards the end of the nineteenth century did not merely, nor even primarily, result from the changes and tensions within Southeast Asia. They reflected changes in Europe and the world at large, in particular the external challenges to Britain's power, as industrialization affected other parts of Europe and the world, and Britain and indeed Europe itself lost their extraordinary primacy. But by the late nineteenth century the major loci of authority in Southeast Asia had been settled, and the revived rivalry of the period affected only the rounding-out of frontiers. In this phase the British moved readily from tolerating others towards compromising with them. The conference on Africa and West Africa that met in Berlin in 1884–5, and included the European powers, Turkey and the United States, provided a principle: European states would accept the frontiers established by their rivals if their claims were backed by effective occupation. The recrudescence of rivalry was thus no more to the advantage of indigenous autonomy than its earlier diminution: indeed it clearly conduced to the establishment of outside control. Intensifying rivalry in Europe and the emergence of non-European powers, the United States and Japan, had the same effect. The former urged on compromise between Britain and France, helping to determine the frontiers of Burma, Malaya, Indochina and Siam. A combination of factors helped to ensure that Spain was replaced in the Philippines by the United States and that the authority of the Moro sultanates was finally destroyed. But in a sense these were adjustments of a system that had developed during the British primacy of the nineteenth century. The system was overthrown only by the Japanese incursion of 1941–2.

The making of the new frontiers in Southeast Asia in the nineteenth century had depended in some sense on British decisions. They in turn were affected by the essentially economic nature of Britain's world-wide interests; by its desire for European stability; by its acquisition of the raj in India; and by the importance attached to its trade with China. These concerns affected Britain's view of different parts of Southeast Asia in different ways. For this reason, though also for others, the outcomes differed. Much depended on the relationship of Britain with specific European powers. Where they were minor, it tended not to displace them, but to connive at their imperialism so as to avoid that of any powers that might be more threatening, and paradoxically that might reduce their immediate need to establish full control. Against major European powers, however, it might have to take more direct precautions, but that did not necessarily mean exclusion.

The attitudes and policies of other European powers have thus to be taken into account. The Dutch, whose dependence was underlined by British conquests and retrocessions, were prompted all the more to con- centrate on Java; on areas that could be made profitable; on development, peace and order. *Onthouding*, or abstention, was possible as well as desirable in the outer islands. The increased rivalry of the later nineteenth century, as well as new economic opportunities, spurred them on to round out their empire. Their concern over Islam was another factor. Generally they tried, as in earlier centuries, to avoid provoking it, and their war with Aceh was a challenge they found difficult to handle. Spain, whose weakness the British had also underlined by capturing Manila in 1762, recognized that it too was dependent on them and permitted them major economic opportunities in Luzon and the Visayas. The international rivalry of the late nineteenth century, and the challenge of Islam, led the Spanish into bloody but indeterminate efforts to make their claims over the Moro lands effective. In the late eighteenth century the French had seen a venture in Southeast Asia as a way of compensating themselves for British success in India and China. Their revival of interest in Vietnam in the 1850s, not opposed by the British, responded to a need to demonstrate the greatness of France overseas. That seemed all the more necessary under the Third Republic, when its position in Europe was under challenge.

The opportunities for these European states were determined not only by the British, but also by the Southeast Asians. Their states might attempt to adjust to new circumstances: they might not; if they did, they might fail; if they began the task, they might not realize that further adjustment would be needed. Even in the early nineteenth century, it seemed that Asian states would have to modernize to survive, and that they might need a greater or lesser degree of European influence to ensure that they did so. Such in itself might destroy ancient authority without replacing it, and make them weaker rather than stronger. The alternative might be piecemeal partition, itself weakening the core structure. If either or both of these outcomes determined their position by the late nineteenth century, the new pressures then exerted by international economic expansion and political rivalry might bring about a final dissolution.

THE DUTCH REALM IN THE INDONESIAN ARCHIPELAGO

While Britain occupied only Fort Marlborough in West Sumatra, two European powers were already established in Southeast Asia at the outset of the period, the Dutch and the Spaniards. Their empires differed in character. That of the Dutch did not involve widespread control. But the determination of the British, at once not to challenge their supremacy in the archipelago, nor to permit that to be done by others, assisted the Dutch to establish their power during the nineteenth century and reduced the possibility that Indonesian states could sustain their independence. An occasional rift with Britain urged the Dutch on, though they were usually careful to provide British merchants with commercial opportunities. More generally, the relationship enabled them to defer their empire-building till they were strong enough, or till they found it necessary or desirable because of the risks of the intervention of others or because of their own needs and urges. The Asian states might enjoy a practical, albeit misleading, freedom from Dutch intervention in the meantime.

In the closing decades of the eighteenth century, the Dutch still retained an Asia-wide empire, with Batavia (Jakarta) as its centre. But their hold even on the Malaysian-Indonesian area fell far short of territorial dominion. Its failure to compete in the Asian textile and opium trades, and the decline in its spice trade, had led the Verenigde Oost-Indische Compagnie (VOC, the Dutch East India Company) to concentrate on Java, and to see the peninsula and archipelago rather as an outwork for its empire there. In any case, the Dutch position rested for the most part on contracts and treaties with indigenous states, more concerned with questions of commerce than questions of government, more with deliveries of produce than transfers of sovereignty. What was critical for VOC, and as a result for the indigenous states, was the exclusion of European rivals. This the Dutch sought to ensure on paper all the more because they found it difficult to ensure in practice: 'they are afraid', said the British statesman Henry Dundas, 'that the communication we may have with the Natives would lay the foundation for their total shaking off of the miserable dependence in which they are held by the Dutch'.[2] The British had good commercial grounds for expanding such communication: their hold on trade with Asia and, through the country traders, within Asia, had improved; the East India Company needed archipelagic goods to amplify its trade to China. But there were other arguments against alienating the Dutch in the context of the European rivalries of the time. It was important not to drive the Dutch into the hands of the French, so expanding their threat to the new dominion in India, undermining the trade to China, and indeed damaging

[2] Quoted H. Furber, *Henry Dundas, First Viscount Melville, 1742–1811*, Oxford, 1931, 103.

the security of England itself. The Anglo-Dutch treaty of 1784 did not go beyond securing the right to navigate in the Eastern Seas. Remaining in West Sumatra, the British did not extend their political challenge except on the periphery of Dutch power, by acquiring Penang from the Sultan of Kedah in 1786.

A pro-French régime nevertheless survived in the Dutch Republic until the Anglo-Prussian intervention of 1787. Then the British attempted to put their interests in the Indies on a new footing while, as they thought, recognizing those of the Dutch, reaching an accord, they hoped, in the East and in Europe. Their concept involved a kind of delimitation—the first time, but not the last, that the notion was to emerge. The Dutch should remain in their settlements on the continent of India and the Malay peninsula; the British would secure the naval base of Trincomalee in Ceylon (Sri Lanka). But the VOC should transfer the right to Riau which it had lately secured from the Sultan of Johor-Lingga; this would afford protection for British ships en route for China and provide an entrepôt for British trade in the archipelago. In return the spice monopoly would be guaranteed: no British traders would operate, and no British settlements be made, east of the easternmost point of Sumatra. These ideas not even a friendly Dutch régime could accept, and the negotiations failed.

In the Napoleonic Wars that followed, the Dutch Republic again fell under French influence, and the British took over a number of Dutch possessions in India, Ceylon and the archipelago, and finally in 1811 Java itself. The defeat of France, and the establishment of the new Kingdom of the Netherlands, were the signal for the restoration of all the Dutch territories but those in Ceylon and at the Cape of Good Hope. But no provision was made in the convention of 1814 for the settlement of prewar disputes over the archipelago. By 1814, indeed, the British East India Company had no real interest in the spice trade; nor even in the archipelago trade in general, since Indian opium now substantially provided for its tea investment at Canton. But the interim administration of Java by Stamford Raffles and the opening of the trade to the East under the Company's Charter of 1813 had led to the establishment of British merchants on that island, interested in distributing British textiles and purchasing coffee. These viewed with concern the restoration of Dutch sovereignty and the prospect of a revived policy of commercial exclusion. The extensive renewal of treaties and contracts with the native states outside Java upon which the Dutch Commissioners-General embarked after the restoration of the colonies in 1816 likewise aroused the apprehension of country traders and of merchants and officials at Penang.

Raffles, like Dundas earlier, had pointed out the weakness of the Dutch position in the archipelago, but, with a wider sense of responsibility, he believed that the British should assure their trade and influence there by themselves establishing settlements and concluding treaties with Indonesian rulers. Indeed, by making the Company's Governor-General in India 'Batara', they should secure 'a general right of superintendence over, and interference with, all the Malay States', so as to support legitimate authority, suppress piracy, limit commercial monopoly and control arms

Map 1.3   The Malay Peninsula

traffic.[3] These views were not accepted in London. In 1815 the Secret Committee of the Court of Directors disapproved of the treaties Raffles made: 'such engagements are impolitic and injudicious; . . . calculated to involve the British Government in the internal concerns of those States, and the perpetual contests which they are carrying on with each other'.[4] Back in the archipelago at Fort Marlborough, Raffles modified rather than abandoned his plans. One argument he now used impressed his superiors in India: the importance of protecting the China route. Thus he gained the authority under which in 1819 he concluded a treaty of friendship with the yet independent Sultan of Aceh at one end of the Straits of Melaka (Malacca) and acquired rights from princes of Johor to a factory on Singapore island at the other.

The Secret Committee deplored 'the extension in any degree to the Eastern Islands of that system of subsidiary alliance which has prevailed perhaps too widely in India'.[5] But now decisions had to be taken on the archipelago, and the British government again moved towards a kind of conditioned delimitation. Raffles's schemes must be used, not to overthrow the Dutch empire, but again to press upon the Dutch a compromise by which its continuance could be reconciled with local British interests. In the view of the Foreign Secretary Lord Castlereagh, the government could not 'acquiesce in a practical exclusion' of British commerce from the archipelago, nor in complete Dutch control of the 'keys of the Straits of Malacca'. The prospects for a compromise would be affected by the preliminary question of 'the extent of the rights claimed by the Government of the Netherlands in the Eastern Seas'. The Dutch must

> distinguish how much of this claim rests upon strict possession, how much upon concession from the native princes, and by what limits in point of space, or by what rules of intercourse the Netherlands Government proposes to consider the rights and authority of that state to be restrained or modified towards the subjects of other powers frequenting those seas.[6]

The Dutch king, Castlereagh wrote, might 'hold Java and any other of his old possessions in direct colonial sovereignty in which of course he will establish the system he thinks the wisest, but which after all, my opinion is, ought not in prudence to be one of exclusive trade'. Beyond these limits he should have an understanding with Great Britain 'which may open the native commerce of the other islands to a fair and friendly competition, without the establishment of any other preponderating military or political

---

[3] Sophia Raffles, *Memoir of the Life and Public Services of Sir Thomas Stamford Raffles*, London, 1830, 59ff.
[4] Quoted John Bastin, 'Raffles and British Policy in the Indian Archipelago, 1811–1816', JMBRAS, 37, 1 (May 1954) 100–3.
[5] Secret Committee to Governor-General, 22 May 1819, Board's Drafts of Secret Letters to India, First Series, L/PS/5/543, 5, India Office Library, London.
[6] Castlereagh to Clancarty, 13 Aug. 1819, secret, FO 37/107, Public Record Office, London; H. T. Colenbrander, ed., *Gedenkstukken der Algemeene Geschiedenis van Nederland van 1795 tot 1840*, 's-Gravenhage, 1915–21, 8, 1. 130–2.

authority in those seas to counterbalance that which the Dutch now and long have exercised'.[7]

The exchanges were complicated by a concern about other powers. Raffles argued for an active policy. But if the British extended their challenge to the Dutch, their example might be followed by others, and that might damage British interests. It would be difficult to insist upon any British rights in respect of the commerce with Indonesian states in contractual relationship with the Dutch, a British negotiator argued,

> without admitting at the same time the equal right of other European nations, and of the Americans, to their share also. Perhaps as the policy of extending British establishments or connexions in the Eastern Islands has hitherto been considered by the British Government as at least extremely doubtful the utmost length to which our preliminary demand ought to go . . . should be a stipulation that the Dutch will form no new engagements, especially on the Island of Borneo.[8]

In fact, the Dutch wished to avoid an inquisition into their 'title deeds'. While, therefore, the British accepted the spice monopolies in enumerated islands of Maluku (the Moluccas)—the fine spices they produced were now in any case also produced outside the Indonesian archipelago—the Dutch agreed that no treaty should be made thereafter by either power with any native power in the Eastern Seas 'tending either expressly or by the imposition of unequal duties to exclude the trade of the other party from the ports of such native power, and that, if in any treaty now existing on either part, any such article to that effect has been admitted, such article shall be abrogated upon the conclusion of the present treaty'. This became Article 3 of the treaty finally concluded on 17 March 1824. Article 2 of that treaty was designed to give Dutch trade 'the sort of protection which the British trade enjoys in the Indian ports' and under limitations allowed protective duties in Dutch possessions. The articles were less than clear. But it was in any case impossible to define the position too elaborately without arousing the jealousy of other powers. 'The situation in which we and the Dutch stand to each other is part only of our difficulties', wrote George Canning, one of the plenipotentiaries; 'that in which we both stand to the rest of the world as exclusive Lords of the East, is one more reason for terminating our relative difficulties as soon as we can'.[9] A challenge to the Dutch must be avoided, for it was felt that this might invite the intervention of other major powers in areas flanking the route to China. But too obvious and too close an agreement with the Dutch might provoke other powers to intervene. Before the war only one other power had been in question: France. Now France was defeated, though not eliminated, and others had penetrated to Asia, including the Americans, and both its victorious role in Europe and its interest in Japan even raised the question of Russia's involvement. At this juncture intervention was less actual than

[7] Castlereagh to Clancarty, 13 Aug. 1819, private, FO 37/107; *Gedenkstukken*, 8, 1. 132–3.
[8] Memorandum, n.d., Dutch Records, I/2/31, India Office Library.
[9] Note by Canning on Courtenay's memorandum of 15 Jan. 1824, Dutch Records, I/2/32.

potential: a blatant statement of overlordship might provoke a challenge otherwise avoidable.

The same consideration throws light on other important articles in the treaty of 1824. The Dutch had at first opposed and then finally accepted the British occupation of Singapore, and they also proposed to leave Melaka provided the British left Sumatra. As the Dutch plenipotentiary, A. R. Falck, put it, a line would be drawn between their respective possessions through the Straits of Melaka and passing north of Riau. In the treaty the proposed line was replaced by articles, effecting this same division in different words, less likely to arouse the jealousy of others. A difference arose over Aceh, which was important for its position at the head of the straits. It was now British policy to resign all Sumatra to the Dutch, and the more effective their control, the more effectively they would be able to exclude other major powers. The recency of Raffles's treaty of friendship with the sultan raised a difficulty, however, which could be overcome only by including, in notes attached to the treaty, stipulations binding the Dutch to establish security in Aceh without infringing its independence.

Falck's dividing line and the non-intervention articles substituted for it did not extend as far as Borneo, though he certainly believed that Borneo was to be left to the Dutch. This, however, was not stated in the treaty, partly because of fears that the British Parliament might object to the 'abandonment' of Borneo as well as of Sumatra, and, once more, partly because such an extended Anglo-Dutch agreement, if it were explicitly expressed, might arouse jealousy among other powers. Indeed the British plenipotentiaries probably felt that the arrangements made over treaty states removed the need, referred to earlier, for an 'opening' on the island of Borneo.

The treaty of 1824 was a form of delimitation: it excluded the Dutch from the peninsula, it admitted their predominance in the archipelago. It should not be seen as a stage in an advance towards a predetermined end, for much was left open and subject to argument, and there was no clear determination that two realms would be set up. Some options were, however, closed off. The precaution over other powers, though not expressed in the treaty, continued to be influential. Apprehension about them continued to restrain the British in handling Dutch relations with Indonesian states. And other powers were on the whole to respect the Anglo-Dutch relationship without always realizing the verbal weakness of the treaty of 1824. The arrangements affected the indigenous states all the more as a result. Britain was unlikely to take their part against the Dutch. The chances of their behaving as international actors, able to enter rela-tions with third powers, was nullified by a combination of Dutch jealousy, British connivance, and European caution. Meanwhile, however, the weakened position of the Indonesian states might not be apparent. The Dutch, with a British guarantee, might often be able to avoid actual intervention.

The merchants of Penang and Singapore were opposed to Dutch exten-sion on any terms, even if unaccompanied by protectionist measures, because they saw it as a threat to their entrepôt traffic, and a constriction of the scope of their operations. They differed not only from Raffles, who opposed Dutch authority but wanted to reform the Malay world and end its fragmentation, but from the government in London which preferred a regular European government administered by a minor power. For a while the Dutch in any case largely avoided expansion: they were deeply embroiled in the Java War of the 1820s, then in the Belgian breakaway struggle after 1830. These events, and the need for revenue, concentrated their attention on Java where they developed the forced-labour Cultivation System and also found a market, despite the treaty of 1824, for Dutch textiles. They were drawn into West Sumatra, however, by local initiative. Batavia had modest plans, Padang expansionist ones; and the authorities there could oblige their superiors to accept faits accomplis.

Returning to Padang after the British occupation, the Dutch committed themselves to helping the Minangkabau *penghulu* (chiefs) against the Padris, Wahhābi-style religious reformers, in 1824. A settlement was made with Bondjol, identified as the central Padri authority, while the Java War was on. On its conclusion, Governor-General Van den Bosch favoured securing the recognition of the Dutch régime throughout the archipelago. In Sumatra, he thought it would be sufficient for the Dutch to occupy ports, river-mouths, selected interior market towns: the aim should be to avoid direct intervention and concentrate on encouraging 'profitable activity'.[10] In West Sumatra, however, he agreed that order must be re-established. One bizarre notion was to use Sentot and some Javanese auxiliaries, but this proved counter-productive. From 1837 the war with the Padris was prosecuted with vigour and Minangkabau was incorporated in the Dutch realm.

Trade had been flowing from the interior to the east coast. There Jambi had acknowledged Dutch sovereignty in 1833–4. Inderagiri followed in 1838, then Panei and Bila, and Sultan Ismail of Siak sought Dutch protection. Merchants in the Straits Settlements protested. Rather surprisingly, the Foreign Office in London took their part. In the case of Siak, the British seemed to be faced with a threat of Dutch conquest. In the absence of any precise stipulation about conquest, as distinct from treaty-making, in the treaty of 1824, they attempted to counter this by reviving a treaty with the sultan made on behalf of the Penang government in 1818. In the case of neighbouring Jambi, they indeed faced the question of a Netherlands treaty with an indigenous power. But suppose, the Foreign Office wondered, the Dutch claimed sovereignty by treaty as they might by conquest? could conditions then be imposed on the exertion of their authority in respect of foreign trade? The Dutch indeed claimed that the stipulation of Article 3 of the 1824 treaty did not apply in such cases, though Van den Bosch's cautious successor, J. C. Baud, withdrew from the east coast pro tem. Palmerston, the British Foreign Secretary, was inclined to agree that Article 2 alone applied; and so the question of sovereignty, initially raised

---

[10] Elizabeth E. Graves, 'The Ever Victorious Buffalo: how the Minangkabau of Indonesia solved their "colonial question"', Ph.D. thesis, University of Wisconsin, 1971, 144.

by the problem of conquest, and then asked in relation to treaties, displaced the basis of the 1824 compromise. The distinction it had tried on Castlereagh's basis to draw between treaty states and possessions was now blurred.

Under the pressures of the Cultivation System and Dutch protectionism, Article 2 had, however, been found to afford little protection for British trade in Dutch possessions. The British Foreign Office endeavoured in the recession of the 1830s to uphold the cause of the merchants in Java, related as their interests were to those of important textile manufacturers at home. It was the failure to obtain any real satisfaction from the Dutch in this respect that was largely responsible for the Foreign Office's decision to take up the Straits Settlements complaints. By 1838 the official view had already shifted far from that of 1824: 'an extension of Dutch Influence, or Territorial Possession', it was remarked, 'would in all probability be attended with consequences injurious to British interest, and should be looked upon with jealousy by the Government of this country.'[11] In the 1840s, indeed, a more positive challenge to the delimitation of 1824 seemed possible. Adventurers were appearing as it were in the niches between actual and potential Dutch extension, in the no-man's-land which the Dutch had felt they could safely neglect. Now, despite the 1824 treaty, or because of the dispute over it, the Dutch feared that these adventurers might secure official backing. Baud ordered an archival survey of Dutch rights and contracts, and special commissioners were sent out to fill the gaps revealed. In general they were, however, only being papered over. Occupation rarely followed, and native rulers still tended to see the contracts more as treaties than as transfers of control. There was more forceful action in Bali, where the Dutch commissioner had secured treaties only by verbal promises of help against the Mataram kingdom in Lombok. The help not being forthcoming, the treaties were not ratified; the Dutch sent three expeditions to deal with the Bali rajas, though still no occupation followed. The renewal of Anglo-Dutch rivalry could indeed only diminish the independence of the Indonesian states, unless the British were prepared to abandon the 1824 settlement. Mere apprehension that they might do so drove the Dutch into affirming their claims over the Indonesian states and in some cases establishing a more formal control over them.

The British challenge to the Dutch in fact never went far. Nor did it last long. The improvement in overall economic conditions in mid-century meant that there was less domestic pressure on the British government, and the Dutch government, headed after 1848 by the liberal Thorbecke, began to liberalize its system. That did not remove the Straits Settlements objections to Dutch extension in Sumatra when it was renewed in the 1860s. In the 1850s Dutch policy had continued for the most part to be of a restrained nature. But after an English individual had responded to a request for help, the Dutch had made a treaty with Siak in 1858, and under it claimed dependencies to the north in the following years. Governor Orfeur Cavenagh supported the Straits Settlements protests, but the

---

[11] Strangways to Barrow, 9 Jan. 1838, FO 37/213.

Foreign Office, preferring regular European rule, used them to secure a new delimitation. This was the treaty of 1871, under which all objections to Dutch territorial control in Sumatra were withdrawn in return for a commercial open door. The appearance of other imperial powers on the scene, now less hypothetical than in the 1820s, only revalidated the pre-Palmerston approach. The extension of the Dutch was generally preferred to the intervention of other powers in the archipelago. As Under-Secretary at the Foreign Office, Lord Wodehouse had written in 1860:

> I believe the policy of Mr. Canning's treaty was much the wisest, *viz.*, to leave to the Dutch the Eastern Archipelago. . . . The exclusive colonial policy of the Dutch is no doubt an evil, but it has been much relaxed of late. . . . It seems to me in many respects very advantageous that the Dutch should possess this Archipelago. If it were not in the hands of the Dutch, it would fall under the sway of some other maritime power, presumably the French, unless we took it ourselves. The French might, if they possessed such an eastern empire, be really dangerous to India and Australia, but the Dutch are and must remain too weak to cause us any alarm.[12]

The means by which the Dutch regained the sanction of the British they now applied to the other European powers penetrating the area, too: an open-door policy. Like Britain, the powers would be less likely to challenge the Dutch territorially if they found their policies acceptable commercially. The further internationalization of the area in the later 1870s and 1880s—especially the arrival of the Germans—again urged the Dutch to strengthen their claims, as did economic opportunity and local ambition. The indigenous states lost the autonomy they had possessed when, largely with British connivance, the Dutch had been content in many places with paper claims. For example, the year following the Berlin conference, J. A. Liefrinck, sent to investigate rumours of the wealth of Lombok, urged an end to the policy of 'benevolent indifference'.[13] In 1887, the raja refused, however, to make a supplementary treaty and accept a Dutch agent. Forceful action, the Council in Batavia urged, lest it should appear that Aceh had broken Dutch power; caution, decided Governor-General Pynacker, lest action resulted in another prolonged conflict, though the Sasaks revolted against the raja in the east of the island, and the local Dutch officials sought to provoke an incident. The next governor-general authorized an expedition. It succeeded only with difficulty.

For the most part Indonesian states had lost their independence by stages, involving treaties, Dutch pressure, British connivance, others' non-intervention or threats to intervene, their own incapacity; they were gradually subsumed into the Netherlands realm, the 'radical and internal weakness' of the Dutch turned to a semblance at least of strength. But Aceh had a tradition of independence, Islamic stiffening, and no real involvement in the treaty system, and the British inhibition in 1824 had made it extra difficult for the Dutch to incorporate it, as it were, from the

---

[12] Memorandum by Wodehouse, 18 Aug. 1860, FO 12/28.
[13] Alfons van der Kraan, *Lombok: Conquest, Colonization and Underdevelopment 1870–1940*, Singapore, 31–2.

top down. At the time of the 1871 treaty Aceh was still independent, and in the context of expanding colonial rivalry, this was worrying. 'The pretension of excluding others where one will not or cannot undertake matters oneself is in the long run, at least for a small power, untenable and ... extremely dangerous.'[14] The Dutch took the kind of action they were to hesitate over in respect of Lombok. 'An end must come to the equivocal policy of Atjeh [Aceh] towards the Netherlands Government. That state remains our weak point as far as Sumatra is concerned. As long as it does not recognise our sovereignty foreign intervention will continue to threaten us like the sword of Damocles.'[15]

Earlier, under Governor-General Pahud, the Dutch had attempted to develop friendship without claiming sovereignty. But piecemeal advance on the west coast during the Padri struggle had made that difficult, and Dutch claims over the east coast under the Siak treaty of 1858 were a direct challenge to the Acehnese. The Acehnese war that ensued after 1873 showed the special qualities of the sultanate and of the role of Islam. But it also showed the general importance for the Dutch of the non-intervention of others and explained their normal preference for an essentially continuous political rather than military process of consolidation. The Dutch in fact did not secure total victory. The long struggle helped to reshape their policy towards Islam in general, and to promote their attempts to rationalize a realm pragmatically built up over several centuries. The British no longer opposed the infringement of Article 3 of the 1824 treaty that the process involved.

RAJ, COMPANY AND RESIDENCY IN BORNEO

In 1824 the British had probably intended that the Dutch should predominate in the archipelago, even in Borneo. But earlier they had been interested in the Brunei-Sulu region, and a combination of personal initiative and dissatisfaction with Dutch policy elsewhere led them back to Borneo in the 1840s. The government established the colony of Labuan and made a treaty with Brunei. It avoided taking over Sarawak, where the Brookes built a raj of their own. In the 1880s British protectorates were established over Sarawak, the territory of the newly-established British North Borneo Company and the remnant of Brunei, and a British Resident was established in the sultanate in 1905. Partly provoked by the Brooke venture and by the founding of the Company, the Dutch established their control more firmly over the rest of Borneo.

The apparent change in British policy towards the Dutch in Borneo derived in part from the partial break between the 'exclusive Lords' in the 1830s: Dutch policies had led Palmerston to declare that Dutch extension was in general not to British advantage. But something more positive was required to turn that shift of policy towards British intervention. Northern

[14] Gericke and Van Bosse to the King, 19 Apr. 1871, quoted A. J. S. Reid, *The Contest for North Sumatra*, Kuala Lumpur, 1969, 86.
[15] Loudon to Van de Putte, 25 Feb. 1873, quoted ibid., 95.

Borneo became of greater interest with the opening of trade to China and, since it possessed coal, with the development of steam communication. More important were the personal intervention of James Brooke, the most effective of the various adventurers in the no-man's-land left between the potential and the reality of Dutch imperialism, and the public support he was able for a time to secure. Even so, the change in official British policy was limited, and there was continual tension between Brooke and the government. With the Dutch excluded, the British needed to avert the intervention of other powers by other means. But they were not keen to take on additional responsibilities; unwilling or unable to displace or abandon Brooke, they became anxious not to be drawn on any further by him.

James Brooke's initial aim was to undo the policy of 1824. He wanted to revive Raffles's concept of a British empire in the archipelago by intervening where Dutch authority was weak or non-existent, and reforming and sustaining the indigenous states. Subjected to no formal relationship with the Dutch, the sultanate of Brunei became a field of activity as well as advocacy. Brooke planned at once to argue for and to demonstrate the validity of his policy by intervening in one of its dependencies, Sarawak, and restructuring its system of government so that law and order would be established and commerce flourish. British power could be involved, in particular because of the commitment to put down piracy, included in the treaty of 1824, and generally regarded as a duty for the British Navy. Support for his native allies in Brunei itself could be justified by arguing, too, that the Brunei region possessed coal which the British needed. With the assistance of others Brooke mounted a campaign at home, designed to influence the government by stressing the philanthropic and commercial objectives of the venture. The British government did not take over Sarawak, but it did give Brooke, raja there from 1841, some support, not only through naval activities, but by appointing him Agent with the Sultan of Brunei in 1844. The intervention produced a crisis with the Brunei élite in 1846. That led in turn to a further instalment of British intervention. Labuan was now made a colony and the treaty concluded with the sultan in 1847 secured a measure of extraterritorial jurisdiction and provided against cessions to other powers. There was still no British take-over, but Brunei was clearly, like states in the Dutch sphere, losing its room for manoeuvre.

There seemed some chance that Brooke might secure further backing for his Rafflesian plans: instructions given him as Commissioner and Consul-General to the Sultan and Independent Chiefs of Borneo in 1848 indicated that the position was designed 'to afford to British commerce that support and protection . . . peculiarly required in the Indian seas in consequence of the prevalence of piracy . . . and by reason of the encroachments of the Netherlands authorities in the Indian Archipelago'.[16] But questions about the possible abuse of British naval power at the raja's instigation reinforced doubts about a more expansive policy, which generally improving economic conditions in any case made less urgent. The extent to which public

---

[16] Palmerston to Brooke, 23 Feb. 1848, FO 12/6.

opinion was involved made the policy particularly subject to change if that opinion changed, and when a new government appointed a commission of inquiry in 1853, the policy, never fully adopted, was almost entirely abandoned.

Brooke was not, however, deprived of his raj, anomalous though it was for a British subject to be a ruler in his own right. Indeed, unable to exert influence over Brunei, he increasingly sought to extend the boundaries of his raj at its expense and to regard Sarawak as an independent state. His realm thus rested on displacing Brunei's, co-opting local Malayo-Muslim leaders, mobilizing, too, the energies of erstwhile Iban enemies, and, still more ambivalently, the energies of Chinese immigrants. It also still rested, despite all the tension and anomaly in the relationship, on British power. The British government would not push him out and so return to 1824— public opinion would not go that far—and indeed it was committed to protecting the lives and interests of British subjects, though not to supporting an independent raj. Nor did it want any other power to step in, especially as the South China Sea became more vulnerable with the establishment of the French in Indochina. The raja at times threatened to look for support elsewhere. Rather paradoxically this—with the assiduous support of friends in high places—produced a kind of recognition of the Brooke régime with the appointment of a British consul in Kuching in 1863.

The raja's successor, his nephew Charles Brooke, had fewer inhibitions about pushing Sarawak's expansion: he had none of the romantic commitment to the old sultanate which the old raja had never quite lost. Brunei itself was, furthermore, open to expansion. It was a realm built in part on regional and ethnic checks and balances: depleted by the advance of Sarawak, they were the more difficult to operate. But the British government was anxious to avoid a further extension of an anomalous raj, and invoked the treaty of 1847 against the new raja's purported acquisition of the Baram in 1868. The weakness of Brunei, however, made this negative kind of intervention policy difficult to sustain. Other powers after all might intervene in defiance of the treaty of 1847. Indeed some United States adventurers secured concessions from the sultanate. That was, however, made to provide a way forward for the British. New concessions led to the founding of the British North Borneo Company, and the British government, seeking a more effectual way of excluding others without directly confronting them, and providing for law and order while limiting its own responsibility, gave the Company a charter in 1881. Brunei was thus smaller still. The British government envisaged its disappearance. The protectorate agreements made in 1888 with all three states, Sarawak, North Borneo (Sabah) and Brunei, were not designed to prevent this. They would prevent others intervening in the interim and damaging a safe and orderly partition.

Though further diminished, Brunei did not disappear from the map. That was partly a result of British decisions, partly of Brunei's. Resentful over the chartering of the Company, Raja Charles pressed ahead, but his acquisition of Limbang in 1890 helped Sultan Hashim of Brunei consolidate opposition to further cessions, and to some extent his policy of playing off raj and Company succeeded. But he would not have won the last respite for Brunei without a shift on the part of the British. From the late 1870s some officials in the Colonial Office had come to think that a more regular exertion of British authority was required in Borneo. At first they considered it could be achieved through the raj, and were critical of the creation of the Company, another anomalous régime. In the 1890s a new prospect seemed to open up: the creation in Borneo of a political system along the lines of that developed on the Malay peninsula. The appointment of a British Resident in Brunei was intended to be the first step. In a sense the British would be replacing one set of anomalies by another: a federation of indirectly-ruled territories. They did not succeed, but created a further anomaly. There were now three régimes in northern Borneo, all in different senses British, each differently constituted, and they were not pushed together like the Federated Malay States. It was thus possible for the bifurcated remnant of Brunei to pursue a political destiny that differed from that of Sarawak and Sabah: oil was to make it more different still.

Among the Dutch, *onthouding* had prevailed in the 1830s: in 1838 senior officials in Borneo were forbidden to set foot outside the immediate area of their Residencies. The activities of Brooke, and of another British adventurer, Erskine Murray, at Kutai, prompted a change of policy. 'Borneo has become the *point de mire* [focus] of all kinds of speculative enterprises', J. C. Baud lamented.[17] The Dutch not only protested but sought to affirm their position in Borneo as elsewhere. 'He who is sparing at seedtime cannot expect to reap a rich harvest.'[18] A number of treaties were made with states on the east coast, and a 'Government of Borneo' was set up in 1846 as a gesture against foreign intervention. The British North Borneo Company was also unwelcome to the Dutch, though they finally assented to an agreement in 1891 designed to settle the frontier between the territories they claimed and the three protectorates the British had now established. The Company venture had also precipitated a delimitation involving the Spaniards and the sultanate of Sulu.

SULU AND THE PHILIPPINES

Spain, with whom Sulu so often clashed, had by the late eighteenth century become a minor power, the presence of which generally caused the British no concern, and the friendship of which was desirable in Europe. The Spanish claim to empire in the Philippines was respected, all the more because like the Dutch—indeed perhaps more readily since their empire was based on different principles—they allowed the British real commercial opportunities. Only in Sulu were the British for a while mildly tempted to uphold indigenous independence from Spain. In the end, however, the choice the powers agreed upon was partition. The intervention of new powers prompted a delimitation and rounding-out of the older Spanish, British and Dutch empires in that region as elsewhere. The fate of

[17] Quoted G. Irwin, *Nineteenth-century Borneo*, The Hague, 1955, 155.
[18] Rochussen's words are quoted in ibid., 156.

Sulu was thus in part determined, not only by the policies of the British, but of those who ruled the Philippines, the Spaniards, and, from 1898, the Americans, who later shared power with nationalists mostly from Luzon and the Visayas.

Britain's relations with the Spaniards in the Philippines bore some comparison to its relations with the Dutch in Indonesia. By the late eighteenth century, Spain was no longer in itself a threat, but it could be a prey or an asset to Britain's rivals, the French. In the Seven Years' War (1756–63), the British took Manila. But it was not retained. It was important, if possible, to restore good relations with Spain in Europe, and Britain's policy overseas had to take that into account. The lesson was not lost on the Spaniards, however. It reinforced the dictates of Enlightened Despotism: if they were to retain their territories, they must rule them more efficiently. They must also develop them, and even open them up to foreign commerce. This would include the trade of the British and that of others, too, partly as a balance against the British, but one of which they could not complain.

Though with them there were no British treaties like that of 1824, the Spaniards, like the Dutch, both opened up commerce and consolidated their territorial control. Manila was formally opened in 1834, but had in effect been opened earlier; other ports followed in 1855, and without, for most of the century, effective Spanish competition, British merchants indeed did especially well, exporting rice from Luzon, then turning the Visayas to sugar. The development of the export trade indeed stimulated the development of a primarily mestizo monied élite. Some Spaniards saw the contradictions in their policy. The very steps taken to assure Spain's role were promoting new challenges to it. The colony, Sinibaldo de Mas predicted, would 'emancipate itself violently with the loss of considerable property and many lives'.[19]

The consolidation of Spanish control meanwhile proceeded with some effect. Military-political governments were extended in the mountainous interior of Luzon and by the introduction of steamers the Visayas were protected from the slave-raiding depredations to which they had been desperately exposed. But the southern islands, the source of many of the attackers, were not effectively brought under control. The footholds on Mindanao were indeed extended and the ancient sultanate of Magindanao virtually eliminated. In the Sulu archipelago, however, the position was different.

There, as in some parts of Indonesia, the position was a tripartite one: the British were involved, and they did not, as in the north, squarely back the Spaniards. Indeed, the Spaniards, apprehensive of them, were driven to a mixture of assertions of control over the inhabitants and diplomatic concessions to foreign powers. Their assertions of control failed to establish a firm position for them in the Sulu sultanate. There was a legacy of hostility between the missionary power and the Islamic sultanate, and the Spaniards had no Dutch-style success with an inveigling network of treaty

---

[19] Extract in E. H. Blair and J. A. Robertson, eds, *The Philippine Islands*, Cleveland, 1903–9, LII, 89.

relationships with what was in any case a segmented state. Treaties were made, but distrust on both sides reduced their effect. Convulsive military incursions were neither supportive nor in themselves decisive. Furthermore, the Sulus were able to engage in relations with other powers, including the British, uninhibited by the formality of a treaty like that of 1824. Even when the British, and indeed other powers, finally abandoned the Sulus to their fate, the Spaniards did not secure effective control.

At the outset of the period, some British authorities had been interested in limiting Spanish control in the Moro lands and in establishing themselves there. Before the conquest of Manila, Alexander Dalrymple, an emissary of the Madras government of the East India Company, obtained the cession of Balambangan, and after the return of Manila the Company determined, after much hesitation, to occupy the island as a base for trade in Southeast Asia. The settlement came to an early end in 1775, attacked by Sulus who were possibly encouraged by Spanish intrigues. It was reoccupied temporarily during the Napoleonic Wars, and Raffles was also interested in the area, in particular in Marudu Bay in northern Borneo. It was again this area that initially attracted James Brooke's attention and, even though he was to concentrate on Sarawak and Brunei, he did not forget the north. In 1849, as commissioner, he visited Sulu, and made a treaty with the sultan along the lines of that he had recently made with Brunei. Spain protested. The British government did not ratify the treaty. They were affected by criticism of Brooke, as elsewhere; they also wished to avoid offending Spain because of its European significance. Spain had indeed pointed out that France had desisted from a challenge in Basilan.

The Brooke venture precipitated a new Spanish expedition to Sulu, but no regular establishment of Spanish control. Piracy, the penetration of Islamic revivalism, the threat of other powers—in particular the evidence of German interest—all prompted the Spaniards to further and unprecedentedly violent action in Sulu in the 1870s. It was in this crisis for the sultanate that the North Borneo concessionaires secured a *pajak* or lease of the possessions the sultan claimed there, and the Chartered Company was seen as ruling initially in the names of the sultans of Brunei and Sulu. The partition was taken further in 1885 by agreement among the European powers. The Spaniards undertook not to support the Sultan of Sulu's claims over northern Borneo. Though critical of Spain's anti-Islamic violence, the British abandoned their half-hearted attempts to sustain the independence of the sultan, already partly compromised in a protocol of 1877. The Anglo-Spanish deal was the more readily made because of the interest of the Germans in the area. They had protested against Spain's violence, but insisted they wanted only guarantees of commercial access. The British went along with this so as to secure such guarantees, but also to prevent more extensive German action. The effect was, however, to spur Spain to greater, though still unsuccessful, efforts to establish effective control. Dalrymple, Brooke and others had talked of sustaining a neutral Sulu, but partition and partial absorption had ensued, substantially because the British had not been prepared to challenge the Spaniards, and had preferred them to the Germans.

The British were interested, too, in the outcome of the Spanish-

American War in the Philippines (1898). As the Spaniards had feared, internal opposition had coincided with foreign intervention, as it had to a degree at the time of the British occupation of Manila in the 1760s. It was not British intervention this time, but American. There was little chance of effectively resisting it. Nor indeed, their predominance damaged, could the British interpose. Their preferred solution was the continuation of Spanish control. If that were impossible, then in their view American control was preferable to German. In the event the Germans were left with the Carolines and Pellews, the Americans with the Philippines. But in Luzon they had to contend with the nationalist opposition, brought under control by a mixture of violence and co-option. In the Moro lands the Americans initially made a new treaty with the Sultan of Sulu, only later proceeding to assertion of direct control—in fact again applying a great deal of violence and leaving the sultan with a nominal religious authority. The nationalist government of Quezon refused to recognize a successor on Sultan Jamal-ul-Kiram's death in 1936, and the sultanate thus ceased to exist, except in respect of a claim to North Borneo. But its lands were not fully integrated into the Philippines. In the 1920s there had been talk of separating them and a Briton had dreamed of a Federated Sulu States Union, in some sense a new version of older neutrality proposals, but equally 'visionary'.[20]

The Germans had assented to the Sulu deal of the 1880s reluctantly. That was the period of Bismarck's colonial ventures and of the Berlin conference, contributing to Britain's establishment of the protectorates in Borneo, in turn leading to the settlement of the Borneo frontier with the Dutch in 1891. German activity also helped to define another frontier. Bismarck's colonial policy had launched Germany into New Guinea. Its demonstration of interest precipitated the Queensland annexation of the southeastern coast and the hoisting of the British flag at Port Moresby late in 1884; a settlement with the Germans followed in 1885. The Dutch had claimed the western side of the territory, in part as appanage of the sultanate of Tidore, and in 1828, apprehensive of British moves in northern Australia, had made a settlement at Triton Bay. In the late 1840s, again apprehensive of the British, they had arrogated rights over the interior. In 1895 they reached a boundary agreement with the British, and the Germans also accepted a boundary line at 141 degrees east. What became yet another post-colonial frontier was established by agreement among colonial powers. In 1902 the Dutch established a post at Merauke, designed to restrain the raids of the Tugeri tribes into their territory. The realm now extended, as the nationalists were to say, from Sabang to Merauke.

BRITISH MALAYA

Some suspicion of German intentions, more certainly a wish to take precautionary steps against foreign intervention, played a part in Britain's

[20] N. Tarling, *Sulu and Sabah*, Kuala Lumpur, 1978, 323–4.

policy towards the Malay peninsula. There the arrangement with the Dutch in 1824 contrived to exclude them from a territory with which they, like previous archipelagic powers, had long been concerned. But if the fortunes of archipelago and peninsula were thus unprecedentedly separated, that did not mean that British rule was necessarily to be established on the peninsula, nor did it prescribe the form such rule might take if it were. British interests could be sufficiently met for a time at least without it: with Penang, acquired in 1786, Melaka, finally transferred in 1824, and Singapore, occuped in 1819, Britain commanded the straits. It had no great economic interest in the interior until the development of a new demand for tin from the 1840s and for rubber at the turn of the century. Nor for some decades was there any risk of intervention by other European powers, which the presence of the British in the Straits Settlements tended to ward off anyway.

There was, however, a sense in which, as with the archipelago, the political situation was a tripartite one: it involved the British, the Malay states, and in this case not another European state, but an Asian one, Siam. Britain's intervention in the peninsula was partly defined by its perception of its relations with Siam and by the policies that Siam itself followed in the increasingly colonial world of the nineteenth century. The effect was initially to contribute further to the removal of the Malay states from the international ambit, but ultimately to produce a partition that, however inappropriate in terms of history or ethnicity, was to form the frontier of a post-colonial state. In a sense indeed the situation was more than tripartite. Siam was seen, and saw itself, in a larger international context: first that of the old Chinese-dominated system of international relations, second that of the new imperialist one. The outcome on the Malay peninsula is not fully explained, therefore, without an exploration of Siam's position.

Nor is it fully explained without recognizing that, though the British avoided formal intervention in the peninsula till the 1870s, and in the case of a majority of states till later still, they did intervene in a number of other less formal ways. Not only did their presence in the Straits Settlements help to insulate the peninsular states from contact with other European powers. Local merchants, local officials, local Chinese interests, Malay aristocrats and rulers themselves, tied the Straits Settlements and some of the states together, and helped to determine the form and scope of intervention and the pace of its arrival. The British-influenced Malay sultanates that provided the framework of twentieth-century Malaya were shaped in the nineteenth century.

In the French Wars, the settlement of the Dutch at Melaka had been taken over, and their prospective return under the convention of 1814 had stimulated the interest of the British East India Company's authorities at Penang in the fate of the neighbouring states: the Dutch might seek to re-establish a monopoly of the tin from Perak and Selangor. But the Thais were another factor. For them Kedah had a strategic importance, in view of their long struggles with Burma; and both the assertiveness of a new dynasty, and the ambitions of its southern viceroy at Nakhon Sithammarat (Ligor), encouraged them to extend their tributary relationship even beyond it. The rulers of Kedah had hoped to secure the support of the English, to whom Penang and later Province Wellesley, a strip of mainland territory, had been ceded, but in vain. In 1816 the Sultan of Kedah, as a Siamese vassal, had been instructed to invade Perak to secure tribute, and he refused to approve the cession to the Company of Pangkor, suggested by John Anderson, an official at Penang, as a depot for the tin trade of that settlement.

In 1821 the Thais themselves invaded Kedah. Some officials in Penang advocated intervention against them.

> We have become a preponderating power on this side of India and we ought to hold in our hands the scales of justice, to protect the weaker power against the usurpations of the stronger, to mediate between them all on every occasion when our interference can be effectual, and even at times to exhibit a tone of superiority to check the extravagant pretensions of the different states.[21]

Anderson himself suggested appointing a Resident in Kedah on the model of the Indian subsidiary alliances. But the government in India, then the immediate superior of the Straits authorities, refused to countenance on the peninsula the kind of policy it adopted on the subcontinent, or the kind of political structure it utilized, though Governor Robert Fullerton now argued that the removal of the Dutch from Melaka under the treaty of 1824 would simply open the way more fully to the Thais.

The war between the Company and Burma led, however, to negotiations between the British and the Thais at Bangkok. Before they began, Anderson was sent to Perak and Selangor, and the sultan of the former offered him Pangkor. At Bangkok, however, the negotiator, Henry Burney, secured less than the Penang authorities wanted. Pattani, which the Thais had overrun, was not brought into the discussions, though the Thais did agree not to obstruct the commerce of Kelantan and Terengganu, which they also claimed, and in effect a kind of frontier was thus delimited. The Sultan of Kedah, whom they had displaced, was not restored, but the Sultan of Perak was left himself to decide whether he would send tribute to Siam or not. A further emissary from Penang, James Low, persuaded him not to do so, and secured the cession of Pangkor. But this agreement was disapproved in Calcutta, as was a subsequent naval-military action, directed against pirates on the Perak coast but also designed to assist the ruler. The prime task, the Governor-General in Council insisted, was to sustain good relations with Siam, now based on the Burney treaty of 1826.

In subsequent years, nevertheless, the straits authorities managed still to intervene in the Malay states. They could do this only by indirect means, and their efforts tended in effect to preserve the states by working on and through them. In fact they enhanced the power of at least some of the rulers, who reacted positively to the changes that were taking place and the approaches that were made. In general the process made it more likely that the future association between the British and the peninsula

[21] Minute by Clubley, 16 Sept. 1823, Straits Settlements Factory Records G/34/91, India Office Library.

would centre on relationships with the Malay rulers. But these relationships, as they developed, differed from state to state.

In the Burney treaty, the British had not only failed to secure the
restoration of the Sultan of Kedah, but had committed themselves to
keeping him away from the vicinity of the sultanate. This they did not
achieve, but the local authorities co-operated with the Thais in dealing
with two 'piratical' descents on the Thai-ruled sultanate that his followers
organized in 1831 and 1838. These attacks helped to persuade the Thais to
change their policy, and the attitude of the British made it easier for them
to accept Governor Bonham's mediation that led to the sultan's restoration
as a Thai vassal. 'England is a great nation', Rama III (r. 1824–53) declared.
'We have made a treaty with her. She has shown herself to possess enough
moral obligations, and is unlikely to undertake any uncalled-for measure.'[22] Kedah thus came to represent the tripartite sharing of authority in
its own way: Thai supremacy, Malay rule, British influence. In Kelantan
and Terengganu, Burney had avoided definitely recognizing Thai
supremacy. The British tried to fend off its effective implementation by
naval deployment ostensibly against pirates in the early 1830s, but they
exerted less influence than in Kedah.

In Johor they exerted more. Ibrahim, the ruler, lived on Singapore
island. He also saw the advantages in an association with British
commerce and influence. He worked with the merchants in developing the
state and with the authorities against piracy. Indeed he persuaded his
neighbour, the ruler of Pahang, also to work against piracy and the slave
trade. From this time, in fact, the rulers of peninsular Johor, though seen
as parvenus by other Malay rulers, had a special association with the
British. Indirectly, however, it provoked another clash with the Thais and
a readjustment of the tripartite relationship.

The association between the British and Ibrahim of Johor was in some
degree self-defeating as a means of extending peace and order on the
peninsula. Other rulers were jealous of his special position. The heir to
the old sultanate of Johor, recognized by Raffles in order to confirm the
occupation of Singapore, had to be bought off in the treaty of 1855. More
significant, the ruler of Terengganu, Omar (r. 1839–76), anxious to develop
his own connexion with the British, resented their focus on Ibrahim.
Governor E. A. Blundell wanted to respond. He solicited the Indian
government's sanction for 'occasional visits to the independent Rajas
around us, thereby establishing a more friendly intercourse and removing
any misapprehension or obstacles that may exist. Such visits should be
wholly devoid of any political aspect, and be merely paid as the marks of
amity and friendship.'[23] He suggested also that Sultan Omar should send
some of his sons to be educated at Singapore, where the Rev. B. P.
Keasberry had established in his boarding school a separate school of
noblemen, to which the rulers of Kedah and Johor were sending their
scions.

---

[22] Quoted Kobkua Suwannathat-Pian, *Thai-Malay Relations*, Singapore, 1988, 90.
[23] Blundell to Secretary, 27 May 1856, Board's Collections 189619, p.67, F/4/2692, India Office
Library.

Civil war in Pahang tested the policy, for Ibrahim and Omar intervened on opposing sides. Blundell's successor, Cavenagh, initially criticized Ibrahim, then backed him. Omar, previously apprehensive of the Thais, changed his attitude. Cavenagh authorized a naval bombardment of Terengganu in November 1862. It was this that helped to produce a new arrangement on the peninsula, though not the one that the governor had sought. Despite the bombardment, Ibrahim's opponents were victorious in Pahang, partly through invoking the support of the ex-sultan of Lingga, descendant of the rulers of the old Johor empire, and he finally accepted a revised frontier between that state and his own. Because of the bombardment, the British accepted the Thai claim to supremacy in Terengganu that they had earlier avoided explicitly acknowledging. The Thais had protested, and the British government listened. Moreover, the Colonial Office, responsible for the Straits Settlements after 1867, ignored the legacy of its predecessors, the Company and the India Office; its governor, Harry Ord, found it convenient to work through the Thais. Though Omar had tried to imitate Ibraham—who opened a direct contact with London in 1866—the northern states were now seen as part of the patrimony of Siam, where indeed by this time the British government had formal representation. The settled condition of Kedah, Terengganu and Kelantan was, Ord even inferred, largely the result of the Thai supremacy.

The violence of 1862, followed by the shift to Colonial Office authority, thus led to a break in the traditional attitude to the northeastern states over which Siam claimed supremacy, and indeed to a misinterpretation of the sequence of events that had created contemporary conditions in those states. This change of attitude did not, however, destroy what previous history had brought about. The northern states had been preserved from Siamese occupation and their rulers had a place in the pattern of Anglo-Thai relations. The ultimate transfer of Siamese rights to the British and the advisory position they assumed in the early twentieth century were thus prepared in the days of the Company and India Office governors. Though arrangements and attitudes changed in the 1860s, that did not obscure the long-term connexion of British and Malay rulers that ultimately prevailed south of the Pattani line that Burney had seen as the limit of negotiation.

Whatever the source of the orderliness of the northern states, it meant Ord was more concerned with Perak and Selangor. Those states had less effective structures and less effective rulers, and the instructions of the superior authorities had prevented intervention on the scale required for dealing with the issues raised by the expansion of tin-mining and Chinese immigration from the 1840s. Cavenagh had contrived to intervene in Perak in 1862 on the basis of the Anderson treaty of 1825, but, though he pressed for increased powers, he could not obtain them from his superiors. Nor could Ord. Only in 1873 did the Colonial Office authorize his successor, Sir Andrew Clarke, to consider intervention in the west-coast states.

The motives of the Colonial Office no doubt included its concern for order, the precondition for trade. Still more, it was concerned over the possibility of foreign intervention, which would undermine the strategic control of the straits that had been one of the main achievements of 1824.

Foreign intervention was perhaps unlikely, given the appearance of British predominance; private interests, benefiting from the very absence of foreign competition, may have exaggerated the risk. Evidence of actual interest in the region on the part of other Europeans is also lacking. There had been rumours back in 1870 that the North German Confederation was seeking a naval station in the Pangkor area; but they were apparently no more than rumours and were not taken seriously. Possibly no definite evidence is needed: the changes in Europe, in particular the creation of the Second Reich (1871), may have aroused apprehensions, or at least suggested a need to take precautions; and that may suffice for motivation in a world that was clearly changing and in which old certainties were being undermined. The concern expressed by Lord Kimberley (previously Lord Wodehouse) over the German presence in Sulu from the early 1870s may, however, have made him more conscious of a need for precaution on the peninsula.

That the Colonial Secretary saw a connexion between events in the Sulu region and events in the peninsula region is again suggested by his attitude to the chartering of the North Borneo Company. A principal aim was to keep North Borneo free of other powers. One possible occupant was Germany and one major objection was its newly-adopted tariff structure. The other issue was security. 'She is not a weak state like the Netherlands whom we can easily influence, and her presence near the Malay Peninsula might seriously weaken and embarrass our position by unsettling the minds of the natives.'[24] 'The Germans would be a too powerful neighbour, and their presence in Borneo would exercise a disturbing influence in the Malay Peninsula.'[25] The security of British interests in the two regions Kimberley saw as indivisible. If these were arguments about Borneo, they were also arguments about the peninsula. In a number of states, however, intervention did not seem to be required at least for the time being: Johor, for example, and the 'Siamese' states, too, though partly because of the concern to sustain Siam's own independence, which others might undermine if Britain showed the way.

Intervention thus was limited in geographical scope: the British went only as far as they needed. It was also limited in form. The Pangkor engagement of 1874 involved the appointment of Residents, who would give advice which the rulers had to take on all matters except religion and custom. The notion had been present with Anderson in the 1820s and had an Indian background. But what was surely in official minds was the example of Johor, the ruler of which seemed readily to accept more informal advice. In fact the experience and conditions of the west-coast states were different, and the assumption that it would be sufficient to give advice albeit on a more formal basis proved mistaken. The murder of the first Resident in Perak, J. W. W. Birch, prompted, however, a punitive expedition. Paradoxically this contributed to the maintenance of the tradition of advice and guidance. The Colonial Office, especially Lord

---

[24] Memorandum by Kimberley, 13 July 1880, FO 12/55; CO 144/54 [10768], Public Record Office, London.
[25] Memorandum, 22 Oct. 1880, PRO 30/29/143, Public Record Office, London.

Carnarvon, blamed the crisis not upon its own or Clarke's mistakes, but on his successor Jervois's advocacy of annexation, and refused to admit that its original conception of Residents was inadequate. The Perak War was in itself an education: it meant that advice would be accepted, and that the idea could be upheld since it was not the practice. So, again, a tradition built up before 1867 remained part of the pattern of twentieth-century Malaya. The installation of a Resident with long experience of Brunei perhaps also contributed to the success of the system, and it was applied to Pahang in 1888, against the background of increasing activity by European powers in Southeast Asia as a whole and by European concessionaires in Pahang in particular. There, however, it produced tension and disturbance. This helped to lead in 1895 to the creation of the Federated Malay States. Although some saw this as a model for Borneo, in fact it created a central government that made the concept of advice ever more myth than reality. When in 1909 Siam transferred its rights over the northern states, they accepted Advisers not Residents, indeed only with reluctance, and did not enter the so-called federation.

BRITAIN AND BURMA

Britain's policy towards Malaya had been affected by its interests in India and China. The former affected its attitude to Burma more deeply, but it was also shaped by the attitude of the Burman monarchs. There were issues relating to trade, and more serious issues relating to possible foreign intervention: but the respective attitudes to interstate relations perhaps presented a greater difficulty even than the latter. The British built a territorial raj in India, which had its own imperatives for foreign policy, differing indeed from those of Britain itself. Within India it could contemplate no challenge; on its frontiers it insisted on compliance. The attitude of the Burmans—particularly in view of the successes of the Alaungpaya dynasty—was too assertive to fit into such a pattern. These differences lay behind the conflicts that marked the course of Anglo-Burman relations. The result was the stage-by-stage annexation of the kingdom to the Indian empire. For a while it had seemed possible that the independence of the core of the old kingdom could have been preserved. But even Mindon Min (r. 1853–78) was reluctant to accept the degree of subordination paradoxically required, and his successor's government, less wise, coincided with a period of general international insecurity and a phase of particular French expansiveness that encouraged the British to take precautionary measures.

British contacts with Burma had been limited by the Dutch in the days of their predominance in seaward Asia. Then they were affected by the eighteenth-century rivalry with the French on the continent of India. The creation of a British dominion in India was greatly to affect British relations with the kingdom that Alaungpaya was recreating and that defeated the Mon revolt of the 1740s. The French threat again precipitated action. From bases in southern Burma they might affect the security of British India. Their settlement at Syriam prompted the British to settle at

Negrais. The opposition of Alaungpaya (r. 1752–60) to both, and the destruction of French power in India, virtually ended the British contacts; though the French were to use bases at Mergui and Rangoon in the next war, the British had few relations with Burma in the subsequent years. But while their power extended in India, the Burman kings, after sacking Ayutthaya, conquered Arakan, and this brought the two empires in contact again. The questions that now arose, difficult in themselves, were more intractable because of the political attitudes fostered in the interim.

One issue indeed arose from the conquest of Arakan itself. Refugees fled into British territory: the British were reluctant to return them, but unable to prevent their using British territory as a base for counter-attacks on the Burmans. A new war with the French led the governor-general to try to improve relations with the Burman court by sending Michael Symes on a mission to King Bodawpaya (r. 1782–1819). He was told that Burma could not deal with a subordinate government like Bengal, and warned the Company's authorities there of the 'characteristic pride and unbounded arrogance' of the Burmans, which might lead to further acts of aggression: they had 'an extravagant opinion of their own power', respecting British power less than the powers of the subcontinent itself. Symes thought that the British should make 'reasonable allowance for their mistaken principles', preserving a good understanding, but avoiding a close connexion: 'it is to our interest to maintain their independence, and to guard it from foreign encroachment.'[26] On the advice of William Francklin, Governor-General Wellesley subsequently considered making a 'subsidiary alliance' with Burma on the Indian model, and Symes was sent on a second mission. It was entirely vain. The Burmans were proud of their success, though also suspicious of British designs: they sought to evade a connection with the British, and with Bengal.

The British were anxious to check French influence. Continued Burman independence might be a sufficient guarantee against it, insulating their empire in India from direct contact with foreign powers. But they really wanted more. The British needed, as Symes had put it even on his first visit, to guard that independence. Further, they could not accept a challenge from the Burmans themselves that might by example undermine subsidiary relations on the subcontinent itself. The Burmans could retain their view of the world only in a kind of isolation that could no longer exist: even a distanced relationship of the kind Symes had at first envisaged was now outdated. Could a new balance be attained, given the very different concepts the two states had of their proper relationship? A subsequent British-Indian emissary, John Canning, reported that the king was not partial to the French: at most they were seen as a counterpoise to the English. In any case the French were soon to be defeated again. The other Burman perception remained. 'It seems that [the king] will treat with no power on earth as an equal ... He will grant a boon but will not make a treaty.'[27] 'It might contribute to the future tranquillity of our eastern territory', the Governor-General in Council ominously commented in

---

[26] M. Symes, *An Account of an Embassy to the Kingdom of Ava*, London, 1800, 463–4.
[27] Quoted D. G. E. Hall, *Europe and Burma*, London, 1945, 96.

1812, if the Burman government were 'led to form a just estimate of the greatness of our power and the weakness of its own'.[28]

Though the issue of the Arakanese refugees died away, additional frontier issues emerged in Assam, Manipur, Cachar, and in March 1824 Governor-General Amherst pre-empted a talked-of Burman invasion by declaring war on Burma. He echoed the attitude earlier assumed in Calcutta: 'no permanent security from the aggression of the Burmese ... can be safely calculated on, until that people shall have been made to feel the consequences of their provoking the British Government to depart from the pacific tone of policy it has hitherto pursued.'[29] The essential aim of the war was not to acquire territory, but 'to produce such an impression of the power and resources of the British Empire in India as will deter the Court of Ava from any attempt again to disturb the friendly relations which may be re-established by the result of the present contest'.[30] Amherst sought a balance: 'The Burmese had to be punished sufficiently so that they would not trouble British security again, and yet not so much as to turn them into a permanent and unreasoning foe who would be persistently troublesome in the future.'[31]

An initially ill-conducted campaign produced no immediate victory. The terms of peace were as a result stepped up to ensure tangible proofs of British success: otherwise 'the powers of India might have been tempted to believe the British Government had at last encountered an enemy which it had failed to humble'.[32] The First Anglo-Burman War ended with the treaty of Yandabo, finally secured in 1826, in which the Burmans ceded Arakan, Assam and Tenasserim, and agreed to cease interference in Manipur and Cachar. They also agreed to pay an indemnity, to receive a Resident at Ava, to send an ambassador to Calcutta. The British thus insulated their empire on the subcontinent from both foreign challenge and native insolence by acquiring much of the Burma coast. But this was hardly consistent with a friendly relationship with the rest of Burma unless, as Amherst had envisaged, the Burmans accepted the other implications of their defeat. In fact the old attitude remained.

Sent to follow up with a commercial treaty, John Crawfurd recommended against appointing a Resident: he would be an object of jealousy to a government 'indescribably ignorant and suspicious'.[33] Better, again, a stand-off, since the alternative was not compliance but conflict; better a distancing in which the Burmans could indulge their fancies. Disputes along the new frontiers led the Company, however, to revise Crawfurd's policy—perhaps conflict, arising anyway, could be thus avoided—and Burney was sent to Ava in 1830. The Manipur boundary was settled in

[28] Quoted G. P. Ramachandra, 'Anglo-Burmese Relations, 1795–1826', Ph.D. thesis, University of Hull, 1977, 279.

[29] Quoted G. P. Ramachandra, 'The Outbreak of the first Anglo-Burmese War', JMBRAS, 51, 2 (1978) 82.

[30] Quoted Ramachandra, 'Anglo-Burmese Relations', 391.

[31] L. Kitzan, 'Lord Amherst and Pegu: The Annexation Issue, 1824–1826', JSEAS, 8, 2 (1977) 182.

[32] Quoted Ramachandra, 'Anglo-Burmese Relations', 433.

[33] Quoted W. S. Desai, History of the British Residency in Burma 1826–1840, Rangoon, 1939, 50.

Burma's favour, though the indemnity remained. But, albeit Burney was able to establish good relations, King Bagyidaw remained 'full of the most ungovernable pride and arrogance . . . most unwilling to admit the British Government as equal to his in pride and strength'. For him the presence of a Resident was 'a proof of our supremacy and a badge of his servility and vassalage'.[34] In a sense he was right: he did not wish to be reminded of it.

Unrealistic in a different way, the king's successor, Tharrawaddy (r. 1838–46), refused to bind himself to his predecessor's treaties. 'I am determined to place the relations between the two countries on precisely the same footing as they were previous to the reign of the late King who committed a blunder in going to war with you, and all of those acts I wish to have annulled and forgotten.'[35] Burney finally left the capital. He thought the king should be made to acknowledge the treaty and the authority of the governor-general, if need be by force, the British taking the opportunity 'of establishing a more extensive influence and control over the Court of Ava, and of placing our relations with this country on a more solid and secure footing'.[36] Burney's successor Benson also advocated force. Lord Auckland, the governor-general, opposed its use. The British had 'to make allowances for the prejudices and the headstrong pride of a new dynasty clinging in its intercourse with foreign nations to the distasteful usages of former times and vaunting its resolution to revert to them'.[37] Moreover, the British had greater problems on the northwest frontier. Auckland's concern with Afghanistan in fact led the Indian government to leave Anglo-Burman relations once more on a stand-off basis.

Complete isolation was not possible, however: there were trade as well as frontier contacts, and it was always possible that the escalation of a dispute would again open up the question of Anglo-Burman relations, laid to uneasy rest by the Afghan war. The Second Anglo-Burman War indeed emerged from a conflict between British traders and the Burman governor at Rangoon, over which the Bengal authorities acted firmly and a combustible commodore highhandedly. The war was the subject of Richard Cobden's critical pamphlet, 'How Wars are Got up in India'. But the governor-general, Lord Dalhousie, though annexationist in India, was perhaps less the aggressive empire-builder in Burma than the defender of British prestige on the subcontinent, which encouraged a concept of policy that differed from that of the commercial and manufacturing interests at home: 'the Government of India could never, consistently with its own safety, permit itself to stand for a single day in an attitude of inferiority towards a native power, and least of all towards the Court of Ava.' 'We can't afford to be shown to the door anywhere in the East.'[38] The second war was far more efficiently conducted than the first. But what was to represent the British victory this time? Dalhousie believed that the retention of Pegu, though ruled out at the end of the first war, was now 'the

[34] Quoted Desai, 71, 196.
[35] Quoted Desai, 296.
[36] Quoted Desai, 309.
[37] Quoted Desai, 390.
[38] Quoted D. G. E. Hall, ed., *The Dalhousie-Phayre Correspondence 1852–1856*, London, 1932, pp. xviii, xix.

only adequate measure for the punishment of the Burmese, for the reimbursement of expenses, and for ensuring future peace by crippling Burman power'.[39] The authorities in London wanted an Anglo-Burman treaty as well. That, however, Dalhousie thought would be superfluous: indeed it would invite further quarrels. The Burmans would, moreover, not readily sign it without a further advance to their capital, possibly involving the occupation of all Burma, which would be difficult and expensive.

Dalhousie's policy was in the event followed: the new king of Burma would in any case sign no treaty. The governor-general clearly implied that, while occupying the rest of Burma would be a burden for the British, it would not be necessary, since the reduced kingdom was likely to be compliant. Though signing no treaty, Mindon Min indeed sought to develop good relations with the British. Complimentary missions were exchanged in 1854–5 between the Burman capital and Calcutta, and new commercial treaties made in 1861 and 1867, so that steamers ran up the Irrawaddy and gained British trade back-door access to China. Mindon Min also engaged in measures of 'defensive westernisation'.[40] In themselves, those need not worry the British. More risky was his decision to develop relations with other powers. The mission to the United States of 1857 resulted in no treaty. The mission to Europe in 1872–3 led to a commercial treaty with France, though the French did not at first ratify it because of British concern over Mindon's desire for arms and for an offensive-defensive alliance. There were overtures to Russia in 1874. Mindon was asserting the status of Burma as an independent power. But he risked losing what remained of it: the British could contemplate only less than full independence for Burma and that the Burmans had to accept, if not formally recognize, if they were not to lose all.

Relations also deteriorated because of the 'shoe question'. Generally, British envoys had removed their shoes before a royal reception. Once an envoy made an issue of it in 1875, however, the British could not continue the practice. While from 1862 the British had a Resident at Mandalay, Mindon's capital, there was as a result less opportunity for him to resolve issues after 1875. In 1879 the Resident was withdrawn after the murder of Sir L. Cavagnari in Kabul. The way was more open than ever to court intriguers; open, too, to the increasing number of European adventurers and concessionaires that were penetrating into still independent parts of Southeast Asia.

The new king, Thibaw Min (r. 1878–85), missed perhaps the best opportunity of putting Anglo-Burman relations back on a satisfactory basis. Lord Ripon proposed a commercial treaty between India and Burma and a friendship treaty between Queen Victoria and Thibaw, which would at least meet the Burman desire for a connection with London, such as Mindon Min had pointed out Siam enjoyed. The opportunity was lost:

[39] Quoted ibid., p. xxv.
[40] Oliver B. Pollak, *Empires in Collision: Anglo-Burmese Relations in the mid-nineteenth century*, Westport, 1979, 113–14.

those at Mandalay opposed to improving Anglo-Burman relations, and so bringing back the Resident, pointed to the challenge that Britain was facing in Egypt as a reason for going no further. Adding rashness to unwisdom, the Burmans sent a mission to Europe, and its negotiations in France aroused British suspicions. The 1873 treaty with France was ratified. There was a supplementary commercial convention which Jules Ferry hoped Britain would interpret as a French 'desire to obtain something in independent upper Burma, where she was so jealous of her influence. This would make her more amenable to a trade-off which would enable us, should the occasion arise, to secure advantages in Siam, or at least a means of holding the British in check in the Malay peninsula.'[41]

Moreover, in January 1885 Ferry gave the Burman ambassadors a secret letter, offering to make arrangements for arms supplies when Tonkin had been pacified by the French. The letter was made public later in the year through the efforts of Andreino, the Italian consul in Mandalay who, as agent for the Bombay-Burmah Timber Company and the Irrawaddy Flotilla Company, had his own reasons for wishing to undermine a French connexion. The British determined on an ultimatum. Lord Randolph Churchill declared:

> It is French intrigue which has forced us to go to Burmah; but for that element we might have treated Theebaw with severe neglect . . . If you finally and fully add Burmah to your dominions before any European rights have had time even to be sown, much less grow up, you undoubtedly prevent forever the assertion of such rights, or attempts to prepare the way for such assertion.[42]

The occasion for the ultimatum was a commercial dispute involving leases by the Bombay-Burmah Timber Company, but the main concern of the British authorities was strategic. There were French and Italian speculators and concessionaires in Mandalay, but it was the political rather than the commercial implications of their activities that aroused concern. Despite the arguments presented by the late D. P. Singhal, the clue to British policy is, as Hugh Tinker pointed out, provided by a later remark of Lord Curzon's:

> India is like a fortress . . . with mountains for her walls . . . beyond these walls . . . extends a glacis of varying breadth and dimension. We do not want to occupy it, but we cannot afford to see it occupied by our foes. We are quite content to let it remain in the hands of our allies and friends, but if rivals and unfriendly influences creep up to it . . . we are compelled to intervene.[43]

The Third Anglo-Burman War relates to 'imperialism', inasmuch as one factor in precipitating it was the growth of European political rivalry and concession-hunting. But it related more clearly to a long-standing Indian

---

[41] Statement by Francois Deloncle, 1897, quoted P. J. N. Tuck, *French Catholic Missionaries and the Politics of Imperialism in Vietnam, 1857–1914*, Liverpool, 1987, 233.
[42] Quoted G. Keeton, *King Thebaw and the Ecological Rape of Burma*, Delhi, 1974, 243.
[43] Quoted H. Tinker, reviewing D. P. Singhal, *The Annexation of Upper Burma*, JSEAH 1, 2 (1960) 106.

political concern than to a movement in British public opinion. Burma
must not challenge British prestige; still less must it be the scene of activity
by another power.

In the days of British predominance, Burma's position had been insecure,
since the rulers of India wanted it to assume a position of less than
complete independence: its failure to do so led to partition. The advent of
European rivals in the later nineteenth century gave Burma a temptation,
not an opportunity: attempts to play off other foreigners against the rulers
of India could bring only disaster. Ferry's scheme did nothing for France; it
led to the end of Burma's independence.

In the two-week Third Anglo-Burman War, the British-Indian forces
quickly occupied Mandalay, and King Thibaw was exiled. Lord Dufferin,
Viceroy of India, now faced the problem which Dalhousie had avoided.
His answer was annexation rather than protectorate. There was a vacuum
in Mandalay and it was essential to provide against European intrigue. The
Viceroy also thought annexation the best means of securing peace and
prosperity. But he was mistaken: a long programme of pacification had to
follow. Snodgrass, who fought in the First Anglo-Burman War, had
criticized those who had thought that the conquest of the capital 'would
have had a good effect upon the whole Eastern world'.[44] Dalhousie,
governor-general during the second war, thought the entire subjugation of
Burma would be 'most injurious to the interests of the British Government'.[45] The contrary view was that the Burmans awaited deliverance at
the hands of the British. Brigadier-General George White, accompanying
the expeditionary force in the third war, again recognized it was wrong. 'It
is a mistake to suppose that these people were anxiously awaiting annexation. The more I see and hear, the more convinced I am that they are very
loyal, in their easy-going way, to the house of Alompra.'[46] 'A considerable
minority of the population to say the least, did not want us', as Sir Charles
Crosthwaite put it.[47] Some resistance was led by real or pretended scions
of the house of Alaungpaya, some by local leaders, and the British could
not realistically see them as mere dacoits. There was reaction in lower
Burma, too.

The establishment of British control in the frontier areas was also a
prolonged process. The Shan rulers, for example, had paid tribute to the
Burman court, though its influence had declined in the closing years of the
dynasty. Their relationship with the new rulers had to be determined.
From the outset the general British policy was to allow them autonomy, 'so
long as they governed well, promoted trade, and paid a moderate tribute'.[48] Though there was some initial resistance, allegiance was secured on
this basis by April 1888. 'The position of the Shan princes was . . . like that
of a team of comparatively fine soccer players suddenly finding themselves
in an American football game.' Mandalay was now in very different hands.

[44] J. J. Snodgrass, *The Burmese War*, London, 1827, 284.
[45] Quoted Muhammad Shamsher Ali, 'The Beginnings of British Rule in Upper Burma', Ph.D.
    thesis, London University, 1976, 139.
[46] Quoted ibid., 41.
[47] Quoted M. Aung-Thwin, 'The British "Pacification of Burma"', JSEAS, 16, 2 (1985) 250.
[48] Quoted Ali, 179.

The British set about drawing boundaries, claiming or rejecting areas 'according to the needs of the moment . . . trotting out Burmese claims whenever it suited them, or ignoring such claims whenever necessary'.[49] The frontier itself had to be settled with the Chinese and the French. China regarded Burma as a tributary state, but the British were concerned to avoid a quarrel, and in a convention of July 1886 agreed to send ten-year missions on a basis of equality. The Chinese had in any case been in no position to act, and saw Britain as an ally against France. The Burman kings had damaged their chance of survival by their failure to comply with British requirements, but their prospects had also been dimmed by the advance of French power in Vietnam. That involved the Chinese, too, and indeed they went to war with France.

BRITAIN, FRANCE AND VIETNAM

The French had shown interest in Vietnam as the British began to exclude them from India. The divisions and civil war in Vietnam in the late eighteenth century seemed to give them opportunity. But, once Gia-long (r. 1802–19) had reunited the empire, he sought to diminish foreign contacts, even with the French, and his successors went further still, in particular in their endeavours to exclude Catholic missionaries. The opening of China brought French warships to the area: with little commerce to protect, but concerned for French prestige, they were disposed to protect Christians. In the conflicts that ensued, the British did not intervene. They had sent a number of diplomatic and commercial missions to Vietnam, both before and after the opening of China, but the response was negative, even though they had endeavoured to play down their aggressive Indian image. The British decided that the French venture was acceptable, so long as it did not trench upon the independence of Siam and Laos, and thus upon the security of their interests in Burma, India and Malaya.

Anglo-French rivalry was the context for European intervention in Vietnam, as in Burma, in the mid-eighteenth century. In their contest with the British, the French looked not only to the Mon regions of lower Burma but to the Nguyen lands. A French mission of 1748–51 sought from Vo-Vuong, the southern ruler, a factory in Danang Bay and a repeal of the ban on Christian missionaries. British success in India and China continued to invite French attention to Vietnam. Vergennes argued that the French should pre-empt the English in Cochinchina, as southern Vietnam was called:

> If they decide on that place before us, we will be excluded for ever and we will have lost an important foothold on that part of Asia which would make us masters by intercepting in time of war the English trade with China, by protecting our own in the whole of India, and by keeping the English in a continual state of anxiety.[50]

---

[49] Chao Tzang Yawnghwe, *The Shan of Burma*, Singapore, 1987, 76–8.
[50] Quoted A. Lamb, *The Mandarin Road to Old Hué*, London, 1970, 64.

The British did indeed decide to send a mission to Cochinchina. But, though European rivalry thus again threatened to involve an independent Asian kingdom, in fact participation in the North American war distracted the French, while Vietnam, with the onset of the Tayson rebellion (1771– 1802), seemed too chaotic to sustain Britain's commercial interest in new approaches to China from the south.

Vo-Vuong's grandson, Nguyen Anh, sought French aid in his contest with the Tayson. Even though the French had regained their Indian possessions, lost in the American war, the authorities there, more cautious than subordinates often were, proved reluctant to intervene. Under missionary pressure, however, Louis XVI's government made a treaty with a Nguyen mission in Paris in 1787, offering aid in return for the cession of Danang. Because of the reluctance of the Pondicherry authorities, no official aid eventuated, but Pigneau, head of the Société des Missions Étrangères, secured some volunteer help for the Nguyen cause.

Probably it was superfluous, and Gia-long, as Nguyen Anh became, would have triumphed in any case. But even in the minds of those it may have helped, it tended to associate division in Vietnam with foreign intervention, enhancing the tendency to associate unity with isolation. The Vietnamese, like the Burmans, were aware of British conquests in India; they were aware, too, that European rivalry might, as there, invite intervention. But the ideological preoccupations of Vietnamese rulers went beyond such tactical considerations and made it difficult to perceive, still more difficult to take advantage of, differences and changes of attitude among the Europeans. The British interest in Vietnam was limited: keeping the French out, perhaps opening up commercial opportunities. Unlike Burma, Vietnam was beyond the ambit of Indian considerations and the realm of Indian prestige. Adjusting to British needs could have been reconciled with, even provided for, Vietnam's independence. But meeting negative responses from Vietnam, and disappointed over its trade, the British were to drop their opposition to French settlement, provided it remained within limits.

Anxious to avert the establishment of French influence in newly-reunited Vietnam, Wellesley sent the Roberts mission to Gia-long. But neither then, nor after the French wars, were the Vietnamese open to the further development of French influence, and Gia-long's successor, Minh-mang (r. 1820–40), indeed tried to limit that of the missionaries. The British sent another envoy, Crawfurd, in 1822. He was unsuccessful, and indeed, going even further than the Burman kings, Minh-mang refused to receive him on the ground that he was emissary only of a governor-general. The British took no further action: their purposes in Vietnam differed from their purpose in Burma. The Vietnamese were, as Crawfurd put it, 'far removed' from the sphere of our Indian politics'.[51] French influence was non-existent. Vietnam, too, was a feudatory of China, which it was desirable not to offend lest the Company's tea trade at Canton be disturbed as a result. In Burma Crawfurd was to recommend a stand-off. More

---

[51] John Crawfurd, *Journal of an Embassy from the Governor-General of India to the Courts of Siam and Cochin China*, London, 1830, I. 473.

realistically he recommended in respect of Vietnam merely an occasional complimentary mission from the king's government, which might help the indirect trade with China. But an additional commercial contact there was no longer really needed, since opium supplied the investment in China, and no move was made.

The change in Britain's relations with China suggested a change in its relations with those states seen and seeing themselves as its feudatories. The Company lost its monopoly in 1833, and under pressure from the free trade relations deteriorated into the first Anglo-China war. As a result the first of the nineteenth-century 'unequal treaties' was made, treaty ports opened, extraterritorial jurisdiction granted, customs duties limited, Hong Kong acquired. Now, the ex-missionary Charles Gutzlaff argued, was the time for a new mission to Vietnam, sent by the king's government. Sir John Davis, his superior, supported the idea: 'the recent example of China, to which the ultra-Gangetic nations of the Continent of Asia have been in the habit of looking with awe and respect, might influence the latter very favourably in the event of any overtures on our part towards a more extended intercourse'.[52] But his mission of 1847 was entirely vain. Heavy rains gave the Vietnamese a pretext to avoid Davis' visiting the Nguyen capital, Hué: 'we shall . . . part on civil terms at least, and if more progress has not been effected it may be attributed perhaps to the impression made on this timid and cautious people by the late conduct of the French'.[53]

Third parties were indeed involved. One reason was continued Catholic activity on the part of missionaries in defiance of the Nguyen régime. An American ship intervened violently in their favour in 1845. More significant were the French. They had no commerce in East Asia, but like the Americans they had, since the opening of China, ships. Moreover, with the British in occupation of Hong Kong, it seemed necessary for the French also to have a base in East Asian waters. One possibility, Basilan, an island in the southern Philippines, was ruled out by Spanish opposition. Another was to secure Danang, allegedly ceded in 1787. In any case the French navy acted in support of the missionaries, and Danang was the scene of the violence to which Davis referred. Earlier he had hoped that this would assist his mission. But both the Chinese war and the actions of the French and Americans had persuaded the Vietnamese rulers to adhere even more closely to an isolationist policy applied indifferently to all the powers. Not altogether surprisingly, they did not distinguish the different nuance in British policy: the British expanded elsewhere, and might well do so in Vietnam. But undoubtedly ideology and fear of subversion obscured the perception that the British were more powerful in general and more restrained towards Vietnam in particular, and diminished the possibility of improving relations with them and so reinforcing their interest in Vietnam's independence. Isolation was not a realistic policy, nor was playing off one European against another. The best option was to come to terms with the British. But for the Vietnamese, as for the Burmans, that proved impossible, though for different reasons.

---

[52] Davis to Aberdeen, 1 Aug. 1845, FO 17/100.
[53] Davis to Palmerston, 26 Oct. 1847, FO 17/130.

Similar factors affected the fortunes of John Bowring who, as Superintendent of Trade at Hong Kong, inherited instructions to open up the East Asian countries, and succeeded in Siam. He sent Thomas Wade to investigate the prospect of a favourable reception from the Vietnamese.

> The manner in which this announcement is received will enable me to judge whether it is best I should proceed alone, or wait the period when I can be accompanied by the Ministers of France and the United States. I am disposed to think their presence might be an embarrassment and not a facility in my proceedings.[54]

Wade landed with a single follower and took up residence, 'my hope being that when the authorities found me fairly planted on shore, they would either forward me to the capital, or bring me in contact with some one deputed by the Prime Minister to receive the [Bowring] letter. In this I was disappointed.'[55] Bowring observed that 'the same repulsive and exclusive spirit which characterizes all the Indo-Chinese populations East of the Ganges was displayed in every possible form'.[56]

Disappointed of a purely British approach, Bowring was now prepared to co-operate with the French. Their policy was, however, becoming more extreme. They resorted to violence to secure the reception of their envoy's letter. Later that year the Emperor Tu-duc (r. 1848–83) had a Spanish bishop decapitated to discourage the rest. Napoleon III had been considering missionary proposals for intervention in Vietnam, and this episode provided the occasion. The commission he appointed argued for expansion.

> Force of circumstances seems to have confined France to the European territories which she possesses today. Hence it would be unacceptable if, denied expansion in Europe, she were forced to restrict her capabilities for action to these narrow confines while other maritime nations try to strengthen their power and resources in regions which Providence seems to have held in reserve to receive the superabundant expansionary capacities of Europe.

Other maritime nations could share in the trade, their opposition, if it existed, being thus counteracted. French rule would be welcome to the Vietnamese, too: 'our domination would be a deliverance for them from a hateful yoke'.[57] Danang should be seized to guarantee the execution of a treaty providing for the protection of missionaries and for commercial concessions and an indemnity.

In August 1858 a joint Franco-Spanish expedition seized Danang, but it could not attack Hué overland. Instead it proceeded to Saigon, captured early in 1859. Despite the protests of the missionaries—who wanted action elsewhere and believed there would be a rising against the Nguyen in the north—the French began to concentrate on founding a colony in the south. Even so there was, as the commission had anticipated, no British

---

[54] Bowring to Clarendon, 7 May 1855, FO 17/229.
[55] Memorandum in Wade to Bowring, 17 Sept. 1855, FO 17/233.
[56] Bowring to Clarendon, 8 Oct. 1855, FO 17/233.
[57] Quoted Tuck, 49–52.

opposition. The tripartite relationship had become a dual one, to the disadvantage of Vietnam.

In Hong Kong the *Register* indeed proclaimed that the Anglo-French jealousies of Pigneau's days had died out.

> We may doubt the success of any commercial settlement at Tourane [Danang], but if it is to form a link in the chain of European intercourse with the East, if it is to aid in spreading western civilisation and a more liberal policy in this quarter of the globe, it is not France alone but the whole of commercial Europe that will profit by the step, and we of all others, should be the first to wish the expedition God speed, even though the motives in which it first originated were those of opposition to our own power.[58]

The official British attitude did not differ. The aim was to provide stable conditions for British trade: if the Vietnamese had failed to respond, the French were acceptable. 'They have long had a fancy for locating themselves there', Bowring wrote. 'It will tend to the extension of Trade and there is perhaps no locality where less mischief will be done as regards our interests.'[59] In Europe the British sought to discover the 'ulterior object', if any, of the French. The major concern the British ambassador expressed was over non-Catholic Christianity in Vietnam. Britain had no special interest in Vietnam's commerce, and Vietnam had failed to interest the British in its political independence. There was no good reason to upset good relations with France in Europe by taking up the cause of Vietnam. The French venture in Vietnam might have advantages: its disadvantages could be provided against.

A memorandum prepared for the Indian government after the capture of Danang suggested that French expansion would open Vietnam to commerce. That expansion must be kept within certain limits but could be tolerated so long as Siam and Laos remained independent of France. A French fleet at Danang might indeed check the Russian fleet in the north; an eastern Cherbourg was not 'cause for serious anxiety'.[60] The British Admiralty, however, was to find that the establishment of the French on one side of the seaway to China added to the importance of Labuan and northern Borneo on the other. Perhaps the major immediate impact of the French expedition on British policy was in fact to strengthen a wavering interest in north Borneo. In the longer term, however, the French seemed to be bursting the territorial limits the British favoured.

The French had secured the three eastern provinces of Cochinchina, and then, under local initiative, took over the western provinces, meeting no opposition from the dynasty, though a great deal from the partisans. The colonial authorities were disposed to move north in the 1870s, especially as they realized that the Red (Hong) River might provide the access to China which, as the French naval lieutenant, Doudart de Lagrée, had shown, the

---

[58] *Hong Kong Register*, 31 Aug., 7 Sept. 1858.
[59] Quoted N. Tarling, *Imperial Britain in South-East Asia*, Kuala Lumpur, 1975, 124–5.
[60] Quoted B. L. Evans, 'The attitudes and policies of Great Britain and China towards French expansion in Cochin-China, Cambodia, Annam and Tongking 1858–83', Ph.D. thesis, University of London, 1961, 41.

Mekong did not, and also because they were apprehensive of the Germans. Paris at first sought to restrain them, then removed its curb. In 1882 a small French expedition was sent to deal with disorder obstructing Red River traffic, and another the following year secured control over lower Tonkin. Defying the Chinese, to whom Hué had appealed, the French established an effective protectorate over the rest of Vietnam. Occupying Tonkin and taking up Vietnamese claims brought the French into Laos, and there they inherited a contest with Siam. By 1893 the crisis of Siam's independence itself seemed to be at hand. In that the British were interested.

THE INDEPENDENCE OF SIAM

Siam was unique in retaining its independence throughout the colonial period. That was a result of its interaction with the policies of the British. Siam was prepared to compromise; and the needs of the British were less urgent than in Burma, less dispensable than in Vietnam. Initially they were restrained by their concern to avoid extension of territory in the Indian style, and to avoid conflict that might endanger the trade to China, to which like Vietnam Siam sent tribute. Local British authorities wanted a more adventurous policy on the Malay peninsula, but were on the whole constrained by their superiors. At the same time the Burney treaty of 1826 showed that the Thais were not entirely negative. The change in the relationship with China suggested a revision of that treaty. But again the British were doubtful and though Sir James Brooke was sent there, they did not take up the intemperate suggestions he made. The result was the peaceful negotiation of a new treaty in 1855. As the Dutch and Spaniards paid a price for their continuance as rulers in Southeast Asia, Siam paid a price for its independence—an 'unequal treaty'. It sought to limit its dependence on the British, without destroying the guarantee offered by a relationship with the strongest of the Western powers, by developing relations with other powers also. In addition it paid a price territorially, in Cambodia, in Laos, in Malaya. But it also effectively sought defensive modernization, again relying primarily, but not merely, on advisers from Britain.

Siam was, to borrow Crawfurd's terms, 'within the pale of our Indian diplomacy' in view of British interest in the 'tributary' states of northern Malaya. But the installation of a British envoy at the Thai capital, Bangkok, would only be a source of irritation, Crawfurd had felt. 'The sea on one quarter, and impracticable mountains and forests on another, are barriers which, together with the fears and discretion of the Siamese Government, will in all likelihood preserve us long at peace with this people'.[61] The Supreme Government in Calcutta had indeed been doubtful about sending Burney to Bangkok:

---

[61] Crawfurd, I. 472.

all extension of our territorial possessions and political relations on the side of the Indo-Chinese nations is, with reference to the peculiar character of those states, to their decided jealousy of our power and ambition, and to their proximity to China, earnestly to be deprecated and declined as far as the course of events and the force of circumstances will permit.[62]

But, under the impulse of the Burma wars, very much part of Indian diplomacy, the governor-general sent the Burney mission. Though no envoy was placed in Bangkok, treaties were made that sought to regulate commerce there and to settle the position of the Malay states in the context of Anglo-Thai relations. Amherst—belligerent over Burma—instructed the Penang officials carefully to abide by the agreements with Siam. They must not exaggerate, he said, the menace involved in the proximity of the Siamese to their settlement.

> Our only national object of policy hereafter in relation to the Siamese should be to endeavour to allay their jealousy of our ultimate views ... and to derive from our connexion with them every attainable degree of commercial advantage, by practising in our intercourse with them the utmost forbearance, temper, and moderation both in language and action, by striving to cultivate a friendly understanding with the Court and its provincial Governors in our neighbourhood, and above all, by faithfully and scrupulously observing the conditions of the treaty which fixes our future relations.[63]

The feudatory status of Siam in relation to China argued, as with Vietnam, for restraint. But it now became in the case of Siam a matter of sustaining an agreement rather than, as in the Vietnamese case, of breaching isolation. The change in the British relationship with China was an argument for a change in the relationship with Siam as with Vietnam and Japan. Trade had developed at Bangkok in the interim, though British merchants complained of high measurement duties and monopolies, and one of them, Robert Hunter, quarrelled with the government. Gutzlaff argued that a mission to Bangkok should seek to revise the commercial parts of the Burney treaty. The India Board was, however, unwilling to risk the relationship established by it: the Burney treaty was 'sufficient for the objects of trade and Friendship', and the Board doubted 'the policy of risking the advantages possessed under the present treaty in an attempt to obtain greater advantages under a new engagement'.[64] The Singapore merchants pressed the idea, however, and the India Board grudgingly gave in. Palmerston also accepted the notion that Sir James Brooke, currently commissioner and consul-general in Borneo, should undertake the task, and he was given instructions that covered Vietnam as well.

The instructions authorized Brooke to visit Siam if he thought that

[62] Governor-General in Council to Governor in Council, 19 Nov. 1824, Straits Settlements Factory Records, G/34/99.
[63] Governor-General in Council to Governor in Council, 23 July 1827, Straits Settlements Factory Records, G/34/142.
[64] Ripon to Aberdeen, 11 Mar. 1846, FO 17/117.

he 'might be able to make some arrangements that would effect an improvement in the British Commercial Relations with that Country'. The commercial stipulations, it was suggested, might bear some relation to those made with other 'imperfectly civilized States', such as China and Turkey. The other stipulations should provide for 'the unrestricted right' on the part of resident British subjects to exercise Christian worship, and for 'the exclusive jurisdiction of British authorities over British subjects', as provided for in Brooke's Brunei treaty of 1847. In conducting negotiations with the Siamese and Vietnamese, Brooke was to 'be very careful not to get involved in any dispute or hostile proceedings which would render our position in Siam or in Cochin-China worse than it now is, or which might compel Her Majesty's Government to have recourse to forcible measures in order to obtain redress'.[65]

Brooke himself appears at first to have contemplated establishing with the next king the kind of relationship he had sought to establish in Brunei.

> I consider that time should be given to the work of conciliation, that their prejudices should be gradually undermined, rather than violently upset, and that as we have delayed for thirty years doing anything, that in the course of this policy we may wait till the demise of the king brings about a new order of things. Above all, it would be well to prepare for the change, and to place *our own* king on the throne [namely Mongkut], ... a highly accomplished gentleman, for a semi-barbarian.[66]

But Rama III, still on the throne, was opposed to a new treaty: why, he ironically asked, was one necessary, since he had one with the Company? Brooke was encouraged to put in formal proposals, and these were rejected. The Siamese ministers had 'never encountered anyone else who came to conduct diplomatic negotiations like a professor giving instructions—instructions that pour forth like waters flooding forests and fields'.[67] Now the envoy advocated a different programme.

> The hope of preserving peace by an expedient Policy—by concession, submission, by indifference, or by any other course, than by rights firmly maintained by power justly exerted, is both a delusion and a cruelty; and after years of embarrassment and the sacrifice of a favourable prestige leads to a sanguinary war.
>
> An adherence to this principle has raised our Indian Empire, and established the reign of Opinion which maintains it; and the departure from this principle has caused the present deplorable condition of our relations with Siam ... there is no other course open to Her Majesty's Government, except to demand ... either a more equitable Treaty in accordance with the observance of civilized nations, or a total withdrawal of British subjects and their property from Siam.
>
> Should these just demands firmly urged be refused, a force should be present immediately to enforce them by a rapid destruction of the defences of

[65] Palmerston to Brooke, 18 Dec. 1849, FO 69/1.
[66] Brooke to Stuart, 17 June 1850, in John C. Templer, ed., *The Private Letters of Sir James Brooke*, London, 1853, II. 304.
[67] Quoted W. F. Vella, *Siam under Rama III*, New York, 1957, 139.

the river, which would place us in possession of the capital and by restoring us to our proper position of command, retrieve the past and ensure peace for the future, with all its advantages of a growing and most important commerce.[68]

Siam, Brooke was arguing, as Penang officials had in 1823, should not only be brought within the pale of Indian diplomacy, but treated, indeed, in subcontinental terms of opinion and prestige.

Abandoning any plan to go to Vietnam, Brooke argued for intervention in Cambodia: it was to be, as it were, the Brunei of mainland Southeast Asia.

> Cambodia . . . is the Keystone of our Policy in these countries—the King of that ancient Kingdom is ready to throw himself under the protection of any European nation, who will save him from his implacable enemies, the Siamese and Cochin Chinese. A Treaty with this monarch at the same time that we act against Siam might be made—his independence guaranteed—the remnants of his fine Kingdom preserved; and a profitable trade opened—The Cochin Chinese might then be properly approached by questioning their right to interrupt the ingress and egress of British trade into Cambodia . . .[69]

The British government did not follow Brooke's recommendations: it avoided the violence he advocated. In respect of Siam, it preferred to await the change of ruler rather than resort to warlike demonstration. This was consonant with the trend of British policy towards Siam as so far conducted by the Indian authorities and the India Board. Brooke had been told that, if he did not succeed, he should at least not make it necessary for the government to engage in a punitive operation. The India Board had opposed any negotiation that might risk relations with a marcher territory for a doubtful advantage. The Foreign Office had finally secured its grudging assent to the mission, but had inherited some of its unwilling-ness to engage in political adventure. Furthermore, it was widely held, as at first by Brooke himself, that the accession of a new king in Siam would in any case bring a more liberal policy. Anglo-Siamese relations would broaden down from the Burney precedent: their narrowing was only temporary, and was not a cause for violent interruption. The Thais benefited from the earlier decision of Rama III in avoiding the consequence of his later decision. But the prospect of Mongkut's accession was also important. As the Phraklang's son told Brooke, the new king 'fully understands the relations of Foreign Nations . . . any intercourse or consul-tation may hereafter be conducted in an easier manner than before'.[70] Though the attacks on Brooke in respect of his Borneo policy meant that he did not go, instructions were in fact again issued to the Hong Kong authorities; Bowring successfully carried out the mission and a treaty was signed in 1855.

The treaty, Bowring rather exaggeratedly told his son Edgar, brought

---

[68] Brooke to Palmerston, 5 Oct. 1850, FO 69/1.
[69] Brooke to Palmerston, 5 Oct. 1850, confidential, FO 69/1.
[70] Letter to Brooke, 23 Apr. 1851, FO 69/3.

Siam 'into the bright fields of hope and peaceful commerce'.[71] It displaced the measurement duties and monopolies by a system of export and import duties, opened the rice trade, and provided for the appointment of a consul and for extraterritorial jurisdiction. But for Siam the 'bright fields of hope' were political as well as commercial. The Thais had again come to terms with the predominant power in Asia and so, by contrast to the Vietnamese, given themselves a guarantee for the future. France and the United States were expected to send missions to Siam also. The Kalahom said he was glad Bowring had arrived first, for the Thais 'had trusted that he would be the pioneer of the new relations to be opened between them and the West, as they could then count upon such arrangements being concluded as would both be satisfactory to Siam, and sufficient to meet the demands that might hereafter be made by other of the Western Powers'.[72] The Thais perceived the nature of European rivalry more accurately than others: the powers could not now readily be played off, but one power being stronger than the others, coming to terms with it would limit what the others could demand. The British secured a strategic interest and commercial opportunity in return for the recognition of Siam's independence. Though at this juncture involving no territorial changes, the deal was not unlike those that they made formally or informally with European authorities in island Southeast Asia. The treaty in this case was, however, based on the 'unequal' model applied to 'imperfectly civilized' states. It was amplified the following year by the Parkes negotiations.

Parkes brought a royal letter from Queen Victoria to King Mongkut (r. 1851–68), however, which reduced Siam's 'inequality'. It 'touched his heart and flattered his ambition'.[73] In fact the king's ambition, and the object of the concessions he made, was to secure the recognition of Siam as an independent state among the European nations. In this he had succeeded, and so given his state a better chance of survival than that of Burma or Vietnam. In Vietnam the opportunity had not been taken; in Burma there was no such opportunity before Ripon's neglected offer.

The 1855 treaty brought other changes in its wake. A British envoy was placed in Bangkok and direct contact established with London. Though Malaya was not covered in the Bowring treaty, the Anglo-Thai relationship in respect of it necessarily altered. Dealing directly with the northern Malay states became more difficult for the government of the Straits Settlements, and the bombardment of Terengganu enforced a change of view the more effectively because of Siam's connexion with the government in London. The strain in relations that the bombardment temporarily created enhanced the French opportunity to step into Cambodia. Now based in southern Vietnam, they challenged Siam's interest in Cambodia by offering its king their protection, which he reluctantly accepted. This outcome in fact the India Office was itself ready to accept, as the French did not move into Siam itself nor into Laos. For the British, Siam now

---

[71] Bowring to E. Bowring, 13 Apr. 1855, English Mss. 1228/125, John Rylands Library, Manchester.
[72] Quoted Tarling, *Imperial Britain*, 180.
[73] Parkes to Clarendon, 22 May 1856, FO 69/5.

became a buffer not a marcher territory. In 1867 it gave up its claims over Cambodia in return for the provinces of Battambang and Angkor. Resented by the Cambodians, that too could be accepted by the British, and another part of the pattern of relations between Siam and the West was set till the turn of the century.

The advance of French power into central and northern Vietnam meanwhile modified the understandings over Malaya. If Siam were after all to fall under French influence, the security of northern Malaya would be threatened. The Thais, however, wished to retain their claims over the states there, and a British challenge to them might incur their hostility and turn them towards France, if not encourage the French to challenge the Thais elsewhere, rather as the Terengganu crisis had occasioned their move into Cambodia. To strengthen British influence without alienating the Thais, a new expression was given to the tripartite relationship in some of the northern Malay states: the Resident Councillor at Penang was appointed Consul to Kedah and Perlis.

The French moves in Laos produced a crisis for Siam but also for the British; they saw it as a buffer, not only now for their Malayan interests and for lower Burma, but also for upper Burma, which they had recently conquered. Pavie, French envoy in Bangkok, indicated in March 1893 that France intended to assert a claim to all territory east of the Mekong, and a naval demonstration at Bangkok in July was designed to secure Thai compliance. Britain urged Siam to accept French demands so as to avoid their being stepped up, and at the same time tried to restrain France. The French government agreed to establish a buffer in the north, where part of the Shan states, tributary to Burma, now British, extended east of the Mekong. The Thais had to renounce their claims over Laos east of the Mekong, but the French did not get Battambang and Siemreap: 'the disgorging is a noble operation', Lord Rosebery congratulated himself.[74] The British then sought the creation of the promised buffer, but in vain. Instead, in 1896 they, too, surrendered their claims east of the Mekong, making the river the frontier of Laos and Burma, and in return secured something of a French guarantee of the independence of Menam valley, inasmuch as each power agreed not to advance without the other's consent. The Thais might well, however, conclude that Britain had stopped short of affording them the support they expected. The agreement may indeed also have been a sign of Britain's diminished predominance: insurance with the major power was no longer sufficient. It had to compromise with other powers. That was no more a guarantee of Asian independence than European rivalry had been: perhaps it promised even less.

The British realized, however, that the agreement of 1896 did not cover their concern with the peninsula, particularly north of the Malay states, where, moreover, there was interest in a canal through the Isthmus of Kra. The French might not intervene there, but, as European rivalry intensified, another power might. German activity was now of renewed concern and

---

[74] Quoted Chandran Jeshurun, *The Contest for Siam 1889–1902*, Kuala Lumpur, 1977, 49.

greater actuality. In April 1897 the British made a secret agreement with
Siam, in which the latter promised to cede no rights on the peninsula
without British consent, in return securing a promise of British backing
against third-power attempts to acquire dominion there. Siam also agreed
to make exclusive commercial concessions in the area subject to British
approval. In order to appease Thai sensitivities, the agreement was so
secret that even Sir Frank Swettenham, as governor of the Straits Settlements, could not be told about it, albeit that the Colonial Office knew,
'though we pretend we do not know, that Sir Frank Swettenham knows of
the Treaty'.[75]
    The development of the peninsula, in particular the impact of the rubber
boom, led to a further regulation of the Anglo-Thai relationship with
northern Malay states. Swettenham planned to assist Siam to secure
written agreements from the sultans, giving it de jure status, if it would
employ British officers as Residents, and this resulted in the joint declaration of 1902, a reformulation of the tripartite sharing of political power in
the states. The agreement did not, of course, cover Pattani, and the Sultan
of Terengganu would not accept a Thai-appointed Resident, seeking,
rather, something like the relationship between Johor and Britain.
    In any case these arrangements all proved transitional. Pressed by
developments in Europe, France and Britain moved closer together, and in
1904 the erstwhile rivals made an agreement resolving many of their
overseas disputes. In the case of Siam, it reaffirmed the understanding of
1896. 'England says to France, "You strip him on one side, I will strip him
on the other. As to the middle, we may leave that alone for the present." '[76]
The editor of *Blackwood's Magazine* was perhaps even more cynical than he
should have been, for the Menam basin continued to be left alone. But
outlying parts of Siam were not. In the same year France had acquired
sections of Luang Prabang on the west bank of the Mekong. Three years
later it returned some of these acquisitions, while Siam ceded back the
Cambodian provinces of Siemreap and Battambang. France also reduced
its extraterritorial rights in Siam. A similar adjustment followed with
Britain. The 1897 restrictions on commercial concessions had proved
inconvenient to the Thais. They wanted funding for the railway system
that would consolidate their kingdom. They again wanted to reduce
extraterritorial rights. To secure these objectives they ceded to Britain their
rights over the northern Malay states, though the British there had the task
of negotiating with rulers whose independence they had done something
to keep alive. Outlying territory could be bargained for greater equality,
the Thais had decided; and they had retained their capacity to do so, while
the lesser states, Laotian, Cambodian, Malayan, had to submit to partition
and changes of allegiance. King Chulalongkorn (r. 1868–1910) had thought
to include Siam's tributaries in his programme of centralization and
modernization: now he abandoned that. The priority lay elsewhere.
    With this agreement the Thais adjusted to a world in which British

[75] Quoted Suwannathat-Pian, 155n.
[76] Quoted in R. S. Stetson, 'Siam's Diplomacy of Independence, 1855–1909', Ph.D. thesis,
New York University, 1969, 176n.

predominance had been further compromised. With it, too, tripartite power-sharing in the peninsular states ceased. Pattani remained part of Siam. To the south the Malay states became part of what was increasingly seen as British Malaya, though it was represented by no single formal political entity.

THE POLICIES OF THE WESTERN POWERS

Analysis of Western policy involves considering the impulses and the motivations behind it; the interest-groups involved, which in fact also affected the policy itself; the shifts over time; the options available to policy-makers; the means at hand; the information drawn on, the perceptions attained.

In a general sense the Europeans, the chief Western actors for much of the century, were impelled by their political and economic strength and strategic advantage, which had increased since their initial successes in Asia, and would increase further with their industrial and technological revolutions and enhanced capacity to mobilize their resources. On these advantages they wished to build. They were also impelled by other purposes, not necessarily mere rationales, nor mere products of the pursuit of wealth and power, though related to their success and to their wish to build upon it: to convert, to civilize, to spread European culture. They were impelled and motivated, too, by their own rivalry, always a compulsive element in the projection of Europe overseas.

For the central part of the period, that rivalry was muffled by the predominance of the British among them and in the world as a whole. It was not of course inconsistent that the British would pursue in such a phase relatively moderate policies. Their economic success, advantaged by their early industrial revolution, also conduced to political moderation. The result was a tendency to temporize with other European powers and to look to non-European powers outside their ambit to modernize themselves. They had a kind of imperium in Southeast Asia, determining or influencing the policies of others, but generally not themselves ruling, allowing those others to take their time over strengthening, modernizing or partitioning as the case might be. All the same, India affected British policy, and its political and strategic needs were quite different from those of a great industrial and commercial power, though it made its contribution to the success of that power. Britain had to provide there for the security of a territorial dominion and for its insulation from foreign menace. Its policy towards Burma was thus quite different from its policy elsewhere in Southeast Asia. Britain's interest in China also affected its view of Southeast Asia. That country should not, indeed, become another India, but its commerce, and the route to it, were important. That made for a strategic interest in the Straits of Melaka and the South China Sea, and also, at least for a while, encouraged a moderate policy in Siam and Vietnam.

The relative moderation of the British was not necessarily shared by

other European powers established in Southeast Asia. They were constrained to treat British commerce fairly, but, a lesser power in the shadow
of a greater, the Netherlands was tempted to follow compulsive economic
practices like those of the Cultivation System. Politically the minor powers
could generally rely on the overall guarantee of the British. But moments
of uncertainty could lead to convulsive and even violent action, and this
increased, in Sulu as in Aceh, when British predominance declined and
other powers seemed likely to intervene. These were some of the effects of
leaving the archipelagic world to minor European powers. The French
were not a minor power, but their enterprise on the mainland was still
driven by a wish to assert their greatness in Europe. They rightly recognized that the British would not oppose their venture on economic
grounds.

With all the Western powers, policy was made not merely, sometimes
not primarily, by central governments, though they often expected non-
Western governments to respond with all the immediacy and coherence
that they failed to display themselves. As a result, its main thrusts could be
given different emphases; they could even be contradicted, particularly
before trans-world communication began to inhibit local initiative and
enhance the input of metropolitan governments. There were several levels
of government, and with all the Western powers—with the British on the
peninsula, the Dutch in the outer islands, the Spaniards in the Philippines,
the French in Indochina—local officials tended to go beyond their instructions or even act in defiance of restraints by superiors. There were also
tensions between official and mercantile interests, again at various levels.
Government and commerce might have different views of the priorities
and purpose of intervention. In the case of the relations of the Straits
Settlements with Sumatra, for example, merchants developed an interest
in the preservation of a status quo not officially seen as advantageous in
the longer term. The expansion of European economies and their increasing
penetration into Southeast Asia in the later nineteenth century expanded
the role of private interests: concessionaires might or might not seek or
receive the backing of governments, local or central. The differing interests
in some sense represented frontiers that might be successive rather than
coterminous. While Britain was predominant and other powers did not
feel pressed to extend their control, there was scope for adventurers,
pursuing their own interests—even, in the case of Raja Brooke, creating
his own sub-colonial order. The effect in most cases was to induce the
neighbouring colonial power to extend its effective frontier. The last
decades of the nineteenth century offered a range of opportunities for
private enterprise, for concessionaires, gun-runners, legal advisers, until a
new series of compromises was reached between older and newer powers
and new frontiers were established or old ones further consolidated.

A time-shift is reflected indeed in the changing balance of these interests
and authorities within states and, as well, in the conduct of their relations
with one another. Before about 1870, Britain's predominance was evident;
after 1870 apprehended and actual challenges increased, partly as a result
of political changes within Europe, partly as a result of shifts in the
distribution of economic power. The Industrial Revolution was indeed

another factor: by 1870 other countries not merely European were effectively following Britain's example or overtaking Britain, often pursuing protectionist policies in order to do so. On both counts increased competitiveness ensued overseas. The patronage of a predominant power was less available: it was moved to compromise with others. More formal demarcation and partition ensued under rules that themselves were formalized at Berlin. The political and economic changes were both affected by the development of communications, including the opening of the Suez Canal in 1869 and the linking of the telegraph in 1870–1. Economically the opening-up of Southeast Asia was expedited and its links with world markets tightened. Politically, the input of metropolitan governments were enhanced, themselves pressed by an increasing variety of interests and pressure-groups, and by an advance of democracy at home that often made for rigidity overseas. The Dutch government had been against the war with Aceh, but found it difficult to pursue peace once it had started. Events in Asia could also influence the metropolis. Ferry fell because of an incident in Vietnam, and the Third Anglo-Burman War was an election issue.

In part as a result of these processes, though also as a result of Southeast Asian policies and reactions, the Western powers adopted different options. There were, of course, a number of patterns. In earlier centuries—even in the eighteenth—Europeans had dealt with states in Southeast Asia in some sense on terms of equality, sometimes ruthless, rarely patronizing. This was so even in the archipelago where there was more involvement than on the mainland. With the increase of European power, and the failure of Asian states to cope with the economic and political pressures to which they were subject, other alternatives were opened up. One option might be to partition a state; another to protect or dominate it and reform it. Partition was not always the resort of the strong, rather, perhaps, the reverse: the Dutch nibbled at the periphery of Aceh, having failed to dominate at the centre, making the prospect of ultimately so doing more difficult. Nor did protection necessarily lead to Raffles-style reform: it might simply be a convenient means of acquiring control and indeed claiming additional territory as the French acquired Vietnamese claims over Laos and Cambodia.

The emphasis in British policy, at least outside areas more or less consigned to the Dutch or the Spaniards, was on the maintenance and reform of Asian states. Some reformed themselves: Siam, most successfully; others, less fully, less lastingly. But the attempt was not always welcome. It might threaten British interests particularly if it involved attempts to diversify international relationships in the context of European rivalry. But even in Burma the British sought a less than independent state rather than absorption of territory into the empire: only when they failed did they resort to partition and incorporation. In Malaya the British accepted the continued integrity of states with which local officials had developed relations that survived the changes of the 1870s, and indeed helped to shape them. Sarawak was in some sense a native state, as at times James Brooke angrily claimed. The British could not allow it to act with the ultimate degree of independence, namely to seek protection from another European state. But for the most part the unrealistic plans which the first raja developed along these lines were not supported by his friends and relatives, and were not carried out. The British finally adopted a form of protectorate, as over North Borneo, that allowed the authorities a very large, and ultimately embarrassing, degree of autonomy. In respect of other areas, especially in the archipelago, officials, and less often merchants, saw advantage in the regularization expected from the expansion of the colonial authorities, the presence of which the British had sanctioned. The same view applied to Vietnam, even on the part of private interests, after its failure to respond positively to British initiatives, and the French began to establish themselves.

More clearly than for the British, for other European powers the establishment of colonial authority was often in itself a desirable objective, and for metropolitan as well as for local officials, at least in the longer term. The Dutch were set on the rounding-out of the realm of Netherlands India and the Spaniards on the control of all of the Philippines. Dominion in French Indochina the Third Republic saw as compensation for disappointment in Europe and elsewhere. But, though their aims might differ from those of the British, they recognized that they could rarely be achieved by the mere application of force. The means they adopted were indeed not unlike those of the British, though the objective might differ.

There were phases of great violence on the part of all the Europeans, and indeed of the Americans, in Burma and Indochina, in the Philippines and Netherlands India. But force was adopted in association with other means, or where they had failed. The British dropped diplomacy in Burma and turned to war in 1824, and again in 1852, in the hope that they could prompt a change of attitude, their main aim throughout. By contrast the Dutch sought the progressive incorporation of native states into Netherlands India. But again force was only part of their method. Their greatest success indeed came over time with the combination of diplomacy, the possibility of force, and the severance of indigenous states from other international contacts: using force was a confession of failure; it was expensive and damaging, as the case of Aceh made dramatically evident. There the Dutch fell into a mode which the Spaniards had never escaped from in Sulu. European powers generally hoped that limited force or the threat of force might be sufficient to produce the political change they sought, making available the native instruments of authority and administration they needed to acquire.

The Europeans were strong at sea: steamers made them stronger. Where land force was used, it was generally not provided merely from the metropolis. The British had the superb resource of the Indian army. Other powers, more riskily, tended, like the British in India itself after the Mutiny, to rely on peripheral or minority elements, the equivalent of the martial races of British India. It was not surprising that two elements — old aristocracies or parvenus who became identified with colonial rule, and minorities who provided soldiers for colonial governments — might find it most difficult to accommodate to the rule of the successor states.

Finally it is clear that the impulses of the Europeans were shaped and their actions affected by the information available to them and the perceptions they brought to its selection and appreciation. In some cases information might be intentionally misinterpreted. Piracy is a case in point. One reason for the frequent use of the term in the nineteenth century was the British commitment to put it down. It was an impediment to trade, and its suppression would promote law and order on the seas. The Anglo-Dutch treaty of 1824 provided for co-operation against it, and other states and rulers were enjoined to work against it, like the Sultan of Brunei in the 1847 treaty. Naval forces could be involved and head money was payable. Since British power was considerable, but British policy relatively restrained, those who wished to use it could readily be tempted to apply the term rather widely, to attempts of the sultanate of Aceh to establish entrepôt trade, to the attacks of Iban upon the core rivers of Sarawak, to the marauding and slave-trading of the Ilanun and Balanini of the Sulu islands and northern Borneo, state-building enterprises though they might be.

European contemporaries themselves disputed the application of the term, for example at trials of captured Ilanun or in criticisms of James Brooke. Were those pirates properly so-called, who acted under authorization from the Sultan of Sulu? Was being an opponent of the extension of the raj of Sarawak sufficient qualification for being treated as a pirate? The issue, indeed, is not merely the intentional misuse of the term. The questions which contemporaries asked marked an extension to the archipelago of a European system of laws, and the response might invite further action. If the Sultan of Sulu had authorized piracy, should he not be held responsible? Or the Spaniards?

Piracy, as earlier in Europe, might indeed be a form of marine warfare, used either in enforcing the rule of an existing state, or establishing the power of a new state, or in displacing one political constellation by another. Indeed contemporaries recognized that, by seeking to put it down, they were interfering in a political process. At times, they had to deny the legitimacy not only of the states involved and their purposes, but of the dynamic of change involved. Putting down piracy involved displacing the states that existed or reforming them.

The outcome sought might again influence the analysis of the origins of the problem. Piracy, Raffles argued, originated in the decay of the native states as a result of Dutch incursions and monopolies, and Brooke and others followed this line, which supported a policy of order by restoration. The argument was more attractive than the notion that Malays were 'inveterate' pirates, and it has helped historians also to probe into the purpose and process of suppression. But again it is dangerous to generalize. The piracy of the Johor empire was clearly related to the 'breaking down of larger government',[77] though demonstratively abandoning it gave Temenggong Ibrahim an alternative source of power. But the analysis fits Sulu less well. Piracy became a source of power and wealth, since, as Warren has demonstrated,[78] it enabled the sultanate in its slave-raiding form to acquire the population that sustained its trade between Borneo and

---

[77] Owen to Ibbetson, 24 Oct. 1830, Board's Collections 52586, p.119, F/4/1331.
[78] J. F. Warren, *The Sulu Zone 1768–1898*, Singapore, 1981.

China for the better part of a century. That was still, of course, a decline in terms of the larger aims of the Moro sultanates of the sixteenth and seventeenth centuries. But it was in some sense a creative response to the conditions of the late eighteenth and early nineteenth centuries. For a time Sulu prospered. But its association with piracy and slave-raiding did not suggest that its further decline could be averted. For it added to the ambivalence over its relations with the British, and gave the Spaniards an argument against them and against Sulu itself.

In the case of piracy, indeed, the application of international law generally worked to the disadvantage of the independent Asian states involved, and generally, though not always, to the disadvantage of the pirates. For the most part, indeed, it was on the European side in this as in other cases. Moreover, it could be invoked or disregarded as seemed convenient. The Sultan of Aceh could not close ports, but Raffles could. The British could challenge or condone a Spanish blockade of Sulu as seemed expedient. It is possible to argue that the application of international law, in those positivist days, was in itself a piece of imperialism. Yet it could at times check the Europeans by acting on their own rivalries and on the tensions among their authorities—the Governor of Penang and the Recorder quarrelled over the treatment of Kedah—or between authorities and private interests, or among private interests themselves. It could also spur them on: pirates would be drowned rather than taken in for trial. Lawyers are found advising indigenous rulers—like J. C. Mitchell in the case of Lombok—though not always to happy effect. In that case it urged the Dutch on.

There was a kind of reverse misconception, that the Asian states were states in a European sense and that their central authorities were as effective as Europeans liked to think their own were. Moderates might thus expect too much of them, and be disappointed; reformers might have to go further than they wanted; extremists might demand too much and rejoice at the outcome. But perceptions of their weakness could also be exaggerated. If central authority was weak, it did not follow that the state was weak. Conquerors might bite off more than they could chew. There was a widespread, but often unfounded view that the masses were awaiting delivery from native tyrants, supported also by the European belief that order and good government would liberate economic enterprise and help to create wealth. There was, at least till the late nineteenth century, only a limited perception of the ideological and religious under-pinnings of the Southeast Asian states. The contemporary reports convey no real understanding of the Confucian preconceptions and purposes of Minh-mang, nor of the Buddhist role of the Burman kings.

In the archipelago Islam was rightly seen as an antagonist, but the European powers each handled it differently. The Dutch had long sought to play down its influence by rather crude methods: towards the end of the century, its post-Suez revival and sophistication made them, under the influence of their frustration in Aceh, and of the Dutch Islamicist Snouck Hurgronje's research and advocacy, more subtle. The Spaniards, building their empire on conversion, were cruder still: there was little chance of the kind of accommodation with Sulu that the Dutch achieved with many of the states of the archipelago. Indeed, the Spaniards' attacks on Sulu in the 1870s helped to inspire Islamic resistance elsewhere: they found Sulu *panditas* travelling to Mindanao 'with the sinister goal of uniting among themselves the Moros, whose disunity had been up to then the greatest advantage the Spaniards had perceived'.[79] The United States, with no commitment to conversion and with the capacity to secure better information, yet behaved with even greater violence in the face of fanatic resistance. The British were more cautious, in part again because of an Indian factor: they had more Muslim subjects than any other state, and the Mutiny there added to their wish to avoid clashes between Europeans and Muslims in general. In Malaya they left Islam—as they hoped—to the sultans. One of their criticisms of Spain in Sulu was that the Spaniards would raise up general jihad against European rule in Asia.

The story is better understood if the other side of it is also borne in mind. The policies, purposes and perceptions of the Europeans have been summarized. What were those of the Southeast Asians?

SOUTHEAST ASIAN POLICIES

The Maritime Region

The indigenous authorities in the archipelago, for the most part long connected with the Dutch and with diminished international personality, had less scope to determine the outcome of the encounter with the nineteenth-century West than those on the mainland. Dundas had suggested that the Dutch might be overthrown, but only with the aid of foreign powers. In fact the British were generally cautious over disturbing the pattern of Dutch power: they might prefer to inherit it than destroy it. What they did in the interregnum and after would certainly not encourage indigenous rulers to think that they could either rely on rivalry among the Europeans or seek the support of the more powerful of them against the less.

Indigenous rulers were not, of course, consulted over the Anglo-Dutch treaty of 1824; they would apprehend its outcome, like that of the convention of 1814, only through the actions that followed it. Dipanagara's aim in the Java War of 1825–30 was, as Ali Basah Penjalasan put it, 'to restore the high state of the Islamic religion throughout the whole of Java'.[80] An appeal to the British would be unlikely. But it would certainly have met a negative response, though the merchant John Palmer might lament the outcome.[81] In western Sumatra, the replacement by the Dutch of the British authorities, who had been in some areas for 150 years, was apparent. 'Our Privilege of Trade at the Dutch Ports seems to supersede the necessity for retaining any Settlement on Sumatra', Palmer commented: 'but the contempt of the Feelings of the Natives and our Engagements

[79] Quoted R. C. Ileto, *Magindanao, 1860–1888: the career of Datu Uto of Buayan*, Ithaca, 1972, 43.
[80] Quoted P. B. R. Carey, 'Javanese Histories of Dipanagara', BKI, 130 (1974) 287.
[81] Quoted N. Tarling, 'The Palmer Loans', in D. P. Crook, ed., *Questioning the Past*, St Lucia, 1972, 116.

with them will deservedly load us with obloquy everywhere.'[82] The position of the states in the outer islands in contractual relationship with the Dutch was less clear. Obviously the renewal of their contracts was the least the Dutch could seek. For a while, however, the indigenous rulers might retain a good deal of autonomy, though they might not know why, and they might feel able to admit foreign merchants and even adventurers without fully realizing the danger of so doing.

Only in the case of Aceh had the British felt that the recency of the relationship with the sultan established by Raffles justified a special reservation in 1824. The Penang authorities did not, however, see fit to negotiate the end of his treaty: any arrangement with Aceh would only encourage its 'tendency to overawe and subjugate the numerous petty states with whom our trade is conducted'.[83] Perhaps as a result, the ruler of Aceh rather paradoxically continued to set some store by the Raffles treaty and was less inclined to turn to the Dutch. He certainly retained an effective independence that encouraged them to proceed by partition rather than by protection, leaving the Acehnese and foreign merchants beyond the frontiers to trade or clash as they might meanwhile. The piecemeal encroachment of the Dutch led Sultan Ibrahim to turn to other powers in the 1850s. But that was to go beyond what the Dutch could allow. When the independence of Aceh was made plain by the Anglo-Dutch treaty in 1871 and the publicity it received, they had to foreclose on the sultanate. The Dutch usually applied force only to back up a system of contractual relations: the latter lacking in Aceh, they needed the force all the more, and that was one reason why they could not bring the war to an early end, even though there was little chance of European help for their opponents, and the sultan's appeal to Turkey elicited only a gesture. In the course of the struggle, a reason for their normal policy became apparent: Islamic elements in society, always strong, secured leadership. The Dutch had precipitately abolished the sultanate and failed to compromise with the *adat*-chiefs or *ulèëbalang* (hereditary chiefs), though these saw that prolonged resistance eroded their position and enhanced that of Muslim extremists. With the latter the Dutch could not readily come to terms, and the struggle had its echoes in other parts of the archipelago. Snouck Hurgronje wrote:

> Had a sultan or scion of the royal house, endowed with exceptional strength of will and clearness of judgment, placed himself at the head of the struggle *à outrance* which took place when the Dutch came to Acheh, and inspired the Achehnese people by precept and example, such a prince would without doubt have been for the invaders anything but a negligible quantity . . . As it is, an ulama who preaches holy war is able to deprive an Achehnese ulèëbalang of the allegiance of a considerable portion of his subjects; how much more could have been accomplished by a raja who was the ulamas' equal in sacred authority, and over and above this was clothed with the legendary traditions of the past greatness of Acheh![84]

---

[82] Palmer to Prince, 10 May 1825, quoted Tarling, *Imperial Britain*, 52.
[83] Memorandum by Fullerton, 21 Mar. 1825, Straits Settlements Factory Records G/34/100.
[84] C. Snouck Hurgronje, trans. A. W. S. O'Sullivan, *The Achehnese*, Leyden, 1906, I. 145.

Previous to 1871 the British had offered some challenge to the Dutch advance from Siak over states on the east coast of Sumatra with a dubious allegiance to it. In the 1860s a number of rulers sought British help, but the support that eventuated was mainly local, and it did little but prompt the Dutch to act more firmly. Even in respect of states where contractual relationships were more continuous, the process of absorption into the Dutch domain was not always smooth. The period of *onthouding* perhaps again gave indigenous rulers a false confidence. The Dutch, however, intervened if economic interference seemed likely to become political, or private interference official, particularly after Brooke's adventure had shown the dangers. The ruler of Lombok, for example, still had a remarkable degree of autonomy in the 1850s, but he could not turn his international connexions to account, for doing so would only prompt the Dutch to act. The Dutch decided to eliminate that autonomy, however, only in a later phase when they resolved to round out their empire under the impact of increasing European penetration and of the impulse of their own imperialism. They could intervene among divided rajas and could undermine the loyalty of the Sasak peoples. But they could not break the bond of raja and followers at the very core of the kingdom, which was expressed in the final suicide attacks, *puputan*.

The sultanate of Brunei, by contrast, was a survivor, but at a price, or several prices. It was not involved in the Dutch network, though perhaps the Anglo-Dutch treaty of 1824 had intended that it should be. A deterioration in Anglo-Dutch relations and a personal initiative on the British side helped to avert that. But it was also the result of a Brunei response. Initially that was dictated in part by the rivalries of the Brunei rulers as much as or more than by their concern to prevent a Dutch take-over. Perhaps indeed they were slow to recognize the threat of European control, poorly informed as they were of the outside world, relatively isolated, kept in touch only by interested parties. It may as a result have been easier to think in terms of playing off outside elements one against another, an adaptation, perhaps, of a traditional diplomatic mode of holding the Brunei empire together. Raja Muda Hassim looked to Brooke; his rival, Pg Makhota, looked to the Dutch. With them Brunei had no contractual relations and less than others need fear provoking them. Hassim still had the wisdom to enquire which was the cat, which the rat. And would the cat act?[85]

The traditional diplomatic view seemed still to prevail among Bruneis when their range of international contacts was narrowed. The Dutch were excluded under the treaty of 1847, the Americans and the Spaniards by their own incompetence and by the demi-official British venture that led to the founding of the British North Borneo Company. Brunei could survive between raj and Company, Briton and Briton. But it was a costly diplomacy: what came to face Brunei was partition between them. Brunei determination to call a halt, though not unanimous, helped to bring about the establishment of the Residency, as it were, for want of something better: Britain against Britons. Sultan Hashim, who achieved this, was one of the party that had destroyed Brooke's allies in 1846, even though

[85] N. Tarling, *The Burthen, the Risk and the Glory*, Kuala Lumpur, 1982, 30.

Brooke's aim had been to restore the sultanate Raffles-style, and one of those who had subsequently sought support by accepting piecemeal partition. But, with the aid of a change in British policy, he managed to avert the total disappearance of the sultanate.

If James Brooke had sought to prod Brunei into reform, he and his successor in the event built up the separate state of Sarawak. But that rested not only on the partition of Brunei, but on a series of accommodations on the part of the chiefs and peoples of the raj as it expanded. The old focus of loyalty was displaced, but the chiefs had other options open to them, since the raj, lacking in external strength especially after the first raja's break with the British government, needed collaborators all the more. The Malayo-Muslims at the river-mouths became in a sense joint rulers with the white raja, while the original Iban opponents of Brooke rule became its doughty warrior class and assisted in its expansion. In some degree the raj became an autonomous actor on the Southeast Asian stage, even an independent state, a Malay state, as Raja James claimed. An alternative is to see it as a pseudo-colonial state, ultimately relying on British power. Perhaps the truth is somewhere in between.[86] The rajas themselves were clear that their system was superior to colonial rule or rule in the style of the Federated Malay States. But neither before nor after the 1888 protectorate agreement was it truly an independent state, and if it was a Malay state, it was one that accommodated to Britain in special ways.

The state of North Borneo was different again. With its creation its peoples were cut off from political contact with other Europeans, though an obligation to the Sultan of Sulu remained: they were faced with an alien government with no traditional basis and no obvious collaborators. It was resisted by Mat Salleh on a largely traditionalist, only partly Islamic, basis: it secured little help from the British government, but the opposition got none from other governments. A kind of compromise was proposed in 1898, by which Mat Salleh would be accepted as a chief in the interior; but this the Company officials ruled out, though the managing director, W. C. Cowie, a man with a local trading background, favoured it. A laborious series of expeditions was required to eliminate the opposition. A more regular system was gradually established, but it took time to build a chiefly infrastructure.

The establishment of North Borneo represented a partition of Sulu as well as of Brunei. For the Sulus the British connexion, though of limited duration, was a decisive factor in their long relationship with Spain. Their aim was to preserve independence in face of Spanish military action, diplomatic blandishment, religious crusade. The Spaniards established a claim, but no effective control, and indeed, following the Balambangan episode, the Sulus were able to build a new prosperity on arms, slaves and the China trade. A relationship with the British developed which could, however, afford little reassurance, given the piracy issue, and the uncertainty of their commitment to Sulu's independence despite the treaties made by Dalrymple and Brooke and their advocacy of its neutrality. The

[86] cf. Sanid Said, *Malay Politics in Sarawak 1946–1966*, Singapore, 1985, 11, 16–17.

Sulus had seized an opportunity to sustain their state and its special balances between co-operation and rivalry, patronage and dependence, centrality and segmentation. But it was no guarantee of a safe future: the sultan's appeals to the British would meet a qualified reception; and sympathy for him and his people was evoked more by the violence and irregularity of Spain's proceedings and the fear that they might provoke an Islamic reaction. The sultan yet retained sufficient independence at the end of the Spanish régime to make a treaty with the United States, and some of those associated with the Company hoped that the British would yet be able to follow in Sulu the kind of policy they followed on the peninsula. Any such hope was destroyed by the Americans. For them the Bates treaty was mere temporizing, while they dealt with the insurrection in the north. Dislodging the sultan's power, however, faced them with bitter Islamic-inspired resistance.

'We have been struck with amazement at the dispensation of the Lord, the Creator of all the worlds, who has accomplished his divine will and decree in a way which is not comprehensible to us, parting brother from brother, father from son and friend from friend.'[87] That was the reaction of the Bendahara of Pahang to the treaty of 1824, which destroyed the unity of the Malay world. Subsequently new patterns emerged on the peninsula, the result not only of British policy or of the different positions and structures of the Malay states, but also of their different levels of perception and statesmanship. No British Resident was ever appointed to Johor, though its example perhaps helped to introduce the system elsewhere. A fragment of the old empire of Johor, its future was deeply influenced by its rulers, the erstwhile Temenggongs. They recognized that no foreign intervention could be sought: the problem was to maximize independence from the colonial neighbour even so, if not turn him to account. They associated themselves with the Straits Settlements government, demonstratively breaking with the pirates of the old régime, but also received advice from British merchants and lawyers, conveniently or otherwise nearby, and even made a connexion with London. Riskily they sought to expand their political influence; realistically they developed Johor's economy by facilitating Chinese immigration and enterprise. In some ways they were a model, and at times, in a sense because of that, a vexation to those governors who sought more formal colonial control: they were, in a sense, native Raja Brookes. They also knew when to give in: finally accepting an adviser, but still carving out autonomy. Perhaps it was the parvenu character of these rulers that led them temporarily to try aggrandizement; it also made them pragmatic.

Other rulers had to cope with the pre-eminence which the ruler of Johor had secured for himself and, disposed to work with the British, eliminate his monopoly of the British connexion. Sultan Omar of Terengganu was one. He, too, broke with the pirates and sought relations with Singapore, and Governor Blundell responded. But Johor's ambition and the Pahang civil war led him, too, into risky policies that, perhaps unexpectedly, paid off. Terengganu was bombarded, but the policies of Blundell's successor,

[87] Quoted B. W. Andaya, *Perak: The Abode of Grace*, Kuala Lumpur, 1979, 2.

Cavenagh, were disapproved. The price was recognition of Thai supremacy, but it did not destroy Terengganu's autonomy.

In Kedah that supremacy was already accepted. The sultan had secured no promises of help against the Thais when he ceded Penang, and indeed the followers of his dethroned successor were officially treated as pirates in the 1830s. But there was private help, and legal obstacles could be turned to account. In any case, whatever their superiors said, the Straits Settlements authorities were anxious to limit effective Thai supremacy on the peninsula. If it could be done by avoiding its theoretical recognition, so much the better. But if it could be done only by avoiding or limiting its practical implementation, even though it was theoretically accepted, that was an acceptable alternative. The Kedah ruler accepted the deal which Bonham promoted. Malay rulers in the northern states swung among the options left open to them as a result of the lack of formal Thai control and the local British unwillingness to second it: side with the Thais, oppose them; side with the British, oppose them; even play off one with the other. Overall they did extraordinarily well. Incorporation in Siam, Pattani-style, was avoided; so was incorporation in the Federated Malay States.

The Burney treaty left the Perak chiefs to decide the question of their allegiance to Siam, and Governor Fullerton sent Low over to make sure that they chose to reject it. That action the superior authorities disapproved, but their disapproval of the Low treaty was never notified to the Perak authorities. The Thai option ceased to be available, but Perak was divided in other ways. The Malay chiefs were alive to the benefits of the tin trade and encouraged Chinese immigration via the Straits Settlements. But it was not done centrally, as in Johor's case, and its impact upset the distribution of power in the sultanate. The governors tried everything: invoking old treaties; dealing direct with local chiefs; using the ruler of Johor; finally installing a Resident. But what that meant for the élite became apparent only with the work of Birch; and what had to be accepted became apparent only with the expedition to avenge his assassination. Better perhaps to accept and work to limit rather than resist. Educated in Malay, Sultan Idris (r. 1887–1916) learned English when he came to the throne of Perak so as to keep open his lines of communication.[88] The fact that the British did not annex but appeared still to advise gave the rulers some scope, though its limits were a warning to Johor and the northern states to avoid a Resident if they could. Pahang accepted one only reluctantly, and some resistance followed. The northern states accepted only advisers. 'The Malays, like other races, hate foreign interference', King Chulalongkorn commented in 1903. 'It is a big misconception when the British say the Malays respect and support them . . . If Malay leaders have sought British assistance, it is because Great Britain is a great power.'[89]

The Mainland

Mainland Southeast Asia, more independent than the archipelago at the

---

[88] J. M. Gullick, *Malay Society in the late Nineteenth Century*, Singapore, 1987, 60.
[89] Quoted Suwannathat-Pian, 157n.

outset of the period, operated with different political dynamics. The great kingdoms were those of the Burmans, the Thais, and the Vietnamese. Each had its own problems of integration, even in regard to the core of the realm: the endemic weakness of patrimonial systems, like those of the Burmans and the Thais; the intractable problem for the Vietnamese of holding a kingdom together through applying a version of the Confucian system of the Chinese. Each kingdom also had an expansive urge, which thrust the Thais, for example, not only into the Malay states, but into Laos and Cambodia; it thrust the Vietnamese also into those luckless states; and brought the Thais and the Burmans into competition over the Shan states. Each state in any case contained minorities: the Burmans loosely integrated or failed to integrate Karens, Arakanese, Mons, Kachins, Chins, Shans; the Thais, Malays and Shans; the Vietnamese, Chams, Khmers, hill peoples. The states were also at times at odds with each other. The Thais and the Vietnamese avoided direct conflict: the conflict was at the expense of the intermediate states of Laos and Cambodia. The Thais and the Burmans had, by contrast, a legacy of direct conflict, and indeed the foundation of the most recent Thai kingdom followed the Burman destruction of Ayutthaya in 1767. Intra-regional dynamics, a more effective and a more comprehensive influence on political life on the mainland than in the archipelago in the late eighteenth century, were all to be altered by the subsequent imposition of the imperial régimes, though to some extent they facilitated it.

Perceiving the advent of the imperial powers clearly and assessing their nature were indeed made more difficult, not only by the traditional preoccupations and relationships of the mainland states—Vietnamese rulers could not believe that trade was an aim in itself[90]—but by the fact that so far the Europeans had had little impact on the mainland. In the archipelago, their presence was of long standing; they could not be dislodged, unless they dislodged each other, and it seems to have been widely, though not universally, recognized that at best it was necessary to compromise with them, to work within the framework they established. The mainland states had no such background. They had more experience of a suzerain power that worked in a different way. China intervened on the mainland with spasmodic violence and with dramatic effect. But for the most part it was content with a confession of vassalage and indeed made that profitable to its tributaries.

The relationship was not nurtured on the Chinese side by mere desire for flattery or mere domestic need: it was also China's means of providing security. It was natural, indeed, for a continental state to seek to insulate itself from outside threat and establish a surrounding zone of what might be called submissive neutrality and diminished independence. The most striking feature of the late eighteenth century was perhaps not so much the increased activity of European traders and empire-builders as the re-emergence (at their initial instance) of a large state on the subcontinent of India, which had the security imperatives possessed by other such states. Of this the mainland states were indeed aware. If Burma fell more outside

[90] A. B. Woodside, *Vietnam and the Chinese Model*, Cambridge, Mass., 1971, 263.

the Chinese sphere than Siam or Vietnam, it fell more inside the pale of an Indian diplomacy. Siam and Vietnam were also aware of the conquests of the British Company and apprehensive of them, but they responded differently. Characteristically too, they changed their relationship with China in different ways as the international position changed.

Burma was the least fortunately placed geographically, so far as India was concerned, and its approach to international relations made it unlikely to accept the diminished independence which essentially was the objective of the new rulers of India. Independence could be retained on the mainland as it could not in the archipelago, but only on conditions. The problems that arose between the states were, as a result, additionally difficult to solve, and helped to lead to two wars that stage by stage partitioned the Burman kingdom. The parties in Burma that favoured compromise could readily be undermined. The British rulers of India found it difficult to avoid taking up otherwise unsatisfactory causes. Even the modernization of this kingdom, otherwise not unwelcome, must have limits. Should it arm itself? should it grant concessions to foreigners? A third war, involving a foreign threat, led to a final incorporation. By this time, partly thanks to a legacy of distrust and the presence of disorder, incorporation seemed preferable to continuing the dynasty in a subsidiary relationship in what may be seen as a more normal pattern for the British in Asia. Resistance continued even so; perhaps indeed it was enhanced. The dynasty had failed to turn it to account.

The Nguyen rulers in Vietnam also failed to turn resistance to account. Their unification of a kingdom difficult to hold together and long divided de facto made them the more anxious over subversion and the more unwilling to modify their version of Confucianism. The approaches of the West offered them nothing that they wanted: commerce was not a general boon but a limited monarchical perquisite. Missionary endeavour recalled civil war and foreign intervention, and undermined assimilation of the great tradition. The conquests of the British in India added to the distrust, since it was far from clear to the Vietnamese that the British in Southeast Asia would behave differently; nor did they in Burma. For the Vietnamese, the best chance was to come to terms with the major power so as better to resist any other, and this option was available in the sense that it was not in the archipelago. But the Vietnamese, poorly informed in any case, were unable to take advantage of the option, and had no ally against the French save their ineffective Chinese suzerains.

Though Minh-mang was curious about the West, neither he nor his bureaucracy could abandon a Confucianist consensus. When the conflict came, there was élite and mass resistance. A French officer recognized 'the existence of a national spirit among the Annamese, whom we have always thought ready to accept and indeed worship any master who would allow them to plant and harvest their rice'.[91] The dynasty, facing a challenge in the north, compromised, vainly hoping to regain Cochinchina by negotiation. The partisans were disavowed: 'the Emperor does not recognise us,

---

[91] Mark W. McLeod, 'The Treaty of Sai-gon and the Vietnamese response to French intervention', Ph.D. thesis, University of California, Los Angeles, 1988, 145.

but it is indeed our duty to carry on our struggle for the safeguarding of our fatherland'.[92] On moving north, the French were able to choose a figurehead Nguyen ruler, and this option they selected, by contrast to the British approach in Burma. They still faced resistance, and it was belatedly invoked by Emperor Ham Nghi. Righteous uprisings or *khoi nghia* were led by scholars and gentry, but at least in Bac Giang Province there was a more lower-class movement led by Hoang Hoa Tham.[93]

The Thai reaction was more positive than the Burman and the Vietnamese. Their position was in their favour: more remote from India than the Burmans, more remote from China than the Vietnamese, less ideologically committed than they were, but more integrated than either. There was a legacy of flexibility, indeed, but perhaps the Ayutthaya conquest was in one sense a piece of good fortune. The new régime, based in Bangkok, was outward-looking and encouraged immigration and commerce. Rama II was unwilling at first to receive Crawfurd, but was persuaded to do so. More aware of British power as a result of the First Anglo-Burman War, Rama III accepted the Burney treaty. He was unwilling to accept one from Brooke, but his successor accepted one from Bowring. Even though it inhibited the full independence of his kingdom, the Bowring treaty preserved it in essence. The dynasty rightly perceived the need in this period not so much to play off the outside powers, as to accept the predominance of the greatest and seek to diminish that predominance without alienating it. King Norodom (r. 1860–1904) of Cambodia rightly envied Chulalongkorn: he had a 'a court of consuls'; in the Cambodian court there was only one representative.[94] The Thai kingdom had also to accept a measure of partition. But it surrendered territory not as the price of non-cooperation or as an alternative to co-operation, but as a complement to a pattern of co-operation which involved successive accommodations, and that sufficed to preserve the essential independence of the core of the Thai realm. 'It is sufficient for us to keep ourselves within our house and home; it may be necessary to forego some of our former power and influence',[95] as Mongkut had realistically put it. A Catholic mandarin, Nguyen Truong To, estimated that Siam was no stronger than Vietnam. 'However, when it engaged in contact with Westerners, that country knew how to wake up to reality immediately.'[96]

An Overview

The European states displayed division and diversity; but they possessed arms, assumptions and technology in common, and rivalry urged them on. Southeast Asian states were also divided among and within themselves, and they displayed no unity in meeting the challenge from outside. Their divisions in fact had long helped the Europeans. By this time,

---

[92] Quoted Truong Buu Lam, *Patterns of Vietnamese Response to Foreign Intervention*, New Haven, 1967, 11.
[93] Woodside, *Community*, 29.
[94] Quoted Milton E. Osborne, *The French Presence in Cochinchina and Cambodia*, Ithaca and London, 1969, 177.
[95] Quoted A. L. Moffat, *Mongkut, the King of Siam*, Ithaca, 1961, 124.
[96] Quoted Woodside, *Vietnam*, 261.

indeed, states in the archipelago had little scope for opposing the Europeans and little chance of acting in common: their internal divisions left them additionally exposed. Islam was to inspire opposition to the West, and be inspired by it; but despite their apprehensions, it did not stop the advance of the Europeans. The mainland states were initially able still to pursue traditional objectives, but that may have distracted them from meeting the new challenge. Traditional divisions among and within them were still strong. Even as his relations with the British deteriorated in 1823, the king of Burma, with his Thai enemy in mind, sent an embassy to Vietnam, headed by a Eurasian 'addicted to intoxication'.[97]

Survival may have been the main task. Some did not even see that, though growing conscious of British dominion in India, and later of Chinese decline; none except perhaps Siam were ready, like the Japanese, to undertake the changes that might be required in society, policy, economy. The impulse may have been to maintain the status quo: and the failure of such a policy, and resultant loss of territory, as in the case of Arakan or Cochinchina, only made adaptation at once more urgent and more difficult. Even those states that went beyond that, like Sulu, pursued a traditional dynamic. That there were answers was shown in Southeast Asia by Siam, elsewhere in Asia by Japan. But they were fortunate in circumstance as well as well-led, though differently led: one by a centralizing monarchy, the other by a post-revolutionary oligarchy. Both were able to see a priority, to formulate a response; both were strong enough to carry through a compromise.

Diverse elements indeed contributed to the making of policy in the various Southeast Asian states. Being a ruler did not mean being an autocrat: generally the ruler's power was strongest at the centre, often even there depending on patron–client allegiances. Where control of the periphery was weak, depending again on patron–client connexions, a unified response to European pressures was unlikely: changes of allegiance were part of the traditional dynamic. At the centre, ministers and court officials would be jockeying for power, often seeing the contacts with the Europeans in terms of factional politics, if not offering advice on the contacts that differed for less interested reasons. In many states there was tension between the religious and the secular. In the mainland Theravāda countries, the king was seen as the protector of Buddhism, an aspiring *cakkavatti*; in the archipelago, Islam at once supported the sultan's rule and sought to shape state and society; in Vietnam the Confucian ethnic was sustained by the Nguyen dynasty as a means of upholding its fragile unity, in effect challenging and channelling village loyalties. The hold of the state on the masses was uncertain: religious leaders might have more hold than the state; secret societies more than the Confucianist élite. The peasants indeed might not be reliable, though there is little evidence that, as Europeans tended to say, they longed for deliverance from native oppressors, and that could not necessarily be said even of minorities. Rather the masses, like the minorities, were an uncertain quantity. Involving the

---

[97] Burney to Ibbetson, 5 June 1824, Straits Settlements Factory Records G/34/95.

masses in politics, even in a resistance struggle, might be socially risky for the rulers and the élite. Mass opposition remained unused till too late in Burma and Vietnam. The minority peoples were less reliable still, though few hastened to shift their allegiance to the Europeans.

The year 1870 appears to offer, on a number of counts, a significant chronological division in terms of the making of European policies. It also affords, in part as a result, a division in terms of their impact. For that reason the date must also be of significance in Asian policy, whether or not it was so perceived. From then on, indeed, there was even less room for manoeuvre. Now on the mainland, as already in the archipelago, the European challenge was unavoidable. Indeed for the most part there could be little hope of sustaining independence, or even autonomy: the interaction would have to continue within the European framework. Within this periodization, other dates were also of significance: outside the archipelago, the establishment of paramountcy in India, the initial British defeat of China, later the victory of Japan over China and Russia. Inside, the crucial historical moments differed from state to state, recognized as such at the time or not: 1873, say, for Aceh, 1824 (or 1885) for Burma, 1826 or 1855 for Siam, 1859 for Vietnam.

Various policy options could be conceived, even attempted, taking more or less account of the Europeans. One conceivable option was to pursue traditional objectives in isolation from them; but that was impossible even for Minh-mang to achieve, though it was the course that, despite his curiosity about the West, he had to favour. Another was to contain or resist them, if need be by force, though after a phase of isolation that was likely to be even more risky than before. In any case long-term resistance might undermine the state, producing peasant rebellion or populist Islamic challenge. The third option was to compromise, 'to adjust our position to circumstances', as Nguyen Truong To put it in the 1860s.[98] But what would represent compromise? Retaining as much of the old customs and culture as possible and as much of the territory as possible? Or proceeding to a greater degree of modernization and avoiding a direct challenge to the interests of the Europeans, but perhaps attempting to operate on their ground, using their expertise, invoking their international law? The latter the Thais managed. Others found it difficult to compromise, perhaps even more so after partition had begun, because of opposition within. It was also difficult to modernize without appearing to threaten European interests, or getting caught among them, like the rulers of Kelantan, making concessions to private interests disapproved by the government of the Straits Settlements.

The methods at the disposal of the Asians for pursuing their options were various. Diplomacy was, of course, one, though it is usually more effective when power is explicitly or implicitly behind it. An isolationist could try politely asking visitors to leave, and later resort to executing those who persistently returned. Diplomacy might also be used to attempt containment: working with a predominant power, perhaps at a cost;

---

[98] Quoted Truong Buu Lam, 90.

playing off the foreigners, though that was a risky policy and could in fact prove provocative. Diplomacy was also a means to compromise, and it was a means, too, of turning the desire to modernize to account and of realizing that objective. Diplomacy was one option, force was another: but still less effective if not backed by power. Prompt submission might avoid catastrophe and include an element of compromise; fuller submision might facilitate modernization, and make possible an eventual come-back. But that was an argument used more by collaborationists after conquest than by negotiators before.

Asian policies were, like European, affected by information available and perceptions applied. Information might be hard to come by, biased, filtered. Monarchs rarely ventured beyond courts—Thibaw had never been more than five miles from Mandalay—and were often apprehensive over invoking popular resistance. Some were illiterate, like Sultan Hashim of Brunei or Bendahara Ahmad of Pahang. Their sources were frequently low-level: adventurers, missionaries, self-seeking consuls, lawyers. What information was available might be recast or obscured by the framework of its presentation: a monarch might not be able to bear receipt of some news or the mode of some approach. Tradition might stand in the way. And yet information was vital. What indeed was Europe? was it one or many? how could you appraise the powers? which indeed was the cat and which the rat? Could you ignore the unbelievable defeat of China sufficiently to avoid less easy options? Did you perceive the difference between the British and British India? Could you distinguish between a European government and subordinate officials or merchants, who often had no reason to emphasize the distinction themselves? Did faction struggles obscure reality? Even the experienced Kinwun got it wrong in Mandalay in 1885. Judgement was vital, too. 'The British and the French can entertain no other feelings for each other than mutual esteem as fellow human beings, whereas the likes of us, who are wild and savages, can only be regarded by them as animals', wrote King Mongkut in 1864. 'The only weapons that will be of real use to us in the future will be our mouths and our hearts constituted so as to be full of sense and wisdom for the better protection of ourselves.'[99]

INTERACTION AND ACCOMMODATION

The European approach to Southeast Asia varied from area to area and time to time. But that was not the sole reason for diversity of response. There was a range of possible 'solutions' or 'accommodations', the availability of which did not depend only on the Western powers. The most pre-emptive of them, conquest, was indeed rarely the first to which the Western powers resorted. Others might serve for longer or shorter periods. But, if there was an opportunity for those others, it had to be perceived and seized.

[99] Quoted Likhit Dhiravegin, *Siam and Colonialism*, Bangkok, 1974, 22.

Certainly the availability of solutions did in part depend on the needs of the Western powers. Those needs, quite often the more vigorously expressed because of the lack of a coherent or overall policy, were diverse. The Europeans might seek to protect merchants or missionaries; they might seek only a measure of law and order; they might seek political dominance. They would be influenced by their own cultural, religious and political traditions and a wish to demonstrate success to constituencies in Europe. They might be driven by rivalries in Europe or be rivals of other colonial powers in Southeast Asia, which they might come to terms with or seek to pre-empt.

For much of the period, particularly before the 1870s, the impact of the Europeans was indeed mediated by the predominant interests of the British. Those were not concentrated in Southeast Asia itself, and they had no interest in conquering it or making further Indias of Further India. The policies of other powers might be made in the shadow of British power, even shaped by it, but Britain left room for a diversity of approach and timing.

There were indeed shifts over time. Britain's predominance was marked up to 1870. Thereafter Southeast Asia was more fully open to the impact of the Industrial Revolution, and other Western powers showed increasing interest in Southeast Asia as in Africa. At Berlin new rules were accepted by the rivals in the absence of an overbearing empire. Rival Europeans would accept as valid only certain minimum forms of control. It was an impulse either to intensification of control, or to partition, or to both. Rivalry among the Europeans now gave Asians fewer options rather than more. De facto autonomy might be curtailed, lest a claim were effectively challenged.

If there were differences in the Western approaches, there were a range of accommodations to them. If those approaches changed over time, there might be phases also in the accommodations to them. One form of accommodation could succeed another, not necessarily in regular steps: resistance sometimes followed a series of adjustments that had turned out to be insufficient. Even resistance, however, did not quite rule out accommodation. The parties came to terms in some sense: the colonial régimes could not rule without collaborators, and collaborators they could find from the old or from new social elements, again with a range of motives, patriotic or personal in ambition. Accommodation continued within the new frontiers. A colonial régime might admire and wish to utilize the native leaders that had fought it, as the Brookes used the Iban, and the Company contemplated using Mat Salleh. It might fear the social disruption that could follow the displacement of traditional leaders. Alternatively, like the French in Cochinchina, it might actively seek an alternative élite.

The kind of accommodation depended in part on the character of the régimes involved at any particular time, as well as on the current position and objectives of the relevant Western power and its relationship with the other powers. The attitude of those régimes varied, of course, with their geographical position. That might mean that they were more exposed to the Western powers, though they might also be better informed about them and have a longer tradition of adaptation. It might give them greater means or hopes of resistance, through mobilizing their own resources in manpower or matériel, or through calling on great neighbours.

The régimes also varied in their nature. Some were more loosely integrated, some more centrally controlled. Neither condition of itself predicted the outcome of relations with the West, though the former perhaps made break-up more likely. Central control was significant for success, provided those with control made the right judgements and continued to make them as conditions changed. But aspiration to central control without its actuality was no substitute: it might indeed make for an unhelpful rigidity of response. There were also different kinds of central control. In monarchical states, central authority might be accepted in theory only, on the understanding of its practical limitations. The coherence of the state, again, might depend less on administrative effectiveness or adequacy than on the projection of modes of behaviour sustained by ritual and observance. Possessors of this kind of authority would find it especially difficult to come to terms with a Western power that went beyond the most minimal demands, for contacts might undermine ideological unity, and indicate insufficiency. If that unity was already insecure, the régime might be among the less adaptable, fearing to lose what control it had. Alternatively, or successively, it might fear actively to resist, lest such authority as it had were lost in the process and an alternative leadership emerged.

There were indeed questions of and opportunities for judgment for the leadership: it was not only a matter of geographical conditions and ideologies on the one hand and of Western interests on the other. The questions related in part to those Western interests. Handling the West depended on knowledge of them. How good was information at hand? Even if information were adequate and adequately interpreted, the problem itself remained. Was it best to resist the West, or to make concessions and preserve what you could, or to submit promptly and resist from within? Could you risk playing one power against another, if that option were open, or would you thereby precipitate a pre-emptive strike?

Decisions about such questions related not only to information and judgment about information. They also related to the domestic situation. Did the relations between the ruler and the ruled permit a choice? Was it constrained by an ideological or religious prescription, breach of which would deprive the régime of sanction or support? Did connections with non-Western suzerains prevent accommodation to the West, or offer a way of avoiding it? Tributaries might take advantage of demonstrated weakness, or they might themselves come to terms with the Western powers, making it difficult to fit them into the traditional pattern. For the tributaries, there were also problems. Coming to terms with the West might on the one hand be obstructed by a suzerain. That suzerain might on the other hand come to terms with the West and so reduce tributary status still further. More generally a state—like Johor—might see advantage in associating with the West so as to increase its influence over a neighbour. The alternative to submission was to resist or—as with Terengganu—to seek direct relationship with the Western power. Rarely, too, was an élite united in its reponse: indeed, the very intractability of the problems faced tended to add to division.

Asian policies, options, methods, have been analysed largely in terms of states, though to adopt that definition of political activity was in some sense itself a piece of Europeanization. To describe the result of the interaction of European and Asian in terms of the loss of independence may also not be entirely apt. It may even be anachronistic, for the sense of identification with a state was often limited, and the state was not necessarily seen as one among others. Even if the establishment of a colonial framework was clearly the outcome, consciousness of the implications might penetrate to the mass of the people only slowly. Not every change was so dramatically signalled as that in Burma.

> The city people had not been fully aware that the king was to be taken away until they saw our troops marching with Theebaw and the royal family in their midst. Then they awoke to the fact and a great cry went up from men, women and children alike. They bowed down to the ground doing shikko ... an enormous crowd ... assembled, ... and at intervals their lament rose up on the night air. A few stones and clods of earth were thrown.[1]

The people of Mandalay felt that their religion was in danger as well as their identity. Colonial powers in Southeast Asia generally avoided such drama. The interaction of Asian and European was a continuum, within a changed framework.

The framework was indeed just that: it allowed for a diversity of relationships, though all testifying to the increased political influence, if not hegemony, of European peoples and ideas. The hegemony of the Europeans, but not their ideas, was to be displaced only by changes outside Southeast Asia, just as it had been brought about so largely by them, though in both cases the outcome was also to a greater or lesser extent the work of Southeast Asian peoples. In the meantime the patterns of the colonial period were various. Some countries came under direct rule, some indirect; minorities and peripheral peoples often had new opportunities; one state indeed avoided the complete loss of political independence.

The reasons for the more or less general imposition of the colonial framework deserve reconsideration if only perhaps because of their apparent obviousness. Clearly it is primarily a question of power. The Europeans had more power at their disposal than before: more indeed, than any other single world centre had ever possessed. It was bound to be felt in Southeast Asia as elsewhere, given that region's locus and its intrinsic interest, its existing conditions and links; given, too, the Europeans' superiority at sea, their hold on India and later China, their traditional determination, their industrial prowess, their advanced technology. In these general terms the Asian states were at a disadvantage. In addition, the impact of the Europeans was not diminished, but if anything increased, by their rivalry; but the divisions among the Asian powers

---

[1] *The Pioneer Mail*, 16 Dec. 1883, quoted Ali, 44.

impeded any opposition they presented, and their individual modernization was spasmodic.

Only one substantial state survived with real independence; and considering features of Siam's history may help to explain why others failed.
Japan, too, may be compared with Southeast Asian states, and perhaps
most obviously to Confucianist Vietnam. At once its greater capacity for
adaptation is revealed in its combination of a deep sense of unity with
divisions, its insistence on tradition with a readiness to learn. Even so
Japan came nearer to a colonial solution than is sometimes realized, and it
benefited from a prevalent moderation among outside powers and a useful
connection with the most important of them.

Few Southeast Asian political entities were in so fortunate a position.
In the archipelago, many were already too entangled with the Europeans
to take political decisions save within that framework, and the British had
less interest in their fate than in that of the Dutch and the Spaniards. On
the mainland, isolationism was clearly not a viable option, though the
Vietnamese sought it. They had something of the sense of the unity of the
Japanese, but without the sophisticated diversity of views with which it
was combined. The Burmans' view of the world was in a sense like the
views some Japanese treasured, an expansionist one informed by a Buddhist ethic, that could only bring them greater humiliation the more
adjustment was deferred. Burma was also less well placed than Siam. The
latter was beyond the influence of Indian diplomacy, and later a buffer
between two empires. But it also acted positively towards the Europeans:
partly because it had an unusual degree of central control, thanks to
Bangkok's position; partly because it had a new and outgoing dynasty;
partly because it had the wit to recognize that the Europeans were at once
one and divisible and that among them the British were for the most part
the most powerful. It was fortunately placed in time, too: it was expanding
after a disaster; it had territory which it could spare, and which it was not
too obstinate to abandon if necessary. It could compromise.

Southeast Asia after all was unlikely to be a centre of world power; it was
likely to be deeply affected by changes in the distribution of power
elsewhere, and placed in a position of responding to them. The Europeans
were indeed to be displaced initially by the Japanese who had adopted
much that was European. In turn they were displaced by the Allies led by
the United States, and the Southeast Asian peoples had to try to determine
their future in yet another international context, that of a world dominated
by the US and the Soviet Union.

Even in such a context there was scope for judgment and decision. So
there had been in the making of the framework the Southeast Asian
peoples so largely inherited. And in turn they had partly depended on the
quality of information available to them, and their ability to interpret it.
The sources available in the nineteenth century were certainly defective.
Another way of appraising the contacts of European and Asian is by
considering them on a personal basis. Michael Symes and Henry Burney
gave lively accounts of their meetings with Burman leaders, and so did the

latter.[2] Those Vietnamese officials who met Thomas Wade, however, found it difficult to convey his message. The influence of the consular writer at Brunei, Enche Mohamed, was the greater because of the illiteracy of the sultan and the absence of British officials. The intermediaries between Europe and Asia were a diverse band, indeed a motley one.

THE COLONIAL RÉGIMES

The colonial framework outlined one of a succession of state systems in Southeast Asia. The statecraft of each had, within the limits of opportunity and judgment, involved a range of devices in endeavours to fulfil the purposes of the state: alliance, allegiance, violence, patriarchal and bureaucratic relationships, the backing of ideology, religion, law. The colonial system, like earlier systems, used elements of the old, combined with new elements, in an attempt to realize its objectives. Its combinations differed in different areas because its purposes differed and because those areas differed. It had some of the features of the contemporary European state system—in particular the emphasis on territory and frontier—and these often distinguished it from a Southeast Asian system that tended to deal in terms of people rather than land. But colonialism stopped short of the ideological association of state and citizens that the Europeans had worked towards. There were elements of modernity in the colonial approach, some indeed pointing that way, but that was not a conclusion the régimes could readily draw. Nationalisms clashed, that in Europe with that in Asia. At the same time the colonial régimes could not utilize fully the kinds of loyalty that earlier régimes had evoked, those based, for example, on Islam or Buddhism, and their attempts to co-opt rulers or aristocracies tended to change, even erode, the position of those leaders. They claimed, with greater or less justification, to offer good government. Even if their claim were justified, its ambit was limited. 'Thakin, you may say she was not a good queen, he was not a good king, but they were our own', Queen Supayalat's maid of honour said to Fielding Hall after Thibaw's removal. 'Do you think we can love a foreign master as we loved our king, who was, as it were, part of ourselves?'[3] In the face of this attitude, we must ask why were the colonial régimes successfully established and why did they endure so long?

An answer to the first question has been attempted in the preceding pages. In the archipelago, even more than on the mainland, the old kingdoms were weak in themselves, and often their hold could be readily undermined, sometimes with aid from within. On the mainland, even more than in the archipelago, the states were at odds with each other, and there were errors of information and judgment among the rulers. These

---

[2] cf. Thaung Blackmore, *Catalogue of the Burman Parabaiks in the India Office Library*, London, 1985.
[3] Quoted Ali, 44.

factors limited the need for European force, though that force was available, particularly at sea, and could, as in India, be enhanced with Asian allies and recruits. It was not realistic, Emperor Tu-duc argued, to fight the French. 'Do you really wish to confront such a power with a pack of cowardly soldiers? It would be like mounting an elephant's head or caressing a tiger's tail. ... With what you presently have, do you really expect to dissolve the enemies' rifles into air or chase his battleships into hell?'[4]

European force was perhaps more effective as a threat than as an actuality: it could get bogged down, sometimes literally, like the *Sphinx* on the bar of the Menam during Brooke's mission, sometimes figuratively, like the Dutch in Aceh. It was certainly more effective unused but available in combination with diplomacy. A further reason for the successful establishment of the colonial framework was its readiness within limits to compromise and turn to account those whose allegiance it needed. Initially at least it often had only limited purposes: to establish and maintain order, to ensure stability. That made it more acceptable, though it is doubtful that its message for the masses was so well received as it hoped. The masses were entitled to ask whether it would really relieve them from 'oppression'. If it did, was it only to install a different sort of oppression, perhaps less mediated by cultural factors and bonds of patron–client reciprocity?

What in any case was to replace it? Those it perforce bred up had their answer: to borrow the nationalism that identified people and state in Europe, and to build support on its basis within the frontiers the Europeans had established. But they could not defeat the colonial régimes on their own: the destruction of those régimes required the intervention of the Japanese and later the United States. Then the nationalists had their opportunity. Their success in gaining independence meant that they faced new problems: they had to consolidate régimes from which more was now expected amid divisions that had been only partially concealed during the fight against the colonialists. And, for good or evil, they had to accept the framework created in the colonial period. It was within that framework that their nationalism had largely emerged, and the Japanese had not effectively broken it down. The new world order was even less likely to welcome changes in it than the colonial powers that had earlier divided most of Southeast Asia among themselves. This was the challenge for a new statecraft.

BIBLIOGRAPHIC ESSAY

The historiography on this subject, perhaps even more than most, is affected both by attitude and by availability. The European sources are exceptionally copious; the stances writers take particularly controversial. In the light of the former, it is difficult to represent the views and policies of Asians. In the light of the latter, particularly in combination with the former, it is difficult to maintain a balance.

---

[4] Quoted Tuck, 175.

Sophisticated historical writing in the field was relatively sparse until the early twentieth century. Even then, it tended to be cast in a heroic or imperialist mould, like the writings of D. C. Boulger (*The Life of Sir Stamford Raffles*, London, 1897) or Henri Cordier (a series of articles in *T'oung Pao* on French colonial policy), or like those of P. H. van der Kemp (a series of articles on Anglo-Dutch relations mainly in *De Indische Gids* and *Bijdragen tot de Taal-, Land-, en Volkenkunde*). It tended to be nationalistic in tone, not merely over against Asians, but other Europeans also.

The application of professional historical values is more obvious in the inter-war period with the writings of D. G. E. Hall (e.g. *The Dalhousie-Phayre Correspondence*, London, 1932), W. S. Desai (*History of the British Residency in Burma 1826–1840*, Rangoon, 1939), and L. A. Mills ('British Malaya, 1824–1867', JMBRAS, 1925, reprinted 1960), and it intensified after World War II, when, moreover, primary sources became more freely available. Writers of the 1950s and early 1960s established a new framework, though still perhaps concerned more with policy than with impact, with one side of the story. They included C. D. Cowan, *Nineteenth-century Malaya The Origins of British Political Control*, London, 1961; G. Irwin, 'Nineteenth-century Borneo, A Study in Diplomatic Rivalry', VKI, XV (1955); Emily Sadka, *The Protected Malay States, 1874–1895*, Kuala Lumpur, 1968; Neon Snidvongs, 'The development of Siamese Relations with Britain and France in the reign of Maha Mongkut, 1851–1868', Ph.D. thesis, University of London, 1961; Walter Vella, *Siam under Rama III*, New York, 1957; Damodar Singhal, *The Annexation of Upper Burma*, Singapore, 1960; and the present author in his earlier books: 'British Policy in the Malay Peninsula and Archipelago 1824–1876', JMBRAS (1957) reprinted Kuala Lumpur, 1969; *Anglo-Dutch Rivalry in the Malay World, 1780–1824*, St Lucia, London, and New York, 1962; and *Piracy and Politics in the Malay World*, Melbourne and Singapore, 1963.

Shifts in attitude began to correct this approach from the early 1960s. At times, however, they could be so severe as almost to dislodge the whole endeavour, and to put the validity of what was seen as purely political or merely diplomatic history in question. The challenge was sometimes associated less with a new research thrust than with a reversal of viewpoint.

Greater balance and nicer nuance quickly followed. The later 1960s saw in this field, as in others, the appearance of work that reached a new level of sophistication, and it continued in the following decade, in, for example, A. J. S. Reid, *The Contest for North Sumatra*, Kuala Lumpur, 1969; John Ingleson, 'Britain's Annexation of Labuan in 1846', *University Studies in History*, V, 4, Perth, 1970; Milton Osborne, *The French Presence in Cochinchina and Cambodia*, Ithaca, 1969; and Peter Burns, *The Journals of J. W. W. Birch*, Kuala Lumpur, 1976. Other examples were Oliver Pollak, *Empires in Collision: Anglo-Burmese Relations in the mid-nineteenth century*, Westport, 1979; Charles Keeton, *King Thebaw and the Ecological Rape of Burma*, Delhi, 1974; Robert Pringle, *Rajahs and Rebels*, London, 1970; Carl Trocki, *Prince of Pirates*, Singapore, 1979; and J. F. Warren, *The Sulu Zone, 1768–1898*, Singapore, 1981. Books by Rollins Bonney, *Kedah, 1771–1821*, Kuala Lumpur, 1971; Eunice Thio, *British Policy in the Malay Peninsula, 1880–1910*, Kuala Lumpur, 1969; and Khoo Kay Kim, *The Western Malay States, 1850–*

1873, Kuala Lumpur, 1972 added to our knowledge of Malaya. Chandran Jeshurun, *The Contest for Siam 1889–1902*, Kuala Lumpur, 1977; Pensri Duke, *Les relations entre la France et la Thailande (Siam) an XIXe Siècle*, Bangkok, 1962; and Thamsook Numnonda, 'Negotiations regarding the cession of the Siamese Malay States, 1907–9', JSS LV (1967) added to our knowledge of Siam. The present author produced his books on the Borneo and Sulu region (*Britain, the Brookes and Brunei*, Kuala Lumpur, 1971, and *Sulu and Sabah*, Kuala Lumpur, 1978), while new light was thrown on the creation of British Burma by Ernest Chew, 'The Fall of the Burmese Kingdom in 1885', JSEAS, X, 2 (1979); G. P. Ramachandra, 'The outbreak of the first Anglo-Burman War', JMBRAS, LI, 2, 1978; and Muhammad Shamsheer Ali, 'The Beginnings of British Rule in Upper Burma', Ph.D. thesis, University of London, 1976.

The 1980s have seen attempts to examine or re-examine Asian sources, in particular by scholars from Australia, Malaysia and Thailand, like A. C. Milner (*Kerajaan*, Tucson, 1982), Alfons van der Kraan (*Lombok: Conquest, Colonization and Underdevelopment, 1870–1940*, Singapore, 1980), Ian Black (*A Gambling Style of Government*, Kuala Lumpur, 1983), Shaharil Talib (*After its own Image: The Trengganu Experience 1881–1941*, Singapore, 1984) and Kobkua Suwannathat-Pian (*Thai–Malay Relations*, Singapore, 1988).

The potential of the subject is far from exhausted: in a way, indeed, it is central to the contacts of Europe and Asia. But that, as the present chapter again suggests, does not make it easier to deal with.

2

POLITICAL STRUCTURES IN THE NINETEENTH AND EARLY TWENTIETH CENTURIES

In the nineteenth and early twentieth centuries profound changes took place in the political order in all Southeast Asian countries. A main feature of these changes was the foundation of European-style state administrations within territories formally defined by European imperialism. Colonial rulers created centrally controlled and functionally organized bureaucracies to govern regions which were delineated with little or no regard for indigenous conceptions of political or cultural boundaries. The personalistic and quasi-feudal complex of arrangements which had been the hallmark of earlier political systems was overridden and often eliminated.

The change was one that began slowly and then began accelerating with almost blinding rapidity as European industrialism and nationalism remade the entire world. At the beginning of the nineteenth century much of the region remained outside the control of any European power. Only Penang, Melaka (Malacca), Java, some of Maluku (the Moluccas), and part of the Philippines could really be said to be under European control. By 1850, the European advance was limited to a few British footholds in Malaya, the beginnings of a French presence in Indochina, a few Dutch treaties and the British occupation of Arakan and Tenasserim. During the next three decades, much of the region was divided into spheres of influence among the various European powers, and the political boundaries which characterize the region today had been fixed. Actual control of population, however, was limited to a few metropolitan centres: elsewhere it was exercised through treaties with otherwise autonomous chiefs or through loosely governed intermediaries. European rule was little more than claims of sovereignty and the rights to certain revenues and economic privileges.

By the 1920s, the whole of Southeast Asia had undergone a radical change. The clear linear borders shown on the map now divided the region into discrete political and administrative units. Networks of roads, railroads, telegraph wires and postal systems connected the economic centres of the various European empires with their hinterlands. The

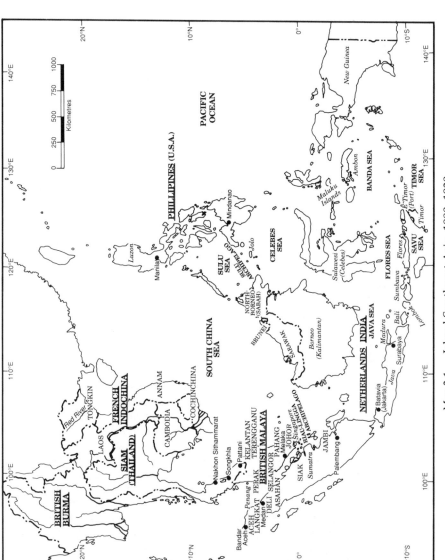

Map 2.1 Island Southeast Asia, 1880–1930

bureaucratic grids of central control had sprung out into respective 'national' hinterlands standardizing laws, languages, currencies, and even weights and measures according to their respective European usages.

The nature of the new political order was a radical departure from what had preceded it. In most areas, for the very first time, the arm of the state was capable of reaching into the daily lives of ordinary villagers on a sustained and intensive basis. Salaried government officials began to undertake the tasks of tax collection, law enforcement, land management, the judiciary, and public works, according to uniform, centrally determined, and very often alien standards. In addition to these accepted functions of government, the newly created administrations came to engage in an ever-increasing range of new activities, including education, public health and sanitation, and social and economic policy. These changes ushered in the era of the modern state in Southeast Asia.

The elimination of the traditional order was often a violent process. Age-old political forms were swept away in a matter of a few short years by fiat, or else were crushed by ruthless suppression. Those who resisted the imperialist advance invariably found it a hopeless, if not suicidal enterprise. Several entire political entities, such as Bali, Aceh and Sulu, perished in paroxysms of frenzied violence. More than once poorly armed but dedicated and often religiously motivated warriors threw themselves against Gatling guns, heavy artillery, repeating rifles and the disciplined infantry forces of industrialized states.

Officially, the new colonial order made no compromise with the Southeast Asian world. Confident to the point of arrogance, European administrators and military leaders in the region possessed both the will and the capability to destroy the old order and thus believed they had the power to create a new one. Unofficially, all was not as it seemed, and the realities of exercising effective administration were far beyond the actual capability of the imperial powers. They could destroy and thwart indigenous political and social initiatives, but they could not create what they imagined. The high tide of European colonialism continued to be characterized by compromise, qualification, half-measures, and inevitably frustrating results. The gap between aims and achievements was usually blamed on the 'laziness', the 'incompetence' and presumed racial, cultural and moral inferiority of the indigenous peoples. Despite the failure of stated European objectives, however, fundamental change was effected although it was often entirely unintended and sometimes contrary to the initial purpose.

The powerlessness of the indigenous peoples was more apparent than real. If active resistance was hopeless in the long run, it could be a very long run indeed as the Dutch discovered in Aceh. More difficult to control was passive resistance, indifference, and even self-interested co-operation which could subvert the best-laid plans. The weight of superior numbers and pure inertia worked to impede European efforts. Nor is it accurate to see Southeast Asians as merely reacting to European initiatives. Individuals, classes and entire ethnic groups took advantage of the opportunities that presented themselves. Many indigenous peoples actively moved, often with surprising alacrity, to align themselves with whatever new

Map 2.2   Mainland Southeast Asia, 1880–1930

centres of power appeared. Nothing was more deceptive than the illusion of total European control, for, in learning from the West, the most ardent collaborators prepared themselves to throw off foreign rule. By the 1930s, indigenous political and administrative élites or subélites in every European colony were beginning the quest for autonomy and independence. Even in Siam, where royal absolutism had created a centralized bureaucracy and military, modern education and the administrative competence of well-trained commoners had created a challenge to the monarchy.

The first section of this chapter is devoted to the role played in these newly created states by the 'collaborating' classes. In each case, it was necessary for the colonial rulers to rely on the co-operation of one or more groups of Asians in order to exercise effective control. A key variable was in the nature and status of the indigenous collaborator class. In some instances, these were the traditional ruling classes who had accepted the reality of Western domination. In other instances, marginal or minority populations came to fill these functions. Whatever the case, the changes directed and organized by Western colonial rulers deeply altered the nature and composition of the indigenous ruling classes. There was a fundamental alteration of the traditional relationship between rulers and ruled, in addition to a redefinition of both the rules and the realm.

In the early part of the nineteenth century, as in the past, colonial governments depended on almost feudal relationships with local collaborating classes. Thus traditional élites were often given some official recognition, and day-to-day government was conducted through them. The slowness of transport and the general isolation of Europeans in the tropics led to the creation of Eurasian or mestizo classes which assumed a life and culture of their own in places like the Dutch and Spanish territories. Even in the British-controlled Straits Settlements, control of the Chinese was accomplished through adaptations of the Dutch system of the *Kapitan China* or through revenue farmers and secret society headmen.

In the years after 1880, most of these arrangements were terminated as they were seen to place too much power in the hands of non-Europeans. Nevertheless, it continued to be necessary to maintain some sort of collaborating class if colonies were to be run effectively. Clerks, runners and minor office functionaries had to be Asians and had to be hired locally. If nothing else, there was the cost factor. European personnel were prohibitively expensive. In some cases the new Asian clerks were simply a new generation that accepted demotion and made the best of it. In other cases, particularly in the many new territories that were annexed or simply taken over after 1880, it was a case either of domesticating the former ruling class or else of creating entirely new classes to perform the mundane functions of colonial government. In Burma, the British came to rely on Indian immigrants to staff the lower levels of the bureaucracy, while in Laos and Cambodia the French used Vietnamese, and in Borneo and Sumatra the Dutch employed Javanese.

Although it was intended that power over policy formulation would be kept in European hands and the functions of primary decision-making were located more firmly in the metropole, considerable influence came to rest in the hands of these local classes, if only on an informal basis.

Moreover, they generally obtained a Western education and were exposed to radically different social and political ideas. In the years after World War I, these people sparked off movements for independence and self-government.

The second section of this chapter approaches the question of direct and indirect rule. Generally speaking, the depth and nature of the changes wrought by colonial rule depended on the degree to which indigenous political and social institutions were retained. In those places where colonial rule occurred as a result of treaties or some form of accommodation with local leaders and institutions, European control was exercised, at least nominally, through the indigenous structures, and was known as 'indirect rule'. This was the case in the Malay states, much of the Netherlands East Indies, and in Cambodia and Laos. 'Direct rule' was said to characterize situations in which the colonial takeover was accomplished by conquest or cession and the former political institutions (if, indeed, any had existed) were abrogated and new ones were created. British Burma, French Cochinchina, the Straits Settlements, and parts of the Spanish Philippines and the Netherlands East Indies represented examples of this variation.

While the legal status of the prior political institutions could be taken as a formal guide to the presence of a system of direct or indirect rule, in practice there was often little to distinguish the systems. During this period, legal niceties were respected only at the convenience of the colonial power, though such technical points once again became of importance when questions arose regarding the structure of the post-colonial state. In the late nineteenth and early twentieth centuries, indirect rule often signified no more than a transitory stage between the inception of a colonial presence and the development of a more comprehensive administrative machine. In most places, by the end of the 1920s, the state had been radically transformed through functionalization, rationalization and the extension of the European presence. On the other hand, in some respects, rule was always conducted through non-European intermediaries.

The third topic of this chapter is the imposition of 'law and order', certainly an ambiguous undertaking by any standard and even more so in colonial Southeast Asia. Initially, Europeans had been content to allow local law and custom to serve as their guide in daily administration. The only exception was the Philippines, where the Spanish friars saw it as their duty to combat paganism and to resist the advances of Islam. Generally speaking, however, the situation in British and Dutch colonies, where business came first, was marked by compromise. By the middle of the nineteenth century Europeans felt themselves drawn into local politics because of 'instability'. Colonial rule thus advanced on the justification of 'restoring order', suppressing piracy and 'protecting' peaceful trade.

These attitudes were gradually transformed by the bourgeois reformist movements of the metropoles in the 1890s. By the end of the nineteenth century all European states had come to see their role in Southeast Asia as one of bringing 'civilization'. Whether they conceived of it as the 'White Man's burden' or as a *mission civilisatrice*, all colonial régimes came to justify themselves as organized to secure the welfare of the native peoples. Such pretensions may seem hypocritical at a time when the most strenuous efforts were simultaneously being made to exploit local economic resources for the benefit of the European metropole and while draconian measures to control labour and restrict indigenous political life were taken with little compunction. Nevertheless, debt slavery, in fact most forms of slavery, were eliminated, as were piracy, head-hunting, cannibalism, trial by ordeal, the arbitrary rule of native chiefs and the power of secret societies. Uniform systems of law and justice were instituted. Taxation was regularized and the administrative norms of the West were established within the various territories controlled by each power. The final stage in the imposition of law and order came as nationalist consciousness and the desire for political autonomy stirred the indigenous peoples. At the same time the new Asian working classes of the region began to organize for economic justice. Each colonial power came to create security forces, secret police organizations and spy networks to suppress political movements and labour unions. These too, became a part of the colonial heritage of the post-imperial order.

In almost every new state of the region, the new colonial rulers created what J. S. Furnivall has styled 'plural societies'. These social formations, which are the topic of the fourth section, came about as a result of a variety of conditions. Sometimes they were caused by the accidental nature of the process of colonial takeovers. At other times, ethnic groups would be separated or thrown together because of the manner in which the border-lines were drawn or redrawn, an exercise often conducted in conference rooms in European capitals, and done in the interest of perceived economic or administrative efficiency, or to satisfy the strategic concerns of the various European powers.

As a result, the political units which emerged from this period frequently included a multiplicity of racial and ethnic groups. Just as often, the new lines split territories which had formerly been the possession of a single ethnic community, or traditional state, between two new political entities. In addition, these years were also marked by significant population shifts. Economic specialization developed along ethnic lines with the 'new' or capitalist sectors being taken over by newcomers. Likewise, social stratification often rearranged and reinforced ethnic barriers.

In addition to social shifts, the colonial régimes sought to impose linguistic uniformity in areas where none had ever existed. This happened in two ways, sometimes both together. European languages became the lingua franca of the new administrative territory as happened in Burma, Indochina, Malaya and the Philippines. In other areas, one of the local languages that already enjoyed widespread use was pressed into service as an administrative language, as was the case with *bahasa melayu* in Indonesia. Even in countries where indigenous languages had official status, European languages became the language of higher education of the élites. As a result, those Asians who sought positions in the colonial bureaucracies studied the European languages and imbibed the cultural peculiarities of the Western metropole. Regardless of the benefits or disadvantages of this change, those who became educated found themselves even further removed from the concerns and everyday lives of their own rural compatriots.

Whatever the cause, however, the results tended to be surprisingly similar. Different racial and ethnic groups found themselves thrown together within the same political units but paradoxically often under separate administrative and even legal structures. Relations between minority populations and groups that would become 'national majorities' after World War II were often 'suspended'. In Burma, British administrators in the minority areas institutionalized the customs and political structures of the Shans, Karens and others, while Christian missionaries put their languages into written forms based on the Roman alphabet, just as Malay, Indonesian, Tagalog and Vietnamese were converted to Roman letters. In other areas of Southeast Asia, Chinese immigrants flocked into the newly created economic sectors while the colonial legal and administrative structure effectively insulated most of the indigenous peoples from the affairs of its Chinese residents. The colonial heritage has left these new 'national' territories with the ambiguous heritage of clearly-drawn national borders enclosing collections of heterogeneous and antagonistic ethnic communities.

The final section offers a study of two contrasting cases. The nineteenth century saw the traditional Burmese state and finally the Burmese monarchy collapse as it sought to resist increasing British pressure. By contrast, the kings of Siam (Thailand) yielded and accommodated themselves to British and other Western demands for open borders, unrestricted trade and extraterritorial privileges. At the beginning of the twentieth century Burma and Siam seemed to represent opposite poles of the 'colonial' experience. In 1886 and 1887, with the conquest of upper Burma and the abolition of the monarchy, the British began the process of totally restructuring the country's administration according to the model of British India. Placed under the most rigorous form of direct rule, Burma became the most thoroughly colonized state in the region. Siam, by contrast, remained technically independent. Its monarch moved beyond compromise with the West and embarked upon a process of administrative reform, centralization and modernization. Although usually treated as an exception in Southeast Asia, since it was not formally taken under European control, Siam may be seen as an extreme example of indirect rule. It can be argued that the combination of unequal treaties, foreign economic predominance and the presence of foreign advisers made the position of Siam quite similar to the situation of one of the unfederated Malay states, such as Johor. In the final analysis, in both countries, regardless of who directed the process, the results were quite similar in certain respects. Like all the other states of Southeast Asia, they found their territories delineated by Europeans and were subjected to the processes of administrative centralization and rationalization according to European models. They found their social and political structures rearranged and transformed by migrants, new economic forces and shifts in the class structures. Nevertheless, by 1930, Burma appeared to have moved further down the road of political modernization and economic development than Siam. The latter was still run by an absolute monarchy, and a traditional élite clung to power through the persistence of quasi-feudal institutions.

The years immediately preceding World War II saw the European order in Southeast Asia under a variety of challenges. The trauma of World War I and the economic stress of the world-wide depression had seriously undermined Western power. At the same time, the social and political order which had been created to serve European interests had taken on a life of its own, and everywhere nationalist movements sought either to overthrow or to succeed to the political order which had come into being. Political liberation of Southeast Asia, however, would occur within the structures created by European colonialism.

INDIGENOUS COLLABORATION

European domination was based on superior military technology, economic strength and the possession of national and mercenary armies. Despite this power, successful European administration needed co-operation from strategic indigenous groups. In the first instance, Europeans themselves were simply too thin on the ground to undertake the tasks of day-to-day administration on any but a fairly high level. In pre-modern times, it was necessary to take Asians into partnership and to allow them a share of power within the colonial apparatus. These groups lost status with the rationalization of the state.

Nevertheless, Asian collaborators were still necessary. As the role of government became both more extensive and more intensive, the demands upon colonial administrative structures increased immeasurably. Language and cultural barriers alone necessitated a class of subordinates whose role it was to convey an increasing number of directives to broader sectors of the local populations. These intermediaries were drawn from a variety of sources, depending on the local situation and historical development of each colony. Sometimes they were members of traditional ruling groups, sometimes they were newly risen classes, in other instances they were immigrants. Whatever its origin, a class of indigenous, or at least local, collaborators was necessary for successful colonial rule.

The Dutch and Spanish empires in Java and the northern two-thirds of the Philippines were pre-modern creations and had come into being in the sixteenth and seventeenth centuries. The conditions of the age necessitated the development of local ruling classes dependent upon European patronage and support. In both areas local élites were brought into the colonial régime and often exercised considerable powers. These included village headmen in the Philippines who became *gobernadorcillos*, or regional chiefs such as the *bupati* in Java whose traditional duties to their former overlords were subsumed by the Verenigde Oost-Indische Compagnie (VOC, the Dutch East India Company) and converted into the delivery of trade produce.

In the Netherlands East Indies, a close association had grown up between the Javanese *priyayi* class and the Dutch. Although each performed specific functions in civil administration, the political partnership between the *pangreh pradja* and Binnenlandse Bestuur was an unequal one but, because of its long-standing nature, it was quite complex. Nor was it the sort of thing that could be diagrammed on an organizational chart.

Throughout the nineteenth century the *pangreh pradja* continued to function both as the successors of the pre-colonial chiefs and as agents of the
Netherlands government.[1]

Heather Sutherland suggests that the relationship between the European civil service and the *pangreh pradja* was characterized by continued
bargaining 'between elites of two races and of two cultures'. The cultural
foundations were important. The *priyayi* did not see themselves as traitors
to the traditional order or as betrayers of their peoples. Rather they were
merely respecting what they understood as 'power'. According to Sutherland, the intellectual base of the *pangreh pradja* was in their perpetuation
of the traditional ideas of status and aristocratic values. These included
'continuing beliefs in supra-human aspects of life and government', the
importance of local family cults, and belief in the importance of graves.
'Belief in the possibility of working with transcendental forces was virtually universal among the Javanese, and the cultivation of power by
mystical exercises was very common, a hallmark of priyayi culture.' The
Javanese thus stressed moral and religious aspects of government. They
perceived a need for an essential harmony between spiritual and physical
environments. The persistence of these beliefs was a reminder that the
priyayi had evolved from feudal chiefs to government administrators
during the nineteenth century.[2]

The relationships that grew up between the European colonial régimes
and these traditional collaborator classes are difficult to typify. They were
ambiguous and complex to say the least, and were marked by compromises and contradictions. It was difficult to tell where the European left off
and the Asian began. In fact, it could be argued that these early colonial
states were more Asian than European. The earlier colonial governments,
such as those in the Philippines and the Netherlands East Indies, were
much like traditional Southeast Asian states. They depended on patron
and client links between several layers of local chiefs whose segmented
polities ultimately gave them a certain standing that was recognized by the
local populations. Tax collections, law and order, public works and religious affairs were seen as the responsibility of the regional chiefs or even
village authorities whose relations with the centre had been essentially
personal.

The rationalization of the state brought a move to revise these relationships. Positive steps were taken to demote those groups who had, in
earlier years, actually exercised power, including those who had facilitated
the imperial advance. Most régimes took steps to deprive these groups of
the spheres of private power they had come to possess within the colonial
political and social order. The new administrative arrangements were also
aimed at removing the traditional social and political cement that had
bound traditional leaders to their peoples. By the beginning of the twentieth century, Southeast Asians were finding themselves declining in status
and power.

---

[1] H. Sutherland, *The Making of a Bureaucratic Elite*, Singapore, 1979, 2.
[2] ibid., 4–6.

Whole classes of the colonial populations that might have been counted as allies in earlier years were likewise demoted or abolished as Europe drew closer to its possessions in Southeast Asia. The Eurasians of the Netherlands East Indies, especially Java, whose decline had begun in the beginning of the nineteenth century, were close to becoming outcasts by the 1880s. Jean Gelman Taylor[3] has traced the process of their displacement in the colonial society and state of the late nineteenth century. For such groups, the imposition of racial and cultural barriers between Asians and Europeans was particularly degrading.

In other countries, however, these classes were not displaced. In fact, they managed to position themselves so as to inherit power when the colonialists ultimately departed. Their success or lack of success in so doing depended largely on their ability to maintain a power base in the local society. This was particularly true in the Philippines where the mestizo classes as well as some of the creoles were already raising the nationalist banner by 1870. The efforts by the Spanish during this time to modernize their administration in Philippine and concurrently to avoid sharing power with the *ilustrados*, led to the Philippine revolution and the takeover by the United States. Not all of these groups went peacefully into oblivion.

In the case of the Straits Settlements, British rule during most of the nineteenth century had rested on the collaboration of the Straits Chinese, especially the *kapitans*, the secret society headmen, the revenue farmers and *baba* merchants who had come to occupy semi-official positions. Similar groups of Chinese also existed in Batavia and other Javanese towns, in Saigon, Bangkok and Manila. Very often, their power within the Chinese communities, or in local society in general, was rooted in secret societies and groups of revenue farm police.

In particular, the opium revenue farms, which were invariably controlled by Chinese, came to be perceived as the most glaring examples of enclaves of the state in private hands. The revenue farmers exercised power over the local population through their own networks of spies, thugs and informers. As a first step in the rationalization process, economic and political power were separated. Between 1885 and 1910, the revenue-farming systems were increasingly restricted and ultimately abolished and converted into government monopolies. This happened first in the French possessions and later in the Dutch and American colonies and finally in the British territories and Siam.

Even where efforts to decrease the influence of these classes in the colonized areas were largely successful, many managed to maintain some footing on the socio-political mountain. In British Malaya the Straits Chinese were well-enough established and often wealthy enough to move into the middle ranks of the expanding bureaucracy as clerks and sometimes even as professionals. Individuals such as Song Ong Siang, Dr Lim Boon Keng and Tan Cheng Lock occupied places of prominence in local society during the first half of the twentieth century. It can even be argued that their cultural descendants did in fact inherit at least Singapore. These

[3] *The Social World of Batavia: European and Eurasian in Dutch Asia*, Madison, 1983.

were the graduates of Raffles Institute and the other English-language schools. The class of 'Queen's Chinese' that formed the Straits Chinese British Association were the predecessors of the English-'stream' Chinese, who, in the case of Singapore, have taken charge of the post-colonial society.

Despite these efforts at rationalization and decreasing traditional power bases, collaborators continued to be particularly important to colonial governments in the years after 1890, when increasing numbers of special-ists were recruited from European civil services to perform technical tasks in fields such as medicine, public sanitation, and engineering in mines, railroads and construction. Unlike earlier colonial officials, who came to Southeast Asia prepared to serve for periods ranging from a decade to life before returning home, the servants of the modern administrations could often expect to return to the metropole after two to three years. Sometimes they could be reposted from a colony in Southeast Asia to one in Africa or Southern Asia or even in the Americas. Their commitment was not to a particular Southeast Asian area or state but to a career in a global imperial bureaucracy.

European officials were expensive. They came with their wives, their children and as much European cultural baggage as they could manage. They expected medical and retirement benefits, paid 'home leaves' for themselves and their families, and of course high-quality education, in European schools, for their children. They needed housing and amenities of a European level as well as staffs of servants to undertake the tasks which were considered unfit for white people in the colonies. The sheer numbers of people needed for efficient administration meant that most of the lower ranks had to be recruited locally. Such a rank of semi-skilled clerks, runners and village-level personnel also served to place a status barrier between the power élite and the menial public employees. It also prevented the appearance of a class of poor, or even average, whites who might dispel the illusion that the Europeans were racially superior to all Asians.

The push for bureaucratic standardization in the Netherlands Indies, which reached a peak between 1910 and 1915, brought a real shift in relations between the Dutch government and the *priyayi*. During these years the formerly independent feudal chiefs were forced to accept their new status as merely a part of a centralized bureaucracy.[4] Although some *priyayi* families gained financially as the government began to promote large-scale economic enterprise, most tended to slip in economic status. They were integrated under centrally directed control and thus became less dependent on popular support than on Dutch approval.[5]

The elimination of Spanish authority in the Philippines by the United States brought the US up against the resistance of the *ilustrado* class which had begun the revolt against Spain in the first place. During the early years of the twentieth century, the American relationship with the *ilustrados* was probably unique in Southeast Asia. Unlike other colonial powers, the

---

[4] Sutherland, 2.
[5] ibid., 11–14.

Americans saw their possession of the Philippines as only temporary. Americans wished to build a benevolent colonial government which would gain the co-operation of the people and at the same time educate them for self-government. The new colonialists were convinced that the *ilustrados* were as yet unprepared for self-government. As William Howard Taft wrote:

> While they [the *ilustrados*] deal in high sounding phrases concerning liberty and free government they have very little conception of what that means. They cannot resist the temptation to venality, and every office is likely to be used for the personal aggrandizement of the holder thereof in disregard of public interest.[6]

Taft would have preferred to place power in the hands of the 'people'. However, it was necessary to solicit the support and co-operation of the élite in order to end the war which frustrated Filipino nationalists and armies of peasants were waging against the United States. American administrators found it expedient to allow the co-operative elements of the Filipino élite an increasingly larger role in government and to look the other way as they enriched themselves at the expense of the peasants and increased their traditional power within the local communities. Norman Owen points out that the contradictory goals of cheap and expedient administration coupled with republican ideals led to a 'perpetual compromise' which ultimately allowed the *ilustrado* class to take power. Taft had warned against the tendency 'merely to await the organization of a Philippine oligarchy or aristocracy competent to administer government and then turn the islands over to it'.[7]

Although the Americans were newcomers to the colonial game in 1899 and 1900, their decision to seek the co-operation of a group within the native society and then to attempt to remould it to their purpose was one that was taken by all colonial régimes throughout the region. Even though not all did so with the intention of training a ruling class to succeed them, most colonial administrative policies achieved the same end. A class of indigenous functionaries was trained to fill the lower ranks of the civil and military services. Groups that had begun as élite classes in pre-colonial or 'early' colonial society, such as the Malay aristocrats, the Filipino *ilustrados* or the Javanese *priyayi*, were converted into civil servants or, as they preferred to be called, government officials.

In other cases, new, non-élite groups were identified by the colonial powers as preferred allies. Traditional leaders were eliminated altogether in Burma. The old circle headmen were abolished and new 'village' headmen were appointed as civil servants. Likewise in Cochinchina, the elimination of the traditional mandarins necessitated the employment of ordinary Vietnamese as government servants. In some instances where,

6 Michael Cullinane, 'Implementing the New Order: The Structure and Supervision of Local Government during the Taft Era', in Norman G. Owen, ed., *Compadre Colonialism: Studies on the Philippines under American Rule*, Ann Arbor: Michigan Papers on Southeast Asia no. 3, University of Michigan, 1971, 15.
7 Norman Owen, 'Introduction: Philippine Society and American Colonialism', in ibid., 5–7.

for a variety of reasons, local leaders were unavailable, 'foreign' Asians came to serve in these roles. In Annam and Tonkin, where the traditional hierarchy of mandarins was left in place, a new civil service, made up largely of Frenchmen, was organized alongside it. On the other hand, the lack of suitable personnel in the Cambodian and Laotian protectorates led the French to employ Vietnamese. In Burma and Malaya, the British often found it convenient to use Indians, and in the case of the latter, Chinese.

In the military services the use of alien or minority populations as soldiers seemed even more prevalent. Following policies that had been developed in India, the British specialized in cultivating certain populations as military allies. Two-thirds of the British military in Burma were made up of Karens, and the other third were mostly Kachins and Shans. In the Netherlands East Indies, the Dutch had long made it a policy to employ Ambonese in the colonial military. In Malaya, the British frequently employed sepoys from India.

A side-effect of the recruitment of local personnel for government service was the establishment, in virtually all colonies, of school systems. These were often followed by the appearance of private schools, generally run by Christian missionaries. The language of instruction was usually the European tongue of the colony. Schools using the vernacular as a medium of instruction were also founded, but these tended to be seen as less prestigious. The impact of the schools was, of course, far-reaching, since it had the effect of creating cultural allies for the colonial powers. This class of individuals began to separate themselves from their native cultures and to adopt not only Western languages, but values, prejudices, life-styles and, most ironically, expectations. Advancement according to merit, an essential element of Western education, was a dangerous precedent in colonial systems founded on the erection of racial barriers. Personal humiliation and the frustration of expectations created by the Western educational experience fuelled the first generation of anti-colonial revolutionaries in the 1930s. The protégés of the European rulers became their competitors.

The increasingly racist aspect of European administrations began after a time to create a backlash, and this profoundly altered relations between European and Asian members of the colonial élites. Theories about the nature of Southeast Asian political thought and political practice developed by scholars such as Benedict Anderson and Anthony C. Milner[8] indicate that indigenous rulers and chiefs might have initially seen it as their duty to collaborate with colonial rule. Because of the rather gradual process of the colonial takeover as well as the fact that groups like the *priyayi* saw themselves as servants of power, they did not see their activity in co-operating with the Dutch government as an act of treason. In other cases, such as in British Malaya, Malay chiefs who collaborated with the colonial advance also saw themselves as continuing to serve the *kerajaan*, the government. The idea that a colonial government was necessarily an

[8] Anderson, 'The Idea of Power in Javanese Culture' in Claire Holt et al., eds, *Culture and Politics in Indonesia*, Ithaca, 1972; A. C. Milner, *Keraja'an: Malay Political Culture on the Eve of Colonial Rule*, Tucson, 1982.

alien entity had not actualy forced itself into the consciousness of local ruling classes. It was really only with the development of nationalism that Southeast Asians came to perceive a fundamental difference between the interests of the state and their own societies. Certainly a part of this awareness of difference came as a reaction to European racism.

In a country such as Siam, where there was no formal colonial government, the monarchy itself can be seen as both the collaborator and the colonialist. So far as foreign powers were concerned, the two Thai monarchs who ruled during the years of European advance, Mongkut (r. 1851–68) and Chulalongkorn (r. 1868–1910), carefully accommodated themselves to European demands. They gave up territories; they signed treaties that compromised their control of customs, foreign nationals and trade; they accepted the advice of foreigners on reforming their own political, economic and social systems; and they went so far as to hire European experts to carry out such changes. The reforms in Siam resulted in the centralization and the enhancement of the monarch's power within the realm.

Internally, Chulalongkorn used the modernization programme to eliminate the hereditary court officials and the *chao muang*, the provincial élites who had made the local governorships their family preserves. They were replaced with the representatives of the Bangkok-based bureaucracy which was under the control of the Western-educated brothers of the king. New officials were recruited from the Bangkok élite and from among the children of provincial families which were willing to accept education in exchange for their loss of hereditary privilege. These provincial élites lost their former military status, and European advisers were hired to train a professional military armed with modern weapons.

The two early twentieth-century Chakri monarchs (Rama VI and Rama VII) were much less adept at managing the apparatus of the central state that Chulalongkorn had created. They may be seen as the first of the colonial rulers to be toppled by their own class of collaborators. The participants in the 1932 coup d'état had a great deal more power vis-à-vis the monarchy, and thus did not need to wait until the imperial military was neutralized by outside forces. They in fact led the military force.

By forming alliances with sectors of the local population, colonial rulers were acting out of expediency. The results of these policies proved to be profoundly dangerous to the colonial governments. The indigenous allies gained an intimate familiarity with the colonial system that ultimately turned them into the most dangerous of enemies, possible replacements for the European rulers. In addition to this peril, Europeans had created a class who excelled at collaboration, who understood instinctively the nature of colonial power, and who were prepared to collaborate with whomever held the balance of military strength. European colonial officials were often stunned by the alacrity with which 'their natives' responded to the Japanese promise of 'Asia for Asians' in 1942.

In the case of the Philippines, as in Malaya, Cambodia and Laos, the traditional élites were fortunate enough to succeed. They followed the path from traditional leadership to colonial ally to post-independence élite, staying on top while the world changed beneath them. In the Netherlands East Indies, the transition was not so smooth. The extent to which these classes found themselves associated with anti-nationalist interests in the midst of revolutionary turmoil was usually a function of how far they had allowed themselves to become separated from their own societies. The new administrative class in Vietnam, often Catholics, strove to become 'French'. In the post-colonial era, the situation would be particularly difficult for those ethnic or social minorities that had served the European state and then found themselves isolated in the years of nationalist revolution.

DIRECT AND INDIRECT RULE

J. S. Furnivall, in his classic work on colonial rule in British Burma and the Netherlands East Indies, noted that the two countries shared many similarities.

> But in respect of colonial practice they show a striking contrast. In Burma the British have from the first relied on western principles of rule, on the principles of law and economic freedom; in Netherlands India the Dutch have tried to conserve and adapt to modern use the tropical principles of custom and authority.[9]

This statement points up the key distinctions Furnivall discerned between systems of direct and indirect rule in Southeast Asia. The rationale for direct rule flowed from the impulse to reform which was an important element in classical eighteenth-century European political thought. It was first attempted in Asia by the English liberals Warren Hastings and Lord Cornwallis in India.[10] The impulse came to Southeast Asia with Thomas Stamford Raffles, who experimented with classical liberal principles in Java and implemented what he called a 'system of purity and enterprise' in Singapore. Western imperialism in Southeast Asia thus created these systems of direct rule as a part of the idealistic effort to reconstruct the world according to a rational design.

The early systems of indirect rule such as that of the Dutch in the Indies and of the Spanish in the Philippines were born of no distinct plan but, according to Furnivall, simply emerged as expeditious methods of extracting economically valuable commodities from unwilling Asian producers. At the beginning of the nineteenth century, individuals like Raffles saw these systems as corrupt and exploitative. By the end of the nineteenth century, the ideological ground had shifted and the difficulties of various sytems of direct rule conduced to the proposition that indirect rule was more humane since it softened the harsh impact of economic freedom and avoided adverse indigenous reactions to unfamiliar codes of law. As a result, indirect rule came to be seen as a method of helping natives to gain independence on their own through slow but genuine development.

These criteria may cover the general distinctions between the two

[9] J. S. Furnivall, *Colonial Policy and Practice*, Cambridge, UK, 1938, reprinted New York, 1956, 10.
[10] ibid., 28.

systems, but there is much more to it. Labels conceal both differences and similarities. Furnivall appears correct in his judgment that there was no sharp line between systems of direct and indirect rule in practice. British rule in the Malay states was called indirect, but was really quite intrusive and bore little resemblance to the administration of the Dutch East Indies. In the Philippines, where the United States instituted a completely new system, they ended up by preserving much of the informal power structure and in ruling through the *ilustrado* and *cacique* classes. On the other hand, French indirect rule in Annam and Tonkin was every bit as intense and intrusive as was the direct rule system of Cochinchina. Thus the labels covered a wide variety of actual practice. Moreover, whatever label was used, the system changed over time as it was adapted to local conditions and revised as a result of pressures from home governments and colonial economic interests. Nevertheless, the distinction is a useful one, if for no other reason that the fact that indirect rule often maintained the legal status of the traditional political system in the post-colonial era.

In its broadest sense indirect rule signified a co-operative relationship between elements of the local ruling or élite classes and the colonial power. European sovereignty, whatever it entailed, was carried on within the context of the traditional political institutions. The old system, as well as its ruling class, retained its legitimacy. In the case of Java, Dutch control had been first grafted on to the top of the old 'feudalistic' system and over time the *bupatis* and regents had been transformed into bureaucrats, but their functions continued to be largely of a police and economic nature. Their charge was to preserve *rust en orde* (peace and order). Until the early years of the twentieth century the Dutch continued to rely on customary law for the arbitration of disputes and on the personal, 'inherited' authority of the *bupati* or regent (the major Javanese officials) to ensure that the functions of government were carried out.

In other situations, such as the Federated Malay States, the British Residential system had come into existence as a result of treaties with the sultans. British officials were installed at the courts of the rulers to give 'advice'. By the 1880s, these 'Residents' had taken over the functions of law enforcement, legislation, tax collection, and had created the foundations of the modern administrations. Regardless of the level to which they were involved in the direction of affairs, however, the de jure sovereignty of the Malay rulers was maintained. This was a contrast to Java, where the alien system was placed above the traditional system, and colonial rule was exerted through the indigenous ruling class. In Malaya, the colonial system came into being as a layer of government between the traditional rulers and the people. French government in the protectorates of Laos and Cambodia was similar in structure to the British system in Malaya.

In the case of direct rule, Furnivall suggested that in practice it involved the attempt by Europeans to impose Western-style administrations and systems of law upon Southeast Asians and simply to abrogate whatever had been before. Legalistically this meant the abolition of pre-existing monarchies and their supporting hierarchies of chiefs and officials. At the same time, provincial, district and village boundaries and other administrative categories were redefined. It meant the introduction of new

definitions of property, court systems and procedures and a redefinition of
the individual's relationship to the state.

In practice, perfectly executed direct rule never really existed, simply
because it would have taken an administration entirely staffed by Europeans to make such a system possible. The rule of the United States in the
Philippines was instituted with what appeared to be the most ambitious
aims of all Southeast Asian colonial régimes. After seizing the islands from
the Spanish in 1899, President William McKinley prayed over the problem
and decided that the United States had a duty to 'civilize' the Filipinos.
Under the administration of William Howard Taft, Americans set out to
remake the Filipino society along American lines. Michael Cullinane has
noted that Taft's administration saw the introduction of 'all the basic
American democratic institutions'. These included an electoral process, a
civil service based on merit, an American-style judiciary, a constitution
with a bill of rights, a three-tiered system of local, provincial and national
government, and an elected Filipino legislature with a political party
system.

The American system began with an emphasis upon local self-government
with the aim of building democracy 'from the bottom up'. Very quickly,
however, American administrators discovered that the Filipino élites who
came to fill posts in municipal government were regularly 'mishandling
public funds' by voting all available revenues to pay their own salaries.
American administrators began tinkering with the system they had superimposed on the islands. On the one hand they moved towards greater
centralization in order to prevent the 'crying evils' of unrestricted Filipino
rule, and at the same time they were forced by rising costs and the need to
encourage Filipino co-operation to permit an increased Filipinization of
local government. In the end, the *ilustrado* class succeeded not only in
taking control of the government from the bottom up, but also managed,
through the electoral process, to organize themselves to protect their class
interests on a national basis. Thus, what began as a system of direct rule
aimed at total reform of society ended as one that confirmed the dominant
position of the traditional oligarchy. In effect, American rule operated very
much like the system of indirect rule in the Netherlands East Indies, where
local and regional élites mediated the impact of foreign influence. But
unlike the Dutch colony, the American administration became a part of
the local system rather than vice-versa. The Javanese *priyayi* lost their
traditional constituency, whereas the *ilustrados*, the *caciques* and large
landowners actually strengthened their position in the Filipino political
and economic order.

Even within specific colonial entities, systems of direct and indirect rule
came into existence alongside one another as a result of a variety of
circumstances. Prior to this period, there had been little cohesion within
traditional Southeast Asian political units. With the possible exception of
Vietnam, the major states of the mainland were what Stanley J. Tambiah
has termed 'galactic polities'. Within the island world the pattern of the
'segmented state', which James Warren has applied to the Sulu sultanate,
best describes the relatively loose pattern of political association among
autonomous Malay *negri*. Throughout the region, there was little distinction

between domestic and foreign relations, so far as the central authorities of the major political units were concerned. The model format for these relations continued to be the 'mandala', whereby the central authority attempted to manipulate the circles of states and principalities around it. And, in fact, initially, the European colonial establishments behaved according to these patterns as well.

The European 'forward movement' in the mid-nineteenth century was the first step in the rationalization of the state apparatus, because it drew a clear distinction between domestic and foreign. The borders which were created in this process, however, did not automatically create domestic uniformity. Despite all of the steps toward rationalization and modernization, the colonial empires were still not much more than haphazard collections of historical 'accidents'. For instance, British-controlled Malaya, as late as 1942, while all of it might have been coloured pink in most maps, was really an ill-assorted administrative patchwork. There were the three Straits Settlements which were a Crown Colony, under direct rule; and the four Federated Malay States under indirect rule, each with its own sultan but actually run by Residents under the authority of a central administration in Kuala Lumpur. The five unfederated states were under even more indirect rule, with each sultan maintaining his own administrative élite with varying degrees of sophistication and efficiency, and the newly-installed British Advisers having far fewer powers than the Residents in the Federated States. In northern Borneo, Sarawak was under the autocratic rule of the Brooke family; North Borneo (modern Sabah) was under a chartered company; and the sultanate of Brunei was a protectorate.

The innovative and truly alien presence in the midst of this hodge-podge was the federation which would, in time, become the core of the successor nation-state. This was a totally new political creation for which there was no historical precedent. As Rupert Emerson was at pains to point out,

> the Federation is in almost every aspect the creation not of Malays, but of the other people who have come into Malaya. It is the latter—the British in the political sphere and the Chinese, British, and Indians in the economic sphere—who found the bounds of the States too small to encompass their activities and reared above them the larger federal structure.[11]

It was this creation of larger political superstructures by all of the colonial powers that remade the map of Southeast Asia and thereby created the vessels for the new states. In almost every case, the administrative apparatus of these new amalgamations was wholly European in inspiration and organization. On this level, rule was always direct, and as time passed, more and more of the political and administrative power was exercised by these central structures. In 1909, within the Federated States a federal council was created under the presidency of a High Commissioner with what Emerson styled 'an invisible grant' giving it unlimited power to legislate.

In the Netherlands East Indies, the Dutch had succeeded in establishing their influence within a vast sweep of islands from Sumatra to New

---

[11] R. Emerson, *Malaysia*, New York, 1937, reprinted Kuala Lumpur, 1964, 175–6.

Guinea. By the 1940s, their territory was a crazy-quilt of individual arrangements, treaties, conquests, protectorates and concessions. Generally speaking, some form of indirect rule characterized most of the colony. The introduction of the 'Short Declaration' made the rapid expansion of the Dutch holdings possible in the early years of the twentieth century. Any chief who recognized the authority of Batavia (Jakarta) was confirmed as the legitimate ruler of his territory. Between 1898 and 1911, some 300 'self-governing' states came under Dutch control.[12] In some of these, a form of the Javanese system was attempted, but on the whole it was quite inappropriate for the relatively lower populations in the outer islands.

The Dutch had moved forward so quickly to affirm their claim to these places, particularly in Sumatra, Sulawesi and Borneo, that they bit off more than they could possibly chew, let alone digest. They lacked the resources to man and finance administrations for these new states. This was especially true in the period after about 1900 under the Ethical Policy which demanded a certain show of interest in the welfare of the people. European economic interests further required the construction of public works and services to support their penetration. As a result, Emerson notes that 'the Dutch were forced into a more or less makeshift acceptance of the widely divergent native institutions which they found at hand, functioning at first under the somewhat casual and unco-ordinated supervision of this improvised corps of Dutch and native officials'.[13] In some cases the Dutch government found it necessary to post Javanese members of the *pangreh pradja* to administrative posts in Borneo and Sumatra.

Furnivall noted that systems of indirect rule usually had a separate system of direct rule which applied to European residents of the colony who lived under some approximation of the metropolitian system. This dichotomy between systems was quite striking in the areas that were subject to large-scale European economic penetration. The Sumatran Cultivation District, the region around Deli and Medan, stands as a case in point. This area, which ultimately grew to constitute a region some 320 kilometres long and about 80 kilometres wide, had been 'purchased' or 'rented' from the sultans of Deli, Langkat and Asahan by European 'planters', actually corporations, and was literally governed by its own system of law standing entirely outside the governments of the traditional Malay sultanates. The area came to be populated by immigrants who made up the labour force, first Chinese and later Javanese. The mixed bag of European estate managers were also outsiders. The sultans grew to be exceedingly wealthy, and the Malay, Minangkabau and Batak subjects continued to live much as they had always lived.

On taking over the Philippines, the United States seems to have assumed that the Spanish claim to the Muslim areas of the south, particularly Mindanao and Sulu, was as strong as the claim to the other portions of the islands. The Americans thus occupied the Moro areas as a part of their entire conquest. In addition to the 'insurrection', as the Yankees called the Filipino Revolution in the north, they also found themselves faced with

---

[12] D. G. E. Hall, *A History of Southeast Asia*, New York, 1981, 622.
[13] Emerson, 426.

resistance from the peoples of Sulu and Mindanao. The Muslim peoples of this region had never considered themselves under Spanish rule in the first place, and thus saw little basis for the American presumption. In the end, American rule in the south was far less direct than it was even in the north, and local administration tended to continue in the hands of the local élites. The introduction of Western concepts of property, however, did lead to the economic development of the region, largely by Christian settlers from the north and by foreigners. These settlers stood outside the jurisdiction of the traditional Moro *datu* or headmen.

French Indochina came to be composed of five major administrative divisions, each ruled with different degrees of intensity. The Laotian principalities and Cambodia, which the French claimed on the basis of their misinterpretation of the concept of Vietnamese 'suzerainty', emerged as indirectly ruled territories. Laos involved the creation of an entirely new state within borders formed by the amalgamation of lands which had never before been under a single administration.

Initially, the only part of Indochina which was directly ruled was Cochinchina. Between 1897 and 1902, under Paul Doumer, the administration was unified and the 'protectorate' of Tonkin became for all practical purposes a directly ruled territory. In Annam, Laos and Cambodia, royal courts continued to exist along with their ministers, officials and 'mandarins', together with a French administration under a *Résident Superieur*, a Privy Council and a Protectorate Council. The states were divided into provinces, each placed under the charge of a Resident and a native official who continued to rule under his guidance. Hall points out that the system came to resemble that of the Netherlands East Indies, particularly in Java. In both cases the distinction between direct and indirect rule was legal rather than practical.

The real distinction often lay in national styles and definitions of what constituted government. It is thus important to examine the impact of the various systems as they affected the indigenous societies, rather than the stated intentions and theories of European rulers. Furnivall contends that in the English system of colonial government the officials, both European and native, became magistrates and tax collectors. They administered judgements under the rule of English law. Even in Malaya where Malay custom and religion were left to traditional authorities, the sphere of *adat* and religious law was greatly circumscribed and redefined. Officials found themselves responsible for large numbers of people and thus encountered them only through the impersonal medium of the court system.

> Thus British colonial administration on the system of indirect rule emphasises the judicial aspect of native authority, encourages greater formality in native courts and insists on close supervision over native judicial procedure by British officials. On the Dutch system even the European officials are policemen, agents of policy; on the British system even native officials tend to become magistrates and judges, servants of the law.[14]

---

[14] Furnivall, 285.

Furnivall's judgment on the British system of direct rule was far from flattering. With the increase in courts came a massive increase in crime in Burma. In comparison to the Dutch system he noted: 'It is a common complaint that under indirect rule, in Java or Malaya, officials coddle the people, treat them as children; but under direct rule, they are apt to treat them as naughty children.' So far as economic development was concerned:

> The Malay, . . . left aside by the main current of economic development, remains stagnating in a backwater, and the progress of the last sixty years has merely changed him 'from a poor man in a poor country to a poor man in a rich country'; relatively at least he is poorer than before.
>
> Burma provides another type of economic development—by native enterprise under direct rule . . . yet the cultivators have been transformed into a landless rural proletariat and the country as a whole is conspicuous for the growth of crime.[15]

Direct or indirect, the general trends of all systems by the end of the first decade of the twentieth century were contradictory. On the one hand there was the movement toward greater centralization, rationalization and efficiency; on the other, there was a contrary movement, both intentional and unintended, leading to the development of indigenous anti-colonial political movements. At the end of the nineteenth century, the Dutch had come to be concerned for the welfare of their colonial subjects. They thus instituted the Ethical Policy, which was to foster both economic development and village self-government. The Americans had taken Kipling's unsolicited advice and picked up the 'white man's burden' and were preparing their 'little brown Brothers' for American-style democracy, while the French developed their *association* with the Vietnamese, Lao, Cambodian and assorted populations of Indochina in pursuit of the *mission civilisatrice*. In Burma, the British were moving toward the creation of a certain level of self-government, and in Malaya they were beginning to train an élite that would replace their own rule.

Paradoxically, the actual movement was toward more direct rule. Indirect rule was, in a sense, a transition. Between 1880 and 1940, Europe grew even closer and communications within the colonies became faster with the construction of railroads, telegraphs and metalled roads. From the metropoles came demands for a growing variety of reforms: on the one hand, toward greater welfare, and on the other toward improved access to local resources on the part of European capitalist interests. Together with these came equally insistent demands from metropolitan legislative bodies to reduce costs and to find local revenues for colonial improvements.

This movement, however, was not necessarily uniform. The patchworks remained. Inaccessible areas, although included within the borders of some state, often remained unchanged by colonial rule. Regions that seemed to offer no immediate financial benefits, or which lacked economic resources, were bypassed by the roads and telegraphs. Rule in these areas

---

[15] ibid., 414, 424.

continued to be indirect. This was particularly true of the highland areas of the mainland states and the interiors of the islands, where a multiplicity of tribal and other peoples continued life in traditional ways. If their lives were changed by the colonial experience it was only because of the arrival of Christian missionaries, and prohibitions against head-hunting, slavery and other such practices.

The debate over what constituted direct or indirect rule may seem irrelevant in the context of the radical nature of the changes that were actually inflicted upon the indigenous social, political, economic and cultural landscapes. In the years after the Pacific War, however, the legalities once again came into play. Where colonial advances had taken place on the basis of treaties and formal agreements with indigenous authorities, then their postwar successors were often able to gain recognition as legitimate and sovereign—as happened in Malaya, Cambodia and Laos. In other areas, such as Vietnam and Indonesia, colonial rule was seen by nationalist forces to have destroyed the integrity of these agencies and they, together with their claims, were swept away by the tides of revolution and civil war.

LAW AND ORDER

Take up the White Man's burden—
  Send forth the best ye breed—
Go bind your sons to exile
  To serve your captives' need.

Rudyard Kipling

Damn, damn, damn the Filipino
Pock-marked khakiac ladrone;
  Underneath the starry flag
  Civilize him with a Krag
And return us to our own beloved home.

American marching song, c. 1900.[16]

During the nineteenth century the mission of bringing 'law and order' formed a major part of the European agenda. This impulse may be illustrated by the British, who began their first real penetration of the region at the beginning of the century with their occupation of Dutch territories during the Napoleonic wars. It seemed to individuals such as Raffles that a kind of endemic chaos existed throughout the island world. Raffles considered the phenomenon of Malay piracy to be the result either of a flaw in the Malay character or else of the 'decay' of earlier Malay empires. This second possible cause was thought to have been brought on by repressive Dutch and Spanish policies of monopoly that restricted

[16] Quoted in R. Roth, *Muddy Glory*, Hanover, 1981, 85.

trade. As a result, impoverished Malay rulers were unable to control their unruly followers who took to the seas and preyed upon peaceful native trade.

While it is probably true that Dutch activities, such as the sack of Riau in 1784, had prevented the formation of powerful maritime states in the islands, it seems that piracy and slave-raiding were an integral part of the maritime Malay political process. It is also possible that the influence of British trade, which initially focused on the sale of guns and opium to places like Sulu, Riau, Makassar and Aceh, might have unleashed opportunistic forces within maritime society. James Warren has suggested[17] that the upsurge of British country trade in the late eighteenth century was a major incentive for Sulu raiders, who increasingly sought slaves to aid them in procuring more trade goods so they could buy more guns and opium.

As a classical liberal, Raffles recommended the promotion of free trade and (after his indifferent success as lieutenant-governor of Java) the establishment of a port, where goods of all nations might be traded under the security of the British flag. This ideal was realized in his foundation of Singapore. While he eschewed the formation of a territorial empire and entanglement in Malay politics, he felt it incumbent on Europeans to enjoin native chiefs to suppress priacy in their domains. They also aimed to end slave-raiding and slave-trading that seemed an integral part of Malay piracy. The subsequent campaign to suppress piracy became a major rationale for the expansion of European power in the island world. As resources became available to the colonial powers, naval expeditions from the 1840s onward swept Southeast Asian waters; where treaties and blandishments were ineffective, search-and-destroy missions followed. British and Dutch gunboats moved from the Straits of Melaka to the Riau archipelago and the coasts of Borneo. Later in the century, Spanish squadrons finally succeeded in reducing the Sulu strongholds to ruins. While the results of these pacification programmes did not lead immediately to intensive colonial control, they did prepare the ground for European and Chinese economic penetration which often set off a new wave of conflict, necessitating further intervention.

Disorder on the borders was almost a constant theme in the history of British take-overs in Burma, as it had been in India. Each step was taken with the stated intention of securing 'law and order' in the neighbouring region, and each annexation was followed by another. As British and Indian economic interests chafed at the continuing recalcitrance of the rump Burmese state, they laid the groundwork for the final step in the absorption of Burma. It resulted in the abrogation of the traditional monarchy.

Cooler heads in the Indian administration and the India Office had counselled against the elimination of the Burmese monarchy. They wished to overthrow King Thibaw (r. 1878–85), but favoured an arrangement which would have permitted indirect control, and maintained traditional structures under a pliable monarch and British protection. They were

---

[17] *The Sulu Zone*, Singapore, 1979.

fearful of increased costs, a labour shortage, and the endemic rice deficit in upper Burma. British commercial interests in lower Burma, however, favoured total take-over. The protectorate scheme failed when the Burmese officials with whom the British had hoped to collaborate fled with Thibaw. As a result, the Viceroy of India, Lord Dufferin, announced on 1 January 1886 that Thibaw's domains had been annexed to Her Majesty's dominions. When he visited Mandalay in February, he abolished the *hlutdaw*, the royal council, put upper Burma under direct administrative control, and made Burma a province of British India.

This led to the total collapse of the old order and set the stage for outright rebellion. The British had decapitated the 'beast', only to discover that it immediately regrew a thousand more heads. In the past, they had fought only the rulers; now they found it necessary to fight the society. With the collapse of civil administration, villagers organized foraging parties to seek rice, money, fuel and provisions for their own communities. Those who gave up their arms at the order of the British-directed *Hlutdaw* became targets for the wandering bands of dacoits, most of them ex-soldiers of the disbanded Burmese army. Foraging bands organized themselves as guerrillas, and the British faced an entire countryside in armed uprising against the colonial forces. What was expected to be a quick and surgical coup had mushroomed out into a big, messy pacification. Quickly, the rebellion spread to lower Burma and then to the Shan who supported a *sawbwa* (a Shan chief) as candidate for the Burmese throne. This was not an organized effort, but a widespread and spontaneous collection of localized uprisings. The major work of pacification took about three years. By the beginning of 1889, there were 233 police and military posts in Burma, and the British forces in upper Burma numbered 18,000.[18]

Ultimately, the entire region from the Shan plateau to Dien Bien Phu was torn by disorder. It was exacerbated by the activities of armed Chinese bands known by the colours of their flags. They had fled from China following the defeat of the Taiping Rebellion. Earlier, Francis Garnier had led a campaign against them in Tonkin. Following his death, French forces were withdrawn, only to return in 1884 when France annexed Tonkin. This move brought France into a costly war with China, while at the same time a rebellion broke out in Cambodia, there was a revolt in Saigon, and Vietnamese troops from Annam crossed the border into Cochinchina. Following the suppression of these revolts, the pacification of Tonkin continued until 1895.

The earlier Dutch campaigns against pirates set the stage for one of the most extended and violent confrontations in the island world. The Dutch had always considered the north Sumatran state of Aceh an irritation. The Dutch official and ethnologist, C. Snouck Hurgronje, put them among 'the least well mannered of the inhabitants of the Archipelago'.[19] By the 1870s Dutch economic interests in the Straits of Melaka had begun a propaganda campaign to undercut Aceh's flourishing pepper trade with

---

[18] C. Crosthwaite, *The Pacification of Burma*, London, 1912, 128.
[19] C. Snouck Hurgronje, *The Achehnese*, Leiden and London, 1906, I. 119.

Penang. Aceh was styled a 'pirate nest' and was said to be threatening commerce in the western part of the archipelago. Having already brought Siak and the neighbouring states of Deli, Langkat and Asahan under their control, the Dutch began to develop what would become the Cultivation District of East Sumatra. An attack on the seat of the Acehnese sultan in 1873 was driven into the sea. The Dutch returned and took the town at great cost to both sides. In the battle the sultan was forced to flee and the Acehnese sultanate was effectively destroyed.

This was a signal for the Acehnese *uleebelang*, or regional chiefs, to rise up and defend their own districts against the invaders. When the Dutch finally succeeded in suppressing these chiefs, they found themselves confronted with a religiously inspired guerrilla war led by the village *ulamā* or clergy. In the end, the war between the Dutch and Aceh lasted nearly four decades, and at times it tied up most of the army of the Netherlands East Indies and nearly bankrupted Batavia. The war transformed Acehnese society as well. Prior to the Dutch invasion, James Siegel has noted, there was little connection between the various institutions of Acehnese society: the sultanate, the chiefs, the villagers and the religious leaders. The *ulamā* succeeded in mobilizing the people. 'They appealed to men to act not as villagers but as Muslims; to the *ulamā*, this meant forgetting traditional social identities.'[20] Although the religious war likewise failed, it did create in Acehnese society a readiness to respond to nationalist appeals in later years.

This conflict taught the Dutch to reshape their own tools of suppression. In 1906, the mobile, lightly-armed strike forces which had proved effective against the Acehnese were sent to Bali, where the island's kings had stubbornly resisted Batavia's attempts to dominate them. Faced with final defeat, many aristocrats despaired and committed ritual suicide rather than submit to Dutch rule. Armed only with spears and lances, they threw themselves, together with their women and children, at the Dutch guns, and perished. Lombok had already been annexed and other chiefs of island and coastal *negri* in the archipelago signed the Short Declaration that accepted Dutch rule.[21]

Thus, between the mid-nineteenth century and the 1930s, from Aceh to Sulu, European governments found themselves engaged in 'pacification' campaigns against traditional states and popular rebellions. In many cases the traditional rulers capitulated quite readily while the ordinary people decided to stand and fight. Colonialists came to realize that Southeast Asian societies were far tougher and far more resilient than their rulers. The rebellions mobilized the military and security forces of the colonial apparatus in almost every territory, whether or not it was a war zone. Colonial powers stood ready to enforce their rule with the sword, or more appropriately, the Maxim gun, the Gatling and the Krag. Because of the lopsided advantage in weaponry, money, communications, discipline, and technology, these contests were invariably won by the colonial forces.

[20] J. Siegel, *The Rope of God*, Berkeley, 1969, 74.
[21] M. C. Ricklefs, *A History of Modern Indonesia: c. 1300 to the Present*, Bloomington, 1981, chs 3–4.

They turned out to be brutal, guerrilla-type struggles which gave full play to European racist sentiments, and generally brought home-town American and European conscripts face-to-face with angry Southeast Asian peasants.

Usually these conflicts took place in the fringe areas and in regions which had not yet felt the force of colonial rule. As such, they were the result of the consolidations of empire that took place as the European powers moved to secure their control over regions which had formerly been only within their spheres of influence. The Dutch war in Aceh began as an attempt to remove the final obstacle to full colonial control over the island of Sumatra. In the early 1880s the four-cornered struggle in the highlands of mainland Southeast Asia began in earnest with the British pacification of upper Burma, the French expansion into the Lao states, and moves to secure their own borders by the Siamese and the Chinese. Finally, the Philippines erupted, with the first nationalist war of liberation beginning in 1896 against Spain and continuing to almost 1910 as the United States came in 1899 and moved against the revolutionaries. Later on, as economic conditions worsened in the years of the Great Depression, new peasant uprisings occurred in the central areas of Vietnam, Burma and the east-coast Malay states.

The American experience in the Philippines was marked by the extremes of the turn-of-the-century European colonial impulses. Framed with the noblest of intentions of 'leading the Filipinos to democracy', it was marked by one of the bloodiest wars in the region. The Americans had, in fact, blundered into the earliest nationalist movement in Southeast Asia when they joined forces with Emilio Aguinaldo in overthrowing the Spanish in 1898. Nevertheless, the enemies they faced were not all *ilustrados*, but a force that was only semi-nationalist and semi-traditionalist. The peasant forces actually constituted a radical popular uprising which was controlled by neither the old élite nor the new nationalists. Russell Roth has with some accuracy styled it one of America's 'Indian Wars'.

In the southern Philippines, where Americans faced the wrath of the Muslim *juramentado* or the *parrang sabbil*, the issue had nothing to do with nationalism. The Moros carried on a religious war against an army largely motivated by racism. From 1902 to 1913, United States forces fought a series of bloody battles with bands of Moro warriors who locked themselves up in coral stone *cotas* and fought to the death. The last major engagement was the battle of Bud Bagsak, fought in a volcano crater on Mindanao. It ended only when all 500 Moros defending the fortress had been killed, but campaigns against the Moros continued until 1935.

Hugh Clifford, who was sent to Pahang as the Resident at the sultan's court in 1888, has described life in the Malay states when Britain began 'moulding their history'. Rule by traditional chiefs was arbitrary, cruel, capricious and unlimited. The peasants were without rights and totally subject to the whim of the raja. The British saw themselves as bringers of law and order.[22] To Clifford, the most pernicious group at the courts of

---

[22] P. Kratoska, ed., *Honourable Intentions*, Singapore, 1983, 227.

Malay chiefs was the *budak raja*, the sultan's bodyguard, made up of young aristocrats.

> They dress magnificently in brilliant coloured silks, with the delightful blend-
> ings of bright blues which Malays love by instinct; they are armed with dagger
> and sword and spear, all beautifully kept and very handsome in appearance,
> and they pass most of their time in making love and in playing games of
> chance. Their duties are numerous but by no means heavy. They follow at the
> heels of the Sultan when he takes his walks abroad to guard him from harm,
> and to give a finishing touch to his magnificence; they row his boat, hunt
> game, and snare turtle doves in his company . . . murder those who have
> offended their master, seize property which he covets, abduct women, spy
> upon chiefs . . . Men such as these, who from their youth are taught to be
> unscrupulous, and to live expensively upon no settled income, quickly dis-
> cover means whereby money may be obtained . . . You must remember that
> this rabble is the only force by which the country is policed.[23]

With the arrival of Europeans, not only Malaya, but all of the other parts of Southeast Asia, shared in the benefits of 'civilization'. Hardworking and incorruptible administrators, such as the indefatigable district officers, travelled the countryside giving patient adjudication for no material reward. For the British in Malaya and the Dutch in the Indies the period was marked by a professionalization of the colonial civil services.

In Malaya the key to the new administrative structure was the Residen-tial system. Hugh Low created the model for it in Perak after J. W. W. Birch was killed. He succeeded by forming a council made up of the Malay chiefs, the Chinese leaders, the ruler and himself. They discussed his proposal for reforms; thus the Malays had a 'sense of influencing policy'. Governor Weld was impressed by Low's accomplishment and he made it the model for administration in all of the Protected States, as they were then called. Within a decade, however, the rather limited advisory role of the Residents was rapidly expanded to include most of the major functions of administration.

Weld also instituted reforms in the personnel selection process. Until 1883, Malayan civil service officers were a mixed bag of European adven-turers and Eurasians who had usually been recruited locally. Weld sacked half of the officials in Selangor during his first two years in office. Thereafter, the civil service officers were recruited in Britain by the Colonial Office and sent out as junior officers. In 1896 the Colonial Office instituted an examination which had to be taken by all potential recruits for official positions, and which really selected for public-school and univer-sity backgrounds.[24]

Similar moves toward professionalization of the colonial civil services were instituted in all the other European possessions of the region. Ultimately, the same impulse to develop a trained corps of administrators came to include indigenous officials as well. In Java, between 1900 and

---

[23] ibid., 233–5.
[24] John Butcher, *The British in Malaya 1880–1941: The Social History of a European Community in Colonial Southeast Asia*, Kuala Lumpur, 1979, 40–2.

1910, Colonial Minister Simon de Graaff introduced a series of reforms aimed at providing training for the *pangreh pradja*. These reforms were attempts to eliminate the old *magang* system, whereby experienced officials would accept the unpaid services of younger *priyayi* who worked with them as apprentices. De Graaff's reforms included an education requirement and the institution of rank lists. He also called for a distinction between functionaries and professional officials. These reforms went slowly because of a desire not to antagonize the *priyayi*, particularly in an era when nationalist political sentiments were beginning to raise their heads.[25] The Javanese *priyayi* ceased, however, to be the lords of individual states and became an élite class of officials operating throughout Java.

The Thai rulers were likewise moved to implement many of the same innovations in the realm of administrative centralization and rationalization as colonial governments undertook. A similar wave of reforms was begun in French Indochina under Governor Paul Doumer (1897–1902). He followed a Napoleonic pattern and unified civil administration throughout the French territories. He also abolished the last vestiges of indirect rule in Tonkin by eliminating the imperial viceroys. At the same time, he organized a unified government for the Laotian territories, creating the basis for the new state.

The French in Vietnam did not enjoy much of a respite between the suppression of traditional resistance and the upsurge of nationalist rebellions. As early as 1912, Vietnamese students and intellectuals had organized a nationalist group at the University of Hanoi: the Association for the Restoration of Vietnam. They were inspired by the successful overthrow of the Qing dynasty in China and the establishment of a republic. Under Phan Boi Chau's leadership they staged a number of demonstrations in Tonkin. These efforts were brutally suppressed, and the rebels were rooted out; many were beheaded and the rest imprisoned on Pulau Condore. At the same time, similar movements were beginning in the Dutch East Indies. Some began as religiously-inspired movements, such as the Sarekat Islam, and others, like the Budi Utomo, were inspired by ambitious bureaucrats; but they all clearly had overtones of nationalism. By the 1920s, the British were facing similar movements in Burma among both the educated élite and the pauperized peasantry.

European dominance was established in the region with military force, and finally reinforced with more rigorous measures to police the societies under their control. As a result, the security forces of the bureaucracy increased as threats to the state were perceived in the local population. Increasingly these came from the areas where administrative innovations had caused the greatest disruption to the majority peasant populations. If the wars succeeded in bringing into place the final elements of the modern authoritarian state, they also sowed the seeds of what would become wars of national liberation in the era after World War II.

In all the areas under European powers the same spectrum of policies, alternating between welfare and warfare, characterized the imperial advance. The attention given to efficiency and profit was generally more

---

[25] Sutherland, 67–85.

pronounced than that given to the welfare of the peoples. The policies reflected a variety of Western agendas: conservative, liberal, democratic, and sometimes socialist. The impulse for humanitarian reform was always tempered by demands for efficiency and functional rationality from home governments and metropolitan economic interests. Programmes which sought order, welfare and profit often led to conflicting measures, the resolution of which was generally decided by 'home' interests rather than those of the indigenous peoples. Colonial business and economic interests wanted ease of access to the resources and markets of the colonies. They wanted barriers against their competitors in the colonies. They wanted land and labour legislation that gave them security of property and an unlimited supply of cheap, well-disciplined workers. These interests had a deep influence on the development of administrative policies and legal frameworks, particularly in terms of labour and contract law and property codes. At the same time the cultural discipline of clocks, railroads, time-tables, and of the civil engineer, swept out from colonial urban centres across the paddy fields, hill farms, forests and seas of the region.

Throughout the region military pacification first destroyed or at least intimidated what remained of the traditional political order, and adminis-trative reform followed. In the end, Western-style law and a kind of order was imposed on the region. Whether individuals were better off, or 'happier' at the end of the process, and whether the costs were worth the benefits achieved are still matters of controversy. If the Europeans did not always do good, at least some of them did well. It is clear that Southeast Asians had little control over what happened to them during these years. Their world was destroyed and rebuilt around them; they had only the choice to accept or resist, and those who resisted usually died. On the other hand, those who accepted often gained control of the very tools which had first destroyed their predecessors.

The wars and the reforms did not put an end to protests. Before 1920, colonial régimes in Burma, Vietnam, Indonesia and the Philippines found themselves confronted with far more dangerous foes than poorly armed peasants led by visionaries promising paradise and invulnerability. The new enemies were of two kinds. On the one hand there were educated anti-colonialists seeking to establish nations inside the very administrative frameworks set up by the imperial rulers. They had in fact been created by the régimes they sought to displace. They were students, bureaucrats and urban workers. On the other hand, there continued to be peasant upris-ings as modern taxes were imposed and the impact of private property struck the villages. These movements, though traditionalist in their incep-tion, were quickly pre-empted by newly organized socialist and communist parties. The modern state had fathered modern peoples.

PLURAL SOCIETIES

Probably the first thing that strikes the visitor is the medley of peoples— Europeans, Chinese, Indian and native. It is in the strictest sense a medley, for they mix but do not combine. Each group holds by its own religion, its own culture and language, its own ideas and ways. As individuals they meet, but only in the market-place, in buying and selling. There is a plural society, with different sections of the community living side by side, but separately, within the same political unit . . .[26]

Furnivall's classic definition of the plural society applies to all Southeast Asian colonies. Together with ethnic, linguistic, cultural and religious differences, he noted that groups were also distinguished by occupational specializations. It was a sort of caste system without the religious sanction it had in India. He saw the plural society as the 'obvious and outstanding result of contact between East and West'.

He presented this type of social formation as one of the typical aberrations of the colonial situation in the tropics. Social and personal relationships had been atomized and commercialized. This rule applied within as well as among racial and religious groups. The force of custom had been eroded by the individual will for economic gain. As a result, the community, the village, the cohesive social and political units, had been transformed into 'crowds'. The play of economic forces, he argued, had been exempt from control by social will.

This analysis, constructed in the 1930s and informed by Marxist views, may place excessive responsibility at the feet of the colonial powers. Certainly custom was crippled by the intrusion of global economic forces. It is also clear that the social will of traditional communities was dispersed and abrogated with the introduction of European law and rational admin-istration. Furnivall, one feels, did not deal adequately with the heritage of ethnic diversity in Southeast Asia in the years prior to European rule. Likewise, his overwhelmingly economic approach really does not touch on the sexual and psychological dimensions of plural societies.

In the traditional Southeast Asian countryside as well as the cities, diversity was the rule rather than the exception. Differences in language were common. Even within populations who spoke the same language, dialects proliferated if for no other reason than the low frequency of contact. The variety of ecological niches necessitated a high degree of regional occupational specialization. Thus, speakers of the same language might have widely diverse subsistence styles and whole categories of dissimilar customs. Contrasts between urban and rural cultures were extreme. Even in the mid-nineteenth century the Malays of the Riau and Johor courts considered groups such as the *orang laut* as barbaric and did not even see them as Muslims, a primary criterion for being a 'Malay'. Lifestyles practised by the various social classes were also widely different. In fact, it might be said that status was a far more significant criterion in the minds of Southeast Asians than was race or ethnicity.

If an argument can be made for the existence of ethnic diversity in pre-colonial Southeast Asia, so too can one be made for the presence of foreign communities. The port cities of the region, whether under indigenous or European control, were always polyglot collections of traders, travellers and adventurers from all over the world. Descriptions of cities such as

---

[26] Furnivall, 304–5.

Melaka, Ayutthaya, Bangkok, and Surabaya as they existed outside or prior to European domination suggest that foreign communities were not only welcomed but were usually permitted to govern themselves under the control of their own 'headmen'. It is clear that such arrangements were perpetuated in the British and Dutch port cities in the nineteenth century.

The traditionally low levels of population in Southeast Asia had made labour one of the scarcest of resources. Anthony Reid observes that the chronic labour shortage and the prevalence of slavery and kidnapping meant that not much security was expected from the state. As a result, patrons and clients relied on each other for support and protection. These conditions had long since given rise to 'systems of bonding based largely on debt, where loyalties were strong and intimate, yet at the same time transferable and even saleable'.[27] Such arrangements also further diversified the ethnic composition of Southeast Asian populations.

One means of off-setting the labour shortage was to encourage the immigration of groups of Chinese labourers, a process that began in earnest as early as the eighteenth century. The histories of G. William Skinner and Jennifer Cushman of the Chinese in Siam, and my own work on Singapore and Johor, have shown these newcomers were encouraged by local rulers. They pioneered the growth of tin and gold mining, and the cultivation of pepper, gambier, sugar and a number of other commercial crops which brought increased revenues to Southeast Asian political leaders. Studies of China have shown that the initial waves of Chinese migration were driven not by European influences but rather by internal economic and social conditions. It may be more correct to view the wave of Chinese migration as an independent movement which met the Europeans halfway in Southeast Asia.

The conditions of social diversity, as well as the tendency to commercialize labour, agriculture and mining, suggest that the foundations for what Furnivall called plural societies were already in place before the nineteenth century and before the intensification of European control. Were these relations substantially altered in the administrative changes that took place during the high tide of European colonial rule? The answer must be affirmative. Despite pre-existing conditions, the colonial experience can be seen as the primary causal factor in the creation of plural societies. Certainly, the levels of social stress and communal tensions which appeared in the twentieth century are evidence that some qualitative change had taken place in the societies of the region.

Two of the differences singled out by Furnivall seem most important. One is in the abrogation of indigenous 'social will' by the imposition of a European administration. The second was in the increase, both quantitative as well as qualitative, in immigration from other parts of Asia, particularly China and India. Not only did more of these groups migrate to the region than ever before, but they came to perform a greater variety of social and economic roles. This migration grew and was transformed within a social context controlled by Europeans. The rulers separated themselves from the indigenous society at large and at the same time

---

[27] A. Reid, *Southeast Asia in the Age of Commerce*, New Haven, 1988, I. 129.

required that immigrants and newcomers likewise maintain identities distinct from 'natives', thus setting new precedents.

Unlike earlier outside conquerors, the European ruling strata in this period ceased to acknowledge any social or legitimate sexual connection with the remainder of the peoples in their colonies. They were, in fact, responsible not to their subjects but to the legislatures, bureaucracies and citizenries of distant nation-states. This disconnection seems to have been a crucial element in the new situation. Colonial régimes were not responsive to the local social will, nor did they need to be. Administration was from the top down and with such a rigour that there is little to compare with it in world history. The relative power imbalance that existed between the colonial régimes and their Asian subjects at the beginning of the twentieth century was a truly extraordinary historical aberration, and one that could not and did not persist. Nevertheless, the imbalance made it possible for Europeans radically to affect the bases of Southeast Asian societies.

An important aspect of the power imbalance was that Europeans imposed their own perceptions of race and ethnicity upon Southeast Asian society. Recent social and anthropological studies of colonial society, particularly those by John Butcher and Jean Gelman Taylor,[28] indicate that Europeans began placing greater distances between themselves and Asian society in the nineteenth century. With the arrival of large numbers of European women and the establishment of European family life in the colonies, sharper lines were drawn against association with other races. Sexual liaisons between Asian women and European men, once accepted as a part of the normal order of things, became objects of scorn, and Eurasian and mestizo classes generally declined in status. This trend was buttressed by pseudo-scientific social Darwinist concepts about racial superiority and inferiority, and about the effect of the climate on culture, history and the quality of 'civilizations' which coloured the views of the societies under colonial rule.

There were also subtler elements, particularly the psychological outlook of the increasingly defensive European community, that increased racist tensions in the ethnic medley. John Butcher has detailed the intensification of anti-Asian prejudices amongst Europeans, both civil servants and individuals in the private sector, at the beginning of the twentieth century. A number of measures created legalized and formal racial segregation in the region for the first time, mostly to bar Asians from European enclaves. This included segregation on the railways, in the civil service, in housing (where possible) and especially in the 'clubs' and even in football teams.[29] Butcher suggests that this development of European racism was a paradoxical result of the 'success' of colonial administration in transforming its Asian subjects:

> at the very time that Europeans were most asserting their superiority the actual cultural differences between them and Asians were diminishing. . . . Far from

---

[28] Butcher, *The British in Malaya*; Taylor, *The Social World of Batavia*.
[29] Butcher, ch. 5.

promoting harmony, however, the narrowing of the cultural gap aggravated relations between Europeans and Asians. On the one hand Europeans wished to inculcate Asians with their values and to introduce them to their institutions and pastimes, but on the other as the gap narrowed they could not feel as certain of their distinctiveness, and by implication, their superiority . . . As the cultural and educational gap between Europeans and Asians closed, the colour bar, however it was justified, was the only remaining means Europeans had of maintaining their superiority over Asians.[30]

The English came to see themselves as a distinctive kind of 'community' and thus set a pattern for others to emulate. Certainly, there is little evidence that any Asians saw themselves as constituting this sort of discrete and racially 'pure' community until much later.

Ethnicity became confounded with social and political roles. A key example is the project in social engineering undertaken by the Brooke régime in Sarawak. Chinese were looked upon as 'economic' subjects and were encouraged to become active in the various subsidiary commercial activities in both retail and wholesale trade, in mining, and in agricultural pursuits such as pepper, gambier, tapioca, rubber and coconut cultivation. Malays were recruited into the lower ranks of the civil service, Europeans into the upper ranks. Iban were brought into the military and police services, also under European leadership. The Brookes, once having established their rule in the region, took steps to 'protect their native peoples' from disturbing outside influences. The same programme of assigned social roles implied also a programme of active discouragement. Thus, Malays, Iban and other indigenous peoples were discouraged from careers in economically profitable pursuits. Their lands were protected from commercial exploitation by Chinese, Indians and other 'greedy' foreigners. Chinese, by the same token, were not welcomed in government service, except as revenue farmers.

While the impulse toward social engineering was less pronounced in the remainder of British Malaya, the virtual paradigm of a plural society came into being with a similar stress on assigned social and economic roles. Whether in the Straits Settlements under direct rule, or in the Malay states under indirect rule, ethnic groups began to separate in economically distinct communities. As Europeans defined themselves as the ruling class, other groups were similarly defined. Chinese were economic, and went to the mines, the plantations and the cities. Malays were protected, and encouraged to remain peasants or fishermen. A variety of legal structures, some quite deliberate, some unintended, led to the same end: a plural society. Land policies, labour laws, natural resource regulations, language policy, educational programmes as well as police and social welfare programmes all moved to separate the various ethnic communities.

The administrative machinery constructed by the British literally built separate structures for the various ethnic and economic groups. Since the British continued to proclaim that these were Malay states under Malay rulers, actual government was always conducted in their names, and even

[30] ibid., 122.

though Rupert Emerson styled this a 'comforting and useful fraud', the official political structure remained a part of the sovereign right of the Malay rulers. This built a barrier against the Chinese and other newly arrived Asian immigrants.[31]

Chinese immigration, which had steadily increased throughout the nineteenth century, became a veritable flood by the beginning of the twentieth century. Immigrants funnelled through Singapore into the western Malay states as well as to the Dutch possessions in Sumatra and Bangka where they supplied a labour force for the expanding tin mines and rubber plantations. Their numbers also swelled the growing urban centres of the British territories both in Malaya and Burma, as well as in the Dutch, French and American colonies.

In Malaya a separate administrative agency was set up, first to deal with particular problems arising out of the presence of secret societies and Chinese women. This was the Chinese Protectorate. It became an entire sub-government, staffed with Chinese-speaking officers and charged with overseeing the 'Societies Ordinance', which in fact regulated all association within the Chinese population. The Protectorate ultimately claimed responsibility for immigration and labour welfare and organization, for Chinese schools, for control of Chinese prostitution, Chinese newspapers and the entire range of Chinese affairs. Not only were the Chinese separated from the other races, but linguistic and regional distinctions between the various Chinese 'tribes' were institutionalized. The only associations that gained government approval were the regional *hui-guan* which stressed differences of language and place of origin.

Indians had been coming to the Straits Settlements since their foundation, primarily as cloth merchants and moneylenders. In the last decade of the nineteenth century and the early years of the twentieth, the subcontinent came to be seen as a source of labour by the European owners of rubber plantations. Despite continuing attempts to control Chinese labour, European estate managers found themselves unable to cross the cultural barriers and were frustrated by the continuing influence of informal organizations among Chinese labourers. They wanted a cheap, abundant and tractable labour force, and they came to see it in India. In the 1880s Hugh Low and Frederick Weld asked the British government to permit the migration of Indian labourers to the Malay states. Most of the new generation of potential planters in the Malay states were British who had already had experience in India and Ceylon (Sri Lanka). The Indian authorities demanded that the Malay states establish 'protectors' of Indian immigrants, and implement a significant body of legislation to regulate the conditions of the new arrivals. These acts, while providing for some measure of welfare for the immigrants, also placed Indians, like Chinese, within a discrete administrative framework. Like the Chinese, the Indians were treated as 'sojourners' in a Malay land.

As rubber cultivation became established, thousands of Tamils came from southern India and Ceylon. In the Malay states they often found themselves isolated on plantations with their families and existing in

[31] Emerson, 140–1.

communities with virtually no connection whatsoever with Malaya at large. The expansion and success of European rubber planting led Chinese entrepreneurs to set up plantations as well, with their own labour resources. In some cases, pepper, gambier, sago and tapioca were inter-planted with rubber. Thus, wealthy Chinese became plantation owners and less affluent planters became small holders. In any case, between 1890 and 1920 large areas of the Malayan countryside (most of it formerly under rainforest) were cleared and populated with isolated proletarian commu-nities of foreign Asians who were more dependent upon the global market than they were upon the weekly market. The same sort of thing also happened in the Dutch possessions in Sumatra and Borneo, as well as in Cochinchina and parts of Cambodia. The Dutch used Chinese and later Javanese in Sumatra and the French began to recruit peasants from the Tonkin area to work on the plantations of Cambodia and Cochinchina.

Within this context, the entire export economy of the region came to be dominated by non-indigenous peoples. Depending on the particular colo-ny, Chinese, Javanese, Vietnamese and Indians formed the migrant labour force and most of the thinly-staffed middle ranks of the new enterprises, while wealthy Chinese and European corporate interests controlled the commanding heights of the colonial economies. Most indigenous peoples found themselves, like the Malays who were left, as Furnivall has pointed out, becoming poor men in a rich land.

The social, administrative or economic role assigned to a specific com-munity by the colonial power ultimately determined a discrete ethnic identity. In traditional Southeast Asian societies it is certain that individ-uals, families and villages were aware of differences between themselves and others, but rarely did their consciousness of kind become broad enough to include individuals and groups beyond their own village or immediate kin, and rarely did this sense of identity give rise to ethnic, religious or racial violence. In the Malay states, for instance, there was little sense of common identity between a Malay of Selangor and one of Kelantan, nor was there a discernible level of ethnic tension between Malays and Chinese, or Malays and Indians in either of those states. Few Malays showed concern with the fact that no Chinese and few Indians were Muslims.

Likewise, Vietnamese of Tonkin found little in common with inhabitants of the Mekong delta. The people of one island in the Netherlands East Indies certainly felt no particular bond to the people of another island controlled by the Dutch. The rigorous division of races, ethnic and linguis-tic groups was often a European colonial innovation. Long-standing colo-nial practices, such as those in Batavia and Manila, were marked by legislated distinctions between the various social, economic and ethnic groups. Although many of the medieval 'dress codes' that characterized early Dutch rule had disappeared by the twentieth century, the impulse to divide by race was everywhere an important aspect of the colonial order, and it was in colonial circumstances that racial violence began to raise its head.

In Burma, ethnic animosity developed much more rapidly than elsewhere. There, primarily because of the connection between Burma and British India, Indian migration into southern Burma was unrestricted. Indians came as agricultural labourers in the newly opened commercial rice production of the delta. More affluent migrants became landowners and moneylenders. Educated Indians and Anglo-Indians moved effortlessly into the civil service. In the towns the migrants came into competition with the Burmese middle class in trading and the professions. The rapid economic progress of the Indian immigrants created an explosive situation by the 1930s. Robert Taylor observes that British colonial rule in Burma had created a situation where there 'was almost an inverse relationship between the size of the various ethnic groups and their hold on political and economic power during the late colonial period'. Government was controlled by the British, Indians and Anglo-Indians. The economy, including banking, landownership, investment, internal and external trade, was dominated by the British, Indians and Chinese.[32]

The combination of pre-colonial conditions together with the particular policies of different colonial powers led to new realignments of the social order. In the case of French Vietnam, religion provided an area of diversity. In Cochinchina several Buddhist and Taoist sects had coexisted with officially sanctioned Confucianism. With the spread of French rule and the growing power of Vietnamese Catholics—if only because some of them knew French—reactions against colonial rule were often led by religious movements. This led to the creation of the peculiarly Vietnamese form of a 'sect' which began to emerge in the 1920s. These groups, the most well-known of which are the Cao Dai and the Hoa Hao, combined Christian, Buddhist, Taoist, Confucian elements as well as secret society ideology and ritual to form separate communities. Ultimately these sought to form their own military and political structures and to control their own territories.

Religion ultimately became a rallying point for Burmese anti-colonialist as well as anti-foreign movements. The influence of Christian missionaries seeking converts among minority peoples such as the Karen and the Shan, together with general British contempt for Buddhism, had a politicizing effect on Burmese Buddhism. Both the *pongyi* and the young people of the new Burmese middle classes responded to issues such as the 'shoe controversy'. As the Buddhist revival took place in the various mainland states, indigenous peoples who had become converts to Christian ideologies found themselves more sharply separated from majority communities.

While Islam as a source of anti-colonialism was only negligible in British Malaya, Muslim peoples in both the Philippines and Sumatra responded to the inroads of colonialism by militant resistance. The peoples of Sulu and Mindanao had a long tradition of defying Spanish Catholicism. Spanish pressure had reinforced the identification of Islam and their political identities. Americans did little to alter a heritage of armed separation.

Educational and language policies were yet another source of division in all colonies. Usually, the language of the ruling class became the language

[32] Robert H. Taylor, *The State in Burma*, London, 1987, 128–9.

of government and business. In Burma, the Philippines and Malaya, areas with complex ethnic landscapes, English became the lingua franca. Those indigenous peoples or Asian immigrants who had some command of the language were in privileged positions when it came to professional advancement. In all these countries there was no incentive for the immigrants and minority peoples to learn the majority tongues, since the language of advancement was the European language. The intrusion of European languages brought other cultural influences as well. The new states themselves were isolated from their neighbours in other colonial states and reoriented toward the European metropoles. Thus by the 1920s, one could visit classrooms in Cambodia and hear students at the *lycée* reciting lessons from books that referred to 'our ancestors the Gauls'.

In the Dutch East Indies language policy took a different track. Education in Dutch itself was pursued by the higher ranks of the Javanese civil service who saw it as a path to advancement within the Dutch system. At the same time, as the Dutch possessions grew in number, the use of Malay as a lingua franca became widespread throughout the Indies, thus providing a basis for unity where in fact virtually none had existed before. What would become *bahasa Indonesia* was a 'modernized' language with a Roman alphabet that spread throughout the Dutch domains. The numerous states which had come under indirect Dutch control by means of the Short Declaration remained 'watertight compartments', each an entity apart, though at the same time open to a wide range of exceptions. The use of a language like Indonesian brought these individual states into a broader community and put their peoples into touch with others who had previously been entirely alien to them.

On the other hand, the terms of the Short Declaration treaties created new kinds of pluralism within these states. The treaties applied only to the relationship between the rulers and their subject people, whomever they were understood to be, and the Dutch government. Virtually all others were not subject to the *adat* of the particular state, but under a different set of regulations. This included Europeans, 'foreign orientals', native civil servants, persons residing on land ceded to the central government, other natives from other states, and natives under labour contract. Each one of these categories was in fact governed under a separate rulebook: more watertight compartments.

The creation of colonial educational systems reinforced the divisions created by the influence of European languages. In Malaya British policies strengthened the barriers between the ethnic communities. The children of Malay aristocratic families received the Malayan version of an English public-school education at the Kuala Kangsar Malay School. For the average Malay, the educational horizon was the Muslim *pesantren* or *pondok* school run by a local teacher, which offered some instruction in memorizing the Koran. As early as 1872, the British realized that even peasants needed some education, and they embarked on the creation of a Malay-language educational system, to provide Malay villagers with at least three years of schooling. Frank Swettenham was of the opinion that instruction should be provided only on a need-to-know basis.

> Whilst we teach children to read and write and count in their own languages, or in Malay ... we are *safe*. Beyond that, I should like to see the boys taught useful industries and the girls weaving, embroidery and mat-making, all profitable and all practised with a high degree of excellence in different states of the Peninsula.[33]

The British lack of enthusiasm for native education was matched by the Malays, who were unwilling to send their children to government schools. Finding qualified teachers was always a problem. In 1920, Richard Winstedt made provision for a teacher-training school. Ultimately the schools were staffed by the graduates of the Sultan Idris Training College for Malay teachers at Tanjong Malim.

For the more ambitious inhabitants of British Malaya, especially the children of Indians, Chinese and Eurasians, there were the private English-language schools set up by various missionary groups, primarily the Catholics. The religious orientation provided a disincentive for Malay attendance, thus creating yet another institutional barrier between the races. Chinese also saw merit in organizing schools to teach their own language, and wealthy Chinese merchants gained status within their communities by supporting Chinese education. Thus yet another separate 'stream' was added to the educational offerings in Malaya. By the 1920s, enlightened estate owners were beginning to provide schooling for the children of their Indian labourers, and thus Tamil-medium schools began to cater to yet another ethnic constituency.

The creation of plural societies seems, in the final analysis, to have resulted from a combination of factors. Ethnic diversity was a fact of life in the region long before Europeans arrived, but with administrative rationality and European racism things changed. The new territorial frameworks of the colonies within which relatively unified administrative structures came into being were in fact the foundations of the new nation-states. The new administration, however, identified and isolated these diverse elements, compartmentalizing some, protecting others and allowing still others greater freedom of action. The impact of market forces and the global economy continued the process by commercializing the ethnic occupational specializations. Language and educational policies drove home the final barriers.

In the example of Siam, a distinction between European and indigenous rule is apparent. The economic role of immigrant Chinese was similar to that in other regions, but the government's policy toward them was not hindered by the erection of exclusionist legal barriers to assimilation as was the case in the European colonies. Although anti-Chinese sentiment was given voice by King Vajiravudh in the years before 1920, it never fully separated the indigenous peoples from the immigrants.

The root of the problem was the creation of 'communities'. It seems that this was the real European innovation. The works of Butcher and Jean

---

[33] Quoted in P. Loh, *The Malay States 1877–1895*, Singapore and Kuala Lumpur, 1969, 169.

Taylor suggest that the Europeans created that notion by making themselves the model for all the other restricted communities. The final stage in
the development of these plural societies came in the 1920s and 1930s, as
nationalist movements began to stir among the various peoples of the
region. In virtually every case the emerging national communities found
themselves facing social constructions riddled with contradictions and
discrepancies. The administrative territories which had been centralized
under the various European powers included a multiplicity of ethnic
groups, both indigenous and of foreign origin, many of which enjoyed
privileged situations, or at least separate systems of control. In some cases,
nationalist sentiments arose among foreign immigrants before they did
among the indigenous peoples.

Thus, in Malaya and Singapore, Chinese nationalism had established
itself before Malay nationalist groups began seeking autonomy. In fact, it
might be said that the spectacle of Chinese political activity actually had
the effect of galvanizing Malay nationalism. In most places, the Chinese
came to be seen as a challenge to indigenous nationalist groups. This was
the case in Indonesia, the Philippines and Vietnam. In Burma, the Indians
bore the brunt of discrimination from nationalist militants. The very
militancy of modern nationalism, arising as it did within the plural
societies created by colonialism, came to see the 'non-national' communities as reminders of foreign domination. These minorities would suffer
as a result of this heritage.

SIAM AND BURMA

These two neighbouring states on the Southeast Asian mainland are a
study in contrasts. The period of state modernization shows these contrasts at their most extreme. Burma was invaded from India, annexed, and
reconstructed according to British will. The entire territory was subjected
to direct rule; no systematic effort was made to work within the traditional
order. Siam, by contrast, escaped invasion and foreign rule. The state was
ushered through its process of administrative and political modernization
by its own traditional rulers. King Rama IV, Mongkut, accepted the
unequal Bowring treaty in 1855 and opened the country to Western
economic and cultural influences, making himself a leader in this process.
His son, Rama V, Chulalongkorn, whose rule (1868–1910) spanned the
period of European colonial expansion, is credited with preserving the
state's independence.

Oddly enough, the goals and models of administrative centralization
and political reform in both states were in many ways similar. The Siamese
were strongly influenced by British methods of government, in both
Malaya and Burma as well as at home. Much of the Thai modernization
was accomplished with the advice of European specialists, and it was
certainly spurred by pressures from British and French diplomats, merchants and missionaries who, in a sense, looked over the shoulders of the
Thai throughout the period.

Nor was Siam free from foreign military threats and intervention.

During the last two decades of the nineteenth century, David Wyatt states, the country lost control of 456,000 square kilometres of territory to Britain and France. It is also true that throughout this period Siam was forced to carry out its programmes while bound by unequal treaties which allowed economic and legal privileges to foreign subjects, and placed restrictions on the type and level of taxes which the government could impose. The Thai were also severely restricted in their freedom of action in their own foreign affairs, particularly in regard to their neighbouring states. In many respects, the international status of Siam was quite similar to that of one of the indirectly ruled Malay states or to many of the outlying island states of the Netherlands East Indies. Moreover, the administrative reforms sponsored by the Thai king merely strengthened the state and really did nothing at all to promote the development of political freedom among the people. Socially, Thai society was very heterogeneous, including Malay, Mon, Lao, and indigenous hill peoples such as the Hmong and the Yao, as well as a significant number of Chinese immigrants. The Siamese social order was likewise divided by traditional distinctions of class and status that remain embedded in the language.

Clearly a major difference lay in the means by which reforms were introduced. The fact that the Thai modernization was 'self-inflicted' meant that the trauma was certainly reduced. Perhaps the Siamese experience is as good an argument as any against colonial rule, no matter how noble the intentions, but it is also clear that Siam's experience in many respects depended on what happened to its neighbours. The fact that an indigenous élite carried through the reforms seems to have allowed the Thai social order to retain a degree of cultural integrity that was stripped from the Burmese and other Southeast Asian peoples. A comparison of the two cases and consideration of some of the social, economic and cultural consequences will help in understanding the processes.

In Burma, where British rule was introduced from India, and was intended to displace the government of the Burmese monarchy, new classes arose to fill the ranks of the administration. After the annexation of upper Burma, British administrators in charge of the pacification moved radically to restructure the civil administration along the lines of the Indian system without regard to prior patterns of village and local government. The British invasion and pacification, accompanied by the immigration of large numbers of Indians and Chinese and the erection of separate administrations for minority populations, were a traumatic experience for Burmese society in general. The collapse of the Burmese social and political order in 1885 was a crisis of enormous magnitude for the culture as a whole.

John Cady has used terms like 'social deterioration' and 'cultural disintegration' to describe the impact of British rule. Virtually every other major historian of Burma in recent times has been in agreement in pointing to the generally detrimental impact of British rule on Burmese society and on its long-term political and social development. Furnivall's critique of the Indian model of direct rule and economic liberalism has been decisive in setting the tone of scholarly debate regarding Burmese development. Hall has criticized Crosthwaite 'who came with firmly fixed ideas of Indian

administration, [and] brought with him a ready-drafted scheme for making the village, as in India, the basic social and political unit'.[34] This was an
innovation that cut the traditional rural socio-political order to the heart.

Furnivall and more recent students make it clear that Crosthwaite really
did not understand the function of the circle headmen, whose positions
were abolished, and village headmen, who were created from virtually
nothing. The latter were given powers and functions that they had never
before enjoyed. The new class of village and local functionaries tended to
be Indian as often as Burman, because of the British view that there was an
insufficient number of trained Burman personnel.

The real problem was not so much the fact that the model for administrative and institutional reform was Indian, but that the officials who
implemented it neither knew nor cared very much about Burma. Their
knowledge and experience were based on what they had learned in India.
Crosthwaite's comments suggest that he really did not understand the
nature of property under Burmese customary law and that he did not have
a clear concept of the manner in which the traditional government had
been able to maintain political communication with its people. Perhaps
Furnivall was incorrect in styling the *myothuggi* as a popularly chosen
representative of the village, but neither was he a centrally appointed
bureaucrat who was periodically reposted. The township officer who more
or less took on his function as a sub-district officer had responsibility for
about a hundred villages. Under the British system his duties were
primarily to hear cases and collect revenue. Other functions of the state
were separated under specialist departments, so that education, sanitation, irrigation and other responsibilities were outside the ken of the
township officer and district officer.

The prolonged pacification programme was a response to the disorder
precipitated by the abolition of traditional rule; Robert Taylor argues that it
had the effect of requiring the colonial state to develop stronger instruments of suppression and social control. In a sense, it can be said that from
1885 until 1942, Burma was always under a form of martial law. Taylor
remarks on the irony that the British who came with the pledge to free the
Burmese from arbitrary government had replaced the 'shackles of custom'
with the 'fetters of regulation'.[35] Their policies resulted in the paradoxical
legacy of the colonial state in Burma:

> the great strength of the colonial state was its external sources of military
> power and administrative organization gained from Britain and India. The
> great weakness of the colonial state was its inability to sustain support, either
> active or passive, from the indigenous population.[36]

Another result of the British pacification of Burma was that there was
little room for mutual trust between Burmans and the English. As a result,
British policy generally favoured minority peoples. Most of the soldiers

[34] Hall, p. 771.
[35] Taylor, *The State in Burma*, 98–9.
[36] ibid., 115.

and police were Indians. Crosthwaite remarked that the failure to train Burmans as soldiers was 'a blot on our escutcheon'.[37] Nevertheless, the British trained Karen and Kachin regiments who, along with Indians, garrisoned the Burman, Shan and Chin districts.

In Siam, the reform of the traditional government on an internal basis presented a wide range of unique problems. In many ways the Thai ruler had to tear down and rebuild the house while he continued to live in it. Ministries in the capital and the palace had become the hereditary holdings of powerful families who controlled their own revenues, provinces, and economic resources through large patronage networks, and sometimes even had their own private armies. Provincial administration was chaotic, with many provinces under the hereditary rule of local dynasties. Other provinces were directly under specific ministries, such as the western provinces bordering Burma which were under the Kalahom and controlled by the ex-regent, Sri Suriyawong, the head of the powerful Bunnag family. Other groups dominated the government and revenues of the south, which was locally in the hands of Chinese *kapitans* and revenue farmers; and still other arrangements held true for the northeast where Lao chieftains enjoyed relative autonomy within their territories. It was necessary for a reformer first to pierce through this entrenched system. Such a government was the kind that the British had swept away in Burma.

The pace of reform in Siam was far slower than in that country. Initially Chulalongkorn's reforms were hindered partly by conservative factions who generally remained in power until 1885. Even though most of the older officials, particularly the leaders of the powerful Bunnag family, had disappeared by 1890, change was impeded by the lack of qualified, educated leadership. Chulalongkorn generally relied upon his own brothers and half-brothers to staff his remodelled administration. They were the only individuals who had received a modern education.

Gradually one ministry after another was reformed or consolidated as the old head died. New ministries and departments were initiated and given operative independence on a piecemeal basis, often functioning as temporary offices within the palace until such time as a ministry was capable of assuming its tasks in a responsible manner. The king first appointed his own choice to the Ministry of the Capital. This was followed by appointments to the Treasury and Foreign Affairs where he placed his own brothers. Most of the transfer of power from the old guard took place between 1882 and 1888, a period which saw the death of Prince Wichaichan, Chulalongkorn's archrival, and the ex-regent Prince Suriyawong. His brother, Prince Damrong, took charge of the Interior Ministry only in 1892, which was also the first year in which the heads of all of the ministries first met as a cabinet. At the same time, it was also necessary to introduce systems of auditing, bookkeeping, filing, registering correspondence and the practice of filing quarterly and annual reports.[38]

The reform of provincial and local government and the centralization of the state apparatus in Siam proceeded along British Indian lines. Local

---

[37] Crosthwaite, 131.
[38] D. K. Wyatt, *Thailand: A Short History*, New Haven, 1984, 193–201.

government was organized under a Ministry of Interior with provincial governors appointed by the ministry and with provinces broken up into districts or *amphur*, under the control of a centrally appointed *nai amphur* or district officer. Below that level, officers such as the village headmen and *kamnan* were chosen from the local communities. However, while the system certainly resembled a British Indian model, there were significant differences.

Reform of the courts and the legal system was an important step in breaking free of the unequal treaties and the consular jurisdiction. In this case, rather than following the British model, the Thai employed French and Belgian jurists as advisers and implemented a version of the Napoleonic code to carry through the changes. This reflected the general policy that governed the use of foreign advisers. Each ministry had several, and they were deliberately chosen from different nationalities (British, French, Belgian, American, Danish, German, etc.) to avoid the impression that one particular European country was unduly influencing the reforms. In many cases they had little experience of local conditions.[39]

The fact that Thai officials controlled the process meant that they were generally free to choose advisers as well as accept or reject their advice. While the reform of the legal system was guided and eventually approved by European advisers, the system was adapted to Thai realities. On the other hand, the introduction of a British legal system in Burma was a disaster. It bewildered the Burmese. British law courts and their judgements had little relevance to Burmese ideas of justice. Cady styled it 'a game of technicalities and rules which only the not-too-scrupulous legal profession seemed to understand and profit from'. Burmans, he said, were more concerned about personal dignity and affronts to status than about infringements against property, which is what concerned the British and Indian magistrates.[40]

Like the British, the Thai monarchs faced problems of resistance as the state was expanded and centralized. This was particularly true in the minority areas. In 1902, when Damrong's reforms were sweeping away the old order, three revolts arose in different parts of the country. In the south, Muslims led by the Raja of Pattani revolted as local governors resisted the transfer of their revenue to the central authorities. The area around Ubon in northeast Thailand erupted into the 'Holy Man's Rebellion'. Although it was led by a messianic monk who claimed that the end of the world was near and that many miracles would occur, the uprising was also supported by members of the old ruling families of the area. In the north, near Phrae, several hundred Shan who had come from Burma to work in logging and gem mining rebelled. They too had the support of local ruling families who resented the loss of their traditional privileges. In each case, the central government was able to suppress the rebellions with relative ease.

One of the major innovations of Chulalongkorn's reforms was the establishment of a professional military. This was a real contrast between

[39] ibid., 211.
[40] J. F. Cady, *A History of Modern Burma*, Ithaca, 1958, 146.

Siam and the colonized states. The Thai were the only Southeast Asians who were in a position to develop their own army before World War II. This, too, was done by royal princes and pioneered first in the Corps of Royal Pages in the palace. A Department of the Army was created in 1888 when the military was separated from the old Kalahom. In 1902, universal military conscription was introduced. Siamese forces had acquitted themselves well when fighting against the French in Laos in 1893. While they were unable to defeat European armies and navies, Thai forces were sufficient to crush domestic revolts. In a sense, Bangkok had become the imperial force, ready to civilize its own unruly 'natives' with modern weapons.

In Burma, the relations between Europeans and non-Burman minorities were one of the forces that helped to create a plural society. The heritage of these policies continues to stand as a block to national unification in Burma today. In the Shan, Karen and Kachin areas, local élites and aristocrats were usually maintained and much of the traditional social structure was left intact. In the hill areas, unlike lower Burma, the British often were quite willing to rely on systems of indirect rule. By contrast, in Siam such peoples were treated as feudal remnants who were reorganized into compartments of the central bureaucracy. By 1905, most of the hereditary chiefs, both Thai, Shan, Lao and Malay, had been relieved of their traditional revenues and administrative powers.

In Burma, while the lowlands were being ruthlessly modernized under direct rule and flooded with aggressive new immigrants, hill peoples were in a sense being put into a museum. But some of these groups were converted to Christianity and taught English. Their own languages were, for the first time, written down, codified and brought into print—usually in the Roman alphabet. This creation of print communities had an important role in strengthening ethnic and 'national' consciousness. While the same missionaries were also active in the hill areas of Siam, their presence did not have the same divisive effect as in Burma.

The numbers of Chinese migrants into Siam grew considerably during this period. By 1910 Chinese amounted to nearly 10 per cent of the total population, numbering about 792,000, most located in the provinces around Bangkok. In Siam, as elsewhere in Southeast Asia, the Chinese moved into the labour market, particularly into the plantations, mines, market-gardening and the urban workforce. They almost totally dominated the retail trade and the domestic and international rice trade. Many Chinese prospered, some gained government positions, and many were assimilated over the course of the nineteenth century. In southern Siam the proportion of Chinese was much higher in relation to the general population, particularly in the tin-mining areas around Phuket, Ranong and Nakhon Sithammarat. Here the Thai rulers had appointed Chinese headmen to become provincial governors. Although many of them were replaced in the administrative reforms of the period, the southern border provinces continued to be dominated by wealthy Chinese families who in many cases were branches of Penang families, such as the Khaw.[41]

---

[41] J. W. Cushman, 'The Khaw Group: Chinese Business in Early Twentieth-century Penang', JSEAS, 17, 1 (March 1986), 58ff.

The Thai situation closely approximated the plural societies of other Southeast Asian states. There was a similar ethnic division of labour. Ethnic Thai, even peasants, were often unwilling to accept low-paying, hard-labour jobs so long as rice agriculture remained a profitable occupation. Those who were more ambitious among the Thai sought advancement in the Buddhist monkhood or government service. The Chinese came to dominate the modern sector of the Thai economy, and as the numbers increased they became more of an identifiable community. The communal differences solidified as bureaucratic realities took effect and the old patronage networks that had formerly served as paths of assimilation disappeared. At the same time, more Chinese women came to Siam, and Chinese families gave greater permanence to the distinction between the Thai and the Chinese. In 1915, King Vajiravudh began to raise the banner of Thai nationalism and in a vitriolic essay singled out the Chinese as 'Jews of the East'.[42]

The growth of Siam's plural society suggests that, despite control by its own monarchs, the country was still subject to many of the same economic and social forces that affected other areas. The vast increase in migration, the arrival of Chinese women, and the pattern of Siam's economic growth depended on the processes of technological change, such as the development of regular steam travel and the growing ease of communications. There were also more liberal migration policies in China. It is also true that many Chinese enjoyed privileged status as the subjects of colonial governments and thus were able to operate under the protection of the unequal treaties. As a result, cities like Bangkok grew, very much like colonial port cities of Singapore, Saigon and Batavia, as Chinese centres.

Although Bangkok did have most of the marks of a colonial port city, it was also the centre of the Thai royal government and it functioned as the cult centre and religious focus of the country. The national shrines such as the Wat Po and the Temple of the Emerald Buddha as well as the royal palaces made the city the spiritual centre of the state. This was in stark contrast to Burma where the economic and political life of the colonial state now focused on Rangoon, while the former capital of Mandalay had been demoted and the former royal palace had become a British club. Perhaps the major difference in this respect was in the status of the Buddhist religion.

In Siam, Buddhism continued as the official religion of the country under royal protection. It thus functioned as a force for national unity and historical continuity. The reformed Thammayutika sect, which had been founded in the nineteenth century by Mongkut while he was in the monkhood, had a major influence. The sect was more rigorously intellectual than customary and less ritualistic. It put a heavy stress on education and took a leading role in promoting village-level education for the layman. Its own intellectual centre was the Buddhist university at Wat Bowonniwet. The sect had strong links to the royal family, and at the turn of the century it came under the leadership of Prince Wachiranan, another

---

[42] W. F. Vella, *Chaiyo! King Vajiravudh and the Development of Thai Nationalism*, Honolulu, 1978, 193–4.

of Chulalongkorn's brothers. When he became the Supreme Patriarch, he led a thorough-going reform of Siamese Buddhism including its religious practices, texts, and rituals, and the status of the *sangha* or monkhood. This created a channel of communication from the king to the village that did not rely on political or administrative channels. The traditional educational role of the village monasteries was vital in spreading the standardized script and literature of 'Bangkok Thai' as well as Western-style mathematics and science.

The contrast between Siam and Burma could not have been greater in this respect. The Burmese monks, who had performed a similar role in traditional education, vigorously resisted the colonial government's attempts to promote a modern syllabus through the monastery schools. The Siamese attempts went forward on the prestige of the monarchy, while in Burma the colonial government's relationship with the *sangha* ranged from outright opposition by the Buddhist monks to contempt on the part of the British. In the uprisings of 1885 and 1886, monks actually joined the fighting against British forces; where Karens were concerned, this had the effect of turning the pacification into religious and ethnic warfare. Vinton, the American Baptist missionary, wrote to Crosthwaite in 1886:

> The strangest of all is the presence of poongyees [Buddhist monks] on the battlefield. This is unheard of in history.
> The Karens universally interpret this as God's sign that Buddhism is to be destroyed forever. They say the challenge of Thebaw could be answered by the British government, but the challenge of the fighting poongyees can only be taken up fitly by Karens under their own missionaries . . . I have never seen the Karens so anxious for a fight. This is . . . welding the Karens into a nation . . . The heathen Karens to a man are brigading themselves under the Christians. This whole thing is doing good for the Karen. This will put virility into our Christianity.[43]

Thus, while in Siam Buddhism acted to unify the country and to strengthen the hand of the central government, in Burma religion served as a real source of division within society while at the same time dividing the Burmans from the government. Because of the abolition of the Burmese monarchy, there was no institution left in Burma with the prestige to regulate the *sangha*. Burmese Buddhist institutions thus fragmented, and it was Western-educated Burmese laymen who used the religion as a rallying point for resistance to colonialism. Significantly, the Burmese *sangha* had little to do with the growth of the Young Men's Buddhist Association.

In regard to language and educational policy, the Thai élite responded to the challenges of modernization with major attempts to reform the educational system and to turn it into an agency of centralization. Even though missionaries were permitted to operate within the country and they often stressed the teaching of English, no dual-language society developed in Siam as happened in Burma and every other colonized

43 Cady, 139.

territory. Since modern literature, science and other general subjects were mediated through the Thai language, the language itself continuously moved forward and did not stagnate. The fact that individual Burmese advanced quickly in Western fields on the basis of English education obscured for a time the retrograde influence that the system had on Burmese in general. In the 1920s and 1930s, it often seemed that Siam was the laggard.

By the 1920s, Burma seemed to be advancing rapidly in terms of political and economic development. The British had created a modern commercial economy, and much of the population had been brought, one way or another, into the modern sector. Burmese exports, particularly of rice, were among the highest in the region, while in Siam economic growth was slower. This was due to a lower level of investment as well as to a less developed infrastructure. Also, despite the modernizing efforts of the monarchy, European-run administrations were much more efficient at protecting property, particularly European property, and at advancing European economic interests.

In terms of the growth of representative institutions and modern-style constitutional government, it also seemed that Burma was moving more rapidly than Siam. By 1921, Burma had, because of its connection with India, begun the process of developing instruments of self-government. Ironically, one of the rallying points for Burmese student activists was separation from India, and it continued to be a focus of protests until the mid-1930s when London decided to break the connection. Burmese pressures on British administrators were apparently quite successful. By 1923, a dyarchy constitution gave Burma a measure of self-rule. Elections were held in 1922, 1925 and 1928, though they seemed to have little relevance to the average Burmese, particularly the rural peoples. In 1937, a reformed constitution gave Burma an increased level of self-rule, but it continued to be too little too late for Burmese student activists.

In Siam as early as 1885 the monarch had resisted calls for a similar move toward constitutional government and parliamentary institutions. Chulalongkorn had been petitioned by a group of returned students to move toward democracy and to prevent the growing concentration of power in the hands of the executive. He refused on the grounds that the country was not yet educated and that the older men were incompetent while the younger ones were not prepared to govern. His successor, Vajiravudh, was able to govern as an absolute monarch, although generally limited by the presence of his father's brothers who continued to dominate the administrative structure. An attempted coup, shortly after he took the throne in 1912, confirmed his inherent reactionary tendencies and turned him firmly against constitutional government. Instead he is recognized as the founder of Thai nationalism and credited with the establishment of the state ideology, which stressed the identification of 'Nation, Religion, King', and left the country with a heritage of official, conservative nationalism. While not a popular force at this time, it later provided the basis for a more militant mobilization of Thai society.

Vajiravudh's successor was less fortunate in dealing with popular demands. Rama VII, Prajadiphok, faced rising demands for constitutional reform and greater responsibility from the non-royal members of the new military and civilian bureaucracy. He found himself confronted with a coup in 1932 led by civil and military 'promoters' such as Nai Pridi Panomyong and Phibun Songkhram. He abdicated, and when the dust had settled Phibun had ousted his erstwhile partners and created a military dictatorship. He embarked upon his own programme of modernization and nationalist reform, which owed much to his appreciation of Japanese and German models.

As war clouds gathered around Southeast Asia, both Siam and Burma, like some of the other countries of the region, had well-established nationalist movements. Most of them were organized largely by Western-educated élites who had first tasted power within the new bureaucracies of the colonial and semi-colonial states of the region. By the late 1930s, all had reason to move toward an anti-European stance, a position which left them well-prepared to welcome the Japanese in 1942.

BIBLIOGRAPHIC ESSAY

The most comprehensive treatment of the region's history remains D. G. E. Hall's *A History of Southeast Asia*, 4th edn, New York, 1981, despite its dated format. The nineteenth and twentieth centuries are covered in a more accessible fashion in David Joel Steinberg, et al., *In Search of Southeast Asia: A Modern History*, Sydney, 1987. In recent years a large number of histories and political studies have appeared focusing on specific countries or regions and based in large part on indigenous sources as well as colonial and other Western-language sources. These include Barbara Watson Andaya and Leonard Y. Andaya, *A History of Malaysia*, New York, 1982; Robert H. Taylor, *The State in Burma*, London, 1987; M. C. Ricklefs, *A History of Modern Indonesia: c. 1300 to the Present*, London, 1981; David K. Wyatt, *Thailand: A Short History*, New Haven, 1984; David Chandler, *A History of Cambodia*, Boulder, 1983. Older, but still useful surveys include Le Thanh Khoi, *Le Vietnam*, Paris, 1955; Milton Osborne, *The French Presence in Cochinchina and Cambodia: Rule and Response 1859–1905*, Ithaca, 1969; John F. Cady, *A History of Modern Burma*, Ithaca, 1958; and J. D. Legge, *Indonesia*, Englewood Cliffs, 1964.

Collaborator Classes

Literature on indigenous collaborator classes is quite recent as a separate topic: nevertheless the rise of local ruling groups since independence, many of which had clear connections to the colonial régimes, has spurred interest in this topic. Much of the literature has focused on the nineteenth and twentieth centuries. Heather Sutherland's *The Making of a Bureaucratic Elite, The Colonial Transformation of the Javanese Priyayi*, Singapore, 1979, and her 'The Taming of the Trengganu Elite', and Onghokham's 'The Inscrutable and the Paranoid: An Investigation into the sources of the Brotodiningrat Affair', both in Ruth McVey, ed., *Southeast Asian Transitions: Approaches through Social History*, New Haven, 1978, are some of the more outstanding works in this genre, the first two focusing on Java and the other on Malaya. Also useful are J. M. Gullick's *Indigenous Political Systems of Western Malaya*, London, 1958, and his more recent *Malay Society in the Late Nineteenth Century*, Singapore, 1989; M. C. Ricklefs, *Jogjakarta Under Sultan Mangkubumi, 1749–1792, A History of the Division of Java*, London, 1974; Anthony Reid, *The Contest for North Sumatra: Atjeh, the Netherlands and Britain 1858–1898*, Kuala Lumpur, 1969. Carl Trocki has examined the relationship of the Johor chiefs and the Singapore Chinese leadership with the British colonial state in the nineteenth century in *Prince of Pirates, The Temenggongs and the Development of Singapore and Johor 1784–1885*, Singapore, 1979; and *Opium and Empire: Chinese Society in Colonial Singapore, 1800–1910*, Ithaca, 1990. Studies of institutions such as revenue farms related to the overseas Chinese also provide important insights into the role of Chinese allies of colonial régimes. James R. Rush, *Opium to Java*, Ithaca, 1989, is an important contribution, as are the studies of the various Chinese communities by Maurice Freedman, G. William Skinner, Wang Gungwu, Wong Lin Ken, Edgar Wickberg, Lea Williams, and Leo Suryadynata. Works such as Anthony Reid, 'Habib Abdur-Rahman Az-Zahir (1833–1896)', *Indonesia*, 13 (1972), approach the question from the biographical point of view. Also of interest is some of the autobiographical work, best represented by Abdullah bin Abdulkadir's *Hikayat Abdullah*. Some work has been done on earlier periods such as the innovative study by Jean Gelman Taylor, *The Social World of Batavia: European and Eurasian in Dutch Asia*, Madison, 1983. The growth of indigenous élite classes in Indochina has been covered in David Marr, *Vietnamese Anticolonialism, 1885–1925*, Berkeley, 1971, and *Vietnamese Tradition on Trial 1920–1945*, Berkeley, 1981, and in Osborne, *The French Presence*.

Direct and Indirect Rule

Analyses of direct and indirect rule have a substantial historiographical tradition. One of the earliest studies, still durable, is Rupert Emerson's of British and Dutch colonial rule in Malaya and the Indies, *Malaysia: A Study in Direct and Indirect Rule*, New York, 1937. Another important and influential early study of this sort is J. S. Furnivall, *Colonial Policy and Practice: A Comparative Study of Burma and Netherlands India*, Cambridge, UK, 1948. Related questions are also raised in the works of Gullick, as well as those of Sutherland, Trocki and Robert Taylor. For the Philippines there is the collection of articles in Norman G. Owen, ed., *Compadre Colonialism: Studies on the Philippines under American Rule*, Ann Arbor, 1971, particularly Michael Cullinane's 'Implementing the "New Order": The Structure and Supervision of Local Government During the Taft Era'. Important studies of other countries in the region are found in McVey, ed., *Southeast Asian Transitions*. There is also a wealth of important material in the biographical works and memoirs of colonial officials in Southeast Asia. Important insights on the systems of rule in the Malay world are found in Anthony C. Milner, *Keraja'an: Malay Political Culture on the Eve of Colonial Rule*, Tucson, 1982, and Shaharil Talib, *After Its Own Image*, Singapore, 1986.

Law and Order

The literature on law and order in Southeast Asia is perhaps the best developed genre of colonial writing on the region. Such works as Sir Charles Crosthwaite, *The Pacification of Burma*, London, 1912; C. Snouck Hurgronje, *The Achehnese*, Leiden and London, 1906; Auguste Pavie, *Mission Pavie*, Paris, 1898–1904; Sydney Cloman, *Myself and a Few Moros*, Garden City, 1923; Victor Hurley, *Swish of the Kris: The Story of the Moros*, New York, 1936; and Henry Keppel, *The Expedition of H.M.S. 'Dido' for the Suppression of Piracy, with extracts from the Journal of James Brooke Esq., of Sarawak*, London, 1846, are representative examples of the memoirs of individuals involved in the colonial takeover of the region and major apologists for the establishment of European-style rule in most of the region. This has been added to by publication of earlier materials such as Paul Kratoska's collection, *Honourable Intentions: Talks on the British Empire in Southeast Asia Delivered at the Royal Colonial Institute*, Singapore, 1983, and Amin Sweeney, *Reputations Live On: An Early Malay Autobiography*, Berkeley, 1980. Studies written in the aftermath of colonial rule have been built upon examinations of the colonial archives: Nicholas Tarling, *Piracy and Politics in the Malay World*, Melbourne, 1963; Jagjit Singh Sidhu, *Administration in the Federated Malay States 1896–1920*, Kuala Lumpur, 1980; Milton Osborne, *The French Presence*; Emily Sadka, *The Protected Malay States, 1874–1895*, Kuala Lumpur, 1968; Anthony Reid, *The Contest for North Sumatra*; Eliodoro G. Robles, *The Philippines in the Nineteenth Century*, Quezon City, 1969; Russel Roth, *Muddy Glory: America's 'Indian Wars' in the Philippines 1899–1935*, Hanover, 1981. More recent studies, written from the perspective of indigenous successor régimes, often present a more critical version of events. Works in the latter category examine the often conflicting mix of indigenous political cultures with the rationalized structures of European colonialism. Examples include Benedict R. O'G. Anderson, 'The Idea of Power in Javanese Culture', in Claire Holt, ed., *Culture and Politics in Indonesia*, Ithaca, 1972; James Siegel, *The Rope of God*, Berkeley, 1968; James Warren, *The Sulu Zone*, Singapore, 1979; Heather Sutherland, *The Making of a Bureaucratic Elite*; and Robert Taylor, *The State in Burma*. Another important analysis of 'pacification' programmes conducted by colonial powers is James C. Scott's *The Moral Economy of the Peasant*, New Haven, 1976.

Plural Societies

J. S. Furnivall coined the term plural society and his works remain the starting point for serious study of the phenomenon, particularly *Colonial Policy and Practice*. This study not only defines the phenomenon, but also remains the only truly comparative study. Most of the literature is country-specific, or limited to a specific ethnic community. Numerous studies focus on groups such as the Chinese, especially where their presence poses serious economic and political questions such as in Malaysia. These include the somewhat dated but still useful work of Victor Purcell, *The Chinese in Southeast Asia*, London, 1965, and C. P. Fitzgerald, *The Southern*

Expansion of the Chinese People, London, 1972. Important views of Malaysia are presented in Philip Loh Fook Seng, *The Malay States 1877–1895, Political Change and Social Policy*, Kuala Lumpur, 1969; his *Seeds of Separatism: Educational Policies and Social Change 1819–1972*, Kuala Lumpur, 1975; K. J. Ratnam, *Communalism and the Political Process in Malaya*, Singapore, 1965; Michael Stenson's study of the Indian community, *Class, Race and Colonialism in West Malaysia*, St Lucia, 1980; and L. A. P. Gosling, 'Migration and Assimilation of Rural Chinese in Trengganu', in John Bastin and R. Roolvink, eds, *Malayan and Indonesian Studies: Essays Presented to Sir Richard Winstedt on his Eighty-fifth Birthday*, Oxford, 1964. For Singapore, there is James Warren, *Rickshaw Coolie: A People's History of Singapore*, Singapore, 1987. A unique approach to communal studies is John Butcher, *The British in Malaya 1880–1941, The Social History of a European Community in Colonial South-East Asia*, Kuala Lumpur, 1979. The classic study of Thailand is by G. William Skinner, *Chinese Society in Thailand: An Analytical History*, Ithaca, 1957; also important is Dorothy Hess Guyot, 'Communal Conflict in the Burma Delta', in McVey, *Southeast Asian Transitions*. The classic work on tribal minorities is E. R. Leach, *Political Systems of Highland Burma*, 1954. A recent addition is Ann Laura Stoler, *Capitalism and Confrontation in Sumatra's Plantation Belt 1870–1979*, New Haven, 1985.

Siam and Burma

The standard studies of Siam include David Wyatt, *Thailand: A Short History*, New Haven, 1984, as well as his *The Politics of Reform in Thailand*, New Haven, 1969; also valuable are the documents collected by Chatthip Nartsupha and Suthy Prasartset, *The Political Economy of Siam 1851–1910*, 1981. David M. Engel, *Law and Kingship in Thailand during the Reign of King Chulalongkorn*, Ann Arbor, 1975, is an important discussion of the reforms of Rama V. Another important view of Thai modernization is Stanley J. Tambiah, *World Conqueror and World Renouncer: A Study of Buddhism and Polity in Thailand Against a Historical Background*, Cambridge, UK, 1976. Recent Thai scholarship has taken a more critical view of the monarchy's role in modernization with the revival of works by the Thai Marxist, Jit Phumisak, translated by Craig Reynolds in *Thai Radical Discourse: The Real Face of Thai Feudalism Today*, Ithaca, 1987.

For Burma see Taylor, *The State in Burma*, and Cady, *A History of Modern Burma*. Other important studies of Burma include Josef Silverstein, *Burma, Military Rule and the Politics of Stagnation*, Cornell, 1977; Frank N. Trager, *Burma, From Kingdom to Republic: a Historical and Political Analysis*, 1966; and the more recent David I. Steinberg, *Burma, A Socialist Nation of Southeast Asia*, Boulder, 1982.

CHAPTER

3

INTERNATIONAL COMMERCE, THE STATE AND SOCIETY: ECONOMIC AND SOCIAL CHANGE

Economic and social change in Southeast Asia in the period from around 1800 to the outbreak of World War II flowed essentially from the unprecedented impact of international commerce on the economic and political structures of the region. Such commerce had long exerted a major role in shaping the nature of Southeast Asian politics and society but, driven by the imperatives of developing Western capitalism and the Industrial Revolution, particularly after about 1850, its global reach and irresistible dominance in this century-and-a-half transformed Southeast Asia with an astonishing thoroughness, rapidity and finality. In a sense, it created the modern state system in Southeast Asia, and in so doing gave rise to the attendant panoply of social change.

STATES AND SOCIETIES IN THE EARLY NINETEENTH CENTURY

Around 1800, the transformative role of this new form of global commerce was still in its infancy; Southeast Asia, accordingly, retained much of its political, economic and social integrity and dynamism. Through most of lowland riverine Southeast Asia, Indic-inspired élites of varying sizes and power, centred on a ruler of prestigious person and impeccable lineage, presided over patterns of social and economic organization that valued control and augmentation of manpower rather than territory or capital. Organized in bonded relationships, formal and informal, with their patrons, most of the subjects of these élites lived in thickly settled clumps which contrasted sharply with the sparsely populated and heavily forested landscape of most of Southeast Asia. 'State', indeed, is a rather grandiose title for what was essentially a knotting together of the leading ends of strands of vertically-shaped personal relationships. The institutions of state and governance were informal, impermanent, personal,

This essay has benefited from the comments of Ian Black, David Chandler and Norman Owen. Most of all I am indebted to John Butcher for his constant encouragement and challenging ideas.

malleable and negotiable, and always prey to contestation from courtly aristocrats or local potentates. Accordingly, administrative control was characteristically weak, diffuse, irregular and decentralized; effective power outside the core of the state was usually the preserve of territorial chiefs or quasi-autonomous tributaries. The varieties of authority were represented at one extreme by the starched and nervous version of Confucian organization employed by the Sino-Vietnamese state, from 1802 centred at Hué. This involved a clearer conception of a state as an impersonal entity and a mandarinal mode of administration, but even though it governed its subjects more formally, busily and efficiently than its Southeast Asian neighbours, the majority of eligible taxpayers still eluded the mandarin's head-tax list. At the other extreme stood locally fragmented chiefly settlements in sparsely populated uplands, lowland interiors and out-of-the-way coasts, free of any pretensions to statehood.

The 'stranded' nature of political and social organization was buttressed by ritual and ideology, but it was substantiated by a leader's ability to acquire wealth and distribute it among his followers. The exchange and redistributive networks upon which this structure depended reached from the remotest upland tribes of Southeast Asia to the busy commercial centres of southern China and west Asia; they provided Southeast Asian leaders with the revenue and reverence they needed to sustain their polities. A state's ruler was typically its greatest trader; to allow others an unrestricted right to trade was to risk the emergence of alternative centres of power. State-sponsored trade was usually organized on a tributary basis, focused on the China market and conducted by Chinese agents. It brought locally produced or collected rice, fish, pepper and exotic forest and marine products (ivory, feathers, sea cucumbers, gemstones, beeswax and resins, for example) into circulation to be exchanged for strategic goods such as weapons, gunpowder and building materials and especially luxury goods—silks, ceramics, fumigants, drugs, precious metals—for the use of domestic élites. State trading monopolies, however, were always difficult to maintain and likely to unravel in the face of competition from rival commercial networks, sometimes foreign, sometimes under the sway of aristocratic or regional élites. Thus the need, both financial and political, for the allied institution of revenue farming, whereby royal monopoly rights to demand produce or impose levies on consumption and other forms of activity such as local trade or gambling were sold off to local power figures (often foreigners who controlled local commerce) in return for a fixed sum and political co-operation.

The focus of this economic activity was the city. Wealthier and more imposing élites projected their power from grand (but sometimes, nonetheless, transferable) urban centres such as Ava, Bangkok, Hué and Yogyakarta. They peopled their capitals with slaves and bondsmen (a status usually acquired by falling into debt) who provided them with prestige, service, income, artifacts, manufactures, entertainment and culture; under the prevailing conditions of low population and physical insecurity there existed no urban free wage-labour market. Foreign merchants, quartered in discrete ethnic areas, provided a cosmopolitan flavour. Such cities aimed to encapsulate the essence of the wider polity and, indeed, larger cosmological forces, so as to represent and endorse the state's greatness and that of its king. The rulers of less prosperous states lacked this grandeur, but shared similar ideological pretensions.

It was the periphery, however, which provided the focal point with its context, significance and the means of its sustenance. The great majority of Southeast Asians lived not in cities but in subsistence-oriented lowland rural communities or fishing villages or, in much smaller numbers and at a further remove from the state's power, as upland or inland swidden peoples or sea nomads. The village was not the placid unit, self-sufficient economically and politically, portrayed in later romantic writings. The peasant economy was built around the production of irrigated rice. Much of the rice was consumed by the growers in combination with vegetables, fish and occasionally meat, but it was also needed to purchase items from outside the village—salt, for example, and porcelain and copper utensils, iron for weapons and for tipping ploughs, musical instruments, draught animals and even opium which, Raffles noted of Java in 1817, 'has struck deep into the habits, and extended its malignant influence to the morals of the people'.[1] To obtain these things, peasants relied on traders, usually Chinese, who ferried in goods from the major towns and exchanged them for rice and other agricultural surpluses or produce which villagers collected from the nearby forests (wood, rattan, gutta percha). Goods were generally moved along rivers, since roads were crude, dangerous, and unreliable, vehicles uncommon, and beasts of burden and porters expensive. Distinct from supra-local trade circuits, there were well-established and busy networks of periodical local markets where peasants exchanged the handicrafts they had manufactured or the tobacco they had grown for rice or dried fish or betel. Most exchange was in the form of barter, but at the same time money, usually in the form of copper or zinc pieces, was well known and used; there was a wide variety of coins scattered throughout rural Southeast Asia, most of them of very small value to suit the peddling nature of rural commerce.

A state's prosperity, as well as the longevity of a particular ruler, depended upon success in milking this hive of production, industry and commerce. Directly or indirectly, the ruler claimed a portion of its produce and levied taxes on its commercial activity, feeding the receipts into the higher circuits of national and international trade for his profit. He also made demands upon the labour power of his subjects to build the infrastructure—waterworks, bridges, roads—needed to enhance production. All this was achieved through the vertical ties of loyalty which aggregated personal followings. A strong, centralizing king necessarily commanded the loyalty and subservience of the bulk of the population; times of weakness and strife inevitably coincided with periods when central control of manpower had dissipated, with followers drifting off to local or courtly competitors. The structural instability inherent in the contest for followings circumscribed the state's demands on its subjects, because it simply did not have the means in these potentially volatile circumstances to enforce unreasonable demands on a regular basis. Thus

---

[1] T. S. Raffles, *The History of Java*, Kuala Lumpur, 1978 [first published 1817], I. 102.

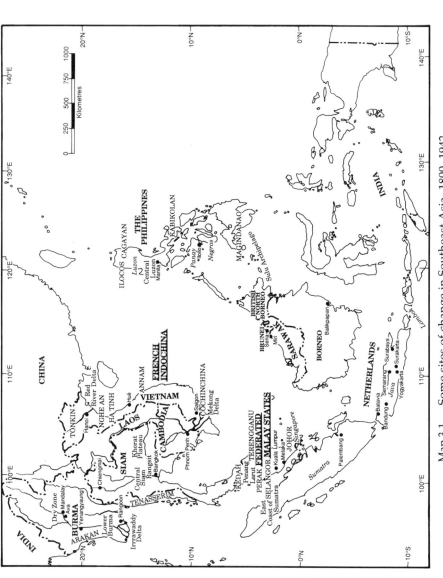

Map 3.1　Some sites of change in Southeast Asia, 1800–1942

its calls upon the village were characteristically light and irregular, and made with a good measure of consideration given to villagers' welfare. Remote settlements often provided little more than an occasional remittance of tribute in the form of a portion of the jungle and sea products they had collected. For their part, in return for their produce and labour services, followers enjoyed the prosperity, security, status and administrative and technological expertise channelled to them by the state, as well as the spiritual privileges of obtaining merit and sharing the glory of the ruler.

With the exception of northern and central Vietnam, peasant communities were not the clearly defined, spatially symmetrical and socially cohesive institutions so common today and, because of instability and the continuing need to forge relationships with new patrons, frequently they were not territorially based or sentimentally attached to specific sites. Peasant villages were somewhat random collections of plaited bamboo and thatch dwellings, most commonly built on stilts, strung along roads or river banks and often separated from each other by forest and fields. Their populations were very small: around 1815, for example, a typical Javanese village numbered between 200 and 300 people. Like the larger society of which it was the largest component, peasant society was hierarchical and stratified. There were relatively wealthy and powerful men in the village (subject to restraints on the exercise of their power like those on that of the state), and economically weak and dependent people; between these two poles were the mass of small landholders. Gender, like economics and politics, was an enduring line of division. The basic unit of peasant society was the male-headed family. While women could, in some peasant societies, hold land, it was generally the case that the male household head was the landholder, and thus formal village politics was the preserve of males. Perhaps reflecting this, most labour fell to women. A relatively strict sexual division of labour left men with the task of preparing fields and guarding the crop. Females, however, were usually responsible for transplanting, harvesting and hulling the crop, on top of their background duties of child-bearing and rearing, domestic labour, and a variety of other tasks such as weaving mats or baskets, or spinning cotton and weaving cloth for their family's use, or taking produce to the market to bargain over its sale. Peasant life was not a continually busy one; there were hectic periods at the beginning of the wet season (planting) and the start of the dry season (harvesting), and at times when corvée duty or military service was required, but a relatively large reservoir of time remained which could be spent in leisure or religious and social activities.

WESTERN MERCHANT CAPITALISTS

In this setting, Western mercantile activity, like that of the indigenous state traders of Southeast Asia themselves, was essentially directed at transporting goods produced by others in order to realize the highest possible profit on their sale in international markets, while protecting that activity from others' competition. It was exemplified most dramatically by the Spanish grasp on the Manila environs as a half-way house for the Acapulco–China trade, by the long and frequently successful efforts of the Verenigde Oost-Indische Compagnie (VOC, Dutch East India Company) to achieve a monopoly of the spices of eastern Indonesia, and by British country traders who, in their own way, linked Southeast Asian to Indian and Chinese trade. A deliberately self-limiting exercise, mercantile capitalism eschewed interference with indigenous polities except to make necessary arrangements for the delivery of desired trade goods; apart from strategically placed forts and 'factories', it avoided territorial conquest and the overheads which administration and defence of such territories involved unless these were deemed necessary to protect its more important commercial interests. While sometimes it superimposed itself upon the indigenous setting through its activities as tribute gatherer and trade director—even to the point, as the VOC did in the archipelago, of destroying previously vibrant indigenous trading networks—mostly it meshed its activities into the practices and routines already well established in Southeast Asia.

Before 1800, the two major exceptions to this pattern were in west Java and central Luzon, where colonial authorities had acceded to extensive territorial control. Both exceptions, however, had resulted from a warping by local circumstance of the logic of European mercantilist practice rather than from the adoption of new policies by the colonial powers involved, for in both cases monopoly, the blunt instrument of mercantilism, was predominant. In west Java, the encumbrance of territory had been as an indirect result of the need felt by the VOC to deal with indigenous potentates who were amenable to its commercial aims. From the 1670s onwards, the VOC had found itself caught up in Javanese dynastic disputes; by siding with winners it was endowed with slices of territory which had to be administered, defended and made profitable. This meant in turn a move from simply collecting produce grown by others to actively directing production, which in this case was achieved by co-opting local Javanese leaders, under limited European supervision, so as to have their peasantries cultivate and deliver large quantities of coffee, and lesser amounts of such items as indigo, cotton yarn and rice.

In the Philippines, the declining importance of the galleon trade, interchanging in Manila vast quantities of Mexican silver for Chinese silks, ceramics and other luxury products and to a lesser extent Indian piece goods, pressed the Spanish colonial government in the late eighteenth century to capitalize upon advances into provincial Luzon made by Catholic missionary friars and attempt to extract revenue by means of a production and marketing monopoly on tobacco. Under the tobacco monopoly specific areas, notably in northeastern Luzon, were set aside for forced peasant production of tobacco under the supervision of local chiefs who had been transformed into colonial agents; the tobacco was delivered at low prices to the government and resold at profit, mostly in monopoly marketing areas within Luzon where the production of tobacco was forbidden.

THE DEVELOPMENT OF INTERNATIONAL COMMERCE
FROM ABOUT 1820

The well-worn patterns of Southeast Asian social and commercial organization began to change rapidly from around 1820, as international
demand, fed directly and indirectly by the early phases of the Industrial
Revolution in Europe and the end of the Napoleonic Wars, brought a
quickening of trade and commercial activity in the region. In Java,
Holland's desperation to halt its dismal slide into financial and political
obscurity saw it intensify its efforts to squeeze profit from its loosely held
territorial control. During the British interregnum in Java (1811–16), Raffles
had already sought to do this by abolishing the role of local aristocracies as
production and labour brokers and introducing a land tax to draw Javanese
peasants into direct contact with the (British) international economy. His
efforts failed, but important aspects of them, notably the land rent system,
were retained by the Dutch. Under the umbrella of mercantile methods
revived from the practice of the now defunct VOC, they became components of the Cultivation System (1830), a virtual state monopoly of production and sale. This scheme, the brainchild of a fierce and complicated
character, Governor-General Johannes van den Bosch, forced peasants,
under the leadership of their own chiefs, to grow specific export crops
(coffee, sugar and indigo were the main ones) to be auctioned in Europe
by the Nederlandsche Handel Maatschappij (Dutch Trading Company), to
which they were consigned by the Indies government. Force was exercised, especially in the early years, by recourse to the moral authority of
indigenous leaders, but with the passage of years the Cultivation System
came to be practised as much through a combination of economic coercion
(taxation) and incentive (for example, the rapidly increasing popularity of
Dutch manufactured cottons amongst Javanese) as through the exercise of
traditional authority. The overall success of this compound strategy is
manifest in the staggering amount of peasant labour employed in the
Cultivation System, around 70 per cent of all peasant households in the
areas of Java under direct Dutch rule in the 1830s and 1840s, gradually
reducing as the system began to be wound back from about 1850 (and all
on a relatively small amount of peasant land, a Java-wide average of
about 5 per cent at its peak in the early 1840s). While the Cultivation
System enjoyed extraordinary commercial success—providing one-third
of Holland's state revenue in the 1850s—it was essentially at odds with the
new tides of commerce sweeping through Southeast Asia; its characteristic
features of monopoly in production and sale, coercion, and the carefully
protective modulation of the domestic economy were increasingly discordant with the emerging economic liberalist theme of the new era.

In the Philippines, by contrast, state monopoly was on the wane as
Spain's imperial might crumbled; the tobacco monopoly endured, albeit in
declining form, until laid to rest in 1882. Side by side with it, however,
came erratic efforts by the colonizers to bring firmer control to the hinterland by tying local élites into the colonial governing apparatus and using

their influence to expand, mostly ineffectively, the range of revenue-gathering devices. Unlike the Dutch, however, the Spanish were too weak and irresolute to stand in the face of changing international circumstances and attempt, by monopoly alone, to withstand more commercially advanced competitors. From late in the eighteenth century, patterns of trade and consequently production began to change significantly. Increasing penetration of the Manila market, first by British country traders and, at the end of the century and thereafter, by British and American merchants, together with the gradual development of a Chinese mestizo entrepreneurial group which moved out of the core towns and into the provincial countryside, opened up the Philippines to the world market (made official by the Spanish for Manila in 1834, and extended to other regional ports in 1855). Accordingly, the focus of Philippine trade swung away from Mexico and towards Asia and the West; its content changed from Mexican silver first to exotic tropical goods like birds' nests, tortoiseshell, sea cucumbers, ebony, and woods, and then to locally produced agricultural commodities, the quantities of which multiplied in response to commercial opportunity. Merchant houses, mainly British and American, were established in Manila from the 1820s; they provided the capital and merchandising facilities which allowed Chinese mestizo groups, now rapidly overcoming or merging with indigenous provincial landholding élites, to establish or expand the production of such cash crops as sugar (in central Luzon), tobacco (in Cagayan) and abaca (in Kabikolan). In time, the Chinese, whose numbers had grown rapidly with the removal of restrictions on Chinese immigration in the 1840s, began to usurp mestizo dominance of regional commerce, acting as retailing intermediaries for Western (especially British) products, of which the most important were textiles, and siphoning out the growing volume of Philippine produce. As far as the Spanish colonial government was concerned, its major contribution to these processes was 'to get out of the way'.[2] This pattern of commercializing agriculture was to remain virtually unchanged in the Philippines throughout the remainder of the colonial period. Its rapid growth, even in these formative years, was manifest in a tripling of the value of exports between 1825 and 1850, and the change in their composition from forest and sea products to sugar, abaca, coffee and tobacco.

The same pressures and opportunities for change were being felt in the wider reaches of Southeast Asia. In Siam, where the royal élite combined significant profits from trade with China with a wariness towards Westerners, the probings of Western traders eager for produce to feed on to the world market were having an effect. Rama III allowed individual Western merchants to operate, and in 1826 conceded some limited liberalization of trade in response to Henry Burney's mission on behalf of the East India Company. The preponderant response of the Siamese élite, however, was not capitulation but a determined effort to increase its economic strength and political control by expanding production and commerce for its own

---

[2] Norman G. Owen, 'Abaca in Kabikolan: prosperity without progress', in Alfred W. McCoy and Ed. C. de Jesus, eds, *Philippine Social History: Global Trade and Local Transformations*, Quezon City, 1982, 194.

benefit. As in the Philippines, immigrant Chinese were made welcome, especially from the reign of Rama III. Free of corvée obligations, they provided manpower to enhance production (in sugar and pepper plantations, in tin mines and on public works such as canal construction) and technical and commercial skills, so as better to service Siam's role in international commerce. On the western Malay Peninsula, tin mining had been long if sporadically carried on by Malay chiefs and, more often through the early nineteenth century, scattered Chinese entrepreneurs, using primitive labour-intensive techniques and financed by wealthy Straits Chinese merchants; now it began to grow in importance. It climaxed with the discovery of a rich detritus of ore at Larut in Perak in 1848 and subsequent important discoveries in the western valleys of the peninsula, which coincided with a rapid rise in world demand for tin which Cornwall's mines could no longer satisfy. To cater for this demand in a sustained way, mine operators could no longer rely on erratic and inefficient production by Malay peasants and small numbers of Chinese workers; increasingly they introduced technological advances such as the chain pump and, most important of all, attracted increasingly large numbers of southern Chinese immigrant labourers to work the mines. In the early 1860s, indeed, it was estimated that there were around 25,000 Chinese labouring in the tinfields of Larut alone.

The changing spirit of the times was most closely captured by Britain's establishment of trading centres at Penang (1786), Melaka (1824) and especially Singapore (1819), occasioning the Dutch to establish similar ports within their sphere of influence. This was the beginning of the age of 'free-trade imperialism', founded on the belief that 'free trade', commerce unhindered by protection and undiverted by the demands of territorial administration, inevitably meant Britain's economic success as well as greater prosperity for those peoples with which it traded.

Paradoxically, however, 'non-intervention' frequently provoked substantial change. The rapid development of the free-trade entrepôt of Singapore was itself a case in point. Its presence as an outlet for international commerce encouraged the growth of Chinese pepper and gambier plantations in Singapore and especially neighbouring Johor. Organized according to the *kangchu* system[3] with Chinese labourers and under a shifting cultivation régime, the plantations required little capital, supervision or skill, and promised rapid returns to the *kangchu* and his investors, not only from produce but from the income generated from the sale of opium to workers. The British in Singapore farmed out the monopoly rights to the sale of opium to Chinese syndicates; the *kangchus* acted as their local agents, a situation which helped them defray wage costs on their plantations. The revenue generated by this monopoly in turn financed Singapore's free-trade status. Thus sustained by reciprocity, Singapore quickly gained prominence as a collection and distribution

---

[3] The *kangchu* ('lord of the river') was a Chinese headman granted lease rights by the local Malay ruler to a stretch of river valley land for shifting plantation agriculture. He organized and controlled the immigrant Chinese who worked the plantation lands (James C. Jackson, *Planters and Speculators: Chinese and European Agricultural Enterprise in Malaya, 1786–1921*, Kuala Lumpur, 1968, 15–22).

centre for regional and international commerce. Trade included European piece goods (slow at first but later increasing to a flood), China tea, Indian opium, Malayan tin, Sumatran pepper, local plantation products such as gambier, pepper, and tapioca, and local forest produce, notably gutta percha. Singapore took over from Siam as the major entrepôt for archipelago produce en route to China and provided (with the industrious assistance of Bugis traders) a focus to reintegrate Asian regional trade in a manner not witnessed since the demise of old Melaka in the sixteenth century. Further afield in the Sulu archipelago, the demand by British country traders for 'Straits produce' like birds' nests, sea cucumbers and tortoiseshell to trade for China's tea provided the necessary conditions which galvanized local rulers to embark on a century of extensive slave raiding throughout the archipelago, procuring the labour power (a total of around a quarter of a million people) which they needed to collect items from the jungle and the sea to service the trade. The fact that at this time the West itself produced relatively little which Asians desired was the key to this style of obtrusive non-intervention. For the most part, Westerners had to acquire in Asia what they needed to trade in Asia; thus they had to attract Southeast Asian produce to nodal points for use in the China trade.

Elsewhere, the impact of developing commerce and closer international contacts was more restrained. In Vietnam, French missionaries and merchantmen nibbled away—sometimes with considerable success in the case of the missionaries (140,000 Catholics in west Tonkin alone by 1855)—for souls and profit without making a significant impact on the empire of the vigorous Minh-mang (r. 1820–41). The Vietnamese court, while evincing an interest in acquiring Western technology (notably steamships), satisfied itself with a small and closely controlled trade focused on China and mostly limited to luxury items (including Chinese books). Vietnam did not remain unaffected, however, suffering an inflation-causing outflow of silver to China, used by the Chinese to pay for their imports of British opium. The Lao and especially the Cambodian kingdoms did, by contrast, remain unaffected by the accelerating pace of international commerce. They were too poor, distant, difficult of access, unimportant, and preoccupied with failing battles to preserve their identities against cultural and political encroachment from Siam to the west and Vietnam to the east. Burma, like Siam, suffered the effects of Britain's importunity, partly in the name of free trade. The First Anglo-Burman War of 1824–6 resulted in the British annexation of Arakan and Tenasserim and some limited privileges for British commerce.

In retrospect, this period of accelerating international commercial contact may be seen as a transitional stage from the older, limited equilibrium of state-sponsored trade, monopolies and privileges to a new and highly complex mode of capitalism. As commercial activity gathered momentum, fuelled by the increasing rapacity of global trade, indigenous and foreign leaders and traders responded in a variety of ways, ranging through indifference, stolid opposition to its new demands, and cautious adaptation, to enthusiastic co-operation. The logic of commercial development, however, would soon limit those options to two: co-operation or ignominy.

THE CREATION OF A NEW ORDER FROM ABOUT 1850

Around the beginning of the second half of the nineteenth century under the powerful example of Britain, the West moved into the phase of high capitalism. Increasingly, the key to wealth and power was to be found in industrial production and not just mercantile commerce. The transformation in the dominant 'mode of production' in the West brought with it an inner dynamism and a consequent international competitiveness which led the West, more particularly Europe, to impose itself in new and dominating ways on much of the rest of the world. The Industrial Revolution placed extraordinary economic and social power at the disposal of the Western powers, and with that came the realization that such power demanded more elaborate and more intensive exploitation of less developed areas. It provoked different and radically heightened demands and patterns of consumption and it provided incentives, opportunities and even the means for that exploitation—developments in manufacturing and processing technology such as tin cans and pneumatic tyres, advanced weaponry, telegraphic communications between Europe and Southeast Asia, and rapid and cheap bulk transport of commodities and labourers by steamship.

The high age of the Industrial Revolution expressed itself in increasing competition among the colonial powers for the territorial annexation of most of Southeast Asia, a process that properly began in a halting and piecemeal fashion around 1850 and climaxed in the rush for empire in the concluding years of the century as Britain's industrial pre-eminence waned. In Indochina, from the pinpoints of influence established in the Mekong delta in 1859, French control expanded westwards to grasp Cambodia in a protective embrace, and north and northwest to the ancient core of the Red (Hong) River delta and the principalities of Laos. The British annexed lower Burma in 1852 and imposed 'free trade' commercial treaties on the Burmese kingdom in 1862 and 1867 which removed (on paper but not in fact) most royal monopolies and allowed free movement of people and goods. The simultaneous response of the increasingly harassed and desperate King Mindon was a programme of reforming centralization. This aimed at expanding the production of rice and manufactured and processed goods, developing foreign trade—much of which still passed through his hands—and amplifying royal revenues (through, for example, granting timber concessions to foreign firms, notably the Bombay-Burmah Trading Corporation), all to strengthen his state. It was too late; in 1886 the British swallowed the old Burman heartland. In Malaya, British 'intervention' in 1874 led to a pattern of action and reaction which saw the creation of the Federated Malay States in 1896 and gradually brought the remaining Malay states under formal colonial control through the second decade of the twentieth century. In the Indies, the Dutch, by dint of war and unilateral 'diplomacy', sewed together the people and lands of the 'Indonesian' archipelago to form a 'Netherlands East Indies'. In the Philippines, Spain and then (after 1898) the United States increasingly brought the disparate communities of those islands under a single state authority. The only exception to this pattern, the Siamese state, was forced to accommodate to British demands for free trade under the conditions of the Bowring treaty of 1855, which set import and export duties at fixed, low levels, and abolished most trading monopolies and internal taxes on goods and trade. Bangkok's response was a rapid elaboration of its already existing 'state strengthening' strategy, in this context involving the formal consolidation of its peripheral territories under centralized state control. By the beginning of the twentieth century, Southeast Asia's complicated and variegated political setting had been reduced to six states working on principles of political organization and political legitimacy quite different from those in force a generation or two before. Five of the states were run by Western colonial powers—the British in Rangoon and Singapore, the French in Hanoi, the Dutch in Batavia and the Americans in Manila. The other state, Siam, was run by a modernizing indigenous élite which shared many of the administrative and legal characteristics of the newly emergent colonial states.

PHASE ONE: LIBERALISM

From our perspective, the construction of a new Southeast Asian economic and political order may seem inevitable and perhaps even necessary. This masks, however, the complex interactions of policy, practice, effect and reaction which led to its creation, and which may best be understood by tracing the phased evolution of Southeast Asia's states from the situation of bewildering and apparently endemic political pluralism in the first half of the nineteenth century to one of centralized dominance at its end. The first phase, liberal capitalism, characteristic of practice in lower Burma, Cochinchina, central Siam, Malaya, Sumatra, and Luzon, was simply to create the conditions which allowed the adjustment, elaboration and incorporation of existing styles of production into global marketing systems. At the same time it spoiled and harassed arrangements obstructive to growth. It began around 1850, reached its apogee around the turn of the twentieth century and, overlapped by its successor phase, endured rather than prospered thereafter, for reasons which will become clear. The key feature of this first phase was its laissez-faire character, a reflection not just of popular ideas about the universal applicability of liberalism but more concretely of the limitations of state power and the lack of private Western investment capital. Its success was achieved with small amounts of capital and depended almost solely upon huge inputs of human labour; its development, unlike Java's under the Cultivation System, was not a last gasp of jealous mercantilism but a result of removing restraints on the penetration of international market forces. The concomitant values propelling growth were the newer ones of individualism and acquisitiveness rather than old customary obligation. These values were increasingly relevant and powerful in circumstances where international commerce could provide a diverse range of consumer goods for peasant producers. The result was change of a more rapid, free-wheeling, uncontrolled and fundamental sort than had previously been encountered. Some Southeast Asians caught up in these developments prospered, at least temporarily; many others suffered grievously. For all of them it was the beginning of a pervasively transformative era. The following are some examples of this stimulating but structurally limited phase in operation.

Rice Smallholding in Lower Burma, Cochinchina and Central Siam

While the region of the Irrawaddy delta was by no means unoccupied or uncultivated in 1852 when it was annexed by the British, it was relatively empty in terms of what was to come later.[4] Contemporary accounts put the population of the delta area at around one million, with about three hundred thousand hectares under cultivation. Then, as later, the production of rice was the central economic activity, with much of the surplus used to feed the population of upper Burma. Before 1852, however, development of the rice industry had been inhibited by the Burmese government's ban on exports; this held prices very low and, coupled with an undeveloped economy, provided little incentive for producers to cultivate surpluses above levels required for subsistence and tribute or to bring more land under cultivation. The British annexation of lower Burma transformed this self-contained, self-sufficient and relatively static peasant society. Almost immediately, the British removed the ban on rice exports and lifted trading restrictions, a decision that happened to coincide with a time when Europe was looking for new sources of rice because of the Sepoy Mutiny in India and the Civil War in the United States. Reflecting the influence of prevailing liberal ideas, the British also decided that the most efficient and reliable way of organizing rice production was to encourage Burmese smallholder rice producers rather than employ a system of large landholdings. This was accomplished by means of a system of land taxation based on small village cultivation, and land tenure laws which sought to maximize the possibility of smallholder ownership. Peasants, for example, came to own land on which they had originally squatted if they occupied it and paid revenue upon it for twelve years. In addition, the British provided stability, milling and exporting facilities, flood control and irrigation works and transport infrastructure (especially riverine), all invigorating the production and marketing of rice and the development by Burmese themselves of retailing networks and capital provision. The response of the Burmese smallholder was a massive development of agriculture in the last decades of the nineteenth century. Population increased fourfold in the last half of the century, predominantly through a high rate of natural fertility but also as a result of a remarkable immigration of poor, young, male peasants (sometimes seasonal labourers) from upper Burma's dry zone, where agricultural conditions and prospects were uncertain and, later, of impoverished peasants and

---

[4] This discussion draws heavily on Michael Adas, *The Burma Delta: Economic Development and Social Change on an Asian Rice Frontier, 1852–1941*, Madison, 1974, and to a lesser extent Cheng Siok-Hwa, *The Rice Industry of Burma 1852–1940*, Kuala Lumpur, 1968.

labourers from south-east India who, recruited and financed by labour-gang foremen (*maistry*), came to toil in Burma for a few years before returning home. The area under cultivation grew by a factor of eight and rice exports by a factor of twelve between 1885 and 1906, transforming lower Burma 'from an undeveloped and sparsely populated backwater of the Konbaung Empire into the world's leading rice-exporting area'.[5] So dominant did rice production and export become in the Burmese economy that rice accounted for up to three-quarters of Burma's exports by value before 1930.

Apart from the normal environmental problems of frontier develop-ment—the toil of land reclamation, dangers from malaria and wild ani-mals, attacks of crop-eating insects, and diseases of plough animals—the major difficulty facing peasant agriculturalists was credit. As the pace of development accelerated toward the end of the century, the provision of credit, previously made available by friends, shopkeepers and a small number of indigenous moneylenders, came to be dominated by Indian Chettiars; establishing facilities in rural areas and greatly increasing the amount of credit available, they acted directly as moneylenders for peasants and also provided finances for the host of indigenous money-lenders. As economic activity increased and finance became more readily available, the large-scale use of credit among peasants became the norm in delta society, a process fuelled by an improving standard of living and rising costs.

This first phase of development before the turn of the century was one of great expansion, growth and social mobility for peasant smallholders. Under prevailing conditions, even the poorest immigrant could aspire to own his own land, build a substantial dwelling, purchase large quantities of imported consumer goods (the quantity of cotton goods imported into Burma grew sixfold between 1873 and 1914) and generally enjoy a stand-ard of living hitherto unknown for a person of his rank. Even tenants shared in the burst of prosperity, because the large amount of available reclaimable land and the general shortage of labour gave them a strong bargaining position against their landlords; in some places, indeed, ten-ants were allowed to work holdings rent free.

Such prosperity, fluidity and development could last only as long as the frontier of opportunity remained open. By the early years of the twentieth century, land began to run out as population continued to expand. Moreover, ecological problems began to make their presence felt: for example, flood control embankments prevented the widespread deposi-tion of silt on farmland, and yields began to drop. Smallholders found the price of land rising steadily, hindering their ability to extend their hold-ings. Declining yields cut into their surpluses and placed them closer to the danger margin; credit became more expensive; inflation raised the costs of goods and services; market conditions became less predictable, especially after World War I. Most important of all, smallholders were firmly enmeshed in relations of credit dependency that limited their ability to respond to market forces—most of them, for example, had to sell their rice immedi-

---

[5] Adas, 4.

ately upon harvest to pay off accumulated debts, rather than stockpiling it until prices improved. Larger landholders and middlemen of various kinds—rice sellers, brokers, merchants—capitalized on these problems to increase their leverage over small producers. The result was that an increasing number of owner-cultivators fell into such extremes of debt that they had to part with their land. This, together with the fact that rising costs made land reclamation the preserve of wealthier producers, meant that a greatly increased proportion of land fell into the hands of larger landholders, many of them absentee non-agriculturist owners. The proportion of cultivated land owned by non-agriculturalists in lower Burma rose from 18 per cent in 1907 to 31 per cent in 1930 (although only a small proportion of them were Chettiars, who generally preferred control of money to control of land), and rates of tenancy increased accordingly. Petty smallholders who managed to retain their land did so only at the cost of dangerously increasing their levels of indebtedness: in one district in 1922, for example, nearly half the cultivators were indebted beyond their surpluses.

The increasing pressure felt by owner-cultivators was also felt by less fortunate classes. Tenants found their profits declining, and thus their ability to strike out on their own as owner-cultivators; moreover, as land began to run out and population thicken, the balance of power swung decisively in favour of landlords. Competition between would-be tenants forced up the rents: at the turn of the century, tenants had not paid much more than 10 per cent of their revenue to landlords; twenty-five years later, 50 per cent was common. At the end of the 1930s, nearly 60 per cent of lower Burma's agricultural land was under full fixed-rent tenancy. Landlords' dominance allowed them to exploit their tenants in new ways as well—by refusing to grant revisions of rent in bad seasons or forcing them to bear more of the costs of rice production. This in turn led to a highly mobile tenant population with a great increase in shorter-term tenancies. Landless labourers were probably in the most precarious position of all, with tough competition between a growing number of workers for a more or less static supply of jobs. Their number grew steadily, not so much from immigration from upper Burma—which dropped off steadily after the turn of the century as conditions there improved through enhanced irrigation facilities and the development of cash cropping—but from the growing number of Indian migrant labourers escaping from poor conditions at home and fanning out into the countryside from the cities where they had first settled, seeking seasonal or permanent work in agriculture, and also from former owner-cultivators dispossessed of their land. As employment possibilities shrank, so did wages, in both absolute and relative terms, and the cost of living kept rising inexorably.

The pattern of change in the Mekong delta of Cochinchina bore some remarkable similarities to that in lower Burma: an empty and unexploited frontier, a free-wheeling response to the quickening demand for rice on international markets following French annexation, a rapid growth of population fuelled by migration from the heavily populated and impoverished north. The French transformed the landscape to the west and south of Saigon by undertaking monumental earthworks and canal construction, using corvée labour until the 1890s but thereafter employing private French firms which used mechanized dredging and suction equipment to perform the task. More than 1300 kilometres of canals were dug, providing not just irrigation water but an excellent means of transportation. Land under rice cultivation in Cochinchina expanded from 274,000 hectares in 1873 to 1,174,000 in 1900 and 2,214,000 in 1930. Between 1860 and 1900, rice exports grew by a factor of ten, and then doubled again over the succeeding three decades. Vietnam became the world's third-largest producer of rice; up to 1931 the staple accounted for two-thirds of Vietnam's exports.

French policy and practice were manifest as early as 1862 when the lands of Vietnamese who had rebelled against or fled from the imposition of French rule were confiscated and sold off to speculators; they served severely to accelerate a pre-colonial trend towards the social polarization of landlordism and landlessness. The French granted ownership to settlers who squatted on virgin land to the east and north of Saigon, cleared it, made it productive, put a claim to it and paid taxes on it; nonetheless, larger landholdings quickly became evident. Partly this resulted from peasants falling behind in their credit repayments; more important, perhaps, was the lack of appropriate mechanisms for ordinary farmers to make legal claim to the land they had cleared and, conversely, the exploitation of land registration procedures by village notables, wealthy peasants, indigenous officials, entrepreneurs, and Europeans. In the virtually unoccupied areas reclaimed from swamp to the west and south, the French deliberately sought to create a rice plantation economy by auctioning off large blocks of land to Europeans and especially to absentee Vietnamese who worked them on the basis of share tenancy. Living from rents and debt repayments, these landlords left the profits from rice milling, transporting, dealing and export almost entirely in the hands of Chinese merchants based in Saigon-Cholon. In contrast to the early predominance of petty smallholders in lower Burma, it was usually the case in the Mekong delta that immigrant peasants began their careers as tenants rather than owners, with no reasonable hope of being able to improve their condition. This important difference apart, however, the fate of peasants in the Mekong delta followed the same general course as in the Burma delta—a combination of decreasing resources, rapidly expanding population, declining terms of trade for rice, dependence upon rural credit, all leading inexorably to impoverishment and landlessness. By 1930, 2.5 per cent of landholders owned 45 per cent of the cultivated land, while only one peasant household in four possessed any land at all. The great majority of peasants in the delta were either tenant farmers or landless agricultural labourers. Indeed, in one recently settled province in the far south in 1930, two-thirds of the cultivated land was in the form of holdings of more than 50 hectares.

In Siam, in response to the Bowring treaty of 1855 which forced Siam to become a participant in the broader world economy, large new areas of rice land in the central plain were opened up for peasant rice cultivation. The volume of Siam's rice exports grew more than twenty-five times between about 1860 and 1930. Thanks mainly to the labour invested in waterworks construction and land reclamation by Chinese wage labourers and Siamese smallholders, the area under rice tripled, expanding from the central plain to the north and northeast. The rapid expansion of rice production and export, however, was not accompanied to a significant degree by the intractable social polarizations evident on the rice frontiers of lower Burma and Cochinchina. This was partly because the Thai nobility were oriented to commerce by their unofficial sponsorship of (and integration with) Chinese entrepreneurs during the nineteenth century, accustomed to feeding off the wealth produced by trade, and distracted by the centralizing efforts of the Thai monarch; they found relatively little attraction in controlling extensive rural landholdings. As well, the capital available for development was mostly home-grown and thus relatively insubstantial, so that development was significantly less rapid, widespread and thorough than in the case of Burma or Cochinchina and potential resources in land remained in abundance. Moreover, because agricultural expansion took place in areas contiguous to the existing centres of activity, peasant pioneers were not dependent strangers in a new land but simply more distant neighbours of their kin, and privy to existing support networks which provided the credit they needed for development. The result was that, except in areas reclaimed under government sponsorship—notably the Rangsit region northeast of Bangkok developed by the private Siam Canals, Land and Irrigation Company from 1889 and sold off to well-connected speculators—absentee landlordism, tenancy, indebtedness and dependency did not become such predominant features of Siam's rice economy as they did elsewhere. Rice trading, transport, and milling became and remained the preserve of the Chinese, often financed by the Siamese nobility; the export business was shared between Western and Chinese brokerage firms with only minimal Siamese participation.

Tin Mining in Malaya

In the western Malay states, the 'rush to be rich' occasioned by growing world demand for tin from about 1850 had produced eager and chaotic squabbling and violence between Chinese entrepreneurial groups organized in secret societies, between them and the Malay chiefs who controlled the tin lands, and between the Malay chiefs themselves who fell into contestation over claims to revenues from tin. This invited a British 'law and order' response from 1874 which in turn provided the political, legal and administrative circumstances for accelerated development. With British intervention, exploitation intensified further; by 1895, the western Malay states were responsible for 55 per cent of world tin production as against 11 per cent in 1874. Increasingly, too, the brokerage role of local Malay chiefs in production was bypassed as Straits investors, no longer dependent upon their political authority (partly because the chiefs were by now frequently and heavily indebted to them), dealt directly with Chinese mine operators who assumed virtually complete control of the tin fields. Apart from their technological skills in mining, drainage and smelting, the dominance of tin mining by Chinese merchants and mine-owners was a function of superior corporate business practices (such as the *kongsi*), socially lubricated capital and marketing networks, and their ability, through wealth and the strategic use of clan organizations and secret societies, to recruit and control ever larger numbers of cheap indentured labourers from southern China. These workers were funnelled through Singapore by 'coolie brokers'; they had come to the tin fields to escape war and starvation at home, to create a new, if temporary, life in Southeast Asia, and eventually to return, newly prosperous, to their homeland. Something like five million Chinese arrived in Malaya in the nineteenth century, and a further twelve million in the first four decades of the twentieth. The nineteenth-century immigrants were mostly tied to three-year contracts legally sanctioned by a discharge ticket system to control mobility; their wages paid for their credited passage, their food (often provided under a 'truck' system), their opium consumption and gambling, and allowed where possible for remittances to family in China. The immigrant participants in this 'pig trade' suffered appalling living conditions and very high rates of morbidity and mortality from malaria, beri-beri, dysentery and industrial accidents; annual death rates of mine workers were sometimes as high as 50 per cent.

Smallholder Rubber in Malaya and Sumatra

Smallholder production for the world market attained probably its most lucrative form in the development of the smallholder rubber industry of Malaya and Sumatra. Taking advantage of the introduction of *Hevea brasiliensis* from Brazil via Kew Gardens in London, peasant cultivators, profiting from the demonstration effect of highly capitalized Western rubber plantations which yielded enormous profits, planted huge areas of rubber trees in individually small plots in west Malaya and in south and east Sumatra: by 1940, for example, 715,000 hectares of Sumatra were under smallholder rubber. The crude latex (or coagulated rubber sheets) which the growers produced was placed on the world market through Chinese marketing chains linked to Singapore. In Malaya, the boom years of rubber in the early twentieth century provided a powerful incentive to peasant smallholders to produce rubber rather than investing their skill and labour in rice-growing to feed the growing population of coolie labourers working on nearby Western plantations, much to the chagrin of British officials who tried various admixtures of inducement and sanction (such as the 'no rubber' condition applied to the use of certain categories of land) to discourage smallholder rubber. In Sumatra, initial development was slower, but the extent of smallholder rubber grew sevenfold between 1920 and 1930 at a time when Malaya, in a bid to turn around a price slump after the post World War I boom, had subjected itself to production restrictions under the Stevenson scheme (1922).

The most interesting aspect of smallholder production was the manner in which peasants integrated rubber growing into already existing cycles of food production. This normally took two forms. The first, most common in Sumatra where smallholdings developed well away from the sites of Western plantation agriculture, was an adaptation of swidden cultivation, whereby agriculturalists cleared stretches of forest and planted food crops, moving on to other sites when the land became too exhausted for food production after two or three crops. Now they planted rubber trees in the disused cropping area. In this jungle environment, the rubber tree proved a great ecological success; planters simply returned to the site to tap the trees when they had matured after about seven years. The alternative method, favoured in Malaya, involved sedentary cultivation. Peasants devoted a portion of their established land to rubber trees. While they waited for the crop to mature, they continued their normal subsistence-oriented lives as rice growers; upon crop maturity, rubber production became a valuable and non-disruptive adjunct to subsistence farming. Under both these régimes, the flexibility of part-time rubber production perfectly suited cultivators who had little capital and who were unprepared and unwilling to commit their futures wholly to the uncertainties of the world rubber market. Smallholder rubber cost little in terms of initial outlay, the risks to subsistence were minimal, labour investment between initial planting and tapping was negligible, and most important of all, cultivators could defer production until the market was at its most favourable. When rubber prices were low, peasants lived on their subsistence; as they rose, it was a simple matter to turn on the latex tap again.

By the end of the colonial period, smallholders in the Netherlands East Indies had more land under rubber trees than did that country's plantation sector, and produced almost as much rubber. In Malaya, they produced almost one-third of rubber exports. This massive contribution to the rubber industry changed the lives of smallholders significantly. The sudden influx of cash from rubber rapidly increased the standard of living of those peasants involved. In Sumatra, for instance, peasant incomes doubled or tripled within a very short time; the new flows of disposable cash were spent on improving houses, building mosques, travelling to Mecca, buying imported textiles and other consumer goods, and sometimes reinvesting in the expansion of areas under rubber. Some smallholders became extensive growers, so that they and their families could not tap all their trees themselves and had to employ rubber tappers who worked in return for a half-share of the product. This relatively high payment indicates a significant demand for labour in these developing areas, and the earnings to be made from rubber tapping produced a large spontaneous immigration to the rubber areas of Sumatra. The prosperity of rubber smallholders relative to that of peasants in Java involved in more controlled and servile modes of colonial production is reflected in income tax data: in 1929, less than 3 per cent of Javanese households earned more than 300 guilders per annum, while the corresponding figure in the outer islands was 19 per cent.

Despite this, there was no widespread structural change in peasant society as a result of the smallholder rubber boom. The role of peasant producers remained limited. They were commonly no more than producers of latex, eschewing involvement in rubber processing or marketing and spending their income on consumer goods—food, cloth, bicycles, sewing machines. Their produce, either latex or sheeting, was passed on to Chinese middlemen who transmitted it to large (usually) Western exporters. While in the Netherlands East Indies substantial Indonesian commercial networks in competition with Chinese had developed by the mid-1920s, even becoming involved in rubber exporting, these were exceptional. Most Malay and Sumatran rubber planters remained peripheral to the world markets they supplied; they remained rice-growing, village-dwelling peasants who also happened to plant and tap rubber trees.

Sugar and Abaca in Luzon

Unlike the Burma and Mekong deltas, the central Luzon plain was already the subject of developing cash crop exploitation for the world market before the mid-nineteenth century. As the pace of economic development quickened after about 1850, the Filipino élite, and particularly the Chinese mestizo element which was gradually merging into it, managed to gain control of huge areas of the central Luzon plain, laying claim to large estates (*hacienda*) for the production of rice as well as tobacco, cattle and sugar. At the same time, peasants migrating in large numbers to the interior of the plain from the regions around Manila in the south and from the Ilocos areas of northwest Luzon claimed and brought under cultivation large areas of land in a fractional, piecemeal and gradual manner. The contest between these two groups for control of the plain's land resources was decided rapidly and conclusively in favour of the élite. Sometimes they managed this by purchasing estates from the original holders or from the government itself. Again, as elsewhere in Southeast Asia, their knowledge of land law and legal procedures, together with their abundant wealth and manipulation of connections, enabled them to lay claim to large holdings and make those claims stick. The most important method of large land acquisition, however, was through the extension of credit to smallholder settlers. Under the mechanism known as *pacto de retroventa*,[6] Chinese mestizos lent money against the security of land titles; one was so successful that he expanded an original holding of 250 hectares to control scattered holdings of some 5000 hectares. The rapidly expanding production of sugar in central Luzon from the middle of the century onwards, stimulated by international demand and facilitated by technological improvements in the form of steam-powered mills, was organized around the *hacienda* institution.

Tenancy was the core of this system. The tenants contracted with landholders to pay a share of the income from the sale of processed sugar as rent for the use of land. Where tenants were scarce and where ample opportunity existed for them to transfer their allegiance to another patron, rents tended to be fixed and low; moreover, tenants enjoyed such favours as free firewood and the right to grow vegetables rent-free on dwelling plots. Under these circumstances, the tenant was 'the planter-capitalist's industrial partner responsible for managing his own farm'.[7] By the turn of the century and thereafter, however, the conditions of tenancy had swung

---

[6] This was a contract under which a landholder handed over his title to a buyer for a specified price with an option of repurchasing the land at a later specified time.
[7] Alfred W. McCoy, 'A queen dies slowly: the rise and decline of Iloilo city', in McCoy and De Jesus, eds, 325.

very much in favour of the landlord. Central Luzon became more tightly attached to the world economy, especially after the American takeover and the general opening of United States markets (notably the Payne–Aldrich Tariff Bill of 1909 which allowed 300,000 duty-free tons of Philippine sugar into the US market); this, together with the intensification of colonial control, the spread and enforcement of Western concepts of ownership, increasing and improving mechanization of cane production and processing, and the rapid growth of population, all contributed to the consolidation of the *hacienda* system and created an impoverished and indebted peasantry saddled with increasingly inequitable share tenancies rather than fixed rents. By the late 1930s, around two-thirds of the cultivated land of central Luzon was farmed by tenants, and much of it was owned by absentee landlords.

Abaca, from which was produced the rope and cordage increasingly demanded by the industrializing West for rigging and binding, was grown predominantly on the large landholdings of local élites in the region of Kabikolan in southeast Luzon, and harvested and processed by a unique combination of peasant wage labour and sharecropping. Although abaca prices were acutely sensitive to cyclical industrial booms and downturns, especially in the United States, the trend line of exports through the nineteenth century was always steep (though gradually flattening), rising from 432 tonnes in 1825–9 to 12,599 tonnes in 1850–4 and 115,985 tonnes in 1900–4. By that time abaca provided about two-thirds by value of Philippines exports.

PHASE TWO: FROM LIBERALISM TO MANAGEMENT

The characteristic feature of the liberal state was its ability to create and maintain circumstances conducive to greatly enhanced traffic in international commerce—evidenced, for example, in a tenfold growth in the nominal value of Philippines exports between 1855 and 1902. Its logic had required the abolition of production and marketing monopolies on export goods and a significant curtailment of customary revenues in kind, especially those levied in the form of corvée labour. Unlike earlier régimes, the liberal state was not afraid for political reasons of encouraging diverse and extensive private economic initiatives. Nonetheless, the state lacked the political and administrative power to manage its subjects efficiently and directly; moreover, in contrast to the monopolist régimes of the early nineteenth century and before, the state's direct profit from the new economic arrangements it had sponsored was meagre. One source of state revenue was duties imposed on the export of produce to Europe, North America and other parts of Asia and import duties on the industrializing West's consumer items, both of which could be levied relatively easily and cheaply as produce and commodities were funnelled through ports under the state's direct control. However, these alone could not fill the revenue void caused by the abandonment of monopoly, nor could they be exploited too hard for fear of prejudicing the trade which generated them. What helped most of all to sustain the state's finances in this intermediate period of relative politico-administrative impotence was its ability to capitalize on the vastly increased buying power of a vastly increased and frequently mobile population, both the products of liberal policies. As with its production strategy, the state resorted to an existing institution, in this case the revenue farm system, adapting and expanding it to fill new needs in a changed environment. Under these new circumstances, revenue farming provided states with a very cheap means of gathering revenue from commerce, consumption and leisure which would otherwise have remained uncollected, without inhibiting economic expansion. In Siam in the reigns of Rama III and Rama IV, for example, imperialist pressure for free trade, together with increasing competition in the China trade, had gradually forced the kings to relinquish their trade monopolies; their response to this financial loss was to skim off a portion of the surplus created by increased economic activity within Siam by farming out to courtiers, local chiefs and Chinese merchant entrepreneurs the right to collect new or reorganized forms of state taxation and to control monopolies on such activities as opium smoking and gambling. This was a more efficient method of collection than the old decentralized tribute system, and it resulted in a spectacular multiplication of revenue from consumption and leisure activities: revenue from these farms grew twenty times in the four decades after 1851. Around the same time, Malay rulers, no longer able to enforce their monopoly on the sale of tin, imposed and farmed out duties on its transit along the river systems they controlled. After 'intervention', the revenue farms put out by the government, mainly to Chinese tin-mine operators, for the collection of import duty on opium and for gambling, alcohol and pawnbroking, provided the state with one-third of its revenue. In other Malay states not yet under British political control such as Kedah and Terengganu, revenue farming was at least as important to rulers anxious to enlarge their revenues (and thus their power) by taxing increasing economic activity; in Kedah, indeed, revenue farms provided more than 90 per cent of the state's revenues around 1900. In Java, the opium farms leased out by the Dutch to Chinese entrepreneurs since the 1830s reached their peak of profitability in the 1870s and 1880s, building on the economic animation promoted by the Cultivation System even as they helped compensate the state treasury (providing as much as one-fifth of its revenue) for the income forgone with its dismantling. In Cochinchina, the French let out the right to sell opium as early as 1861, first to two Frenchmen and later to a Chinese consortium.

But revenue farms were not just an ancillary means of revenue collection and, as sometimes happened, a convenient means for rulers to obtain cheap loans from suppliant farmers. They served two other vital roles as well. First, they were themselves an indispensable component of the liberal drive for economic development. Revenue farming in the Federated Malay States, for instance, helped finance and sustain tin mining. The major Chinese tin miners who generally held the farms used them as a means of lowering their labour costs by regaining from their workers a considerable proportion of what they had paid out in wages; this increased their profits when tin prices were high, and saw them over difficult patches when prices dipped. Indeed, the revenue farms served to enhance production by providing incentives to mine operators to increase the number of workers at their mines who could produce tin and at the same time consume opium or gamble. In a similar way, revenue farming provided a stimulus for export production in the countryside in Siam, particularly since the great bulk of farm revenue came from opium smoking and gambling, activities in which the Chinese labouring class figured prominently. It made their labour cheap, kept them indebted and kept them working. Second, the revenue farms were the single major source of state revenue in many of Southeast Asia's states by the late nineteenth century, partly through their ability to extract money relatively painlessly from alien and mobile populations who would otherwise have been difficult to subject to taxation. This phenomenal success provided the financial wherewithal for constructing the operating mechanisms of the modern state, such as expanded bureaucracies, roads and railways, armies and police forces, allowing for the vertical and horizontal extension of state control characteristic of the second phase of management.

Around the turn of the century, all these legacies of liberalism made for the ripening of conditions—economic, ideological, political, administrative—which allowed the structural imperatives of modern Western imperialism to play themselves out fully. The result was the creation in Southeast Asia of modern centralized states, with the will and the means to manage, exploit and 'improve' their subjects systematically, rather than simply oversee, motivate or cajole them.

THE MODERN STATE IN SOUTHEAST ASIA

The organizational principles and practice of these new states differed from those of their predecessors in five major ways. First, bureaucracies grew enormously in size with the management requirements of the new order. This was partly because the numbers of European civil servants expanded; in Indochina, for example, they doubled in the four years after 1907 as a consequence of Governor-General Doumer's creation of a separate and overarching 'federal' administration to oversee the affairs of the Indochinese states. But the greatest growth was found in the number of indigenous officials who filled positions in the middle and lower ranks of government service. Official numbers swelled with the incorporation of previously independent or semi-independent political entities into the colonial state—for example, the absorption of what is now Laos into French Indochina in the 1890s or the southern Philippines into the American colonial state based on Manila.

Second, the scope of bureaucracy became far wider than before. In 1855, for example, the central administration of the Netherlands East Indies had been divided into five departments: Finance; Revenue and Lands; Produce and Civil Stores; Cultivations; and Civil Public Works. Thus 'the general administration in those days resolved itself into a financial administration and care of the country came down above all to care for lining the treasury'.[8] By 1911, however, there were seven departments with a much broader range of functions: Justice; Internal Administration; Education and Worship; Civil Public Works; Finance; Agriculture, Industry and Trade; and Government Enterprise. In Burma at the turn of the century, a series of bureaucratic reforms saw the creation of a number of functionally specific areas—jails, hospitals, land revenue and registers, excise, justice—which had previously been only vaguely distinguished; hand in hand with this went the creation of a host of other administrative institutions to promote economic and social development—for forestry, agriculture, veterinary affairs, fisheries, communications, education, credit, public health. This elaboration indicates the broadening of what government saw as its interests and responsibilities. Unlike its colonial and indigenous predecessors, the new colonial state, as well as the royalist state in Siam, was interested not just in embodying revered values, keeping the peace and promoting revenue and income, but in a whole range of activities which were aimed both at controlling and benefiting the peoples it now considered its 'subjects'. Thus, in the Netherlands East Indies, government expenditures increased by about seven times between the 1860s and the end of the colonial period; indeed, they outstripped revenues to such an extent that the government very often ran at a deficit during the three-quarters of a century before World War II, making up the shortfall by floating international loans which left it with a consolidated debt of more than a thousand million guilders by the 1920s. In Siam, government expenditure grew at an annual rate of nearly 14 per cent through the 1890s; 45 per cent of expenditure in the early twentieth century was spent on defence and internal administration. In the general budget of Indochina, expenditures rose from 17 million piastres in 1899 to 108 million in 1931.

    Third, the expanded size and broader scope of government produced an intensity in governance which had never previously been experienced by Southeast Asians. There were more officials doing a much greater range of jobs, and they were doing them more frequently, more regularly and much more efficiently. This growing control was, moreover, facilitated by competition among indigenous élites at all levels for state patronage; their efforts to curry favour tended to build a culture of mutual denunciation which was sadly destructive of their own roles and identities but splendidly consonant with the state's requirements. One scholar describes the process thus:

> To follow the development of the colonial régime is to follow the inexorable progress of cadastral surveys, settlement reports for land revenue, censuses, the issuance of land titles and licences, identity cards, tax rolls and receipts, and a growing body of regulations and procedures. . . . Nets of finer and finer official weave caught and recorded the status of each inhabitant, each piece of land, each transaction, each activity that was assessable. . . . there is little doubt that, compared to the kingdoms they replaced, they left few places to hide.[9]

[8] Ph. Kleintjes, cited in A. D. A. de Kat Angelino, *Colonial Policy*, Chicago, 1931, II. 51.
[9] James C. Scott, *The Moral Economy of the Peasant: Rebellion and Subsistence in Southeast Asia*, New Haven, 1976, 94.

According to Furnivall, the celebrated scholar-official of Burma, 'even up to 1900 the people saw little of any Government officials, and very few ever caught more than a passing glimpse of a Western official. By 1923 the Government was no longer remote from the people but, through various departmental subordinates, touched on almost every aspect of private life.'[10]

Fourth, all this government activity no longer placed such a premium on the refined manipulation of personal ties and followings but required a new style of administration, characterized by clearly defined, formal and impersonal institutions, specificity of bureaucratic function, regular procedures, and huge amounts of paper. It demanded Western-style administrative skills and formal Western education, and Westerners' approval. In 1913, for example, the Dutch colonial government introduced the requirement that those who were to be promoted to the highest indigenous rank of Regent in the colonial bureaucracy had to have a minimum of formal Western education and had to be capable of speaking and understanding Dutch. In Vietnam in 1903, a knowledge of French was made a prerequisite for admission to the mandarinate in Tonkin and Annam, and in 1919 the anachronistic Confucian civil service examination system was finally dispensed with. In Siam, modern education rather than ascribed rank increasingly became the passport to promotion and senior appointment within government service. Throughout most of Southeast Asia, the old system of managing local Chinese communities through their own headmen (*Kapitan China*) either fell into disuse or was altogether abandoned, to be replaced by direct and formal control. Such developments also brought with them a major transformation in the basis of political legitimacy. One's right to rule was no longer a function of divine anointing, or extraordinary wealth and display, or possession of the palace or regalia, but rather of secular administrative efficiency, formalized order, and getting things done. The political potency of the old values was receding in the face of new needs and new demands.

Fifth, the shape of rule was transformed from a fragmented and localized sprawl into a centrally controlled, regular and compact hierarchy. In Siam, for example, Chulalongkorn's reform of tax farming after 1873 was not simply aimed at increasing the efficiency and regularity of revenue collection, but also at curbing the powers of semi-independent aristocrats, powerful families and provincial chiefs to whom he had previously farmed out revenue-collection rights in the transitional period of state formation. The reduction of their revenue powers starved them of their followings and made them dependent upon, rather than just supporters of, the state. At the same time, the personal administrative fiefdoms of members and clients of the royal family gave way to twelve formal and functionally specific departments, organized on Western—indeed, colonial—principles. In their recently 'annexed' territories, the new Southeast Asian states gradually and carefully set up their own administrations to incorporate (and control) already existing indigenous bureaucracies; thus, in the

---

[10] John S. Furnivall, *Colonial Policy and Practice: a Comparative Study of Burma and Netherlands India*, New York, 1956, 77.

Khorat plateau in what is today northeast Thailand, regional lords (*chao muang*) were transformed into salaried provincial governors. By degrees, such local lords were often replaced by the centre's own appointees. This process of centralization was perhaps symbolized most starkly in the transformation of legal practices and systems. In the Indies, for example, Dutch persistence and ingenuity attempted to codify the permeable, locally variant and constantly evolving *adat* law; in doing so, they corrupted its essential mutability, but this was a small and unnoticed price to pay for the knowledge by which the Dutch hoped to control the frustrating variety of their new subjects. Especially in areas of commercial significance, village land, the control of which had previously been based on loose, communal arrangements of usufruct, was transformed into a commodity item by new laws which ensconced a notion of private, individual right, providing protection and incentive for increased production. In the realm outside the village, so as to reinforce and sustain their political dominance and smooth the path of economic development, Westerners imposed or inserted their own versions of law—in their eyes fair, rational, impersonal, humane, independent—above or in place of older formal legal systems such as the Vietnamese code or the Islamic codes of the Malay states which were seen as manipulated or arbitrary or venal; and they instituted formal police forces (and jails), as well as encouraging the emergence of professional advocates, to oversee their implementation and operation. As a result, according to one scholar of Cochinchina, 'justice became less accessible, less certain and more costly'.[11] Indigenous law and, indeed, the religion from which it issued, was shuffled off into the residual category of the 'personal', to take care of those necessary but unimportant things which did not affect the colonial purpose, to remind Southeast Asians of their cultural inferiority and immaturity, and to provide a facade of undisturbed 'custom'. Religion, itself increasingly subject to state supervision, was to be a matter for 'priests', not law-makers and rulers.

This growing intensity and purpose of government activity were most obvious—and most forcefully felt—in the realm of taxation. From the consolidation of the new states until the Great Depression, taxation receipts, now payable in cash rather than kind, increased sharply. In Cochinchina, for example, in the wake of Doumer's fiscal and administrative reorganization, tax revenues rose from 5.7 million piastres in 1913 to 15.7 million in 1929. In the Netherlands East Indies, the amount collected grew from 57.3 million guilders in 1900 to 361 million guilders in 1928; one Dutch official, surveying the revenue system, felt moved to assert in the mid-1920s that Java's peasants were being taxed to the limit. In Siam, revenues rose from 15.4 million baht in 1892 to 117.4 million in 1927. In the Philippines, the value of internal revenue collections rose by 170 per cent between 1906 and 1916. Such increases were a function of heightened efficiency in collection (as in the systematization of Java's land rent system in the early twentieth century) and a broadening of the tax base which tighter control allowed, as well as the continuing growth of

[11] Milton E. Osborne, *The French Presence in Cochinchina and Cambodia: Rule and Response (1859–1905)*, Ithaca, 1969, 268.

export-oriented economic activity and the population's magnified dependence upon it; under these circumstances, taxation was both a prod and a stimulus to increasing production. A notable indicator of the changing nature of governance in this realm was the growth of revenue from direct personal and company taxation and the levying of import and export duties, in contrast to the decline of income from the sale of government products, and from indirect taxes and revenue gathering, particularly revenue farms.

A revolution in financial and commercial practices accompanied this administrative transformation. Of major importance were the gradual restriction and then rapid termination of revenue farming, especially the lucrative opium farms. Paradoxically, the growth of centralized and powerful states, partly paid for by revenue farming, rendered it an anchronism. The instability of tax farms made them 'ultimately volatile and unhealthy for the economy',[12] not to mention politically dangerous; the state now had the wherewithal to collect revenues directly and on its own account. In Indochina between 1897 and 1904, the French established state monopolies on the sale of opium, alcohol and salt; this confirmed and at the same time centralized earlier and generally unsuccessful local French initiatives to abolish revenue farming, and greatly increased the weight of these consumption taxes so that they formed the major revenue item for the French colonial state. As in Siam, this development was at least partly political in the sense of curbing local and sectional pretensions to wielding independent and unsupervised power over the population. Contemporaneously the Dutch abolished the farming out of opium and pawnbroking and replaced them by government monopolies and licences, as did the British in Malaya with opium and gambling.

Other less dramatic but nonetheless important changes were also afoot. Governments constructed regular, stable and national currency systems, pegged to the gold standard in most places shortly after 1900 and expressed as paper money, to replace the enormous variety of coins of different weights and standards. To sustain and monitor the currency, they established national banks. Increasingly, they organized or sponsored (usually inefficiently, inconveniently and thus ineffectively) the provision of credit for the small-scale needs of peasants and petty traders and manufacturers, such as mutual loan associations in Cochinchina and people's banks in Java.

In the private sphere, previously peopled by adventurous individual merchants and entrepreneurs, banks and commercial houses—mostly Western but Asian ones as well—sprouted in the centres of colonial control and in Bangkok to act as agents for government, providers of credit and other facilities to private investors and shippers and insurers of goods. Nowhere was this activity more noticeable than in the development of the agency houses of Singapore; they flourished on the virtues of vertical integration, investing in local production, organizing and overseeing the

---

[12] Hong Lysa, *Thailand in the Nineteenth Century: Evolution of the Economy and Society*, Singapore, 1984, 129.

floating of new companies, providing management expertise for plantations, importing and exporting commodities, granting insurance, and
lubricating their operations with credit. They were the beachheads of
corporate enterprise, the local agents and managers of a vast financial
network ultimately controlled from the boardrooms of Europe and North
America.

Hand in hand with this enormous administrative and financial endeavour came the construction of roads, bridges, offices, railways, new
ports and port facilities, shipping services, irrigation works, telegraph
services and other infrastructure designed to bring government hard up
against the people, to 'pacify' them, to develop and monitor their productive capacities, to siphon out the commodities demanded by the West, and
to profit more efficiently from them. It was no coincidence that the first
state railway in Java connected the rich sugar regions of east Java with the
great port of Surabaya, nor that the first tracks laid on the western Malay
peninsula (from 1885) linked the separate tin-mining regions laterally to
coastal ports and later pushed north and south to integrate expanding
rubber plantations. In Burma, the state-subsidized Irrawaddy Flotilla
Company and the newly constructed railways (2500 kilometres of line by
1914) provided cheap and easy transport for rice exports and consumer
imports. Between 1900 and 1935 in Indochina, more was spent on economic infrastructure development than on any other single item in the colonial
budget, providing almost 3000 kilometres of railways, canals and waterworks, vast areas of reclaimed land, ports, offices and a remarkably
extensive system of metalled roads. Even the maladministered and demor-
alized Spanish régime (boasting fifty governors-general in the fifty-two
years after 1835) managed to establish an embryonic modern transport
infrastructure in Luzon, including a railway tying the central plain to
Manila. A developed and controlled polity and a developing economy
were two sides of the same colonial coin, something exemplified by the
development of Indies inter-island shipping by the Koninklijk Paketvaart
Maatschappij in the early twentieth century and the expansion of the
Siamese railway system into the north and east of the country.

Plantations and Mining

All these developments provided the conditions for a wholly new form of
economic activity: production which was relatively capital-intensive, privately financed, corporately managed and technologically advanced. Its
most common manifestation was the modern plantation, a system of
production which was the symbol and the direct result of intrusive high
colonialism. Large and powerful concerns, sometimes indigenous but
generally of European or North American origin (for example, Harrisons &
Crosfield, Michelin, US Rubber, SOCFIN), usually working under long-term
leases and benefiting from colonial infrastructures and land improvement
measures, put vast areas of hitherto virgin Southeast Asian countryside
under export crops. In Malaya alone, in response to the extraordinary
growth of the motor-vehicle industry in the West, the plantation rubber

area grew from 2400 hectares in 1900 to almost 570,000 hectares by 1921, the result of an investment of over £70 million. Attempts to define this mode—'a capital-using unit employing a large labour force under close managerial supervision to produce a crop for sale'[13]—conceal the great diversity with which plantation systems operated in Southeast Asia. Plantations on the frontier most closely approximated the stereotyped ideal. They were developed in sparsely populated and often virgin regions of Southeast Asia for the cultivation of crops like rubber, sugar, oil palm and tobacco, radically transforming vast forest environments into neatly segmented and orderly arrays of fields with ecological repercussions that have yet to be properly appreciated. In the grey and red lands north and northwest of Saigon, powerful French companies built extensive rubber plantations, pouring in huge sums of speculative money in the 1920s: between 1925 and 1929, investments in rubber totalled 700 million francs and the area under crop increased from 15,000 to 90,000 hectares. The land was worked by indentured Vietnamese, most of them from the poor and overpopulated north. A similar pattern evolved in Cambodia, where rubber plantations worked by Vietnamese labourers under the control of large French companies dated from 1921. In the outer islands of the Netherlands East Indies, plantation agriculture became the focus of colonial economic activity from the late nineteenth century on. In the fabled plantation area of the east coast of Sumatra, there arose great plantations of tobacco (grown under a shifting régime), rubber, palm oil, tea and sisal in virtually unsettled areas which required the importation of huge numbers of indentured coolie labourers to service them. The coolies came originally from China through an immigration bureau established by the Deli Planters Association, but most, by around 1915, were from Java. In Malaya, rubber, starting from virtually nothing in the 1890s, rapidly came to dominate the country's agricultural export economy, replacing Chinese shifting cultivation of gambier and pepper; to secure the labour they needed, Malayan plantations used some Chinese labour but mostly relied on importing 'free' southern Indian workers. In the Philippines, the hub of sugar production moved gradually from the early 1880s from Luzon, with its *hacienda*–smallholder complex of production, to Negros, where true plantations emerged around the end of the century. Chinese mestizo planters, previously entrepreneurs in the once booming, now fading, Iloilo textile industry on neighbouring Panay, carved out large *haciendas*, often by means of fraud and sometimes force, from existing peasant smallholdings. Their activities were financed by large foreign firms which dominated sugar exports; their workforce comprised debt-bonded labourers and seasonal workers, organized in work gangs, who grew and harvested cane for delivery to large modern steam-powered centrifugal mills, called centrals, which were rapidly replacing the numerous light steam and cattle-driven mills in the 1910s and 1920s. The Java sugar industry—gradually moving from government control to private enterprise in the forty years after 1850—contrasted in organizational style and environmental setting with the frontier plantations. Set in the lush and heavily populated rice

---

[13] Eric R. Wolf, *Europe and the People without History*, Berkeley, 1982, 315.

districts of north, central and especially east Java, the industry was based on hiring peasant wet-rice land for cane growing for periods ranging from three to (after 1918) 21½ years. Peasants were granted access to their land between cane crops to grow rice and other staples. Cane was grown, harvested and transported by hired hands—often, indeed, the land-holders themselves—under close factory supervision, and manufactured into sugar at technologically advanced mills mostly owned by Dutch limited companies. Having endured the difficulties of depression and crop disease in the 1880s, the industry moved from a style of individual enterprise control to one of corporate management and, with huge capital inflows, began a phase of rapid expansion from the turn of the century, doubling its cropping area between 1900 and 1929.

Notwithstanding the value of scientific inputs in improving seed and rootstock, cultivation techniques and processing, the profitability of such concerns lay essentially in their recruitment and tight control and super-vision of large numbers of workers to clear and prepare land, plant and tend the growing crops, harvest them on maturity, and work in processing centres on the estates. Recruiting labour was the central problem. Not only were plantations generally in remote and lightly populated regions, but managers often found it impossible to obtain the services of local peasants. Thus frontier plantations depended almost wholly on recruitment from afar, sometimes employing private recruiting agencies to deliver them the numbers they needed, and sometimes relying on their own efforts. In Vietnam, the great reservoir of labour lay in the crowded lowlands of Tonkin and Annam; by the late 1920s, some 17,000 workers per annum were introduced into the plantations from those regions. They generally worked under indigenous foremen (cai) who recruited them, managed their affairs and subcontracted their services to plantation managers. In Malaya, Chinese workers were in short supply and Indians deemed more docile for plantation work; estate-based Tamil foremen-recruiters, called kangany, travelled to southern India, usually to places whence they them-selves had come, and recruited villagers—often their kin—for periods of service by advancing credit and promises. After 1907, recruitment was financed by a government-sponsored fund to which all plantations con-tributed. In 1910 alone, 91,723 Indians arrived in Malaya, and the figure peaked in 1913 at 122,583; smaller proportions of Chinese and Javanese were also employed. Javanese from the crowded villages and towns of central and northeastern Java were drawn to Sumatra by similar methods, but under indenture. Between 1913 and 1925, 327,000 contract coolies departed Java for the plantations and work sites of the outer islands. To service the Negros sugar plantations, estate foremen recruited permanent or seasonal workers from the western regions of neighbouring Panay (fallen on hard times with the demise of the Iloilo textile industry), or caught up dispossessed local smallholders by playing on their need for credit.

Most recruits were males in their twenties and thirties, although some-times, as on Malayan rubber estates, they brought their families with them. A much smaller proportion of young females was also recruited and frequently forced into prostitution. Like the Chinese of an earlier period, all these labourers came to make their fortunes and return home (although large numbers did remain as settlers, especially in Malaya and east Sumatra). They were generally housed in barrack-type accommodation in a discrete area of the plantation, although this tended to give way to individual dwellings as the proportion of female workers increased (in 1938, 37 per cent of east Sumatra's plantation labour force was female) and as permanent labour settlements were established. Their lives were ordered (and sometimes ended) by their closely supervised work. Their wages were low (for women only half to three-quarters those of men), and what little disposable income remained men often spent on gambling and prostitutes; systematic indebtedness was a useful means for plantation managers to maintain their workforces. With appalling living conditions, disease was rampant and death never far away; in 1927 in Cochinchina, one in twenty plantation workers died, and local death rates were often much higher than that. This was double the overall mortality rate for the colony, and among a population of workers supposedly in the prime of life. To ensure a docile or at least compliant workforce, plantation managers could call upon the authority of the state, embodied in such legislation as the Netherlands East Indies Coolie Ordinances of 1880, 1884 and 1893, which imposed fines, imprisonment or extra labour obligations for those who transgressed the conditions of their contracts; less formally they employed physical beatings and financial penalties, or exploited ingrained habits of regimentation. Nonetheless, brutal mistreatment and mean conditions sometimes led workers to attack supervisory personnel and, intermittently, to conduct strikes. 'They are men, so are we. How can we accept that they continually beat us?', remarked Nguyen Dinh Tu, a participant in the 1927 assassination of a French overseer at the Phu-Rieng plantation in Cochinchina.[14] Desertion was quite common; 4484 coolies—around one in ten of the workforce—ran away from Cochinchina plantations in 1928.

Under the new management-oriented régimes of high colonialism, resource extraction, like agricultural production, took on wholly new forms. By the turn of the century in the Malayan tin industry, the rich surface tin deposits for which Chinese labour-intensive methods of extraction had been appropriate were close to exhaustion, and labour was becoming more expensive with the end of the opium revenue farms, and more mobile with demand rising elsewhere. These problems blunted the edge of Chinese competitiveness and, allied to increasing European dominance of tin smelting and the appearance of huge and expensive bucket dredges from 1912, saw control of the industry flow more and more from Chinese into Western hands. The failure of the Chinese to adapt was partly a result of the fact that dredges required huge capital sums which Chinese were either unable or, more likely, disinclined to procure for this purpose, and partly because the colonial government provided Westerners with large land leases and geographical and geological advice to make this expansive form of mining workable and profitable. The result was that by 1937 dredges produced half Malaya's tin. A trend to highly capitalized and

---

[14] Cited in Martin J. Murray, *The Development of Capitalism in Colonial Indochina (1870–1940)*, Berkeley, 1980, 311.

mechanized mining was not, however, evident everywhere. In Vietnam, where coal production had quadrupled to 2 million tonnes by 1930, only 6 per cent of Tonkin coal production was mechanized at the end of the 1930s.

Oil production, in contrast to tin, relied from the very outset on capital-intensive operations; as a result, the oil industry, established in the vicinity of such places as Yenangyaung (central Burma), Palembang (southeast Sumatra), Balikpapan (east Borneo), Seria (Brunei) and Miri (Sarawak) came to be the monopoly of a very few large international companies such as Royal Dutch-Shell, Standard Oil and Burmah Oil. Similarly, the timber industry, equally demanding of capital to exploit remote sites in such locations as northern Burma, northern Siam and British North Borneo (even when employing traditional extraction techniques and local ethnic minorities as workforces), became largely the preserve of a small number of large Western firms such as the Bombay–Burmah Trading Corporation.

ASPECTS OF SOCIAL CHANGE

Southeast Asia's gradual incorporation into a global system of commerce, together with the consequential accelerating impetus for new forms of state control, economic development, and invigorated local, regional and international trade, reshaped patterns of social life in the region in momentous ways. The social change typical of the period, however, was not a matter of simple, discrete and direct responses to specific events; rather, it evolved from conjunctions of developments that were sometimes interconnected and mutually reinforcing and sometimes contradictory and ambiguous, all stimulated and sometimes dictated by the general pattern of economic growth. One useful way of unravelling the complexities of this social transformation is to examine, against the general contours of change already outlined, especially its last and dominant phase, how these conjunctions affected those aspects of Southeast Asians' lives—their reproductive activities, their places of residence, their occupations and modes of work, their gender, their states of health—that affected them most deeply.

People: Growing and Moving

One of the most readily obvious changes which coincided with Western-inspired economic change was rapid population growth. The classic case of rapid and sustained population growth is, of course, Java, where a population of between three and five million at the end of the eighteenth century had grown to 40.9 million by 1930, a rate approaching 1.9 per cent per annum. But statistics from other parts of Southeast Asia show similarly spectacular growth: in Malaya, a population of 250,000 in 1800 had risen to 3.8 million in 1931. In the Philippines, one of 2.5 million in 1830 had grown to 16.5 million by 1940. Burma's population more than doubled between 1891 and 1941. The component parts of French Indochina grew at rates around 2 per cent per annum from the late nineteenth century on. Siam witnessed a similar rate of increase after the turn of the twentieth century.

In some settings, especially where plantation modes or labour-intensive resource extraction were common, a considerable proportion of this growth came from immigration. As early as the 1820s, the Chinese population of west Borneo was estimated at between 30,000 and 50,000. Especially from the mid-nineteenth century, Chinese flocked to the Malay states as indentured labourers or 'paid immigrants' and perhaps as many as three million Indian Tamils were brought to Malaya as rubber workers in the early decades of the twentieth century. Under less iniquitous circumstances Chinese (not to mention Mons, Khmers, Laotians and other ethnic groups) were encouraged through the nineteenth century to settle in Siam, and Chinese flowed into the Philippines in such numbers that, despite persistent counterflows home, the Chinese population rose from around 6000 in 1840 to 100,000 by 1890. Malays from Sumatra, Java and other parts of the archipelago migrated in large numbers as free settlers to the largely empty western Malay peninsula from the late nineteenth century onwards. Indians flocked into lower Burma, especially after the beginning of the twentieth century, to work stints as labourers; Indian traders, moneylenders and prostitutes landed with them. About 2.6 million Indians migrated to Burma between 1852 and 1937; by 1931, 10 per cent of lower Burma's population was Indian.

Immigration alone, however, cannot explain the rates of growth which, despite some earlier scholarly scepticism, seem to be remarkably high, to stretch over long periods of time, and thus to constitute a dramatic new phase in Southeast Asia's demographic history. Nor can Southeast Asian states' greater efficiency in controlling, incorporating, settling and enumerating disparate and distant populations. Attempts to explain the mechanism of this surging growth and to discover what sustained it have polarized around the views that either increased fertility or reduced mortality were responsible. Arguments for increased fertility generally attribute population expansion to indigenous attempts to reduce the state's labour impositions by augmenting the available workforce through natural means or, alternatively, to the development of circumstances that promoted higher fertility, such as a large-scale transformation from shifting to sedentary cultivation or a more settled and certain future. The mechanisms adumbrated to explain higher fertility also vary. Some look to a significant decline in female celibacy, others to reduction in female age at marriage; one ingenious suggestion locates the mechanism for increased fertility in shorter periods of breast-feeding and amenorrhea caused by greatly increased labour demands upon women. Those who propose reduced mortality cite the reduction of warfare and especially the devastating consequences which flowed from it (crop destruction, disease, the capture or flight of populations), increased nutrition, better standards of health care and even perhaps a transition to endemicity of previously epidemic diseases. The key to a solution seems to lie in identifying the characteristic demographic pattern before the period of intensive colonial rule. From the scanty research thus far performed, it appears that the prevailing trend was one of regularly high natural fertility interspersed with frequent periods of catastrophic mortality which were for the most part the result, direct and indirect, of warfare (as, for example, in the depopulation of Kedah resulting from the Siamese attack of 1821). If this was so, it seems difficult to adduce argument and evidence that a rate of fertility which was already very high could be expanded to an extent sufficient of itself to explain the high and sustained rates of growth of the nineteenth and twentieth centuries. At the very least, there is little evidence to suggest the widespread adoption of behaviour which might increase fertility to a higher and demographically significant plane, such as earlier or more frequent marriage, the forsaking of previously widely used and effective fertility-control practices, or increases in coital frequency. By the same token, however, apart from the imposition of peace there is little evidence, either precise or suggestive (and sometimes evidence quite to the contrary) of higher levels of nutrition or radically changed environments more conducive to health which might be adduced as positive support for the reduced mortality thesis. Under such circumstances, the most plausible picture is perhaps one of a significant reduction in mortality, possibly augmented by a small increase in fertility resulting from more settled and regular times. Since a dearth of appropriate data renders the relevant variables intractable to satisfactory empirical evaluation, it seems unlikely that a solution will emerge that goes much beyond this.

Population growth was spectacular, as was the large-scale introduction of new ethnic groupings. However, a similarly profound demographic trend, internal migration, has lain almost unnoticed and its impact little investigated. One reason for this is that colonial governments (as well as the Siamese élite) treasured a stable and docile workforce just as much as their predecessors did. Characteristically, they sought to register and immobilize sedentary cultivators, to domesticate wandering swidden cultivators as rice farmers who could be counted and regularly taxed, and to play down exceptions to their purpose. Their efforts at control were only partially successful, because despite an enduring stereotype of the territorially-rooted peasant household, mobility rather than permanency seems to have been a keynote of peasant life in this era as well as in earlier ones; indeed, the opening of new economic opportunities accelerated mobility. There were a number of great peasant migrations. The opening of the Burma delta through the later nineteenth century attracted huge numbers from the dry zone; thus in 1901, 10 per cent of lower Burma's 4.1 million people was made up of people born in upper Burma, an important ingredient in the process of 'Burmanizing' the Irrawaddy delta region. The opening of Siam's central plain attracted large numbers of peasants from the northeast. In Vietnam, the long southward movement of Vietnamese reached its conclusion with the opening up of the Mekong delta lands under French rule; thousands of Vietnamese moved into Laos and Cambodia as well (there were 60,000 of them in Cambodia by 1908). In the Philippines, the vast plain of central Luzon attracted and was gradually brought under the plough by immigrants from the Manila region and from Luzon's northwestern edge. The east Java frontier was pushed back by people from the northeast coast and the thickly settled volcanic valleys of central Java; this was part of a more general pattern of movement which left more than one Indonesian in ten living outside the region of his or her birth in 1930.

As well as these dramatic movements, there was a persistent and probably rapidly accelerating 'background' movement, often of a circular or sojourning nature. Everywhere, as the pace of commercialization increased and transport infrastructure improved, seasonal wage labour flourished, bringing peasants in great numbers from the Khorat plateau of upper Burma to harvest rice in the lands around Bangkok or the Burma delta, or from Panay to cut cane on Negros sugar plantations. As many as 50,000 Tonkin peasants regularly sought seasonal work in the region's coal pits. Itinerant labour gangs traversed the Cochinchina ricefields in search of harvesting work. Statistics on railway passenger traffic convey something of the intensity of this moving around; Malaya's railways, for example, carried 4.8 million passengers in 1904 and 14.7 million by 1916, while Burma's carried 8.4 million passengers in 1896 and 27 million by 1928. Social customs and obligations, as well as opportunity and oppression, helped to feed the persistent movement. Thus in lower Burma there was a great deal of internal migration within the delta region itself, partly caused by the practice of equal splitting of inherited lands among the family offspring; one member would frequently buy out the others, who then proceeded to the frontier to establish themselves anew on larger holdings. Again, people often fled to new regions to escape from debts and obligations incurred in longer-established areas of the delta. In Luzon, deteriorating tenancy conditions encouraged mobility as peasants searched for more secure and satisfactory arrangements; one unreflective *hacendero* later complained that 'peasants around here were forever moving around before the Japanese occupation. I don't know why, but they did.'[15] Peasants in the Federated Malay States at the turn of the twentieth century have been characterized as 'restless people in search of elusive fortunes'.[16] Patterns of incremental movement were evident everywhere as people slowly and relentlessly radiated out from points of settlement to form satellite communities, mostly as household units rather than pioneering individuals. Alien minorities were no exception to this pattern; whereas 92 per cent of Chinese in the Philippines were resident in Manila in 1848, the figure was only 48 per cent by 1894. All these movements of people, ranging from dramatic and permanent surges to bit-by-bit reclamation and modest local commuting, contrived to transform radically the landscape and ecology of previously sparsely inhabited and thickly forested plains.

Villagers

The characteristic flux of populations annoyed and perplexed governments who sought ever more closely to control their peoples. In general, they attempted to do this by investing the village community with state

---

[15] Cited in Benedict J. Kerkvliet, *The Huk Rebellion: a Study of Peasant Revolt in the Philippines*, Berkeley, 1977, 26.
[16] Lim Teck Ghee, *Peasants and Their Agricultural Economy in Colonial Malaya 1874–1941*, Kuala Lumpur, 1977, 55.

power, in order to supervise their subjects more closely. The village, previously a rather loose amalgam of peasant households, often with no fixed territorial attachment, and subject to a competing array of patrons, became an administrative institution of the state. In Burma, the British were puzzled at what they saw as the vague, personal and untidy style of administration provided to lower-level communities by local traditional chieftains, *thugyis*. Their response was to 'create' the village as an artificial administrative entity, often in the form of an arbitrary amalgamation of formerly discrete settlements. In Cambodia, when the French found no institutionalized villages (as they understood them), they responded by inventing 'artificial proto-villages'[17] called *khum*. A similar though not quite so fundamental process of artifice was evident in Java as well. Such changes in administrative mentality were reflected in the spatial organization of villages. Mobile, vaguely integrated, higgledy-piggledy settlements slowly became firmly attached to specific sites, their dwelling compounds fenced, their houses compacted together in more or less orderly patterns, their rights to surrounding fields and forests ever more precisely demarcated.

Previously, village politics, like those of the larger state, had been built around the notion of consensus, a broad understanding of the limited rights and powers of the village leadership group over against those of the village community. Under the press of the developing and ambitious state, however, leadership tended to become focused in one person, a village chief, and the authority he held came not from community consensus but from the increasingly intrusive state. Under the régime of the Cultivation System in Java, for example, the village chief was required, regularly and frequently, to make demands which would previously have been unacceptable. In this situation, the importance of consensus, of mediating and balancing between the two poles of the village and the state, fell into disuse. In order to maintain his position (and the lucrative rewards which went with it, such as a percentage of the taxation receipts he collected and a controlling hand over land allocation), the chief came more and more to rely on the coercive power of the state, and less and less on his own political ability. This meant, in fact, that his formal power (and the privileges that went with it) increased, but also that because that power was so dependent on the state he became estranged from his villagers; while the rank of village chief was never officially a governmental position, in practice it became so. In the frontier environment of Cochinchina, where peasant communities were less spatially integrated and authority correspondingly more diffuse than in long-settled and heavily populated regions like Java and Tonkin, a similar thrust in French policy had rather more confusing results. As the French attempted to bring the village under administrative control, they tended to saddle the ruling body of the village, the council of notables, with a huge range of specific administrative tasks and roles, and to transform the village chief, previously no more than the executor of the council's decisions, into a power figure in his own right. Because of the more 'open' nature of villages in Cochinchina,

---

[17] Alexander B. Woodside, *Community and Revolution in Modern Vietnam*, Boston, 1976, 129.

however, power remained relatively unconcentrated. Authority within Cochinchina's villages had customarily been a function of age, learning and especially the wealth that came from controlling land. But the French interference laid such burdens upon village life that the 'natural' leaders of the village were reluctant to take up an office which was full-time, unsalaried and expensive, and which harmed their relations with other villagers. This meant that those who took up village office were often less esteemed than those they replaced—'the more ambitious and unscrupulous'[18] members of the village, as one writer puts it, who relied for their power totally on the backing of French force, and who used their office as a means of advancement. For example, they might allow fellow villagers to clear virgin land, and then lay claim to it themselves, because they controlled the village-level process of making land claims. The result was an acute crisis in village government, in which those who had customarily provided leadership went their own way, and those appointed by the French generally used their office in an exploitative rather than protective manner.

As commerce grew in scale and intensity and as land increasingly became a commodity in its own right, the new or enhanced configurations of authority both above and within villages resulting from the greater reach of state power were reflected in a mountingly uneven and exploitative distribution of productive resources among peasants. At the top, there emerged a group of large landlords, frequently and increasingly of the absentee variety, who had capitalized on their attachment to the state to assume control of much of the village's land. Beneath them was a layer of households who possessed enough land to provide for their own upkeep. Beneath them lay a large component of villagers—as much as 70 per cent of the village population in the case of Tonkin, often more than 60 per cent in Java—who had insufficient land to sustain themselves, or no land at all. The lot of this last group was an ever more insecure and impoverished style of life; to make ends meet they relied on tenancy, field-labour paid in cash or kind and, increasingly, in off-farm work: small-scale industry, such as the manufacture and marketing of handicrafts, petty trade, and especially the varieties of wage labour thrown up by developing economies. Many of these people fell into or approached a meagre, proletarian mode of life.

What was novel about this situation was not inequality nor privation nor exploitation—these had always been natural aspects of village life—but rather their permanence and pervasiveness. The new centralized state drove further, deeper and more efficiently into village life than any of its predecessors. Characteristically nervous about 'unrest', it deprived villagers (those at the bottom of the heap as well as those above them who now perceived their interests as unacceptably compromised) of their previous ability either to negotiate tolerable livelihoods with a range of competing potential patrons or to flee their antagonists altogether. As time went by, as the old physical frontier disappeared and as the new political frontier was confirmed, the avenues for evading impositions or redressing

---

[18] Murray, 427.

perceived wrongs were narrowed and almost eliminated.

The result was that peasants' attempts to protect their livelihoods and styles of life, while not necessarily increasingly in volume, took on a more organized, public and confrontationist style and tone. 'Everyday resistance' endured, as it always will—earthy jokes at the expense of a landlord, small-scale theft, strategies of absenteeism or footdragging, isolated arson, the adoption of various forms of religious cults, the use of folk theatres or other forms of art and culture as protest vehicles. But the range of such measures was continually circumscribed more tightly by a state which could construct efficient intelligence services and which made a virtue of punishing those it saw as dangerous to 'public order' so as to set an example to others. Under these circumstances, attempts at withdrawal or refusal to acknowledge the state's authority—as with the frequent cases of social banditry and, best known of all, the Saminist movement of north-central Java—resulted, paradoxically, only in confrontation. Peaceful organized protest—associations for mutual aid, both material and spiritual, petitions, marches, demonstrations, even strikes—could be ignored or smugly tolerated. Most often it was easily and arrogantly dismissed by targeting ringleaders, threatening force, or buying off dissent. In the end, peasants were frequently moved to physical violence in a final and desperate means to redress what they perceived as intolerable oppression. Sometimes this took the form of uncoordinated and spontaneous outrage, as in the assassination of the tax-collecting Resident Bardez by Cambodian peasants in 1916. In its more developed modes—such as the Muslim communist rebellion of 1926 in west Java, the millenarian nationalist Saya San movement of lower Burma in 1930–1, and the defiance of the 'red soviets' of Nghe An and Ha Tinh in northern Annam of the same period—resistance was often shaped and hardened by disaffected non-peasant intellectuals. In the short term all these movements were tragic and futile, trampled unforgivingly by the technological and political superiority of the state.

City Dwellers

The village and the countryside were the characteristic focuses of Western-inspired economic development; they were the production sites for primary produce and resources. Change, however, affected not only the sites of production, but also the places from which production was directed, the newly developed colonial capitals and Bangkok. Under the new régime of Western-inspired production and trade, the two great tasks of cities were commerce and territorial administration, combined in ways that had never previously been possible in Southeast Asia. The cities of the high colonial period possessed, unlike their classical antecedents, the skills and technology to marry both these functions effectively.

One way of appreciating urban change in this period is to analyse a freeze-frame of Southeast Asian cities at the zenith of their transformation. In 1930, there were sixteen cities with populations of 100,000 or more. They can be divided into three groups: first, the 'old' indigenous capitals of

Mandalay, Bangkok, Hanoi, Yogyakarta and Surakarta, mostly modelled on the principles of the old sacred city; second, old colonial cities with their origins in the merchant capital era of the Western presence, cities founded or settled by Westerners essentially as trading posts: Batavia, Semarang, Surabaya, Manila, Penang and Singapore; third, the new colonial cities of Rangoon, Saigon, Kuala Lumpur, Palembang and Bandung, cities which owed their importance to being sites of the commercial expansion which marked this period of high colonialism. Comparing this freeze-frame to one taken a century or so before reveals a number of crucial developments. Pre-eminence had passed from the old sacred city to the city based on commerce—Mandalay gave way to Rangoon, Yogyakarta to Batavia, Hué to Saigon. A city's vitality was a function of its unrelenting commercial orientation; with the exception of Kuala Lumpur and Bandung, the new colonial cities were port cities, and even these two exceptions owed their size to their commercial significance. Commerce and territorial adminis-tration had been welded together; capitals now stood at the termini of infrastructural grids through which produce was moved out of the interi-or, and administrative control of the hinterland established, maintained and enhanced.

More spectacular than this change in the functions of cities was the late, rapid increase in their sizes. Before the last part of the nineteenth century, urban populations in Southeast Asia generally grew more slowly than rural ones, a reflection of the limited, perhaps stultifying, effect of Western merchant capital on urban development. The development of state territo-rial control and more pervasive forms of economic activity, however, saw the beginnings of rapid and continuing urbanization; now all the major cities grew in population much faster than the rural areas that surrounded them, partly because of relatively poor conditions in the local (and inter-national) countryside, and partly because the city seemed to promise a better life of expanding economic opportunities. Thus, for example, Batavia's population increased at an average annual rate of 5.5 per cent between 1905 and 1930, and Bandung's at 5.2 per cent; over the first three decades of the twentieth century, Bangkok's rose at an average annual rate, respectively, of 3.5 per cent, 4.0 per cent and 4.0 per cent. Rangoon's population grew by a factor of 3.5 between 1872 and 1921. In Malaya in 1911, one person in ten lived in a city of more than 10,000 inhabitants; by 1931, it was one in seven. In the Philippines, the level of urbanization rose from 12.6 per cent to 21.6 per cent between 1918 and 1939.

Such growth in numbers manifested itself in the spatial expansion of cities, rendering them considerably larger than their pre-colonial and early colonial predecessors. This occurred not just because economic activity and population growth expanded, but also because Westerners tended to move out from the centre of the city and establish their residences in more commodious and expansive regions on the peripheries. In Batavia, for example, the Dutch established a large residential suburb, evocatively named Weltevreden ('contented') on the southern outskirts of Batavia, away from the congested and disease-ridden old port centre; in Surabaya, large areas to the south were established for the exclusive habitation of Europeans. This practice tended to expand city boundaries, so that previously rural settlements often found themselves part of the urban environment; in 1927, for instance, the city of Semarang included 137 villages within its boundaries and took up an area larger than 100 square kilometres.

Westerners dominated city space. In Bandung in 1930, for example, they made up 12 per cent of the population but occupied more than half the urban space. Maps of other colonial cities reveal a similar disproportion with large areas set aside for Westerners' offices, residences and recreation (clubs, race tracks, cricket grounds). Their dominance was partly reflected, too, in the rigid racial compartmentalization of the city—Westerners in one quarter (the most salubrious), Chinese in another, Arabs in another and various ethnic indigenous subgroups in others—something already present in pre-colonial times but exacerbated and refined under more intensive colonial rule. Colonial governments, especially in Java and also Manila (where the Spanish believed it was 'healthier' to keep the races apart), often forced ethnic groups, especially Chinese, to live in separate areas, so better to police their activities and to protect the indigenous people from their alleged rapacity. By the same token, segregation was sometimes the result of historical circumstance—Kuala Lumpur's China-town was the site of the early Chinese tin-mining camp—and sometimes it arose because ethnic groups in cosmopolitan cities tended to congregate together where they could share language, and profit from family or clan support. Discrimination based on ethnicity and relative poverty also ensured that city populations were unevenly distributed. Despite the expansive dimensions of cities in the high colonial era, their centres tended to be exceedingly densely populated. The suburbs were occupied by peasants whose urban status sprang from administrative accident; by squatter immigrants combining urban employment with market gardening; and by wealthier (mainly Western) people who could afford to commute to the city centre every day. Most occupants of cities, however, were poor, too poor to live far from where they worked, so that as the population of cities grew, more and more people packed more and more tightly into the inner urban commercial cores. In Bandung, for example, the area of urban kampongs decreased by 25 per cent between 1910 and 1937, but the population rose from around 45,000 to about 160,000; one part of Semarang had a population density of 1000 people per hectare. The excruciating congestion was exemplified in a report from Surabaya of a dwelling which measured 3 metres by 8 metres, was 1.7 metres high, and which housed 23 workers. In another house 120 workers were crammed, each of whom paid three cents a night for the privilege. In Singapore, the lodgings of rickshawmen were often owned by rickshaw owners; they sometimes contained (if that is the appropriate word) 16 people in one room or, again, 175 in a house. Over a thirteen-year period, the number of tenants in one house in Singapore rose by more than 300 per cent.

While the focus of the colonial city was commerce, it was commerce of a limited kind. In the industrializing urban centres of nineteenth-century Europe, cities produced goods, employment, and income, and exercised a modernizing influence in the surrounding areas; in contrast, the Southeast Asian cities were agents rather than actors in the process of production.

Although all these cities had some industry—metal, cigarette, furniture, tile and batik factories, coconut-processing plants, cement works, printeries, railway maintenance yards—such activities were ancillary to the real focus of the city's life and existed to service machinery, to process agricultural goods or manufacture small-scale commodities which were cheaper than or not competitive with imports. There was no call for substantial industry where the industrialized West already enjoyed a tremendous advantage in terms of technology, capital, social organization and amenities. More particularly, the rulers and merchants of these cities had little desire to encourage industrialization which would compete with imports from metropolitan Europe, nor did they wish to encourage a demand for urban wage labour which might vie with the requirements of mines, plantations and smallholder food production. Least of all did they want the political problems which might arise with the growth of a clamorous indigenous middle class or a discontented proletariat. Consequently, the role of the city in late colonial Southeast Asia was not that of an industrial dynamo but rather a channel, pushing the products of its hinterland on to the world market and distributing Western consumer imports and Westernized administration into the hinterland.

The peculiar nature of the Southeast Asian capitals led (with such notable exceptions as Batavia and Hanoi) to the phenomenon of the primate city. This was not in itself, it must be added, a new feature of Southeast Asian urbanization. Directing economic development and the process of administrative integration and control, and channelling the fruits of its activities on to the world market, the capital came to dominate each state, with its size at least twice as great as the next biggest city. Bangkok, indeed, became the greatest primate city in the world: in 1940 it was fifteen times bigger than Siam's next biggest city, Chiengmai. In these capital cities were concentrated the various component parts of this endeavour; the major offices of the bureaucracy, the head offices of banks, agency houses and shipping and insurance firms, the ports and great warehouses, the centres of education (such as they were), the termini of the transport networks. Some of these cities became so huge that they contained a significant proportion of the population of the whole nation, a paradoxical realization of the pre-colonial concept that the central city *was* the nation.

An emphasis on urban morphology tends to distract attention from the lives and fates of the people who inhabited these cities, particularly the less fortunate ones. Apart from Westerners, they fell into three general categories. There was an élite comprising the traditional aristocracy, absentee landlords and powerful members of non-indigenous groups, especially wealthy Chinese. Below them in the social hierarchy came an indigenous middle class which, while growing rapidly—especially in the Philippines where Western education was relatively widely available—was proportionately only a tiny segment of the total indigenous population; it was peopled by government white-collar workers, private merchants and entrepreneurs, and professional people like teachers, doctors and engineers. The great mass of the urban population, however, was made up of the working class, those who made their living through manual labour. A large number of them were either immigrants to the cities or the immediate descendants of such immigrants, and sometimes they came from far afield, often making the capital city an alien enclave—Indians in Rangoon, Chinese in Singapore and Saigon and, to a lesser degree, in Bangkok and even Phnom Penh. Only one-third of Rangoon's 1931 population had been born in the city; more than half Batavia's 1930 population was born outside the city; in Manila, over one-third of the population increase of the city between 1903 and 1939 came from immigration. Alongside those permanently settled in the cities were the considerable numbers of circular migrants—comprising perhaps as much as 40 per cent of the adult indigenous population—who normally resided in the countryside and came to the cities for temporary or seasonal work. Characteristically, they worked at their urban occupations for two or three months before returning to their rural environment.

Many members of the working class found employment in formal occupations, which were characterized by wage labour, regular hours and a certain degree of security. Some worked as construction labourers; some worked in factories, producing such things as embroidery, cigars, cigarettes and sandals. Many more worked in formal service industries, as train or tram drivers or conductors, domestic servants and cooks, repairmen, waitresses, dock workers. A very large number, perhaps even the majority, did not have formal employment at all, but worked in the so-called informal sector, as rickshaw pullers (20,000 of them in Singapore in the early twentieth century), pedicab drivers, roadside barbers, or prostitutes, or selling food and drink at the roadside or along railway tracks, or recycling rubbish from dumps. The characteristic feature of work in the informal sector was that it was highly labour intensive and consequently less productive than formal employment; it tended, then, to reinforce and entrench the poverty of its practitioners.

The most remunerative jobs in the formal manual workforce—as car mechanics, electricians, bus drivers—went to older, more literate males.[19] Poorly paid jobs, such as domestic service, went to those who were youngest and least literate, that is, those most likely to be newly arrived in the city; they were disproportionately occupied by women. Again, people working in the informal sector tended to be younger and less literate than those employed in the formal sector. Female employees had high rates of job turnover, probably because of childbearing and childrearing duties. Most manual workers were also subject to persistent bouts of unemployment or underemployment. The importance to newcomers of personal contacts and networks for gaining employment, informal on-the-job training and a place to live meant that career trajectories were notable for their lack of vertical mobility and sometimes for their ethnic or regional character: a young female who began employment as a domestic servant might in later life find employment as a washerwoman or cook or peddler, none of which required much literacy; less literate male servants would frequently move on to become porters or dockworkers or market vendors; an illiterate

---

[19] This section is mostly based upon Daniel P. Doeppers, *Manila, 1900–1941: Social Change in a Late Colonial Metropolis*, Quezon City, 1984.

servant could not generally aspire to become a relatively well-paid tram conductor. For this reason, ethnic and locality groups tended to be concentrated in certain occupations and certain residential areas.

Enduring poverty manifested itself most obviously in the squalid living conditions of manual workers in all colonial cities in Southeast Asia. Very few members of the urban working classes owned their own houses and land; most had to pay high rents for miserable conditions, without sanitation, refuse disposal facilities or drainage. Often accommodation was shared with others. Most suffered seriously and often mortally from the baleful effects on their health of such conditions, and morbidity and death were exacerbated by heavy exertions and poor or inappropriate nourishment.

Although many city dwellers were materially poor and indebted, retained strong links with their rural origins, and were strangers to urban life, they did not necessarily form a culturally lost or misplaced group. To replace the social life and supports they had left behind in the countryside, they often created energetic and highly organized urban proletarian cultures, expressed in such things as a multiplicity of community self-help groups like the *sinoman* of Surabaya, oral information networks, folk theatre like Iloilo's *zarzuela*, and local newspapers (read aloud in groups). Much of this energy was eventually directed into labour unions to improve wages and conditions at work sites and ultimately and naturally (as workers began to appreciate the structural reasons for their poverty and hardships) into variants of nationalism. In this way, the colonial city, the key symbol and means of Western dominance, became the site from which the ending of that dominance was engineered.

Entrepreneurs and Traders

The development of government enterprise and, later, sophisticated banking, merchant and agency institutions by Western concerns was one of the major aspects of Western dominance in Southeast Asia in this period. The commercialization they fostered penetrated deeply into the indigenous world to tap the wealth of agriculture and resources at the base of society. Under the Cultivation System, for example, peasants were moved to labour for the Dutch exchequer not just through physical or moral coercion but also to acquire the cash income to meet their taxation demands, pay debts and purchase the goods they increasingly came to need and desire. The exponential growth of rice production in the lowland river basins of mainland Southeast Asia and of smallholder rubber in Malaya and Sumatra was similarly fuelled by the need to meet taxation, service debt and purchase commodities; in Siam, for example, consumer goods consistently made up more than 70 per cent of all imports, drawn in to meet the demands of smallholding peasants. The trend towards regional crop specialization also fuelled demand for enhanced commodity merchandising; the attachment of the Bikol region to intensive abaca production, for instance, made it a permanent rice deficit area after 1850. Throughout Southeast Asia, incentive and need fuelled production;

money flooded into villages, accentuating individualism and providing a powerful stimulus to the growth of petty commerce.

In most parts of Southeast Asia, the means through which the village, the mining camp and the plantation were tied to the world economy was the various tiers of Chinese entrepreneurs and middlemen. The wealthiest and most influential of them, men like Loke Yew of Selangor and Oei Tiong Ham of Semarang, enjoyed close working relations with Western capital and government (or with the royal élite in Siam, where they were sometimes ennobled and incorporated into the regional bureaucracy). They operated as tax-farming entrepreneurs through much of the nineteenth century and thereafter as compradores, collecting and managing goods and business for Western financial and agency institutions and importers and exporters. Some became exceedingly successful independent merchant capitalists in their own right, accumulating vast fortunes in the process: Yap Ah Loy, for example, the Kapitan China of Kuala Lumpur from 1868 to 1885, owned 150 houses in Kuala Lumpur as well as substantial mining and plantation interests. Connected to these men through complex arrangements of credit, and often by kinship and clan links as well, were multiple networks of Chinese agents and petty traders, who carried consumer items and cash into the countryside and exchanged it on exploitative terms for the produce of the hinterland: rice, rubber, tobacco, sugar, abaca. The lowest formal link in the chain was the little Chinese retail store set in the village or small town, its modest appearance contrasting sharply with its vital economic importance, and its every inch crammed with consumer items. These stores (*sari-sari, kedai, toko* were three of the names they went under) provided peasants and workers with credit to finance their crops, replace their tools, and celebrate their festivities, and consumer goods (textiles, metalware, non-local foods) to keep them going. In return, shopkeepers obtained the promise of a later repayment, at substantial interest, on their investment, in the form of either a portion of the harvest or a cash payment. Chinese penetration, indeed, went even lower than the retail store. Peripatetic petty traders visited indigenous periodical markets and even individual village producers, disbursing goods and credit and collecting produce to pass up the export chain. In this way, local trade came to be dominated by the Chinese.

Explaining Chinese pre-eminence in these aspects of commerce has always been difficult and controversial, all the more so because the vast majority of Chinese in Southeast Asia enjoyed little success of any sort, commercial or otherwise, and were frequently fortunate to escape the experience of Southeast Asia with their lives. Contemporary Western observers customarily attributed Chinese success to such 'inherent' qualities as preparedness to endure hard work and discomfort and devious cunning, characteristics in which 'natives' were thought to be seriously deficient. More appropriate explanations, however, look to the social structure and commercial organization of overseas Chinese communities and the long history of Chinese trade with Southeast Asia. Organized in tightly-knit and carefully controlled language, clan and kinship groups, sometimes organized as secret societies and guilds, Chinese communities provided identity and support to both newcomers and old hands. They were a source of capital, credit, connections, labour power and markets. These things, not to mention the patronage Chinese enjoyed from Western and Siamese élites, were the building blocks of Chinese economic predominance. By contrast, indigenous entrepreneurship was fragmented, lacking in capital and commercial links, and often stunted by the forced diversion of the most powerful and able members of indigenous society into colonial bureaucracies; it could offer only the weakest opposition.

Developments in Burma provided something of a contrast to this pattern. On the one hand, domestic agricultural credit was dominated by Chettiars; to their well-established and trusted links with the Western banks and companies who provided them with operating capital, Chettiar moneylending firms coupled a longstanding tradition of expertise in credit provision and bookkeeping, sustained and elaborated by tightly sanctioned family and community networks that passed on their knowledge and business structures generation after generation. On the other hand, however, the Chettiars did not generally involve themselves directly in collecting produce and marketing consumer goods. This was left to the Burmese themselves, usually fuelled by Chettiar credit; despite competition from Indian and Chinese middlemen, they played a major role in the domestic economy as up-country rice millers, paddy brokers and petty commodity merchants, advancing credit, collecting produce, and distributing consumer goods from Indian and Chinese wholesalers to peasant producers.

Slaves, Bondsmen, Coerced and 'Free' Labourers

Notwithstanding the occasional existence of small pockets of early capitalist enterprise and wage and contract labour, such as the use of Chinese workers on canal construction in Siam during the reign of Rama III, the characteristic feature of the way most Southeast Asians organized scarce labour in the early nineteenth century was their preference for slavery and forms of bondage. This probably reached its pinnacle in the Siamese practice of tattooing dependants. Through the course of the nineteenth and early twentieth centuries, albeit gradually and unevenly, both these forms gave way to more 'modern' forms of organization.

Slave trading was abolished in English possessions in 1807; slavery as such was abolished by the Dutch in the Indies from 1860 and by the French in Cambodia in 1884. In Siam, King Chulalongkorn proclaimed a gradual phasing out of the practice in 1874. Slavery's demise, however, was much less a result of legislation (humanely intended or otherwise) than of changing social and political realities across the region. In Java, its decline in the eighteenth century had been partly a consequence of the gradual disappearance of a previously prosperous indigenous commercial class as a result of Dutch economic strangulation; in short, few people could now afford the luxury of maintaining slaves. At the same time, the growth of an impoverished peasantry had devalued the importance of formal slaveholding since, in circumstances of increasing state control, labour could be acquired more readily and cheaply through other means such as labour taxation. In Siam, the major forces at work were perhaps more complex. They involved the presence of large numbers of wage-labouring Chinese; the desire by the royal élite to centralize political control in its hands, a process which required that non-royal élites in both capital and regions be disqualified from independent control of large numbers of what Bangkok now considered to be 'its' subjects; and the need to increase the supply of peasant rice farmers for the purposeful development of rice monoculture, by now the great motor of the Siamese economy. The French reforms in Cambodia were a thinly disguised attempt to destroy the patronage style of Cambodian politics, reduce regional leaders to impotence and dependence, and affirm their own unambiguous control. More generally throughout Southeast Asia, the development of 'law and order' made redundant the services of personal retainers or bodyguards, while with the expansion of economic opportunity, bondage became a less attractive option for peasants. It is notable, however, that where economic and political environments were not conducive to reform—particularly in regions where Western-inspired efforts at centralization and economic development were sporadic or slight, such as the more remote parts of east Borneo and Magindanao in the early twentieth century—slavery stubbornly endured despite sporadic efforts to eradicate it.

Economic development and the elaboration of state control similarly provided conditions for the gradual elimination of the many varieties of traditionally coerced labour, many of which differed only in degree from the styles of slaveholding long practised in Southeast Asia. Where economies were increasingly reliant upon regular peasant production of commodities like rice and sugar, the maintenance of recurrent labour imposts upon peasants constrained them from these productive tasks, and sometimes reinforced their loyalty to provincial élites; it was counterproductive to state revenues and politically dangerous to boot. Moreover, in circumstances where landlessness and impoverishment were growing, as in Java, economic need transformed peasants into reliable wage labourers. Thus it was that, from the last part of the nineteenth century, service demands for the indigenous élite and state corvée labour were gradually phased out in Java, the latter replaced by a head tax. In Siam, the obligation of peasants to provide three months or more of their labour for the king was eliminated in 1899 and a money tax put in its stead. It was, perhaps, for similar reasons that corvée obligations were considerably lower in Cochinchina than in Annam or Tonkin.

It would be wrong, however, to assume that markets and modern state formation definitively and naturally led to the superseding of all forms of 'unfree' labour. As if to demonstrate that the general process of emancipation was not a lineal progressive movement from slavery to the 'freedom' of wage labour, old forms of bonded or coerced labour endured: corvée's abolition in Vietnam came only gradually after 1937, and it continued into the 1930s in the outer islands of the Netherlands East Indies. Moreover, new ones were developed, particularly by Westerners themselves who sought to people labour-scarce plantations with foreign indentured labourers bound under penal contracts to work for three-year periods; indeed, the conditions of such servitude were much harsher than those generally suffered by slaves in early centuries. Outcries occasioned by the revelation of abuses brought formal reform in the shape of a somewhat grudging abandonment of indenture—the British in Malaya abolished Indian indenture in 1910 and Chinese in 1914, while the Dutch legislated to remove its last vestiges in the Indies only in 1942. Despite this, the methods of labour recruitment and control suffered relatively little change. In Malaya, for instance, Chinese indenture was replaced by private recruitment or by the lodging-house system where Chinese could be recruited on arrival—in both cases, the labourer's indebtedness brought him or her under an employer's control rather than just into his employment.

To the end of the colonial period, there was little real evidence of a transition to a system of free wage labour. While opportunities for wage labour expanded greatly—for example, two-thirds of Indochina's rural population relied on some form of wage labour to make ends meet—the characteristics of a bonded society remained. This was evident even within the new and modern environment of the city, flushed with immigrant landless peasants desperate for a livelihood. Workers remained personally attached to agents, managers and foremen who contracted them out as labour gangs; low wages and poor conditions proliferated; the use of debt obligations as a means of direct economic coercion endured; opportunities for vertical or horizontal employment mobility remained limited; ethnic and familial networks determined occupation; and a real wage-labour market refused to emerge. Economies structured along colonial lines could not afford to have it any other way.

Women

Southeast Asian women customarily enjoyed comparatively higher status than those in many other regions of Asia. Even the Chinese-influenced Le legal code of Vietnam, for instance, endorsed a significant measure of property and inheritance rights for females; again, women in central Luzon could inherit, buy, sell and pass on land in their own right. Southeast Asian women did not incur seclusion or separation (with the partial exception of women of high-born class), and enjoyed substantial esteem as carers, organizers, providers, financial managers and spiritual intermediaries within the household and village. It was significant that whatever savings a peasant household might have accumulated were frequently held in the form of female jewellery. Sexual equality was most nearly approached in poorer families where all had to contribute substantially for the unit to survive. Nonetheless, women generally did not approach the status of males. The structured inequality of the sexual division of labour awarded women the major share of domestic duties (cooking, washing, cleaning, spinning and weaving the household's clothing, collecting firewood and water) and a considerable array of tasks outside the home (transplanting and harvesting crops, pounding rice, manufacturing handicrafts, selling and purchasing goods at market). Women were perennially prey to the whims of better-off men, and at times of crisis it was their daughters who were sold off as slaves and prostitutes.

The demands and effects of the period of Western domination affected women in complex and sometimes ambiguous ways. Demeaning attitudes to women allowed Westerners, particularly in the years before their political dominance was complete, to have easy recourse to prostitutes, house servants and concubines. Paradoxically, however, these women frequently achieved substantial influence by exploiting the accidental roles they acquired as cultural mediators of the strange new world encountered by their Western partners. More important than this transitional role, however, was the manner in which Western economic power contrived to change significantly the place of women in the social and domestic order of things.

This transformation was perhaps most marked in the realm of textile production. Colonialism's twin goals were to increase agricultural production from Southeast Asia and to use the region as a market for the products of industrial Europe, machine textiles most of all; these were linked in a mutually supportive and particularly disruptive way as far as women's roles and perceptions were concerned. Clothing for a Southeast Asian family had nearly always been spun and woven by the women of that household: virtually every Western traveller's account of Southeast Asia in the early nineteenth century refers to a loom in every household. Through the later nineteenth century, however, the enormous growth in peasant consumption of cheap European manufactured textiles bit deeply into household production and even into more commercialized textile industries like the remarkably successful enterprise based on Iloilo. Peasants and urbanites were increasingly purchasing cheap European cloth at market rather than weaving it in their own houses. In Java, an early example of the trend, the value of imported textiles rose from 3.8 million guilders in 1830 to 13.1 million guilders ten years later; in Burma by 1930, around three-quarters of the country's textiles were imported, while the nominal value of cotton manufactures imported into Siam rose seven times between 1864 and 1910. Vietnam, where the French established their own manufacturing industry, was the only exception to this pattern.

The key to this development was that the levies and tasks required of peasant societies in general were greatly increased: they included demands on males for corvée or paid labour for infrastructure development; more intensive or extensive cropping or the enhancement of household income in other ways in order to cater for a rapidly growing rural population; and the need to increase agricultural production for the market to pay taxes and buy consumer goods. In these circumstances, female labour could be put to comparatively better use in other tasks than slow and laborious weaving. Women increased their already considerable inputs into domestic agriculture, in part to compensate for male absences; they sought greater income from agricultural labour or petty trade; and they gained employment in the off-farm wage-earning sector (domestic service and factory work were two popular spheres). In other words, in an economic régime where cash was relatively freely available and the terms of trade favoured crop production and ancillary industry, it made better economic sense to the household for women to be employed in these ways.

A similar displacement of women from time-honoured duty, in this case the pounding of rice, occurred with the introduction of mechanical rice milling. This development resulted from improvements in steamship technology as well as the opening of the Suez Canal; the consequent rapid transport allowed rice to be clean milled (making it lighter) and to reach a far-off destination without the risk of spoiling. Thus, while there were just 13 commercial rice mills in Lower Burma in 1869, there were 83 by 1900 and 538 by 1930. The result for women was a considerable contraction of employment in this sphere.

In one scholar's view, displacement of this sort reduced women's social status; it caused something of a deterioration in their cultural identity; and it prejudiced their economic position vis-à-vis men.[20] This is a true assessment, but it over-emphasizes the negative. More and more women were driven by opportunity or need from their domestic milieu of agricultural production and exchange. Pressed hard against the ragged edges of social and economic change, they sought work wherever they could in both formal and informal sectors, often with considerable success. They comprised a surprisingly large proportion of the wage-labour sector, especially in light manufacturing work such as embroidery or cigar rolling where they were deemed to be more reliable, careful, docile and dextrous (and, of course, cheaper) than men, and increasingly in mines and on plantations as well. Yet their income, despite its importance to the household unit, was poor (usually around half that of men) and perceived as ancillary; their status was low, their positions dispensable. The best-paying and most prestigious jobs went to men; as the urban workforce grew and modernized, and as competition for work increased, it seems likely that jobs occupied by women declined in status, conditions and remuneration, and perhaps in number as well. Notwithstanding all this, however, these developments had an incipiently emancipatory flavour. As two (male) Vietnamese Marxists put it in 1938:

> In order to survive, women are now forced to leave families to work in factories and mines. Daily they rub shoulders with men and toil as men do, and thus come to understand their true value. Knowing that they must work to eat, women no longer simply *follow* their fathers and mothers, *follow* their husbands and sons, as though they were in a state of perpetual bondage.[21]

The Sick and the Dead

Before the beginning of the nineteenth century, Westerners were generally highly impressed with the physical well-being of Southeast Asians.[22] Thereafter, they began to comment increasingly unfavourably upon Southeast Asians' health, their lower rates of longevity and their smaller

[20] Norman G. Owen, 'Textile displacement and the status of women in Southeast Asia', in Gordon P. Means, ed., *The Past in Southeast Asia's Present*, Ottawa, 1978.
[21] Cuu Kim Son (Tran Duc Sac) and Van Hue (Pham Van Hao), cited in David G. Marr, *Vietnamese Tradition on Trial, 1920–1945*, Berkeley, 1981, 242.
[22] This section draws substantially on the essays in Norman G. Owen, ed., *Death and Disease in Southeast Asia: Explorations in Social, Medical and Demographic History*, Singapore, 1987.

physical stature. In retrospect, these changing appreciations reveal less about Southeast Asians' health than about rapidly increasing Western vitality. The average age at death for Southeast Asians then and earlier was around twenty-five or thirty years of age; infant and child mortality were certainly very high, and once people had survived past the age of five they could probably expect to reach the age of fifty or fifty-five. Southeast Asians suffered from a wide range of diseases: malaria, typhoid fever, tuberculosis, venereal diseases, and possibly bubonic plague as well. Typical of pre-modern, pre-industrial societies, the most frequent causes of death by illness were infective gastro-intestinal diseases or fevers.

So tenuous a grip on life affected their behaviour in ways one can only surmise: parents' knowledge that many of their children would not survive infancy surely affected fertility patterns, while the relatively short span of years available to most people must have influenced fundamentally their beliefs and how they organized and managed their social and working lives. In general, Southeast Asians attributed diseases to two frequently intertwined causes. The first was personal spiritual forces—spirits, demons, ghosts—which attacked individuals or communities. The second, most common in Vietnam but evident elsewhere as well, was behaviour not in harmony with the preordained order of things. These understandings governed the way Southeast Asians responded to disease; just as they were always ready to seek the causes of their ailments at a variety of levels in a syncretistic way, so this multi-layered approach was carried over into the realm of curing. So, for example, to fend off the horrifying cholera epidemic of 1820 in Bangkok which killed about one-fifth of the city's population, the king proposed a whole series of actions which were meant to cover every contingency: cannons to be fired off all night to frighten away the spirits, special formulas sung and religious processions held to ward them off, and everyone to stop work and engage in merit-making to placate them. Since the proximate variables which could cause illness and death were so numerous, and since they were impossible to identify with any precision, there was no sense of there being a single correct treatment for a particular ailment; people customarily took refuge in a range of different methods to cure themselves, sometimes concurrently, sometimes sequentially—drugs, prayer, holy water, consulting various medical practitioners, adopting a more moral style of behaviour. What helped in one case might not necessarily help in another: in Vietnam, for example, the time at which the sickness or injury occurred was crucial in deciding the outcome and the form of treatment.

The accelerating intrusion of the West in Southeast Asia through the nineteenth century had no directly devastating effect upon the health of the indigenous population, as it did in Australia and Africa. Westerners introduced no new diseases, at least none on a scale to be socially or demographically significant, because Southeast Asia's long involvement in international commerce had already opened it to international disease. On the other side of the ledger, however, Westerners' efforts to improve Southeast Asians' health were unhelpful, with the notable exception of the vaccination campaigns (begun in Java in 1804) which eventually reduced smallpox to an insignificant disease. The Dutch, like the Siamese, had no answer to cholera which was introduced into Java in 1821 and which often had a case mortality of 60 per cent; the best they could come up with was opium-based drinks that were little more than panaceas. American medical therapy was similarly unsuccessful in combating the Philippines cholera epidemic of 1902–4. Indeed, the Western presence probably had damaging indirect effects on health standards. Demands on the subject population's labour and food supplies led in some cases to poverty and malnutrition, and consequently lowered resistance to infection from existing pathogens. Again, the development of infrastructure and the increasing commercialization of agriculture which came with Western-inspired economic growth allowed for the far easier spread of pathogens, particularly to virgin populations which had previously been isolated from them and among whom, consequently, the effects of infection were particularly disastrous. Deforestation for crop production, mining, and public works, as well as the expansion of artificial irrigation, promoted the incidence of malaria. Increased commercial rice milling made polished rice more readily available for non-agricultural workers, and a surge of beri-beri resulted. Finally, the expansion of urban centres provided an extraordinarily unhealthy environment, with cramped and unhygienic housing and insufficient clean water and sanitation; in the first decade of the twentieth century, the death rate among Indonesians in Batavia was 64 per 1000; during epidemics, it went as high as 400 per 1000 in some parts of the city.

For much of the nineteenth century the colonial impact on indigenous health was probably minimal and possibly damaging. In contrast was the period of high colonialism, when Westerners seemed dominant on every front—political, technological, economic. Their sense of superiority, as well as their need for political legitimacy, commonly embodied the notion of a paternalistic duty to look after the people whom they were destined to rule: the application of 'imperial medicine' was one component of this attitude. Imperial medicine was particularly interested in controlling, by medical research and eradication campaigns, the most spectacular manifestations of ill-health, epidemic sicknesses. The continued outbreak of such epidemics was an affront to Western dominance; moreover they had serious economic consequences because they killed so many labourers and rendered so many others incapable of work. A second thrust of imperial medicine was to improve sanitation and general hygiene; by the early twentieth century, significant progress in medical science had brought a recognition of the relationship between environment and disease: between pooled water and malaria, drinking water and cholera, poor sanitation, bare feet and hookworm. A third area of activity was in the training of indigenous doctors, nurses and midwives. However, notwithstanding the establishment of medical schools such as STOVIA (School tot opleiding van inlandsche artsen) in Batavia, the number of people trained was pitiably small; they were generally clustered in the main towns, and socially alien to most of the population; moreover, the medicine they practised was unfamiliar and expensive. In Penang in 1930, there were only fourteen trained midwives for a population of 190,000; Vietnam in

1930 boasted one Vietnamese auxiliary doctor or pharmacist for every 67,000 people; in Lombok in 1931, three qualified doctors served a population of 790,000. A fourth area of activity was to provide routine inspections and medical and educational services. Clinics were established to combat venereal disease. Drug dispensaries were opened in towns to provide medication for the population. In Malaya, a network of infant-welfare centres was established to provide medication and advice for mothers and their children. There were also, of course, hospitals, but where these catered for indigenous people rather than Westerners they were turned to only as a last resort, confirming 'their reputation for burying rather than curing people'.[23]

Overall, the impact of Western medicine in Southeast Asia after the beginning of the twentieth century was mixed. During the influenza pandemic of 1918, which has been described by one author as 'probably the greatest single natural disaster ever to hit this earth',[24] and which killed about 1.5 million Indonesians, Dutch medicine could treat only symptoms and was helpless to control the progress of the disease. In Malaya between 1910 and 1930, half a million people died of malaria, despite great advances in scientific knowledge of the disease's cause. Nonetheless, Western medicine eventually made important strides towards understanding and containing major diseases such as beri-beri, cholera and malaria by vaccines and drugs and better control of the environment. Infant mortality rates, especially the dreadfully high ones encountered in cities, were significantly reduced, at least in some parts of Southeast Asia. Despite these triumphs, the effect on general mortality rates seems to have been limited. As far as morbidity is concerned, one can only guess that its incidence also declined somewhat. One reason for this apparent lack of success was that medical strategies were designed to cure and control rather than to prevent. Imperial medicine was essentially interventionist in character; it sought to stop or control particular manifestations of disease, especially spectacular ones, rather than to change the root conditions which allowed those diseases—as well as 'background' ills like infantile diarrhoea and tuberculosis—to emerge and flourish. A second reason was the lack of appropriate resources in money and personnel. Budgetary constraints on 'welfare' items—except, as on the plantations, where there were obvious and demonstrated connections between spending, health and profit, something that emerged only around 1930—ensured that progress was partial and halting.

Westerners

If numbers alone were the measure, the Western presence in Southeast Asia in this period was insignificant. The development of Westerners' influence and power was at first gradual and finally rapid and comprehensive by the turn of the twentieth century. In contrast, their numbers

---

[23] Susan Abeyasekere, 'Death and disease in nineteenth century Batavia', in ibid., 199.
[24] Colin Brown, 'The influenza pandemic of 1918 in Indonesia', ibid., 235.

remained proportionately tiny, for instance 0.4 per cent of the total population of the Netherlands East Indies and 0.18 per cent of Indochina's population. A more appropriate indicator of emerging Western dominance—political and economic—was the changing organization of their social existence. In the early and mid-nineteenth century, the West, in those places where it enjoyed at least formal territorial control or substantial commercial influence, was represented not only by stolid grey officialdom but also by a colourful collection of freebooting adventurers, inventive evangelists, romantics, crooks and eccentrics. To get where they needed and obtain what they wanted—and sometimes just to keep their lives and minds in a hostile environment—Westerners had to adapt themselves to the styles and practices of the region. They were obliged to compromise in the face of superior authority and numbers, and to manage and exploit commercial and social structures as they found them. Thus it was with Speedy of Larut or Bozzolo of Upper Perak, not to mention the numerous Scotsmen who proved extraordinarily effective in appreciating and working the Southeast Asian system.

All this changed with the achievement of political supremacy by the new states. Control, once attained, had to be maintained, and this meant the fabrication of a new myth of authority. Thus developed the claim of Westerners to innate cultural, technological and moral superiority over the peoples and societies they ruled; a superiority manifested and sustained by the importance attached to prestige, to 'maintaining standards', to keeping one's proper distance from the subject population. This had numerous important repercussions. It meant the thinning from government service of the flamboyant individualist who disdained accountability, to be replaced by 'properly' organized and standardly trained bureaucrats whose patronizing attitudes and mountainous paperwork often meant they understood 'the native' less intimately than their predecessors. It meant the development of a relatively homogeneous, prosperous and insulated enclave society of Westerners, organized above all around the ritual of the club, where one could 'drop one's guard' without prejudice to prestige. It meant the influx of Western wives (when Western men could afford to take them), a development which itself reinforced the sense of separateness and dominance; where Western men could not afford to support wives, the Asian concubine was replaced by the Asian prostitute, and mestizo culture evaporated under the heat of formal racial separatism. In some places, notably the Netherlands East Indies, it meant that Westerners began to consider the colony as their home rather than a place of sojourn. Most interesting and paradoxical of all, it increased the anxiety and constrained the freedom of action of Westerners, particularly when indigenous voices (mostly Western-educated ones) began feebly questioning the future of Western political dominance; witness the bored, lonely and unsettled lives of wives entrapped by the social and political demands of their environment, and Orwell's police officer who, against his best instincts, felt forced by a hooting crowd of Burmese to shoot the elephant.[25]

[25] George Orwell, 'Shooting an Elephant', in Sonia Orwell and Ian Angus, eds, *The Collected Essays, Journalism and Letters of George Orwell*, London, 1968, I. 235.

The Prosperous, the Poor, and the Underdeveloped

Material prosperity and underdevelopment are not always and necessarily mutually exclusive; in the short term, and in some places on a more permanent basis, colonial-style production frequently brought prosperity to indigenous societies. Thus, despite the demands made on their land, labour and other resources, Javanese peasants who grew sugar for the Dutch under the Cultivation System were considerably better off than they had been before 1830. The extra purchasing power from crop payments and wages served to enhance their commercial contacts beyond the village itself; increasing prosperity expressed itself in expanding purchases of salt and European cloth, in higher levels of consumption of rice and meat, and in a much busier commercial life. Those who grew, harvested and stripped abaca in Kabikolan similarly enjoyed nearly a century of hitherto unknown (though sometimes irregular) prosperity as a result of the rapid growth in demand for cordage fibre in the West. Peasants growing rubber to augment rice cultivation in Malaya or Sumatra profited from new and more regular sources of income. The rolling back of the frontier of lower Burma by Burmese rice smallholders was based on the realization that increased production brought greatly increased prosperity and heightened social mobility.

Nonetheless, at the outbreak of the Japanese war, most Southeast Asians were poor and many of them were falling ever deeper into poverty, losing their land and suffering from a declining availability of foodstuffs. To explain the existence and persistence of poverty, some observers have adumbrated a wealth of cultural inhibitors to economic development among Southeast Asians. These included 'natural slothfulness' or at least passivity; aversion to risk and a parallel need to invest surplus in informal and unproductive social and spiritual insurance; religious strictures on usury and wealth accumulation; and an overwhelming submission to the uncertainties of fate. Explanations of this type, however, beg questions about the origins and endurance of these alleged patterns of behaviour, especially given persistent evidence of Southeast Asians' enthusiastic responses to material incentive in colonial times, not to mention the zest with which they have recently taken to capitalism.

The key to Southeast Asian poverty lies rather in the fact that the widespread prosperity engendered by Western-inspired economic growth did not lead to fundamental structural change in the economies and societies of the region. Of those Southeast Asians who profited from investment in crop production or mining, few showed much interest in converting their wealth into upward social mobility or radically different varieties of economic pursuit. Those who succeeded in these activities— sometimes making extraordinary fortunes—did not have the political power nor probably the desire to change or develop the structure of the economy. However, the peculiar structure and nature of production was in its essence inimical to the longer-term interests and prosperity of the vast majority of Southeast Asians.

There were two mutually reinforcing components in this scheme of things. The first was that Southeast Asia's comparative advantage in the

international economy lay in the production of a narrow range of unpro-
cessed or simply processed raw materials: rice, sugar, tin, coal, oil, rubber,
timber, fibre, tobacco; moreover the particular comparative advantage of
each component state tended to narrow the range of goods produced even
more severely. Economies structured in this way were highly susceptible
to damaging cyclical price fluctuations: partly because of the relative ease
with which competition from other sources of supply could be mounted,
and partly because they depended on the health and needs of the more
developed economies which purchased their goods. Such was the trend
endured from the late nineteenth century onwards: depression in the
1880s and 1890s, recovery in the decade after 1900, the disruption of World
War I, a short-lived boom, and a downward spiral into the Great Depression. To make things worse, superimposed on this picture was a general
downturn in the international terms of trade for these commodities from
the early twentieth century onwards. For the same general reasons, these
forms of production did not have the capacity to provide long-term
expanding profits for their producers or investors. They were also constantly subject to supersession: sometimes for economic reasons, like the
expanding world production of cheaper forms of fibre, replacing Bikol
abaca; sometimes at the whim of fashion, as in the Western preference for
cigarettes rather than cigars wrapped in Deli's exquisite leaf.

Consequently, investors, both indigenous and foreign, sought to outlay
as little as possible in fixed capital and to recover it from profits with the
utmost rapidity. Where production was based around elaborating existing
systems of peasant labour organization—for example rice in lower Burma
or on the Mekong delta, or sugar in Java and central Luzon, rubber
smallholding in Malaya and Sumatra—it settled into static forms that
depended upon an increasingly intensive exploitation of those labour-
intensive and poorly capitalized systems. Investors devoted their attention
to increasing the size of the pie (through lateral extension of cropping) and
their slice of it (through increasing rents and crop shares) without building
up any substantial long-term flexibility or self-sustaining capacity. Technology, as in the introduction of steam-driven centrifugal sugar mills,
steam rice milling or the application of the results of scientific research on
agriculture, was meant to make the prevailing systems of production more
efficient rather than raising production to a new and higher plane. The
admittedly beneficial spin-offs from this development in the form of small-
scale ancillary industries—transport, machine shops, packaging—were
similarly elaborations on an existing theme. This meant, of course, that
once the structural limits of this method of production were reached,
peasant welfare inevitably nose-dived. This happened when, for example,
reclaimable land began to run out or became more marginal, or the number
of residents seeking employment increased rapidly, or irrigation systems
decayed, or prices fell abruptly.

The second and more important component, of course, was that these
were Western-dominated economies. They were, in the last analysis,
intended for the benefit of the metropolitan power and its allied interests.
Improved prosperity was available and obtainable for Southeast Asians if
its pursuit did not collide substantially with the economic interests of the

metropolitan state. The colonized status of Southeast Asia's economies manifested itself in various ways. One was the 'colonial drain', repatriating profits from entrepreneur investments (these were estimated at $US3007 million in 1930) which might otherwise have been reinvested in productive enterprise. A variation of this, especially in the Philippines, was the diversion of wealth to an indigenous entrepreneurial class which invested in conspicuous consumption, and there was also the repatriation of earnings by sojourning Chinese and Indian labourers. A second was taxation systems which bore most heavily upon poorer indigenous classes, effectively subsidizing the Western sector of the economy. Yet another was policy decisions which discriminated against peasant enterprise, such as banning smallholder sugar production for Western factories in Java in 1923 because of the threat it was seen to pose to the Western-controlled industry; or casting the major burden of lowering production on to smallholders in the Malayan rubber restriction of the 1920s ('a total sell-out of peasant interests',[26] according to one writer); or regulating to prevent smallholders growing tobacco in the vicinity of the east Sumatra plantations. Peasant production could survive side by side with Western capitalist enterprise while economies grew and while there was still slack to be exploited, but it was immediately dispensable if it competed too well. A fourth manifestation of the colonial nature of such economies was the introduction of harmful tariffs. Those in French Indochina served to subsidize metropolitan manufacturers at the expense of the indigenous population; Indochina imported more goods from France and its other colonial possessions than any other country. United States tariffs discouraged Americans from investing in Philippines processing industries. A fifth manifestation was the pattern of domestic expenditure. Characteristically this invested heavily in sustaining the state (bureaucratic expansion to control and tax the population, transport inputs for defence purposes) and servicing the existing economic structure (ports, roads, railways for the transit of export goods) rather than productively investing in education, manufacturing or the technology of peasant agricultural production such as seeds, fertilizers and irrigation. This was perhaps most notable in Siam where the élite saw little short-term personal gain from such improvements. Colonialism and colonial-style production were organized to perpetuate the circumstances which made it profitable, not to ensure an economically independent and sustainable future for the indigenous population. Under these circumstances, even such well-intentioned efforts to 'protect' Southeast Asians from the effects of economic change as the Malay Reservations Act of 1913 served rather to confirm their status as poor, dependent and peripheral.

THE GREAT DEPRESSION

Since about the middle of the nineteenth century, the economic life of the Southeast Asian colonies and Siam had been structured around supplying

---

[26] Lim Teck Ghee, *Peasants and Their Agricultural Economy*, 144.

food and raw produce to world markets; the wealth that had accrued to those in charge had been a function of their ability to sell these products on world markets at profitable prices. This unsophisticated and undiversified structure had survived numerous crises visited upon it by the vagaries of the world market, but these were as nothing compared to the Great Depression, which devastated the markets of virtually all the products upon which Southeast Asia's economies were based. World commodity prices tumbled: the average wholesale price of Java sugar fell from 13.66 guilders per quintal in 1929 to 9.60 guilders in 1930, reaching a low of 5.61 guilders in 1934; rice prices in Cochinchina declined from 7.15 piastres per quintal in 1929 to 1.88 piastres in 1934; rubber prices on the London market from 10.25 pence per pound to 2.3 pence between 1929 and 1932. Thus the value of exports—the economic lifeblood of the colonies—declined precipitously in the years after 1929. In the Federated Malay States, the value of rubber exports fell from 202 million Straits dollars in 1929 to 37 million in 1932; in the same period, the value of tin and tin-ore exports dropped from 117 million dollars to 31 million. The value of Indochina's rubber exports fell from 62 million francs in 1930 to 27 million in 1932. In the Netherlands East Indies, the value of agricultural exports declined from 1237 million guilders in 1928 to 294 million by 1935. The Philippines, protected by its special access to American markets, avoided the worst effects of the slump until the United States imposed import quotas on Philippines commodities in the mid-1930s.

Declining exports seriously affected the revenues and activities of the colonial states and Siam. The state revenues of the Federated Malay States and the Netherlands East Indies, for instance, were roughly halved between 1929 and 1932, as was the size of the general budget of Indochina. Nevertheless, governments were initially unaware of the seriousness of the situation, and were generally slow to react. It was only when it became clear that this depression was something entirely new in both its severity and its duration that governments began seriously to cast about for solutions. In the economic area, the main thread of their efforts involved attempts to protect their primary-product export industries so as to ensure their survival. This meant joining world-wide schemes such as the Chadbourne Plan for sugar and the International Rubber Regulation Agreement which sought to limit production and thereby raise prices. These measures were largely successful in their aims, but they could do little more than provide long-term solutions to problems that were being immediately felt, especially as government expenditures could not at once be cut back proportionately. In some cases, indeed, colonial policies exacerbated problems caused by the Great Depression. The Indies government, for example, in deference to the policies of the metropolitan government, steadfastly refused to devalue its currency until 1936 and had to compete for declining markets with nations which had devalued much earlier.

Private commercial concerns suffered even more severely; because they could not sell their products, or could sell them only at ridiculously low prices, their incomes virtually disappeared. As a result, many companies were simply wiped out; in Java, only 45 of the 179 Western sugar factories continued to operate, while the area planted to cane fell from 200,831 hectares in 1931 to 27,578 in 1935. Some enterprises were more fortunate than others; in Indochina, rubber companies received large doses of aid from the government to see them through their problems. Through the region, most companies managed to survive, usually by cutting back heavily on their costs of production. In the Malayan rubber industry, for example, more effective machinery and higher-yielding plants were introduced, the number of expensive European supervisors cut back, wages, salaries and commissions reduced; by 1932, the costs of the highest-cost producers were only five-eighths of those of the lowest-cost producers in 1929. Operating costs on east Sumatra's rubber plantations were halved between 1928 and 1932 by increasing the efficiency of tapping systems and rubber processing.

The effects of this reduced activity, reduced income, and the range of economizing and support measures struck at every level of Southeast Asian society. The number of Western government officials was reduced (in the Malayan civil service, for instance, from 270 in 1929 to 213 in 1935); further recruitment was stopped; and salaries were reduced sometimes by as much as 25 per cent. Companies were much more ruthless in cutting costs than government; in Malaya, between 30 and 40 per cent of the planting community was retrenched between 1930 and 1933, while half the 1700 European employees on east Sumatra's plantations were dismissed. These people were repatriated or, alternatively, provided with government or community support to prevent them falling into a penury that might prejudice Western prestige. Indigenous employees of government bureaucracies and private companies also suffered significant wage cuts and severe levels of retrenchment. Where those dismissed were able to find work, it was often far beneath their accustomed station; many were forced to return to the countryside from which they had originated. Paradoxically, those who retained salaried employment—usually more senior and experienced men—often prospered because the cost of living fell much more quickly and precipitately than their salaries: the real income of Filipino civil servants, for instance, doubled between 1929 and 1932. Their spending power sometimes manifested itself in countercyclical booms in spheres like the construction industry. The income differential between such people and the bulk of the population increased markedly in these years. It was also true that some indigenous workers moved up the social scale as they replaced more expensive Western or Chinese employees in bureaucratic and service industries.

Non-Western unsalaried employees did much less well, although the extent of their impoverishment has probably been overstated. Most regular wage labourers were employed in mines and plantations. Those not under indenture were the first victims of retrenchment. In Malaya between 1930 and 1932, nearly 200,000 Indians and 50,000 Chinese plantation workers were repatriated at the cost of the Federated Malay States government. Moreover, poor employment prospects led many foreign labourers to leave the country voluntarily. All told, more than 240,000 more South Indians left Penang (the port of arrival and departure for Indians) than arrived between 1930 and 1933, and between 1931 and 1933, nearly a quarter of a million more Chinese left Singapore than arrived. Between

1930 and 1934, the number of estate workers in east Sumatra fell from 336,000 to 160,000, with most of those dismissed repatriated to Java. Those who remained on such enterprises, whether 'free' or indentured, had to make do with wages which gradually fell to half those of 1929, reduced working hours and sometimes even unemployment: the wages paid to non-Europeans on east Sumatran tobacco plantations, for instance, fell from 29.4 million guilders in 1929 to 10 million guilders in 1934. Their struggle to make ends meet was eased by the fact that the cost of living also dropped appreciably—in some places and times to half its pre-depression level—but many still had families to feed in circumstances where there was little or no ancillary work for wives and children. They took up substitute activities to see them through—fishing, hunting, or cultivation of rice and vegetable crops to provide extra sources of food and income, often on urban outskirts or on allotments made available by the plantations.

The years of depression brought two important changes in the social composition of plantation and mine labourers. The first was the development of a much more balanced sex ratio. In Malaya, for instance, where there were 225 Chinese men for every 100 Chinese women in 1931, by 1939 the ratio was 144 to 100. The change sprang partly from ordinances that restricted the inflow of male Chinese from 1933 but left female immigration untouched until 1938; moreover, unemployed females were not repatriated. Foreign workers who had refused repatriation began to think of themselves as permanent residents of Malaya, and sent for their wives to join them. In Sumatra's plantation belt, a similar trend towards more equal sex ratios was evident, reflected in a more family-oriented style of residential accommodation; this was a response, perhaps, to the decline of indenture and the consequent need for plantations to establish a permanent retinue of settled workers rather than transient, difficult labourers. The second aspect of change was the rapid decline in indentured service in those areas where this form of recruitment was still practised. Whereas 76 per cent of labourers on east Sumatran plantations had been indentured in 1929, all but 7 per cent were 'free workers' by 1934.

Smallholder producers had periodically prospered from the rapid growth in international demand, especially in industrial produce. By 1929, 41 per cent of the Netherlands East Indies' rubber output came from smallholders, as did 96 per cent of its kapok, 45 per cent of its tobacco, 73 per cent of its coffee, and 22 per cent of its tea. Everywhere, however, the depression cut deeply into incomes from cash cropping. Where smallholders competed for markets with Western plantation agriculture, legislation restricting production burdened peasants much more than the estates, leaving them few options to sustain their incomes. Even where ecological conditions were favourable for it, there was no point in smallholders trying to diversify their cropping patterns because the prices available for the whole range of cash crops were disastrously low; in the absence of alternatives, many continued to produce their accustomed cash crops at high levels despite crashing prices. In the great rice-producing deltas, the depression served to confirm and entrench existing modes of life. In Cochinchina, the rapid drop in rice prices after 1929 affected landlords

just as it did peasants. Landlords themselves were usually large users of
credit from urban rice markets and moneylenders; they had commitments
to meet, and the only way they could meet them was by reducing
production costs and increasing production. They dismissed large numbers of wage labourers and cut the wages of those who remained: perhaps
as many as 40 per cent of the wage labour force was sacked, and the
salaries of employed workers were halved in the first few years of depression. The result was that half a million hectares of rice land remained
uncultivated in 1934. Despite this, the amount of rice exported actually
rose during the depression, a reflection of more exploitative collection of
produce by landlords. Such pressures served also to accelerate the existing
trend towards land alienation and concentration, and the growth of a
substantial tenanted class. In lower Burma, too, the most obvious sign
of rural distress was the huge climb in the rate of land alienation. The
proportion of land held by non-agriculturalists climbed from 31 per cent in
1930 to nearly 50 per cent by 1935; Chettiar moneylenders, previously keen
to eschew landholding in favour of liquid capital, controlled 25 per cent of
lower Burma's cropped area by 1937. Many of those who lost their land
took up as tenants, just as conditions were making tenancy increasingly
insecure. Tenants owned nothing of substance and depended for their
survival on the flow of credit; unable to service debts with rapidly falling
rice prices, they were frequently forced from their holdings which landlords rented out to new tenants under much harsher conditions. Landless
labourers found themselves competing for an ever-shrinking number of
jobs. According to one estimate, rice consumption in Burma fell by nearly
25 per cent in these years as the amount of rice exported grew at the
expense of the domestic consumption. In contrast to these dislocating
developments on the Mekong and Irrawaddy deltas, distress and deprivation were much less evident in Siam's central plain. As we have seen, the
pace of expansion in rice cultivation had been much slower because of a
relative lack of capital and a less elaborate and formal credit network. The
factors of production in the rice economy, particularly land, remained
relatively undeveloped and there was, accordingly, much more slack:
there were many more options which could be exploited at times of need.

Java's situation was somewhat different from the previous cases because, by the twentieth century, peasant participation in the export economy was much less direct than in, say, Burma or Malaya where an owner or
cultivator could sell the product of his labour for cash. Few Javanese
peasants produced export goods for sale on their own initiative and sold
them to middlemen; their involvement with export cropping, large though
it was, was mediated through the Western-controlled economy where
foreigners initiated and directed the productive process. Under such
circumstances, peasants for the most part were dependent servants of
Western enterprise rather than active participants in the colonial economy
itself; they had, then, little or no control over their fates when the Great
Depression hit. Their situation was made all the worse by the fact that
Java's domestic economy (as distinct from its export economy) was already
stretched critically tight. Rapidly increasing population and a declining
availability of land had pushed ever larger numbers of people out of the

village in search of either full-time or part-time employment; increasingly, peasant society was unable fully to support all the people it produced, and Western agricultural enterprise had come to sustain large numbers of them. Java's sugar industry, for example, provided permanent employment for tens of thousands of Javanese, and seasonal and temporary employment for three-quarters of a million of them, as well as providing huge sums for land rental. Income from such sources had provided a level of welfare which would not otherwise have been available. Its virtual removal in the depression years (payments for land rental and wages by the sugar industry declined from 129.6 million guilders in 1929 to 10.2 million in 1936) cast the Javanese back on already inadequate domestic resources. There was, however, little sign of the increasing land polarization evident elsewhere, in part because of the peculiar structure of rural credit in Java. The general pattern of peasant adaptation was a significant intensification of domestic agriculture. Peasants expanded the area under cultivation (partly by utilizing the substantial areas previously under Western export crops, particularly sugar) and, more important, they used available land much more intensively: the cropping ratio of wet-rice land increased from 1.31 in 1928 to 1.41 in 1937, while dryfield cropping was substantially elaborated. The employment this generated within villages, together with shifts in the allocation of village labour, helped to absorb most of the people released from Western enterprises.

Later episodes like the subsistence crises of 1944–5 in the Philippines and Vietnam were probably more troubled and painful for their victims than the years of depression; there were, moreover, significant regional variations in the degrees of hardship suffered through the early 1930s. Overall, however, it was a time of considerable distress for rural Southeast Asians, with widespread unemployment or underemployment, a substantial decline in the amount and quality of food available for consumption, and a general fall in living standards. The latter was expressed in terms of reduced expenditures on leisure, religious and other celebrations, non-consumables, and travel, and perhaps even a decline in marriages. While all were exposed to difficulties, the poor were hit hardest. According to one estimate from Indochina, landless wage labourers and those who had land but were forced to seek occasional wage work, often far from home, made up two-thirds of the rural population and 'form[ed] a miserable mass of workers who only satisfy their hunger at the time of plentiful work or during the harvest'.[27] Hardship bred frustration which often vented itself in crime and banditry and, in Burma, communal violence against Indians.

CONCLUSION

By the late 1930s, Southeast Asia was showing signs of severe strain. The duration and intensity of the Great Depression had made manifest in the clearest terms the unsophisticated, narrow, structurally stagnant and

---

[27] Rene Bunout, cited in Murray, 615.

dependent nature of the region's economies. In the Western-dominated drive to integrate them into international circuits of commerce, they had been cast as pliant invalids; the great majority of Southeast Asians who relied on them were left with their livelihoods compromised. In this scheme of things, they could be sustained only so long as Western-inspired export production supported them, and when that support evaporated in the years of depression the restricted and unbalanced nature of their relationship with the global economy became clear.

Meanwhile, other structural flaws were appearing. The economic development of Japan in the commercial life of Southeast Asia, with its genuine industrial capability, its ability to produce cheap goods of reasonable quality such as textiles and bicycles, its aggressive marketing, and its unpegged yen, served notice that Western control of imports was no longer assured. By 1934, Japan had outstripped Europe as a supplier of imports to the Netherlands East Indies, holding nearly a one-third share of that sector. In the context of the Great Depression, and in the face of Japanese and other commercial infiltration, the long-held dogma of free trade was coming under severe attack. In the Indies, this first exhibited itself in the creation of regulations in 1933 to control the import of rice into Java and, later, into other parts of the colony; this was an attempt to stop the Indies being used as a dumping ground for surplus Asian rice and to upgrade the Indies' rice production capability by keeping prices at relatively high levels. The measures, however, soon extended to protection against Japanese manufactures such as cement, cloth, utensils and light industrial products. The French in Indochina and the British also had recourse to similar policies.

Hand in hand with this development, the notion that colonial possessions were not just convenient appendages for the metropolitan powers was also gaining strength. The Great Depression had brought home with some urgency that the interests of mother country and colony were not necessarily identical, and that the commercial needs of the former could have serious detrimental effects upon the economy of the latter. Indeed, the Governor-General of Indochina was moved to remark in 1937 that 'it is impossible to conceive that Indochina should remain forever in a state of economic vassalage, under the pretext that it must not compete with French products either in France or at home'.[28] The experience of the depression had shown how the subservience of colonies to metropolitan interests had left their economies with dangerously limited bases, and thus exposed to socially devastating conditions over which the colonies themselves had no control. Thus, the need to diversify activities by moving away from a concentration on the provision of food crops and raw industrial materials to the development of a more elaborate industrial base became more thoroughly accepted. Among the most spectacular examples of this was the extraordinary growth of the west Java weaving industry in the mid- and late 1930s: it made use of vastly improved mechanical and handlooms (the numbers of handlooms in use grew from 500 in 1930 to 35,000 in 1940), it employed huge numbers of women in factory and

---

[28] Cited in Joseph Buttinger, *Vietnam: A Dragon Embattled*, London, 1967, I. 185.

(part-time) cottage industry, and it produced four-fifths of the Indies' needs in woven sarongs.

Where this pattern might have led is impossible to know, for the age of colonialism in Southeast Asia had nearly run its course. Over the previous century and a half, in the context of revolutionary changes in the world's economic and social order, Southeast Asia had been thoroughly transformed by its incorporation into the emerging global system of commerce. Around 1800 its physical resources and environment were pristine, their value unrealized and barely exploited; its people, small in number, diverse in culture, were scattered among innumerable polities of varying sophistication and uneven economic stature. By 1940, there was a wholly new Southeast Asia. It was fixed fast to global commerce. Its polities were simplified according to the centripetal pattern of the modern nation-state while subservient to more powerful Western states. Its economies were organized to reflect this new conception and distribution of power. Its demographic, cultural and ecological patterns were irreversibly altered, frequently in detrimental or dislocating ways. The ambiguous and often contradictory legacies of these years of elemental change guaranteed that succeeding generations of Southeast Asians would face a trying and combative future.

BIBLIOGRAPHIC ESSAY

Most general studies that discuss this period, such as D. G. E. Hall, *A History of South-East Asia*, London, 1955, John F. Cady, *Southeast Asia: Its Historical Development*, New York, 1964, and, the best and most stimulating of them, David J. Steinberg, ed., *In Search of Southeast Asia: A Modern History*, New York, 1971, rev. edn, 1987, are showing their age. There are numerous country studies of varying quality, including M. C. Ricklefs, *A History of Modern Indonesia*, London, 1981; Barbara W. Andaya and Leonard Andaya, *A History of Malaysia*, New York, 1982; David Joel Steinberg, *The Philippines: A Singular and a Plural Place*, Boulder, 1982; David P. Chandler, *A History of Cambodia*, Boulder, 1983; David K. Wyatt, *Thailand: A Short History*, New Haven, 1984: they provide useful introductions, but their concerns are mostly political rather than economic or social. Until quite recently, the dearth of serious research on the history of social and economic change meant continuing reliance on such classics as J. S. Furnivall, *Netherlands India: A Study of Plural Economy*, Cambridge, UK, 1944; Charles Robequain, *The Economic Development of French Indo-China*, London, 1944; J. Russell Andrus, *Burmese Economic Life*, Stanford, 1948; James C. Ingram, *Economic Change in Thailand since 1850*, Stanford, 1955; G. C. Allen and Audrey G. Donnithorne, *Western Enterprise in Indonesia and Malaya*, London, 1957; and G. William Skinner, *Chinese Society in Thailand: An Analytical History*, Ithaca, 1957.

Over the last couple of decades, progress has been made on a number of fronts using different techniques of analysis to uncover or reinterpret Southeast Asia's experience. One popular approach has been the analysis

of a specific industry or crop and of the ways it influenced those who
serviced its various needs. Important works of this sort include Wong Lin
Ken, *The Malayan Tin Industry to 1914*, Tucson, 1965; Cheng Siok-Hwa,
The Rice Industry of Burma: 1852–1940, Kuala Lumpur, 1968; Michael Adas,
*The Burma Delta: Economic Development and Social Change on an Asian Rice
Frontier, 1852–1941*, Madison, 1971; John Drabble, *Rubber in Malaya 1876–
1922: The Genesis of the Industry*, Kuala Lumpur, 1973; Ed. C. de Jesus, *The
Tobacco Monopoly in the Philippines: Bureaucratic Enterprise and Social Change,
1766–1880*, Quezon City, 1980; R. E. Elson, *Javanese Peasants and the Colonial
Sugar Industry: Impact and Change in an East Java Residency, 1830–1940*,
Singapore, 1984; and Norman G. Owen, *Prosperity without Progress: Manila
Hemp and Material Life in the Colonial Philippines*, Quezon City, 1984. Often
closely allied to this approach has been regional history, allowing closer
and often more fruitful investigation of social relations than national-
or industry-level studies permit. Stimulating examples of this are John
A. Larkin's classic, *The Pampangans*, Berkeley, 1972; James Francis Warren,
The Sulu Zone, Singapore, 1981; Shaharil Talib, *After Its Own Image: The
Trengganu Experience 1881–1941*, Singapore, 1984; and the summaries of
regional research contained in Alfred W. McCoy and Ed. C. de Jesus, eds,
Philippine Social History, Quezon City, 1982. Another popular object of
analysis, encouraged by the desire to write 'Asia-centric' history and to
enquire into Southeast Asian poverty as well as to draw out the poorly
documented fates of the bulk of the region's people, has been the notion
of 'peasant'; work in that area has led to spirited controversy, initiated
in particular by James C. Scott's *The Moral Economy of the Peasant*, New
Haven, 1976, and extended by Samuel Popkin's *The Rational Peasant: The
Political Economy of Rural Society in Vietnam*, Berkeley, 1977, and numerous
other commentaries: for example, a symposium on 'Peasant Strategies in
Asian Societies: Moral and Rational Economic Approaches', JAS 42, 4
(1983). For similar reasons, there have been important developments in
urban studies: Alfred McCoy's work on Iloilo (summarized in *Philippine
Social History*); John Ingleson, *In Search of Justice: Workers and Unions in
Colonial Java, 1908–1926*, Singapore, 1986; James Francis Warren, *Rickshaw
Coolie: A People's History of Singapore*, Singapore, 1986; and Daniel P.
Doepper's fascinating study of career trajectories in *Manila: 1900–1941:
Social Change in a Late Colonial Metropolis*, Quezon City, 1984. Notable, too,
in this context, is David G. Marr's study of Vietnamese intellectual life in
the early twentieth century, *Vietnamese Tradition on Trial, 1920–1945*, Berk-
eley, 1981. Related questions of population growth, mobility and mor-
bidity have been discussed in Norman G. Owen, ed., *Death and Disease in
Southeast Asia: Explorations in Social, Medical and Demographical History*,
Singapore, 1987.

Other work has focused on changing bureaucratic structure as a key to
understanding changing conceptions of power and hierarchy, perhaps
most revealingly in Heather Sutherland, *The Making of a Bureaucratic Elite:
The Colonial Transformation of the Javanese Priyayi*, Singapore, 1979, and 'The
Taming of the Trengganu Elite', in Ruth T. McVey, ed., *Southeast Asian
Transitions: Approaches through Social History*, New Haven, 1978, and also in
Alexander B. Woodside, *Vietnam and the Chinese Model: A Comparative Study*

of Vietnamese and Chinese Government in the First Half of the Nineteenth Century, Cambridge, Mass., 1971; Onghokham, 'The Inscrutable and the Paranoid: An Investigation into the Sources of the Brotodiningrat Affair', in *Southeast Asian Transitions*; Jan Breman, *The Village on Java and the Early Colonial State*, Rotterdam, 1980; Jean Gelman Taylor, *The Social World of Batavia: European and Eurasian in Dutch Asia*, Madison, 1983; Akin Rabibhadana, *The Organization of Thai Society in the Early Bangkok Period, 1872–1873*, Ithaca, 1969; and Constance M. Wilson, 'The Nai Kong in Thai Administration, 1824–68', *Contributions to Asian Studies* 15 (1980).

Changing labour, ethnic or gender relations in the context of broader economic transformations have been explored in Edgar Wickberg, *The Chinese in Philippine Life: 1859–1898*, New Haven, 1965; K. S. Sandhu, *Indians in Malaya: Immigration and Settlement, 1786–1957*, Cambridge, UK, 1969; John Butcher, *The British in Malaya 1880–1941: The Social History of a European Community in Colonial South-East Asia*, Kuala Lumpur, 1979; Ann Laura Stoler, *Capitalism and Confrontation in Sumatra's Plantation Belt, 1870–1979*, New Haven, 1985; and numerous articles by G. R. Knight, including 'Peasant Labour and Capitalist Production in Late Colonial Indonesia: The 'Campaign' at a North Java Sugar Factory, 1840–70', JSEAS, 19, 2 (1988). Dependency theories and structural varieties of Marxist thought have encouraged study of the organization of production; apart from Martin J. Murray's monumental *The Development of Capitalism in Colonial Indochina (1870–1940)*, Berkeley, 1980, this strand has been particularly noticeable in work on Thailand, such as Chattip Nartsupha and Suthy Prasartset, eds, *The Political Economy of Siam, 1851–1910*, Bangkok, 1981, and Hong Lysa, *Thailand in the Nineteenth Century: Evolution of the Economy and Society*, Singapore, 1984. More recently, attempts to understand the region as a dynamic and interconnected whole and to establish a firmer understanding of the transformative role of the state have led to the analysis of revenue collection and farming as analytical devices; notable pioneering works include Carl Trocki, *Prince of Pirates: The Temenggongs and the Development of Johor and Singapore*, Singapore, 1979; James R. Rush, 'Social Control and Influence in 19th Century Indonesia: Opium Farms and the Chinese of Java', *Indonesia*, 35 (1983); John Butcher, 'The Demise of the Revenue Farming System in the Federated Malay States', MAS, 17, 3 (1983); and Ian Brown, *The Elite and the Economy in Siam, c. 1890–1920*, Singapore, 1988. Invaluable sets of statistics have been published in the series of W. M. F. Mansvelt and P. Creutzberg, eds, *Changing Economy in Indonesia*, since continued by other scholars, and Constance M. Wilson, *Thailand: A Handbook of Historical Statistics*, Boston, 1983.

4

RELIGION AND ANTI-COLONIAL
MOVEMENTS

The period from the mid-nineteenth to the early twentieth centuries in Southeast Asia was one of increased turmoil concomitant with intensified European penetration, political consolidation by the dominant states, and the economic transformation of the countryside. European records of this period evidence a multitude of resistance movements, popular rebellions, acts of insubordination and other assertions on the part of the colonial 'other'. Since wars and rebellions have always been the stuff of which traditional histories have been written, it should be of no surprise that many of the charismatic leaders and their movements in the present study have already been mentioned in the general histories of Southeast Asia. But, in general, they have not been treated in their own terms; they figure as momentary interruptions of the grand sagas of colonial conquest, nationalism, modernization or state construction. In colonial records these phenomena are simply 'disturbances', sometimes 'aberrations', their per- petrators reduced to the status of dacoits or fanatics often led by crazed monks, popes, and prophets. Post-colonial writers, on the other hand, have appropriated such movements for their narratives of nationalist opposition to colonial rule.

More recently, such movements have been viewed as primitive precur- sors of modern, more successful, sociopolitical movements. Harry Benda must be credited with establishing a hierarchy of types that has provided subsequent scholars with a persuasive means of classifying the otherwise confusing and regionally-diverse data. The most primitive form of peasant movement, of which the 1890s Samin movement in Java is cited as an example, is characterized as rural-based, backward-looking, lacking organization, spontaneous and irrational. The most advanced are urban- based, progressive, organized, and consciously political. Benda points to the 1930s Sakdal movement in central Luzon as gearing towards the latter form since it had an educated, nationalist leader and a party structure, as well as a distinct independence goal.[1]

The evolutionary perspective that has been brought to bear on the nineteenth-century peasant unrest already knows the end-point—modern movements—toward which they were presumably 'groping'. What this

[1] Harry J. Benda, 'Peasant movements in colonial Southeast Asia', in *Continuity and Change in Southeast Asia*, New Haven: Yale University Southeast Asia Studies Monograph Series no. 18, 1972, 221–35.

perspective does is to bring these movements into line with a theory of human emancipation and social change, rather than enable us to listen to them and give them their due. The concept of 'millenarianism', it must not be forgotten, was developed during the era of high colonialism when cargo cults and the like were reduced to irrational and ultimately subhuman forms in order to suppress them more easily.[2]

Rather than reduce diversity and difference to general types like 'primitive', 'millenarian', and the like, our task ought to be the pursuit of the different meanings of such concepts in different contexts. Instead of merely classifying peasant movements and reducing them to techniques for coping with the hardships of life, we might ask how they were informed by thought: their shapes of the future, notions of community, and perceptions of change and leadership. Here is where religions can be seen to function as crucial matrices for peasants' interpretations of their experience.

In many of these stirrings from the countryside, religion can be seen to have provided both a language for articulating discontent and the social forms for mobilizing adherents against their perceived enemies. By 'religion' we do not mean an unchanging corpus of key doctrines and practices or the classical statements that define a particular belief-system. Once implanted in Southeast Asia, the universalizing faiths became localized as Thai, Filipino, Vietnamese, or whatever. Core doctrines entered into play with older local preoccupations, such as ancestor worship, invulnerability magic, healing, worship of village and mountain spirits, and ideas of power. Furthermore, as these localized religions functioned in popular movements they were already readings 'from below' in line with the material and symbolic interests of the subordinate classes. A distinction should be made between official interpretations of religion that tend to emphasize the fatedness, immutability or unchangeability of the social order, and popular views that acknowledge the possibility of change and reversal in the social order.[3] Images of ordered Southeast Asian hierarchies and state systems are presented in officially-sanctioned monuments and documents, but these must be seen as constructions posited and consolidated in relation to potentially subversive millennial and utopian visions.

The millennial strains inherent in the various dominant religions of Southeast Asia produced not just a counterculture, but a counterstructure as well to the dominant polities. The possibility of interpretations involving the subversion of the existing order is inherent in the doctrines and traditions themselves. The processes of localization and assimilation by subordinate groups have led to certain, often minor, themes in these religions coming into play at times of rebellion, or being built up by cult and sect leaders into an ideological or ritual system that was perceived to

[2] Benedict R. Anderson, 'Millenarianism and the Saminist movement', in *Religion and Social Ethos in Indonesia*, Clayton, 1977, 48–9.
[3] See James C. Scott, *Weapons of the Weak: Everyday Forms of Peasant Resistance*, New Haven, 1985, 332–4; Reynaldo C. Ileto, *Pasyon and Revolution: Popular Movements in the Philippines, 1840–1910*, Quezon City, 1979, ch. 1; Andrew Turton, 'Limits of ideological domination and the formation of social consciousness', in Turton and Shigeharu Tanabe, eds, *History and Peasant Consciousness in South East Asia*, Osaka: National Museum of Ethnology, 1984, 63–5.

threaten the legitimacy of the state or the official interpretations of the faith. The sects and movements that will be discussed here should be viewed as emanating from traditions perhaps less visible but no less vibrant than dominant, state-sponsored ones. In view of the difficulty in obtaining or comprehending statements from within the movements themselves in such a broad study as this, there are bound to be obvious disparities in the depths to which we can take our discussions of individual movements and regions. It is thus important to keep in mind the above-mentioned perspectives which are being brought to bear on the subject, despite the limitations of the sources.

THE RELIGIO-POLITICAL LANDSCAPE

The sensational and prolonged anti-colonial movements of the late nineteenth century—e.g. the Can Vuong movement, the Katipunan rebellion, the Aceh War—can be understood only in terms of the internal dynamics of the societies that produced them. Resistance, evasion, assertion, withdrawal, and even self-immolation were possible modes of action in Southeast Asian societies even prior to the crises of the late nineteenth century. In this section, we examine the tensions between centres and peripheries, and the cultural systems—which we call 'religions'—that facilitated state-building as well as provided the idioms of resistance to the state. Quite often, as we shall see, the individuals who led groups of pupils, adepts or ordinary villagers against the colonial forces were the very same ones who had been opponents, critics or simply shadowy 'others' of rulers and officialdom. Despite the differences in doctrinal content between, say, Thai Buddhism and Filipino Christianity, the religio-political terrains in which they operated were very similar, leading to striking regularities in the style of anti-colonial resistance throughout Southeast Asia.

The Thai polity, to take our first example, was built upon an accepted tradition of contracting and expanding mandalas. The empire of Rama I in 1809 consisted of a large number of power centres which can be imagined as a series of concentric circles, only the 'inner core' of which, close to Bangkok, can be said to have been ruled directly at the outset. The actual processes by which the Chakri kings transformed such a polity into a modern territorial state in response to a changing geopolitical order is treated elsewhere in this volume. What concerns us here is the nature of the popular resistance to such centralizing moves.

Buddhist states in Southeast Asia had always been plagued by centrifugal tendencies and internal unrest. The nature of the mandala system itself, in which local and subordinate identities were never erased, contributed largely to this. But the political geography was also complicated by the presence of individuals or groups dwelling in forest hermitages or wandering about holy mountains. This activity was an extension of the early Buddhist practice of 'going forth', distancing oneself from society in order better to achieve the strict disciplining of mind and body demanded by the eightfold path. Around the more charismatic forest-dwellers have formed cults or associations, the aim of which was usually the self-fulfilment of the adepts, although at times these cults were charged with a more political mission.

The role of holy men, men of great merit (*phumibun*) in the founding of Thai kingdoms and settlements and the strengthening of 'official' Buddhism is well known. As monasteries grew, so did their dependence on the generosity of the rich; on the other hand, the legitimacy of kings rested in great part on their fulfilment of the precepts of the *dhamma*, the body of teachings zealously guarded by the *sangha*. The triangular relationship between the *dhamma*, *sangha*, and monarch enabled the state-centre to appropriate much of Buddhist activity for its own ends. As much as possible, holy men were kept under the supervision or surveillance of officially recognized abbots.

Village monasteries and temples, however, tended to be ambiguous signs of central control, potentially subversive under charismatic abbots. Because the *sangha* was also a grass-roots phenomenon to which lay people became attached at some point of their lives, it was the vehicle for the dissemination of popular Buddhist literature and practices. The everyday preoccupation with the accumulation of merit is evidenced in the popularity of accounts of the former lives of the historical Buddha. Another favourite theme of such literature was the coming of the future Buddha, the Maitreya, and his glorious reign. The sanctuaries of monasteries all over Thailand are decorated with wall paintings, many of which are inspired by the *Traiphum*, a text which promotes expectations of coming *cakkavatti*, men of great inner power, and the Maitreya.

Official Buddhism continually sought to co-opt ideas and expectations of the coming of a righteous ruler and saviour, often fused in one person. Millennial expectations were 'short-circuited' by the Chakri kings' assumption, in the folk mind at least, of Bodhisattva status: they were the men of greatest merit in the kingdom, approximating the *cakkavatti* ideal. While the court appropriation of karmic theory tended towards the stabilization of the existing sociopolitical order, the absence of a caste system in Burma and Siam nevertheless created a tension between social experience and religious expectations as far as karma was concerned. An individual's high karma, and consequent abundance of merit, could be demonstrated in various ways—such as the performance of healing and magic—and shared with or transferred to others. While kings sought as much as possible to reserve this role for themselves, in actual fact villagers often turned to alternative and more localized men of merit for leadership.

The Thammayut movement, founded by Mongkut around 1833, is often seen as part of Siam's drive to modernize, to adapt Buddhism to the age of science. This movement, though, should also be seen in terms of bolstering the power of the centre by arresting the proliferation of popular Buddhist texts, or at least controlling the public consumption of such. By marginalizing the potentially subversive, millennial side of Buddhism, the dynastic state would be strengthened. However, the Thammayut movement appealed mainly to the Thai middle class. The popular Buddhism, through which villagers continued to organize their experience, contained a potential critique of the monarchy and offered alternative figures—

phumibun and *phuwiset* (person with extraordinary power) around whom they could gather particularly in times of natural calamities, profound political changes, or intensified economic demands of the state.

The politico-religious terrain in Burma was much the same. Since the time of Anawrahta in the eleventh century, the establishment of the *dhamma* ran parallel to the unification of kingdoms. Kings often had to suppress renegade groups of monks and the persistent worship of indigenous spirits called *nat*, eventually reaching a compromise by incorporating the latter into popular Buddhism. More than the Siamese, the Burmese kings exercised considerable control over religious affairs through their sponsorship of an ecclesiastical hierarchy headed by a Thathanabaing, a title which literally meant 'lord or owner of the Buddhist religion'. In theory the primate exercised authority through a chain of command reaching down to the head of the village monastery. But because monks were, after all, individual ascetics who had not vowed obedience to any superior, royal and ecclesiastical control over them was ambiguous.

The tensions that perennially existed between the officially backed hierarchy and individual monks and sects arose also from the fact that, to villagers, supposedly animistic and anti-Buddhist figures such as the *weikza* (a magician, one who has overcome death and has supernatural powers) were not really much different from monks in an advanced stage of meditation and merit-accumulation.[4] The invulnerability, curative powers, and prophetic wisdom of *weikza* and *pongyi* alike made them attractive to villagers and townspeople fleeing from corvée exactions and other hardships or simply seeking a more meaningful existence. Undoubtedly, as in Siam, the transformation of such groups of teachers and followers into more militant movements can be attributed at least partly to the popularity of Buddhist texts which provided villagers with images of the coming Maitreya and the ideal Buddhist ruler (*Setkya-min*, a Burmanization of *cakkavatti*).

The popularity of Burmese kings lay in part in their ability to identify themselves with these potent figures and the ideal conditions of existence they represented. King Kyanzittha (r. 1084–1112), for example, announced that the era of rule he inaugurated would mirror the magnificence of heaven. Not only would the highest moral order prevail, but there would be freedom from all sickness and pain, calamity and misfortune. 'Even the poor old women who sell pots and potlids . . . They shall become rich . . . Those who lack cattle shall have plenty of cattle . . . Even poor people who have difficulty in getting food and clothes shall wear gold ornaments.'[5] Much of the attraction of popular Buddhism obviously lay more in such promises of the satisfaction of earthly wants, than in an escape from them. It is thus not surprising that King Bodawpaya (r. 1781–1819) should have proclaimed himself as the Buddha Mettaya (Maitreya), destined to be a world conqueror. His successor Bagyidaw used the title Setkya-min, while Bagyidaw's heir apparent was actually named Setkya-min.

---

[4] Stanley J. Tambiah, *The Buddhist Saints of the Forest and the Cult of Amulets*, Cambridge, UK, 1984, 315.

[5] Cited in Emmanuel Sarkisyanz, *Buddhist Backgrounds of the Burmese Revolution*, The Hague, 1965, 60.

The other side of the Burmese kings' identification with millennial Buddhist figures was their continual attempts to purify the faith and to suppress heretical movements. In the eighteenth century King Hsinbyu-shin persecuted a heretical sect called the Paramats, while his successor Bodawpaya occasionally executed heretics. Purification of the order implied not merely an attack on monastic indiscipline, but a drive to unify a *sangha* that tended to fracture into many contending sects, with the ensuing danger that such groups might articulate grievances against the throne. The threat such sects offered to the king could be compounded if they aligned themselves with some pretender to the throne, or *min-laung* (lit. king-to-be, embryo king) who happened to claim special powers.

The crisis of the Konbaung dynasty, brought about by internal rivalries compounded by British threats and conquests, encouraged precisely the dispersal of the *sangha* and the flourishing of small, increasingly militant, groups led by monks, *weikza*, and *saya* (experts in esoteric lore). Millennial expectations gravitated towards these figures, particularly after the loss of the centre of the realm and the physical disintegration of the Konbaung polity. The very sorts of holy men, cult centres, and popular energies that the Thai kings managed to contain and draw towards the centre became, as we shall see, the sources of resistance to the politico-economic order imposed by British rule in Burma.

As we move to the eastern part of mainland Southeast Asia, we find Confucian rulers experiencing very much the same problems as their Buddhist counterparts. Having overcome the Tayson centres of rebellion and established themselves at Hué in the beginning of the nineteenth century, the Nguyen emperors were finally able, for the first time in history, to unify the north and the south, and even to establish control over the Cambodian court at the expense of the Thai. But the Confucian state's control over the vast empire was plagued with problems from the start. Gia-long's reliance on French support resulted in the spread of Catholic missions which would eventually provoke religious conflicts among Vietnamese villages. The incorporation of the south, with its Cham and Khmer traditions, posed the complex problem of integrating diverse ethnic and religious groups into an idealized Confucian political and moral order. And as always, there was resistance posed by the strong autonomous tradition of the villages, which were tantamount to religious congregations centred on cults of guardian spirits.

Although the official religion of Vietnam was, like China's, an amalgam of the 'Three Teachings'—Confucianism, Taoism and Buddhism—the need for national integration spurred the scholar-gentry to fashion the Nguyen polity more in accordance with the Confucian ideal. This involved the closer integration of villages in the central polity through the grant of patents to village guardian spirits—the imperial document to be housed in the main shrine (*dinh*). National integration also spurred a continuation of the old and well-documented 'war' on Buddhism. Since Buddhist monks had often served as advisers to their patrons in secular matters, and since monastic centres often served as havens for disaffected nobles and peasants alike, the war on Buddhism was meant to neutralize potential sites of rebellion against the Nguyen court. The Buddhist monkhood was pressured into adhering to the monastic ideal of withdrawal from the world of men. And as far as they could, without alienating the peasantry, the scholar-gentry attacked the superstition and fanaticism which they associated with popular Buddhist and animist practices. Emperor Minh-mang himself was visibly contemptuous of such beliefs as invulnerability magic. In 1834, to disprove the Thai faith in amulets, he tied one to the neck of a duck, shot at it himself, and reported the duck's death.

The emperors and mandarins of traditional Vietnam thus saw them-selves as the guardians and agents of a superior, secular civilization both surrounded, and threatened from within, by barbarism. However, their drive to impose this Confucian order was punctuated by rebellions and other acts of resistance. It is estimated that 105 separate uprisings occurred during Gia-long's reign (1802–19), and 200 during Minh-mang's (1820–40). Specially in the north, where the Tayson rebellion, Chinese invasion, floods, typhoons, crop failures, and official abuses all wreaked their havoc, many villages were abandoned. Drifting peasants contributed to a spate of rebellions, led by bandits who were often advised by men of scholarly background. Remote sacred mountains provided bases of operations, and the popular imagination was fired by the appearance of omens promising a new and better society in the aftermath of rebellion.

One source of instability was intrinsic to the system itself. The legitimacy of the Vietnamese state rested on the emperor's possessing the mandate of heaven and ruling through purity of example. The Confucian-educated élite composed of mandarins and scholars generally looked up to the emperor as the exemplar of moral behaviour, and transmitted to the populace at large the values of obedience to superiors and veneration of the ruler. However, as in other parts of Southeast Asia, this élite could function as an ambiguous sign. In troubled times, such as after serious floods or famines, the mandate of heaven could be perceived to be lost by the emperor, leading to popular unrest. In such situations local scholars, in particular, because of their close ties with villagers in their roles as teachers, scribes and physicians, could lead rebellions against the reigning monarchy.

Confucian scholars did not derive their power and influence from the accumulation of merit or virtue, as did Buddhist monks. They were simply superior men acting in accordance with Confucian ideals. Vietnamese villagers, however, never ceased to be attracted to individuals who could tap the power of spirits and gods. Partly this was due to the failure of the examination system centred at Hué to produce enough scholar-gentry to achieve a uniform Confucianization of society—a situation particularly serious in the south. Since, in the Confucian ordering of things, common people had no religious function, they continued to be attracted to prac-titioners of the Taoist, Buddhist and other religions who offered, aside from notions of personal salvation, practical skills in healing, divination, geomancy and so forth. The officially sanctioned belief in an impersonal heaven always existed in tension with theistic beliefs in ancestral and guardian spirits.[6] In some areas of traditional Vietnam, challenges to

[6] Charles F. Keyes, *The Golden Peninsula*, New York, 1977, 201.

the authority of the state were mounted in the name of a spirit or god, such as a Bodhisattva, who was perceived to have greater power than that of the emperor. If the state was triumphant, then here was proof that greater power resided in heaven rather than with spirits and gods.

One theistic belief that greatly perturbed the Confucian court from the early nineteenth century on was Christianity. The conversion to French Catholicism of whole Vietnamese villages—by 1848 there were 68,000 converts—was tantamount to a challenge to the Confucian social order itself. Of course, the panoply of Christian beliefs was itself subjected to a certain amount of 'Vietnamization'. Popular culture was given an added dimension through the Gospel story, the sacraments, and other basic elements of the Christian faith. But in relation to the totalizing Confucian order, Christianity was subversive. Christians were oriented to the after-life; they counted time in linear fashion from Christ's birth; they recognized a potentate in Rome; they dressed and behaved differently. In areas affected by this new religion, 'canton teachers' were recruited from among local scholars to lecture on Confucianism. In the second half of the century the persecution of Vietnamese converts and priests, coupled with mission-ary ambitions, were to a great extent responsible for the massive French intervention.

In the southern part of Vietnam (Nam Bo) Christianity was only one of several religions competing for the allegiance of the populace. This was a frontier area which the Confucian court sought to populate and incorpo-rate into the realm. These two aims were not exactly compatible: in seeking to attract manpower to the area, the court found it necessary to refrain from policing the religious beliefs and practices it suppressed elsewhere. In any case, because land-ownership tended to be valued more highly than a bureaucratic career in the south, rising families did not generate enough scholar-gentry to do the policing. For various reasons Nam Bo, especially its western part bordering on Cambodia, became a haven for defrocked monks, political dissidents, heretics, bandits, Chinese secret society elements and a diverse immigrant population, all of which could carry on their 'proscribed' rituals. Sects and movements inherently subversive of the existing order thus often began there and spread beyond their confines through the work of itinerant apostles.

By the 1850s, Vietnamese authorities were quite alarmed by the growth in the region of a popular religious tradition called Buu Son Ky Hong (Strange Fragrance from Precious Mountain). The name is derived from the characters inscribed in the amulets distributed by the sect leader Doan Min Huyen, who held the title of 'Buddha Master of Western Peace'. The Buddha Master had put together themes and practices culled from different religious currents among the Vietnamese, Khmer, and Chinese 'floating' populations. He and his disciples were 'holy men' who could prophesy the future and perform rituals, medicinal curing, divination, and the like. Like the *phumibun* and *weikza* of the Buddhist polities, apostles of the sect formed small groups of adherents without much organizational structure and concerned mainly with self-cultivation in accordance with the Buddha Master's precepts. At times of unrest, however, these groups had the potential of feeding into a wider rebellion or anti-colonial movement.

Much of the Buddha Master's attraction lay in his ability to provide more specification to eschatological ideas already familiar to the populace. 'The Low Era is at an end' was the slogan of Buu Son Ky Hong in the nineteenth and early twentieth centuries. Upon a time base of cycles of eras (High, Middle, Low), the end of each marked by cataclysmic events, the Buddha Master based his specific prophecies. The world was reaching the end of a cycle, an apocalypse would occur, and the Maitreya Buddha would descend to initiate a new era and cycle. The attractiveness of the Maitreya's advent can be gleaned from the following prophecy:

> When the Buddha descends into An Giang,
> The people of the Six Provinces will know an easy life.
> Every home will have things in plenty,
> Everywhere will be peaceful and happy,
> The roads to Heaven will be wide open,
> We will follow in the steps of emperor Shun and the Sages,
> There will be harmony in the Three Spheres.[7]

The message of the Buddha Master was understood by a population that included ethnic Khmers, Vietnamese, and Chinese who lived in a kind of no-man's-land beyond the control of the centres of state power at Phnom Penh and Saigon. This region of unrest in fact also constituted the southern and eastern edges of the Cambodian mandala. Since the seventeenth century the Nguyen overlords of the south had intruded into space formerly under Cambodian control, starting with the occupation in 1620 of Saigon (still known to Cambodians today as Prey Nokor). Large chunks of territory and thousands of ethnic Khmer were subjected to progressive Vietnamization for over two hundred years. Vietnamese intervention extended to the throne itself, forcing the Cambodian royal family to split into pro-Thai and pro-Vietnamese elements. Dynastic squabbles and foreign invasions diminished whatever control the throne had over the countryside. Thus, in the eighteenth and early nineteenth centuries, much of the countryside was under the control of 'holy men' (*nak sel*) endowed with magical powers and able to tap the millennial strains of popular Khmer Buddhism.

The *nak sel* were particularly active in the southeastern borders, where anti-Vietnamese feelings were particularly intense. In the first half of the nineteenth century intensified Vietnamese control over this region sparked several rebellions against the throne. In 1820 a monk named Kai declared himself king in the vicinity of a sacred mountain in southeastern Cambodia called Ba Phnom. The economic grievances are clear: Kai was rebelling against the exactions of the Vietnamese who had been in virtual control of the court since 1811. Politically he sought to displace the feeble monarch and restore the potency of the centre. But what actually drew

[7] Cited in Hue Tam Ho Tai, *Millenarianism and Peasant Politics in Vietnam*, Cambridge, Mass., 1983, 29.

adherents to his cause was his possession of special powers deriving from his great merit, his connection with the sacred mountain, his distribution of amulets, and his millennial message of a new and pure society free of the Vietnamese. A mixed Vietnamese-Khmer force sent against Kai failed because the Khmer commanders deserted with their troops and turned against the Vietnamese. Eventually the rebellion was crushed by a purely Vietnamese contingent.

The receptivity of Khmers in southeastern Cambodia and Nam Bo to the preachings of the Buu Son Ky Hong apostles in the 1850s can be attributed more specifically to the turmoil occasioned by a massive anti-Vietnamese revolt from 1840 to 1847. High-ranking officials (*onkya*) had interpreted the Vietnamese exiling of the Cambodian queen and her entourage, and the confiscation of her regalia, as the virtual dismantling of the monarchy. Vietnamese actions aimed at rationalizing the Cambodian administration were seen as attacks on the very foundations of the Buddhist state and social order. The *onkya*-led revolt that ensued was similar in many respects to the Burmese guerrilla warfare against the British following the Konbaung dynasty's fall in 1885. No overall leader emerged. Although estimates of rebel strength ran to thirty thousand men, these were fragmented into hundreds of small bands armed mostly with knives, cross-bows and clubs.

It seems an inescapable conclusion that millennial ideas informed the response of Khmer villagers to the call of the *onkya*. Originating along the east bank of the Mekong, the revolt had spread farther inland and to parts of southern Vietnam inhabited by Khmer—terrain over which *nak sel* had great influence. Who were leading the small band of rebels? And why were they pitting their puny weapons against the Vietnamese war machine? The disappearance of the queen and her regalia would have been interpreted as a sign of the approaching Low Era. Monks were undoubtedly involved, for it was the Buddhist order itself, patronized by the monarch, that was threatened with extinction. As one rebel wrote, 'We are happy killing Vietnamese. We no longer fear them; in all our battles we are mindful of the three jewels [of Buddhism]: the Buddha, the law, and the monastic community.'[8]

The ending of the rebellion was, not surprisingly, marked by the restoration of the monarchy under Thai sponsorship, and with Vietnamese acquiescence. The elaborate ceremonies that took place in 1848 signified the restoration of Theravāda Buddhism as the state religion. Monasteries were subsequently rebuilt and monks encouraged to assume their 'normal' roles in society. But all this activity merely confirms that what had transpired in the recent past was the loss of official Buddhism's control over the monks in the countryside, many of whom were in fact identical to the *nak sel* rebel leaders. Despite these restorative gestures, Khmer monks and disciples of the Buddha Master would continue, in the decades to come, to provide leadership and inspiration for movements aimed at bringing about the ideal Buddhist polity in the face of alien intrusion.

[8] Cited in David Chandler, *A History of Cambodia*, Boulder, 1983, 131.

As we move to the island world of Southeast Asia, the religio-political terrain becomes somewhat more complex. One is struck by the diversity of the Malayo-Indonesian world owing to the varying degrees of accommodation with Hindu, Buddhist and Islamic influences, the dichotomy between coastal-commercial and inland-agrarian principalities, and the different levels of state formation that had been reached by the end of the eighteenth century. The Philippines seems to be altogether different, owing to centuries of Spanish colonization and the widespread adoption of Christianity. Despite such complexities, however, certain regularities can be discerned. Pilgrimage sites, rural prophets, gurus, millennial messages, and invulnerability magic all had their role to play in opposition to the establishment. One finds in them pronounced slippages between older ideas of power and the universalizing faiths of Islam and Christianity. The Philippines, it turns out, is no exception to the rule.

In studies of the Indic states of Java, the bulk of the attention has been paid to the *negara*, the site of the royal palace and shrine, the axis of the universe and thus the very source of power of the kingdom. The interior of Java can be visualized as a conglomeration of such power centres whose influence and authority rose and fell in a succession of periods of order and disorder. Local chiefs and villagers became incorporated into one or another *negara*, depending on which was in the ascendancy, as evidenced in its ruler being in possession of the *wahju* (divine radiance).

In the peripheries of the Javanese kingdoms where the power of the centre was weakest, we can identify another set of élites, of individuals powerful in their own right yet outside the sociopolitical order. In pre-Islamic times these were the hermits and sages (*resi, adjar*) who inhabited remote mountain sides and caves. They had withdrawn from society to live a life of isolation and asceticism in order to penetrate the secrets of the universe and acquire the powers of a seer; they were able, among other things, to call attention to the state of decay of a kingdom. Because of their prophetic powers, *adjar* were respected and feared by rulers. They were also attractive to other seekers of knowledge, who became their pupils. And in times of crisis, they could be the foci of rebellious activities. The hermit tradition is conveyed to villagers through the *wayang* shadow play, in which the advice of an *adjar* is sought because he is able to offer alternative views that might otherwise be missed. At times these alternatives pointed to messianic ideas, such as the appearance of a *ratu adil* (just king).

With the advent of Islam and colonial rule, the traditional *adjar* largely disappeared. Since the conversion to Islam in the Javanese interior had been achieved without destroying the basic features of the old Indic polity, the new Islamic-titled rulers simply harnessed the doctrines and functionaries of Islam to enhance the power of the state or centre. But the official appropriation of Islam, which would carry over into the Dutch colonial period, was confounded by the presence of independent, rural religious leaders who played a role quite similar to the *adjar* of old. The *kyai* (venerated teacher of Islam) established reputations and followings in *pesantren*, or schools, often located in remote villages beyond the administrative control of the state. There were also the gurus or masters of Sufi brotherhoods called *tarekat*, which mushroomed in Java and parts of Sumatra in the nineteenth century. In times of crisis these Islamic teachers, leading bands of their pupils, would emerge from their isolated *pesantren* and *tarekat* to play a role, albeit temporary, in the collapse of an old order and the emergence of a new.

The popular appeal of the *kyai* went beyond his Islamic learning and holiness. Many of the best-known *kyai* were also healers and prophets. They were deemed to be men of immense potency, which was dispensed to their adherents in the form of invulnerability and cures. They also operated in a cultural milieu that could readily interpret unusual occurrences, such as volcanic eruptions and foreign intrusions, in terms of a Javanese amalgam of Hindu and Islamic ideas of time. The message of the *kyai* could, and often did in the nineteenth century, mesh with beliefs in the imminent coming of the *ratu adil*, the just king who would institute an age of justice and plenty after a period of decline; or with the appearance of the Mahdi who would bring a temporary end to suffering and oppression by restoring order and founding a new kingdom.

Before the Dutch incorporated the *priyayi* (Javanese hereditary aristocracy) into the colonial bureaucracy from the mid-nineteenth century on, there was tension but not really a chasm between court *priyayi* and religious figures beyond the state's control. It was part of the aristocratic tradition for the youth to withdraw from *kraton* life at some point of their lives, in order to engage in study, meditation and asceticism in isolated places under the guidance of sage-hermits and Islamic teachers. Aristocrats often negotiated the pilgrimages to holy graves alongside travelling *santri*, the 'students of religion', thus coming into contact with prominent Islamic teachers as well as crowds of ordinary pilgrims. As with all passages through sacred sites in Southeast Asia, the Javanese practice of visiting holy places fitted very well into scenarios of rebellion. This is exemplified in the career of Prince Dipanagara, chief protagonist in the Java War fought against the Dutch (1825–30). Dipanagara had in previous decades spent much time wandering about the hills in the environs of Yogyakarta, visiting shrines, caves and other holy places. Such activities would have been undertaken by him, and interpreted by other Javanese, as a way of strengthening his inner being in preparation for some difficult and historic task. At the same time, some of his wanderings would, at the very least, have made groups of teachers and pilgrims in those holy sites aware of the issues that informed his acts of defiance against the Dutch.

Though led by a scion of the Yogyakarta royal family, the Dipanagara rebellion attracted all levels of Javanese society to its cause. But it was not necessarily the interests of the *priyayi* that the peasant rebels sought to defend against colonial intrusion. Through his links with religious figures and centres in the countryside, his act of defiance came to be interpreted by the society at large in moral and even millennial terms. It was outside a cave where Dipanagara had often meditated that the standard of revolt was raised in 1825. He claimed to be a champion of Islam, not merely of its formal institutions but in the sense of purifying the whole of Javanese society that had become degraded by the presence of the Dutch and their collaborators. By assuming the title of Sultan Erucakra, which is a name of the *ratu adil*, he gave concrete form to the society's widespread familiarity with images of struggle and change as transmitted through popular art forms such as the *wayang*. Not just the *kyai* and their adherents, but even bandits and peasants as well, recognized in Dipanagara the fulfilment of their aspirations.

After the war, the anti-feudal policies of the Dutch were abandoned and the *priyayi* became increasingly part of the colonial edifice. The courts were stripped of their vast territorial holdings and became reduced to 'ritual establishments'. Dipanagara's was thus the last of the *priyayi*-led rebellions. Meanwhile, the conditions were created after 1830 for the heightened involvement of *pesantren* and *tarekat* in protest movements. The expansion of the civil service and the colonial penetration of rural areas threatened the traditional religious leaders while providing them with a wider base of economically-dislocated villagers from which to draw adherents. In an attempt to control the directions of popular religiosity after the Java War, the Dutch and *priyayi* administrators organized a parallel religious bureaucracy with prescribed roles from the regency down to the village level. This, however, served only to increase the resolve and solidarity of the independent *kyai* and *ulamā*. In the spate of minor anti-colonial uprisings that immediately followed the Java War, some of which looked to Dipanagara's return, leadership was mainly in the hands of *kyai* and other holy men, rather than scions of the nobility. The increasing identification of *priyayi* with Dutch rule is evidenced in an 1843 uprising led by Amad Daris, a commoner, who sought to expel all officials from Java and inaugurate a new era in which the hierarchical social order would be overthrown.

In the coastal-commercial states of the archipelago, the *ulamā* and their *pesantren* played an even more crucial role in unrest and resistance. The idea of kingship evolved quite differently in these coastal principalities: not, as in interior Java, from a divine-kingship model with the palace as the centre of the universe, but from the notion of ruler as the regulator of commerce in the market, and the Protector of Islam. The Acehnese sultan, for example, did not symbolize the overriding unity of the Acehnese people. Islam, however, was used to strengthen his position vis-à-vis the district chiefs. His relation to Islam made the sultan culturally superior, a magical figure even, but without real power.

The Acehnese *pesantren* were always separate from the villages and were even economically self-sustaining. The *ulamā* were not rivals of the chiefs, and challenged the latter only on moral or reformist grounds. In normal times, *pesantren* simply coexisted with the villages, making no attempt to impose themselves on the flawed society around them. Yet they were potent foci of unrest. In the first place, villagers could be attracted to the *ulamā* for the 'wrong' reasons: because they had power to command a blessing or a curse, to cure sickness, and to provide invulnerability. But on a wider scale, men were attracted to the *pesantren* because of the opportunity offered them to leave their villages and kinfolk behind in order to unite as Muslims. The *ulamā* himself symbolized this movement towards supra-kinship unity. Furthermore, in times of unrest or when action was necessary to purify and defend the Faith, the *pesantren* offered an avenue towards an alternative form of existence in Paradise. This, as we shall see, made the *ulamā* a powerful leader of resistance against the Dutch.

Beginning in the nineteenth century, attitudes of Islamic teachers towards their secular surroundings and the intrusions of the colonial state were shaped to a large degree by radical developments in the wider Islamic world. The pilgrimage (hajj) was a conduit for reformist impulses that initially shook Mecca in 1803 when it was invaded by the Wahhabis, a militant group from the deserts of eastern Arabia. The Wahhabis preached the return to the pure teachings of the Koran and the tradition of the prophet. They declared a jihad (holy war) on lawlessness, irreligion, and heresy—a kind of Islamic puritanism. Pilgrims from Southeast Asia could not but be impressed by this revitalization of their faith. Although they rejected some aspects of reform that clashed with popular practices—such as the worship of saints and holy places—many hajjis (pilgrims from Mecca) returned to their communities bent upon combating corruption and imposing strict Islamic laws.

The new Islamic orthodoxy had direct political repercussions as well. Previously the pilgrimage could readily be incorporated into a *raja*-centred polity; it was an extension of the royal domain, enhancing popular perceptions of rulers as 'Shadows of Allah on Earth'. By the nineteenth century the pilgrimage was nurturing other ideas of where political and communal life ought to be centred—such as Islamic law, or national identity. This development coincided with the Dutch and English consolidation of their claims to the archipelago. The effects were particularly dramatic in the relatively more complex polities of Java and Sumatra. Since the *priyayi* and other traditional aristocracies eventually collaborated with the Dutch, the reformist attack on 'official' Islam (i.e., that patronized by the aristocrats) was readily broadened into an anti-colonial struggle. As the militant reformists saw it, not only was official Islam in an abysmal state, but the Dutch *kāfir* (unbelievers) were actually working through the system to establish their control.

The first major outburst informed by such sentiments occurred in the Minangkabau region of Sumatra. Early in the nineteenth century Minangkabau pilgrims initiated what came to be called the Padri movement (from Pedir, whence most of them had sailed for Arabia). The Padris gained control of many *tarekats* based in the foothills of Merapi and other mountains, fortified them and put them on a war footing. Their goals were to cleanse the lowland communities of such practices as cockfighting, gambling, and alcohol consumption, and uniformly implement the Islamic legal code; their attempts were resisted by the royal family and many local communities. Declaring a *jihad*, the Padris at times resorted to the use of armed groups of teachers and students to effect their reforms. Eventually, they clashed with the Dutch who, aided by the royal family and some chiefs, were determined to wrest control of the coffee trade which was then in the hands of the Padris. Hostilities began in the early 1820s and did not really end until 1838.

The Padri war illustrates how a religious impulse from the outside— reform Islam—was able to radicalize existing *tarekat* and *pesantren*, thus transforming groups of teachers and pupils into insurgent armies that fought the 'corrupt' Islam of the villages as well as the expanding colonial state. There would be more such confrontations, particularly after the opening of the Suez Canal in 1869—increasing the traffic to Mecca—and the advent of the high colonial period. It must be borne in mind, however, that the terrain on which hajjis preached determined the character of the movements as much as the reformist ideals did. As more and more peasant villagers were drawn into such movements, particularly on Java, millennial expectations and demonstrations of magical power became the overriding concerns.

As stated earlier, the religio-political terrain of the Christianized Philippines was not much different from those of 'traditional' or pre-colonial states elsewhere in Southeast Asia. Spanish colonial rule had delineated cities, towns (pueblos) and provincial boundaries within an administrative structure that looked good on paper. In actuality, a mandala-type situation existed wherein the prestige and power of the parish priest and indigenous town élite (*principalía*) determined a pueblo-centre's hold over the peripheries. Up to fairly late in the century, there was ample scope for non-pueblo elements—called hermits, bandits, wanderers, curers, heretics and the like—to operate almost at will, attracting people to them during periods of natural calamities or annual pilgrimages, or forming permanent communities beyond the pueblos. The movement of people away from the Spanish centres could be due to a variety of reasons ranging from exorbitant tax and corvée demands to the rumoured calls of a prophet to prepare for a coming new era.

Each Spanish religio-political centre, located in the church-*convento* complex, in effect had a rather less visible and less structured 'other' that mimicked its ritual practices while retaining many of the features of pre-Spanish religion; it competed for manpower, and in times of crisis flared up in rebellion. The more intense manifestations of an 'other side' to the Spanish ordering of Indio life were to be found in areas difficult to penetrate by the police and army, and a multitude of them existed in the nineteenth century. Even such a heavily 'Hispanized' region as central Luzon had the sacred Mount Arayat at its centre, and was bordered by the Zambales mountains to the west and the Sierra Madre to the east. Almost every major island had tall mountains—some of which were regarded as sacred—the slopes of which served as havens for individuals or communities fleeing from pueblo control or simply wishing to practise alternative lifestyles, as hermits or sectarian adepts.

Officially, the spread of Catholic doctrine among Filipinos of all classes was supposed to tie them to the Spanish-Christian world. The Spanish priest was the agent of the Christian god, whose superiority to the local sorcerers and spirits was repeatedly demonstrated during the period of conversion. The institutionalization of the Catholic faith in the colony coincided with the birth and growth of pueblo centres, and a native élite that saw themselves as children of Mother Spain. However, the popularization of Catholic teachings through hymns, poems, dramas, and particularly the epic of Christ's passion, death and resurrection (*Pasyon*) produced a popular view of the world in which the human and divine dimensions could not be kept entirely separate. Thus, there became available for appropriation such figures as that of *Kristo* (Christ), a man of power (*kapangyarihan*), yet lowly and humble, the leader of a group of ordinary men and women who are infused with a knowledge far superior to that of the learned priests of the establishment. While functioning to integrate the indio into a social and ritual circuit leading upwards to the parish priest and the Christian god, the *Pasyon* also created the possibility of *separation* from family and pueblo life to heed the call of a sorcerer, prophet, or rebel and 'head for the hills', to die for this leader's cause and thus to see heaven. A conception of the biblical unfolding of time was also introduced: a notion of the eras (*panahon*) of the Father, Son and Holy Spirit, the winding down of the latter marked by catastrophic events preceding the apocalypse and the return of Christ the King. Prophets were expected to be able correctly to read the extraordinary events in human time in terms of this over-arching conception of changing eras.

Such non-official readings of the Christian master text provided the ideological conditions, at least, for certain forms of opposition to the Spanish colonial order. Often, these radical movements were originally Church-approved sodalities and confraternities which changed their character under the influence of prophetic leaders and extraordinary circumstances such as famines and the appearance of comets. The most sensational of these was the Cofradía de San José (Confraternity of St Joseph) which began in 1832 as one of dozens of sodalities throughout the islands devoted to the practice of piety and the performance of works of charity. But under the leadership of Apolinario de la Cruz, an articulate lay brother attracted to Catholic mystical literature, the Cofradía expanded and began to function as a separate church. As small groups of its preachers and adherents continued to sprout all over the southern Tagalog region, the Cofradía was proscribed by the Spanish church in 1840. This native holy man and prophet was drawing whole congregations away from the official church. Furthermore, it was discovered that portraits of Apolinario depicted as a saint were being venerated at secret meetings.

Apolinario retreated to the slopes of Mount Banahao, a sacred mountain, where he managed to attract thousands of lowlanders to join him in forming an independent commune that would prepare for the impending cataclysm and the new church that would arise from the ashes. His success can be attributed in part to the Spanish friars themselves. They had implanted in the region a religious vocabulary that the Tagalogs infused with their meanings. To his brethren Apolinario promised superior knowledge, equality, material abundance, victory over illness and even over death. Take, for example, the following excerpt from a devotional text written by a friar:

> That day most eagerly awaited
> becomes even more joyful
> should the source of fulfillment
> be seen with our eyes.

All goodness and truth
that people aim for
but never quite attain
will be granted in heaven.

... High-born or low,
rich or poor,
all will look alike
this is God's vow.[9]

A note in Apolinario's copy states: 'This is what will be seen by those who ascend beginning 19 February 1840.' Familiar images of Paradise beckoned villagers to join this particular event. Apolinario himself was recognized early in his career as a saintly figure, then later as a Tagalog Christ and, finally, king—a title he vigorously denied ever arrogating to himself. At the same time, he had the 'traditional' attributes of a curer and a practitioner of invulnerability magic.

The violent suppression of the Cofradía did not stamp out the movement. Survivors of the revolt simply withdrew to their villages or to isolated settlements in the hills, secretly continuing to adhere to their beliefs and practices and spreading the tradition to other islands to the south.

One crucial factor that made such sects attractive was the Spanish failure to develop a satisfactory corps of native clergymen. If Apolinario de la Cruz had not been barred from entry into the Franciscan order, the illicit Cofradía would probably not have developed. In the late eighteenth century a serious shortage of Spanish priests had forced the archbishop to ordain native Filipino priests. But by the 1820s their increasing numbers and intellectual sophistication had become a matter of grave concern to the Spanish clergy, who imagined the native priests leading their flock against Mother Spain. By the 1830s the tide had turned against the Filipinos, and more and more of their parishes were turned over to the Spanish orders. Not surprisingly, a Filipino priest was incriminated in the Cofradía rebellion of 1841. As the rift between Filipino and Spanish priests deepened through the rest of the century, it was bound to instill a religious dimension to anti-colonial agitation from *within* the pueblos themselves.

ANTI-COLONIAL MOVEMENTS FROM 1850

The second half of the nineteenth century saw an acceleration of the European imperial advance into Vietnam and Burma, the imposition of a 'protective' net around the Malay states, and territorial and bureaucratic consolidation in Siam, the Netherlands East Indies and the Philippines. Political independence was surrendered in varying degrees to the Europeans, as economies were increasingly tied to the global economic system

---

[9] Cited in Ileto, 49.

centred in Europe; villages experienced the steady penetration of the money economy as well as central administrative and fiscal control. Such revolutionary transformations in the politico-economic order were accompanied by a series of disasters like cholera epidemics, armed invasions, and fluctuating commodity prices leading to a depression in the 1880s. Given the intensity of the changes taking place around them, Southeast Asian villagers during this period showed a readiness to follow individuals who could organize their experience and point to a better future. Whether led by kings, gentry, religious teachers or sage-prophets, whether they called for armed resistance or withdrawal from society, the popular movements that emerged reveal striking similarities in form, a reflection no doubt of the religious experience that animated the bulk of them.

Siam would at first glance appear to be exempt from the phenomenon of anti-colonial resistance. In a broader sense, however, the Chakri kings were practising a form of colonialism when they transformed their realm in the image of the European colonial states elsewhere. Faced with foreign economic penetration and the loss of royal trade monopolies after the signing of the 1855 Bowring treaty, the Chakri kings were compelled to intensify the production of rice and other crops for export, as well as exploit their teak and tin reserves. The need to streamline the economy, and to collect taxes and duties efficiently, necessitated the consolidation of boundaries and the direct control of far-flung provinces. Always the worry was that the British and French would enlarge their domains at Siam's expense.

In the process of transforming the basically feudal, *mandala* polity into a centralized, bureaucratic one, the former tributary states and semi-autonomous provinces were forced into line by commissioners sent from Bangkok from 1874. This form of internal colonialism not only eroded the power of local ruling families, but imposed hardships on villagers through the rapid dismantling of their subsistence economy and the imposition of various taxes in cash, collected mainly by Chinese agents. Under such circumstances, not surprisingly, several revolts or assertions against Bangkok broke out in various parts of the kingdom.

Around August 1889, there were various protest actions against the new taxes in the north around Chiengmai, a region with a centuries-old identity as the site of the Lannathai kingdom. A month later, a peasant rebellion broke out led by Phaya Phap (Phraya Prapsongkram), a petty official linked to the Chiengmai royalty. Significantly, Phaya Phap used to be called *Nan* Techa, *Nan* being a title held by a person previously ordained as a Buddhist monk. His ability to mobilize up to 3000 peasant followers (mostly Khoen people), including a large number of Buddhist monks, in open rebellion against the Thai and Chinese was no doubt due to his ability to articulate their discontent within a popular religious idiom. He was perceived to be a man of extraordinary powers, owing to his great accumulation of merit. He shared his invulnerability to enemy bullets with others through the ritual of bathing in sacred water. In normal times, he would have been one of dozens of holy men surrounded by adepts in search of self-fulfilment. But in this particular context he articulated popular expectations of a new era: he was expected to reign as the ideal

Buddhist king of a revitalized Chiengmai that was independent of Bangkok and free of taxes.

Similar reactions to Thai practices occurred in the northeast and in Laos. Beginning in 1899, there were reports of *phuwiset* and *phumibun* distributing sacralized water and medicine to peasants and performing various purification rituals. Most of these white-robed ascetics had had monastic experience; some had been forest dwellers and hermits, others had the ability to cure. They prophesied imminent disasters such as howling windstorms and darkness for seven days and nights. Some remarkable transformations were to occur: pebbles would become gold and silver, while gold and silver were to become pebbles; gourds and pumpkins would become elephants and horses, and so forth. The *phumibun* preached that the people should be pure of heart and join them in order to be saved or to become rich. Monks and ordinary villagers alike began to gather around these charismatic figures, often prefixing their names with the honorific 'Ong'. By 1901 the *phumibun* or 'holy man' phenomenon had escalated; the total emerging in 1902 alone numbered well over 100. By this time it was clear to the Thai and French authorities that the *phumibun* and their followers were intent upon defying the new politico-economic order and establishing their own kingdom. As these movements became threatening, Thai officials called them by the pejorative term *phi bun*.

Most of the 1901–2 *phumibun*-led movements did not lead to armed clashes with the state. The large groups of people who gathered around the holy men were taught to observe the Buddhist precepts, not to cause harm to others. However, the simple fact of their separateness from the official Buddhist *saṅgha*, plus the tendency of *phumibun* to be ordained with semi-divine status, was subversive enough of the established order.

The threat to the state was multiplied when millennial expectations were generated among the populace. The case of a *phumibun* named Ong Keo illustrates this. In several wats of the Saravane region in southern Laos there appeared, in 1901, white cotton panels depicting Ong Keo as a *thevada* (god) enjoying the blessings of a Buddhist paradise—suggesting the invocation of the Maitreya tradition. Himself an Alak tribesman, Ong Keo initially attracted mainly the Kha hill people of southern Laos to his movement, but eventually large numbers of Lao joined as well. The following year, the Lao on the Thai side of the border also became involved. They were led by Ong Man, a lieutenant of Ong Keo, who publicly declared himself *Phaya Thammikarat Phumibun*, a celestial being descended from heaven to save mankind from sin.

At this point, in 1902, the *phumibun* phenomenon had reached the point of armed rebellion. Each fighting unit was led by a *phuwiset* who wore multicoloured robes in monkish fashion, his head wrapped around with palm leaves inscribed with magical formulae. In March Ong Man's forces captured the Thai governor of Khemarat, but they were eventually defeated by the repeating rifles and powerful cannon of the Thai army. In late April, the forces of Ong Man and Ong Keo surrounded the French Commissariat in Savannakhet, convinced that they were in no danger since the French militia's ammunition would turn into frangipanni flowers. When the French did open fire, a hundred and fifty of them were killed. Ong Keo was later shot dead after he was lured to the negotiating table.

The *phumibun* movements that directly challenged the state, or were perceived to be doing so, were quickly suppressed by the vastly superior Thai and French forces. But this does not mean that the ethos that sustained these movements also disappeared. After all, the king of Siam himself claimed the status of *phumibun*. The difference between him and the others was that only he was empowered by the state to share his merit. Significantly, the captured rank and file were made to drink the water symbolizing their allegiance to the Thai king. But how could there be any guarantee that some other *phumibun* would not come along to capture their imagination and loyalty?

The problem for the Chakri kings was that, in the eyes of the ordinary villager, power resided not just in the rich and the mighty, but in poor, forest-dwelling ascetics as well. Whether they liked it or not, these recluses attracted followers and seekers of wisdom, and were often invested with attributes which they themselves denied. Such was the case with a monk named Siwichai, from the province of Lamphun in the north, who had the title *khru ba* (venerated teacher). Having emerged from a period in the forest, Siwichai founded a new monastery atop a hill outside his village where he taught the ways of the forest-dwelling tradition. Soon he began to attract large numbers of people from the provinces of Lamphun and Chiengmai—not just Thai but Karen, Meo and Muser as well. His reputation grew by leaps and bounds; soon he was rumoured to have the unusual powers characteristic of a Bodhisattva.

By the end of the nineteenth century, *Khru ba* Siwichai had become more than just a venerated ascetic and teacher. Stories of his various acts of defiance against the enroachments of the national *sangha* were becoming caught up in the wider narrative of the north's attempt to preserve its identity and heritage. The issue that provoked most concern was the government's attempt in 1902 to integrate monks and wats into a single, unified organization controlled from Bangkok. Since resistance was articulated in the Buddhist idiom, it is not surprising that there should be widespread rumours—which Siwichai apparently refused to discourage—that he was a Bodhisattva: the appearance of this sort of figure would have signalled the coming of a new era of righteous rule for the north. Like Phaya Phap farther to the north, and the *phumibun* rebels in the northeast, Siwichai had become a vehicle for the articulation of popular sentiments against the internal colonialism practised by the Chakri dynasty.

The 'disturbances' and uprisings in Siam during this period pale in comparison with those in Burma and Vietnam, which experienced a direct foreign invasion. Since the British and French represented alien cosmologies which threatened the Buddhist and Confucian orders, widespread resistance could be generated through appeals for a 'holy war' to preserve the integrity of a civilization or to restore its greatness. Let us first examine Burma, where the British dismantling of the kingdom of Burma provided the setting for resistance in the idiom of popular Buddhism.

The destruction of Konbaung Burma proceeded in three stages. Finally, in November 1885, the British captured Mandalay and early the following year annexed the rest of the kingdom to the empire's Indian province. The gradual loss of royal authority in the south beginning in 1824 had the effect of widening the gap between the monarchy's claims to actualizing the ideal Buddhist state, and the reality of its decline under the British onslaught. The less the actual ruler displayed the characteristics of a *cakkavatti*, or Setkya-min, the wider the space was for royal or Setkya-min claims to be made by other men of merit and power such as *weikza*, *saya* and monks. Furthermore, the series of wars, military defeats, and foreign occupations could not but have been viewed in terms of the Buddhist conception of history—as signs of the age of world decline, which would be followed by a new age. Thus, the retreat and fall of the Konbaung dynasty, while causing dislocation and a sense of loss, also pointed towards a future in which the kingdom and a perfect Buddhist society would arise, and the Future Buddha—the Maitreya—would finally descend. This ideological context helps explain the forms and intensity of popular resistance to British occupation.

It was after Burma's losses in 1824 that the Setkya-min claim became a potent force for galvanizing peasant uprisings. King Bagyidaw's heir apparent, as we have seen, was a prince actually named Setkya-min who was executed under the next king in 1838. But there were rumours that this prince was actually saved by the magician Bo Bo Aung, and was going to reappear at any time to restore the greatness of the Buddhist kingdom. The folk expectations of a return of Setkya-min were subsequently tapped by a series of claimants to his identity and mission. In January 1839, the very use of the name Setkya-min by a certain Maung Tsetkya enabled him to collect followers for a revolt in Pegu, a predominantly Mon area. This phenomenon was repeated several times, despite severe repression in the offending districts by the Konbaung forces.

The appearance of Setkya-mins and other Buddhist messiahs became intensified after the annexation of lower Burma in 1852. Although this may be attributed mainly to the British-Indian presence, a contributing factor was the withdrawal to Mandalay of many of the more ecclesiastical monks—i.e. those who recognized the Thathanabaing's authority and the king's patronage. This left the supervision of Buddhism in the villages to independent, local *sangha* which could very well have supported the Setkya-min claims of rebel leaders. In any case, the recognition of such figures largely rested upon the populace. In 1858, a mere fisherman, who had received a portent, was recognized as the Mettaya (Maitreya) destined to expel the *kalas* (Western strangers, barbarians) from Rangoon. His followers then proceeded to capture the local colonial commissioner. Two years later, a Future Buddha (Paya-Alaung) appeared, threatening the British position in Toungoo. Although these revolts were quickly put down by the superior British-Indian forces, the sentiments that propelled them endured. In 1861–2 the German ethnologist Bastian heard Burmese songs which seemed to be about a prince of victory who was expected to drive out the invaders.

Just before the third and final war with the British, King Thibaw himself donned the armour of world conqueror, announcing to all of his subjects that he would march forth with his army to expel the English heretics and *kalas*. His mission to uphold the honour of religion and country would, he said, 'gain for us the notable result of placing us on the path to the celestial regions and to Nirvana, the eternal rest'.[10] Thibaw's fight ended in disaster, but the framing of the struggle in Buddhist terms ensured a continuance of popular resistance despite the loss of the monarchy. It took another five years of campaigning from 1886 to subdue the country. At one point, the British deployed an army of 32,000 troops and 8500 military police against various guerilla groups.

The British conquest entailed the exiling of the king and the removal of the royal throne from Mandalay Palace to a museum in Calcutta. The British knew that this would mean for the Burmese the collapse of a whole cosmological and moral order anchored in the royal capital. As a senior monk expressed it in a *ratu* poem:

> No more the Royal Umbrella,
> No more the Royal Palace,
> and the Royal City, no more . . .
> This is indeed an Age of Nothingness
> 'Twere better we were dead.[11]

Indeed, this was widely perceived as the end of an era, for at the end of a Buddhist World Age, the throne is the last part of the whole world to disappear. But the British strategy underestimated the forces that could be generated by this period of dislocation and uncertainty in between world ages.

The fall of the centre saw a flurry of activity from various claimants to a restored throne. Some, like the Myinzaing and Limbin princes, had established ancestries, but many others were pretenders with dubious claims to royalty. British reports mention, without going into much detail, individual foci of resistance who went by the names of Buddha Yaza (Buddha Raja), Dhamma Yaza (Dhamma Raja), or Setkya Mintha (Setkya Prince). In the past, the Burmese state had harnessed the notion of *cakkavatti* to legitimize its conquests and reigns. Now the field was open to practically anyone who could successfully claim to be an Embryo or Future Buddha who would restore the traditional Buddhist monarchy. Having a direct, genealogical link to the old royal family was an advantage, but in the end what mattered most were one's leadership qualities and ability to address millennial expectations. District chiefs (*thugyi*), *weikza*, *saya* and *pongyi* were able to gather bands of fighting men around them by demonstrating their possession of inner power and claiming to hasten the coming of the new Buddhist age.

The role of monks and ex-monks was crucial in the resistance movement. The British attempted to neutralize the monks by acting through the Buddhist ecclesiastical authority in the same way the kings had done. But although the Thathanabaing offered to preach submission to the British if his traditional authority was upheld, in fact he no longer commanded the

---

[10] Cited in Donald Smith, *Religion and Politics in Burma*, Princeton, 1965, 84; and Ni Ni Myint, *Burma's Struggle against British Imperialism*, 1885–1895, Rangoon, 1983, 42.
[11] Cited in Ni Ni Myint, 42

respect of the majority of monks, his proclamation being regarded as a betrayal of the cause. All over upper and lower Burma men in yellow robes were reported to be advising rebel leaders, or actually bearing arms at the head of guerrilla bands. Among those who rejected the Thathana-baing's advice to surrender to the British was U Parama, a Shan. The Thathanabaing had appointed him the district *saṅgha* official for the Hsipaw region in the Shan States. But he joined the Myinzaing prince's resistance movement, then on the latter's death joined the faction of the Limbin prince, who made him 'Thathanabaing of the Shan States'. Even when Limbin surrendered in 1887, U Parama continued to hold out until he was captured. The significance of his rejection of the Thathanabaing is not just that he was against the British takeover, but that the fall of Mandalay, the old centre, had created the possibility of the peripheries—in this case, the Shan States—reasserting themselves.

There were some colourful rebel monks whose careers drew more than the casual mention in British records. In 1886 U Ottama, who had cast off his yellow robe, unsuccessfully attacked Salin, in Minbu District, with more than 3000 men. He established a small principality of his own north of Minbu and controlled it until the end of 1888, when British counterin-surgency measures succeeded in depriving him of village support. The military police found him, with only one follower, sitting despairingly by the Chaungdawya pagoda. Then there was U Kelatha, a self-proclaimed Setkya-min, who with eighteen followers attacked Fort Dufferin in 1887. Now this fort was actually the old Mandalay palace which U Kelatha attempted to occupy in order to cosmologically turn the tide of war against the British. Finally, there was the ex-monk U Po Lu who declared himself a *min-laung* (king-to-be) and led a ragtag band of peasants into Sandoway in 1889. Assisting him was a blind monk renowned as an expert in invul-nerability charms.

Effective police action by the British saw to it that these uprisings were contained and finally suppressed. Conflating all such disturbances to the category of 'dacoity'—a tactic used by the colonizer all over Southeast Asia—was one way of excluding such activities from the realm of 'normal' politics. As the British consolidated their gains, they encouraged the development of a new, non-hereditary, urban-based and Western-educat-ed élite; from this group would spring the nationalists of the twentieth century. The monkhood, now more fragmented than ever, had to relin-quish much of its educational role beyond the village and was encouraged to confine its activities to 'religion'. However, the expectations that an ideal Buddhist king—a Setkya-min, perhaps, or Buddha Yaza—would someday restore Burma's greatness never really faded in the rural areas. In the following century armed uprisings continued to break out in the old areas of Setkya-min activity. And when urban nationalists arrived in the villages to preach their anti-colonial message, their success would depend very much on tapping Buddhist notions of change.

The French occupation of Vietnam differed significantly from the British occupation of Burma in that the Confucian court was not the object of destruction. By gradually turning the monarchy into a facade, however, the French upset the harmony between heaven and earth that the emperor ritually sustained. Resistance to French rule was evoked in the name of the emperor, who stood for an idealized existence on earth; in this sense, one can speak of a millennial dimension to the event. For the sectarian movements in the south, the slippage between Confucian appeals and the Buddha Master's prophecies spawned another flurry of activity that would remain fairly constant through to the next century.

The French forward movement began in September 1858, when an invasion force sent by Napoleon III seized Da Nang. Early the following year the Gia Dinh defence complex around present-day Saigon (Ho Chi Minh City) fell. In late February 1861 the defence complex at Ky-Hoa, outside Gia Dinh, was overrun by the French. After this battle, the formal, organized Vietnamese defence deteriorated progressively. The French wove a net of treaties and concessions around the court at Hué, continued to recognize it as the legitimate source of local authority, then propped it up against those who angrily turned against the imperial collaborators.

Meanwhile, popular resistance in the Mekong delta, under the banner of the Popular Self-Defence Movement, developed mostly under the leadership of local scholar-gentry and landowners who ignored the Hué court's compromise dealings with the French. That elements of the scholar-gentry should become foci of resistance was to be expected, given the popular regard for them as the 'soul' (*linh hon*), the spiritual locus of society in times of great crisis. Truong Dinh, for example, could count on a fighting force of about a thousand tenants and peasants armed with spears and swords. The pompous title he adopted, Binh-Tay Sat-Ta Dai Tuong (Western Pacifying, Antiheresy General), bespeaks the Confucian order which he sought to upheld against the Catholics and barbarians.

The *nghia quan* - 'righteous armies' or partisans—of Truong and others repeatedly ambushed French strongholds and rivercraft, assassinated collaborators, and taunted court representatives to go out and fight the enemy. Among the populace there circulated the now famous eight-character epithet: 'Phan and Lam sell out the country; the court doesn't care for the people.'[12] The guerrilla partisans, however, drew a careful distinction between the actual, reigning king and the moral principle of loyalty to the monarchy. While condemning the court, they repeatedly pledged loyalty to the monarchy as an idealized institution. In the past, the defence of this political and moral order often demanded the sacrifice of their lives in fighting Chinese invasions. This became part of a tradition of martyrdom. As the great poet Nguyen Dinh Chieu wrote of the peasants killed fighting the French near Saigon in 1861: 'You are dead, but temples and shrines have been erected for your cult, and your name shall be cherished by thousands of generations to come.'[13]

The seemingly interminable resistance in the delta, and the breakdown of mandarin rule, were largely responsible for the French decision to seize all of its provinces and establish direct rule in 1867. The departure of most of the patriotic scholar-gentry after 1867 did not, however, usher in

---

[12] Cited in David G. Marr, *Vietnamese Anticolonialism*, Berkeley, 1971, 32.
[13] Cited in Alexander B. Woodside, *Community and Revolution in Modern Vietnam*, Boston, 1976, 29.

the tranquillity expected by the French. For while scholars drew upon Confucian ideals to mobilize the peasants behind the throne, a good many of the armed partisan units, even under the Popular Self-Defence Movement's banner, were actually religio-political or sectarian in nature. Confucian scholars and emergent Buddha-Masters had found common ground in the anti-colonial struggle. The French realized this when their attention was drawn in 1867 to the person of Tran van Thanh, who had been an officer in the regular army but later emerged as the leader of the Dao Lanh sect which was determined to continue the fight.

Tran van Thanh had built up his base near the border with Cambodia, where he communicated with the spirits, practised healing, and distributed amulets to his hodgepodge of followers who had come from all parts of southern Vietnam. The Buu Son Ky Hong tradition, ever powerful in this region, was expressing itself in a distinctly anti-colonial form. It is significant that the struggle here transcended ethnic divisions. Tran's closest ally was a Cambodian monk and 'holy man' named Pou Kombo. The French by 1864 had gained a firm foothold in King Norodom's court. In 1865 Pou Kombo rallied the Khmers in eastern Cambodia and southern Vietnam around him by claiming to be a grandson of King Ang Chan, who would restore the greatness of the kingdom. At one point his followers numbered ten thousand and even threatened the court at Udong. He and Tran van Thanh together raided French military positions in Chau Doc until Pou Kombo's death in 1867.

In 1872, the Hué court, which in the past would have attempted to neutralize the sect's influence, sent Tran van Thanh a banner bearing the characters *Gia Nghi* (Resolute and Righteous)—a signal to step up the struggle. But the following year the French killed Tran, exposing his body for three days to demoralize the sect. Unfortunately they had not reckoned on the popular belief in reincarnation. The Dao Lanh apostles spread the word that Tran had merely disappeared from the world of the living. In the midst of a cholera epidemic followed by the threat of famine in 1877, an apostle announced that a spirit had told him that the time had come to expel the French. This spirit would descend from heaven and actually lead the faithful into combat and make them invulnerable. The embodiment of this spirit was a certain Nam Thiep.

Nam Thiep was able to unify the Dao Lanh groups and mount a rebellion in 1878. He announced that the Low Era was ending, and that the reign of the Emperor of Light (i.e. the Maitreya) was being established. Peasants armed with bamboo spears and amulets attacked French garrisons, only to be driven back decisively by rifle fire. But this did not faze Nam Thiep, who in 1879 proclaimed himself a living Buddha and built a new community on Elephant Mountain, in the region of the Seven Mountains.

The year 1882 must have been a particularly ominous one for the peasant populace of the region. Rumours spread of the French occupation of Hanoi and their operations throughout the Red (Hong) River delta. Then late in the year the cholera struck, and a comet appeared in the sky. These events triggered fresh expectations of a cataclysm. The comet was interpreted by Dao Lanh preachers as a sign of the impending French departure. Not

surprisingly, various sects began to mobilize, swelling the population of
Nam Thiep's base on Elephant Mountain. Khmers, Vietnamese, and
Chinese alike could be counted among the adherents. However, no long-
term plans were made for a revolt, the assumption being that the court
would send in reinforcements and the rest of the populace would join in as
groups of sectarians traversed the villages.

Like his predecessor Tran van Thanh, Nam Thiep became involved
in Cambodian affairs in 1885. Soon after the French had succeeded in
pressuring King Norodom into signing a treaty that, among other things,
installed French Residents in provincial cities and threatened to dismantle
the Cambodian feudal order, a rebellion broke out under the leadership of
Prince Si Votha, Norodom's half-brother. Significantly, the provincial élite
was able to rally popular support by comparing French treatment of
Norodom with the way the Vietnamese had treated the Cambodian royal
family in the past. In other words, the French were seen to be threatening
the very foundations of the Buddhist polity and social order. In such a
situation, as in Burma around that time, claims to power by someone with
dynastic links would have fused with popular beliefs in the coming of a
messiah Buddha who would restore the political, economic and religious
integrity of the kingdom after a period of disorder. This may also explain
why Nam Thiep was enthusiastic about supporting Si Votha's cause, to
the extent of enlisting Dao Lanh members in the Cambodian forces. The
rebellion began to subside only when the French allowed King Norodom
to travel around the countryside to convince the insurgents that the
reigning monarch was still in control of the centre.

With the Cambodian rebellion over by 1886, the Vietnamese volunteers
returned to their base. At this point, however, the French noted an
increase in sectarian activity coinciding with the circulation of decrees
calling for the population to rise in support of Emperor Ham Nghi. Peasant
restiveness was, in fact, noted all over Vietnam and must be seen in the
overall context of the collapse of the monarchy.

The death of Tu Duc in 1883 had precipitated a crisis of succession,
which enabled the French to negotiate a treaty turning Vietnam into a
French protectorate. On 5 July 1885 the boy Emperor Ham Nghi fled the
capital and called for an all-out struggle to expel the French. The numerous
scholar-gentry and peasants who had been organizing local resistance in
previous years without royal sanction were elated to find their ruler
amongst them. This did not mean that other members of the royal family
ceased their collaboration with the French. However, henceforth the
succession of kings on the Hué throne would be regarded as mere puppets
by the anti-French activists and their peasant supporters. With the centre
spiritually empty, resistance could galvanize, in the traditional manner,
around the person of the 'real' king, or around various pretenders to
the throne.

The circulation throughout Vietnam of the edict of Can Vuong (Loyalty
to the King) considerably widened the terrain of anti-French resistance.
Now, for example, central Vietnam, Ham Nghi's base, was in turmoil as
well. The history of the Can Vuong movement is too complex to be
detailed here. The pertinent question to ask is why ordinary villagers

responded to this royalist, scholar-gentry affair. The edict provides some clues: while it was addressed mainly to the scholar-gentry, it also had great emotional impact when read or interpreted to the populace at large. 'With luck,' it said, 'Heaven will also treat man with kindness, turning chaos into order, danger into peace, and helping thus to restore our land and our frontiers. Is not this opportunity fortunate for our country, meaning fortunate for the people, since all who worry and work together will certainly reach peace and happiness together?'[14] We get the sense here that popular participation in the movement was a way of restoring the harmony between heaven and society that was so crucial for prosperity and happiness. Without a proper emperor, there was no one to mediate between heaven and earth through the proper performance of rituals, no one to assure that agriculture, society and state were properly attuned to the workings of fate.

In a sense the Can Vuong movement was also a popular, religious one. Tenants and peasants who joined the scholar-gentry can, of course, be seen as merely fulfilling their traditional duties towards their intellectual and social betters. However, the scholar-gentry also represented, at the local level, the link between the human and divine planes of existence. The political situation after 1885 would have been construed by many as the imminent end of the dynastic cycle, precipitating a tumultuous period during which the mandate of heaven might shift to another claimant. And this was precisely one of those times when the scholar-gentry assumed leadership of popular movements. But the scholar was only one type of figure around whom the peasantry traditionally gathered. To those informed by Buddhist notions of history, the very same events—the Can Vuong manifesto even—would have intensified perceptions of the Low Era. Thus the attraction of messianic figures like Nam Thiep.

There is a Javanese parallel to the French co-optation of the Vietnamese court aristocracy and the stiffening of resistance towards the centre which this engendered. The identification of the *priyayi* and their 'official Islam' with the Dutch during the second half of the nineteenth century exacerbated the tensions between centres and peripheries in Java, whose history during this period is filled with accounts of disturbances, illicit gatherings, and uprisings. Some of these were located in areas haunted by the potent spirits of past kingdoms; such were the 'illicit' gatherings around the graves of the Mangkunegara dynasty on Mount Lawu's slopes. A desire for wholeness in this age of colonial economic penetration and political reordering made millennial appeals and messianic figures attractive; at the very least, groups of people could seek to withdraw from the colonial order and its money economy in order to maintain their self-worth. To Dutch officials, at least, the most serious threat came from the Islamic figures who wandered about preaching jihad and the imminent arrival of a new era. As the Dutch *kāfir* presence intensified, village Koranic schools and *pesantren* increased in number, injected with anti-colonial sentiments by *ulamā* and hajjis circulating through a network of *pesantren* and *tarekat*.

14 Cited in Marr, 50–1.

The spread of anti-colonial sentiments can be traced in part to the intensification of the pilgrimage to Mecca. The liberal policies following the dismantling of the Cultivation System in the 1870s brought increasing wealth to those able to respond to new economic opportunities. For these fortunate ones, success was to be capped by fulfilling the last religious duty: the pilgrimage. Despite restrictions placed by the Dutch, the numbers of pilgrims increased dramatically after the opening of the Suez Canal in 1869. Although only a select few stayed long enough to study under a great teacher and be initiated into a *tarekat*, even the masses of pilgrims could not but be transformed by the experience of the pilgrimage. In Mecca they mingled with co-religionists of all classes and races and learned about the crisis being faced by Islam as a result of Western expansion.

Hajjis returned to their towns and villages aware of the need for purification, renewal, and even outright assertion against the colonizer. It was common to find hajjis and their circles of followers constituting small communities within the wider Muslim community and yet set apart from it through their puritanism, austerity, and condemnation of *adat*. A notable example in the 1850s was Hajji Mohamad Rifangi who started a movement of sorts, called the Budiah movement, among the rural populace of Pekalongan and Kedu residencies. There was nothing outwardly 'anti-colonial' about this movement, but the members' withdrawal from the collective social and religious life of their villages, plus Hajji Rifangi's constant disruption of 'official' religious services in the Kalisalak mosque, were subversive enough to local officials, who secured his exile to Ambon.

Reformist and pan-Islamic sentiments spread by the hajjis had the potential of being translated into mass action. For the majority of Javanese, the last two decades of the century saw a drastic decline in living standards. This, combined with ever more regulations and tax exactions from a more efficient bureaucracy, made the peasantry receptive to appeals for a rejection of the colonial order. As stated earlier, however, such appeals were never received in pristine form, for they had to operate within a field of older expectations and traditions. The activities of itinerant hajjis prior to the 1888 uprisings in Banten are illustrative. When Hajji Abdul Karim, a guru in the Kadiriah *tarekat*, returned to Banten in 1872, he not only established a religious school in his home village but travelled through Banten, holding purification rites, *dhikr* (short prayers with ritualized body movements) and processions. In the religious revival that ensued, he came to be regarded as a saintly figure with curative and invulnerability powers, his prestige outshining the local *priyayi* officials. He predicted an imminent jihad, the arrival of the Mahdi and the 'Last Judgement'. Says the Dutch Islamicist Snouck Hurgronje, 'Every evening hundreds eager for salvation flocked to where he was staying, to learn the *dhikr* from him, to kiss his hand and to ask *if the time were at hand* and how long the Kafir government would continue.'[15]

Other holy men, all hajjis, circulated through the branches of the Kadiriah *tarekat* in the Banten region, propagating the message of jihad

---

[15] Cited in Sartono Kartodirdjo, *The Peasants' Revolt of Banten in 1888*, 's-Gravenhage: Martinus Nijhoff, 1966, 180.

and the coming of the Imam Mahdi to packed audiences in the mosques, at the same time dispensing or selling amulets, rosaries and copies of the Koran brought back from Mecca. When hostilities broke out in Cilegon in July 1888, the ragtag rebel army was composed largely of peasant disciples or devotees of the *kyai* who marched against superior government forces, convinced that they were invulnerable in waging the holy war. In less than a month the rebellion was crushed, but the spirit of revolt was not extinguished. Despite the indiscriminate persecution of hajjis, Islamic teachers and mystics continued to circulate surreptitiously throughout the *tarekat* and *pesantren* networks; bands of gurus and pupils re-emerged from time to time threatening new insurrections.

The impact of the pilgrimage and orthodox Islam in shaping popular opposition to the Dutch-*priyayi* colonial order is clearly demonstrated in other Javanese movements and disturbances, and need not be mentioned individually here. It needs to be stressed, however, that colonial officials tended to exaggerate the Islamic element in the various movements and 'disturbances' they discovered. When, for example, a certain Djasmani was arrested together with his armed band in the residency of Kediri, there was an attempt to link him to the Banten rebellion then raging. Actually, he had absolutely no connection with hajjis or *tarekat*, his aim being to establish a new kingdom and be proclaimed Sunan Hrutjokro or Sultan Adil. Another popular leader, Kasan Mukmin, did visit *pesantren* and famous *kyai* but was not recognized by religious leaders with authority. He was regarded as an ordinary curer (*dukun*), yet to his enthusiastic followers in the 1903 revolt he was an incarnation of Imam Mahdi. There were numerous sectarian movements that had nothing to do with Islam, but were manifestations of a much older search, through Javanese mystical practices (*kebatinan*), for equilibrium and fulfilment in a world gone out of kilter.

The difficulty of neatly classifying Javanese resistance to colonialism shows up in the Samin movement. From about 1890 Surontiko Samin, an illiterate villager, began to attract a following in the Blora regency. No notice was taken of this movement until about 1905, when local officials reported the Saminists' withdrawal from common village activities. More seriously, they either refused to pay taxes or regarded payments as voluntary contributions. They also insulted the local *priyayi* officials by replying in *ngoko* (low Javanese) during interrogation. The government could not quite gain a clear picture of the movement. Samin's teachings were interpreted differently by individual gurus and their followers. There were said to be expectations of a new era and the *ratu adil* or Erutjakra, and Samin himself was to assume the title of *raja* while two followers would get names from *wayang* mythology. But these attributes of a 'typical' Javanese messianic movement were denied by the leaders, and appear rather to have been various readings of the movement's aims by followers or outsiders.

It is clear that the Saminists rejected outside interference, government restrictions and demands, and the money economy. Furthermore, their religious beliefs had much in common with Javanese mystics—such as, for example, their notion of 'God is within me.' But although they did not mount an armed insurrection, their movement was plainly subversive. Whilst their immediate targets appeared to be the *priyayi*, Chinese middlemen, and European officialdom, in a wider sense they were opting out of the whole social order based on the Islamized *abangan* village, with its normalized traditions and hierarchies. They refused the ritual mediation—such as at weddings—of Islamic officials, not out of doctrinal difference but because they eschewed altogether the notion of an official hierarchy.

In a situation wherein new alien ideologies were penetrating the Javanese hinterland, it is not surprising that Christianity, too, would figure in uniquely Javanese forms of protest. Conversion to Christianity, of course, implied submission to Dutch rule in most cases. It was the religion of the Dutch, and conversion was seen as *masuk belanda* ('entering Dutch society'). However, as in the Philippines, Christianity could lead to dissatisfaction with colonial rule and offer an idiom of resistance to it. In 1817 Protestant converts in Maluku (Moluccas) led by an Ambonese Christian soldier, Thomas Matulesia (known as Pattimura), rose against the Dutch; they invoked biblical themes to legitimize their action. In the Batak region, as we shall see, the Christian God was seen as a source of power to counter missionary hegemony. The relative paucity of Christian-inspired protest movements can perhaps be attributed to the Dutch reluctance to allow missionary proselytization, especially in Java. It was only after 1850 that the government reluctantly granted permission to missionary organizations to operate in some residencies.

The most remarkable example of nineteenth-century Javanese adaptation to Christianity and the latter's use as a vehicle of protest was the Sadrach movement in central Java. Sadrach might be regarded as a typical rural religious leader trained in Javanese and Islamic mystic traditions. In the late 1860s, however, he discovered in Christianity a superior *ngelmu* (faith or knowledge). He won a following by displaying his superiority to other gurus. By the 1870s he was regarded as *guru kuasa*, a 'powerful teacher,' as well as a famous healer (*dukun*); he used Christian formulae in addressing his followers. Large groups came under his leadership. Some were of *santri* background, some *abangan*. The gathering of various Christian groups around him partly fitted into the pattern of *guru* and *murid* (teacher and pupil). By 1887 Sadrach's circle involved seventy local and seven regional groups. This congregation was independent of the Christian church, the members being loyal to Sadrach personally as in the case of pupils in a *tarekat*.

Javanese messianic expectations found specific expression among a good number of Sadrach's followers in the *ratu adil*, who was none other than Christ. Sadrach himself was expected to participate in the restoration of Javanese society and the expulsion of foreigners. In fact, Sadrach should be counted as one of several Javanese religious leaders who resisted Dutch dominance—specifically that of the church and the missionary orders—at that time. Eventually he was denounced by Dutch missionaries as a false teacher, and intense efforts were made to integrate him and his flock into the official church.

The Dutch forward movement in Sumatra had begun in Minangkabau in the 1820s, precipitating, as we have seen, the Padri War. In the 1850s and 1860s, Dutch 'pacification' efforts extended to Palembang, Jambi and other small states where opposition to the Dutch and their local allies was fanned by hajjis and local *ulamā*. The Dutch advance northward brought them to Batak country and to Aceh, where the most spirited and long-lived resistance took place.

Batak resistance to colonial rule centred on the Si Singa Mangaraja ('great-king-kind-of-lion') figure. Although Batak traditions acknowledge the existence of such a dynasty, the Si Singa Mangaraja was not normally a political figure among the Batak. He was revered as a divine king and an incarnation of Batara Guru. He had the ability to summon rain and control rice-growing, to drive evil spirits away, and so forth. His main political function was to maintain harmony among the Batak people as well as stable relationships with the outside world. When the Padris spilled over from Minangkabau territory in the 1820s, the tenth Si Singa Mangaraja (Ompu Na Bolon) became the symbol of Toba Batak unity against the intruders.

The economic and political transformation wrought by the Dutch presence in the Toba area tested the power of Si Singa Mangaraja. Also, missionary activity from the 1850s began to divide the local chiefs, some of whom had come to terms with the new religion in order to consolidate and extend their power. Although not personally opposed to the Christian missionaries, Si Singa Mangaraja XI and his son (the twelfth) were pushed by anti-missionary chiefs and Acehnese agents into confrontation with the Dutch. In 1878, Si Singa Mangaraja XII held a religious ceremony to unify his people, and then went off to fight the Dutch in what amounted to a holy war. Defeated, he consolidated his forces and struck again in 1883, with Acehnese aid. This time the Dutch wounded him, destroyed his most important shrine, and drove him off his land. He was killed in a skirmish in 1907.

The Batak, however, believed that the Si Singa Mangarajas did not die but just disappeared. Even upon Si Singa Mangaraja XII's death, his *tona*, (real or imagined commands) and those of his son Raja Buntal were still widely obeyed. Moreover, the call to restoration of this legendary god-king inspired Bataks from all over the region, not just the Toba, to join sects and movements which often turned against Dutch rule. From 1890 on, the Batak region experienced the rise of the Parmalim, Na Siak Bagi and Parhudamdam movements, all proclaiming the restoration of Si Singa Mangaraja's ideal kingdom.

In the Parmalim (from the Batak *malim*, 'to be different from others') movements, Si Singa Mangaraja spoke through various local gurus. However, by this time many Christian concepts and names—God, Jesus and the Virgin Mary being prominent—had entered into the vocabulary of the movement. Although their God was the same as that of the Dutch, the Parmalim preached that they offered a superior means of access to the Supreme Being Jehovah. Parmalim groups refused to accept the terms of subordination imposed by the Dutch government, so from around 1890 various Parmalin gurus promising God's protection and Si Singa Mangaraja's reappearance, were able to gather disaffected Batak around them to protest against the Dutch measures. The inevitable suppression of these movements did not extinguish Parmalim beliefs which, however, underwent revision in an attempt to tap the power of the Europeans. Conversion to Christianity practically decimated its ranks in the early 1900s.

The Na Siak Bagi ('man suffering from misfortune') movement took a slightly different turn. Si Jaga Simatupang, a prominent leader of the later stage of the Parmalim, preached a return to the Toba High God, Muladji Na Bolon, as their source of power. However, this revival was heavily influenced by Christian moral injunctions. Si Jaga, who assumed the name Na Siak Bagi, convinced his followers that the poor and humble were to share in God's power, and that even Si Singa Mangaraja might appear to them in humble garb. By 1910 Na Siak Bagi had attracted a wide following, including a few chiefs, and people came to him for amulets and to undergo rituals of purification. Many thought of him not just as a messenger of their High God, but as a new Si Singa Mangaraja himself. The Dutch, rightly perceiving Na Siak Bagi as a potential focus of rebellion, had him arrested in November of that year.

The only serious challenge to the Dutch consolidation of Sumatra came at the hands of the Acehnese. Aceh was wealthy, organized, well armed, and fully determined to remain independent. The Dutch force that first invaded Kota Raja (Banda Aceh) in 1873 was driven out. And when Kota Raja was finally occupied the following year, the sultan and much of the populace fled to the hills to begin a guerrilla war that formally ended only in the early 1900s. The parallels with Burma after the British capture of Mandalay, or the Philippines after the United States army overran Malolos, are striking. The loss of the capital, the centre, triggers a more bitter and prolonged conflict because charismatic local leaders and their followers enter the fray, releasing the tremendous though often short-lived energies of a populace experiencing a violent transition between two eras. In the Aceh War the familiar themes of pan-Islamism, jihad, millennial expectations and *ulamā* leadership are clearly manifested. Although the Ottomans never really provided the assistance expected of them, their moral support and that of Muslim centres throughout the archipelago sustained the Acehnese through the first two decades of the war. Also, events like the Russo-Turkish War of 1877–8, the Mahdist rebellion in the Sudan, and the passage of a Turkish warship through Singapore in 1890, were perceived as signs of forthcoming success in the protracted jihad.

Clearly, the tenacity of the Acehnese resistance can be attributed to the efforts of the *pesantren*-based *ulamā*, the most distinguished among them being Teungku Cik di Tiro. By the time guerrilla warfare commenced in 1881, he had taken over leadership from the *hulubalang* or *uleebalang* (hereditary chiefs) and their religious officials. The *ulamā* constructed ramparts in the mountains, collected 'holy war contributions', and even succeeded in reconquering areas which were returned to the *hulubalang*. What constituted the basis of their popular appeal? The *ulamā*, who counted among them Arabs of Hadhramaut Sayyid descent, were the links to the reformist and anti-colonial currents in the Islamic world. Committed to the goal of a revitalized Islamic community, they and their pupils lived in perpetual tension with the chiefs and ordinary villagers, who had other visions of their own. It was the circumstances of war that enabled the *ulamā* successfully to draw peasants away from their traditional kinship obligations, in order to unite as Muslims. But even then, what appealed most to the guerrilla fighters was not the image of a community of believers but the fulfilment of their desires in a heavenly existence. As the *Hikayat Prang Sabil* (Epic of the Holy War) put it,

> The blessings of God are unlimited for those who serve,
> who fight the *prang sabi*.
> To those He gives Paradise full of light,
> Seventy heavenly princesses.
> More than can be counted He gives . . .
>   You will get a new face, a young one . . .
> God will give you wealth and life . . .[16]

By 1903 the royal family and the *hulubalang* had been completely subdued. But the guerrilla war continued in the form of attacks by small bands under the guidance or outright leadership of *ulamā*. These *muslimin* (Muslims), as the Acehnese called them, were prepared to die a martyr's death rather than submit to the rule of *kāfir*. It was only in 1913 that the two main centres of resistance were broken, by which time tens of thousands of Acehnese had died in the war. The Dutch attempted to neutralize further outbreaks by propping up the authority of the *hulubalang* as district chiefs, in the same way that they established collaborative ties with the Javanese *priyayi* chiefs and the Minangkabau *penghulus*. At the same time, the *ulamā* were to be restricted to purely religious affairs. This strategy, however, merely deepened the divisions, aggravated by the war, within Acehnese society. Up to the 1930s local *ulamā* continued to attract groups of followers around them. Together they would recite the forbidden *Hikayat Prang Sabil*, take an oath of resistance, and then go off to attack some Dutch outpost. At times, individuals took this path to Paradise by attacking Dutchmen in the towns, a phenomenon the Dutch called *Atjeh-moord*.

Dutch expansion into Kalimantan (Borneo), a response to the growing presence of the Englishman James Brooke and his successor, produced significant resistance in the west and southeast of the island. In 1859 Pangeran Antasari, a prince from a branch of the Banjermasin royal house that had lost out in an internal power struggle, rose against the Dutch and their client ruler. Although major hostilities had ceased by 1863 (Antasari was killed the previous year), the conflict persisted up to 1905. Antasari was fortunate in having by his side a popular peasant leader called Sultan Kuning, who was a healer and practised invulnerability magic. The Banjermasin War was, in fact, another holy war. At one point

---

[16] Cited in James T. Siegel, *The Rope of God*, Berkeley, 75.

the movement's centre was located in a village which was perceived as a transplanted Mecca. Small bands of men armed with charms and cursing the *kāfir* would emerge to attack the Dutch working in the nearby coal mines. Not only did the rebels hope to revive Banjermasin's past glory: they looked to a future without taxes and where all their wishes would be fulfilled.

In the peninsular Malay states the tensions between 'official' and 'rural' Islam which often fuelled anti-colonial resistance in Java and Sumatra was largely absent. The political structures of the small riverine principalities never evolved to such an extent that an elaborate hierarchy of religious officials was ever deemed necessary. Religious authority thus resided largely with whomever among the rural *ulamā* were seen fit to exercise it. By the end of the century, these *ulamā* were being brought into the new religio-legal bureaucracy then developing in the court centres under British protection. This relatively benign reorientation of *ulamā* activity towards the new, British-supervised order may explain the absence of widespread resistance movements in the Malay states. However, it would be a mistake to equate this with universal acceptance of the new system. The relative absence of millennial movements in the Malay peninsula points to a basic problem in dealing with the interconnection of religion and unrest: we only get to know about the subject when it becomes embodied in a movement or disturbance that becomes visible and threatens the state. Rumoured prophecies, visits by itinerant preachers and curers, unprescribed rituals, irreverent language—such manifestations of 'resistance' tend to evade documentation.

At the more visible level, the late-nineteenth-century intensification of the Mecca pilgrimage did have a pronounced impact upon religious life in Malay communities. The spread of *tarekat* such as the Naksyabandiyya and Kadiriah, coupled with pan-Islamic anti-colonial sentiments transmitted via Singapore, ensured the circulation of millennial visions and prophecies in the margins of the Islamic court centres. The potential was there for these images to be drawn upon for religious mobilization against an intruder or overlord. Resistance to Thai suzerainty is a case in point. In the early 1800s, following Siam's conquest of Kedah, a protracted jihad was declared on the Thai infidels. By the turn of the century, the Chakri consolidation of its territorial claims vis-à-vis the British resulted in a redrawing of lines which left Pattani, by 1909, as the only Malay state within the Thai ambit. The incorporation of this famed 'cradle of Islam' into the Thai state beginning in 1902 met with resistance from the disempowered nobility and particularly the *ulamā*. From 1903 *ulamā* and their followers engaged in tax boycotts and other acts of insubordination. In 1910 public offices were burned down by a group led by To'Tae, an elderly mystic claiming invulnerability. The following year, the Thai authorities with difficulty put down another uprising led by a certain Hajji Bula. By far the most widespread uprising occurred in 1922, when *ulamā* successfully appealed for a jihad against the Buddhist régime.

The British success in working gradually through the traditional leadership probably explains why anti-British uprisings were rare in the Malay states. However, there were at least two instances where open conflict, with religious overtones, did break out. One was in Sabah where local opposition to new taxes imposed by the North Borneo Company found expression in Mat Salleh's rebellion which began in 1895 and simmered till 1905, taking on the aspects of a jihad. Mat Salleh's use of Islamic standards as well as symbols of royalty attracted a wide following. To Muslims he was the Mahdi, the coming saviour.

A more significant movement against British control occurred in Pahang. Only grudgingly did the sultan accept the presence of a British Resident, and even then the interior chiefs refused to concede. Things came to a head in 1891 when the Resident persuaded Sultan Ahmad to sign a decree depriving a district chief, Dato Bahaman, of his title. The latter came out in open defiance, initiating a series of armed confrontations known as the Pahang War. Pan-Islamic anti-colonial appeals were in evidence at this point. However, the rebel chiefs always claimed that they were defending the ruler's interests. It was Sultan Ahmad's tacit support that gave the movement much of its initial momentum, attesting to his role as the moral and religious centre of Pahang Malay life. This role subsequently came under threat owing to collaboration with the British. As Sultan Ahmad bowed to British pressure, Bahaman and his allies were perceived as the defenders of their heritage against infidel threats. The rebels came to be influenced by a Terengganu holy man, Ungku Sayyid Paloh, who imbued the movement with the spirit of jihad.

During the second half of the nineteenth century, the Spanish colonial state attempted to establish uniform control over the territory it claimed. In part it had the same problems as the other European powers which were drawing the boundaries of Southeast Asia. The army encountered resistance from some of the semi-independent hill peoples of the northern Luzon Cordillera, while the navy was barely able to capture the Muslim capitals of Jolo and Cotabato. Spanish accounts of the wars in the south, beginning with the campaign against Sulu in 1851, are quite clear about the religious dimension as seen from both sides. As a Dominican friar put it in 1876: 'The war against Jolo is now a just war, a holy war in the name of religion.'[17] The *ulamā* of Sulu, naturally, were proclaiming the same cause, calling for its support as an expression of loyalty to the Sultan. The holy war also raged in Mindanao, where Datu Utto had rallied the Magindanaoan chiefs of the interior against the advancing Spaniards. The independent areas showed many signs of an Islamic revival spearheaded by hajjis and foreign-trained *ulamā*, some of Arab origin. Thus, the Spanish conquest of the major towns meant little to a populace that was becoming ever more conscious of its Islamic identity in the face of a direct Christian assault.

The intensity of Islamic fervour in Mindanao and Sulu was brought home to Spanish soldiers and missionaries through the phenomenon they named *juramentado* ('one who has taken an oath'), known as *sabil ullah* to the Sulus. The *juramentado* were groups of men who fearlessly threw themselves upon companies of Spanish soldiers—or Christian civilians

---

[17] Cited in Cesar A. Majul, *Muslims in the Philippines*, Quezon City, 1973, 292.

in marketplaces—inflicting great damage until each one was killed. Although there are few *pesantren* and no *tarekat* on record in Sulu and Mindanao, a close examination reveals that *juramentados* were groups in the *tarekat* tradition. The adepts underwent a period of fasting and meditation under expert *ulamā* or *pandita*. They were then initiated into the teachings of the *parang sabil* (holy war), and offered a vision of Paradise that they would enter upon death. The *juramentado* phenomenon intensified as the sultans increasingly failed to hold their own against the better-equipped Spaniards.

While the 'Moro Wars' captured headlines in the Manila press, the Spanish establishment was actually more preoccupied with consolidating the Christianized territory they supposedly had held for over 250 years. With the loss of much of America and Spain itself in crisis, the colony had to be economically self-sustaining and potential trouble had to be eliminated. In a sense Manila's problems were the same as Bangkok's. The last of the old royal monopolies were abandoned and various port cities— notably Manila, Iloilo and Cebu—were subsequently opened to international commerce. British, French and United States capital joined up with Spanish and mestizo interests to open new areas to commercial crop cultivation. Such ventures, aided by the new network of ports and roads and the termination of Moro slave-raiding, allowed people in heavily populated areas to migrate to unsettled territory. Unfortunately, few of these pioneers ended up as independent farmers. The funds advanced to them by mestizos and foreigners in order to establish themselves almost certainly dragged them into a cycle of debt, a problem specially acute in the sugar-producing areas. As elsewhere in Southeast Asia where capitalist agriculture took root, peasants took the brunt of declining commodity prices. And as elsewhere, they were increasingly attracted to leaders who promised them a new and better era.

Quite common from the 1860s on were combined police and church actions against illicit gatherings, both in the towns and in the hinterland. What were these proscribed groups up to, and how did religion function in their assertions against the colonial state? Among the dozens of movements discovered in Luzon, let us take just three examples. In 1865 three men addressed at various times by such appellations as *Dios* (God), *Kristo* (Christ) and *Maestro* (Teacher) were reported to be circulating in the Camarines provinces, southeastern Luzon. At secret gatherings in various homes, including a few of the wealthy, people gathered to hear one or the other of the trinity speak about certain doctrines contained in a sacred book. Claiming to have descended from heaven and based on nearby Mount Isarog, they promised to cure sufferers of the cholera and smallpox, relieve the land of locust plagues, and create an abundance of food.

In 1870, the Spanish discovered that a certain Januario Labios had stirred up townspeople around Mount Banahao, in the southern Tagalog region, by claiming to have communicated with the spirit of the dead rebel Apolinario and the Virgin Mary, who had instructed him to rebuild the Cofradía de San José and revive its religious rituals. Those who responded to the call would be rewarded with heavenly bliss in the after-life, but meanwhile they would enjoy independence and freedom from tribute.

Labios, like his model Apolinario, was drawing people away from the town centres toward a 'New Jerusalem'—a complex of sacred caves and springs—in Mount Banahao's foothills. When the police arrested Labios, they found in his possession several notebooks of Tagalog writings about the life of Christ, and some medicinal prescriptions.

The third Luzon example takes us to the provinces north of Manila. Beginning in 1887, Gabino Cortes, a man 'of very small fortune', started to preach to the peasants around Mount Arayat that a worldly catastrophe was imminent. By getting together in small groups to pray and perform communal rituals, they would receive divine protection as well as an abundance of wealth. Considerable numbers of mainly poor peasants from Pampanga and Bulacan provinces gathered in the homes of Cortes's disciples. Since they were dedicated to nonviolence and, after all, recited Christian prayers, the local authorities decided to leave them alone. Gabino, however, was no ordinary lay preacher. Stories circulated that he possessed a magic ball, given to him by an old man on the mountain, with which he could cause money, food, and male attendants to appear. When he was crowned king in 1888, the subversive nature of the movement became all too apparent, and the civil guard moved in to disperse it.

The Visayan islands experienced much the same sorts of assertions against the colonial order. After the great cholera visitation of 1882 and the appearance of a comet in that same year, Spanish officials in Samar and Leyte provinces became preoccupied with a rash of 'disturbances' in inland settlements only recently incorporated into the colonial state. Certain sites—distant from pueblo centres—where images of Catholic saints were venerated for their healing and other miraculous powers, were found to be quartering groups of pilgrims who had come originally to fulfil certain vows made in order to be saved from the cholera. The problem was that these groups of people, who claimed to be there to pray, engage in trade, or merely to satisfy their curiosity, were being won over by itinerant preachers who distributed miraculous cures and prophesied a cataclysm and the coming of a new era.

The rumours that coincided with the appearance of these *Dioses* (Gods) reveal some of the preoccupations of the crowd. Isidro Reyes, who was arrested in early 1884 for promising magical cures, was believed to be a messenger sent by God to announce the coming of a Bisayan king. There was to be a great catastrophe, such as the sinking of the islands or the end of the world. Various groups led by gods or saints armed themselves with primitive weapons and retreated to the hills to await the appearance of a new city ruled by their own king, under a new era in which ancient customs and dress would be revived and the prices of goods would decline. Leaders distributed amulets and magical prayers (*oraciones*) to render protection from enemy bullets and the cholera. In November 1884 three to four hundred rebels attacked Borongan, a major town, but their knives and clubs were no match for Spanish bullets. Police operations, supported by Spanish priests and the local *principales*, continued until 1886.

Just who were these *Dioses*? In the Visayas they were practically identical to the *babaylan*, male and female sorcerers dating back to pre-Spanish society. The *babaylan* had always been around since the conquest, as the shadowy rival of the Catholic priest, attracting people to their haunts beyond the pueblo where they practised their sorcery which in time accommodated many of the symbols and rituals of Catholicism itself— hence their continued attraction to the wider populace. Towards the end of the nineteenth century, the *babaylan* became particularly active among peasants in the islands of Panay and Negros who were suffering from massive indebtedness and from the vagaries of the world economy. Spanish reports of the 1880s, in particular, provide the identities of dozens of men and women arrested for gathering people into 'illicit associations' which practised illegal curing and sorcery, refused to pay taxes, and so on.

Among those with more substantial documentation is Ponciano Elofre, better known as Buhawi (Waterspout, God of the Four Winds), who attracted Spanish attention in 1887 when people from all the towns along the southeastern coast of Negros started trekking to his independent community in the adjacent mountains. Buhawi had all the trappings of a *babaylan*: curing powers, invulnerability, the power to change shape, command of fire, flood and rain. Lest these attributes be regarded in some sort of binary opposition to Christianity, there is also strong evidence that Buhawi had been a devout Catholic, fond of religious processions, and never without a cross hung around his neck. Buhawi's massive following originated as a small, private novena prayer group, which expanded as word spread about his special powers and talents. But there was something else about his message that was attractive: his prediction that the world would be destroyed by a great flood and cast into utter darkness. Those who did not heed his call would perish. Thus Buhawi also came to be called 'The Redeemer' by his followers.

Like the 'holy man' phenomenon in Siam, the movements described above were centred on extraordinary religious leaders: preachers, prophets, gods and Kristos. Their utterances circulated among a populace familiar with traditional animist practices, as well as with figures in the Old and New Testaments who bridged the gap between the divine and human planes of existence. The millennial strains are evident: these men and women pointed to a coming change of era, as heralded by such signs as epidemics (particularly the cholera), comets, and hardships caused by a collapse in the world sugar price.

As the century wore on, the Spanish pueblos themselves became the sites of unrest. While undoubtedly the majority of Spanish priests outside the friar estates continued to be respected, if not revered, the continued ejection of Filipino priests provoked racial tensions that would grow to national proportions. In 1862, there were only twelve parishes left for some 400 secular priests, mainly Filipinos. Brief periods of liberal government, coupled with the influx of the ideas of the Enlightenment specially after the opening of the Suez Canal, accelerated the demands of the native priests for equality. Spanish reaction was firm and unrelenting, from surveillance in the late 1860s to the actual execution of three reformist priests in 1872.

The inadvertent creation of a triad of Filipino martyr-priests gave a more 'national' focus to the popular movements that followed. Even the above-mentioned *Dioses* movements in the Visayas called on followers to pray for the soul of one of the slain priests, Father Burgos. The involvement of ordained priests in some of these religio-political movements is clear, if not yet fully documented. Certainly Filipino priests would be actively involved in the massive rebellion of 1896, and in the resistance to United States occupation from 1899 their behind-the-scenes exhortations would produce comparisons with Indian medicine men.

The rebellion of the Katipunan (Highest and Most Venerable Association of the Offspring of the Land) in 1896 is usually seen as the climax of a liberal awakening, when Enlightenment ideas imbibed by Europeanized Filipino intellectuals since the 1880s finally became translated into a mass movement. When viewed 'from below', however, the religious dimension of this movement is unmistakeable. In exhorting the lower classes to participate, the Katipunan leadership juxtaposed events of colonial history with biblical images of the Fall from Eden; joining the rebellion was interpreted as a redemptive act; the rallying cry *kalayaan* ('liberty') reverberated with meanings of a return to a condition of wholeness and prosperity. Furthermore, the execution in December 1896 of the celebrated propagandist Dr José Rizal gave the movement a martyr to focus on. Rizal's own words and behaviour ensured that his final hours would be interpreted in terms of Christ's passion and death, a story familiar to every Christianized Filipino. And sure enough the image of a 'Filipino Christ' was seized upon equally by the revolutionary leadership and independent sectarian leaders. Henceforth, Rizal would be incarnated in many a peasant rebel leader until well into the next century.

By 1897 the Katipunan uprising was widely interpreted as a sign of an impending change of eras. True, the pueblo élites in all but a few provinces around Manila remained aloof from the fray or loyal to Spain. But, significantly, all over the islands those illicit associations in the peripheries of the pueblo centres re-emerged to fight the Spaniards. The descendants of the Cofradia on Mount Banahao—now the 'Katipunan of San Cristobal'—with their saints and magical ropes, attacked the Spanish garrison at Tayabas. The movement of Gabino Cortes resurrected as the Santa Iglesia of Felipe Salvador. The followers of Buhawi became a Katipunan under the leadership of Papa (Pope) Isio. One movement—the Guardia de Honor—originally recruited to defend friar interests against the 1898 republic, became imbued with millennial expectations and was broken up by the Americans. Movements such as these led by prophets, saints and curers certainly saw the war years as part of the great cataclysm preceding the end of the world. By the end of the century, then, the religio-political movements of earlier decades had largely reappeared as 'nationalist' ones. Yet they remained distinct from, and subversive of, the 1898 republican order and the mainstream independence movements during United States rule.

The wars of conquest now largely over, the early twentieth century is generally viewed as a new period marked by various manifestations of the 'modern'. The privileged native actors are now the urban-educated élites speaking the languages of progress and national unity. The organizations which they established are readily contrasted with the more 'traditional' and 'backward-looking' movements characteristic of the previous century. Yet the latter continued to thrive in their rural environments during the period of high colonialism. Not only that, but the course of 'modern' movements was profoundly shaped by older terrains and discourses.

As the Americans discovered in the aftermath of the Philippine war (1899–1902), military victory and the co-optation of the élite did not terminate the event called 'the revolution'. Macario Sakay, a veteran of the Katipunan secret society and sometime actor in passion plays, continued the resistance in Luzon until 1906. Priests of the Philippine Independent (Aglipayan) Church which had broken off from Rome in 1902, preached on the theme of the 'unfinished revolution' to congregations which continued to grow through the 1910s. In Aglipayan and other sectarian churches throughout the islands there evolved a religious iconography which juxtaposed Christian and revolutionary figures. A messianic figure was generated in 1910 when the exiled General Artemio Ricarte promised to return with the aid of the Mikado's fleet, bringing independence. Secret societies allegedly under Ricarte's direction attempted to rise upon the outbreak of the Great War in 1914.

Among the most effective resistance leaders of this period were the curers, sorcerers and sectarian preachers of old who now promised to obtain that magical condition called 'independence'. In the Visayas, Papa Otoy and Papa Isio held out until 1907. Felipe Salvador, variously hailed as king, pope or Christ by his peasant followers, continued his proselytizing in central Luzon until his capture in 1910 after he had occupied a town in the belief that the appearance of Halley's Comet signalled the advent of independence. But, after Salvador's execution, others readily filled the void. The proliferation of rural sects went largely unnoticed until the early 1920s when police fought skirmishes with sectarians led by a preacher known as Lantayug, who claimed to be a reincarnation of Rizal. Thousands of peasants from the eastern Visayas and northern Mindanao had converged on the island of Bucas Grande, where the 'Eternal City' was to emerge after the holocaust. The sect refused to pay taxes, rejected the Catholic Church, and threatened to confiscate the property of the rich. A similar set of events unfolded in Negros and Panay where, in 1921, Flor Yntrencherado declared himself Emperor of the Philippines, as well as a reincarnation of the martyred priest José Burgos and a successor to the patriots of 1898. Like all the others, Yntrencherado vowed to finish the revolution and realize the utopian dream of 'independence'.

The situation was little different elsewhere in Southeast Asia. In Burma the *pongyi* largely ignored or resisted government attempts to institutionalize a system of monastic schools wherein English subjects would be grafted onto the traditional, mainly religious, curriculum. The British thought the 'backward' *kyaung*, or village schools, to be the losers, since the brightest and most ambitious students gravitated towards government and mission schools. On the other hand, this meant that from 1900 to 1920 the *kyaung* remained largely free of state interference. Peasants circulating through them continued to be reminded of the impermanence of alien rule and the return of kings who would protect Buddhism and restore unity and prosperity. Another locus of resistance was the semi-secret sect or *gaing*, where *weikza* and *saya* practised the traditional arts of sorcery and curing, powers which made them potential 'embryo kings' or *min-laung*. The Filipino Rizals and popes had their Burmese equivalents in *min-laung* and Setkya-mins—such as the *min-laung Buddhayasa*, Nga Myin, who in 1907 attacked the police station at Sedaw, or the *min-laung* Maung Than who underwent the ceremony of accession in 1910 and forthwith attempted to attack Shwebo. Rumours periodically surfaced of *min-laung* prophecies, and the police had to break up crowds gathering at sites where the birth or the return of a king was expected.

The Dutch administrators were no less preoccupied with 'disturbances' in their domains. The *ulamā*-led resistance in Aceh continued to smoulder through to the 1920s. In west Sumatra the *guru tarekat* and mystics, heirs to the Padris, were largely behind the anti-tax rebellions of 1914. Between 1915 and 1917 the Batak countryside again responded to leaders bearing the potent title 'Si Singa Mangaraja', but this time drawing inspiration from Islamic prayer and purification rituals. The Parhudamdam, as this latest Batak movement was called, urged a holy war against the Dutch, yet was entirely separate from other Islamic movements of the time. Java, of course, had its fair share of unrest centring on expectations of the *ratu adil*. Kyai Dermadjaja was typical: an itinerant santri who received mystical training in various *pesantren*, attracted a circle of disciples, and proclaimed himself *ratu adil* in 1907. His followers went bravely to battle expecting the *wayang* figures Togog and Semar to aid them, just as in the Philippines the aid of heroes of *awit* (metrical romance), Bernardo Carpio and Don Juan Tiñoso, was invoked during the revolution.

Similar hopes for the restoration of ideal kingship animated Vietnamese popular movements, particularly in the south. Despite the French hold over the court, it continued to provide signs that the cosmic order it represented would return. In 1912 the Confucian revolutionary Phan Boi Chau, who had earlier canvassed the sentiments of sectarian preachers in the Mekong delta, founded the monarchist 'Revival Society' (Quang Phuc Hoi) and formed an interim revolutionary government with exiled Prince Cuong De at the helm. In 1915 the prince's army moved out from bases in China to attack some towns in the north, but was badly defeated. The following year, the young Emperor Duy Tan, heeding the advice of a Taoist scholar, mounted a coup against the French which quickly ended with his arrest in a Buddhist temple south of Hué. Duy Tan was, in fact, just one of three Vietnamese emperors who were deposed and exiled by the French between 1885 and 1926. Such gestures of resistance were of immense significance to villagers looking to the old centre for sustenance and hope.

Not surprisingly, peasant rebels in the Mekong delta responded to the monarchist signals in their own way. As in Burma, the de facto absence of the emperor opened up the field to any pretender promising a new order. Around 1912 a mystic and healer, known as Phan Xich Long (Phan the Red Dragon) and claiming to be a descendant of deposed emperor Ham Nghi, called for an overthrow of the French, precipitating an attack on Saigon in 1913 by his white-garbed followers. In 1916 the delta experienced another wave of rebellions, this time centred on the monk Bay Do who lived on

Forbidden Mountain. Whether or not there was a connection with Emperor Duy Tan's coup, as the French suspected, the Maitreya myth
circulating at this time certainly presumed a monarchical order: 'How have
you paid the Four Debts since you have not even fulfilled a tenth of your
duties? How can you pretend to be faithful toward the King and toward
your father and mother? . . .'[18]

In a sense, the colonial wars of the previous century had never ended.
The ethos of resistance continued to be nurtured in concealment, taking
the shape of uprisings only when the state excessively intruded into village
life, or when signs of cataclysmic change appeared—Halley's Comet, the
Great War, the Great Depression, or even something local like the major
flood of 1926 in Terengganu or the 1927 eruption of Mount Canlaon
in Negros. Rizal and other heroes of the revolution were worshipped
in sectarian chapels from Mount Banahao in Luzon to Bucas Grande in
Mindanao. From Shwebo in central Burma emerged a series of embryo
kings who urged non-payment of taxes and attacks on British government
offices. As late as the mid-1930s photos of the deposed Emperor Duy
Tan were being venerated in a temple on Forbidden Mountain. Mang-
gadua in downtown Batavia—the very heart of the Dutch empire—was
the locus of saint worship focused on holy graves which served as the
catalyst of certain *ratu adil* movements. These sites were part of extensive
circuits of communication traversed by troubadour singers, seekers of
esoteric knowledge, itinerant curers and fortune tellers, and ordinary
pilgrims. At certain junctures flourished secret societies, cults, peasant
associations, and circles of teachers and followers where 'independence'
or 'freedom' was experienced in communal relationships, mutual help
arrangements, the practice of martial arts, religious rituals, and the like.
Even entire villages, usually under the sway of anti-colonial *pongyi*, *kyai*, or
priests, could be sites of hidden resistance.

In most, if not all, of these cases, the emergence of a righteous and
just leader was the catalyst of rebellion. The past had been mythologized
as a condition in which society revolved around ideal kings and selfless
patriots. Popular hopes of their reappearance signified the lack of a
spiritual centre, a source of power, in an age of economic dislocation and
alien rule. One would, therefore, expect to encounter fewer instances
of popular anti-colonial movements in. societies where the monarchies
retained their vitality, as in Siam and, to a lesser extent, Cambodia and the
Malay states.

The ghosts of a lost past certainly did not haunt the Thai kings, who
successfully assumed the roles of protector of religion, helmsman of the
state, and national talisman. Vajiravudh, in a 1911 speech, saw himself as
possessor of the power of the nation, using it for the benefit and happiness
of everyone. To the Thai peasant, such statements only confirmed the
view that the king was the fount of merit and energy. Even the occasional
Thai-led *phuwiset* rebellion, such as that which occurred near Saraburi,
north of Bangkok, in 1925 did not challenge the centrality of the monarch:
it was to him that the rebel leader Ai Kan presented his grievances, all

18 Cited in Hue Tam Ho Tai, 75.

stemming from foreign interference in Siam's economic life and religion. More extensive *phumibun*-led movements there certainly were, but these developed in the northeastern provinces where artificial boundary lines had pushed into the Thai sphere peoples who naturally looked to Vientiane. Thus during the 1924, 1933 and 1936 uprisings the coming of the Maitreya was seen as a prelude to the re-establishment of a Lao kingdom.

Like their Thai counterparts, the Cambodian kings continued to be the symbols of national identity, protectors of Buddhism and, at the village level, semi-divine figures. But French protection was bound to exact its price. Excessive colonial demands on corvée labour and taxation particularly from 1912 on, spawned rural unrest which peaked in 1916 when tens of thousands of peasant demonstrators converged on Phnom Penh, compelling King Sisowath to address angry crowds outside his palace. Later, he travelled through the most disturbed rural areas by automobile in order to evidence his power and reassure the population. Not unlike Norodom during the 1885 rising, Sisowath by his royal presence managed to calm the protesters, for it was *Luong*, the king, and not the French from whom they expected relief. But where the royal gaze failed to reach, there were attacks on plantations, government offices, and foreigners. As in the past, monks and holy men were often the instigators of such actions. Predictably, the southeast provinces were almost certainly 'disturbed' by holy men with links to the sects based across the border in Cochin-China. In fact, in 1927 thousands of Cambodian peasants were reported to have trekked to the Cao Dai centre at Tay Ninh—before the French closed the border—in order to prostrate themselves before a statue of a prince on a white horse whose imminent reincarnation would mark the renewal of the Cambodian kingdom. There were expectations, after all, of a saviour-king who would replace the pro-French one at Phnom Penh!

The nature of British protection—non-interference in religion and custom, encouragement of courtly grandeur—meant that the world of the Malay sultans and their subjects remained largely intact. Peasants, furthermore, were shielded from the export economy and its concomitant dislocations through the importation of Chinese and Indian labour. But there were limits to peasant toleration of colonial demands, and to the restraining influence of the sultan and his entourage of Islamic officials. The 1915 uprising at Kelantan began on the fringes of the sultan's authority where hajjis and imams—representing non-official Islam—continued to exercise local leadership. The rebels sought the expulsion of foreigners and a change in the tax system. They were emboldened by the conviction that Britain was losing the war in Europe, and by the fact that their leader Hajji Mat Hassan, alias To' Janggut, was *keramat*—a holy man armed with supernatural powers. Neighbouring Terengganu experienced even more intense conflict a decade later. In the upriver regions, rural religious teachers, *sayyid* (descendants of the Prophet) and *keramat* persons had always provided an alternative focus to the sultanate in times of crisis. Thus when a peasant revolt, provoked by new land restrictions, erupted in 1928 it was framed in terms of a holy war against the *kāfir*. A new sultan and other officials would replace those who had become colonial servants or *orang neraka*, people of hell, as one Hajji Drahman put it.

Thus far we have looked at protest movements originating in older sites of unrest and opposition to the centre. But one obvious phenomenon of the early twentieth century was the emergence of urban-based leaders and movements with increasingly strident nationalist voices. Colonial régimes, in their liberal phases at least, considered sectoral representation in their fledgling Assemblies and Legislative Councils an important aspect of native progress and encouraged or at least condoned it within limits. The new, educated élites, on the other hand, grabbed these opportunities to voice their aspirations. Now in appealing for unity through their newspapers and rallies, urban organizers soon found themselves grappling with, and usually drawn into, more deeply rooted idioms of change. In the Philippines by 1909, Partido Nacionalista stalwarts Manuel Quezon and Sergio Osmena had become adept at tapping memories of the 1896 revolution and transposing this to the electoral struggle. When the Sarekat Islam first began to spread throughout Java in 1913, its most eminent propagandist, Oemar Said Tjokroaminoto, used familiar images from the *wayang* and Islam to call for native solidarity in the attainment of progress and equality with the Dutch. In Burma during the 1920s, the urban leaders of the General Council of Burmese Associations (GCBA), backed by the General Council of Sangha Samaggi (GCSS, the monks' association), took their message to the countryside, forming rural nationalist associations called *wunthanu athin*. In writings and speeches directed to village audiences, references to the life and teachings of the Buddha were regularly interspersed with the *wunthanu* political message.

Partido Nacionalista, Sarekat Islam and GCBA rallies were huge and colourful affairs. Politicians and organizers spoke of progress and unity, harangued against discrimination and unfair laws; there was talk of 'freedom', '*kemerdekaan*', '*independencia*' and the like. To the illiterate majority in attendance what often registered were images of Paradise, the earthly nirvana (*lokka nibban*), a just and moral order, a world in perfect harmony with Heaven's laws, a future with no taxes and no corvée labour. The drifts of meaning often turned millennial: imminent independence, the 'Djayabaya prophecy' concerning a Javanese liberator, the restoration of Burmese kingship. As these memorable rallies became the subject of rumours, the politicians themselves were seen in an entirely different light. Tjokroaminoto was thought to be none other than Prabu Heru Tjokro, the awaited *ratu adil*. Quezon, arriving from the United States in 1916 after having lobbied successfully for eventual self-rule, was hailed as the redeemer bringing independence. U Chit Hlaing, the GCBA president, was followed around by adherents holding aloft a golden umbrella, and was greeted by peasants with a royally caparisoned elephant.

The legal mass movements, of course, were in no position to sanction moves that might actually subvert the political status quo. Quezon and Tjokroaminoto—in close contact with their colonial patrons and advisers—were anxious to prevent popular energies from diverting their organizations from the goals of native progress *cum* loyalty to the mother country. Furthermore, participation in colonial politics promised a stable career and personal rewards to the bulk of the new, Western-educated élites. Certainly, in the Philippines campaigning for independence did not preclude the accumulation of wealth. In Burma many prominent leaders of the central GCBA soon stood for election to the Legislative Council, effectively quitting their roles in boycott and non-cooperation activities. Even the rehabilitated Buddhist primate—now an ally of the British— tried in vain to prevent *pongyi* from engaging in political agitation. Thus, while politicians generally capitalized on millennial expectations to win the crowds, their actions tended to fall short of their words and this made them vulnerable to criticism from radicals who also employed religious ideas in their arguments.

A blistering critique of the politicians Quezon, Roxas and Osmena runs through the literature of Philippine peasant movements from the Ricartistas of the 1910s to the Sakdal of the 1930s. The tapping of revolutionary memories in electoral campaigns had its limits, since peasant leaders from Pedro Calosa in Luzon to Lantayug in Mindanao were doing the same thing in claiming to be messengers or outright reincarnations of Rizal and Bonifacio. The difference is that, consistent with the careers of past heroes, they lived out their convictions by defying the state. As Calosa put it, they rebelled in 1931 in order to show the Americans that there was 'no town, no matter how small, without *real* people'.[19] 'Real' meant, as the Sakdalistas repeatedly stated, having a *loob* (inner being) that matched the *labas* (externalities). Quezon and company were 'accused' (*sakdal*) of hypocrisy rather than genuine inner commitment. 'The leader of a subject country', the newspaper *Sakdal* declared, 'should be the first in making the sacrifice ... No liberty was ever obtained happily ... nobody ever triumphed without passing over Golgotha and being nailed at the cross of Calvary.'[20]

Tjokroaminoto, as well, came under attack for his personal ambitions and alleged mismanagement of funds. A more serious charge was made in the early 1920s by militants, some prominent *ulamā* and *kyai* among them, that the Partai Sarekat Islam, Central Sarekat Islam, and Muhammadiyah were merely using the appeal to Islamic unity in order to camouflage their retreat from the struggle. Hajji Mohammad Misbach, a leading *pesantren*-educated *muballigh* (Islamic propagandist), in his attacks drew a distinction between *Islam sedjati* (true Islam) and *Islam lamisan* (pseudo-Islam), or between *mukmin* (the faithful) who sacrifice everything for God and *munafik* (hypocrites) whose claim to be *mukmin* is only for show. Islamic propagandists in Banten, Minangkabau, Aceh, and Terengganu echoed the same refrain.

At the local branches of the Partido Nacionalista, Sarekat Islam and GCBA, the programmes of the central organizations were not necessarily adhered to. Strikes and demonstrations were mounted without official permission by more radical leaders, who eventually gravitated towards less compromising organizations like the Democrata, Indische, and of course the Socialist and Communist parties. Some of the branches were really secret societies and sects which had adopted the forms of the 'modern' organizations. Such was the case with Thet Kywe, leader of eleven *wunthanu athin*, who proclaimed himself the Setkya min-laung in 1922.

---

[19] Pedro Calosa interview, in David R. Sturtevant, *Popular Uprisings in the Philippines, 1840–1940*, Ithaca, 1976, 274.
[20] Cited in *Tribune*, 12 May 1935; copy in the US National Archives, file 4865–93, BIA.

It could be the other way around, of course: Western-educated radicals used traditional forms to gain a mass following. In 1927 the French-educated lawyer Nguyen An Ninh started to organize peasants in his home province of Gia Dinh, using rituals and oaths patterned after the Heaven and Earth secret society, and promising a more equitable sharing of wealth. By 1928 he had attracted a sizeable following made up of people who commonly joined sects. To his dismay, however, he found that some members wanted to become mandarins, and he himself was venerated as a divine figure. The French, nonetheless, tagged the movement as 'communistic' and suppressed it. A similar experience befell Patricio Dionisio, a Filipino lawyer and journalist who in 1927 formed a patriotic society to propagate, through legal means, the goals of the 1896 hero Andres Bonifacio. His rhetoric was akin to that which pervaded Partido Nacionalista rallies, yet by reviving the rituals and symbols of the Katipunan secret society Dionisio struck a chord among peasants all over Luzon during the Depression years. By 1931 Dionisio's attempts to restrain his Tanggulan Society proved futile; talk of armed rebellion prevailed and the inevitable arrests followed. With the dissolution of the Tanggulan, most of the members simply drifted towards other, rising groups such as the Sakdal, Socialist and Communist parties which also spoke of the 'unfinished revolution' and the 'new era' on the horizon.

The success of Socialist and Communist parties in establishing mass memberships from the mid-1920s on can be attributed to the 'adaptationists' among the organisers who allowed party principles to be carried by 'traditional', mainly religious, idioms of protest. The extremely popular *Pasyon of the Workers* (or 'Red Pasyon'), for example, composed in the mid-1930s by Socialist Party member Lino Dizon, used the story of Christ's life and death as a springboard for an attack on wealthy landlords, the government, the institutional church, and capitalism. In Java and Sumatra, which witnessed widespread PKI (Partai Komunis Indonesia) rebellions in 1926–7, a turning point was reached when Islamic teachers like Hajji Misbach and Hajji Achmad Chatib embraced the cause. They preached that the trials devised by God in this day and age took two forms: capitalism, which promoted greed and distance from God, and imperialism, which threatened the world of Islam. Interspersing their arguments with Koranic passages, they stressed the religious meaning—proving one's faith—of resisting the *kāfir* government and its local allies. To the dismay of doctrinaire party leaders, the *ulamā* even called for the holy war to be waged, since capitalism was seen as being no different from Satan. But such 'excesses' had to be tolerated, for the hajjis, *ulamā* and *kyai* who preached revolution were highly respected—some even revered for their secret knowledge. In Aceh, Minangkabau and Banten, the mosque, *tarekat*, and *pesantren* became—as in the past—centres of revolutionary activity.

The Indochina Communist Party (ICP) also succeeded in organizing large numbers of peasants in the 1930s and thereafter. The cultural explanation for this is not hard to find: peasants accustomed to sorcerers or holy men predicting the future decreed by heaven did not have much trouble accepting the Marxist notion of a historical process that would guarantee victory to the revolutionaries. After all, this was the teaching of cadres who behaved in a manner reminiscent of the village Confucian scholars, whether in crusading against corruption, displaying a superior morality, or practising stoicism in the face of adversity. The mandate of heaven was envisioned as passing from class to class rather than from dynasty to dynasty; images of the civilizing action of this mandate even pervaded the language that articulated the notion of 'socializing landed property' (*xa hoi hoa*). In the Mekong delta, where Confucianism had been weak, the apostles of the Buu Son Ky Hong and other folk Buddhist sects, and to a lesser extent the Cao Dai, had nonetheless paved the way for some communist successes. Decades of anti-colonial agitation and periodic expectations of the Maitreya had made the sectarians receptive to suggestions of violent and total change, in the aftermath of which would emerge a society without greed, taxes and alien rulers.

The establishment of communist organizations over older terrains of rebellion meant that the ensuing uprisings tended to take on a life of their own. The rebellions in Java and Sumatra by all appearances were fought as jihads and *parang sabil* by peasants nursing their red party membership cards like precious amulets. The arrests of key PKI organisers in Banten throughout 1925–6 meant that when the revolt started in November 1926, the *ulamā*, aided by men of prowess called *juwara*, were indeed the *only* leaders around. The revolt took on meanings quite different from what the party intended; *kemerdekaan* meant freedom from taxes, but it could also signify the establishment of an Islamic state, or the restoration of the old sultanate. Like their poorly armed compatriots in Minangkabau, Aceh, and elsewhere, the Banten rebels were mowed down by Dutch reinforcements. The defeats everywhere testified both to the firepower of the state and the failure of Communist Party policy. But from another perspective, the outcome was not unexpected; the rebels were, as the Acehnese put it, *muslimin*—men who had put their faith in God and died a martyr's death.

There was a similar slippage between the party and the mass membership in the Nghe-Tinh 'soviet' movement of 1930–1. All sorts of contradictory actions were taken in the name of socialism. The ICP had to admit its difficulties in dealing with 'superstitions and anachronistic customs' in Nghe-Tinh itself. In the south, the communist cadres guiding fraternal organizations called 'Committees of Action' found it next to impossible to extinguish millennial expectations among the rank and file. As soon as government repression began to take its toll in 1931, peasants abandoned the committees and sought refuge in the sects. When a charismatic figure in Huynh Phu So appeared, the committees in traditional Buu Son Ky Hong areas practically turned over their mass membership to the Hoa Hao sect.

In the context of what was happening elsewhere in Southeast Asia, the 1931 Saya San rebellion does not seem to be all that 'fantastic' and 'backward'. Saya San was the perfect leader of a Burmese mass movement. He had been an itinerant fortune teller, curer (*se saya*), *gaing* member, practitioner of invulnerability magic, and sometime *pongyi*, before joining the GCBA in 1924. In other words, he had traversed the older terrain of resistance before joining a modern organization. His concerns in the GCBA focused on the rural miseries caused by taxes and police abuses.

Like other truly committed activists elsewhere in Southeast Asia, he witnessed with dismay the abandonment of militant action by the élite— the central GCBA leaders in this instance—prodding him to form his own Galon association to resist the collection of head tax. By 1930 the ingredients of a mass uprising were all there: unbearable taxes, plummeting paddy prices, a great earthquake that shook lower Burma in May. A great cataclysm was about to happen, and Saya San stepped in to fulfil the scenario. He proclaimed himself a *min-laung* and, subsequently, Setkya-min; he adopted the whole paraphernalia of kingship, the most significant of which was the building of a palace to serve as the new centre, the source of potency of the realm. Once the rebellion was launched in December 1931, it spread rapidly and without much central control over twelve of Burma's twenty districts, with *pongyi* and *saya* making up the bulk of local leadership. This was no longer just a tax revolt, but a holy war against the enemies of Buddhism and the monarchy. Aeroplanes and machine guns were needed to turn the tide of rebellion in mid-1931, by which time around 1300 rebels had been killed.

It could be said that Saya San was merely turning back the clock, that his revolt was disorganized, ill equipped and doomed to failure. But such a verdict is based on a certain view of what constitutes success, and involves locating the rebellion within a linear history that moves towards our 'modern' present. Alternatively, the rebellion can be understood in its own terms—as a religious experience, perhaps, or an intense moment in the lives of its participants. In this light, we might ponder the meaning of that memorable event during the Banten 'communist' rebellion, when five hundred poorly armed rebels emerged from the Labuan mosque dressed entirely in white, except for a black-clothed septuagenarian waving a flag bearing a quotation from the Koran: 'With God's help everything can be achieved.'[21] Little, in fact, separates these rebels from Salud Algabre, a Sakdal organizer in Cabuyao, who said of her experience in the 1935 rebellion: 'That was the moment. Everything led up to the uprising. That was the high point of our lives. . . . No uprising fails. Each one is a step in the right direction.'[22]

BIBLIOGRAPHIC ESSAY

Several comparative and theoretical studies of rebellion have made extensive use of Southeast Asian materials. The earliest example of this, written in 1965, is Harry Benda, 'Peasant movements in colonial Southeast Asia', in *Continuity and Change in Southeast Asia*, New Haven: Yale University Southeast Asia Studies, 1972. The Saya San rebellion and the Nghe Tinh soviets are case studies in James Scott, *The Moral Economy of the Peasant*, New Haven, 1976. In neither work is the role of religion particularly noted. However, Scott explores the culture of popular protest in 'Protest and profanation: Agrarian revolt and the Little Tradition', *Theory and Society*, 4, 1–2 (1977). And Michael Adas, *Prophets of Rebellion*, Chapel Hill, 1979,

---

21 In Michael C. Williams, *Sickle and Crescent: The Communist Revolt of 1926 in Banten*, Ithaca: Cornell Modern Indonesia Project, 1982, 55.
22 Algabre interview, in Sturtevant, 296, 299.

underlines the importance of millennial visions for the Diponegoro and Saya San rebellions.

That peasant consciousness and ritual action can be given at least equal play in a Marxist analysis is demonstrated in Andrew Turton and Shigeharu Tanabe, eds, *History and Peasant Consciousness in South East Asia*, Osaka: National Museum of Ethnology, 1984. Here, Tanabe uses the 1889–90 Chiengmai rebellion as a case study of peasant ideological practice. Other relevant chapters are Chatthip Nartsupha's on the ideology of 'Holy Men' revolts; Masaya Shiraishi's on rural unrest in early Nguyen Vietnam; and Joel Kahn's on the 1927 communist uprising in west Sumatra.

The best introductions to the religio-political terrain of the Buddhist states are Stanley Tambiah, *The Buddhist Saints of the Forest and the Cult of Amulets*, Cambridge, UK, 1984, and Charles Keyes *The Golden Peninsula*, New York, 1977. For Thailand, specifically, see Yoneo Ishii, *Sangha, State and Society: Thai Buddhism in History*, trans. Peter Hawkes, Honolulu, 1986. On Buddhism and popular religion in Burma, see Melford Spiro, *Buddhism and Society*, 2nd edn, Berkeley, 1982; and E. Michael Mendelson, *Sangha and State in Burma*, Ithaca, 1975.

Other studies of the 'Holy Man' rebellions besides Chatthip Natsupha's are Ishii, *Sangha*, ch. 9; John Murdoch, 'The 1901–1902 Holy Man's rebellion', JSS, 42, 1 (1974); and Charles Keyes, 'Millennialism, Theravada Buddhism, and Thai society', JAS, 36, 2 (1977). For the Laotian side of these rebellions see Francois Moppert, 'Le révolte des Bolovens', in Pierre Brocheux, ed., *Histoire de L'Asie du Sud-est: Révoltes, Réformes, Révolutions*, Lille, 1981. Popular perceptions of Khru Ba Siwichai are examined in Charles Keyes, 'Death of two Buddhist saints in Thailand', *Journal of the American Academy of Religion*, Thematic Studies, 48, 3–4 (1982).

Accounts of the Burmese resistance to British-Indian occupation tend to be dominated by British perspectives. Nonetheless, some useful introductions are John Cady, *A History of Modern Burma*, Ithaca, 1958; and Trevor Ling, *Buddhism, Imperialism and War*, London, 1979. The millennial aspects are best brought out in the sympathetic study by Emmanuel Sarkisyanz, *Buddhist Backgrounds of the Burmese Revolution*, The Hague, 1965. Ni Ni Myint, *Burma's Struggle Against British Imperialism, 1885–1895*, Rangoon, 1983, further uncovers the Burmese side of the story.

Sarkisyanz, *Buddhist Backgrounds*, is still the most illuminating work on Burmese religion and nationalism. Donald Smith, *Religion and Politics in Burma*, Princeton, 1965, is more lucid but overly dwells on Burmese Buddhism's failure to adjust to the 'modern' world. A wealth of information, though skewed towards the élites, is found in U Maung Maung, *From Sangha to Laity: Nationalist Movements of Burma, 1920–1940*, Canberra: Australian National University Monographs on South Asia, 1980. The Saya San rebellion finds a place in all of the abovementioned works. Patricia Herbert's paper, 'The Hsaya San rebellion (1930–1932) reappraised', Clayton: Monash University Centre of Southeast Asian Studies, 1982, portrays Saya San as less of a *minlaung* than a mainstream nationalist, but for an opposing view see T. Ito, 'Pre-Saya San peasant uprisings in colonial Burma', paper presented to the 31st International Congress of Human Sciences, Tokyo, 1983.

The tradition/revolution nexus in Vietnam is succintly presented in Keyes, *Golden Peninsula*. Paul Mus's seminal ideas on the subject can be gleaned from John McAlister and Paul Mus, *The Vietnamese and their Revolution*, New York, 1970. If one can ignore its dated exaltation of scientific thinking, the chapter on Confucianism and Marxism in Nguyen Khac Vien, *Tradition and Revolution in Vietnam*, Berkeley: Indochina Resource Center, 1974, is an excellent introduction to the culture of the scholar-gentry class. Alexander Woodside sensitively reflects upon the modern transformation of this élite in *Community and Revolution in Modern Vietnam*, Boston, 1976, which marks a pinnacle of sorts in wartime attempts to understand the Vietnamese 'enemy' on its own terms.

The limits of state control in Nguyen Vietnam are analysed in Masaya Shiraishi's chapter in Turton and Tanabe, as well as in Hue Tam Ho Tai, *Millenarianism and Peasant Politics in Vietnam*, Cambridge, Mass., 1983. The latter is a fascinating study of the persistence of the Buu Son Ky Hong tradition, in the light of which Vietnamese—and to some extent Cambodian—anti-colonial movements are reassessed. A more top-down approach is taken in David Marr's indispensable sourcebook, *Vietnamese Anticolonialism, 1885–1925*, Berkeley, 1971. Most of the abovementioned works address the vital but problematic relationship between the communist movement and more deeply-rooted mentalities among both gentry and villagers.

David Chandler, *A History of Cambodia*, Boulder, 1983, presents a useful overview of Khmer manifestations of unrest. But the 'Holy Man' phenomenon is better described in Chandler's 'An anti-Vietnamese rebellion in early nineteenth century Cambodia: Pre-colonial imperialism and a prenationalist response', JSEAS, 6, 1 (1975). For detailed accounts of the 1916 demonstrations see Milton Osborne, 'Peasant politics in Cambodia: The 1916 Affair', MAS, 12, 2 (1978); and Alain Forest, 'Les manifestations de 1916 au Cambodge', in Brocheux, *Revoltes*.

As an introduction to the historical complexities of Indonesia, Claire Holt *et al.*, eds, *Culture and Politics in Indonesia*, Ithaca, 1972, has stood the test of time. Benedict Anderson's chapter, 'The idea of power in Javanese culture' offers a convincing explanation of charisma and centre–periphery relations. Also important are the chapters by Sartono Kartodirjo on agrarian radicalism in Java and Taufik Abdullah on Minangkabau. Peter Carey offers the best accounts of Javanese millennial expectations focused on Diponegoro; see his 'The origins of the Java War (1825–30)', *English Historical Review*, 91 (1976), and 'Waiting for the "Just King": the agrarian world of south-central Java from Giyanti (1755) to the Java War (1825–30)', MAS, 20, 3 (1986).

Post-1830 assertions against Dutch–priyayi rule are examined in Sartono Kartodirjo, *Protest Movements in Rural Java*, Singapore: ISEAS, 1973, which, however, is marred by an attempt to locate Javanese movements in an evolutionary series. Sartono's earlier work, *The Peasants' Revolt of Banten in 1888*, 's-Gravenhage (*Verhandelingen van het Koninklijk Instituut voor Taal-Land- en Volkenkunde*, Deel 50), 1966, is a classic in the field. On the Samin movement, see the pathbreaking study by Harry Benda and Lance Castles, 'The Samin movement', in *Continuity and Change*. The limits of their analysis are underlined in Benedict Anderson's provocative essay, 'Millenarianism and the Saminist movement', in *Religion and Social Ethos in Indonesia*, Clayton: Monash University Centre of Southeast Asian Studies, 1977. On the incorporation of Christianity into Javanese religion, see Ph. Quarles van Ufford, 'Why don't you sit down? Sadrach and the struggle for religious independence in the earlist phase of the Church of Central Java (1861–1899)', in R. Schefold *et al.*, ed, *Man, Meaning and History*, The Hague, 1980. The *ratu adil* theme appears in nearly all studies of Javanese protest movements, but nowhere does it figure more centrally than in Bernard Dahm, *Sukarno and the Struggle for Indonesian Independence*, trans. Mary F. Somers Heidhues, Ithaca, 1969, which also looks at the Sarekat Islam.

A useful guide to the major uprisings and wars throughout the Dutch East Indies is Merle Ricklefs, *A History of Modern Indonesia*, London, 1981. Christine Dobbin, *Islamic Revivalism in a Changing Peasant Economy in Central Sumatra, 1784–1847*, London, 1983, is the authoritative work on the Padri Wars. On Batak resistance see Lance Castles, 'Statelessness and stateforming tendencies among the Batak before colonial rule', in *Precolonial State Systems in Southeast Asia*, Kuala Lumpur: Monographs of the Malaysian Branch of the Royal Asiatic Society, 1975; and the comprehensive study by Masashi Hirosue, 'Prophets and followers in Batak millenarian responses to the colonial order: Parmalim, Na Siak Bagi and Parhudamdam, 1890–1930', Ph.D. thesis, Australian National Univeristy, 1988. The most comprehensive account of Acehnese resistance to the Dutch is Anthony Reid, *The Blood of the People*, Kuala Lumpur, 1979. James Siegel, *The Rope of God*, Berkeley, 1969, links social structure and categories of perception to the Aceh war.

The classic study of the communist-led rebellion in west Sumatra is B. Schrieke, *Indonesian Sociological Studies*, part one, The Hague, 1966. On east Java see Michael Williams, *Sickle and Crescent: The Communist Revolt of 1926 in Banten*, Ithaca, 1982. The main shortcoming of these works is their lack of attention to language and discourse. This problem is brilliantly overcome in Takashi Shiraishi, *An Age in Motion*, Ithaca, 1990, which deals with popular radicalism in Java from the rise of the Sarekat Islam in 1912 to the rebellions of 1926.

The spread of pan-Islamic sentiments in the archipelago is documented in Anthony Reid, 'Nineteenth-century Pan-Islam in Indonesia and Malaysia', JAS, 26, 2 (1967), and William Roff, 'South-East Asian Islam in the nineteenth century', in *The Cambridge History of Islam*, II, Cambridge, UK, 1970. On the 1915 Kelantan uprising, see Ibrahim Nik Mahmood, 'The To' Junggut rebellion of 1915', in William Roff, ed., *Kelantan*, Kuala Lumpur, 1974; and J. de V. Allen, 'The Kelantan rising of 1915: some thoughts on the concept of resistance in British Malayan history', JSEAS, 9 (1968). The 1928 Terengganu rebellion is treated extensively in Heather Sutherland, 'The taming of the Trengganu elite', in Ruth McVey, ed., *Southeast Asian Transitions*, New Haven, 1978. However, a better perspective 'from below' is provided in Shaharil Talib, *After its Own Image: The Trengganu Experience, 1881–1941*, Singapore, 1984.

Islam's role in mobilizing resistance to Thai suzerainty is detailed in Surin Pitsuwan, *Islam and Malay Nationalism*, Bangkok: Thai Khadi Research Institute, 1985. For the analogous case of resistance to Spanish conquest in Mindanao and Sulu, the best introduction is Cesar Majul, *Muslims in the Philippines*, Quezon City, 1973. Samuel Tan takes the story up to the American invasion in *The Filipino Muslim Armed Struggle, 1900–1972*, Manila: Filipinas Foundation, 1977.

Centre–periphery relations in the Spanish Philippines are discussed in Reynaldo Ileto, 'Outlines of a non-linear emplotment of Philippine history,' in Lim Teck Ghee, *Reflections on Development in Southeast Asia*, Singapore: ISEAS, 1988. The Cofradia de San José is treated extensively in Reynaldo Ileto, *Pasyon and Revolution: Popular Movements in the Philippines, 1840–1910*, Quezon City, 1979; and Setsuho Ikehata, 'Popular Catholicism in the nineteenth-century Philippines: The case of the Cofradia de San José', in *Reading Southeast Asia*, Ithaca: Cornell University Southeast Asia Program, 1989, 109–88.

David Sturtevant, *Popular Uprisings in the Philippines, 1840–1940*, Ithaca, 1976, provides an extensive coverage but falls prey to stress-strain and linear classification theories. The Dios-Dios phenomonen in Samar is described in Bruce Cruickshank, *Samar: 1768–1898*, Manila: Historical Conservation Society, 1985. Western Visayas movements are examined in Don Hart, 'Buhawi of the Bisayas: The revitalization process and legend-making in the Philippines', in Mario Zamora, ed., *Studies in Philippine Anthropology*, Quezon City, 1967; and Alfred McCoy, '*Baylan*: Animist religion and Philippine peasant ideology', in David Wyatt and Alexander Woodside, eds, *Moral Order and the Question of Change*, New Haven: Yale University Southeast Asia Studies, 1982.

The religious aspects of the 1896 revolution are discussed in Ileto, *Pasyon*; his 'Rizal and the underside of Philippine history', in Wyatt and Woodside, *Moral Order*; and John Schumacher SJ, 'The religious character of the revolution in Cavite, 1896–1897', *Philippine Studies*, 24 (1976). In *Revolutionary Clergy*, Quezon City, 1981, Schumacher thoroughly documents the Filipino clergy's role in nationalist movements to 1903. Post-1910 peasant radicalism is treated in McCoy, '*Baylan*'; Reynaldo Ileto, 'Orators and the crowd: Philippine independence movements, 1910–1914,' in Peter Stanley, ed., *Reappraising an Empire*, Cambridge, Mass., 1984; and Brian Fegan, 'The social history of a central Luzon barrio', in Alfred McCoy and Ed. de Jesus, eds, *Philippine Social History*, Honolulu, 1982. The Sakdal movement occupies a chapter in Sturtevant, *Popular Uprisings*; however, new ground is broken in Motoe Wada, 'The Sakdal movement, 1930–34', *Philippine Studies*, 36 (1988).

CHAPTER

5

NATIONALISM AND MODERNIST REFORM

Throughout Southeast Asia, the early twentieth century produced reformist
activity directed toward altering established practices, whether indigenous
or colonial in origin. This modernist impulse accepted the need for change,
recognized benefits to be gained from some of the new arrangements
introduced under colonial régimes or by Western advisers, and generally
worked within the framework of bureaucratic systems of administration,
creating organizations and promoting principles that owed little or nothing
to indigenous traditions and much to ideologies and techniques introduced from outside the region. Many modernist reformers had Western
educations and held ideas concerning how governments ought to be run
that were similar to the views of the officials whose régimes they opposed.
They often had somewhat less in common with the mass of the people, for
the most part semi-literate peasants, in whose name they professed to act.
    One strain of modernist activity led to the formation of governments for
the states that succeeded colonial régimes after 1945, and part of the task of
this chapter is to explain the role of modernist political movements in
events leading up to the creation of these successor states. Such movements are conventionally called nationalist, but most of them represented
nationalism of a particular sort, based on territories containing heterogeneous populations rather than on groups of people with shared cultural
characteristics. A second strain of political activity represented the interests of collectivities with good nationalist credentials. The members of
these groups thought of themselves as part of a larger whole sharing a
common language, religion, or culture ('imagined communities' in the
terminology of Benedict Anderson[1]), but they did not form independent
states and their unsatisfied nationalist aspirations would remain a source
of political conflict in post-colonial Southeast Asia. There was also modernist reform in Southeast Asia which did not pursue independence and
showed little interest in political nationalism, but addressed religious or
social concerns, generally through measured social programmes, occasionally in religiously inspired revolutionary activity.
    What lay behind this reformist impulse? The answer can be traced to

[1] Benedict Anderson, *Imagined Communities: Reflections on the Origin and Spread of Nationalism*,
London, 1983, 15–16.

several more or less concurrent developments. One was the provision of education to small but growing segments of the local population, for it was this educated group, tiny though it remained, that provided leadership and new ideas throughout the region. Other sources of impetus included increased mobility and improved communications facilities; the introduction of Western-style bureaucratic administrations; the inspiration provided by reformist activity elsewhere, first in Japan and later in China and India; a growing race consciousness on the part of colonial officials; and the spread of anti-colonial ideologies. Finally, the policies adopted by colonial régimes toward local political activity had much to do with the tactics and objectives of reformers, and the timing of developments.

The significance of education in the development of reformist movements can be seen in the fact that virtually every major indigenous political thinker and leader in Southeast Asia during the first half of the twentieth century received, by the standards of the time, an exceptional education. Most obtained what might be called 'Western education', referring to the teaching of skills—basic literacy and arithmetic and sometimes craft-related techniques as well—in a classroom, and the awarding of certificates which qualified the holder for certain types of employment. Students who continued their education in Europe often encountered a curriculum and a university environment that stimulated political awareness and introduced them to Western concepts of nationalism, democracy, socialism and constitutionalism. Many became painfully aware that the political ideals and aspirations of the peoples of Europe or America were far from being realized in their homelands. Moreover, while higher degrees in principle opened opportunities at higher levels of bureaucracy, senior posts were monopolized by Europeans and the local aristocracy, and in many instances a formal or informal 'colour bar' prevented non-Europeans from advancing in the civil service.

Government educational programmes were closely related to the motives that lay behind Western intervention in Southeast Asia. Economic and strategic considerations were of fundamental importance, though public explanations of imperialism tended to emphasize humanitarian motives. Frank A. Swettenham captured the situation nicely when, having written that British intervention in Malaya was 'a duty forced upon England' and 'imperative from motives of humanity alone', he added that it was also certain to be 'highly beneficial to British interests and British trade'.[2] One important function of education was to train subordinate administrative and clerical staff for government offices and commercial houses. Social Darwinism, which pictured a world in which some races were advanced and others backward, provided an additional motive for education by introducing the idea that more advanced (that is, Western) nations had a duty to assist less advanced nations, a concept reflected in slogans such as the White Man's Burden and the *mission civilisatrice*. The Malay peninsula in the 1880s, according to Hugh Clifford, was 'in the Middle Ages, surrounded by all the appropriate accessories of the dark centuries',[3] and

2 Frank A. Swettenham, *British Malaya*, London, 1907, 174.
3 Hugh Clifford, *The Further Side of Silence*, New York, 1916, 40.

Britain was attempting 'nothing less than to crush into twenty years the revolutions in facts and in ideas which, even in energetic Europe, six long centuries have been needed to accomplish'.[4] Drawing on this perception, Western régimes justified intervention by taking on the role of parent or teacher, providing education and working to bring local communities closer to the 'modern', or Western, world.

In most colonies, these ideas never reached the level of fully developed administrative policy and most colonial governments carried out very modest programmes of education. The principal exception was the American administration in the Philippines which made public education widely available, reflecting the egalitarian educational philosophy of the United States, and also a fervent desire in some quarters to prepare Filipinos for self-government on a democratic model as quickly as possible in order to be rid of the risks and obligations of colonial rule. Elsewhere in Southeast Asia, the need to economize and the fear that education would create a troublesome class of people who held diplomas but were unemployable slowed the development of education. Educational expansion was also impeded by a lingering romantic notion that extolled the virtues of cultures unspoilt by civilization, and led to efforts to protect communities against disruptive intrusions.

As the twentieth century progressed, non-government education became an important focus of nationalist sentiment. Religious schools, particularly Muslim *pesantren* or *madrasah*, and in some places private secular education programmes, taught practical skills, but many also promoted nationalist feeling, at least indirectly. Colonial administrations were acutely aware of the dangers which unfettered educational institutions might pose. French authorities closed the independent and nationalist Dong Kinh Free School shortly after it was founded in Hanoi in 1907; Britain imposed tight controls on Chinese schools in Malaya; and the Dutch authorities passed a number of restrictive measures to regulate private education in the Netherlands East Indies.

The receptivity of Southeast Asian peoples to Western education varied. The obvious efficacy of European technology posed a challenge that could not be ignored, and those concerned with self-strengthening welcomed the chance to gain access to that technology. However, the need to master a foreign language and operate within a foreign culture in order to go beyond the elementary level of study was a major obstacle, while costs were beyond the reach of most of the population.

The relationship between Western education and the political development of Southeast Asia is easily traced, since nationalist leaders came from this background and drew many of their ideas from European political traditions. More difficult to assess is the extent to which those who opted for Western education were unusual individuals. The question whether exceptional people acquired Western education, or whether Western education produced exceptional people, is probably unanswerable, but a great many of those who formed the new élite came from the lesser aristocracy

[4] Hugh Clifford, 'The east coast', in *Stories by Sir Hugh Clifford*, ed. William R. Roff, Kuala Lumpur, 1966, 11.

or its equivalents, and there must be a strong suspicion that education provided an outlet for talent and ambition.

Although education was important to the process of introducing new ideas, other sources also played a critical role. Southeast Asian travellers, among them traders and seamen, young people who left their homelands seeking work and experience, and Muslims who participated in the hajj or studied in the centres of Muslim learning, contributed to the pool of ideas. European administrators themselves added new political understandings, as did others from outside the region, a broad category that included missionaries and traders, immigrant labourers, trade union organizers and Comintern agents.

Improved transport and communications contributed significantly to the development of political thought. Two leading nationalist figures, José Rizal in the Philippines and Raden Adjeng Kartini in Java, shaped their thinking in part through letters exchanged with correspondents in Europe. In many parts of Southeast Asia the rate of basic literacy was fairly high owing to instruction given as part of religious training, and information spread rapidly through print media. Radio broadcasts and increased mobility further facilitated social interaction and exposure to new ideas.

Western-style bureaucratic systems of administration, introduced to the region in the last half of the nineteenth century, brought major innovations, centralizing authority to an unprecedented degree and eliminating many of the traditional prerogatives of indigenous leaders. The changes resulted in increased and more stable revenues for the state, as well as more efficient (and less flexible) ways of collecting taxes. They allowed the state to become involved in a wider range of activities, and to legislate in areas previously left to the workings of local custom.

Modernist reformers recognized the utility of bureaucracies and, while they objected to many features of colonial rule, their intention was generally to take over rather than to eliminate the mechanisms of the colonial state, and to turn them to new purposes. This approach distinguishes modernist reform from two other sorts of opposition to colonial rule, the one a defence of the old régimes and traditional methods, the other consisting of millenarian religious movements and peasant uprisings. Both traditionalist and millenarian opponents of colonial rule objected to the intrusive administrative procedures that accompanied Western domination, but neither mounted a serious threat to any established government. When nationalist reformers eventually came into power, they retained these aspects of colonial rule.

Events elsewhere in Asia and the world were a source of inspiration for modernist reform. The example of the self-strengthening movement in Japan greatly influenced anti-colonial activity in Southeast Asian territories, as did later nationalist struggles in China and India and within the region itself. Japan, where the Meiji restoration was followed by a reformist movement which borrowed from abroad to defend indigenous traditions, inspired many political activists in Southeast Asia, notably in

Vietnam and the Philippines. Japan's victory in the Russo-Japanese War of 1904–5 had an extraordinary impact in the region, since it represented the triumph of an Asian over a Western power. The nationalist struggle in China also served as a model, particularly after Japan abandoned anti-colonialism to improve relations with the European powers in the wake of the Anglo-Japanese Alliance of 1902 and the Entente Cordiale of 1904, and embarked on its own course of imperialist expansion. The 1911 revolution placed China under an administration sympathetic to nationalist causes elsewhere, and the country subsequently provided a refuge for a number of political exiles from Southeast Asia.

Developments outside Asia, particularly World War I and the Great Depression, also greatly affected Southeast Asian politics in the decades leading up to the Pacific War. Direct Southeast Asian involvement in the European conflict was limited: a German cruiser, the *Emden*, raided Penang in October 1914; the Straits Chinese contributed substantial sums of money to the British war effort; the French government requisitioned Vietnamese labour to serve in Europe. A few Burmese labourers were sent to Iraq, while Siam (Thailand) entered the war on the side of the Allies in July 1917, despatching a small expeditionary force to the European front. Indirect effects of the war were of greater importance. The unprecedented scale and carnage of the hostilities served to undermine any pretensions that Western civilization possessed inherent moral superiority, while on a more concrete level, Britain and France, despite emerging as victors, both suffered a serious (and, it would prove, irreversible) erosion of economic and military power. The war led directly to the Russian Revolution, which in turn transformed Marxism-Leninism from a somewhat abstract European ideology into a force on the Asian political scene, with the rapid formation of embryo communist movements in the Dutch East Indies, China, and other parts of the region. The war also brought about the breakup of the great multinational empires of Europe and Eurasia (Austro-Hungarian, Ottoman, and Russian) along roughly ethnic lines, giving self-determination and the nation-state formally sanctioned recognition as the accepted basis of the international political order. And on an ideological level, the fifth of President Woodrow Wilson's famous Fourteen Points asserted that on colonial questions 'the interests of the populations concerned must have equal weight with the claims of the government whose title is to be determined'—a partial recognition of nationalist aspirations accepted by the colonial powers in principle if not, as Ho Chi Minh discovered at Versailles, in practice.

The Great Depression, with its disruption of capitalist trading networks, profoundly affected colonial or semi-colonial commodity producers as well as the more industrialized nations. The prices of rice, rubber, tin, coffee, sugar and other major Southeast Asian exports fell drastically, driving down both government revenues and personal incomes. In Burma, Vietnam, and the Philippines the economic hardships of the early 1930s contributed to outbreaks of rural violence, while the economic crisis was also a major factor in the 1932 coup which ended the absolute monarchy in Siam. However, the effects of the depression were uneven in Southeast Asia: the impact fell mainly upon areas where the colonial period had brought into being a commercialized export-oriented agriculture or commodity production linked to world markets, notably the extended river deltas of Burma, Siam, and Vietnam, and parts of Malaya, the Dutch East Indies, and the Philippines. More remote areas, where a semi-subsistence mode of production still prevailed, were less affected by the economic crisis, and consequently by the political repercussions which accompanied it.

Racial consciousness is deeply embedded in Asian history, but it took on new significance during the early twentieth century. European visitors to Southeast Asia in the seventeenth century approached Asians as equals, displaying an openness and readiness to learn that was often lacking in the nineteenth century, when scientific and industrial developments had produced a technological gulf between Europe and the rest of the world. Even nineteenth-century accounts of colonial life portray a relatively easy mixing and camaraderie between the limited number of Europeans resident in the region and the local population. By the early twentieth century a substantial increase in the number of European officials had begun to make it possible to emulate a European lifestyle, a tendency reinforced by the arrival of significant numbers of European women in the colonies. Europeans and Asians increasingly met only in their working capacities, and then often in an unequal relationship.

New ideologies further enhanced the significance of race. Social Darwinism provided a 'scientific' explanation for racial inequality, and nationalism brought race into matters of state. Discrimination on racial grounds was a grievance upon which nationalist politicians could readily capitalize, and it provided a useful focus for their programmes.

Anti-colonial ideologies derived from a number of sources, and sometimes promoted inconsistent goals. The term 'nationalism' is commonly used to characterize much of the opposition to Western rule, but the equating of nationalism with anti-colonialism, although enshrined by long usage, obscures important distinctions. Some anti-colonial movements (notably those based on Islam and socialism) promoted transnational ideologies and were intrinsically hostile to nationalism, while others represented the interests of non-national groupings, such as the aristocracy or traders or those professing a certain faith.

In nineteenth-century Europe, 'nationalism' referred to the idea that humanity was divided into discrete groups—peoples or communities distinguishable by differences of language, religion, culture, and physical appearance—and to the argument that these 'nations' should be the basis of sovereign states. The doctrine also implied that the nation, the people, as the ultimate source of power and authority, should participate in the governing of the state through representative institutions. Nationalism of this sort did not provide an appropriate model for a stable political order in areas such as Southeast Asia, where a profusion of groups that differed in language, religion, culture and physical appearance intermingled. It was, however, the most successful political idea in nineteenth-century Europe and, since imperialism in Southeast Asia violated all the basic tenets of nationalism, it had obvious attractions for opponents of colonial rule.

The defects of nationalism as a political ideology for Southeast Asia were apparent. Some reformers saw socialism or religion, doctrines which transcended ethnic and cultural differences (and opposed the way nationalism divided the working class, or the community of believers), as better foundations upon which to build in the future. Marxism provided a comprehensive explanation and critique of imperialism, along with a rationale for action and an assurance of success in the long term, but the confrontational style adopted by communist parties was alien to the cultures of the region, and control of the communist movement by Moscow seemed suspiciously like imperialism in another guise. Marxism's hostility to religion, although played down by exponents within the region, also limited its appeal.

Religion and culture were another source of opposition ideas. For many people, the most objectionable feature of colonial rule was that it involved the subjugation of Muslims, or of Buddhists, to non-Muslims or non-Buddhists. The payment of taxes and other levies, although sometimes harsh, may have been little different from what the population had endured under indigenous rule, but the spectacle of non-believers, of barbarians, ruling the state and failing to respect indigenous custom was new. It provided a clear symbolic expression of a world that needed to be changed. However, from a tactical point of view one fundamental consideration was that the colonial régimes were (or appeared to be) militarily too strong to be dislodged by force, particularly since efficient intelligence services enabled the colonial authorities to act against opposition groups while they were in a formative stage. And if the anti-colonial struggle was to be carried out in the political sphere, the idea of nationalism, which enjoyed legitimacy in Europe and was accepted in principle by many colonial officials, offered greater leverage than socialism or religious movements which lacked powerful constituencies in Europe and were viewed with intense suspicion by colonial administrations.

Anthony D. Smith has suggested that nationalist movements require: 'an easily identifiable territory and location' together with 'a single political authority and bureaucracy'; a population sharing both a 'myth of common origins and history' and other distinctive cultural features such as language or skin colour; and an urban intelligentsia acting as the bearer of the nationalist idea. In Southeast Asia, as in many colonial contexts elsewhere, the territorial basis for nationalist movements (along with the unified political authority and the centralized bureaucratic administration) was largely provided by the colonial powers, a situation characterized by Smith as 'territorial nationalism', or 'nationalisms without nations'. In these circumstances, a nationalist movement 'arises among heterogeneous populations [and] is based upon the territorial unit in which they are forcibly united and administered, usually by a colonial power',[5] while the people concerned 'possess no common and distinctive cultural identity to

[5] Anthony D. Smith, 'Introduction: the formation of nationalist movements', in Smith, ed., *Nationalist Movements*, New York, 1977, 5, 9.

protect . . . The main aim is to take over the alien's political machinery and adopt his administrative unit as the basis of the projected "nation".[6]

The territorial divisions produced by colonialism in Southeast Asia coincided neither with indigenous political units nor with groups possessing myths of common origins and distinctive cultural features. Borders sometimes divided groups which shared national characteristics, and nearly always embraced various groups which did not. As a consequence, nationalism based on a common cultural identity, and anti-colonialism among those subject to a colonial state, were distinct and sometimes conflicting concepts.

Instances of what Smith calls 'ethnic nationalism', political activity undertaken by culturally distinct populations, also occurred in the region. Examples include the Thai of the Chao Phraya basin of central Siam, the Muslims of southern Thailand and the southern Philippines, and the Malays in British Malaya. In British Burma some non-Burman or non-Buddhist peoples developed ethnic nationalist movements and opposed integration with other communities living in the territory.

In the Netherlands East Indies, ethnic nationalism was largely subsumed by territorial nationalism, although local, ethnically-based organizations developed before the Japanese Occupation, and ethnic loyalties produced a divisive regionalism after independence despite official emphasis on unity and an Indonesian identity. Within the Philippines, too, ethnic loyalties derived from dialects or cultures remained potent, but posed little threat to the unity of the state except in the Muslim south, where the Moros combined ethnic and territorial nationalist appeals. Non-territorial ethnic nationalisms also emerged in Southeast Asia, based on groups of people distinguished by cultural features but lacking a clearly defined territorial base, among them the Chinese, Indian, and Karen communities.

Some populations which did possess shared cultural characteristics ultimately came to identify themselves with territorial nationalism and attempted to co-opt it as their own. The Burmans in British Burma, the Khmer in Cambodia, and the Vietnamese, and after 1945 the peninsular Malays, tended to give territorial nationalism an ethnic flavour and to define other peoples within their territories as ethnic minorities.

Governments within the region, most of them colonial administrations, varied greatly in their degree of tolerance for indigenous political activity. At one extreme the United States régime in the Philippines co-operated with an elected Filipino legislative body which actively promoted the cause of independence. In the Netherlands East Indies the Dutch administration adopted the so-called Ethical Policy at the start of the twentieth century which officially encouraged local involvement in administrative affairs, and in 1918 launched a partially elected parliamentary body, the Volksraad. However, the Volksraad was limited to an advisory role, and the government permitted only modest criticism, suppressing organizations that ventured beyond these limits. British administrations in Burma and Malaya also operated legislative councils with some local participation but

---

[6] Anthony D. Smith, *Theories of Nationalism*, London, 1971, 216–17.

provided no latitude for effective opposition to the régime from this source. The French in Indochina were intolerant of all but the mildest expressions of dissent. Where political activity went beyond what a government was willing to countenance, colonial régimes dismantled organizations, banished and imprisoned leaders, and effectively stifled opposition. By acting before opposition movements had built up momentum, colonial administrations usually managed to prevent the mounting of major challenges to their authority.

Anti-colonial groups faced a difficult choice in deciding whether to seek reforms by co-operating with colonial administrations, or to refuse co-operation and face the possibility of suppression. Filipino political parties co-operated, but also had a growing measure of real power, and any advocate of non-cooperation would have been in the invidious position of opposing a Filipino administration. Elsewhere in the region the question whether to co-operate with colonial administrations to achieve reforms was a divisive issue, but by the 1920s and 1930s the failure of colonial régimes to address suggestions raised by reformers had led more and more to confrontation, and to increasingly repressive counter-measures.

Beyond these general considerations the character of modernist reform movements varied according to local circumstances, and must be discussed individually. Attention will first be given to movements that were territorially based, directed at taking over control of a colonial régime, and then to movements that were ethnically based. Finally, reference will be made to loyalist activity that does not fit neatly into either category.

TERRITORIAL NATIONALISM

The Philippines

The first major modernist movement directed against colonial rule in Southeast Asia developed in the Philippines. Its origins lay in issues related to the Catholic faith shared by a majority of Filipinos and the Spanish. The initiative for political reforms came from younger, educated members of the élite, the *ilustrados*, who were inspired by the ideals of European liberalism and sought political participation through democratic institutions.

During the 1890s a revolutionary movement to secure independence from Spain developed, but the decade ended with the United States displacing Spain as a colonial power within the archipelago. Under American rule the Philippines differed from the rest of Southeast Asia in two fundamental ways. First, the Americans gave Filipinos a substantial and increasing role in the administration, as part of a stated policy to grant the colony independence at an early date. In connection with this policy, the government made education widely available in order to develop a populace capable of involvement in public affairs and able to participate in democratic institutions of government. Second, the Filipino élite owned large tracts of land, giving them a base of power and wealth outside the government, and a clear stake in sustaining the country's agricultural export economy.

The population of the Philippines occupied numerous islands, and was further fragmented by mountainous terrain. These physical divisions were reinforced by linguistic differences, regional loyalties and religious conflicts. During the nineteenth century, however, a shared 'national' identity began to develop, and a small number of people became politically active in the cause of bettering the political and social situation of the Philippines as a whole.

Some historians have attempted to place this change earlier, pointing to a long series of conspiracies and uprisings during the Spanish period as evidence of a nascent Filipino nationalism. The interpretation was rejected as long ago as 1889 by the nationalist leader José Rizal on the grounds that such revolts were isolated and directed against local grievances, and that Filipinos became conscious of themselves as a nation only during the nineteenth century.

Why did a Filipino identity emerge at this time? Rizal traced the change to a new Spanish attitude toward the population of the archipelago. While the Filipinos had once been treated 'as a subject, but not an inferior people', during the nineteenth century Spaniards began to show contempt for the Filipinos. According to Rizal, 'They made the race itself an object of insult. They professed themselves unable to see in it any admirable quality, any human trait',[7] and this insult, directed at the entire 'Indio' population, gave rise to a 'national' response.

One key episode in generating Filipino political consciousness was a mutiny at the Cavite Arsenal in 1872 and its aftermath. The mutiny lasted only two days and was easily suppressed, but Spanish authorities claimed it was part of a larger conspiracy and used the opportunity to crack down on various proponents of liberalization. The government imprisoned or exiled a number of Filipino priests, and three dissidents—Fathers José Burgos, Mariano Gomez, and Jacinto Zamora—were sentenced to death. The executions, by garrotte and carried out publicly, had a deep impact that was far from what the Spanish administration intended. Many considered the priests innocent of the charges laid against them, and the Archbishop of Manila refused to defrock them, lending credence to the idea that the three men had been executed to intimidate others who might be moved to challenge Spanish authority.

The executions shifted the focus of what had been a grievance against the friars to the Spanish administration as a whole, and following this event a political movement took shape among the Filipino élite, and particularly among the small group of Filipinos studying in Spain. Because their principal activity consisted of drafting articles and pamphlets calling attention to conditions in the Philippines, this initiative is known as the Propaganda Movement. The best-known writings produced by the group were a fortnightly newspaper called La Solidaridad, which appeared be-

---

[7] Quoted by Horacio de la Costa, SJ, 'Rizal's political ideas', in his The Background of Nationalism and Other Essays, Manila, 1965, 33–4.

tween 1889 and 1895, and two novels (*Noli Me Tangere* and *El Filibusterismo*) written by Rizal.

[In general, the objectives of the Propaganda Movement reflected the ideals of nineteenth-century liberalism] They included equality before the law for Filipinos and Spaniards alike, and political rights for Filipinos comparable to those enjoyed in Spain. Far from advocating independence, the Propaganda Movement sought recognition of the Philippines as a province of Spain with representation in the Spanish parliament, the Cortes. Rizal wrote in a private letter in 1887 that 'in the present circumstances we want no separation from Spain; all we demand is more care, better instruction, better officials, one or two representatives, and more security for ourselves and our property.'[8] In an article in *La Solidaridad* he put the matter more colourfully, writing of 'the stainless patriotism and the loyalty of the Filipinos who since [the sixteenth century] have been joined to Spain, not for reasons of religion nor of traditionalism but, at the beginning, for reasons of high political convenience, and later, for love, for affection for the Mother Country'.[9]

Filipino demands generated sympathy in Europe but the friars resident in the Philippines, drawing on anti-liberal statements in the Syllabus of Errors issued in 1864 by Pope Pius IX, rejected the proposals. In 1889 Gregorio del Pilar, the editor of *La Solidaridad*, took a stronger line in urging assimilation of the Philippines with Spain. Rizal, however, was revising his position and increasingly diverged from this viewpoint, looking instead toward working for change within the Philippines itself: 'The error all make in thinking we can help here [in Europe], far away, is a great mistake indeed. . . . The field of battle is in the Philippines; there is where we should be.'[10]

Rizal returned to Manila on 26 June 1892, and on 3 July helped set up an underground organization called the Liga Filipina to work for unity, mutual protection, and reforms. Less than a week later he was arrested by the Spanish authorities, who sent him into internal exile in Mindanao. Within a few months, the Liga Filipina was dissolved. One faction continued to support Del Pilar's propaganda work in Europe, but another helped establish a secret society known as the Katipunan, which laid the groundwork for an insurrection that broke out in 1896 against Spanish rule.

The Katipunan was founded and led by a former Liga Filipina member named Andres Bonifacio (1863–97). For its structure and symbolism, the organization drew heavily on Freemasonry, indigenous mysticism, and Catholicism. Politically, the Katipunan worked to secure independence, and prepared for violent revolution to achieve this objective. Rizal declined to support this endeavour, arguing that conditions were not yet right, but plans went ahead. Fighting broke out on 26 August 1896 when the plot was revealed to the Spanish authorities. The government responded by trying and executing Rizal for his supposed involvement.

---

[8] Cited in John N. Schumacher, SJ, *The Propaganda Movement: 1880–1895*, Manila, 1973, 226.
[9] 'How to deceive the native land', *La Solidaridad*, II (15 May 1889), 72–3, reproduced in José Rizal, *Political and Historical Writings (1884–1890)*, Manila, 1989, 27–30.
[10] Schumacher, 223.

The Katipunan proved ineffective against Spanish forces, but Emilio Aguinaldo (1869–1963) had some success in Cavite and emerged as a rival to Bonifacio for leadership of the revolutionary cause. The two agreed to resolve the issue through an election, which Aguinaldo won. Bonifacio refused to accept the outcome and, accused of treason, was executed by followers of Aguinaldo.

On 1 November 1897, the revolutionary movement, located at Biak-na-bato in Bulacan Province, established a government and promulgated a constitution to formalize independence from Spain. Spanish forces continued to achieve successes, but the colonial government, concluding that the defeat of Filipino forces was likely to lead to protracted guerrilla warfare rather than peace, negotiated a settlement. The Pact of Biak-na-bato stipulated that fighting would cease, that rebel forces would surrender their arms, and that Aguinaldo and his supporters would receive a payment of three million Mexican dollars and leave the Philippines. This extraordinary agreement reveals the weakness of the Filipino forces, constantly harassed by the Spanish and unable to attract the backing of the landed Filipino élite, the *principalia*, whose wealth and control of manpower would have appreciably strengthened the revolutionary cause. The terms were not wholly carried out by either party, but Aguinaldo did depart for Hong Kong, only to return with American forces which invaded the Philippines in 1898 following the outbreak of the Spanish–American War.

Back in the Philippines, Aguinaldo, with growing support from the *principalia* now that success appeared to be at hand, issued a decree setting up a government to replace that established at Biak-na-bato, and on 12 June 1898 proclaimed Philippine independence. A congress convened at Malolos prepared a constitution for the Philippine Republic. This document, promulgated on 21 January 1899, embodied a bill of rights which barred arbitrary arrest or detention; prohibited taxation except by a legally authorized body; guaranteed Filipinos 'the full enjoyment' of 'political and civil rights'; established rights of *habeas corpus*, property, and domicile; and guaranteed freedom of expression and association. The Malolos administration also adopted measures (such as a civil marriage law) aimed at reducing the powers of the friar-dominated Catholic Church, and on 23 January, the day the Philippine Republic was inaugurated, President Aguinaldo issued a decree expelling all regular Spanish clergy from Philippine territory. The Malolos constitution also declared forfeit all properties of the religious corporations, claiming them for the government. However, the republic soon found itself at war with the United States, a struggle which it ultimately lost, and these measures were not carried out.

Relations between American and Filipino forces around Manila, already uneasy, deteriorated in early February and fighting broke out between the two sides. At the time, ratification by the US senate of the Treaty of Paris, drafted to settle the Spanish-American War and providing for cession of the Philippines to the United States, had been delayed owing to protracted debates between pro- and anti-imperialist interests. With the outbreak of hostilities, the Senate proceeded to ratify the treaty by a narrow margin, making the Philippines an American colony. Fighting continued until 1902, but the Americans were substantially in control by 1900. The character of the Philippine revolution has aroused heated debate. Large numbers of Filipinos supported the cause of the republic, but questions have been raised concerning whether popular participation resulted from mobilization by élites using patronage networks, or was a free expression of popular feeling—a revolt of the masses. If the latter, there is also a question whether the inspiration lay in nationalism, folk beliefs, or Catholicism. John Schumacher has suggested that no single explanation will apply to all participants, an observation in keeping with the evidence and with common sense. He rejects generalizations concerning the behaviour of social classes during the revolution on grounds that élite characteristics and behaviour varied widely, and that mass support for the conflict was tempered in some instances by hostility toward the élite.[11] Another criticism has been advanced by Reynaldo C. Ileto, who argues that some historical accounts impose a spurious continuity on events, placing the Katipunan in a sequence of developments leading to the formation of a Philippine Republic with a Western-style constitution. Ileto suggests that those 'who swelled the ranks of the Katipunan had certain ideas about the world and their places in it, ideas quite different from those of the "better classes" of society', and that some of these ideas survived the transition to élite, *principalia* leadership under Aguinaldo, forming an undercurrent of political thought directed toward national rebirth and redemption that persisted under American rule.[12]

While fighting was still under way, a Philippine Commission carried out a fact-finding exercise. A second commission, with William Howard Taft as chairman, was appointed in September 1900 and established civil government in July of the following year. Initially, the second Philippine Commission served as the country's legislative body, but the Philippine Organic Act of 1901 accepted the principle of Filipino participation in government, and in 1907 a new arrangement was introduced which gave lawmaking powers to a bicameral legislature consisting of the Philippine Commission and a Philippine Assembly made up of Filipino delegates selected from the provinces.

From the beginning Filipinos occupied positions of authority as municipal officers and provincial officials, and two political parties took shape during the first decade of American rule. The Partido Federalista was instrumental in securing a peace settlement in the Philippine–American War, but it adopted an assimilationist posture—advocating American statehood for the Philippines—that cost it popular support. Although the Federalistas shifted their stance in 1907 (adopting the name Partido

[11] The issues are debated in Milagros Guerrero, 'Understanding Philippine revolutionary mentality', reviewing *Pasyon and Revolution: Popular Movements in the Philippines, 1840–1900*, by Reynaldo C. Ileto, *Philippine Studies* 29 (1981) 240–56; Reynaldo C. Ileto, 'Critical issues in "Understanding Philippine revolutionary mentality"', ibid., 30 (1982) 92–119; and John N. Schumacher, SJ, 'Recent perspectives on the revolution', ibid., 445–92.
[12] Reynaldo Ileto, *Pasyon and Revolution: Popular Movements in the Philippines, 1840–1910*, Quezon City, 1979, 99, 139.

Nacional Progresista), a newly formed Partido Nacionalista, which backed immediate independence, dominated the new Philippine Assembly, and remained pre-eminent in Philippine politics throughout the period of American rule.

Despite the activities of opposing political parties and superficial resem-blances to political arrangements in the United States, Philippine politics became a clash of contending personalities within a dominant one-party system. Theodore Friend has written of this period that 'the Philippine political party was unideological and only loosely institutionalized, tend-ing to form around charismatic persons rather than special programs'.[13] The key figures were Manuel L. Quezon, Sergio Osmeña, and Manuel Roxas. Osmeña, an aloof and cautious man, initially dominated the Partido Nacionalista, but during the 1920s the colourful and tempera-mental Quezon outmanoeuvred him, becoming the leading political fig-ure, and the country's first president when the Philippine Commonwealth came into being in 1935. The younger Roxas, an ambitious and aggressive man, entered politics during the 1920s as a protégé of Quezon, who secured for him the position of Speaker of the House in 1922. Roxas later aligned himself with Osmeña, completing an uneasy triumvirate at the top of the Philippine administration.

A Democratic Party victory in the 1912 United States presidential elec-tion portended faster progress towards political change, and President Woodrow Wilson stated in 1913 that United States policies should be formulated 'with a view to the ultimate independence of the Islands and as a preparation for that independence.'[14] Filipinization of the government administrative services proceeded apace under Governor-General Francis Burton Harrison (1913–20), placing substantial power in Filipino hands, and in 1916 the Jones Law established an administrative structure modelled on that of the United States, with a strong executive (for the time being the American governor-general with an appointed Cabinet) and an independ-ent judiciary alongside the bicameral legislature, the Philippine Commis-sion being replaced by an elected Senate. The Jones Law stated that the United States would recognize independence for the Philippines 'as soon as a stable government can be established therein', a declaration of good intentions that left much latitude for negotiation and disagreement.

With independence promised in principle, the outstanding question was when it would be granted. Nationalism remained an emotive issue and politicians made what capital they could out of the demand for early progress in that direction, though public opinion so clearly favoured independence that no significant disagreements were possible on this central point. Historians have, however, questioned the devotion of the Partido Nacionalista to achieving this goal. Lewis E. Gleeck Jr, for exam-ple, argues that when independence seemed to become a real prospect under Harrison, the Partido Nacionalista employed 'two different policies,

---

[13] Theodore Friend, *Between Two Empires: Philippine Ordeal and Development from the Great Depression through the Pacific War, 1929–1946*, New Haven, 1965, 27.
[14] This statement is quoted by J.S. Furnivall in an unfinished manuscript published post-humously under the title *Experiment in Independence: The Philippines*, Manila, 1974, 24.

one of independence for public consumption, and another of autonomy under American sovereignty and protection, in private'.[15] Publicly the party pursued the issue by sending a series of independence missions to Washington, beginning in 1919 with one led by Quezon. But the 1920s brought Republican administrations that did not wish to press ahead with independence, and Leonard Wood, the governor-general for most of the decade (1921–7), took steps to reassert American control of Philippine affairs. He had as a result a stormy relationship with Quezon.

The Great Depression produced a difficult situation for nationalists in the Philippines. Philippine sugar and tobacco competed with domestic production in the United States and its possessions elsewhere, and there was a strong lobby in the United States seeking to place Philippine imports on an equal footing with those from foreign countries. Under pressure from this quarter, a number of members of the United States Congress moved to offer full and immediate independence to the Philippines. However, the proposals envisaged subjecting imports from the Philippines to American tariffs, a potentially disastrous provision given that over 75 per cent of Philippine exports went to the United States, and that the depression had severely reduced the demand for tropical agricultural products world-wide.

The response of the Filipino leadership was to negotiate a transitional period when a Filipino administration would take responsibility for the affairs of the country, and tariffs would be increased gradually to allow the economy to adjust. There has been much criticism of the policies pursued during the 1930s. Some historians have accused the élite leadership of the Partido Nacionalista of betraying Filipino nationalism to benefit their social class. In the words of Norman Owen, 'wealthy agriculturalists succeeded in defining their own interests as those of the Philippines'.[16] This case rests on the fact that the Filipino élite was composed of landowners who derived the major part of their income from agricultural exports, and stood to lose if the country did not have free access to the United States market. However, had Filipino leaders agreed to the more radical independence proposals, the sudden loss of the United States market for agricultural exports would surely have had a deleterious effect on the general welfare of the country.

Personal considerations also helped shape the tactics of leading politicians. In 1933 the United States Congress overrode a veto by President Hoover to pass the Hare–Hawes–Cutting Act, providing for independence after a ten-year transition period. During this time a Philippine Commonwealth constitution was to be drafted and elections held, while on the economic side quotas would be imposed on duty-free Philippine exports to the United States, and a graduated tariff would be introduced. Independence was to take effect automatically after ten years, but the United States

[15] Lewis E. Gleeck, Jr, *General History of the Philippines, Part V, I: The American Half-Century (1898–1946)*, Manila: Historical Conservation Society, 1984, 97.
[16] Norman Owen, 'Philippine economic development and American policy: a reappraisal', in Norman G. Owen, ed., *Compadre Colonialism: Studies on the Philippines under American Rule*, Ann Arbor: University of Michigan Center for South and Southeast Asian Studies, 1971, 113.

would retain commercial rights and military bases in the Philippines. Quezon opposed this legislation, ostensibly because of the provisions relating to military bases but in large part because it had been negotiated by Osmeña and Roxas, and he wanted to be personally responsible for independence. Following Quezon's lead, the Philippine legislature rejected the Hare–Hawes–Cutting Act, and Quezon then renegotiated the agreement, achieving slight modifications, and accepted the Tydings–McDuffie Act on much the same terms the following year. Quezon's faction triumphed in elections held in 1934 to select delegates to the Constitutional Convention, and the transition period commenced in 1935 with a national plebiscite approving the new constitution and the country's first presidential election, which Quezon won.

In the broader sphere of modernist reform, the Philippines was relatively quiet until the 1930s. With substantial educational opportunities available, with a Filipino Congress writing the laws of the country, and with a predominantly Filipino civil service, there was little scope for opposition nationalist political groups. The Catholic Church, which had been closely identified with the Spanish régime, underwent a somewhat difficult adjustment after 1898. The Church had to submit to the principles of religious liberty and separation of church and state, and to the forced sale of lands held by the religious orders. Moreover, it faced a loss of support to a schismatic religious movement called the Iglesia Filipina Independiente (the Philippine Independent, or Aglipayan, Church), formed by Bishop Gregorio Aglipay in 1902. This Church had its origins in an initiative of the revolutionary period to form a Filipino Church loyal to the Vatican, but later took shape as a body outside the Catholic Church. Initially the Philippine Independent Church attracted about a quarter of the Catholic population.

During the 1930s, in part as a result of the Great Depression, political activity intensified in the Philippines. An opposition movement took shape under the name 'Sakdal', a word meaning 'to accuse' or 'to strike' and the name of a newspaper critical of the Nacionalista administration. The Sakdal leader, Benigno Ramos, a former Quezon protégé, at first directed the movement along orthodox political channels, forming a Sakdal Party that capitalized on divisions within the Nacionalista leadership and contested the 1934 general election with some success. By 1935, however, the transition to the Commonwealth government was strengthening the Nacionalista position, and the Sakdal Party responded with increasingly strong rhetoric and overtures to the Japanese for support. When the government applied repressive measures, Sakdal supporters staged an uprising in early May 1935. Government troops quickly defeated the rebels, destroying the party if not the spirit of Sakdalism.

At the beginning of the decade both a Socialist Party (formed by Pedro Abad Santos in 1929) and a Communist Party (publicly launched on 7 November 1930) had also entered the political picture in the Philippines. The Communist Party was declared an illegal organization in 1931 (a decision confirmed by the Supreme Court in October 1932) and went underground. The socialists concentrated on trade-union activities and peasant causes, and after 1935 recruited supporters of the discredited Sakdal Party into an increasingly effective political movement. In November 1938, Quezon released communist leaders from provincial exile, and the communists joined the socialists in creating a new Communist Party of the Philippines, which participated in a Popular Front against Fascism and did well in the 1940 elections.

Peasant unions, such as the Kalipunang Pambansa ng mga Magsasaka sa Pilipinas (National Society of Peasants in the Philippines), were also a significant force during the 1930s. The unions challenged the authority and supremacy of the landed élite, but it has been argued that in many respects their objectives were conservative or even reactionary, oriented toward preserving or restoring traditional social arrangements that provided welfare guarantees, rather than achieving radical change.

The Filipino Independent Church also took up the cause of the peasant, and Bishop Aglipay stood against Quezon in the 1935 election to select a Commonwealth President. This challenge was not a serious threat, and the Nacionalista leadership drew together to produce a comfortable victory in the election. Their success is conventionally seen as a triumph of Philippine nationalism, but it has also been characterized by Alfred W. McCoy as a triumph of Philippine authoritarianism based on 'a system of clientelist politics' that was to be 'institutionalized and perfected' under the Commonwealth.[17]

Under United States rule, Philippine nationalism was a political weapon deployed by the dominant Partido Nacionalista. Because independence had been conceded in principle by the American régime, opposition groups did not and could not take shape around this issue, but by the same token nationalism did not provide a focus to draw together the disparate groups that made up the Philippine population. Regional sentiments remained important and politicians derived support based on their linguistic and regional identifications. Efforts to devise a national language or other all-embracing national symbols were half-hearted and largely ineffective throughout the American period. While support for the Commonwealth government and for independence was widespread, regional loyalties and the authoritarian pattern of administration would create difficulties in the postwar era.

The Netherlands East Indies

In its early days, the Dutch régime adopted the administrative style of the kingdom of Mataram which preceded it in Java, and made extensive use of members of the Javanese aristocracy as regional administrators. Opposition to Dutch rule likewise drew on indigenous patterns of political behaviour, employing traditional symbols and working toward objectives that fitted within the traditional political order.

---

[17] Alfred W. McCoy, 'Quezon's Commonwealth: the emergence of Philippine authoritarianism', in Ruby R. Paredes, ed., *Philippine Colonial Democracy*, New Haven: Yale University Southeast Asia Studies, 1988, 118–20.

Toward the end of the nineteenth century, the Dutch increasingly replaced this quasi-royal system with a bureaucratic administration, and a new form of political opposition developed. Based in part on racial or 'national' distinctions, it accepted the conventions of statecraft that under-lay the colonial government, and competed for the right to participate in or to run the administration. The beliefs and traditions of the archipelago, the mysticism and the cosmology that drew on indigenous as well as Hindu-Buddhist concepts, did not disappear, but they no longer lay at the heart of the political process.

Reformers pursued a variety of goals, including modest cultural asser-tion, economic development, religious purification, and independence. For the most part the tone was modernist, reflecting dissatisfaction both with Dutch rule and with long-established indigenous practices, and there was an emphasis on the application of reason to solve problems or shape new initiatives, rather than reliance on faith or traditional authority. Inspiration came from a variety of sources, including a reformist tendency within Islam, and the conceptual and technical innovations that reshaped production, trade, and administration throughout the world during the nineteenth century.

Some specialist prewar accounts of nationalism in the Netherlands East Indies exist, but serious writing for a general readership paid little atten-tion to Indonesian opposition politics. Nor was this lack of emphasis wholly unwarranted in view of the modest accomplishments of prewar Indonesian political activity. Bernhard Dahm has observed that a great majority of the population of the Netherlands East Indies knew nothing of the nationalist movement, and the movement itself 'did not constitute a threat to the colonial government'.[18] On the other hand, the Dutch administration was extremely concerned with local political activities dur-ing the 1930s, and an extensive and effective system of surveillance contributed to the reformists' lack of success.

The issue of wartime collaboration, and the nationalist struggle against reimposition of Dutch rule after 1945, led to a reassessment of prewar political activity in the archipelago. An Indonesian study of the nationalist movement appeared in 1947,[19] and George McTurnan Kahin published a classic English-language account in 1952.[20] Kahin adopted a chronological approach, briefly describing the history of opposition to Dutch rule before 1900 and then tracing modern nationalism from the early twentieth cen-tury, portraying it as the activities of a series of organizations of different ideological persuasions. This portrait of the nationalist movement remains standard,[21] although subsequent in-depth studies have altered percep-tions of some of the organizations concerned. However, it seems possible that these divisions have been overemphasized. The nationalist leader Mohammad Hatta considered Indonesian Marxists to be nationalists at

---

[18] Bernhard Dahm, *History of Indonesia in the Twentieth Century*, London, 1971, 77.

[19] L.M. Sitorus, *Sedjarah Pergerakan Kebangsaan Indonesia*, Jakarta, 1947.

[20] George McTurnan Kahin, *Nationalist and Revolution in Indonesia*, Ithaca, 1952.

[21] Secondary-school texts used in Indonesia provide an account that follows much the same lines as that of Kahin.

heart, and Sukarno glossed over the differences between nationalism, Marxism and Islam. Such interpretations might be said to reflect an imperfect understanding of Marxism or nationalism, but alternatively might be seen as reflecting a deep understanding of Indonesian society, and as illustrating the inadvisability of relying on foreign categories to interpret Indonesian events.[22]

Modernist reform activity in the Netherlands East Indies can be divided into four phases, based on the goals and activities of local organizations and the stance adopted by the Dutch government. An initial phase of co-operative activity between 1900 and roughly 1918 was followed by a radical period, a non-cooperating phase, and in the 1930s by a period of grudging co-operation dictated by restrictive Dutch policies. Alongside this politically oriented activity, there was also a reform movement that largely disregarded the Dutch administration and used education and social welfare activities to work for change.

Reformist activity benefited from the Ethical Policy inaugurated by the Dutch administration in 1901. Designed to redress past injustices, the Ethical Policy brought the introduction of measures to promote economic development, improve health and welfare, and to encourage indigenous participation in professional life and in social and administrative affairs. However, during the 1920s relations between the Dutch administration and Indonesian activists became increasingly acrimonious, and the Ethical Policy was effectively discarded.

During the nineteenth century the influence of the *bupati*, the *priyayi* or aristocrats who served as Regents within the Dutch administration, underwent a decline. In response, some among the *bupati* advocated self-strengthening through education, both for the aristocracy in their capacity as leaders of Javanese society, and ultimately for non-nobles as well, to enable them to participate in the administration of the country. Notable for their efforts in this regard were R. M. A. A. Hadiningrat, *Bupati* of Demak, and his niece, Raden Adjeng Kartini, whose interest in modernization and in education for women made her a nationalist icon after her death in childbirth in 1904.

Indonesians who had obtained an education through the two principal Dutch institutions available to them, the Opleidingscholen voor inlandsche ambtenaren (OSVIA), a school to train native officials, and the School tot opleiding van inlandsche artsen (STOVIA), a school for training native doctors, took the lead in proposing political initiatives. STOVIA graduates in particular felt that their education and work received insufficient recognition, and in May 1908 a group of them formed an organization with the name Budi Utomo (Glorious Endeavour) to promote social reform. The founders, who expressed a wish to help ordinary people, planned to extend their movement throughout Java and ultimately throughout the

---

[22] Drawing on this perspective, Takashi Shiraishi has re-examined political activity in Java prior to 1926 with a view to abandoning conventional categories and considering political groupings not as representing distinct ideologies but as a part of a broad 'movement', or *pergerakan*. See his *An Age in Motion: Popular Radicalism in Java, 1912–1926*, Ithaca, 1990.

Netherlands East Indies, but an older and more conservative element of the aristocracy soon took control of Budi Utomo, diluting its reformist character and stressing Javanese culture and Javanese values.

Three organizations dominated Indonesian reformist activity during the 1910s: Sarekat Islam, created to encourage economic activity among the indigenous Muslim population; Muhammadiyah, a modernist reforming Muslim organization; and the Indische Sociaal-Demokratische Vereeniging (ISDV, the Indies Social-Democratic Association), a radical Marxist group. None of these organizations was ethnically based, although all originated in Java and had their greatest strength there.

Another body, the Nationale Indische Partij, founded in 1912, directed its appeal to all races and called for racial equality, socio-economic justice and ultimate independence. As an organization the group accomplished little, for the government suppressed it within a year and sent its principal leaders, E. F. E. Douwes Dekker, Suwardi Suryadiningrat and Tjipto Mangunkusumo, into exile in the Netherlands. All returned within a few years and played a further role in the nationalist movement, but their fate gave some indication of the limited range of political activity the government was prepared to countenance. The membership of the Nationale Indische Partij regrouped as Insulinde, a predominantly Eurasian organization which had limited appeal in other sectors of the society.

Formally constituted in September 1912, Sarekat Islam grew into a mass movement claiming a membership in excess of two million. The organization proposed to promote a commercial spirit, act as a mutual aid association for members, serve the spiritual and economic interests of the people, and combat misunderstandings concerning Islam. Its key figure was an aristocratic OSVIA graduate, Raden Umar Sayed Tjokroaminoto. Although Sarekat Islam benefited from the modest latitude given indigenous organizations under the Ethical Policy, overt political activity was disallowed, and the movement accordingly adopted a co-operative stance in dealing with the Dutch government. For its part, the Netherlands East Indies administration sanctioned Sarekat Islam activities at the local level but did not authorize a central organization until 1916, by which time local branches had developed to such a degree that they were not amenable to central control.

A charismatic leader, Tjokroaminoto rapidly became a cult figure, and popular identification of him with the messianic Javanese tradition of the *ratu adil* (just king) contributed to the movement's early growth. After 1915 this approach was criticized by, among others, Agus Salim, a member of the Central Sarekat Islam who helped turn the organization towards an increased emphasis on Islam and modernism. In 1917 the Sarekat Islam formulated a Declaration of Principles that focused on Islam as the source of democratic ideas and spiritual education, and stressed a need for intellectual and moral development to enable the people to participate in politics. It also produced an Action Programme which called for transformation of the Volksraad into a true legislature, establishment of regional councils and extension of the franchise.

In the first Volksraad elections, held in 1917, only two nationalist figures won seats, Abdul Muis of Sarekat Islam and Abdul Rivai of Insulinde. The

NATIONALISM AND MODERNIST REFORM

governor-general, who had hoped to draw the nationalist opposition into the political process, subsequently selected other activists to serve as appointed members, including the Sarekat Islam leader Tjokroaminoto, and Tjipto Mangunkusumo. Nationalist representatives formed a bloc called the Radical Concentration, but the Volksraad did not become a major forum for Indonesian opinion and efforts to turn it into a true parliament failed. By the 1920s Indonesian leaders were beginning to favour a non-cooperative approach and withdrawal from the Volksraad.

Around 1918, Indonesian political activity entered a radical phase, owing to a lack of substantive concessions on the part of the Dutch administration and to pressure from ISDV members who joined Sarekat Islam in the latter part of the decade. The Marxist ISDV had been founded in 1914 by Hendricus J. F. M. Sneevliet. Owing to its European make-up and the novelty of its political stance, the group had only limited popular appeal, but Sneevliet attempted with considerable success to acquire a mass base by linking his movement with Sarekat Islam. Although Sneevliet was expelled from the Indies in 1918, ISDV supporters in the Sarekat Islam grew in strength, and became increasingly extreme in their demands, clashing with moderate elements in the leadership. The ISDV was particularly strong in the city of Semarang, and the Semarang branch of Sarekat Islam, under the leadership of two ISDV activists, Semaun and Darsono, pressed for implementation of a programme of revolutionary action.

In 1918 the Dutch administration uncovered a secret revolutionary 'Section B' of the Sarekat Islam, leading in 1920 to prison sentences for various figures associated with it. The episode caused defections from Sarekat Islam, notably among the peasant membership, and also deepened divisions within the organization as a conservative religious faction led by Agus Salim and Abdul Muis began trying to counter radical influence. At the sixth Sarekat Islam Congress, held in 1921, the leadership moved against the ISDV faction, pushing through a resolution that called for party discipline and barred joint membership in Sarekat Islam and other organizations. As intended, the measure resulted in a communist withdrawal.

The ISDV group (which in 1920 had adopted the name Perserikatan Komunis di India, PKI, or the Indies Communist Organization) retained control of a number of local branches and made these the basis of a Red Sarekat Islam, but the Dutch administration was monitoring events and in 1922 began expelling communist leaders from the Netherlands East Indies. Faced with increasingly effective government surveillance, one faction within the PKI laid plans to stage a revolt. Efforts to secure Comintern support failed, and most PKI branches refused to participate, but uprisings took place in Banten in November 1926, and in the Minangkabau lands of west Sumatra early in 1927. Although instigated by the communist leadership, these uprisings owed much to local grievances and, lacking widespread support, were quickly put down. However, in the aftermath the Dutch administration suppressed the PKI so effectively that the party did not again become a political force in Indonesia until after 1945.

The communist uprisings of 1926–7 confirmed the views of those in the Dutch administration who felt the Ethical Policy had gone too far, and effectively ended the ethical period. A new Indische Staatsregeling, in essence a constitution, introduced in 1925 provided added controls, and while nominally giving concessions to the nationalists ensured that power remained in Dutch hands. However, while Dutch attitudes toward Indonesian political activity hardened during the 1920s, under Governor-General A. C. D. de Graeff (1926–31) the Dutch administration maintained a moderate stance. De Graeff's conservative successor, Jonkheer Mr B. C. D. De Jonge (1931–6) was less tolerant of opposition. When Indonesian political activity became increasingly non-cooperative, his administration took strong action, sending the principal figures into internal exile.

Islam provided the rationale for a non-nationalist activism based on the principle that all Muslims formed part of an *Ummat Islam* or Islamic community that transcended political and ethnic divisions, but it served nationalist purposes as well, raising objections to rule by non-Muslims over Muslims and offering the prospect of support from outside the region. However, a substantial proportion of the Muslim population held beliefs that combined Islamic doctrines with elements of local tradition, some arguably in conflict with orthodox Islam. Reformists had attacked this sort of syncretism in the Minangkabau area of Sumatra in the early nineteenth century, precipitating the prolonged and traumatic Padri wars, and anti-colonialism based on Islam inevitably brought such matters to the forefront once again. Divisions within the Muslim community as well as the presence of a significant number of non-Muslims in the archipelago made Islam a questionable basis for national unity, while many reformist leaders saw economic and political modernization as their primary objectives, and had little interest in religious dogma.

Muhammadiyah, formed in Yogyakarta in November 1912 by Kijai Hadji Ahmad Dahlan, was a principal component of the modernist, reform-minded faction known in Indonesia as the *kaum muda* (lit. young group). In the religious sphere, Muhammadiyah attacked heterodox religious practices, the influence of *adat* (customary law) and the associated aristo-cratic *priyayi* society, and Westernization. The *kaum muda* advocated a purified Islam purged of accretions derived from Indian and Indonesian sources, and applied reason to basic textual materials such as the Koran and the Sunnah so as to deal with contemporary issues. Muhammadiyah, which favoured a religiously-oriented programme of modernization, con-centrated on education and social welfare, and generally did not become involved in political activity.

This reformist programme eventually drew a response from those who practised the syncretic form of Islam that had long prevailed in the archipelago. In 1926 this faction, generally known as the *kaum tua* or elder group, formed a rival organization called Nahdatul Ulama (The Rise of the Religious Scholars) to defend established religious practices. Like Muham-madiyah, Nahdatul Ulama tended to stay out of politics during this period.

Sarekat Islam, after its split with the ISDV, attempted to establish itself as a major voice for Muslim interests, but the organization had been compromised by its association with communism. During the 1920s, religiously oriented moderates tended to turn to established non-political groups such as Muhammadiyah, while on the political side, the communists and later a newly formed nationalist organization, the Perserikatan Nasional Indonesia (PNI), seized the initiative. In 1929 Sarekat Islam reconstituted itself as the Partai Sarekat Islam Indonesia, but the organization never recovered the influence or pre-eminence it had once enjoyed.

During the 1920s, reformist activity that concentrated on religious or educational matters but was not overtly political grew increasingly significant, and bolstered the nationalist cause. Education was a concern of Indonesian intellectuals of all persuasions, and grew in importance as Dutch monitoring and suppression of political activity became more intense. Schools and study groups provided a forum for disseminating new ideas and creating a politically aware population, while avoiding direct action that might provoke a Dutch response. One major educational movement, called Taman Siswa or the Garden of Students, was founded in 1922 by Ki Hadjar Dewantoro (the former Indische Partij activist Suwardi Suryadiningrat) who had developed a strong interest in education during his period of exile in the Netherlands. Like Nahdatul Ulama, the Taman Siswa represented an assertion of Javanese identity, combining Javanese culture and a modernist Western-oriented curriculum as an alternative to modernist Islam. Muhammadiyah also devoted a great deal of attention to education, sponsoring schools that taught the ideas of reformist Islam together with practical skills. Reformers in the outer islands similarly used education to spread modernist and nationalist ideas, notably in the Minangkabau area where the Sumatra Thawalib organization established a school system that became an intellectual centre for anti-government activity.

Indonesian students in the Netherlands became politically active during the 1920s. Their vehicle was Perhimpunan Indonesia (the Indonesian Association), which had its origins in a student society formed in 1909. In 1918 the group began expressing nationalist political views, and in 1925 was reconstituted as a political body which, although never large, became a fertile source of ideas and launched many of its members, including Mohammad Hatta—Perhimpunan Indonesia's moving force—Sutan Sjahrir, Soetomo, and Sartono, on careers as political activists. Perhimpunan Indonesia advocated a unified archipelago-wide effort against the Dutch, with non-cooperation as a tactic, and it formulated the concept of 'Indonesia', an essential step in moving away from the colonial 'Netherlands East Indies' and creating a new national identity.

In Europe, Perhimpunan Indonesia worked together for a time with Marxist groups, but the high degree of control exercised over the communist movement by Moscow made Perhimpunan Indonesia members fear that following this path might simply mean the replacement of one form of imperialism by another. In 1926 Hatta, as head of Perhimpunan Indonesia, and the PKI leader Semaun signed a convention under which the two groups would co-operate. The agreement was in effect for only two weeks before the Comintern instructed Semaun to repudiate it, but the arrangement became known to the Dutch security service and coloured its view of Hatta and the Perhimpunan Indonesia.

Another development of the 1920s was the emergence of a second generation of political activists within Indonesia, and of new political organizations that displaced Sarekat Islam as the leading secular nationalist association. The younger leadership, disillusioned with the lack of progress to date, adopted a more confrontational style. Study clubs, the first established in Surabaya by Dr Raden Soetomo, a founding member of Budi Utomo and a Perhimpunan Indonesia member while studying in the Netherlands, provided a common meeting ground for returned students and local activists. The most important of these groups was the General Study Club of Bandung, where the membership included established leaders such as Tjipto Mangunkusumo and Douwes Dekker, and also Sukarno, an engineering student in Bandung when the group was formed in 1925. Sukarno, who rapidly became one of the key nationalist figures in the Netherlands East Indies, argued for unity in opposing the Dutch, and attempted to produce a synthesis of nationalism, Islam and Marxism. However, government pressure had caused the Bandung Study Club to distance itself from Marxism even before the abortive uprisings, and the alliance between secular modernizers in the nationalist movement and the religious faction was always uneasy.

In 1927, the study clubs and returned members of Perhimpunan Indonesia formed a new political organization called the Perserikatan Nasional Indonesia (PNI, the Indonesian National Association) to promote the cause of Indonesian nationalism by fostering unity, eliminating reliance on the Dutch, and working towards independence. The Bandung Study Club took the lead in setting up the organization, and Sukarno occupied a prominent place in its executive body. The Dutch government monitored the situation but for the moment tolerated these developments as a means of containing nationalist sentiment and preventing the growth of extremist tendencies.

John Ingleson has observed that the leaders of the PNI, although describing themselves as radicals, adopted moderate demands:

> There was a noticeable lack of radicalism in the party's social and economic policies, particularly when compared with the platform of the banned PKI. There was nothing which would lose it support among the wealthier Indonesian elite. Scant attention was given to urban workers, there was no mention of peasant rights nor of land reform and no suggestion of any redistribution of wealth or resources after independence, beyond the cessation of Dutch drainage of the economy. This was partly in order to retain as wide a spectrum of support as possible but at the same time it was also a reflection of the essential social and economic conservatism of the PNI leaders.

By way of mitigation, Ingleson notes that government sensitivity in the aftermath of the PKI uprising made a moderate programme expedient to avoid suppression. This moderation notwithstanding, the Dutch security service associated the PNI with Marxism, and accordingly treated it as a very dangerous movement.[23]

[23] John Ingleson, *Road to Exile: The Indonesian Nationalist Movement, 1927–1934*, Singapore, 1974, 56–7.

Sukarno, who considered unity to be of paramount importance, was also instrumental in creating a federation of anti-colonial parties called the Permufakatan Perhimpunan-Perhimpunan Politik Kebangsaan Indonesia (PPPKI, the Association of Political Organizations of the Indonesian People). The major political organizations joined this front, but the PPPKI was rent by conflicts (in particular over the appropriateness of a non-cooperative approach, and the role of religion) and played only a minor part in subsequent events.

The nationalist movement did succeed in gaining acceptance for a number of key symbols in the late 1920s. One was a red-and-white national flag, another the national anthem, entitled 'Indonesia Raya'. The movement also pressed for use of Indonesian—based on Malay, the lingua franca of the ports—as a national language, and for new terminology: Indonesia for the Netherlands East Indies, and Jakarta for Batavia. A youth congress that met in 1928 adopted a slogan to the effect that Indonesia comprised one people, one language, one homeland, and this youth pledge provided a rallying cry for the nationalist struggle.

The PNI flourished until the end of 1929, building its organizational base while using Sukarno's extraordinary gifts as an orator to attract mass support. As the membership grew, Sukarno became increasingly bold in his speeches, and the government began to intervene, banning some meetings and forbidding the use of emotive terms relating to freedom and independence at public gatherings. The PNI's growing extremism, which many members opposed, led in December 1929 to the detention of a number of leaders including Sukarno, who was subsequently tried and sentenced to four years' imprisonment, although he was released after serving half the term.

During the 1930s the reformist movement was characterized by grudging co-operation. Dutch authorities under the influence of De Jonge, and the conservative H. Colijn, who became Minister of Colonies in 1933, conceded little to nationalist sentiment and made it clear that non-cooperating groups would not be tolerated. The Dutch security service identified five sources of danger to the colonial régime: extremist movements (indigenous messianic activity); trade unionism; foreign movements (a category that included both international communism and Perhimpunan Indonesia); nationalist and Muslim movements; and the Chinese movement (arising from the influence of political developments in China on Chinese living in the Indies).[24] During the 1920s and 1930s, the government took strong and generally effective action against organizations in all categories.

After Sukarno's conviction, the new PNI leader, Sartono, suspended PNI political activity, and in April 1931 dissolved the organization. Two successor parties were formed. Partai Indonesia (Partindo) attempted to carry on PNI activity under a new name, while the Pendidikan Nasional Indonesia (Indonesian National Education, known as the PNI Baru, or New PNI), a body which reflected Hatta's philosophy, sought to educate a

[24] Theodore Friend, *The Blue-Eyed Enemy: Japan against the West in Java and Luzon, 1942–1945*, Princeton, 1988, 39.

cohort of future nationalist leaders and to cultivate a political base among the proletariat and the peasantry. Upon his release at the end of 1931, Sukarno resumed his attempt to foster nationalist unity through the PPPKI, but he found divisions too deep to overcome and on 1 August 1932 joined Partindo, just twenty-four days before Hatta returned to Indonesia to take control of PNI Baru after spending eleven years as a student and political activist in the Netherlands.

A year later, on 1 August 1933, the government again detained Sukarno, this time banishing him to Flores without a trial. Hatta and Sjahrir adopted a conciliatory approach, but nonetheless were arrested in February 1934 and banished to Boven Digul in New Guinea. By the end of 1934, most prominent anti-colonial leaders had been detained, and non-cooperating nationalism had ceased to be a viable option. For the remainder of the prewar period, the nationalist cause was represented by cautious, co-operating groups such as the Partai Indonesia Raya or Parindra (The Greater Indonesia Party), formed in 1935 by drawing together members of various moderate organizations, and the Gerakan Rakyat Indonesia or Gerindo (Indonesian People's Movement), a nationalist organization sympathetic to socialism which was founded in 1937. Partindo dissolved itself in 1936, and PNI Baru ceased to play a significant role after its leaders were detained.

One of the most important nationalist figures of the 1930s was Mohammed Husni Thamrin, chairman of the PPPKI during the 1930s and head of the political section of Parindra. A close friend of Sukarno and a strong critic of colonial rule, Thamrin was sufficiently co-operative with the Dutch to retain his independence, and as a member of the Volksraad had a forum for openly and effectively criticizing abuses. His death in Dutch custody in January 1941, although due to natural causes, helped to mobilize anti-Dutch opinion in the last months before the Japanese invasion.

The rise of fascism in Europe and Japan during the 1930s altered the political situation, and proponents of a loyalist posture made a number of efforts to reach an accommodation with the Dutch government as war approached. In October 1936 Sutardjo Kartohadikusumo, president of an Association of Native Civil Servants founded in 1929, initiated a petition in the Volksraad addressed to the queen and requesting that an imperial conference be convened to draft a reform programme leading towards Indonesian self-government within a Dutch commonwealth. The Dutch government did not respond until late 1938, and then rejected the petition.

Gerindo, reflecting the growing concern about the growth of fascism in Europe, also offered co-operation with the Dutch internationally against this threat, while pursuing nationalist objectives domestically; but it found the Dutch unreceptive. In 1939 the main nationalist organizations (including Gerindo, Parindra, and Partai Sarekat Islam Indonesia) formed an umbrella group called the Gabungan Politik Indonesia (GAPI, the Indonesian Political Federation). GAPI offered to work with the Dutch against fascism in return for a promise of autonomy for Indonesia, and attempted to get the Dutch to agree to the formation of a true Indonesian parliament, but the Netherlands rejected these proposals. After the German invasion of Holland, the Dutch government-in-exile declined to consider the status of Indonesia while the war was in progress, and rebuffed further suggestions by Indonesian leaders.

Another development of the late 1930s, and a significant portent for the future, was an agreement by Muhammadijah and Nahdatul to join forces in a Council of Muslim parties (the Madjlisul Islamil A'laa Indonesia, or MIAI). Created to co-ordinate religious affairs, MIAI was soon drawn into politics and supported GAPI's proposals to establish an Indonesian parliament, but with the proviso that it should be based on Islamic principles.

The involvement of peoples living outside Java in modernist political reform varied considerably. Many societies in the archipelago fulfil the classic definition of a nation, possessing unique languages, cultures, and historical traditions, and some developed nationalist activity based on these characteristics. In the case of the Minangkabau, one of the most distinctive societies owing to its matrilineal traditions, regional loyalties were subsumed by involvement in a broader nationalism, and Java-based organizations such as the Muhammadiyah and the PKI were well received. Minangkabau, however, was unusual among territories outside Java in having a long history of colonial rule (Dutch control dated from the 1820s), and was exceptionally aware of extra-local events owing to the *merantau* tradition which took young men away from the Minangkabau heartland to trade or study elsewhere. By way of contrast, the Acehnese, who also had a long history of external contacts with traders from outside the archipelago, were preoccupied with local issues and showed no great interest in political developments in Batavia or elsewhere. Political organizations formed around Acehnese leaders, and national Indonesian organizations had little appeal.

Other societies and groups also had parochial concerns that competed with the political objectives of the small, urban-based, Western-educated nationalist élite in Java, as reflected in a large number of youth organizations operating during the 1920s (including besides Jong [Young] Java, Jong Sumatra, Jong Celebes, Jong Bataks Bond, Jong Ambon, and Jong Minahasa). The Eurasian community, attracted initially to the multi-racial Nationale Indische Partij which the Dutch suppressed in 1913, subsequently turned to Insulinde, which supported a moderate programme of reform. The Chinese and Peranakan communities likewise formulated political programmes, a development discussed elsewhere in this chapter. Finally, in the Indies as elsewhere, there was an element of loyalist sentiment. The *priyayi* who served the Dutch administration, the Ambonese in the Dutch military forces, some of the Eurasians in government service, and the Chinese in the archipelago had good reason to fear Indonesian nationalism, for it was directed against themselves as well as against the Dutch.

The Dutch administration itself developed an initiative to shape and channel reformist sentiment in a benign way. Marxism, secular nationalism and Islamic reform were all directed against both colonial rule and indigenous traditions within the archipelago. In an effort to counterbalance these movements and build political support, the Dutch promoted the study of *adat*, or customary law, attempting to transform it into a set of principles that would provide a foundation for a modern state and society. The Dutch had identified the indigenous aristocracy as their natural allies within Indonesian society, and *adat* had the added value of enhancing the importance of the aristocracy. This approach underlay a postwar Dutch initiative to create a federal Indonesia which would safeguard the interests of less powerful cultural groups within the archipelago, and certainly had some appeal in areas which saw Jakarta-based nationalism as a new form of imperialism.

French Indochina

There is general agreement that nationalism developed in Vietnam considerably earlier than in Cambodia or Laos. When, however, is another question. Particularly in a country such as Vietnam with a long history of active resistance to foreign domination and colonialism, it is difficult to draw a dividing line between traditional patriotism or national consciousness and what may be regarded as modern nationalism. One standard study, covering the period 1885–1925, avoids the problem by using the more elastic term 'anti-colonialism'.[25] Another Vietnam specialist has written that 'if nationalism in the Southeast Asian context means ideologies that simultaneously stress the rediscovery and preservation of a distinctly non-Western cultural identity and the assimilation of modern Western techniques and revolutionary ideas, then Vietnamese resistance to French colonialism before the 1900s was not nationalistic but a compound of xenophobia and Confucian loyalism', adding however that such resistance 'was nonetheless a vital forerunner of Vietnamese nationalism'.[26]

The issue arises out of Vietnam's centuries-old tradition of resistance to attempts to impose Chinese hegemony, and the fact that early anti-French activities often seemed to fit into much the same mould. Divided loyalties, for example, were an old issue, and as the French seized control of Cochinchina in the 1860s, bitter debates engulfed the Confucian literati as to whether collaboration afforded an acceptable alternative to non-cooperation. The moral dilemma was complicated by the fact that in the early years of French advance the imperial court at Hué adopted a compromising, concessionist policy, signing agreements recognizing French authority in various regions, so that in theory at least open resistance to the French meant opposition to court policy as well. Nonetheless the early French advance into Cochinchina in the south and then Tonkin in the north was met with at least sporadic, if not centrally co-ordinated armed resistance.

The moral dilemma was temporarily resolved in the mid-1880s when a group of hardline anti-French officials seized control of the court and fled inland with the boy-emperor, in whose name an edict calling for a general uprising against the invaders was issued. The French soon placed a more

---

[25] David G. Marr, *Vietnamese Anticolonialism*, Berkeley, 1971.
[26] Alexander Woodside, in David Joel Steinberg, ed., *In Search of Southeast Asia: A Modern History*, rev. edn, Honolulu, 1987, 312.

pliant member of the imperial family on the throne, and eventually captured and sent into exile his refugee predecessor, thus ending royal sanction for the Can Vuong ('aid the king') movement. Nonetheless this example served as the inspiration for a series of scattered anti-French, and at times anti-Catholic, uprisings in the years to come, the latter directed primarily at Vietnamese who had adopted the Catholic faith.

Such resistance did not prevent the consolidation of French rule over all of Cochinchina, Tonkin, and Annam, under somewhat differing for-malistic legal arrangements but in effect amounting to a unitary colonial administration. The task of evolving a coherent colonial policy was made more difficult by the notorious political instability in France itself, which in the half-century from 1870 to 1920 went through two major wars and numerous changes in cabinets and ministers responsible for its Asian empire. The frequent shifts of political line were to some degree reflected in Vietnam itself, with relatively short tenures for top colonial administra-tors (some twenty governors-general between 1887 and 1920) and long-running debates over such questions as whether cultural policy should aim at 'association' or 'assimilation'. Economic policy was more firmly and consistently pursued: the resources of Vietnam should be exploited for the benefit of France and the empire. This included the development of an infrastructure of roads, railways, ports, and the like; the opening of new lands, particularly in the less-populated Mekong region in the south and southwest, and a great expansion in the cultivation of rice and, at a somewhat latter date, rubber, mainly for export; the recruitment of labour from the densely populated north to work as rice planters or on rubber estates; a limited industrial development in certain products which would not compete with French imports in the local market; and a burdensome tax system that relied heavily on excise taxes on a range of consumer items, including such necessities as salt. While the large plantations were mainly French-owned, Vietnamese with capital and connections also acquired extensive tracts of land, and particularly in the south there emerged a class of indigenous absentee landowners who depended for their well-being on the colonial system. The existence of such a dependent élite inevitably hindered the development of a broadly-based nationalist movement.

In the first decades of the twentieth century, Vietnamese anti-colonialism underwent a gradual transformation as it assimilated and incorporated a variety of foreign influences. At the beginning of the century anti-French agitation was still dominated by 'Confucian scholar activists', of whom Phan Boi Chau (1867–1940) and Phan Chu Trinh (1871–1926) are perhaps the best known. They were much influenced by the abortive late Qing reform movement of Kang Youwei, Liang Qichao and their followers. Through the medium of Chinese-language translations and adaptations (which this early generation read more easily than French) they also came in contact with French liberal thought and such current Western doctrines as Social Darwinism. Another major external influence was the example of Japan, which by its victories in the Sino-Japanese and Russo-Japanese Wars (1894–5; 1904–5) and the 1902 conclusion of the Anglo-Japanese Alliance had clearly demonstrated its emergence as a technologically modern state, able to deal with the Western powers on a basis of equality.

Various pan-Asianist elements, and Chinese reformers living in exile in Japan, encouraged Vietnam to follow Japan's path in adopting Western science and technology in order to throw off Western domination. In particular Vietnamese students were encouraged to study in Japan, and short-lived attempts were made to establish proto-nationalist schools in Vietnam itself.

On several major questions, Phan Boi Chau and Phan Chu Trinh differed. One, which was to prove a divisive issue in Vietnamese nationalism down to the 1950s, was the role of the monarchy. Chau at this stage still favoured retaining the monarchy as a unifying symbol, hoping to find a suitable member of the imperial family willing to provide leadership, at least in name, to an anti-French movement; Trinh, however, was an uncompromising critic of the collaborationist court and an advocate of republicanism. He also, in contrast to Chau, rejected any resort to violence as part of the independence struggle. He was impressed by the liberal aspects of French culture and humanist philosophy (he spent most of the latter part of his life in France), and he had a belief, not shared by Chau, that the French presence in Vietnam could be a positive force if it led to the introduction of progressive aspects of Western civilization and ultimately to concession of the political rights and ideals of the Enlightenment.

The second decade of the century was, on the surface, and despite another abortive plot involving a young emperor, a period of relative calm. France was absorbed in the great conflict in Europe, and in Vietnam a liberal governor-general, Albert Sarraut, who served two terms which together covered nearly half of the decade, seemed to offer hope of progressive policies and gradual change. In this atmosphere there emerged moderate reformers willing to work within the colonial system, constitutionalists, and cultural nationalists. But there were also developments which would prove to be of greater long-range significance. In Asia, Japan began to lose its appeal as a model. Responding to Western diplomatic pressures, official Japanese policy became increasingly hostile to the presence of anti-colonial activists and students. Japan had annexed Taiwan in 1895 and Korea in 1910, and during the war tried to impose the Twenty-One Demands on China and laid claim to former German rights in Shantung; it was increasingly perceived as having embarked on an 'imperialist' path, as likely to be a threat as a source of support. But an alternative model, both geographically and culturally closer to Vietnam, emerged with the 1911 Revolution in China. While fragmented and unstable, the new China offered both a republican ideology and the possibility of bases of operation adjacent to Vietnam itself.

Further away, the upheaval of World War I in Europe gave rise to more radical impulses. The war itself seriously challenged the notion that Western civilization was in any way inherently progressive and superior, while it brought in its wake the Russian Revolution and the emergence of communism as a world political force, rather than a European ideology. In 1911 the man who would ultimately become known as Ho Chi Minh had left Vietnam for Europe. From a Confucian, if anti-French, upbringing he moved in France to involvement in, and then disillusionment with socialist movements. Finally, like many young Asian nationalists, he was drawn to

Marxism and ultimately to the communist centre, Moscow. The appeal of Marxist-Leninist thought for anti-colonial activists was strong: it offered an explanation (through the imperialist stage of capitalism) of the fate which had befallen their countries; it offered the hope, even assurance, that the present colonial status was temporary; and perhaps most importantly, it offered a modus operandi, in terms of party organization, strategy, and the stages of revolution through which independence would be regained and a socialist society achieved. It has also been argued that certain structural similarities between Confucianism and Marxism—such as their this-worldly orientation, their claims to represent a rational, scientific doctrine of universal applicability, and their hierarchical nature and strong emphasis on political relationships and the state—facilitated moving from the former to the latter; in any case, it is largely in areas of traditional Confucian influence that popular communist revolutions have, to the present, succeeded in Asia.

These more radical strands in the anti-colonial movement gained strength in the 1920s as the age of the Confucian scholar activists drew to a close and Confucianism itself, increasingly identified with the court and collaboration, ceased to be a major force in Vietnamese nationalism. Secular groups, lacking strong ties to a traditional religion or ideology, came to the fore, in some ways differentiating Vietnam from the rest of Southeast Asia. There established religions such as Buddhism (Burma, Siam), Islam (Indonesia, Malaya), and an indigenized Christianity (the Philippines) played an important part in nationalist movements in the early decades of the century, and in a number of cases well beyond. A partial exception in Vietnam was the Cao Dai sect, which from the mid-1920s rapidly gained a large following in the south. It proclaimed a syncretic theology, and a form of conservative anti-colonialism which ultimately veered toward pro-Japanese sentiments.

The mid-1920s saw another leftward swing in the French political scene, and consequently in the colonial leadership, but the relatively mild reforms that resulted disappointed those who hoped for change within the colonial system. The failure of moderate, co-operative parties, such as the Constitutionalists, to achieve significant concessions and progress toward at least a measure of internal autonomy predictably left the field open to more radical groups. French intransigence and repression increasingly meant that there appeared to be no alternative between outright collaboration and clandestine, subversive activity.

The first of the radical groups to make a major, though brief, impact was the Viet Nam Quoc Dan Dang (Vietnamese Nationalist Party), usually known by the acronym VNQDD. The VNQDD was founded in 1927, modelled upon the then-triumphant Kuomintang in China. Based in the cities, with most of its following in the north, the VNQDD was organized along the lines of a secret society. Without attempting to build a mass base, it plotted to subvert Vietnamese garrison forces and hoped for revolutionary insurrection sparked by spectacular but isolated acts of violence. The assassination of a French official in 1929 resulted in harsh French repression, leading to a desperate, premature uprising at Yen Bai in February 1930. After brief initial success the revolt was put down, and the severe French reprisals which followed effectively put an end to the party. The decimation of the VNQDD, coupled with French suppression of more moderate forms of political activity, left the communists well placed to compete for leadership of the anti-colonial movement. Ho Chi Minh from the mid-1920s had been operating from South China or Siam, and in 1925 had organized the Vietnamese Revolutionary Youth League. After various factional vicissitudes, in 1930 he succeeded in bringing together several left-leaning groups to form the Indochina Communist Party (a name insisted upon by the Comintern, which objected to the 'overly-nationalistic' tone of the originally proposed 'Vietnamese Communist Party').

The party's inception coincided with the onset of the Great Depression, which brought sharply lower world prices for rice, rubber, and other commodities, and in Vietnam itself increased tenancy, indebtedness, and unemployment, all seemingly favourable conditions for a revolutionary struggle. Indeed in mid-1930 large-scale rural uprisings did take place in the Nghe An and Ha Tinh provinces of north central Vietnam, and, with local officials killed or taking flight, for a time colonial authority broke down. As the rebellion progressed it took on definite communist over-tones, with the formation of 'soviets' and the adoption of various revolu-tionary symbols. There has been debate as to whether the communists were instigators of the uprisings or opportunistic, and possibly reluctant, late-comers whom the force of circumstances thrust into the leadership of what had started as essentially spontaneous movements.

In any case the French found it expedient to place the responsibility on 'Bolshevik' agitators, and when after protracted military operations the uprisings were put down, the expected repression and reprisals followed. In the short term the result was a serious set-back for the party, with much of the leadership inside Vietnam jailed or executed; for the longer term the uprisings did demonstrate the village revolutionary potential, suggesting a strategic orientation that the party would later adopt.

For the next few years the communists maintained a low profile, working to evolve a coherent strategy amid a number of conflicting pressures. Moscow still claimed the right to dictate worldwide communist doctrine, and Comintern policy went through unpredictable shifts be-tween 'united front from above' and 'united front from below'. Theoretical debates centred on the role of the peasantry, which Marx in his European-oriented analysis had virtually written off. Lenin had put somewhat more emphasis on the peasantry in the revolutionary scenario, but had still given a leading role to the industrial proletariat. But in Vietnam the industrial proletariat was quite small, and the 1930–1 uprisings had shown the rural revolutionary potential. There was also the example of China, where under Mao's leadership the communists were establishing them-selves in bases in the countryside. The end result was to place greater emphasis on the actual internal conditions of Vietnam, rather than foreign theoretical formulations, and by the end of the decade the party had adopted a rural strategy of revolution.

The communists were also handicapped by internal divisions. Ho's Indochina Communist Party (ICP) faced strong competition, particularly in the urban areas of south Vietnam, from 'Trotskyite' factions, reflecting a further importing of global communist schisms and polemics into the Vietnamese context.

In the late 1930s a number of developments on the world scene sharply affected and altered the prospects of the ICP. Germany and Japan emerged as aggressive, expansive nations, while in France a left-of-centre government came to power resulting, for a time, in a somewhat freer political atmosphere in Vietnam. Faced with the growing threat of the Axis powers, international communist strategy now dictated a 'united front from above', in which the peasantry and proletariat would join with the 'national' bourgeoisie and small capitalists in a broad anti-fascist coalition. This policy line came to an unexpectedly abrupt end in August 1939, with the shock announcement of the Nazi–Soviet non-aggression pact. Within days war broke out in Europe, followed some nine months later by the fall of France and the subsequent establishment of the pliant Vichy régime. The Indochina part of France's empire recognized in name, if not always in fact, Vichy's authority; it soon came under strong Japanese diplomatic pressure and the threat of military moves. The result was 'negotiations' in which the colonial authorities had little choice but to yield to demands for the stationing of Japanese military forces in northern Vietnam (September 1940) and subsequently in the south (July 1941). Meanwhile Thailand took advantage of the weakened French position, and a degree of Japanese support, to reclaim areas of western and northern Cambodia and trans-Mekong Laos that had earlier been ceded to France.

This blinding whirl of international developments radically transformed the internal situation in Vietnam, and the communists were quick to take advantage of the opportunities that seemed to have arisen. Early in 1941 Ho, who had lived abroad since sailing for Europe thirty years earlier, crossed from China into northern Vietnam, where he presided over the establishment of a new organization, the Viet Nam Doc Lap Dong Minh (League for the Independence of Vietnam), known as the Vietminh. Though it was dominated by communists, the Vietminh was a front which aimed at creating a broad coalition of anti-colonial, anti-Japanese elements; to this end it played down the more radical aspects of social revolution, stressing instead such 'national' goals as the achievement of independence.

The eve of the outbreak of the Pacific War found the communists well placed to take the leading role in the anti-colonial struggle. They had strong organization and leadership. They were beginning to develop rural base areas, especially along the northern Vietnam–China border, which included some tribal regions. These were areas in which they were strongest and their opponents—whether French colonial authority, Japanese, or rival 'nationalist' groups—were weakest. And because until the last stages of the war, the Vichy colonial administration and the Japanese were in 'alliance', the Vietminh had the unique advantage of being able to be anti-colonial and anti-Japanese at the same time. In other parts of Southeast Asia where the Japanese overthrew colonial rule, nationalists often confronted the awkward choice of supporting the new order against the West, or supporting their former colonial rulers against Japan's imperial designs. Men like Laurel, Sukarno, Aung San and others who for

whatever tactical or expedient reasons chose temporary co-operation with
the Japanese inevitably, with Japan's decline, faced possible charges of
'collaboration'. In Vietnam the Cao Dai and certain other would-be nationalists were also to some degree compromised, but for the Vietminh
collaboration was not an issue, and their anti-colonial, anti-Japanese stance
appealed to a wide spectrum of Vietnamese who wanted to see their
country freed from foreign influences.

Thus the unique political configuration in Vietnam at the outbreak of the
Pacific War meant great complexities but also great opportunities for the
newly-formed Vietminh. Their leaders might well have echoed the Maoist
dictum, 'All is chaos under the heavens; the situation is excellent.'

For Cambodia and Laos, discussion of pre-1941 nationalism is likely to
emphasize the negative: why were there so few visible manifestations of
nationalist activity? Certainly forerunners of postwar independence movements were not totally lacking. In Cambodia there were isolated instances
of popular discontent over various colonial policies, while a Buddhist
Institute established in 1930 under French and royal patronage turned,
contrary to its sponsors' intentions, into something of a centre for cultural
nationalism and revival. This reassertion of traditionalism was encouraged
by Thailand which, particularly after the 1932 change of government, tried
to expand its influence in its former vassal state, based upon a shared
religion and Indic cultural heritage. From the other direction, politically-
oriented south Vietnamese religious sects attracted Cambodian adherents
from both sides of the Cambodian–Vietnamese border; and the Vietnamese-
dominated Indochina Communist Party had from an early stage a small
Khmer component, though relations between Cambodian and Vietnamese
communists for much of the period since the 1930s have been more stormy
than fraternal.

In Laos there was a long tradition of anti-French (and at times anti-Lao)
tribal rebellions, particularly in the southern highlands, which later
became an important component of the postwar communist movement.
Thailand also again tried to extend its influence at French expense, aided
not only by the religious and cultural affinities which applied to Cambodia,
but also by the ethnic and linguistic kinship between Thai and Lao. And
again the Vietnamese, through the ICP, patronized a small Lao communist
movement, which would play a role in the Lao Issara group of the 1940s
and ultimately find its own identity in the Pathet Lao.

Nevertheless, when contrasted with the case of Vietnam, the paucity of
pre-1941 Cambodian and Lao 'nationalist' activity is striking. It is difficult
to point to any organized parties, other than the Vietnamese-initiated ICP,
and only a handful of individuals emerge as identifiable 'nationalists',
compared to the scores of prominent figures in histories of the early
Vietnamese anti-colonialist and nationalist movements.

A number of factors would seem to account for this relative colonial calm
in Cambodia and Laos. In both territories the French ruled with a fairly
light hand, at least when compared to the economic exploitation and
political repression which characterized the colonial régime in Vietnam.
Cambodia had only limited resources of interest to the French, mainly

rubber and rice, while Laos had even less to offer in the way of economic potential. Indeed the colonial administration in the latter perennially ran at a deficit, requiring subsidies from other parts of Indochina.

In a sense, the French could claim to have 'saved' Cambodia, which at the height of its power had extended its rule over the Mekong delta and large areas of modern Laos and Siam. The southward and westward advance of the Vietnamese and the eastward expansion of the Thai had by the nineteenth century reduced Cambodia to a shadow of its former imperial glory, paying tribute to the courts of both Bangkok and Hué, and if the French had not appeared on the scene it is possible that Cambodia might have been completely absorbed by its stronger neighbours.

If the French can be said to have saved Cambodia, they virtually created Laos in its modern form. Pre-modern 'Laos' was composed of a number of rival principalities, often in conflict with one another and all subject to varying external pressures. From north to south, the major traditional centres included Luang Prabang, Xieng Khouang, Vientiane, and Champassak, though an unsuccessful attempt by Vientiane princes in the 1820s to throw off Bangkok's sovereignty had resulted in a harsh Thai retribution that left Vientiane devastated and depopulated. French interest in what would become modern Laos was only minimally strategic (after the early discovery that the unnavigable upper Mekong would not provide a 'river road to China') or economic. Rather it was in considerable measure the result of the initiative of enterprising individuals—romantic adventurers such as Henri Mouhot and Auguste Pavie—coupled with an almost compulsive drive to compete with the British for the grandeur of empire. The latter concern was alternately restrained or reinforced by the erratic shifts of French domestic politics but, particularly after the humiliating defeat France suffered in the Franco-Prussian War, pressures grew in some quarters to compensate for lost prestige at home by expanding possessions abroad—even in regions which might promise little in the way of tangible benefits.

Not surprisingly, many among the Cambodian and Lao élite could view the French as benevolent protectors, or at least a lesser of evils. The recent pre-colonial histories of both Cambodia and the areas which came to form Laos suggested that the realistic alternative they faced was not between French colonialism and independence, but between French colonialism and domination by one or another, or a combination, of their stronger neighbours. France at least was far away, and there was no danger of French immigration on a significant scale. French culture was also remotely alien, and while a very limited circle of the élite acquired some French education and a taste for French luxuries, the great majority of the population remained little affected by the French 'civilizing mission'; indeed, in the encounter of cultures the process was often reversed, with Frenchmen being attracted to the traditional Buddhist cultures of the Cambodians and the Lao.

This combination of a relatively benign French presence with a potential threat, should the French leave, of Thai or Vietnamese domination, obviously militated against the development of anti-colonial sentiment and contributed to the late emergence of any identifiable modern 'nationalism'.

Nevertheless, French rule inevitably did at times intrude into the lives of the people and, as noted above, there were occasional popular protests, particularly in Cambodia, and ethnically based uprisings in Laos. Amongst the élite also, not all accepted the French presence as beneficial. Factionalism and personal rivalries were common, and at times took the form of political opposition or outright rebellion. By the eve of the Pacific War even some of those who had benefited most from the colonial system were moving towards an anti-French nationalism: the soon-to-emerge Lao Issara and Pathet Lao movements were both headed by princes of a collateral line of the royal house of Luang Prabang, while in Cambodia the mercurial Prince Sihanouk, elevated to the throne in 1941 because of his youth and presumed malleability, was to prove to be much more independent-minded than his French sponsors had anticipated.

Burma

In Burma, as in Vietnam and Siam, certain unique factors specific to the country and operative throughout the period under consideration significantly affected the course of development of nationalism. Among the most important of these was the large number of ethnic groups, whether 'traditional', i.e. long present in the country, or relatively recent arrivals. The former include, among the more numerically prominent, the Burmans, the Mon, the Arakanese, the Karen, the Shan, and the Kachin, and the latter the Indians and, to a lesser degree, the Chinese. This multiplicity of ethnic groups has been a centrifugal force in Burmese history, resulting in political fragmentation and posing a constant obstacle to the establishment and maintenance of any strong, unitary authority. Similarly in the twentieth century ethnic questions were a divisive issue in the nationalist movement, especially as certain of the minority groups, fearful of the domination of an ethnic Burman majority, looked to British colonial authority for protection. In this regard, Burma has less resembled relatively more homogeneous Vietnam or Siam than parts of insular Southeast Asia, most notably the Dutch East Indies with its examples of ethnic minorities also seeking the protection of the colonial rulers. Many such groups, whether in the Dutch East Indies or Burma, were unenthusiastic about the prospect of independence within the boundaries of the colonial state and deeply concerned about the conditions under which it might be achieved. In the final postwar negotiations leading to Burmese independence, the most intractable issues were not between the Burmese and the British but between the Burmans and various other ethnic groups.

Several British actions taken immediately following the annexation of upper Burma in the Third Anglo-Burmese War (1885–6) also profoundly affected future political developments. Foremost perhaps was the abolition of the Burmese monarchy, apparently undertaken in the light of immediate circumstances with little consideration of the long-term consequences. Royal misrule had been one of the British justifications for the war, so the removal of King Thibaw was inevitable. There was no obvious candidate to succeed him, in part because Thibaw and his clique had eliminated most potential rivals when he first came to the throne. Nevertheless, many Burmese, even if critical of Thibaw personally, favoured maintaining the monarchy as an institution, and some British officials and others with experience in Burma also questioned the wisdom of abolishing what had traditionally been a central focus of Burmese politics and society, and a source of legitimacy for the state. Other colonial examples show that preserving a traditional élite, as in Vietnam, Cambodia and Laos under the French, Malaya under the British, or the Indies under the Dutch, could lend a degree of legitimacy and acceptability to colonial rule. And though it might require a Machiavelli to foresee it, the continued existence of traditional élites in a number of cases served as a divisive force within nationalist movements. Early would-be reformers often split over the question of goals, whether to seek to restore some element of the traditional élite or to establish a new order. The dilemma was particularly acute when the traditional élite actively collaborated with colonial rule, as illustrated by the differing early 'nationalist' agendas advocated by Phan Boi Chau and Phan Chu Trinh in Vietnam.

A second British action which had major consequences for the development of nationalism in Burma was the decision to link Burma administratively to India. This led to the introduction of Indian models of administration, whether or not suitable to Burmese conditions. Moreover, the Indian anti-colonial movement was chronologically far in advance of that of Burma, or of any area of Southeast Asia outside the Philippines (the Congress Party had been established in 1885); and it became an important influence on early nationalism in Burma. The Indian political experience served as a model for the Burmese, and there were also some direct contacts, with activists from Burma spending time in India, where they were exposed to new techniques of organization and strategy, and visits to Burma by Indian nationalist leaders.

The administrative tie also meant that any reforms or moves toward self-government conceded by the British in India were considered for Burma as well, potentially giving Burma the benefits of India's progress. And finally, linking the two led to virtually unrestricted Indian immigration, with the result that ethnic Indians came to play an important role in the middle and lower levels of administration and in the economy of Burma. At least in the economic sphere, the position of the Indian minority was somewhat analogous to that of the Chinese in such countries as Vietnam, Siam, and the Dutch East Indies. Census data from 1931 showed about 7 per cent of the total population of Burma to be Indian, concentrated particularly in Rangoon (which was 53 per cent Indian, and about two-thirds immigrant) and other urban centres, compared to a figure of less than 2 per cent for the Chinese; overall, ethnic Burmans totalled more than 60 per cent, and other indigenous groups about 25 per cent. As will be seen, the nationalist movement in Burma was at times to take on an 'anti-Indian' orientation, paralleling 'anti-Chinese' sentiments evident in certain other parts of Southeast Asia in the period.

The British annexation of upper Burma sparked off widespread resistance, initially in traditional guises. Members of the deposed royal house, local chieftains, and other traditional élites led an uncoordinated series of rebellions, while various ethnic groups, following long-established histori-cal patterns, took advantage of upheaval at the centre to assert their autonomy. Despite superiority in arms and organization, it was more than five years before the British could claim to have achieved the 'pacification' of Burma, particularly the newly-annexed upper regions.

By the early years of the twentieth century these traditional forms of resistance largely gave way to new types of anti-colonial activity, conform-ing to what in other Southeast Asian contexts has been termed 'national-ist'. In Burma this early nationalist activity was closely linked to the Buddhist religion, which provided a powerful rallying focus against British rule but also proved in some ways a divisive issue within the nationalist movement. A number of the ethnic minorities were non-Buddhist, while in decades to come even a number of Buddhist Burmans would be attracted to Marxist-socialist thought, leading to the problem—given Marx's strictures on religion—of reconciling Buddhist traditions with secular Western ideologies.

Best-known of the early 'modernist' organizations was the Young Men's Buddhist Association (YMBA), established in 1906 (though deriving from some small, localized precursors) with obvious echoes of the West's YMCA. Initially the YMBA was largely non-political, focusing on cultural, and especially religious, revival. This programme reflected a widely per-ceived decline in traditional Burmese social norms and formations, in part attributed to the disappearance of the monarchy and the court, which historically had been major patrons of the arts and religion, and a con-comitant deterioration in the standards and influence of the Buddhist sangha (monkhood).

The YMBA, however, became increasingly politicized in the 1910s as a result of the long-running shoe controversy, the question whether British and other foreigners should be required to conform to the traditionally unquestioned practice of removing shoes when entering the precincts of a Buddhist temple or monastery. While ostensibly religious, the issue was also political in that it challenged the right of the British overlords to determine what constituted proper behaviour in a Burmese setting; it drew the line of division clearly between the British on one side and the Buddhist communities, principally the Burmans, Mon and Shan, on the other. Despite its political overtones, the religious origins of the contro-versy made it a relatively safe yet formidable strategic issue on which to challenge colonial authority. The final resolution—with the British con-ceding to each abbot the right to determine acceptable practice for his monastery—left the power of decision in indigenous hands and was seen by nationalists as a major, if somewhat symbolic, victory.

Despite such successes, the YMBA soon succumbed to the factionalism endemic in Burmese society and politics, and a split in the movement led to the emergence in 1921 of a new umbrella organization, the General Council of Burmese Associations (GCBA). The name itself, incorporating 'General' and 'Burmese' (rather than 'Buddhist') was indicative of the intention to forge a broader anti-colonial front than had been feasible within the YMBA. One of the GCBA's first initiatives was to support a strike of students at the new University of Rangoon, beginning a long tradition of political activism among university students.

Following the end of the war in Europe, British concessions to nationalist pressures in India resulted in a dyarchy constitution allowing for a very circumscribed degree of indigenous participation in the colonial government. Burma was excluded from the arrangement, setting off a wave of nationalist protests and strikes, and the British Parliament in 1921 extended dyarchy to Burma, a change which took effect two years later. The issue raised two major questions which were to exercise Burmese nationalists throughout the 1920s and most of the 1930s. The first was whether they should continue to seek, as had hithertofore been almost unquestioned in the nationalist agenda, separation from India. This step would bring with it, *inter alia*, the prospect of restrictions on Indian immigration, but such separation now might mean that Burma would fail to share further British concessions to nationalist demands in India. Secondly, there was the question whether nationalists should participate in British schemes of limited self-government, such as partially elected councils, or adopt an uncompromising stand of electoral boycotts, non-cooperation and non-participation. Of the two questions, the latter was a more immediate and practical issue for Burmese nationalists: in the short run, only the British could define the relationship between Burma and India, but Burmese were forced to decide for themselves whether to pursue their goals within or outside the new constitutional arrangements. The debate within the nationalist movement on both questions was acrimonious, with major leaders frequently shifting position as circumstance and opportunity seemed to dictate.

These and other issues resulted in an increasingly divided nationalist movement during the 1920s. The factional rivalries that had plagued the YMBA soon surfaced in the GCBA, leading it to split over questions both of policy and personalities. Long standing urban–rural divisions also became more marked. Urban nationalists on the whole, essentially accepting the modernizing aspect of imperialism, wanted to oust the British and take over the colonial state. Many of the rural constituency wanted not only to oust the British but also to abolish the colonial institutions that had come in their wake—the bureaucratic, economic and other structures that impinged upon and interfered with traditional village life. Controversy also surrounded the increasingly open involvement of the Buddhist *saṅgha* in politics, whether in the form of ecclesiastical domination of certain factions of the GCBA, or the activities of individual monks such as the charismatic U Ottama, who after developing contacts with the Indian nationalist movement launched a campaign severely criticizing the colonial administration in Burma and calling for self-rule.

Nationalist organizations during the 1920s and 1930s sought support from all ethnic groups, yet in many respects reflected Burman interests that were not in harmony with the feelings of other groups. An emphasis on Buddhism, of little interest to non-Burman animists and a source of concern to the Christian Karen, remained a feature of Burman nationalism, and this tendency was reinforced by the political activity of Buddhist monks. Also, when Burman students during the 1920s undertook the creation of a national school system, the Burmese language was proposed as the medium of instruction, and Burmese literature and history figured prominently in the curriculum.

The Great Depression, in Burma as in Vietnam and other areas of Southeast Asia, marked a watershed in the nationalist movement. The prices of rice and other commodities collapsed, and with them much of Burma's export market, leading to severe economic hardships, particularly in areas which in the course of the vast expansion of rice cultivation since the 1850s had become dependent upon a commercialized, largely mono-crop agriculture. Economic hardship brought heightened communal tensions: violence was directed against Indians, who competed in the labour market and also figured prominently as moneylenders and, as a result of mortgage foreclosures, increasingly (if not designedly) as land-owners. To a lesser extent resentments were directed against the Chinese as well. And as in Vietnam, the economic crisis gave rise to rural rebellion, in the form of the Saya San uprising—the most spectacular, if perhaps not ultimately the most significant manifestation of anti-colonial activity between 1885 and the Pacific War.

Saya San was a former monk and a practitioner of 'native' medicine, and the traditional aspects of the revolt have attracted much attention: the reliance on amulets and magic spells, Saya San's professed goal of restoring the monarchy, complete with makeshift replicas of a palace and the royal regalia, and so forth. But Saya San also had extensive experience in more modernist anti-colonial movements, in particular in a faction of the GCBA especially concerned with peasant grievances. The main targets of the rebellion were representatives of the colonial administration, colonial taxes, land rents, and what was generally perceived as increasing bureaucratic interference in traditional life. Given that these were the targets, it has been argued (although not by the British authorities) that more fundamental social and economic causes, which had given rise to widespread village-level nationalist activity in the 1920s and were exacerbated by the depression, underlay the facade of reactionary superstition. In any case the rebellion, beginning in late 1930, spread over wide areas of lower and central Burma; while it never seriously threatened British rule, it was not completely put down until 1932.

If Saya San stood at one pole of Burmese nationalism in the 1930s, an opposite strand was developing in the form of an urban, secular, radical movement, attracting in particular young university students influenced by socialism, Marxism, and other currents of Western thought. The mid-1930s saw another major student strike at the University of Rangoon, and also young activists taking over the Dobama Asiayone (We Burmese Association), a nationalist organization originally founded in 1930 by older leaders. The student leaders appropriated to themselves the title *thakin* ('master'—the appellation usually reserved for the British rulers). They included the charismatic Aung San (whose assassination in 1947 would have severe consequences for the future of Burma, because he was virtually the only major nationalist leader who had the confidence of the non-Burman minorities), and U Nu, who later became the first prime minister of post-British (and post-Japanese) Burma and remained an active political figure down to the upheavals at the end of the 1980s. Like the student activists of the preceding decade, the *thakin* sought to unite all ethnic groups in a Burmese nation, but as before their conception gave priority to Burman elements and envisioned the assimilation of minorities. The *thakin* adopted as their slogan: 'Burma is our country; Burmese literature is our literature; Burmese language is our language. Love our country, raise the standards of our literature, respect our language.'[27] A related issue was an initiative to unify the frontier areas with Burma proper. Burman nationalists argued that Britain, practising a policy of divide-and-rule, had disrupted a historically unified state, and rejected the British contention that the limited administrative unity introduced during the 1920s was an innovation.

As nationalist agitation increased in the late 1930s, including frequent demonstrations and strikes by both students and workers, the British responded with another round of administrative reforms. The Indian Statutory Commission (known as the Simon Commission) which reviewed dyarchy in the late 1920s had recommended the separation of Burma from India, as did the Burma Round Table Conference held in London in 1931–2. In Burma, anti-separationist sentiment had been growing in strength, fuelled by a general distrust of British motives. Action on the issue was delayed until 1937 when Burma was finally separated from India and a new constitution gave the Burmese considerably greater powers of self-government. Ba Maw, a veteran nationalist figure, became prime minister in a 'Burmese administration' responsible for such less critical matters as health and education, but the British still reserved to themselves a number of key spheres of administration—notably defence, foreign affairs, major issues of finance, and control of the 'excluded areas', the Shan states and border regions inhabited by minority ethnic groups.

The more radical, and particularly the younger members of the nationalist factions were dissatisfied with these limited British concessions, and continued to demand more fundamental changes and a commitment to full independence in a foreseeable future. Frustrated both with the British and with what they saw as the compromising, collaborationist attitude of many of the older Burmese leaders, some young activists began to think in revolutionary terms and to look abroad for possible sources of support. Initial contacts were established with Kuomintang elements in China, who by the late 1930s were not notably anti-British but could at least claim anti-imperialist credentials, but it was ultimately in Japan that a source of tangible support was found. There was a considerable element of opportunism in this: many of the young Burmese who turned to Japan were politically leftist, if still Buddhist, and not particularly sympathetic toward the right-wing militarism and emperor system dominant in Japan (the Saya San episode had marked the last pale shadow of monarchism in the

---

[27] Cited in Josef Silverstein, *Burmese Politics: The Dilemma of National Unity*, New Brunswick, 1980, 39.

Burmese context). But despite such ideological differences, radical Burmese nationalists and conservative Japanese militarists had a common interest in overthrowing Western rule in Southeast Asia. Japan was willing to provide arms and financial support, and the Thirty Comrades, including Aung San, accepted the offer of aid and secretly went abroad for Japanese-sponsored military training in Hainan. The Thirty Comrades were to return to Burma with the invading Japanese in 1942 as leaders of a Burma Independence Army, although as Japan's fortunes declined they ultimately switched sides, 'allying' themselves with their former British adversaries; from this small group would come many of the major political and military figures of postwar Burma.

This brief sketch of anti-colonial and nationalist activities in Burma in the decades leading up to the Pacific War suggests three general themes. One is that the nationalist movement was disrupted by recurrent factionalism based upon personalities, policy disagreements, and such discordant dichotomies as the urban–rural, traditional–modernist, and religious–secular. Compounding these causes of factionalism was the problem of incorporating other ethnic groups, whether traditional or recent arrivals, into Burman-dominated political movements and ultimately into a Burman-dominated polity, a problem which remained unresolved in the post-independence period. A second theme which emerges is the rise of a relatively radical secularism at the expense of the more traditional, religious orientation of the early nationalist movement, although there would be later attempts at a synthesis of the two strands (most notably under U Nu), and an official post-independence ideology of 'Buddhist socialism'. Finally, compared to other colonial powers such as the French, the British in Burma were on the whole more moderate and compromising. This encouraged at least parts of the nationalist movement to work for change within the system, and contributed, along with historical, cultural, and other factors, to producing a type of nationalism less politically radical than that, for example, in Vietnam. While Burma nominally adopted a form of socialism, communism failed to become a major force; indeed the Burmese communist movement was split by the endemic political factionalism that affected other ideological groupings, and spent much of its energies on internal struggles rather than providing a viable political alternative.

ETHNIC NATIONALISM

Differences of language, social and political arrangements, and local customs are conventionally seen as the markers of a nation, as primordial attachments delineating a natural unit of association for political purposes, but the experience of Southeast Asia challenges the assumption that ethnic identity is immutable. Various peoples are known to have altered speech, social and political arrangements, and modes of family life as personal circumstances changed. The compilers of the 1931 census of Burma took note of the 'extreme instability of language and racial distinctions in Burma'.[28]

The general tendency in Southeast Asia was for anti-colonial activity within territories defined by European control to provide the impetus for state formation, and 'nations' in the region accordingly tended to be communities defined by territorial and administrative systems. Ethnically-based nationalism did, however, occur, although the only state to take shape on this basis was Thailand, the sole country not subjected to direct colonial rule and the various influences which that experience entailed. Malay nationalism, although culturally based, developed within a territory where the Malay population was economically disadvantaged and barely constituted a numerical majority, and did not become a major political force until after 1945. Many culture-groups in Southeast Asia were numerically too small or lacked sufficient resources to form a viable state in their own right, and some ethnic nationalisms were directed toward securing the position of a group within a larger political entity. Other communities, such as the Karen and Shan, the Muslims in Burma and in Pattani, and the Moros, opposed the predominant nationalist political tendencies in the states where they resided. None succeeded in forming a recognized independent state, but each did form an 'imagined community' that perceived itself as a nascent nation-state.

Thai Nationalism

From the late nineteenth to the mid-twentieth century, nationalism in Southeast Asian contexts is often seen as being virtually synonymous with anti-colonialism. Siam, which retained a formal, if highly circumscribed independence throughout the period of Western imperialist expansion, could not develop a nationalism in any narrowly defined anti-colonial sense. Thai 'nationalism' was necessarily in many ways unique in the Southeast Asian region, and as such offers instructive comparisons and raises questions about definitions and models of 'nationalism'.

The beginnings of modern 'nationalism' in Siam, as opposed to traditional patriotism or national consciousness, may reasonably be dated to the mid-nineteenth century and arose, as throughout much of Asia, in response to perceived external threats. This incipient nationalism was both backward-looking and forward-looking. Backward in time it focused on the great disaster of recent Thai history, the capture and destruction of Ayutthaya by the Burmese in 1767. By the 1830s the British had effectively eliminated Burma as a threat to the Thai state, but the fall of Ayutthaya continued (and continues) to have a strong hold on the Thai historical consciousness. The moral drawn from Ayutthaya's fall was that it had been caused by a lack of *samakkhi*, an Indic-derived term meaning roughly 'to have unity' or 'harmony') among the élite. The need for *samakkhi* among royalty and the nobility, with the assumed consequent acquiescence of the rest of the population, became a recurrent theme in Thai thought as new threats emerged in the nineteenth century.

[28] *Census of Burma, 1931*, 178, cited in Silverstein, 8.

These threats came, as foreseen by Thai rulers as early as Rama III (r. 1824–51), not from Siam's long-standing major rivals, Burma and Vietnam, but from the West. For a period in the seventeenth century, European powers, and particularly the French, had played a major role in Siam's economy and politics. But an anti-foreign reaction in the 1680s had virtually eliminated Western influence, and for the next century and a half European interests and energies were largely focused on the more commercially promising islands of the region, and on rivalries in other areas of the world. Left largely to itself, Siam concentrated on traditional dynastic interests and intrigue, a foreign trade oriented particularly toward China, and wars with Burma and Vietnam.

The 'second wave' of Westerners who began to arrive in Siam with increasing frequency in the early nineteenth century differed considerably from their predecessors. In the wake of political and industrial revolutions in Europe and the Americas, they were imbued with new political and economic theories, and armed with technologies that were the product of a period of rapid advance. Mainland Southeast Asia now became a major focus of interest for its trade potential—both as a market for Western goods and a source of various commodities, for strategic reasons, and for such illusory but tenaciously pursued hopes as the discovery of new routes to the supposed riches of China.

The Thai response to the perceived Western threat has been described as a 'concessionist' policy, ceding not only economic and political privileges but increasingly giving up territory as well. Because unequal treaties were concluded with a number of states, and foreign advisers employed by the Thai government were deliberately drawn from a range of countries, the policy is often seen as a 'balancing' one, attempting to play the competing imperialist powers against one another. In practice it came closer to relying on Great Britain, which was perceived as the dominant power in the region, and as a nation whose interests were primarily economic and whose demands could thus be met without a total sacrifice of sovereignty. The French, on the other hand, were seen as having not only economic but strong religious and political motives, a quest for 'glory of empire' (especially after the European debacle of 1870–1) that could be satisfied only by territorial expansion. King Mongkut in a famous metaphor said that the choice facing Siam was whether 'to swim upriver and make friends with the crocodile [the French] or to swim out to sea and hang on to the whale [the British]'.[29] It is clear that he and his royal successors down to 1932 opted for the whale, with the result that Siam in some degree became a part of Britain's informal empire, in which British interests, particularly economic, predominated without the exercise of formal sovereignty.

Thai policy was concession and accommodation to the perceived strongest regional power (i.e. from the mid-nineteenth to the mid-twentieth century, Britain followed by Japan followed by the United States). The policy has been praised as flexible and pragmatic, and condemned as

[29] Quoted in M. R. Seni Pramoj and M. R. Kukrit Pramoj, *A King of Siam Speaks*, Bangkok: Siam Society, 1987, 177–8.

unprincipled. A nineteenth-century American visitor to Siam cited approvingly the opinion of a seventeenth-century French writer regarding the Thai: 'as enemies they are not dangerous, as friends they cannot be trusted'.[30] That such sentiments were not purely the product of Western prejudices is suggested by Prime Minister Phibun's alleged reply when asked, early in the Pacific War, against what potential foe Thai military planning should be directed: 'Which side is going to lose this war? That side is our enemy.'[31]

A more positive response to the Western challenge came in what, by analogy with contemporary developments in China and Japan, might be called a 'self-strengthening movement', a programme of internal reforms intended to transform Siam into a modern, stable state capable of resisting external pressures. Begun on a modest scale by Mongkut, the reform measures were considerably, albeit at an uneven pace, intensified in the long reign of his successor Chulalongkorn (1868–1910). The range of areas covered was broad, with finances, administration, and communications perhaps showing the most immediately visible results. Various Western technologies were introduced, including weaponry, as well as organizational and institutional structures. But there was also an ideological element, including a consciously promoted 'official' nationalism focusing on loyalty to the throne and introducing new terms to the Thai political vocabulary. One such was the Indic term *chat*, which began to expand from its traditional meaning of something like 'caste' or 'tribe' to 'people' or 'race' and ultimately to the Thai equivalent of 'nation' (conceived in terms of both people and territory).

This 'official nationalism', also variously referred to as 'élite nationalism' or '*sakdina* nationalism',[32] had its beginnings under Chulalongkorn; it was greatly intensified, formalized, and institutionalized by his successor Vajiravudh (r. 1910–25). The first Thai king to be educated abroad, Vajiravudh during his long stay in England and extensive travels in other parts of Europe, America and Japan had acquired many of the Western ideas and prejudices of his day, which he mixed with more traditional Thai elements into a rather eclectic national ideology. While continuing the promotion of various aspects of Western science and technology, he put a new emphasis on 'Thai-ness', a kind of cultural nationalism which stressed alleged Thai values and traditions, and a somewhat romanticized vision of the Thai past. Where Chulalongkorn and his generation had, with only

---

[30] Quoted in Howard Malcolm, *Travels in South-Eastern Asia*, 2nd edn, Boston, 1839, II. 129.
[31] Quoted in Benjamin A. Batson, 'The fall of the Phibun government, 1944', JSS, 62, 2 (July 1974) 100 n. 23.
[32] 'Official nationalism' is used in such works as Anderson, *Imagined Communities*, ch. 6. and Kullada Kesboonchoo, 'Official nationalism under King Chulalongkorn', paper presented at the International Conference on Thai Studies, Bangkok, 1984, and 'Official nationalism under King Vajiravudh', paper presented at the International Conference on Thai Studies, Canberra, 1987; 'élite nationalism' in David K. Wyatt, *Thailand: A Short History*, New Haven, 1984, ch. 8; '*sakdina* nationalism' in Chatthip Nartsupha, Suthy Prasartset, and Montri Chenvidyakarn, eds, *The Political Economy of Siam 1910–1932*, Bangkok, 1978, 31. '*Sakdina*' refers literally to the traditional elaborate hierarchical system of manpower control; as used by modern revisionist critics it has taken on such connotations as conservative, exploitative, and (somewhat loosely) 'feudal'.

occasional reservations, confidently assumed that Western techniques and methods could be assimilated without affecting the fundamental nature of Thai society, Vajiravudh now warned that with excessive and indiscriminate borrowing from Western culture the Thai might cease to be 'Thai'. Another perceived threat was the sizeable Chinese minority, rapidly growing numerically and in economic power and, particularly in the wake of the 1911 Revolution in China, the bearers of what Vajiravudh saw as alien political and cultural values.

Vajiravudh sought to counter such threats, Western or Chinese, through a promotion of martial values, intense patronage of the Buddhist religion, and, most insistently, a hierarchical élitism which above all stressed loyalty to the monarch and throne. Indeed, Vajiravudh argued that the status of the Crown was so high that Siam, in contrast to the West, had no class distinctions, only the king and 'the rest'. This ideology was summed up in the motto 'King, Nation, Religion', the officially sanctioned 'three fundamental institutions' which in subsequent decades would continually be publicized as the guiding principles of state and society. This programme was personally and vigorously promoted by Vajiravudh himself, through prolific writings, public addresses, the establishment of such organizations as the para-military Wild Tiger Corps, and numerous other channels of propaganda.

In foreign relations, Vajiravudh in 1917 led Siam into World War I on the side of the Allies. Siam's modest military involvement was motivated primarily by pragmatic diplomatic considerations, such as the desire to become a founder member of the League of Nations and the launching of a campaign, ultimately successful, to abolish extraterritoriality and other privileges that had been ceded to the Western powers under the treaty system.

Vajiravudh was and has remained a controversial figure, both in his broader role as monarch and, more narrowly, for the type of 'nationalism' he propounded. To his admirers, and in subsequent official historiography, he is the revered 'father of Thai nationalism'. Critics have pointed to the strongly élitist nature of his nationalism, in which the people are very much subjects rather than citizens, with social bonds that run vertically rather than horizontally; to the ethnically and religiously exclusive character of this nationalism, in spite of its being formulated in an existing political entity with a long history of cultural pluralism; and to Vajiravudh's lack of sympathy for other nationalist movements, which he scathingly criticized, arguing that Asians were generally unsuited for self-rule, except, perhaps, under traditional, authoritarian élites.

Following Vajiravudh's death in 1925, his rather flamboyant brand of state-sponsored nationalism took on a much more subdued tone. This was partly due to personalities: his successor, Prajadhipok (r. 1925–35), disliked pomp, ceremony, and the public eye as much as Vajiravudh had gloried in them. But it was also due to policy, for the new reign faced serious economic problems, brought on in part by Vajiravudh's excesses, and a perceived decline in the prestige of the monarchy. It responded with a deliberate dismantling of many of Vajiravudh's programmes, including the Wild Tigers and a number of other aspects of the royally-inspired nationalism. Some elements, such as the 'King, Nation, Religion' formula, were retained, but with a much lower public profile, and the more assertive 'Siam for the Siamese', heard occasionally in earlier years, was increasingly invoked. In a few areas, such as restrictions on Chinese immigration, the new reign went beyond Vajiravudh's strident but merely rhetorical condemnation, although Prajadhipok in his public pronouncements reverted to the stress on ethnic harmony and friendship which had characterized Chulalongkorn's policy. But all in all the last reign of the absolute monarchy saw a virtual abandonment of Vajiravudh's nationalist programme; it was, however, to be vigorously revived by the military leaders who rose to power in the years following the 1932 coup that ended royal absolutism.

There were in Siam, even well before 1932, those with other visions of the future, not endorsing an indefinite continuation of benevolent autocracy or a Vajiravudh-style 'nationalism from above'. As early as 1885 a group of princes and officials with experience in Europe had petitioned Chulalong-korn, calling for relatively radical changes in the system, including the introduction of a constitutional monarchy and a parliament. The king responded and showed some sympathy for their ideas, but argued that Siam was not yet ready for such innovations. The social critic Thianwan (1842–1915), with at times a certain degree of princely patronage, similarly called for wide-ranging Westernization and political modernization. On a different level, a series of rural rebellions in the 1890s and 1901–2 challenged central authority and the political ideology of the state, though now looking less to foreign models than an idealized past and a millenarian reordering of society.

In Chulalongkorn's reign such challenges were fairly easily answered, ignored, or suppressed; in the reigns of Vajiravudh and Prajadhipok they became more insistent, undermining and ultimately overthrowing the traditional order. The clearest pre-1932 manifestation of growing discontent was the 'R.S.130 [1912] conspiracy', a plot among a group of lower-ranking military officers and a few civilians to end the absolute monarchy and remove Vajiravudh from the throne. Significantly, in addition to personal grievances, the plotters cited the examples of Europe, Japan, and the recent overthrow of imperial rule in China as standards against which Siam's 'backwardness' should be measured. Revealed to the government and quickly aborted, the 'R.S.130 conspiracy' was nevertheless symptomatic of deeper stirrings among a new emerging middle class in the bureaucracy and certain trades and professions. A key group in this new class, which was to play a role disproportionate to its relatively small numbers in determining Siam's future development, consisted of students returned from abroad. Study overseas, once almost exclusively limited to the sons of royalty and the traditional nobility, had gradually become available to a broader spectrum of society. The experiences of non-élite students abroad, particularly in France, increasingly differed from those of the earlier generation of students. In Chulalongkorn's time the government had deliberately discouraged study in France, both because of traditional enmity, dating from the seventeenth and reinforced in the nineteenth century, and because of suspicion of France's liberalism and republican institutions. But World War I brought a change: Siam and France had been 'allies', and French prestige in military sciences had been much enhanced, while in Germany and Russia, traditional destinations of a number of Thai students, the monarchies had been swept away. There was also the practical consideration that the Thai legal codes were being redrafted on the basis of Napoleonic law, with the aid of French legal advisers. Thus in the 1910s and 1920s growing numbers of Thai students, particularly in law and military studies, were sent to France, most of them on government scholarships. Typically they were from the less élite elements of this privileged minority; royalty and the higher nobility, mainly private students, overwhelmingly maintained their traditional preference for study in England.

As some conservatives had feared, the students in France did come in contact with 'subversive' influences—republicanism and more radical doctrines of French socialist and Marxist thought, and a range of Asian nationalists dedicated to achieving independence for their respective colonial homelands. The result was the formation in the mid-1920s of an embryo organization committed to bringing about political change in Siam. The handful of student founders saw Siam as relatively backward socially, politically and economically; the absolute monarchy, one of the last in the world, as increasingly an anachronism; and, at a more personal level, limited career prospects in Siam's semi-feudal system, despite their high level of technical expertise.

The latter situation had in part to do with the rather convoluted course of royal politics. Chulalongkorn, in an extended power struggle with the traditional noble families who had long dominated the court and major ministries, had of necessity filled key positions with those he thought he could trust, his relatives—originally brothers and half-brothers, and in the latter part of his reign his sons. Vajiravudh, who was on bad terms with most of the senior members of the royal family, including his mother, had reversed the process, relying much more on commoners. But the basis on which many were chosen, including artistic talents and personal ties to the king, hardly produced a meritocracy, and the rapid rise of royal favourites to high official titles and positions inevitably caused resentments among disgruntled princes and veteran bureaucrats. The inexperienced Prajadhipok not unnaturally turned back to the senior relatives whom Vajiravudh had largely ignored, but the perceived result was a 'régime of the princes' in which talented commoners found their career paths blocked by the royal near-monopoly of top bureaucratic positions, particularly in such fields as the military. The students in France watched these trends with growing concern, the more so because of the strongly Anglophile sympathies of the king and most of his royal advisers.

Prajadhipok, despite his relative youth and inexperience, was generally perceptive in seeing the problems faced by the régime. Unfortunately he was less effective in taking measures that might have overcome them. In a confidential memorandum written in the first year of his reign he noted: 'The position of the King has become one of great difficulty. The movements of opinion in this country give a sure sign that the days of Autocratic

Rulership are numbered. The position of the King must be made more secure if this Dynasty is going to last.'[33] In the following year, when the political activities of Pridi Phanomyong, the chief instigator-organizer of the students in France, had brought him to the attention of the authorities, Prajadhipok, in granting a petition revoking Pridi's recall, commented that he did not believe that Pridi would become 'a serious danger to the government' as the Thai Minister in Paris had reported, but 'if the government doesn't use him in a manner commensurate with his knowledge, then things might develop in an undesirable way'.[34] And in contrast to Vajiravudh's criticisms on general principle of Asian nationalist movements, Prajadhipok's views were more ambivalent, mixing a degree of sympathy with a pragmatic assessment of Thai self-interest:

> As long as French rule continues in Vietnam it is a 'safeguard' for Siam. No matter how much we sympathize with the Vietnamese, when one thinks of the danger which might arise, one has to hope that the Vietnamese will not easily escape from the power of the French.[35]

In response to the perceived problems and discontent which the régime faced, Prajadhipok formulated a range of proposals for political change, including representative institutions at both the local and national levels and the introduction of a constitution limiting royal powers. Drafts of such measures were debated at the top levels of government, but in the face of strong opposition from the senior princes and a number of key foreign advisers the king hesitated, until the proposed reforms were overtaken by events in the form of the economic crisis brought on by the Great Depression and then the 1932 coup itself.

The last years of the absolute monarchy also saw the development of more radical political movements, both modernist and traditionalist in orientation. At one end of the spectrum, communist groups for the first time appeared in Siam, although being small in numbers and drawing their membership almost entirely from ethnic Chinese or Vietnamese, with only very limited Thai involvement, they were not seen by the authorities as a serious threat. At the other extreme were isolated outbreaks of millenarian, 'holy men' rebellions in rural areas, similar in some respects to the rural uprisings of 1901–2 and earlier periods. What is striking is how the two types of movements, so different in their underlying ideologies, should come to rather similar conclusions about the problems of Siam, i.e., the exploitation and growing impoverishment of the rural classes, and the cause of these problems—the collusion of the ruling élite, and particularly royalty, with the Western imperialists.

In June 1932, a group calling itself the People's Party, organizationally deriving from the student activists in France in the 1920s, overthrew royal absolutism. In fact 'the people' were scarcely involved, and public reaction to the coup was more indifference or incomprehension than enthusiasm. The People's Party itself had only about 100 members when it seized

---

[33] Quoted in Benjamin A. Batson, *The End of the Absolute Monarchy in Siam*, 1984, 288.
[34] Quoted in ibid., 79.
[35] Quoted in ibid., 177.

power (a number that then increased markedly); it was divided between a
more liberal civilian faction and a generally conservative military faction,
and there was considerable initial uncertainty as to the direction in which it
would lead Siam. A brief radical phase saw the issuing of a six-point
programme which included the promise of a comprehensive national
economic plan, and a strongly worded manifesto criticizing the previous
government and suggesting the possible complete abolition of the monarchy. These early pronouncements were drafted by Pridi, and alarmed not
only supporters of the old régime but the more conservative elements
within the People's Party. The manifesto was disavowed, with apologies,
constitutional monarchy became the official policy, and within scarcely a
day the radical phase of the upheaval was largely over. When some nine
months later Pridi did present his draft economic plan, calling for the
nationalization of large sectors of the economy and highly centralized
economic planning, it set off an acrimonious debate within the government in which the conservative faction ultimately triumphed: as a result
the economic plan was labelled 'communistic', the National Assembly
(Pridi's power base) was dissolved, and certain provisions of the constitution were suspended. Pridi himself was sent into exile in France.

A second coup in June 1933 brought *Phraya* Phahon to the prime
ministership as leader of a more moderate military faction, resulting in the
recall of Pridi (but not the revival of the controversial economic plan). In
October an attempted counter-coup by conservative elements, concerned
in part by alleged leftist influences in the government, was unsuccessful.

In fact the régime moved not leftward but rightward, particularly with
the rising influence of *Luang* Phibun Songkhram, who as a military student
in France in the 1920s had been an early member of the coup group and in
1934 became Minister of Defence. Increasingly, the reluctant Phahon
served as a moderating and balancing force between the rival military and
civilian factions, until finally, after having been dissuaded in several
previous attempts, he stepped down from office in late 1938.

Phahon's resignation resulted in the elevation to the prime ministership
of the ambitious Phibun, and inaugurated a new phase in Thai nationalism. Basically, Phibun revived many elements of Vajiravudh-style nationalism, but often carried them to extremes beyond anything Vajiravudh
himself had envisioned or implemented. Furthermore, advances in education and literacy meant that print-media could now reach a far larger
audience than in Vajiravudh's time, while the new technology of radio,
introduced in Siam in the 1920s and 1930s, made official propaganda
accessible even to considerable numbers of those not functionally literate.

Philbun's programme, like Vajiravudh's, was élitist, with the difference
that the focus of loyalty was no longer the monarch, now a boy-king living
in Europe, but Phibun himself, as prime minister cum commander-in-
chief. Indeed, the intensively promoted cult of 'The Leader' meant not
only the downplaying of 'King' but also to some degree of 'Nation' and
'Religion', the other two original elements of Vajiravudh's triad, and of
'Constitution', which in the early post-1932 euphoria had often been
added as a fourth 'fundamental institution'. Phibun in a statement to the

cabinet early in 1942 justified his 'follow The Leader' philosophy by
pointing to the contrasting frailty of the 'fundamental institutions':

> The Japanese have the Emperor as their firm guiding principle. We have
> nothing. What we have are Nation, Religion, Monarch, and Constitution.
> Nation is still a vision; Religion is not practised devoutly; the Monarch is still a
> child, only seen in pictures; the Constitution is just a paper document. When
> the country is in a critical situation we have nothing to rely upon. Thus I ask
> you to follow the prime minister . . .[36]

A second aspect of the ideology of the Phibun era that harked back to
Vajiravudh was a form of cultural nationalism. This included a range of
measures, from the promotion of 'traditional' Thai values to the forced
imposition of certain Western cultural practices, particularly in the form
of a series of twelve *ratthaniyom* ('state conventions') regarding various
aspects of behaviour and dress.[37] At the same time there was selective
discrimination against some other 'alien' cultures, including in particular a
severe repression of Chinese-language media and education. The Thai
language itself was 'modernized', and various other cultural traits adjusted
to conform to real or imagined antecedents. This programme of cultural
propaganda was in large measure co-ordinated by *Luang* Wichit Wathakan, chief ideologue of the régime, who as director-general of the Department of Fine Arts composed and sponsored the performance of a plethora
of nationalistic plays and songs based predominantly upon idealized
historical themes.

Cultural nationalism was accompanied by economic nationalism, militarism, and an aggressive promotion of the Buddhist religion. Economic
nationalism was most particularly directed against Western and Chinese
domination of the modern, commercialized sector of the economy. Under
the slogan of 'nation-building', fascist-style state enterprises and monopolies were established in a number of fields, and various professions and
occupations were restricted to Thai nationals. Militarism was another
prominent strand of the official ideology, with large budget increases for
the armed forces and a general glorification of martial values, reflecting
in part contemporary trends in Germany and Japan, and the perceived
waning of the influence of the Western democracies in the late 1930s.
Military youth groups were also formed, again obviously patterned on
foreign models. And, as in Vajiravudh's time, Buddhism received intense
official patronage. While this, with rare exceptions, did not reach the point
of outright repression of other religions, the message was clearly conveyed
that to be Thai and to be Buddhist were virtually synonymous.

Finally, the Phibun régime was actively expansionist, in the form of a

---

[36] Thai text quoted in Thamsook Numnonda, *Fyn Adit* [Reconstructing the Past], Bangkok,
1979, 139–41.
[37] English translations of the twelve *ratthaniyom* (1939–42) are given in Thak Chaloemtiarana,
ed., *Thai Politics: Extracts and Documents 1932–1957*, Bangkok, 1978, 244–54. The *ratthiniyom*
and related decrees mandated such Western modes of dress as hats and gloves, and
specified in detail what hours of the day should be devoted to various activities.

'pan-Thai' movement which sought to recover 'lost' territories and peoples (including some not ethnically Thai) who had once formed part of the extended Thai empire. The symbolic confirmation of the Thai irredentist drive came in 1939 with the change of name from the ethnically-neutral 'Siam' to 'Thailand', intended internally as a declaration of Thai domination vis-à-vis Chinese or Western influence, and externally to advertise Thailand as the natural home of all of the 'Thai' peoples. The first tangible steps toward fulfilling the 'greater Thailand' dream came with war against the weakened French régime in Indochina in 1940–1 and the resulting recovery of former Thai territories in western and northern Cambodia and trans-Mekong Laos, one of the rare instances when the 'official' nationalism fostered by either Vajiravudh or Phibun received any substantial mass support. Later, in 1943, Japan transferred additional Malay and Burmese territories to what proved to be temporary Thai control.

Thus on the eve of the outbreak of the Pacific War, Thailand's military-dominated régime was aggressively pursuing a type of nationalism in many ways unique in the Southeast Asian context. And with only brief interruptions, such as Pridi's return to power in 1944–7 or the 'democratic era' of 1973–6, a form of this conservative, élitist, 'official' nationalism would continue to be the dominant state ideology down through the 1980s.

Malay Nationalism

The character of nationalism in the Malay peninsula derived from economic, social and political transformations of the late nineteenth and early twentieth centuries. Before this period, Perak was a state of some importance, but the major concentrations of Malay population were in Kedah on the west coast, Pattani-Kelantan-Terengganu on the east, and Johor-Riau in the south. Selangor had come into being as a Bugis state during the eighteenth century, while the area that became the Negri Sembilan contained a collection of small Minangkabau states that were united as a single entity only under British pressure toward the end of the nineteenth century. Pahang, which the British in 1896 drew into a confederation along with Perak, Selangor and the Negri Sembilan, was a thinly populated outlying region of the Johor-Riau empire.

Within Perak, Selangor and the Negri Sembilan, the period of British rule brought enormous changes. Tin-mining, a long-established enterprise which expanded rapidly after discovery of the Larut tin fields in the 1840s and the Kinta Valley deposits in the 1880s, was the principal source of income and of government revenue until the second decade of the twentieth century when it was overtaken by the burgeoning rubber industry. Johor, too, developed a major export economy based on commercial agriculture, although there the driving force was the Malay ruling house. Labour for the export economy came from China and from India, while rice to feed the workforce was imported from Burma and Siam and Cochinchina, a situation with exact Southeast Asian parallels only in the East Coast Residency of Sumatra and in North Borneo. Export industries in British

Malaya did not draw any major inputs from the indigenous population. Technically, Kedah, Kelantan, Terengganu and Perlis were client states of the Thai king until 1909, when Siam surrendered its rights in the area to Great Britain, although as early as 1897 a secret agreement between the two powers had given Britain a degree of influence over affairs in southern Siam. One consequence of this history was that political and economic changes came later and were much less intrusive in Kedah, Kelantan, Terengganu, and Perlis than in areas with a concentration of mines and estates, and these 'Unfederated Malay States' retained a significant degree of local administrative autonomy. The northern states tended to retain rice-based subsistence economies, and were less congenial places for non-Malay immigrants than Perak or Selangor or Johor, where tin-mining and commercial agriculture had already attracted large and growing non-Malay communities.

Malaya thus presents a picture different from most parts of Southeast Asia, where colonial administrations had to deal with large numbers of people whose lives had been substantially disrupted and whose traditional beliefs had been called into question. In making arrangements for the Malay population, the British administration saw its task as limiting dislocation rather than coping with pressures to produce increasing amounts of labour or food.

Colonial régimes lacked the status and the local knowledge of indigenous élites, and most found it necessary to seek the collaboration of some element of the local population, and to provide training in Western-style schools for junior clerical and administrative staff. In Malaya this process started somewhat later than elsewhere in the region and, with the export economy concentrated in non-Malay areas, was less pressing. A Malay College established in 1905 cultivated conservative opinion, serving the traditional élite and producing candidates for a Malay Administrative Service, subordinate to the almost exclusively British Malayan Civil Service. A second institution, the Sultan Idris Training College, founded in 1922 to conduct teacher-training programmes, drew students from village vernacular schools. By promoting the study of Malay literature, the college created an environment that encouraged political awareness and a critical evaluation of Malay society, and its graduates played a prominent role in the development of a nationalist critique of British rule in Malaya.

Modernist reform in the Malay peninsula before 1940 concentrated for the most part on religion and education, drawing on regional developments as well as ideas derived from the Arab Middle East and Turkey. The Malay press published extensive discussions of religious issues, and as in the Netherlands East Indies those involved divided into a reformist *kaum muda* (young group), seeking to purify Islam in Malaya and to set aside heterodox accretions, and a conservative *kaum tua* (elder group) seeking to maintain the status quo. One commentator on Malay nationalism has identified 1926 as a watershed in the development of Malay political attitudes.[38] In that year a group of activists formed a Malay political party

---

[38] Radin Soenarno, 'Malay nationalism, 1898–1941', JSEAS, 1 (1960) 9ff.

called the Kesatuan Melayu Singapura (Singapore Malay Union), providing a forum for the development of Malay thought. In that year too, Malays came into contact with Indonesian radicals, fleeing their country after the failure of the communist uprising in 1926, while Sukarno's PNI, with its demand for immediate independence, gave further impetus to this emerging strain of radical thought.

The Malay critique identified three problem areas: the Malay rulers who collaborated with the colonial government, the colonial administration itself, and the growing alien population. Criticism of the rulers was difficult to sustain among a population that traditionally gave the sultans unquestioned loyalty, and it produced a counter-movement calling for greater attention to Malay culture and identity and emphasizing the importance of the rulers. The British administration, the obvious target for nationalists, was generally sympathetic toward the Malays during the 1920s and 1930s, stressing the need to ensure adequate representation of the local population in the cohort of government employees, and taking steps to protect the interests of the Malays when they seemed threatened by an immigrant population that outnumbered them in some states of the peninsula. During the 1920s, a group of British administrators, arguing that not enough had been done for the indigenous population, began pressing the government to take stronger action to promote Malay interests. The tenor of this pro-Malay policy can be seen in comments by the High Commissioner, Sir Shenton Thomas, criticizing in 1936 proposals that Malayan-born Indians be given a greater role in the administration: 'I do not know of any country in which what I might call a foreigner—that is to say, a native not a native of the country or an Englishman—has ever been appointed to an administrative post.'[39] This left the immigrant population as a focus for Malay grievances.

When the Great Depression reduced demand for Malaya's exports, the government repatriated a number of Indians and Chinese, while an Aliens Enactment restricted new immigration and made it clear that those allowed to come were to remain only for the duration of their contracts. However, the administration soon came to doubt the wisdom of this policy. To sustain the economy, Malaya manifestly needed Indian and Chinese labour, and on-going recruitment of workers posed a number of difficulties. In India there was growing hostility within the Congress Party to the sending of unskilled labourers abroad, and it was by no means certain that this source would remain available. The continued recruitment of Chinese workers was also problematic, since conditions were unsettled in southern China, the traditional source of labour, and it was unclear whether arrangements to obtain workers would continue to function smoothly. Another negative aspect of the situation was that political agitators could easily gain entry to Malaya by coming as labourers. Accordingly the government began to explore the idea of maintaining a permanent Chinese and Indian population in the peninsula, a policy

---

[39] W.R. Roff, *The Origins of Malay Nationalism*, New Haven, 1967, 109–10, citing Federal Council Proceedings, 1936, B18.

which aroused Malay fears of being swamped in their own homeland by foreigners.

Toward the end of the 1930s the situation changed dramatically. Anti-Japanese activity among the Chinese population, as well as strikes and labour unrest, heightened Malay concerns about foreign domination. In 1937 the Singapore Malay Union formed branches in Melaka and Penang, and Malay associations took shape in other states as well. A Brotherhood of Pen Friends (Persaudaraan Sahabat Pena), which examined political affairs and particularly the position of the Malays, was formed in the same year, as was a radical group called the Kesatuan Melayu Muda or Malay Youth Union, the outgrowth of an informal student group at the Sultan Idris Training College. The Kesatuan Melayu Muda 'neither professed loyalty to the Sultans and the British nor spoke of non-cooperation, but worked to promote nationalist feelings and teachings among its members, whose strength lay in the lower classes'.[40] A Pan-Malayan Conference of Malay state associations met in Kuala Lumpur in August 1939 to attempt to draw these disparate Malay groups together in a single movement; the effort failed, but it laid the groundwork for a more successful postwar organization, the United Malays National Organization. The political initiatives of these years, both the radical tendency represented by the Kesatuan Melayu Muda and a conservative nationalism oriented toward Malay culture and traditions, survived the Japanese Occupation to inspire opposition to Britain's proposals to reconstitute the administration of the country after the war.

Moro Nationalism

The Moros, the Muslim population of the southern islands of the Philippine archipelago, strenuously opposed Spanish rule; effective Spanish control of many areas, particularly the Sulu archipelago, came about only in the mid-nineteenth century. American policy toward the Moros was set down in an 1899 agreement between General John C. Bates and the Sultan of Sulu, in which United States sovereignty was acknowledged but the Moros were assured of non-interference in matters of religion and custom. The agreement did not, however, specify the dividing line between civil and religious affairs, and the first ten years of American rule brought numerous disputes and armed rebellion.

In 1903 a Moro Province was created, and in the following year the United States abrogated the Bates Agreement, assuming direct authority over the region and imposing military rule. A number of military operations were undertaken against the Moros, culminating in the bloody battle of Bud Dajo on 6 March 1906. Following this episode the Americans adopted a more conciliatory approach, but in 1911 undertook complete disarmament of the Moros, after which a civilian administration took over.

American reforms related to education, taxes, family law and public

---

[40] ibid., 222, citing Ibrahim Yaacob, *Nusa dan Bangsa Melaju*, Jakarta, 1951, 59–60.

health measures, issues which the Americans considered strictly secular but which impinged in various ways on Islamic principles and Moro custom. During the first two decades of the twentieth century the Moros viewed the American administration as inimical to their interests, but this perception changed when American concessions to Philippine nationalism brought Christian Filipinos into positions of authority over the Moro area.

Accelerated Filipinization of the administration during Francis Burton Harrison's term as governor-general gave Christian Filipinos a majority in both houses of the Philippine Assembly and a growing proportion of civil service posts, in Mindanao as well as in Luzon and the Visayas. The avowed intention of American policy was 'the amalgamation of the Mohammedan and Christian native population into a homogeneous Filipino people',[41] and the Moros, doubtful about Christian Filipino intentions, viewed these developments with considerable apprehension. The Jones Law of 1916 removed remaining distinctions between Christian and non-Christian areas, and gave the new all-Filipino legislature full law-making powers over the entire country. It also created a Bureau of Non-Christian Tribes, responsible for Muslim and 'pagan' affairs, which the legislature placed under the Secretary of the Interior.

Filipino nationalists, accusing the Americans of pursuing a divide-and-rule policy in the south, promoted the notion that Christians and Muslims alike constituted the Filipino people, and encouraged united action against colonial rule. American officials generally accepted this argument, adopting the idea that Moros were 'substantive Filipinos', who had no 'national thought or ideals' and were likely to come into 'increasing and eventual homogeneity with the highly civilized Filipino type', producing a 'national existence' in which religious distinctions were immaterial.[42] The Americans had hoped to reduce cultural differences by appointing Christian Filipinos to administer non-Christian areas, and creating agricultural colonies for Christian Filipinos on public lands in Mindanao and Sulu (a policy initiated in 1913), but these measures only increased tension within the area. During the 1920s and 1930s American authorities received a number of appeals from Muslims for protection from Christian Filipino rule. One complained that the Philippine legislature had made no provision for the customary practices of the Moros:

> The Philippine Legislature has ... failed to recognize our religion. They have failed to pass any laws recognizing our marriages ... and according to the present laws in force in the Philippine Islands, and also the decisions of its Courts, our wives are concubines, and our children illegitimate.[43]

When preparations were under way for formation of the Philippine Commonwealth, the Moros sought to reach an accommodation with the

[41] Frank Carpenter, Governor of the Department of Mindanao and Sulu, quoted in Peter Gordon Gowing, *Mandate in Moroland*, Quezon City, 1983, 292.
[42] Carpenter, in ibid., 275.
[43] Quoted in Peter Gordon Gowing, *Muslim Filipinos—Heritage and Horizon*, Quezon City, 1979, 168–9.

new government, requesting that the Constitutional Convention make special provisions for the practices of the Moros and the provisions of Islamic law. The convention disregarded these suggestions, and the succeeding Commonwealth government took a number of steps which posed a grave threat to the Moros. Christian Filipinos were given strong encouragement to migrate into Muslim areas, special legal provisions contained in the Administrative Code for Mindanao and Sulu were repealed, and President Quezon declared the 'so-called Moro problem' to be 'a thing of the past'.[44] From the Moro point of view, the Americans had disarmed them, disrupted their political organizations, and then handed them over to their enemies. Armed resistance resumed in 1936, the beginning of a very long campaign to assert the claims of the 'Moro nation'.

Shan Nationalism

The leaders of the Shan states, the *sawbwa*, following British military expeditions to 'pacify' the territories during the 1880s, signed agreements establishing a political arrangement that left most administrative, judicial and revenue affairs in the hands of local chiefs. The agreements did, however, establish the subordination of the *sawbwa* to the government of Burma on the grounds that they were 'formerly subject to the King of Burma'.[45] Following the dyarchy reforms of the early 1920s, which divided Burma into two parts, central Burma (or 'Burma proper') and the 'frontier' or 'excluded' areas, the British government created an entity known as the Federated Shan States which was placed under a British Commissioner appointed by the Governor. The Shan Chiefs sat as a Federal Council, but this body served in an advisory capacity and had no executive or legislative powers, an arrangement that substantially reduced the authority of the *sawbwa*.

During the 1930s, when Britain undertook reforms in the system of limited self-government in central Burma, the *sawbwa* attempted to regain some of their lost powers, and to persuade the British administration to place individual Shan states on the same footing as the princely states of India, making them independent entities under the British Crown but separate from federal Burma. Although supporting protection of the Shan Federation from 'Burman encroachment', the British government rejected these initiatives, citing their understanding of historical relations between the Shan rulers and Burma as well as the arrangements in effect during the past forty years of British rule as precedents. British officials anticipated the eventual development of 'some form of union' between the Shan States and the government of Burma.[46]

[44] ibid., 176–7.
[45] 'Form of Sanad granted to Sawbwas', in Sao Saimong Mangrai, *The Shan States and the British Annexation*, Ithaca, 1965, a pp. VII, xxxi.
[46] Robert H. Taylor, 'British policy and the Shan States, 1886–1947', in Prakai Nontawasee, ed., *Changes in Northern Thailand and the Shan States 1886–1940*, Singapore: ISEAS, 1988, 36–8. The quotation is taken from Burma Office file 1506/1937.

Toward the end of the 1930s Burmese nationalists became increasingly critical of arrangements segregating the Shan States from Burma, and sought to draw the area into the nationalist movement. The Dobama Asiayone passed a resolution in May 1940 that 'powers under the Constitution should lie not only with the people of Burma proper but also with the people in excluded areas and that the interests of the *Sawbwas* should not be allowed to obstruct the way to freedom for Burma'.[47] The *sawbwa* for their part continued to press their case with Britain in 1940 and 1941, but had little success apart from obtaining approval for raising a military force. Britain continued to pursue a policy shielding the Shan States from Burmese nationalist interference, without making concessions to Shan aspirations, but during the war a scheme was devised for drawing the Shan States into a federal Burma. These plans were overtaken by events after the war, particularly the early granting of independence to Burma, but the issue of national integration and the role of the Shan remained one of the key issues with which the new Burmese government had to contend.

Karen Nationalism

The Karen established a Karen National Association (KNA) in 1880, one of the earliest nationalist groupings in Southeast Asia and anticipating Burman nationalist bodies by several decades. The unifying element behind the KNA was Christianity, fostered by missionary activity from early in the nineteenth century, and the association sought to preserve and promote the Karen identity.

Many Karen supported British rule,and the KNA gave its backing both to British pacification efforts during the 1880s and to the British cause during World War I. After the administrative realignment of the 1920s in Burma, the KNA pressed Karen claims to special consideration under the British administration, arguing that their numerical strength and loyal support entitled them to 'advance step by step along with the Burmans'.[48] The position of the Karen seemed especially precarious because they lived intermingled with other ethnic groups, and in few areas constituted a majority. In 1928 Karen leaders sought to rectify this situation by calling for formation of a Karen state, saying in a classic nationalist formulation that they wished 'to have a country of their own, where they may progress as a race and find the contentment they seek'.[49] This initiative placed the Karen squarely at odds with Burman efforts to subsume ethnic loyalties within a single Burman-dominated state. Coupled with the past loyalty of the Karen to Britain it produced a hostile response from the Burma Independence Army, which killed a number of Karen, among them a cabinet minister, in the early days of the Japanese Occupation, laying the ground for a long-running and bitter postwar conflict.

---

[47] ibid., 41.
[48] Silverstein, 45, quoting the Karen leader Sidney Loo-Nee.
[49] ibid, 46, quoting the Karen leader San C. Po.

Burmese Muslim Nationalism

Burmese Muslims, many descended from Indian, Persian or Arab stock and distinguished from the bulk of the Burmese population by racial characteristics as well as religion, appear in some of the earliest European accounts of Burma. They formed a distinct community, and retained strong connections with South and West Asia. After the British conquest, large numbers of Indians came to Burma, about half of them Muslim. The Muslim population of Burma followed political developments in India, forming a branch of the All-India Muslim League in 1909 and a branch of the Khilafat Movement. There were also organizations devoted to Muslim interests within Burma, notably the Burma Moslem Society, founded in December 1909, which made submissions during the discussions of constitutional reforms that led to dyarchy, and to the Simon Commission, as well as to the Legislative Council in Burma.

As the Burmese nationalist movement gained force, it adopted a distinctly Buddhist orientation, describing Burmese Muslims as *kalas*, 'foreign immigrants'; the Muslim community responded by turning to Britain for protection. In discussions of the proposed separation of Burma from India, Burmese Muslims sought an arrangement which would give a formal political role to their community. Burmese Buddhists objected to this proposal, with one leader arguing that in the context of 'Burmese-Buddhist tolerance' there was 'no reason whatsoever to entertain any anxiety on the part of the religious denominations who form the minorities in Burma'.[50] The Simon Commission recommended that special places in the Legislative Council be reserved for Muslims, but the British government did not accept this proposal and the terms of the arrangement separating Burma from India in 1937 made no special provisions for the Muslim community. A new General Council of Burma Moslem Associations was formed in 1936, and a 'Renaissance Movement' took shape in 1937 which represented the interests of Burmese Muslims, stressing the Burmese identity of this community and blaming Indian Muslims, who were excluded from membership even if they had settled permanently in the country, for sowing discord within the Burman community.

Hostility between the Burmese and the Indians, heated in any case, was particularly virulent in the case of the Muslim community. Issues relating to marriage laws and economic competition led to the outbreak of violent anti-Indian riots in July 1938, first in Rangoon and then in rural areas, leaving large numbers dead and wounded and over a hundred mosques burned, and creating enmities that remained unresolved when Burma became independent.

Pattani Nationalism

The population of Pattani, a major trading state that had been subordinated to Siam, consisted largely of Muslims of Malay stock, whose affinities lay

---

[50] 'Note of Dissent' by U Ba U, published as an appendix to the Report of the Simon Commission, cited in Moshe Yegar, *The Muslims of Burma*, Wiesbaden, 1972, 60.

with the Malay states to the south. Relations with Bangkok were often strained, and in 1817 an attempted rebellion against Thai authority led to the division of Pattani into seven provinces. Bangkok also adopted assimilationist policies for the area—Prince Damrong, the Minister of the Interior, had written to King Chulalongkorn as early as March 1896 that those entering government service, 'even though they are foreigners and uphold a different religion', should 'acquire Thai hearts and manners just as all other [of] His Majesty's servants'.[51] Administrative reforms carried out between 1902 and 1906 integrated Pattani more fully with the rest of Siam, while agreements with Britain during the same decade led to a 1909 treaty that transferred Thai rights over the neighbouring Malay states of Perlis, Kedah, Kelantan and Terengganu to Great Britain.

The 1902 reforms assigned Thai civil servants to staff the newly revamped administrative services in the area, and stripped the local nobility of their powers to levy taxes and perform other government functions. These measures provoked resistance in the Malay areas of southern Siam, and Muslim leaders sought support from Britain as well as from other Malay states. In 1901 the Malay rulers had 'bound themselves to make a united resistance to any forcible exhibition of authority on the part of the Siamese',[52] and they responded to the 1902 reforms by instituting a boycott of government activities that brought about mass resignations of local officials and led to a series of uprisings. The Raja of Legeh wrote to the Governor of the Straits Settlements complaining that Malay chiefs were forced to kneel and bow before portraits of the King of Siam and before idols. 'To worship idols is . . . strictly prohibited in Mohammadan Religion. This causes a feeling of disgust and discontent among the whole inhabitants of Legeh.'[53] Three rajas were removed from office by the Siamese as a result of this agitation, and a fourth, Raja Abdul Kadir Kamaroodin, ruler of the rump state of Pattani, was given a ten-year jail sentence, two years and nine months of which he served before being released and going into exile in Kelantan. Heightened Siamese nationalism under King Vajiravudh, with its emphasis on king, nation, and [Buddhist] religion and the promotion of Thai education, led to further unrest, and Raja Abdul Kadir was behind a major uprising in 1922. After his death eleven years later, his youngest son, Tengku Mahmud Mahyideen, succeeded him as leader of the Pattani independence movement.

The uprising of 1922 brought a moderation of Thai assimilationist policies, and after the coup of 1932 replaced the absolute monarchy with representative institutions, the Pattani area cautiously began to participate in the Thai system of parliamentary government. During the 1930s the government pushed ahead with compulsory education for the region, an initiative which many Muslims associated not with political development, but with Buddhism and recruitment into the Thai army. However, Pattani

---

[51] Quoted in Surin Pitsuwan, *Islam and Malay Nationalism: A Case Study of the Malay-Muslims of Southern Thailand*, Bangkok, 1985, 40.
[52] ibid, 46, citing F. A. Swettenham to N. Chamberlain, 20 Nov. 1901.
[53] ibid., 54, citing Tengku Ngah Shamsooden, Rajah of Legeh, to F. A. Swettenham, 18 Jan. 1901.

nationalism was quiescent until Phibun became prime minister in December 1938 and introduced a policy of forced assimilation in the south. Phibun's emphasis on race, and his depiction of Siam as a state for the Thai race, appeared to exclude the non-integrated Malay-Muslims of the south. Traditional Malay dress was disallowed, as were Malayo-Arabic names, use of the Malay language, and Malay marriage and inheritance practices. Malay nationalism, dormant for a number of years, came alive and as before looked for assistance to Malaya, where Tengku Mahyideen attempted to enlist both Malay and British support to defend Muslim interests. During the war, the Far Eastern Committee of the British War Cabinet discussed the possibility of uniting Pattani with Malaya in a postwar settlement, but by the war's end Bangkok had adopted a more conciliatory policy, and Britain did not pursue the matter.

The Pan-Thai Movement

The pan-Thai movement, which flourished briefly in the late 1930s and early 1940s, envisioned the political and cultural unification of peoples living in at least five distinct political units. Its objective was to dissolve existing territorial demarcations, products of the colonial order, in favour of a vaguely defined greater Thai state based upon somewhat idealized historical precedents.

For nearly a century prior to the 1932 change of government, the Bangkok régime had adopted a largely defensive posture and worked to cultivate friendly relations with its British and French colonial neighbours; as late as the 1920s Thai authorities had actively discouraged any criticism of French rule in Laos and Cambodia, or displays of Thai chauvinism. The end of the absolute monarchy brought to power, within a few years, a more aggressive, military-dominated leadership; 'Siam' became 'Thailand', and with Phibun as prime minister and *Luang* Wichit Wathakan as chief ideologue of the régime, an ambitious campaign was launched to reclaim 'lost territories' and unite the various Thai peoples. The word 'Thai' was loosely construed to include all those over whom the monarchs of Ayutthaya or Bangkok had once claimed sovereignty, whether linguistically related peoples such as the Lao and Shan or the linguistically distinct Khmer and Malays.

War in Europe, and then in Asia, temporarily favoured the attainment of pan-Thai objectives, and parts of colonial Cambodia, Laos, Malaya and Burma were incorporated into a greater 'Thai' state. With few exceptions, Bangkok's irredentist campaign was not warmly received by the peoples affected, for historical memories of earlier periods of central Thai rule were often negative, and dominant identities were likely to be localized rather than 'Thai'. The more nationalistic of the Lao, for example, saw large parts of old Siam as properly not 'Thai' but 'Lao', producing a counter irredentist impulse. In any case the outcome of the war ended the dream of a greater Thailand; pan-Thai aspirations were abandoned, at least publicly, and Thailand returned to its borders as they had been defined by the colonial powers in 1909.

Pan-Islam

Political activity based on Muslim unity appeared to have the potential to become a serious threat to the administrations of the Netherlands East Indies and British Malaya, and was closely watched. Islam is a way of life, and divisions between a religious and secular sphere, or between church and state, are unacceptable, as is a situation in which non-Muslims rule Muslims. However, the potential threat went beyond the fact that substantial proportions of the populations of the two areas were Muslim. All Muslims consider themselves part of a single Islamic community, the *ummat Islam*, that transcends divisions of race or culture, and this concept gave rise to the spectre of a vast international movement mounting a holy war to displace non-Muslims, fears which were reinforced by myths and misunderstandings about Islam, particularly regarding a supposed fanaticism among its followers.

If the possibility of a united Muslim opposition was real enough, mobilizing the community to take concerted action, even in the absence of state interference, would have been extremely difficult. Within Islam there was no central figure who could speak with authority on behalf of the *ummat Islam* or command their undivided loyalty. The Caliphate, based in Istanbul and nominally the religious and temporal centre of the Islamic world, had become 'the well-nigh powerless symbol of the nonexisting unity of all Muslims',[54] an ineffectual institution even before its abolition by the Turkish government in 1924. In 1915, when the Ottoman Empire aligned itself with the Central Powers and declared war on the Western Allies, the Caliph called for a holy war against his enemies, including the colonial powers in the Netherlands East Indies and Malaya. The Dutch, neutral in the war, protested and the Netherlands East Indies was subsequently excluded from this call, but it also had little impact in Malaya where it remained in effect. Elimination of the Caliphate attracted some attention in Southeast Asia. Colonial security services kept a close watch on public opinion, but little came of the matter, although contending factions in Indonesia and Malaya used the Turkish reforms as examples of what ought or ought not to be done locally.

The elusiveness of the pan-Islamic ideal was a result of divisions within the Muslim community on religious matters, and the strength of alternative, secular concerns. Religious divisions separated those who advocated a purified Islam, those who defended Muslim practices as they had developed in Southeast Asia, and the substantial number of nominal Muslims who had little interest in such matters. Secular concerns included racial and cultural issues, and in some quarters a desire to achieve modernization and self-strengthening by means of Westernization.

Pan-Chinese Nationalism

Nationalism in China called upon the Overseas Chinese to reassess their political loyalties and, beyond that, their basic identity insofar as they

---

[54] Harry Benda, *The Crescent and the Rising Sun*, reprint edn, Dordrecht, 1983, 21, citing the views of C. Snouck Hurgronje,

might have abandoned elements of 'Chinese-ness'. Southeast Asia, with its large and prosperous Chinese communities, was a particular focus of this effort, and as various initiatives took shape, governments in the region became concerned about the development of a pan-Chinese perspective and the possible consequences of a growing sense of loyalty to China.

The size of the Chinese communities in Southeast Asia ranged from a few hundred thousand to well over a million, but with the exception of British Malaya, where the 1,700,000 Chinese constituted nearly 40 per cent of the population, the Chinese were small minorities. During the 1930s the Chinese population of the Netherlands East Indies exceeded one million people but made up only about 3 per cent of the population. The Chinese population of Vietnam was about 1 per cent of the total, of Cambodia probably around 10 per cent, and of Burma 1.3 per cent of the total, or 1.8 per cent of the ethnic Burman population.

A nationality law passed in 1909 by the imperial government of China claimed all persons born of a Chinese father or a Chinese mother as Chinese subjects. The people embraced by that definition were otherwise extremely diverse. A majority of the Chinese migrants in Southeast Asia came from southern China, but numerous dialects were represented. Most were merchants or labourers and the society in general encompassed a narrow range of social classes, although wars and rebellions in China had introduced a scattering of other social elements as losing factions fled into exile. Some Chinese in Southeast Asia lived in enclaves where the language and diet were Chinese, and where political authority was exercised by Chinese headmen. Others were isolated, routinely speaking a local language and rarely mixing with other Chinese. In most territories the Chinese communities consisted of young men, and the family life which figures prominently in Confucianism was largely absent, leading to an attenuation of Chinese customs, while some Chinese immigrants married local women and they or their offspring became integrated with the local community, learning indigenous languages and adopting local customs. The degree of assimilation achieved in succeeding generations depended to a great extent on the receptivity of the indigenous peoples. In the Philippines and Siam, children of mixed Chinese–local marriages tended to merge with the local population and in many cases became indistinguishable from them. In Muslim communities Chinese assimilation was less readily accomplished, and Baba or Peranakan communities which combined features of Chinese and indigenous culture developed in the Malay peninsula and Indonesian archipelago.

Colonial rule added yet another layer of complexity. Most colonial administrations followed the principle of *jus soli* or place of birth in determining nationality, which taken in conjunction with the policy of the Chinese government gave the Chinese in Southeast Asia dual nationality. Moreover, colonies offered education in European languages and attractive opportunities for those able to interact with the European community. G. W. Skinner has pointed out that the natural tendency was for Chinese immigrants to adapt themselves to the élite environment of the country in which they lived. Where colonial rule prevailed, they were inclined to learn Western languages and adopt Western ways. In Siam, where an indigenous aristocracy retained power, the Chinese learned Thai and adopted Thai ways.[55]

After 1900 increasing numbers of Chinese women emigrated to Southeast Asia, making it easier for male migrants to set up families which retained Chinese traditions. At the same time, however, the number of males who came for limited periods, lived in Chinese enclaves and maintained a Chinese identity also increased dramatically. In the years before 1940 three types of Chinese communities were found in Southeast Asia: China-oriented groups, Western-oriented groups, and communities which combined Chinese and Southeast Asian characteristics. It was within this context that Chinese nationalism developed in the region.

Culturally, Chinese nationalism produced a movement to reassert a Chinese identity. Politically, it stood for opposition to foreign domination and participation in the revitalization of economic and political life in China. For Chinese with a Southeast Asian orientation, or who were Westernized, these tendencies created dilemmas. Some underwent a process of re-sinification, learning Mandarin and seeing that their children secured a Chinese education. Others opted to identify with the colonial régime or to come to terms with indigenous nationalism. With regard to the latter, the anti-Western stance of the Chinese nationalists would seem to make them natural allies of local opponents of colonial rule, but nationalism in Southeast Asia was partly directed against the Chinese, who were seen as a foreign presence in the region.

In 1905 Sun Yat-sen founded the Tung Meng Hui (Common Alliance Society), and over the next six years established branches across Southeast Asia with Singapore as regional headquarters. Nationalist sentiment among the Chinese in Southeast Asia was considerably heightened by a trade boycott against the United States, a response to renewal of America's Chinese Exclusion Act in 1904. The Philippine Chinese who lived under American rule were most directly affected by the issue, but Chinese communities elsewhere in the region supported the boycott, an experience that increased political awareness and helped develop a sense of unity that transcended regional borders. Subsequent political developments in China, such as the fall of the Qing dynasty in the 1911 Revolution, the Twenty-One Demands issued by Japan in 1915, and the Sino-Japanese conflicts of the 1930s, which led to widespread anti-Japanese boycotts in Southeast Asia, further strengthened this feeling of participation in a larger Chinese community.

The deep political divisions in China—prior to the 1911 Revolution between republicans and Qing dynasty loyalists, subsequently between the Kuomintang nationalists and the Chinese Communist Party—also affected the Chinese in Southeast Asia. The Kuomintang and the communists both recruited support throughout the region, opening clubs and other organizations and establishing newspapers, and their activities met with a hostile response from colonial administrations. The Kuomintang attempted to operate as an orthodox political movement, establishing

[55] G. William Skinner, 'Change and persistence in Chinese culture overseas: a comparison of Thailand and Java', in *Journal of the South Seas Society*, 16, 1–2 (1960) 86–100.

party branches and inviting Chinese communities in Southeast Asia to elect delegates to party conferences in China. Colonial authorities considered involvement in Chinese politics on the part of the Overseas Chinese unacceptable and made protests to China over this issue, and also over a conscription law making all men of Chinese descent liable for military service in the Chinese armed forces. China did not have the power to enforce these regulations in Southeast Asia, and in fact made no effort to do so, but in the eyes of the region's administrations the involvement of Southeast Asia's Chinese population in Chinese politics raised questions of political loyalty.

Efforts to promote Chinese education with a curriculum derived from China, attempts to draw the Overseas Chinese into Chinese politics, the activities of Chinese consuls in Southeast Asia, the formation of Chinese chambers of commerce and other organizations serving Chinese interests, and a clear feeling within Chinese communities that they were participating in a national awakening aroused fears among colonial governments and the non-Chinese inhabitants of Southeast Asia alike of the possible effects of pan-Chinese political activity. The centre was China, but the sphere of activity took in the entire region of the Nanyang, the South Seas.

Governments within the region kept a close watch on Chinese political activity, and most enacted new regulations to contain the situation. In British Malaya the administration imposed controls over Chinese educational materials, took action against political and secret society activity, and introduced limits on immigration that were largely applied to the Chinese. In Siam the strident Thai nationalism prevailing after the 1932 coup had an anti-Chinese tone: Chinese schools and newspapers were suppressed to encourage assimilation, and a variety of restrictions were imposed on Chinese economic activity. The Commonwealth government in the Philippines adopted anti-Chinese policies, and the constitution as well as subsequent legislation severely limited the capacity of non-Filipinos to carry out economic activities within the country. In the Netherlands East Indies the administration considered the Chinese community largely pro-Dutch and, while restricting direct involvement in Chinese politics, imposed relatively few new restrictions on the Chinese during this period.

Baba or Peranakan Nationalism

Chinese families long resident in the Malay peninsula and Indonesian archipelago formed distinct cultural groups, known in the archipelago as Peranakan and in Malaya as the Baba or Straits Chinese. While these communities retained elements of Chinese culture, their language, dress, customs and food were an amalgam drawn both from Chinese and local traditions.

Confronted with growing Indonesian nationalist sentiment directed in part against itself, the Peranakan community in the Netherlands East Indies responded in different ways. Overtures to Indonesian nationalists offering cooperation against Dutch rule bore no fruit. The alternatives were to assert the rights of the Peranakan as a long-established community within the archipelago, using the considerable wealth of the community to support these claims, or to look to China for support. These tactics were pursued with some success, but both had serious drawbacks. The economic dominance of the Peranakan community was itself a nationalist grievance, and leverage derived on this basis had to be applied with much discretion, while the intercession of China was objectionable from the perspective of Indonesian nationalism and Dutch colonial rule alike. The Peranakan group in some respects enjoyed preferential treatment, and, facing a potentially hostile Indonesian nationalist movement, could ill afford to alienate the Dutch.

In Malaya the Babas were of less political significance than a broader category of 'Straits-born' Chinese, who retained more of Chinese culture than the Babas but shared their Southeast Asian orientation. With Malay nationalism generally unaggressive, the concerns of this group were directed toward deciding what stance should be adopted regarding China, and on this matter the community divided, some identifying with China and others with the colonial administration. However, while the distinction between China-oriented and Straits-oriented loyalties helped shape prewar political attitudes, it diminished in importance after 1945, when Singapore began the odyssey that led to independence in 1965 under a leadership in which the Straits-born Chinese played a prominent role.

Indian Nationalism

Developments in India also had important consequences for Southeast Asia nationalist movements, both in the model they provided and and, more directly, in influences on reformist and nationalist activity in areas with significant immigrant Indian populations, such as Burma and British Malaya. Indian communities in Southeast Asia remained relatively unassimilated, at least compared to the Chinese in Siam and certain other areas. Indians by and large maintained their distinctive and multi-faceted identities, reflecting the great ethnic, linguistic, and religious diversity within the Indian subcontinent. They generally supported one or another faction of Indian nationalism, but remained largely apart from, and to some degree fearful of, the major Southeast Asian nationalist movements.

Outside Burma and the Malay peninsula, Indian immigration was limited and of little political significance. In Burma, Indians constituted about 7 per cent of the total population in 1931, but their predominance in Rangoon and high profile in the economy made them a target of Burmese nationalists. In Malaya 10 per cent of the 1911 population was Indian, a figure which rose to 14.3 per cent by 1931, but most lived and worked on estates and were of less concern to Malay nationalists than the more visible Chinese community. As a result of marriages between Indian Muslims and Malays, a 'Jawi Pekan' group developed in British Malaya, adopting some of the cultural characteristics of both communities.

Nationalist activity among Indians in Southeast Asia in the first decades of the twentieth century, as in the case of Chinese communities, was oriented primarily towards the home country; indeed some sections of the Indian population, particularly those classes which enjoyed relative prosperity under the colonial order, were fearful of the possible consequences of Burman or Malay nationalism, and thus tended to see British rule as a protective shield.

Nonetheless, the example of the nationalist movement in India had repercussions in Southeast Asia which extended beyond the overseas Indian communities. India offered a case of opposition to direct colonial rule, in contrast to China where 'imperialism' was more amorphous. Perhaps most significantly, Indian nationalist activity dated from an early period relative to the emergence of nationalist movements in most of Southeast Asia. The Congress Party had been founded in 1885, at a time when some parts of the Southeast Asian region, such as Annam and upper Burma, were just coming under European rule.

As in the case of Chinese nationalism, various factions competed for the loyalties, and the financial support, of the overseas communities. Though the Congress would ultimately become the main vehicle for achieving Indian independence, much early Indian political activity in Burma and in major urban centres was oriented towards more radical strands of the nationalist movement. A prominent example was the Ghadr (Mutiny) Party, based abroad, especially on the west coast of North America, which hoped to spark revolts against British rule in India and Burma. However, early militant radicalism was predominantly a north Indian phenomenon with limited appeal in Malaya, where most of the substantial Indian population derived from south India.

Radical nationalists were particularly active in times of apparent European vulnerability, for example during World War I, which seemed to offer promising opportunities to challenge British or French rule. Diplomats and agents of the Central Powers actively encouraged militant Indian nationalists, offering arms and financial support to Indian (and Vietnamese) anticolonial movements. In Southeast Asia these German-sponsored attempts to incite insurrection in British and French colonies were directed particularly from Bangkok, where the Thai remained neutral until July 1917, and from Batavia, where the Dutch remained neutral throughout the European war. Southeast Asia became a major channel for Ghadr Party attempts to infiltrate propaganda and arms to India.

In Southeast Asia itself, the most dramatic event of this period was the February 1915 mutiny by part of an Indian regiment stationed in Singapore, resulting in a number of deaths in the uprising itself, and in the retaliatory executions which followed. The British authorities, fearful of possible repercussions in India and elsewhere, tried to play down any political motivations among the mutineers. The weight of evidence shows, however, that the regiment had been strongly affected by nationalist propaganda, by contacts with German prisoners of war (whom the mutineers were assigned to guard), and (the regiment was almost totally Muslim) by the entry of the Ottoman Empire in the European war on the side of the Central Powers.

The mutiny was quickly suppressed, with French, Japanese and Russian naval contingents coming to the assistance of the depleted British forces, but the uprising foreshadowed the situation during the Pacific War. Then, with the British again 'vulnerable', Congress dissidents and others formed the Indian National Army and fought alongside Japanese forces on the Burma front, against British and 'British Indian' troops.

More moderate strands of Indian nationalism were also influential in Southeast Asia, with growing support (as British compromises escalated) for the Congress and Gandhi's leadership; in particular, some important Burmese nationalist leaders had personal contacts and experience in the Indian nationalist movement from the 1910s to the 1930s. Such contacts also operated in the other direction, with prominent Indian leaders such as the nationalist poet Rabindranath Tagore making visits to Southeast Asia in the interwar period, and the Congress Party, on both practical political and humanitarian grounds, taking an active interest in the welfare and working conditions of emigrant Indian labourers.

The Indian example influenced some Southeast Asian nationalist movements, but for the most part Indian communities in Southeast Asia focused primarily on the evolving situation in India itself, and there was little importing of Gandhian methods of non-violent resistance. Indeed, Southeast Asian nationalism on the whole tended to become increasingly militant and revolutionary, except in cases where a colonial power such as the United States encouraged forms of collaboration which offered the prospect of a real transfer of power to indigenous groups.

THE LOYALIST OPTION

As anti-colonial and other reformist activity developed, various groups throughout the region began to perceive disadvantages to themselves inherent in independence, or in the leadership of particular opposition groups. Emerging from this tendency was what might be termed a loyalist option among people who supported or benefited from a colonial relationship.

In the Netherlands East Indies the loyalist option had a particular appeal for various groups: the Chinese, whose overtures to local nationalists met with indifference and mistrust; the Ambonese, who provided the Dutch military with much of its manpower in the archipelago; parts of the Eurasian community which inclined toward Dutch civilization and held aloof from Indonesian culture; and the aristocracy, many of whose members had participated in the Dutch administration and were accordingly a nationalist target. It was this loyalist element that the Dutch attempted to strengthen by promoting customary law (*adat*) as a basis for administration and law, and by promoting federalism after 1945.

Muslims in the southern Philippines also adopted a loyalist stance during the 1920s and 1930s as Filipinization of the administration placed Catholic Filipinos in positions of authority in the south. In British Malaya the Straits Chinese, some of whom described themselves as 'the King's Chinese', generally comprised a loyalist community. Dominant in the port cities of Singapore and Penang, this group felt threatened by the large and growing group of China-born Chinese, and potentially by nationalism in the Malay world which surrounded them. The British administration could count other potential allies among the Anglicized Indians and Malay aristocracy, and the Malay population as a whole tended to view the British as a source of support against the substantial Indian and Chinese communities in the peninsula. In Vietnam the Constitutionalist Party, the Catholic community and particularly that element of the Vietnamese population which had adopted French citizenship, formed a loyalist element. However, in contrast to the situation in Burma, where the response of the Shan and Karen to nationalist pressure from a numerically dominant group was to turn to the colonial power for protection, minority ethnic groups in Vietnam found a source of patronage in the Communist Party.

CONCLUSION

Southeast Asia before World War II produced a wide range of reformist activity, some of it directed against colonial régimes, some toward religious change, and some toward modernization and social development. The reformist strain that can be described as anti-colonial nationalism was based on a broad racial distinction between white colonizers and non-white colonial subjects. Beyond this stark division the substance of nationalism was problematic, for the people drawn together within the boundaries of colonial states were otherwise diverse in their cultures, religious practices, economic activities, social organization, and behaviour.

The period 1900 to 1940 produced three types of political movements in Southeast Asia: one based on particular social or cultural characteristics; a second based on the territories defined by the colonial powers; and a third on religious or ideological principles that transcended those boundaries. The first bore fruit in Siam, but elsewhere ethnic nationalist goals were rarely achieved. The third produced religious movements as well as socialist and communist parties. The most difficult to advance was the second, since there was little basis for unity beyond the shared experience of colonial rule, but territorially-based administrations offered a concrete political objective and became the basis of independent states after 1945.

Part of the significance of reformist organizations during this period lies in their structure, for voluntary organizations based on particular interest groups or promoting certain concepts were a departure from previous Southeast Asian practice. They provided a forum for the development of new lines of thinking, and produced the leadership that ultimately took control of the independent states that came into being after 1945. However, to some degree organizations revolved more around leaders than ideologies, and the personalities and ambitions of various individuals played a major part in determining the success or failure of the ideas they advocated and the groups they led.

The underlying racial basis of anti-colonial movements produced a heightened awareness of ethnic identities. After the war numerically predominant groups in Burma, Thailand, and Malaya would lay claim to nationalism as the vehicle for promoting their own cultural aspirations,

while in the Philippines and Indonesia the governments made conscious
efforts to avoid identifying national culture with any one group, as did the
Communist Party in Vietnam. A paradoxical feature of both approaches
was that political movements based on prototypical nationalist criteria—
a shared language, culture, or set of religious beliefs and the wish to
nurture and protect an identity based on these qualities—found little place
within the region. They stood condemned by anti-colonial movements,
and by the independent successor states after 1945, for posing a threat to
'national unity'.

In sum, modernist reform activity in Southeast Asia between the late
1800s and 1940 embraced issues that went beyond the struggle against
colonial rule: more was involved than simply political independence.
Changes arising from a variety of circumstances—including the Industrial
Revolution, the development of a world market, responses of different
elements within local societies to new opportunities, and colonial rule—
had disturbed established social and political arrangements, and had set in
motion a protracted debate among the peoples of the region. Colonial
governments were the agents for some but by no means all of these
changes, and what was at stake went beyond the question of whether
outsiders or domestic élites were to hold power. The issue was to decide
which of the contending visions of the future would prevail.

BIBLIOGRAPHIC ESSAY

Material on the Philippines is scattered amongst diverse sources. The study
by Lewis E. Gleeck Jr, of the American period in Philippine history, *The
American Half-Century (1898–1946)*, is part 5, vol. 1 of a proposed *General
History of the Philippines* (Manila: Historical Conservation Society, 1984).
John N. Schumacher, *The Propaganda Movement: 1880–1895—The Creators of
a Filipino Consciousness, the Makers of the Revolution*, Manila, 1973, shows
how the foundations for modern nationalism were laid. The writings of
Teodoro A. Agoncillo on the Philippine revolution (his 1956 *The Revolt
of the Masses* and his 1960 work, *Malolos: The Crisis of the Republic*, both
published in Quezon City by the University of the Philippines) describe
the development of nationalism, and Cesar A. Majul, *The Political and
Constitutional Ideas of the Philippine Revolution*, New York and Quezon City,
1967, sets down the philosophical and ideological underpinnings of events
during this period. Reynaldo Ileto, *Pasyon and Revolution: Popular Movements in the Philippines, 1840–1910*, Quezon City, 1979, offers a different
perspective on this period, and three essays published in the journal
Philippine Studies, the first a review of Ileto's work, provide a contentious
but extremely useful discussion of the revolution: 'Understanding Philippine Revolutionary Mentality' by Milagros C. Guerrero (29, 1981), Ileto's
rejoinder entitled 'Critical Issues in "Understanding Philippine Revolutionary Mentality"' (30, 1982), and a magisterial overview, by John N.
Schumacher, 'Recent Perspectives on the Revolution' (30, 1982). Maximo
M. Kalaw, *The Development of Philippine Politics*, Manila, 1926, and Peter W.
Stanley, *A Nation in the Making: The Philippines and the United States, 1899–*

1921, Cambridge, Mass., 1974, focus on the period up to the mid-1920s. Theodore Friend, *Between Two Empires: Philippine Ordeal and Development from the Great Depression through the Pacific War, 1929–1946*, New Haven, 1965, and his later *The Blue-Eyed Enemy: Japan against the West in Java and Luzon, 1942–1945*, Princeton, 1988, provide intriguing interpretative accounts of the 1920s and 1930s, a period also covered perceptively by Bernadita Reyes Churchill in *The Philippine Independence Missions to the United States, 1919–1934*, Manila: National Historical Institute, 1983. David R. Sturtevant, *Popular Uprisings in the Philippines, 1840–1940*, Ithaca and London,1976, deals with a variety of non-institutionalized reformist movements. Two volumes have been published specifically on the subject of Philippine nationalism: Usha Mahajani, *Philippine Nationalism: External Challenge and Filipino Response, 1565-1946*, St Lucia, 1971, and Teodoro A. Agoncillo, *Filipino Nationalism*, Quezon City, 1974; and Horacio de la Costa, *The Background of Nationalism and Other Essays* Manila, 1965, contains a thoughtful analysis of this topic. José Rizal's writings appear in numerous sources, including *Rizal: Political and Historical Writings (1840–1890)*, Manila: National Heroes Commission, 1963, reissued by the National Historical Institute as part of a comprehensive centennial edition of Rizal's works. Renato and Letizia R. Constantino's provocative accounts of Philippine history, *The Philippines: A Past Revisited*, Quezon City, 1975, and *The Philippines: The Continuing Past*, Manila: Foundation for Nationalist Studies, 1978, offer interesting if controversial interpretations. 'Quezon's Commonwealth: The Emergence of Philippine Authoritarianism', by Alfred W. McCoy, along with the other papers collected in Ruby R. Paredes, ed., *Philippine Colonial Democracy*, New Haven: Yale University Southeast Asia Studies, 1988, and Norman Owen's *Compadre Colonialism*, Ann Arbor: University of Michigan Center for South and Southeast Asian Studies, 1971, give useful details on the prewar era.

Accounts of the development of Indonesian political thinking are numerous. The classic Dutch account is J. Th. Petrus Blumberger's three-volume work, *De Communistische Beweging in Nederlandsch-Indië*, Haarlem, 1928; *De Nationalistische Beweging in Nederlandsch-Indië*, Haarlem, 1931; *De Indo-Europeesche Beweging in Nederlandsch-Indië* Haarlem, 1939. The classic account in English is *Nationalism and Revolution in Indonesia* by George McTurnan Kahin, Ithaca and London, 1952. *Politiek-Politioneele overzichten van Nederlandsch-Indië*, 1: *1927–1928*, II: *1929–1930*, III: *1931–1934*, compiled by Harry A. Poeze (The Hague, 1982; Dordrecht, 1983 and 1988) contains exhaustive detail on nationalist organizations. Other valuable overviews include Robert Van Niel, *The Emergence of the Modern Indonesian Elite*, The Hague, 1960, and Bernhard Dahm, *History of Indonesia in the Twentieth Century*, London, 1971. Van Niel's article 'From Netherlands East Indies to Republic of Indonesia, 1900–1945', in Harry Aveling, ed., *The Development of Indonesian Society*, St Lucia, 1979, provides a compact summary, as does John D. Legge, *Indonesia*, Englewood Cliffs, 1964. More specialized accounts include: Takashi Shiraishi, *An Age in Motion: Popular Radicalism in Java, 1912–1926*, Ithaca and London, 1990; Friend, *Blue-Eyed Enemy*; *Perhimpunan Indonesia and the Indonesian Nationalist Movement, 1923–1928*, Clayton: Centre of Southeast Asian Studies, Monash University,

1975, and *Road to Exile: The Indonesian Nationalist Movement, 1927–1934*, Singapore, 1979, both by John Ingleson; Akira Nagazumi, *The Dawn of Indonesian Nationalism: The Early Years of the Budi Utomo, 1908–1918*, Tokyo: Institute of Developing Economies, 1972; Harry J. Benda, *The Crescent and the Rising Sun*, The Hague and Bandung, 1958; Deliar Noer, *The Modernist Muslim Movement in Indonesia, 1900–1942*, Kuala Lumpur, 1973; Alfian, *Muhammadiyah: The Political Behavior of a Muslim Modernist Organization under Dutch Colonialism*, Yogyakarta, 1989; Mitsuo Nakamura, *The Crescent Arises Over the Banyan Tree*, Yogyakarta, 1983; Kenji Tsuchiya, *Democracy and Leadership: The Rise of the Taman Siswa Movement in Indonesia*, Honolulu, 1987; and Susan Abeyasekere, *One Hand Clapping: Indonesian Nationalists and the Dutch, 1939–1942*, Clayton: Centre of Southeast Asian Studies, Monash University, 1976. Harry J. Benda and Ruth T. McVey provide a useful introduction to events of the 1920s in *The Communist Uprisings of 1926–1927 in Indonesia: Key Documents*, Ithaca: Cornell University Southeast Asia Program, 1960, and McVey, *The Rise of Indonesian Communism*, Ithaca, 1965, is the definitive work on this subject. Extremely useful material is also found in biographies of Sukarno by J.D. Legge (*Sukarno. A Political Biography*, Sydney, London, Boston, 1972), Bernhard Dahm (*Sukarno and the Struggle for Indonesian Independence*, Ithaca, 1969), and C.L.M. Penders (*The Life and Times of Sukarno*, Kuala Lumpur, 1975). Sukarno's own views, as filtered through journalist Cindy Adams, are found in *Sukarno: An Autobiography, as Told to Cindy Adams*, Hong Kong, 1965, and an edited translation of Mohammad Hatta's memoirs has been published under the title of *Mohammad Hatta: Indonesian Patriot—Memoirs*, Singapore, 1981. *Portrait of a Patriot. Selected Writings by Mohammad Hatta*, The Hague and Paris, 1972, is also a valuable source and Mavis Rose has published *Indonesia Free: A Political Biography of Mohammad Hatta*, Ithaca: Cornell University Southeast Asia Program, 1987. Useful accounts of developments outside of Java include Taufik Abdullah, *Schools and Politics: The Kaum Muda Movement in West Sumatra (1927–1933)*, Ithaca: Cornell University Southeast Asia Program, 1971, and Anthony Reid, *The Blood of the People: Revolution and the End of Traditional Rule in Northern Sumatra*, Kuala Lumpur, 1979.

Events in Vietnam after 1945 drew attention to antecedents of the Vietnamese independence struggle, and the literature on pre-war Vietnamese reform efforts is now substantial. Among the major accounts are Joseph Buttinger, *Vietnam: A Dragon Embattled*, I, London, 1967; David G. Marr, *Vietnamese Anticolonialism, 1885–1925*, Berkeley, Los Angeles, London, 1971, and its sequel, *Vietnamese Tradition on Trial, 1920–1945*, Berkeley, Los Angeles, London, 1981; William J. Duiker, *The Rise of Nationalism in Vietnam. 1900–1941*, Ithaca and London, 1976; Daniel Hémery, *Révolutionnaires Vietnamiens et pouvoir colonial en Indochine*, Paris, 1975; and Alexander Woodside, *Community and Revolution in Modern Vietnam*, Boston, 1976, partly superseding Paul Isoart's still useful *Le phénomène national Vietnamien de l'indépendance unitaire à l'indépendance fractionnée*, Paris, 1959. Pierre-Richard Féray, *Le Viet-nam au xx siècle*, Paris, 1979, provides a general history of modern Vietnam, as do Nguyen Khac Vien, *Histoire du Vietnam*, Paris, 1974; Thomas Hodgkin, *Vietnam: The Revolutionary Path*, London,

1981; and Ken Post, *Revolution, Socialism and Nationalism in Viet Nam*, I, Aldershot, 1989, from a leftist perspective. Studies of the Communist Party include Pierre Rousset, *Le parti communist vietnamien*, Paris, 1973; and *Vietnamese Communism, 1925–1945*, Ithaca and London, 1982, by Huynh Kim Khanh. Ralph Smith, *Viet-Nam and the West*, Ithaca, 1971, and Paul Mus in an extended interpretative essay, *Viet-Nam: Sociologie d'une guerre*, Paris, 1952, examine the encounter between Vietnamese culture and the West. Helpful on specific topics are the essays in *Aspects of Vietnamese History*, Honolulu, 1973, edited by Walter F. Vella; Megan Cook, *The Constitutionalist Party in Cochinchina: The Years of Decline, 1930–1942*, Clayton: Centre of Southeast Asian Studies, Monash University, 1977; Hue-Tam Ho Tai, *Millenarianism and Peasant Politics in Vietnam*, Cambridge, Mass, 1983; and Jayne Susan Werner, *Peasant Politics and Religious Sectarianism: Peasant and Priest in the Cao Dai in Viet Nam*, New Haven: Yale University Southeast Asia Studies, 1981.

Materials on nationalist reform in Cambodia and Laos are sparse. For Cambodia, David P. Chandler, *A History of Cambodia*, Boulder, 1983, provides an accessible summary, and Alain Forest, *Le Cambodge et la colonisation française: historie d'une colonisation sans heurts*, Paris, 1980, gives thorough coverage to the period 1897–1920. For Laos, Geoffrey C. Gunn in *Political Struggles in Laos (1930–1954)*, Bangkok, 1988, covers the 1930s in some detail.

The most comprehensive recent account of political developments in Burma is Robert H. Taylor, *The State in Burma*, London, 1987, but John L. Christian's *Modern Burma*, Berkeley and Los Angeles, 1942, a thorough and well-documented account of pre-war political developments in Burma based primarily on official British sources, remains extremely useful. Four works examine nationalist activity during the 1920s and 1930s in considerable detail: U Maung Maung, *From Sangha to Laity: Nationalist Movements of Burma, 1920–1940*, Canberra: Australian National University, South Asia History Section, 1980; Surendra Prasad Singh, *Growth of Nationalism in Burma, 1900–1942*, Calcutta, 1980; Albert D. Moscotti, *British Policy and the Nationalist Movement in Burma, 1917–1937*, Honolulu, 1974; and Khin Yi, *The Dobama Movement in Burma (1930–1938)*, Ithaca: Cornell University Southeast Asia Program, 1988. Patricia Herbert, *The Hsaya San Rebellion (1930–1932) Reappraised*, Clayton: Centre of Southeast Asian Studies, Monash University, 1982, is stoutly revisionist.

The standard work on Malay nationalism is W.R. Roff, *The Origins of Malay Nationalism*, New Haven, 1967, but very useful discussions are also found in Radin Soenarno's 'Malay nationalism, 1896–1941', JSEAH, 1,1 (1960) and the articles collected in *Nasionalisme: Satu Tinjauan Sejarah*, edited by R. Suntharalingam and Abdul Rahman Haji Ismail, Petaling Jaya, 1985. Firdaus Haji Abdullah explores the relation between Islam and politics in his *Radical Malay Politics: Its Origins and Early Development*, Petaling Jaya, 1985, as does Clive S. Kessler in *Islam and Politics in a Malay State: Kelantan, 1838–1969*, Ithaca and London, 1978. The pseudonymous *Class and Communalism in Malaysia: Politics in a Dependent Capitalist State* by 'Hua Wu Yin', London, 1983, examines Malaysian history and pre-war political activity from a Marxist perspective.

With the 'reign mentality' still imposing a heavy hand on Thai historiography, a comprehensive study of pre-war Thai nationalism has yet to be
written. The most substantial work specifically devoted to the subject is
Walter F. Vella, *Chaiyo! King Vajiravudh and the Development of Thai Nationalism*, Honolulu, 1978, in which the richness of data contrasts with a lack of
critical analysis. An earlier, more indigenous lineage for Thai nationalism
is posited in Eiji Murashima's somewhat iconoclastic 'The Origin of Modern Official State Ideology in Thailand', JSEAS, 19,1 (1988). 'Official
nationalism' in the Seventh Reign is discussed in Benjamin A. Batson, *The
End of the Absolute Monarchy in Siam*, Singapore, 1984. Less élite strands of
nationalism, culminating in the 1932 coup, have also received extensive
treatment. In terms of events, perhaps the most detailed (if not always
accurate) account is Thawatt Mokarapong, *History of the Thai Revolution:
A Study in Political Behavior*, Bangkok, 1972; the intellectual underpinnings
of the coup are well discussed in Pierre Fistié, *Sous-développement et utopie
au Siam: Le programme de réforms présenté en 1933 par Pridi Phanomyong*, The
Hague and Paris, 1969, and in the early sections of Yuangrat Wedel,
*Modern Thai Radical Thought: The Siamization of Marxism and its Theoretical
Problems*, Bangkok: Thai Khadi Research Institute, Thammasat University,
1982. General studies aside, the period between the coup and the Pacific
War is poorly covered. However, useful contemporary works include M.
Sivaran, *The New Siam in the Making*, Bangkok, 1936; Kenneth P. Landon,
Siam in Transition, Chicago, 1939; Virginia Thompson, *Thailand: The New
Siam*, New York: Institute of Pacific Relations, 1941; and the last historical
chapters of the first edition of Phra Sarasas, *My Country Thailand*, Tokyo,
1942. An important, thoroughly revisionist critique of all English-language
scholarship on Thai nationalism, and on modern Thai history in general, is
Benedict Anderson, 'Studies of the Thai State: The State of Thai Studies' in
E. Ayal, ed., *The Study of Thailand*, Athens, Ohio: Ohio University Center
for International Studies, 1978. Various relevant documentary materials
are provided in Chatthip Nartsupha et al., eds, *The Political Economy of Siam
1910–1932*, Bangkok: Social Science Association of Thailand, 1978; Benjamin A. Batson, ed., *Siam's Political Future: Documents from the End of the
Absolute Monarchy*, Ithaca: Cornell University Southeast Asia Program,
1974; and the first sections of Thak Chaloemtiarana, ed., *Thai Politics:
Extracts and Documents 1932–1957*, Bangkok: Social Science Association of
Thailand, 1978. New directions in historical research, revealing the multi-
faceted perceptions of 'nation', are explored in Shigeharu Tanabe, 'Ideo-
logical Practice in Peasant Rebellions: Siam at the Turn of the Twentieth
Century' and Chatthip Nartsupha, 'The Ideology of 'Holy Man' Revolts
in North East Thailand', in Andrew Turton and Shigeharu Tanabe, eds,
History and Peasant Consciousness in South East Asia, Osaka: National
Museum of Ethnology, 1984.

Accounts of 'minority' groups in mainland Southeast Asia include Josef
Silverstein, *Burmese Politics: The Dilemma of National Unity*, New Brunswick,
1980; Chao Tzang Yawnghwe, *The Shan of Burma: Memoirs of a Shan Exile*,
Singapore: ISEAS, 1987; Sao Saimong Mangrai, *The Shan States and the
British Annexation*, Ithaca: Cornell University Southeast Asia Program,
1965; Moshe Yegar, *The Muslims of Burma: A Study of a Minority Group*,

Wiesbaden, 1972; and Robert H. Taylor, 'British Policy and the Shan States, 1886–1942', in Prakai Nontawasee, ed., *Changes in Northern Thailand and the Shan States, 1886–1940*, Singapore: Southeast Asia Studies Programme, ISEAS, 1988. Pattani is dealt with by Surin Pitsuwan, *Islam and Malay Nationalism: A Case Study of the Malay-Muslims of Southern Thailand*, Bangkok: Thai Khadi Research Institute, Thammasat University, 1985, and the careful but for the twentieth century far less complete notes accompanying the edition of the *Hikayat Patani* prepared by A. Teeuw and D.K. Wyatt, The Hague, 1970. Gerald Cannon Hickey, *Sons of the Mountains: Ethnohistory of the Vietnamese Central Highlands to 1954*, New Haven, 1982, examines the modern history of Vietnam from a minority perspective. The position of the Muslims in Pattani and in the southern Philippines is compared in W. K. Che Man, *Muslim Separatism: The Moros of Southern Philippines and the Malays of Southern Thailand*, Singapore, 1990, while Peter G. Gowing provides accounts of the Moros in his *Mandate in Moroland: The American Government of Muslim Filipinos, 1899–1920*, Quezon City, 1983, and *Muslim Filipinos—Heritage and Horizon*, Quezon City, 1975. Further information is found in *The Muslim Filipinos: Their History, Society and Contemporary Problems*, edited by Peter G. Gowing and Robert D. McAmis, Manila, 1974.

The Indian community in Southeast Asia is described by Nalini Ranjan Chakravarti, *The Indian Minority in Burma*, London, 1971; Usha Mahajani, *The Role of Indian Minorities in Burma and Malaya*, Bombay, 1960; Kernial Singh Sandhu, *Indians in Malaya*, Cambridge, UK, 1969; and Sinnappah Arasaratnam, *Indians in Malaysia and Singapore*, Bombay and Kuala Lumpur, 1970.

The literature on the overseas Chinese in Southeast Asia is enormous. Victor Purcell, *The Chinese in Southeast Asia*, London, 1951, remains useful but can hardly be described as a definitive work. The effects of the 1911 revolution are considered in Yen Ching Hwang, *The Overseas Chinese and the 1911 Revolution*, Kuala Lumpur, 1976, and in a volume edited by Lee Lai To entitled *The 1911 Revolution—the Chinese in British and Dutch Southeast Asia*, Singapore, 1987. The Chinese community in Indonesia has been studied by Leo Suryadinata in a number of works, including *The Chinese Minority in Indonesia*, Singapore, 1978, *Peranakan Chinese Politics in Java*, Singapore, rev. edn, 1981, and his edited collection of documents entitled *Political Thinking of the Indonesian Chinese, 1900–1977*, Singapore, 1979. For the Philippines, Edgar Wickberg, *The Chinese in Philippine Life, 1850–1898*, New Haven and London, 1965, provides essential background information, and Antonio S. Tan, *The Chinese in the Philippines, 1898–1935*, Quezon City, 1972, brings the account forward to the beginning of the Philippine Commonwealth. For Cambodia, W.E. Willmott's two books, *The Chinese in Cambodia*, Vancouver, 1967, and *The Political Structure of the Chinese Community in Cambodia*, London, 1970, provide a thorough account, as does G. William Skinner's *Chinese Society in Thailand: An Analytical History*, Ithaca, 1957. Skinner's 'Change and persistence in Chinese culture overseas: A comparison of Thailand and Java', *Journal of the South Seas Society* 16, 1–2 (1960) is a well-known attempt to explain variable rates of assimilation among Chinese communities in Southeast Asia. Material concerning

Malaysia and Singapore for the period 1900–40 is surprisingly sparse, given the importance of the Chinese community in British Malaya, and Victor Purcell, *The Chinese in Malaya*, London, 1948, is seriously dated. Yoji Akashi, 'The Nanyang Chinese Anti-Japanese and Boycott Movement, 1908–1928—A Study of Nanyang Chinese Nationalism', *Journal of the South Seas Society* 23 (1968) deals with one aspect of Chinese nationalism. C.F. Yong, *Tan Kah-kee: The Making of an Overseas Chinese Legend*, Singapore, 1987, is a rare biographical account of a major figure, and Chui Kwei-chang's article 'Political Attitudes and Organizations c. 1900–1941' in Ernest Chew and Edwin Lee, eds, *A History of Singapore*, Singapore, 1991, provides a substantial account of political developments among the Chinese in pre-war Singapore. C.F. Yong has combined with R.B. McKenna in *The Kuomintang in British Malaya*, Singapore, 1990.

General works cited in this chapter include Benedict Anderson, *Imagined Communities: Reflections on the Origin and Spread of Nationalism*, London, 1983, Anthony D. Smith, ed., *Nationalist Movements*, London, 1976, and *Theories of Nationalism*, London, 1971, by the same author.

TWO

FROM WORLD WAR II
TO THE PRESENT

Writing a history of Southeast Asia as a region presents many challenges: the diversity the region displays in so many fields of human endeavour makes its history exciting but intractable. But if this is true throughout, the period since World War II presents the historian with special problems. By contrast to much of the earlier history, the period is copiously covered in written and printed documents. But they tell only part of the story. The period is, too, relatively recent, so that, in assimilating and analysing the material, it is hard to be sure that the right themes have been chosen. Even determining the date at which to stop is fraught with difficulty. The authors of this part have accepted that their approach must be tentative. At times they must content themselves more with narrative than interpretation.

The period indeed opens with an event the impact of which is still clearly being felt, the Japanese invasion and the collapse of the European empires. This is the subject of Chapter 6. Once more the fortunes of Southeast Asia were profoundly affected by forces outside the region. Once more its peoples reacted in a variety of ways. The colonial régimes were destroyed. In the Japanese phase new social and political opportunities were opened up for some, new constraints placed on others. The economy of the region, damaged in the Great Depression, was profoundly dislocated. Parts of it were fought over, parts not. The attempts of the colonial powers to return were again variously successful. Nationalist movements contended for power. They faced not only returning colonial rulers, but new local rivals. Their success was also partly dependent on the impact of changes outside the region, the decline of British and the rise of US power, the Cold War, the triumph of Chinese communism, the independence of India.

In general the nationalist élites inherited the colonial states. Their task was now to govern them. The political structures that they used are surveyed in Chapter 7. It argues that some structures were particularly shaped by war and revolution. Others were plural in nature, particularly those set up in the early years of independence. A third category the analysis discerns is maximum government. Its emergence may at least in part relate to the impact of and opportunities offered by the Asia-Pacific economic boom from the 1960s.

Chapter 8 discusses economic and social change in Southeast Asia. The leadership of the new states had to argue that independence would mean the end of poverty and developmental backwardness. Most sought growth, generally involving a good deal of direct government involvement in the economy. Different ideologies affected government policy. But so did the changing international environment, to which as ever Southeast Asia had to respond. That in turn was affected both by the economic policies of particular outside powers and by global economic trends. The search for growth met varying success, but urbanization and industrialization were often accompanied by degradation of the environment. Traditional hierarchy and community were challenged, sometimes enthusiastically, sometimes more doubtfully. Most Southeast Asians achieved some compromise between the old and the new. The other options were protest and, rarely successful now that the state was unprecedentedly strong, rebellion.

The region remains a site of encounter between divergent world-views, and its peoples experience a rich variety of religious experiences. Earlier transformations in Southeast Asian history had been attended by changes in religion, and, Chapter 9 suggests, pragmatic utilitarianism may be the most powerful missionary force in the Southeast Asia of the late twentieth century. But older patterns persist, particularly at the village level. They have also been taken up by the state, as governing élites seek to turn them to account, and in particular to integrate the states they have inherited. They continue, however, to have a vitality of their own. In effect, traditionalism, magic, millenarianism, mysticism, scripturalism and fundamentalism exist within all the world religions of the region. The experience of the spiritual among Southeast Asians remains intense, but increasingly they are likely to have faith in religion rather than accept it as an integral part of a whole system.

Throughout this work the authors have sought to adopt a regional approach to the history of Southeast Asia. The majority of them come from outside Southeast Asia, and it may be easier for those who live elsewhere to conceive of it as a region than for those who live in a Southeast Asian country. Chapter 10, which is the last chapter of the work as a whole, suggests that regionalism was slow to develop both because of the concern of the nationalist governments with consolidating the new states and because of the continued intervention of outside powers. But by the last decade of the century Southeast Asia had substantially determined the character of its nations and established a degree of regional cohesion. Though the region was as ever an object of interest to the great powers, its states had secured some control over their fate.

CHAPTER

6

SOUTHEAST ASIA IN WAR AND PEACE: THE END OF EUROPEAN COLONIAL EMPIRES

So marked is the diversity of Southeast Asia that even the recent history of each country, indeed of each community, possesses its own periodization and invites examination as a more or less autonomous entity. Nonetheless, the separate territories and societies do have sufficient shared experiences to allow a level of generalization for the area as a whole. The developments which provide a degree of regional coherence are not themselves, however, necessarily unique to the region. On the contrary, the outstanding landmarks in the closing chapter of Southeast Asia's colonial period are also features of the broader terrain of world history, notably the rise and fall of the Japanese empire, the postwar restoration of European colonialism and the achievement of national independence during the Cold War. Indeed, given that the focus of this chapter is upon the end of European empires in Southeast Asia, it is only to be expected that the momentous events and key decisions which are both the determinants and the symbols of its periodization are of major significance for, since they partly emanated from, the world beyond Southeast Asia.

WORLD WAR II AND JAPANESE OCCUPATION

World War in Southeast Asia, 1941–1945

Few historical events in the history of Southeast Asia appear so definitive as the Japanese invasion in December 1941.[1] By a stroke more compelling than the fall of Melaka to the Portuguese in 1511, the balance of power between Europe and Asia seemed to have been immediately and permanently transformed. The reasons for this invasion are to be found largely,

---

[1] A selection of titles on the outbreak of World War II in Asia and on other topics covered in this chapter is to be found in the bibliographical essay.

but not entirely, in events outside the region; in, for example, the growth of militarism in Japanese society during the 1930s, in the imperialist expansion of Japan and the course of the war in China, and in Japan's economic needs and the ideology of Co-prosperity. One must also take into account the weaknesses of European powers which, despite the apparent confidence and stability displayed by their governments in the colonies during the late 1930s, were at home distracted, and in the case of France and the Netherlands overwhelmed, by the war in the West. An additional dimension to any explanation of Japanese success and European failure in 1941–2 is that of the 'imperial periphery'. Amongst its more noteworthy features were, first, the raw materials which the region itself offered to the Japanese; second, the realities of the colonial position which, in contrast to appearances of virtual omnipotence, was marked in all instances by a fundamentally rickety network of collaborative ties with local peoples; and, third, the absence of any co-ordinated resistance to the Japanese advance.

In June 1940, when first the Netherlands and then France fell to Germany, Japan signed an agreement with Phibun Songkhram's government in Siam and also began to demand special privileges whereby it might land forces in French Indochina. In August the new régime of Vichy France permitted the Japanese the use of ports in Indochina and in September Japan joined the Axis in a ten-year tripartite pact, although this would not prevent it from upholding a neutrality agreement with Moscow (concluded in April 1941) when Hitler invaded the Soviet Union in June 1941. Early in 1941 Japan acted as 'mediator' between France and Siam in Indochina. One result of these negotiations was the convention in March whereby Siam regained territory on the west bank of the Mekong which it had lost to France in the Paknam incident of 1893. A second consequence was the further extension of Japan's territorial position in the region and the consolidation of its position for another leap forward, since it had succeeded in obtaining supplies of rice, rubber, coal and other minerals from Indochina, and also had won the formal confirmation of its military occupation of French territory. By the end of July Japan had effectively occupied Indochina, and the army and navy were preparing for operations in Southeast Asia and the Pacific. Japan nonetheless held back from military hostilities while at the same time Western powers, and especially the USA, attempted to block its advance with a combination of negotiations and embargoes.

The period of expansion through diplomatic means ended soon after mid-October when Prince Fumimaro Konoye was replaced as premier by General Hideki Tojo, the Minister of War, who had previously served as chief of staff with the occupation force in China. Feeling the pressure of the economic blockade, particularly as regards oil supplies, determined not to lose international status and mindful that the US would be likely to assist Britain and the Netherlands in the defence of their colonies, Tojo's government decided at the start of November on an early military strike. During the night of 7–8 December Pearl Harbor, Malaya, the Philippines and Hong Kong were attacked, and on 8–9 December the United States, Britain and the Netherlands declared war on Japan. But the US Pacific Fleet had been crippled in Pearl Harbor, half the American air force in the Far East was destroyed at Clark airfield, and British naval power in Asia was wiped out when HMS *Repulse* and HMS *Prince of Wales* were sunk off the coast of Pahang on 10 December. Japan had achieved supremacy in the air and at sea.

The military advance continued remorselessly and in several directions at the same time. On 2 January Japanese troops captured Manila and Cavite, though the island-fort of Corregidor at the entrance to Manila Bay held out some months longer. British and Commonwealth troops were unable to make an effective stand in the Malayan peninsula; Kuala Lumpur was captured by troops of General Yamashita's Twenty-fifth Army on 11 January, and 'fortress Singapore' came under siege on 31 January when the causeway between Johor Bahru and the island was blown up by departing Commonwealth forces. The Japanese had for a time hoped to occupy the Netherlands East Indies in the same manner that they had taken over French Indochina, that is without a military campaign which would waste Japanese resources and endanger the most valued of Indonesia's assets, namely the oil industry. Dutch stubbornness, however, forced Japan in January to launch a campaign for the occupation of the Netherlands East Indies. Towards the end of the same month a two-pronged invasion of Burma was mounted from Thailand which, having revised its relationship with Japan in the form of a ten-year alliance on 21 December, declared war on the Allies on 25 January.

The climax of the blitzkrieg came with the fall of Singapore on 15 February. Secure in the air, at sea and on land, controlling the major strategic point in the region, divested of effective enemies, Japan could now proceed to mop up residual colonial resistance. The battle of the Java Sea (27 February—1 March) opened up the Netherlands East Indies to the Japanese who, having captured Batavia on 6 March, virtually completed their occupation of Dutch possessions by early May. Meanwhile the British had evacuated Rangoon on 7 March, and the conquest of Burma culminated with the seizure of Mandalay on 2 May; the campaign in the Philippines ended with the fall of Corregidor on 6 May. This was the furthest extent of the Japanese conquests.

Surprise is said to have been a key reason for Japan's military successes. Tokyo recognized the need to avoid at all costs a war of attrition which would have allowed its enemies, and particularly the USA, a breathing space during which they could have blocked the Japanese advance upon the prime targets of Southeast Asian mineral supplies and the region's defensible strategic points. Second, though some of Japan's triumphs were close-run things—even the victory in Singapore was one of these—we must not underestimate what so many purblind decision-makers in Western governments did at the time, namely Japan's real strengths. During the months before armed conflict, Japanese diplomats displayed immense skill in obtaining Russian neutrality in the Far East, in exploiting American isolationism for as long as possible and in taking advantage of Thai territorial revanchism. Preparations for war were thorough, military morale was high, and the conduct of the campaigns themselves benefited from knowledge of local conditions. Conversely, and here is a third factor in Japan's success, Europeans were insufficiently mindful of the threat of war in the East and their response was further weakened by the lack of co-ordinated resistance on the part of colonial governments in Southeast Asia. More important still in determining the outcome of events in the East was the impact of the war in the West: the gathering storm in Europe from the late 1930s onwards distracted Europeans from forearming themselves in Southeast Asia, while Hitler's military success in 1940–1 prevented an adequate response to Japan from Britain, France and Holland. In the end, revelations of the fragility of the power and the superficiality of the support which Europeans enjoyed in Southeast Asia provoked an outcry at home. In addition to military scapegoats, 'effete' colonial rulers and 'treacherous' colonial subjects were blamed in turn, although in fact fifth-columnists made an insignificant contribution to the outcome of the campaigns of 1941–2.[2]

Almost as soon as it had reached its greatest extent, the Japanese empire was forced on to the defensive and soon afterwards into retreat. The day after the fall of Corregidor, Japan's advance was arrested at the Battle of the Coral Sea (7 May 1942). A month later came the turning-point of the Pacific War when, by their victory at Midway (4–7 June), the United States established ascendancy at sea and in the air. Cutting two swathes across the Pacific, the Americans launched the Allied counter-offensive. General MacArthur, at the head of the Southwest Pacific Command, advanced through the Solomon Islands (August–November 1942) and the eastern archipelago (1943–4) to land on Leyte in October 1944, while the Central Pacific Command under Admiral Nimitz pursued a similar 'island-hopping' course through the Marshall Islands, Guam and the Carolines. Both forces converged on Okinawa and the home islands in the spring of 1945.

On the Burma front the campaign was at first more sluggish. In the summer of 1942 General Wavell proposed Operation Anakin to retake Rangoon. This came to nothing. Although Orde Wingate's First Chindits demonstrated in early 1943 the possibility of survival behind Japanese lines, albeit at enormous human cost, the Allies were dogged by disease, low morale and poor liaison between the British, American and Chinese contingents. The appointment of Louis Mountbatten as Supreme Allied Commander Southeast Asia (SACSEA) in August 1943 breathed new life into this theatre. Although Plan Culverin for the reconquest of Sumatra in 1944 was not proceeded with owing to Anglo-American disagreements, General Slim's Fourteenth Army withstood Japanese offensives at Imphal

---

[2] Major Iwaichi Fujiwara was, for example, the leader of a special agency (the F Kikan) set up to recruit overseas Indians to the Japanese side, but its contribution to the 1941–2 campaign was negligible. As regards Malaya, an enquiry by the non-official Association of British Malaya concluded that there was little evidence of fifth-column activity: see Sir George Maxwell, ed., The Civil Defence of Malaya, London, 1944. It appears that the only significant outbreaks of local armed opposition to Europeans in Southeast Asia during the Japanese invasion were the activities of Aung San's Burma Independence Army and the Muslim rebellion in Aceh in Feb.–Mar. 1942: Jan Pluvier, South-East Asia from Colonialism to Independence, Kuala Lumpur, 1974, 195. See also Eric Robertson, The Japanese File: Pre-war Japanese Penetration in Southeast Asia, Hong Kong, 1979.

and Kohima in March–June 1944. Then, destroying the resistance of the Japanese Fifteenth, Twenty-eighth and Thirty-third Armies, and expecting support from Aung San's Anti-Fascist Organization, Allied troops swept south and entered Rangoon early in May 1945. Southeast Asia Command (SEAC), whose headquarters had moved from New Delhi to Kandy in April 1944, now set about preparing Operation Zipper, the seaborne invasion of Malaya which was to be assisted from within the peninsula by Force 136 in liaison with the Malayan People's Anti-Japanese Army (MPAJA).

The war came to an end, however, before Operation Zipper got under way. Air-raids upon Japan from November 1944 onwards reached a crescendo in the massive offensive on Tokyo and other cities in May–August 1945. On 6 August the first atomic bomb was dropped upon Hiroshima, and this was followed by the second on 9 August. On 8 August 1945, the USSR declared war on Japan and swept into Manchuria. On 10 August Kuniaki Koiso's government offered to surrender provided the emperor kept his throne. Four days later the Japanese accepted the Allied terms of capitulation and on 15 August the emperor announced his surrender. Territorial expansion had brought them military burdens without commensurate economic gains, and the Japanese were in the end worn down by the economic, military and technological power of the Allies, who turned their full might upon the Pacific theatre after victory in Europe.

The Japanese Occupation

A decade of expansion had resulted in the creation of the 'Greater East Asia Co-Prosperity Sphere' embracing Japan itself, Manchuria, Korea, and territories of China and Southeast Asia. 'Asia for the Asians' was the avowed objective of Japan's mission to eradicate Western influence over, and bring freedom and prosperity to, all races living in the Sphere, and many Southeast Asians at first hailed the Japanese as liberators. This ideology was intended both to inspire front-line troops and to win local support. In fact it meant the subjection of Southeast Asian communities to the Japanese way, including the veneration of the emperor, mass celebrations of anniversaries in the imperial calendar and compulsory language classes in *nippon-go*, as well as the subordination of their interests to Japanese military and material requirements.

Directing affairs on behalf of Emperor Hirohito, Premier Tojo was the architect of imperial policy until July 1944. Conquered territories in Southeast Asia immediately came under military control. The commander of the Southern Army, Field Marshal Terauchi, established his headquarters at Saigon. Java, Sumatra and Malaya were in the charge of the army (Sumatra and Malaya being united under the Twenty-fifth Army until 1943) while the rest of the Dutch East Indies was placed under the navy. Although it was their intention, and well within their capacity, to retain as a colony the strategically vital island of Singapore (renamed Syonan or Light of the South), the Japanese clearly lacked the manpower to rule all their

dependencies directly. As regards Siam, attempts were made to subordinate the country's economy to Japanese needs—which were resented by
the Thais—but the Japanese made no move to intervene in the internal
government of the country. Elsewhere the pragmatic adaptation of the
institutional structures and administrative methods of the previous colonial régimes was a feature of the new colonialism. In each state vacated by
Europeans, the Japanese inherited and utilized institutions and instruments that came to hand, though their task was made difficult by wartime
damage to administrative fabric and the lack of experienced personnel.

Former Dutch and British territories, where Europeans were interned,
were bereft of senior administrators; but in Indochina the Japanese retained French officials until March 1945, Governor-General Decoux arguing that in this way France saved its colonies. In the Philippines, where
Filipinos had managed affairs since the inauguration of the Commonwealth in 1935, the local élite continued in post, and in other parts of the
region where Southeast Asians had occupied junior echelons of government, local officials were advanced to fill gaps at higher levels. So, too,
were former critics of colonialism and nationalist politicians who previously had either been imprisoned by Europeans or fled from them.
Sukarno and the Malay radical Ibrahim Yaacob, for example, were released
from detention and each was active in the mobilization of grassroots
support for the military objectives and economic policies of the Co-
prosperity Sphere in Indonesia and Malaya respectively, while Aung San,
having returned to Burma from exile as one of the Thirty Comrades, placed
the Burma Independence Army at Japan's disposal. The younger generation was also groomed for public duties. In Malaya, for example, some of
the more able young men were sent for training at the *Kunrensho* colleges at
Melaka and Singapore, or participated in paramilitary organizations such
as *Giyu Gun* and PETA (a Malay acronym for Defenders of the Fatherland),
or were even sent for further education in Japan itself.[3]

In June 1943, as the Japanese took the strain of a war on several fronts
and anticipated Allied counter-offensives, Tojo declared his intention to
delegate civil administration. Consequently on 1 August Burma became
'independent' under Ba Maw as 'Adipadi' (or Fuehrer); in September the
Central Advisory Council was set up in Java under Sukarno; a Malayan
Consultative Council was established in Singapore; and on 15 October José
P. Laurel became head of an 'independent' régime in the Philippines. At
the same time Japan rewarded Siam with the restoration of land: in July
1943 the four northern Malay states (Perlis, Kedah, Kelantan and Terengganu) were added to the territory of two Shan states and parts of Cambodia and Laos which Siam had already regained thanks to Japan. In 1944
continuing military reverses led to further political changes: in July Tojo
was replaced as prime minister by General Koiso and in the same month
Phibun Songkhram was forced to resign as Thai premier; he was replaced
by Khuang Aphaiwong who served until September 1945 more or less
under the direction of Nai Pridi Phanomyong and the anti-Japanese and

---

[3] See Yoji Akashi, 'The Japanese Occupation of Malaya' in Alfred W. McCoy, ed., *Southeast
Asia under Japanese Occupation: Transition and Transformation*, New Haven, 1980.

American-sponsored Free Thai. In September 1944 Koiso promised, though he was never to have the time to grant, independence for Indonesia. In the following March the administration of Indochina was removed from French hands, and a nominally independent government was set up in Vietnam under Emperor Bao Dai.

Although these changes reflected Japanese needs rather than any sympathy for the aspirations of nationalist movements or, indeed, any acknowledgement of the latter's strength, the Japanese accepted that they risked damaging their own position by the gratuitous alienation of communities upon whose co-operation day-to-day rule depended. After all, the imposition of Japanese culture and insistence on emperor-worship were affronts to local customs and beliefs, particularly of the Buddhist and Moslem communities. With respect to the latter, the Japanese, like the Dutch and British before them, took account of these feelings by institutionalizing consultative processes. Towards the end of 1943 they sponsored the formation in Java of the Majlis Sjuru Muslimin Indonesia or Masjumi (Consultative Council of Indonesian Muslims).[4] Similarly the régime expressed respect for Islam in Malaya: the sultanates were left intact and a convention of religious councils was held at Kuala Kangsar in December 1944. The religious movement in Malaya, however, was anodyne compared with that in Java, which, having been legitimized by the régime, came to compete for the soul of the Indonesian nation with *priyayi* administrators, politicians such as Sukarno and Hatta, and the militant youth of PETA.

The primary objective of the military occupation of Southeast Asia had been economic, but the systematic exploitation of the region's assets was baulked from the outset by the wartime disruption of communications and devastation of shipping. The invasion and, more particularly, the scorched-earth tactics of the retreating Allies had destroyed or badly damaged much of the infrastructure of colonial states and wrought considerable havoc in the estates and mines of the colonial economy. The basis of the former colonial economies of Southeast Asia was further undermined by the different demands which the new colonial power made of the region. According to Japan's Commodity Materialization Plan the value of Malaya, for example, lay in its coal and iron rather than its rubber and tin, while the intention was to extract oil, nickel and bauxite from Indonesia. The effectiveness of Japan's command economy, however, rested on command of the sea and air; yet this was shortlived, being rolled back day by day after the US victory at Midway in June 1942. The consequent collapse of trade in turn resulted, as far as Southeast Asian countries were concerned, in a surfeit of traditional exports and a dearth of vital imports. There were gluts of rice in Burma and Thailand but dire food shortages elsewhere, especially in those areas which had become dependent upon food imports during the prewar period. Insufficient goods led to rationing, hoarding, a rampant black market and galloping inflation. This economic upheaval meant that, except for the small minority who won contracts

4 See H. J. Benda, *The Crescent and the Rising Sun: Indonesian Islam under the Japanese Occupation*, The Hague, 1953.

with the forces of occupation, Southeast Asians in general suffered unemployment, poverty and the loss of basic necessities. In desperation government dragooned people into agricultural schemes, while former plantations were given over to food programmes.

The social consequences of war and occupation cannot be quantified with any degree of accuracy, though the loss of life was on a scale unknown in the region since the beginning of modern government records, and the atrocities committed by occupying forces upon Southeast Asians verged on genocide in the case of Singapore's Chinese.[5] Subsequent food shortages reached starvation proportions in some areas and diseases (particularly malaria) were on an epidemic scale throughout the region by the time of the Allied reoccupation. In addition, communities were uprooted. Families fled the towns to escape direct contact with the régime and squatted on forest fringes to scrape together a livelihood from subsistence cultivation. Labour was forcibly recruited from, for example, the Burmese, the overseas Indian community and amongst Indonesians in order to build such projects as the Burma railway or military defences. In addition, men were conscripted for military or paramilitary service or for the Indian National Army.[6] Furthermore, the occupation aggravated the latent hostility between ethnic communities (between, for example, Malays and Chinese or Burmans and Karens) and also provoked struggles between competitors for power within individual communities. Communal conflict was less the result of deliberate policy or totalitarian manipulation on the part of the Japanese—on the contrary, the Japanese practice of divide-and-rule was grossly exaggerated by their enemies. Conflict was far more the outcome of economic hardships, changes in political patronage, the erosion of local government, and the sheer mutual mistrust of those unaccustomed to indigence. These were the conditions which would spawn violent conflict whenever Japanese rule was relaxed or after it had finally disintegrated.

Southeast Asian Nationalism, 1941–1945

Violence and oppression, the ideology of liberation and the taste of opportunity, the experience of arbitrary rule in some parts of the region and the collapse of government in others, all these features of 1941–5 sharpened political perceptions and stimulated nationalist activities in Southeast Asia.[7] War and the Japanese occupation, however, contributed as much to the dissipation of political energy as to its generation, and as

---

[5] See C. M. Turnbull, *A History of Singapore 1819–1975*, Singapore, 1985, 190–4, though see also Yoji Akashi, 'Japanese policy towards the Malayan Chinese 1941–1945', JSEAS, 1, 2 (1970).

[6] For an account of this army recruited from amongst the Indians of Southeast Asia see J. C. Lebra, *Japanese-trained Armies in Southeast Asia*, Hong Kong, 1977, and K. K. Ghosh, *The Indian National Army: Second Front of the Indian Independence Movement*, Meerut, 1969.

[7] The young Ahmad Boestamam in Malaya, for example, later recalled the exciting challenges of these years whereas the experience of 'Co-prosperity' taught the older U Nu in Burma to 'beware of Pied Pipers!'. See Ahmad Boestamam, trans. W. R. Roff, *Carving the Path to the Summit*, Athens, Ohio, 1979, and Thakin Nu, *Burma under the Japanese. Pictures and Portraits*, London, 1954.

much to the fragmentation of nationalist movements as to their consolidation. Rather than square up directly to alien control, the nationalists' priority was the cultivation of local support; this they often pursued in competition with each other. Since at this time none possessed the strength to achieve power unaided, most accepted the need to seek outside assistance; the result was that the calculations of nationalist leaders and their capacity to act largely hinged on the outcome of the war and the fates of their respective sponsors.

Although they may not have assessed their long-term interests and those of the communities they aspired to lead purely or even primarily in terms of the aims of the principal combatants in World War II, Southeast Asian political activists nonetheless faced up to the questions as to whether they stood to gain or lose by supporting the Axis or the Allies, and whether their fortunes would be further advanced through painstaking negotiation or armed struggle. Such issues caused debate, frequent divisions and long-lasting feuds within their ranks. In Indonesia Islamic élites and militant youths came to jostle for Japanese favours with nationalists of the prewar Indonesian National Association (PNI), whose leaders anyway hedged their bets on the outcome of the war: Sukarno openly co-operated with the Japanese, while Mohammed Hatta acted as intermediary with Sutan Sjharir's small underground organization. Asian communists were particularly taxed by the ideological and practical implications of collaboration and resistance, and split over the Comintern directive (issued after Hitler's invasion of Russia in June 1941) to ally with imperialism in opposition to fascism. Of Burma's Marxist Thakins, some, like Thein Pe Myint, were prepared to form an anti-fascist alliance with Britain whereas others, notably Aung San, argued that the interests of the Burmese pointed to joining with the enemies of Britain.[8] Meanwhile the perfidious secretary-general of the Malayan Communist Party (MCP), Lai Teck, kept his options open, following Moscow's line of 'united front' yet betraying his anti-Japanese comrades when it suited him.[9]

The choice between collaboration and resistance at any given time was determined by a mixture of considerations. Some were attracted by the prospect of rewards, seduced by the ideology of the Co-prosperity Sphere or bewildered by the apparent omnipotence of the Japanese empire. Selection of sides was also affected by ethnic allegiances, kinship ties and conflicts far more localized than the global struggles between fascism, communism and imperialism. Collaborators were not necessarily drawn from those who had previously opposed Western rule; as we have seen, Asian functionaries of European governments, who may be thought to have had vested interests in the old régime, generally submitted to employment under the new one. Moreover, the critics of colonialism who at first were eager to espouse the Japanese cause grew to doubt Japan's willingness and ability to transfer power to Southeast Asians.

---

[8] See Robert H. Taylor, *Marxism and Resistance in Burma 1942–1945. Thein Pe Myint's 'Wartime Traveler'*, Athens, Ohio, 1984.
[9] Cheah Boon Kheng, *Red Star over Malaya. Resistance and Social Conflict During and After the Japanese Occupation of Malaya, 1941–1946*, 2nd edn, Singapore, 1987, 56–100.

To be effective, a collaborative relationship must bring advantages to both parties involved. The Japanese used Southeast Asians to run routine administration and mobilize support for political demonstrations, public works and agricultural schemes. The extent to which Southeast Asians themselves derived political benefits from these activities is, on the other hand, difficult to measure. Co-operation with the régime did not in itself guarantee concessions from it. Aung San, for example, lost faith in Japanese promises so much so that in 1944 he formed the Anti-Fascist People's Freedom League (AFPFL) whose services he offered to Mountbatten in June 1945. Sukarno was abandoned by the Japanese before they were able to inaugurate Indonesia's independence, and it was the Pemuda (youth) who forced him to declare *merdeka* (independence) two days after the emperor's surrender. Moreover, Japanese patronage could not for long compensate adequately for lack of local support and credibility. Parties, like Masjumi in Indonesia, which represented significant constituencies were able to capitalize on the relationship, but shallow-rooted organizations failed to survive if the Japanese prop was removed. Whereas Sukarno's republican movement had the ballast to ride the storms of 1945, Ibrahim Yaacob's KRIS (Union of Peninsular Indonesians) was flat-bottomed and easily overwhelmed: Ibrahim, who tried to take over the helm in mid-August, was powerless to guide the Malayan vessel and soon abandoned ship for refuge in Jakarta. Similarly, when the Japanese replaced the French-manned administration of Vietnam with an 'independent' government in March 1945, it was not the incumbent Bao Dai but the revolutionary Ho Chi Minh who made the most of Japan's weakening grip upon Vietnam.

If collaborators were not synonymous with the opponents of European colonialism, then resisters were by no means its natural allies. The backbone of anti-Japanese resistance movements was, on the contrary, provided by historic enemies of Western imperialism, namely Kuomintang cells and especially Southeast Asia's communist parties, who shrewdly calculated on an eventual Allied victory, but also set their faces against the restoration of European rule.[10] Their first priority, however, was to muster lasting local support and they did this by harnessing rural unrest and concealing their communist creed within a nationalist front of more widespread appeal. Thus in Burma communists were active in the AFPFL until the Burma Communist Party was expelled from the League in 1946. In Malaya the Chinese-dominated MCP, influenced not least by ingrained Sino-Japanese enmity, followed the Comintern line, setting up the Malayan People's Anti-Japanese Army and making contact with Force 136 agents. In Vietnam between May and October 1941, Nguyen Ai Quoc (Ho Chi Minh) launched the Vietminh (League for Vietnam's Independence) as a broad-based resistance organization comprising all anti-Japanese nationalists. Although the Vietminh's programme was not communist (its goal

---

[10] For local resistance movements see Taylor, *Marxism and Resistance in Burma*; Cheah Boon Kheng, *Red Star over Malaya*; Benedict J. Kerkvliet, *The Huk Rebellion. A Study of Peasant Revolt in the Philippines*, Berkeley, 1977; and Greg Lockhart, *Nation in Arms: The Origins of the People's Army of Vietnam*, Sydney, 1989. Cf. Charles Cruickshank, *SOE in the Far East*, Oxford, 1983.

was a democratic republic of independent and united Vietnam) and although the Indochinese Communist Party was officially disbanded, communists like Ho Chi Minh and Vo Nguyen Giap were nonetheless its principal leaders. Seeing the danger of nurturing communists on their southern flank, Chiang Kai-shek's Kuomintang detained Ho between 1942 and 1944; the Vietminh trod a difficult path between allaying the suspicions of the Kuomintang and other non-communists and succumbing to neutralization. In the struggle for power in Tonkin, the Vietminh secured their position by developing the tactics of guerrilla warfare, appealing to the peasantry and cultivating US assistance. In the Philippines Luis Taruc led the Hukbalahap (or People's Anti-Japanese Army) which turned out to be the best-organized and most effective of the resistance forces in Southeast Asia. Furthermore, capitalizing on the polarization of Filipino society and particularly the peasant discontent of central Luzon, the Huk went much further than either the Vietminh or the MPAJA (the one being impeded by continuing French colonialism and the other by Sino-Malay communalism) in implementing a programme of social revolution aimed at breaking the economic power of great landlords. By the end of 1944 the Huk were in undisputed control of most of central Luzon. They undermined Japanese power elsewhere in the Philippines too, and greatly assisted the USA in its reconquest of the country. Finally we might mention 'non-occupied' Siam where the left wing, led by Nai Pridi, kept in touch with the Free Thai in exile and, after the enforced resignation of Phibun in July 1944, controlled the governments first of Khuang Aphaiwong and then of Seni Pramoj (the former leader of the Free Thai in the USA), who became prime minister in September 1945.

Although resistance armies received military supplies from the Allies and were able to establish control over certain rural areas, these country-based and largely communist-led organizations were something of an unknown quantity in the calculations of Americans, British and Chinese. We have noted Kuomintang mistrust of the Vietminh; the Allied commanders in the SEAC and Philippines theatres were similarly suspicious of the reliability and intentions of the AFPFL, MPAJA and the Hukbalahap. They were wary of making any great use of them, though in this respect Mountbatten was of necessity as well as temperamentally more inclined to be accommodating than was MacArthur. Whereas Aung San's offer of cooperation was accepted by Mountbatten whose officers also liaised with Chin Peng's MPAJA force, MacArthur rounded up the Huks despite the fact that they had mounted the most strenuous resistance to the Japanese. Like the Katipunan in 1898, the Hukbalahap was unable to thwart an American invasion. On his return, MacArthur immediately disbanded the Huk and imprisoned Luis Taruc. Although resistance armies seemed poised to seize power and were in actual control of some areas by August 1945, they were not in a position to prevent the reoccupation of the region by the Allies. Indeed, their leaders hoped to enhance their claims for a place in the postwar world by facilitating that reoccupation, and it is clear that their influence upon the course of the European return was more marked than had been the contribution of fifth columnists to the Japanese advance in 1941–2.

Neither collaboration nor resistance invariably brought their expected rewards. The fortunes of nationalists rested on the amount of assistance they received from outsiders and the extent of support they enjoyed locally; the absence or the removal of either factor could bring about their eclipse. Great Power patronage on its own was not enough to secure a party's success, although Great Power opposition could block its progress. Nationalist activity, on the other hand, did not determine the outcome of the campaigns of 1941–2 and 1944–5, although it did affect the manner of Japanese rule and Allied reconquests. Allegiances were volatile during World War II since nationalists were as anxious to distance themselves from their sponsors as the latter were inclined to ditch them.

While it is generally accepted that the Japanese invasion and occupation turned Southeast Asia upside down,[11] the nature, extent and permanence of the changes of these years have all been viewed from sharply differing angles. While many have judged it to have been the climacteric in the modern history of Southeast Asia, contrasting images jostle for attention. One is of a dark age of barbarism quenching the 'Roman' legacy of colonial government; another is of the dawn of a new age, heralding the triumph of national self-determination. On the other hand, those who are less inclined to be startled by big bangs and prefer an interpretation that places more emphasis on continuous development, if not a steady state, have kept in mind the deep-rooted patterns and particularities of the region's past when making their assessment of what was, after all, but a brief chapter in its history.

So far as the place of Europeans in Southeast Asia was concerned, the military disasters of 1941–2 were profoundly humiliating as well as materially damaging. Furthermore, the Japanese invasion, occupation and eventual defeat vitiated those conditions which had been fundamental to the viability of the old-style colonial régimes. The international isolation and economic equilibrium of the region disappeared; the fabric of government was eroded; and political relations became more intense. In short, the events of 1941–5 led to the destabilization of every country in the region: the circumstances of August 1945 were not propitious for the restoration of colonial systems. So intrusive and extensive was the disruption that the collaborative networks as well as the infrastructure of pre-colonial states were now in disarray. In addition, the demands of world war, and not just those of the Southeast Asian campaigns, dramatically affected the ability of Europeans to regain their colonial territories. It was clear that the restoration of colonial rule would be impossible without the deployment of men, materials and military power on a far larger scale than Europeans had ever found the need to wield before or were likely to be in a position readily to command in the straitened circumstances of the postwar world.

In considering the impact of war upon the colonial empires one should not focus on the Southeast Asian 'periphery' to the exclusion of the European metropole. Just as loss of colonies in Southeast Asia undermined

[11] cf. the near contemporary account by Chin Kee Onn, *Malaya Upside Down*, Singapore, 1946.

European pretensions to empire in other parts of the world, so the war in the West had a major impact upon the future of Europeans in the East. By weakening the economies of European states, it reduced their capacity to fulfil an imperial role. Paradoxically, it also increased their determination to resurrect their overseas empires in order to compensate for injuries inflicted upon the wealth and the prestige of the nation. Thus it was that the Japanese period did not put paid to colonial empires for ever, and that after 1945 there were vigorous and not completely unsuccessful attempts to reassert the European presence in the region.

The notion of a watershed in the imperial relationship, a turning-point in the relative positions of Europeans and Southeast Asians, is illustrated in those studies of nationalist movements which emphasize the changes that occurred in political ideology, leadership and organization during a period whose significance for the region was, it has been argued, out of all proportion to its length. Conversely, other writers have drawn attention to the large measure of continuity in indigenous political activity and state development, and have claimed that the Japanese made few initiatives and left little lasting impact in these areas.[12] In distinction from either of these interpretations—the one suggestive of a clean break, the other of linear progression—this discussion has stressed the veritable confusion that engulfed Southeast Asia in 1941–5. Up to a point, of course, the problems encountered by the returning Europeans invited nationalists to assert themselves more defiantly in the face of any attempt to restore colonialism. Indeed, all demonstrations of over-rule, it might be thought, could only have been counterproductive, encouraging amongst Southeast Asians the very resistance which they were intended to contain. But the havoc of war had added to the difficulties of nationalists too. It had shorn rungs from the ladder they hoped to climb and had damaged the citadel they aspired to take. Furthermore, since the upheaval had also multiplied the contestants for power, there was the prospect of the struggle for national independence dissipating itself in civil strife. The race was on, but in the stampede following the Japanese surrender few winners and losers were yet discernible.

COLONIAL RESTORATION AND STRUGGLES FOR INDEPENDENCE, 1945–1948

Colonial Planning for Postwar Southeast Asia, 1942–1945

Almost as soon as they had lost their empires, Europeans began to draw up plans for their recovery. They did so according to their respective assessments of their joint and individual interests, and in the light of their

---

[12] The emphasis laid by, for example, H. J. Benda on the significance of the Japanese period (e.g. *The Crescent and the Rising Sun* and 'The Japanese Interregnum in S.E. Asia' in Grant K. Goodman, comp., *Imperial Japan and Asia. A Reassessment*, New York: Occasional Papers of the East Asia Institute, Columbia University, 1967) has been reconsidered in Alfred W. McCoy, ed., *Asia under Japanese Occupation: Transition and Transformation*, New Haven, 1980.

perceptions of the region's future. Two factors in particular determined the planning for colonial restoration: the value of overseas possessions, and the capacity to tap their worth. Indochina and Indonesia had formed the core of the overseas empires of France and the Netherlands before the war, and their governments-in-exile had no doubts about their importance for national recovery. De Gaulle's colonial policy was geared to the re-establishment of French power in a postwar world, while the identity as well as the well-being of the now hapless Holland had been nurtured by three and a half centuries in the East Indies. Britain's possessions in Southeast Asia were, by contrast, on the fringe of an imperial system which centred upon India. Nevertheless, Churchill made no secret of his belief that the recovery of Singapore was 'the supreme British objective in the whole of the Indian and Far Eastern theatres . . . the only prize that will restore British prestige in this region'.[13]

If it was clear that Europeans had not yet lost the will to rule non-Europeans, in 1942 it was still uncertain how they would set about realizing their intentions, especially since to a greater or lesser extent the restoration of British, Dutch and French colonies in Southeast Asia hung on the might of the United States, whose president was convinced that the age of imperialism was dead. Running through the wartime Grand Alliance was a vein of mistrust born of the colonial issue. Americans were predisposed to regard European colonialism as a mark of decadent societies, as ideologically misguided because it stood in the way of national self-determination, and as an obstruction to the pursuit of the American way and especially American trade. Britain's 'imperial preference' had particularly galled Americans during the 1930s and US anti-imperialism came to focus upon the British imperial record, although the Dutch and the French were by no means immune. Europeans, for their part, dismissed their colonial critics as, at best, naive or, at worst, mischievous. Trans-Atlantic sententiousness and ready-made blueprints, it was held, failed to disguise American self-interest; nor did they make a constructive contribution to the solution of the more intractable colonial problems. As the British were keen to point out at the time, the Americans themselves had had colonial responsibilities in Southeast Asia and the Pacific which they had singularly failed to meet in 1941–2.

Differing approaches to the issue of European imperialism were apparent, for example, in divergent Anglo-American interpretations of the Atlantic Charter of August 1941, particularly of Article 3 which recognized 'the right of all peoples to choose the form of government under which they will live'. These differences affected the conduct of military operations. Because of his avowed commitment to the integrity of the British empire, Churchill was suspected by well-placed Americans of being less than whole-hearted in the pursuit of Allied war aims and was accused of delaying the second front in Europe until circumstances were suited to the preservation of the British empire. Likewise in the Southeast Asian theatre Mountbatten's American deputy, General Stilwell, was a bitter

---

[13] Quoted in John Darwin, *Britain and Decolonisation. The retreat from empire in the postwar world*, London, 1988, 42.

Anglophobe, and a number of operation plans (for example, Culverin in 1944) snagged on Anglo-American differences. In the closing stages of the war the US administration, preferring to treat the French as an associate rather than an allied power, placed all sorts of obstacles in the way of the participation of Free French units in the battle for Indochina. These misgivings infected joint planning for postwar Southeast Asia. In 1942–3 Roosevelt (echoing Woodrow Wilson in the closing stages of World War I) advocated some kind of international trusteeship council to administer former Southeast Asian colonies on behalf of subject peoples. The French and Dutch would have been powerless to resist had the White House pressed ahead with such a scheme while even Britain, it was feared in some quarters of Whitehall, might have been pushed to the point of sacrificing its colonial claims on the altar of the Anglo-American 'special relationship'.[14]

As it happened, American anti-imperialism moderated with the prospect of peace. Its fire faded with the death of Roosevelt in April 1945. Moreover, as their forces hopped across the Pacific in 1943–5 the United States swept up new islands (such as the Marianas and Marshalls) which they would be reluctant to relinquish. In addition, the demands of global policing and the residual American inclination to return to hemispherical isolation contributed to growing indifference in Washington to the recovery of 'colonial' Southeast Asia once the fighting stopped. We should not anticipate the sea-change in American attitudes to both European colonialism and regional security caused by the advent of Cold War in Asia several years later. Nevertheless, American military planners came to accept that the strategic interests of the USA would be better served in several turbulent regions of the world (Southeast Asia included) by the restitution of the apparently stable order of colonialism than by the institution of potentially fragile nation-states. One consideration in this respect was the opportunities which colonial governments, starved of funds from home and hungry for American investment in the postwar rehabilitation of devastated territories, might afford American business. Furthermore, the US administration recognized that in the end it could not afford to antagonize or, more seriously, to undermine those Allied leaders like De Gaulle and especially Churchill who were implacable imperialists. Finally, US antagonism to European empires diminished as Americans allowed themselves to be persuaded that Europeans were revising the ideology and reforming the structures of their empires.

For these reasons, although colonial régimes would be subject to unprecedented international scrutiny by the United Nations after the war (and increasingly so as more Afro-Asian countries became members of the organization) and although their survival in postwar Southeast Asia would hang in large measure upon the acquiescence (if not the active support) of the USA, the acid seeped out of Washington's strictures. Thus, while the

[14] For extensive examinations of Anglo-American differences over empire see Christopher Thorne, *Allies of a Kind: The United States, Britain and the War against Japan, 1941–1945*, London, 1978, and Wm Roger Louis, *Imperialism at Bay 1941–1945: the United States and the decolonization of the British Empire*, Oxford, 1977.

Yalta Conference in February 1945 set up new mechanisms of accountability to the United Nations with respect to the administration of certain trust territories in Africa and reaffirmed the principles of the Atlantic Charter, it abandoned the demand for the general internationalization of colonies.

So it was that during their three and half years of exile from Southeast Asia the Americans, British, Dutch and French considered their respective roles in the region in an atmosphere of interdependence yet mutual mistrust. All planning took place within military parameters in the first instance, but policy-makers looked beyond the requirements for successful invasion, reoccupation and military administration to the longer-term objectives of civilian rule.

Despite Britain's scuttle from Burma in 1942, plans for the restoration of colonial rule were drafted with confidence. Governor Reginald Dorman-Smith, supported by a staff of British officials who had evacuated the country as the Japanese had marched in, set up his court-in-exile at Simla, and it was here rather than in London that much of the preparation for reoccupation was laid. Separation from India and the inauguration of the ministerial system in 1937 had amounted to a radical departure in British policy for Burma: the priority of the wartime planners was Burma's economic rehabilitation, not its political advance. Consequently, the proposals which were published in May 1945—after the reoccupation of Burma and victory in Europe but when the war in Asia still seemed to have a year or two to run—merely held out the prospect of eventual dominion status for Burma (i.e. self-government within the British Commonwealth, which at this time was also the British intention for India). If anything, the white paper regressed beyond the *status quo ante bellum*, since it envisaged suspending the ministerial system of 1937–42, putting the country under the direct rule of British officials until December 1948, and allowing the Scheduled Areas of ethnic minorities to remain under British control until they themselves opted for amalgamation with 'Burma proper'. In short, wartime plans for Burma aimed at the restoration of British power and commercial interests, but were justified by reference to the well-being of Burma and the Burmese.

British preparations for postwar Burma and the Malayan region followed dissimilar courses. The circumstances in which policy was worked out for British Malaya and Borneo were very different, and the planning itself was far more radical than in the case of Burma. Fewer colonial officials had escaped Japanese detention in Malaya and Borneo, and the initiative was seized in London by the Colonial Office (and the Malayan and Borneo Planning Units). The result was a fresh departure designed to bring about the administrative consolidation of British territories, facilitate the economic development of the region and eventually lead to the creation of a self-governing nation (or nations) out of the plural societies of the 'Malaysian' region. The first steps down this road were taken during the war: in May 1944 the Cabinet approved proposals for, first, a Malayan Union of the peninsular Malay States and the former Straits Settlements of Penang and Melaka; second, for Crown Colony rule in Singapore, Sarawak and North Borneo; and third, for a governor-general supervising British colonial interests throughout the region. Although these proposals were drawn up in secret and were destined to arouse considerable local opposition, they were part of a radically different and avowedly more progressive approach by the British to colonial affairs.

In December 1942, when Britain was itself making great efforts to present the acceptable face of imperialism to the American government and people by publicizing the ideology of 'partnership', Queen Wilhelmina delivered a speech which promised the convention of a postwar conference for the reorganization of the Kingdom of the Netherlands into a Commonwealth. This was to consist of the Netherlands itself, the Netherlands East Indies, Surinam and Curaçao, and was based on the principles of 'complete partnership' and 'self-reliance' (or internal self-government). The East Indies were the centrepiece of Dutch overseas interests and the Dutch government-in-exile was determined to return there, even at the cost of giving hostages to fortune. The scheme had a considerable impact in the West and went a long way to counter US criticism of European overseas empires. Indeed, Americans held up the Dutch as exemplars to the British. In Indonesia, however, Queen Wilhelmina's speech went unnoticed at the time it was delivered. Moreover, it was overtaken by the events of the next three years and, although used by the Dutch as their point of departure in postwar negotiations with Indonesians, in the event it contributed little to the postwar restoration of Dutch colonialism in Southeast Asia. Thereafter, the Dutch government-in-exile—most prominently Dr H. J. van Mook who was Minister for Colonies and Lieutenant-Governor of the provisional government of the Netherlands East Indies—was hamstrung in its planning by its material weakness. When it became clear that the British and not the Americans would be responsible for the Allied reoccupation of the Netherlands East Indies, the Dutch were aggrieved that their interests were increasingly neglected.

The emergence of De Gaulle as undisputed leader of the Free French by mid-1943 confirmed Roosevelt in his opposition to entering into any commitment to restore Indochina to France in advance of the Japanese defeat. On this issue the French government-in-exile and the British government maintained a common front: it was, after all, as much in Britain's interests to build up a strong France, as well as a strong Holland, for the rehabilitation and security of Western Europe, as it was to safeguard the generality of European colonialism in postwar Asia. De Gaulle, however, did little to endear the French to progressives, let alone to critics of colonialism. The Brazzaville Declaration of January 1944 ruled out 'all idea of autonomy and all possibility of development outside the French Empire'.[15] The Japanese coup replacing residual French administration in Vietnam with the 'independent' régime of Emperor Bao Dai only stiffened French imperial resolve. On 24 March 1945 De Gaulle's government issued a statement spelling out a future in which an Indochinese Federation (of Tonkin, Cochinchina, Annam, Laos and Cambodia) would rest within a French Union concentrated upon and controlled from Paris.

---

[15] 'Brazzaville Declaration of 1944' quoted in Anthony Short, *The Origins of the Vietnam War*, London, 1989, 40, and J. D. Hargreaves, *Decolonization in Africa*, London, 1988, 64–6.

The statement of 24 March seemed to reinforce the antipathy of the Americans (whose Office of Strategic Services or OSS had recently discovered Ho Chi Minh) to French participation in the war against the Japanese. Nevertheless, in the longer perspective, the beginning of the end of American resistance to the restoration of French rule in Indochina can be dated from this point. De Gaulle was later persuaded by colonial reformers and American critics to moderate the strongly imperialist sentiment of the March statement and modify the structure of the Union Française in such a way that the status of a number of French colonies was altered to that of 'Associated States'. According to this formula the more 'advanced' dependencies outside tropical Africa, such as Morocco, Tunisia and Indochina, would be set on the road to internal autonomy within the French Union. 'Reculer pour mieux sauter': the French government believed that these concessions would do nothing to undermine the international standing of France, and anyway many French people, including senior army officers, did not foresee a genuine loosening of ties between Paris and the colonies. In order to work, however, these constitutional arrangements required a large degree of metropolitan control over local colonial affairs, and this the postwar Fourth Republic was not destined to enjoy.

The Western powers returned to Southeast Asia determined to impose a colonial system of some kind. For Burma the British prepared for an immediate period of direct rule, while they planned a similarly assertive role for themselves in Malaya and Borneo. Over-rule in both areas was intended to be preliminary to the construction of eventually self-governing members of the British Commonwealth. Building on Queen Wilhelmina's declaration of 1942, the Dutch also drew up a Commonwealth arrangement allowing for a degree of local autonomy within a Netherlands-centred imperial system. The French Union was, in theory, an even more coherent arrangement for the integration of an overseas empire. Of the colonial powers in Southeast Asia, only the USA expected to make an early transfer of power to its subject peoples once they had been liberated from the Japanese. The American commitment to grant independence to the Philippines on 4 July 1946, however, did not come about in response to developments since Pearl Harbor, nor did it amount to the surrender of imperial control. It was, in fact, a stipulation of the Tydings–McDuffie Act of 1934, which had established the Commonwealth of the Philippines, and was intended to secure American interests and continuing influence in the country beyond the date of formal independence.

Colonial Restoration and Nationalist Resistance: Confrontation and Negotiation, 1945–1948

The brevity of the colonial reoccupation and the speed with which the colonial empires were cleared out of Southeast Asia has tempted commentators on the immediate postwar years to present nationalists as the victors, colonialism as a lost cause, and Malaya as a temporary exception to the inevitable success of region-wide resistance to European rule. Such blunt conclusions, however, cannot be allowed to stand without important modifications. First of all, although it would be misleading to underrate the difficulties faced by Europeans bent on restoring their power in Southeast Asia in 1945–8, we should beware of anticipating the end of their empires. It is true that their homelands were bled white, their colonies were broken-backed and that reoccupation turned out to be neither smooth nor permanent. It must also have been the case that scarcely any Europeans in positions of authority could have expected to find their colonial inheritance unmarked by the tumult of war or imagined that they would reconstruct old forms of control. Indeed, the British took care to dress up their plans in progressive language, and the Dutch and French were persuaded to modify the methods and rhetoric of prewar colonialism. Nonetheless, European morale had recovered sufficiently since 1941–2 to foster a widely-held belief that the obstacles in the way of their return were surmountable and that the re-establishment of their régimes would be in the best interests of Southeast Asians as well as to their own advantage.

In arguing that there was something resembling a common colonial purpose in Southeast Asia, we should not forget the nuances, sometimes tensions, between European viewpoints. Not only did discussions between London, Paris and The Hague often lack unanimity, but the policies of each of these governments themselves frequently changed tack. Government policy, of course, is rarely doctrinally coherent, since the art of the possible necessitates compromise. Inconsistencies in the respective British, Dutch and French positions become more intelligible when reference is made to personality clashes and the complexities of decision-making. There was a variety of interested groups—including politicians and civil servants, military officers and businessmen, metropolitan authorities and those on the spot—and they adopted different approaches to the problems of reoccupation. For example, directors of rubber and tin companies requested more public expenditure than British Treasury officials could contemplate; Governor Gent was keenly disliked by 'old Malayan hands', and Governor Dorman-Smith in Burma was sacked by Attlee; van Mook in Jakarta occasionally tried to rush The Hague into decisions; and Léon Blum, the premier of France, juggling with a precarious coalition, found himself presented with a fait accompli in Indochina by Admiral d'Argenlieu in November 1946.

A factor that assisted the European return was the distraction of Great Power attention from Southeast Asia by problems in Europe, the Middle East and South Asia. Palestine and India were the major imperial issues where Britain risked (and, in the case of the former, actually suffered from) American criticism, while Greece and Iran levered apart the superpowers of the wartime Grand Alliance, thus paving the way for Cold War. If the USA took an interest in Southeast Asia in 1945–8, it was largely to give encouragement (but not, at this stage, material assistance) to Europeans, rather than lend support to their nationalist challengers.

In querying familiar assessments of colonial weakness we should likewise be careful not to exaggerate the strength of nationalist movements in the immediate postwar years. Nationalism did not carry all before it to complete the business which had been started, but left unfinished, in the upheaval of 1941–2. On the contrary, there is a strong case for arguing that Southeast Asia experienced a 'new imperialism' in the immediate postwar years and that colonialism was not the preserve of the mentally inert and those who had lost touch with the reality of world affairs. Neither in the Philippines, where independence was transferred with apparent grace, nor in Indonesia and Indochina where it was bitterly contested, did the Western presence show signs of abatement. Since nationalist movements were themselves fragmented, it would be as unwise to present them as unstoppable forces in Burma, Indonesia and Vietnam as it would be to assume the immovability of colonialism in Malaya. It was the best and the worst of times for all and everywhere.

Given the similar ends and shared problems of Europeans seeking to restore the fundamentals, if not the prewar forms, of colonial control in the unstable circumstances obtaining throughout the region, and bearing in mind the unprecedented efflorescence yet diffusion of nationalist movements in every territory, it is not surprising that Europeans and Asians explored ways of advancing their respective positions by striking bargains with each other. From September 1945 to early 1948, the British, Dutch and French were engaged in attempts to enlarge their political control, subdue rebellion and rehabilitate their dependencies. One of their tasks was to win the co-operation of nationalist leaders who, for their part, showed a similar willingness to collaborate in order to gain valuable European assistance in the competition with rivals, the consolidation of power and the quest for legitimacy. Indeed, if one is to identify a common theme in the confused politics of Southeast Asia during the aftermath of war, it is the pattern of alternate phases of confrontation and negotiation as Asians and Europeans sought a modus vivendi.

Malaya is sometimes cited as the exception to a trend best exemplified by Burma during the aftermath of war. In Malaya, it is said, colonialism was reinstated without apparent difficulty, while elsewhere nationalism forced it into retreat. Although we now know that the British position in Malaya was more secure than that of the Dutch or French in their territories, we should beware of drawing too stark a contrast between these colonial experiences by underplaying the difficulties of one in order to highlight those of others. Instead of the 'triumph of nationalism', 1945–8 witnessed—to borrow a phrase from the historiography of postwar Africa— 'the second colonial occupation' of Southeast Asia.[16] Since it was the case that, in spite of the constitutional changes that occurred in the Philippines after the war, Burma was the only territory from which Western imperialism had been eradicated by 1948, colonial Malaya rather than nationalist Burma might well be taken as the paradigm of the period.

It was decided at the Potsdam Conference in July 1945 to divide the responsibilities for the military administration of Japan's empire between American, British and Chinese commands. According to these arrangements the United States would repossess the Philippines, occupy Japan, liberate Korea and assist Chiang Kai-shek in China, while the British-led

---

[16] See, for example, D. A. Low and J. Lonsdale, 'Towards the New Order, 1945–1963' in D. A. Low and Alison Smith, eds, *History of East Africa*, III, Oxford, 1976, 12–16.

SEAC would assume charge of 'colonial' Southeast Asia (apart from North Vietnam which was to be occupied by Chinese troops as far south as the sixteenth parallel).

Independence in the Philippines

The Americans were confident that the Philippines would remain within their informal empire in the Pacific whatever constitutional concessions were made to Filipinos; they had set up the Commonwealth of the Philippines in 1935 with the promise that independence would follow after ten years. The Japanese Occupation did not deflect them from this strategy, principally because it scarcely altered the social basis and composition of the Filipino ruling class through which American influence had been exercised. On their return, the Americans ignored both the claims of guerrillas who had resisted the Japanese and the misdemeanours of élites who had assisted them. As we have seen, General MacArthur swept aside the pretensions of the Hukbalahap, relegating them to the status of rebels. Moreover, he did not pursue the punishment of enemy collaborators but went about restoring civil administration as early as February.

MacArthur at first worked through President Sergio Osmena who had been a leading member of the government-in-exile and represented the pro-American leadership that had dominated Filipino politics before 1942. Meanwhile, however, Manuel Roxas, a member of the land-owning oligarchy who had managed to serve the Japanese régime without breaking his links with the Americans, was officially cleared of the taint of treachery and encouraged to mount a challenge to the Osmena administration. Flush with funds, Roxas and his Liberal Party conducted a vigorous campaign against Osmena's Democratic Alliance which reluctantly fell back on left-wing, even Huk, support. In the April elections the Liberals won majorities in the House of Representative and Senate, and Roxas beat Osmena for the presidency. So far as the Americans were concerned, Roxas proved more compliant than Osmena might have been; he could be relied upon to secure the country against radical social change and to provide for American economic and strategic requirements. After the passage of the Bell Act, ensuring free trade between the two countries, and the Tydings Act, providing financial aid to the Philippines, the Philippines was proclaimed an independent republic on 4 July 1946. The strong links between Washington and Manila which survived both the Japanese Occupation and the achievement of independence suggest that, as Pluvier has commented, 'there was, in fact, hardly any fundamental difference between the policy of the United States in South-East Asia and that of the European colonial powers'.[17] The grant of formal independence to the Philippines, however, did signify a greater willingness on the part of Washington than of Paris, The Hague or even London at this time to experiment with informal methods of imperialism in postwar Southeast Asia.

Southeast Asia Command (SEAC), 1945–1946

As soon as Emperor Hirohito surrendered, SEAC's frontier was extended to embrace Thailand, southern Indochina and the greater part of Indonesia

[17] Pluvier, 386.

in addition to Burma, Malaya and Sumatra, and its headquarters were transferred from Kandy to Singapore. SEAC's task was to accept the Japanese surrender and repatriate Japanese personnel, to evacuate Allied prisoners of war and others in detention, to keep the peace and assist the restoration of colonial rule at least until the future status of liberated areas had been fully worked out. It appeared, therefore, that the extension of SEAC's authority guaranteed not only British interests in the region but those of the Dutch and the French as well. In fact, however, the assumption of sole responsibility for the reoccupation saddled Britain with heavy burdens and obligations, some of which it would be hard-pressed to fulfil.[18]

Though an enormous enterprise by any standard, SEAC's resources were inadequate to its tasks. The Americans were not willing to make substantial contributions to it and the British government found that its own resources were already overstretched by military commitments in Europe, the Middle East and South Asia. Loss of initiative in India meant that Britain could no longer freely deploy Indian troops in policing imperial territories elsewhere in the world, as it had done, for example, in the Middle East after World War I. Moreover, the need to place Britain's economy on a peacetime footing and the promises made to the electorate meant that the Labour government was under domestic pressure to demobilize Britain's conscript army as soon as possible.

Furthermore, despite the contemporary reports of joyous welcomes accorded to the returning Allies, their reoccupation of the region was something of a shabby scramble. From the outset SEAC was wrong-footed by the unexpected swiftness of the war's end. Its troops were deprived of the opportunity of redeeming their military reputation in the eyes of locals by force of arms; its administrators were called upon to set up military governments over the whole region immediately instead of step by step. An understandable lack of preparedness largely accounted for that anarchic hiatus between the Japanese surrender and the Allied 'liberation'. The landings on the coast of Malaya (Operation Zipper) could easily have turned into a military debacle had SEAC met with resistance, and when British troops eventually arrived in Java they encountered armed opposition and lawlessness on a large scale.

SEAC's position did not improve significantly after headquarters and a framework of military administration had been established in each territory. Throughout the region food shortages, worthless currency, political uncertainty and administrative collapse resulted in SEAC's having few footholds from which to assert itself over profiteering and banditry, vigilantes and kangaroo courts, communal conflict and competing bids for power of various nationalist groups. The army of occupation was unable, therefore, to confine itself to military administration *tout court*; it became increasingly involved in regional politics both at local and international levels. In September the British government, through Mountbatten, put heavy pressure on Thailand for the return of lands wrested from Burma

[18] See Peter Dennis, *Troubled days of peace. Mountbatten and South East Asia Command, 1945–46*, Manchester, 1987.

and Malaya, the full restitution of British property, trading privileges, free rice and the right to station troops indefinitely. These punitive 'Twenty-one Demands' struck Pridi, who had been leader of the wartime Free Thais and was now acting as regent, as a blatant attempt to reduce his country to colonial or neo-colonial status. The Americans who had other ideas about winning the co-operation of postwar Siam (as the country was again called in 1945–7), intervened to secure a substantial dilution of the terms of the Anglo-Thai treaty. The Anglo-Thai treaty, which was eventually signed in December 1945, was one aspect of SEAC's contentious political role in postwar Southeast Asia.[19] As regards 'colonial South-East Asia', Mountbatten appeared more liberal than he did to many Thais but his position was made the more onerous by diplomatic pressure from the governments of France and the Netherlands. They suspected that a British supremo who could bring himself to accept for an ally the 'war criminal' Aung San in Burma and to decorate the communist Chin Peng in Malaya was half-way to endorsing the claims of Sukarno and Ho Chi Minh as well.

Transfer of power or struggle for independence in Burma?
On 17 May 1945, a fortnight after Rangoon had fallen to Slim's Fourteenth Army, the British government published the White Paper announcing its postwar policy towards Burma. Full self-government within the British Commonwealth was accepted as Britain's long-term objective for Burma as it was for India, but no timetable for political advance was spelled out. Instead, as we have seen, it was proposed to return, for the interim at least, to the position established by the 1935 constitution except in one major respect: the ministerial system would be temporarily replaced by direct rule in order to facilitate the speediest economic reconstruction of the country. The British were, however, soon forced to abandon this measured approach. Mountbatten was particularly sensitive to the local appeal and nationalist demands of AFPFL, and recognized that it was imperative to reach an understanding with Aung San. Well aware that the White Paper for Burma was inappropriate to the circumstances which reoccupation revealed, he tried to push Dorman-Smith faster and further down the road to self-determination than the governor was inclined to go. In August 1946 Dorman-Smith, who had only antagonized Aung San, was replaced by Sir Hubert Rance.

The police strike in Rangoon soon after Rance's inauguration as governor revealed the poverty of British imperialism in no uncertain terms. Government was on the verge of breakdown and the political initiative fast slipping from Britain's grasp. Rance was convinced that he would have to bring Aung San into his Executive Council, and that the White Paper had to be scrapped. Thereafter British rule was rapidly wound up. An AFPFL delegation went to London in January 1947 and reached an agreement with Attlee's government on the election of a constituent assembly to draft the constitution for independent Burma. When AFPFL won a resounding victory in these elections in April, it seemed that the British had achieved a stay of execution: they had found a strong man with whom to do business

[19] See Judith A. Stowe, *Siam becomes Thailand. A Story of Intrigue*, London, 1991, 337–59.

and looked forward to a future of cordial relations with the new Burma.

Such hopes soon receded. The Aung San–Attlee agreement on independence triggered a struggle for the spoils between a myriad of Burmese groups, notably AFPFL itself, the Burma Army, the Burma Communist Party, the Karen National Union, and others besides. The assassination in July 1947 of Aung San and six Cabinet colleagues removed the one nationalist leader who might have had a chance of uniting Burma and maintaining close relations with Britain.[20] As it turned out, AFPFL remained in office and fashioned the constitution for independent Burma. However, its commitment to both republicanism and centralism ensured, in the one case, complete severance of Commonwealth membership and, in the other, the hostility of Burma's minorities. Moreover, Aung San's successor, U Nu, was unable to establish his authority effectively beyond Rangoon when civil war, not least communist insurrection and Karen secessionism, engulfed the Union of Burma following the achievement of independence on 4 January 1948.

Why had British interests and influence in Burma been overturned so precipitately? Part of the explanation, but not the whole of it, lies in the strength of the nationalist challenge. AFPFL's struggle for independence, it should be noted, succeeded because it conjoined with other major developments in and beyond Burma. First of all, Aung San's bid for power was launched at a time when conflict among the Burmese themselves placed overwhelming strains on Britain's ability (and ultimately its military capacity) to determine political advance. As Hugh Tinker has commented, 'Power was surrendered by the British to the Burmese long before the Union Jack was lowered on 4 January 1948.'[21] The British might well have coped with opposition had it come from a single source; what undermined the structure of the colonial state and British efforts to keep it in good repair was the extensiveness of the damage and rapidity of its deterioration. What weakened the landlord's determination to hang on to that which he felt was his entitlement was the apparently unanimous opposition of tenants who otherwise squabbled with each other to secure the whole property or squat in parts of it. This political confusion was to AFPFL's immediate advantage since, short of old-time collaborators, Britain realistically negotiated with the strongest of its opponents; the result was that, of the several competitors for the colonial inheritance, AFPFL manoeuvred itself into the best position to win possession of the tottering structure of British Burma. In the longer term, however, Burma's confusion was to AFPFL's disadvantage; the paint and plaster that had been slapped on to get a quick sale soon peeled away, and disagreement abounded amongst the new owners over the question of multiple occupancy.

---

[20] For fresh light on the assassination of Aung San see Louis Allen, 'The Escape of Captain Vivian. A Note on Burmese Independence', *Journal of Imperial and Commonwealth History*, 19, 2 (1991).

[21] Hugh Tinker, 'Burma: power transferred or exacted? Reflections on the constitutional process' in R. B. Smith and A. J. Stockwell, eds, *British Policy and the Transfer of Power in Asia: Documentary Perspectives*, London: School of Oriental and African Studies, 1988, 24; see also Tinker, 'The Contraction of Empire in Asia, 1945–48: The Military Dimension', *Journal of Imperial and Commonwealth History*, 16, 2 (1988).

WAR AND PEACE: THE END OF EMPIRES

A second factor to take into consideration is the British Labour government's reappraisal of the importance of Burma as an imperial asset. Although the reforms of 1935–7 had cut the constitutional ties between Burma and India, Burma still remained an appendage of the Indian Raj in the official mind, and British policy for Burma continued to shadow developments in South Asia. Having decided in the winter of 1946–7 upon an early withdrawal from India, Attlee's administration looked at Britain's other Asian dependencies in a new light. Whereas the strategic and economic value of Malaya had never stood higher, Burma, which had been acquired and maintained in the interests the Indian empire, now lost its imperial raison d'être.[22] The end of British rule in India was publicly announced on 24 February 1947, when the deadline was set for June 1948 (a date later brought forward to 14–15 August 1947), and coincided with the decision to seek escape from formal empire in Burma as well. That the escape route turned out to be an uncomfortable one is indicative not so much of the British reluctance to leave, as their inability to determine the manner of their going.

Although a certain amount of Anglo-Burmese goodwill was for a time retained, not least because the new leadership required outside assistance in coping with its internal problems, the British were soon citing the transfer of power to Burma as an object-lesson whose repetition in other territories was to be avoided at all costs. For Britain decolonization in Burma proved to be a failure on economic and strategic grounds: civil war, neutralism and isolationism threatened the rice trade and weakened Western defence in the gathering Cold War. An exception so far as British decolonization was concerned, British policy towards Burma did not altogether reflect the new colonialism which was a feature of the postwar settlement of Southeast Asia as a whole. Between September 1945 and early 1948, Burma was the only territory where the former colonial power failed to secure its position even in an informal capacity.

New imperialism in Malaya
Withdrawal from South Asia was matched by swings to the Middle and Far East in Britain's interests and influence. As regards their dependencies in Southeast Asia, the British returned with plans for direct rule and promises of self-government. In addition they assumed responsibility for supervising the restitution of colonialism in Indonesia and Indochina, and for co-ordinating the rehabilitation of the region as a whole.

The British Military Administration was established in Malaya in September and lasted until the inauguration of the Malayan Union under Governor Gent on 1 April 1946. Just as he was identified with liberal colonialism in Burma, so with regard to Malaya, Mountbatten was anxious that the British should command the moral high ground by giving full publicity to the progressive aspects of the Malayan Union scheme which appeared to meet the eight-point programme of the Malayan Communist Party on every count. Even so, however, the period of military occupation

<hr>

[22] See R. B. Smith, 'Some contrasts between Burma and Malaya in British policy in South-East Asia, 1942–1946' in Smith and Stockwell, eds, *British Policy*, 30–76.

was costly in terms of local goodwill as well as in manpower and material resources. Like Burma, Malaya was plagued by lawlessness and ethnic conflict. Malaya differed from Burma, however, in three important respects which go a long way to explain the differing outcomes of colonial reoccupation in the two countries. First, Malaya acquired an enhanced value after 1945 and even more so after the demission of empire in India; Malayan rubber and tin were major commodities feeding British factories and, more importantly, earning dollars for the sterling area. Secondly, Malaya (together with Singapore) was the base of British power in a region of contiguous Great Power rivalries. Thirdly, the British were not under the same economic, political and military pressures in Malaya as they were in Burma: Malayan mines and plantations were swiftly rehabilitated; the unprecedented Malay opposition to the Malayan Union was readily appeased; Indonesian-inspired radicalism fizzled out; and the leadership of the MCP for the time being chose to pursue the 'united front' strategy of infiltration in preference to armed struggle.[23] While the self-determination of a Dominion of Southeast Asia, embracing the Malayan peninsula, Singapore and the Borneo territories, was Britain's ultimate objective, the time-scale of political advance was indistinct and nationalist forces were inchoate. In any case Britain was on its guard against making any move which might suggest repetition of the humiliating scuttle of 1941–2.

This is not to say that the wartime plans for a Malayan Union in the peninsula or for Crown Colony rule in Singapore, North Borneo and Sarawak were implemented without protest. The surrender of Sarawak by the Brookes to the Crown in 1946 provoked anti-cessionist protest, principally from Malays in the Kuching area. This opposition failed to deflect the British from their course of action, and died away when the assassination of Governor Stewart in 1949 induced Anthony Brooke to renounce all claims to his patrimony. More significant was the unprecedented Malay opposition aroused by the Malayan Union and especially the proposal to award citizenship to non-Malays. Frightened by the prospect of the loss of traditional Malay support on the one hand and the emergence of Indonesian-inspired or communist-led opposition on the other, the British decided to appease the Malay Rulers and Dato Onn bin Jaafar's newly formed United Malays National Organization (UMNO). In July 1946 constitutional negotiations got under way; insistent that a strong central government and some form of common citizenship should be retained, the British nonetheless accepted the Malay case as regards the Rulers' sovereignty and a more restrictive citizenship scheme. Although the British never lost sight of the multiracial principle underlying the Malayan Union, the Federation of Malaya, which was inaugurated on 1 February 1948, was essentially a reaffirmation of Anglo-Malay collaboration, ensuring British domination at the centre, securing Malay control over the separate states, and further alienating Malaya's Chinese community.

The island-colony of Singapore resumed its role as the headquarters of British military power in the region. It also became the centre for the diffusion

---

[23] See Cheah Boon Kheng, *The Masked Comrades: A Study of the Communist United Front in Malaya, 1945–1948*, Singapore, 1979.

of Britain's political, economic and cultural influence throughout postwar Southeast Asia. The systematic disposition of British interests and activities, which had been the priority of Duff Cooper's short-lived ministry in 1941–2, was the major recommendation of Mountbatten's political adviser, M. E. Dening. When SEAC was wound up, Lord Killearn was appointed as the Foreign Office's special representative having the prime task of restoring the region's rice trade, while Governor-General Malcolm MacDonald supervised the affairs of Britain's various colonial dependencies. Between them they sought to secure the postwar settlement of the region, bringing pressure to bear on colonial partners in some instances and wooing the leaders of emergent Asia in others. In 1948 Killearn left Southeast Asia and thereafter MacDonald, as Britain's Commissioner-General 1948–55, fulfilled the dual function of co-ordinating British colonial and foreign policies in addition to chairing the British Defence Co-ordinating Committee.[24] Since the USA was comparatively indifferent to the region's affairs at this time, 1945–8 amounted to Britain's moment in Southeast Asia.

Negotiation and war in Indonesia, 1945–1948
The reassertion of imperial power by the Dutch was made difficult—some would say impossible—by the changes which had occurred during their absence and Dutch inability to make adequate adjustments to them. First among these we must count the fragmentation of the colonial state under the looser control which the Japanese had exerted over the archipelago. Added to this was the emergence of correspondingly divisive nationalist forces and anarchic, albeit highly localized, groups such as those who toppled the sultanates in east Sumatra or plunged into civil war the Javanese town of Bandung.[25] Dutch problems were further compounded by the hiatus that was allowed to intervene between the Japanese surrender and the arrival of the SEAC reoccupation force. This was delayed by troop shortages, with the result that General Christison did not land in Java until late September 1945, some six weeks after Sukarno had proclaimed *merdeka*. In response to the nationalists' partial establishment of an independent republic of Indonesia, the furthest van Mook was prepared to go was to offer a variation on the theme of Queen Wilhelmina's 1942 speech, that is the creation of a Netherlands Commonwealth or imperial federation in which semi-autonomous colonial states would remain bound to Holland. The Dutch, for their part, have apportioned blame differently: Prime Minister Attlee, Supreme Allied Commander Mountbatten and General Christison between them failed to provide an adequate platform

---

[24] For aspects of Britain's postwar regional policy see N. Tarling, '"Some Rather Nebulous Capacity": Lord Killearn's Appointment in Southeast Asia', MAS, 20, 3 (1986), and Tilman Remme, 'Britain, the 1947 Asian Relations Conference, and regional co-operation in S.E. Asia', in A. Gorst, L. Johnman and W. S. Lucas, eds, *Postwar Britain, 1945–1964. Themes and Perspectives*, London, 1989.

[25] See Benedict R. O'G. Anderson, *Java in a Time of Revolution: Occupation and Resistance, 1944–1946*, Ithaca, 1972; John R. W. Smail, *Bandung in the Early Revolution 1945–6. A study in the social history of the Indonesian Revolution*, Ithaca, 1ᶜ64; Anthony Reid, *The Blood of the People: Revolution and the End of Traditional Rule in Northern Sumatra*, Kuala Lumpur, 1979; and R. B. Cribb, 'Jakarta in the Indonesian Revolution 1945–1949', Ph.D. thesis, University of London, 1984.

from which Holland might mount its return to the Indies. In contrast to General Gracey's firm action allowing General Leclerc's early take-over in Vietnam, Christison appeared to sympathize with Indonesian nationalists, while shipping shortages and other problems so delayed the return of the Dutch in adequate numbers that some bitterly complained that the British deliberately conspired to prevent the restoration of the Dutch empire in Southeast Asia.

It is true that in 1945–6, as in 1815–16, the Dutch were dependent on the British for the restoration of their possessions in the East. The British, it should be noted, were as anxious to assist the Netherlands after the surrender of Emperor Hirohito as they had been after the defeat of Emperor Napoleon; on both occasions the British were largely motivated by the need to assist in the resurrection of the Netherlands in Europe. In 1945 Attlee's Labour government had no wish to be associated with any action which added to Holland's appalling plight of penury and near starvation. On the other hand, the British government was not keen to commit men and materials which they could ill afford to a prolonged and debilitating military operation and one which also threatened to damage Britain's international reputation. Moreover, since the theory and practice of Dutch colonialism did not altogether coincide with their own, they were embarrassed by, and increasingly resented involvement in, actions that pointed to the return of Indonesia to unreconstructed Dutch colonialism. Mountbatten and Christison, like their masters in London, were predisposed to seek the political co-operation of the nationalists rather than risk military confrontation with them; but Lieutenant Governor-General van Mook refused to countenance dealings with Sukarno, while Sjharir, who presented the Dutch with a slightly more acceptable face of nationalism, rejected outright the Dutch olive branch of 'partnership' within the Netherlands 'Commonwealth'. Bogged down in political stalemate and a maelstrom of disorder, Christison and his men were distracted from the task of evacuating internees and repatriating Japanese. They found themselves in some instances relying on Japanese to hold the line against lawlessness, while in others, they formed the target of nationalists' resistance, as in the bitter fighting over Surabaya where General Mallaby was murdered in October 1945. Indeed, the British looked forward to the end of this rather tawdry episode and, though they had had little influence on the way the Dutch approached the political problems, it was with relief that they transferred authority over the outer islands to the Dutch in July 1946 and completed the evacuation of Java and Sumatra by the end of November.

Like Europeans elsewhere in the region, until 1948 the Dutch significantly advanced their position in Indonesia. Being beneficiaries as well as victims of times that were out of joint, they were able to call upon the allegiance of the outer islands whose leaders were mistrustful of the Java-centred republic. Such indeed was their hold over the outer islands by mid-1946 that van Mook went ahead with the 'Commonwealth' scheme, and at the Malino conference with Indonesian leaders of the Dutch sector in July he set about organizing 'autonomous' states which would form components of a Netherlands Federation. Controlling the outer islands, the Dutch could bring economic pressure to bear on the Republican government (now based in Yogyakarta) since the latter were desperate for food imports and also lacked the necessary exports to generate foreign exchange. Parleying with rebels and traitors did not appear to come naturally to the Dutch, who resented yet succumbed to British pressure to negotiate with nationalists; but it was the relative strength of the Dutch rather than their weakness which induced republicans to come to the conference table at Hoge Veluwe in the Netherlands in April 1946 and at Linggajati near Cheribon (Cirebon) in November 1946. By the Linggajati agreement (provisionally signed on 15 November) the Dutch recognized the Republican government's writ in Sumatra and Java, and both sides agreed to co-operate in establishing a sovereign, democratic and federal 'United States of Indonesia'. Linggajati saw the Dutch relax their previous insistence upon the 'imperial' connection, and ensured that future debate would revolve round the distribution of power within the proposed federation. Nonetheless the Dutch emerged from the talks materially unscathed and in no mood to abandon their claims to the East Indies. Had they worked harder at cultivating nationalist leaders, it is conceivable that they might have won genuine collaborators in their commonwealth experiment. Instead, they preferred to play upon the divisions within the nationalist movement while preparing to do battle with it should the agreement come to naught.

The Dutch were assisted by the structural diversity of the nationalist movement and by feuds between Republican politicians. As in many another 'nationalist revolution', the ideology of struggle (*perjuangan*) against imperial rule was propagated in order to distract attention from simultaneous conflicts between Indonesians. From within the fledgling government Sukarno, Sjharir and Hatta respectively appealed to the populist, socialist and Islamic strands of Java-centred Indonesian nationalism. Even so, the tapestry which they wove, or rather their attempt at patchwork, did not entwine all colours of opinion without some violent clashes, nor did they succeed in stitching together such a variety of political textures without rents and tears here and there. The movement threatened to come apart at the seams, indeed, under the strain imposed on it by the *pemuda*, the Indonesian Communist Party (PKI) and Masjumi. Moreover, if the Dutch were initially dependent upon British troops, the Republican government had fewer resources at its command. Its legitimacy was in dispute, its military strength unreliable, its economic base was in shreds; it was forced to withdraw from Jakarta to Yogyakarta early in 1946.

The fissiparous tendencies within the nationalist movement were encouraged, and the Republic was further weakened, by a long-running disagreement between those who urged *diplomasi* or negotiation with the Dutch and the advocates of *konfrontasi* or armed confrontation. That Sjharir was willing to negotiate at all indicated in the first place his lack of confidence in the nationalists' ability to repulse the Dutch by military means; it also evinced his preparedness to co-operate in the creation of some kind of a federation and an appreciation of the value of Dutch assistance in the fashioning of a viable successor state. As it was, the Republicans' failure to extract Dutch recognition of their claims to independence and sovereignty fostered mutual mistrust, aggravated political feuds within the nationalist camp, and undermined Sjahrir's authority; the result was that he was forced out of office in June 1947 and the Linggajati agreement lapsed. The Dutch turned these divisions to their advantage and followed up the collapse of the agreement by deploying some 150,000 troops in the Police Action or First Military Action. Their forces made territorial inroads into the Republican heartland of Java, and the stranglehold they managed to impose upon Yogyakarta strengthened their hand at a further round of talks which got under way at the end of the year and culminated in the Renville agreement (January 1948). The Republic could do no other than accept the current lines of demarcation and the plan to set up a United States of Indonesia in advance of any Dutch commitment to withdraw militarily. Like the conference at Linggajati, that of Renville exacerbated fissures within the nationalist movement and forced the resignation of a major politician, this time the foreign minister Amir Sjarifuddin.

Another aspect of the survival of Dutch colonialism during this period was its resilience in the face of 'world opinion'. It is true that Britain was instrumental in persuading the Dutch to open negotiations towards the end of 1946; Lord Killearn played an important part in setting up the Linggajati conference. Similarly, it was criticism in the United Nations of the Police Action which persuaded the Dutch to mount the Renville talks. Nevertheless the Dutch made few significant concessions to their opponents at either encounter, and their ability to withstand international opprobrium at this time is in marked contrast to the constraints placed by the United States on their freedom of action after the abortive Madiun coup later in 1948.

Revolution and resistance in Vietnam
In Vietnam the respective positions of nationalists and imperialists were more rapidly staked out and more firmly entrenched than in Indonesia, with the result that war between them occurred sooner and became more prolonged. The Vietminh moved fast in order to anticipate colonial reoccupation and to confront the Chinese entering from the north and the French in the south with a fait accompli. The key moments in the August revolution were the election of Ho Chi Minh by the Vietminh Congress as chairman of the National Liberation Committee in Hanoi on 13 August; the enforced abdication of Emperor Bao Dai as head of state on 25 August; and the proclamation in Hanoi of the independent Democratic Republic of Vietnam (DRV) on 2 September. At the same time the Vietminh in Saigon established a Liberation Committee which sent representatives to meet General Gracey when he flew into Saigon on 13 September.

Gracey's objectives were to disarm the Japanese in SEAC's sector (that is south of the sixteenth parallel); to restore order in the Saigon area; and to assist in the restoration of French control. General Leclerc, who reached Saigon on 5 October, was looking forward to an early revival of the French colonial régime which was assumed to have been merely in abeyance since the Japanese coup of the previous March. This task was not complicated to the same extent as was Christison's in the Netherlands East Indies by the

problems of finding, liberating and repatriating large nun
pean detainees. Still, Gracey was troubled by indiscipline an
troops who provoked a good deal of Vietnamese unrest,
activities of guerrillas who dominated the countryside in the :
and French officers saw eye to eye in rejecting the claims of
in Saigon, and, soon after his arrival, Gracey set about disarmi͏   .. ᴜᵑᵘ
re-establishing French control over Cochinchina. Firmly, though not un-
disputedly, based on the Cochinchina bridgehead, the French proceeded
to reassert themselves in Cambodia, Laos, Annam and Tonkin. By the first
week in March, Gracey was in a position to hand over the civil administration to Governor-General d'Argenlieu, and the military command to
General Leclerc.

During the next nine months relations between the French and the
Vietminh deteriorated from uneasy negotiations into outright war. At first
Ho tacitly accepted the reimposition of French authority over Indochina,
while the French did all they could to avoid military engagements with the
Vietminh. Since Ho Chi Minh was consolidating his support, he also
avoided armed confrontation and hoped to win advantages through
diplomacy. Like the Dutch, the French tried to restore their power (though
not the prewar colonial order) by building up a coalition of collaborators
and hemming in their opponents. Within the projected Federation of
Indochina (which itself would lie within the French Union) they envisaged
direct control over the most economically valuable area of Cochinchina and
effective, if less formal, control over the monarchies of Cambodia and
Laos. This, they felt, would more than compensate for political concessions to the Vietminh in famine-stricken Tonkin. On 6 March Ho Chi Minh
and Jean Sainteny concluded an agreement whereby the former accepted
the deployment of French troops in Tonkin, while the latter recognized the
DRV as a free and self-governing state, though with the proviso that it
remained a part of the Indochinese Federation and the French Union. The
French also promised to hold a referendum on the issue of the territorial
unity of the three parts of Vietnam. France appeared magnanimous, but in
reality it made more gains than did the Vietminh by this arrangement: in
exchange for paper promises it had achieved a distinct military advantage
in the north. Further conferences—at Dalat from 17 April to 11 May and at
Fontainebleu from 6 July to 10 September—did not, however, break the
stalemate over three vexed issues, namely: French insistence on the
integrity of the Union, the Vietminh's demand for the reunification of
Vietnam, and the place of Vietnam in the federation of Indochina.

This diplomatic phase ended dramatically when d'Argenlieu ordered
the bombardment of Haiphong on 23 November 1946. The Vietminh
retaliated by blowing up the power station in Hanoi on 19 December, and
the next day Ho Chi Minh declared a 'war of nationwide resistance' against
the French. So began the First Vietnam War.[26] Its opening offensive,
known as the battle for Hanoi, lasted until mid-February 1947, when

[26] But R. B. Smith has written: 'One of the most remarkable features of the Vietnam War is that
no one can say precisely when it began': *An International History of the Vietnam War,
I: Revolution versus Containment, 1955–61*, London, 1983, 3ff.

Vietnamese resistance collapsed and the French completed their occupation of the city.

It is generally supposed that the French *coup de main* was intended to force Ho Chi Minh back to the conference table, not on to the battlefield. The bombardment, indeed, can be interpreted as the continuation of diplomacy by other means, rather than its abandonment. The French had witnessed both the steady reinforcement of Ho's position in the north (following his electoral victory, the inauguration of a new constitution and the appointment of a new cabinet earlier in November) and the growing disruptiveness of Vietminh units in the south. The longer he was allowed to consolidate his position, it was argued, the less amenable he would be politically and the more elusive he would become militarily. The resort to force was, however, a cardinal error. The short, sharp shock neither extracted political concessions from Ho Chi Minh, nor did it knock out his army. French troops may have succeeded in taking Hanoi and other towns, but in so doing they drove the Vietminh into the hills whence came their strength. That the French failed to foresee Ho Chi Minh's reactions — he was provoked into doing the very things which violence was intended to prevent — reveals a profound lack of understanding of both Vietminh strategy and the deep rural roots of their support, for, whereas the French cultivated anti-communist élites in the towns, the Vietminh fomented social revolution in the countryside.

French actions in Vietnam at the end of 1946, like their intervention ninety years earlier, are to be explained largely by reference to three factors: the fluidity of metropolitan politics, the impetuosity of the military on the imperial frontier, and the poor control exerted by Paris over the man on the spot. The socialist premier of France, Léon Blum, laid the blame on d'Argenlieu, but Blum's commitment to peaceful methods was also compromised by the imperialism of his coalition partners and even that of the generation of 'radicalized socialists' who had emerged in postwar France.[27] This war was no exception in arising from the miscalculations of decision-makers and their uncertain grip on events. The battle for Hanoi, once joined, committed France to a war which during the next seven and a half years would come to dominate its overseas policy, debilitate its postwar economic recovery, and jeopardize its position in the defence of Western Europe. On occasions it would determine the fates of governments and shake the very foundations of the republic.

All this was for the future, however, for 1945–8 witnessed the colonial reoccupation of Southeast Asia. In the aftermath of war the British, Dutch and French were determined to regain their assets and influence in the region, notwithstanding domestic problems and the progressive vapourings of some politicians. During these years the British may have relinquished Burma but they established direct rule over the 'Malaysian' territories; the French in Indochina, like the Dutch in Indonesia, managed to match local resistance, and refused to let expressions of international disapproval deflect them from their chosen course.

[27] See Miles Kahler, *Decolonization in Britain and France. The Domestic Consequences of International Relations*, Princeton, 1984, 165ff., 171–6.

REVOLUTION AND DECOLONIZATION IN THE COLD WAR, 1948–1957

The Cold War did not break upon the world like a clap of thunder but rather, it came like rolling fog. It gradually enveloped first Europe and then Asia from the time when the Big Three partitioned the world between them at Yalta (February 1945) and Potsdam (July 1945) to the invasion of South Korea by the North in late June 1950.[28] During these five years the wartime Grand Alliance was replaced by two hostile blocs. In 1947 the Truman Doctrine (March) committed the United States to the defence of Greece, and Zhdanov's 'two-camp' doctrine (September) replaced the communist strategy of 'united front' with a call to world revolution. A communist coup in Czechoslovakia, the Brussels Treaty and the Berlin airlift during 1948 marked a hardening of lines in the West, while communists in Burma, China, Indonesia, Malaya, the Philippines and Vietnam sought power through the barrel of the gun. In 1949 the establishment of the North Atlantic Treaty Organization (NATO) represented a triumph for regional containment, but the defeats and retreat of Chiang Kai-shek in China convinced the US Secretary of State, Dean Acheson, of the need to prevent 'further communist domination on the continent of Asia or in South-east Asia'.[29] At first it seemed that the strategy of containment gave the European colonial empires a reprieve; if so, it was to be brief, for the last scenes in the drama of decolonization in Indonesia, Vietnam and Malaya were played out against the backdrop of Cold War.

The Achievement of Indonesian Independence, 1948–1949

At the Renville conference (named after the warship on which it took place in January 1948) it was agreed to set up the United States of Indonesia *before* the Dutch withdrew their forces from the country and to accept for the time being the current lines of demarcation between Dutch (or Malino) territory and that held by the republic. The Dutch had, therefore, established a strong position and they pressed home their advantage in August during talks in The Hague, where they worked out details of the USI with the BFO (the Federal Consultative Council of representatives from Malino territories). Their hand was reinforced, in the short term at least, by dissension in Republican ranks which came to a head the following month in the attempt by the PKI to hijack the nationalist movement. The Madiun coup of September, led by Musso who had recently returned from the Soviet Union, proved unsuccessful and, as we shall see, enhanced the non-communist credentials of Sukarno and Hatta in the eyes of the Americans. The immediate effect of this conflict between Republicans,

---

[28] See, for example, Robert L. Messer, *The End of an Alliance. James F. Byrnes, Roosevelt, Truman, and the Origins of the Cold War*, Chapel Hill, 1982; Richard M. Freeland, *The Truman Doctrine and the Origins of McCarthyism. Foreign Policy, Domestic Politics, and Internal Security 1946–48*, New York, 1985; and Marc S. Gallicchio, *The Cold War Begins in Asia: American East Asian Policy and the Fall of the Japanese Empire*, New York, 1988.

[29] Memorandum by Dean Acheson, 18 July 1949, cited in Short, *Origins*, 73.

however, was to weaken their resistance to the Dutch. It correspondingly encouraged the Dutch to take an even tougher line against the Yogyakarta government. Further negotiations in The Hague in October between the Dutch and the BFO revealed the determination of the Netherlands to employ counter-revolutionary nationalists in the imposition of a settlement upon Indonesia.

The initiative in Dutch policymaking had by now shifted from Batavia to The Hague. Van Mook was forced to resign (being replaced as governor-general by Louis Beel) and in November Hatta could do little other than agree to place the Republican army under the control of the federal authorities until the USI was formally inaugurated. The Dutch were nonetheless uneasy about Republican participation in the interim government; as a result, not content with the sizeable political gains they had won since the beginning of the year, they determined on a course of action which would crush the republic once and for all. On 18 December the Dutch government revoked the Renville agreement and the next day launched the Second Police Action (or Second Military Action). It was startlingly successful in military terms: Yogyakarta was occupied and key Republican leaders, including Sukarno and Hatta, were detained.

The year 1948 appeared to have been a good one for the Dutch offensive against the Republic of Indonesia. The Second Police Action, however, revealed the inadequacy of military imperialism—whatever the military superiority the Dutch enjoyed over the republicans—for securing their political objectives. Immediately after they launched their offensive, the Dutch were subjected to international criticism which reached such a pitch as to have a decisive effect on the decolonization of Indonesia. On Christmas Eve the United Nations passed a resolution calling for a cease-fire in Indonesia, and at the end of January the Security Council decided to set up the UN Commission for Indonesia to supervise the provision of an interim federal government. The Dutch bowed to this pressure to the extent of officially calling off their military action. Although operations continued against Republican forces, nationalist guerrillas succeeded in making inroads into Dutch-controlled territory, upsetting Dutch communications and tying down their 140,000-strong army, with the result that by August the Dutch accepted the impossibility of bringing off a conclusive military victory. They now took the diplomatic path, and in mid-April informal negotiations got under way with republican leaders.

The Second Police Action, however, had scarcely improved Holland's political position. In their dealings with Indonesians the Dutch had become over-dependent upon the support of the 'Malino group' (as represented in the BFO) whose influence, hitherto confined to the outer islands, was increasingly challenged even there by growing support for the republic. Nor did the Dutch fully extract the potential of an alliance with an alternative, albeit counter-revolutionary, coalition of nationalist interests. On the contrary, Holland's resort to armed aggression tarnished any legitimacy the Malino group may have enjoyed in Indonesia and also alienated its leaders. Suspicion of Dutch federalism was aroused, and this in turn cut the chances of Holland achieving its objectives at the negotiating table.

Republican leaders, by contrast and despite the setbacks of the Second Police Action, entered the talks politically more buoyant than they had been in the conferences that had produced the short-lived Linggajati and Renville agreements. In 1947–8, as we have seen, unity in the cause of home rule had been offset by disunity over the question of who should rule at home with the result that Indonesian divisions had assisted the restoration of Dutch colonialism. As 1949 unfolded, however, the Republican movement suffered less fragmentation and its leaders asserted themselves more confidently over rebels and revolutionaries. After the PKI's abortive coup at Madiun and the suppression of the attempt by Darul Islam (launched at the time of the Second Police Action) to pursue its goal of the Islamic state, Indonesian opposition to the Dutch became firmly non-communist and secular. The Republican leaders did not shrink from employing harsh methods in rooting out opposition to their authority and, in the twin struggles against Dutch colonialism and challenges from within, the army established itself as guardian of the state.

The publication of the Roem–Van Royen statement on 7 May 1949 marked a significant shift in the relative positions of Holland and the republic and a milestone in the decolonization of Indonesia. In being a party to it the Dutch accepted the need to seek a political settlement. Moreover, in contrast to the Renville agreement, they were now prepared to adopt the nationalist line that transfer of power should take place in advance of the integration of the republic into a federation. The political impact of this was momentous: the hardliner, Beel, resigned as governor-general and the BFO of Malino leaders now shifted from supporting the Dutch to cultivating the Republicans.

Thereafter the Dutch retreat was inexorable. An agreement on military withdrawal was reached on 22 June 1949 and Dutch troops pulled out of Yogyakarta a week later (30 June). The armistice was signed on 1 August and the peace conference opened in The Hague on 23 August. The major issues here concerned the extent of the financial obligations with which the successor state should be saddled, and the position of West New Guinea (West Irian). At the same time as the Dutch–Indonesian negotiations were going on, talks were taking place between Republican and BFO delegations; there was an inter-Indonesian conference between 20 July and 2 August, and by the end of October the two sides had reached agreement on the federal structure of the USI. On 2 November agreements on the transfer of sovereignty were signed by Dutch and Indonesian leaders. They provided, first, for the federation of a Republican unit (embracing Java and Sumatra) with the fifteen outer islands which the Dutch had sponsored; second, a prospective Netherlands-Indonesian Union; third, guarantees for Dutch property and personnel; and, fourth, the assumption by the new Indonesian régime of some four million guilders of debt. On 28 December 1949, the day after the instruments of transfer had been signed, Sukarno entered Jakarta as president of the United States of Indonesia.

The way in which power had been transferred provoked much nationalist criticism; the economic arrangements and the project for a loose union with the Netherlands were attacked as forms of neo-colonialism. In fact, the constitutional arrangements were soon superseded; in August 1950 the federal scheme came to an end and, except for continuing Dutch claims over West Irian, Indonesia emerged free of alien control. Even so, the extent to which the country was set on a new course by these events became the subject of much scholarly debate, as well as remaining the stuff of polemic.[30]

The Indonesian revolution meant the overthrow of Dutch rule. Coming on top of the Japanese Occupation, the upheavals of 1945–9 left indelible marks on the political consciousness of Indonesians, the social relations between them, and the policies of their leaders. The ideology of the struggle (*perjuangan*) was, because of its real potency, more than a useful political myth: it has fashioned the shape of the modern history of Indonesia. On the other hand, with the removal of the Dutch, nationalists were robbed of a common enemy, and what had been a temporarily unifying factor: in adopting the motto 'Unity in Diversity' the new régime was in large measure whistling in the dark. Moreover, the structural weaknesses of the state were by no means removed on the achievement of independence; nor did the post-colonial government launch a transformation of government or society. Firmly ensconced in Jakarta and heir to colonial institutions, it faced in the rest of the archipelago the perennial problems encountered by the Dutch and resorted to the techniques of its predecessors in order to suppress opponents and safeguard the régime against political, regional and religious dissent. In short, pre-colonial patterns, the Dutch legacy and the experience of the struggle for independence combined to determine the political history of Indonesia in the first decade of independence.

Another point of contention is more central to the subject of this chapter than is the nature of the post-colonial Indonesian state: it concerns the relative significance of nationalist and international pressure in forcing the pace of Dutch decolonization in 1949. Those who adopt the perspective of an area-study are inclined to stress the importance of 'developments in Indonesia itself' rather than 'the actions of the Security Council' in New York.[31] Nonetheless, it should be noted that in 1949 the Dutch were better placed in Indonesia both militarily and possibly politically than were the French in Indochina, yet a colonial war was to be prosecuted in Vietnam for four and a half years after the departure of the Netherlands from Indonesia. More significant than UN actions in themselves, however, was the US line on Indonesia; this partly guided, and was partly reflected in, the UN resolutions. That Holland's colonial régime collapsed earlier than that of French Indochina cannot be explained without reference to the international politics of 1948–50.

In 1949 neither France nor Holland was able to continue its colonial campaign without at least the approval and preferably the tangible support of the United States. Each, however, carried different weight in world affairs: French influence was reduced at this time by the instability of the Fourth Republic, but Holland was much weaker still, displaying to a

---

[30] For introductions to this debate see M. C. Ricklefs, *A History of Modern Indonesia*, London, 1981, 200–21, and Anthony Reid, 'Indonesia: revolution without socialism' in R. Jeffrey, ed., *Asia, The Winning of Independence*, London, 1981, 113–62.
[31] Pluvier, 487.

greater degree than at any time in the past two centuries the characteristics of 'a colonial giant but a political dwarf'.[32] Moreover, in the foreign policy calculations of the US administration for the conduct of the Cold War and the containment of communism, France and Holland were assigned dissimilar roles. While Washington argued that a French victory in Indochina would allow France to play a fuller part in the defence of Western Europe and was, therefore, prepared to allocate Marshall Aid to the war in Indochina, the same concern for European security led the Truman administration to a very different line on the resolution of the Indonesian conflict. Convinced that the overseas venture was draining Holland's lifeblood and impairing its domestic recovery as well as its contribution to the stability of Europe, the United States not only refused to assist the Dutch in Southeast Asia but went so far as to threaten to withhold Marshall Aid from programmes for the rehabilitation of the Netherlands.

Thus European affairs went a long way in determining US policies to (and, hence, the fates of) Dutch and French colonialism in Southeast Asia; American attitudes were reinforced when Asian circumstances were taken into account. In 1948–50 European colonialism continued to jostle with Asian nationalism in the competition for American approval, and, as in the earlier 1940s, the US administration was still more inclined to frown on the one and smile on the other. In the late 1940s, however, neither ideology commanded as much American attention as did communism, the existence or threat of which came to determine the disposal of American favours in the world and in Southeast Asia in particular. It became an axiom of US foreign policy that American interests in Asia rested on the survival of non-communist régimes, and, whereas the momentum of the CCP advance in China persuaded the US administration to regard French Indochina as the front line of the free world, Sukarno's stand against Indonesian communists at Madiun won for the republic the seal of American approval. From the middle of 1949, US policy shifted from non-intervention to intervention in Southeast Asia; in early 1950, with Mao Zedong (Mao Tse-tung) established in Beijing (Peking), Washington was persuaded that 'Southeast Asia was the fulcrum on which the recovery of the developed nations rested'.[33] This meant offering assistance to the non-communist Republic of Indonesia as well as to the French in their war against the Vietminh.

The End of the French Empire in Indochina, 1948–1954

Neither the French nor the Vietminh attracted significant outside assistance during the first two years of the Vietnam War. Far from the battle for

---

[32] Because of this unique position amongst European imperial powers, the makers of Dutch foreign policy during the twentieth century 'knew all too well that in a world full of dangers a small nation can only walk on tiptoe'. H. L. Wesseling, 'The Giant that was a Dwarf, or the Strange History of Dutch Imperialism', *Journal of Imperial and Commonwealth History*, 16, 3 (1988) 69.

[33] Andrew J. Rotter, *The Path to Vietnam. Origins of the American Commitment to Southeast Asia*, Ithaca and London, 1987, 2.

Hanoi (1946–7) being provoked by a conspiracy of international communism, the Vietminh found themselves neglected by the Soviet Union, the
Chinese Communist Party and the Communist Party of France, while
the French were too obviously pursuing colonial goals for the comfort of
the United States. The aims of the Vietminh were to force the French out
of Indochina as a whole (hence their support for Son Ngoc Thanh in
Cambodia and Prince Souphanouvong's Pathet Lao insurgents in Laos)
and to unify Vietnam as an independent sovereign state. Neither their
programme nor their support was starkly clear-cut, however. There were
disputes amongst Vietnamese communists over tactics, differences being
particularly in evidence as regards operations in the north and the south,
whereas their nationalist goals attracted Vietnamese of all persuasions and
backgrounds except French-trained army officers, some Catholics, and
those with personal stakes in a continued French presence. French objectives were, by contrast, to construct an Indochinese federation within the
French Union and maintain the regional distinctiveness of the territorial
components of Vietnam. Victory against the Vietminh was regarded as
essential for the survival of their wider empire and for the revival of French
influence in Europe.

In September Bollaert, who had replaced d'Argenlieu as French High
Commissioner soon after the battle for Hanoi, attempted a political initiative with his 'final offer' of 'freedom and autonomy within the French
Union'. This was rejected by the Vietminh with the result that Bollaert
began to cultivate the 'Bao Dai solution'. On 7 December 1947 he concluded the so-called Along Bay accord whereby Vietnam would become
'independent' as an 'associated state within the French Union', and
Cochinchina would be reincorporated within the other two parts of Vietnam preparatory to the return of Emperor Bao Dai from self-imposed exile
in France. The Along Bay accord signified a concession on the part of
Bollaert who referred to Vietnam's right to independence and territorial
unity—objectives shared by Vietminh and anti-Vietminh nationalists
alike. It failed, however, to outflank the Vietminh or to bridge the gap
between them and Vietnamese non-communists, or even to provide the
foundations for the construction of a solid alternative to the DRV. It led,
instead, to the formation of General Xuan's provisional government which
proved to be ineffective. Its 'independence' was compromised from the
outset by the obligation to co-operate with the French in restoring peace to
Vietnam, its authority was disputed by Bao Dai's adherents, and its very
existence finally put paid to the possibility of co-operation with Ho Chi
Minh. No nearer to breaking the deadlock, Bollaert resigned in September.

The war continued. By the end of the year the French were not only
bogged down in Tonkin but fearful that the Chinese might intervene to tip
the military balance in favour of the Vietminh who, for their part, were no
nearer to attaining their objectives. They felt that their cause was neglected
by nationalist sympathizers in the United Nations, while the mounting
successes of Mao Zedong had not led to substantial military aid flooding
south across China's border with North Vietnam. In any case, they were
wary that indebtedness to the Chinese communists might result in the
CCP taking over the direction of the Vietnamese liberation struggle or

provoke American intervention on behalf of the French. Throughout 1949 the French government worked at the Bao Dai formula. In March President Auriol and Emperor Bao Dai concluded the Elysée agreement whereby France formally acceded to the Vietnamese goals of national unity and national independence. On Bastille Day, Bao Dai returned to Vietnam as 'head of state'; on 30 December talks, which had been going on in Paris since 1 September, resulted in the Convention of Saigon (ratified by the French Assembly on 2 February 1950) providing for the transfer of sovereignty to the 'State of Vietnam'. The extent of the independence now granted to Bao Dai, however, was as limited as the support he enjoyed in Vietnam. Whatever traditional allure the emperor may have exuded, he lacked a base in popular politics and was in any case too tainted by a long record of equivocation to command the respect of either Vietnamese nationalists or French imperialists. The latter were half-hearted in support of him, suspecting that he might attempt a deal with the Vietminh or, alternatively, claim more concessions from the French than were compatible with the lingering dream of French Union. Real power, therefore, remained with the French who continued to shoulder the burden of the war.

At the same time, however, the dimensions of the war were expanding. Between the spring of 1949 and the end of 1950 international polarization was distinctly etched by various events: the formation of NATO (April 1949), knowledge of Russia's possession of the hydrogen bomb (30 September 1949), the inauguration of the People's Republic of China (1 October 1949), the Sino-Soviet Treaty (14 February 1950), the Schuman Plan (8 May 1950), the outbreak of the Korean War (25 June 1950) and the entry of China into the Korean War (November 1950). Against this background, the USA and China committed themselves to help Bao Dai and Ho Chi Minh respectively. The lines of Cold War, of Great Power confrontation and containment, now underscored the demarcation between the forces of colonialism and the 'liberation struggle' in Vietnam. The USA recognized Bao Dai's Vietnam as an 'independent state within the French Union' on 7 February 1950, and on 8 May Dean Acheson announced Truman's programmes of $13 million of military assistance to Southeast Asia, $10 million of which were being allocated to the French.[34] China had recognized the DRV on 18 January 1950 (being followed by the USSR twelve days later) and by the middle of the year had drawn up an aid programme involving the supply of arms and military training. China contributed to the preparations for the Vietminh's Le Hong Phong II offensive in northern Tonkin in the autumn of 1950 which resulted in defeats for the French (notably at Cao Bang) and left the People's Army of Vietnam in control of the border area of central Tonkin.[35]

Although established in Hanoi and the Red River delta, the French had failed to dominate the countryside of Tonkin where Giap pursued guerrilla

---

[34] This was the beginning of a commitment which would rapidly expand; by 1952 the US was funding 40 per cent of the French war effort; two years later its share had risen to 70 per cent.

[35] Laura Calkins, 'Sino-Viet Minh Relations, 1948–52', Ph.D. thesis, University of London, 1990, 120ff.

tactics effectively and prolonged the war to France's ultimate disadvantage, for time was not on the side of the French. Yet, while the military debacle of the autumn of 1950 revealed real weaknesses, the French presence was now sustained by America. Once they learned to present themselves as the defenders of a legitimate Vietnamese régime in its struggle against world communism, the French were able to exploit the geopolitics peculiar to Indochina and, somewhat fortuitously, to identify their cause with that of the 'free world'. At the end of 1950 the French military position was desperate; had they not won US assistance (taking the form of an extension of the Marshall Plan to Indochina) and had the Vietminh not called off their general offensive (in deference to China's anxiety over border security), their chances of survival would have been slim.

Of the three options in Indochina—colonialism, communism or monarchy—the Americans relished none, though they were persuaded to stomach the last when it was garnished with the rhetoric of self-determination. That the US administration shifted its position from opposing French colonialism to supporting the puppet of French colonialism is not to be explained totally or even primarily by reference to French machinations or to French needs. Of central importance in US calculations was their diagnosis of what the administration, Congress and American public all took to be an underlying global conflict between communism and the 'free world'. In 1949–50 Americans felt threatened by the Sino-Soviet bloc in Asia as well as in Europe, and the survival of France appeared crucial to US interests in, indeed to the very security of, both continents. Assistance to France in Indochina would not only block the advance of Chinese communism, it was argued, but would also release French troops for the containment of Soviet expansion in the West. The American strategy of containment in Southeast Asia, therefore, arose both from the seeds of West European union and from 'the ashes' of its policy in China.[36]

Although American military involvement in Vietnam would not become irrevocable for several years to come, in May 1950 the US entered into a momentous commitment to grant military assistance to the French. Whether the turning-point in US policy towards Vietnam is to be identified with the May decision itself or whether the switch occurred a year earlier with the collapse of Chiang Kai-shek in China and the unfolding of NATO in Europe, it is clear that by May 1950 US support for the French was out in the open and that the connections between Western defence and the stability of Southeast Asia were as firmly established in the official mind of Washington as in the political consciousness of the American public. The conjuncture rather than coincidence of developments in the West and East, so far as US policymaking went, is illustrated by the fact that, in order to win Congress support for NATO, the administration was prepared to accede to the request of Congress for a military budget covering the 'general area of China'. Again, it is noteworthy that Acheson announced the grant of American aid to Indochina on the same day that Schuman published his plan for Franco-German reconciliation.

---

[36] Robert Blum has argued that 'the American containment policy in South-East Asia arose from the ashes of its failed policy in China': cited in Short, *Origins*, 74.

The emergence of American anti-communism in 1949–50 had, therefore, decisive and contrasting effects on the colonial fortunes of the Dutch and the French. US pressure upon the Dutch from late 1948 hastened the arrival of Indonesian independence, while US support for the French gave a lease of life to the colonial régime. Whereas Madiun established a congruity between the anti-colonialism and anti-communism of the Indonesian Republic, with regard to Indochina the US had for some years oscillated between sympathy for the Vietminh's anti-colonialism and hostility to their communism. There are, indeed, grounds for arguing that until the middle of 1949 American policy towards Indochina suffered more tensions and contradictions than did their Indonesian policy. For example, although an American commitment to intervention in Indochina was shaping up as early as 1947, there was to begin with something of an even-handedness in American approaches to the French and Vietminh and a residual mistrust of French colonialism. Bit by bit, however, the US managed to reconcile its hope for a 'democratic' Vietnam with support for the new-style colonialism professed by the French, and was persuaded that the French Union would shore up the French position in Europe's defence and stand as a bastion against communism in Asia. After May 1950 France relied upon the Americans for the tools, while the US expected it to finish the job. It was an awkward division of labour and, as the prospects of French victory faded following the false dawn associated with de Lattre de Tassigny, Franco-American co-operation was dogged by mutual recrimination.

The US administration decided to support the French position in Vietnam against a probable Vietminh offensive launched with the full-blooded backing of the Chinese Communist Party and People's Liberation Army. As is now well known, at the time their judgment rested on an incorrect assessment of the homogeneity of the communist world and a misreading of the likely effects of Mao's victories upon the fighting capacity of the Vietminh. Despite the Sino-Soviet treaty and expressions of solidarity between Asian communists, each party had its individual needs and interests, and there were wide variations between communist organizations in the tactics and even the strategies which they adopted in the liberation struggle. Contrary to the expectations of Western powers, and it should be added those of the Vietminh too, the Chinese undertook no major assistance to the Vietnamese between mid-1948 and early 1950, while the extent of support afforded by the USSR at the same time was insubstantial. It was only after the outbreak of the Korean War that Chinese military aid to the Vietnamese was expanded. When this occurred, it became clear that Chinese and Vietnamese communists had different views on its deployment, stemming from their separate strategic perspectives on the Far East and Southeast Asia.

The road to Geneva
Following China's entry into the Korean War (November 1950) the Vietnam conflict entered a new phase. Fear of Chinese intervention stiffened the US commitment which in turn led to the transformation of General Giap's army and his greater dependence upon outside assistance. The arrival of de Lattre de Tassigny as civil and military supremo in December

had an inspirational effect upon the French war effort. By June 1951 he had halted the Vietminh offensive in Tonkin, thereby encouraging the French to demand further assistance from the Americans and to resist political concessions to the Vietnamese. By the end of the year, however, de Lattre was dead. In February 1952 the Vietminh, benefiting from military aid which now reached them on an unprecedented scale from China, forced French forces to withdraw from Hoa Binh. The build-up of communist military strength now made victory in Tonkin a distinct possibility.[37]

The French were trapped in a dilemma. Upon the outcome of the war appeared to hinge the future of the French Union and the fate of the Fourth Republic, yet war-weariness progressively enveloped the nation and its leaders. The loss of life and economic strain were taking their toll. The public, disillusioned by what they increasingly took to be sacrifices for an American cause, opposed suggestions of conscription for Indochina, while successive governments were only too aware that Vietnam was aggravating political instability at home and weakening them in relation to a reviving and rearming West Germany. As their inability to continue the fighting on their own was revealed day by day, the French played upon the convergence of the Vietnam War and European defence to extract further assistance from the USA. In exchange for their participation in the European Defence Community (which was agreed in May 1952 but never ratified by the French Assembly) they demanded such aid in Indochina as would enable them to win the war or at least to release sufficient troops to ensure French military equality with West Germany. Nonetheless, doubts grew as to the reliability of American support, for not only did the US administration make aid conditional upon French participation in the EDC but in Southeast Asia it was becoming ever more fixated by communist China. Moreover, it seemed to many French people that the ironic logic of military victory meant political defeat, since the confirmation of the independent state of Vietnam would spell the end of the French empire.

At the end of Truman's term as president the United States' involvement in Vietnam was not yet direct, inevitable or irrevocable and, like the French, it was uncertain in its approach to the war. Before it could decide whether to respond to the communist threat directly or through surrogates, it had to identify the enemy and choose between the Vietminh and the Chinese as the target. In theory, four courses were open to the US government: it could ungrudgingly assist the French effort; it could shift its support to Bao Dai and focus on the Vietnamization of the war; it could intervene directly and unilaterally; or, fourth, it could work for an international solution either militarily or at a peace conference. Each option had its drawbacks. In identifying with a French war, for example, the US risked losing the war itself or alienating Asians who would be essential to a permanent political settlement. Yet the second course was no less hazardous, since the Vietnamese preferred 'to sit on the fence' rather than support Bao Dai. The third and fourth options were not seriously contemplated by Truman's administration, but they received considerable attention from his successor.

[37] Calkins, 'Sino-Viet Minh Relations', 211–37.

In January 1953 Eisenhower was inaugurated President of the United States. The Republican administration and especially the secretary of state, John Foster Dulles, seeing the French flagging and the Vietminh expanding into Laos, determined to take over the direction of the war. They became irrevocably committed to victory in August–September 1953; when the Navarre plan of the summer of 1953 to throw more French troops into the campaign fizzled out, they began to contemplate the possibility of direct military involvement. Throughout the period from the start of the battle of Dien Bien Phu to the conclusion of the Geneva Conference (March–July 1954) the Eisenhower government discussed the feasibility and, in particular, the objectives, preconditions and extent of US armed intervention. Each of these issues raised a host of questions. Should American aims be to keep France in the war, or support 'independent' Vietnam, or again to take over completely from the French? Should intervention depend upon the prior grant by the French of independence to the Associated States or on 'united [i.e. international] action'? As regards the preferred or permissible level of military activity, the spectrum ranged from the existing programme of providing weapons and advisers to the despatch of land, sea and air forces through to bombing operations, the actual engagement of ground troops and the use of nuclear weapons. Vice-Admiral Davis summed up their problem: 'One cannot go over Niagara Falls in a barrel only slightly.'[38]

As the French reeled under the Vietminh onslaught at Dien Bien Phu, the US attempted to draw others, especially the British, into a joint military operation. Internationalizing the war by involving other Southeast Asian states and members of the British Commonwealth became the prerequisite of US entry as Dulles announced in his 'united action' speech on 29 March 1954. However, America's allies had different approaches to the problem. The UK in particular resisted the internationalization of the war; it refused to participate in Dulles' proposal for a joint air-strike on the grounds that this would alienate Asian nations, provoke China, activate the Sino-Soviet pact and risk a third world war. Whereas Britain suggested an international conference on the Indochina question, Dulles argued that only 'united action' in advance of talks would ensure an acceptable political settlement. In January 1954 at the Berlin Conference of foreign ministers, Anthony Eden, in the face of US resistance, managed to include Indochina on the agenda for the conference on Korea scheduled to take place a few months later at Geneva. When it became clear at the end of April (on the eve of the Geneva talks) that the British government would not participate in joint military action over Indochina, Eisenhower acted decisively to prevent the US administration sliding into unilateral intervention.[39]

The Geneva settlement, 1954

In the 1950s Southeast Asia was a less important region in British global strategy than, say, the Middle East; until the spring of 1954 Britain had shown comparatively little interest in the Vietnam War, nor had it prepared a coherent policy with regard to Indochina. Britain was, however,

[38] Cited in Short, *Origins*, 126.
[39] ibid., 146–7.

eager for a settlement one way or another in order to safeguard its own interests in Southeast Asia (notably Malaya which appeared threatened by the escalating conflict) and strengthen the position of France in the arrangements for European defence. When the reports from Dien Bien Phu ruled out the possibility of a French victory, the British government pushed for a negotiated settlement rather than risk Great Power conflict over the issue. Britain's role at Geneva was not, therefore, the outcome of a long-considered strategy for Indochina, nor did it reflect its power to influence events in the region. That the conference took place and managed to produce any agreement at all was due as much to the compliance of France, the USSR and China. It was these four powers, not the Americans nor the Vietnamese, who were the principal participants in the talks and the architects of the Geneva settlement.[40]

Pierre Mendès France, who became French prime minister in June, declared his aim to achieve peace within a month. He instilled decisiveness and direction into the French quest for an escape route from Indochina by which it would yet retain access to influence and interests. In the somewhat more relaxed international atmosphere following the death of Stalin (March 1953), Molotov and Zhou Enlai were anxious to find a peace formula; each needed to avoid antagonizing the other in Southeast Asia and both wished to contain American expansionism. It has been suggested that Russia was induced to go along with the Geneva settlement by a French promise to sabotage the European Defence Community (EDC), though there is little, if any, evidence of such a conspiracy.[41] The DRV later claimed (in 1979) to have been betrayed by China at Geneva, arguing that Zhou Enlai had been primarily concerned with the security of China's southern perimeter and, as a consequence, had been agreeable to the more or less indefinite partition of Vietnam so long as the Geneva settlement was guaranteed by the United States. If this was China's objective, then the outcome of Geneva must have been a disappointment to it, for Dulles, thoroughly frustrated by the proceedings, chose to have nothing to do with the conference agreements. In the early summer of 1954 Dulles was resisting a negotiated settlement in Vietnam and urging the launch of the European Defence Community with equal passion, and he acquiesced in the conference as the price for the prospect of French ratification of the EDC treaty. In the event he was disappointed on both fronts: unable to call the shots at Geneva, the US dissociated itself from the final declaration, while the following month the French Assembly threw out the EDC.

Although its proceedings were irritable and hesitant, the conference did in the end produce a ceasefire agreement between France and the DRV; it established an International Supervisory Commission (to implement the cessation of hostilities); and it issued a final declaration on behalf of all delegations excluding the United States. As a result, a provisional military demarcation line was drawn across the country at the seventeenth parallel and French military withdrawal was put in train. At the same time the independence, integrity and security of Cambodia and Laos were

[40] See James Cable, *The Geneva Conference of 1954 on Indochina*, London, 1986.
[41] ibid., 129ff.

underwritten, while the prospect of the political settlement and reunification of Vietnam was held out, once elections (proposed for July 1956) had
been held. Beyond this the conference is said to have prevented the
internationalization of the war, brought to an end the French colonial
empire in Southeast Asia, and contributed to the long march of the
peoples of Indochina towards self-determination.

The Geneva settlement marked a pause in the conflict, however, not an
end to it. In international relations it represented the pursuit of war by
other means. Predicated upon a Manichean division of the world into two
hostile blocs, it reinforced belief in the existence of Western and communist monoliths. Instead of providing for the agreement of the Great Powers,
it set the scene for another phase in their future confrontation. None of the
participants (including the co-chairmen, Britain and the USSR) had either
the will or the means to stand firm on the implementation of the Geneva
settlement and to convert the ceasefire into a political agreement. The
United States came to hate everything Geneva stood for; China soon
claimed it had been duped as regards the position of Cambodia and Laos;
and the opposing Vietnamese felt betrayed by their respective sponsors.
Some weeks later the creation of the Southeast Asia Treaty Organization
(SEATO) at the Manila Conference (September 1954) introduced a new
phase in the conduct of containment in the region by replacing the
outworn structures of French colonialism and military imperialism with a
system of 'collective security'. Geneva may have prevented the internationalization of the Vietnam War in the summer of 1954, but it provided
for the formal entanglement of Indochina in the international relations of
Cold War.

A second consequence of the Geneva Conference was the end of the
French colonial empire in Southeast Asia. Usually portrayed as truculent
imperialists, atavistically seeking to revive a glorious past and oblivious to
postwar realities, the French failed to construct a viable alternative to the
DRV. The Vietminh were militarily vigorous—winning battles in Tonkin,
conducting guerrilla operations in the south and extending their campaign
elsewhere in Indochina—and Ho Chi Minh established an alternative
administration not only in the territory directly under his control but also
clandestinely in the south; in contrast, the claims of the Bao Dai régime to
be nationally representative rang hollow. It is true that there was considerable tension within the Vietminh over optimum military strategies for
Tonkin and Nambo (Cochinchina) and that they needed external military
assistance if they were to win decisively; but the internecine feuding on
Bao Dai's side was indicative of its divorce from popular forces, while his
very survival (let alone any military success) depended upon French
troops and American money. As regards Indochina as a whole, the French
attempt to build up a bloc of Associated States was half-hearted and came
too late to have a material effect upon the war in Vietnam. Here, although
they managed to cling to the towns and the Red River delta, the French
had surrendered the northwest of Tonkin by the middle of 1952, and the
costly sacrifices incurred in holding their position thereafter destroyed
the commitment back home to continue the fighting. All that said, however, the French did manage to curb the Vietminh advance and, when they

departed, they in effect transferred to the United States the responsibility of sustaining the non-communist State of Vietnam.

While the Geneva settlement may have given respite to the peoples of Indochina, it did not provide a lasting peace; nor did it achieve the goals of national self-determination in Vietnam. The questions of the independence and sovereignty, the unity and integrity of the country remained the unfinished business of the conference. To the Vietnamese contestants Geneva was a postponement, not the fulfilment, of their respective programmes for the achievement of national liberation. Ngo Dinh Diem, who became prime minister in South Vietnam in June 1954 and would remain leader until his assassination in 1963, was as bitterly anti-French as he was anti-communist. He resented the fact that his government was not a party to the Geneva arrangements. The ambiguity of his consequent position—was it the government of the state of Vietnam or its temporary administration which he led?—riled him, and he protested against the partition of his country. The DRV were similarly dissatisfied; the Vietminh had made huge sacrifices to win resounding victories, yet the liberation of a united Vietnam had eluded them. Giap's military campaigns had been greatly assisted by supplies from China in particular; now at the peace talks the DRV felt diplomatically repressed by China and the USSR, which insisted on the subordination of the national liberation struggle to the wider interests of the communist world. The Vietminh struggle had only half succeeded. The fact that the independence and unity of Vietnam remained unresolved meant that the programme for social revolution would continue to be subordinated to military objectives. Yet their military position was not promising, since they were now directly confronted by the United States.

A comparison with the Indonesian struggle may be instructive here; while Ho and Giap were more successful militarily than Sukarno and Hatta, yet the Dutch were hustled out of Indonesia and the Vietminh were thwarted in victory. In both instances, however, it was wider international issues that determined the way colonial empires ended. In the case of Indonesia, Great Power involvement was one-sided: concerned for the defence of Western Europe and convinced by the anti-communist credentials of the republic, the United States took it upon itself to force the pace of decolonization. In Indochina, by contrast, the Great Powers were in competition with each other: in blocking the moves of their rivals' satellites they also blunted the aspirations of their own clients without assuming responsibility for the implementation of the arrangements which were cobbled together at Geneva in the summer of 1954.

Malaya: Decolonization and Counter-insurgency, 1948–1957

By the time the Geneva Conference had ended, the Malayan communists were a spent force militarily and Malaya was well on course for independence within the British Commonwealth. At the end of May 1954, Sir Gerald Templer, who had broken the Malayan Races Liberation Army, was succeeded as High Commissioner by Sir Donald MacGillivray, who swiftly met the constitutional demands of the non-communist Malayan Alliance. A year later the Alliance won a landslide victory in the federal elections, formed a government under Tunku Abdul Rahman, and, having refused to make political concessions to the Malayan communists in talks held at the end of 1955, conferred with the British on the early conversion of internal self-government into complete independence. The extent to which there are discernible connections between insurgency and decolonization on the one hand, and between local and international developments in Southeast Asia on the other, are themes central to a discussion of the Malayan Emergency.

Enquiry into the outbreak of the communist uprising in Malaya has been dominated by two debates. One has been over the relative significance of local and international factors in determining the course of events; the other concerns the extent to which either the Malayan communists or the British authorities were prepared for the outcome.[42] Following hard on the heels of the Calcutta Youth Conference (February 1948), which issued the call for 'armed struggle' in Asia, and more or less coinciding with the uprisings of the Burma Communist Party, Hukbalahap and PKI, the decision of the MCP to take to the jungle and resort to armed violence was interpreted from the outset as part of the Cominform's pursuit of world revolution. The causal links between deliberations in Calcutta and decision-making within the MCP have, however, been largely discounted by some historians. Focusing upon Malayan circumstances, they have emphasized the importance of the economic hardships and political marginalization of Malaya's Chinese; of changes in party leadership with the flight of the 'moderate' Lai Teck and the emergence of Chin Peng as general secretary; and of MCP frustration with the 'united front' strategy in the face of counter-revolutionary activity by the police and the reformed trade union movement. They have also drawn attention to the almost accidental manner in which the Sungei Siput murders committed the MCP to 'armed struggle', tipped the scales against British toleration of the party, and triggered a twelve-year Emergency. Accurate intelligence was to be vital to the eventual success of counter-insurgency, but it is doubtful whether in 1948 the authorities were provided with sufficiently precise warnings as to MCP intentions or information which could be relied upon as the basis for appropriate action. The High Commissioner, Gent, whose reputation had suffered from the Malayan Union debacle, was blamed for failing first to anticipate and then to counter MCP violence. At the end of June he was recalled for 'consultations', but he died in an air accident as his plane approached London.

During the next three and a half years the British mood swung between hope and despair as a force of some 4000 guerrillas tied down increasing numbers of police and troops. Malaya's strategic position and its economic

---

[42] See A. Short, *The Communist Insurrection in Malaya, 1948–1960*, London, 1975. For a recent review of the outbreak of the Emergency from the perspective of Malaya see Richard Stubbs, *Hearts and Minds in Guerrilla Warfare: The Malayan Emergency 1948–1960*, Singapore, 1989, 42–65, and for a discussion of China's involvement in communist-led uprisings in Southeast Asia see R. B. Smith, 'China and Southeast Asia: The Revolutionary Perspective, 1951', JSEAS, 19, 1 (Mar. 1988).

importance—it was the sterling area's largest dollar-earner—meant that its surrender was unthinkable to the British government. Periodically parliament was reassured that there would be no repetition of 1941–2, that the strike-rate against insurgents was improving, that plans for the long-term development of the territory were in hand, and that Britain would not withdraw until conditions were ripe for Malayan self-government within the Commonwealth. At the same time, however, the Cabinet worried about the increasing costs of the Emergency when Britain was hard-pressed to repay loans, rehabilitate the domestic economy, create a welfare state at home, and meet its commitments to global security. The Korean War aggravated their problems: by January 1951 defence estimates for 1951–4 stood at approximately double the level envisaged before the outbreak of the conflict, yet, given the fear of tumbling Southeast Asian dominoes, Malaya offered no prospect of retrenchment. The new High Commissioner, Henry Gurney, appeared to fare little better than Gent in the suppression of insurrection; the military, police and administration, and liaison between them, were all subjects of grave concern, while the authorities made little progress in winning the active co-operation of the Chinese community. British morale reached its nadir with the assassination of Gurney in October 1951.

The apparent drift in Malaya, which some attributed to the lack of direction provided by Britain's Labour government, seemed to end when the Conservatives under Churchill returned to office and General Templer was appointed High Commissioner and Director of Operations early in 1952. Like General de Lattre de Tassigny in Indochina, Templer was put in charge of both military matters and civil administration, and he had an immediately electrifying impact upon the war. In contrast to the French experience, however, the arrival of the new supremo coincided with a lasting improvement in British fortunes.

Clearly personalities and their policies had a role to play in the ebb and flow of the Malayan Emergency and the eventual defeat of the communist insurgents. Nevertheless, it should be noted that the Conservatives continued the policies of their Labour predecessors in all essentials: both parties emphasized the need for political development and nation-building, and both set great store on the Malayan Union principles of the consolidation of the discrete territories of the region (particularly the closer association of Malaya and Singapore) and the growth of multiracialism as opposed to communal politics.[43] Moreover, Templer himself brought to fruition plans whose seeds had been sown during Gurney's time, notably Briggs's scheme to resettle in New Villages half a million Chinese squatters upon whom the communists relied for supplies and information. Indeed, Templer's 'hearts and minds' strategy, with its accent upon the political and social advance of the Malayan people, had been foreshadowed by various moves made under Gurney: they included the quasi-ministerial Member system (April 1951); the bill to increase the number of non-Malays eligible for federal citizenship (which came into effect in September 1952,

---

[43] A. J. Stockwell, 'British imperial policy and decolonization in Malaya, 1942–52', *Journal of Imperial and Commonwealth History*, 13, 1 (1984).

seven months after Templer arrived); and attempts to improve the economic lot of the Malays (for example through the Rural and Industrial
Development Authority set up in 1950).

The British never lost sight of the fact that, as Eden put it, 'Communism
in Asia cannot be checked by military means alone.'[44] The press statement
made by Colonial Secretary Oliver Lyttelton during his visit to Malaya in
December 1951 stressed the prime need to restore law and order and was
welcomed by some as a commitment to reassert British authority, but in
fact it did not breach the bipartisan pledge 'to guide Colonial people along
the road to self-government within the framework of the British Empire'.
The directive issued to Templer a few weeks later started with the
declaration that '[t]he policy of His Majesty's Government in the United
Kingdom is that Malaya should in due course become a fully self-governing
nation'; it expressed the hope that 'that nation will be within the British
Commonwealth'; it pointed to the need to 'achieve a united Malayan
nation . . . [through] a common form of citizenship for all who regard the
Federation or any part of it as their real home and the object of their
loyalty'; and it instructed the High Commissioner 'to guide the peoples of
Malaya towards the attainment of these objectives and to promote such
political progress of the country as will, without prejudicing the campaign
against the terrorists, further our democratic aims in Malaya'.[45]

If the aims of British policy were not in doubt, the timing, manner
and very chances of their realization were by no means certain. 'Nation-
building' involved the cultivation of multiracial as well as popular politics,
and a British precondition for the transfer of power was the emergence of a
responsibly-led, democratically-endorsed and multiracial party of government. Alarmed at the politicization of communal antagonisms resulting
from the successive crises of the 1945 interregnum, Malayan Union and the
Emergency, Commissioner-General MacDonald sponsored the Communities Liaison Committee and approved of Dato Onn's attempts to broaden
the appeal of the communally exclusive United Malays National Organization (UMNO). But neither of these initiatives put down firm roots in the
political subsoil, while Onn's avowedly non-communal Independence of
Malaya Party flopped within a year of its inauguration in the second half of
1951. Like the Americans in their attitude to the Vietnamese, the British
were dismayed by the propensity of Malaya's Chinese community to 'sit
on the fence'. To win their allegiance, Gurney had encouraged the launch
of the Malayan Chinese Association (MCA) in 1949, although until his
death he remained unconvinced that its leaders possessed sufficient determination effectively to counter the MCP appeal to the poor and disenfran-
chised majority of Malaya's Chinese. In short, from its start in June 1948 to
the end of 1951 the Emergency appeared to retard the prospects of British
withdrawal and to constrain the development of Malayan politics.

From 1952, the essential ingredients of counter-insurgency operations—
intelligence, policing and civil-military co-ordination—all improved and,

[44] Sir Anthony Eden, *Memoirs: Full Circle*, London, 1960, 109.
[45] Public Record Office, PREM 11/639, 1 Feb. 1952. See also John Cloake, *Templer. Tiger of Malaya. The life of Field Marshal Sir Gerald Templer*, London, 1985, 457–8.

with the achievement of more tangible successes against the guerrillas, the pace of political advance resumed. In order to prevent victory by the Independence of Malaya Party in the Kuala Lumpur municipal elections of February 1952, the local branch organizations of UMNO and MCA struck an ad hoc alliance. In March 1953 this arrangement was formalized by the central leadership of both parties, and the Alliance was augmented by the accession of the Malayan Indian Congress in 1954. As Templer rolled back the insurrection, declaring the first 'white area' (where Emergency regulations were relaxed) in Melaka in September 1953, so the Alliance pressed for the early grant of independence. The British were mistrustful of a political coalition, which if it survived at all threatened to institutionalize communalism, and dubious of the ability of UMNO and MCA leaders to discipline their respective supporters; for these reasons the British at first cold-shouldered Alliance exuberance. Though not severely shaken by the non-cooperation campaign which the Alliance mounted in May–June 1954 in order to hammer home their demand for an elected majority on the Federal Legislative Council, the British were nonetheless conscious of the absence of any popular alternative. The upshot was that High Commissioner Donald MacGillivray (1954–7) reached a compromise with the Alliance on the composition of the new Federal Council in July 1954.

The pace of decolonization hereafter gathered such momentum as to leave officials breathless. By the end of 1955 the Alliance appeared to have met British requirements in bridging racial divides, commanding electoral support in the federal elections of July 1955, and standing firm against communism at the Baling talks with Chin Peng in December. When British and Malayan delegations conferred in London in January–February 1956, the former conceded the Alliance timetable for independence by the end of August 1957, while the latter accepted the need for a continuing British presence in post-independent Malaya for the defence and economic well-being of the country. The next eighteen months saw a hectic round of negotiations with respect to the financial aspects of independence, the Anglo-Malayan Defence Arrangement, and the balances to be struck between Malay privileges and non-Malay rights and between state autonomy and central powers in the constitution of the new state. All these issues provoked disagreements and there was some hard bargaining over the defence treaty, but on the fundamentals of security and subversion both sides thought alike.

If the communist insurrection had forced the pace of political change in Malaya, it had fortuitously played into British hands by throwing up a staunchly anti-communist leadership which not only valued continuing close relations with Britain but also enjoyed overwhelming popular support. This had not occurred in either Indonesia or Vietnam, where the Dutch and French had failed to find secure footholds in the shifting sands of local politics. The contrast in the respective fortunes of European colonial régimes, however, is not to be attributed solely or even mainly to British skill in manipulating nationalist politicians. After all, the Alliance was not a colonial stooge but a product of ingrained communalism, for which the activities of British colonialists in the past may have been partly responsible, but to which British decolonizers were now forced to reconcile themselves. The structure of Malaya's plural society, indeed, virtually predetermined the failure of the Chinese-dominated MCP to rouse anything more than token Malay support; this in turn explained their inability to sustain a rural revolution or to present a convincingly nationalist programme. In addition, and in contrast with the Vietminh, the Malayan communists did not receive significant help from outside the country; they waged the 'armed struggle' more or less in isolation. In view of its meagre triumphs and the slow progress towards victory, the MCP leadership decided in October 1951 to end indiscriminate violence (but not to abandon the military campaign) and to focus on the political organization of the masses. In this area, too, it could not compete with the Anglo-Malayan authorities at federal, state and district levels. What support the MCP had once mustered slipped away, and Chin Peng had no trump cards to play when he parleyed with Tunku Abdul Rahman, chief minister of the elected Malayan government.

Just as the MCP waged the liberation struggle without significant aid from China or the USSR, so Britain was left more or less to its own devices in this theatre of the Cold War. Although Malaya was central to British influence in the region, it was peripheral to the interests of other Great Powers. The Malayan Emergency did not attract international attention to nearly the same degree as did Indonesia in 1948–9 and Indochina in 1950–4. The British were not eased out of their colony by American political pressure, as the Dutch were; nor, like the French, were they propped up by US military assistance. Of course, the British government was gratified by Washington's approval of its efforts and more material expressions of support in the form of non-military supplies. The costly Malayan operation also carried some advantages for British diplomats treading the tightrope of the special relationship; on the one hand, it demonstrated British anti-communist bona fides while, on the other, it provided an excuse for not joining the US in a strike on Indochina. As time went on, indeed, the British became increasingly worried by American militarism which, as the events surrounding the Geneva conference revealed, jeopardized good relations with the independent and emergent states of Asia.

The closeness of Anglo-Malayan relations in the aftermath of the transfer of power raised all sorts of questions as regards the degree of independence which was actually achieved by the successor state. Although Malaya refused to join SEATO, it remained central to British interests in Southeast Asia for at least another decade. It participated in the internal security of colonial Singapore, and then provided the stem of Malaysia on to which the remaining colonies of Singapore, Sabah and Sarawak were grafted as Britain relinquished responsibility for them in 1963. Britain, for its part, directly assisted Malaya in Emergency operations until they officially ended in 1960; it rushed to the defence of Malaysia in its Confrontation with Indonesia in 1963–6; it was the dominant partner in the Anglo-Malayan Defence Arrangement[46] (to which Australia, New

---

[46] See Chin Kee Wah, *The defence of Malaysia and Singapore. The transformation of a security system 1957–1971*, Cambridge, 1983.

Zealand and Singapore also adhered); and it took charge of the defence of Western interests in maritime Southeast Asia. In the 1960s, however, the Wilson government decided on economic grounds to run down its military commitment east of Suez and to embark upon a phased withdrawal from the Singapore naval base. Domestic realities forced post-imperial Britain to come to terms with the regional realities of post-colonial Southeast Asia, whose international affairs were by now dominated by the US presence.

CONCLUSION

Since the main theme of this chapter has been the ending of European empires in Southeast Asia, it is appropriate to conclude with some general reflections on their decline and fall. Libertarians through the ages have detected philosophical lessons in the hubris and subsequent nemesis of successors to Ozymandias King of Kings, the glory and grandeur of their rise being followed by the folly and degeneracy of their fall. In unravelling the tangled skein of imperial fortunes over centuries, determinists have, in contrast, constructed cyclical historical models; others, seeing neither rhyme nor reason in these ephemeral phenomena, have concluded that if, like Topsy, empires 'just growed' or were acquired 'in a fit of absence of mind', then it might follow that they waned as they had waxed, it being neither a morally justifiable nor a rationally predictable process.

Perhaps the key to an understanding of the decline and fall of empires lies in the essential nature of empire itself, the suggestion here being that such gangling growths somehow carry within them the seeds of their own destruction. Or perhaps it is rather to be discovered in the systematic analysis of individual cases: some empires being things of shreds and patches swiftly succumbed to adversity, whereas more elaborate structures collapsed under their own weight as territorial responsibilities increased beyond the metropolitan capacity to sustain them. A different explanation would connect the strength of a state's commitment to the expansion and retention of its overseas empire with troubles and weaknesses on the home front. In some instances domestic policies eroded the imperial bond; in others they served to strengthen it. As we have seen, metropolitan difficulties after 1945 did have the effect of enhancing the value of overseas possessions and of stiffening British, Dutch and French determination to hold on to them. In times of national crisis, imperialists perceived a route to salvation through the development of the deceptively prodigious potential of colonies; reactionaries opposed any concessions which suggested lack of imperial spunk; progressives and pragmatists advocated tactical retreat as the best means of saving trade, investments, the goodwill of emergent nations and prestige in the international community. Indeed, there is a case for arguing that empires never ended but merely changed their form as colonialism was succeeded by neo-colonialism, as formal imperialism gave way to informal imperialism, and as the baton of Western dominance passed from Europe to the USA and USSR.

If the reasons for the ebb and flow of Europe's influence overseas are located by some in the metropole, others focus on developments on the periphery and challenges from outside.[47] Thus, as war and peace swept across Southeast Asia in the 1940s and 1950s, so there were dramatic twists in the fortunes of alien régimes and nationalist movements, and major adjustments in the 'collaborative relationship' between local élites and foreign forces. Indeed, a more obvious explanation for the fall of empires would appear to lie in the force of local and nationalist movements provoked by prewar colonial rule and unleashed in the disturbed conditions of world war and its aftermath.

Imperial weakness is sometimes regarded as a cause, and sometimes as an effect, of nationalist strength. Colonialism and nationalism often appear in the mind's eye to be positive and negative images of a single phenomenon, repellent poles, opposite ends of a spectrum, extremities of the arc described by a pendulum. The juxtaposition of colonialism and nationalism through scientific metaphor is, however, too mechanistic to bear an exact resemblance to the historical experience. Those who highlight the force of nationalism in the deposition of colonial empires have an obligation to peer into the penumbra of such presumptions in order more precisely to identify its nature and assess its power.

Nationalism, like class, is a boundary phenomenon, a social category easy to recognize yet difficult to define.[48] Its characteristics are imprecise and subjective, varying over time and from place to place. Ethnicity and race, religion and language, geography and the concept of 'homeland', history and an awareness of shared traditions, all these are among the main features of nationalism, though their mix and relative significance vary from case to case. It is generally accepted that nationalism is expressed through political organization and that nations aspire to, or actually enjoy, separate statehood. In some cases the nation-state might include several ethnic and linguistic groups, as in Switzerland or Indonesia; in others the political movement may be the creature of just one such group, as in Zionism or Malay nationalism. Again, it is usual for the nation to occupy a distinct territory, for example in Ireland or Thailand, although some movements embrace a number of states and gather a momentum from the very absence of any clear territorial frontiers as in the case of pan-German or pan-Malay nationalism. Conversely, groups which some identify as 'minorities', 'clans', 'tribes' or 'districts' might, like the Karens of Burma or the Ambonese of Indonesia, claim separate nationhood and strive to secede from a larger so-called 'national' entity. The nationalist has, indeed, a dual concern to safeguard the nation from the fissiparous tendencies of its parts and from external threats to its autonomy.

Nationalism is associated with the struggle for independence, the concept originating in Europe's political ferment of the 1840s. We will

---

[47] Recent literature on European decolonization includes: R. F. Holland, *European Decolonization 1918–1981: an introductory survey*, London, 1985; Darwin, *Britain and Decolonisation*; A. N. Porter and A. J. Stockwell, *British Imperial Policy and Decolonization*, I: *1938–51*, II: *1951–64*, London, 1987 and 1989, and Franz Ansprenger, *The Dissolution of the Colonial Empires*, London, 1989.

[48] For a recent essay on this much discussed subject see E. J. Hobsbawm, *Nations and Nationalism since 1780. Programme, myth, reality*, Cambridge, UK, 1990.

leave aside the question of the applicability of European terminology and political categories to non-European circumstances; there are to hand, anyway, a number of models of national identity specifically derived from Afro-Asian case-studies, ranging from the 'primordial' to the 'functional-ist', from 'resistance' to 'collaboration', from 'traditional' to 'modern' and from 'élitist' to 'mass'. The mobilization of peoples as nations owes much to their sense of alienation, that is their experience of political, economic and cultural subjugation.

Before World War II colonialism, in its political and economic forms of power and ownership, had already become the target of protest in South-east Asia. Wars in Java and Aceh, risings in Perak and Pahang, the disaffection of Vietnamese scholar-gentry and Saya San's millenarianism in the Irrawaddy delta are a few examples of traditionalist resistance. With the extension of Western influence, however, forms of nationalism devel-oped not so much in opposition to the colonial state but in many ways as a function of it. Here, Western-educated élites, having espoused European values and being eager to manage their own affairs, were essentially 'collaborators'. They wrestled with their colonial masters in the hope, not of destroying, but rather of wrenching from them the panoply of state power. Both manifestations of nationalism resembled each other in being reactions to imperial authority. The nationalist activity of 1941–57 still bore the hallmarks of 'collaboration' and 'resistance', yet was clearly distin-guishable from the prewar responses to colonial rule by the administrative disintegration, economic dislocation and social maladjustment that scarred the later period. Conditions which oscillated between arbitrary rule and anarchy, such as obtained throughout Southeast Asia between 1942 and 1946, and in many parts of the region in the decade that followed, spawned a host of nationalisms as communities struggled to survive through the articulation of identity and common cause. The disturbed conditions which impeded the restoration of colonial rule also, therefore, added to the problems of those wider nationalist movements that aspired to inherit the colonial state in its entirety and envelop it in the mantle of the nation-state.

Related to the termination of colonial empires in Southeast Asia and the achievement of national independence was the transformation of the region's position in international affairs. On the eve of our period South-east Asia had been isolated from the major trouble-spots of the world and, if anything, had stood as a buffer between the spheres of interest of the Great Powers. In international affairs Southeast Asia was then little more than a geographical expression; its separate countries had been closely linked to their various colonial masters but scarcely at all with each other.

War and its aftermath resulted in attempts to create a regional order in Southeast Asia first by the Japanese, then by the Allies and subsequently by opposing Cold Warriors. In the 1940s, for the first time in modern history, the area acquired an international identity. The Allies matched the ideology and organization of the Co-prosperity Sphere with the principles of the United Nations and the machinery of Southeast Asia Command. After the defeat of Japan it was clear that world war had brought about major changes in the relative influence which individual Western powers were able to assert, and in the relations that subsisted between them, in Southeast Asia. Although the Japanese occupation did not prevent the restoration of former colonial régimes, following the 1941–2 debacle the European presence hinged on US military and economic power and on decisions taken in Washington. After 1945 West Europeans to a greater or lesser degree became clients of the USA through the Marshall Plan, within NATO and, by extension, in Southeast Asia as well. Conversely, the emergence of nation-states in the 1950s was moulded by the political, economic and military assistance received from America or China or Russia. While it is true that, even after the demise of formal colonialism, Britain in particular was able to exert considerable influence over its former dependencies and the region beyond, the international relations of Southeast Asian countries now revolved round Cold War rather than neocolonial considerations. By the time of the Geneva Conference, Southeast Asia had emerged as one of the world's major trouble-spots largely because Great Power rivalries abutted there.

BIBLIOGRAPHIC ESSAY

A general survey is contained in Milton Osborne, *Southeast Asia. An Illustrated Introductory History*, Sydney, 1988. John F. Cady, *The History of Post-war Southeast Asia*, Athens, Ohio, 1974, is fuller on the period after 1957, but more detailed coverage is provided by Jan Pluvier, *South-East Asia from Colonialism to Independence*, Kuala Lumpur, 1974. Developments in specific countries are introduced by Alfred W. McCoy, 'The Philippines: independence without decolonisation', Anthony Reid, 'Indonesia: revolution without socialism', David Marr, 'Vietnam: harnessing the whirlwind' and Lee Kam Hing, 'Malaya: new state and old elites' in Robin Jeffrey, ed., *Asia. The Winning of Independence*, London, 1981. European decolonization is introduced by R. F. Holland, *European Decolonization 1918–1981: an introductory survey*, London, 1985, and Franz Ansprenger, *The Dissolution of the Colonial Empires*, London, 1989.

For World War II see Akira Iriye, *The origins of the Second World War in Asia and the Pacific*, London, 1987; S. Woodburn Kirby et al., *The War against Japan*, 5 vols, London, 1957–69; Christopher Thorne, *Allies of a Kind: The United States, Britain and the War against Japan, 1941–1945*, London, 1978; Wm Roger Louis, *Imperialism at Bay 1941–1945: the United States and the decolonization of the British Empire*, Oxford, 1977. There is a mass of published material on the failure of British naval strategy and the fall of Singapore 1942, for example: W. David McIntyre, *The Rise and Fall of the Singapore Naval Base, 1919–1942*, London, 1979; James Neidpath, *The Singapore Naval Base and the Defence of Britain's Eastern Empire, 1919–1941*, Oxford, 1981; Malcolm Murfett, *Fool-proof relations: the search for Anglo-American naval co-operation during the Chamberlain years, 1937–40*, Singapore, 1984; Arthur J. Marder, *Old Friends, New Enemies: The Royal Navy and the Imperial Japanese Navy, Strategic Illusions, 1936–41*, Oxford, 1981; Louis Allen, *Singapore 1941–1942*, London, 1977. For the Burma campaign see R. Callahan, *Burma 1942–1945: the policies and strategy of the Second World*

War, London, 1978; Louis Allen, *Burma: The Longest War 1941–45*, London, 1985, and *The End of the War in Asia*, London, 1976. See also Charles Cruickshank, *SOE in the Far East*, Oxford, 1983.

The Japanese occupation and its impact on Southeast Asia are discussed in the following: F. C. Jones, *Japan's New Order in East Asia, 1937–1945*, London, 1974; W. H. Elsbree, *Japan's role in Southeast Asian Nationalist Movements*, Cambridge, Mass., 1953; Josef Silverstein, ed., *Southeast Asia in World War II*, New Haven, 1966; H. J. Benda, *The Crescent and the Rising Sun: Indonesian Islam under the Japanese Occupation*, The Hague, 1953; Alfred W. McCoy, ed., *Southeast Asia under Japanese Occupation: Transition and Transformation*, New Haven, 1980; Robert H. Taylor, *Marxism and Resistance in Burma 1942–1945. Thien Pe Myint's 'Wartime Traveler'*, Athens, Ohio, 1984; J. C. Lebra, *Japanese-trained Armies in Southeast Asia*, Hong Kong, 1977; Benedict R. O'G. Anderson, *Java in a Time of Revolution: Occupation and Resistance, 1944–1946*, Ithaca, 1972; John R. W. Smail, *Bandung in the Early Revolution 1945–6. A study in the social history of the Indonesian Revolution*, Ithaca, 1964; Cheah Boon Kheng, *Red Star over Malaya. Resistance and social conflict during and after the Japanese occupation, 1941–1946*, Singapore, 1983; Benedict J. Kerkvliet, *The Huk Rebellion. A Study of Peasant Revolt in the Philippines*, Berkeley, 1977; Judith A. Stowe, *Siam becomes Thailand. A Story of Intrigue*, London, 1991.

Aspects of Allied wartime planning for postwar Southeast Asia and reoccupation of the region are covered in the following works: Hugh Tinker, ed., *Burma: The Struggle for Independence, 1944–48*, I, London, 1983; Nicholas Tarling, '"A New and a Better Cunning": British Wartime Planning for Post-War Burma', JSEAS, 13, 1 (1982), '"An Empire Gem": British Wartime Planning for Post-War Burma', ibid. 13, 2 (1982), and 'Lord Mountbatten and the Return of Civil Government to Burma', *Journal of Imperial and Commonwealth History*, 11, 2 (1983); C. Mary Turnbull, 'British Planning for Post-war Malaya', JSEAS 5, 2 (1974); A. J. Stockwell, *British policy and Malay politics during the Malayan Union experiment, 1942–1948*, Kuala Lumpur, 1979; R. B. Smith, 'Some contrasts between Burma and Malaya in British policy in South-East Asia, 1942–46', in R. B. Smith and A. J. Stockwell, eds, *British Policy and the Transfer of Power in Asia: Documentary Perspectives*, London, 1988; F. S. V. Donnison, *British Military Administration in the Far East, 1943–45*, London, 1956; Peter Dennis, *Troubled days of peace. Mountbatten and South East Asia Command, 1945–46*, Manchester, 1987.

For postwar developments culminating in the independence of Burma see Hugh Tinker, ed., *Burma: The Struggle for Independence, 1944–1948*, 2 vols, London, 1983–4, and 'The Contraction of Empire in Asia, 1945–48: The Military Dimension', *Journal of Imperial and Commonwealth History*, 16, 2 (1988); Robert H. Taylor, *The State in Burma*, London, 1987; Louis Allen, '"Leaving the Sinking Ship". A Comment on Burma and the End of Empire' in D. K. Bassett and V. T. King, eds, *Britain and South-East Asia*, Hull: Centre for SE Asian Studies, 1986; and Smith, 'Some contrasts between Burma and Malaya' in Smith and Stockwell, eds, *British Policy*.

Of the wealth of literature on the tumultuous aftermath of war in Indonesia and the Indonesian revolution, the following are particularly important: Anderson, *Java in a Time of Revolution*; Smail, *Bandung in the*

Early Revolution; George McT. Kahin, *Nationalism and Revolution in Indo-nesia,* Ithaca, 1952; and Anthony Reid, *The Blood of the People: Revolution and the End of Traditional Rule in Northern Sumatra,* Kuala Lumpur, 1979. See also Reid, 'Indonesia: revolution without socialism' in R. Jeffrey, ed., *Asia.*
Indochina has been examined from a number of angles although the focus has been the First Vietnam War, viz: French decolonization, the origins of American involvement, the Vietminh struggle for liberation, and the international settlement of 1954. These different perspectives are reflected in the following selection of titles: Marr, 'Vietnam' in R. Jeffrey ed., *Asia;* Bernard B. Fall, *Street without Joy,* Harrisburg, 1961; R. E. M. Irving, *The First Indochina War,* London, 1975; R. B. Smith, *An International History of the Vietnam War, I: Revolution versus Containment, 1955–61,* London, 1983; Peter M. Dunn, *The First Vietnam War,* London, 1985; James Cable, *The Geneva Conference of 1954 on Indochina,* London, 1986; Andrew J. Rotter, *The Path to Vietnam. Orgins of the American Commitment to Southeast Asia,* Ithaca and London, 1987; Anthony Short, *The Origins of the Vietnam War,* London, 1989; Greg Lockhart, *Nation in Arms: The Origins of the People's Army of Vietnam,* Sydney, 1989; Laura Marie Calkins, 'Sino-Viet Minh Relations, 1948–1952', Ph.D. thesis, University of London, 1990.
Imperial policy and Malayan politics from the inauguration of the Malayan Union to the achievement of independence are discussed in the following: Mohd. Noordin Sopiee, *From Malayan Union to Singapore Separa-tion,* Kuala Lumpur, 1974; J. de V. Allen, *The Malayan Union,* New Haven, 1967; Stockwell, *British Policy and Malay Politics,* and 'British Imperial Policy and Decolonization in Malaya, 1942–52', *Journal of Imperial and Common-wealth History,* 13, 1 (1984); Anthony Short, *The Communist Insurrection in Malaya, 1948–1960,* London, 1975; R. Stubbs, *Hearts and Minds in Guerrilla Warfare. The Malayan Emergency 1948–1960,* Singapore, 1989; Heng Pek Koon, *Chinese Politics in Malaysia: A History of the Malaysian Chinese Associa-tion,* Singapore, 1988. For the cession of Sarawak to the Crown in 1946 see R. H. W. Reece, *The Name of Brooke: The end of White Rajah Rule in Sarawak,* Kuala Lumpur, 1982.

CHAPTER

7

THE POLITICAL STRUCTURES OF THE INDEPENDENT STATES

Writing about recent history can be an incautious exercise. The closer the past gets to the present, the more insecure it is for the historian. The natural instinct is to withdraw from the present, which is precariously perched on the edge leading to the future, and find that comfortable distance between the writer and the brink. The aim is to gain the security that is often professionally called 'perspective'. From the historian's point of view, the trouble with the contemporary past is that it is still happening and there are no reliable records ('primary sources') to cite. Equally problematic is the possibility that the people described in the narrative may still be alive, and writing about living personalities can be notoriously insecure for the historian. Another dilemma is the fact that readers— fellow historians and others—bring to bear on that same narrative their own experiences and interpretations.

Couple these built-in disabilities in writing contemporary history to a description of the political structure of the independent states of Southeast Asia and there will emerge a veritable nightmare. So much needs to be discussed. So many themes can be presented. It is like a Balinese painter at work. He tries to depict as much as possible so that the canvas is completely covered, including the corners. The viewer then faces the task of relating the numerous features to each other. Very often, especially to the uninitiated, the end product merely registers as a patchwork of colours and shapes with no discernible message.

Within each state of Southeast Asia are legislative and executive institu- tions: the military, the bureaucracy, religious hierarchies, interest groups and others. All these constitute 'political structures'. However, they often bear little relationship to one another, much like the variety in a Balinese painting. The Balinese style is therefore not the preferred mode of expres- sion. Rather, like Chinese calligraphy, a few strokes here and there on a broad canvas will be applied in order to suggest to the reader what can be perceived.

How should political structures in Southeast Asia be studied? Should they be simply described? But if that alone is attempted, the links connect- ing those structures would be lacking, and those interlinkages are them- selves a matter of historical truth. The structures cannot be viewed simply

The author is grateful to those who evaluated the draft of this chapter and made comments for improvement. In particular, the following were especially helpful: Associate Professor Cheah Boon Kheng and Dr Abu Talib Ahmad, both of Universiti Sains Malaysia, and Professor Sombat Chantornvong of Thammasat University.

as external expressions of human behaviour: the milieu in which they function must also be studied.

For analytical purposes, it is convenient to identify three categories of political structures: those affected by revolution and war; the 'plural' ones; and 'maximum' government. Structures affected by revolution and war are relatively unfamiliar because they have been obscured by the more recognizable, distinctive and newsworthy 'events' of violence characterizing those phases of history. In Southeast Asia, those structures were largely found in the Indochina states and Indonesia during the early postwar years. To a large extent, they were fashioned by the milieu of war and violence that imposed constraints and demanded makeshift arrangements. Plural political structures were initially predominant in the first flush of independence. They catered for various elements of stresses and strains in society, allowing for dominant and subordinate structures not necessarily sharing common value systems to exist side by side in a plurality. In such political structures, attempts were made to accommodate counter-structures or counterpoints.[1] With the passage of time, however, conditions emerged which rendered these plural structures less than efficient. Apart from the Indochinese states, most of the other societies experienced a period of history during the years of independence that coincided with the great Asia-Pacific economic boom. Further research on its impact on political structures is required. However, for present purposes, it can be argued that political structures had to change in scale to adjust to the demands of the new economic conditions. Plural structures with their niches for local interest groups began to make way for maximum governments—pervasive, omniscient, all-powerful, often the fount of authority.

REVOLUTION AND POLITICAL STRUCTURES

Revolution impacted on the political structures by providing the consensus that transformed society from disparate and separate units into a united whole. It was possible to achieve consensus through revolution because, in the main, Southeast Asian leaders exploited nationalism and focused attention on eliminating a common enemy—usually the colonial power. This nationalism was still very much an extended version of the old anti-colonialism that was prevalent before the states of Southeast Asia became independent. It was especially widespread in Vietnam where the contest against the French and the United States was carried out in a continuous struggle, and it is to Vietnam that attention should first be given.

Northern Vietnam

Vietnam is not an easy country to understand. Much of what transpired in the society was so enveloped in mystery and secrecy that one could be forgiven for failing to delineate the specific segments of the political structure and give each part its due importance. For a great part of its

---

[1] The term was used in W. F. Wertheim, *East-West Parallels: Sociological Approaches to Modern Asia*, The Hague, 1964, 26, 34.

history as an independent state, from 1945 till well into the 1980s, Vietnam was, moreover, at war. The military enemies included France, the United States, China, and then the Cambodian guerrillas. How the constant warfare shaped the political structures is particularly difficult to ascertain: given the nature of war, it is difficult to collect data about most issues. Moreover, Vietnam experienced war for such a long period that analytical approaches applicable to other states at peace cannot be simply grafted on to the Vietnamese case.

In other Southeast Asian states, leaders played significant roles in moulding political structures. In Vietnam, during the formative years from 1945 to 1960, this does not seem to have been the case. Although Ho Chi Minh remained the towering nationalist leader, there appeared to be no personality cult and no attempt by him to adopt a high profile. Similarly, the communist party kept in the background. The reasons for this state of affairs are not difficult to fathom. The need to reconcile differences among the splintered Vietnamese élite meant that Ho had to work behind the scenes until the situation was sorted out. Also, in the years from 1945 to 1960, the leader of Vietnamese communism—Ho himself—was not firmly established and he had to depend on the support of the non-communists. Much of the work of government was therefore carried out by committees which formed the main segments of the political structure.

As long as matters did not get out of hand, Ho took a back seat. Before 1960, he emerged only twice to decide on matters of national importance. The first was the partition of Vietnam into north and south along the seventeenth parallel in 1954. It is still not clear why Ho settled on this concession to the French, especially when the military victory of Dien Bien Phu (1954) clearly promoted the Vietnamese cause at the negotiating table. Most likely, he was under pressure from the Soviet Union to make concessions to the French in order to induce Paris to oppose the creation of a European defence community. Equally probable was a pragmatic decision taken by Ho to settle for the northern half of Vietnam in order to win some years of peace for reconstruction after a long period of war and destruction.

The second occasion when Ho showed his hand was his intervention during the November 1956 Nghe An peasant rebellion which arose principally over discontent with land reform. Issues like land reform reveal more about political structures than a plain description. From the earliest days of its inception, the party had concerned itself with the issue of land and the related problems of indebtedness, fragmentation of plots, rents and loans. In 1955, a major attempt at land reform was launched. In accordance with its goals, some cadres were specially designated to expropriate land without compensation, to redistribute the lands of the Catholic Church, and to confiscate communal lands which village elders could assign, thus boosting their prestige and power. Poor peasants were invited to classify their neighbours, denounce them and then move to have their lands confiscated. In the confusion, many people—including party members, government officials and supporters of the revolution—were branded as landlords and thus lost their properties, positions and sometimes their lives. The Nghe An rebellion was the result.

The opposition that was aroused led Ho to discontinue the forced collectivization of peasant land. Again, it was a crucial situation that he felt required his intervention. But Ho intervened without at the same time alientating the hardliners in the party: they were soon rehabilitated. Ho's role in the political structure before 1960 was not therefore a pervading presence. In fact, interestingly enough, the task of explaining the errors of the land reform programme was given to General Giap, the defence minister.

The low profile Ho assumed could be traced to the historical development of the Vietnamese revolution. Ho's quick action to correct the mistakes of the collectivization programme was an honest admission of the fact that the enemies of the revolution were not a feudal society and a feudal tradition. The French had already destroyed elements of the old feudal régime by reducing the royal court to insignificance and by commercializing agriculture. At the same time, the French did not contribute to the formation of a capitalist régime. In this environment, Ho could afford to de-emphasize class conflict and class struggle. His aim, before and after 1945, was to emphasize continuity with peasant opposition to foreign rule led by the gentry. What was important was the formation of an anti-foreign united front in the interim. Given these basic premises, most political structures remained essentially makeshift wartime innovations.

The Vietminh, a united front with the non-communists, was one example. The exigencies of war meant that party and state apparatus had to be decentralized, and this gave the middle and lower level cadres some impression of broad-based participation. This coincided with the traditional political structure which was decentralized with the village as the basic unit. The village was therefore the real political structure, and in 1945 the Vietminh made the wise decision to consolidate its control of the country by exploiting this traditional institution. As each village fell under Vietminh control, a committee of liberation was set up there. Following this decentralized approach, similar committees were established for 'liberated' factories, mines, barracks, towns, districts or provinces. As expected, the duties of the committees concentrated on gathering support for the national liberation movement. By ensuring that each local committee had its share of Vietminh cadres, the entire system guaranteed that a political infrastructure was developed by the Vietminh that could constitute the basis of a nascent authority.

However, as peace returned to the countryside after the Nghe An rebellion and after a spate of good harvests in 1958 and 1959 (always an important factor in the food-deficient north cut off from the rice granaries of the south), the stage was set for changes to make the political structure more permanent. But, even when communism was stressed, provocative issues like class conflict were not emphasized.

At the level of the central government in Hanoi, Ho commissioned and, in fact, played a personal role in the framing of a new constitution which was finally adopted on 1 January 1960. The new constitution was noted for the prominence it gave to commmunism. No longer was the facade of a broad national front with the non-communists deemed necessary. However, there was also no evidence that the constitution established a fanatical, class-conscious political system. The other distinguishing feature was the recognition it gave to the contribution of Ho to the Vietnamese nation. As president, Ho was invested with absolute powers. However, he practised collective leadership. The principal party leaders were given charge over major power bases. Pham Van Dong was given control over the government machinery; Vo Nguyen Giap control over the defence forces; and Truong Chinh control over the National Assembly. Elections for the Assembly were held after the promulgation of the new constitution. The powers given to this body did not suggest, however, that it would wield much influence.

It must be noted that the history of national assemblies as a political structure in north, as well as south Vietnam, was chequered. The first colonial council had been formed in the 1880s in Tonkin. When independence was declared in 1945, one of the earliest actions taken was the formation of a National Assembly to provide an institution in which all political groups could be represented. With the partition in 1954, the north elected a new assembly, the south following in 1956. However, whether north or south, national assemblies were co-optative bodies appended to an élite or party decision-making process, not totally unlike the bodies set up by the French colonial authorities. Thus Vietnam in 1960 emerged as a totalitarian political structure with a dominant president, a disciplined party and the largest army in Southeast Asia to boot.[2] The system remained essentially unchanged through the 1960s and as the war intensified; further administrative changes were placed on the back burner until after the reunification of the north and the south in 1975.

The significance of the National Assembly as a component of the political structure, however, should not be dismissed just because the institution appeared powerless. Since the election of the first National Assembly in January 1946 and through the subsequent elections of 1960 and 1964, there were always southern deputies who supposedly represented constituencies in the south. The National Assembly therefore presented a powerful symbol of Vietnamese political unity. However, in 1971, for the fourth National Assembly, these deputies were not re-elected and the National Assembly became a strictly northern body. This was probably a consequence of the formation in 1969 of the Provisional Revolutionary Government (PRG) by the Vietcong in the south. The re-election of the southern deputies was therefore rendered irrelevant. This move was also designed to give credibility to the PRG as a political structure independent of Hanoi.[3]

The party and the army were also important segments of the political structure. The Vietnam Dang Lao Dong (Workers' Party) had always claimed to be the sole legitimate leader of the proletariat and the instrument of the will of that class. All other interests must be subordinated to the party and even professional military interests and attitudes had to conform to the party ideology. The party grew in strength from 1946 to

---

[2] Bernard B. Fall, 'North Vietnam: a Profile' in Robert O. Tilman, ed., *Man, State, and Society in Contemporary Southeast Asia*, New York, 1969, 382–92.
[3] Tai Sung An, 'The Fourth National Assembly of North Vietnam: Significant Developments', *Asian Survey*, XII, 4 (1972).

1960. Numbers and ubiquity alone, though, are insufficient criteria for an appreciation of the important role of the party in the political structure. Several key members of the Lao Dong's central committee also doubled as important leaders of the north Vietnamese government. Thus party beliefs could easily be translated into national policies. The party itself was not a homogeneous monolith: internal differences related to the Sino-Soviet conflict. In 1956, when Ho replaced Truong Chinh as Secretary-General of the Lao Dong, this was interpreted as a setback for the pro-Chinese wing. In September 1961, when Ho relinquished this top political post in favour of Le Duan (who was not considered objectionable by the pro-Chinese wing), this was viewed as a renewed sign of weakness of the pro-Moscow wing. There were also generational differences. Ho and Ton Duc Thanh belonged to the 'old Bolsheviks' who had fought the French. Le Duan belonged to the group of party bureaucrats who were not combatants in the revolution.

According to Marxist theory, the army was the handmaid of the party in the political structure. Control over the army by the Lao Dong was exercised by recruiting the commanders as party members. In fact, promotions in the military had to be approved by the party. Also, party cells were organized within the military for surveillance. Notwithstanding the theory, it would be difficult to understand how the Lao Dong could exercise authority over the army. After all, the army's magnificent victory at Dien Bien Phu against the French in 1954 gave it a high status. It was also more representative of the population than the Lao Dong because its soldiers were mainly peasants, and its officer corps consisted of a sprinkling of intellectuals (General Vo Nguyen Giap) and minorities (e.g. Major General Chu Van Tan from the Tho tribe). However, the fact that it agreed to the division of Vietnam along the seventeenth parallel in 1954 suggested that its impact as a political structure could be blunted by other political forces, notwithstanding its power. Furthermore, although the army was often described as pro-Moscow because of its dependence on the Soviet Union for weaponry and its modernization during the initial years, it also needed support from the population to compensate for its technological and material deficiencies. For this, the party was important for it helped to organize the people into labour gangs and military welfare groups. Party propaganda was also needed to stress the prestige of military work.

Ho's death on 3 September 1969 did not change the political structure to any significant extent. In accordance with the constitution, the aged vice-president, Ton Duc Thang, succeeded as president. However, Ho's powerful position as chairman of the Central Committee of the Lao Dong Party was left unfilled. Ton Duc Thang was old, and in poor health; his incumbency was largely ceremonial, and the presidency became a symbol, especially since he was a southerner—an important qualification in Hanoi's drive for reunification. If a change in the political structure was evident, it was the devolution of power to a quadrumvirate comprising of Le Duan (First Secretary of the Lao Dong Party), Prime Minister Pham Van Dong, Truong Chinh (the Chairman of the Standing Committee of the National Assembly) and Vo Nguyen Giap (the Defence Minister). In general, although power was divided among members in the quadrumvirate, the sharing was not even. At a time of war, it would not be surprising if Giap was in ascendance. From the early 1960s to late 1968, his influence was in fact very evident. The military strategy that was current then stressed the 'main-force' approach that would result in a 'final glorious victory'. When that failed, strategic planning was transferred to the National Defence Council where the non-military leaders also made decisions on military affairs. Truong Chinh, a vice president of that council in 1971, was able to push for a protracted 'people's war' strategy.

The post-Ho political arrangements were formalized in the new constitution adopted in mid-December 1980. This replaced the earlier constitution of 1969 in which the presidency—held by Ho—was the highest office. Now it was replaced by the Council of State whose members would form a collective presidency. The administrative arm of the Council of State remained the Council of Ministers headed, as before, by the prime minister.

Southern Vietnam

War and revolution in the south failed to galvanize the population as in the north. Nationalism served to widen the chasm between the ruling élites and the population at large. However, as in the north, the combination of war and revolutionary changes also contributed to the confusion of political structures in south Vietnam. On the one hand, there were the constitutional trappings of elections, referenda, new constitutions, and constituent assemblies. On the other hand, the extra-constitutional forces were the 'real' structures that deserve attention. These included the personal family rule of Ngo Dinh Diem and later the military oligarchies that emerged, with or without civilian participation. Also, the counter-élite of the National Liberation Front was a major structure.

Diem first came into power during the crisis following the partition of Vietnam in 1954. He deposed the emperor, Bao Dai; a referendum on 23 October 1955 resulted in his being chosen as chief of state; finally, his rise was completed with the proclamation, three days later, of Vietnam as a republic with himself as president. The hallmark of Diem's government was authoritarianism. Diem chose this option partly because of his personal disposition but also because he believed that the Vietnamese nationalist élite was hopelessly divided and only an authoritarian structure could overcome its weaknesses. Indeed, Vietnamese history demonstrated that the élite was split, manipulated, enticed and used by French, Japanese, communists and Americans.

However, there was still the need to secure the support of various sectors of the society for the national leadership. Following the Vietminh model, Diem and his supporters formed the National Revolutionary Movement, the Republican Youth, the Vietnamese Women's Solidarity Movement, and the Personalist Revolutionary Labour Party which was supposed to be the counterpart of the Indochinese Communist Party. These organizations were used in a top-down approach as propaganda and political control mechanisms. They had no life of their own.

The most significant characteristic of Ngo Dinh Diem and the rulers who followed was their position in the spectrum of Vietnamese leaders. They were the allies of the foreign powers. Diem was sponsored, installed and supported by the United States. At least eight out of fourteen cabinet ministers in the Diem government were civil servants (or collaborators) in the pre-1945 French colonial régime. All the military leaders who ruled from Saigon after Diem—Duong Van Minh, Nguyen Khanh, Nguyen Van Thieu, Nguyen Cao Ky—began their military careers fighting on the French side during the so-called First Indochina War, 1946–54. In contrast, all the top-level leaders of the north began their revolutionary careers fighting for Vietnamese independence.

A consideration of the role of the military oligarchy within the political structure in south Vietnam can start with the place of the military in society. As a general observation, it can be noted that the heavily Confucian-influenced environment in Vietnam did not accord the soldier much prestige. Bearing arms was not held in high regard. Rather, scholarship and intellectual pursuits offered better alternatives. Also, the military in Vietnam was not prominently associated with the nationalist movement. In fact, there were examples of Vietnamese military leaders within the living memory of people in the independent period who had fought with the French against the Vietnamese. Thus, there was no institutional base upon which the military could develop as a component of the political structure of which it was very much a part.

The governments that followed the fall of Ngo Dinh Diem on 1 November 1963 demonstrated the lack of roots in society by their short life span:

1. The Nguyen Ngoc Tho (civilian) government, in fact a facade for the military, lasted 86 days. Three generals were appointed to the cabinet in recognition of the military's role in deposing Diem.
2. The General Nguyen Khanh government lasted 260 days. Its aim was to forestall the neutralist tendencies of some army generals. Although its core group was the military, it tried to include lay leaders of the Buddhist movement.
3. The Tran Van Huong (civilian) government lasted 84 days. It represented an army-sponsored effort to restore south Vietnam to civilian rule.
4. The Nguyen Xuan Oanh (civilian caretaker) government lasted 19 days. This government marked the re-entry of the military into active political life. The cabinet members included Major General Nguyen Van Thieu and Vice Air Marshal Nguyen Cao Ky.
5. The Phan Huy Quat (civilian) government lasted 112 days. It was only a transitional government that emerged in the midst of political upheaval following a coup attempt, paving the way for the takeover by Thieu and Ky.
6. The Nguyen Cao Ky–Nguyen Van Thieu government lasted from 9 June 1965 till the fall of Saigon to the north Vietnamese forces. Although it showed more staying power, it had to be reshuffled many times.[4] Generally, the ultimate power holders under this military régime organized themselves into the Armed Forces Council (or Congress). A directorate served as the executive body of the council.

---

[4] I. Milton Sacks, 'Restructuring Government in South Vietnam', ibid., VII, 8 (1967).

By 1967, the Chairman of the directorate was Nguyen Van Thieu and, by virtue of this position, he was also head of state.

One aspect of the political structures created by these leaders was the lifeline provided by the United States. Their tenure and maintenance were made possible by the awesome power provided by this external body, which though not part of the domestic political structure, was certainly a great source of assistance. The American air-strikes, the search and destroy missions, the defoliation programmes, the Phoenix programme which applied 'selective terrorism' to ferret out the communists, the forced resettlement programme, all constituted an American presence which was a political structure in its own right.

The military governments after 1963 also permitted political parties to function. By the end of 1969, there was a total of twenty-seven active political parties and groups in south Vietnam. Most of them were based on personal ties and loyalties rather than specific programmes to mobilize mass support. Their divisiveness would have rendered them ineffective. But in any case mass participation was limited: President Thieu had made the conscious decision by the end of 1969 to limit his basis of support to the army, the Catholics and the parties rather than the population at large.[5]

The shallow roots of the Saigon authorities require the study of a counterpart political structure, but this is shrouded in obscurity. From what can be pieced together, it seems that Ho believed that the effort to recover territory in the south would be most decisive in the urban areas, either by elections or in the event of anarchy. This city strategy required a political structure that could realize Ho's objectives. Prior to 1951, the Central Committee of the Communist Party of Vietnam had been represented by the Nam Bo Regional Committee, then located in Ca Mau in the deep south. Difficulties of communication led to the reorganization of the Nam Bo Regional Committee into the Central Office for South Viet Nam (COSVN) in 1951. The COSVN headquarters was moved to Tay Ninh, just a short distance from Saigon. The establishment of the COSVN marked a considerable increase in its status and authority. While the Nam Bo Regional Committee was also an advance guard of the Central Committee, the COSVN included a number of Central Committee members assigned to permanent duty in the south.

The decision in 1954 to abandon the south was viewed with disappointment by the communist cadres there. It was not till 1959 that the relatively low profile recommended by Ho was jettisoned in favour of limited armed activity. Whether this change of strategy was responsible for the creation of the National Liberation Front (NLF) is not clear. The view that the NLF was a creature of Hanoi appears to be an oversimplification, while the idea of a southern organization acting independently or in spite of Hanoi is also difficult to stomach.

The NLF represented a counter-elite to Saigon's leadership. However, the fact that the former succeeded in ultimately defeating the latter tended to give the impression that it had roots in society that the Saigon government (both military and civilian) did not enjoy. That may not necessarily

5 Allan E. Goodman, 'South Vietnam: Neither War Nor Peace', ibid., X, 2 (1970).

be the case. In Vietnam, the basic political structure was the village. Government had always been viewed as the predator, the tax collector, the police, the undisciplined soldier-bandit. At the time when the Saigon authorities tried to exercise control over the Vietnamese countryside, the NLF represented the protection of society against the government. It had the advantage of being local, though in the end, it too had to behave like a government, exercising its power of tax and control.

It is still necessary to explain the support the NLF enjoyed that made it a viable component of the political structure. Apart from the abuses of the Saigon government and other factors, the prospect of acquiring more land constituted another important motive for villagers to support the NLF. The NLF, after all, was a patronage organization, redistributing land from the well-to-do to poorer farmers. It should be noted, though, that the NLF did not issue deeds of ownership.

The issue of land distribution brings into focus the problem of the dynamics of the NLF and its antecedent, the communist movement in the south. Was the central engine of the political structure the appeal of issues and causes, or was it the organizational technique with its attendant administration and methods of coercion? There is no reason for accepting one and rejecting the other. The communists in the south had always combined both. During the period 1954 to 1960, organization and discipline were important. With the formation of the NLF and the beginnings of factionalism in the Saigon government, the communists could rely on economic and social programmes to generate support. However, as the pressure of war increased after 1966, more reliance had to be placed on the organizational infrastructure. Worse still, as the tide turned against the communists with heavier American military involvement, the communists were compelled to depend on the northern parent organization for survival.[6]

Dependence on its organizational superiority of course did not mean abandonment of political reform. In 1967, the NLF promulgated a new programme after the presidential election held by the Saigon authorities. This programme was modelled on the early Vietminh platform of a united front of all interest groups. The salient promises included land purchase for equitable distribution; property rights for religious institutions; protection of indigenous industries through restrictions on and prohibition of foreign manufacturing interests; ethnic and religious liberties; equal rights for women; and provisions for a social security system. A victory policy was envisaged rather than negotiations with the Saigon authorities. Reunification of north and south Vietnam was accepted as a long-range goal.

The prospects of reunification were enhanced when the death knell for the Saigon government under President Thieu was sounded at the signing of the Paris Peace Agreement in January 1973. The agreement was the culmination of efforts by the United States government to disentangle itself gracefully from military involvement in Vietnam. Little was said about the fate of the Vietnamese, whether north or south. The only

---

[6] Hammond Rolph, 'Vietnamese Communism and the Protracted War', ibid., XII, 9 (1972).

political structure provided in the agreement was the National Council for National Reconciliation and Concord which was to be formed for the purpose of enabling the contending Vietnamese sides to thrash out their differences. The council was never established.

Thieu also ignored the third force groups, a collection of non-communist opposition groups that had coalesced with the hope of forming some kind of coalition government with the communists within the framework of the Paris Peace Agreement. Rampant corruption within the Thieu government also resulted in the alienation of the Catholic Church which had been one of its strongest supporters. Nor did Thieu's narrow political structure embrace the Buddhist hierarchy or religious sects like the Cao Dai and the Hoa Hao. During the earlier years, especially under the presidency of Diem, these religious groups were principal players, operating within political structures in their own right.

With the Peace Agreement signed, the north Vietnamese increased their military activities in the Mekong delta and the border provinces of Tay Ninh and Phuoc Long. In January 1975, the entire province of Phuoc Long fell to northern control. The United States response was only the threat of possible retaliation. Encouraged, the north continued the offensive. The last great battle was the twelve-day long struggle for the control of Xuan Loc, a small town less than fifty kilometres from Saigon, in April 1975. When Xuan Loc fell, Thieu resigned and the northern troops with their southern allies finally captured control of Saigon on 30 April 1975.

The reunification of Vietnam opened the way for setting up new political structures. However, the rapidity with which Saigon fell took even Hanoi by surprise. Initially, the decision was taken to soft-pedal the reunification process. It was Truong Chinh who explained why Vietnam was still divided into two states. In November 1975, he reported:[7]

> On the State plane, although Vietnam is one country but [sic] nominally it is still divided into two states: in the North it is the state of the Democratic Republic of Vietnam while in the South it is the state of the Republic of South Vietnam. In the North, there is the Government of the Democratic Republic of Vietnam. In the South, there is the Provisional Revolutionary Government of the Republic of South Vietnam. The North has a national assembly, while the South has no National Assembly but an Advisory Council besides the Government. The North has a socialist constitution and legal system, while the South has no socialist constitution and legal system but only the programme of the National Front for Liberation and a number of regulations having the character of laws promulgated by the Provisional Revolutionary Government.

However, the decision to speed up reunification was taken soon after. When the war against the United States ended, there were only a few southern cadres left who could staff the political structure of a southern state. The northern leaders (including Truong Chinh) wanted to take advantage of the southern preparedness for change soon after the fall of

[7] Quoted in Huynh Kim Khanh, 'Year one of Postcolonial Vietnam', *Southeast Asian Affairs 1977*, Singapore, 1977, 300.

Saigon rather than allow the development of inclinations for independence. Also, the desire of the aged northern leaders quickly to realize their
dream of reunification could not be discounted.[8]

Towards this end, a Political Consultative Conference was held in
Saigon in November 1975 to discuss plans for reunification. It was decided
to conduct nationwide elections for a unicameral National Assembly which
would be the supreme organ of power, and which would write a new
constitution. The elections were duly held and the new National Assembly
met in June 1976, proclaiming the founding of the newly reunified Vietnamese state on 12 July 1976.

What can be said of the political structure in this new state by way of
conclusion? All through the postwar history of Vietnam until the invasion
of Kampuchea (Cambodia) in 1978, the party was perceived as the 'rock of
ages' that could not be eroded. A monolithic party, an omniscient leadership—these were the lodestars. Even when Ho was alive, the politburo
adhered closely to the principle of collective leadership. This continued
after his death, although in daily administration there were now two key
figures—Le Duan and Le Duc Tho. These two, together with three
others—Truong Chinh, Pham Hung and Pham Van Dong—formed the
inner circle of five. Whether it was one or two or five, the party remained
united. Yet this too could not last. The Kampuchean invasion, the economic
mess in the country, its isolation in the world, and an increasing dependence on the Soviet Union which undermined the much-vaunted Vietnamese sense of independence for which they had fought for decades to
win—all these began to coalesce in the 1980s to force upon the party
leadership acceptance of political changes.

Cambodia

Cambodia and Laos were drawn into the orbit of the revolution in
Vietnam. However, unlike the revolution in Vietnam, where nationalism
was the powerhouse, the revolution in Cambodia had to contend with
Prince Sihanouk whose monopoly over nationalism was almost unassail-
able. Before 1970, any mention of Cambodia must necessarily involve the
name of its ruler—Sihanouk. Given Sihanouk's charm and his capacity to
absorb opposition, the casual observer would be forgiven if the impression
was gained that there were no other political structures available to
Cambodia apart from that offered by the prince himself. Yet the lessons of
hindsight—especially obvious after his deposition—would demand studying the alternatives to Sihanouk: only thus can any attempt be made to
understand the chaos and diversity that emerged after 1970.

A Democratic Party (Krom Pracheathipodei) had been led by Prince
Sisowath Yuthevong (1912–47). Educated in France and married to a
French lady, Yuthevong wanted to establish democratic institutions à la
France in Cambodia itself. For this, of course, independence from France
was important. The party drew its support from Son Ngoc Thanh, an

8 Ibid., 302.

erstwhile opponent of Sihanouk then living in exile, supporters of the Issarak movement (the nationalist group based in Bangkok that fought for independence from France), and other members of the Cambodian intellectual élite. The inclusion of Son Ngoc Thanh in the party naturally did not win the approval of Sihanouk. Nevertheless, in the September 1946 election for the Consultative Assembly to advise Sihanouk on a constitution, the Democratic Party won fifty of the sixty-seven seats. With this mandate, the party proposed a constitution in 1947 which gave power to the National Assembly, where the party was certain to hold the majority of seats. However, by that time the French had returned to Cambodia and were comfortably ensconced once more. In Phnom Penh, street names in honour of French heroes and events were restored. Holidays to commemorate Sihanoukist events were cancelled. Thus the power that the Democratic Party could amass, notwithstanding its electoral majority, was limited to what the French were prepared to grant. Not even the aura of Thanh's return in 1951 to join the Democratic Party helped. The intransigence of the French, the opposition from Sihanouk, and the death of the party's leaders (Yuthevong died in 1947 and his successor was assassinated in 1949) all conspired to ensure the lack of an alternative in the political structure in Cambodia.

Thanh himself left the Democratic Party and went underground in 1952, setting up his headquarters in Siemreap, somewhere near the Thai border. Within this zone, Thanh tried to establish political institutions that resembled those found in prewar Japan. His shadowy existence placed him outside the mainstream political structure throughout the 1950s and 1960s. In fact, his political strength was drained when Sihanouk pre-empted his nationalist appeal by a dramatic and successful 'crusade for independence'. Throughout 1953 and 1954, the population rallied to Sihanouk and essentially reduced Thanh's support to the minimum.

Sihanouk realized that with independence, new political structures would be necessary. In particular, the maintenance of the monarchy would require it to be revolutionized and linked to the people. At the same time, the prestige of the monarchy, a valuable input in the political structure, must not be left unexploited even though, by tradition, the throne was above politics. Therefore, in order to ensure that his political objectives were achieved, Sihanouk abdicated on 2 March 1955 in favour of his father, Prince Norodom Suramarit.

One of the most important contributions to the development of political structures in Cambodia made by Prince Sihanouk was the creation of the Sangkum Reastre Niyum (Popular Socialist Community), the mass movement that was born in March 1955. The Sangkum won every single seat in the elections of 1955, 1958 and 1962, each time with very high percentage votes. In the 1962 election, the Sangkum won all the seventy-seven seats in the National Assembly and garnered between 75 and 100 per cent of the votes depending on the constituencies.

Within Cambodia, there was no other political group that had the appeal of the Sangkum by 1955. The Sangkum was Sihanouk and his picture was its symbol. Independent candidates were frowned upon, and opposition to Sihanouk could mainly be found in the Sangkum. Indeed, Sihanouk used the Sangkum to absorb his opponents in the Democratic Party. However, even by 1962, the process of assimilation had not been entirely successful. Within the Sangkum, the young educated members complained of discrimination in favour of the old and corrupt. Hou Yuon was one of the younger members who criticized the cult of personality advanced by Sihanouk. There was also rivalry between the politically conservative and the radical élites within the Sangkum. Sihanouk's original intention in including both groups was to preserve national unity and to check the dominance of any one side. However, rebellions instigated by the radicals in April 1967 led Sihanouk to suspect that the left was getting the upper hand. When he warned that the rebel leaders would be severely dealt with, the two most prominent and vociferous of the radicals, Khieu Samphan and Hou Yuon, went underground.

The consolidation of the left-wing resistance to Sihanouk was a stage in the development of an alternative political structure. The left viewed the creation of an independent Cambodian state quite differently from Sihanouk or the earlier Democratic Party. For the latter two, independence was an end with hardly any effect on the political or social structures. For the left, independence was a pause in the Cambodian revolution after which complex issues of Cambodian nationalism and Cambodian socialism would have to be accommodated, domestically as well as at the regional level, in the history of Indochina (especially Vietnam) and at the international level, within the historically-determinist laws of Marx and Lenin.

The structure that harboured the Cambodian communists was the Khmer People's Revolutionary Party, founded in September 1951 after the dissolution of the Indochinese Communist Party earlier that year. At that time, the war against the French in neighbouring Vietnam was raging, and Vietminh combatants were using Cambodia as a staging area. With the support of these Vietminh, the Cambodian communists were able to control considerable portions of territory—estimates range up to one-half of Cambodia—including the power to levy taxes and contributions. The French military command estimated that the taxes they controlled equalled half the entire Cambodian budget and three times its expenditure on national defence.[9] By the time the Geneva Conference took place in 1954, the Cambodian communists and the Vietminh were significant forces.

The same Geneva Conference was to reduce the Cambodian left to insignificance. Sihanouk insisted that the indigenous communists should not be admitted to the Geneva Conference. At the same time, the Vietminh were prepared to abandon the cause of the Cambodian communists in order to earn the best concessions for Vietnam.

Right-wing political groups and the anti-communist military gained support from the United States which wanted an active anti-left government that would allow the open destruction of communist sanctuaries in Cambodia. The right-wing coup launched by Lon Nol who toppled Sihanouk in 1970 proved, however, only an interruption in the drive to establish a left-wing government that would provide protection for the communists. Lon Nol was toppled in 1975.

[9] J. L. S. Girling, 'The Resistance in Cambodia', *Asian Survey*, XII, 7 (1972).

The fall of Lon Nol and the emergence of the new communist leader, Pol Pot, marked an important phase in the development of political structures in Cambodia, now called Kampuchea. It was Pol Pot's aim to uproot society and reconstitute anew the existing political structures. His Communist Party of Kampuchea (CPK) was compelled to draw upon radical classist and anti-traditional themes because the mildly reformist and nationalist avenues were already monopolized by Sihanouk. The CPK was founded in 1960 and launched its armed struggle only in 1968. By then, a highly nationalistic home-grown autocracy had developed under Sihanouk. Sihanouk's credentials as the national liberator were almost impeccable. The CPK therefore had to out-do the nationalism of Sihanouk in order not to be tainted as anti-national. Thus radical classism and extreme forms of nationalism were embraced.

This position distinguished the CPK from the Vietnamese communists. In practical terms also, the experience of the Cambodian communists in co-operating with the Vietnamese was not encouraging. The fall of Sihanouk and his replacement by Lon Nol should have helped to cement relations between the CPK and the Vietnamese, but this was not the case. In 1973, when the Vietnamese signed the ceasefire agreement with the United States, the CPK found itself abandoned once again in its struggle against the pro-American Lon Nol régime. When internal opposition to the rigours of Pol Pot's rule became widespread, it was easy for other Cambodian leaders like Heng Samrin to seek Vietnamese support in order to depose Pol Pot. This happened in January 1979 when Vietnamese-led forces captured Phnom Penh and installed Heng Samrin at the head of a People's Revolutionary Committee to administer Kampuchea.

The invasion by the Vietnamese forces naturally had its own impact on the political structure in Kampuchea. However, its effects were not clearly seen because the invasion was not a clean surgical action. Rather, it degenerated into protracted guerrilla warfare. There was evidence, though, of the grand design of Vietnam. In 1980, there were meetings of foreign ministers in Phnom Penh (January) and Vientiane (July) to ensure more co-operation between Vietnam, Laos and Kampuchea.

Within Kampuchea itself, the Vietnamese-supported Heng Samrin régime appeared to be ensconced in power and capable of developing its own political structures to replace those of the old Pol Pot forces. In January 1979, a People's Revolutionary Council had been established, with Heng Samrin making it clear that there was no place in the new political structure for non-communist Cambodian groups. That ended any chance of an alliance with such groups as the Khmer People's National Liberation Front led by Son Sann, an opponent of Sihanouk, on the common basis of opposing Pol Pot—at least for the time being.

Meanwhile, a flurry of activities took place among the groups opposed to Heng Samrin to establish an alternative political structure. In a situation of war, this was extremely difficult. Son Sann's faction was militarily weak. The Khmer Rouge of Pol Pot and Khieu Samphan was a political embarrassment, but was better equipped and well trained. Sihanouk himself stood aloof. What emerged in the end was a coalition that allowed the

three main opposition factions to maintain their own identity, organization, structure and policies.

Laos

The theme of war and revolution is more difficult to pursue in respect of
Laos. There, the struggle against foreign influence—Vietnam, Thailand,
the United States—merged with an internal struggle among family-led
political structures. For the greater part of Laos' history as an independent
entity, war and revolution failed to produce the unity that would reverse
its earlier history of petty kingdoms and on-going diaspora of the Laotian
people. Seen from this perspective, the study of political structures should,
willy-nilly, start with the princely familes or Laotian élite that controlled
the kingdoms. The patterns that can be discerned should provide a picture
of the political institutions that emerged.

In the Lao political structure family-based centres were indeed prominent. Most of the Lao élite were descendants of the old royal families and
courtiers of Champassak, Vientiane, Xieng Khouang and Luang Prabang.
Only a limited number came from the provinces of Khammouane and
Savannakhet. None came from Nam Tha, Phong Saly, Sam Neua, Attopeu or
Sayabouri, areas not populated by the Lao. The élite was given access to
preferential education by the French colonialists and, after independence,
members of this privileged group occupied key government positions.
They included Prince Phetsarath; his brother, the neutralist Souvanna
Phuoma; and the communist sympathizer Prince Souphanouvong.

A second characteristic worthy of note was the kinship ties between the
various leaders. The three princes—Phetsarath, Souvanna Phouma and
Souphanouvong—were half-brothers, the first two having the same mother.
These kinship ties also extended into the bureaucracy and the armed
forces. The ties were not sacrificed even though Souphanouvong was
identified with the Pathet Lao which opposed the royal family.

These similarities did not result in the emergence of homogenous
political structures over all the territory that is currently called Laos. In
fact, two different types of structures could be identified, one symbolized
by the Royal Lao Government and the other by the Pathet Lao. The first
continued to rely on the traditional sources of power—the royalty, the
military and an obedient peasantry. All these were primarily Lao institutions and in fact, the royal leaders, Phetsarath and Souvanna Phouma,
were imbued with a traditional attitude of superiority toward the non-
Laotian tribal peoples. Their policy towards the latter was 'Laotianization',
though this policy was not pressed aggressively. As a result, a major
chasm existed between the Lao and non-Lao peoples under their leadership. Their preference for close relations with the United States also
tended to distinguish them from the rural Lao and even the Buddhist
monkhood. The Pathet Lao, on the other hand, was different. Souphanouvong operated in areas not heavily populated by the ethnic Lao, Xieng
Khoung, Phong Saly and Sam Neua. He was therefore compelled to carve
out new sources of support by appealing to the non-Lao as well as the

unorganized groups of disaffected intellectuals, youths and workers. Such different constituencies of support could not but affect the political structures of both sides.

At the same time as these different structures began to pull Laos into two main divisions, the French were led into a convention with Laos in 1949 which granted the territory autonomy within the French Union. Negotiations were therefore started to bring about a reconciliation between the Pathet Lao and the Royal Lao Government. For the latter, the problem was the method of accommodating Souphanouvong, whose dominant personality would overshadow any arrangements for co-operation. For Souphanouvong, the aim was to preserve his power base in the non-Lao ethnic areas as well as the continued control of his military units and influence over the cabinet.

The negotiations at Geneva in 1954 to settle the war in Vietnam after the French debacle at Dien Bien Phu provided the first opportunity for compromise. Laos was cast for a neutral role. The Pathet Lao was regrouped in the northern provinces of Sam Neua and Phong Saly. Plans were drawn up to integrate the armies of Souphanouvong and Souvanna Phouma. These were viewed as provisional arrangements pending an internal all-Laotian political settlement which was concluded only in 1957; but very quickly any semblance of political compromise ended in 1958 when seats for the National Assembly were contested in an election provided for under the 1957 settlement.

The pro-Pathet Lao parties won narrowly but this victory was pyrrhic because, instead of settling political differences, the prospect of communist control of Laos attracted the attention of the United States which began to interfere in the Laos political structure. The manoeuvring of the United States resulted in the establishment of the Phoui Sananikone government in Vientiane which was less accommodating than the earlier one led by Souvanna Phouma. The Sananikone government was succeeded by the pro-American Phoumi government. Prince Souphanouvong then terminated his connections with the government in Vientiane and returned to his territorial base. In 1960, in a bid to end the civil war, Captain Kong Le from the army paratrooper battalion staged a coup to bring Laos to a neutralist position. Far from achieving reconciliation, the coup segmented Laos into three parts: the neutralists joined by Souvanna Phouma in Vientiane, the pro-Americans led by Phoumi who retreated to Savannakhet in the south, and the Pathet Lao in the north.

From then on, the intrusion of foreign forces in Laos became a semi-permanent feature of the political structure. The Americans continued to supply arms to Phoumi, thereby enabling him to maintain his position in Savannakhet. At the same time, US economic aid to Vientiane continued, but Souvanna Phouma also decided to open another 'lifeline' to the Soviet Union, which soon came forward with assistance in the form of food and fuel. Such aid became even more important after Thailand imposed an economic blockade on Vientiane in protest against the neutralist coup which had ousted the pro-American Phoumi. In December 1960, the latter's military forces marched on Vientiane, forcing Souvanna Phouma to form a government-in-exile in Cambodia and pushing Captain Kong Le's forces to the Plain of Jars, at which place he was joined by the Pathet Lao forces and provided with Soviet military aid. The Pathet Lao, now also actively supported by the Soviet Union, then embarked on a vigorous campaign to capture territory controlled by Phoumi's forces.

The support given to the respective Laotian allies by the contending external powers led to a dangerous situation that required resolution. The result was the convening of the second Geneva Conference in 1962, where attempts were made to form a coalition government based on the warring factions. In June 1962, this was achieved. Foreign assistance was terminated and military personnel were ordered home. Superficially, the situation in 1962 suggested that there was a return to the arrangements of 1957, but in fact foreign intervention had completely altered the political structures. The coalition government that was formed boosted the power of the pro-American Phoumi: he was given the post of Minister of Finance in control of foreign aid funds for the payment of salaries of civil servants and military personnel. Souphanouvong's Pathet Lao had by 1962 become very much a pawn in the hands of the powerful Vietnamese in the north who needed control of the part of Laos through which their soldiers traversed to the south. The weakest chink in the armour of the coalition government was Souvanna Phouma, who had to balance the ambitious Phoumi and the powerfully-backed Souphanouvong. It should be noted that Souvanna himself did not enjoy any regional or genuine mass base of support. However, he was able to remain as part of the political structure because he cemented alliances with powerful families like the Sananikones of Vientiane and Sisouk na Champassak in the south. Also, he was the symbol of neutralism which was the anchor of the 1962 Geneva agreement. Thus foreign derivatives were also important in strengthening that segment of the political structure in Laos.

The coalition government did not last long. In 1963, Souphanouvong and his ally, Phoumi Vongvichit, left Vientiane abruptly. However, Souvanna Phouma was still committed to retain the tripartite system that had become frozen as a result of the 1962 Geneva agreement. He was also desirous of keeping the door open for the return of Souphanouvong and Vongvichit. This meant that the posts previously held by the two were left vacant and these were the important portfolios of deputy prime minister, minister of economy and planning, and minister of information and tourism. Government was largely hamstrung.

Meanwhile, plans to hold elections for fifty-nine deputies to the National Assembly proceeded apace and they took place on 18 July 1965. These elections were important because they marked a phase of new developments that cast considerable strain on the existing political structure. While the entire structure had previously been dominated by feudal or leading families, the elections introduced a new middle class which had benefited considerably from the economic aid furnished by the United States after the 1962 Geneva agreement. A commodity import programme was started by the United States, in which goods were made available for local merchants to import at a low rate and sell in Laos at a high rate. The difference represented a profitable source of new wealth which contributed to the emergence of the middle class. Their representatives were elected to the National Assembly as deputies in 1965 and they thus had a stake in government policy. When government became paralysed because of the differences explained above, irritation among the deputies increased. In 1966, Souvanna Phouma was forced to dissolve the National Assembly when it rejected the budget, and new general elections were called for 1967.[10]

By that time, political labels had become less important on the non-communist side. In 1967, Kong Le was compelled by his own men to go into exile in France. The right-wing leader, Phoumi Nosavan, was also forced to take refuge in exile in Thailand as his hopes for a political return faded. Laos became divided *de facto* into two roughly equal parts contested by the Pathet Lao and the Royal Lao Government. The military struggle that ensued till 1975 followed a predictable pattern: during the dry season from October to May, the Pathet Lao (backed by the Vietnamese, who probably totalled 40,000 in Laos by 1968) tended to take the initiative in order to seize tactically important positions and replenish their food supplies; during the wet season, the royalist forces appeared to have the advantage because of their greater mobility, thanks to American-supplied equipment and the use of aeroplanes.

The effect of this internal conflict on the political structure could only be guessed. Evidently, the longer the fighting, the more difficult it was to create a structure that would suit both the contenders. In fact, the Third Congress (1968) of the NLHS—the political arm of the military Pathet Lao—indicated that it planned to lay the groundwork for a broad political front having as a common programme the elimination of American influence from Laos, but it also made clear that cooperators with the United States, like Souvanna Phouma, would have no place in it. Thus the price for rejoining the coalition government that Souvanna was still trying to preserve was stated clearly.[11]

The signing of the Paris Peace Agreement on 23 January 1973 presented a new opportunity for the Laotian leaders. Article 20 of the agreement called on the signatories to abide by the 1962 Geneva agreement. This led to the signing in Vientiane on 21 February 1973 of the Agreement on the Restoration of Peace and Reconciliation in Laos. The agreement was encouraged by the Americans, the Soviets and the north Vietnamese. It provided for the establishment of a provisional government of National Union and a National Coalition Political Council. Specifically, both sides agreed that Souvanna would be prime minister of the provisional government. Each side also agreed to provide a vice-premier and five ministers. Each minister would be assisted by a vice-minister chosen from the other side. However, a minister's absence would be filled only by his own party and not by the other party's vice-minister. It was agreed that the Pathet Lao would chair the council which would operate on the principle of unanimity. Troops and the police from both sides would be used to ensure the neutralization of Vientiane and Luang Prabang. All other foreign forces would be withdrawn. However, pending an election, the date for which was not fixed, each side would retain control over its own territory. The

[10] Arthur J. Dommen, 'Laos: the troubled "neutral"', ibid., VII, 1 (1967).
[11] Paul F. Langer, 'Laos: preparing for a settlement in Vietnam', ibid., IX, 1 (1969).

careful balance that was struck ensured that only matters of consensus would be implemented.[12]

In hindsight, it is obvious that this was only a temporary arrangement. In 1975, after the fall of Saigon, the Pathet Lao seized power. Prince Souvanna Phouma, the prime minister, was appointed adviser to the government. The Lao king was deposed in December that year and the Lao People's Democratic Republic was proclaimed and ruled by leaders of the Pathet Lao.

Indonesia: The Revolution

Revolution did not occur only in the Indochina region. It also took place in Indonesia and there it shared some major similarities with that in Vietnam. Both aspired to overthrow colonial rule. Both were self-reliant and eschewed dependence on foreign aid. Both sought to unite their respective nations. Both revolutions reached a terminal point when the colonial or foreign powers made their official exit. This last feature had special meaning for the Indonesian case. The revolution in Indonesia ended in 1949 after a relatively short struggle of four years, compared to that of the Vietnamese which lasted from 1945 to 1975; the brief period of struggle meant that there was no need for long-drawn contention, agitation or dispute of the kind that would produce revolutionary dogmas. Unlike the Vietnamese revolution, the Indonesian revolution was not one phase in a series with each episode terminating on an expectant note because the continuation would unfold later. In Vietnam there was a pause in 1954 with the signing of the Geneva agreement and the division of Vietnam at the seventeenth parallel. Another pause—albeit a very short one—took place in 1973 after the signing of the Paris Peace Accords between the United States and north Vietnam. Each pause was succeeded by a renewed effort to complete the revolution. In contrast, the Indonesian revolution was completed at one go. There was no need for challenges to constituted authority to be repeated. A sovereign Republic of Indonesia—the antithesis of the Netherlands East Indies—was firmly established. Put another way, the Indonesian revolution did not require a sequel with its attendant ideological baggage beckoning towards a revolution yet to come and suggesting what form it might take.

Throughout its duration, revolution in Indonesia was almost a seamless web of political and armed struggle. Revolution imposed upon and demanded from the independent state of Indonesia a unity that was not previously possible. This unity was realized by the co-operation of two well-known leaders of the prewar nationalist movement—Sukarno and Mohammad Hatta. Together, they constituted a political structure that lasted for as long as that co-operation was required.

Sukarno was the president of the Republic of Indonesia proclaimed in 1945 and Hatta was vice-president. The 1945 constitution provided for a powerful executive president. However, during the early years of the

---

[12] MacAlister Brown and Joseph J. Zasloff, 'Laos 1973: wary steps toward peace', ibid., XIV, 2 (1974).

revolution, Sukarno could not exercise his constitutional powers. He was compelled to let Prime Minister Sjahrir take precedence because, in the immediate postwar world, it was not practical for Sukarno—tainted by collaboration with the Japanese—to deal with foreign powers. Sjahrir was noted for his non-collaborationism. Symbolically, however, the co-operation between Sukarno and Hatta was a significant political structure that fashioned consensus during the revolution. Indonesian society was sorely lacking in unity because it was a matrix of communal, ethnic, religious and cultural segmentation. Broadly speaking, Sukarno repre-sented the Javanese syncretistic religious strain; Hatta was Sumatran and more emphatically a Muslim. Sukarno was skilled at oratory, agitation and mass politics, whereas Hatta, an economist by training, was interested in restoring economic and administrative order to the chaos created by revolution.

Their co-operation provided the mechanism for driving a revolution towards its goal. On the one hand, Sjahrir and Hatta took up the task of hobnobbing with the Dutch and the post-1945 British occupation forces to negotiate international agreements, the Linggajati and Renville Agree-ments of 1947 and 1948 respectively. In particular, Sjahrir was publicly identified with the decision to concede many areas in the outlying territories to the Dutch as the latter's military strength increased in the islands outside Java. What Sjahrir and Hatta achieved turned out to be unpopular though necessary. On the other hand, Sukarno concentrated on propaganda, mobilization and agitation. Such a programme of activities encouraged guerrilla warfare against the Dutch, sabotage, revolutionary fervour and bravado. Sukarno was identified with the popular and attention-grabbing actions.

To be sure, the Sukarno–Hatta combination met considerable opposi-tion. The Dutch launched two military strikes (Police Actions, 1947 and 1948) against the Republic of Indonesia. The second one resulted in the arrest of Sukarno and Hatta. Internally, the national communists carried out an unsuccessful coup in 1946. The revived Communist Party of Indonesia (PKI) launched an abortive revolt at Madiun in east Java in 1948. Carried out during the Second Police Action, it was viewed by all as a stab in the back of the republic at its hour of need. Fundamentalist Muslims (Darul Islam) led a rebellion to establish an Islamic state in west Java, an uprising that was not crushed till 1962. Again, its timing—launched as it was in 1948—was unfortunate. Moreover, it inflicted casualties on the Indonesian army and impressed upon it an extremely unfavourable image of militant Islam. The revolution also meant different things to different groups. While Hatta and Sjahrir conceived the revolution in terms of a colonial uprising, there were independent and separate attempts at social revolution, e.g. overthrowing traditional aristocrats who had previously enjoyed the support of the Dutch. These took place in northern Sumatra and parts of Java.[13]

By and large, notwithstanding the opposition, consensus prevailed.

[13] See Benedict R. O'G. Anderson, *Java in a Time of Revolution: Occupation and Resistance, 1944–1946*, Ithaca and London, 1972 ch. 15.

Apart from the Darul Islam, the Muslims made concessions in the constitu-tional discussions just before the Japanese surrendered, and agreed not to include the specific mention of Islam in the state ideology of Pancasila. Instead, they settled for the Jakarta Charter, a draft prologue to be tagged on to but not part of the constitution, enjoining those who professed Islam to abide by Islamic laws. The Indonesian army was another political structure that acted as an instrument of consensus uniting the diverse population. In the dark days of 1948, during the Second Police Action, the army was the only source of hope and national authority in the republic.

PLURAL POLITICAL STRUCTURES

In the polyglot world that was Southeast Asia, revolution as a vehicle for consensus was not the remedy adopted by all the independent states. For many others, revolution conjured images of agrarian radicalism, a topsy-turvy world of political intrigue and conspiracy. A way to avoid revolution was to forge political structures that would win the support of large sections of a given population.

Burma: Aung San

The Burmese attempted to create political structures based on consensus of a kind. Post-colonial Burma (called the Union of Myanmar from 1989 onwards) can be studied in terms of its leaders' attempting to forge a civil ideology or a national culture that would provide the legitimacy needed for a consensual political order. Consensus was a vital ingredient if Burma was to exist as a state. In fact, Burma's independence was granted by the British only when an amicable settlement had been reached between Burma proper and the surrounding upland territories populated by ethnic minorities. Negotiations between Aung San on the one hand and the Shan *saw-bwas* and leaders of the Chins and Kachins on the other hand led to the formation of a Union federal government. In 1947, the frontier areas and the Shan states pledged their loyalty to the Union in the Panglong Agreement. Four states were envisaged in the non-Burmese territories, Shan, Karenni, Kachin, Karen, and also a Chin Special Division.

The first Burmese leader, General Aung San, visualized Burma as a plural society in which diverse political structures coexisted within a framework of overarching consensus. He was a prewar student leader later given military training by the Japanese. He had returned to Burma as the leader of the Thirty Comrades, who arrived in Burma at the head of the Burma Independence army, and whose achievements became legendary. Aung San was careful to avoid the development of political structures that would prove divisive in Burma. In his view, an authoritarian structure based on a resurrected and absolutist Burmese monarchy could not attract support. In a country where Buddhism played a central role in the lives of individuals and in the struggle for independence, Aung San was also noted for having argued for the separation of religion and state: 'In politics there is no room for religion inasmuch as there should be no insistence that the president of the Republic should be a Buddhist or that a Minister for Religion should be appointed in the cabinet.'[14] On the ethnic minorities, an important subject that plagued the later years of independent Burma, Aung San's position would have won much support. Never was there a more liberal political structure for the minorities than that proposed by Aung San in May 1947. He proposed that the status of 'Union State', 'Autonomous State' or 'National Area' should be conferred on those territories that possessed the following characteristics: (1) a defined geographical area with a character of its own; (2) unity of language different from the Burmese; (3) unity of culture; (4) community of historical traditions; (5) community of economic interests and a measure of economic self-sufficiency; (6) a fairly large population; and (7) the desire to maintain its distinct identity as a separate unit. It does not require much imagination to realize that Aung San's relatively relaxed views, if accepted, would lead to considerable autonomy for the important minority communities. Fortunately or unfortunately, for reasons that are not clear, Aung San omitted such detailed provisions from a later pronouncement in June 1947 on the same subject. He died soon after, the victim of an assassin's bullet, and his vice-president, U Nu, succeeded him.

Malaysia before 1969

Like Burma, Malaysia (and before 1963, Malaya) was also a multiethnic plural society. In both cases, the British delayed granting independence until suitable arrangements were made to provide for the accommodation of the ethnic minorities in the independent state structure. In Burma, the solution was embodied in the Panglong Agreement. In Malaya, arrangements were less formal but the Alliance 'formula' proved to be a more durable structure.

The evolution of the Alliance formula was an exercise in arriving at some sort of consensus among the principal races in Malaya. Malaya was not an entirely logical grouping of territories and peoples. It inherited from its colonial order several loosely linked administrative units: the Straits Settlements, the Federated Malay States and the unfederated Malay States. In 1963, Sabah, Sarawak and Singapore were added to the political state structure to constitute the new Federation of Malaysia. There were, of course, some common denominators. All of the above-mentioned states had experienced a history of British colonial rule. There was also a core of Malay nationalism in the peninsular part of Malaysia. However, the disintegrative forces were sufficiently potent. In 1948 and 1953, secessionist movements emerged in Penang, and the same happened in Johor and Kelantan in 1955. Singapore was forced to leave Malaysia in 1965. In Sabah, the Chief Minister—Tun Mustapha—acted like an autonomous head of state till he was toppled from power. As for the population, communal conflict was always lurking near the surface. From 1948 till

[14] Cited in *The Political Legacy of Aung San*, compiled by and with an introductory essay by Josef Silverstein, Ithaca: Cornell University Southeast Asia Program, 1972, 3–4.

1960, there was also a revolt launched by the Malayan Communist Party aimed at establishing a government led by communists, principally Chinese. This environment of discord and conflict was temporarily tamed by the development of an alliance between the Malays and the Chinese. In effect, a consensual environment evolved whereby communal issues were not debated in public but settled through compromises in private. Essentially, this consensus operated on an avoidance principle—avoidance of open, public debate. It was called the Alliance because in 1952, the principal party organs of the Malays and the Chinese—the United Malays National Organization (UMNO) and the then Malayan Chinese Association (MCA) —entered into a co-operative alliance to contest the first municipal election held in Kuala Lumpur. The contested seats were allocated on the basis of an informal agreement. In this celebrated event, the Alliance won nine out of the twelve seats contested, showing that Sino-Malay co-operation was possible under this political structure. Similar arrangements in subsequent elections brought more electoral gains. The parties were so confident of its potency that the Alliance formula of private compromise was employed to produce the informal 'bargain' that lay at the basis of the independent state structure of 1957. An independent Malaya in which Malays and non-Malays were roughly equal in numbers was not viable unless the major ethnic groups agreed on the manner of sharing political and economic power. This bargain ensured the political primacy of the Malays by entrenching the position of the Malay Rulers in the political structure; by weighting rural electoral constituencies; by favourable admission ratios in the key sectors of the civil service and educational institutions; by special allocation of licences and other privileges. All these provisions were embodied in Section 153 of the constitution in the phrase 'special position of the Malays'. In return, the Chinese were allowed to retain their economic power. Also, they could attain limited political power through generous citizenship provisions.

For the Alliance to succeed in an independent state, several conditions had to be met. Leaders had to enjoy substantial support in their respective communities. For UMNO, this condition was fulfilled during the early years of its history. As a political structure, UMNO was *the* Malay party. Its branches reached the Malay village where it was not surprising to find village elders, teachers, or religious leaders holding membership in UMNO as an example to their followers. These party branches in turn followed the dictates of the *mentri besar* (chief minister) of each state in peninsular Malaya; since most of the states had *mentri besar* who were pro-UMNO, virtual bloc votes were ensured. Until the mid-1970s, votes at the crucial UMNO General Assembly were usually cast as a bloc in accordance with the wishes of the *mentri besar*. The considerable influence of the *mentri besar* meant that the votes of each state could be delivered to support the UMNO leaders at the national level. (From 1975 onwards, the formal bloc vote was replaced by the secret ballot, but the *mentri besar* were still able to influence the way votes were cast.) The relationship between the national leaders like Tunku Abdul Rahman and the state leaders remains an important area for further research but generally the latter tended to act in accordance with the dictates of the former, at least in the case of peninsular

Malaya. This pyramid-like political structure in UMNO, with the national leaders commanding rural votes, was a veritable phalanx. The MCA leaders also enjoyed undisputed control of Chinese votes during the early years of independence. The MCA began as a welfare organization in 1949 dedicated to help the Chinese squatters who were zoned to live in New Villages as part of a programme to isolate them from the influence of the MCP. The latter was the only party then that could pose a challenge to the MCA. When it was declared illegal in 1948, the MCA enjoyed the monopoly of legitimate political recruitment among the Chinese.

This is not to suggest that support for the Alliance formula was undiluted. In fact, the partners in the Alliance network were not the only political structure of note. For example, there were Malay groups which opposed the UMNO, considering it as an organization representing largely the administrative élite, scions of the royal houses and others who were willing to accommodate multiracialism. The religious ingredient, Islam, seemed to be under-represented in their scheme of things. There was, in fact, a vibrant tradition of Malay Muslim education since the colonial period, centred on the private institutions of the Maahad II-Ehya Assyarif Gunung Semanggul (Miagus) in the northern part of the state of Perak, and similar *pondok* and *madrasah*. The products of these educational institutions constituted a political structure that embarked on more radical politics than those represented in the Alliance network. Their religious training and their belief in God's reward for life after death contributed to the development of an altruistic and sacrificial attitude that led to radical politics. The Miagus was the educational institution which provided the seedbed for the birth of the Partai Islam se Tanah Malaya or PAS (Pan-Malayan Islamic Party or PMIP) and Partai Rakyat (People's Party). These parties formed an alternative political structure because, unlike those in the Alliance, their major characteristics were *bangsa* (race), *agama* (religion) and *tanah Melayu* (land of the Malays). The PAS, in particular, sought the establishment of a theocratic state, the recognition of Malay as the only official language and nationality, and the restriction of non-Malay privileges. The Partai Rakyat espoused an ideological amalgam of Malay nationalism, agrarian socialism and egalitarianism.

A remaining condition for the Alliance formula to work was the need for the leaders to enjoy close personal relations with one another. The Tunku was comfortable in non-Malay circles. He had a wide circle of non-Malay friends. His own mother was half Thai. It was also well known that he had adopted Chinese children. However, in the course of time and especially with the formation of the Federation of Malaysia in 1963, a more business-like and formal relationship replaced the hitherto informal and personal pattern of interaction among leaders. A whole new generation of Malays and non-Malays had grown up with no inkling of the 'bargain' struck by their elders. The formation of Malaysia in 1963 introduced new political forces into the structure that did not meet some of the conditions mentioned above. The proposal to bring Malaya, Singapore, Sabah, Sarawak and Brunei into a federation was a major change of and challenge to the political structure.

The entire sequence of events began with an almost innocuous announcement by the then Malayan prime minister, Tunku Abdul Rahman, on 27 May 1961, at a Singapore press luncheon:

> Malaya today as a nation realizes that she cannot stand alone and in isolation ... Sooner or later she should have an understanding with Britain and the peoples of the territories of Singapore, North Borneo, Brunei and Sarawak ... We should look ahead to this objective and think of a plan whereby these territories can be brought closer together in political and economic cooperation.[15]

Expanding the Federation of Malaya would seriously affect the communal nature of the political structure. The Bornean territories were populated by ethnic communities like the Iban who, apart from being 'sons of the soil', had little in common with the Malays. Singapore was predominantly Chinese with ideological tendencies towards the left. The nature of party politics was also different. In Borneo, parties had an ethnic emphasis and they were ephemeral. In Singapore, the dominant party was the People's Action Party (PAP) which was urban, socialist, non-communal, and used to governing a fairly homogenous island. It practised open debate on most important issues. The Alliance, as already suggested, was communal, non-ideological and used to private discussion of sensitive issues.[16] A political structure founded on Malay primacy could not but feel the strains.

All the leaders were in fact aware of the changes that the political structure would sustain, and they sought to find ways to limit the stresses. Again, the search for a consensus among the major communities became the main task. On the issue of representation in the House of Representatives, the inclusion of two million Chinese from Singapore would mean an allocation of some 22 seats compared to the 104 for peninsular Malaya, 12 for Sarawak and 7 for Sabah. This would boost the influence of the Chinese in federal policy-making. In the negotiations that followed, Singapore agreed to a reduced representation of 15 seats in return for autonomy in matters pertaining to labour and education, the latter a core issue in communalism. At the same time, the representation of Sarawak and Sabah was increased to 24 and 16 seats respectively. This assuaged the fears of the Borneans that they would be submerged or eclipsed by the Malays, who were considered more experienced in politics.

Closely related to representation was, of course, the matter of citizenship, which was a contentious issue on which consensus was difficult. The extent to which the people in Singapore and the Bornean territories would be accepted as Malaysian citizens would impact on the political structure, since the communal balance under the Alliance would need readjustment. For the Malay peninsula alone, before the formation of Malaysia, the citizenship issue was not complicated. All persons who were citizens of any state in the federation (mainly Malays), automatically became citizens on independence day, 31 August 1957. In addition, all persons born in Malaya after that date also became citizens (*jus soli*). Citizenship by

[15] Peter Boyce, *Malaya and Singapore in International Diplomacy: Documents and Commentaries,* Syndey, 1968, 8.

[16] John S. T Quah, Chan Heng Chee and Seah Chee Meow, *Government and Politics of Singapore,* Singapore, 1985, 155–6.

naturalization was also available. In 1962, the provisions regarding citizenship were redefined, effectively making it more difficult for non-Malays to qualify. In addition to *jus soli, jus sanguinis* (the condition that one of the two parents had to be a citizen or a permanent resident at the time of the child's birth) was also required.

The negotiations leading to the formation of Malaysia complicated the citizenship issue further. Two aims had to be satisfied, namely, Singapore politics had to be restricted to the island so that the communal balance in peninsular Malaya would not be upset, and Borneo had to be protected from the flood of Malay or Chinese entrepreneurs who might want to exploit the opportunities there. The latter aim was achieved quite simply. Travellers to Sabah and Sarawak, as it turned out, were required to obtain prior approval from the government of the state concerned. To achieve the former aim, provisions were enacted to ensure that Singapore citizens (who were mainly Chinese) could vote only in Singapore. Furthermore, Singapore citizens could stand for federal office only in a Singapore constituency. These features were necessary in order to make the inclusion of a predominantly Chinese Singapore acceptable to the predominantly Malay government of Malaya.

Money is the life blood that sustains any political structure. In peninsular Malaya before the formation of the Federation of Malaysia, the federal government in Kuala Lumpur controlled all the finances and did not hesitate to disburse funds in accordance with political criteria. With the formation of Malaysia, it was expected that Singapore and Brunei would contribute their revenue surplus while Sabah and Sarawak would be deficit states. (It was the management of finances that constituted one of the hurdles resulting in Brunei's refusal to join Malaysia. Sultan Omar of Brunei would not concede that the central government had the right to impose duties on Brunei's oil, while Kuala Lumpur insisted on that prerogative.)

In the end, almost on the eve of Malaysia Day, Singapore was given the right to collect and retain its own taxes, but 40 per cent of these had to be remitted periodically to Kuala Lumpur. The net effect of this arrangement was to grant considerable autonomy to Singapore within the new political structure, while Sabah and Sarawak also enjoyed some autonomy because they were granted the right to collect and retain export revenues on minerals and forest products.

The financial arrangements continued, however, to bedevil relations between Singapore and the federal government in Kuala Lumpur and formed one of the reasons leading to the former's eventual exit from the federation. While allocation of funds constituted a distinct area of disagreement and discord, it was not totally divorced from the communal issues because, indeed, Singapore's contribution gave the new member state a voice in how the money would be spent. In Singapore's view, the concept of the equality of races meant the practice of racial *laissez faire* which would allow equal treatment for all in order for the best to emerge unaided. That understanding of racial equality ran counter to the traditional practice of the Alliance in general and UMNO in particular. In the communal scheme of things, the government harboured no intention to change the heavy investment of public funds to support the Malays, believing that such preferential treatment would help them to become the equals of the non-Malays. Singapore's views therefore posed a direct challenge to the conventional approach to communalism. That, in itself, could have been accommodated if the views were confined to Singapore. However, Singapore's PAP also considered itself the representative of the Chinese in peninsular Malaya in addition to its multiracial constituents within Singapore.

In 1964, elections were called for the peninsular states; the PAP decided to contest several selected seats, hoping that success in six or seven would convince UMNO leaders that it would be more popular with the Chinese and therefore a more appropriate alliance partner than the MCA. This attempt to poach on Alliance territory failed, and the PAP won only one seat.

Meanwhile, even before the 1964 polls, the UMNO—in an act that foreshadowed the PAP's election participation—had also decided to enter the 1963 Singapore elections in an effort to present itself as the representative of the Malays there. Although it did not win any seats, UMNO continued its campaign for Malay support in Singapore. The vehicle used by UMNO was the Jawi-script, Malay-language daily—the *Utusan Melayu*—in which the PAP was vilified as a Chinese chauvinist party led by Lee Kuan Yew. The Malays in Singapore were encouraged to rely on Kuala Lumpur as the big brother who would protect them. Such constant harping on communal issues during 1963 and 1964 resulted in racial riots in Singapore on the occasion of the Prophet's birthday celebration on 21 July 1964. The bloodshed was stopped, but this event signalled the beginning of the end. Communal tension continued to be high.

In particular, the PAP's participation in politics in Malaya in 1964 and 1965, especially its programme of 'Malaysian Malaysia' (as distinct from the implied but unstated 'Malay Malaysia'), struck at the roots of the bargain. The only sensible way to avoid racial conflict was the separation of Singapore from Malaysia on 9 August 1965. This epochal event defused the communal threat somewhat, but the opposition towards the special position of the Malays was continued by the Democratic Action Party (DAP, successor to the PAP) and in a somewhat muted form by the Gerakan Ra'ayat Malaysia.

What was the effect of the separation on Malaysia's political structure? It showed the important role of leadership because the separation was decided by the Tunku while in London without consulting UMNO. Indeed, the Tunku had not held prior discussions with UMNO when he first broached the idea of Singapore joining the Federation of Malaysia.

If anything, the separation also strengthened the central control of the federal structure. No longer were attacks on the practice of communalism launched in the halls of parliament. The leadership provided by Singapore in criticizing Malay primacy also disappeared almost as it were overnight. However, communal problems did not then disappear.

In fact, one of the greatest legacies of the early experience of Malaysia was the increase in communal discord. Many Malays felt that their interests were pushed aside in order to accommodate the Chinese. For example, they felt that policies like the sole use of Malay as the official language by 1967 were not supported strongly enough. In fact, their demands for economic uplift could not be satisfied without affecting the non-Malays. The latter also felt discriminated against by what they discerned as pro-Malay policies. Slogans like 'Malaysian Malaysia' ignited heady visions of a new racial order. Dissatisfaction with the Tunku and the MCA leadership naturally emerged. The former was disliked for his relaxed attitude of multiracial tolerance. The MCA leaders were considered as unsuitable champions of Chinese rights. For the Malays within UMNO, opposition began to coalesce around the person of the Tunku's deputy, Tun Abdul Razak. The PAS also emerged as an alternative promoter of Malay rights. When general elections were held in 1969, opposition parties like the DAP and the PAS made significant inroads into the Chinese and Malay support of the MCA and UMNO respectively. Extremists from both races, the Chinese encouraged by the gains of the DAP and the Malays incensed by perceived Chinese betrayal of and defection from the Alliance, took to the streets on 13 May 1969 in an orgy of killing. The political structure of the Alliance was in sore need of repair.

The prospects for developing political structures designed to enhance consensus among the ethnic groups in Malaysia and Burma were not good. In both states, leaders who favoured plural structures under an overarching unity did not survive. Aung San was assassinated, while the Tunku was discredited by the 13 May riots. Future attempts at consensus-building proved to be less liberal and generous.

Burma: U Nu

In Burma Prime Minister U Nu tried to develop a political structure based on a synthesis of Buddhism and socialism, with an especially heavy dose of the former. The programme appealed to many Burmese who were Buddhists, but it also aroused the fear of the ethnic minorities who suspected that they would be marginalized since they were not Buddhists. Buddhism also opened the way to Burmanization and the demise of the non-Burman ethnic traditions. The programme also failed to receive support from the socialists.

U Nu's intended political structure of the state was therefore not akin to Aung San's. In fact, U Nu's tenure of office was marked by pressures from ethnic groups seeking greater autonomy. The ostensibly federal political structure that was granted to Burma at independence conferred statehood on the Kachin, Kayah and Shan frontier regions. In addition, Shans and Kayahs were given the right to secede after 1958. The Chins were administered in a special division, while the Karens were allowed to create a state in 1951. However, these liberal provisions for separate political structures were more form than substance. All the states or divisions were dependent on the central government for funds. Their governments were responsible not to state legislatures but to councils made up of members of the central parliament, albeit drawn from their states.

The ethnic minorities tolerated U Nu, if only because his government was so ineffective that proper exercise of authority was not consistently applied. In part, U Nu's erosion of power was due to the challenges posed to his leadership after 1948. For example, in March 1948, the communist party (later known as White Flags) revolted. A paramilitary force, the People's Volunteer Organization, joined the communists. The communists enjoyed considerable support because they championed popular causes in order to redress peasant grievances, such as cancellation of agricultural debt (owed mainly to Indians), returning ownership of land to the cultivators, reserving exploitation of natural resources to the Burmese. The ensuing civil war between the communists and Rangoon resulted in the collapse of the central administration. In the districts, local bosses (*bo* in local parlance) emerged, exercising control with their own paramilitary bands to defend their fiefs. By the time the civil war ended, the *bo* were managing local affairs and in fact operating a government structure parallel to the centre.

A challenge to U Nu's control of the government also emerged from his own party, the Anti-Fascist People's Freedom League (AFPFL). The AFPFL was the ruling party but U Nu's control over it was weak at best. Founded by Aung San, it was, in any case, not a monolith but merely an alliance of mass organizations (e.g. the All-Burma Peasants Organization, Federation of Trade Organizations), ethnic groups (e.g. Karen Youth League), independent individual members (e.g. U Nu, the prime minister) and at least one political party, called the Socialist Party. Many of the organizations were in fact the personal followings of certain leaders who jealously held tight control over them. The followers were often territorially based, and this feature and the fact that the leaders had to divide the spoils among the followers, only encouraged rivalries within the AFPFL. Cohesion as a party was lacking.

The large majority won in two national elections (1951–2 and 1956) tended to hide the fissures within the party, but these emerged at the third All-Burma AFPFL Congress in January 1958. At that meeting, U Nu declared that the AFPFL would be transformed from a coalition to an unitary party. All affiliates, henceforth, had to adhere to the party ideology and accept a status subordinate to the party hierarchy. At that time, U Nu rejected Marxism as the party ideology but opted for a form of socialism.

These developments resulted in the split of the AFPFL into two factions—the U Nu group and the Kyaw Nyein–Ba Swe group. The split led to a severe drop in the parliamentary majority for U Nu. The latter feared a vote of no-confidence in a forthcoming budget session. In an unconstitutional move, U Nu promulgated the budget without debate. An atmosphere of political tension followed. U Nu asked General Ne Win to form a caretaker government to restore order so that a climate of confidence could be created for elections to be held. Ne Win's caretaker government was in full control of the country for eighteen months. During this time, it stabilized the cost of living and increased exports and foreign-exchange reserves. It also attempted to exert central control over the various regions of Burma by eliminating the power of the *bo* and replacing them with the authority of appointed district officers and security and administrative committees.

When U Nu's faction won a resounding victory in the February–March 1960 elections and returned to power in the first peaceful transition from military to civilian rule, U Nu named his faction the Pyidaungsu or Union Party. His rivals retained the name AFPFL. The Union Party did not live up to its name. It soon succumbed to squabbling among the leaders. Two groups emerged. One called itself the Thakins, consisting of the leftist party members who had supported U Nu in the earlier 1958 split. The other group was the U Bo's who were relative newcomers and more conservative in their ideology. The internal divisions resulted in the party losing its credibility and this was in part responsible for the military takeover by Ne Win in 1962.

The parties in opposition to U Nu's earlier AFPFL (before 1958) and the later Union Party (after 1960) were not far different. Before 1958, the chief opponent of the AFPFL was the National Unity Front (NUF). It was also a coalition, but the members were almost equally strong constituent parties—ranging from the non-communist Justice Party to the Marxist Burma Workers and Peasants Party. Its only reason for cohesion rested on its opposition to the AFPFL. After its electoral failures in 1960, the coalition disintegrated leaving behind as its anchor group the Burma Workers and Peasants Party which was renamed the Burma Workers Party. By the time of the military takeover, it was clearly a Marxist-controlled coalition.

The other main political party in opposition to U Nu was the Kyaw Nyein–Ba Swe group which had retained the name of AFPFL. It never really posed a challenge to U Nu, being largely a party of personal followers of the principal leaders.

Two specific policies adopted by U Nu after 1960 were responsible for his downfall. The first was the call to establish Buddhism as the state religion. The Buddhist hierarchy was a substantial political structure because it provided a refuge from state laws but at the same time could pose as the conscience of the people. Relations between church and state could therefore be viewed in terms of contest or co-optation. Religion was a field in which U Nu appeared to have interfered most conspicuously from the 1950s. He believed that Buddhism was the means of making socialism possible because the economic system could not be changed unless human hearts were first transformed. In 1950, when the Buddha Sasana Council Act was enacted, U Nu created a state-financed agency for the promotion and propagation of Buddhism. Nu's support for Buddhism at that time was in part a programme to provide an ideological challenge to the left-wing forces. In 1954, in response to pressure from abbots, instruction in Buddhism was begun in state schools. Later, in 1961, he vowed to declare Buddhism as the state religion because of his own strong desire to perform this deed of merit, among other reasons. This move was of course opposed by the non-Buddhist minorities, and by the army which wanted the state religion to be limited to Burma proper. In essence, U Nu's proposal would have made little real difference since Buddhism was already so widely practised. However, the non-Buddhist ethnic minorities were incensed that an attempt to strengthen Buddhism was even made.

The second reason for Nu's downfall was the impact of his policies on the maintenance of the federal structure. In 1960, as an election promise,

U Nu proposed the establishment of separate states for the Arakanese and Mons. After the elections, he reneged and delayed the statehood bills, thus alienating the Arakanese, Mons and others. Insurgency increased and by the end of 1961, U Nu even admitted that the minority rebels controlled one-tenth of the country.[17]

It was the danger of the disintegration of the state structure that led to U Nu's being deposed by Ne Win in 1962. With Ne Win's accession to power, the focus shifted definitively from tolerance of plural political structures towards the creation of maximum government.

The Philippines before Marcos

Plural political structures were found in the Philippines at the inception of independence. However, the study of these structures presents a difficulty that historians must surmount, namely, the need to purge the mind of contemporary preoccupations in the analysis of the past. In the case of the Philippines, this advice is difficult to follow. In February 1986, President Marcos was overthrown in a peaceful, democratic revolution, called the 'second Philippine Revolution', in recognition of the first one that occurred in 1896 against Spanish colonial rule. On both occasions, the continuous trend of patriotism and the desire for democratic government with room for diverse political structures were the distinguishing features. The historian cannot but reflect on the similarities.

The key to understanding political structures in the Philippines is the family. Its importance had historical roots. The pre-Hispanic local settlements were kinship groups. The Spanish colonialists did not destroy the family ties but in fact strengthened them considerably. The Spanish government alienated the Filipinos because it was predatory, negative and burdensome. Without an ally in government, they had no alternative but to provide for their own welfare. The American colonial period and independence thereafter did not change this situation. The American régime gave the traditional élite opportunities for extending the family structure into politics. Aided by its economic strength, this élite was able to control the government upon independence. The result of this marriage of political leadership and economic power was the entrenchment of conservatism and family influence in government. The extended Filipino family system in which both paternal and maternal relations are considered as belonging to the family provided a made-to-order political structure.

What values did the family impart to the political structure? They included the priority given to the satisfaction of particularistic needs and the importance of personal and daily relationships. These ethics and norms were largely internalized in the individual. The head of the family therefore assumed importance as a leader with social and political clout. Members of the family and other retainers were able to share the good fortunes of the leader. A structure of dependency soon developed.

This aspect of a family-based political structure was further augmented by colonial legacies. Both Spanish and American rule bequeathed a highly

---

[17] Quoted in Richard Butwell, *U Nu of Burma*, Stanford, 1963, 227.

unequal system of land tenure. In the agricultural sector, this meant that there was a large exploitable class of tenants susceptible to influence by a politically powerful landowning class. Such a situation promoted a client framework. Leaders were supported because they were able to satisfy the demands of their followers: the former were patrons and the latter clients. Leaders themselves had patrons and in this way the entire political structure was vertically linked from the *barrio* to the national capital.

Two features of this patron–client relationship particularly marked the political structure. First, national leaders were not generally required to maintain direct ties with the population. For election to the presidency, the most important condition was the ability to dispense rewards to command the support of the voting blocs. Second, party loyalty was not important and therefore there was no need for parties to present identifiable programmes. Parties were never distinct ideological entities. They resembled fiefdoms allied together. Party leaders could not therefore campaign on the basis of programmes because these would endanger the alliances within the party. After elections, the party leaders were sustained by local voting blocs controlled by local leaders who had to be rewarded. Such a situation encouraged the formation of two grand parties, the 'ins' and the 'outs'. This two-party feature distinguished the party political structure in the Philippines and extended even into the Muslim south.

This two-party political structure was interrupted only briefly by the Japanese occupation. When the ageing Sergio Osmena returned with General MacArthur to restore the Partido Nacionalista, his claim to leadership was challenged by Manuel Roxas—once the lieutenant of Osmena and a much younger, prominent prewar Nacionalista leader—who remained in the Philippines through the occupation. The result was a split in the party in the run-up to the presidential election in 1946, with Osmena's faction reconstituting itself as the Nationalist Party and Roxas' supporters calling themselves the Liberal Party. The sources of party alignment, however, remained the same and what Osmena and Roxas achieved was the splitting of support in each province.

As was to be expected, the two parties did not greatly differ. Both were conservative in the defence of private property and the existing social system. Both parties tried to win the middle ground, with neither going to the extremes so as to alienate the mainstream voters. Within this broad framework, there were certain regional differences. The Nationalist Party appeared to be strong in the Tagalog-speaking coconut-growing southern Luzon and in Cebu. The Liberal Party enjoyed strong support in the rice-growing Pampanga region of central Luzon and in the Ilocos provinces of the north where the people were members of the Philippine Independent (Aglipayan) Church and employees of the extensive tobacco industry. However, these regional links were very tenuous. For the purpose of the 1965 presidential election, Ferdinand Marcos, a Liberal Party member who was also Ilocano and Aglipayan, joined the Nationalist Party. As a result, the Nationalist Party, which was previously strong in southern Luzon, overnight became a heavyweight in the north. Thus regional identification was no sure indicator of the strength or weakness of the political party structure. On the whole, regional distinctions were not important because regional differences were slight, except for the stark but general contrasts between the Muslim south and the Christian north. Regional rivalry invariably meant rivalry for favours.

This line of analysis suggests that individual leaders could swing votes in very material ways. It should also be noted that these individuals were often heads of influential families which served as major components of the political structure. The Filipino tradition of authoritarianism probably had its origins in these hierarchically structured families. It was not uncommon to find political leaders and office-holders at the national and local levels of government wielding authority as if they were dominant patriarchs. Examples include scions of the Lopez, Aquino–Cojuangco, Osmena and Romualdez clans.

The independent state of the Philippines was therefore characterized by continuous political struggle between élite families represented in political parties which controlled votes from the *barrio* (village) through the patron–client system. The regular change of leaders in government through elections gave the impression that democracy was at work in the Philippines. In fact there was an almost monotonous political struggle between the élites. Two exceptions merit mention. The election of Ramon Magsaysay was significant because he was the first Filipino presidential candidate to employ the grassroots approach. The election in 1961 of Diosdado Macapagal was also noteworthy as the first real contest between the party machine and the grassroots. Macapagal's victory was viewed by some observers, prematurely as it turned out, as ending the domination of the upper class, not least because Macapagal was born of lower-class origin in Pampanga.

However, if democracy implies space for other political structures to exercise influence and control national policies, this was not the case in the Philippines. The political élite was small, and thus personal relations were important. Intimacy also served as a bulwark that prevented other structures from challenging the political élite families.

Of these, one that emerged as most important in the 1980s was the Catholic Church. With the population 85 per cent Catholic, it is not difficult to imagine how the Church can exercise considerable influence within the political structure of the Philippines and, indeed, be a part of it. The bishops exercised authority over the educated, the wealthy, and the masses alike. The clergy managed schools, welfare and other institutions. The Church also launched action programmes aimed at mass relief, thus providing a viable alternative to government. Above all, the Catholic Church was rich. The Archdiocese of Manila, first founded in 1579, was indeed reputed to be one of the wealthiest dioceses in the world.

During Spanish colonial rule, the church had been a partner of the state. The two co-operated to extend the empire and spread the faith. American colonial rule stressed the separation of church and state. After independence, this separation continued.

Organizationally, the Catholic leadership was centred principally in a body known as the Catholic Bishops' Conference of the Philippines, an alliance of eighty-one prelates with the power to decide official policy for 5000 priests in the country. Its long-term leader was Cardinal Jaime Sin, Archbishop of Manila from 1974 and a cardinal from 1976. He held a central moderating role between the conservatives on the one hand and the radical clergy on the other, the latter being supporters of socio-political activism. Traditionally, the bishops' conference had given its support to the government in power as long as its interests were not affected. Generally, the wealth of the Church implied that it was one of the social pillars of support of the status quo. But when martial law was proclaimed in 1972, and Marcos had suppressed all other opposition, the Church was to act as the conscience of the political structure.

Another political structure enjoying mass support was typified by the Hukbalahap. By any definition, the Huk movement was the best illustration of the widespread rural discontent in the independent period of Philippine statehood. From 1946 to 1953, the Huks were able to launch a full-scale rebellion in central Luzon, in part because the movement derived considerable support from the peasants who had been severely disadvantaged by the breakdown of the mutual support system between the upper and lower classes. According to traditional practice, the élite was expected to act as patrons, for example by contributing to community activities and providing help to their tenants in times of distress. In return, a member of the lower class was expected to show deference. In central Luzon, this two-class system was breaking down because of the increase of absentee landlords. The widespread use of the leasehold system instead of share tenancy also meant that the lower class was exposed to a less protected life. The backbone of the Huk movement was broken by President Magsaysay who offered land in the south to those Huk who surrendered. He also enacted agrarian reform legislation in 1954 and 1955.

Apart from the Huks, there seemed to be no political structure representing labour or the working class. This could be due to the reform measures of Magsaysay. The presence of strong family ties was also another explanation. In urban areas, splinter parties to woo the labour vote were not successful because the discontented among the working class tended to return to the *barrio* where relatives could provide subsistence.

Arguably, the propensity for conflict between political structures was greater in the Philippines than other Southeast Asian states. Society tended to be more adversarial than consensual. The most potent source of conflict was agrarian unrest which pitched peasants against landowners in a classic structural conflict of masses versus élite. The links between the structures in the Philippines are therefore characterized by discord. One of the principal explanations for this state of affairs lies in the failure of the élite in Philippine history to transcend its class affiliation.[18] For example, in 1896, this élite separated itself from the Katipunan, a populist movement. In 1899, many élite leaders abandoned the revolutionary government of Emilio Aguinaldo and opted for political freedom from Spain but not social or economic democracy. Later, in 1900–1, élite leaders collaborated with the United States to establish a colonial counter-revolutionary régime. The subsequent American policy of free trade meant an added economic advantage to them as producers of cash crops with open access to the

---

[18] Leslie E. Bauzon, *Philippine Agrarian Reform, 1880–1965*, Singapore: ISEAS Occasional Paper no. 31, 1975, 17.

United States market. At the same time, rural grievances were left unresolved. This situation continued little changed in the 1950s and 1960s. Agrarian unrest continued to loom as a major theme in government policies. Reform measures failed because of intense opposition by the landlords, and the lack of supporting infrastructure that should have accompanied declarations of sincere intent, for instance provision of credit facilities, marketing outlets, co-operatives, attacks on bureaucratic obstruction and so on. When reform measures failed, governments adopted coercion. In the early 1950s, during the height of the Huk rebellion, President Elpidio Quirino even suspended the writ of *habeas corpus*—a drastic measure for a state often described as the showcase of democracy.

Indonesia: The Political Parties

There was a time after the end of the Indonesian revolution when pluralistic political structures abounded in Indonesia. One of the conditions for the relinquishment of Dutch sovereignty in 1949 was in fact the establishment of a federal state structure in the republic so as to accommodate the diverse interests of a far-flung archipelago. The federal state did not last more than a year: each of the constituent states elected to join the unitary Republic of Indonesia by the end of 1950. Meanwhile, a provisional constitution of 1950 was enacted to accommodate the transition from federal to unitary structures. It was a measure of the intense dislike for colonial-inspired schemes that led to the rapid demise of the federal state. Anti-Dutch feelings, however, soon lost potency as a cementing force contributing to consensus. Attention had to be given to sorting out the chaos left by the revolution. Economic stabilization was urgent. Then, too, decisions were needed regarding the future of the Dutch investments, the return of West Irian (which remained in Dutch hands), the conduct of foreign relations, the demobilization of the revolutionary fighters. These problems challenged the consensus that was achieved during the revolution.

The task of solving them was entrusted to the political structure of party-based cabinet governments. The early cabinets were headed by Hatta and leaders of similar outlook. Their approach to the problems facing the independent state was technocratic. Economic rationalization was emphasized. Foreign investments were encouraged. Forms of extreme nationalism were eschewed. Their actions flowed from the assumption that the revolution had ended and the task of organizing the new-born nation beckoned. Sukarno opposed this approach because it relegated him to a back seat, requiring skills with which he was less familiar. After 1953, he supported cabinets that adopted a more militant approach to nationalism. This meant renewed emphasis on foreign policy issues or the recovery of West Irian or programmes on which consensus could be easily obtained. At the same time, economic rationalization or courses of action that would invite disagreement were avoided. The political élite was divided on these lines.

This division, however, was linked to more fundamental cleavages in political structures. Many of the Hatta-type leaders were members of the Masjumi (Federation of Muslim Organizations) representing the reform wing of Indonesian Islam. The Sukarno-type supporters identified with the Indonesian National Party (PNI) and the Muslim Scholars' Association (Nahdatul Ulama, NU) representing the more traditional Muslims. Each of these parties was the centre of a matrix of culturally discrete groups (called *aliran*) that extended from the level of national politics to schools or organizations at the village level. The dichotomy between the two groups of leaders also tended to parallel the division between the outer islands and Java. In short, party, cultural, ideological and geographical divisions reinforced each other. The independent state that emerged from the revolution appeared to be more fragmented than ever, and consensus was nowhere to be found.

The first nationwide election held in 1955 confirmed this fragmentation. The PNI obtained 22 per cent of the vote, the NU 18 per cent; both derived their votes from Java. The Masjumi obtained 21 per cent, most of its votes coming from the outer islands. A fourth party, the Indonesian Communist Party (PKI), netted 16 per cent. The strong showing of the PKI and the concentration of its votes in Java showed that it was a strong contender for the same religio-cultural community as the PNI and NU. The election therefore failed to fashion the political structures that would provide consensus.

The next measure taken to achieve consensus was the convening of a Constituent Assembly to draft a new constitution on which common agreement on the nature of the state could be achieved. Almost immediately, the structural cleavages represented by the political parties expressed themselves in argument over the kind of state structure Indonesia should adopt. Should it continue to be based on Pancasila formulated by Sukarno in 1945, in which religion was recognized by reference to belief in one's own God? Or should it be revamped to become a state explicitly expressed in terms of Islam, ostensibly the faith of the majority? The debates lasted from 1957 to 1959. They demonstrated how difficult it would be for an ostensibly Muslim-majority state to coalesce around a single, unified political structure under the banner of Islam.

Sukarno, despairing at the cleavages represented by diverse political structures, proposed a solution, namely, the establishment of a new structure called Guided Democracy under his leadership. A non-party leader, believing that his Javanese syncretism could be usefully employed to reconcile opposing viewpoints, Sukarno felt that Guided Democracy would eliminate the fundamentally divisive character of party-based cabinet governments. The PKI and a dominant faction in the army led by the Chief-of-Staff, Colonel Nasution, supported him, each with their own motives. The Masjumi strenuously opposed any attempt to establish Guided Democracy, considering the scheme inimical to the protection of Islam and other party-sponsored interests.

The proposal to establish a new political structure under the aegis of Guided Democracy also aroused the opposition of the inhabitants of the outer islands who saw it as another ploy by Javanese leaders to impose colonialism under a new name. Fear of growing communist influence in Java was also worrying to the outer islanders who were mainly Masjumi Muslim supporters. The result was the outbreak of regional revolts in

Sumatra and south Sulawesi, led by anti-communist and anti-Javanese army officers. By 1958, the rebellion had spread to the extent that a counter-government with its own prime minister was proclaimed in west Sumatra. The Masjumi and the Socialist Party (PSI) supported the rebellion. However, with the help of Nasution, Sukarno was able to crush the rebellion quickly.

Thus by the following year, 1959, the political structure had changed considerably. Political parties either were discredited by identification with the rebellion, or had agreed to accept Sukarno's superior role in Guided Democracy. Hatta had resigned from the vice-presidency in December 1956 and was no longer available to check Sukarno. The regional revolt had been crushed and unity had been restored, albeit one that was Java-oriented. The military had once again become a major political structure when martial law was proclaimed in 1957 on the outbreak of the regional revolts. Sukarno was now in a position to apply pressure on the Constituent Assembly to produce a constitution to his liking. When this body refused, he dissolved it and proclaimed the reinstatement of the 1945 constitution in 1959, thus heralding the era of Guided Democracy. In brief, a new political structure emerged in 1959 based on the narrow foundation of power-sharing between Sukarno and the military. The hoped-for consensus of diverse political structures contending in an overarching liberal system had proved beyond Indonesia's grasp.

MAXIMUM GOVERNMENT

While revolution continued in Vietnam, the other parts of Southeast Asia experienced a period of history that coincided with an economic boom. This boom meant a broad-based economic take-off for most of the independent states. Leaders emerged to take advantage of these conditions, many of them creating new political structures or refashioning existing ones. This they believed was essential in order to benefit from the boom. By and large, the political structures that emerged tended to concentrate power in the hands of a few. The ruling élite shrank in size, but at the same time government acquired the maximum influence possible.

Maximum government, of course, had its defenders. The most articulate was S. Rajaratnam, the former Foreign Minister of the independent state of Singapore, who argued that power was essential for many purposes, including legitimizing and modernizing the régime. Suitable political structures allowing for maximum government were therefore necessary. Certain political attributes, like separation and balance of power, multiplicity of political parties, and proliferation of opposition groups, were seen as inappropriate.[19]

---

[19] S. Rajaratnam, 'Asian Values and Modernization' in Seah Chee Meow, ed., *Asian Values and Modernization*, Singapore, 1977, 99–100.

The Philippines under Marcos

Another important defender of maximum government was President Ferdinand E. Marcos of the Philippines. Some credence should be given to the view that Philippine political structures experienced a major transformation when Marcos was re-elected president in 1969. During his second term, in 1972, Marcos declared martial law, suspended the writ of *habeas corpus* and closed the era of pluralistic politics that had existed since 1935. The political structures that emerged allowed for maximum government. This was a major change compared to the period before 1972 when government could not help but be minimal, faced as it was with serious differences within the élite as well as divisions between the élite and the masses.

Marcos' own explanation for dismantling democratic structures so entirely was simple. When declaring martial law, he cited the constitutional provisions that supported him. Such action was sanctioned 'in case of invasion, insurrection, or rebellion or imminent danger thereof'. He went on to note that lawlessness was perpetrated by Marxist–Leninist–Maoist elements. At the same time, he accused the Muslim minority of fomenting rebellion in the south and Christian vigilantes, like the Ilagas, of contributing to insecurity in that region.

Contemporary accounts attest to increased insurgency in Mindanao from 1969. This phenomenon, however, was not new. For the past four hundred years, there had been a simmering struggle to defend the Muslim heartland of Mindanao from the control of the Christian north. The Muslims themselves numbered only 8 per cent of the total Philippine population, and were concentrated largely in Mindanao, Sulu and Palawan. Such a small minority could have been accommodated in a Philippine polity but for government policies since the 1950s that exacerbated Muslim (or Moro) and Christian relations. The Muslim grievances were an expression of opposition to the continuing Christian migration to the south. This migration threatened to christianize the south as well as posing a danger to the Muslim control of land. The local economic infrastructure also came to be heavily dominated by the local Christian sector. Thus the Muslims formed the Moro National Liberation Front (MNLF) with its goal of secession from the Philippines.

The MNLF was to go to war against the Marcos martial-law government in late 1972 with the support of Libya, members of the Islamic Conference and the Malaysian state of Sabah. By the end of the 1970s, this war had resulted in the deaths of thousands of Filipinos, and many had become refugees. Excesses committed by the Philippine military units sent to fight the Muslim rebels did not endear Manila to the population in the south. In 1976, the MNLF was able to force the Manila government to sign an agreement in Tripoli in which the government agreed to grant the Muslim Filipinos an autonomous region. A ceasefire was proclaimed, but it was short-lived because both sides accused each other of bad faith. In particular, the Manila government appeared to have undermined the agreement regarding autonomy by holding plebiscites in the areas of the proposed autonomous region. War resumed in 1977.

The MNLF was not, however, able to meet the challenge. In addition to its military weaknesses, its political structure was also divided. The organization was a marriage of convenience between traditional Moro élites and Marxist-inspired radicals led by Nur Misuari who was the MNLF chairman. Ethnic antagonisms compounded the complications. When the Marcos government offered concessions as part of its autonomy programme, the MNLF split. Misuari and the radicals vowed to continue the struggle, while the traditional élite abandoned the secessionist goals in favour of working with Manila. In the end, the MNLF could not overcome the semifeudal and communal structure of the Muslim community.

At the same time as the outbreak of the Muslim rebellion there had been increased insurgency in the central plains of Luzon under the leadership of the Marxist New People's Army (NPA). Drawing on the same roots of agrarian discontent as the Huks, the NPA provided an alternative political structure that had grave implications for the future of the Philippines.[20] The insecurity motivated many Philippine families to organize their own vigilantes. Since firearms were readily available, armed clashes occurred frequently. Investors were frightened off. The economy took a dive, made worse by the unfortunate coincidence of natural disasters and the lavish use of funds in the election year of 1969. The fear of a general insurrection in Luzon was also fuelled by two huge explosions on 21 August 1971 at the Plaza Miranda (Manila), killing and injuring many at a political rally. This incident provided the occasion for Marcos to proclaim martial law.

Under martial law, Marcos wanted to create a political structure called the 'New Society'. What this meant could be understood if juxtaposed against the pre-1972 situation. In a classic statement on the need for maximum government, he said: the 'old society was individualistic, populist. It tended to gravitate around rights. Naturally it was self-centred. Society broke down on the Jeffersonian principle of concentrating on rights instead of duties. It became a popular saying that that government was best which governed the least. Well, that is no longer valid.' In the New Society, people were expected to think 'more and more of the community . . . This communality of feeling and spirit does away with the individualist, the selfish, and even class interest.'[21]

The common good demanded urgent attention to land reform. Within one month of the declaration of martial law, Presidential Decree No. 27 for the emancipation of the tiller of the soil from bondage was formulated in

---

[20] What would have been the nature of NPA control? Only glimpses are available from areas already under NPA authority. Peasants were allowed a share of their produce determined by the NPA. Exactions of local industries were fed into a network that transhipped food and supplies to party cadres. See the statement cited by Jose P. Magno and A. James Gregor, 'Insurgency and the Counterinsurgency in the Philippines', *Asian Survey*, XXVI, 5 (1986) 516: A lawyer whose region was subject to NPA control reported that its rule was 'terrible'. He recounted that 'when the NPA takes over an area, its control is absolute. They control thinking, behaviour, and the way of living . . . At least under the military one may survive—under the NPA there is no question, they just liquidate you if you oppose them. There is no rule of law, just "people's courts" and executions.'

[21] *Asiaweek*, 1 Oct. 1976, no. 40, 17–18.

consultation between the president and a few close advisers. The decree conferred ownership of family-sized farms on all tenants on rice and corn land. However, promulgation was again not matched by implementation. The Department of Agrarian Reform charged with the task failed to clarify many points in its administrative policy. This itself raised questions on the extent to which the president, a major landowner, himself wanted to push land reform. Vagueness was also a weapon of the strong: the landlords could adopt evasive measures. The entire process of land reform—involving agricultural credit, legal manoeuvres, crop conversion to avoid land acquisition, vagaries in the compensation scheme—was also massively complicated for the tenants who simply wanted to own a piece of land for their livelihood.

In pursuit of the 'communality of feeling', Marcos also used martial-law powers to destroy the power of rival families. The fiercest opponent of martial law was Benigno Aquino. He was soon arrested and exiled. In the case of the Lopez clan, family business assets were seized. Marcos also tried to curb the powers of families which derived wealth from sugar. In this endeavour, he was assisted by a decline in world sugar prices and falling demand. He set up the Philippine Sugar Exchange to control all the marketing of sugar abroad: all sugar produced had to be sold to that authority. Land holdings exceeding 100 hectares were also purchased at low prices, resulting in huge losses to families with wealth based on land.[22]

As for the civil political structures, such as the constitution and the Philippine Congress, restructuring was the answer. Even before martial law was proclaimed, a Constitutional Convention had met in June 1971 to write a new constitution which would not contain unpopular American-inspired features found in the existing 1935 constitution. One of the most important topics discussed was executive power. The new constitution in its final approved version provided for a prime minister who shared power with a president. The precise division of powers is unimportant in this context, except to note that Marcos would continue to enjoy the powers of the presidency under the existing 1935 constitution as well as the powers of the prime minister under the new constitution during an interim period. Since the length of this interim period was indeterminate, Marcos could continue to exercise undiminished power. Given the regular change of leaders during the pre-1969 era to which people were accustomed, this marked a significant change in the nature of the political structure.

To replace Congress, Marcos organized a new political structure called People's Assembly, established in each *barangay* in the Philippines. Its membership included all citizens over the age of fifteen. It was intended to be consultative and was designed to provide a home-grown political structure that would draw its sustenance from indigenous sources. This structure would be free from the weaknesses and corruption of the liberal democratic system of the period before martial law that was modelled on the United States system. Marcos also organized his own political party, the Kilusang Bagung Lipunan.

[22] For details, see David Wurfel, 'Elites of Wealth and Elites of Power, the Changing Dynamic: a Philippine Case Study', *Southeast Asian Affairs 1979*, Singapore, 1979, 233–45.

The establishment of new structures would not have been possible without the support of the military. Under martial law, the military extended its influence in society. It was given control of the media, public utilities, and industries like steel.[23] The field campaigns against the NPA and the MNLF inevitably meant that the army had a greater decision-making role in the political structure. However, the emergence of the military as a structure with political significance was not an overnight affair: it had historical roots. In the 1950s, the Philippine military assumed an internal peacekeeping role, in addition to its customary duty of external defence, when it became clear that the Huks would challenge the Manila government. Magsaysay allocated non-military socio-economic activities to the defence establishment. Under the name of civic action, the military embarked on projects like land resettlement. It was also used to police the electoral processes in the 1950s and counter the influence of the Huks.

However, the intervention of the military in government was not an unmixed blessing for Marcos. Its growing influence later made it a decisive factor in the overthrow of the régime.

The maximum government of Marcos' political structure seemed to be impregnable and beyond challenge. Even when martial law was lifted in 1981, that facade of power remained. All proclamations and orders issued under martial law continued in force. It was therefore a significant event when, in February 1986, a hitherto unknown homemaker, albeit the wife of the slain Senator Benigno Aquino, was able to topple Marcos in a peaceful 'revolution'. The first sign of a crack in the facade of the New Society was the assassination of Aquino in 1983 as he was returning from self-imposed exile. The inability of Marcos to contain the NPA revolt also pointed to the danger of the extension of communist influence. This was unsettling for the United States, which maintained two military bases in the Philippines. American reluctance to support Marcos wholeheartedly, coupled with dissension within the military over Marcos' policies regarding the communists, provided the encouragement for opponents of the New Society to coalesce in a common endeavour. The Catholic Church was also outspoken. It supported Marcos' contention that the NPA posed a threat to security. It also endorsed attempts to combat corruption and to restrict the illegal use of firearms. However, it felt that the implementation of martial law was immoral. The heavy-handed treatment of Marcos' political opponents and the failure to satisfy the needs of the poor were considered as violations of human rights. It soon began to condemn the abuses of the New Society and in fact publicly proclaimed its withdrawal of support from Marcos.

An analysis of the downfall of Marcos might be started by asking why he, unlike Suharto and Lee Kuan Yew, was unable to create political structures that provided lasting maximum government. The answer probably lies in the fact that Suharto and Lee were developers of structures but Marcos was a destroyer.[24] The political structure that emerged to topple

---

[23] See Soedjati Djiwandono and Yong Mun Cheong, eds, *Soldiers and Stability in Southeast Asia*, Singapore: ISEAS, 1988, chs 8-9; Carolina G. Hernandez, 'The Philippines', in Zakaria Haji Ahmad and Harold Crouch, eds, *Military–Civilian Relations in South-East Asia*, Singapore, 1985, 157–96.

[24] William H. Overholt, 'The Rise and Fall of Ferdinand Marcos', *Asian Survey*, XXVI, 11, (1986).

Marcos was almost spontaneous—a Parliament of the Streets: a mass uprising that immobilized the functions of government. It disappeared as soon as its objective was attained and although Corazon Aquino rode to power on the back of this Parliament of the Streets, she no longer relied on it when she faced political challenges from the military during her presidency. While President Aquino actively tried to dismantle the objectionable political structures of the New Society, what emerged still remained fluid. Power was dispersed. Maximum government was clearly on the retreat and the emergence of private vigilante groups was indicative of a return to the old days of pluralistic political structures.

Malaysia after 1969

If 1972 was a watershed for political structures in the Philippines, the racial riots of 1969 in Malaysia also provided the occasion for a drastic overhaul of the structures in that country. The riots immediately resulted in the suspension of parliament, and in its place a National Operations Council, chaired by the deputy prime minister, was formed. The council had branches at the state level, and its membership included the armed forces. Its relationship with the cabinet was not clear but none of its decisions was ever over-ruled. With regard to the political structure, its principal contribution was the establishment of a National Consultative Council in January 1970 to examine the ethnic, political, economic and cultural problems affecting national unity. Its sixty-seven members included representatives from the trade unions, professions, religious bodies and most political parties, but it was boycotted by the Democratic Action Party and the left-wing Partai Sosialis Rakyat. It was intended as a forum for the government and other groups to discuss communal problems while parliament was suspended. Its deliberations resulted in the far-reaching decision to ban public (and parliamentary) discussion on first, the special position of the Malays and other indigenous groups; second, the use of Malay as the national language; third, the citizenship rights of any ethnic group; and fourth, the position of the Malay rulers. With this groundwork completed, parliament—now somewhat reduced in legislative authority—reconvened in 1971 as the nation's supreme law-making body. The National Operations Council was renamed the National Security Council, dealing mainly with security (principally communist) affairs. The armed forces returned to their strictly military role. The National Consultative Council was retained to discuss communal issues which parliament could not consider. A Department of National Unity was also set up to formulate a national ideology, called Rukunegara, to serve as a focus for the multiethnic population.

It was not, however, a simple return to the *status quo ante*, before 1969. It was the view of the National Operations Council that the riot originated from economic causes related to the communal distribution of wealth. One of the results of the riot was the launching of the New Economic Policy to eradicate poverty among all races and to eliminate the identification of race with occupation. Although the policy was socio-economic in orientation, it had serious implications for the political structure. Before 1969, the focus of Malaysia's economic policy was on rural development programmes that aimed at reducing disparities of income between the Malays and the urban Chinese. After the inauguration of the New Economic Policy, the objective was transformed so as to concentrate on the large-scale uplift of the *bumiputra* (son-of-the-soil) through urbanization and the creation of a *bumiputra* middle class.

Such a policy had major effects upon the political structures. It immediately aroused the suspicion of the non-Malay middle class which was established through the colonial economic system. The strengthening of the *bumiputra* middle class could not but undermine the support previously given to the Alliance by the non-Malays. Although this did not *ipso facto* mean a switching of allegiance to non-Malay parties in the opposition, like the DAP, it tended to weaken the personal links, trust and camaraderie shared by the Alliance leaders. Moreover, the emergent middle class was wholly dependent on the government for its continued growth. The process of urbanization itself would not have been possible without government support. Furthermore, the complex technologies, the expansion and accumulation of capital, and the sophisticated marketing operations—characteristic tasks facing the middle class in the late twentieth century—all tended to point towards the need for strong government, a strong bureaucracy, and a defined hierarchy within the political structure.

In later years various other political structures began to assume greater importance. One of these was the institution of the monarchy and the sultans in each state. The Malaysian king and his colleagues in the states occupied largely ceremonial positions. Under the constitution, they were required to act in accordance with the advice of the elected prime minister. There appeared to be no occasion for this role to change from 1957 till about 1981. During that period, the prime ministers were either scions of the royal houses or closely related to them. In 1981, with Mahathir bin Mohamad as prime minister, this changed. Mahathir was the son of a commoner. He believed that there should be less emphasis on a feudal style of government which stressed loyalty, and that more attention should be paid to ability, skill and achievement.

Friction soon appeared between the state rulers and the elected government. Sultan Haji Ahmad Shah of Pahang, who later became the Yang di-pertuan Agong (king), was one example. In 1978, he opposed the appointment by the prime minister of a *mentri besar* who was not supportive of the palace. After Sultan Haji Ahmad Shah became king, his son—the regent and heir apparent—withheld royal approbation from several state bills. In Johor, relations between the sultan, Mahmood Iskandar, and the *mentri besar* were also sour. In 1980, the latter had questioned the former's right to succeed to the Johor throne. Following the state and federal elections of 1982, another *mentri besar* was appointed in deference to the sentiments of the sultan.

Such interference in the political structure invited concern. What would happen when the strong-willed sultans of Perak and Johor had their turn to become king? Reaction to that possibility came in 1983 when constitutional amendments were submitted to reduce the powers of the king. A Conference of Rulers rejected the amendments. Go-betweens were sent to find a solution to the impasse. A compromise was finally reached without a face-to-face confrontation between the rulers and the elected government. This was entirely in keeping with Malay cultural norms because even Mahathir, a commoner, had to observe form and ritual when dealing with the rulers. After all, it was Mahathir himself who wrote in 1970, years before he became prime minister: 'Formality and ritual rate very high in the Malay concept of values. What is formal is proper. To depart from formality is considered unbecoming, rude and deserving of misfortune or punishment by God and man. This is essentially a conservative attitude.'[25]

Another political structure was the state. Constitutionally, a strong federal authority reduced the importance of the state as a political structure, but there was also sufficient diversity among the states in the whole of Malaysia to enable them to pull in different directions. Since money was often the lubricant that made a federal system workable, the viability of a state as a political structure independent of the central government depended on the revenue available. For peninsular Malaysia, subventions were critical for all the states, and offers of money for development were often used to attract votes in elections. A state like Kelantan which elected PAS-led governments might be denied federal assistance.

Unlike the other states in peninsular Malaysia, both Sabah and Sarawak joined the federation of Malaysia with safeguards which included a delay in switching to the use of Bahasa Malaysia and the control of immigration. In Sabah, the chief minister, Tun Mustapha, almost succeeded in creating a state within a state, asserting his independence to the extent of providing sanctuary as well as armed assistance to the Muslim secessionists in Mindanao, and, if the accusations of his opponents were to be believed, entertaining thoughts of secession. The central government dealt very patiently with Mustapha. It was not till September 1975 that he was forced to resign. In Sarawak, a three-tier political structure of councils ensured that a degree of state autonomy was retained. Essentially, a system of twenty-four district councils, directly elected by the population, formed the first tier. The second tier consisted of five divisional advisory councils made up of representatives elected from the district councils. The third tier was the Council Negri (State Legislative Council) in Kuching, consisting of representatives elected from the divisional advisory council. The Council Negri then proceeded to elect twenty-four representatives to sit in the federal parliament in Kuala Lumpur. This system was unlike that found in the other constituent states of Malaysia. It was established to provide training for representatives inexperienced in political practices. It ensured that the representative who finally secured a seat in the federal parliament would have served in all tiers. The structure therefore allowed local interests to be represented all the way up to Kuala Lumpur. Although that did not prevent the central authorities from interfering in the state political structure, the Sarawak case was unique. But it should be noted that, on 14 September 1966, a state of emergency was declared in Sarawak on the grounds that the political situation was being exploited by the communists. All state powers were immediately transferred to the federal

25 Mahathir bin Mohamad, *The Malay Dilemma*, Singapore, 1970, 157.

authority and overnight the political structure in Sarawak was refashioned. The Sarawak constitution was amended to give substantially more powers to the governor (a federal appointee) over the chief minister, the Council Negri and its speaker.

Lastly, mention must be made of more populist political structures. Communism, though significant in its own right before 1960, failed to strike roots in Malaysia because it failed to overcome obstacles like Malay nationalism and communalism. In 1975 and early 1976, after a period of inactivity, there were reports of selective assassinations by communist hit squads in urban areas. But these ended in 1976, and guerrilla warfare also appeared to be on the decline. The MCP itself had split in 1970 and 1974, and by 1976 the three factions that were left were contending among themselves as much as against the government. The late 1970s and the early 1980s were also years of active *Dakwah* movements by Muslims to intensify the spread and practice of Islam. Various pressure groups also provided alternative centres of focus, e.g. the Aliran Kesedaran Negara (National Consciousness Movement), ABIM (Malaysian Islamic Youth Movement), and the Consumers' Association of Penang. They became well known because of their outspoken comments on government policies, but whether they had the potential to emerge as political structures in their right had yet to be seen.

Indonesia from Sukarno to Suharto

The development of maximum government was also most evident in Indonesia under the rule of presidents Sukarno and Suharto. The existence of maximum government was implied by the type of political structures that allowed Sukarno to dismiss the Constituent Assembly in 1959; to dissolve the legally-elected parliament in 1960; and to ban political parties like the Masjumi and the Socialist Party (PSI). Similarly, how else did Suharto derive the power to declare the mass communist party (PKI) illegal; to declare certain influential Muslim leaders disqualified from assuming leadership of the reconstituted Muslim political party (PMI); to manipulate the leadership of other political parties; and to dismiss fellow army generals from powerful positions? While charisma could have helped Sukarno to get his way, the same could not be said of Suharto. The more likely answer lies in the power of maximum government in the political structures available to the two leaders.

Sukarno had made his first move at establishing maximum government in 1956, when he proposed a new form of democracy, which he called Guided Democracy, to replace the liberal '50 per cent plus one' democracy then existing in Indonesia. Guided Democracy was finally proclaimed in 1959. Founded on the constitution of 1945 which provided for a strong executive presidency, Guided Democracy was seen by Sukarno as a political structure which would save the nation from the drift and purposelessness that had characterized Indonesia from 1949 to 1959. As president, he would 'guide' the nation to its proper path. In a speech in 1959, he said:

It was felt by the whole of the People that the spirit, the principles and the objective of the Revolution which we launched in 1945 had now been infected by dangerous diseases and dualisms.

Where is that spirit of the Revolution today? The spirit of the Revolution has been almost extinguished, has already become cold and without fire. Where are the Principles of the Revolution today? Today nobody knows where those Principles of the Revolution are, because each and every party lays down its own principles, so that there are those who have departed from even the principles of the Pantja Sila. Where is the objective of the Revolution today? The objective of the Revolution—a just and prosperous society—is now, for persons who are not sons of the Revolution, replaced by liberal politics and liberal economics. Replaced by liberal politics, in which the votes of the majority of the people are exploited, blackmarketed, corrupted by various groups. Replaced by liberal economics, in which various groups want only to grab wealth at the expense of the People.

All these diseases and dualisms were conspicuous in this period of invest-ment, particularly the four kinds of disease and dualism of which I have several times warned: Dualism between the government and the leadership of the Revolution; dualism in men's perspective on society—a just and prosper-ous society or a capitalist society; dualism between 'the Revolution is over' and 'the Revolution is not yet completed'; and dualism as regarding democracy: Shall democracy serve the People, or the People democracy? . . .[26]

Although the opposition to Guided Democracy was weak, presidential power within the political structure was not unlimited. Sukarno depended on the military's tools of coercion. In return for its support, the military was given key positions in civil administration and economic management under the aegis of martial law. To balance the dependence on the military, Sukarno was forced to cement ties with the PKI. The latter supported Guided Democracy because it needed Sukarno's protection from persecu-tion by the military. In return for this favour, the PKI provided the mass audience as well as the encouragement for Sukarno's increasingly strident and militant campaigns. Whether it was a question of the formulation of ideology (e.g. Political Manifesto or Manipol, Usdek, Nasakom), the anti-Dutch campaign to recover West Irian, or the confrontation against the newly-formed state of Malaysia, the PKI mobilized the crowds and sup-plied the adulation that Sukarno needed. In return, the party's programme of activities was allowed to proceed almost uninhibited. For example, the PKI pressed ahead with its *aksi sepihak*, a unilateral course of action to seize land for the landless. This alienated the landowners, many of whom were supporters of Muslim parties. By late 1964, the rural scene in Java was polarized between a radical left that purported to join Sukarno in continuing the revolution and a military–Muslim alliance that was fearful of a com-munist takeover. The consensus that Sukarno thought Guided Democracy could bring was only an illusion. Guided Democracy marked one further step towards maximum government.

[26] Speech reproduced in Roger M. Smith, ed., *Southeast Asia: Documents of Political Development and Change*, Ithaca, 1974, 197–8.

The military's opposition towards the communists was not only ideological and historical, harking back to the days of the Madiun revolt in 1948. The PKI represented a departure from the structure of the other political parties. These latter parties were élite organizations with little mass participation: the PKI was different. Once in power, non-élite masses were expected to succeed in redistributing political and economic privileges previously available only to a relatively small cohort. The PKI's support for Sukarno in fact doomed the latter because it alienated him from the rest of the élite: he was hobnobbing with a mass party. When an abortive coup took place on 1 October 1965 resulting in the murder of six generals, enough was enough. The PKI was accused of orchestrating the coup. Despite pressure from the military, Sukarno still refused to ban the PKI. A relatively unknown soldier, General Suharto, was given the task of restoring security since he was in charge of Kostrad, the military's strategic reserve; he emerged as the leader opposed to Sukarno. In an extended power struggle in which student and other groups participated, Sukarno was effectively deposed on 11 March 1966. The PKI was then banned. Suharto was named acting president in 1967, and in the following year became president. Meanwhile, the military allowed PKI supporters in central and east Java and Bali to be massacred by Muslims in a *jihad*. There were estimates of half a million to a million killed.

When Suharto became acting president in 1967, the political structure that he inaugurated came to be called the New Order. However, it shared certain similarities with the Old Order of Sukarno's Guided Democracy. Like Sukarno, Suharto kept political parties at arm's length. While Sukarno used the PKI to counter-balance the military and other political parties, Suharto employed the same tactic to play off the Muslims against the nationalist parties. In both cases, Suharto and Sukarno betrayed their Javanese religio-cultural bias against Islam, especially its militant version. Suharto refused to sanction the reconstitution of the banned Masjumi, even though its leaders quite logically expected that they would be permitted to resume their political activities, because they were the only ones who had dared to challenge Sukarno's Guided Democracy. In the end, Suharto agreed to allow the formation of the PMI, but insisted that its leaders should not be drawn from the ranks of the old Masjumi executive.

However, the differences between Suharto and Sukarno were equally significant. When Sukarno was president, attempts were made to mobilize the population for campaigns like the recovery of West Irian, confrontation against Malaysia and agitation for land reform, though such mobilization was not long-term but restricted to specific transient goals. When Suharto was president, the watchword was political passivity. Suharto's political structures were designed to reduce mobilization. Political parties were not permitted to organize in the villages and sub-districts, the home of 80 per cent of Indonesia's population. Instead, the population was conceived as a 'floating mass', free from the disintegrative pulls of party politics. To fill the political space that political parties were required to vacate, Suharto sponsored the organization of a functional group, popularly known as Golkar. Organizing the population into political structures that pivoted on parties embracing different ideologies tended to emphasize cleavages in society. It was believed that it would be less divisive if the population was organized in accordance with the function each sector served in society. Golkar was therefore an agglomeration of civil servants, the armed forces, intellectuals, women, youths, workers, farmers, veterans and even pedicab drivers. It was the instrument to mobilize votes in general elections. In July 1971, the country's second national election was held. With the help of some heavy-handed tactics, the Golkar won 236 seats out of the total of 360. The NU won 58 seats, making it the most important of the non-government parties. The revamped PMI followed with 24 seats while the PNI only garnered 20. In its election activities, the Golkar was no different from a political party.

The emphasis on political passivity also guided Suharto's handling of the student political structure. During the struggle to topple Sukarno, the students emerged as the moral conscience of the nation. They led demonstrations. The student organizations (KAMI, KAPPI) helped to bring down the old order. However, by 1969, the students were no longer a credible political structure. Suharto did not tolerate an independent moral authority and although students emerged again in later years to question the wisdom of some of Suharto's policies, for example in the 1974 anti-Japanese riots, they did not constitute a structure of long-term stamina and significance.

Political passivity was taken a step further in 1987 when all societies, including political parties, were required to declare as their sole guiding principle the state ideology of the Pancasila. This move was rationalized as the de-ideologization of the Indonesian political structure. Political parties were thus forcibly divorced from their primordial and traditional sources of power. Even Muslim groups, for example, had to acknowledge the Pancasila as their lodestar. The result of this move was to force all groups to subscribe to one ideology—the one approved by Suharto.

This measure was preceded by an earlier attempt to restructure the remaining nine political parties into two groups. All Muslim parties were forced to coalesce under the banner of the Development Unity Party (PPP). Similarly, the PNI was forced to co-operate with the Christian parties under the banner of the Indonesian Democratic Party (PDI). The result was more internal bickering and growing ineffectiveness. In the end the NU withdrew from the PPP and ceased to continue as a political party in 1985.

With the emasculation of the political parties, parliament—already weakened—ceased to be of major importance. During Suharto's presidency, the more important structure was the People's Consultative Assembly (MPR) which comprised the parliamentarians and appointed delegates. The assembly was empowered to elect and fire a president. It deliberated on the broad guidelines of state policy. The president was responsible to the assembly, but the latter's effectiveness was limited by the fact that it met only once in five years.

Another distinction between Sukarno and Suharto was the source of legitimacy. Sukarno's activist policies led to economic ruin. Suharto's distaste for political activism accorded with his view of the function of an independent state. He was deeply convinced that the New Order could be justified only by promoting orderly government, the rule of law, economic rationalization and internal consensus.

Given the concentration of power under Suharto, an ex-soldier, it is

relevant to examine the extent to which the military constituted a significant political structure. The Indonesian military embraced a cohesive
ideology for the greater part of its history. During the revolution, the army
commander, General Sudirman, described the military as belonging to the
people of Indonesia. This meant that it would not participate in the power
struggle of the political parties of the day. This position was widely
accepted and was instrumental in the military's contribution to the consensus achieved during the revolution.

With the end of the revolution, Sudirman's dictum was ignored. The
military became entangled in party politics. Pro-Sukarno officers intrigued
to sabotage the civilian government's attempts to demobilize soldiers. In
1952, Nasution led a group which tried to dissolve parliament for obstructing measures to professionalize the military. The divisions in the military
were not bridged till 1955. Shortly thereafter, regional revolts broke out,
with some army officers providing leadership to the rebels.

However, the dominant group of officers was opposed to the rebellion.
Led by Nasution, they realized that the military's role as a political
structure had to be accommodated in some manner. In 1958, Nasution
reinterpreted Sudirman's dictum to mean that the military would embark
on the 'Middle Way'. In his view, the Indonesian military would not follow
the path of coups widely practised by the Latin American military forces
in the 1950s. On the other hand, it would not be a lifeless tool of
the government.

In practical terms, the Middle Way could not be defined exactly. When
martial law was proclaimed, the military became a political structure in its
own right. This was also the time when the military assumed an economic
role in the country by seizing the management of Dutch investments.

The post-1965 situation provided a larger field for the expansion of the
military's political role. The term used to describe this new role was
'dwifungsi' or dual function. Army seminars constantly reiterated that the
military now had two roles to fulfil: a strictly defence role and a socio-
political role.

Perhaps the best example of an exponent of dwifungsi was Suharto
himself. By 1967, he occupied the top position in both military and civil
hierarchies. Until 1973, he was also the Minister of Defence and Security
in control of combat troops; he was commander of the armed forces too.
In themselves, the postings were not sufficient to ensure Suharto's control.
The Indonesian military had been plagued by warlordism since its inception, and top brass did not automatically exercise authority. The chain of
command had to be developed. Organizational changes were implemented in 1969 and 1973–4. The overall result was the transfer of operational
control of combat troops to Suharto. Other military organizations designed
to enhance security by removing opponents to the New Order were
strengthened. These included the Operations Command for the Restoration of Security and Order (Kopkamtib),[27] Special Operations Service
(OPSUS) and State Intelligence Agency (BAKIN).

In turn, military officers were given appointments in the judiciary, the

---

[27] In 1988, Kopkamtib was replaced by the Bakorstanas which had weaker authority.

executive branch of the civil administration, the top ranks of the diplomatic and consular corps, and business enterprises like Pertamina, the oil conglomerate. The provincial and local governments were also opened to military officers, including the post of village headman which usually went to army sergeants or policemen.

Thus benefits were allocated in exchange for control. The political structure of the military demonstrated the operations of a patron–client relationship. Its history demonstrated that as long as consensus was maintained, benefits would flow from the centre outwards.

Thailand

Not all states were rent by the same extent of communal or ethnic divisions as Indonesia or Malaysia. In Thailand, for example, there is a single tradition accepted by a unified nation, usually expressed in terms of Buddhism and the monarchy. This does not deny the existence of 'counter-structures'. The Muslims in southern Thailand represent a distinctly different tradition. Thailand is also not without its share of upland minority tribespeople. On the whole, however, these 'counter-structures' did not alter the major configurations of the Thai state.

Thailand has been called a 'consensus polity'.[28] For the greater part of Thai history, the monarchy was the focus of this consensus; it continues to be the source of political legitimacy and the reference point for national unity. The military-led revolution of 1932 displaced the political influence of the monarchy as a structure, although there was little change in the relationship between the monarch and the subject. Its incumbent since the end of World War II, Phumiphon Adulyadej, was able to mould the monarchy as an effective political tool. He ascended the throne in June 1946, after the death of his brother, the king, under mysterious circumstances. In 1950, he was crowned King Rama IX. By that time, the army was in control of the nation's political process and it was led by Field Marshal Phibun who had participated in the events of 1932 which led to the overthrow of the absolute monarchy. For the first seven years, the king distanced himself from the government.

In terms of executive power, the monarch was displaced by the bureaucracy—another political structure of note. The bureaucracy consisted mainly of ambitious civil servants and military officers. Its expansion took place under the early modernizing rulers of Thailand. A number of reasons account for its importance and continued prominence after 1945. Since Thailand was not colonized, and in fact embarked on a large-scale modernization programme under its kings, the bureaucratic élite remained in power and its influence was enhanced by its expansion. Its economic strength remained intact because its traditional role of extracting tribute on agricultural production and trade remained unaffected. Despite the commercialization of rice production, no new socio-political groups emerged to challenge the bureaucratic élite. For example, a landlord class did not

---

[28] David Morell and Chai-anan Samudavanija, *Political Conflict in Thailand: Reform, Reaction, Revolution*, Cambridge, Mass., 1981, Part 1.

emerge since tenancy was not a serious problem. Peasants without land did not have to seek patronage from a landlord class since there was land aplenty to exploit. The Thai political structure therefore remained in essence the same for a considerable length of time after 1945—a bureaucratic élite lording it over a large peasant mass.

This pattern of political structures—the monarchy and the bureaucracy—operated on the organizing principle of hierarchy. It has been said that 'Thais accept the fact that there are two categories of people: the powerful and the powerless, the important and the unimportant, the older and the younger . . .'.[29] Any analysis of political structures cannot evade the problem of authority. The sense of superordination and subordination constituted an intrinsic part of interpersonal relations. This notion of authority could even be detected in linguistic patterns of address in the Thai language.[30] It is therefore not strange that in Thailand, consensus was expressed by its leaders acting through the bureaucracy or the monarchy. Personalism remained the preferred expression of political action. What was important was not the institutionalization of new organizations or structures but the existence of leaders who could command confidence. The leader became the focal point. Such were the cases of King Chulalongkorn, Field Marshal Phibun, Field Marshal Sarit Thanarat. These leaders all fulfilled the function of a reference point in their lifetimes.[31]

Political activities were limited to a small ruling élite. The greater part of the Thai population had no share in the court intrigues or political manoeuvres. The dominance of this élite can also explain the weakness of radical alternatives to it. Because the commercialization of agriculture was confined to rice, which was the staple crop grown since time immemorial, there was little disruption to traditional patterns of political structure. This, coupled with the fact that land was relatively easily available, meant that radical intellectuals could not hope to attract the peasantry. Indeed, the Communist Party of Thailand was already formed in the early 1940s; it did not gain much support from the central plains area till the 1960s when tenancy began to pose a problem and the ratio of people to land began to worsen. Its base was confined to the northeast, which was poor and populated by people different from those in the central plains.

From 1947, it was the military group within the bureaucracy that was dominant. In that year, a coup on 8 November paved the way for the return of Phibun. The coup was a reaction against the former civilian government's concessions to the Allied war powers. These were viewed as damaging to the economy and humiliating to the monarchy. Moreover, that civilian government's recognition of the Soviet Union, the repeal of the anti-communist act, and the increased agitation in the Chinese community smacked of communism with its radical agrarian tendencies.

The 1947 coup was also important because it marked the emergence of Sarit Thanarat in national politics. Sarit was then a colonel and military commander of the 1st Regiment in the army's strategic First Division,

[29] Cited in Morell and Chai-anan, 22–3.
[30] Herbert P. Phillips, *Thai Peasant Personality: the Patterning of Interpersonal Behavior in the Village of Bang Chan*, Berkeley and Los Angeles, 1966, 143.
[31] Chai-Anan Samudavanija, *The Thai Young Turks*, Singapore: ISEAS, 1982, 2.

based in the Bangkok region. Knowing that many of his fellow officers wanted to take part in the coup, he realized that he had to lend his support if he wanted to retain his popularity among them. Sarit himself launched a coup in 1957 which put him in power. Sarit's coup of 1957 marked the start of a 'revolution' in the sense that he tried to re-examine the political concepts that Phibun had borrowed from the West and give them a Thai flavour. This was not at all surprising because the promoters of the coup were the products of indigenous training. Sarit and his colleagues had started their careers during the Great Depression of the 1930s when there were no funds for study abroad. It was only in the 1950s that military officers were sent to the United States for training.

Sarit's own view of democracy centred on the need for it to be indigenous. He made a colourful analogy: 'Let us hope that our democracy is like a plant having deep roots in Thai soil. It should grow amidst the beating sun and whipping rain. It should produce bananas, mangoes, rambutans, mangosteens, and durians; and not apples, grapes, dates, plums, or horse chestnuts.'[32] The fundamental values he wanted to protect were the three ideals of king, religion and nation.

Sarit deliberately set out to cultivate the throne. None of the coup leaders could afford to offend the monarchy but it was clear that tension existed between the king and the country's leaders at various times after 1945 until Sarit became the sole leader in 1957. Phibun had been able to sideline the king because his own credentials dated back to the 1932 revolution, and because the king was still young and inexperienced. Sarit, however, treated the monarchy differently. He had no other credentials except that there were popular demands to remove the corrupt Phibun régime. He was therefore compelled to turn to the monarch for support and, indeed, one of his stated aims in the coup of 1957 was the need to protect the throne. Under Sarit's leadership, the king was given a greater role domestically and internationally. Through this exposure, the king was made to identify with the policies of the régime and thus enhance its prestige.

Domestically, for example, Sarit tried to identify the monarch with the army. The swearing of allegiance by the troops to the throne and flag became major military occasions under Sarit. The army's 21st Regiment was transferred to palace duties, and the queen became its honorary commanding colonel. The king also accepted various honorary command positions. Traditional ceremonies associated with the monarchy and also with Buddhism, discontinued since the 1932 revolution, were revived. The royal *kathin* procession, a Buddhist monarchist ceremony, was one such example. The exposure of the king to foreign countries began in late 1959 and early 1960. Three neighbouring countries were toured, south Vietnam, Indonesia and Burma. The visits were a major public-relations success for Sarit, who was not considered as 'sophisticated' in the Western sense because, totally trained and educated in Thailand, he did not have a good command of English. On the other hand, Rama IX had grown up in many foreign countries and was used to foreign ways. His beautiful consort was

---

[32] Thak Chaloemtiarana, *Thailand: the Politics of Despotic Paternalism*, Bangkok, 1979, 158.

another advantage. From 1960 till 1963 when Sarit died, the king made many trips, especially to those countries with monarchies.

Religion was another pillar in the Sarit political structure. The state religion in Thailand was Theravāda Buddhism which was different from the Mahāyāna Buddhism of Vietnam, Japan and China. An estimated 93.4 per cent of the Thai were Buddhists. This meant that the network of masses, monkhood and monarchy was very strong. The layman enters the monkhood and the monarchy has been a principal supporter of the monkhood for centuries. However, while the relationship between the masses and the monkhood was based to a large extent on personal ties, that between the monkhood and the monarchy (or the constitutional government after 1932) could not be taken for granted.

The religious order could be abused and used as a place for political refuge by anyone who merely shaved his head or donned the saffron robe. For the purpose of studying the hierarchy of the Buddhist Church in the postwar period, reference must be made to the Buddhist Order Act passed earlier in 1941. Under this scheme, a Supreme Patriarch was appointed by the king. The former would preside over an Ecclesiastical Assembly, an Ecclesiastical Cabinet and the Ecclesiastical Courts, each with separate powers to balance the influence of one another. This worked well, until two sects started squabbling over the appointment of a successor to the Supreme Patriarch who died in 1958.

The quarrels started shortly after Sarit came to power. As he was trying to enhance traditional Thai values of which Buddhism was one, the discord within the Buddhist hierarchy took place at an inappropriate moment. In 1962, he initiated measures to bring the monkhood under control. He pushed through the establishment of a centralized system under a Supreme Patriarch with strong authority. He abolished the checks and balances within the structure. As the Supreme Patriarch was a royal appointee, control over the Buddhist hierarchy was ensured.

Sarit believed that the ideal was a hierarchical political structure of three segments: government, bureaucracy and people. His preference was definitely not for a system of political parties with vertical links to the constituents. The three segments that constituted his political structure were intended to be static, and Sarit's policies and programmes were designed to maintain the boundaries between the hierarchical sectors.

Government, Sarit's first-order segment, must be paternalistic, despotic and benevolent. This was his expressed view at the 1959 Conference of Vice-Governors and District Chiefs:

> The principle to which I refer is the principle of *pho ban pho muang* [father of the family, father of the nation]. The nation is like a large family. Provincial Governors, Vice-Governors, District Chiefs are like the heads of various families. So it should be engraved on the minds of all administrative officials that the people under their jurisdiction are not just other people but their own relatives.[33]

---

[33] Quoted in Toru Yano, 'Political Structure of a "Rice-Growing State"' in Yoneo Ishii, ed., *Thailand: Rice-Growing Society*, Honolulu, 1978, 143.

POLITICAL STRUCTURES 441

Bureaucracy, Sarit's second-order segment, was the loyal servant of his benevolent paternalism. An oft-quoted statement attributed to him illustrates this view:

I feel all of you [the bureaucrats] are my eyes and ears and heart toward the people. I am deeply concerned for the happiness and well-being of my people and I would like you to represent my concern. I want you to offer the people love and enthusiasm. I want you to help me hear, see, and above all think ... You occupy the same position as the old *khaluang tangcai* [local governors representing the king]; in short, I want you always to remember that you are representatives of my feelings. I love the people and I intend to devote myself to them and in the same way I want you to love the people and devote yourselves to them.[34]

Concerning the people, Sarit's idea of their position in the nation was clear and simple. They should have a livelihood and a place to live.[35]

Finally, if this static political structure could not continue in existence, there was always the army as another political structure to depend upon in the last resort. By Sarit's time, the Thai army had assumed the character of an internal force to be deployed for internal security. Even in the nineteenth century, there was no need for an army to defend Thailand from external invasions.

However, the army's importance was not solely as an internal political structure. It also served as a conduit by which foreign inputs were injected into the domestic political structure. This characteristic could first be observed soon after World War II. At that time, the British recommended that sanctions be applied to the Thai armed forces for fighting with the Japanese. However, the United States viewed this as continued interference in Thailand's domestic affairs. Thus the structure of Thailand's armed force remained intact after World War II and the unreconstructed army, used to power, could be expected to demand a major share of the government. Prime Minister Phibun immediately exploited the favour shown by the United States, then the world's superpower, by aligning Thailand with the fight against international communism. The United States accepted this support because the period after 1948 was characterized by the Cold War, and by communist successes in Czechoslovakia, China, Malaya, Vietnam and elsewhere. It was important for the United States to support strong, stable régimes, and military-led governments seemed to fit the bill.

The Thai–American relationship became mutually reinforcing. In July 1950, Phibun offered to send troops and rice to support the American war effort in Korea. The Americans responded by instituting the Fulbright educational exchange agreement and the Economic and Technical Cooperation Agreement of 19 September 1950. World Bank loans were secured for Thailand and military assistance was initiated in October 1950. In 1954, Thailand joined SEATO. When Sarit became prime minister, the United States viewed him as the perfect strongman with the power to act

34 Quoted in ibid., 143.
35 ibid.

decisively, often in their interests. Sarit's tough no-nonsense approach to government confirmed the American opinion of him. Strikes were banned; unions were dissolved; branches of foreign corporations were permitted to purchase land, gain exemption from taxation and freely import technicians, often bypassing the existing immigration laws. In turn, the United States decided to make Bangkok its regional headquarters for various activities. This support continued after the death of Sarit. In fact, under the latter's heirs—Thanom and Praphat—Thailand became a huge American base. By 1968, there were 50,000 American servicemen on Thai soil and this visible presence generated a boom in the construction, service and other sectors.[36]

The extended discussion on Sarit[37] is necessary because the consequences of his policies had a serious impact on the political structures in Thailand in subsequent years. They helped to create a new economic bourgeoisie. One of the most important of the policies was the lifting of the existing limit of 50 *rai* (about 8 hectares) on landholding. This policy laid the basis for large-scale speculation, especially in those areas where Americans intended to build major strategic highways. Land speculators with inside information bought huge tracts of strategically located land and sold them at high profits. Subsistence farmers were turned into tenants. By the 1960s, an increasingly large number of farms in the Bangkok area were no longer owner-operated. Thailand began to experience the dislocating effects of rural indebtedness and absentee landlordism that it had escaped because it was never colonized. The dispossessed led the exodus to Bangkok where they were unemployed, underemployed, or worked in the service sectors. Simultaneously, the new prosperity originating from American and Japanese investments created a great demand for education. In 1961, there were 15,000 students enrolled in a total of five universities. By 1972, the total was to reach 100,000 in seventeen universities.[38]

By the year of Sarit's death in 1963, an increasingly volatile situation both in the rural and urban areas was bequeathed to three strongmen: Field Marshal Thanom Kittikachorn, Field Marshal Praphat Charusathien and General Kris Sivara. This triumvirate, with Thanom as the prime minister, continued Sarit's policies. However, their weakness became evident as the forces of change impinged upon Thailand. Thanom, for example, did not exercise the same degree of control over the army as Sarit had. Praphat's commercial activities led to his being tainted with corruption and shady business deals.

With Sarit's passing, opposition began to coalesce around various alternative political structures. One of these was the revolutionary insurgents in the rural areas, mainly those identified with the Communist Party of Thailand. Communism, it should be noted, had always been regarded as contrary to traditional Thai values and Buddhist principles. Sarit and his

---

[36] Ben Anderson, 'Withdrawal Symptoms: Social and Cultural Aspects of the October 6 Coup', *Bulletin of Concerned Asian Scholars*, 9, 3 (1977) 15.
[37] The discussion on Sarit is based largely on Thak, *Thailand: the Politics of Despotic Paternalism*, Bangkok, 1979, *passim*.
[38] Anderson, 'Withdrawal Symptoms', 16.

successors were strong anti-communists. However, their neglect of the territories in the northeast broadened the basis for party recruitment. By 1973 the party constituted an alternative political structure that expressed an ideology different from king, religion and nation.

Farmers in the north and central plains of Thailand also experienced greater rural indebtedness, high rates of tenancy and rocketing land rents. Low productivity, low incomes, and land fragmentation became bugbears that somehow would not disappear. To be sure, these problems did not suddenly erupt in the 1970s. However, they simmered near the surface— neglected by a Bangkok government that never considered farmers in terms of meaningful political structures.

In the urban areas, students provided the framework for another political structure. Although students were not always politically passive, they were more concerned with problems on their own campuses prior to 1972 than with national issues. In that year, the National Student Centre of Thailand, an organization that had been revived in late 1969, spearheaded a public campaign to boycott Japanese goods. This move earned the centre its nationalist credentials, because Thailand was then suffering from a trade deficit with Japan. In October 1973, against a background of rice shortages in Bangkok, rising cost of living, and graft, the students led demonstrations in Bangkok. Violence erupted, and on 14 October, the nation was stunned when the king ordered Thanom, Praphat and Narong (Thanom's son and Praphat's son-in-law) into exile.

It is not the intention here to give the impression that the military-led government could be easily demolished by student groups feeding on general dissatisfaction in the country. The pressure from the students would not have produced results if the king had not intervened on their behalf. By 1973, King Phumiphon had ruled for twenty-seven years. Meanwhile, elections had been held, constitutions had been written and discarded, and cabinets had been formed and dissolved. The king continued in office through all these political vicissitudes. When he recognized that the military-led government was unpopular because it was unresponsive, he withdrew his support and it fell.

The downfall of Thanom and Praphat and the passing of the old Sarit order marked the onset of a three-year interregnum of open politics. This period was characterized by violence and conflict, against a background of aggressive communist threats. It was also marked by a bold experiment in democracy, the like of which Thailand had never experienced before. A new draft constitution was written in 1974, and it was decidedly ultra-liberal. It provided for the removal of many institutional devices by which the bureaucracy—civil as well as military—had dominated the mainstream political structure since 1932. To approve the draft constitution, a new National Assembly was elected pending national elections for a new legislature. Members of the new National Assembly, however, turned out to be no different from the representatives of the old élite, although the number of military and police representatives that were chosen was remarkably small. The liberal provisions of the draft constitution did not survive the review of the National Assembly.

The return to conservatism showed that the downfall of the military-led government in October 1973 was at least as much a result of internal military intrigues as of student pressure. From November 1971 onwards, the Thanom government had become faction-ridden mainly because of the likelihood that the unpopular Narong would succeed Thanom. General Kris Sivara led the faction that opposed Thanom and Praphat on this matter. The students served his faction well. In late 1973 and early 1974, they continued to attack those politicians and military leaders who supported Thanom and Praphat. This again was welcomed by Kris as a measure to enhance the power of his own faction.

The king's support for the students was also not a sign of disapproval of the military. In fact, by 1976, the monarchy was firmly in support of the military again. To a large extent, this was due to the king's perception that open politics as pursued since 1973 were tearing the fabric of the nation and undermining the monarchy. The post-1973 period was a golden opportunity for political parties—hitherto subservient to military dictates—to emerge as power brokers. Political parties of the right, left and centre proliferated. A coalition government, formed after the 1975 election, consisted of three parties—Social Action, Thai Nation, and Social Justice. However, there was no co-ordination and, in fact, three 'minigovernments'[39] existed. As a result of pressure from the military an election was called in April 1976. This turned out to be a bloody affair, augmenting the popular conviction that politics was disreputable (*'len kan muang'*, a pejorative phrase suggesting that politics was an unprofessional, dirty and treacherous game). It should be noted that Thai political parties were not mass parties but parliamentary clubs that gave prominence to personal interests and individual links. Ideology or platform did not constitute the basis of party organization. When interests changed, party affiliation also changed. Permanent attachment to a party could be ensured only if there were incentives (monetary or otherwise) to stay. One Thai cabinet minister said: 'politicians are like birds sitting on a tree. The tree is analogous to the political party. When the tree bears lots of fruits, i.e, plentiful money and privileges, MP's will leave their parties and join it.'[40] To make things worse, the period from October 1973 was characterized by widespread strike action in Bangkok. All these events occurred against a backdrop of the reunification of north and south Vietnam, the frenzied retreat from Saigon by United States forces, and the fall of Laos and Cambodia to communist control. The profound sense of insecurity and uncertainty could not but influence the nation in general and the king in particular. The message was clear: insecurity threatened, and even the Chakri dynasty might be swept aside.

The reaction to open politics encouraged rightist groups like the Nawaphon, the Red Gaurs and the Village Scouts to be active. They were supported by the military and business groups, the latter fearful that the confusion in Thailand would harm their finances. The Village Scouts even received royal patronage. In October 1976, bloody clashes took place between students and rightist groups. On 6 October 1976, military units

[39] Morell and Chai-anan Samudavanija, 261.
[40] Thak, 63.

seized power from the civilian Seni government. Thus Thailand returned to military dominance and royal legitimacy after only three years.

However, the period after October 1976 was not merely a return to the consensual polity of the monarchy and the bureaucracy. The military had become faction-ridden in the absence of strong men. Its leaders no longer served their early years in the strategic command of the Bangkok troops, as had been the case with Sarit, Thanom, Praphat and Kris. In fact, the leader of the October 1976 coup was an admiral, Sangad Chaloryu. The new prime minister who was eventually appointed, General Kriangsak Chomanand, did not have experience in army troop commands. His power base within the military was extremely narrow. The same was true of the next prime minister, General Prem Tinsulanond. He had to rely on the politicians, especially the members of the Social Action Party, for support. That made it necessary for him and for other military leaders to get entangled in the strange world of political bargaining and compromises. The machinations that abounded gave the impression that the military was weak and losing direction. Factions within the military began to manoeuvre in an attempt to save the situation. A faction known as the Young Military Officers Group (or more popularly the Young Turks) was formed to find a solution. The group argued that the executive should be given strong political power to solve the problems of social and economic injustice. Only after that could a more open and participatory political system be gradually established. In 1981, the Young Turks led a coup against the Prem government, hoping to get their viewpoint accepted. However, they failed to prevent Prem from establishing a counter-coup headquarters in Korat, 260 kilometres northeast of Bangkok, with the royal family accompanying him. From Korat, General Prem made repeated broadcasts that the royal family was safe with him. That sealed the fate of the coup leaders, and ensured Prem's continuance in power. The abortive coup demonstrated that the monarchy was confirmed as the most significant political structure in Thailand. The leader who received royal endorsement was the one accepted by the state as the ruler.

This returns the discussion to the point made earlier that Thailand was a consensual polity with the monarchy as a principal focus. The pluralistic political structures of 1973–6 were an interregnum in Thailand's history of maximum government.

Burma: Ne Win

If Sarit was in full control of a monolithic structure, the neighbouring state in Burma was in disarray when General Ne Win assumed power after the coup of 1962. Ethnic consensus was lacking. Political feuds had racked the previous government of U Nu. Ne Win considered it his task to overcome the disintegrative tendencies. In the course of establishing political structures to achieve that goal, maximum government was also developed.

While U Nu's government was partisan, sectarian and communal, Ne Win planned to recast the political structures as non-partisan, non-sectarian and non-ethnic.[41] To a large extent, Ne Win's political models were drawn from his civil-war experience in the late 1940s.

The political structure that was created immediately after the coup of 1962 was the Revolutionary Council. The council combined all the powers of the state. It ruled by decree till 1974 when a new constitution was promulgated. The chairman was Ne Win.

Soon after the coup, the Revolutionary Council issued an ideological statement, The Burmese Way to Socialism (BWS), which served as a guide to government policies. The statement of belief read as follows:

> The revolutionary council of the union of Burma does not believe that man will be set free from social evils as long as pernicious economic systems exist in which man exploits man and lives on the fat of such appropriation. The Council believes it to be possible only when exploitation of man by man is brought to an end and a socialist economy based on justice is established; only then can all people, irrespective of race or religion, be emancipated from all social evils and set free from anxieties over food, clothing and shelter, and from inability to resist evil, for an empty stomach is not conducive to wholesome morality, as the Burmese saying goes; only then can an affluent state of social development be reached and all people be happy and healthy in mind and body.
>
> Thus affirmed in this belief the Revolutionary Council is resolved to march unswervingly and arm-in-arm with the people of the Union of Burma towards the goal of socialism.[42]

The purpose of the statement was to focus loyalty on as well as to mobilize popular support for the political structures of the state. Generally, the BWS specified that the state rested upon the people and not on a narrow capitalist or landlord class. The anti-capitalist and anti-imperialist rhetoric was derived from the civil-war experiences of the military. The BWS was also against parliamentary democracy, noting that it had failed to achieve unity under the previous government led by U Nu. A week after the proclamation of the new ideology, Ne Win commented that 'parliamentary democracy contains too many loopholes for abuse to be of value to a country like Burma'.[43] Inherent in the plan of action was the establishment of a single party that would lead the state to socialism.

The BWS was non-partisan because its socialist roots were indigenously Burmese. Drawing on experience of the civil war from 1948 to 1949, Ne Win tried to reconcile warring factions divided on ideology. When the Burmese Communist Party revolted against U Nu's government in March 1948, army officers had been compelled to support one against the other. This tore the army apart. Although Ne Win identified himself with U Nu, he appreciated the necessity of seeking accommodation with the communists too. The BWS can therefore be viewed as an attempt to establish consensus among opposing factions. He tried to unite the three major political parties in an effort to form a single national party, somewhat

[41] Robert H. Taylor, 'Burma' in Ahmad and Crouch, eds, 36.
[42] Roger M. Smith, ed, *Southeast Asia*, 134.
[43] Fred R. von der Mehden, 'The Burmese Way to Socialism' *Asian Survey*, III, 3 (1963) 132.

in the image of Aung San's AFPFL of 1945. The poor response led Ne Win to create a new party in 1962 called the Burma Socialist Programme Party (BSPP), also called the Burmese Way to Socialism Party or Lanzin in Burmese. Its aim was to steer the country towards the ideological goals of the BWS. At the beginning, it was not conceived as a mass party. Its members were individual cadres drawn mainly from the police and the military. Because of its urban bias, the Lanzin did not succeed in recruiting peasants. Minorities did not join, because they favoured a multi-party system which would ensure the articulation of their own interests by ethnic-based groups. In 1971, Lanzin was reconstituted as a mass party in an attempt to project a national image in a one-party political structure, but apparently this move only brought in members less committed to the party's ideology and more interested in securing favours or positions of power.

In his search for non-sectarian political structures, Ne Win showed that even during the caretaker period of 1958–60, he was against the religious practices of U Nu by lifting the ban on cattle slaughter and *nat* (spirit) worship. In 1959, Ne Win launched the 'Buddhism in Danger' campaign to prevent communist subversion of the Buddhist Church. However, this was seen as a cynical attempt to rally the Buddhists against U Nu, since only the monks who supported U Nu's political opponents participated in the campaign. Ne Win's non-sectarian stand led to the overwhelming electoral gains of U Nu in 1960. From 1962, however, Ne Win remained undaunted in pursuing his non-sectarian goals. He was firmly convinced that U Nu's promise to make Buddhism the state religion was divisive. Thus he was most intent on restricting the political activities of the Buddhist monks. In 1962, for example, he required all monks to register. This was aimed at the individual who wished to pass himself off as a monk by merely shaving his head and donning the yellow robe. In April 1964, the Revolutionary Council decreed that all Buddhist organizations must vow not to engage in political activities, though this had to be rescinded in May after protests. In March 1965, the Revolutionary Council sponsored a Buddhist conference which, among other things, outlined a programme of religious education reform. Several monasteries and individual monks objected to the results of the conference and Ne Win had to move forcefully against them. Subsequently Buddhist clergy were excluded from voting or holding office in many kinds of organizations.

Ne Win was also intent on destroying the autonomous ethnic political structures that U Nu had allowed to develop. Again, his civil-war experience reinforced his distaste for organizations based on ethnic grouping. In 1948, the army was still organized on a communal basis, and ethnic loyalty rather than loyalty to the state was the operating principle. In December of that year, Karen and then Kachin units revolted. They even succeeded in controlling the northen town of Mandalay briefly in 1949. Ne Win was left with the task of fighting the ethnic army rebels at the same time as fighting those army units that had joined the communists in revolt.

Therefore, it was understandable that shortly after the coup in 1962, Ne Win ordered the arrest or removal of hereditary leaders, especially among the Shans. Then the state councils with their chief ministers were abolished. In their place, state supreme councils consisting of local civilian leaders and military commanders were established, and these were linked in a hierarchy all the way up to the Revolutionary Council. The success of this administrative measure depended, of course, on whether the new leaders could displace loyalty to those who were jailed or leading the armed struggle. As well as the new administrative structure, the mailed fist was also employed as Ne Win deployed the Burmese army against the insurgents. However, military campaigns were never really successful, in part because of the difficult terrain. The continued challenge posed by the ethnic minorities can therefore be viewed as providing an alternative political structure to that of Ne Win. But the minorities were ultimately a peripheral, not mainstream, structure. They did not try to exploit the situation when the military government broke down for two to three months in 1988. The power structure ultimately lay in central Burma.

The potency of the ethnic political structures should not therefore be overstated. For example, secession especially among the Shan states was a much publicized threat to consensus in Burma. But what secession really meant is not easy to explain. True, the Shan were close linguistic relations of the Thai. In the nineteenth century, some Shan princes were sent to Bangkok to be raised and trained. However, the Shan ethnic and political identity also depended historically on the claim that the Shan system of principalities was connected with the Burman kingdom of Pagan. Shan Theravāda Buddhism was more akin to the Burmese style rather than the Thai. Much of the Shan language was influenced by Burmese, which made it less understood in Thailand.[44]

Despite the facade of non-partisanship, non-sectarianism and non-ethnicity, the enigma of Ne Win remained. Until the coup of 1962, Ne Win portrayed himself as a reluctant leader. Yet it was clear that Ne Win was the Revolutionary Council. Although there was a small military oligarchy in the council, it was Ne Win who called the shots. At the beginning, Ne Win's closest advisers were Brigadiers Aung Gyi and Tin Pe. However, when Aung Gyi disagreed with Ne Win over the pace and direction of socialism in Burma, he resigned in 1963 and was retired from the army. When the economic policies of Tin Pe failed, he too resigned in 1968. The next confidant until 1974 was Brigadier San Yu. Some civilians like U Ba Nyein and Dr Maung Maung were also appointed to the Revolutionary Council. The ease with which Ne Win dropped an individual from the council and supported another suggested the power he exercised. Even though he retired from the military in 1971 and entrusted the civil administration to a prime minister in 1974, he was still acknowledged as the leader in control. Ne Win himself did not promote a personality cult. Though his portrait was hung in government offices, it was always next to Aung San's. Indeed, it could be conjectured that a principal political structure in Burma was the Aung San–Ne Win complex. Ne Win was one of the Thirty Comrades and, indeed, a syndrome akin to that of China's Long March had been created in Burma, drawing upon the reputation of Aung San. This reservoir of legendary exploits was a major source of legitimacy for Ne

[44] F. K. Lehman, ed., *Military Rule in Burma since 1962*, Singapore, 1981, 2.

Win's political structures. When Ne Win established the Revolutionary Council in 1962, the inspiration was attributed to Aung San:

> The correctness and sagacity of the action of the Revolutionary Council will be fully appreciated if we consider only for a moment what the Founder of our Independence *Bogyoke Gyi* Aung San himself would have done in the situation that has just obtained if he were alive today. *No sane person would have doubted that the same steps would have been taken by that indomitable leader.*[45]

In the same vein, the BWS, the 'Revolution' (Ne Win's name for his period of rule) and the Lanzin were all attributed to the inspiration of Aung San. In fact, the Socialist Republic of Burma was the greatest tribute to Aung San. Since 1962, Aung San had also been cast as the fourth Great Unifier of Burma (after Anawrahta, Bayinnaung and Alaungpaya), and since Ne Win's portrait was often posted in government buildings in the company of Aung San, it could be argued that, by extension, Ne Win was identified with Aung San as a unifier.[46]

The power that Ne Win exercised in the political structure was, of course, backed by the Burmese army. The latter was a very confident group. It had overcome factionalism within itself. At the same time, it saved the civilian government of the day from the threats of the communist and ethnic rebels. With no or little foreign help, Ne Win's army was forced to rely on its own resilience to discharge its duties. The civilian politicians had little to offer by way of assistance. This accounted for the substantial claims throughout the 1950s on the national budget for internal security, one-third or even half of the total amount. The army budget was not challenged[47] and the army remained well-treated and well-provided compared to the rest of the population.

The Burmese army, however, was not impervious to change, even though the political leadership remained unchanged. Since 1962, the population in Burma had doubled. Large sectors of the official economy had disintegrated—a testimony to Ne Win's preference for self-reliance. In its stead a black market flourished. Opposition groups within Burma proper—principally students[48]—proliferated in an inchoate mass. Amidst all these changes, one thing became clear: Burma under Ne Win had hardly begun to address the economic issues that neighbouring Southeast Asian countries had tackled years before. Questions about Ne Win's leadership emerged.

In 1988, students launched massive demonstrations in Rangoon in a bid to topple Ne Win. For a period, Burma's government was paralysed or disintegrated. Ne Win resigned but in September 1988, the military made

[45] Jon A. Wiant and David I. Steinberg, 'Burma: The Military and National Development' in Soedjati Djiwandono and Yong Mun Cheong, eds, 301.
[46] ibid.
[47] Taylor, 'Burma', in Ahmad and Crouch, eds, 27.
[48] Students posed the strongest urban challenge to Ne Win. In 1974, students combined with workers to protest against inflation and food shortages. In the course of ending the protests, schools and universities were closed. Protests occurred again in December 1974 at the funeral of the former United Nations Secretary-General, U Thant, and again in 1975 when students camped at the Shwedagon Pagoda in protest.

a come-back and formed a Council for the Restoration of Law and Order. The events of September 1988 were likened to the military's taking over from the U Nu government in 1958. In both cases, the military intervened to re-establish political and economic order so that elections could be held.[49] However, the military in 1988 was no longer the same as that of 1958 or even 1962. The events in 1988 revealed that the military as a political structure was not the monolith of the earlier years.

In 1962, the Revolutionary Council comprised military officers who had forged bonds during the days of the Thirty Comrades. There was also a common desire to consolidate political power. These factors bound the Revolutionary Council together as a solid political structure.

However, as the years progressed, old comrades died, and the shared experience in the independence struggle disappeared as a bonding agent. Current issues also overshadowed history. After 1962, the Burmese military was required to second officers to new party organizations and government postings. Commanders who were then concentrated on fighting the insurgents took the opportunity to transfer their unwanted officers to administrative and party positions. This practice turned out to be a mistake. When the BSPP was transformed from a cadre to a mass party in 1971 and the First Party Congress was convened, combat officers found that their seconded party officers were now in charge. Much of the political manoeuvring in the subsequent party congresses was a reflection of this contest between combat and party officers, culminating in the victory of the combat officers after 1973. The latter, after all, commanded the field units and they would be pivotal in determining policy.[50]

In 1988, effective power lay with the combat officers. They had earned their spurs fighting against ethnic insurgents, not against British or Japanese soldiers as in Ne Win's generation. Many of these officers had observed that the old BWS had contributed to the economic mess that led to the student riots from the mid-1970s. Observers did not, however, rule out Ne Win's continued influence.

Singapore

Singapore shares with some other Southern Asian states political structures which allow for maximum government. However, while states like Indonesia, Burma, and the Philippines under Marcos fashioned their political structures in accordance with domestic needs, Singapore's political structures were shaped to a large extent by the external environment. Because the population was overwhelmingly ethnic Chinese, the communal pressure to identify Singapore with nearby China—a legitimate regional power—was very strong. Yet Singapore had always been located in a Malay world. Close affinity with China could interfere with the search for a consensus and arouse the suspicion of minorities. More cogently, it would definitely colour the perception of neighbouring states of what nationhood in Singapore meant.

[49] See Robert H. Taylor's article reprinted in the *Straits Times* (Singapore), 13 Feb. 1989, 20.
[50] Jon Wiant, 'Tradition in the Service of Revolution: the Political Symbolism of Taw-hlan-ye-khit', in Lehman, ed., 70–1.

The choice of a merged political structure within Malaysia was compelled, in part, by this external environment. There were, of course, domestic economic reasons why Singapore chose to join Malaysia. However, equally if not more important was the need to correct the leftward drift of communal politics among the Chinese-educated in Singapore. The most vibrant pre-Malaysia political structure of Singapore consisted primarily of the masses—students and workers—mobilized by the communist united front acting within the People's Action Party. Overt communist activities were declared illegal in 1948 and remained outlawed. It was hoped that with membership in a Malay-led Federation of Malaysia, the radical agitation of the Chinese-educated left wing would be circumscribed and even reduced to manageable proportions by a government in Kuala Lumpur which had fought communism since 1948. The Malaysia strategy was pushed by the English-educated Chinese leader, Lee Kuan Yew, together with non-Chinese colleagues in the moderate wing of the PAP. Even before Malaysia was formed, there were detentions without trial under the draconian Internal Security Act in 1961 with the connivance of the Kuala Lumpur government; these were harbingers of what could happen once Singapore entered the federation and internal security became a federal concern.

The Malaysian experience had a considerable impact upon the political structures of Singapore. First, for the PAP—the dominant political party—the emasculation of the left-wing resulted in the consolidation of a more cohesive political structure controlled by the English-educated moderates alone. Second, the confrontation between the communal structures of peninsular Malaya and the non-communal 'Malaysian Malaysia' group convinced Singapore leaders that multiracialism was the key to consensus. Third, it confirmed that Singapore's political structures could not be isolated from the external environment. Singapore joined Malaysia with restrictions on the rights of its Chinese citizens to vote other than in the island only. Despite this, Malay extremists in UMNO attempted to discredit Lee and participated in the Singapore general elections of 1964 to win the support of the Malay minority, thereby gaining a foothold in the political structure. Also, the structure of Singapore as a member state in a federal entity was challenged by Sukarno's *konfrontasi* (confrontation). The confrontation was a mixture of issues like neo-colonialism, ethnicity, hegemony and leadership in Southeast Asia, and Chinese dominance over trade. Thus it seemed that even changes in the political structure of Singapore could not be implemented without the endorsement of regional neighbours. Finally, with Singapore's exit from Malaysia, the issue of survival became imperative. In a crisis of that magnitude, political structures that stressed consensus and agreement on broad common goals found a fertile field for development. The economic security that statehood in Malaysia had conferred evaporated overnight. Yet Singapore had to make a living. Its only recourse was to plug into the global network of trade and investments. This meant further entanglement in an external environment that its political structures would not be able to control. The most it could do was to put its own house in order. Thus the management of its domestic political structures was crucial.

Lee began a programme of action to ensure that the dissent that characterized the 1950s would not be repeated. In the end, the measures adopted were so thorough that Singapore as a whole resembled a monolithic political structure in support of the leadership of Lee. Lee's no-nonsense style of government gave the structure an effectiveness that would not be possible under another kind of leadership. He stressed that there must be a core group within the cabinet to take tough and immediate decisions. In an interview with the *International Herald Tribune*, Lee had this to say about decisiveness: 'If you like good, you've got to oppose bad. If you want honesty, you fight and kill corruption. If you want men with principles, you must destroy men without principles. There are no halfway houses.'[51] Lee's use of the Internal Security Act to nip in the bud dangerous sources of opposition that would undermine the existing political structures was likened to a karate chop—clean, specific, direct and, of course, effective.

Parallel with this management style was the extension of Lee's control over parapolitical and parastatal structures.[52] One group of parapolitical bodies was the trade unions. In the 1950s, it was the control of the trade unions by the left-wingers within the PAP that gave them such great influence within the party. By 1965, the PAP-supported National Trades Union Congress (NTUC) had gained control over the trade unions from the left-wing Singapore Association of Trade Unions. The NTUC's main platform was to call upon the trade unions to discard their narrow self-interest and to 'modernize' by working towards accommodating rather than confronting government and the employers. Thereafter, with the support of the PAP, the NTUC leadership—which itself was drawn from the PAP ranks—reduced emphasis on its collective bargaining role and expanded upon its social role to provide members with educational, recreational and business opportunities. In 1972, the government set up the National Wages Council which was a tripartite wage-negotiation body consisting of labour, employers and the government. This further eroded the collective bargaining role of the trade unions. Thus, by 1972, the trade unions assumed a role within the political structure in which industrial relations were not the only concern.

Lee was emphatic that new forms of mass organizations be formed. He insisted that all members of parliament be faithful in conducting their weekly meet-the-people sessions which provided constituents with the opportunity to voice their problems. This also allowed the MPs to get a 'feel' of people's concerns. The exercise constituted a major component of the political structure. Cabinet ministers were also instructed to conduct 'walkabouts' in all constituencies on Sundays to provide a further channel between people and the government. MPs were required to chair residents' committees and management committees in community centres. All these links ultimately became more important than the formal structures that could be identified.

---

[51] Quoted in *Straits Times*, 14 Sept. 1988, 1.
[52] The terms 'parapolitical' and 'parastatal' were used in Seah Chee Meow, 'Parapolitical Institutions', in Jon S. T. Quah, Chan Heng Chee and Seah Chee Meow, eds, *Government and Politics of Singapore,*, Singapore, 1985, ch. 8.

What of the political structures within the government itself (the legislature and the bureaucracy)? The civil service was a parastatal institution that Lee thought should be integrated into the political structure in order to facilitate the achievement of government objectives. In 1959, the groundwork had been established by setting up the Political Study Centre to impart political education to civil servants and to raise their understanding of the problems of the people. After 1965, the importance of the civil sevice was further increased by a system of recruitment which emphasized talent and qualifications. Coupled with salaries and benefits that approximated those in the private sector, this served to promote the civil service as an important component of the political structure. The civil service also became a vital training ground for future members of parliament on the PAP ticket. The link thus established could not but enhance the role of the civil service within the political structure.

Extending maximum government controls through political structures, however, was not the same as building the structure of a nation. Nation-building was a particularly urgent task because of the abrupt circumstances in 1965 that surrounded the birth of an independent state. Singapore's exit from Malaysia left a residue of Malays who now found themselves a minority community in the Malay archipelago. Although the Malays constituted less than 10 per cent of the population, their existence made it probable that any fissures in a multiracial society would occur along ethnic fault lines. Notwithstanding the image of monolithism that Singapore's political structures portrayed, the Malay community contained the seeds of dissent and separation. An important issue relevant for the study of political structures had always been the representation of Malay interests in parliament.

As the dominant party in parliament, the PAP was always careful to field a sufficient number of Malay candidates. The experience of Lee and his senior colleagues in the communal politics of Malaysia and the importance they placed on the external environment demonstrated to them the crucial need to preserve multiracialism. However, various conditions emerged to threaten the continuance of this parliamentary tradition. The housing policy of the national Housing and Development Board tended to promote non-Malay residence in hitherto Malay-majority areas. In other words, there were no more electoral constituencies that could deliver block votes for a Malay candidate. At the same time, an increase in the number of younger non-Malay voters with no memories of the 'Malaysia' experience tended to place a premium on parliamentary candidates with professional skill, education and technocratic abilities, qualifications with which Malays were less equipped.

Such a situation could lead to a decline in the number of Malay representatives in parliament. In a political structure with elections based on one-person-one-vote and the first-past-the-post principle, there were very real dangers for the representation of the Malay community. If not resolved, these could render Singapore's position in a Malay archipelago untenable.

Indeed, results from several consecutive elections showed that the number of votes that Malay candidates could command was dropping compared to Chinese candidates in the same constituency. Chinese voters tended to vote for Chinese candidates. As a result, there was a trend towards a non-Malay parliament or a parliament with disproportionately low Malay representation. In short, Singapore's political structure was moving towards one in which the Malay minority would be marginalized and, of course, alienated. Given the geopolitical factors, this would send the wrong signals to Singapore's neighbours.

There were, of course, safeguards within the existing political structure to rectify the situation. In December 1965, soon after separation from Malaysia, a Constitutional Commission was appointed to provide for multi-racialism within the constitution. Generally, Article 89 recognized the 'special position' of the Malays. The commission also recommended the creation of a non-elected advisory body called the Presidential Council on Minorities. With members appointed at the discretion of the president, it was expected that this body would be able to check on any adverse impact of legislation in respect of racial issues.

Another solution was the Team-Member-of-Parliament concept and the creation of the Group Representation Constituency (GRC) in 1988. Under this scheme, certain constituencies were designated as GRCs. This meant that contestants for those electoral wards must include a member of the minority race (Malay or Indian as the case may be) as one of the candidates. This ensured that there would be a minimum number of representatives in parliament from each minority group. The GRC scheme was duly adopted in the amended constitution. In this way, multiracialism was legislated into the political structure. At the same time, all political parties, including the small or weak ones, were required to field at least three candidates on a single slate in order to contest the designated constituencies. This could be construed as a step towards the further development of maximum government, because only the stronger parties could fulfil the conditions.

Earlier, to ensure that all the measures taken to develop suitable political structures were not in vain, Lee had ordered the formation of the Singapore Armed Forces to defend the achievements that had been registered. The first decisive moves in this direction came soon after Singapore separated from Malaysia. When the July 1969 racial riots took Kuala Lumpur by storm and threatened to spill over into Singapore, Lee ordered the armed forces to display their tanks at the August national day parade in a show of force designed to instil confidence that the political structures in Singapore were sufficiently resilient to withstand any external pressure. Subsequently, in November 1972, in a move to pre-empt any attempt at merger with Malaysia which would change the political structures in Singapore, Lee persuaded the Parliament to amend the constitution so that thereafter any merger or any surrender of sovereign power over the police and the armed forces would require a referendum with two-thirds majority of the people voting. After that, the armed forces became an important component of the political structure, with 'bridges' linking them to the civilian segments. The stress on a citizen army, total defence, and the creation of a conduit by which high-ranking officers could cross over to participate in national politics or be seconded to the bureaucracy, all ensured that the armed forces would have a major role in the political structure but not a dominant one.

Brunei

Discussion on independent Brunei can best begin with the official view that the tiny state had never been colonized by the British. It had always been a protectorate. Hence, Britain's grant of independence to Brunei on 1 January 1984 was not similar to the independence experienced by its other colonies. It was in order to fulfil diplomatic requirements that Brunei needed a formal proclamation of independence.

This perspective provides for a 'longer view' of Brunei's political structures, in respect of which the year 1984 was not a watershed. Of these, the most important was of course the Malay Islamic sultanate.

An indication of the sultanate's importance was already revealed before Brunei became independent when it was negotiating with the Federation of Malaya on the terms of admission into the new state of Malaysia. The question of precedence of the Sultan of Brunei in the Conference of Rulers was evidently a major cause of the disagreement that brought about the breakdown in the Malaya–Brunei negotiations. Precedence, however, was not only an issue of protocol and ceremony. The sultanate of Brunei was one of the oldest in the Malay world and naturally the sultan thought it would be justified to claim a degree of pre-eminence in the line-up for the post of Yang di-Pertuan Agong, the titular head of state in the proposed Malaysia. The existing provisions stipulated that the incumbent should, generally, be selected on the basis of precedence. This in turn was determined by the date of accession to the throne. The Sultan of Brunei would have to wait his turn. The proceedings of the negotiations were not made public, but it was likely that the sultan asked for a position higher than his due in the hierarchy. When objections were raised, the discussions faltered.

The negotiations suggested that the sultan recognized the crucial importance of protecting the sultanate at all costs. Indeed, the history of modern political structures in Brunei was almost a history of the work of two sultans, the late Sir Omar, who was the twenty-eighth ruler of Brunei, and his son Sultan Hassanal Bolkiah.

In 1959, when a constitution was drafted to confer internal autonomy on Brunei, the decision was made to strengthen the sultanate by ensuring that power was transferred not to the people but to the ruling dynasty. For Sir Omar who negotiated the constitution, that was the principal way to replace the influence of the British resident with his personal rule. In his view the Islamic sultanate was the only political structure that could protect the non-Islamic ethnic groups. In an independent Brunei, the 1961 Citizenship Regulations would continue in force, allowing non-citizens (principally the Chinese who formed 23 per cent of the population) to enjoy residence rights and to travel on papers of identity after 1 January 1984. Moreover, applications for citizenship would continue to be entertained.[53]

---

[53] Roger Kershaw, 'Illuminating the path to independence: Political themes in *Pelita Brunei* in 1983', *Southeast Asian Affairs 1984*, Singapore, 1984, 69.

Maximum government in a political structure centred on the person of the ruler was the principal feature in Brunei. However, to counter criticisms against the accumulation of absolutism, measures were taken after 1984 to develop political structures apart from the sultanate and thus a ministerial cabinet was formed. But the substance remained the same. Sultan Bolkiah held a tight grip on the entire structure by assuming the offices of Prime Minister, Home Affairs and Finance. He appointed his father Minister of Defence, and two brothers also held important ministerial positions. When his father died on 7 September 1986, Sultan Bolkiah assumed the post of Minister of Defence. A new revised constitution was also promulgated. Based on the earlier 1959 document, it consolidated royal power further because it abolished the Legislative Council. Under the 1959 constitution, there were four other councils: the Council of Ministers, the Privy Council, the Religious Council, and the Council of Succession. There were also village and district councils linked with these councils. Such formal structures aside, it is also important to note that after 1980, the sultan made personal visits to the villages to hear grievances and this was an important political structure, albeit an informal one.

Since the granting of independence was not conditional on either elections or representative government, there was a limited role for the Legislative Council to play in the political structure. Up to 1962, this council had been controlled by the Party Ra'ayat, the party that formed the majority in fifty-four of the fifty-five district councils. In 1962 the party leader, A. M. Azahari, led a revolt against the sultan in order to launch his programme of re-establishing the former glory of Brunei. Azahari's action contributed a great deal to the monarchical distaste for such representative institutions as the Legislative Council. In theory, this council could exercise some powers. According to the 1959 constitution, all revenues were paid into the Consolidated Fund and the council must give its approval before monies could be spent. With the abolition of the council, state finances and reserves could in fact be treated as the personal wealth of the sultan.

There was some limited toleration of parties within the political structure, even after the Azahari revolt. In May 1985, the Brunei National Democratic Party was registered. The chairman was related to the sultan. In late 1985, a second party—a splinter group from the first—was registered as the Brunei National United Party. Despite these signs of change, Brunei's political structure remained essentially a modernizing autocracy.

An alternative political structure was therefore difficult to identify. If one existed at all, it was the Brunei Armed Forces, but even this institution was so closely associated with the sultan that it formed an extension of his authority.

CONCLUSION

The reference to the Sultan of Brunei returns the discussion to the importance of the leaders within the political structures in the independent states of Southeast Asia. It is submitted that in many instances, the exercise of power by several individuals, separately and independently of each other, gave meaning to the political structures.

In practically all the Southeast Asian states, leaders emerged to assume control of the political structures. Many of them were institution-builders. As creators rather than destroyers, they developed structures which endowed the societies they led with form, continuity and predictability. The study of Southeast Asian political structures cannot but mention the relatively long tenure of many leaders of governments whose extended role in office gave life and vigour to the structures. Indeed, leaders and the governments they led constituted a political structure of primary importance, sometimes to the exclusion of other structures, but endeavouring to absorb the diverse peoples in each of their states to achieve the elusive goal of nation-building.

Ne Win was credited with having said: 'There is no miracle worker. But a willing man with a stout and true heart can accomplish a lot. Placed in bad conditions, he can make them good. Placed in good conditions, he can make them better. With a few hundred of such men we can push the revolution through.'[54] Lee Kuan Yew, reminiscing about the past, spoke of the need for at least three persons who would not be moved under pressure.[55]

The study of political structures in Southeast Asia can therefore justifiably deal with the leaders who shaped the political structures almost in an *ad hoc* manner in response to problems and situations that emerged. A cursory survey of these leaders, by way of conclusion, reveals various interesting features that validate the need to study them in order to understand the political structures.

Of that breed of 'founding fathers' of the independent states in Southeast Asia, attention here focuses on four who were still alive at the end of the 1980s. The doyen of these must be Lee Kuan Yew of Singapore, who argued: 'I belong to that exclusive club of founder members of a new independent country ... Those who believe that when I have left the Government as Prime Minister, that I've gone into permanent retirement, really should have their heads examined.'[56]

Then there was Ne Win, who ruled Burma for twenty-six years (from 1962 to 1988, not including the short caretaker government that lasted from 1958 to 1960). Although he had resigned from the presidency of Burma in the wake of student-led unrest and riots, he was allegedly the *eminence grise* who appointed Sein Lwin as his successor and then, after eighteen days of further violence and killing, removed him from office. It was still believed that he was calling the shots even after the military coup of September 1988 although erstwhile close associates like Maung Maung thought that he had really retired.[57]

The third 'founding father' who still hankered after some degree of influence was Tunku Abdul Rahman, the first prime minister of Malaya and later Malaysia. Although wheelchair-bound and advanced in age, he

---

[54] Maung Maung, *Burma and General Ne Win*, Rangoon, 1969, 300.
[55] *Straits Times*, 16 Aug. 1988, 10.
[56] ibid., 15 Aug. 1988, 1.
[57] Seminar given by Maung Maung, 28 Feb. 1990, National University of Singapore.

flew from Penang to Johor (the southernmost state of peninsular Malaya) to campaign on behalf of a candidate who opposed the UMNO Baru (or New UMNO) party in a 1988 by-election. The Tunku, of course, was a strenuous opponent of the decision by Dr Mahathir, the incumbent prime minister, to replace the old UMNO (the Tunku's party which he led from 1955 till 1969) with the new UMNO. The outcome of the by-election is irrelevant to this discussion: the action of the Tunku suggested the strong determination of founder-leaders to exercise influence over the shape of political structures.

The last 'founding father' of note is, of course, the mercurial Prince Sihanouk. At the time of writing, this leader was still working towards a resolution of the Cambodia conflict despite many threats of retirement.

This survey of recent activities of the early leaders of independent Southeast Asia demonstrates their attachment to those political structures they had so painstakingly created. As Lee Kuan Yew said at a Singapore National Day rally on Sunday, 14 August 1988, 'And even from my sick bed, even if you are going to lower me into the grave and I feel that something is going wrong, I'll get up.'[58]

Not all the Southeast Asian leaders, of course, thought on the same wavelength as these men. Aung San, the Burmese leader who led the nationalist struggle against the British, was one of these. Shortly after the end of the Japanese occupation, he spoke on leadership:

> No man, however great, can alone set the wheels of history in motion, unless he has the active support and cooperation of a whole people. No doubt individuals have played brilliant roles in history, but then it is evident that history is not made by a few individuals only. I have already mentioned to you ... how history develops as the cumulative creation of generations of men responding to the demands of ever growing logical events. I am well aware that there is such a great craving in mind for heroism and the heroic and that hero-worship forms not a small motif in his complex. I am also aware that unless man believes in his own heroism and the heroism of others, he cannot achieve much or great things. We must, however, take proper care that we do not make a fetish of this cult of hero-worship, for then we will turn ourselves into votaries of false gods and prophets.[59]

It is not necessary to evaluate this view held by Aung San, save to say that its importance compared to the ones expressed by the other leaders was diminished because Aung San was assassinated while the others lived to establish structures of consensus.

What then were the circumstances that permitted the dominance of leaders and governments as a political structure? The low levels of political institutionalization in Southeast Asia allowed leaders, defined as those responsible for the orientation of their respective polities, to concentrate unto themselves influence and patronage by means that bore relatively little relationship to the formal political structures provided by the consti-

---

[58] *Straits Times*, 15 Aug. 1988, 1.
[59] Quoted in Roger M. Smith, ed., *Documents of Political Development and Change*, Ithaca, 1974, 93–4.

tution of each state.[60] The environment also increasingly made it easier for leaders to concentrate power in their hands. In the decades after the Southeast Asian states became independent, the pace of change was intense. One of the transformations that took place was the emergence of an international economy that was closely interdependent and becoming more and more integrated. The genesis of this transformation could be sensed even before the Southeast Asian states became independent. The colonial economies were meshed with the metropolitan economy. Various parts of Southeast Asia had already been drawn into the world system. However, this interdependence became more pronounced as the independent states grappled with the immense problems of heavy capital flows, demographic changes, commodity imbalances and unemployment problems. National markets increased in size. Transnational business corporations became prominent. In short, there was a change in scale, and only those political structures that could match the scale or forge links with other structures were big enough to adjust. Government power in Southeast Asia increased in every area because governments were placed in an advantageous position to adjust to the changes taking place in the world.[61] Leaders were thus provided with opportunities for amassing power.

However, this is not to suggest that the process was inexorable, sweeping everything to the side as leaders became more prominent. As Southeast Asia moved into an era in which states and their economies became more integrated, the role of the leaders could well be dwarfed by a change in scale. The narrow nationalism of the early leaders and the political structures they helped to shape may well have to adjust to the fit the globalization of the new era.

BIBLIOGRAPHIC ESSAY

The knowledge explosion has unleashed a torrent of publications on contemporary Southeast Asia history. Not all of them deal directly with political structures—the focus of the preceding pages—but collectively, they succeed in delivering a picture of the composition and dynamics of those structures. What is the basis of selection for mention in this bibliographic note? Standard works in English are cited and the new materials that have emerged in recent years are mentioned, especially those that can contribute to the quantum of primary sources.

Few authors have attempted on their own an encyclopaedic coverage of Southeast Asia. In the few instances where the whole of Southeast Asia is the subject, e.g. John F. Cady, *The History of Post-War Southeast Asia*, Athens, Ohio, 1974, the approach tends to settle along the fault line of a country-by-country analysis. Primary documents sourced from each country can be found in Roger M. Smith, ed., *Southeast Asia: Documents of*

---

[60] See Mohammed Ayoob and Chai-Anan Samudavanija, *Leadership Perceptions and National Security: The Southeast Asian Experience*, Singapore: ISEAS 1989, ch. 11.
[61] Daniel Bell, 'The World in 2013', *Dialogue*, 81, 3 (1988) 2–9.

Political Development and Change, Ithaca, 1974. Those who attempt compara-
tive regional studies usually seize upon a theme that could be pulled
thread-like across Southeast Asia. Examples include Fred R. von der
Mehden, *Politics of the Developing Nations,* Englewood Cliffs,. 1964; Lucian
W. Pye, *Southeast Asia's Political Systems,* 2nd edn, Englewood Cliffs, 1967;
Milton Osborne, *Region of Revolt: Focus on Southeast Asia,* Rushcutters Bay,
NSW, 1970; Michael Leifer, *Dilemmas of Statehood in Southeast Asia,* Sin-
gapore, 1972; Lucian W. Pye with Mary W. Pye, *Asian Power and Politics: the
Cultural Dimensions of Authority,* Cambridge, Mass., 1985.

Collective efforts have more often been the norm. Useful contributions
include John T. McAlister, Jr, ed., *Southeast Asia: the Politics of National
Integration,* New York, 1973, which has a section on national political
leadership.

Unavoidably, the student of contemporary Southeast Asia, whether of
political structures or other topics, is invariably referred to country studies
of which there is an abundant and exciting growth.

Vietnam

The continuing conflict in Indochina has spawned numerous publications.
Scholarship on Vietnam has developed far beyond the circle of writings
delimited by Paul Mus, Bernard B. Fall, P. J. Honey or Dennis J. Duncan-
son. On the impact of international dimensions of war on domestic
structures, see R. B. Smith, *An International History of the Vietnam War,*
London, 1983. An useful analysis of how a revolutionary movement was
able to gain ascendancy, albeit in one province only, is Jeffrey Race, *War
comes to Long An: Revolutionary Conflict in a Vietnamese Province,* Berkeley,
1972. Since the village is such an important unit in the political structure,
one useful reference is Gerald Cannon Hickey, *Village in Vietnam,* New
Haven, 1964. An extremely arresting account of events in Indochina after
1975 can be found in Nayan Chanda, *Brother Enemy: the War after the War,*
San Diego, New York, London, 1986.

Vietnamese writers have also published in English. Reading them will
give an impression, however superficial, of the workings of the political
structures in Vietnam. The writings of Vo Nguyen Giap are well known.
There are also *Ho Chi Minh: On Revolution. Selected Writings, 1920–1966,*
edited and with an introduction by Bernard B. Fall, New York, 1967;
Nguyen Cao Ky, *Twenty Years and Twenty Days,* New York, 1976; *No other
road to take. Memoir of Mrs Nguyen Thi Dinh,* Ithaca: Cornell University
Southeast Asia Program, 1976; Vo Nguyen Giap, *Unforgettable Days,*
Hanoi, 2nd edn, 1978; Nguyen van Canh with Earle Cooper, *Vietnam under
Communism, 1975–1982,* Stanford, 1983; Truong Nhu Tang, *Journal of a
Vietcong,* London, 1986; Tran Van Don, *Our Endless War: Inside Vietnam,*
San Rafael, 1978; Bui Diem with David Chanoff, *In the Jaws of History,*
Boston, 1987. There are interesting articles of tangential interest to political
structures written by Vietnamese in *Vietnamese Studies* (Hanoi), a review
founded in 1964.

Laos and Cambodia

For Laos and Cambodia, the offerings are as few as their respective territories are small. For Laos, the field is no longer confined to the writings of Fall, Langer and Zasloff. Significant contributions include the following: Martin Stuart-Fox, ed., *Contemporary Laos: Studies in the Politics and Society of the Lao People's Democratic Republic*, St Lucia, 1982; Martin Stuart-Fox, *Laos: Politics, Economics and Society*, London, 1986; MacAlister Brown and Joseph J. Zasloff, *Apprentice Revolutionaries: the Communist Movement in Laos, 1930–1985*, Stanford, 1986. Because much information readily available in respect of most countries is difficult to come by in the case of Laos, any contribution is welcome.

On Cambodia, a reliable account is Milton Osborne, *Politics and Power in Cambodia: the Sihanouk Years*, Camberwell, 1973. See also Ben Kiernan and Chanthou Boua, eds, *Peasants and Politics in Kampuchea, 1942–1981*, London, 1982: David P. Chandler and Ben Kiernan, eds, *Revolution and its aftermath in Kampuchea: Eight Essays*, New Haven, 1983; Michael Vickery, *Cambodia: 1975–1982*, Boston, 1984; Ben Kiernan, *How Pol Pot came to Power: a History of Communism in Kampuchea, 1930–1975*, London, 1985; finally, an account by a journalist, William Shawcross, *The Quality of Mercy: Cambodia, Holocaust and Modern Conscience*, London, 1984.

Few native Laotians or Cambodians have written about their respective countries, but Prince Norodom Sihanouk has published a defence of his role as leader in *My War with the CIA: the Memoirs of Prince Norodom Sihanouk*, New York, 1972, and *War and Hope: the Case for Cambodia*, New York, 1980.

Burma

In order to understand Burma's leadership as a core political structure, there are a number of useful publications by Burmese themselves, some of which must be read with care: Maung Maung, *Burma and General Ne Win*, London, 1969; U Nu, *Saturday's Son*, New Haven, 1975; Maung Maung Gyi, *Burmese Political Values: the Socio-Political Roots of Authoritarianism*, New York, 1983; Chao Tzang Yawnghwe, *The Shan of Burma: Memoirs of a Shan Exile*, Singapore, 1987.

However, the seminal contributions are still made by Western scholars, and their writings include those of Josef Silverstein who has published widely e.g., ed., *The Political Legacy of Aung San*, Ithaca: Cornell University Southeast Asia Program, 1972; ed., *The Future of Burma in Perspective: a Symposium*, Athens, Ohio, 1974; *Burma: Military Rule and the Politics of Stagnation*, Ithaca, 1977; *Burmese Politics: the Dilemma of National Unity*, New Brunswick, 1980. Others have also made substantial contributions, e.g. Frank N. Trager, *Burma: From Kingdom to Republic: a Historical and Political Analysis*, London, 1966; and Robert H. Taylor, *The State in Burma*, London, 1987.

Malaysia

One outstanding feature about publications on Malaysia is the recent prolific output of reminiscences and other accounts by former leaders and participants in the political process. These are led by Tunku Abdul Rahman Putra, the first prime minister: *Looking Back: Monday Musings and Memories*, Kuala Lumpur, 1977; *Viewpoints*, Kuala Lumpur, 1978; *As a Matter of Interest*, Kuala Lumpur, 1981; *Lest we Forget: Further Candid Reminiscences*, Singapore, 1983; *Something to Remember*, Singapore, 1983; *Contemporary Issues in Malaysian Politics*, Petaling Jaya, 1984; *Political Awakening*, Petaling Jaya, 1986; *Challenging Times*, Petaling Jaya, no date; *May 13 Before and After*, Kuala Lumpur, 1969. Except for the last three, most of the aforementioned were reproductions of articles previously published in the *Star* newspaper in Penang. The following are also worthy of note: *Strategy for Action: the Selected Speeches of Tun Haji Abdul Razak bin Dato Hussein Al-Haj*, Kuala Lumpur (?), 1969; Mahathir bin Mohamad, *The Malay Dilemma*, Singapore, 1970; Abdul Aziz Ishak, *Special Guest: the Detention in Malaysia of an ex-Cabinet Minister*, Singapore, 1977; Lim Kit Siang, *Time Bombs in Malaysia*, Petaling Jaya: Democratic Action Party, 1978; Tan Chee Khoon, *Malaysia Today: Without Fear or Favour*, Petaling Jaya, 1985; *Rukunegara: a Testament of Hope, Selected Speeches by Ghazali Shafie*, Kuala Lumpur, 1985; Lim Kit Siang, *Malaysia in the Dangerous 80s*, Petaling Jaya, 1982 and the later *Malaysia: Crisis of Identity*, Petaling Jaya: Democratic Action Party, 1986; A. Samad Ismail, *Journalism and Politics*, Kuala Lumpur, 1987. The writings of Chandra Muzaffar, winner of the 1989 Henry J. Benda Prize in Southeast Asian Studies, can also be included in this genre of participant-observer, e.g. *Protector? An analysis of the concept and practice of loyalty in leader-led relationships within Malay society*, Penang, 1979; *Freedom in Fetters: an analysis of the state of democracy in Malaysia*, Penang, 1986; *Islamic Resurgence in Malaysia*, Petaling Jaya, 1987.

Several doctoral dissertations have recently been revised and published. These include one on non-Alliance radical parties, one on centre–state relations, and one on the MCA, respectively: Firdaus Haji Abdullah, *Radical Malay Politics: its origins and early development*, Petaling Jaya, 1985; B. H. Shafruddin, *The Federal Factor in the Government and Politics of Peninsular Malaysia*, Singapore, 1987; Heng Pek Koon, *Chinese Politics in Malaysia: a History of the Malaysian Chinese Association*, Singapore, 1988.

Useful insights on political structures from a more narrow focus include Harold Crouch, Lee Kam Hing and Michael Ong, *Malaysian Politics and the 1978 Election*, Kuala Lumpur, 1980. Apart from Muzaffar's contributions, two of the few publications on Islam are Judith Nagata, *The Reflowering of Malaysian Islam: Modern Religious Radicals and their Roots*, Vancouver, 1984; and Mahathir Mohamad, *The Challenge*, Kuala Lumpur, 1986.

The standard reference works include K. J. Ratnam, *Communalism and the Political Process in Malaya*, Kuala Lumpur, 1965; James C. Scott, *Political Ideology in Malaysia: Reality and the Beliefs of an Elite*, New Haven, 1968; R. K. Vasil, *Politics in a Plural Society: a study of non-communal political parties in West Malaysia*, London, 1971; Mohamad Noordin Sopiee, *From Malayan Union to Singapore Separation: Political Unification in the Malaysia Region,*

1945–65, Kuala Lumpur, 1974; James P. Ongkili, *Nation-building in Malaysia, 1946–1974*, Singapore, 1985, with important contributions on Sabah and Sarawak.

Indonesia

Western scholarship has contributed immensely to an understanding of the political structures of Indonesia after 1945. The standard references must be repeated here: Herbert Feith, *The Decline of Constitutional Democracy in Indonesia*, Ithaca, 1962; Ruth T. McVey, ed., *Indonesia*, rev. edn, New Haven, 1967; Herbert Feith and Lance Castles, *Indonesian Political Thinking, 1945–1965*, Ithaca, 1970; J. D. Legge, *Sukarno: a Political Biography*, New York, 1972; Rex Mortimer, ed., *Showcase State: the Illusion of Indonesia's 'Accelerated Modernisation'*, Sydney, 1973; and Oey Hong Lee, *Indonesia facing the 1980s: a Political Analysis*, Hull, no date, for alternative views; C. L. M. Penders, *The Life and Times of Sukarno*, London, 1974; J. A. C. Mackie, *Konfrontasi: the Indonesia-Malaysia Dispute, 1963–1966*, London, 1974; Karl D. Jackson and Lucian W. Pye, eds, *Political Power and Communications in Indonesia*, Berkeley, 1978; Clifford Geertz, *Negara: the Theatre State in Nineteenth-Century Bali*, Princeton, 1980, which provides fascinating insights into political structures.

In particular, the cultural dimensions of political structures are studied in Claire Holt, ed., *Culture and Politics in Indonesia*, Ithaca, 1972.

More recent publications on very contemporary events include: Tengku Hasan M. di Tiro, *The Price of Freedom (The Unfinished Diary)*, Norsburg, Sweden, 1981; Heri Akhmadi, *Breaking the Chains of Oppression of the Indonesian People: Defense Statement at his Trial on Charges of Insulting the Head of State*, Ithaca, 1981; David Bourchier, *Dynamics of Dissent in Indonesia: Sawito and the Phantom Coup*, Ithaca, 1984; David Jenkins, *Suharto and his Generals: Indonesian Military Politics, 1975–1983*, Ithaca, 1984.

There continue to be major gaps in the literature on political structures. Standard references on Islamic and non-Islamic political structures are few. Studies of political parties include that of J. Eliseo Rocamora, *Nationalism in Search of Ideology: the Indonesian Nationalist Party, 1946–1965*, Quezon City, 1975. There is one recent publication on Golkar, David Reeve, *Golkar of Indonesia: An Alternative to the Party System*, Singapore, 1985. The political structure of communism has been studied by various scholars, but the one published with the hindsight of the PKI debacle was Rex Mortimer, *Indonesian Communism under Sukarno: Ideology and Politics, 1959–1965*, Ithaca, 1974. A major contribution on the military as a political structure is Harold Crouch, *The Army and Politics in Indonesia*, Ithaca, 1978.

Philippines

The events of martial law and the subsequent overthrow of President Marcos in 1986 have tended to affect the selection of materials to read on the Philippines and overshadowed political biographies of those leaders (e.g. Jose V. Abueva, *Ramon Magsaysay: a Political Biography*, Manila, 1971) who were dwarfed by the cataclysmic events from 1969 onwards. Pre-1972 books (e.g. Jose Veloso Abeuva and Raul P. de Guzman, eds, *Foundations and Dynamics of Filipino Government and Politics*, Manila, 1969) and materials published between 1972 and 1986 (e.g. David A. Rosenberg, ed., *Marcos and Martial Law in the Philippines*, Ithaca, 1979) therefore must be read in conjunction with those publications that used hindsight to advantage when discussing political structures. These include those collected in Carl H. Lande, ed., *Rebuilding a Nation: Philippine Challenges and American Policy*, Washington, 1987, and P. N. Abinales, *Militarization in the Philippines*, Quezon City: Third World Studies, 1982.

However, some of the standard studies remain reliable despite the political shifts: Carl H. Lande, *Leaders, Factions, and Parties: the Structure of Philippine Politics*, New Haven: Yale University Southeast Asia Studies, 1964; Onofre D. Corpuz, *The Philippines*, Englewood Cliffs, NJ, 1965; Jean Grossholtz, *Politics in the Philippines*, Boston, 1964. Various journals remain a valuable source of materials on political structures, e.g. *Philippine Studies* (Quezon City) and *Solidarity: Current Affairs, Ideas and the Arts* (Manila).

It should also be noted that the excitement of the 1986 overthrow of President Marcos resulted in the appearance of a number of publications providing personal accounts of martial law experiences. A most significant contribution was Benigno S. Aquino, *Testament from a Prison Cell*, Manila: Benigno, S. Aquino Jr Foundation, 1984. Not to be omitted from mention is Marcos' own defence of martial law: *Notes on the New Society of the Philippines*, 2 parts, Manila(?), 1973.

Thailand

Any attempt to study political structures in Thailand cannot ignore the following publications: John L. S. Girling, *Thailand: Society and Politics*, Ithaca, 1981; David L. Morell and Chai-Anan Samudavanija, *Political Conflict in Thailand; reforms, reaction, revolution*, Cambridge, Mass., 1981; Chai-Anan Samudavanija, *The Thai Young Turks*, Singapore, 1982; David K. Wyatt, *Thailand: A Short History*, New Haven, 1984.

Singapore and Brunei

Both Singapore and Brunei suffer from a lack of materials that can be recommended in a bibliographic essay of this nature.

In recent years, with the passage of time, the first-generation leaders of Singapore have become the source of publications, e.g. *Not by Wages Alone: Selected Speeches and Writings of C. V. Devan Nair, 1959–1981*, Singapore: National Trades Union Congress, 1982; and Chan Heng Chee and Obaid ul Haq, eds, *S. Rajaratnam: The Prophetic and the Political*, Singapore, 1987. Only one biography has been attempted: Chan Heng Chee, *A Sensation of Independence: a Political Biography of David Marshall*, Singapore, 1984.

Since 1970, when Thomas J. Bellows completed his study on the PAP, others have been published, e.g. Chan Heng Chee, *The Dynamics of One Party Dominance: the PAP at the Grass Roots*, Singapore, 1976. More survey-like accounts of the dominant structures in Singapore are Raj K. Vasil,

Governing Singapore, Singapore, 1984 (based, in part, on interviews with Lee Kuan Yew and S. Rajaratnam); and Jon S. T. Quah, Chan Heng Chee and Seah Chee Meow, eds, *Government and Politics of Singapore*, Singapore, 1985.

For Brunei as well as the rest of Southeast Asia, the reader is referred to the annual essays of *Southeast Asian Affairs* (Singapore) and *Asian Survey*. These publications rank with those which publish materials on Southeast Asian political structures occasionally: *Journal of Southeast Asian Studies* (Singapore), *Contemporary Southeast Asia* (Singapore), *Journal of Asian Studies* (Ann Arbor), *Modern Asian Studies* (Cambridge, Mass.).

One promising source of materials on political structures in Southeast Asia is the various publication series produced in the newer centres of regional studies in Australia and Southeast Asia. Examples include the Southeast Asian Studies Program of the Institute of Southeast Asian Studies in Singapore which produced three relevant books on Singapore (mentioned above), Malaysia and Thailand; the institute's Field Report Series (e.g. Lee Ting Hui, *The Communist Organization in Singapore: its Techniques of Manpower Mobilization and Management, 1948–66*, Singapore, 1976); and the Research Notes and Discussion Papers Series (e.g. R. William Liddle, *Cultural and Class Politics in New Order Indonesia*, Singapore, 1977; Ismail Kassim, *The Politics of Accommodation: an Analysis of the 1978 Malaysian General Election*, Singapore, 1978; Leo Suryadinata, *Political Parties and the 1982 General Election in Indonesia*, Singapore, 1982; Harold Crouch, *Malaysia's 1982 General Election*, Singapore, 1982; Albert D. Moscotti, *Burma's Constitution and Elections of 1974: A Source Book*, Singapore, 1977).

In Australia, the Centre of Southeast Asian Studies at Monash University has a series called Working Papers, e.g. Robert S. Newman, *Brahmin and Mandarin: a Comparison of the Cambodian and Vietnamese Revolutions* (1978) and Ivan Molloy, *The Conflicts in Mindanao. 'Whilst the Revolution Rolls on, the Jihad falters'* (1983). Another series is entitled the Monash Papers on Southeast Asia, e.g. Ken Ward, *The 1971 Election in Indonesia: an East Java Case Study* (1974). James Cook University of North Queensland also has an active Occasional Paper Series which has provided, for example, W. F. Wertheim, *Fissures in the Girdle of Emeralds* (1980); W. F. Wertheim, *Moslems in Indonesia: Majority with Minority Mentality* (1980); Ernst Utrecht, *The Military and the 1977 Election* (1980); R. Kreutzer, *The Madiun Affair: Hatta's Betrayal of Indonesia's First Social Revolution* (1981); Peter Burns, *The Decline of Freedom of Religion in Indonesia* (1985).

The Centre of South-East Asian Studies at the University of Kent at Canterbury also has an Occasional Paper series and a relevant publication is C. W. Watson, *State and Society in Indonesia: three papers* (1987).

Although many of the occasional papers appear to be preliminary expositions published in formats that are far from slick, they are useful accounts for those who wish to augment their knowledge on particular aspects.

CHAPTER

8

ECONOMIC AND SOCIAL CHANGE

World War II reduced the Southeast Asian economies, already weakened by the Great Depression, to their lowest levels in modern times. Warfare itself accounted for much of the destruction, particularly in Burma and the Philippines, where the Allied forces resisted longest and returned soonest. When the British retreated from Burma they blew up railways and refineries as they withdrew, and the American liberation of the Philippines employed massive concentrations of naval and aerial firepower; these operations probably accounted for most of the physical destruction in those two countries. By the end of the war Burma had lost all its oil refineries, 90 per cent of its boats, and 85 per cent of its locomotives (along with most of its rolling stock and bridges), while 70 per cent of its roads and most of its docks and factories were severely damaged. As one scholar put it, 'both in internal transport and external trade, Burma was thrown back a century, without warning or previous preparation'. The Philippines was scarcely better off; much of the damage occurred during the 1945 liberation of Manila, in which the country's industrial and modern services sectors—factories, warehouses, power plants, radio stations, telephone exchanges, newspapers, hospitals and universities—had been concentrated. By the end of the battle, the city was 80 per cent destroyed.[1]

Even where there was little or no combat, however, the war took its toll. Throughout the region, the Japanese demand for cotton and other war matériel, along with the extraction of labour and the destruction of draught animals, reduced food production dramatically. At the same time, however, the occupation forces requisitioned rice, leaving the people hungry and driving the death toll up. Many Southeast Asians fled the urban areas, where the food distribution system had virtually collapsed, to live in the villages, or even the forests, as best they could. Those without local connections, such as the Chinese and Indians, were peculiarly vulnerable. In terms of human lives, however, probably the greatest cost was paid in northern and central Vietnam, where 1–2 million perished in the great famine of 1944–5, while surplus rice from the south was shipped to Japan or used for fuel.

I am grateful for comments on earlier drafts of this chapter by George L. Hicks, Ronald D. Hill, Benedict J. Kerkvliet, Elfed V. Roberts, Ronald Skeldon, and all my colleagues on the *Cambridge History* project, particularly Robert Elson. Note that all monetary expressions in this chapter have been converted to current US dollars, and 'billion' is used to mean 'thousand million'.

[1] J. Russel Andrus, *Burmese Economic Life*, Stanford, 1948, 335; David Joel Steinberg, *Philippine Collaboration in World War II*, Ann Arbor, 1967, 114.

Everywhere there were local horror stories of assault, rape, and murder by the occupying Japanese forces, but there was also more systematic exploitation. In Indonesia, Malaya, and Burma, there were hundreds of thousands of *rōmusha* (literally 'labourer in the war effort', but glossed in Java as 'involuntary worker or convict');[2] they were recruited by force or deception for labour far from home on such projects as the 'Death Railway' between Thailand and Burma. Ill-fed, working in appalling conditions under brutal masters, denied any but the most rudimentary medical attention, a majority of them never returned.

Although mortality levels generally rose during World War II they do not seem to have exceeded fertility levels, except in certain subgroups (e.g., the predominantly male Indians of Malaya, whose numbers declined by around 100,000—15 per cent of their pre-war population—during the war). Even in Vietnam, Burma, and the Philippines the total population continued to grow, albeit slowly. Southeast Asians were survivors. When the monetary system was devastated by the issue of vast amounts of occupation currency (called 'Mickey Mouse money' in the Philippines) to pay for requisitioned goods, they turned increasingly to barter and the black market. Imported consumer goods—textiles, matches, needles, cooking oil—were often unavailable, so they did without or reverted to earlier arrangements, such as using coconut oil instead of kerosene in their lamps. The absence or inaccessibility of external markets virtually shut down several major export industries—tin, sugar, tea, coffee, pepper, coal, abaca—so workers turned to subsistence cultivation instead.

Not many Southeast Asians directly benefited from World War II, though a few black-market profiteers came out ahead. In a structural sense, however, the war created some of the preconditions for postwar change. Some Southeast Asians rose to positions of higher responsibility, both in government and production, than they had previously enjoyed. Others formed military and political alliances that led to later peasant and labour unions; where such groups were strongest, as in central Luzon and parts of Vietnam, there were even the beginnings of land reform during the war. The lack of trade helped to break the imperial nexus and push local economies toward greater self-reliance; Chinese tin-miners in Malaya, for example, were forced to diversify into farming. On balance, however, it is clear that the war did the Southeast Asian economy much more harm than good.

Not all of the hardships of Southeast Asians and the long-run damage to the regional economy can be blamed on Japanese iniquity, however. Many of the occupying troops were brutal and there was often a chilling lack of concern for the welfare of the local population, epitomized in the decision of one army command in 1944 to 'maintain the natives' standard of living at the lowest possible level'.[3] Some Japanese also looted gold and gems, with a total value estimated in billions of dollars.[4] At the same time, it must

[2] Theodore Friend, *The Blue-Eyed Enemy*, Princeton, 1988, 162–6.
[3] Quoted in ibid., 162.
[4] Sterling Seagrave, *The Marcos Dynasty*, New York, 1988, 99–119, 296–359, introduces the shadowy subject of 'Yamashita's gold' and suggests that much of it eventually wound up in the hands of Ferdinand Marcos.

be remembered that in wartime the Greater East Asia Co-Prosperity Sphere could not operate as it was designed to. The Sphere was to be based on the exchange of Southeast Asian raw materials for Japanese manufactured goods, a system no less workable in principle than Western colonialism, as the example of prewar Taiwan suggested. From 1942 to 1945, however, Japan's industrial capacity was devoted to the war effort and its shipping was devastated by American submarines. Thus it was unable to supply Southeast Asia with consumer goods in return for the primary produce it demanded, and what had been envisaged as a relationship of exchange (albeit unequal) turned out to be sheer exploitation.

After the surrender of Japan, economic reconstruction and political independence were frequently linked by Southeast Asians. Independence seemed to offer the opportunity to undertake economic policies designed to benefit themselves, not the colonial metropole. To many Westerners, however, rehabilitation of the economy was a priority that ought to precede any consideration of decolonization. Among the colonies of Southeast Asia only the Philippines, despite the lobbying efforts of advocates of 'reconsideration', was so far advanced along the road to independence as to make it inevitable. Even there, the perceived need for rehabilitation made post-colonial economic ties much closer than originally planned. The United States offered $620 million in aid, back pay for tens of thousands of guerrillas, and privileged access to the American market for Philippine goods. In return, it demanded the right of Americans to invest on the same basis as Philippine citizens, insisted that the peso be pegged to the dollar, and retained its military bases.

In Burma, British plans for reconstruction of the pre-war economy soon foundered on the intransigence of Aung San and his Anti-Fascist People's Freedom League (AFPFL). Postwar Britain was unable to provide substantial economic assistance, and hardships were created by its clumsy efforts to collect taxes, impose wage and price controls, and import and distribute essential commodities (through a Civil Supplies Organization that favoured British commercial interests); in view of this, most Burmese preferred independence to a continued colonial connection, and London soon acceded to their wishes. Even before independence the Burmese had established a national Economic Planning Board, and thus started to take policy into their own hands, though they were careful at first to avoid any talk of expropriation or restrictions on foreign investments.

France and the Netherlands, on the other hand, used the need for postwar reconstruction as part of their rationale for attempting the forcible reimposition of imperial control over Indochina and Indonesia, and thus precipitated renewed warfare, postponing effective independence for several years. The Indonesian Revolution (1945–9) was shorter, but probably more disruptive of the local economy, with trade paralysed and production virtually stagnant throughout the period. The First Indochina War (1946–54) lasted longer, but permitted some restoration of the export economy in rice and rubber, particularly in Cambodia and southern Vietnam. In both cases there are few precise data, but it is clear that there were high mortality (though relatively few died in actual combat), much destruction of physical infrastructure, interruption of trade, and rampant inflation; these were often accompanied by social conflict among indigenous forces, sometimes more violent than the war against the colonialists.

Britain's colonies in maritime Southeast Asia, on the other hand, were generally willing to accept rehabilitation rather than insist on independence on the immediate postwar period. Such conflict as did occur had more to do with disputes over the structure of the economy than the question of sovereignty. The British aimed to restore a cheap-labour export-oriented plantation economy, co-opting or suppressing incipient trade unionism; in this they succeeded, thanks to communal divide-and-rule tactics and the postwar rubber boom. They restricted the economic damage caused by the Emergency (1948–60) and eventually reached an understanding with a conservative coalition of Malay aristocrats and Chinese and Indian businessmen, leading to a peaceful transition to independence for Malaya in 1957. Radical nationalists protested that the profits from the rubber boom went primarily to finance the postwar reconstruction of Britain, desperate for dollars—it was later estimated that $720 million was remitted abroad, between 1947 and 1950[5]—but they were not successful in convincing a majority of their compatriots that they would be better off insisting on immediate independence. The comparative weakness of local nationalism ensured a late and smooth transition to independence in Singapore and the Borneo colonies.

Within a decade after the end of World War II, therefore, most of Southeast Asia was in a position to take control of its own economic destiny. Although most indigenous leaders were astute enough to admit, as Aung San did, that desired changes could not be achieved 'by the stroke of a magic wand, as he ... [did] not possess one',[6] they had of necessity to imply that the solution was on the way. No-one could afford to admit that independence, so long sought, might not provide the answer to the continuing problems of poverty and developmental backwardness.

ECONOMIC POLICY IN INDEPENDENT SOUTHEAST ASIA

Although they differed in many other respects, the governments of independent Southeast Asia generally shared broad aims of economic growth, equity and nationalism, along with a belief that central planning and state intervention in the economy were necessary to achieve those aims. Growth—an increase in national wealth—was almost universally desired. Despite talk of other social and spiritual values, there were few Southeast Asian sympathizers for a Gandhian resistance to change or the deliberate abandonment of growth in favour of higher principles. There was no such clear consensus on the means to achieve growth, but it was generally acknowledged that they would have to include restructuring the

---

[5] Michael Stenson, *Class, Race and Colonialism in West Malaysia: The Indian Case*, St Lucia, Qld, 1980, 165–6, citing calculations by V. V. Bhanoji Rao.
[6] Quoted in Andrus, 85–6.

economy, particularly by expanding industry, which was believed to be the key to the wealth of the West. All postwar governments, even that in Democratic Kampuchea (1975–8), believed in economic growth and were at least rhetorically committed to industrialization.

Beyond contributing to a general sense of civic pride, economic nationalism tried to indigenize wealth and production, reduce foreign influence, and establish national self-sufficiency. In practice, this involved a number of different policies: discrimination against local aliens, usually Chinese or Indian, coupled with restrictions on further immigration; restrictions or restraints on foreign investors and transnational corporations; efforts to foster certain crucial sectors of the economy (particularly heavy industry) perceived as necessary to national strength and identity; and attempts to formulate an overall strategy that would somehow be distinctively indigenous.

Equity, at a bare minimum, implied lip-service to some kind of 'moral economy', particularly the belief that every person had a right to survive. What survival entailed, beyond mere physical existence, was not always clear, but some talked of 'basic human needs', including the right to employment, education, health care, and a 'decent' standard of living. Free compulsory elementary education was recognized in the Universal Declaration of Human Rights (1948) and ratified as a regional goal at the 1959–60 UNESCO conference in Karachi; the principle of medical care for all enjoyed similar widespread official backing in Southeast Asia. Only Democratic Kampuchea, in 'an excess of romantic peasantism', systematically downgraded education and Western (though not local) medicine.[7] For some Southeast Asians equity meant more: the right of all to share in the profits of development. Taken to the extreme, this implied an absolute equality of benefits for all, a time when there would be no rich and no poor. Many, however, accepted the differential distribution of rewards as just, or at least inevitable, though they hoped that the gap between rich and poor could somehow be narrowed. At most they envisaged an equality of opportunity, not one of wealth.

To achieve their stated aims of growth, nationalism, and equity, most of the new régimes became directly involved in the economy, both in planning and in direct participation. Despite a few flirtations with laissez-faire ideas, no Southeast Asian government ever seriously attempted to emulate the non-interventionist models praised by free-market ideologues. Instead they took over and expanded the managerial state of the late colonial period, enthusiastically if not always efficiently. Even Singapore, often cited as an exemplar of free-trade liberalism, consistently obtained nearly one-third of all its investment from the public sector and established the most comprehensive public housing programme in the world, accommodating three-quarters of the entire population by the early 1980s.

The process of state control began with the establishment of central banks in Thailand (1942) and most of the other states. In 1955 the World Bank acknowledged that 'a central bank has become a symbol of monetary independence, without which political independence is thought to be

---

[7] Michael Vickery, *Cambodia: 1975–1982*, Boston, 1984, 170–3.

incomplete'.[8] Centralized economic planning, always a feature of socialism, was also urged on capitalist states by the World Bank in the 1950s and
early 1960s. Soon almost every government in the region was issuing
national plans, specifying growth targets (by sector) for the next few years.
At times these merely represented wishful thinking, 'an expression of
intent rather than a rigorous exercise in economic forecasting',[9] but increasingly they came to be important instruments of social engineering.
Planning in Southeast Asia can be said to have come of age at the
beginning of the 1970s. Indonesia's *Repelita I* (First Five-Year Development
Plan) in 1969 was followed by the First Malaysia Plan, implementing the
New Economic policy, in 1970. In 1972 came Burma's Twenty-Year Plan,
subdivided into four-year plans; Thailand's Third Five-Year Plan, which
signalled the shift to export-oriented industrialization; and the Four-Year
National Economic Plan of Republic of Vietnam (RVN). The next year, the
RVN announced a new Eight-Year Plan and the Philippines created its
National Economic Development Authority; in 1976 the Socialist Republic
of Vietnam (SRV), free at last from war, was finally able to introduce its
Second Five-Year Plan.

Even before the rise of central planning, some Southeast Asian governments were acquiring or developing state corporations in utilities, energy,
and industrial development. State corporations were not confined to
nominally socialist governments, but were also undertaken by such stoutly
capitalist states as Thailand under Prime Minister Phibun Songkhram.
Generally they were motivated more by concerns for growth and nationalism than by whatever equity was implied by public ownership. By and
large these ventures did not involve acquisition of, or even competition
with, existing enterprises—Indonesia's expropriation of Dutch capital in
1957 was a notable exception to this general rule—but filled perceived
national gaps, particularly the weaknesses of inherited infrastructure and
industrial base. Few of the pioneering enterprises were well managed or
lasted long, but they set a precedent for greater state participation in the
economy. In Burma after 1962 and in communist Indochina the state
virtually monopolized formal economic activity, but even in the nominally
capitalist countries of the region great state enterprises developed: Singapore's Jurong Town Corporation and Singapore Technology Corporation; Malaysia's FELDA (Federal Land Development Authority), PERNAS
(State Trading Company), and Majlis Amanah Raayat (Council of Trust for
the Indigenous People); Indonesia's Pertamina (the state oil corporation)
and Bulog (National Logistics Board); the Philippine Sugar Commission
(Philsuco) and the Philippine Coconut Administration (Philcoa); and
Thailand's Eastern Seaboard Development Committee.

Such enterprises, combined with the expansion of welfare services,
made the state far more important economically in independent Southeast
Asia than it had ever been in colonial times. Public consumption and

---

[8] *Report on the Economic Development of Malaya*, Singapore, 1955, 168, as quoted in Siew Nim
Chee, 'Central Banking in Malaya', in S. Gethyn Davies, ed., *Central Banking in South and
East Asia*, Hong Kong, 1960, 111–27.
[9] Hal Hill and Sisira Jayasuriya, *An Inward-Looking Economy in Transition: Economic Development
in Burma since the 1960s*, Singapore: ISEAS, 1986, 11.

expenditures in the Philippines, Thailand, and Indonesia rose to almost 10 per cent of the gross national product (GNP) within a decade after World War II, and continued climbing until they averaged nearly 20 per cent by the late 1980s. In Brunei, Burma, Malaysia and Singapore, as well as the communist states of Indochina, they reached at times 40 per cent or more. Thus the modern Southeast Asian states were not mere arbiters in the economic arena, but potent players in their own right. Despite their growth, however, many remained what Gunnar Myrdal called 'soft states', unable or unwilling to implement the decisions they made, though over the course of the postwar period most of them noticeably hardened.

Although the governments of Southeast Asia shared the same broad goals, they varied sharply in their ranking of the priorities of these goals and their choices of strategies designed to achieve them. It was on the axis of attitudes toward equity that the clearest distinctions could be seen, though they were sometimes clouded by rhetoric. Pol Pot, Ho Chi Minh, Ne Win, Norodom Sihanouk, and Lee Kuan Yew each claimed to be a 'socialist', which suggests how empty of meaning that term could be. Nevertheless, we can distinguish on the one hand governments that viewed the great disparities of wealth that existed throughout the region as intrinsically unjust and set about dispossessing the rich, and on the other, those that accepted the basic principle of property rights and believed that the incentives offered by private ownership were necessary for development. Differences in commitment to specific growth strategies, to 'nationalist' policies, and to state enterprise were generally secondary to this fundamental distinction. Redistributionist policies, for example, inevitably involved increasing the size of the state apparatus and were in practice difficult to combine with openness to foreign trade and investment.

It is useful, therefore, in attempting to discern policy trends within Southeast Asia over the past four decades, to distinguish broad clusters of states by their basic orientation to property: capitalist, socialist, and 'third way'. At one end of the spectrum were those governments fundamentally committed to the preservation of private property: the Philippines, Malaysia, Singapore, Brunei and Thailand throughout almost the entire postwar period; southern Vietnam under the republic (1954–75), the Khmer Republic under Lon Nol (1970–5), and Indonesia under the New Order (after 1965). At the other extreme were Democratic Kampuchea (1975–8), which actually attempted the elimination of private property, northern Vietnam after 1954, Burma after 1962, southern Vietnam and Laos after 1975, and the People's Republic of Kampuchea after 1978. Somewhere in the middle were those governments that professed vaguely socialist principles, often explicitly interpreted in terms of local culture, but did little to redistribute wealth: Burma under U Nu (1948–62), Indonesia before 1965 (particularly under Guided Democracy, 1957–65), Cambodia under Norodom Sihanouk (1953–70), and perhaps Thailand under Nai Pridi Phanomyong (1945–7) and later civilian régimes (1973–6) or Laos under various of the coalition governments of the 1950s and 1960s.

Of these three clusters, the capitalist was the largest and achieved the most conspicuous economic success, to the point where it often came to represent the region as a whole. Many recent studies of the regional economy in fact tend to exclude the communist states of Indochina, and often Burma as well, thus effectively defining 'Southeast Asia' as equivalent to the Association of Southeast Asian Nations (ASEAN). Among the capitalist régimes, we can discern three major phases in postwar economic planning: first, rehabilitation and the reconstruction of a primary-producing export economy on the colonial model; second, beginning in the 1950s, the attempt to develop import-substitution industrialization, often accompanied by overt economic nationalism; third, starting with Singapore in the mid-1960s, the effort to convert to export-oriented industrialization. Differences between countries in the details and timing of these policy shifts have been the object of considerable study by economists. Over the whole postwar period, however, it is not the differences of policy within this bloc that are striking, but the broad similarities.

It is much harder to discern a general policy pattern among the socialist governments of Southeast Asia, beyond the immediate reconstruction required in the Democratic Republic of Vietnam after 1954 and the rest of Indochina after 1975 (and Cambodia again in 1979). Over the long run both Burma and Vietnam tended to follow periods of doctrinaire socialism with periods of relative pragmatism and greater scope for private enterprise. Over-enthusiastic land reforms in the DRV in 1953–6, for example, gave way to the public admission of errors and excesses, as did efforts in the late 1970s to impose a strong command economy on the southern half of the SRV. Similarly, the trend toward state ownership and international isolation of the Revolutionary Government in Burma after 1962 was reversed in part by the Twenty-Year Plan of 1972, which emphasized increasing production and re-establishing broader international economic relations. Only Democratic Kampuchea did not survive long enough to repent of its excesses.

The 'third way' economies of Southeast Asia are no more. Burma before 1962, Indonesia before 1965, and Cambodia before 1970 tottered the tightrope between capitalism and socialism as far as they could. The fact that all eventually succumbed to military coups prompted in part by their disappointing economic performances should not blind us to the fact that each managed to survive for more than a decade with ideologies that defied simple categorization and Cold War pressures. Their theories were syncretic and their policies were *ad hoc*, without any discernible tendency except a proud assertion that they were distinctively nationalist: the *Pyidawtha* (literally 'sacred-pleasant-country') welfare state of Nu's Burma, the 'Khmer Socialism' of Sihanouk, and Sukarno's Pancasila and 'Marhaenism'. As emblems of the intellectual history of modern Southeast Asia these formulations are fascinating, representing the rejection of Western economic thought, both classical and Marxist. They did not, however, represent a coherent guide to economic policy or embody a recognizable set of local or Asian principles leading to specific tendencies in decision-making.[10]

---

[10] Such rhetorical rejection of Western models was by no means limited to 'third way' states, as shown by Democratic Kampuchea's 'Angkar' (echoing classical Angkor), Ne Win's 'Burmese Way to Socialism', Mahathir's advice to Malaysians to 'Look East' and Lee Kuan Yew's evocation of Confucian values in Singaporean development.

Another aspect of the nationalism of these economies was a growing touchiness about 'foreigners', both internal and external. At times this xenophobia manifested itself in discrimination against local aliens (particularly the Chinese in Indonesia and the Indians in Burma), at times in rejection of foreign aid that diminished local dignity and autonomy. Such attitudes were certainly not absent from other Southeast Asian countries, but they seemed particularly significant in 'third way' economies, perhaps because of the absence of clear competing economic principles. 'To hell with your aid', Sukarno finally told the United States. 'We prefer to live in poverty, because at least we will be free', Sihanouk proclaimed, in repudiating American military aid in October 1963, asserting a month later that 'the most elementary dignity forbids Cambodia to accept any form of American aid, no matter how small'.[11]

Some scholars of postwar Southeast Asia distinguished 'inward-looking' from 'outward-looking' approaches to development; in terms of economic logic, the former emphasized self-sufficiency and sequestration, while the latter favoured expanded trade as the path to long-term growth. But the rhetoric of Sukarno and Sihanouk, along with the persistent pattern of Southeast Asian discrimination against local aliens, suggests that nationalism was the root, autarky just a rationale. New régimes sometimes attempted to legitimate themselves by carrying such chauvinistic practices even farther: revolutionary Burma by drastically reducing all contact with the outside world, New Order Indonesia by cutting off relations with China and sponsoring the 1965–6 pogrom of local Chinese, Democratic Kampuchea by expelling all Vietnamese and provoking a war with Vietnam, as well as by persecuting Chams and other ethnic minorities. Isolation was in practice more a manifestation of nationalism than a coherent development strategy.

Southeast Asian choices of development strategies were based on both ideology and self-interest. The appeal of capitalism included its resonance with traditional mercantile behaviour in the region and its association with the visible wealth and strength of the West and Japan. Socialism, on the other hand, connected with local ideas of mutual assistance (*gotong royong*, *bayanihan*), charitable redistribution of wealth, and usufruct, rather than absolute ownership, of land. Southeast Asians were also regularly exposed to the conventional wisdom of international economists, a wisdom which itself was evolving throughout this period, from restoration of primary production through to import substitution and then to export-oriented industrialization, accompanied by a growing recognition of the need for increasing agricultural productivity. Occasionally Southeast Asians anticipated these intellectual shifts; Burma's Hla Myint was perhaps the most distinguished regional contributor to the international world of development economics. More often they followed the trends as they evolved, through their exposure to Western advice and education. So heavily, in fact, did graduates of a certain American university dominate the shaping

---

[11] J. D. Legge, *Sukarno: A Political Biography*, rev. edn, Sydney, 1984, 292; Sihanouk, *My War with the CIA: The Memoirs of Prince Norodom Sihanouk as Related to Wilfred Burchett*, rev. edn, Harmondsworth, Mdx, 130, 134.

of economic policy under the New Order in Indonesia that they came to be known as the 'Berkeley Mafia'. Southeast Asian technocrats also shared ideas with each other under the auspices of such agencies as the United Nations Economic Commission on Asia and the Far East (ECAFE; later Economic and Social Commission on Asia and the Pacific, or ESCAP), ASEAN, and the International Rice Research Institute (IRRI), based in the Philippines.

Those who opted out of capitalism also had foreign models from which to choose. The evolving conventional wisdom of Marxism-Leninism clearly influenced Vietnam and its client states. Their emphases on heavy industry in the late 1950s and 'reform' in the 1980s (including the renewed exchange of tropical produce for manufactured goods from the Soviet bloc) were at least in part responses to Moscow's changing orthodoxy, while the original model for the DRV land reform was Chinese. They also, like their capitalist counterparts, had these orthodoxies reinforced by technocrats returning from education in more advanced communist states. Democratic Kampuchea and Revolutionary Burma, on the other hand, staked out more idiosyncratic economic strategies, based partly on indigenous concepts, partly on differing foreign influences—French academic Marxism and Maoism in the former case, Fabian socialism in the latter. The advocates of a 'third way' had no conventional wisdom of either the right or the left to refer to for guidance, and so drew on an eclectic range of sources.

Everyone favoured growth in the abstract, but not everyone was in a position to capitalize on it. Industrialization aimed at import substitution in particular lent itself to the support of vested interests, as it depended on tariff protection or the allocation of special licences or foreign-exchange quotas for its profitability. (Ironically, the Philippines, which pioneered import substitution in the 1950s, became the slowest-growing capitalist state in the region two decades later in part because entrenched interests resisted the full implementation of an export-oriented strategy.) In other contexts, other sectors or industries—oil, export agriculture, transport and communications—were favoured not because of what they were but because of who owned them. There is ample documentation of the link between policy-makers and favoured industrialists throughout the region. Richard Robison's study of ownership patterns in Indonesia—including the extensive holdings of the Suharto (Cendana) group and various military commands—is the most comprehensive, but there are also studies of the 'crony capitalists' of the Philippines and the 'Sino-Thai rapprochement' between businessmen and bureaucrats in Thailand.[12] Ne

---

[12] Robison, *Indonesia: The Rise of Capital*, Sydney: Asian Studies Association of Australia, Southeast Asia Publication Series no. 13, 1986; John F. Doherty, 'Who Controls the Philippine Economy?', in Belinda A. Aquino, ed., *Cronies and Enemies: The Current Philippine Scene*, Honolulu: University of Hawaii, Center for Asian and Pacific Studies, Philippine Studies Program, Occasional Paper no. 5, 1982, 7–35; G. William Skinner, *Leadership and Power in the Chinese Community of Thailand*, Ithaca: Cornell University, Association for Asian Studies Monograph no. 3, 1958; cf. Kevin Hewison, 'National Interests and Economic Downturn: Thailand', in Richard Robison, Kevin Hewison, and Richard Higgott, eds., *Southeast Asia in the 1980s: The Politics of Economic Crisis*, Sydney, 1987, 52–5.

Win of Burma became far more wealthy than his official salary could possibly justify, and three presidents of the Republic of Vietnam, or their close relatives, promoted the flourishing opium traffic there in return for a share of the profits. Decision-makers in communist Vietnam were less likely to enrich themselves substantially (though petty graft was rampant), but often fought for entrenched bureaucratic interests. Whether all this is regarded as simple corruption or seen as accepted 'patrimonial' practice, it cannot be ignored in the analysis of policy formation.

Nationalist policies, too, were reinforced by vested interests. Anti-Chinese and anti-Indian campaigns almost always received backing from indigenous traders and financiers, who genuinely wished to eliminate competitors, as well as from many officials and frontmen, who welcomed the opportunity to squeeze the outsiders more. Campaigns against trans-national corporations similarly were favoured by many local entrepreneurs and officials, such as the outspoken Filipino businessman Alejandro Lichauco,[13] though they were resisted by others who profited from their connections with these corporations.

Equity, insofar as it implied redistribution of wealth, was not usually in the interests of the country's rulers, except perhaps in Indochina. They might expropriate foreign plantations or discriminate against Chinese merchants, but they could not readily advocate serious land reform without jeopardizing their own class base. Of the non-socialist states, only the RVN introduced any effective land reform, and there it was imposed and financed by the USA. Public campaigns for social justice elsewhere defused potential violence and thus benefited the whole proprietorial class, as well as the politicians who proposed them, though in this respect a well-run public relations exercise, such as accompanied most Philippine 'land reforms', could achieve almost as much as genuine redistribution, at much lower cost. To the extent that equity implied public spending on schools, roads, clinics, government credit agencies, etc., it of course created vested interests among those who obtained the contracts to build or manage them.

The state also came to be an interest group in its own right, growing in response to its own imperatives as well as the perceived needs of the country. The absence or weakness of competing interests had made it possible to erect state enterprises in the first place. As there was no strong indigenous bourgeoisie, Southeast Asian governments did not have to placate the private commercial sector by promises of non-interference, and there was no popular insistence on the sanctity of market forces. Once established in business, the bureaucracy tended to expand; this was particularly true of military enterprises in Thailand, Indonesia, Burma, and Vietnam, both capitalist and communist. Despite the arguments of econo-mists who claimed that state-run ventures were always inefficient, Southeast Asian governments showed little interest in privatization until the 1980s, when Singapore started to undertake it (on a limited scale) and other governments started to talk about it. In general, however, the public proportion of national wealth always tended to grow.

[13] The Lichauco Paper: Imperialism in the Philippines, New York, 1973.

The danger in focusing on policy trends is the implicit assumption that they were wholly responsible for all that happened. Certainly much of the political debate within and about the region was framed in terms of legitimation by economic performance; it was implied that 'winners' won simply because they made the right choices, while 'losers' blundered. In practice, however, policy choices were often severely constrained, and performance depended to a considerable degree upon factors beyond the control of Southeast Asian governments. The decentralization of urban development in the DRV was primarily a response to the American bombing campaign; the forced evacuation of Phnom Penh in 1975 could be explained partially in terms of the inability of that swollen city to feed itself after five years of war; and the prosperity of Indonesia, Malaysia, and Brunei after 1973 was largely based on the global oil boom that began in that year. Policy-making in Southeast Asia was not simply the product of ideology and self-interest; it emerged from experience, from trial-and-error responses to a changing international environment.

ECONOMIC IMPLICATIONS OF INTERNATIONAL POLITICS

The world into which the independent states of Southeast Asia emerged was one that would not leave them alone. Governments outside the region persistently tried to influence local affairs. Such 'neo-colonialism' was not the principal determinant of modern Southeast Asian history, as its critics often implied, but its effects cannot be ignored. In the political sphere it ranged from attempts to manipulate local elections to full-scale military interventions. Economic assistance was often the handmaiden of political intent, though the gradual diminution of bilateral aid in favour of multilateral lending nominally depoliticized it. A host of cultural and educational institutions, from the Peace Corps to training programmes for Southeast Asian bureaucrats, officers, and academics, tended to reinforce these links at personal and intellectual levels.

    In the immediate postwar period, the most significant attempts to influence Southeast Asia came from the former colonial powers. Once they had recognized Indonesian independence, however, the Dutch soon faded from the scene. The process of decolonization had left them with a bitter taste: many of their remaining investments were withdrawn or nationalized, and they were not in a strong position to supply much aid or advice. The French in Indochina and the British in Burma were little better off; economically shaken themselves, their continuing influence tended to depend on the goodwill of the new nationalist governments, which was never great. Britain did somewhat better in its former maritime possessions, at least until the 1970s, when it closed its naval base in Singapore and the Malaysian government began to indigenize foreign investments. The French and the British also retained some influence (in non-communist Indochina and Malaysia, respectively) in the field of education, capitalizing on what remained of the prestige of their language and culture through advisers for local ministries of education and study grants for some of their better students.

The USA, on the other hand, emerged from World War II with enhanced wealth and strength, becoming the dominant external influence on the region's economic affairs, the major agent of 'neo-colonialism' in the 1950s and 1960s. It acted not just on behalf of American trade and investment, but as the defender of capitalist interests in general against the perceived threat of global communism. It fought directly against overtly communist movements, particularly in the Second Indochina War, when it deployed over half a million troops; it engaged in the subversion of nominally neutralist but potentially left-leaning governments in Indonesia, Laos, and Cambodia; and it subsidized right-wing movements throughout the region, thus laying the groundwork for military coups in Indonesia (1965) and Thailand (1976) as well as for martial law in the Philippines (1972).

Economic assistance from the United States was generally correlated with political aims rather than need or prospective profitability. The countries of Indochina, where the Cold War became hot, were the most heavily subsidized. Over the course of twenty years (1955–75) the RVN received $16.8 billion in military aid and $8.5 billion in economic aid.[14] In proportional terms, the other non-communist states received even more: the Khmer Republic got aid in 1974 amounting to more than half its GNP, while in 1972 Laos was able to import twenty times as much as it exported, thanks to $250 million military aid (which actually exceeded the entire GNP by 16 per cent) plus another $50 million in economic aid. Thailand, as a site of major American military bases, was also rewarded handsomely for its co-operation. Between 1950 and 1975 Thailand received $650 million in economic aid, $1 billion in regular military assistance (nearly 60 per cent of the total Thai defence budget for the period), and another $1 billion in military operating costs, equipment transfers, subsidies for Thai troops in Vietnam, and base construction costs. In neutralist Burma and Indonesia, however, early efforts to use aid to sway them to the American cause were not particularly successful, although the 1965 coup in Indonesia was, like the imposition of martial law in the Philippines, rewarded by greatly increased aid over the next few years.

The Philippines was unique in the length and depth of its economic dependence upon a single external patron. In the immediate postwar period its government had little choice but to accept American imposi-tions, but over time the United States became less overtly imperious. Direct economic and military aid peaked in real terms between 1949 and 1952, when it totalled over $600 million, and though it continued at substantial levels thereafter it never represented a determinant component of the national budget; by the 1970s, it began to give way to multilateral and private lending. Individual Filipinos also benefited from military and

[14] Douglas C. Dacy, *Foreign Aid, War, and Economic Development: South Vietnam, 1955–1975*, Cambridge, UK, 1986, 200. Nguyen Anh Tuan, *South Vietnam: Trial and Experience: A Challenge for Development*, Athens, Ohio: Ohio University, Monographs in International Studies, Southeast Asia Series, no. 80, 1987, provides a slightly different breakdown, but the same total of just over $25 billion assistance.

civilian pension disbursements from the United States, which averaged over $120 million a year in the late 1970s. The Philippine demand for 'rent' for the military bases (though Americans refused to call it that) escalated from the 1970s onward and resulted in aid promises that rose from $50 million a year in 1979 to nearly ten times that a decade later; at the same time, bases-related spending slid from 2.3 per cent of GNP in the mid-1960s to 1.25 or 1.5 per cent in the mid-1980s.[15] The American share of Philippine trade and foreign investment also declined significantly over time, and by 1974 mutual special tariff concessions were finally terminated.

In spite of the diminution of direct leverage over the Philippine economy, the United States retained a disproportionate influence there, derived in part from the dominant American role in purveying advice to decision-makers and educating technocrats. Filipinos studied American textbooks, undertook postgraduate study at American universities, and engaged in joint research and planning projects with American counterparts; to a considerable extent, the hold that the USA had over the Philippine economy did not reside in ownership, but in the minds of the Filipinos themselves. The USA also attempted to exercise the same kind of personal influence elsewhere in the region, especially in the 1960s. One-fifth of the top level officials in the Thai bureaucracy in the 1970s had earned degrees from American universities, and roughly the same proportion of general officers in the Indonesian army had received training in US service schools.[16]

By the 1970s, however, the position of the USA in the region was changing. Imminent withdrawal from Indochina reduced its influence both there and in neighbouring Thailand, while the oil shocks of 1973 and 1979 reduced its economic strength relative to some of its capitalist rivals. Japan, in particular, emerged as a countervailing economic force in the region. Globally, its official development assistance rose from $244 million (6 per cent of the USA's) in 1965 to $3353 million (47 per cent) by 1980. Like its trade and investment, moreover, Japan's aid tended to be heavily concentrated in Asia, and before long Japan had become the major donor to most Southeast Asian countries. Japan outdid the USA in tying its aid to the utilization of its own goods and services; unlike American aid of the 1950s and 1960s, however, this was not usually accompanied by demands for ideological conformity. Members of the European Community, particularly the Federal Republic of Germany, also converted some of their rising prosperity into aid to Southeast Asia, as did Australia, newly aware of its near northern neighbours, and oil-rich Middle Eastern states, increasingly

[15] David Wurfel, *Filipino Politics: Development and Decay*, Ithaca, 1988, 193–5; Robert Pringle, *Indonesia and the Philippines: American Interests in Island Southeast Asia*, New York, 1980, 58–9; Charles W. Lindsey, 'The Economics of U.S. Military Bases in the Philippines', paper presented at Third International Philippine Studies Conference, Quezon City, 1989. Using a simple Keynesian-multiplier model of the Philippine economy, Lindsey estimated that the impact of this spending on the GNP declined from 3.5 to 2.0–2.3 per cent.
[16] Likhit Dhiravegin, *The Bureaucratic Elite of Thailand: A Study of Their Sociological Attributes, Educational Backgrounds, and Career Advancement Patterns*, Bangkok, 1978, 106–27; Bryan Evans III, 'The Influence of the United States Army on the Development of the Indonesian Army (1954–1964)', *Indonesia*, 47 (1989) 37.

conscious of their Islamic brothers around the world. Meanwhile, petro-dollars flooded international banking circles, and cheap loans, rather than direct grants, became the dominant form of foreign aid in the region.

As time went by, more and more economic assistance to Southeast Asia was channelled through multilateral organizations, such as the World Bank (International Bank for Reconstruction and Development), the Asian Development Bank (ADB), and the International Monetary Fund (IMF). In part this represented an acknowledgment that bilateral aid was perceived as manipulative. To many critics, however, the all-but-compulsory advice of the World Bank and IMF was no less an infringement of national sovereignty and a constraint on independent decision-making than the more overt 'neo-colonialism' of earlier years. To receive or renegotiate major loans, it was necessary to accept a package that almost invariably included devaluation, labour discipline, reduced government spending on social services, and greater opening to imports and foreign investment. Such measures were welcome to investors and often conducive to increased trade, but frequently they were also the cause of short-term hardship, particularly for the poorer classes.

Although the USSR and China inspired and supported revolutionary movements within the region, they had little economic impact outside Indochina. They made occasional efforts to influence Indonesia (before 1965) and Burma through offers of foreign aid, but to little avail; only in Vietnam, Laos, and Kampuchea did their contributions make a real difference. By the best estimates they contributed nearly $90 million a year to the Democratic Republic of Vietnam during 1955–65, rising to over $400 million a year in 1965–75.[17] In the earlier period, much of the aid was in the form of capital goods, but after 1965 it shifted to war matériel, food, and basic consumer goods. The breakdown of relations between Vietnam and China in the late 1970s drove the SRV into deeper economic dependence on the USSR and its Council for Mutual Economic Assistance (COMECON) bloc, to the tune of over a billion dollars a year by the mid-1980s. China, meanwhile, increased its support for Democratic Kampuchea and, after 1978, for the Khmer Rouge in exile. Communist aid, like that from the West, carried with it constraints; mostly it could be used only for goods from the donor countries and implied the acceptance of donor advice.

INTERNATIONAL MARKETS AND TECHNOLOGY

Beyond these governmental initiatives, Southeast Asia was also exposed to independent trends in markets and technology. The quarter-century after World War II was one of unprecedented global prosperity, with international trade growing at an average rate of well above 10 per cent a year and economic production increasing at the highest rate in modern history. This was due in part to improved productivity and lower transport costs,

---

[17] Melanie Beresford, *Vietnam: Politics, Economics and Society*, London, 1988, 143–4.

but there were political factors as well. Along with the absence of war between the major powers there was also a general worldwide reduction of trade barriers, mediated through such institutions as the General Agreement on Tariffs and Trade (GATT) and the United Nations Conference on Trade and Development (UNCTAD). Despite some efforts within UNCTAD to legislate in favour of the developing world, a disproportionate share of the expanded trade and wealth was claimed by the industrialized countries, as the terms of trade tended to move in their favour from the early 1950s onward. Globally, however, there was enough for everyone; even non-oil-producing Third World countries enjoyed an average increase in exports of more than 7 per cent a year.

Tropical products, on which Southeast Asia had depended so heavily during the colonial era, performed well in the first postwar decade. After a dip in the late 1940s, the Korean War created an enormous boom—'a period such as commodity markets in general had never previously known'[18]—in the early 1950s, which helped regional recovery, particularly in Malaya and the Philippines, where productive capacity had largely been restored. Thereafter, however, prices tended to slip, although individual commodities rallied occasionally, particularly in the 1970s. Minerals generally held up better than agricultural products, despite enormous price fluctuations; ventures in copper, tin, bauxite, nickel, zinc, tungsten and chromium all proved profitable from time to time.

The major exception to the general downward trend, however, was oil, which shot to unprecedented heights when the Organization of Petroleum Exporting Countries (OPEC) discovered in 1973 how to flex its economic muscles, quadrupling world prices. Despite later fluctuations, including a second price hike in 1979 and a significant drop in 1982–3, oil prices thereafter were always far higher than they had ever been before. In many respects the first oil crisis marked a watershed in modern economic history, the end of a postwar golden age for world trade. Economic growth did not stop in 1973, however. Though OPEC had caused a short-term global recession and presented new challenges to importers of oil and petroleum-based commodities (such as fertilizer), it also brought substantial new wealth to countries with a surplus of oil or natural gas and supplied the international banking system with more money to lend to worthy—and unworthy—borrowers.

Another major development in the global economy was the growth of transnational corporations and banks. Between 1960 and 1980 the sales of the world's 200 largest industrial corporations increased from $200 billion to $2 trillion, or from 18 per cent to 29 per cent of the entire gross domestic product of the non-socialist world. Much of their investment was underwritten by huge transnational banks, the hundred largest of which had assets of $4.4 trillion by 1981. Their sheer size tended to give these firms substantial influence on multilateral agencies and governments, so that despite their non-official status they had to be taken into account in any analysis of 'neo-colonialism'. Although American corporations and

---

[18] J. W. F. Rowe, *Primary Commodities in International Trade*, Cambridge, UK, 1965, 103.

banks, such as Unilever, General Motors, and National City Bank of New York (later Citibank), were dominant in the early postwar period, from the 1960s onward Japanese and European firms began to gain ground. The share of USA-based firms in the total sales of the world's 200 largest corporations declined from 73 per cent in 1960 to barely 50 per cent in 1980, by which time Japanese banks actually owned greater total assets than their American counterparts.[19] Mitsubishi, Matsushita, Sumitomo, Toyota, Nippon Steel, and the Bank of Tokyo emerged among the major investors in Southeast Asia, where they often outstripped their Western rivals; at the same time, Japan became the leading trade partner of several countries in the region.

As they broadened their horizons, the transnational corporations took advantage of improved communications and tariff reductions to internationalize their operations. To them, Third World countries had once been simply sources of raw materials or markets for manufactures; later they were fields for import substitution investment; finally they became critical elements in a truly global economy, under a 'New International Division of Labour'. The corporations provided basic technology, sourced their production wherever labour was cheapest and taxes were lowest, and marketed the output globally, often taking advantage of special tariff concessions for goods from developing countries. Oil-rich banks, backed by their governments, were happy to supply the necessary capital for such investments. Third World countries bid against each other for the right to participate in manufacturing for the global market. The simple division between primary producers and industrial countries eroded; taking advantage of cheap labour, American department stores ordered children's garments from the Philippines, and Japanese computer firms subcontracted silicon chips from Malaysia.

Those Third World countries, including Singapore, that were first to establish export-oriented light industries, especially in the 1960s, became known as the newly industrializing countries. The manufacture of textiles, garments, toys, electrical goods and electronic components and the processing of primary products (e.g., canning tuna and pineapples, petroleum refining) became for these countries and those which wished to emulate them an opportunity to compensate for declining terms of trade. Another area of compensation was services, sold abroad or to visiting foreigners: banking, ship repair, personal services, and tourism. The Second Indochina War, particularly between 1965 and 1973, boosted such sales in Southeast Asia by the overspill from American military expenditures (e.g., from refitting of naval vessels and 'rest-and-recreation' spending by American troops) to Vietnam and nearby nations, particularly Thailand and the Philippines. By the 1980s Southeast Asia, which had been a net importer of labour and services in the colonial period, was exporting construction workers to the Middle East, maids to Hongkong, doctors and nurses to North America, and entertainers to Japan. Diversification had

[19] Robin Broad, *Unequal Alliance, 1979–1986: The World Bank, the International Monetary Fund, and the Philippines*, Berkeley, 1988, 38–43.

become a key to economic success in the postwar world. Except for the oil-producers, no Southeast Asian country in the 1980s was as dependent on a single commodity as Malaya once had been on rubber or Burma on rice; this helped cushion the effects of global market fluctuations, generally greater for primary commodities than for manufactures and services.

Technological developments also had significant consequences for the economies of postwar Southeast Asia. Perhaps the most significant of these were in the area of health. Beginning with the development of penicillin, sulfa drugs, and DDT in World War II, they led to a spectacular drop in mortality throughout the region. National crude death rates fell by an average of close to 20 per thousand in the four decades following the war, as annual population growth rates climbed to rates unprecedented in human history. New technologies of birth control also became available in this period, but as their utilization depended not just on accessibility but on motivation, which varied widely, the decline of fertility was not as rapid or universal as that of mortality.

The 'green revolution'—actually a complex package of new high-yielding variety seeds, irrigation, fertilizers, and pesticides—was the best-known example of technological innovation in postwar Southeast Asian agriculture. It was developed in the mid-1960s at IRRI and soon communicated to the rest of the region; within a decade traditional rice-deficit countries such as Indonesia and the Philippines became self-sufficient. Southeast Asian agriculture also profited from the development of high-yielding varieties of other crops, particularly rubber—Malaysian yields improved over 120 per cent between 1954 and 1970—and of farm machines such as tractors, combine harvesters, and water-pumps. Along with the extension and intensification of cropping, such technological developments enabled agricultural production in the region to remain ahead of population growth. At the same time, however, other improvements in technology—from the increased mechanization of Western agriculture to the development of synthetic rubber and nylon rope—drove down international market prices for many Southeast Asian crops.

Global developments in industrial technology also had both positive and negative effects on the postwar Southeast Asian economy. Although the computer industry was highly sophisticated at its core, it required components made by a large semi-skilled workforce, often located where labour was relatively cheap, such as in Singapore and the export-processing zones of the Philippines, Malaysia, and Thailand. Other innovations, however, were capital-intensive and extremely complex, reducing the likelihood that a labour-surplus economy could ever be independently competitive. Even when Third World countries obtained modern factories through foreign aid or investment, they often had difficulty keeping them up to date; the heavy industry introduced into Burma, Vietnam, and Indonesia in the 1950s was virtually obsolete two decades later. Southeast Asia was also affected by advances in transportation (cheaper trucks, buses, jeepneys, scooters, and motorboats) and communications (radios, televisions and telephones) which greatly increased the flow of people, goods, and information. Jumbo jets carried tourists, silicon chips, luxury imports and perishable export commodities across the oceans. All these different technologies had different local effects, but in general they tended to facilitate the creation of larger economic networks—provincial, national, and global—in which the wealthier centre tended to dominate the poorer periphery. Within Southeast Asia, national governments enormously increased their capacity to speak to and control distant rural populations; internationally, foreign governments and corporations enhanced their ability to plan globally and so override local initiatives.

The most spectacular new military technologies were those deployed by the USA in the Second Indochina War, which certainly caused more physical damage than any human agency in the history of Southeast Asia, including dropping five times the tonnage of bombs that fell globally in all of World War II. Advanced military technology was also used by Southeast Asians against local rebels and rivals. The campaigns of Jakarta against East Timor and of Manila against Sulu in the 1970s featured jets and helicopter gunships; rumours of chemical warfare also circulated about both of these campaigns, as well as those of the SRV in Cambodia and Laos. The state did not always prevail, as the forty-year Karen resistance in Burma indicated, but each advance in military technology tended to increase the extension of central control.

As independent states, of course, the countries of Southeast Asia could in theory control their exposure to international markets and their access to technology as well as their relations with foreign governments. What they encountered in practice was a package: trade, aid, investment, technology and compulsory advice on how to use them all. The developed capitalist countries accounted for 60–70 per cent of the world's trade and an even larger proportion of international aid and foreign investment, as well as most of the major technological innovations of the postwar period. To reject any element of their package was to risk losing the rest of it, as the 'third way' states came to realize.

The access of the socialist countries of Southeast Asia to new technologies was quite uneven, restricted sometimes by self-imposed quarantine, sometimes by foreign blockade, and always by the effects of war and poverty. After 1954 the DRV opted for the alternative package offered by the communist bloc, which controlled only about 10 per cent of the world's trade and a comparably reduced share of total aid, investment, and advanced technology. Revolutionary Burma and Democratic Kampuchea chose isolation instead, proclaiming self-reliance as a supreme virtue. This had certain benefits for Burma, which was buffered from the full effects of global market fluctuations and possible foreign intervention in its internal politics and cultural life, but it was not an optimal strategy in the postwar economic environment. The enormous expansion of world trade and the extraordinary advance of technology represented a unique opportunity for development, which Southeast Asian states missed out on at their own cost. The efforts of Indochina and Burma in the late 1980s to attract more non-communist trade, aid, investment and technology suggested both how attractive these were and how difficult they were to obtain without compromising national sovereignty.

ECONOMIC GROWTH AND STRUCTURAL CHANGE

There were many technical problems in defining and measuring growth in postwar Southeast Asia. Real GNP or gross domestic product (GDP) had to be calculated, making appropriate adjustments for inflation, the value of non-market production (always a sizeable proportion of local economic activity) and illegal trade (smuggling being a major industry in many of the region's borderlands). These figures were then converted into real income (or GDP per capita), allowing for rapid population increase. National economists and international agencies devoted a great deal of effort to all these calculations, yet admitted that the results were far from perfect.

The available data suggest, nevertheless, that the real income of most Southeast Asians grew in the postwar period, a pattern corroborated by other indicators, such as declining infant mortality and expanded literacy. Only for the countries of Indochina is this conclusion in doubt, in part because warfare and maladministration disrupted economic record-keeping as well as growth. In broad terms the capitalist economies clearly grew faster than the socialist economies, but that is at least partially explained by the fact that they suffered less from warfare and enjoyed greater access to foreign aid and trade. At the same time, it must be acknowledged that growth was usually neither as rapid nor as regular as Southeast Asians had hoped, and that most countries experienced extended periods of stagnation or decline, especially Democratic Kampuchea, 1975–8; but also Malaya, 1951–8; Indonesia, 1959–65; Burma, 1964–74; the DRV, 1965–72; the RVN and the Khmer Republic, 1970–5; the SRV and Laos, 1976–80; and the Philippines, 1981–6. Moreover, the increased prosperity implied by the gross data was not experienced by a substantial number of Southeast Asians, who would have been amazed to hear that they were better off than they had ever been before.

Singapore was the great Southeast Asian success story; over the whole postwar period it was second only to Japan in per capita growth and ranked with Hong Kong, Taiwan, and the Republic of Korea as one of Asia's four 'little dragons'. The British had developed it as an entrepôt, not an industrial centre, and its average annual growth rate through the troubled 1950s was under 2 per cent, though this figure may not fully reflect local earnings from the smuggling trade with Indonesia. With no agrarian sector to speak of, and an inconsequential domestic market after its departure from Malaysia in 1965, independent Singapore had no delusions of economic self-sufficiency. Its leaders realized that it would have to depend on export-oriented industrialization and services, financed by foreign investment if necessary, and set about planning to achieve those ends. A strategic location, an efficient and apparently incorruptible bureaucracy, a well-disciplined labour force (once the independent trade unions were broken), and a tough population planning programme contributed to Singapore's success. By the efficient development of modern banking and the stock market it not only mobilized its own domestic capital but tapped into regional resources as well, standing at the centre of a great Chinese financial network. It served (along with Hong Kong) as a clearing house for all manner of international financial transactions, legal and otherwise. Real per capita income grew at an average annual rate of over 7 per cent in the quarter-century after independence and reached $7500 a year by the late 1980s. Only Brunei did better, emerging from obscurity in the oil boom of the 1970s; its huge oil revenues, divided among a tiny population, gave it a per capita income of over $15,000 by the late 1980s.

Malaya based its postwar recovery on the restoration of primary production, and remained heavily dependent for two decades on the export of rubber and tin and the importation of rice. Its wealth per capita had long been among the highest in the region, and in the immediate postwar period high commodity prices and rapid recovery of production brought it to the top again. In the 1950s the Emergency disrupted production and real per capita growth was negligible, averaging barely 1 per cent a year over the decade. In the 1960s, however, import-substitution manufacturing grew rapidly (averaging 17 per cent a year, 1959–68) and earlier state investment in rubber replanting and the extension of oil palm cultivation began to pay off; GNP growth per capita climbed to average annual rates of 3–4 per cent. In the long run the new Federation of Malaysia was also to benefit from the natural resources of Sabah and Sarawak, especially oil and timber, though some of the proceeds had to be spent in raising the living standards of the poor farmers, fishermen, and hunter-gatherers of these states.

The New Economic Policy of the 1970s was designed to increase indigenous (*bumiputra*) ownership and participation in the economy; the only way this could be done without directly dispossessing the Chinese and Indians was by accelerated growth. One component of this was promotion of non-plantation agriculture through the green revolution, extension of cultivated area, and the introduction of new cash crops. Another was export-oriented industrialization; in the absence of indigenous entrepreneurs, this was operated by the state in trust for the *bumiputra* community. Foreign capital, particularly Japanese, was invited to participate in joint ventures (with 30 per cent of the stock reserved for *bumiputras*) and operate in special free-trade zones. Along with the oil boom, which made its offshore reserves and natural gas worth exploiting, these measures lifted Malaysia's per capita growth rates above 5 per cent in the 1970s, and growing diversification kept the average around 4 per cent in the 1980s, despite a mid-decade recession. With income per capita over $2000 and life expectancy approaching seventy years, Malaysia was clearly the most prosperous of the sizeable Southeast Asian nations.

After some early experimentation with state enterprises, the Thai government under Sarit Thanarat switched in the 1960s to infrastructural investment on behalf of private import-substitution industry and agriculture. Industry, primarily Sino-Thai in ownership, did in fact grow rapidly (averaging over 10 per cent annually); but the sustained growth of the economy as a whole—averaging over 3 per cent per capita in the 1950s, 5 per cent in the 1960s—was possible only because agriculture, from which most of the population still earned their living, also grew steadily. This was due in part to the expansion of irrigation (from 600,000 hectares in 1947 to 2.2 million by 1969) and the increased use of tractors and fertilizers, particularly in the central plain. Most of the growth, however, was attributable to the extension of cultivation, abetted by improved roads, rather than to increased yield. Some of this expansion was in traditional crops such as rice and rubber, but much of it was in new crops, particularly for the Japanese market: maize, kenaf, and cassava. By 1968 the export value of other crops passed that of rice for the first time in modern Thai history, having quadrupled in value over the previous fifteen years. Thailand also benefited from substantial American aid throughout the 1950s and 1960s.

The early 1970s, however, brought political instability, the oil crisis, and the end of most American aid, as well as signs that import substitution was reaching its ceiling. To the surprise of most experts the Thai economy kept growing, with GNP per capita increasing at an average annual rate of 4 per cent through the 1970s and 1980s. The civilian governments of the 1970s did not survive long enough to alter the broad development strategy pursued by the military and the technocrats. This was to promote agricultural development (the green revolution eventually arrived) and export industries, inviting foreign corporations, particularly Japanese, to participate along with local capitalists and a friendly government. Such new exports as textiles, computer components, prawns, and precious stones joined greatly increased tourism to diversify the economy and cushion it against commodity downturns. Thailand also benefited from a population planning programme that slowed demographic increase substantially in the 1970s and 1980s. By the end of the latter decade per capita income had reached $1000, passing the faltering Philippines. During the entire postwar period, in fact, Thailand was second in the region only to Singapore in average rate of growth.

Over the first decade and a half of the postwar period the Philippines was a regional leader in economic growth, thanks to American aid, a well-educated population, and relatively sophisticated institutional infrastructure. It was the Southeast Asian pioneer of import-substitution industrialization; between 1949 and 1957 this sector grew at over 12 per cent a year. The Korean War boom helped to pull GNP growth per capita to an average annual rate of nearly 4 per cent; per capita income remained higher than Taiwan and South Korea as late as 1960. During the 1960s, however, manufacturing growth slowed, due to limited demand and the chronic inefficiencies of over-protection. With commodity prices also sliding, and population increase climbing above 3 per cent a year, GNP per capita growth fell to just 2 per cent. Vested interests in import substitution (American as well as Filipino) prevented the serious implementation of an export-manufacturing strategy urged by both indigenous and foreign experts.

After the declaration of martial law in 1972, partially justified by the poor performance of the economy, growth did in fact pick up somewhat. Over the next eight years it averaged 3 per cent per capita—still the lowest rate in ASEAN—thanks to the green revolution, a construction boom, surging commodity prices, and above all to increased foreign borrowing. The total Philippine foreign debt, public and private, rose from $2.2 billion in 1972 to $9 billion in 1979; along the way, government borrowing passed private indebtedness for the first time. Much of this capital went directly into the pockets of Marcos and his 'cronies' rather than into productive investment, however. With the second oil shock of 1979 and the subsequent collapse in commodity prices, the 'debt trap' started to close. The Philippines had to borrow more than ever, and at worse terms; in just three years (1980–3) foreign indebtedness rose from 6.6 per cent to 49.4 per cent of the GNP, while growth per capita slipped from 2 per cent to zero. In the aftermath of the assassination of Benigno ('Ninoy') Aquino, Jr, public confidence collapsed, and the economy with it. The GNP actually fell over the next three years; by the February Revolution of 1986, it was back at the level of 1980, down 20 per cent on a per capita basis. Under Corazon Aquino there was an immediate improvement in both private investment and foreign aid, but even her most optimistic advisers acknowledged that it would be many years before the economy made up the ground it had lost. Before ameliorative 'restructuring' the foreign debt approached $30 billion and the ratio of debt-service to exports was estimated at close to 40 per cent, double what was usually considered the danger level for developing countries. Population growth also remained high, as planning efforts were left in disarray by the pro-natalist bias of the new régime.

The Indonesian economy, by contrast, began the postwar period poorly and achieved sustained growth only after 1965. The Revolution forced postponement of reconstruction to the 1950s, when the young republic had to struggle with problems of high mortality, food shortages, inflation, and the destruction of physical capital. A GNP growth rate of nearly 2 per cent per capita for much of the decade, though respectable under the circumstances, was disappointing to many Indonesians, particularly Sukarno, who took over effective control of the state apparatus between 1957 and 1959. His answer was nationalism: expropriation of Dutch property; discrimination against the Chinese; major state investment in heavy industry (to make Indonesia self-sufficient); and a rhetorical barrage levelled against 'neo-colonialism' in all its forms, culminating in 'confrontations' over Irian Jaya and Malaysia that increased military spending and reduced foreign aid and trade. The results, in economic terms, were disastrous: trade collapsed, industrial production plummeted, and hyper-inflation (over 2000 per cent a year by the mid-1960s) set in. GNP per capita actually declined between 1957 and 1965, as did food consumption in this already hungry country.

Between 1965 and 1967 the military wrested control from Sukarno and turned the economy over to the technocrats, who immediately sought and received the foreign aid and investment that had been frightened away in the period of Guided Democracy. The emphasis was on curbing inflation, promoting rice production (through the Bimas ['mass guidance'] agricultural extension programme, which provided physical inputs and credit), and fostering import-replacing industries (often with military participation). By the end of the 1960s the economy was well on the road to recovery, and even before the oil boom, annual growth per capita had climbed to 5 per cent. It maintained this rate for the remainder of the 1970s, despite the Pertamina scandal of 1975—possibly the largest defalcation in Southeast Asian history—but fell back to around 1 per cent after the decline of oil prices in 1982–3. To a considerable extent, moreover, this growth continued to depend on the exploitation of primary resources (including timber and minerals as well as oil) rather than on the manufacture of exports, which was always hampered by vested interests in import-substitution industries and an affinity for the ideal of national self-sufficiency. On the positive side, population planning slowed demographic growth somewhat, though Indonesia continued to have over two million new mouths to feed each year. By the end of the 1980s per capita income approached $600 and life expectancy approached sixty years, both the highest in Indonesian history but still the lowest in ASEAN.

Devastated by World War II and the civil war that followed independence (1948–52), Burma entered the 1950s as perhaps the poorest sizeable country in Asia, with a per capita income of less than $50 a year. From this low base it grew rapidly—over 4 per cent a year—throughout the decade, yet by 1960 the production of rice and teak, its two main exports, still had not reached prewar levels, while oil production was barely half what it had been in 1939 and other minerals fared even worse. Meanwhile, the prices of rice and other commodities kept slipping, and endemic insurgency inhibited the development of many outlying districts. Though its tiny manufacturing sector grew rapidly Burma, after more than a decade of independence, had not regained prewar income levels, much less started to catch up with the developed world.

As in Indonesia, disappointment at the performance of the economy led toward radical nationalism. Ne Win went even farther than Sukarno in cutting ties (aid, trade, and investment) with the outside world, discriminating against resident aliens, and plunging down the path of autonomous development, with an emphasis on heavy industry. Within two years of the 1962 coup the government had nationalized almost all mineral development, commerce in timber, import–export transactions, wholesale and brokerage trade, and banking. By the end of 1965 it controlled 60 per cent of manufacturing and 90 per cent of legal trade. Many Chinese and Indians, squeezed by 'inexorably comprehensive restrictive laws … strictly applied',[20] emigrated. GNP per capita scarcely grew over the next decade, as external trade collapsed (dropping more than 10 per cent a year), agricultural production stagnated, and industry and mining suffered from the lack of expatriate expertise, capital goods, spare parts, and co-ordinated planning. Only a vast illegal trade, both internal and external, kept the economy afloat at all.

Adoption of more pragmatic policies in the early 1970s got the Burmese economy moving again, with GNP per capita growing at nearly 4 per cent a year for a decade (1973–83). External assistance, particularly from Japan and multilateral agencies, helped finance major projects in the extractive industries, though at a cost of increasing the ratio of debt-service to exports to 55 per cent by 1986. Agriculture, meanwhile, was boosted both by improved fertilizer supply and a revised marketing system that restored producer incentives; manufacturing also expanded, though it remained

[20] Yuan-li Wu and Chun-hsi Wu, *Economic Development in Southeast Asia: The Chinese Dimension*, Stanford, 1980, 88–9.

unbalanced and underdeveloped by regional standards. In the mid-1980s, however, growth was slowed by rising debt, reduced aid, and recession, even before political turmoil in 1988–9 led to the suspension of most foreign aid and declining GNP per capita once more. Burma remained in monetary terms among the poorest countries in the world, with per capita income under $200, though indicators of health and education suggested that the actual standard of living was not quite as low as this ranking implied.

The economic history of postwar Indochina was dominated and clouded by warfare: against the French, the Americans, the Chinese, and among its peoples. No reliable data are available for the period of the First Indochina War; descriptive evidence suggests a distinct improvement over the desperate conditions of 1945, but not much advance on the prewar economy. In the decade following the departure of the French, however, GNP per capita generally rose. The DRV rebuilt its economy almost from scratch, first with remarkable agricultural recovery (to 1959), then, as collectivization disrupted agriculture, with sustained increases in industrial output; the result was per capita rates averaging around 5 per cent. Growth rates in the RVN were comparable, and massive American aid enabled consumption (which regularly exceeded total GNP) to rise even faster. Even in Cambodia, GNP per capita grew at over 2 per cent a year between 1959 and 1964.[21]

The American military intervention ended this epoch of growth. Total RVN production continued to rise, thanks in part to the green revolution and a booming import trade, but it was only the aid-financed doubling of real expenditures on public administration and defence between 1965 and 1972 that enabled it to keep pace with population growth. DRV production declined under the impact of American bombing, 1965–8, and never fully recovered. Cambodia's GNP, already slowed by recession in the late 1960s, plummeted after Lon Nol took over in 1970, and fell more than 10 per cent a year over the next five years. The economy of Laos was brought almost to a standstill by American bombing, which made refugees of one-quarter of the population.

After 1975 the SRV fully expected a rapid recovery and dramatic transformation of its economy. 'Because we won the war, we thought we could do anything successfully', one official later admitted.[22] The government was aware of, and believed it could handle, the physical and demographic devastation of the south: fields and forests sprayed with herbicides, shattered infrastructure, food shortages, millions of refugees, an estimated three million unemployed, 500,000 prostitutes, 100,000 drug addicts,

[21] Calculated from data in G. Nguyen Tien Hung, *Economic Development of Socialist Vietnam, 1955–1980*, New York: Praeger Special Studies in International Economics and Development, 1977; Andrew Vickerman, *The Fate of the Peasantry: Premature 'Transition to Socialism' in the Democratic Republic of Vietnam*, New Haven: Yale University Southeast Asia Studies, 1986; Dacy, *Foreign Aid, War, and Economic Development*; Nguyen Anh Tuan, *South Vietnam*; and Remy Prud'homme, *L'economie du Cambodge*, Paris: Collection 'Tiers Monde', 1969. No comparable data are available for Laos.

[22] Quoted in Sue Downie, 'Shattered Vietnam on Road to Recovery', *South China Morning Post*, 25 June 1989.

800,000 orphans. What they failed to take into account was how much the economy and society had changed since 1954, and how difficult the 'socialist transformation' would therefore be. Farmers resisted collectivization, urban settlers sent to New Economic Zones returned to the cities, industrial and agricultural production fell, and efforts to crack down on private trade resulted only in the exodus of hundreds of thousands of boat people (mostly Chinese), taking with them both skills and capital. War with Kampuchea (Cambodia) and China in 1979 strained the economy further. On a per capita basis, national income declined at nearly 2 per cent a year during 1976–80. By late 1979 the government had embarked on an erratic series of 'reforms' intended to increase economic efficiency by restoring incentives in agriculture and accountability in industry. These were never whole-heartedly adopted, however, and recovery in the 1980s was uneven: steady growth (around 4 per cent per capita) in the first half of the decade was reversed by triple-digit inflation, agricultural stagnation, and general economic decline between 1985 and 1988.

Like Vietnam, Laos suffered in the late 1970s from the loss of aid, the departure of refugees and an abortive attempt at agricultural collectivization. It also recovered (at an annual rate of around 2 per cent per capita) in the 1980s, benefiting from rising agricultural production and expanded trade with Thailand, particularly the export of electricity from the Nam Ngum project. Both Laos and Vietnam remained heavily dependent on foreign aid, primarily from the Soviet bloc. Even with many loans on concessionary terms, their ratios of debt-service to exports were the highest in the region; Vietnam was 'in a position of de facto default' by the late 1980s.[23] Since much of their national wealth was still produced by agriculture, they were also extraordinarily vulnerable to unfavourable weather conditions. Estimates of per capita income by the late 1980s ranged around $150–200, although, as in Burma, indices of health and literacy were comparatively high.

The devastation of the Cambodian economy in the 1970s is well known, though the notorious atrocities committed by Democratic Kampuchea after 1975 tend to overshadow the deaths (at least half a million) and economic decline under the Khmer Republic before that date. By the most reliable calculations, excess mortality between 1975 and 1979 was in the order of 740,000 to one million—perhaps half of them executed, the rest dying of starvation or illness. Another half million Khmers and some 200,000 Vietnamese fled the country.[24] The harassment, execution, or exile of most engineers, teachers, and medical personnel ruined what there was of industry, education, and modern health care. The country, a surplus rice-producer as late as the 1960s, fell into enormous deficit in the early 1970s; efforts to reverse this by sheer force of political will failed, and famine ensued in some districts. Income estimates were meaningless, but there was little doubt that Cambodia was worse off in 1979 than it had ever been

---

[23] Economist Intelligence Unit, *Country Profile: Indochina: Vietnam, Laos, Cambodia: 1988–89*, London, 1988, 24.
[24] Vickery, *Cambodia*, 184–8, Vickery, letter to editors, *Bulletin of Concerned Asian Scholars*, 20, 1 (1988) 70–3.

in modern times. Recovery through the 1980s was slow, hampered by continuing insurgency and an embargo by most potential aid-donors and trade partners outside the Soviet bloc. In agriculture, industry, and infrastructure, the 1980s never even caught up to the 1960s. By most indicators— food supply, estimated GDP per capita (under $100), infant mortality (over 150 per 1000 births) and life expectancy (under fifty years)—Cambodia remained the poorest country in the region and one of the poorest in the world.

Growth in postwar Southeast Asia was generally connected with the shift from agriculture to industry, one of the defining characteristics of the era. In 1950 manufacturing accounted for 12 per cent of Philippine GDP; elsewhere in the region, 5–10 per cent or even less. Forty years later only in Brunei, Laos, and Cambodia did the proportion remain below 10 per cent; in Burma and Indonesia it had climbed into the 10–15 per cent range; in the Philippines, Malaysia, Vietnam, Thailand, and Singapore it averaged 25 per cent or more. The inclusion of mining, construction and utilities raised the total for all industry to 30 per cent or more in the ASEAN countries. 'Services'—a catch-all category that lumped together public administrators, petty traders, professionals and prostitutes—also tended to grow, except where a strong shift toward socialist autarky shrank the contribution of commerce, as in Burma after 1962 and Indochina after 1975. Agriculture (including fishing and forestry), which had once produced well over half the wealth of the region, slipped steadily in the non-socialist states to one-quarter or less of GDP, though it remained around 40 per cent in troubled Burma and Vietnam, much higher in Laos and Cambodia.

The shifting composition of the GDP was due in part to the movement of labour out of agriculture, which had employed an average of 70–80 per cent of the workforce before the war and in the immediate postwar period. As late as 1960 it still accounted for over 80 per cent in Thailand and Indochina and over 70 per cent in Indonesia. By the late 1980s, however, it had fallen to 60 per cent in Thailand, 55 per cent in Indonesia, 45 per cent in the Philippines, and below 35 per cent in Malaysia; only in Burma (65 per cent) and the states of Indochina (65–80 per cent) did it remain high. The transition from import substitution to export industry helped in this process, as the latter, more dependent on international market forces, was impelled to capitalize on the comparative advantage of cheap local labour, and therefore tended to generate more employment.

Industry's share of GDP also grew because of rising productivity, as output per industrial worker regularly grew faster than output per farm worker. In services, on the other hand, productivity tended to lag, as the numbers of featherbedding civil servants and underemployed street people increased almost as fast as total production; even so, output per worker remained substantially higher than in agriculture. Although some attributed differences in productivity to cultural values ('indolence' or the 'work ethic'), they were clearly due less to differential effort than to differential access to capital, including the technology that capital could buy. This was most obvious in heavy industry, transportation, communications, and utilities, but was true in other sectors as well. Agriculture soon regained prewar production levels using traditional technology, and continued to expand as long as land was available, but yields could not rise indefinitely without capital investment. Beyond a certain point (around two tons of paddy per hectare) further increases depended on costly new technologies, particularly the introduction of high-yielding varieties, chemical fertilizers, pesticides and improved water control. The inability to supply these inputs was, along with pricing and procurement policies that discouraged expansion, a major cause of the retardation of agricultural development in Burma and Indochina.

The formation and deployment of capital was thus a critical variable in postwar Southeast Asia. Some development capital was obtained from abroad, though this brought with it not only foreign influence but also, except in the case of outright grants, an eventual outflow of resources in the form of loan repayments or corporate profits. Only in Indochina did foreign aid represent more than half of capital formation; by the early 1970s, in fact, it accounted for 100 per cent of it in the RVN and the Khmer Republic. Elsewhere in the region domestic savings, including those provided by local Chinese, accounted for from 60 per cent to more than 90 per cent (in Thailand) of gross capital formation.

Throughout the region the state was responsible for a substantial portion (often one-third or more) of domestic capital formation, through taxation and such forced-savings institutions as Singapore's Central Provident Fund. Governments also tried to influence private savings by guaranteeing the security of savings institutions, facilitating the creation of profitable investment opportunities, and using taxes and foreign exchange controls to discourage unnecessary consumption. The traditional emphasis of Southeast Asians on the redistribution of wealth, creating or displaying merit through largesse, tended to reduce somewhat their propensity to save, whereas the traditional Chinese ethic placed greater value on accumulation for the good of the clan. This helped explain the disproportionate weight of Chinese capital in the region; it has been calculated—admittedly on rather tenuous grounds—that by 1975 some $16 billion in Chinese capital was invested in Southeast Asia, roughly twice the amount of foreign direct investment.[25]

Class was also a factor, as the poor understandably spent a much higher proportion of their income on necessities than did the rich, leaving less surplus for possible investment. Redistributionist policies therefore tended in the short run to reduce capital formation. One way or another, however, gross capital formation seems to have increased in the postwar period. In the ASEAN countries it rose steadily from an average of 8–15 per cent of GDP in the 1950s to around 25 per cent (40 per cent in Singapore) two decades later, before falling slightly in the 1980s. In Burma it fluctuated wildly, but averaged under 15 per cent for the postwar period. Vietnam, north and south, achieved levels of around 15–20 per cent in the decade of peace after 1954 and 10–15 per cent in the decade of reunification after 1976, though it suffered net losses during the wartime years.

Not all of this capital was invested to optimal developmental advantage. Much of it, particularly in the capitalist states, was simply 'rent-seeking';

25 Wu and Wu, *Economic Development*, 31–4, 161–72.

the profitability of money-lending and landlordism, particularly in an era of rapid population growth, often outweighed the risks of investing in more productive ventures. Among productive investments, some turned out in practice to be more conducive to development than others. In postwar Southeast Asia growth was correlated most clearly with investments in basic infrastructure, agriculture, and light industry. Heavy industry rarely paid for itself. Energy was a high-risk venture; when a major power project or oil field was fully developed, it could boost the economy substantially, but before that there were usually years of uncertainty and delay. Import substitution, though important in early industrialization, soon ran up against market limits and developed inefficiencies which tended to cascade down to other industries. Export-oriented industrialization then provided a profitable alternative, though it became increasingly competitive over time; the early NICs found it easier than those who later hoped to emulate them.

Substantial investments in 'human capital'—health, education, and social services—were also common throughout the region, but cannot be clearly linked to economic growth. Most independent Southeast Asian states allocated 10–20 per cent of their budgets to education, with another 5 per cent or so for health and related services: inadequate to the task, but far more than had been spent in these areas before. The fastest-growing states in Southeast Asia generally provided the best and most extensive health and educational services, but this was as much a result of their greater wealth as a cause of it. On a proportional basis, relatively poor and slow-growing states such as Revolutionary Burma and the SRV often spent more of their available resources on human services than did such high achievers as Singapore and Malaysia, suggesting that the commitment to equity was even more powerful than the hope of growth.

Though differences in health and literacy remained, they were scarcely comparable in scale to differences in income and capital formation. By the late 1980s, average life expectancy in the region (Laos and Cambodia aside) ranged from around fifty-five years (Burma) to over seventy (Singapore and Brunei), with Indonesia, Vietnam, Thailand, the Philippines and Malaysia all within ten years of each other. Enrolments in primary school, which had ranged from under 10 per cent to over 70 per cent of the appropriate age group in 1950, were approaching 100 per cent throughout the region. Adult literacy rates climbed from well under 50 per cent to 80 per cent or more in most countries. Only in secondary and tertiary education were international discrepancies still wide, yet the cases of the Philippines and the SRV, with relatively strong educational (and health) systems but weak economies, challenged any simplistic 'human capital' interpretation of growth.

NATIONALISM AND EQUITY

Except in Singapore, a distinction was usually made between indigenous peoples and those identified as 'alien', even though some of the latter had been locally resident for several generations and were citizens of the newly independent states. The aliens were widely perceived as profiting at the expense of the indigenous population, a problem which governments took different approaches to solving. Where immigration had not already been severely restricted or prohibited before World War II, this was usually undertaken soon after, thus bringing to a close a century in which Southeast Asia had been open to a massive influx of foreign labour. The more drastic action of expelling resident aliens was rare, however; only Democratic Kampuchea undertook it on any significant scale. More common was a pattern of systematic discrimination that encouraged voluntary emigration, particularly of South Asians from Burma in the 1950s and 1960s, and of Chinese from Vietnam and Laos in the 1970s and 1980s. In Southeast Asia as a whole, however, the number of ethnic Chinese and Indians continued to increase, though it declined as a proportion of the total population (to around 5 per cent), since their fertility tended to be lower than the regional average.

Discrimination against aliens took a wide variety of forms: outright exclusion from certain occupations and industries; requirements that specified proportions of capital, management, or labour in private firms should be indigenous; restrictive quotas on business licences, foreign exchange allocations, and university places; insistence on the exclusive use of the national language in schools and official transactions, etc. Nominally non-discriminatory policies affecting specific industries or sectors of the economy were also employed. The nationalization of retail trade, for example, was particularly hard on the aliens in Burma and Vietnam, where they had previously held a near monopoly in such commerce, while the promotion of rice-growing in Malaysia favoured Malay peasants at the expense of non-Malay urban and plantation sectors.

Despite such policies, the Chinese continued to play a dominant role in the modern sectors of Southeast Asian economies. Recognizing the capabilities of Chinese capital and entrepreneurship, national need and individual greed combined to circumvent anti-alien regulations through legal technicalities or 'Ali-Baba' arrangements, in which an indigenous businessman or official ('Ali') served as frontman for a Chinese capitalist ('Baba'), who continued to manage the enterprise. In response to governmental pressure some Chinese investment did shift from commerce toward manufacturing, but it remained strong in trade as well. Estimates from the 1980s that ethnic Chinese owned 70–75 per cent of private domestic capital in Indonesia and 85 per cent in Malaysia suggested their staying power.[26]

An alternative strategy was to deny the existence of a problem by expanding the definition of 'indigenous' to include naturalized immigrants and their descendants, allowing them full citizenship rights. This was Singapore's position from the start; official nationalism was carefully separated from ethnicity. Thailand started to adopt a similar policy in the late 1950s, with ethnic Chinese encouraged to take Thai names and participate as Thais in economy and society; the achievements of Sino-Thai

[26] Robison, *Indonesia*, 276; Yoshihara Kunio, *The Rise of Ersatz Capitalism in South-East Asia*, Quezon City, 1988, 51.

entrepreneurs in industry came to be regarded more as a source of national pride than as a target for discrimination. During the 1970s and 1980s, with the liberalization of citizenship laws under the Marcos régime, the Philippines seemed to be moving in the same direction. Throughout the region the process of assimilation was facilitated by the end of easy immigration, reducing 'resinification' and the flow of remittances out of Southeast Asia, which had always antagonized local nationalists.

The problem presented by foreign investment was comparable to that posed by resident aliens: popular nationalism insisted that it should be diminished, or even abolished, but the need for capital and technology, as well as the greed of individual decision-makers, argued for retention. In every independent state domestic enterprises were nominally favoured over foreign competitors, though until the 1970s the Philippines was virtually bound to treat American investments as domestic. In some cases there were actual attempts to dispossess foreign investors: communist Vietnam, followed in due course by Laos and Kampuchea, expropriated almost all foreign firms, though it found itself in the 1980s negotiating for investment again. Under Guided Democracy Indonesia abruptly nationalized Dutch holdings and threatened other investors, though after 1965 it reversed policy and welcomed foreign capital once more. Burma also effectively rid itself of most foreign capital by the mid-1960s, and later begged to get some back. In the 1960s and 1970s Malaysia and the Philippines both introduced legislation mandating a higher indigenous stake in the corporate sector, and were generally successful in achieving this within a few years, as foreign firms sold out, wholly or in part, to local investors or the government; at the same time these countries continued to solicit new investment. Only Thailand, Singapore, and Brunei did not at one time or another embark on a systematic attempt to diminish foreign investment; only Democratic Kampuchea did not sometime welcome it back.

The policy debates often became heated, with all sides claiming the mantle of nationalism. Even those who, like Marcos in the Philippines and Mahathir in Malaysia, advocated greater foreign investment in the short run justified it as necessary for increasing national strength and pride in the long run. In practice, the critical question had to do not with whether or not foreign investment existed, but on what terms. Unless they actually intended to expropriate or ban foreign firms, Southeast Asian governments could not simply dictate conditions. To tame transnational corporations they had to negotiate tariffs, taxes, wage rates and labour rights, infrastructural provision and costs, and a hundred other variables; often they wooed potential investors with promises of tax holidays and other special incentives. Foreign corporations in turn tried to prove that they were worth wooing, offering to train more local managers here, pay higher fees or royalties there. Joint ventures were negotiated with all the wariness that surrounded traditional marriage arrangements, and improbable unofficial alliances between transnational corporations, local Chinese entrepreneurs, and indigenous government officials often succeeded where more straightforward endeavours failed. Where their direct ownership was curtailed, foreign corporations often continued to control local production through subsidiaries or subcontractors.

Behind the bargaining lay the possibility of coercion, although it was rarely invoked. Britain did not fight to preserve its direct investments in Burma or Malaysia, nor the USA its in the Philippines, and though the Second Indochina War may have had economic roots, they did not involve direct foreign investment in Vietnam. More common were efforts to subvert governments, such as that of Sukarno, seen as hostile to foreign investment in general; Southeast Asian leaders came to realize that although advocating a tough line on foreign investment might evoke popular support, it also risked arming the opposition. Much of the postwar investment, however, came from Japan, Taiwan, Hong Kong, and Germany, which had no military presence in the region. What influence they exercised came from money, whether on the table or under it.

Over time direct military intervention became less likely, advice was rejected as often as accepted, and efforts at bribery and subversion became more expensive and less effective. In their dealings with foreign governments and corporations, local politicians (including military officers) and businessmen (including aliens) came to be manipulators, not just victims of manipulation. If they co-operated with foreigners, it was not because they were coerced, but because it was in their own interest—though not always that of their countries—to do so. It is impossible to assess who got the best of a myriad bargaining sessions in which all parties tested their ingenuity to the fullest. It would appear, however, that over the course of the postwar period the relative strength of the Southeast Asians improved, if only because as time went by their governments were more stable and their negotiators more experienced. Although they rarely bargained from a position of real strength, they were often able to play off one investor against another or borrow from multilateral institutions, and so escape from the direct dependency that characterized colonialism and the immediate post-colonial years. Certainly many foreign corporations in the 1980s made concessions that they would not have dreamed of making thirty years earlier.

The problem of foreign influence was inevitably tied up with the quest for economic autonomy. Many Southeast Asians hoped to restructure their economies so that they became more diversified and self-sufficient, capable of relying on their own resources rather than depending upon access to stronger economies, but this proved far more difficult than imagined. It was not sufficient simply to decree that the country should produce everything it needed. Heavy industry was inefficient; light industry could sustain prosperity only when it was aimed at international, rather than domestic, markets; and agricultural self-sufficiency generally depended on access to foreign inputs, particularly fertilizer. No Southeast Asian state became self-sufficient in machinery or advanced technology; only the oil producers were self-sufficient in energy; and there was little regional complementarity on which a common market might be constructed. The urge for autarky remained strong, yet almost every effort to achieve it resulted in retarding economic growth. This need for foreign capital, technology, and trade set effective limits on the progress of economic nationalism in postwar Southeast Asia. Though the independent states made some advances in dealing with individual corporations and foreign governments, they were unable to free themselves from the international economy as a totality—a 'world-system'—without sacrificing some of their hopes for rising national prosperity.

Equity was a prime goal of the socialist régimes of postwar Southeast Asia but only a secondary consideration for most of the capitalist bloc, with the 'third way' countries dithering in the middle. To judge by the descriptive evidence, the socialist régimes generally succeeded in reducing, though not eradicating, the gap between rich and poor. In practice this often meant levelling down rather than up; Democratic Kampuchea was the extreme in this regard, as in so many others, with most of the population reduced to an equality of grinding poverty. In Vietnam, land reform and the nationalization of most industry and trade removed the major source of disparities of income, though there remained differentials based on accumulated wealth (sometimes converted into gold, as the accounts of the boat people testify), occupation, and location. In Burma, the softest of the socialist régimes, there was significant accumulation in the hands of the powerful, but the general distribution of wealth within the country was more equal than it had been in colonial times or than it was in the capitalist countries of the region. The departure of many Indian landlords and moneylenders eliminated one of the major existing sources of inequality. Despite a rather half-hearted land reform that left 42 per cent of cultivators in tenancy in 1970–1, data from 1972 showed the top quintile of income earners earning just five times as much as the lowest quintile, as compared with ratios of 8:1 in Indonesia and 10:1 in the Philippines.[27]

The record of the non-socialist countries of Southeast Asia was much less clear. In part the problem was ideological: decision-makers tended to believe that directly redistributionist measures were inimical to growth. In the short run, they thought, a persistent or even increasing imbalance of wealth was one of the necessary and acceptable costs of growth. As Thai technocrat Puey Ungphakorn put it: 'If we pay too much attention to social justice, overall growth would be slowed down, therefore we should put economic development first. Even though the rich will get richer, and the poor get poorer, soon growth will filter down to the poor automatically.'[28] In part the problem was structural: many technological innovations, particularly those arising from foreign advice or investment, were capital-intensive, which resulted in rising unemployment, with a growing gap between possessors of the technology and those displaced by it. In part the problem was social: the régimes were controlled by men who had a vested interest in existing structures and no intention of dispossessing their own class. Even land reform, widely touted as a politically expedient prophylactic against insurgency, was not implemented with any enthusiasm outside the socialist bloc.

The linkage between capitalist policies and income inequality was reflected in the fact that the rural poor tended to be better off, relatively speaking,

---

[27] Robert H. Taylor, *The State in Burma*, Honolulu, 1987, 341–53; Hill and Jayasuriya, 64.

[28] *Glancing Back, Looking Forward* (1977), as quoted in John L. S. Girling, *Thailand: Society and Politics*, Ithaca, 1981, 84. Note that Puey also admitted that 20–30 years of practice of this method had been 'without success', however.

when central governments were weak. During World War II and postwar insurgencies in Vietnam, Malaya, the Philippines and Indonesia, tax collections fell, squatters occupied abandoned estates, many landlords were unable to collect rent, and popular pressure set limits on unfavourable tenure arrangements. Similar conditions prevailed under Guided Democracy in Indonesia, in parts of rural Cambodia under the beleaguered Khmer Republic, and generally in upland areas remote from central control. In such situations the restoration of stability and 'law and order' often meant the payment of back rent and back taxes, expulsion of squatter settlements, and the enforcement of contracts on terms unfavourable to the weaker parties.

Throughout capitalist Southeast Asia, those already wealthy held on to what they had. They benefited from the new opportunities offered by the postwar world, investing in land, producer goods such as fertilizer and machinery, modern services such as banking and tourism, and access to state power through vote-buying, bribery, and education, which opened up the legal system and the technocracy. Statistical measures of income-distribution tendencies, where they exist, show the inequality was already high by international standards in the 1960s and generally tended to rise thereafter, particularly in Thailand, though the Philippines remained the worst. Singapore was the major exception to this trend, having by 1970 reached that level of development at which (as Simon Kuznets predicted) inequality started to drop, though it was still very high. Data for Indonesia were ambiguous, with inequality tending to rise in some sectors and decline in others, but it was clear that overall income distribution, though somewhat better than in other ASEAN states, was badly skewed and little improving.

These gross measures of national income distribution incorporated imbalances of wealth along geographic, ethnic and gender lines, which persisted throughout the postwar period, even in the socialist bloc. The usual geographical bias was in favour of the 'core area' (inhabited by the dominant political group) over outlying hills, islands, and minority areas, urban over rural, and the capital city over everything else. In part this was deliberate, the rulers rewarding themselves for ruling. In part it was the consequence of the creation of centralized infrastructure and government pricing policies tilted against agriculture, such as the notorious 'rice premium' in Thailand, an export tax (of 25–35 per cent) imposed in 1955 that had the effect of reducing prices paid to farmers over the next two decades. In part it was simply the failure to envisage or implement policies that might have led to the decentralization of wealth.

Urban bias was particularly striking in the ASEAN states, where the political centrality of the capital cities combined with nascent industrialization there. (The cities of non-communist Indochina, where foreign aid dominated national income, may have been even more favoured over the countryside.) The average income in Bangkok around 1970 was nearly three times the average rural income, four times that in the impoverished northeast; differentials in the Philippines and Malaysia were not much better. The ratio between urban and rural income in Indonesia was lower at the time, but caught up substantially by 1980, while inequality within

Jakarta reached new heights. Comparable data are not available for the socialist states, but the slow growth of their industry and their occasional attempts to favour the peasantry suggest that urban dominance was probably less pronounced there.

Seen from the periphery, all central governments appeared to be exploiting local resources, such as plantations, mines, forests, and hydroelectric potential, while ignoring local needs and trampling on local rights. Perceived economic discrimination against fringe areas underlay the Indonesian regional rebellions of 1957–8, Muslim insurgencies in the Philippines and Thailand, persistent civil warfare in Burma, and outbursts of upland protest throughout the region.

Ethnic differentials in wealth received most public attention when certain minorities enjoyed a higher standard of living than the politically dominant group. Such minorities became, as we have seen, the object of deliberate nationalist discrimination, most systematically in Malaysia, where the income gap between Chinese and Malays widened throughout the 1950s and 1960s.[29] In the aftermath of the 1969 riots the government embarked on a long-term programme favouring the *bumiputra* (literally 'princes of the land') at the expense of citizens of Chinese and Indian descent; the second 'prong' of the New Economic Policy openly aimed at 'restructuring Malaysian society to correct economic imbalance, so as to reduce and eventually eliminate the identification of race with economic function'.[30] Though falling short of its targets, the policy succeeded to some extent in closing the ethnic income gap in Malaysia over the next two decades. Elsewhere in the region the outcome of racially discriminatory policies was visible only when they resulted in emigration.

Where minorities were poorer than the dominant ethnic group, very little was done to bridge the gap. They were not, in most cases, deliberately discriminated against, just overlooked in the process of development. Temporary exceptions occurred when the districts they inhabited became politically strategic; during the Second Indochina War the peoples of the Annamese Cordillera received economic as well as political attention both from the Americans and from the Pathet Lao and Vietnamese communists. By and large, however, fringe minorities tended to fall further behind, except as they could profit by their own efforts, such as growing opium in the Golden Triangle or smuggling in the Sulu Sea. Their access to national and international markets was enhanced through improved transport; but the same roads and boats brought in lowland settlers and entrepreneurs, who tended to seize new economic opportunities at the expense of local residents, often reducing the latter to wage labourers.

The economic gender gap also apparently widened in the postwar period, though the evidence is sometimes ambiguous. Among the rural majority men generally had better access to new technologies and the new

---

[29] It should be noted, however, that ethnicity alone accounted for only a small proportion—calculated at around 10 per cent—of economic inequality within Malaysia: Sudhir Anand, *Inequality and Poverty in Malaysia: Measurement and Decomposition*, New York, 1983.

[30] *Second Malaysia Plan, 1971–1975*, 1, quoted in V. V. Bhanoji Rao, *Malaysia: Development Pattern and Policy*, Singapore, 1980, 160.

political institutions that determined economic success, while women were more likely to be left in the subsistence sector. The spread of combine harvesters and labour gangs hired by middlemen cut into the income of rural women, who had traditionally seized opportunities for communal harvesting, and when rice hullers displaced hand-pounding it hurt the poorer women who had previously pounded rice for hire. As with other kinds of inequality, the gender gap tended to narrow in times of political stress and widen when 'normality' was restored. In the DRV, women gained administrative experience in agricultural co-operatives and village councils while men were away fighting, but demobilization brought a reversion to traditional roles. A Javanese landlord in the conservative 1970s justified ending the 'open' harvest: 'We can't allow women to get such high wages and even to sneak off with part of the rice: that's not just [*adil*]. Previously, [between 1955 and 1965] . . . the women received far too much. Then we couldn't do anything about it. But now everything is back to normal.'[31]

Not all changes in the postwar period were disadvantageous for women. The expansion of education was accompanied by a much better balanced sex ratio within schools and universities, and in some countries females actually came to outnumber males among both students and teachers. Government service provided employment for some women, though they tended to be shunted away from the key ministries of defence, justice, foreign affairs, and the treasury toward health, education, and tourism. Light industry, particularly exports, often employed young women because their wages were low and they were thought to be docile. Women also participated in the expanding services sector as clerks, shop assistants, waitresses, and entertainers; in the RVN, Thailand, and the Philippines women had superior access to the profitable market for 'services' to American military personnel. In Singapore, high employment and the rise of modern service industries during the 1970s and 1980s greatly increased female participation in the labour force, and helped bring the average wages of women slightly closer to—though still significantly below—those of men. By and large, women with education or urban connections stood a good chance of improving their lot in the postwar period.

For the region as a whole, however, the differential between average male and female incomes remained high throughout the postwar period, and probably tended to increase slightly. Official efforts to establish greater equality between the sexes were generally feeble; communist Vietnam seems to have done marginally better than the rest, with women obtaining child care, health care, and broader employment opportunities as well as rhetorical support from the government. Unlike imbalances of class, geography, and ethnicity, however, that of gender produced no rebellions in postwar Southeast Asia, perhaps because the majority of women operated within family environments in which basic resources

---

[31] Ann Stoler, 'Class Structure and Female Autonomy in Rural Java', *Signs*, 3, 1 (1977) 74–89; Beresford, *Vietnam*, 131; Frans Hüsken, 'Landlords, Sharecroppers and Agricultural Labourers: Changing Labour Relations in Rural Java', *Journal of Contemporary Asia*, 9, 2 (1970) 140–51.

were shared reasonably equitably (if not equally), as reflected in the fact that women still tended to live longer than men.

Though there is no doubt that the rich got richer in capitalist Southeast Asia, the question of whether the poor got poorer remains in dispute. There is some evidence that the living standards of the very poor—the rural landless and urban jobless—actually declined during much of the postwar period, sometimes even when GDP per capita was growing. The real incomes of a majority or a very substantial minority of the population fell during the 1960s in Malaysia and the 1970s in Indonesia and the Philippines; in the last of these food consumption per capita dropped to levels comparable to those in Bangladesh. Even by official definitions (which varied from country to country), the proportion of the population of ASEAN countries said to be living in 'poverty' in the mid-1970s varied from 30 per cent (Singapore) to near 60 per cent (Indonesia), which suggested the magnitude of the problem. If the data existed they would probably indicate that the proportion—perhaps even the number—of Southeast Asians in absolute poverty fell between the 1930s and the 1980s, but this would be of little consolation to the tens of millions of Southeast Asians who were still destitute, suffering real malnutrition as well as relative deprivation. However defined, equity remained more an aspiration than an achievement in most of postwar Southeast Asia.

POPULATION AND THE ENVIRONMENT

Unlike economic growth, nationalism and equity, population and the environment were not objects of serious consideration for planners in early postwar Southeast Asia, though the former began to become a policy issue in the 1960s and the latter in the 1970s. Population growth stemmed from reductions in mortality of 50–80 per cent, brought about largely by improved medical and health technology. Prewar crude death rates averaged around 25–30 (per thousand population); in the immediate postwar period they remained high, particularly in Vietnam and Indonesia. By the late 1980s, however, they had dropped to between 5 and 10 except in Burma, Laos and Cambodia, where they averaged about 15. Wars and spates of fratricidal violence, such as the massacres in Indonesia in 1965–6, reversed the downward trend at times, but rarely produced net population decline. World War II did not prevent demographic increase; the population of Vietnam, north and south, continued to grow throughout the entire postwar period; only in Democratic Kampuchea and East Timor in the late 1970s did deaths actually exceed births.

Detailed analysis shows that mortality varied by country, region, and class in a predictable manner, always favouring the wealthier. This was most evident in infant mortality, where by the 1980s the number of deaths of children in their first year (per thousand births) in Cambodia and Laos was more than ten times as high as it was in Singapore. Nevertheless, the pattern of overall mortality decline suggests a break with the past that can only be explained by technological advances. Even inhabitants of poor countries enjoyed better health in general than most Southeast Asians had ever enjoyed before.

When rates of natural increase reached 2.5–3.5 per cent a year—implying a doubling of population in 20–28 years—a 'population problem' began to be perceived. Planners soon realized that substantial economic growth would be required just to keep people fed and maintain incomes at the same level, to say nothing of improving welfare. The rapid rate of increase also altered the age structure of the population, with far more young people than ever before, often 40–45 per cent of the total population being under the age of fifteen. Besides increasing the dependency ratio (proportion of non-workers to workers), this meant an accelerating demand for schools and, a decade or so later, for jobs, adding to the headaches of planners.

The attitudes of Southeast Asian governments toward the population explosion varied widely. Some welcomed it as a contribution toward national strength—Sukarno once boasted that Indonesia could support 250 million inhabitants.[32] In other countries there was draconian state intervention in family planning—in Singapore fertility actually fell below replacement levels in the 1980s. Over time, there was a growing conviction that population ought to be controlled, a viewpoint consistently pushed by international agencies, which also funded many population planning efforts. Sometimes, however, other economic and political considerations outweighed this commitment. The hope of expanding the internal market (and of increasing the demographic edge of the faster-reproducing Malays over other ethnic groups) inspired Mahathir in the early 1980s to announce an ultimate target of 70 million people for Malaysia, which had just 15 million at the time; the opposition of the Catholic Church to most forms of birth control weakened the commitment of the Philippine government to population planning, especially under the Aquino administration. In Burma and communist Vietnam, population programmes, like many other state initiatives, tended to founder in a morass of contradictions and confusions. In Thailand and Indonesia after 1970, on the other hand, the state was unambiguously committed to population control, which helped reduce birth rates to 25 and 30 (per thousand population), respectively, by the late 1980s.

Throughout the region, in fact, fertility fell substantially after 1960, clearly reflecting not just official sponsorship of family planning but a phase of the global 'demographic transition'. It was a consequence of development, not simply a precondition for it. In broad terms the 'transition' was correlated with such economic and social indicators as rising per capita income and expanded education, particularly of women. In postwar Southeast Asia many women were postponing marriage for a few years while they took advantage of new opportunities for education and employment. They were also more inclined to control their fertility deliberately

<hr />

[32] Terence H. Hull and Ida Bagus Mantra, 'Indonesia's Changing Population', in Anne Booth and Peter McCawley, eds, *The Indonesian Economy During the Soeharto Era*, Kuala Lumpur: East Asian Social Science Monographs, 1981, 264.

and, in some cases, to leave unsatisfactory marriages, though both contraceptive use and divorce rates generally remained much lower than in the West.

Differentials in the timing of the demographic transition between countries were paralleled by differences within countries: fertility fell faster in cities than in rural areas, in wealthier than in poorer districts, and among Chinese than among indigenous populations. Since mortality also continued to fall, annual rates of natural increase slowed only slightly, from a 1960s peak of over 2.5 per cent for Southeast Asia as a whole to around 2.0 per cent in the 1980s—somewhat more manageable, but still higher than in any earlier era. Thus the regional population kept climbing, from just over 150 million at the end of World War II to well over 400 million by 1990.

Among the rural majority, the population boom meant increased competition for land and for opportunities to labour; at these rates even sparsely peopled agricultural landscapes soon became crowded. Some of the increased number remained in the villages, farming smaller and smaller plots of land or trying to underbid other hungry claimants for tenancy rights and the chance to harvest wealthier peasants' rice. Others moved on to open new fields, but wherever they moved, they were likely to impose upon terrain previously used for shifting cultivation or hunting and gathering by earlier inhabitants, forcing them in turn to abandon or modify their traditional way of life, often at considerable human cost.

Urbanization was also associated with population growth. Before World War II the largest cities in the region—Manila, Bangkok, Singapore, Rangoon, and Batavia (Jakarta)—had between half a million and a million inhabitants; by 1980 Jakarta had nearly 7 million, Metro Manila nearly 6 million, Bangkok-Thonburi nearly 5 million, Ho Chi Minh City (Saigon) and Singapore over 2 million, and Rangoon, Hanoi, Surabaya, Bandung, Medan, Semarang and Metro Cebu between 1 and 2 million inhabitants. Kuala Lumpur would also pass 1 million early in the 1980s, and Phnom Penh had swollen to more than 2 million by 1975, though it fell dramatically later that year. Regional centres such as Davao, Chiengmai, and Danang also grew far faster than their rural hinterlands, and the proportion of the total population officially classified as 'urban' doubled between 1950 and 1980, when one out of every four Southeast Asians lived in a city. There were positive aspects to this urban growth, including the expansion of consumer demand and the accumulation of that critical mass of human and financial resources needed for development. Against this could be set the constant need to provide more jobs in industry and services, as well as crowding, pollution, and a recurrent drain on rural resources.

With the closing of borders to most migrant workers, immigration declined in demographic significance in postwar Southeast Asia. The RVN received nearly a million refugees from the north, many of them Catholic, after the division of the country in 1954, integrating them reasonably well into local society, though not without some political strains. Thereafter only Thailand, which accepted hundreds of thousands of refugees from Laos and Kampuchea during the 1970s and 1980s, recorded significant immigration. Even there it was of little demographic consequence in a population increasing naturally by over one million per year; in any event the refugees were generally kept in camps (financed by international agencies) rather than allowed to mingle with the Thai.

In the quarter-century after World War II there was almost no significant emigration from Southeast Asian countries except the exodus of Catholics from the DRV and the repatriation of Indians from Burma. In the 1970s, however, all of the states of Indochina suffered extensive emigration, with Vietnam probably losing the most in absolute terms (over one million), Laos and Kampuchea more proportionally (roughly 10 per cent and 20 per cent of their total populations, respectively). Continued natural increase and some return of emigrants in the 1980s compensated for these losses in demographic terms, though it hardly replaced the talent and capital the refugees took with them. There was also much emigration of skilled and semi-skilled workers from other Southeast Asian states, particularly the Philippines and Thailand, though it, too, was of more economic than demographic consequence. Remittances from Filipinos overseas became by the early 1980s the Philippines' largest single source of foreign exchange, yet cumulative migration amounted to just 1–2 per cent of the total population, less than the number added by natural increase every year.

Internal migration, meanwhile, became more widespread and extended than ever, as structural changes altered the job market and improved transport facilitated mobility. Millions upon millions of Southeast Asians left their farms for the city or the frontier or wherever opportunity shone brighter. Much of this migration was circular, often on a seasonal basis, which had important social implications both for the villages that sent out the migrants and welcomed them back and for the cities and 'industrial' areas that received them temporarily and gave them new ideas. Traditional migration in Southeast Asia had been predominantly male, but as services and light industry developed, female migration, especially to the cities, became more important; women actually outnumbered men among migrants in several countries. Young people of both sexes often relocated to provincial or national capitals for secondary and tertiary education. Sometimes they returned, often they did not; one survey of 150 Thai intellectuals showed 145 of them living in Bangkok, though fewer than half had been born and raised there.[33]

Throughout the region cities swelled and previously forested areas were opened for settlement and agricultural development, while older farming districts lost young workers. People also moved because of war (particularly in Indochina, where almost one-fourth of the population were refugees of one kind or another by 1975), because a new dam, airport, or other development project was planned for their village, or because they worked for an ever-growing government that assigned them to service far from home. Whenever possible, Southeast Asian migrants retained ties to their places of origin, visited them at festival time, summoned families or recruited friends from them when new needs or opportunities arose, and even remitted funds to them, but in practice they became part of new social and economic communities.

---

[33] Girling, *Thailand*, 89–90.

Although the state often inadvertently impelled migration, most South-east Asian governments did not have a clear policy toward it. Officials were well aware of the imbalance between overcrowded cities and rural districts in some areas and apparently underpopulated districts elsewhere, but only Democratic Kampuchea, Indonesia, and communist Vietnam attempted seriously to alter population distribution. The Khmer Rouge simply evacuated the inhabitants of Phnom Penh into the countryside; this was arguably a rational policy, but it was made quite irrational by the speed and brutality with which it was undertaken. The demographic effects were drastic, enormously costly in human terms, and relatively short-lived; after 1978 the new régime encouraged re-urbanization.

Elsewhere efforts were more restrained and sustained. The attempt to relieve population pressure in Java by transplanting its inhabitants to the outer islands actually dated back to the colonial period, but was always difficult to implement on a significant scale. Through the 1950s and 1960s Indonesia's 'transmigration' programme moved only about 400,000 people, but it accelerated in the 1970s and 1980s, transferring over 4 million Javanese to South Sumatra, Kalimantan, Sulawesi, and Irian Jaya. At the same time, however, immigration from the outer islands continued, and Java's total population grew by over 45 million between 1950 and 1990. From 1961 onward the DRV promoted New Economic Zones in the uplands as target areas for migrants from the cities and crowded Red River delta; around one million were resettled over the next fifteen years. After reunification, the SRV extended this system, aiming to develop new zones in the southern highlands with settlers from the north and the bloated cities of the south. Though falling far short of their target figures, they succeeded in moving more than 2.5 million people within the next decade —but the national population grew by nearly 14 million. As with smaller resettlement schemes in Thailand, Malaysia, and the Philippines, the impact on those who moved and the sites to which they moved was profound, but the alleviation of general population pressure was minimal.

Population growth and urbanization, along with the expansion of manu-facturing and extractive industries, accelerated what became a major regional problem during this era: environmental degradation. Visitors were often most struck by the noxious air and precariously potable water of such cities as Bangkok and Manila, which contributed to the incidence of disease and undermined the quality of life of all urbanites. Even greater damage, however, was done by massive deforestation, over-fishing, irresponsible mining, and the pollution of previously productive lands and waters.

Supporters of the state tended to put most of the blame for deforestation on shifting cultivators, while its critics cited loggers as the prime culprits. In practice the relationship was often symbiotic. Large local or trans-national corporations, well-connected with the national élite, obtained legal concessions from the central government for the extraction of limited amounts of timber. This was a major area of investment throughout the region, financing development programmes and political campaigns from upper Burma to Mindanao, by way of northern Thailand, Sabah and East Kalimantan. These legal concessionaires opened roads which were used in turn by illegal loggers, often backed by venal provincial and local officials, to finish stripping the primary growth. Shifting cultivators, including many former peasants who had lost their lands to economic and demographic pressure, then followed the same roads, slashing and burning whatever was left in order to create fields where they could scratch out a living. The collection of firewood also nibbled away at the forests; dam construction drowned them; and in southern Vietnam 12 per cent of the total forest area was bulldozed or sprayed with powerful herbicides during the Second Indochina War.

Definitions and estimates of deforestation varied widely, but all suggested losses on an unprecedented scale: half of the total forest area of Thailand, the Philippines, and Java was lost within twenty or thirty years; much of the rest was degraded from primary stands of hardwood to secondary softwood; and some experts projected the complete disappearance of the Southeast Asian tropical rainforest within a generation or two. Besides losses that could be dismissed as the price of development—disfigurement of the landscape, displacement of long-time forest-dwelling peoples, and depletion of the planetary atmosphere and gene pool—forest degradation also had immediate economic consequences. It meant greatly increased erosion, which exhausted the soil within previously forested areas and led to silting and flooding in the catchment area below. By the 1970s a few planners began talking about reforestation, but it was clear that this was at best a makeshift and stopgap measure. Even in the rare cases where it was implemented, the new forests were not in any biological sense a substitute for the rich diversity of the original growth which they replaced, though they did reduce the effects of erosion and provide some pulp and firewood.

The destruction of the marine environment was less visible than that of the forests, but no less costly. High-technology oceanic fishing fleets, including huge Japanese trawlers, destroyed the piscine population indiscriminately. Local shore-based fishermen in return resorted to such techniques as blast fishing (using dynamite or percussion grenades) and chemical poisoning, which helped maintain their livelihood temporarily at the cost of destroying coral reefs and further thinning marine life. By the 1980s 95 per cent of all Philippine coral reefs had been damaged, and 75 per cent were at least half destroyed; other maritime countries lagged behind in this destruction derby, but were catching up fast. The coastal environment, including mangrove swamps, was also damaged by mine tailings, great piles of mineral debris that were swept by rains down on to agricultural lands as well, turning previously productive valleys into desolate moonscapes. Pollution from pulp mills and other processing and industrial plants flowed down rivers, into lakes and across fields, poisoning freshwater fish, who were also adversely affected by the run-off of chemical fertilizers from the rice paddies.

In their search for economic growth (and, in many cases, personal profits) the policy-makers of Southeast Asia were generally unwilling to limit the profitable extraction of resources, in spite of the fact that most were non-renewable, at least at the rate at which they were being exploited. At times they actually 'imported' pollution; the Kawasaki sintering plant in northern Mindanao, for example, existed only to process iron ore bound from Australia to Japan without offending Japanese environmentalists, who had objected to its unhealthy presence in their own country. In the short run, Southeast Asian choices may have been economically defensible, though the costs of increased health care and of agricultural production lost by pollution, siltation, and flooding have never been adequately reckoned.[34] In the long run, however, the half-century after World War II may chiefly be remembered as the beginning of the end for the natural environment of Southeast Asia.

SOCIAL STRUCTURES AND STRATEGIES

World War II and postwar developments constantly challenged traditional Southeast Asian belief in natural hierarchy and community, already eroded by colonialism and capitalism. Natural hierarchy—the assumption that all living things existed in an innate relationship of ranked inequality—was challenged first by the rhetoric of democracy, which emphasized participation in decision-making rather than obedience and spoke of the equality of all men (and, in its extreme versions, women as well). Distinctions based on birth were increasingly difficult to uphold, at least in public; the deference due to kings, nobles, and hereditary headmen did not disappear, but it was no longer unquestioned.

The vision of a harmonious community of reciprocal obligations, beginning with, but not limited to, kin and the village, also came under ideological attack in postwar Southeast Asia. In the traditional ideal, any accession of wealth ought to be shared within the community; any unexpected need might be met from the resources of the community. (Outsiders were different; one economic advantage that aliens, such as the Chinese, were believed to have, in fact, was that they were not bound by local constraints.) Now this community was challenged by attempts to invoke higher values to which local obligations would be subordinate. Individual liberty—the right of a person to earn, to speak, to worship, and to do whatever else he or she saw fit, regardless of other claims—was preached by foreign advisers and enshrined in modern education. American-trained social scientists told Filipinos that they could achieve their potential only if they left their home villages, where personal obligations wore them down: 'If you want to get up, get out!' Larger entities such as the nation itself, the international proletariat, and the global brotherhood of Islam, also laid claim to Southeast Asian loyalties.

Southeast Asians encountered these ideological challenges amid political, demographic and economic changes that in themselves tended to undermine traditional institutions. Once, according to Vietnamese proverb, the emperor's laws had stopped at the village wall, but in the postwar era nothing could impede the penetration of the state apparatus into the

---

[34] Even in terms of maximizing the economic exploitation of forest resources, it has been shown that state policies in Malaysia, Indonesia, and the Philippines were extremely ill-advised. Robert Repetto and Malcolm Gillis, eds, *Public Policies and the Misuse of Forest Resources: A World Resources Institute Book*, Cambridge, UK, 1988.

village, undercutting local self-sufficiency and making access to higher political power more important than ever. On the national level, men who commanded mass support or the loyalty of troops or party cadres vied for power with traditional aristocrats, generally winning except when charismatic royal or princely rulers like Sihanouk and Tunku Abdul Rahman were able to exploit their own populist appeal. Locally, traditional élites had to forge links with the national apparatus or lose out to more adaptive rivals. As the state also engrossed an increasing share of production through taxation, it could reward its favourites through redistribution of central revenues, thus making them less dependent upon the communities in which they resided.

Demographic developments attenuated traditional community ties in various ways. Migration, facilitated by improved transportation, removed many Southeast Asians to cities or frontiers where they lived among strangers who did not recognize the same hierarchies or share the same values. The villages from which the emigrants departed were also affected by the loss of community members (particularly young adults), and if some of their places were filled it was by newcomers with strange customs and unpredictable loyalties. Meanwhile, rapid population growth not only increased the sheer size of almost all communities, weakening face-to-face contact, but also made labour abundant, and so caused it to depreciate relative to land and capital. Landlords and factory owners felt less necessity to maintain relations of reciprocity and respect with individual tenants or workers when they could easily replace them.

In the economic sphere, there was not only increasing inequality but an attrition of the personal relationships that had traditionally reinforced community ties. More and more Southeast Asians, previously accustomed to flexible working conditions arranged on an individual basis, were drawn into wage labour, which demanded the disciplined acceptance of impersonal rules. This was particularly true in extractive industries and the booming cities, where wage labour dominated the lives of miners, factory workers, construction labourers, and government clerks, and came to shape the outlook even of many who were employed in the 'informal sector'.[35] Though it often involved health risks and exploitative practices (particularly for women and children), it generally represented a profitable alternative to unemployment or precarious self-employment. Wage labour also made considerable inroads in rural areas, as a rising proportion of Southeast Asians lost regular access to land, even as tenants, and had to earn their living by selling their labour to the highest bidder. Since double-cropping tended to increase the demand for hired help, those who exchanged marginal subsistence farming for wage labour were not necessarily worse off in monetary terms. Socially, however, the gap widened between those with access to land and those without.

The decline of local markets similarly counterpoised economic gain with loss of social cohesion. In these markets, traditional gathering points for

<hr />

[35] Michael Pinches, ' "All that we have is our muscle and sweat": The Rise of Wage Labour in a Manila Squatter Community', in Pinches and Salim Lakha, eds, *Wage Labour and Social Change: The Proletariat in Asia and the Pacific*, Clayton: Monash University Centre of Southeast Asian Studies, Monash Papers on Southeast Asia no. 16, 1987, 103–40.

local produce and distribution points for consumer goods, raw economic forces were socially mediated. Prices were arrived at in discrete bargaining sessions that reflected not just supply and demand but personal relationships between buyers and sellers. In the postwar period these markets became less and less relevant: wholesalers or government agencies contracted for farmgate delivery of produce, and consumers sought a better selection of goods in nearby towns or even city supermarkets. Prices tended either to be fixed, or to be negotiated between virtual strangers, so the role of markets in structuring human interdependence was reduced.

Great disparities of power and wealth were not new to Southeast Asia, but traditionally they had been softened by respect, reciprocity, and redistribution, at least in theory. In the postwar capitalist states, however, economic inequality was growing even as traditional status markers were weakening, with the result that people were increasingly defined by their economic position. This new stratification was most visible at the top, where a class of Southeast Asians (including local Chinese) with spectacularly conspicuous wealth emerged, more reminiscent of pre-colonial kings than the prosperous but subordinated élites operating under colonialism. Some of these super rich, like the Sultan of Brunei, were traditional rulers, but others found their way to great wealth through politics (Marcos), the military (Ibnu Sutowo), export production (Lee Kong Chian), retail trade (the Chirathivat family), banking (Chin Sophonpanich), utilities (the Lopez family) or even entertainment (the Shaw brothers). The visible discrepancy between such concentrations of wealth and the misery in which so many other Southeast Asians lived was an obvious source of social tension.

More significant in terms of overall social structure was the increasing number of Southeast Asians who lived comfortably from property, salaries, or business, and did not have to worry about where their food or rent was coming from. (There was some upward mobility, but in most cases those who rose farthest not only exhibited commercial and political acumen, but chose their parents well. Very few exemplars of 'rags to riches' actually started out in anything resembling rags.) Even when their income was rurally derived, they tended to congregate in the growing cities. The urban élite, though small and weak by comparison with the middle classes of the West, was still larger, richer, and politically more consequential than any such group the region had known before. Much intellectual effort, especially on the left, was devoted to defining the precise relationship of this class to the means of production, but they were actually easier to identify in terms of consumption: Western-style clothes, access to tertiary education and private vehicles, occupation of solidly-built houses with modern conveniences, and employment of domestic servants. Many of them also enlivened their discourse with a smattering of English, the new lingua franca of the region. Often they worked in the high-rise international-style office buildings that characterized the great cities of Southeast Asia, which little by little became more like each other and less like the countrysides from which they had originally sprung.

Without the need to struggle for mere survival, the urban élite developed concerns that increasingly overlapped with those of the bourgeoisie elsewhere: education, culture, democracy, development, fashion, law and order, and the quality of life. Some of them evinced liberal values, which took political form in the non-violent revolutions in Thailand in 1973 and the Philippines in 1986, as well as movements for greater democratic freedoms elsewhere. Their concerns were reflected in Intje Hassan's lament over Jakarta:

> Jakarta . . .
> This is no slum
> Only a village
> Four hundred years old
> Dipped in modernity
> Granted a . . .
> Quantum of kilowatts
> For streetlamps
> To chase shadows . . .
>
> Prostitutes . . .
> in darkness, waiting
> Nightclubs and casinos opening
> To pass the leisure time
> School, as partial gift
> To develop ambitions later
> Still empty and unanswered
> And tomorrow . . .
> The frustrated generation, waiting—
> Of enormous problems to overcome—
> in the developed city.[36]

Another example is Catherine Lim's gentle satire on official values in Singapore:

Mr Sai Koh Phan . . . looks at the many campaign posters around, and the pride and gratitude once more surges into his heart, in recollection of years of total fidelity to their admonitions:

> Don't litter
> Don't spit
> Don't stop at two
> Don't dirty public toilets
> Don't sniff glue
> Don't waste water
> Be courteous
> Eat more wheat
> Eat frozen meat
> Don't breed mosquitoes
> Don't change lanes while driving

---

[36] 'The Developed City' (1972), quoted in Gerald H. Krausse, 'From Sunda Kelapa to Jabotabek: A Socio-Cultural Profile of Indonesia's Capital City', in Krausse, ed., *Urban Society in Southeast Asia, II: Political and Cultural Issues*, Hong Kong: Asian Research Service, Asian Studies Monograph Series, 1988, 159–60.

Say 'Good morning' and 'Thank you' in Mandarin
Don't fill your plates to overflowing at buffet lunches
Don't be 'kia su'
Plant a tree
Don't grow long hair
Don't grow
Don't[37]

Below this comfortable class were the numerous urban poor, who, like the élite, to some extent emulated the fashions of the West by wearing T-shirts, drinking Coca-Cola, and listening to pop music. There was no real economic convergence, however; the gap between rich and poor actually widened, with the juxtaposition of luxury and squalor particularly glaring in Manila and Bangkok. The poor were divisible in terms of both level and security of income; in many cities the proletariat who received regular wages or salaries in the formal sector were a minority of the labour force, with the majority being casuals or self-employed, fitting into the interstices of the urban economy as best they could: day labourers, street hawkers, taxi and pedicab drivers, piece-work producers, beggars, guides and would-be gigolos. Some lived in huge government-built blocks of flats, others in squatter settlements; some were brand-new immigrants from the provinces, others were city-born and bred. Along with differences in employment and ethnicity, this made for a wide diversity of interests and a corresponding lack of social and political unity most of the time.

Social stratification was generally less visible in rural areas, where even the well-to-do were often poor by external standards and the consumption of modern goods and services was less conspicuous. Out in the provinces it was sometimes still possible to believe in the pure 'traditional' village, unchanged from time immemorial, sharing poverty as it shared everything else. Local studies throughout the region, however, suggest that in the course of economic development the gap between the relatively well-off and the truly poor was widening, exacerbated by state policies that deliberately courted the rural élite at the expense of their tenants and neighbours. This was accompanied by a general deterioration of relationships of reciprocal obligation within the village, which struck at the heart of the traditional sense of community.

The local community—that face-to-face group in which all knew each other and accepted their mutual responsibilities to each other—had already been attenuated by migration to the frontier and the city. Within the village, however, there persisted conventions of a 'moral economy' in which custom and propriety set limits on avarice. This ideal had long been honoured in the breach, but seems to have been eroded even further in the postwar period, particularly in the 1970s, when new agricultural technologies and enhanced state power allowed landowners, no longer dependent on local labour or goodwill, to ignore the claims of the poor. In Java, harvests that had once been open to all were reserved for a selected few; in

---

[37] From 'The Malady and the Cure' in *O Singapore*, Singapore, 1989. *Kia su*, literally 'afraid to lose', may also be translated as 'afraid of getting involved' or 'afraid of losing face'.

Malaysia, machinery replaced casual local labour; in the Philippines, tenants were evicted to make room for export plantations; everywhere there were complaints that alms and low-interest loans were less frequently bestowed. The logic of capitalism tended to reduce previous patron–client reciprocity to account-book calculations of profit or loss.

The concepts of 'dual economy' and 'plural society' were hard to sustain in postwar Southeast Asia, as both economic and cultural links between various segments of national populations became stronger and more visible. Subsistence farmers were forced into the market economy by higher taxes and rents, or lured in by education and consumer goods; soft drinks and rubber-soled sneakers reached where development experts could not penetrate. The diffusion of national cultures through schools, movies, and the radio tended to homogenize previously diverse societies, and led to the decline of many local arts, customs and dialects.

Even in the remotest hills and islands, traditional structures and values were under attack. Upland communities generally lacked the military capacity to cope with the private armies of logging companies, the legal resources to cope with intrusive government agencies, and the commercial acumen to cope with lowland merchants. The result was often economic dislocation and demographic decline. The only way some of the smaller groups could physically survive was by accepting deculturation and the eventual extinction, not just of individual communities, but of their entire tribal identity. ·

In socialist Southeast Asia, the challenges to hierarchy were even stronger. Ideological attacks on aristocracy and customary rights were pressed more vigorously than under capitalist régimes, as the militant egalitarian state claimed uncontested supremacy over all rivals. Temporary tactical accommodations were sometimes made with 'patriotic' mandarins, monks, or minorities, but the logic of socialism implied the eventual reduction or homogenization of these groups. The prerogatives of traditional élites were systematically whittled away, along with most of their economic base. In their place emerged an 'official class' of bureaucrats, military officers, and party members, whose prestige and economic base derived from their position in the state apparatus. Our information on this new class remains extremely sketchy, but it seems to have enjoyed, like ruling élites elsewhere, privileged access to travel, education, and certain consumer goods. Unlike them, however, it could not overtly accumulate great wealth or reinvest in profit-making enterprises. Whether, as is likely, its members found ways of transmitting their privileges to their descendants is something that at present we simply do not know; the party represented a hierarchy that was supposed to be self-renewing but not actually hereditary.

As for the traditional community, in principle it too had to be sacrificed for the greater good of the nation and the socialist future, as the imposition of agricultural collectivization on the various states of Indochina made clear. The Khmer Rouge in particular were ruthless opponents of the claims of the village and the extended family. Upland societies in socialist Southeast Asia were also profoundly challenged by war, economic strains, and intrusive officials preaching the priority of development and the superiority of lowland civilization. If some of these societies remained slightly less transformed and deculturated than their counterparts in the capitalist states, it reflected differences in communications and effective political and economic penetration more than in actual policy.

Although challenges to hierarchy and community in Southeast Asia were often triggered by Western contact and associated with Western values, they were primarily mounted by Southeast Asians who had internalized the ideas and institutions that they were propagating. Some scholars overlooked this fact, their own judgements distorted by romantic prejudices. In moving from rural to urban poverty, for example, many Southeast Asians gave up picturesque bamboo houses in a lush green landscape for rude hovels made out of packing crates and corrugated iron in apparently unmitigated squalor. Observers tended to interpret this as a clear worsening of circumstances, yet such moves were often viewed by the migrants as steps toward a better life for both themselves and their children; there were 'slums of hope' as well as 'slums of despair'. Similarly, *kerajaan* (royal government) in northern Sumatra was swept away in the 'social revolution' of the 1940s not by Westerners or conscious Westernizers, but by local Acehnese, Bataks and Malays who had no use for their traditional rulers.[38]

To some Southeast Asians the weakening of hierarchy and community implied a number of desirable ends: equality, personal freedom, dignity, mobility, and, above all, economic opportunity. This was most visible among national leaders and the prosperous urban élites, who were almost unanimous in favour of 'modernization', despite occasional lamentation for their vanishing cultural heritage. Capitalists and socialists argued bitterly with each other on many other points but agreed that the future was different from, and more important than, the past. Farther down the social scale, a similar outlook was implied when the poor voluntarily left their villages to seek a better life elsewhere or forsook traditional rituals in favour of modern (often Western) icons. The rising demand of women for education and greater participation in the public sphere represented another aspect of the indigenous challenge to traditional authority.

Social scientists of the 1950s and 1960s devoted much attention to this topic, seeing in 'modern' values the key to automatic improvement both in economics and politics. Secularism and rationality were contrasted with 'traditional' beliefs in supernatural powers and mystical processes; their eventual triumph was assured, though it might be hastened or retarded. The hindsight of twenty years has suggested that this triumph was neither inevitable nor necessarily beneficial, and the debate over exactly how the spread of 'modern' values might be monitored and promoted was in certain respects one of the least productive Western intellectual efforts ever devoted to Southeast Asia. (Recent studies have focused instead on the economic advantages putatively associated with 'Confucian' culture, an

---

[38] Aprodicio A. Laquian, 'The Asian City and the Political Process', in D. J. Dwyer, ed., *The City as a Centre of Change in Asia*, Hong Kong 1972, 41–55 (employing a distinction first articulated by C. Stokes); Anthony Reid, *The Blood of the People: Revolution and the End of Traditional Rule in Northern Sumatra*, Kuala Lumpur, 1979.

equally dubious endeavour.) But the phenomenon that they attempted to analyse was no less real for being difficult to define; in the postwar period significant numbers of Southeast Asians did in fact perceive the world, and their role in it, in new ways.

Although there were some efforts to retain symbolic hierarchy in the political sphere—particularly in the systematic glorification of the Thai monarchy—there was little evident desire to revert to a world of ascriptive authority. In its place, where there was not actual equality, stood an implied hierarchy of achievement, based on military prowess, political dedication, education or entrepreneurship. When skilled politicians like Suharto and Ne Win could invoke a regal style of rule, radiating 'natural' authority capable of either great benevolence or irresistible anger, they got the best of both worlds. Socialists and feminists also attempted to use history to justify their own visions of the future, arguing that in the good old days before colonialism and 'feudalism' there had been no private property and women were the equal of men. For many Southeast Asians traditions of hierarchy and community had been reduced to symbols to be manipulated toward more modern ends.

When traditional communities faltered, Southeast Asians invented new institutions to serve in their place. Migrants often created new locational groups based in urban villages (*kampung*) and squatter settlements or frontier towns. Such groups were weaker than traditional villages, as they lacked the full weight of custom and authority and possessed no village shrine or common burial ground. In time, however, some of them developed a vitality of their own, sponsoring ritual feasts, providing local services, building community projects, organizing youth activities, and creating networks of credit, alliance, and kinship almost as complex as those in the villages left behind. Normally these groups operated with state tolerance or backing, but upon occasion they could help the neighbourhood defend itself against government-backed intruders or developers, as Manila's Zone One Tondo Organization (ZOTO) demonstrated in the early 1970s.[39]

Other Southeast Asians devoted their energies to vocational groups, including professional organizations, labour unions, and student movements. Some found that religious organizations, whether based in relatively new sects (such as Hoa Hao or the Iglesia Ni Kristo) or in revitalized older faiths, gave them a home beyond their home. These provided, in addition to whatever deeper religious significance they embodied, an opportunity for regular contact with other like-minded people, a chance to share worldly goods and stand shoulder-to-shoulder in a worthy struggle. For some adherents they were a kind of enclave within an anonymous urban environment; for others they represented a counter-culture within villages dominated by those who professed a majority faith.

Politics served the same social functions for other Southeast Asians.

[39] Patrick Guinness, *Harmony and Hierarchy in a Javanese Kampung*, Singapore: Asian Studies Association of Australia, Southeast Asia Publications Series no. 11, 1986; *Reason to Hope: A Study of Five Urban Poor Communities in Metro Manila*, Manila: Share and Care Apostolate for Poor Settlers, 1983.

Belief in the 'imagined community' of the nation found institutional expression in political parties ranging from the Vietminh to UMNO (the United Malays National Organization), each with auxiliary women's groups and youth groups as a framework for social gathering. For those to whom the nation—despite state sponsorship and the dissemination of official culture—was an unwieldy or uncongenial focus for the community they sought, the politics of opposition sometimes offered affiliation with a set of associates sharing an ideal. Indigenous minorities found and reasserted their identity as 'Moros', 'Igorots', 'Isan', 'Karen', or *ana chu* (sons of the mountain) through supra-village organizations in the postwar period. The potential of local branches of political parties to offer social cohesion and cultural meaning independent of state orthodoxy was suggested by the ban on them in New Order Indonesia.

To the extent that all of these groupings were voluntary, they allowed greater freedom of self-definition. Those who had once been simply 'Chinese' or *orang Kelantan* (people of Kelantan) now had the option of trying instead to define themselves primarily as residents of a certain urban neighbourhood or as 'Malaysians' or 'socialists' or 'Muslims' or 'professionals'. A few of the new organizations attempted to replace the traditional community entirely, creating spiritual and economic brotherhoods complete unto themselves; but most simply supplemented or combined with it, adding a dimension that had been erased or eroded by other pressures. Many of the groups tended to be unstable; Filipinos described the speed with which they appeared and disappeared as like grass fire (*ningas kugon*).

In socialist Southeast Asia, the range of permissible alternatives was more limited. Religious and political organizations outside the state orthodoxy were discouraged or prohibited entirely, and all other groupings were brought under state or party control as much as possible. Anecdotal evidence suggests that the results of this attempted state monopoly of 'community' varied widely. Sometimes an agricultural collective, a neighbourhood committee, a military unit or a women's group would be infused with a genuine sense of harmony and give meaning to people's lives. More often such organizations were subject to manipulation by party officials or petty bureaucrats, and so became, in social terms, hollow shells. Descriptions of life in communist Vietnam suggest that in times of war (1946–54, 1965–75) patriotism tended to fill state-sponsored organizations with a sense of fellowship and purpose that emptied rapidly once the fighting was over.

Along with welcoming the new, many Southeast Asians clung to the old, retaining what they could of traditional hierarchy and community. At a national level, though royalty and aristocracy lost their power to command, they retained considerable influence. In rural areas millions of people lived in ancestral villages and reaffirmed ancestral ways, exhibiting not blind traditionalism but prudent conservatism. Most Southeast Asians were well aware that new opportunities and arrangements did not in fact benefit everyone equally. Opposition to the introduction of farm machinery was based on the sound calculation that it would displace labour;

scepticism as to the wisdom and benevolence of public officials was all too frequently justified; and the perception of modern education as a potential threat to customary values was largely correct.

The most vocal reassertion of traditional community values came from certain religious groups. Islam, they claimed, meant giving alms and not profiteering; Buddhism implied charity and the rejection of material accumulation; Christianity included the gospel of social justice, in which all believers were brothers. This kind of appeal lent force to such organizations as the Partai Islam (PAS) in Malaysia, the Federation of Buddhists in Thailand, and the Basic Christian Communities in the Philippines. They had only limited success, however, and to some extent their position as defenders of tradition was paradoxical. They were themselves modern organizations, designed to fight modern political and economic battles, and when they did win, it was a victory for a new community, not the old one.

With virtually all other political leaders favouring modernization, overt resistance to it was difficult, and most Southeast Asians could deploy only what James C. Scott described as the 'weapons of the weak': avoidance, non-compliance, sabotage, and veiled insolence.[40] To a considerable extent they succeeded in slowing down the march of what passed for progress, as shown by comparisons between the visions of planners (indigenous and foreign) and what actually happened to their plans. The village proved far more resilient than anyone had imagined. Southern Vietnamese peasants resisted both the 1960s 'strategic hamlet' programme of the RVN and the collectivization efforts of the SRV a decade later, and throughout the region efforts of landlords to alter traditional leasing and harvesting arrangements had to be postponed or reversed, at least temporarily. Over the long run, however, this was a rearguard action fought against a force advancing on many different fronts: official policy, educational expansion, population pressure, the extension of transport and communication networks, and the imperatives of economic growth, from the green revolution to hydroelectric and mining development. Eventually most of the landlords and planners and developers had their way.

When they were unable to ward off the challenges to traditional hierarchy and community, Southeast Asians had to adapt to the new. At worst, violent crime, prostitution, drug addiction, and psychological disorders suggested anomie. Certainly no description of the region that did not include the armed gangs of Mindanao, the bar girls of Bangkok, and the heroin addicts of Saigon could be regarded as complete. It is not easy, however, to confirm that such activities were actually on the increase in the postwar ear (compare banditry and opium use in the colonial period); nor can it be assumed that they were all dysfunctional. If a waitress or an armed guard was an aspirant to upward mobility, why not a prostitute or a professional 'goon'? Deculturation, drug abuse, and severe mental disturbances, on the other hand, were clearly unhealthy concomitants of change.

---

[40] Scott, *Weapons of the Weak: Everyday Forms of Peasant Resistance*, New Haven, 1985; cf. Scott and Benedict J. Tria Kerkvliet, eds, *Everyday Forms of Peasant Resistance in South-East Asia*, London, 1986.

Most Southeast Asians, however, achieved some kind of compromise between retaining old communities and accepting the new. They still lived in the village, but sometimes travelled beyond it, or even worked elsewhere for a while. They kept going to the *wayang* (puppet theatre) and temple festivals, but also listened to transistor radios and read *komiks*. They formed patron–client alliances with local officials, not as an anachronistic holdover from the past, but as a creative response to the fact that the state was a growing source of benefits. They increased the flexibility of their discourse, using deferential styles to those who still appreciated it and more democratic forms of address where appropriate. They ploughed behind water buffaloes and rode Hondas; they participated in *slametan* (ritual feasts) and mass political rallies; they attended both the herbalist and the government clinic. Even under communism they adapted traditional institutions to their needs, regardless of official policy:

> If you come to Thai Nguyen City
> You will see an awful sight,
> For the market, morn till night,
> Bustles with venality.
> Anything you want to buy
> On the sidewalk is displayed—
> Even what the state forbade.
> God may know how, but not I![41]

One element of continuity in their lives was kinship. The Southeast Asian family had been subjected by migration to the strain of distance. It had been denigrated by modernizers and attacked by the Khmer Rouge. But it survived the decline of the village community and permeated many of the newer organizations that replaced it. Politically, postwar Southeast Asia was characterized by nepotism, even incipient dynasticism; Ferdinand and Imelda Romualdez Marcos merely carried to excess what other regional leaders more quietly aspired to. In business, family loyalties accounted for much of what unsympathetic Westerners saw as 'corruption', but locals regarded as simple fulfilment of familial obligations. Micro-studies of geographic and social mobility show the importance of kinship there; most Southeast Asians who moved to cities or frontiers did so along 'chains' of kinship, while those who found new work often did so through the good offices of relatives. Where family connections were not widespread enough to achieve social ends, they were extended artificially; 'kinship', noted Jeremy H. Kemp, '[was] far too valuable to be limited to the facts of biology!'[42] The persistence of traditional kinship does not refute the significance of social change, any more than the persistence of scholastic philosophy and witch-burning in seventeenth-century Europe refutes the significance of the Renaissance. If anything, it acts as confirmation;

---

[41] Nhu Van Lo, 'Flea Market in Thai Nguyen' (1977), quoted in Nguyen Van Canh (with Earle Cooper), *Vietnam Under Communism, 1975–1982*, Stanford, 1983, 43–4.

[42] 'The Manipulation of Personal Relations: From Kinship to Patron–Clientage', in Hans ten Brummelhuis and Kemp, eds, *Strategies and Structures in Thai Society*, Amsterdam: Universiteit van Amsterdam, Antropologish-Sociologisch Centrum, Publikatieserie Vakgroep Zuid- en Zuidoost-Azie, no. 31, 1984, 55–69.

kinship may have persisted simply because it was the only constant in an otherwise kaleidoscopic world. Its reliability, at a time when old values were being questioned and old institutions were crumbling, gave kinship its ongoing importance.

PROTEST AND REBELLION

A final strategy was open to Southeast Asians who could neither sustain the old ways nor tolerate the new: protest and—when protest was unavailing—rebellion. Perhaps at no time in its history had the region heard so many expressions of discontent as in the postwar era, though some of these undoubtedly reflected rising expectations and improved communications rather than declining socio-economic circumstances. Protests took a variety of forms, including petitions, rallies, strikes, marches, boycotts, and a host of symbolic actions. Buddhist monks in Saigon burned themselves to death to protest against the policies of Ngo Dinh Diem; white-collar workers in Makati shredded telephone directories for yellow confetti to honour the martyrdom of 'Ninoy' Aquino. Riots, which rocked most of the great cities at one time or another, may also be considered as a form of protest, though once under way they often seemed to transcend the specific grievances that sparked them.

Protest movements were more common in cities than in rural areas, in part because of such safety from reprisal as the relative anonymity of urban activism might provide. Mostly they were reactive responses to developments seen as harmful to the immediate interests of urbanites, rather than part of a coherent strategy for long-term change. Southeast Asians protested against rising rice prices, bus fares, and school fees; the presence of exploitative aliens (Chinese traders, Japanese investors, American troops); and threats to political or religious freedom (stolen elections, invasions of monasteries). Such unrest rarely escalated into full-scale rebellion, though when it was supported or instigated by elements of the élite it was capable of toppling already shaky governments, as happened in the RVN in 1963, Thailand in 1973, and the Philippines in 1986. Usually, however, the police and armed forces were able to contain or roll these protests back while higher authorities conceded little or nothing.

In rural areas the success rate of peaceful protests was even lower, as it was generally more difficult for the protestors to co-ordinate their actions and easier for the state to suppress them without fear of offending national or international opinion. For many Southeast Asian peasants, therefore, there appeared to be little middle ground between employing the 'weapons of the weak' (including migration) and actual armed rebellion; those without military capacity had little choice but to be polite and avoid direct confrontation.

Although many protest movements in Southeast Asia began as spontaneous responses to local grievances, those that were sustained over the course of years generally had a core identity based on religion, ethnic minority status, or economic class. Armed challenges to the state by religious movements ranged in scale from Darul Islam, which mobilized millions of Sundanese against the Republic of Indonesia for fourteen years (1948–62) to cults like Lapiang Malaya, which engaged the Republic of the Philippines in a single day of conflict (in 1967), at a cost of fewer than one hundred casualties.[43] Other religious leaders—Buddhist monks, Muslim *ulamā*, Catholic priests—also engaged in non-violent protests against the state from time to time. The spiritual meaning of these movements is not the concern here: all that is noted is the possible, though generally unacknowledged, link between religious protest and diffuse socio-economic discontent.

The causes of most separatist movements were relatively easy to discern, as were the limits to their strength. Ethnic minorities far from the national capital felt—often correctly—that they were politically slighted and economically exploited by the dominant ethnic group, and believed that only through independence or communal autonomy could justice be achieved. By virtue of the fact that they were minorities, outnumbered and outgunned, they could hardly hope to win, yet the strength of their commitment (often reinforced by the excesses of government forces) and their familiarity with local terrain allowed some of the movements to persist over decades. Parts of Burma were in a state of active rebellion during the entire postwar period. Separatist activities elsewhere were intermittent but virtually inextinguishable, now flaring up, now in remission, but never wholly healed. Rebellion seemed particularly recurrent where physical remoteness from the centre was coupled with religious differentiation, as among Muslims in southern Thailand and the Philippines, Christians in Maluku, and animists in Irian Jaya and the highlands of Indochina.

Rebellion based on class, rather than ethnicity, potentially had a wider demographic base, as well as access to a systematic ideology and structure of resistance, which most separatist movements lacked. By any calculation most Southeast Asians were poor, and the presence of wealthy landlords and capitalists in their midst must have suggested that their poverty was due in part to exploitation. Marxist logic indicated as early as the late 1940s that Southeast Asians should be ready to throw off their chains, yet of the many rebellions that occurred throughout the region at that time only those in Indochina ultimately succeeded. Elsewhere the early uprisings were defeated; though some of these movements made later comebacks—particularly in Indonesia in the early 1960s and the Philippines in the 1970s and 1980s—the history of postwar Southeast Asia in general confounded those whose analysis was predicated on the centrality of class and the class struggle.

Class, as a category of analysis, can be useful to scholars of Southeast Asia, provided that it does not capsize on the attempt to specify the precise relationship between 'feudalism' and capitalism and makes due allowance for the occasionally opposing interests of class fractions: 'national' and

[43] Karl D. Jackson, *Traditional Authority, Islam, and Rebellion: A Study of Indonesian Political Behavior*, Berkeley, 1980; David R. Sturtevant, 'Rizalistas—Contemporary Revitalization Movements in the Philippines', in *Agrarian Unrest in the Philippines*, Athens: Ohio University Monographs in International Studies, Southeast Asia Series no. 8, 1969, 18–30.

'comprador' bourgeoisies, poor tenants and landless labourers, etc. Where it falters is as a phenomenological category, a representation of indigenous consciousness. Southeast Asians were certainly aware of gradations of prestige and social ranking, and at the most basic level consistently distinguished between 'big people' and 'little people'. What they did not do, by and large, was identify their own interests with those of a broader class and then act in accordance with those collective interests.

Although they avoided the term itself, there was probably greater 'class' solidarity within the upper strata than among the masses. Despite rhetorical flourishes in favour of democracy, and the occasional defection of individual members, the ruling élites were essentially unified on basic principles of governance. Land, they agreed, should not be redistributed without compensation; no need to look further for an explanation for the failure of land reform in most of Southeast Asia. Labour should be disciplined and denied effective participation in either economic or political decision-making—and so it was, even in nominally progressive states such as Singapore. Temporary deviations from these principles in Thailand after 1973 and the Philippines after 1986 were corrected when it was fully recognized just what was at stake. Perhaps the most successful demonstration of upper-class solidarity was the Alliance (and its successors) in Malaya, which overrode ethnic differences to maintain a political system based firmly on the protection of property and order.

Among the masses it was more problematical. Widespread horizontal solidarity was extraordinarily difficult to achieve, even in peaceful protest movements, and in the search for new forms of social organization most Southeast Asians seemed to prefer either vertical links based on patron–client relationships, or limited egalitarian groupings based on personal acquaintance. Even when a vanguard party spelled it out for them, most Southeast Asian workers and peasants were reluctant to accept the abstraction of a 'working class', or at any event to commit themselves to its defence. The Malayan Communist Party was unable to transcend its ethnic base in the Chinese community, and the PKP (Partido Komunista ng Pilipinas) and PKI (Partai Komunis Indonesia) had great difficulty transcending their geographical bases in central Luzon and Java, respectively. Similarly, whereas local strikes were occasionally successful, general strikes and boycotts were not, and those legal political parties that professed a class basis rarely accomplished much in the electoral arena.

Why did such movements fail? To some extent it was the weight of traditional cultural values. Class consciousness was profoundly strange; to understand human relations as based primarily on the opposition of economic roles required overcoming centuries of Southeast Asian thinking about the nature of the world. To some extent it was due to the complexity of new economic and social structures. In the cities there were many different kinds of workers with different interests, while even in rural areas landless labourers, seasonal workers and part-time proletarians were mixed in with the familiar class of tenants. At the same time the expanded involvement of the state and large corporations in the local economy increased the physical and social distance between ordinary workers or peasants and those who controlled their means of livelihood. It was harder to comprehend and confront a governmental development agency, a transnational corporation, or the World Bank than an exploitative landlord or factory owner, and it was harder to develop solidarity with workers five hundred miles away than with fellow tenants.

Class consciousness was also undermined by rising prosperity, in that many of the poor, though more exploited than ever (in the sense of retaining less of the value they helped to create), were actually better off in material terms than they had been before. A different kind of prosperity helped to explain why most military personnel failed to identify with the labouring classes into which they were born. (Officers were usually recruited from the propertied classes.) The state was usually a reliable paymaster, sometimes even a generous one, and in much of the region soldiering also offered occasional opportunities for the receipt of bribes or even armed robbery. It was thus in the economic interest of the troops either to support the government or to try to remove it in favour of one that might treat them even more kindly.

It was official mystification and repression, above all, that inhibited the development of class consciousness in Southeast Asia. At an intellectual level the capitalist states followed colonial precedent in denying that 'class' existed as a significant social factor. In its place they offered either myths of national unity or divisions based on ethnicity which left the rulers among the majority (e.g., Malays) rather than the minority (e.g., landlords). In a sense, every discussion of race or 'the Chinese problem' was a distraction from more dangerous questioning of the socio-economic structure. Many governments censored publications that openly challenged the official orthodoxy, and often persecuted the authors as well. The term 'class' itself became suspect, associated with Marxism and therefore, by implication, with subversion.

Even where the press was relatively free, however, as in the Philippines (before and after martial law), those who tried to translate class conscious-ness into action were subject to harassment or worse. Almost the surest way to invite trouble in Southeast Asia was to be a union or community organizer, even one committed to peaceful change. Effective unions, both industrial and agrarian, were systematically broken up by legal restriction, bribery or violence; some were replaced by tame unions that could be trusted not to ask more than the government or the company was willing to concede; others simply vanished. Organizers were fired, beaten up, blacklisted, imprisoned, or even killed; if they enjoyed some kind of religious immunity, they were put under great pressure to stay out of politics. The human rights record of the independent states of Southeast Asia, never bright, was particularly dim when it came to activities designed to empower ordinary workers or peasants.

In the face of implacable hostility to peaceful change, actual rebellion was an act of desperation. The most convincing analyses of leftist insur-gencies—e.g., Jeffrey Race's study of the National Liberation Front in southern Vietnam and Benedict J. Kerkvliet's study of the Huk rebellion in the Philippines—suggest that they were rooted in local economic and social injustice. Those who joined the movement and risked their lives for it (not necessarily the party leaders, who were often from the disaffected élite) did so because they saw the modicum of economic security and dignity that they had traditionally enjoyed being eroded, while their pleas for justice and attempts to ameliorate their lot within the system proved fruitless. 'We wanted the landlords or the government to guarantee us enough to eat and a roof over our heads', one former Huk told Kerkvliet, while another claimed: 'I didn't want to fight for my life and my share of the harvest. These bastards—landlords, civilian guards, soldiers—they all made me take up a gun.'[44] Most of the rebels were not wild-eyed fanatics deluded into grandiose utopian dreams; they fought to retain basic human rights.

That they lost more often than they won in postwar Southeast Asia is largely attributable to the sheer state power they confronted, a power frequently reinforced by external assistance. The state not only had superior firepower and communications, but the resources to wage effective public relations campaigns and to grant judicious concessions. It could build roads, fly in medical teams, monopolize the media, and sometimes buy off rebel leaders or factions. It could also stir up popular violence against its enemies, particularly in Indonesia, where village lanes ran red with the blood of suspected PKI sympathizers in 1965–6.

In this context the victory of the Vietnamese Communist Party was all the more remarkable, and many books have been devoted to explaining it. (The success of the communists in Cambodia and Laos is easier to comprehend, as those societies were radicalized by the overspill of the Second Indochina War.) Some of the explanations emphasized the strengths of the party itself—continuity of leadership and a sophisticated organization combining central direction with strong local initiative—but the more interesting focused on the sources of its appeal to ordinary Vietnamese. First, the party successfully identified itself with Vietnamese nationalism, offering a new framework for the sense of cultural community that many believed had been lost and portraying its opponents (first the French, then the USA-backed RVN) as the enemies of that community. Second, it appeared to be working on a local level in the concrete interests of ordinary people by reducing rents and allowing the people a greater voice in decision-making.

Unrest did not disappear once socialist or communist régimes were established, however. Continuing insurgencies in Burma, the clumsy and brutal land reform campaign in the DRV in the 1950s (even if it was not the full-scale 'bloodbath' its detractors claimed), the flight of the boat people from the SRV in the 1970s and 1980s, and the horrors of Democratic Kampuchea all suggested that the new régimes had altered, rather than removed, the bases of social conflict. The one-party state replaced the landlord and capitalist as the main source of oppression and the primary target of protest. Official mystification and repression were even stronger than in capitalist Southeast Asia. In communist Indochina the significance

---

[44] Kerkvliet, The Huk Rebellion: A Study of Peasant Revolt in the Philippines, Berkeley, 1977, 164–5; cf. Race, War Comes to Long An: Revolutionary Conflict in a Vietnamese Province, Berkeley, 1972.

of 'class' was officially acknowledged, but only as something exterior or rooted in the past; the suggestion that the state and party apparatus itself represented a new kind of exploitative class structure was taboo. Alternative parties and non-official unions were proscribed; suspected resistance led to severe chastisement, extended 're-education', or even death. Burma was less systematic in extirpating resistance than the Indochinese states, but no less savage toward opponents who fell within its grasp.

The half-century after the outbreak of World War II saw more rapid and drastic social and economic change in Southeast Asia than any comparable period in its history. Starting almost from scratch after the war, the states of the region became politically independent just as the global economy was becoming increasingly interdependent, and this paradox framed much of the debate over specific economic policies throughout the region. Eventually, some states chose to defend property and open themselves to international aid, trade, and investment; they achieved unprecedented but extremely uneven growth, with rising GNP per capita frequently concealing persistent poverty. Others opted for enforced equality and attempted to distance themselves from the capitalist world-system; the price they paid was much slower economic growth and endemic warfare. Throughout the region population grew; agricultural production (thanks to the green revolution) grew even faster; industrial production grew faster yet; and the state apparatus grew fastest of all, while the physical environment began to deteriorate visibly.

The social consequences of these economic changes were complex. Traditions of hierarchy and local community were challenged not just by new ideologies of equality, individualism (or socialism) and nationalism, but by major changes in demographic patterns and economic structures. In the postwar era very few Southeast Asians spent their lives where basic human values and relationships were constant and shared by the entire community. If they themselves did not move, or undertake some different kind of work, or accept the new ideas, they were surrounded by others who did. Although some rejoiced in the liberty and opportunity offered by the new order, most evinced a certain unease as they attempted to uphold traditional institutions or invent new ones.

The limited participation of Southeast Asians in movements of protest and rebellion reflected contentment by some, but simple prudence by many others. Faced by the strongest states—capitalist or socialist—that had existed in Southeast Asian history, they chose to acquiesce and adapt, rather than confront state power. (The recent work of Scott and others on 'everyday' resistance is a useful corrective to the assumption that silence automatically signifies assent.) Yet the minority who chose open defiance left important clues as to how the kinds of changes that occurred in postwar Southeast Asia were perceived by those at the bottom, as well as by planners at the top. They show that, despite nominal prosperity, for many Southeast Asians independence led not to social harmony but to injustice so great that it had to be challenged, sometimes even at the risk of death.

BIBLIOGRAPHIC ESSAY

Information on economic and social change in postwar Southeast Asia has been compiled from a myriad of monographs, articles, and official publications; those listed here did not provide all the data, but suggested ways of viewing them. Gunnar Myrdal, *Asian Drama: An Inquiry into the Poverty of Nations*, A Twentieth Century Fund Study, 3 vols, New York, 1968; Hla Myint, *Economic Theory and the Underdeveloped Countries*, London, 1971; Lloyd G. Reynolds, *Economic Growth in the Third World, 1850–1980*, New Haven, 1985; and Harry T. Oshima, *Economic Growth in Monsoon Asia: A Comparative Survey*, Tokyo, 1987, offer useful comparative perspectives on economic growth. Frank H. Golay et al., *Underdevelopment and Economic Nationalism in Southeast Asia*, Ithaca, 1969, is the best introduction to economic nationalism in the region. Yoshihara Kunio, *The Rise of Ersatz Capitalism in South-East Asia*, Quezon City, 1988, is helpful on sources of investment; cf. Yuan-li Wu and Chun-hsi Wu, *Economic Development in Southeast Asia: The Chinese Dimension*, Stanford, 1980. Robin Broad, *Unequal Alliance, 1979–1986: The World Bank, the International Monetary Fund, and the Philippines*, Berkeley, 1988, analyses the political implications of multilateral aid.

Data on the socialist states are particularly likely to be faulty or biased. A reasonably balanced view can be found in Melanie Beresford, *Vietnam: Politics, Economics and Society*, in the series Marxist Regimes, London, 1988; see also Michael Vickery, *Kampuchea*, and Martin Stuart-Fox, *Laos*, in the same series (both 1986). For Burma, Hal Hill and Sisira Jayasuriya, *An Inward-Looking Economy in Transition: Economic Development in Burma since the 1960s*, Singapore: ISEAS, Occasional Paper no. 80, 1986, is most useful. Douglas C. Dacy, *Foreign Aid, War, and Economic Development: South Vietnam, 1955–1975*, Cambridge, UK, 1986, is the best analysis of official data for that controversial country, but see Alfred W. McCoy et al., *The Politics of Heroin in Southeast Asia*, New York, 1972, for a dimension otherwise overlooked.

For the rest of Southeast Asia the actual economic data are somewhat less problematic. Insightful interpretations are provided in Richard Robison, *Indonesia: The Rise of Capital*, Sydney: Asian Studies Association of Australia Southeast Asian Publications Series no. 13, 1986; Michael Stenson, *Class, Race and Colonialism in West Malaysia: The Indian Case*, St Lucia, 1980; Jomo K. Sundaram, *A Question of Class: Capital, the State, and Uneven Development in Malaya*, East Asian Social Science Monographs, Singapore, 1986; Richard Higgott and Richard Robison, eds, *Southeast Asia: Essays in the Political Economy of Structural Change*, London, 1985; and Robison, Kevin Hewison, and Higgott, eds, *Southeast Asia in the 1980s: the Politics of Economic Crisis*, Sydney, 1987.

Among the hundreds of local studies of social and economic change in postwar Southeast Asia, a few may be singled out: James F. Eder, *On the Road to Tribal Extinction: Depopulation, Deculturation and Adaptive Well-Being among the Batak of the Philippines*, Berkeley, 1987; Clifford Geertz, *Peddlers and Princes: Social Change and Economic Modernization in Two Indonesian*

Towns, Chicago, 1963; Patrick Guinness, *Harmony and Hierarchy in a Javanese Kampung*, Singapore: Asian Studies Association of Australia Southeast Asia Publications Series no. 11, 1986; Gillian Hart, *Power, Labor, and Livelihood: Processes of Change in Rural Java*, Berkeley, 1986; Gerald Cannon Hickey, *Village in Vietnam*, New Haven, 1964; Hickey, *Free in the Forest: Ethnohistory of the Vietnamese Central Highlands, 1954–1976*, New Haven, 1982; Benedict J. Kerkvliet, *The Huk Rebellion: A Study of Peasant Revolt in the Philippines*, Berkeley, 1977; Manning Nash, *The Golden Road to Modernity: Village Life in Contemporary Burma*, New York, 1965; Jeffrey Race, *War Comes to Long An: Revolutionary Conflict in a Vietnamese Province*, Berkeley, 1972; James C. Scott, *Weapons of the Weak: Everyday Forms of Peasant Resistance*, New Haven, 1985; Lauriston Sharp and Lucien Hanks, *Bang Chan: Social History of a Rural Community in Thailand*, Ithaca, 1978; G. William Skinner, *Leadership and Power in the Chinese Community of Thailand*, Ithaca: Cornell University Association for Asian Studies Monograph no. 3, 1958; Ann Laura Stoler, *Capitalism and Confrontation in Sumatra's Plantation Belt, 1870–1979*, New Haven, 1985; and Maria Cristina Blanc Szanton, *A Right to Survive: Subsistence Marketing in a Lowland Philippine Town*, University Park, PA, 1972.

CHAPTER

9

RELIGIOUS CHANGE IN CONTEMPORARY
SOUTHEAST ASIA

Seagoing trade made Southeast Asia a fertile meeting ground from early
history, and at the close of World War II Landon aptly characterized the
region as a 'crossroad of religion'. He emphasized that up to then imported
religions had been subordinated to ancestral spirit cults which were
grounded in relatively autonomous villages, and noted that even the
Westernized élites had adapted modern ideas within a world-view shaped
by local traditions. In the same breath he suggested that the middle of this
century marked a turning point because the closing years of colonial rule
and the disruptions of the war had definitively shaken the foundations of
local life.[1] Despite the range of changes since then, the region remains a
site of encounter between deeply held and widely divergent world-views.
A rich tapestry of ancient local traditions is still sustained with remarkable
force, and significant communities derive their practices from all of the
major world faiths in many of their forms. The diversity, vitality and depth
of religious commitments within the region combine so that it remains an
especially rich laboratory for the exploration of religion.

   The region is filled with vibrant ritual enactments, such as those in
Hindu Bali, and many people routinely enter altered states through
ritualized trance, as in Malaysia's annual Thaipusam festival, touching
realms of consciousness which are remote for most people in industrialized societies. Meditation practices of Javanese syncretic mystics and the
Theravāda forest monastries counterpoint orthodox Islam and ritual Buddhism. Vigorous communities of new Christians exist alongside animists
and some, mainly in urban contexts, who live without knowing religious
meanings. These diverse experiences of reality, shaped by magical animism,
esoteric mysticism, traditional piety, scriptural literalism and modern
scepticism, intersect routinely in villages, markets and offices. At the same
time, because most people feel their religion is both substantive and
significant, contention over spiritual convictions in relation to other
spheres of life is regularly in the foreground of the cultural politics of the
region.

   Every major historical transformation in Southeast Asia has been attended
by changes in religion, and some have been especially facilitated by the
emissaries of new faiths. In the late twentieth century pragmatic utilitarianism

[1] K. P. Landon, *Southeast Asia: Crossroad of Religions*, Chicago, 1949, 202–3.

may be the most powerful missionary force and the communities of that faith are expanding. But focus on the urban surfaces of local life can obscure the persistence of patterns which are rooted in the animistic and rice-growing village substratum of the region. Beneath surface transitions the structures of popular perception and belief remain remarkably cohesive. Changes have generally had their greatest impact on the élites linked to trading ports and temple cities. Even in those contexts whenever local peoples domesticated imported tools of thought and organization, including religious systems, they gave local flavour to patterns which were used otherwise elsewhere. The idioms of imported religions accommodated local meanings. Indian deities came as universal terms for spirit forces known already by different names; Confucianism shaped Vietnamese courts while villagers self-consciously retained ancestral culture.

On the other hand the past fifty years have brought previously unimaginable challenge to the spiritual beliefs and practices rooted in regional prehistory. The depth of social transformation has immense implications in every sphere, and the population explosion has compounded the pace of change. Most people may still live in villages but recently urban populations have mushroomed dramatically. The demographic revolution means that an increasing majority has grown up in a postwar world dominated by modern states rather than ethnicity, by education in schools rather than village ritual religion, and by monetarized economies rather than communal co-operation. Changes occur not only through the ways in which geographically distinct communities are being tied together, but also through transformations in generational, class and gender relations. At the same time the radical transitions of mid-century ensured that the generation which came of age during and after World War II has dominated socio-political institutions through most of the region since then, establishing the predominant tones of cultural evolution into the 1980s.

Change is channelled through metropoles which exemplify the trends they mediate. Pre-modern capitals, such as Mandalay, Chiengmai, Surakarta or Klungkung provide contexts for limited maintenance of traditional arts, but insofar as they do they are like the eye of a cyclone. It is the capital cities which provide a paradigm for the nature of wider changes. Their early colonial centres were already superseded by prewar expansion in the late colonial period. The initial bursts of construction in the 1950s, dramatic as they seemed then, now appear hesitant. Singapore, Bangkok, Manila, Kuala Lumpur and Jakarta have seen such profound expansion in the 1970s and 1980s that their origins have been overwhelmed. Where there were canals and tree-lined avenues in 1950, we see cement in Bangkok. Skyscrapers and multilane highways reshape the spaces of Jakarta so that suburbs like Kebayoran, created only in the 1950s, are now almost unrecognizable. Though restructuring is especially concentrated in these metropoles, they also reach out to reshape the ambience of their hinterlands; changes in cities properly indicate the depth and pace of wider transformation in the past half-century.

In this context, recent reformulations of religion are evident through representations in politics as well as through participation in institutions which are conventionally recognized as religious. Spiritual impulses are implicit within national political culture, cultural policies, and popular practices. We will start by considering religious change at the macro level and in its external dimensions, by dealing with patterns of cultural change and the institutional levels of religious life. In the most general terms recent political cultures have often aimed to reconstruct essentially religious meanings through neo-traditionalism. Resonance with earlier meanings can be surprising and religious nuances are quite clear, but whenever contemporary élites invoke indigenous spiritual cultures it is within new frameworks which make the process one of reinvention rather than strictly of preservation. It is viewed in that light, as a process of creative reinvention, that neo-traditionalism must be considered a theme of cultural politics in the independent states of the region.

Policies of integration, related to education and the formation of national ideologies, threaten tribal and ethnic minorities such as the Karen and Chin of Myanmar (Burma), the Meo of Thailand, the Jarai in the hills of Vietnam and the Mentawai, Punan or Asmat in remote parts of the archipelago, jeopardizing what were until now relatively autonomous identities. Implicitly these policies lead to homogenization, to inadvertent or intended cultural genocide. This mirrors the green revolution in rice agriculture. In that field the spread of new hybrid species increases uniformity of genetic stock, making crops at once more productive and more vulnerable to pests. Through the self-confident modernism of national governments, monocultures extend in the social domain with vigour and the same double edge. Even within the dominant ethnic communities, the restructuring of recognized religion is influenced by instruments of control which facilitate previously impossible regulation, extending to licensing of folk healers, and new forms of opposition, including militant fundamentalisms.

The micro level involves identification of the major types of religious expression in Southeast Asia and exploration of changes within explicitly religious communities. After considering the varieties of recent local religious expression, we will move toward reflection on the ways in which 'experience of what is real' has been evolving. In the innermost dimension this leads toward probing the nature of shifts in the experiential sphere of individual consciousness. Religious changes are not simply a matter of shifting objects of belief or ideology, of altered allegiance to clearly designated organizations, or even of changes in the degree to which people are spiritual in orientation. Religion, as we now understand increasingly, is a matter of what we experience as real, of how we know truth—indeed of whether we can believe there is such a thing—and equally of how our ways of knowing influence our interactions. This account will outline the diversity of explicitly religious movements and then move beyond that. Symbolic structures, on the surfaces of cultural life, have been either evolving, as old symbols accommodate new contexts, or shifting, as new systems replace old ones. At the same time and at a deeper level we can also note that the very nature of the relationship between individual experience, cultural structures and social life is also changing. New contexts and mediations have brought new modes of access to what Southeast Asians of this era are able to know or believe as real.

APPROPRIATIONS OF INDUSTRIAL CULTURE

It is most instructive to view the second half of the twentieth century as the period in which Southeast Asian peoples have been gaining control over and creatively adapting their cultures to industrially derived structures. Though usually considered as the era of independence, this historical phase ironically involves the consolidation of interdependence. Local peoples may directly control their domestic politics once again, but their context is clearly one of increasing interdependence and emergent internationalism. Whether through extended warfare, as in Vietnam, or commitment to trade, as in Singapore, new networks of communication and tools of organization connect people ever more profoundly into world patterns. Where there have been counter-currents, such as those ostensibly aiming to establish locally self-sustaining systems in post-1962 Burma or the Kampuchea of the Khmer Rouge in the late 1970s, they have had the flavour of rearguard actions. Focus on movements of local élites to replace colonial masters directs attention away from critical continuities between colonial and independent systems.

Increasing authoritarianism, economic interdependence, and monocultural modernism are all aspects of the Southeast Asian situation. Early anti-colonial resistance movements, such as the Aceh or Java wars in the archipelago in the nineteenth century or the Saya San rebellion in Burma during the 1930s, centred on revival of social harmony through traditional institutions. In those instances opposition was filtered through and identified with ethnicity, language, or kinship, and we thus see peasant, court and religious movements as the dying gasps of traditional entities. Though they were connected with nationalism through common underlying aspiration and in the mythologies of subsequent activists, they contained no vision of a modern state. In contrast nationalists have competed to create and control modern integrating institutions and Westernized local élites appear as their cutting edge. As the first to experience themselves as members of multi-ethnic states, their target has consistently been control of the apparatus which produced them.

In social historical terms the consolidation of modern state systems and increasing interpenetration are powerful themes which cross the boundary between the eras of colonialism and independence. Governments are now connected with populations through extensions of the very legal systems, bureaucratic networks, educational and military channels that were established in the first half of the century under colonialism. The second half of this century has seen forces of transformation which were only hinted at in the colonial era assume increasing pace. The fruits of the Industrial Revolution at once tie local states to global patterns and bond peoples to each other with new force. Systems of government and taxation; warfare, trade and tourism; state-run education and electronic media; all these intrude increasingly in the lives of even remote peoples. Modern states entail instruments of intervention, through the mechanics of printing and the reach of electronic communications, far more pervasive than those available to earlier systems of power.

Southeast Asian appropriations of new communications media and the apparatus of statehood have been taking place within a context of severe limitation. Everywhere the legacies of colonialism, extremes of political contention, international imbalance, dislocations attending warfare, poverty and rapid urbanization have imposed heavy costs. To grasp recent changes in religious culture, we must understand how economic shifts and population movements threaten the capacity of village communities to sustain old rituals. Warfare, internal migration, new agricultural régimes and deforestation have restructured the physical as well as social environments of tribal minorities and shifting cultivators. Javanese transmigrants to Kalimantan, factory women in Malaysia, Visayan street people in Manila or prostitutes from the northeast in Bangkok cannot imagine cosmological realities or relate to ultimate meanings in the way their relatively settled rice-farming grandparents did as they bowed to Indic-style royalty. In extreme cases, minorities like the Muslim Chams under Pol Pot's Kampuchea (Cambodia) from 1975 to 1979, and others elsewhere, have been faced with apparently genocidal policies.[2] These factors deeply condition cultural process and establish a vital gestalt for understanding changes in popular culture and religion.

Putting cultural and religious history in the foreground facilitates recognition of local volition in a way even social history may not. The appropriation of new media is not simply a matter of the obvious, of acquiring indigenous control over print, radio, film and television. It is also a way of talking about the wider correlates of new industries, forms of entertainment, militaries, bureaucracy and government. As in earlier phases of evolution, adjustments in world-view occur as local peoples enter wider circles of contact beyond the region. Earlier cultural and religious changes have been comprehensible only as shifts in vision accompanied by social changes as intensified commerce brought Sinic, Indic and Islamic vocabularies into the region. In those instances, as their environment changed local peoples found their own purposes fulfilled more clearly through new modes of cultural discourse. Recent trajectories of local development do not match expectations dictated by political economic logic alone, and events are still shaped by or refracted through persistently religious cultures. Southeast Asians are once again claiming to speak with a new voice, though now through their adaptation of industrialized media.

An overview is naturally more easily attained for early and thus distant appropriations of systems of government, writing, trade or agriculture. Insofar as we can achieve such a perspective on the present, it marks a distinctive phase of cultural evolution; there is a change at least as profound as the emergence of states, made more dramatic by the compression of time. Recent changes do not seem incremental, as changes may through earlier history: time itself stops appearing as a constant as interpretation nears the present, appearing to accelerate along with technological innovation and population growth. Just as early societies adapted new patterns in unique ways, contemporary peoples now adapt technological

[2] B. Kiernan, 'Orphans of Genocide: The Cham Muslims of Kampuchea under Pol Pot', *Bulletin of Concerned Asian Scholars*, 20, 4 (1988).

structures and rework their world-views through a modernity which is not static in any of its manifestations. The undercurrents of indigenous cultural voices are not always obvious, especially as political and economic realities tend to dominate our perception of recent social life. Nevertheless localization continues even when the warping pressures of circumstance, including extremes of social dislocation and international intervention, are pervasive.

The extension of modern media into village societies has been remarkable. Newspaper and radio communications began to be widely disseminated before World War II, and now television and films have been reaching villages as well as towns. Increasing consumerism in Thailand, Malaysia and Indonesia has fed the communications revolution from the 1970s onward. Burma has been less affected by modern media, as it has been relatively isolated under Ne Win. Radio programmes, extension education and new farming methods have all changed cultural attitudes and social relations as well as agricultural practices. In Java some villagers report that only the older strains of rice are connected to spirits; the realms of the *devas* become distant and the connections loose as new miracle strains and chemical fertilizers move in. Spirits are also less central to social life as customary law is replaced with rationalized and centrally administered justice. Formerly village heads and councils interpreted customs with a view to resolve disputes in an atmosphere theoretically guided by sensitivity to local spiritual atmospheres. Now decisions are coded by parliaments and, at least in principle, interpreted through bureaucratic representatives.

Every structural reorganization crystallizes new classes, and the germinal intelligentsias of the late colonial era, mainly drawn from earlier élites, became the seed for rapidly expanding and increasingly cosmopolitan supercultures. The revolutionary transitions of the postwar era brought other groups into the new élite. The economic strength of migrant Chinese and Indians has given them a central position, however ambiguous and uncomfortable, in major cities. In most parts of the region the military has became a prime channel for upward mobility, allowing some villagers into the newly forming national élites. Secular education, though still underpinned by patronage systems and thus tied to older class divisions, has offered a channel for others who had less scope through traditional monastic or religious schooling. The extent of their socio-economic and political power gives the new élites a magnetic influence in their cultural environment. As the prime mediators of advanced industrial culture, the new élites are mediators of foreign influence and produce modes of modernity which are distinctive and local.

National boundaries have been sharply defined on maps only in this century, and nationalism is only the political face of response to modernity as mediated by imperialism. Similarly sharpened lines characterize other spheres, as every facet of organization and consciousness is modernized. As literatures and religions have been articulated increasingly through print, they also become defined as text. This has militated against the performance modes and syncretic styles which were predominant in earlier local practices. Scripturalist emphasis on vernaculars brought a shift from an intuitive and participatory ritual style to intellectual sermonizing and a contingent preoccupation with ideologically defined purity. Boundaries between worlds of symbolic meaning have sharpened as much as have those between spheres of power. Other domains also become distinct. To question how religion relates to nationalism, as we may wish to do, reflects a mentality once entirely foreign to the region. Traditional validations of power construed politics as one aspect of a process that was also spiritual; their apparent separability, increasingly institutionalized, is one consequence of recent changes.

SPIRITUAL VISIONS OF REVOLUTION AND INDEPENDENCE

From a spiritual perspective, colonialism was a magical spell as well as a mechanical mastery of institutions, guns and economies. In magical idiom the suppression of will, as in any hegemony, rests on tacit convictions about the way things are, and can thus shift suddenly. So in Southeast Asia at the end of the war, as in Europe more recently, change was a matter of how human will was mobilized and perceptual gestalt configured as well as of who held what instruments of social control. Thus an opening through glasnost led to a dramatic shift in perspective on Soviet dominance and this rapidly reconfigured social realities in Eastern Europe at the end of the 1980s. Similarly the enforced quiet of colonial twilight in the years of the Great Depression was broken dramatically when the Japanese punctured the myth of white supremacy. As the occupation drew to a close in mid-1945 for most Indonesians, Burmese, Vietnamese and Filipinos the prewar order was definitely past, and they prepared for an independence which seemed both imminent and cosmologically destined. European blindness to the spiritual depth and nature of this popular sentiment contributed to the protracted and painful transitions which ensued. It is not surprising that the millenarianism of many Southeast Asians has been difficult to grasp for many Westerners. Such systems appear simply irrational unless it is recognized that the reference is to shifts in atmosphere which everyone registers through different idioms.

Only remote minority groups were untouched by the disruptions of the depression and war years. For the urban-based intelligentsias, independence meant opportunity to replace Europeans in controlling modern communication infrastructure. The political narratives which constitute most histories focus on contention between those élites, but social historians have been consistently drawing attention to the plurality of motives and crosscurrents in the transition years. However sweeping the changes of the postwar years, most people nevertheless retained continuing social practices, wanting mainly to be left alone. For them the grand narratives of political drama appeared as tangents which only occasionally intruded. Insofar as most subsistence-oriented rice-cultivating villagers considered independence, it usually meant aspiration for what was imagined as return to an idealized normality and balance in a context of minimized demands from the state. For many other people, whether embracing Christianity as an appropriation of modernity or celebrating established faiths, the momentous shifts at the end of the war opened new spiritual, as well as social and economic, territories.

From most established religious perspectives in the region the transitions and revolutions have been the outer layers of a reshaping which was also taking place spiritually. In the Theravāda, Confucian, Muslim and Catholic regions there has been widespread assent to notions that the state is responsible for regulating or providing a positive context for spiritual life. Reformation-style separation of political and religious spheres touched prominent élites, but at the roots of social life traditional visions predominated. Thus, among the plurality of interests and ideologies shaping transitions to independence, we register powerful groups who pursued visions dominated by spiritual senses of purpose. These resonances are most apparent in the movements toward an Islamic state, termed 'Darul Islam' in Indonesia. But similar convergence was also evident in Buddhist senses of the Burmese revolution, in Confucian spirituality implicit within Vietnamese communism, and in widespread peasant-based millenarianism. These perspectives influenced the transitions to independence, and moulded social trends of the postwar era.

The strongest root of religious tension in Indonesia lay in Dutch efforts designed precisely to prevent Islam from becoming a focus for nationalist sentiment, to emasculate it by forging strong bonds between the colonial and *adat* élites. This alliance had deepened an existing polarity between religious and political élites, for instance in Java continuing the subordination of mosque officials (*penghulu*) to the bureaucratic élite (*priyayi*). Under the Japanese, however, Islam gained momentum through efforts to orchestrate anti-Western sentiments. Recognizing the influence of religious teachers, the Japanese aimed to mobilize Islamic support throughout the archipelago. By giving separate authority to the Office of Religious Affairs and creating the forerunner of Masjumi (Masyumi), with authority over local Islam, they established a basis for postwar Muslim power, as Masjumi was to became the leading Muslim party during the Indonesian struggle for independence.[3] Thus, in the lead-up to independence, Islam was able to assert a claim toward establishment of an Islamic rather than secular state. Throughout the occupation, Japanese reliance on Sukarno gave him access to radio other nationalists did not have and, as that tool was well suited to his oratorical strengths, his domination of it elevated him to primacy in the public eye. Though secular nationalists thus regained relative strength as the occupation came to an end, the new institutional basis of Islam irrevocably altered the balance of local power.

Anderson suggested that Japanese training of a local militia served, like earlier religious training in hermitages or Islamic schools (*pesantren*), spiritually to prepare youth for the revolution. The deprivations of the occupation focused senses and concentrated energies; it was like an enforced asceticism tempered by conviction that freedom (*merdeka*) would follow.[4] This imagery suggests the special qualities of the energies which were unleashed during the period of suspension and excitement in which the republic was

---

[3] H. Benda, *The Crescent and the Rising Sun*, The Hague, 1958.
[4] B. R. O'G. Anderson, *Java in a Time of Revolution: Occupation and Resistance, 1944–1946*, Ithaca and London, 1972.

born. Though different participants hold variant views, certainly the early days of the revolution were a turning point many have looked back on with nostalgia. Most leaders of the republic since then have recalled what seemed a spiritual unity of purpose which, however momentarily, drew diverse classes and ethnic groups into united effort and aspiration. Whatever the degree of actual unity, most were touched by the intensity of the time and those of formative age remained indelibly marked as they moved on to assume leading roles in the republic. Stringent wartime circumstances and policies combined with chauvinism eventually to alienate most locals, but many Javanese initially saw the Japanese as liberators, those predicted by the prophecies of Joyoboyo, a thirteenth-century king of Kediri.[5]

Their imagery presented the revolution as a momentary vacuum, a phase of upheaval resulting from the departure of divine sanction (*wahyu*) from those in power, a time of craziness which sets the stage for a new golden era. Defeudalization was a prominent theme alongside decoloniza-tion, millenarian senses of the revolution underpinned populist idiom, and many new mystical sects crystallized during the revolution.[6] The collapse of the outer walls of the Yogya palace (*kraton*) was read by some as a physical parallel to a symbolic opening which was connected to deep spiritual changes. Power (*kasekten*), which had been concentrated in kings and courts, flowed outward so that the communion between human and cosmic planes, previously mediated through royalty, became accessible for all who could receive it. Traditional imagery, as throughout Indianized Southeast Asia, consistently presented events within the human micro-cosm as interwoven with and parallel to changes in the social and natural orders of the macrocosm. Thus, in the idiom of some of these movements, the spiritual struggle within the revolution was directed at unseating the imperialism of the mind within the body, an internal reorganization which was seen as simultaneous with the displacement of Dutch power over national culture.

At the same time more orthodox Muslims' aspirations had been long suppressed and were already tuned, through longstanding contacts with Mecca and Cairo, to awareness of European colonialism as a dampening force throughout the Islamic world. Throughout the archipelago Japanese appeals to Islam enhanced conviction that the occupation foreshadowed the creation of the *dar-al islam* (the house of Islam). Movement toward an Islamic state had already been a leading current in prewar nationalism and played an especially consistent and powerful role in Aceh, which was never regained by the Dutch. Elsewhere, in Sumatra, Sulawesi, west Java and even along Java's north coast and within its heartlands, Islamic teachers (*kyai*) and the ideal of Islamic statehood sparked movements which competed with secularism at local and national levels right through the 1940s and 1950s. At their roots these movements were not simple expressions of purism: they also drew from millenarian and magical

---

[5] B. Dahm, *Sukarno and the Struggle for Indonesian Independence*, Ithaca, 1969, ch. 1.
[6] C. Geertz, based on fieldwork in an East Javanese town in the early 1950s, in *The Religion of Java*, Chicago, 1976, notes both the emergence of sects (pp. 112–18, 339–52) and the fact that activists connected changes in spiritual practices to the revolution.

strands of Islam. In the Darul Islam there was common emphasis on the internal spiritual facet of the holy war, the jihad. It was not only highly educated leaders such as Kartosuwirjo, but also many followers who understood that the establishment and expansion of the house of Islam involved an inner purification rather than only an external war.[7]

Though framed as banditry by the victors, from an internal perspective both the Darul Islam movements and the Moro nationalism of Mindanao and Sulu have expressed widespread conviction that national revolutions remained unfinished so long as the resulting states built on European rather than Islamic models. Like Marxists, for whom the revolution was incomplete without radical social transformation, some Muslims fought for a revolution they never won. In Aceh and along the north coast of Java changes were deep rooted, often spontaneously reflecting populist or religious impulses qute contrary to the thrust of what European cultures could register as national political development. In the southern Philippines the Muslim struggle began later, but it parallels the Darul Islam in representing revolutionary nationalism in an Islamic mould. The Indonesian nationalist leadership contained these aspects of revolution by standing against changes which could have jeopardized negotiations. The relatively secularized *priyayi* were heirs to Indic court traditions but Dutch educated; since they controlled the bureaucracy, they ensured limits to social and religious versions of the revolution, especially those of the Darul Islam.

Implicitly religious conflict contributed to the elimination of communism as a component of Indonesian nationalism. In 1948 Sudirman's guerrilla armies threatened to break with Sukarno, and in the same year enforced demobilization of communist regiments precipitated killings, particularly in the Madiun area of east Java. The Indonesian Communist Party (PKI) was eliminated, as it had been by the Dutch in 1926, and many thousands died in local conflicts, this time overseen by the firmly Muslim West Javanese Siliwangi division. By surmounting these populist guerrilla and communist 'threats to nationalism', the leadership gained ground for negotiation, but at the expense of elevating the cleavage between Islam and Javanism to a new order of intensity which persisted into the 1960s. The post-independence period witnessed a divergence between Muslim parties—the traditionalist Nahdatul Ulama and modernist Masjumi—and the syncretic or secular parties—the nationalists (PNI) and communists—which certainly coincided with difference in cultural orientation and related to differing underlying spiritual senses of what the national revolution aimed to accomplish.

In Vietnam traditional images presented the end of the war as implying an irrevocable end to the French order, one which had still held a place for imperial rituals. According to local spiritual culture the name for 'village' (*xa*) itself meant at root 'the place where people come together to worship the spirits'. In the Vietnamese variant of the Chinese model it had still been held, even within the French order, that imperial rituals such as

---

[7] C. van Dijk, *Rebellion Under the Banner of Islam*, The Hague, 1981, 34, 391–6.

the Nam Giao drew on the power and goodwill of ancestors, especially those of the royal clan, to guarantee both crops and the social welfare of the population. Rulers had to be tuned to nature and changed according to rhythms which, even when not apparent on the surface, were felt in the tight village communities. When Emperor Bao Dai abdicated on 22 August 1945 he sanctioned the Democratic Republic led by the Vietminh and entrusted it with the maintenance of his ancestral temples. To villagers, still bound to the land through cults of tutelary spirits focused on ancestral founders, this act represented more than a change of dynasty. It did not stop all ancestral practices, as festivals like Tet, the lunar New Year celebration of ancestors, continued to have symbolic force as a way of reforging bonds between the ancestors, nature and society. Nevertheless it foreshadowed the end of a profound constellation of relationships between heaven and earth.[8]

Their deeply imbued vision of social order implied for Vietnamese contestants that the tensions at the end of the war would lead to the emergence of one victor from among the many who initially appeared as candidates, not to pluralistic accord. In the end it appeared that the communists had made the most successful effort to assimilate modern Western notions to the universe of Vietnamese discourses. This implied that their victory was not only tactical, but also cultural. In local idiom it was cosmologically determined, a shift in the mandate of heaven which could not be reversed by ploy or strategy. According to Mus's argument the revolution was decided in popular eyes in the critical period from August 1945 to March 1946 and this marked a whole generation of leadership, as the same period also did in Indonesia.[9] This culturally rooted sense of the revolution remained largely invisible to French or American analysts and strategists. By focusing on ideologies, institutional structures and urban centres, they consistently failed to register that the mobilization of popular will, conceived locally as spiritual even when communist, influenced events more than formalized ideologies.

Imperial powers did note that in the Mekong delta the Hoa Hao variant of Buddhism attracted a following, as did analogous Javanese movements, around the founder's visionary projection of the colonialists' defeat in 1940. Within it practices of individual spiritual enlightenment clearly intermeshed with the impending revolution. As Woodside noted, 'classical culture had been more discredited at the upper levels of society than at the lower and ... the eighth-century Chinese poet Li Po (whose spirit regularly entered Cao Dai mediums in the 1920s and 1930s) still touched the hearts of more Vietnamese peasants than did the Paris commune'.[10] Within the movement much was made of ethnic myths of origin which saw the primordial spiritual strength of the people as lying in a magical prowess which would defeat the technical advantages of modern powers. The strength of the Hoa Hao movement, which had an independent military-administrative structure in the villages of the Mekong delta, provoked violent elimination of its leader in 1947. Hoa Hao prophecy held

---

[8] Landon, 194–7.
[9] D. McAlister and P. Mus, *The Vietnamese and Their Revolution*, New York, 1970, 118, 126.
[10] A. B. Woodside, *Community and Revolution in Modern Vietnam*, Boston, 1976, 188.

true in the end, but as a statement about communist rather than syncretic Buddhist power.

In urban centres a vigorous but limited modern revival of Buddhism (with in 1935 some 2000 adherents) competed with Marxism in attracting intellectuals to a vision of independence in Vietnam. These new movements, though rooted in older Mahāyāna Buddhism, emphasized the explication of original scriptures in the vernacular. They especially competed with Catholic missionaries, who had begun to succeed in communicating to villagers through local language, at a time when local Buddhists seemed esoteric and technical, making Mahāyāna appear as a preserve of monks. At the same time and on another front, examination of how communist intellectuals were drawn together led Marr to note significant resonances between communism and ingrained millenarianism. Terms in prison functioned to politicize many who had not previously been radical, forging spiritual bonds which underpinned revolutionary cells.[11] While for many millenarian religious impulses converged with revolutionary commitment, at the same time intellectuals also opted for Marxism as a liberation from what appeared as a stasis-oriented Confucian traditionalism.

In Burmese theorizing the interchange between Marxism and Buddhism was more direct and profound. Sarkisyanz established that underpinning the ideology of U Ottama in the 1920s there were notions that political struggle for independence paralleled the stages of Buddhist progression toward enlightenment. Pursuit of 'nirvana within this world', what appeared as a Buddhist 'social gospel', evoked ideals of how the state houses spiritual endeavour which can be traced as far as the Indian Emperor Asoka. Communal values of selflessness and an ethos of levelling were related at once to Buddhism and communism within the Thakin movement of the 1930s.[12] Even popular readings of terms such as 'revolution' and 'liberation' were shaped at critical junctures by Buddhist imagination and constraints. While diverging radically in other respects, this convergence fed into the thinking of most nationalists. Aung San's leadership of the revolution brought emphasis on separation of religion and politics and on socialist militancy in modern secular terms. But the culturalist anti-Western traditions of U Ottama and Saya San became especially relevant again under U Nu's leadership, after Aung San's death and up to 1962.

Shifts to national sovereignty in both Burma and Indonesia saw movement from the relatively Westernized ethos of Aung San, Sjahrir and Hatta to the culturalist orientations of U Nu and Sukarno. In Burma this shift happened quickly. Overt dedication to fostering the Buddhist basis of the state was foreshadowed in 1950 and firmly in place by 1951. U Nu reasserted the traditional role of the state as the protector of religion, seeing it as embodying the cultural values which, following the era of colonial suppression, needed to be enhanced to facilitate spiritual liberation. Socialism continued to be invoked in Burma and Indonesia, but communism was disavowed by the political philosophies which became

[11] D. Marr, *Vietnamese Tradition on Trial*, Berkeley, 1981, 305–6, 316.
[12] E. Sarkisyanz, *Buddhist Backgrounds of the Burmese Revolution*, The Hague, 1965.

dominant in both contexts. From 1949 onwards the presence of communist insurgents in the hills led governments, first under U Nu then Ne Win, to emphasize the incompatibility of Buddhism and Marxism, even while they have consistently advocated a Burmese Buddhist socialism.

Revolutionary transitions to independence, as in Indonesia, Vietnam and Burma, sharpen collective focus on spiritual issues in the same way that the prospect of death does for individuals. But even where the political order was relatively stable or transitions less violent, we can see a parallel configuration in that religious aspirations have been interwoven with revolutionary movements. In the Philippines the hierarchical organization of the Catholic Church tied its leadership closely to the state. This paralleled the social link between the Thai *sangha* and royalty, those cases being more aligned in this respect than either was to the pattern of Muslim organization in the archipelago. But at the grass roots of society, Catholic idiom was often also appropriated to converge with calls by the poor for social justice. Within the Church liberation theology, influenced by currents from Latin America from the 1960s onward, appealed to sectors of the priesthood who identified their mission simultaneously with social and spiritual welfare. The people-power revolution, which contributed to the end of the Marcos era in 1986, involved even the hierarchy of the Church and made candlelight prayer vigils a weapon of protest.

In the Thai context it is especially clear that religious purposes inspire modern state construction. Ironically the strength of continuities there have allowed a less ambiguous pursuit of modernity. Some correllates of modernity, repudiated aggressively as too Western elsewhere, have been embraced. Nevertheless, as Tambiah has argued, religious purposes continue to inspire government visions of progress:

> From early times Buddhism has been positively related to a conception of an ideal politico-social order, whose cornerstone was a righteous monarch who would promote a prosperous society and religion. ... Given this interlaced totality of religion and politics, of national consciousness and religious identity, of righteous morality and politics, it is difficult to see in Thailand a secular nationalism dispensing with Buddhist referents in the near future.[13]

Variations of this image of the relationship between religious and socio-political domains have continued to apply throughout the region.

The fundamentalist revivalism of the 1970s and 1980s make nonsense of assumption that either Muslims or Buddhist populations would distinguish, any more than Confucianists ever did, between spiritual and social spheres. Religious impulses intersect with political-economic purposes in postwar state construction throughout the Islamic and Theravāda regions. Political process has been consistently construed by most local peoples as a sphere of cultural and spiritual contention. This has often remained the case even when revolutionary actions and political ideologies have appeared to be secular on the surface. At the rice roots of village societies, even ostensibly secular ideologies such as Marxism have intersected with

---

[13] S. J. Tambiah, *World Conqueror and World Renouncer*, Cambridge, UK, 1976, 431.

millenarian spirituality. Nevertheless, it is apparent that economic concerns and secular politics have appeared to be increasingly separable from spiritual concerns during the past decades.

THE GENERATION OF NATIONAL CULTURES AS RELIGIOUS CONTENTION

Religious and ethnic identities within each state have been multiple, and competing claims to national identity have thus produced prominent fracture lines within all postwar societies. The relationships which were consolidated implicitly in the territories mapped by colonialism have carried into national structures. States like Aceh and ethnic groups such as the Karen and Meo were drawn, more through colonialism than by any earlier states, into social units dominated by Burmese, Thai, Vietnamese, Javanese, Malay and Tagalog speakers. These majorities are for the most part the occupants of core areas, the centres from early times of intensive rice cultivation, dense population and state formation, and those areas now house the dominant populations of most of the new states. At the same time the social boundaries between local peoples and migrant Indian, Arab and Chinese groups hardened from the turn of the century onward. The fragility of unity and fragmentation of identities have been self-evident. Throughout the region postwar constructions of national culture have self-consciously aimed to produce a dominant mould which would override these profound differences.

   Most of the dominant political philosophies of the postwar period can be characterized as 'neo-traditional', and insofar as they are they infuse religious meanings within modern politics. Confucianism resonated in Diem's South Vietnam; U Nu's socialism was also Buddhist; and Sukarno's Nasakom suggested how Javanist impulses could guide the formation of national ideologies. This is to speak of a positive rather than strictly negative process—when these modern actors appeal to Buddhism or the *wayang*, they are actively constructing, rather than cynically manipulating older popular symbols. Even Vietnamese communists have prioritized communal values, usually in a manner consonant with Confucian-tinged spirituality which some Western Marxists have found hard either to grasp or to correlate with their politics. Suharto built his striking family grave next to the grave complex of the Mangkunegaraan court, to which his wife is distantly related, and modelled it on the temples of Indic Majapahit. By doing so he clearly aimed to memorialize his role as the man who has guided the nation into modernity, but his manner of doing so emulates the way Indic kings commemorated their accomplishments. New national rituals, including ostensibly Western elections, build on senses of ceremony embedded within local society; religious holidays are designated state holidays, and new memorial rites commemorate revolutionary heroes as founding ancestors. These patterns reflect choices guided by deeply worn tracks, even if what was once a dirt path may now have become concrete.

   Though the power of kings is circumscribed, royalty is a continuing centrepoint of ceremonial life in significant parts of Southeast Asia, and wherever it remains it carries religious significance. Kingship remains a central institution in Thailand and Brunei; it continued in Laos through the 1950s; and it existed in modified form in Cambodia until 1975. When Sultan Hamengku Buwono IX, of Yogyakarta in Java, died in 1988, the commemoration of his passing drew extraordinary crowds and was widely noted. Ironically he had maintained the magical power of royalty precisely by the strength of his support for the revolution and his role as vice-president of the republic in the 1970s. In Cambodia Sihanouk evoked similar sentiments, and for similar reasons, throughout the 1950s and 1960s. By adjusting to constitutional monarchy, he preserved the sacral power of royal tradition, accepting homage as had been the due of earlier kings. Considered more widely, as complexes of belief relating to courts and in terms of their residual roles within society at large, traditional courts retain significance in Yogyakarta, Surakarta and in the Malay sultanates, where they still retain religious influence, as well as in Thailand and Brunei, where they are obviously vigorous.

Modernization was spearheaded by royalty in the Thai case and the nexus bonding the court to the *sangha*, to village and to distant regions has been gaining strength consistently. The 1932 constitutional revolution turned what was Siam into today's Thailand and repositioned, but did not eliminate, the kingship. Kings have thus retained a powerful ritual and ceremonial place within Thai society. In the postwar period Buddhism has been even more firmly enshrined, theoretically at least, than ever. Along with the monarchy it is a key ideological basis of the nation. Field Marshal Sarit Thanarat, whose views dominated the 1950s and early 1960s, reinstated some of the lapsed ceremonial functions of kingship and looked to Buddhism as a bulwark against what he perceived as the threat of communism. On the other hand the modern forms of Buddhism which have been promoted by the state have also reflected twentieth-century adaptations. The most prominent modernist forms, within all of the religions in the region, bring a shift of emphasis toward social action. In any event in Thailand traditional institutions have been reformed and enhanced, now underpinned as they are by modern media, as a basis for the cultural integration of the state.

In Burma virtually all residues of the monarchy were eliminated by British colonialism. Nevertheless the independent state resurrected traditions rooted in local religious notions of kingship. U Nu, who was premier for most of the period from 1948 to 1962, adhered to a version of socialism which departed from that of his more secular Thakin colleagues of the 1930s. Observers uniformly note the genuine qualities of a personal spiritual commitment which he underpinned with a simple lifestyle. U Nu's Buddhism was inseparable from the cult of the *nats*. He justified propitiation ceremonies through references to the scriptures; his Pyidaungsu Party gave annual offerings to the spirits and he spent lengthy periods at sites sacred to them, even when deciding economic matters. In 1961 he initiated the construction of 60,000 sand pagodas with iron spires and, as opposition to the declaration of Buddhism as the state religion grew, he spent forty-five days in spiritual retreat on the sacred Mount Popo.[14] Elements of the *sangha* accused him of prioritizing the cults at the expense of Buddhism, but there is no doubt that he sincerely believed the spiritual health of the population would be enhanced by proclamation of a Buddhist state.

National regeneration and the enhancement of Buddhism were seen as coterminous within a vision of the socialist state framed by Buddhist values. The revival which U Nu led emphasized the Buddhist nature of Burma and the importance of its world role as 'the strongest home' of its contemporary practice. The Ministry of Religion was established in 1950, and from 1952 onwards the government employed monks to facilitate the incorporation of hill tribes into the nation. It sponsored Mahasi Sayadaw's insight (*vipassana*) meditation centre in Rangoon, a showpiece of modern Buddhist practice to which foreign visitors of the time were regularly introduced. The Sangayana, the Sixth Great Buddhist Council of 1954–6, was the centrepiece of revivalism, and associated activities coloured the whole decade. It marked the 2500th anniversary of the Buddha, and to some extent became the world event it was intended, as representatives from thirty countries met. Building of the Kaba Aye Peace Pagoda began in 1950, on a site selected on the basis of a visionary experience, and the council took place in the Great Sacred Cave, constructed next to the Peace Pagoda to house 10,000 representatives. At the same time the rebuilding of old derelict pagodas became an object of government policies.

When U Nu campaigned for re-election in 1959, he announced preference for establishment of Buddhism as the state religion, but the ensuing controversies divided even Buddhists. Recurrent disciplinary and factional problems, a residue of the fragmentation resulting from the colonial removal of royal patronage, plagued the *sangha*, the monastic order, throughout the 1950s. In 1951 a fight followed a refusal to allow *pongyis*, Burmese monks, free admission to a theatre; in 1954 two *pongyis* died in a clash over control of a temple school (*kyaung*); in 1956 factionalism led to rioting of monks in Mandalay; and in 1959 the police resorted to tear gas, arresting eighty-nine monks after student rioting in Rangoon. When legislation was pending to amend the constitution, monks objected to the protection it offered to minority religions. It appeared to allow them increased scope for growth by promising minority religions a share of state religious funds. In November 1961 monks went so far as to burn down mosques on the outskirts of Rangoon.[15] When the constitutional change went through in 1961, the minorities seethed because the bill did not bring the unexpected counterbalance of federalism. On the other hand, because the final version of U Nu's legislation proclaiming Burma as a Buddhist state was a mild statement, the Buddhist *sangha* remained divided over endorsing it.

State-sponsored revival of Buddhism lost momentum with Ne Win's coup of 1962. The philosophy of the military has been relatively secular, though even it has theoretically prioritized material development only 'in balance with spiritual life'. The Revolutionary Council announced its guiding philosophy through the Burma Socialist Programme Party

[14] M. Mendelson, *Sangha and State in Burma* (ed. J. P. Ferguson), Ithaca, 1975, 273–4, 350.
[15] D. Smith, *Religion and Politics in Burma*, Princeton, 1965, 206–7, and Mendelson, 353.

in January 1963. Elements of both Marxism and Buddhism found a place in that philosophy, but key traditional notions relating to the *nats* (guardian spirits), Buddhist philosophy of *samsara* (the 'wheel of rebirth') and *kamma* (karma) were omitted. Its thrust was humanistic, appealing to spiritual values and affirming that the state had responsibility for the improvement of the spiritual life of its citizens. Ne Win has not tolerated respect for *nats*. His government launched a concerted attack on spirit beliefs, even banning film productions centring on them. Following Ne Win's coup, the proclamation of a Buddhist Burma was rescinded to pacify minorities and the government made new and concerted efforts to exclude *pongyis* from politics. After 1962 the Union Buddha Sasana Council was abolished; in 1965 the Vinasaya Act of 1949, the Dhammacariya Acta of 1950 and the Pali Education Board Act of 1952 were all repealed, and thus the major elements of U Nu's legislation to strengthen the *sangha* were all eventually eliminated.

Among Vietnamese activists, articulate spokespeople like Thien Minh held that Buddhism represented a choice of values not present in either Western or communist countries. He commented that 'we are convinced that Buddhism can build up a nation because it represents a unified force and because it teaches the doctrine of tolerance and understanding.'[16] Represented by a relatively small *sangha*, Buddhists were strongest in central Vietnam. The postwar revival of Buddhism there began in 1951, when a national conference was attended by fifty monks and lay people in Hué. They joined the World Fellowship of Buddhists, which had been formed in Sri Lanka in 1950. Buddhists took issue with the Diem government because it so often appeared unwilling to recognize a role for them. Diem's policies appeared to be based on patronage models of government, common throughout the region, more than on Catholicism as such, and the Vatican was at pains to dissociate Catholicism from them.

Tensions mounted around the ceremony of Waisak, the celebration of the Buddha's birth, enlightenment and passing, in early May 1963; crowds in Hué were met with tanks and nine died, precipitating lengthy petitioning and a series of demonstrations in Saigon as well. The self-immolation of Thich Quang Duc on 11 June followed a lengthy period of unsuccessful petitioning to Diem on behalf of the Buddhists that year. In August 1964 Buddhist antagonism to the Saigon government led as far as rioting in Danang, where Buddhist-led mobs burned down the huts of Catholic refugees. Buddhist neutralists pressured the Saigon government continually. As General Ky assumed power in mid-1965 and the war situation worsened, lay Buddhists reduced their activism in order to concentrate on education and social welfare activities. They published magazines and periodicals, ran 135 primary and 35 secondary schools and a Buddhist university, and also recruited youth to show their strength.[17]

Throughout 1966 tense negotiations continued between Catholic, Hoa Hao, Cao Dai and Buddhist groups and the Ky government over the holding of elections and prospective representation in the constitutional

[16] J. Schecter, *The New Face of the Buddha*, New York, 1967, 160.
[17] ibid., 210.

assembly. Periodic violence between the military and Buddhist student groups in Danang and Hué failed to bring responses from the government. In May Thanh Quang, a 55-year-old nun, immolated herself before the Dieu De pagoda in Hué. Her action unquestionably indicated the spiritual depth of distress at United States support for Ky's government, making her death an appeal to the hearts of Americans and symbolizing commitment to the spirit of non-violence. But the power of Buddhist activism, strongest in 1963, dissipated gradually in 1966. The appeal to Buddhism as a basis for nationalism was undermined by Cao Dai dominance of Tay Ninh Province, Hoa Hao power in the western Mekong delta and the semi-autonomy of the Montagnard animists, Khmer border people, and Muslim Cham remnants.

In Indonesia the Western notion of division between secular and religious spheres has had only narrow purchase. The few genuinely secular nationalists have always had to address religious—especially Muslim—people, movements and interpretations. At the same time, though 90 per cent of the population profess to be Muslim, the nation is not characteristically Islamic in the way its cousins of that religion's heartlands are. Variants of animism and mysticism remain significant counterweights to the strength of Islam. Within Sukarno's PNI, Javanese spiritual philosophy underpinned political thought; even the communist PKI converged with millenarianism insofar as it extended into Javanese rural life. The place of Islam was a major issue in the lead-up to the proclamation of independence, resulting in an ambiguous compromise called the Jakarta Charter. Some Muslims thought this draft preamble to the constitution, stating that Muslims would be legally required to adhere to Islamic law, would be official. Secularists prevented acceptance of the compromise, arguing that it would have endangered the revolution, but until the 1970s recognition of the charter remained an active objective for Islamic politicians.[18]

Subsequent social tensions have often corresponded with cultural and religious cleavages. Divergence between Muslim orthodoxy and Javanism underlay the rhetoric of the 1950s and remained an explicit focus of tension into the 1970s, as the New Order effectively required membership in a recognized religion. Most Indonesians do believe in God and experience a spiritual dimension as real; one corollary is that they see the national identity as palpable, as a spirit rather than just an abstraction. Insofar as identities are seen as spiritual, the reflexive implication has also been that national reconstruction involves a spiritual struggle. For some this has meant movement toward collective realization of submission to the will of Allah; for others it means repetition of the endless tension between desires, linking us to the material plane, and impulses toward spiritual release. These views, the one Islamic, the other Indic, are suggestive of the major contenders which have been asserting the right to define the spiritual identity of the national entity in independent Indonesia.

Both the Ministry of Religion and the Islamic parties have had a clearly

---

[18] Important discussions of the Islamic perspective are presented in van Dijk, 45–58, and in B. J. Boland, *The Struggle of Islam in Modern Indonesia*, The Hague, 1982, 17–39.

Muslim interpretation of the national commitment to freedom of religion. As Van Nieuwenhuijze observed, at the time of independence many Muslims viewed religion as synonymous with Islam and interpreted religious freedom as meaning 'freedom for Islam', since 90 per cent of the population was supposed to be Muslim. Even purist Muslims now realize that this assumption was superficial, but the notion of Islamic domination remains strong. Muslims have gradually and reluctantly accepted that they remain a fractional element within a plural religious scene. Many Muslims continued to feel, as they had under the Dutch, that only political repression prevented them from setting the mould for a nation they ought to have dominated. Until the 1955 elections the leading Islamic parties assumed that all Muslims would vote for them. They were shocked to find that in the event only 42 per cent of the population voted for them, and this contributed to Islamic and outer island separatism in the late 1950s.

The elections of 1955 and 1957 remain markers of religious commitments in the country. Masjumi, representing modernist Islam, was strongest in the outer islands, in west Java and in urban areas. The traditionalist Muslim Nahdatul Ulama, the nationalists (PNI) and communists (PKI), all had their roots in the heartlands of Java. After the elections, both Muslims and Christians feared growing PKI strength, and resented Java-oriented economic policies. The Darul Islam movements had been continuing in Aceh, west Java, and south Sulawesi intermittently through the 1950s. The association of Masjumi with the PRRI rebellion in Sumatra and the Permesta revolt in north Sulawesi in 1958 was used to push modernist Islam to the political margins. The suppression of Darul Islam, the PRRI and Permesta revolts and nationalization of businesses, all in the late 1950s, drew the military into civilian administration, transforming it also into the primary new vehicle of national integration and reducing Islam's political relevance.

The concept of Guided Democracy elaborated by Sukarno framed politics from 1959 to 1965 and tacitly revived the ethos and style of *kraton* culture[20] Both purist senses of Islam and Western pluralistic notions of democracy were excluded in favour of syncretic thought and the politics of consensus. Magical senses of power underlay the effort to concentrate energy on glorification of the capital and on unifying struggles to liberate Dutch New Guinea and confront 'neo-colonialist' Malaysia. Sukarno recalled the traditional glories of Majapahit as a peak of the past and model for the present. His populist images of the primal peasant (*marhaen*) and of principles of cooperation (*gotong-royong*) and consensus (*musyawarah-mufakat*) were elevated as national ideology. Nasakom (the acronym for 'nationalism-religion-communism') was proclaimed as a synthetic and transcendent ideology, and Sukarno presented himself as the mouthpiece of the people, meaning that he conceived of his personal consciousness as being linked to the collective as its prime mechanism of representation. His charismatic invocations of the spirit of 1945 came with opposition, inflation

---

[19] C. A. O. van Nieuwenhuijze, *Aspects of Islam in Post-Colonial Indonesia*, The Hague-Bandung, 1958.

[20] B. R. O'G. Anderson, 'The Idea of Power in Javanese Culture' in Claire Holt et al., eds, *Culture and Politics in Indonesia*, Ithaca, 1972, and C. Geertz, *Islam Observed*, Chicago, 1972.

and unresolved ills, so that in retrospect even usually sympathetic Javanists felt that it fell short in practice.

Social tensions led toward the coup and counter-coup of 1965. The land-reform laws of 1959 were never implemented, leading communist cadres to stimulate unilateral seizures which provoked a powerful Muslim counter-offensive. The Aidit PKI implicitly remained a vehicle for *abangan* expression, finding numerical strength mainly as a counter to rural Islam. Suharto consolidated control when he manoeuvred Sukarno into providing an authorization to re-establish order on 11 March 1966, through a letter known by the acronym 'SuperSemar'. If Sukarno aimed to transcend ideology through synthesis, Suharto has aimed to purge politics of ideology; if the 'theatre state' resurrected Indic courts, the New Order can be represented as a surfacing of village temperament. Suharto is a committed Muslim, but in Javanist terms—a foster father; and several of his early advisers participated in a prominent cult of the guardian spirits. The group emphasizes pilgrimage to the power points of Dieng and Srandil, both linked to Semar as the guardian (*danhyang*) of Java, as a route to power. Ironically this Javanist ethos is obscured by cultural defensiveness: it is less articulate than either Indic-style syncretism or traditional religions, and the official status of mysticism remains insecure.

Thus the underlying spiritual ethos of the governments led by both Sukarno and Suharto have been inspired by a Javanism within which Islamic sensibility is framed by syncretism. There has been self-conscious emphasis on a corporatist 'family principle' which rationalizes a consensual basis for the politics of the state. That philosophy was clearly articulated in the nationalist educational philosophy of Dewantoro in the 1920s, and it remains relevant. Dewantoro's prewar Taman Siswa movement fed into the national educational system, but has much more significance at present through its relation to national political philosophies. In it a holistic emphasis on collective corporate identity and consensual politics was tied to commitment to develop the whole person in balance by engaging the mind, feeling and will through awareness of all of the senses. Taman Siswa philosophy was connected to mystical theories through Suryomataram, one of the most famous prewar mystics of Yogyakarta, and resonated with the teachings of the Theosophical Society and Maria Montessori.[21]

This philosophy converged with what was to become the dominant philosophy of the nation as expressed in the 1945 constitution, the Pancasila (the five principles articulated by Sukarno which underlie the state philosophy), Guided Democracy in the late 1950s and, not least, the Golkar organization under Suharto. It is pointedly stressed in the exclusive emphasis on the Pancasila demanded by New Order in the 1980s. In 1981 Suharto conflated criticism of himself with that of the Pancasila and in 1983 the MPR (parliament) formalized the separation of religion and politics, undermining Islamic parties implicitly in the process, by legislating the requirement that all political organizations had to adopt the Pancasila as their basis. This was extended to all social organizations and is tied to consistent and self-conscious argument that democracy had to be tuned to

[21] D. Reeve, *Golkar of Indonesia*, Singapore, 1985, 355–6.

the 'Indonesian soul'. Islamic parties commanded about 30 per cent of the vote, despite adverse circumstances in elections in the 1970s, making Islam the clearest oppositional force to the New Order. But recent assessments of Islam in Indonesian politics point out that Muslims have become a majority with a 'minority mentality' and that the faith is 'an outsider'.[22]

STATE REGULATION AND INSTITUTIONAL RELIGION

The consolidation of new states has led to increasing centralized control over institutional religious life; the same powers which limit smuggling or collect revenue have been exercised in regularizing religious hierarchies which are increasingly articulated at national level. This trend is a corollary of the general process of reorganizing social life and it is also due to special interest in mobilizing religious institutions for political, cultural and economic purposes. At the same time it is linked to the view, which governments share even when they are ostensibly secular, that the ambit of state authority includes the spiritual welfare of its population. As many prominent neo-traditionalist political philosophies carry religious senses of purpose, intervention by governments in the religious sphere has usually been sanctioned by postwar states.

Within the Theravāda states the spread of modern education, as a reorganization of *saṅgha*-based education or as a vehicle of new national values, contributes to the reshaping of even popular perceptions of Buddhism. There has been notable progress in this area, with massive rises in adult literacy being achieved during the 1950s. Despite the fact that governments have emphasized secular education, religious schooling continues to be strong. At the same time the lines between traditional religious and modern secular education have also blurred in the postwar period. Religious schools give increasing attention to secular subjects, government sponsorship has extended to religious education, and religious education has even expanded within secular systems.

Burma's first constitution, of 1947, recognized only a 'special place' for Buddhism; this was in deference to the Karen, Kachin and Chin minorities and with a view to induce them to join the union. Naturally neither Christian Karens nor animists elsewhere were attracted to the prospect of Buddhism as a state religion. Once U Nu was in office in 1948, he concentrated on promoting the Buddhist revival as part of his vision of the national revolution, notwithstanding that Burma was not declared as a Buddhist state. The Vinicchaya–Htana Act of 1949, for example, aimed to remove religious disputes from the jurisdiction of civil courts by establishing ecclesiastical courts at the town level throughout the country. It was modified in 1954 to take account of the strength of divergent sects within Burmese Buddhism, as sectarian fissures are prominent and abbots have

---

[22] W. F. Wertheim, 'Moslems in Indonesia: Majority with a Minority Mentality', Townsville: James Cook University, Southeast Asian Studies Committee, 1980, and R. McVey, 'Faith as the Outsider: Islam in Indonesian Politics', in J. Piscatori, ed., *Islam in the Political Process*, Cambridge, UK, 1983.

had more power within their temples (*kyaungs*) than their colleagues elsewhere.

The Ministry of Religious Affairs was established in 1950, partly to restore cohesion to what had become a fragmented religious structure. Meanwhile the Ministry of Education engaged actively in regulating and supporting monastic examinations and standards within the larger monastic universities. From 1947 onwards there was discussion of establishing a Pāli university. On the one hand these moves were designed to counterbalance the long period of absence of royal sponsorship, on the other they served to strengthen government intervention in the affairs of the *sangha*. This combined with periodic debates through the 1950s over registration of monks and the holding of monastic parliaments. These interventions provoked some Buddhists, such as the Anti-Hlutdaw Association, to demand the abolition of the Ministry of Religious Affairs in 1959. Registration was a touchy issue partly because revolutionaries in many instances worked through the *sangha*, gaining a mobility through that they would not otherwise have had.[23]

One notable intervention in Buddhist developments, the Institute for the Advanced Study of Buddhism, was founded through collaboration with the American Ford Foundation in 1954. It implied a mixture of secular and religious objects which sat uncomfortably within Burmese traditions, which did not separate those spheres. Emphasis on English-language learning and both the domestic and international missionary expansion of Buddhism went hand in hand with what became a Burmanization of the curriculum and personnel.[24] This new style of government- and foreign-sponsored training was tied to social service. Promotion of Buddhism was directly linked at once to consolidating the state internally and to projecting its image in the international environment. In Burma by 1962 there were eighty-four temple schools which had enough highly trained monks to register as colleges. The Ne Win government has given no encouragement to *kyaung* schools. They nevertheless remain a vital component of Burmese education, even if the 70 per cent who attended religious schools in 1952 must have declined signficantly since.[25]

In Thailand in 1967 half the primary schools were still *wat* schools where teaching was done by monks. Monastic examination regulations which came into effect in 1910 remain in force and there were 6634 Nak Dhamma schools and 615 Pāli schools. The two *wat* institutes in Bangkok, Mahamakuta Rajavidyalaya and Mahachulalongkorn Rajavidyalaya, became the basis of modern universities in 1945 and 1947, from that point offering a wide range of modern studies along with Buddhist Pāli studies.[26] All of these schools served not only to link the modern state to religious institutions, but also to introduce religious specialists to secular modes of learning. According to figures from 1968 there were about 25,000 *wat* and 185,000 monks, perhaps one-third of them 'temporary', in a Thai population of around 34 million. The hierarchy of monastic institutions, leading

[23] Mendelson, 240–62, 341–5.
[24] ibid., 299–306.
[25] F. von der Mehden, *Religion and Modernization in Southeast Asia*, Syracuse, 1986, 136.
[26] R. Lester, *Theravada Buddhism in Southeast Asia*, Ann Arbor, 1973, 97.

up toward the élite 'university *wat*' of the capital, matched the socio-political hierarchy of cities. In this context, as often in earlier times, the *sangha* offered a prime channel for upward mobility and high status, especially for the relatively poorer villagers of the northeast.[27]

The Thai government has been in the strongest position to patronize Buddhism and it has not held back from fostering and attempting to manipulate the very strong local *sangha*. The government attitude was reflected in a 1963 pamphlet which indicated that 'the complexities of living in the modern world ... necessitate a close cooperation and mutual understanding between the State and the Sangha working harmoniously together for the economic and spiritual well-being of the people'.[28] The 1963 Sangha Act, initiated under Sarit, constituted a powerful intervention in the life of the *sangha*. The previous Acts, of 1902 and 1941, had ironically contained significant democratic features. The 1963 Act centralized power in the name of defusing sectarian rivalry between the cohesive, and hence relatively better represented, modernist Dhammayut and more diffuse Mahanikai sects within the *sangha*. This restructuring reflected Sarit's recognition that Buddhism and the monarchy remained critical to the achievement of modernizing objectives. Each adjustment in state policy with regard to the *sangha* has matched modernizing reforms, relating first to the reforms of the nineteenth century, then to the 1932 revolution, and finally to Sarit's coup of 1957.[29] Continuous strengthening of the bonds between religion and the state, as hierarchical ties have tightened through the Ministry of Religion, has decreased the prestige and autonomy of local *wat*.

It is recognized in all village studies of the Theravāda countries that throughout the period since the war monks continued to play a key role as counsellors and advisers, as well as officiating at religious ceremonies. Now their traditional centrality in this respect has been counterbalanced by community development training. In Cambodia Sihanouk held that 'our 70,000 monks are the "officers" conducting our people to work, just as the officers conduct the troops into combat'.[30] In the late 1960s Maha-chulalongkorn University in Bangkok sponsored community development training for monks in centres dispersed through the country. Monks who attended were expected to return to their villages and apply the skills and perspectives gained in whatever way they could, and there is little doubt that many, as in the purely secular cadre training programmes in Vietnam, absorbed and applied the lessons learned.

In Laos roughly 25 per cent of schools were religious and in 1962 there were ninety-five Pāli schools. There were only a few vernacular high schools up to the time of Pathet Lao victory in 1975. The French did not cut the tie between royalty and the *sangha* in Laos or Cambodia, and it remained relatively tight until the socialist revolutions of the mid-1970s. In Cambodia, as in Laos and Thailand, the state and *sangha* were also much

[27] S. J. Tambiah, 'Sangha and Polity in Modern Thailand', in Bardwell Smith, ed., *Religion and the Legitimation of Power in Thailand, Laos, and Burma*, Chambersburg, 1978, 123–4.
[28] Quoted in Lester, 104.
[29] Tambiah, *World Conqueror*, 252–5.
[30] Lester, 126.

closer than in Burma. There Buddhist schools included 600 primary, two secondary and one tertiary, the Preah Sihanouk Raj Buddhist University of Phnom Penh.[31] Traditionally schooling reached young males in most villages through the *wat*, but by 1967 all but 10 per cent of schools were in the government system and enrolments were increasing rapidly.[32]

The French and Americans looked to the *sangha* as a potential counterweight to communism in Laos throughout the 1950s and 1960s, and its strength was undermined as a result. The *sangha* was particularly deeply divided between Mahanikai and Dhammayut sects, a tension lending itself to factionalism, and at the same time strongly committed to a vision of itself as the prime vehicle of Lao culture, a mission easily construed as counter to American secularism. By the early 1970s, especially as the Pathet Lao gained strength through growing anti-Americanism, the politicization of the *sangha*, ironically facilitated by its own initiatives to broaden its base through encouraging lay missionizing and meditation, had undermined its role within Lao society. With its victory in 1975, the Pathet Lao made every effort to use monks in order to extend its message to the population. It announced policies of religious freedom; there was already a strong basis for collaboration, as notions of Buddhist socialism were well established. At the same time the new government set out to re-educate monks, restrict their privileges and bypass their central social and symbolic role. By 1979 the number of monks was said to have dropped from 20,000 to 1700, and the subordination of the *sangha* to politics appeared to be complete.[33]

A subordinate position in political terms has limited Muslim influence over national institutions in Indonesia, but in the cultural and religious arenas the balance of power differs. In that domain other parties respond increasingly to Islam in the sense that discourses about religious issues are framed increasingly in Islamic idiom. The state endorses an Islamic sense of God and requires citizens to identify with a religion Muslims can acknowledge as such; it sees itself as having an active responsibility in the religious sphere in terms no secular Western state does. In each of these spheres Islamic discourses define the context of Indonesian spiritual life, influencing other strands of religion implicitly and pervasively. Even Suharto was always guarded in reference to his early Javanist preferences, and Muslims still associate related practices with the residue of pre-Islamic traditions. International *tarekats* have remained active but at the national level their significance declined until the 1980s, when a revival became noticeable. Mysticism is often seen now as irrational, a projection or fantasy contrary to the realities of development and modernity, and related practices have been consistently on the defensive, certainly vis-à-vis government agencies.

Though it failed to claim the Indonesian nation fully for Islam, the strength of Masjumi as an umbrella Muslim party was sufficient to ensure rapid establishment of a Ministry of Religion. This was dominated by the

[31] ibid., 96–7.
[32] C. Keyes, *The Golden Peninsula*, London, 1977, 293.
[33] M. Stuart-Fox and R. Bucknell, 'Politicization of the Buddhist Sangha in Laos', JSEAS, 13, 1 (1982) 78.

Nahdatul Ulama until 1971, at which point the New Order effectively displaced that party as the dominating force behind the ministry. Though it is responsible for all religious communities, funds within it are allocated according to census statistics and Islam has thus dominated it heavily. The ministry administered government subsidies to more than 13,000 primary, 776 secondary and 16 higher *madrasas* in 1954 and to a total of 22,000 *madrasas* and *pesantren* by 1965, and these figures kept increasing in the 1970s.[34] The separate Islamic educational network has come increasingly into its own, especially since the 1970s through the tertiary level IAIN (State Islamic Institutes), when substantial oil money went toward it, and this network established the basis for a new wave of nationwide Islamization. The ministry became the main stronghold of Muslim influence within the bureaucracy and a counter to Javanist domination of the Ministries of Information and of Education and Culture.

Given the importance of law within Islam, the establishment of the Ministry of Religion had immense practical implications for local religious life. Islamic courts came under its jurisdiction rather than that of the Justice Department. In issues of family law, notably divorce and inheritance, a legal basis for religious authority was established. From the mid-1950s to 1974 there was intermittent and severe controversy over marriage legislation, especially concerning polygamy and non-Muslim marriages. Muslim reaction to the government's proposed civil legislation of 1974 provoked such extreme reaction that the bill was withdrawn. For Muslims frustration has often focused on the codification of customary (*adat*) law undertaken by the Dutch. The ministry channelled funds and created institutions in a way that strengthened Islamic organizations. At the same time it also implicitly limited the potential for Muslim activists to challenge the basis of the state, as its very establishment implied Muslim endorsement of the state. NU control of the ministry, which was firm by 1954, led it to endorse the state which underpinned it. Other Muslims protested because they wanted to challenge the basis of the state more fundamentally.[35]

Dominance of Islam within the Ministry of Religion is reflected in its definitions of religion and in its role in promoting Islamic senses of what can be religious. When the ministry was established in 1946, it was acknowledged that Protestants and Catholics deserved places, as even in the strictest Islamic terms Christianity is legitimate, a religion of the Book. Other religions were initially lumped under the rubric of 'ethnic'; those of Asian origin had to struggle for recognition, their status remaining problematic in some respects to the present. Each had to reorganize to match essentially Semitic senses of what constitutes religion—they are legitimate now to the degree that they emphasize belief in one God, a clear system of law, a holy scripture, and a prophet. To date, the official list of acceptable religions is largely that promulgated in Sukarno's presidential decree of 1965: Islam, Protestantism, Catholicism, Hinduism, Buddhism and Confucianism. The only exception is Confucianism, which has been relegated to the status of Judaism, being viewed essentially as an ethnic faith rather than an international religion.

---

[34] Boland, 117.
[35] D. Lev, *Islamic Courts in Indonesia*, Berkeley, 1972, 50.

This restricted sense of the term does not allow animism, folk spirit cults, new religions or independent mystical practices as 'religion'. Even the Balinese had to struggle actively before gaining official recognition in the 1950s. Hindu, Buddhist, and Confucian communities were forced to conform to monotheistic conceptions of divinity. The recasting of Buddhist idiom gave an advantage to Mahāyāna groups, as Theravāda Buddhists faced particular difficulty before they agreed finally that the Adi Buddha, roughly referring to the innate Buddha nature in everything, could be identified as 'God'. In the process of gaining recognition, scriptural factions within each community gained strength at the expense of traditional syncretists. Whether in scholarly debate, public discussion or government legislation, the accepted Indonesian definition of religion now accords with the Islamic model of what can constitute one.

Perhaps more critically, Islam conditions government views of its responsibility in the religious arena. The Indonesian government sees itself as having the responsibility to ensure that its citizens follow an acceptable religious faith as an obligation of citizenship. In the Five-Year Plan for 1969–74 (in Chapter IX on 'Religion') it is stated that 'the Government of the Republic of Indonesia has the responsibility of giving guidance and assistance to facilitate the development of each religion according to its own teachings, and to maintain supervision such that each citizen maintains their religious practice according to their beliefs'. This sense of responsibility distinguishes Indonesian views of religious freedom from those held by Western liberal régimes. In secular Western states professions of belief in God play a passive role, mainly meriting rhetorical invocation. Indonesia may not be an Islamic state, but it nevertheless takes from Islam its sense that authorities should intervene to guide the spiritual lives of citizens. Under the New Order the first principle of the Pancasila, that the nation is founded on belief in the one God, is read as a programme for action, and all citizens have generally been required to list an accepted religious affiliation on their identity cards. This view of religious freedom, obviously in marked contrast to that which pertains in the West, is essentially consistent with the Muslim view of the responsibility of the state vis-á-vis religion.

Government regulation of mystical movements extends colonial policies. Traditional courts were transformed through colonialism into an element within the new state, but policies aimed mainly to contain Islam. This alliance, with what were coincidentally the syncretic, mystical and Indic segments of the population, continued an opposition between Islamic and court powers of the pre-colonial era. That opposition is consistent again with the tension between Islam and the New Order. However, the Dutch were also sensitive to the dangers of millenarian and mystical movements, and surveillance has been continued since independence through Pakem, an agency of the Department of Justice since 1954. Offices in major cities supervise meetings and keep records. Even routine sessions of a spiritual nature in individuals' homes and the practices of traditional healers (*dukun*) require licence and registration. The Ministry of Religion also researched folk practices, indicating until 1978 that mysticism lay within its authority. It aimed to guide adherents toward orthodoxy by clarifying that mysticism originated from Islam.

In the New Order lobbying centred on winning legitimacy independent of religion. In opting for designation as *kepercayaan* in 1970, the movements staked a claim to legitimacy within the provisions of the 1945 constitution. That had been readopted by Sukarno in 1959 and remains sacred, together with the Pancasila as the essence of national political philosophy, under Suharto. During the hasty sessions in which the provisional 1945 constitution was drafted discussion of paragraph 29 of part XI (religion) was extended. The paragraph reads: 'The nation is based on faith in God [*Ketuhanan Yang Maha Esa*]; The nation guarantees each citizen the freedom to choose their own religion and to pray according to his own religion or faith (*kepercayaan*).' For independent-minded mystics the key was inclusion of the term 'faith' (*kepercayaan*); they read it as legitimizing practices outside religion so long as those were also directed toward the one God. Golkar, the government functional grouping, indirectly sponsored a congress in Yogyakarta in late 1970 in which mystics argued that they had been wrongly deprived of their rights, that their status was in principle already supposed to be equal to that of the religions. In 1973 the independent movements were recognized as legitimate options within the terms of the 1945 constitution, making it legal for citizens to list a mystical movement instead of a religion on their identity cards. In practice local authorities viewed it as subversive to broadcast this legislation, and when the census took place in 1980 no record of mystical affiliation was registered.

Then the marriage law of 1974 resulted in broader guidelines, easing the requirement for Javanese to adhere to Islamic ritual. Though the government attempt to establish civil marriage was withdrawn, some mystical groups conducted their own marriage ceremonies after 1974. In early 1978, responsibility for supervising the independent mystical sects, until recently usually called *kebatinan* (literally 'the science of the inner') was shifted from the Ministry of Religion to that of Education and Culture, weakening the legal claim of Islam to jurisdiction over them. Legislative changes had limited effects, and in many areas it has been considered provocative to publicize the new laws. The laws have provoked Islamic polemics and confusion in practice. Subud, the Javanese movement which is best known internationally, withdrew from the umbrella organization in early 1978 after its east Javanese SKK officers appeared to pressure adherents to identify themselves only as such, rather than by religious affiliation.

The establishment of a Directorate in the Ministry of Education and Culture theoretically ended subordination of *kebatinan* to religion. It began an inventory of movements, published significant documentation and initiated contact with non-Javanese movements. Recently changes within the Directorate coincide with what appears to have been a shift in government thinking about the relationship between *kebatinan* and religion. During the 1970s activists argued that identification with *kebatinan* was sufficient to fulfil requirement that citizens pursue belief in God. Recently interpretation has become more narrow, and affiliation with mystical movements is separated from the question of religious membership, which is still essential. The pendulum has swung back toward the position of the late 1960s. Most Javanists continue to hold that their mystical practice is interior and separate from religious identification. Pressure for members of movements also to maintain religious identification is again increasing.

Elsewhere in the Islamic zone, as in Sulu and Mindanao, changes have been coloured by social dislocation. In the largely Catholic Philippines, the Church has been basically conservative and closely tied to élite-dominated governments. Notwithstanding currents of liberation theology from Latin America and the critical stance of some Church leaders, such as Cardinal Sin in respect of President Marcos, the general tenor of the church has been conservative. This stance is rooted both in the social origins of its leadership and its staunch anti-communism since the Huk movement of the 1950s. From the vantage point of the Manila government, its policies in the south were strategies for development and national integration, associated with the migration of northern Christian settlers and businesses into what seemed a relatively underdeveloped south; for Muslim locals these programmes represented imposition of intense colonialism in the guise of nationalism.

It is impossible to separate changing religious practices, in this context of intermittent bloodletting, from the socio-economic and political strains of relations between poor Muslim southerners and relatively rich northern patronage powers. Marcos' policies provoked the founding of the Philippine Muslim Nationalist League in 1967. That became the Moro National Liberation Front (MNLF), with a military arm which grew rapidly through the 1970s. Misuari, the most public and astute leader of the movement, eventually sought support from Libya and blended Islamic nationalism with Marxist populism. Religious connections also became a bridge, along with ethnicity, complicating relationships between Manila and Kuala Lumpur. The Tausug, living in both Sulu and Sabah, established a working relationship across the border. Between 1973 and 1978 important steps were taken to regularize trade between Sulu and Sabah and to adjust the national legal system to account for local Muslim law. These steps took some of the fire from separatism, but it remained a running sore, among the many inheritances of the Marcos era which also plagued the Aquino government.[36]

In the Malaysian context, Islamization has been intensified through its role as a vehicle of Malay cohesion. Governments have contributed by proclaiming Muslim holidays, by upholding Islamic values in education and economics, and by encouraging internal conversion (*dakwah*) movements. The relationship between Islamic and national law in Malaysia remains complex, partly due to variations between states. In the sultanates colonial policies allowed distinct religious rights to remain with sultans, and in the modern states local authorities still retain significant powers in this area. Tun Mustapha made especially notable appeals to Islam when he was chief minister in Sabah, working against Christian influences and promoting conversion to Islam.

[36] T. J. S. George, *Revolt in Mindanao*, Kuala Lumpur, 1980, 195–207, 234–5, 266-7.

Since 1960 the government had administered collection of the *zakat*, the religious tithe. States administer the collection of 10 per cent of the paddy and at the same time villages levy their own *zakat*. In urban areas people pay an extra tax instead. In 1968 roughly $US3.5 million was collected: funds have gone to religious buildings and education, in direct subsidies to the poor, even to some business-oriented programmes.[37] Elsewhere national governments have no direct involvement in collecting religious taxes. In Indonesia it is only through private organizations, such as the Muhammadiyah, that *zakat* is collected and disbursed at a local level.

Throughout postwar Southeast Asia, the *haj* has been facilitated by increased air travel and, in Indonesia and Malaysia, it has been encouraged by centralized government co-ordination of arrangements. By the 1980s over 70,000 Indonesian pilgrims went to Mecca annually; Malaysian pilgrims increased from about 5000 to 15,000 between 1965 and 1980 and in the same year over 7500 pilgrims went from elsewhere in Southeast Asia.[38]

Christian missions and churches have remained active through most of Southeast Asia, representing an avenue of continuity for Western influence through education and health work. In areas like Timor, Irian Jaya or among the Karen, as noted already, Christian institutions have constituted independent networks which may threaten, or at least appear to undermine, state control. In this respect churches may parallel the function of Muslim networks in Mindanao and Sulu. In Indonesia and Malaysia, governments have been pressed to respond to Muslim sensitivity by actively restricting Christian missions, especially in areas like Aceh, where there have been popular protests against even locally initiated Christian church construction. In the late 1970s the Indonesian government pressed overseas missions to replace foreign missionaries with local people.

Even in the secular and materialistic city state of Singapore, the government has actively concerned itself with both promoting and regulating religious life. By the late 1970s Confucianism was promoted as an ethos convergent with government interest in social stability; in the 1980s this encouragement was underlined as a way of promoting extended family support for the elderly—to reduce welfare demands on the state. By the end of the 1980s the government was concerned with the rise of fundamentalisms and contingent discord. A white paper on the 'Maintenance of Religious Harmony' was tabled in parliament in December 1989 and noted incidents of social conflict in the late 1980s involving aggressive Protestant and Muslim fundamentalists. Muslims reacted indignantly when Protestants used the term 'Allah' for 'God', a translation which had already been banned by the Malaysian government. Dravidian and Aryan Hindus complained of each other and they also complained that the Christians were too aggressive. At the same time Sikhs and Hindus brought the tensions of South Asia into Singapore.

Resonances of religious difference continue to underlie or interlink with politics, and tensions have been most explicitly religious within the nations of the archipelago. The Muslim south and Catholic north have been at odds throughout the history of the modern Philippines. Religion

[37] von der Mehden, 58.
[38] ibid., 62.

converges with race in Malaysia—the requirement that Malays practise Islam implicitly reflects tension between Chinese and Malay groups. Indonesian politics have certainly been shaped significantly by the underlying division between syncretic traditional and modern orthodox Islam. In the 1950s the communists drew support mainly from syncretic Javanese, and opposition was strongest among the Muslim youth who helped the army eliminate it in the 1960s. Though less prominent, similar tensions have been clear through the mainland states as well. Religious issues wove into the politics of the thirty-year-long Vietnamese revolution. Catholics from the north sometimes worked together with syncretic southern cults during the 1950s and 1960s in opposition to the socialist revolution. In Burma, Buddhist Burmese speakers from the lowlands have been resisted by Christian Karens even since independence. In Thailand the Malay-speaking Muslim minority of the south has not easily endorsed or been integrated into a state which makes so much of the conjunction of Thai ethnicity, Indic-style royalty and Theravāda Buddhism.

REFORMULATIONS IN POPULAR PRACTICE

On the whole, colonial rule did not integrate tribal minorities into states any more than earlier indigenous lowland states had. On the peripheries or margins of centralizing colonial states, modern forces took effect mainly through channels such as missionizing. From the late nineteenth century Protestant missionaries brought communities like the Karen in Burma and the Batak and Sumatra into contact with both Christianity and, not incidentally, modern education. In the postwar era the independent states, dominated by speakers of Burmese, Thai, Vietnamese, Tagalog and Javanese, have spearheaded vigorous new policies of cultural integration. These threaten, ironically often more than earlier Western systems did, to lead to the disappearance of the hundreds of tribal or ethnic minority groups which have inhabited the less-trafficked zones of the region. The residual autonomy of tribal communities in remote parts of the Shan plateau and Mindanao, the Mentawi islands, and interior Borneo or New Guinea have all been brought into direct and increasingly routine contact with new institutions of government, foreign capitalized businesses, national education, and modern health care.

Thus we may observe that if colonialism defined our current maps of the region, the independent states have been left to effect the policies which aim culturally to integrate the peoples living within those boundaries. Similarly in rice-growing village society, still the foundation for the dominant populations of the region, there has been a penetration of state control in the postwar era far surpassing colonial interventions. Through most of the region, village heads and councils had functioned to represent local communities; by their mediation they muted the intervention of outside forces in the village sphere. Now village heads are increasingly the bottom rung of bureaucracies; their responsiveness to local demands has weakened, along with the claims of residents to land and the related strength of contacts with local spirit realms.

Notwithstanding these interventions, traditional and explicitly religious activities remain rich and varied. Many tribal and village cultures remain vigorous, and their commitment to rituals still goes with respect for the spirits of sacred sites. Spiritually linked healing practices remain widespread, as are possession cults and magical undercurrents. Ordinary people everywhere still use amulets and folk medicines; rituals at sacred springs help people find lovers; and students still visit the graves of grandparents to contact spirits, if now to aid success in modern examinations. In village societies the maintenance of traditional beliefs is associated with continuing agricultural and life-cycle rituals.

Continuities within ritual life can be remarkable: even in Bali, long inundated by tourism, ritual practices still mirror those of the prewar era.[39] In the Philippines fiestas celebrate not only holy days and national holidays but also harvests and life-cycle events. Patron saints occupy a position similar to that of guardian spirits in other parts of Southeast Asia. Even among Southeast Asia's widespread Chinese migrant population, the cohesion of spirit-medium cults remains.[40] In Java village life continues to centre on communal rituals, despite the fact that they have become expensive. Financial stresses have not stopped villagers in Kalimantan (Borneo), Bali or Burma from competing to outdo each other in funeral or initiation ceremonies, and often these lead hosts into severe debt. While orthodox Muslims in Indonesia or Malaysia are less likely to overextend in this fashion, the same impulse is displaced among them into excesses of giving in conjunction with Hari Raya, at the end of the fast month of Ramadan.

The syncretic traditional religions, notably local versions of Buddhism, Islam and Christianity, blended with these undercurrents of local culture, and still remain the largest formal communities of believers. But, according to Gourou for example, the central social focus in every village of the Red River delta in northern Vietnam was never the Buddhist temple, but the *dinh*. As the site for major agricultural rituals and other communal celebrations, it is the building in which ritual meetings aim to establish or maintain harmony with deities, the patron spirits of the village. For the populace in general, ancestral spirits have appeared unquestionably real; though Buddhist monks were usually also present, they were not often central to village life. The resilience of such village beliefs was evident in the 1970s when, even after several decades of communist rule, 'village elders were found to be restoring the old ritual processions to the *dinh*, the village communal house, whose mystique—and the politics associated with it—had supposedly been transformed and transposed with the downfall of colonialism'.[41]

In the archipelago periodic conflict in Mindanao relates to government efforts to subordinate the Moros within the Catholic- and Manila-dominated state. In Malaysia the so-called 'Emergency', a war between Chinese,

[39] This remarkable continuity is evident in the three-part documentary film by John Darling, 'Bali Triptych' (Bozado Pty Ltd, 1988). Part two, 'The Path of the Soul', especially compares footage of rituals performed in the 1930s, taken by Mead and Bateson, with his own from the 1980s.

[40] Cheu Hock Tong, *The Nine Emperor Gods*, Singapore, 1988.

[41] A. B. Woodside, *Community and Revolution in Modern Vietnam*, Boston, 1976, 259.

British and Malays, extended through the 1950s and drove guerrilla fighters into the forest areas of the Semang, forcing some to cross the border into Thailand and others into resettled villages.[42] Indonesian confrontation with Malaysia in the early 1960s similarly drew armies to the boundary of Sarawak and Kalimantan. Indonesian military action against the Dutch, in what became Irian Jaya, had already established a military channel for integrating Irian into the state. Christian missions and churches became intensely active there only in the 1950s, in the last decade of Dutch control, and since its *de facto* incorporation into Indonesia in 1962 they have remained the major alternative network to the government in Irian Jaya. Subsequently the protracted war against Fretilin in East Timor, beginning in 1975, has had a similar complexion, aiming to subsume ethnic identities into the nation and facing resistance which has sometimes drawn on Catholic networks. The resettlement of Visayans in Mindanao or of Javanese in Sumatra, Irian Jaya, Sulawesi and Kalimantan, like the rapid expansion of forestry, has also worked to destroy the shifting lifestyles which underpinned the earlier rich diversity of local cultures.

Traditional ceremonial, political or economic exchange between hill and valley peoples had built-in mechanisms to moderate inequities and maintain distance; modernizing governments work to incorporate local chiefships or village councils into national administrations. As in the colonial era, conversion to Christianity sometimes appeared an attractive option. Even in Thailand, where extension of Theravāda into the hills is under way, some hill groups have become Christian instead. Missionary work directed at Biblical translation has facilitated conversion of predominantly oral traditions into writing, providing a route to literacy which is especially relevant for minorities interested in maintaining their language while accessing modern education. This competed with nationalist policies which have usually emphasized literacy through schooling in the language of the dominant ethnic group. Among the Karens, many of whom were converted by Baptists or Buddhists during the past century, natural (*Y'wa*), ethnic cultural (*Mu Kaw Li*) and ancestral (*bgha*) spirit forces continue to interact even among the large number who became Christian. Since 1962 the Ne Win government has actively pursued a policy of assimilation, but militant Karen nationalism remains in residual form along the Burmese–Thai border. In the Democratic Republic of Vietnam, which adopted Chinese policies with regard to ethnic minorities, promotion of literacy was channelled through indigenous tribal languages.[43]

Warfare and its attendant disruptive modes of central intervention have shaped the experience of most tribal areas of the mainland through much of the past four decades. The Vietminh defeated the French in the hills at Dien Bien Phu only through alliance with hill peoples whom they had depended on throughout their struggle. This alliance laid the basis for an unusual degree of autonomous tribal power in the Democratic Republic of Vietnam. The Annamite chain, bordering Vietnam, Kampuchea and Laos, has for decades been a key channel supplying guerrilla armies: first for

---

[42] C. Keyes, *The Golden Peninsula*, London, 1977, 38.
[43] ibid., 28–9.

Vietnamese against the French and then Americans, then for the Khmer resistance to the Vietnamese. In the Shan plateau the mainly Christian Karens, separate communist groups and opium warlords have been fighting intermittently since 1948. Similarly until the early 1970s at least, Sihanouk self-consciously considered Theravāda Buddhism as the prime instrument of national integration for Cambodia. In Thailand's northeast, north and south there have been periodic communist or ethnic guerrilla movements, and since the war the Thai government has felt that the security of its borders depended on assimilating the minorities into lowland Theravāda culture.

Thus in 1963 the Dhammajarig (travelling *Dhamma*) programme began self-consciously to promote the extension of Buddhism to the hill tribes with an assimilationist objective. By 1967 one hundred monks had been sent and instructed to explain their practices whenever local people inquired.[44] Observers of lowland villages uniformly note that the village *wat* remains the prime socially integrating institution of rural Thai society. Some have argued that the bounds of the village in central Thailand are defined by participation in specific *wat* communities. Everywhere participation involves both explicitly religious rites, associated with agricultural cycles, and normative Buddhist celebrations. Village monks are commonly youth who involve themselves increasingly in labour projects as well as with spiritual or secular teaching. While they may now help build roads or advise local military officers, the respect which villagers and officials alike demonstrate is still both strong and rooted in religious sensibilities. Villagers view monks as a separate class, despite the fact that most men have, if briefly, been ordained themselves.

Throughout the village societies of the lowland, Theravāda Buddhist Lao, Burmese, Khmer and Thai regions villagers maintain animistic as well as Buddhist beliefs. Students like Spiro have seen animism and Buddhism as though they are separate systems interacting, but most now concur with Tambiah, who presented them as sub-complexes within one system.[45] Rites oriented toward summoning and ensuring the presence of the 'vital essence' of life (*leipya* in Burmese, *khwan* in Tai, *pralu'n* in Khmer) represent ongoing animistic conceptions. Respect for village guardian spirits and interest in the sacred power of places and amulets or ritual objects combine with indigenous systems of astrology, tattoos and sexual magic and those with systems of merit making, monastic schooling and the doctrine of karma. These are most elaborated in the *nat* cults of Burma, but everywhere through the region practices of spirit possession and healing, linked to beliefs in life essence, remain powerful at the village level.

In Kampuchea and Laos the *saṅgha* lost ground under communist governments, but did not disappear. The proportion of monks relative to the overall male population halved in Thailand between the 1920s and 1970s, but remained high, at about 1:34. In Burma and Thailand the number of village youth ordaining for the annual rain retreat is still high, though expanding secular education has competed with the *saṅgha* as a

44 Lester, 123–5.
45 M. Spiro, *Buddhism and Society*, New York, 1970, and S. J. Tambiah, *Buddhism and the Spirit Cults in North-east Thailand*, Cambridge, UK, 1970.

vehicle of social mobility and thus fewer choose the monkhood as a long-term vocation. In Burma it was claimed that the *sangha* had declined from some 100,000 in royal times to 70,000 in 1941 and then, even more rapidly, to 45,000 in 1958.[46] In the Philippines, where the Catholic priesthood has a very different relationship to the general population, there were fewer than 4000 priests in the 1960s. Nevertheless there too the role of religious specialists at the local level has been changing: they have functioned more directly as agents of change, whether on behalf of the government or through their own perception of themselves as agents of change in the social, as well as specifically religious, spheres.[47]

This sort of shift in the role of religious specialists was noted in the Indonesian context by Geertz, who observed that in the 1950s the politi-cization of rural life through parties led the rural *kyai*, Javanese Islamic teachers, to become brokers for modern politics and ideas as well as continuing to function as teachers within the religious schools, the *pesan-tren*, which housed them.[48] At the same time the *penghulu*, in charge of mosques, and *hakim*, religious judges, have become even more directly part of national structures through their integration, via the Ministry of Religion, into the national bureaucratic network. In Indonesia at the local level the prewar Muhammadiyah has remained a powerful organization through its school system. It has been joined since the 1970s by a series of newer *dakwah* movements. Religious impulses of all sorts were strength-ened in Indonesia through the coup of 1965, as they had been earlier through the revolution. A combination of political pressure and personal trauma led many Javanese to fill the mosques for Friday noon prayers. Many people since the 1970s have undoubtedly found renewed commit-ment to a more purely Islamic faith in the process.

Islamic efforts to purify Javanese Islam of syncretic beliefs and the insistence that all Muslims must rigorously obey the injunctions of their faith had the unintended effect of pushing committed Javanists to define themselves in non-Islamic terms. In the late 1960s several hundred thou-sand converts joined Christian churches. Hindu, Buddhist, and mystical movements were also injected with a new vitality. Hinduism, Hindu Dharma in Indonesia, was exclusively Balinese until 1965, when scattered villages, especially in the mountainous regions of east and central Java, chose to identify themselves as Hindu. Whether opting for Hinduism or Buddhism, villagers in Java have often done so out of conviction that, among the alternatives presented, the Indic religions are closest to the reality of their continuing traditional practices. At the same time new requirements have challenged most local religious communities to redefine themselves in scriptural terms in order to gain recognition from the new national bureaucracy.

This challenge forced Balinese Hindus to redefine their practices during the 1950s. A new generation of postwar Balinese began to establish direct

[46] Mendelson, 336.
[47] von der Mehden, 86.
[48] C. Geertz, 'The Javanese Kijaji: the Changing Role of a Cultural Broker', *Comparative Studies in Society and History*, II (1959–60).

contact with Indian Hindus in order to gain recognition from the Ministry of Religion. Geertz observed, on the basis of his studies in the late 1950s, that this reformation of Balinese religion resulted in the formalization of teachings on a more literal basis, the invention of new rituals, and the construction of sometimes bizarre new temples.[49] At the same time the continuing strength of earlier ceremonial religion is exemplified in Bali, where temple ritual cycles have been maintained. Associated dramatic performances and artistic activities have as often been strengthened as weakened by tourism, since foreign audiences supplement income for hamlets which channel new money into old rituals. The most spectacular demonstration, exceeding even the drama of royal cremation, was the Ekadasa Rudra ceremony at the mother temple of Bali at Besaki. This two-month-long ceremony was initiated in 1963, as 8 March of that year was the end of the Saka year 1884, and marked a 100-year cycle from the previous ceremony. Because that ritual cycle was interrupted by the eruption of Mount Agung, it was only 'completed' through cleansing rituals in 1979. The successful second attempt showed the markings of New Order Society as well as a powerful depth of local commitment to enact a traditional magical ceremony.[50]

Changes have been necessary within all the other Asian-based religions in Indonesia. Several of the small, previously exclusively urban, modern Buddhist movements have become mass movements.[51] Modern Indonesian Buddhism has roots within both the local Chinese communities and in *priyayi* circles, as some of them came to identify with it through the Theosophical Society in the prewar period. Even within the reformed Hindu and Buddhist spheres there have been rebels. Some Javanists hark back to syncretic Majapahit, looking to mysticism rather than scriptural modernism. In the 1970s the Surakarta-based Sadhar Mapan advanced Javanist Hindu yogic rather than Balinese ritual practice, as contained in the mainstream Parisada Hindu Dharma; Kasogatan, a small Tantric-style group, also looked to the Majapahit text *Sanghyang Kamahayanikan* rather than to the purism of many modern Buddhists.

'Religion' had meant the nexus of ritual magic and mystical theory which everywhere wedded private and communal practices with performance and textual traditions. In opting for the new versions of Hinduism or Buddhism, villagers were often expressing their sense that even modernist versions of those conformed to their actual tradition of practice more than modernist versions of Islam did. From village perspectives or for traditionally minded Javanese or Balinese, religious identification was never an exclusive matter. In any event, all of the dominant national organizations of the world religions in Indonesia are now modernist in tone and exclusive in structure, emphasizing ritual, text, and doctrine to the exclusion of mysticism and traditional magical praxis.

[49] C. Geertz,' 'Internal Conversion' in Contemporary Bali' in his *The Interpretation of Cultures*, New York, 1973.

[50] A. Forge, 'Balinese Religion and Indonesian Identity' in J. Fox, ed., *Indonesia: the Making of a Culture*, Canberra, 1980, 227–32.

[51] J. D. Howell, 'Modernizing Religious Reform and the Far Eastern Religions in Twentieth Century Indonesia' in S. Udin, ed., *Spectrum*, Jakarta, 1978.

MAGICAL, MILLENARIAN AND MYSTICAL PRACTICES

Just as modernizing governments have established powerful channels to integrate, dominate and reform the cultures of geographically remote peoples, so they have intruded with increasing directness on the magical practices of villagers even within the centrally positioned lowland societies. The postwar communications revolution has reconfigured cultural relations both horizontally, through space as it were, and vertically, cutting downward across social classes. Most new national governments have actively suppressed the most obviously magical and millenarian elements of local religion, in effect favouring formalized orthodoxies—not surprisingly, as those usually have hierarchies which can be manipulated by centralizing powers. Whether they have been socialist or capitalist in orientation, recent governments have all endorsed older imperial views of folk practices as reflections of 'pre-scientific superstition' which impede 'modern progress'.

In socialist Vietnam there has been willingness to compromise with Buddhism, allowing it a central committee. Support has even extended to the establishment of a High Level School of Vietnamese Buddhist studies. The government is nonetheless actively hostile to anything representing popular millenarianism, which it sees as representing a throwback to definitely outdated superstitions.[52] Folk rituals combined spiritualist séances with Buddhism. An element of animism, through the contacts with spirits implied, made local traditions similar to many others throughout the village cultures of the region. About 10 per cent of the population in southern Vietnam were Catholic in the early 1960s; an estimated 35–40 per cent were considered strong believers in Mahāyāna Buddhism; the remainder were regarded as nominal, meaning that they adhered to a mixture of animism, Taoism and Confucianism.[53]

Alongside traditional religious practices there have been substantial new sectarian movements everywhere in Southeast Asia. In Vietnam the Hoa Hao sect, founded in 1939, claimed a membership of 450,000 in 1964 in Ang Giang Province alone, and two million overall. It has been essentially a local form of Buddhism, but with emphasis on traditional folk practices rather than the more scriptural style of the Thien (Zen) revivalist monks, who began to gain strength from the 1930s onward. Teachings included not only a strong element of millenarianism, but also emphasis on moral reform. In 1966 the Cao Dai, founded in 1925, was estimated to have between one and two million members. It recognized the revelations received by the prophets of all the major world religions, somewhat in the fashion of Ba'hai, presenting them all as vehicles of God's purpose in the world in the past. In it, presence of belief in the one God stands above notions of karma and reincarnation, as is also the case in many Javanese movements. Sect activities were most notable during the 1950s through their political implications, but the indications are that the syncretic sects remained healthy under socialism. Recent visitors have reported not only that attendance at Sunday mass in the cathedrals of Hanoi and Ho Chi

[52] D. J. Steinberg, ed., *In Search of Southeast Asia*, Sydney, 1987, 465.
[53] Schecter, 180.

Minh City has been spectacular, but also that sect temples in the delta are in excellent repair.

In Burma large numbers of the Chin followed a syncretic movement which, like other millenarian movements since the late nineteenth century, adopted aspects of Christianity. The Pau Chin Hau can be interpreted as a movement which adopted elements of Christianity as an indigenous democratization movement which countered both traditional chiefly authority and the intensification of Burmese control.[54] While sectarian cults have been important in Burmese villages, new forms of vipassana meditation have been notable in cities and of more international significance. This movement had roots early in the century, but after 1950 was formally encouraged, particularly by state sponsorship of meditation centres. These were recognized in varying grades and then registered and granted subsidies. From an early stage these centres catered to foreign students of Buddhism. Since the 1950s small groups of foreign students have always been present, and in this sector Burma has never been completely closed. Within that sphere Mahasi Sayadaw occupies a special place, due especially to the patronage provided to him during the 1950s by the U Nu government.

In Thailand the most internationally known exponent of modern Buddhist meditation has been Bhikkhu Buddhadasa, who has presided over the forest hermitage of Suan Mokh in the South. While doctrinally orthodox and borrowing from Zen, he presents a view of Buddhism grounded in 'this-worldly' action. His view is that Buddhism is relevant not only cosmologically, as though only in some future life, but also in terms of its relation to continually evolving living situations. He emphasized, as core doctrines of Buddhism in fact always have, that the states of *samsara*, the worldly condition of attachment, and *nirvana*, the bliss of release, are interiorized conditions in the here and now. Setting himself early on against the notion that Buddhism was fatalistic, he stressed in relation to the teachings of all world religions that they focused ultimately on the practical realization of principles. In a political context his teachings can be styled a form of Buddhist socialism, one which rejected both communist and capitalist materialisms. He has been able to speak to many young educated Buddhists who aim to reconcile traditional faith with modern civic action.

Popular stereotypes of Buddhist monks as intensive meditators have long been dismissed. Though the forest tradition of intensive insight meditation practice has an ancient history with lineages into the present, the vast majority of Theravāda monks in Thailand neither teach nor even practise meditation. Nevertheless several significant schools of *vipassana* practice have emerged from the *sangha*, extending to lay followers who may undertake ten-day retreats on a regular basis. Several teachers have gained overseas followings. In the early twentieth century the meditation master Achaan Mun, who spent most of his career in the northeast of Thailand, revived the longstanding tradition of forest monastic disciplines. His disciples are scattered throughout the country, having founded their

[54] Keyes, 49.

own schools of meditation and catering to both monks and laity. His most noted follower, Achaan Chaa of Wat Pah Pong in Ubon Province, attracted continuous patronage from Bangkok and has sent disciples to establish forest meditation centres in England and Australia.

Whether through modern forms of meditation or in other ways, through education and community action, increasing numbers of monks are actively concerned with trying to reconcile their practices with modern life. Many who aspire to move upward socially also show serious commitment to meditation. The overall effect of modernizing meditative practices is a new strength of emphasis on the possibility of contributing positively through social action by being more tuned and egoless. Whatever the traditional conjunction, it appears increasingly that in contemporary Buddhism there is a positive evaluation of ameliorative social action. The gap between monk and laity, at least with respect to spiritual practices, is also being reformed and in certain respects closed. The meditation movements, both within and beyond the *saṅgha*, represent an active repositioning and continuation of commitment to spiritual realization.

In Malaysia the formal status of Islam as *the* religion of 'Malays' militates powerfully against syncretic cults of the type allowable in Theravāda or Javanese environments; local healers and urbanites nevertheless participate in magical practices or in marginal 'new' religious movements. Just as the *dakwah* movements represent a reinvigoration of Malay identity through strengthening of a pure Islamic commitment, among local Chinese and Indians there have been many followers not only of charismatic Christianity but also of the Indian saint Satya Sai Baba and of the Baitiangong. The latter, founded by Zhao Chongming after a vision in 1976, attempted to unite spirit-medium cults in middle-class Kuala Lumpur.[55] These movements indicate, just as do the urban followers of *vipassana* meditation in Rangoon and Bangkok or the adherents of faith healers in Manila, that magic, millenarianism and mysticism remain popular among Western-educated middle-class Southeast Asians as well as in villages, where it is easier to see such beliefs as a residue of earlier tradition.

Within Indonesia the relationship between politics, religion, and mysticism has been transformed since independence, in the process altering both the context and internal structures of local variants of mysticism. Sukarno's voice had joined others in warnings against black magic, which was a recurrent focus of public debate throughout the 1960s. Since the mid-1960s recognized movements have had firmly to abjure interest in political power, giving official legitimacy only to movements which were at least ostensibly apolitical. In the classical context such a separation was inconceivable; mysticism, culture, and politics were inextricably interwoven in theory and practice. The modern context of religious plurality, Islamic strength, and outwardly secular government all worked to pressure Javanists, those who tended to be the most mystical in their spirituality, into formal organizations. Within this context such organizations

---

[55] S. E. Ackerman and R. L. Lee, *Heaven in Transition: Non-Muslim Religious Innovation and Ethnic Identity in Malaysia*, Honolulu, 1988, 127–36.

have to be defined as purely mystical, in the classical sense that the core of all mysticism is union with the divine, and this separates mysticism from the magical and millennial elements to which it was bound by tradition. The term *kejawen* now most often refers specifically to the traditional styles within which spirit relations, magic powers, and millennial expectations were fundamental. This style remains powerful, even though it is restricted in organizational expression, as a substratum of popular outlook and cultic movement. At the same time new forms of mysticism have risen out of Javanist orientations.

Repression of millennial movements has been continual, constituting a continuing theme of religious politics in the postwar period. In 1967 the Mbah Suro movement was suppressed after it spread rumours of radical change from its centre near Ngawi; in 1968 the Java-wide Manunggal movement was outlawed after a public trial. Tens of thousands of members, some of them highly placed military and civilian officials, paid homage to their guru, Romo Semana, in a style that the government felt evoked Indic courts. Defenders argued that their behaviour merely reflected ordinary expression of respect for an elder. This incident demonstrated the extent to which power-oriented and magical spirituality, tied closely to normal social patterns, had become problematic in a context of commitment to modernizing and centralizing state power.

When the Suharto government announced that it had uncovered an attempted coup in September 1976, it became clear quickly that it centred on a mystic, until then unknown, named Sawito. He had visited power points and, at Gunung Tidar at the centre of Java, claimed to have been given the authority previously held by Semar, the guardian of Java. Subsequently he gathered a remarkable collection of signatures to attach to a document criticizing the moral fibre of Suharto. Former Vice-President Hatta and all the prominent religious leaders whose signatures appeared on the document quickly denied having known what was in it, but it was nonetheless taken seriously. From the Western standpoint Sawito's threat seemed trivial, but the magnitude of Suharto's response demonstrated his sense of vulnerability in those Javanist terms. This special fear, in the face of mystical claims that he lacked the *wahyu*, the divine sanction on which power is supposed to rest, itself indicated the continuing wider relevance of the underlying complex of beliefs to which the challenge related.

Kebatinan movements have been noted since independence in Indonesia. Generally emphasizing experiential realization of the Absolute, they are mainly Javanese in origin and composition, and see their practices as rooted in an ageless indigenous wisdom which predates Indian influences. In this context mysticism refers, as everywhere in its classical meaning, to the inner, spiritual and esoteric dimension within all religion, and also more especially to beliefs, practices and movements which are defined by their focus on individual realization. There are hundreds of identifiable movements in the country. Subagya listed 288 in 1973; an inventory in 1980 registered 160; but there can be no definitive listing.[56] Many groups are so small, local, ephemeral and informal that they never merit note, though some of them may be quite significant. The *tarekats*, the Sufi movements,

[56] R. Subagya, *Kepercayaan dan Agama*, Yogyakarta, 1973, 129–38.

are also mystical, but their affiliation with Islam is intrinsic and they are thus not generally bracketed with the independent movements. Several dozen movements have Java-wide or genuinely Indonesian membership. These include Pangestu, Subud, Sapta Darma, Ilmu Sejati, Sumarah and Hardopusoro. A few of those claim more than one hundred thousand members, but most have at best several thousand who are centrally motivated by their practice.

Kebatinan groups existed within the Dutch colonial framework, but were necessarily secretive in that context. They came into public view during the revolutionary fighting of the late 1940s. Then, paralleling the organizing process of the 1950s through all sectors of society, major movements adopted formal patterns with elected officers, minutes and conferences. This process was in part spontaneous, in part a response to the new demand for records of membership and meetings on the part of government agencies. In the early 1950s a number of movements argued that they deserved recognition as separate religions, suggesting that in the context of national independence it would be an anomaly if only 'imported' religions received government approval. Sapta Darma maintained that argument into the 1970s, but most accepted early on that they were unlikely to be recognized as religions because of the violent response which that would have brought from Muslims.

In the traditional setting, mystical consciousness and social power were cosmologically bound together. Both the Indic notion of the *devaraja* and the Islamic ideals of the state as guardian of religion implied that the ruler had a special relation to the sacred. Insofar as mystics claimed direct contact with divinity, they walked a delicate line to avoid appearance of separate claim to secular authority. Under the Dutch such movements attracted surveillance as potential focal points of rural unrest; in the period since independence the political sensitivity of, and pressures on, religious life have increased. Increasingly autonomous and exclusive definition of each element in the religious scene naturally extended into intensified competition, both to participate in the newly established power structures of the state and to determine how the national identity would relate to religious convictions.

Popular association of *kebatinan* with occultism, no less than analytical association of mystical gnosis with instrumental effects, represents confusion of forms with essence. All of the major national movements dissociate themselves from *kejawen* occultism, emphasizing direct consciousness of God rather than culturally rooted symbols and spirits. This shift of emphasis from powers to consciousness is not simply a response to the politicized context of Javanese mysticism. The same polarity is rooted within early Indic culture; it also represents a penetration of Semitic forms of monotheism, which stress distinction between magic and divine revelation, into the Javanist world. Although Javanist tradition still prioritizes a Tantric-style identification of consciousness and powers, it also already contained a Buddhist-style emphasis on the void as a powerful counter to that; the extension of monotheism resonated with that existing strand of local spirituality. Tantric patterns continue implicitly to have strength in village practices, the *danhyang* cults, and in movements such as Sadhar Mapan and Manunggal. But the Buddhist tradition and mystical separation of consciousness from any visible effects are profoundly rooted in a tradition extending back over a millennium, one which has dovetailed with modern pressures to produce more exclusive emphasis on consciousness.

The movements are not equivalent to Sufism, which is integrally tied to a 'world religion', but rather to culturally based traditions such as Taoism or Shinto. Sufism and Zen place emphasis on lineages connecting living masters to Muhammad and the Buddha. In Javanism such lineage is denied not just as a counter to Islamic claims that it is derivative, but also as an assertion that religious knowledge comes direct from God: in short, an assertion that *kebatinan* is mystical in the fundamental sense of the term. Throughout the 1970s public tension frequently focused on the manoeuvring, partly inspired by the Suharto government, to confer greater legitimacy to the mystical movements. Islamic reaction has been intense and each step toward independent legitimacy has been geared, as much as possible, to avoid stirring reaction. Related debates, such as those surrounding the effort to bring in secular marriage laws in 1973 and 1974, have touched the same sensitive area of religious conflict. In 1973 it became legal to belong to mystical movements without also claiming membership in a 'world religion'; in 1978 these movements were given a new basis of legitimacy when they were released from the jurisdiction of the Ministry of Religion and given their own Directorate within the Ministry of Education and Culture.

Members use Javanese in daily life and group meetings, but Indonesian is used for organizational matters. Traditional cults focused on a charismatic guru; modern movements have semi-rationalized structures. Leaders are distinguished from spiritual teachers; if the patronage model remains strong in practice, theory no longer places it at the heart of organization. Organizations adopt the administrative hierarchy common to all national organizations, but growing care in the keeping of membership lists is often mainly to facilitate relations with supervising bodies. Major sects are relatively open in structure and streamlined in practice, and esoteric tendencies decline together with the decreasing emphasis on instrumental magic, ancestral spirits, and occult powers. Healing plays a major role in sects such as Subud and Sapto Darmo, but is balanced by emphasis on 'God's responsibility' for effecting cures. Monotheistic emphasis is reflected in often puritanical distaste for the possession cults characteristic of most local traditions. Similarly, people in most movements speak of meditation as *sujud* (surrender) or *panembah* (prayer) rather than *semadi*. The Indic resonance of the latter renders it suspect to Islam, which sees *semadi* as implying entry into a 'Godless void', because it usually comes without a notion of personalized divinity.

The strongest evidence of an essentially Islamic framing of discourse about religion lies in the very extent of public debate about and between 'Islam and *kebatinan*'. The relationship has been problematic from the earliest days of the republic in formal contexts of legal clarification; in the press; and down to the village level in relations between branches of mystical movements and local authorities. Umbrella organizations emerged in the 1950s when the leading national spokesperson for them was Wongsonegoro. He headed the Congress of Indonesian Mystics (BKKI), which petitioned Sukarno to request status equal to religions in 1957. In Malang in 1960 a subsequent congress stressed that *kebatinan* and religion differed only in emphasis—mysticism focused on perfecting the individual spirit while the latter emphasized prayer to God. In 1961 a seminar considered the relationship between *kebatinan* and Sukarno's political philosophy; in 1962 another stressed the relationship between spiritual practice, national struggle and world peace. The BKKI aimed to clarify that *kebatinan* represented an indigenous spiritual tradition of high standing, not a jumble of superstition and magic. Participants felt a special relationship to the national identity, arguing that the foundation of the nation's belief in God lay in the strength of *kebatinan* within it. In 1958 the BKKI affirmed that the 'essential characteristic of the Indonesian national identity lies in emphasis on life of the spirit'.

There is strong pressure behind the growth of a literalist monotheism. The first principle of the Pancasila is an underscoring of the profession of faith in one God, though omitting reference to Muhammad, in Islamic terms. Islam may not have established itself as the religion of Indonesia, but there is no doubt that its sense of religion defines, shapes and constrains discourse about religion and spiritual life. This pressure is conveyed through the government bureaucracy, and has influenced private practices as well as public expression of religious life. A disposition to rearguard action, rationalization and justification of practices, pressures even mystics toward literal Islamic terms of discourse. At the same time, as a separate vector of change, there is growing emphasis on a restricted range of dimensions. Indonesian Muslims define religion increasingly in terms of its socio-cultural dimensions. From the perspective of the mystics it appears that orthodoxy itself loses sight of the fact that religion and spirituality are not only mediated and expressed through human symbols and actions but also exist as a sphere in themselves.

In reflecting generally on the range of magical, mystical and millenarian movements through the Southeast Asian region, we can note strong common patterns. Differences relate partly to varying dominant 'world religions' and national governmental policies, as those appear as moderating forces shaping local expression. Everywhere an explicit ideology of scientific modernism colours dominant formal perspectives on folk magic. Conversely, whether in Filipino faith-healing practices in Luzon or in the thinking of the Cao Dai in the Mekong delta of Vietnam, local sects attempt to 'domesticate' science both by incorporating reference to it in magic and by attempting to validate practices by pseudo-scientific criteria. In any event folk magical healing, related to shamanism, remains present, however substantially reformed and defensive.[57]

Like magical healing, millenarianism also remains powerful as a framework for folk perception and practice. An underlying conviction in the

---

[57] The strengths of these currents are evident in studies such as R. W. Leiban, *Cebuano Sorcery*, Berkeley, 1967; M. E. Spiro, *Burmese Supernaturalism*, Englewood Cliffs, 1967; and L. Golomb, *An Anthropology of Curing in Multiethnic Thailand*, Urbana and Chicago, 1985.

cosmological meaning of earthly events, implicitly always including politics, continues to lead people throughout the region to frame social process within their spiritual senses of what constitutes humanity, implying ultimately that life leads toward resolution and balance within nature and that that may be expressed socially through radical shifts in power. These impulses are expressed through national political philosophies as 'neo-traditionalism', as we noted in observing the convergences which relate Marxist and millenarian formations in both Vietnam and Java. The same forces have also operated separately, as a distinct pattern evident through the region, in the form of purely local expressions centring on charismatic teachers who have eschatological visions of social process.

While the magical and millenarian strands of postwar religious practice are most rooted in and pervasive through the villages of the region, newly formed mystical sects and meditation practices cross the urban–rural divide and have often been urban-based. Within them the reformed contemporary élites have essentially rescued aspects of their traditional esoteric spirituality; but they have done it by disentangling consciousness-raising practices (as we may reframe meditation) from the magic and hierarchies of older orthodox Buddhism or Islam, within which such practices had earlier been embedded. *Vipassana* practitioners following the Burmese master Mahasi Sayadaw or the Thai Achaan Chaa, Javanese members of Pangestu, Subud or Sumarah, Tagalog disciples of faith healers, and Vietnamese followers of Cao Dai, have all practised meditation or entered trances; these are new ways of exploring essentially the same spiritual domains which older local traditions have accessed through the mediation of religious specialists such as village shamans, Catholic priests, Islamic *ulamā* or Buddhist monks.

PURIST REVIVAL AND SECULAR MODERNISM

The breakdown of communal structures by rapid socio-economic change has brought a variety of responses. Nevertheless the majority of Southeast Asians still pursue folk customs or syncretic traditional religions. Those derive from practices which were fully formed in earlier periods of history, including the variations of orthodoxy and mysticism already alluded to. Distinctive new currents, such as secularism and fundamentalism, may appear as stark counterpoints to each other, but they equally embody the specifically modern situation. Earlier scriptural modernism was a feature of prewar religious reform and paralleled nationalism in the political arena: it arose essentially as a correlate of the print media.

Now new fundamentalisms, like contemporary areligious secularism, are more especially a reflection of electronic mass media. Fundamentalist revivalism, popular purist movements of regeneration and internal conversion, may be especially apparent in the Islamic sphere, but similar movements appear in all other local communities. The groundswell of revivalist religion calls into question the assumption that industrialization and the pressures of urban life would decrease the social role of religion.

Just as the intensity of fundamentalism in the United States and Iran has confounded expectations, so in Southeast Asia one of the clearest responses to the pressures of modern life has been intensified literal faith. These belief patterns are not, as some secularists imagine, explicable mainly as a residue of earlier traditional faith. They are facilitated by the effectiveness of electronic media and are a specifically modern phenomenon. Earlier forms of reformism were 'modernist' rather than areligiously secular or fundamentalist.

Extending outward from urban areas, and reflecting the outlook of those educated in Western styles, many variants of the scriptural modernism which have prewar origins can still be identified. Rationalizing reformists have emerged separately from within each local Southeast Asian community: they have certainly not been only reflections of the activity of missions from beyond the region, as indigenous modernism arose beyond the sphere of direct colonial impact as a process of independent innovation. Generally they have argued at once for adjustment to modernity and for a return in more critical and rational terms to the original canons of their religion. In the process they attempt to disentangle scripture from myth and faith from magic, claiming a rationalism almost in the terms of modern science.

In Thailand the continuing link between the *sangha* and royalty has meant that modernist forms of religious consciousness were pioneered through dominant religious and political institutions rather than as a counter to them. Mongkut, king of Siam in the mid-nineteenth century, had been a monk for two decades before he assumed the throne. Through contacts he pursued with missionaries he undertook studies of Latin, English, mathematics and astronomy, and he became critical of monks, including those who had trained him: he felt they engaged in chanting without understanding the scriptures. The emphasis on comprehension of texts he initiated through the Dhammayutikaya movement, first founded in 1833, aimed to reduce the related 'confusion' of orthodoxy with popular magic, and the related reformist sects which resulted have become especially important in all of the mainland *sanghas*.

In Thailand, Laos and Cambodia the traditionalist group is known as the Mahanikaya, or 'Great Order', and the reformists belong to the Dhammayuttikaya. In Burma the traditionalists generally belong to the Sudhamma, the 'Good Dhamma' order, while the reformists belong to the Shwegyin, also founded in the nineteenth century. The modernist groups are more committed to emphasis on the study of Pāli texts and the practice of meditation, and are more strict with regard to prohibitions on the handling of money. Only a small minority of monks belong to the reformist orders, but they have strong royal patronage and greater influence than numbers alone would suggest.

Where Western imperialism had divided religious and secular power from each other, politics and religious reformism nevertheless went hand in hand. Because the link between politics and established religion had been cut by imperialism in Burma, with the elimination of the traditional state, the *sangha* was weakened due to the absence of royal patronage. As a result, lay movements, such as the Young Men's Buddhist Association, became the most visible foci of anti-colonial resistance. Religious issues nevertheless remained prominent within political nationalism, as suggested by the fact that its first notable victory early in the century came when agitation gave abbots the right to insist that even the British had to take their shoes off upon entering temple compounds. The prominence of lay practices of *vipassana*, insight meditation, through teachings such as those of U Ba Kin and Mahasi Sayadaw, reminds us of the internal and non-political aspects of modernizing religion. Religious styles self-consciously adapt to changing urban lifestyles and modern education, without always being a response to political issues and objectives.

Malay Islamic modernism has had roots in Cairo, where Al-Azhar University housed Mohammad Abduh's influential effort to reconcile religious doctrine with scientific thought, making it a focus of Islamic intellectual life worldwide. Nationalism went hand in hand with renewal of religion; since independence Malay ethnicity has been identified increasingly with Islam, adding force to purism, and influencing the complexion of religious practices on the ground. In one sense this recent trend is simply a continuation of the longstanding process of '*masuk Melayu*', that is of 'becoming Malay'. Whether in Indonesia, especially in Kalimantan, or in Malaysia, as minority groups come increasingly into contact with urban currents they often adopt Malay-Indonesian language and Islam simultaneously. The modern context extends a longstanding process, but now usually with more direct movement to purist forms of Islam.[58] In Indonesia the Muhammadiyah movement, founded in Yogyakarta in 1911, established a network of schools with a curriculum including mathematics, science, and social studies. Most Javanese, even in cities, have experienced Islam as part of a synthesis including deeply rooted Indian thought and animistic spirit beliefs. Muhammadiyah, like other modernisms, stressed revamping of Islam to expunge what it saw as outdated elements, setting itself against the syncretism present within the *pesantren* pattern of tradition.

Contemporary purism is not simply a continuation of prewar scriptural modernism; it takes a sharper form. In Malaysia the *dakwah* movements do some external missionizing but can be generally characterized as movements of internal conversion. Notable groups within this ambit include Darul Arqam, a small group centring on a commune near Kuala Lumpur; Jemaat Tabligh, an international movement originating in India; and, most importantly, ABIM, a nation-wide and locally rooted movement. Like Muhammadiyah in Indonesia or the Dhammayut sect in Thailand, the Darul Arqam has power beyond its numbers due to tight organization and the high profile of its school and clinic. In both it draws strongly from traditional practices. The Jemaat Tabligh came to the peninsula in the 1950s and exists throughout the country, but with little formal organization. ABIM, the Muslim Youth League of Malaysia, was founded in 1971 and now has a membership of over 35,000. It sponsors rallies and is well

[58] D. Miles, *Cutlass and Crescent Moon*, Sydney: University of Sydney, Centre for Asian Studies, 1976, and R. Hefner, *Hindu Javanese*, Princeton, 1985.

organized throughout the school and university system. It has been strongly connected with international revivalism in Iran and the Arab Middle East, raising consciousness of those areas locally. It attracted a young and well-educated membership under the leadership of Anwar Ibrahim and continues to emphasize internal purification of practices.

Generally in Malaysia during the 1970s and 1980s, explicit and publicly indicated adherence to Islamic practices has been strongly on the upswing within the Malay community. The conflation of Malay ethnic and Muslim religious identity has been longstanding, but it is only recently that it has become a focus of constant invocation. Muslim holidays have become more definitively national in scope. Civil servants dress more conservatively, moving away from the British conventions which many had adopted in the colonial era. Religious issues have converged with ethnic conflict to a remarkable and uncomfortable degree. As Malays have moved increasingly into urban environments, largely facilitated by patronage through the bureaucracy but also by movement toward factory labour and away from the farms, they have confronted Chinese domination of the economy and conflict with Western values more directly. These contexts have sharpened, rather than decreased, movement toward local values in a more purist form. Local movements have also been powerfully influenced by the increase in self-confidence throughout the Islamic world since the oil boom. In part this is related to a worldwide Islamic movement to reject the philosophical baggage which appears to accompany Westernization. The new strength of economies throughout the Islamic world provided an underpinning for this revival.

Indonesian *dakwah* movements have been increasing in strength since the early 1970s. The government has promoted renewal and re-emphasis on Islam, almost in spite of itself. Though significant elements of the national leadership might be privately otherwise inclined, contributions from Suharto's discretionary funds to the *pesantren* have been consistently high from the late 1970s onward. The Ministry of Religion, still preponderantly Muslim in composition and orientation, carries out missionary activities, produces publications, and co-ordinates legal and educational offices which encourage purism. Government ironically goes farther in this respect than even many of those it is presumably catering to would want. Now that the policy in all government buildings is to have a prayer room to cater to Muslims, there is social pressure for those present to appear to be using these new facilities. Muhammadiyah continues to be active through its many schools and hospitals and, while relatively moderate by the standards of many groups, it contributes to continuing Islamization. The Dewan Da'wah Islamiyah Indonesia has been under the leadership of Muhammed Natsir, former Masjumi leader and one-time Prime Minister.

The previously apparently conservative Nahdatul Ulama has been reinvigorated since the 1970s. A dynamic new generation of activists, including Abdurrahman Wahid and Nurcholish Madjid, both thoroughly cosmopolitan products of highly charged modern *pesantren* education, present it with a radically new image. The *pesantren* networks have been revitalized; the *tarekats*, which were linked strongly to them earlier on, have recently regained a new legitimacy, which has perhaps strengthened as the lingering predispositions of Protestant Christian imperialists fade. It appears as though the modernist disdain for mysticism of the prewar era, one which drove those so inclined to distance themselves from Islam by associating with independent and explicitly syncretic movements, has shifted. Since the late 1970s radical movements have increased the political sensitivity of Islam. One indication of the government's attitude is that Libya and Iran are listed, along with Israel and China, among the countries which citizens may not enter with an Indonesian passport.

While from many points of view the government has, in the past two decades, made powerful gestures to neutralize Islamic fundamentalism, within the Islamic community dissatisfactions have remained strong. Many have certainly felt that the New Order's willingness to accommodate mysticism (*kepercayaan*) by legitimizing it in 1973, threatened the position of Islam within the country. There have been only a few public demonstrations, but the incidents which have come to the surface have attracted a great deal of publicity. The 'Kommando Jihad' movement was banned in the late 1970s through association with movements to overthrow the government. In 1978 the Gerakan Pemuda Islam (Islamic Youth Movement) was banned. Libyans were associated with movements in Aceh; in 1981 another group was accused of having support from the Ayatollah Khomeini; a Bandung group commandeered a plane in 1980; and in 1985 the bombing of Borobudur was blamed on Muslim extremists.[59]

Reformism and fundamentalism have appeared in every religious community. Vietnamese Buddhism has been a syncretic blend of spirit beliefs and Confucianism, but was reshaped during the 1920s and 1930s. In the most dynamic phase of the postwar period for Buddhists there, a Vietnamese Buddhist Reunification Congress took place in the week of the New Year of 1964 at Xa Loi Pagoda in Saigon. The congress aimed to unite the South's Mahāyāna and Theravāda followers through a new modern structure, but only perhaps a million joined the resulting United Buddhist Association.[60] Six regional groups of monks and two million estimated Theravāda followers (mainly from provinces along the Cambodian border) remained unconnected to the federation.

Migrant Chinese Buddhism was so emphatically syncretic in Indonesia that it was officially called 'Tridharma', meaning 'the three teachings' and referring to a blending of the philosophies of Lao-tzu, Confucius and the Buddha. Local temples, *klenteng*, have generally invoked all three while emphasizing one, and at the same time housed spirit-medium practices related to folk ancestral cults. While increasing numbers of Indonesian Chinese have converted to Christianity, many have remained within the ambit of their own traditions. A few opted for modernized versions of Confucianism, which had a brief and tentative flowering but which is now discouraged in Indonesia, as it is viewed as an 'ethnic' rather than 'world' religion. More often local Chinese communities have effectively converted to new forms of Buddhism, some even to Japanese offshoots of Nichiren or to an Indonesian version of the Taiwanese-based Unity Sect.

[59] von der Mehden, 110.
[60] Schecter, 204.

Southeast Asian 'Hindus' have also experienced significant reformation. Just as folk practice of Balinese Hinduism is now complemented by a nationally administered orthodoxy, reflecting postwar contacts with India, elsewhere Hinduism has taken new forms which reflect the Hindu renaissance of the Indian homeland. Spillovers from the religious tensions of the South Asian subcontinent, such as those between Tamils, Sikhs and Hindus, have already been noted, as even in Singapore local communities extend the religious politics of new fundamental versions of their faiths. Movements such as the Arya Samaj, which allow non-Indians to convert to Hinduism, have been active in Malaysia. Just as South African experience shaped Gandhi, Malaya was the home of one particularly noted modern Indian teacher. Swami Sivananda, many of whose disciples have a worldwide following, worked initially as a medical doctor in the peninsula early in this century. Revivals of Vedantic philosophy such as his now complement Tamil trance rituals such as Thaipusam.

To indicate the full extent of scripturalism and fundamentalism, we can note that as a style of religious commitment it is identifiable even within some ostensibly mystical religious communities. In Indonesia modernism is usually associated with Muslim organizations, but some Javanese movements are equally defined by revealed texts. Even their practices, as in the large and well-established Pangestu movement for instance, can be more intellectual than meditative; in this they resemble Protestant, Muhammadiyah or Dhammayut groups more than they do stereotypes of mysticism. If our purpose is to identify major strands of religious sensibility at the local level within Southeast Asia, it is certainly important to note that traditionalism, magic, millenarianism, mysticism, scripturalism and fundamentalism crosscut and exist as types of religiosity within all of the varied world religions and ethnic communities of the region.

Even in contexts of radical modernization, traditional practices are often reformulated rather than dropped, as is evident in the vicinity of Kuala Lumpur through the way spirit possession works among factory women from village origins.[61] Though modernity does appear to lead to a streamlining of beliefs, it clearly does not always lead to secularization. However, if we are considering religious and cultural change in the broadest sense, we must be consistent with the suggestion at the outset that 'religion' refers fundamentally to any mediating system which connects people to what they can imagine as 'really real'. In those terms it is important to touch, however briefly, on aspects of world-view and conviction which fall beyond the spheres conventionally designated as 'religious'.

Implicitly this survey has already done so, through suggesting some of the ways in which the national revolutions and the construction of new cultures resonate with traditional spiritual and religious senses of social life. In dealing with variants of local practice, with new Southeast Asian ways of knowing what is real, it is equally important to note the power and extent of secularism, even if ironically framing that here as a variant 'faith community'.

---

[61] A. Ong, *Spirits of Resistance and Capitalist Discipline*, Albany, 1987.

The extension of basic literacy to the general population through modern schools must be considered one of the great achievements of the postwar states. The temple schooling of Thailand and Burma had effected levels of literacy well above those of premodern Europe; it has already been noted that religious schools remain influential throughout the region and that religious subjects remain prominent in the curriculum of state schools, excepting in the socialist states of Indochina. Conversely it can even be argued that religious senses of knowledge suffuse the theoretically secular schools. Secular schools present knowledge virtually as a 'substance' which is communicated through mantric-style rote repetition. Sometimes it is seen virtually as passed by osmosis from teacher to pupil, and the pattern of learning thus echoes the patronage model of discipleship which characterized earlier transmissions of craft skills or sacred lore.

At the same time it can be argued that, just as capitalism may be the most revolutionary force in transforming local societies, in the cultural sphere secularism is the most aggressive of the new faiths. Middle-class urbanites are increasingly cosmopolitan through the nature of their lifestyles, with white-collar jobs, extensive travel and education in increasingly secular systems both at home and abroad. These new middle classes are composed of people who are situated to control new economic activities, the apparatus of states and local adaptations of modern communications; naturally they have power and prominence well beyond their statistical strength. As they are also often in the cultural vanguard, farthest removed from the mystical and magical inheritance of their traditional religions, the forces of genuine secularism are undoubtedly increasing in significance.

However, even modern art forms which appear quite secular on first glance can be read as the new social rituals of everyday life in urban contexts. *Ludruk* theatre, a proletarian drama still popular in Java, teaches the urban public in the postwar era in the same way that the older *wayang* still carries a spiritual message to villagers. Traces of the earlier arts remain present within even such radical steps into new urbanism. So Peacock's study of *ludruk* theatre presented it as a 'rite of modernisation'. In both thematic content and dramatic form the theatre invoked formulaic visions of material progress, now for urbanites. But the modes of presentation nevertheless replicated traditional dramatic codes, even in the nature of the concentration displayed by actors as they virtually unconsciously drew on bodily modes of learning and dance forms which resonated unselfconsciously with the traditional court-derived arts.[62]

Radical though the changes of the postwar period have been, spiritual values and issues remain pervasively important. It is instructive, for example, that in the secular state of Vietnam a self-conscious appeal to spirituality remains. Vietnamese communist literary critics commented in 1970 on the American Susan Sontag's critique of the *Tale of Kieu*, the classic of the early 1800s. They observed without reservation that she was deeply socialized into the individualistic consciousness of the modern West and thus unable to grasp the 'limitless richness' of the Vietnamese soul and with that the value and emphasis within its culture on cummunal

[62] J. Peacock, *Rites of Modernization*, Chicago, 1968, 242–3.

sharing.[63] Spiritual values can thus appear to remain prominent even within cultures which adhere to what most Westerners identify as a materialistic ideology.

TRAJECTORIES OF CHANGING ACCESS TO THE REAL

Through the cycles of history Sinic, Indic, Islamic, and European forces have been superimposed on Southeast Asia. Each worked in some sense to claim it, to recast society within borrowed models. Local cultural memories nevertheless preserve senses of primal identity, and at the moment struggle to assert that through modern forms. Nationalist culture began to take root at the turn of the century, just as the colonial framework defined the boundaries of the contemporary state. Now metropolitan super-cultures radiate from the new national centres, promoting new languages and the growth of a supra-ethnic identity spread through the bureaucracy, schools, literature, electronic media, and, not least, the military. National revolutions have not been just a matter of achieving political and economic independence: they also involve the assertion of identity in autonomous rather than derivative terms. Following the revolutions, the forces of modernity appeared to define national governments through models borrowed from the West; the dominant élites, whether secular or religious, comprised the most Westernized Southeast Asians. Tension between trajectories of growing global integration and resurgent primal identity combine to generate the extraordinary pressures under which contemporary Southeast Asians still labour.

Everywhere clearer demarcation of religious communities has paralleled the modern establishment of national boundaries which was mediated initially by colonialism. Syncretic styles of religion had not focused on boundaries, but on courts, schools or monasteries. Those had existed in a hierarchical world conceived as requiring progress through layers of knowledge, guided by apprenticeships analogous to those in other domains of traditional learning, to a mystically conceived centre. Scripturalism redefined individual experience as literal, and social identification as exclusive; thus tensions increased, intersecting also in new ways with political process. Buddhists felt their faith as an element of revolution in Burma, and many Muslims held that their revolutions should lead to an Islamic state. Paradoxically the strength of adherence to exclusivism undermined its realization in a context crosscut by social and religious pluralism.

There has been a clear trajectory within the religious sphere in postwar Southeast Asia, and it has been a major area of domestic concern. The dominant trend has been that of increasing scripturalism, the strengthening of outlooks associated with the West but reflected locally in a wide range of unique adaptations. Colonial students of Theravāda or of Islam often suggested that the Thai or Javanese were not 'really' Buddhist or Muslim. Their view derived from a textual sense of religion, and in the face

[63] Woodside, 307.

of animistic practices they could see claims to membership in world religions only as a facade. The traditional syncretism of Southeast Asians did not mean that they did not belong within the sphere of the world religions they associated with: it meant that the religions themselves were syncretic. The nature of tensions between communities was transformed through the growth of the scripturalist community. Scripturalism has meant that religion has been defined in increasingly concrete terms. Scriptures, rituals, and doctrines are definable; the mystical is not. Modern structures have meant that definition and distinction have been of increasing importance. This has highlighted differences and increased tensions by sharpening the lines of contrast.

In the traditional context it seemed possible to be what modern syncretist leaders like U Nu or Sukarno said they were—in the latter's case at once mystic, Muslim, and Marxist. Now some can accept those possibilities, but many cannot. Within the traditional religious world there was a very clear sense of a layered cosmos, a hierarchical structure in nature and within human consciousness. Traditionally Indianized states were defined cosmologically and by their centres; now states are defined geographically by their borders. The same shift has taken place within religions as modernity has flattened even local senses of religious space. Religious communities tend now to be closed and with clear boundaries, not open-ended and fluid; the boundaries have arisen in precisely the same way that political boundaries have, and as a result of the same forces.

New meditation movements and styles of mystical, millenarian and syncretic spiritual practice have appeared throughout the region, counterpointing the equally vigorous emergence of secular modernism. At the same time the spirit realms, once central to local maintenance of balanced relations with ancestral culture and the physical environment, now appear to be receding along with the forests as a modern developmental worldview advances. Finally we must note the emergence of secular practices within the urban middle classes and among industrial workers and itinerant traders. For the first time there is a vigorously growing sphere of agnosticism but modernity does not necessarily lead to secularization. Changes are not confined to shifts of membership from one religion to another, or from being religious to becoming agnostic or atheistic. Those shifts are significant and allegiances have been fluid in the region. But at the same time notable internal transformations have occurred within every community of belief. Though the nexus between cultural and spiritual life has been weakened, this has led more often to restructured belief than to secular disbelief.

In the development of tourist industries there is also an ironic rebound affecting local cultures. Even the urban and internationally oriented Southeast Asians are themselves increasingly positioned as tourists in relation to village communities who retain what is now packaged, for tourist purposes, as 'indigenous' and authentic culture. In areas particularly geared to tourism, such as Bali or Toraja in Indonesia, production of art is usually separated in new ways from its previous ritual context. This has an effect also, inadvertent but nevertheless profound, on those who create the works of art. They begin to imagine themselves as, even to become, museum specimens; this is what the commodification of culture, through packaging of tourism as a national industry, aims to turn them into.

Within some sectors of the modernizing élites of the region there is strong and often repeated support for the view that continuing adherence to beliefs in the supernatural is a prime inhibitor of development. This belief is common throughout the Third World as a borrowing from the scientism of the developed world. It applies particularly with respect to modernizing medical systems, which are one of the strongest forces contesting traditional beliefs and practices relating to healing. There is, apart from the self-confidence evident in specific radical and especially religious and mystical circles, little confidence that Western systems of knowledge can be challenged on their own grounds. But much of this is strictly rhetoric. This is to say that, in public life within modern institutions, educated people often play the roles they believe they are expected to according to the logic 'modernity' appears to represent. Tambiah argues that the commitment to Buddhism, for example, has not declined, though its expression in social organizations, such as numbers in the monkhood, may have dropped as a proportion of the male population.[64] It is most likely that it is not the extent and depth of religiosity which has changed, but the way it is socially articulated and publicly expressed.

Modernist styles of commitment have implications for personal experience. Traditional practices emphasize the intuitive aspects of religion; modern styles give priority to the intellectual. The Dhammayutikaya and the Muhammadiyah movements demythologize Buddhism and Islam respectively, echoing themes in contemporary Christian theology. Each modernism presents the essence of religion, disentangled from the ritual, mythic participatory, and intuitively apprehended aspects which used to be fundamental. Traditional education in Theravāda *wat* or Islamic *madrasah* was defined by attunement through sacred language. The significance of chanting in those contexts lay not in whether words were understood but in the act itself: emphasis was on experience as such, not on understanding of or abstraction about it. Within modernism emphasis falls on written words which everybody has equal access to, and the defining features of belief are outside and apart from inner experience— emphasis on rational apprehension is a natural corollary. As community is defined increasingly through literally seen and logically understood forms, there has also been a shift in emphasis from the heart to the head, from the intuition to the intellect within individual experience. Using Geertz's terminology, we can note that people are now more likely to have faith in religion rather than accepting it implicitly as a system everyone belongs to.[65]

The intensity of Southeast Asian experiences of the spiritual remains, despite the challenges of materially directed ideologies from above and social stresses from below. The most significant changes have been occurring not in outward allegiances, but more subtly in the ways in which cultural symbols now mediate access to what Southeast Asians in this era are able to know or believe as real. The most obvious axis of change in this

[64] Tambiah, *World Conqueror*, 267–8.
[65] C. Geertz, *Islam Observed*, Chicago, 1972, 61.

respect has been in the nature of adherence to beliefs, in the growing tendency to hold religious convictions as though they are ideological systems. In earlier periods most peoples of the region breathed their religion, experiencing it as an integral and multidimensional part of an inevitable social atmosphere. Within the now more obviously pluralistic world, religious experiences in the region assume increasingly distinct conceptual and institutional forms. In this era of internationalization and cultural encounter no specific culture or religion, indeed no system of symbols, appears able comfortably to claim the exclusive grip it used to.

BIBLIOGRAPHIC ESSAY

The information explosion of the postwar era is reflected in scholarship on Southeast Asian religions. This is thus strictly a preliminary guide to monographs in English which focus on religious changes in postwar Southeast Asia, and the concentration is on works which connect religion to general processes of cultural change. Only especially critical ethnographies have been included, though almost every ethnography contains important sources of insight into practices of and changes in religion. Many important contributions to the subject are contained in collections which appear here only as such.

For the Southeast Asian region as a whole the study by Kenneth Landon, *Southeast Asia: Crossroad of Religions*, Chicago, 1949, remains important both as an introduction and for the insight it provides into the state of religion at the close of the war. The most helpful recent general work of synthesis is Fred von der Mehden's book on *Religion and Modernization in Southeast Asia*, Syracuse, 1986. Two important collections, one edited by Alton Becker and Aram Yengoyan, *The Imagination of Reality*, New Jersey, 1979, and another by Mark Hobart and Robert Taylor, *Context, Meaning and Power in Southeast Asia*, Ithaca: Cornell University Southeast Asia Program, 1986, contain excellent insights. Relevant related shifts in communications systems, especially in media and drama, are covered in the survey by James Brandon, *Theatre in Southeast Asia*, Cambridge, Mass., 1967.

Charles Keyes' study, *The Golden Peninsula*, New York, 1977, is a superb survey treating social and religious changes on the mainland, including Vietnam, and Robert Lester's introductory survey, *Theravada Buddhism in Southeast Asia*, Ann Arbor, 1973, is a reliable starting point for exploration of the Buddhist countries. A more technical collection, edited by Manning Nash, *Anthropological Studies in Theravada Buddhism*, New Haven: Yale University Southeast Asian Studies, 1966, contains essays which map the field as it has been explored by postwar students of Theravada, and the journalist Jerrold Schecter's work, *The New Face of the Buddha*, New York, 1967, is grounded enough to trust and useful for the scope of its coverage of postwar changes in Asian Buddhism.

There are excellent studies of the interplay between religion and politics in the Theravāda countries. Emanuel Sarkisyanz, *Buddhist Backgrounds of the Burmese Revolution*, The Hague, 1965; Michael Mendelson, *Sangha and*

State in Burma, ed. J. P. Ferguson, Ithaca, 1975; Donald Smith, *Religion and Politics in Burma*, Princeton, 1965; and Stanley Tambiah, *World Conqueror, World Renouncer*, Cambridge, UK, 1977, are each landmark works with very wide relevance. Similar themes are touched on in the essays in Bardwell Smith's edited collection, *Religion and Legitimation of Power in Thailand, Laos, and Burma*, Chambersburg, 1978, and in a symposium on religion and society in Thailand in the *Journal of Asian Studies* 36, 2 (1977), including essays by Kirsch, Reynolds, Keyes and Tobias. A more recent study by Peter Jackson, *Buddhism, Legitimation, and Conflict*, Singapore: ISEAS, 1989, includes particularly instructive material on urban sects in Thailand.

Notable ethnographies deal with the interface between normative Buddhism and folk magic in the postwar era. These include Manning Nash, *The Golden Road to Modernity*, Chicago, 1965; Melford Spiro, *Buddhism and Society*, London, 1971, and *Burmese Supernaturalism*, Englewood Cliffs, 1967; Stanley Tambiah, *Buddhism and the Spirit Cults in Northeast Thailand*, Cambridge, UK, 1971; and Bas Terweil, *Monks and Magic*, London, 1975. Louis Golomb's fine and ranging study, *An Anthropology of Curing in Multiethnic Thailand*, Urbana and Chicago, 1985, and Ruth-Inge Heinze's more narrow one, *Tham Khwan*, Singapore, 1982, deal more exclusively with folk religion on its own terms. Apart from studies of village practice, there are a number of sources for insight into forest meditation practices. The most prominent is by Stanley Tambiah, *The Buddhist Saints of the Forest and the Cult of Amulets*, Cambridge, UK, 1984. Excerpts from the teachings of these teachers are well presented by Jack Kornfield in *Living Buddhist Masters*, Santa Cruz, 1977, and pertinent commentary on the same movements can be found in Donald Swearer, 'Thai Buddhism: Two Responses to Modernity', *Contributions to Asian Studies*, V.4 (1973).

Studies of Islam in Southeast Asia have only recently begun to achieve the depth the subject deserves. Ahmad Ibrahim, Sharon Siddique, and Yasmin Hussain have collected many of the most important postwar essays or excerpts on the subject in their *Readings on Islam in Southeast Asia*, Singapore, 1985. Michael Hooker's edited collection, *Islam in South-East Asia*, Leiden, 1983, is solid and the essays in it by Roy Ellen, on the ethnography of Islam, and Deliar Noer, on politics, are especially pertinent to exploration of postwar religious change. Taufik Abdullah and Sharon Siddique present a more patchy but still useful selection of essays in *Islam and Society in Southeast Asia*, Singapore, 1986. Like the latter, the collection edited by Raphael Israeli and Anthony Johns, *Islam in Asia: Southeast and East Asia*, II, Boulder, 1984, is uneven, but includes useful works.

Because Indonesia has been relatively open to Western scholars, a huge range of studies deals with social and religious change there. Rita Kipp and Susan Rogers have edited a collection of excellent recent studies, *Indonesian Religions in Transition*, Tucson, 1987, and an earlier book edited by Claire Holt, *Culture and Politics in Indonesia*, Ithaca, 1972, remains critical reading for any student of religion, society and politics in Indonesia. Three less uniform collections, each also containing much that is useful, are Gloria Davis, ed., *What is Modern Indonesian Culture?*, Athens: Ohio University

Center for International Studies, Southeast Asia Program, 1979; James Fox, ed., *Indonesia: The Making of a Culture*, Canberra: Faculty of Asian Studies, Australian National University, 1980; and Paul Alexander, ed., *Creating Indonesian Cultures*, Sydney, 1989. There are a number of highly useful survey articles on cultural change and religion in Indonesia. The most notable include Hildred Geertz, 'Indonesian Cultures and Communities', in Ruth McVey, ed., *Indonesia*, New Haven, 1963; Gavin Jones, 'Religion and Education in Indonesia', *Indonesia*, 22 (1976); and Julia Howell, 'Indonesia: Searching for Consensus', in Carlos Caldarola, ed., *Religion and Societies: Asia and the Middle East*, The Hague, 1982.

The political face of Islam up to the 1970s is treated at length by B. J. Boland in *The Struggle of Islam in Modern Indonesia*, The Hague, 1982, and recent currents are covered by Ruth McVey's essay, 'Faith as the Outsider: Islam in Indonesian Politics', in J. P. Piscatori, ed., *Islam in the Political Process*, Cambridge, UK, 1983. Deliar Noer's monograph on the *Administration of Islam in Indonesia*, Ithaca: Cornell University Modern Indonesia Project, 1978, and Daniel Lev's exploration of *Islamic Courts in Indonesia*, Berkeley, 1972, deal with the most important institutional changes in Islamic life. The most valuable study of militant Islam in Indonesia in the immediate postwar period is C. van Dijk, *Rebellion Under the Banner of Islam*, The Hague, 1981. Clifford Geertz provides the most probing suggestions about internal changes within the Muslim community in *Islam Observed*, Chicago, 1971. James Peacock, *Muslim Puritans*, Berkeley, 1978; Douglas Miles, *Cutlass and Crescent Moon*, Sydney, 1976; Mitsuo Nakamura, *The Crescent Arises over the Banyan Tree*, Yogyakarta, 1983, and Mark Woodward, *Islam in Java*, Tuscon, 1989, each bring grounded local perspectives which open insights into important aspects of change.

The most outstanding treatments of Javanese religion are Clifford Geertz's classic, *The Religion of Java*, Chicago, 1976, and Koentjaraningrat's *Javanese Culture*, Kuala Lumpur, 1985. Robert Jay's monograph, *Religion and Politics in Rural Central Java*, New Haven: Yale University Southeast Asian Studies, 1963, broke ground in connecting village religion to national politics. Studies by Niels Mulder, *Mysticism and Everyday Life in Contemporary Java*, Singapore, 1978, and Harun Hadiwijono, *Man in the Present Javanese Mysticism*, Baarn, 1967, concentrate on syncretic mysticism in Java. Robert Hefner's book, *Hindu Javanese*, Princeton, 1985, provides a historically and ethnographically grounded exploration of Tengger society and its interaction with Islam. Frank Cooley's *Indonesia: Church and Society*, New York, 1968, outlines the postwar position of Christian churches and Paul Webb, *Palms and the Cross*, Townsville: Southeast Asian Studies Centre, James Cook University, 1986, has explored the changing position of Christians in the lesser Sunda islands.

John McAlister and Paul Mus, in *The Vietnamese and Their Revolution*, New York, 1970, treated the intersection between spirituality and politics in Vietnam; Gerald Hickey's *Village in Vietnam*, New Haven, 1964, includes a solid account of village ritual and the local chapter of the Cao Dai sect; and Jayne Werner's monograph on *Peasant Politics and Religious Sectarianism: Peasant and Priest in the Cao Dai in Viet Nam*, New Haven: Yale

University Southeast Asian Studies, 1981, concentrates on the organizational face of the same sect. Martin Stuart-Fox and Rod Bucknell, in the 'Politicization of the Buddhist Sangha in Laos', JSEAS, 13, 1 (1982), and George Condominias, in 'Phiban Cults in Rural Laos', in G. W. Skinner and A. T. Kirsch, eds, *Change and Persistence in Thai Society*, Ithaca, 1975, provide insight into Lao practices. Ben Kiernan's essay, 'Orphans of Genocide: The Cham Muslims of Kampuchea under Pol Pot', *Bulletin of Concerned Asian Scholars*, 20, 4 (1988), chronicles the particularly disastrous experience of one of Southeast Asia's many pressed minorities.

Important aspects of religious change elsewhere are treated by Clive Kessler, *Islam and Politics in a Malay State*, Ithaca, 1978; Aihwa Ong, *Spirits of Resistance and Capitalist Discipline: Factory Women in Malaysia*, Albany, 1987; Susan Ackerman and Raymond Lee, *Heaven in Transition: Non-Muslim Religious Innovation and Ethnic Identity in Malaysia*, Honolulu, 1988; Alfred McCoy, 'Baylan: Animist Religion and Philippine Peasant Ideology', in D. Wyatt and A. Woodside, eds, *Moral Order and the Question of Change: Essays on Southeast Asian Thought*, New Haven: Yale University Southeast Asian Studies Program, 1982; Peter Gowing, *Muslim Filipinos*, Quezon City, 1979; Richard Lieban, *Cebuano Sorcery*, Berkeley, 1967; Michelle Rosaldo, *Knowledge and Passion*, Cambridge, 1980; John Blofeld, *Mahayana Buddhism in Southeast Asia*, Singapore, 1971; Tham Seong Chee, 'Religion and Modernization: a Study of Changing Rituals among Singapore's Chinese, Malays, and Indians', *East Asian Cultural Studies*, 23, 1–4 (1984); and Cheu Hock Tong, *The Nine Emperor Gods*, Singapore, 1988.

REGIONALISM AND NATIONALISM

For Southeast Asia the immediate postwar years (1945–8) were a time of change and turmoil. Dominating this era were problems of rehabilitation and aspirations for independence in the face of returning colonial régimes. The Philippines and Burma, along with India, Pakistan and Ceylon (Sri Lanka), parted from their paramount powers in a comparatively amicable way, and guidelines were laid down for an orderly advance to independence by Malaya and British Borneo; but there was little prospect for a peaceful transfer of power in Indonesia and Vietnam, and decolonization was to come to those countries through violence.

Between 1949 and 1959, Indonesia, Cambodia, Laos, Vietnam and Malaya attained independence, while Singapore acquired internal self-government, but these years coincided with the Cold War's spillover into Asia. While this was cold war between the superpowers, there were active war and revolution in many parts of Southeast Asia, where countries were often aligned with Western or communist blocs and faced internal struggles which moulded them according to rival ideological models. Intense power-bloc rivalry in Southeast Asia added to the strains of newly won independence. This contest led to the formation of the South-East Asia Treaty Organization (SEATO), backed by the United States, on the one hand and to Russo-Chinese support for left-wing movements on the other. Superpower competition accentuated internal divisions between radicals and traditionalists, subversives and constitutionalists. It also deepened rifts between states: communist and anti-communist, 'non-aligned' and 'neo-colonialist'. While the 1955 Afro-Asian Bandung conference was a significant step in the emergence of the non-aligned movement, in which Third World nations attempted to develop an independent stance in international affairs, this failed to spread harmony in Southeast Asia.

The following period, up to 1975, covered the Second Indochina War, which brought foreign involvement on a massive scale and dominated developments throughout Southeast Asia. It also coincided with the Cultural Revolution in China. But during this time the first steps were taken to develop regional co-operation. An Association of South-East Asia and aspirations to Malay brotherhood (the Maphilindo concept) foundered on the creation of Malaysia, which led to disputes about Sabah and to armed confrontation between Malaysia and Indonesia (1963–6). The first major breakthrough came with the formation of the Association of

South-East Asian Nations (ASEAN) in 1967. In the early 1970s the sharp divide of the East–West Cold War began to blur. The beginnings of détente between the United States and the Soviet Union were overtaken by the more dramatic rapprochement between the United States and China, the American withdrawal from active participation in the Vietnam war, and subtle changes in Japan's policies towards the region.

The communist victories in the three Indochinese countries in 1975 were seen as a major turning point at the time, and indeed had immediate repercussions for the rest of Asia. But in some ways the events of 1975 only confirmed certain trends already under way. China's Cultural Revolution came to an end soon afterwards, with the death of Chairman Mao Zedong (Mao Tse-tung) in 1976, followed by the beginnings of China's open-door policy, which would have significant effects on Southeast Asia. The new situation, intensified by Vietnam's invasion of Kampuchea (Cambodia) in 1978, put pressure on ASEAN to improve regional co-operation and achieve stability. By the late 1980s the communist countries of Indochina, the non-communist countries of ASEAN, and non-aligned Burma showed promise of peaceful co-existence.

THE CONCEPT OF SOUTHEAST ASIA

The concept of Southeast Asia as a political entity emerged almost by accident from World War II when, at the Quebec Conference in August 1943, the Western Allies decided to establish a separate South East Asia Command (SEAC), embracing Burma, Malaya, Sumatra and Thailand. The Potsdam Conference in July 1945 extended SEAC's responsibility to cover the rest of the Netherlands East Indies and Indochina south of the sixteenth parallel, excluding only northern Vietnam, the Philippines and Laos.

This military expedient provided a cohesive framework for a region which had never previously been seen as a distinct geopolitical area. No single empire had dominated the whole region in pre-colonial times. At the outbreak of the Pacific war, apart from Thailand, Southeast Asia comprised a collection of colonies and protectorates under the tutelage of Western imperial powers. And even Thailand's sovereignty and freedom of international action were limited. The external relations of the region were determined as part of each metropolitan country's foreign policy, without heed to pre-colonial feuds or friendships.

Although the period of consolidated colonial rule in Southeast Asia was comparatively brief, it produced fundamental effects not only on the various subject states but on their relationships with each other and the outside world after independence. Occasionally colonial rule strength-ened existing political structures and tried to take over their regional relationships, but more often Western rule had the opposite effect. The divisiveness was most notable in the separation of Sumatra and the Malay peninsula by the Anglo-Dutch treaties of 1824 and 1871. Elsewhere it smothered bitter feuds such as the traditional enmity between Burma and Thailand, or stemmed age-old developments like the southern expansion of the Vietnamese people and the waning of Cambodia. Often it encouraged the immigration of people from outside the region, notably Chinese and Indians who found opportunities in the colonial economies.

While there were stirrings of nationalism before World War II, the similarities of the imperial experience did not provide a stimulus for co-operation, and nationalism developed at a varied pace and in different forms in the individual countries.

The closest to a regional association before World War II was the Nanyang Chinese National Salvation Movement. The Chinese term 'Nanyang' or Southern Ocean had long been in use but acquired a new significance as Nationalist China tried to bind its overseas compatriots together in the service of the motherland. The Nanyang Chinese National Salvation Movement, which reached its zenith in 1938 in opposing the Japanese invasion of China, had its headquarters in Singapore and branches throughout Southeast Asia. For a short time Japanese aggression against China drew the Nanyang Chinese together in unprecedented unity. This was not proof against the political and cultural divisions within the Chinese community, but the concept—or spectre—of the Nanyang Chinese was a potent force in shaping postwar regional policies and attitudes of newly independent states.

Other external ideological and religious influences exerted some sway at certain periods but were generally divisive. Communism in Southeast Asia was fragmented and weak after the disastrous communist revolt in Java in 1926, followed by the split between the Kuomintang and the Chinese Communist Party in 1927 and the failure of the Comintern to establish an effective Nanyang Communist Party. The pan-Islamic movement, which played a dominant role in early Indonesian nationalism, lost credibility with the downfall of Sarekat Islam in the 1920s, while international Buddhism could not transcend ethnic and sectarian differences.

Yet despite the divisions, Western imperialism stamped a pattern across Southeast Asia. After wars of resistance by subject people and friction among the colonial powers themselves during the early days of their takeover, by the twentieth century territorial boundaries were clearly delineated and civil wars were over. Western imperialism brought peace and stability to the region, which was broken only by occasional upheavals, such as the Saya San rebellion in Burma. The various colonial régimes had many similar features: secular administration, a modernized bureaucracy and judiciary, Western-educated élites, an urban middle class, and economies partially geared to the international world system.

The colonial pattern was shattered by the Japanese invasion and interregnum. The Japanese Greater East Asia Co-prosperity Sphere, in which Southeast Asia was to play a vital role, proved to be more a political firebreak than a catalyst for regional cohesion. It disrupted colonial economies and political administrations without substituting an enduring new system. Nations emerging in the postwar world had to establish their own identity and create a new regional order. The variety of ethnic, cultural and religious differences added complexity to the situation, as did the revival of some traditional issues. Once more the region came under the influence of its powerful neighbours, India and China, which were themselves undergoing great changes. Southeast Asia was drawn into the superpower struggle between the United States and the Soviet Union. And later still it was to fall under the economic influence of Japan.

THE POSTWAR SCENE

A number of factors complicated the immediate postwar scene: the unexpectedly sudden end of the Pacific War, the problems of reconstruction and reorganization in war-torn Southeast Asia, the varied circumstances in which independence was attained, and the desire to create unity. All these were bound to complicate the regional and international relationships of inexperienced new states. There were additional problems: the presence of minorities with external links, the inertia of colonialism which continued after formal political independence had been achieved, the beginning of the Cold War, the communist victory in China in 1949, and the growing involvement of the United States in the area.

In the last stage of their occupation, the Japanese encouraged dialogue between Indonesian and Malay nationalists. Tokyo gave nominal independence to Burma and the Philippines in 1943, to Indochina in March 1945 and to Indonesia on the eve of the surrender in August 1945. But no metropolitan power was prepared to accept this, nor did the nationalists feel themselves strong enough to resist outright the return of colonial rule. While insisting on real independence within a short space of time, initially they preferred negotiations. This was true even in Indonesia among moderate nationalists, such as Mohammad Hatta, and in Vietnam, where in 1946 Ho Chi Minh was prepared to accept membership in the French Union for his Democratic Republic of Vietnam as a 'bourgeois democratic republic' in the first stage towards communism.

The 'firebreak' effect of the Japanese occupation made it nigh impossible to revive the ancien régime, even in places such as Malaya and the Borneo territories where the British were at first welcomed back. The Japanese victories revealed the vulnerability of the colonial powers, which were further weakened by the wartime drain on their economic resources. Japanese rule alienated the Nanyang Chinese vis-à-vis host ethnic groups, some of which collaborated with the Japanese. The occupation had given a taste of pseudo-freedom, while the Atlantic Charter and the founding of the United Nations provided international legitimacy for nationalism. This was further encouraged by disillusionment among the liberated peoples over economic difficulties, shortages and hardships in the aftermath of war.

Although all the Western powers attempted to reimpose their rule after the war, within twelve years most of the area had gained independence. Singapore, Sarawak and Sabah were to follow in 1963 as part of Malaysia, and two years later Singapore became a separate republic. Portuguese East Timor was annexed by Indonesia in 1975 and Brunei became independent in 1984. By that time the region comprised ten independent nation-states:

Brunei, Burma, Cambodia (Kampuchea),[1] Indonesia, Laos, Malaysia, the Philippines, Singapore, Thailand and Vietnam.[2]

The new nations were almost invariably the successor states of former colonies and dependencies and, with the exception of Timor, modern frontiers largely followed the lines laid down by the colonial powers at the high noon of empire. Despite Thailand's initiative during World War II in reclaiming sovereignty over parts of the Shan states, the northern Malay states and territory on the eastern border with Cambodia, the winning of independence did not lead in general to a reversion to the pre-colonial scenario. Indeed working out external policy was determined by many new factors: domestic needs; economic priorities; the continuing relationship with the former colonial powers; the reactions to the great powers; and the evolution of intra-regional relationships, which might involve both conflict and co-operation.

The two most important factors affecting regionalism and international relations in the immediate postwar years were the decolonization process itself, and the problems of creating national identity within the (often artificial) former colonial boundaries.

THE IMPACT OF DECOLONIZATION

The colonial powers returned with different approaches towards their dependencies in Southeast Asia. The United States and Britain had the advantage of returning as liberators against a repressive Japanese régime, but France and the Netherlands, themselves occupied during the war, appeared as imperial masters after the euphoria of liberation had dissipated. The United States honoured its prewar pledge to grant independence to the Philippines, but continued close economic and defence links, which were to be of new significance when the United States came to play a wider role in post-colonial Southeast Asia. France and the Netherlands planned to give their colonies equal status in a French or Netherlands Union. But the vagaries of domestic politics in Paris and The Hague, and the failure to meet Asian nationalist aspirations, led in both cases to wars of liberation. These ended with the breaking of political links—and, to a great extent, economic links—with the paramount power.

The British connection lasted longer, partly because colonial policy in Southeast Asia was not a matter for political rivalry in London, and also because legitimate movements to independence were allowed to

---

[1] The country adopted a variety of names in this period. Known as the Royal Kingdom of Cambodia when it attained independence in 1953, it became the Khmer Republic after Lon Nol took over in 1970. The Khmer Rouge adopted the term Democratic Kampuchea in 1975. The Heng Samrin régime established a People's Republic of Kampuchea in 1979 but reverted to the name Cambodia in 1989. For convenience, the name Cambodia is generally used here.

[2] Papua New Guinea, which became independent in 1975, is excluded from this study as being more traditionally linked with Australasia, although it has had observer status in ASEAN since 1976.

take a more peaceful constitutional path. Thus British economic links and defence responsibilities continued beyond political independence. Further, the Commonwealth concept was already well tried in the case of the old Dominions, and was sufficiently flexible to attract most newly independent countries, except for Burma.

Despite its legal independent status, prewar Thailand had suffered quasi-colonial infringements of its sovereignty, and its declaration of war on the United States and Britain and seizure of British and French colonial territory in World War II left the country in a vulnerable position in 1945. The resignation of premier Phibun Songkhram in 1944 helped to soften Allied hostility, since the successor civilian government was a front for Pridi Phanomyong's Free Thai resistance movement, which was closely in touch with the British and Americans. Nevertheless Britain and France wanted to penalize Thailand for its pro-Japanese wartime role, but were overruled by the United States, which in the early postwar years adopted an anti-imperial stance when it suited national interests. Britain insisted on compelling Thailand to supply rice at fixed low prices to the rest of Southeast Asia—a measure considered essential for the stability of the region—but otherwise the country's integrity was not infringed. In 1946 Thailand was admitted to the United Nations, where it aligned itself with the West. Bangkok welcomed American protection against Anglo-French retribution, and this broadened into a more general reliance on the United States in the difficult postwar world. After Phibun took over once more in 1948, the American alignment became even closer.

While Washington kept its promise of political independence for the Philippines, nothing had been done about the islands' economic reliance on the United States. In July 1946 the Americans transferred power to a conservative oligarchy, and for nearly thirty years the country remained their firm ally, economic dependant and military collaborator.

The British came back to Southeast Asia with new policies of advancing former dependencies to self-government. For Burma, which had achieved a fair measure of autonomy in the 1930s, the British War Cabinet proposed full independence as part of the Commonwealth as soon as the country was ready and the interests of non-Burman minorities assured. In the Malay states, the Straits Settlements and the Borneo protectorates, where there had been little overt nationalism before World War II, the British had approved schemes to streamline the political structure and prepare the way for eventual self-government.

In 1946 Britain separated Singapore as a Crown Colony and organized the peninsula into a Malayan Union, which in 1948 became the Federation of Malaya. Sarawak and British North Borneo were brought under direct colonial administration, but Britain deferred plans for changing the status of Brunei, which continued to be a protected sultanate. Subsequently the orderly transfer of power in Malaya and Singapore and the constitutional incorporation of Sarawak and British North Borneo into the Federation of Malaysia facilitated continuing military and economic links with Britain and membership of the Commonwealth.

But in Burma the apparent strength of the nationalists largely deter-mined the pace of political events. Aung San's Anti-Fascist People's

Freedom League (AFPFL) emerged from the war with such ostensible popular support that the British, with too many other priorities on their hands, went along with Burmese demands without securing adequate safeguards for minorities or achieving the degree of preparedness London had considered necessary. A constitution was agreed in April 1947, but three months later Aung San and most other AFPFL cabinet leaders were assassinated, and the premature granting of independence in January 1948 immediately plunged the country into civil war. Vulnerable and weak, the Union of Burma Republic was preoccupied with its internal problems. It joined the United Nations but not the Commonwealth, and to a large extent reverted to its traditional pre-colonial policy of isolation from the outside world.

Dutch attempts to force its colonies into a Netherlands Union and to isolate and undermine the newly declared Republic of Indonesia soured the independence settlement negotiated at The Hague in 1949. Provision for continued Dutch investment and commercial links laid down in the agreement foundered during the ensuing troubled years.

In Indochina the returning French administration did not recognize the independent régimes created by the Japanese. Paris re-established its authority in Cambodia and Laos in 1946, signing agreements with both countries providing for constitutional monarchies. But in Vietnam the French were unable fully to reimpose their power or come to terms with Vietnamese nationalism. By the end of 1946 France was engaged in outright war against the Democratic Republic of Vietnam, which was dominated by the Vietminh.[3]

NATIONAL IDENTITY AND UNITY

While international frontiers were a consequence of imperialist interests and not necessarily designed to create nationhood, they proved to be the least contentious issue in the post-independence period. With the notable exception of the Philippines claim to Sabah and the multinational claim to the Spratly Islands, there were few serious territorial disputes. Nevertheless the variety of sometimes incompatible racial groupings, including immigrant communities, formed during the colonial period left problems and tensions which affected regional and international relationships.

Some political leaders stressed cultural nationalism. They tried breaking free from the colonial past to build up a sense of national cohesion by using the language, religion or ethnic affinity of the politically dominant group as a unifying factor. This happened with the Buddhist religion in Burma and the Malay language in the Federation of Malaya. But such emphasis highlighted minority differences and tended to look back to conservative tradition. Elsewhere, as in Indonesia, or later in Singapore, nationalist leaders stressed a unity in diversity, acknowledging ethnic, religious and linguistic distinctions but adopting a secular approach with such common

---

[3] Vietminh: Vietnamese Independence Brotherhood League, founded in 1941 as a front organization of the Indochina Communist Party.

goals as modernization. On occasions independence meant transferring power from foreigners into the hands of a traditional élite or Westernized privileged class, which tried, at least in the early years, to maintain the economic and social status quo with the minimum disruption, as in the Philippines and Malaya. But more radical nationalists aimed, in over-throwing alien rule, to restructure society, eliminate poverty, and redis-tribute wealth more equitably.

Even Thailand, which had never been colonized, needed to establish an identifiable nationalism, which it had failed to do despite the 1932 revolu-tion. While the British and French had annexed many of the ethnically non-Thai border areas, postwar Thailand still had to come to terms with Malay Muslim separatism in its southern provinces and the influx of hill tribes in the north. Meanwhile, in Bangkok the pendulum continued to swing between military and civilian bureaucracy, usually in bloodless coups which caused little internal upset but made for unstable and shifting government policies.

Before World War II the Muslim Moro population of the southern Philippine islands had raised objections to the proposed granting of independence, which might subject them to the rule of the Christian majority, and indeed communal problems were to flare up later. But the immediate concern of the newly independent régime under President Manuel Roxas was to cope with agrarian unrest and communist Huk guerrilla warfare. For this the Roxas régime needed aid and recognized its economic reliance on the Americans, both for the immediate needs of postwar rehabilitation and for long-term development. In March 1947 the Philippines granted the United States military bases on 99-year leases and made a mutual defence assistance agreement. The interdependent questions of military bases and economic assistance would continue to dominate Philippines foreign and domestic policy.

Burma's chief need was to absorb non-Burman states and defeat com-munist guerrillas, while at the same time avoiding provoking its poten-tially dangerous neighbour, China. Prime minister U Nu, the AFPFL vice-president, who took over the leadership after Aung San's murder, was respected as an individual but did not command the allegiance of either the army or the left wing of his party. Within a year of independence Burma was torn apart by the insurgency of communists, former Burma Independence Army soldiers, Karens and hill tribes, so that the U Nu government exerted little control outside the urban areas. The consequent instability and preoccupation with establishing national cohesion, com-bined with its vulnerability, reinforced Burma's inclination to isolationism.

Some sense of Indonesian nationality evolved through the long struggle for independence, yet at the same time the bitterness of those years left many divisions, a fragile federal organization, a ravaged economy, and a dearth of administrators. The unleashing of guerrilla warfare during the anti-Dutch campaign bequeathed a legacy of violence, which was to characterize the new nation and perpetuate rifts between moderate secular nationalists, aggressive *pemuda* (youths), left-wing socialists, and Muslim fundamentalists. Indonesia's experiences during the fight for independ-ence made it suspicious of the West—not only of the Netherlands but also of the United States and Britain. British troops had reoccupied the Indies on behalf of the Dutch at the end of World War II, and Britain had withdrawn from the scene after helping to produce the unsuccessful Linggajati agreement.

Since the majority of Indonesians were Muslims, there was a natural inclination to look to fellow Islamic countries for moral support. In 1947, during the struggle against the Dutch, Haji Agus Salim, Vice-Minister of Foreign Affairs for the Republic of Indonesia and a fluent Arabic speaker, toured the Middle East. He negotiated a treaty of friendship with Egypt and obtained recognition for the republic from Syria, Saudi Arabia, the Lebanon and Iran. But Indonesia's internal needs meant tolerating diversity in order to achieve national unity, which led it to play down an Islamic image.

In Indochina the French and Vietminh remained at war, while independence for Malaya and Singapore still seemed a distant prospect in the late 1940s. Progress in the Federation was complicated by the outbreak of a communist uprising in 1948, and by the need to provide for the various racial groups in a country where the indigenous Malays were now outnumbered by Chinese and Indian immigrant communities.

REGIONAL LINKS IN THE IMMEDIATE POSTWAR ERA

Widespread anti-colonial sentiment in the immediate postwar years did not prove a regional bond since Southeast Asian nationalism was fragmented. This was true even before the lines were under-scored in the Cold War and the area became involved in superpower rivalry. In these early days independent countries often found that pressing internal needs precluded the ability to devise sound foreign policy, so that what policy there was usually stayed in a state of flux, engendering a fluid and complex international situation. Regional ties among the newly independent countries were slow to develop.

There was no obvious regional leader. While the Philippines boasted a nationalist movement dating back to the 1870s and was the first Asian colonial territory to gain independence—predating even India in this respect—its ongoing links with the United States made it a spokesman and docile ally of that country rather than an acknowledged pace-setter of regional nationalism. This was accentuated by the strong social and cultural influence of the Spanish and American colonial period, which left a Christian majority and the largest Western-educated community in Southeast Asia. Filipino statements praising the United States at an Asian Relations Conference held in New Delhi in March 1947, only months after the Philippines became independent, shocked other delegates, as did a statement at the Manila Treaty conference in 1954 that Filipinos did not regard themselves as Asians.

Thailand's status as the only traditionally independent country in Southeast Asia and the first to become a member of the United Nations, might have qualified it for a leadership role in the rest of the region. During the decade prior to World War II Thailand had shaken itself free of extra-territorial jurisdiction and in the period from 1938 to 1944, under Phibun Songkhram, had pursued an aggressively nationalist policy. Pridi Phanomyong, who headed the immediate postwar civilian government in Thailand, was a forward-looking radical intellectual, sensitive to the forces of nationalism in the region. Critical of the way the French were reimposing their rule in Vietnam, he showed sympathy with Vietminh aspirations and gave coun-tenance to a large Viet-Nam News Service, which was the Vietminh's spokesman in Bangkok. Thai ministers joined the executive of a Vietminh-sponsored South-East Asia League, formed in Bangkok in 1947, which collected together nationalists from Vietnam, Laos, Cambodia, Burma, Indonesia, Malaya and Thailand.

Sutan Sjahrir, then leader of the Republic of Indonesia, visited Bangkok in April 1947 and the Pridi government appeared ready to recognize the Republic of Indonesia. But Pridi was ousted in November 1947 and Phibun Songkhram returned to power, first as Supreme Commander of the Armed Forces and three months later as prime minister. A practical patriot, anxious to preserve his country's safety, as he had done so skilfully during World War II, Phibun took a more simplistic and less visionary view of foreign affairs than his predecessor. The South-East Asia League was banned as an alleged instrument of communist subversion, and the Phibun government refused to recognize or aid the Indonesian Republic in its struggle against the Netherlands, or to assume responsibility as a neighbour for the nationalist movement in Vietnam, insisting these were matters for the United Nations and the Great Powers to determine. In effect Thailand turned its back on left-wing movements and became increasingly aligned with the United States.

Despite the Union of Burma's genuine sympathy towards the Republic of Indonesia in its struggle for independence, the Rangoon government's general weakness and relative isolation prevented it from giving concrete assistance or playing any significant regional role.

Indonesia was the largest and most populous of the new states and gained prestige through its independence struggle. When the ill-fated Linggajati Agreement in late 1946 was seen as heralding the emergence of a United States of Indonesia, the Republic's Prime Minister Sjahrir was fêted in Malaya and Singapore. But the Indonesian leaders at that time eschewed any ambitions to link the Malay peninsula with Indonesia, and such a union would have been anathema to non-Malays and to many Malay nationalists in the peninsula. Indonesia hosted the Afro-Asian Bandung conference in 1955; it was to be acknowledged later as *primus inter pares* in the Association of South-East Asian Nations (ASEAN); and it had a special regard for Vietnam which it saw as the only other Southeast Asian country which was forced to fight the former colonial power to achieve independence. But Indonesia was too deficient both in men of stature and in resources to give any immediate regional or international leadership.

In the unstable and fragmented situation of Southeast Asia, the concept of regionalism in the immediate postwar years was a reaction to events rather than some preconceived plan. It was shaped in the main by a variety of sometimes conflicting external influences, ranging from personal initiatives to the activities of United Nations agencies and of foreign governments.

Individuals needed to be brought together before organizations could be formed, and often this was easier to do in Europe than in Southeast Asia itself. In the late 1940s the Malayan Forum, established by Asian students in London, provided a meeting place for the future leaders of Malaysia and Singapore and helped introduce them to prominent European left-wingers. In the same period the London-based Union of Democratic Control, run by Dorothy Woodman, attracted Indonesian, Vietnamese, Burmese and Thai nationalists and gave them a voice through radical members of parliament and the *New Statesman* journal. Indeed John Coast, a protégé of the Union of Democratic Control who worked for the Indonesian revolutionaries, claimed to have masterminded the Bangkok-based South-East Asia League, as a means of bringing together nationalists from the various countries.[4]

The United Nations provided an effective forum for Southeast Asia during this period, notably in Indonesia through the work of its Good Offices Committee in promoting the January 1948 agreement, and by channelling international pressures to secure the eventual transfer of power. The United Nations' Economic Commission for Asia and the Far East (ECAFE), which was set up in March 1947 with its headquarters in Bangkok, was important in providing a regional organization.

But the major force encouraging co-operation at this stage came from the overlapping and sometimes contradictory initiatives of Britain and India. In the closing stages of World War II the British government had envisaged a postwar regional commission in Southeast Asia, involving collaboration with France and the Netherlands, as part of a worldwide scheme for colonial development. But this concept was set aside in view of the strength of anti-imperialist sentiment, and concern that a regional organization might open the way to interference from the United States or the United Nations. Instead, in February 1946 Britain appointed a Singapore-based Special Commissioner, whose main function was to co-ordinate the distribution of essential supplies for the area. In May 1948 this post was upgraded to Commissioner-General for the United Kingdom in South-East Asia, whose parish embraced the whole region, apart from the Philippines which were seen as an American sphere of interest. His role would be to build up political influence so that—as the British Foreign Office saw it—Southeast Asia would look to Britain for 'spiritual leadership'.[5] At the same time Britain shifted the focus for co-operation from the other colonial powers to the Commonwealth, hoping that Australia, New Zealand, and newly independent India, Pakistan and Ceylon would become involved.

While the British considered that India in particular was essential to its plans for co-operation, Prime Minister Jawaharlal Nehru preferred to adopt the role of independent champion against imperialism. New Delhi

[4] John Coast, *Recruit to a Revolution: Adventure and Politics in Indonesia*, London, 1952, 52.
[5] Foreign Office minute, 9 Oct. 1948, FO 371/69683, Public Records Office, London.

tried to play a positive part, with varying success, in sponsoring national-ism in other parts of Asia through its embassies and by leading the anti-colonial lobby in the United Nations. In March 1947, in the run-up to its own country's independence, the Indian Council of World Affairs called an Asian Relations Conference in New Delhi, assembling representatives from more than thirty Asian countries, including Thais, Indonesians, Malayans, Burmese and Vietnamese.[6] While disclaiming any ambitions on the part of New Delhi, Nehru stressed that India was 'the natural centre and focal point of the many forces at work in Asia' and that to create '"One World" we must . . . think of the countries of Asia co-operating together for that larger ideal'. But the small Southeast Asian countries were reluctant to come under the thumb of India or the rival Asian giant, China. There was no support for Nehru's proposal to create a permanent Asian organization, and the communist defeat of the Nationalists in China killed the plan to hold a second conference there in 1949.

In January 1949 Nehru called another inter-Asian conference to deal with the situation in Indonesia at a time when the Dutch had seized Yogyakarta and arrested Sukarno, Hatta, Sjahrir and Agus Salim. The New Delhi conference demanded the release of the Republican govern-ment leaders, the withdrawal of Dutch troops from the whole of Indonesia and the transfer of sovereignty to a United States of Indonesia by 1 January 1950. A few days later the United Nations Security Council ordered an end to hostilities, the restoration of the Yogyakarta government and the reopening of negotiations; they led to The Hague agreement and inde-pendence. While many Asian countries were sympathetic towards the Indonesian struggle for independence, only India gave concrete support. The two countries shared a cultural heritage, and Nehru knew and respected both Hatta and Sjahrir. In turn the Indonesian leaders admired the Indian National Congress and were also attracted by New Delhi's independent policy in steering clear of power blocs. Nevertheless, neither Indonesia nor other Southeast Asian countries wished to pass from West-ern imperial rule to domination by an Asian neighbour, and Thailand, for instance, sent only an observer and not a representative to the January 1949 conference. Despite the bitterly anti-colonial tone of the proceedings, the delegates did not respond to Nehru's call to form a South and Southeast Asian body to oppose Western imperialism.

THE BEGINNING OF THE COLD WAR, 1948–1954

The effects of the Cold War soon spread to Asia, compounding the confusion and turbulence of the period, when governments were buffeted by conflicting ideologies and the backlash of Great Power rivalry. The

---

[6] Asian Relations Organization, *Asian Relations—being a Report of the Proceedings and Documen-tation of the First Asian Relations Conference, New Delhi, March–April 1947*, New Delhi: Asian Relations Organization, 1948. For a detailed account of the conference see Tilman Remme, 'Britain, the 1947 Asian Relations Conference, and regional co-operation in South-East Asia', in T. Gorst, L. Johnman and W. S. Lucas, eds, *Postwar Britain, 1945–64: Themes and Perspectives*, London, 1989, 109–34.

superpowers sought to manipulate newly emerging countries, which were faced with a choice between the conflicting role models of communism and capitalism as the means of achieving national cohesion and general development. Thus the dominating factor became ideology rather than the welding of different ethnic and religious groups into a national entity: it was the contest between left-wing and moderate nationalists that determined the character and international ties of these states.

Up to that point the Soviet Union and the United States were only peripherally involved in mainland Southeast Asia. Even after the formation of the anti-imperial Cominform in September 1947, Stalin dismissed Southeast Asia as a region of low priority. This view seemed to be confirmed by the speedy collapse of the Madiun revolt, staged by the Indonesian Communist Party in 1948. Nor, prior to 1954, did Russia see any advantage to be gained from the war in Vietnam.

While American activities were such that the thirty years from 1945 to 1975 have sometimes been described as 'the American era', in fact the United States was not significantly involved on the mainland until the advent of the Cold War, and even then it was a slow build-up. As the colonial systems crumbled, a relatively untried State Department was groping for a viable policy towards Asia. For a time, despite their anti-colonial bias, the Americans deferred to Britain's longer experience and greater immediate stake in Southeast Asia. In its global defence strategy the United States saw the British forces in Singapore and Malaya as a regional stabilizing factor.

Indeed in the early days it was Britain who tried to persuade the United States to become more involved. Despite lack of direct evidence, London suspected Moscow's prompting behind the communist risings which took place in Burma, Malaya and Indonesia in 1948. In November 1948 the Commissioner-General for the United Kingdom in South-East Asia warned London about the consequences of a communist victory in China, which would make Southeast Asia 'a major theatre in the Cold War'. In May 1949 he predicted that once China fell, Indochina would probably succumb in six months, followed by Siam (Thailand), then Burma and Malaya. By this time the British government was convinced of the roll-on effect of communist subversion, whereby the triumph of communism in one country would destabilize its neighbour, each falling in turn until the region was engulfed by communism. This was to crystallize as the 'domino theory' after President Eisenhower drew this analogy in April 1954. But in 1948–9 Washington rebuffed repeated British urgings to offer aid to South and Southeast Asia along the lines of the Marshall Plan in Europe.

Washington also discouraged the idea of an American-backed anti-communist Pacific Pact, which was mooted by President Elpidio Quirino of the Philippines as a parallel to the North Atlantic Treaty Organization (NATO), created in 1949 to contain communism in Europe.[7] President Syngman Rhee of South Korea and Generalissimo Chiang Kai-shek supported the idea, hoping to bolster their own flagging régimes. Chiang and Quirino met at Baguio in July 1949, when, with South Korea's support,

<hr/>

[7] Charles M. Dobbs, 'The Pact that Never Was. The Pacific Pact of 1949', *Journal of Northeast Asian Studies*, 3, 4 (1984) 29–42.

they agreed to invite India, Australia, New Zealand, Thailand and Indonesia to form an anti-communist Pacific front, as 'our answer to the threat of Red imperialism'. Australia, New Zealand and Thailand showed some initial interest, but from the start the Truman administration poured cold water on this scheme, and Quirino argued his case before the American Congress to no avail. Subsequently Quirino organized a conference in Baguio in May 1950, but felt compelled to exclude South Korea and Taiwan and to change from an anti-communist to a non-communist stance. Economic, social and cultural matters were discussed, but not security issues, and no organization was set up.

But behind the scenes the Americans were secretly reviewing their policies towards Southeast Asia, while keeping their options open on establishing relations with the new communist régime in China. In November 1949 Washington gave the first indication of its willingness to send aid to the region, and as Cold War battle lines became entrenched, United States policy became dominated by its commitment to contain communism.

China's intervention in the Korean War seemed to confirm American fears about a master plan for communist expansionism. At the end of World War II Korea had been divided into two states. When the communist north invaded the south in June 1950, the United States responded immediately and persuaded the United Nations Security Council to rally behind the south. China's entry into the war in support of North Korea, in November 1950, brought it into conflict with United States and other United Nations forces.

Deep-seated Sino-American hostility persisted for the next twenty years, throughout the Eisenhower, Kennedy and Johnson administrations. Washington backed Taiwan against the People's Republic of China, encouraged the British suppression of communist insurrection in Malaya, and gave considerable material support to the French in their fight against the Vietminh. In August–September 1951, the secretary of state, John Foster Dulles, main architect of American anti-communist foreign policy, negotiated three treaties: a mutual defence pact between the United States and the Philippines; a tripartite treaty with Australia and New Zealand (ANZUS); and a security pact with Japan. These were all part of the worldwide race between the two superpowers to secure the support of the Third World.

Meanwhile Britain pressed ahead with its plan to use the Commonwealth to build up regional co-operation against communism. Commonwealth Foreign Ministers, meeting in Ceylon in January 1950, resolved on a plan to provide economic and technical aid for South and Southeast Asia. Initially the Colombo Plan[8] was confined to a six-year programme for economic aid with a Commonwealth focus, but Britain hoped that it would extend its scope to include security matters and enable London to wield political influence in the region.

In every Southeast Asian country colonial or independent governments already faced communist-led subversive movements, which attracted a

---

[8] *The Colombo Plan* (Cmd 8080), HMSO 1950; Colombo Plan, *Report of the Consultative Committee on Economic Development* (Cmd 8529 of 1951–52).

strong following among some patriots, discontented minorities, and the poor. As an ideology, Marxism-Leninism had little relevance in Southeast Asia except in the minds of a small number of intellectuals. There was no large urban proletariat. Communism often conflicted with religious beliefs and the traditional order of society, including the attitude of both land-lords and peasants towards property rights. Prewar communism generally made little headway whenever the Comintern insisted on hardline ortho-doxy, which precluded a united front with religious groups, traditional élites or nationalists. But communism flourished during the 1937–45 Sino-Japanese War, when the Chinese Communist Party contrived to identify itself with Chinese patriotism. And during the Pacific War communist-led guerrilla armies attracted followings of patriots and used nationalist resist-ance as the foundation on which to build up a disciplined organization with a detailed political programme, as in the case of the Hukbalahap (the People's Anti-Japanese Army in the Philippines), the Vietminh, the Malayan People's Anti-Japanese Army, or the Burmese Anti-Fascist People's Freedom League.

In postwar nationalist movements the role of communism was ambiva-lent: in theory the international aims of communism negated nationalism, but nationalist movements in the region were often useful tools. During the long years of struggle against the French, for instance, the communist-led Vietminh and Pathet Lao attracted a large following of nationalists and anti-colonialists who were not necessarily communists themselves. Some-times communists failed to keep their hold over nationalist movements. In Burma, for example, although the Anti-Fascist People's Freedom League grew out of the Burmese Communist Party, the decision of Hubert Rance, the British governor, to appoint non-communist AFPFL leaders to the executive council in 1946 split the nationalists, and when Burma became independent in 1948 the communists took up arms against their former comrades. The Malayan Communist Party, which had provided leadership for the Malayan People's Anti-Japanese Army, found itself divorced from the mainstream of Malayan nationalism by the outbreak of the 1948 Emergency. But communism had special appeal for some minority com-munities, as in Laos and Burma. To many people in Southeast Asia, communism was the hope of the underdog, promising a fairer society with freedom from foreign domination, land for the peasants, and a better standard of living for the poor. It was difficult to rouse similar popular enthusiasm for anti-communism, particularly if this was identified with foreign rule or a wealthy indigenous élite. Also newly independent countries became disillusioned when they discovered that political inde-pendence did not remove economic dependence on the industrialized nations.

In the late 1940s communism appeared to be in the ascendancy, and many in the Third World perceived it as the way to the future and modernization. The major international communist conference held in Calcutta in March 1948 focused attention on communist activity in South-east Asia at a time when the communists were gaining the upper hand in China. The West feared the Chinese communists would support revolu-tions in neighbouring territories, either by direct military intervention or by logistical and moral support, particularly through their Nanyang Chinese compatriots. While rooting out communism, the colonial authorities and their non-communist successors needed at the same time to allay the political, economic and social discontent on which communism thrived.

In fact the period was one of confused ambitions for the communists. Their various revolts and wars in Indonesia, Malaya, Vietnam and Burma, were no part of a grand pre-planned Soviet strategy, such as Lenin's dream of communist revolution in Asia, or the Comintern's ambitious design to use China in the 1920s as the means of realizing this dream.

While the Soviet Union had shown little interest in Southeast Asia, apart from the 1920s Comintern interlude, the Chinese Communist Party posed a more immediate threat. From the late Ch'ing and Kuomintang régimes the People's Republic inherited the tradition of harnessing the Nanyang Chinese to China's cause. But as early as the mid-1950s Beijing (Peking) began to find the Overseas Chinese more an embarrassment than an advantage, and the People's Republic put its own foreign policy interests before concern for its overseas compatriots. Nothing approaching the prewar Nanyang Chinese National Salvation Movement re-emerged, and these expatriates remained divided by education, dialect, ideology and local loyalties. Nevertheless the perception of them as a potential danger and fifth column continued to play a significant part in shaping the attitudes and policies of Southeast Asian governments.

As the Cold War intensified, so did competition between Western and communist blocs for support in Southeast Asia. Direct interference further complicated the independence process and the task of nation-building. Ideology was not merely a question of the nationalists' chosen path in developing their states; it was also a reflection of Great Power influence. Southeast Asian countries faced often conflicting demands to counter militant insurgency while seeking constitutional advance, economic development and an improving quality of life.

Many nationalist leaders claimed to be socialists, although their interpretation of socialism could range from orthodox Marxism-Leninism to a liberal mixed economy. While the Democratic Republic of Vietnam looked to the communist world as its model, Malaya, Singapore, the Philippines and Thailand adopted a market economy as part of the international capitalist system. Others, such as Sukarno's Indonesia, while avoiding communism at home, wanted to break free from Western-style economies. Burma followed its own unique brand of Buddhist socialism.

Despite the obvious dangers of the Cold War, small nations could extract benefits in the form of economic and military aid as the price for their support for the superpowers. But often countries came to rely on foreign aid and put too much emphasis on suppressing dissidence and insurgency and not enough on fostering development.

The Philippines, for instance, relied on American military aid to suppress the Huk insurrection, which reached its height in 1950 and was only gradually brought under control over the next five years under the leadership of Ramon Magsaysay. As secretary of defence and from 1953 as president of the republic, Magsaysay succeeded in overcoming Huk resistance by a combination of military firmness, resettlement and amnesty. But transferring landless Christian peasants from Luzon to Muslim Mindanao promised trouble for the future. And while Magsaysay himself was a guerrilla leader and man of the people, United States support for suppressing communism had the effect of bolstering the ruling oligarchy even further. After Magsaysay was killed in an aeroplane crash in 1957, the Philippines returned to élitist dominance under his successors.

Manila became a natural anti-communist ally of Washington during the Cold War, and in January 1950 Dean Acheson, the American secretary of state, described the Philippines as a vital link in the world-spanning island chain that was the forward defence line of the United States. Filipino troops, financed by the United States, fought in the Korean War from August 1950, and in August 1951 the two countries signed the further Mutual Defence Treaty. For many years the United States tended to take the Philippines for granted. The republic gained considerable advantage from the relationship with the United States, but at the cost of economic and military dependence, which became increasingly unpopular at home and detracted from its standing abroad.

Meanwhile in Thailand Phibun's government moved steadily to the right and gained further American approval by sending Thai troops to fight in the Korean War, while keeping Thailand comparatively stable. The loyalty of the two million ethnic Chinese in Thailand was suspect, particularly in the wake of the 1949 communist takeover in China and because the Thai Communist Party at that stage was predominantly ethnically Chinese. Consequently Phibun revived some of the anti-Chinese measures which had characterized his earlier 1938–44 administration.

The bitter struggle for independence preoccupied Indonesia in the late 1940s to the exclusion of any concern about international Cold War politics. While the Indonesian Communist Party (PKI) was the largest in Asia outside China, it had recurrent problems because of its anti-religious bias. The 1948 Madiun revolt, which endangered the nationalists at a critical time in the anti-Dutch struggle, discredited the party for some years, branding communists as traitors to the national cause in league with foreign interests.

The PKI slowly rebuilt its strength in the early 1950s but was only one of several elements—albeit a major one—in Indonesia's precarious political balance. Within a year of independence the federal structure was abandoned in favour of a unitary state, and a provisional constitution was promulgated in August 1950. Agreement on a permanent constitution was delayed for years, since the provisional parliament was hampered by party discord and frequent changes of cabinet. With the end of the economic boom arising from the Korean War, political conflict became more intense.

The communist insurgency in the Federation of Malaya in 1948 resulted in the declaration of a state of Emergency which lasted for twelve years. Although guerrilla warfare did not extend to Singapore, the colony was subject to the same emergency regulations, which enabled the colonial government to counter communist guerrillas and left-wing organizations. At the same time the British and local establishment wished to undermine the Malayan Communist Party's claim that its Malayan Races' Liberation

Army was fighting for independence on behalf of all communities. For a time official policy discouraged legitimate radical dissent as well as driving extremists underground. But behind the scenes in 1949 the Commissioner-General convened a Communities Liaison Committee, which brought together the leaders of the different ethnic groups and, over a period of many months, hammered out agreements on the question of citizenship and economic development. The British also encouraged the formation of an anti-communist Malayan Chinese Association. From this developed a pact between the United Malays National Organization (UMNO), the Malayan Chinese Association and the Malayan Indian Congress, which formed a national Alliance to demand independence. A further part of the Commissioner-General's remit was to draw Singapore and the Federation of Malaya together and to create a Borneo federation comprising Sarawak, Brunei and North Borneo, as a prelude to forming a wider confederation embracing all five territories. But these plans proceeded slowly in the early 1950s.

While Burma's communists were strongly entrenched neither Russia nor China gave support to the insurgents at this stage, and with help from India by 1953 the Rangoon government was able to contain the communist rebels. Thus Burma seemed to be relatively immune from early Cold War tensions, immersed in its own internal problems but keeping a wary eye on its powerful Chinese neighbour. Burma was the first non-communist country to recognize the People's Republic of China, which it treated with particular circumspection, despite the fact that many of its border minority guerrillas were identified with communism. The end of civil war in China added to Burma's troubles when defeated Kuomintang troops fled across the frontier, taking to banditry which plagued the northern provinces for more than ten years. The authority of the AFPFL declined steadily as internal unrest persisted and the economy stagnated.

Indochina assumed increasing importance to the United States. In the last stages of World War II, the Americans were de facto allies of Ho Chi Minh's anti-Japanese guerrillas and were critical of French measures to reassert their rule in Vietnam. But after the People's Republic of China confronted the Americans in the Korean War, the United States saw the French régime in Vietnam as the best bulwark against the southern expansion of Chinese communism, and by 1954 Washington was paying two-thirds of the cost of the 'French' war.

But the French failed in their attempts to establish a non-communist nationalist government in Vietnam, which would attract the support of moderate nationalists favouring parliamentary democracy as an effective alternative to the Vietminh. The only leader with the ostensible standing for such an administration was the former emperor Bao Dai, whom the French persuaded to return to Vietnam in April 1949. Despite a series of weak coalition governments in Paris giving inadequate support to Bao Dai, he became widely regarded as a Westernized French puppet. The United States and Britain tried to persuade other independent Asian countries to recognize his régime. But neighbouring Thailand felt too vulnerable itself to take the risk. And India, whose approval would have carried the most weight with other Asians, refused to accept the legitimacy of a government which was backed by French troops.[9] Britain hoped the conference of seven Commonwealth countries, which was held in Ceylon in January 1950 to launch the Colombo Plan, would agree to support Bao Dai, but Pandit Nehru remained adamant in his stance.

Cambodia and Laos became Associated States within the French Union in 1949, but King Sihanouk sought more independence in defence and foreign affairs. He assumed the premiership in 1952 and the following year France transferred full control of military affairs to his government. A few Khmer Issarak (Free Khmer) guerrillas launched sporadic attacks in Cambodia, but in neighbouring Laos the situation was more tense. Refusing to recognize the country's status as a constitutional monarchy within the French Union, left-wing nationalists formed the Pathet Lao (Patriotic Front) under Prince Souphanouvong to fight for complete independence. By mid-1953 Pathet Lao troops, in conjunction with Vietminh forces, had overrun half of the country.

The People's Republic of China gave substantial help to North Vietnam, where the whole population was marshalled into conducting a people's war, under the brilliant leadership of General Vo Nguyen Giap, and in 1954 Hanoi inflicted a crushing defeat on the French at Dien Bien Phu.

While the fighting was still going on in Vietnam and Laos, negotiations were in train at Geneva to settle the future of Indochina. The Geneva Agreement of July 1954 ended French rule but did not bring a lasting peace, and Hanoi failed to get the immediate reunification of Vietnam. Instead the country was partitioned along the seventeenth parallel, with provision for nationwide elections to be held two years later. Assuming that the agreement would exclude American military interference in Indochina and that the elections would reunite the country, Russia and China persuaded the Vietminh to accept less than their spectacular military victory might justify. But these assumptions did not materialize. Failure to fulfil the Geneva Agreement perpetuated the division of Vietnam for more than twenty years and led eventually to massive direct American intervention.

THE SOUTH-EAST ASIA TREATY ORGANIZATION

The South-East Asia Treaty Organization (SEATO), brain-child of John Foster Dulles, the US secretary of state, was formed consequent to the 1954 Geneva Agreement on Indochina. Delegates from Australia, France, New Zealand, Pakistan, the Philippines, Thailand, Britain and the United States, meeting in Manila in September 1954, agreed on a South-East Asia Collective Defence Treaty.[10] At the same time, at the urging of President Magsaysay of the Philippines, they promulgated a Pacific Charter, which undertook to uphold the principle of equal rights and self-determination under the United Nations and to try by peaceful means to promote self-government and independence of 'all countries whose peoples desire it

---

[9] C. M. Turnbull, 'Britain and Vietnam, 1948–55', *War and Society*, 6, 2 (1988) 102–24.
[10] South-East Asia Collective Defence Treaty (Miscellaneous No. 27 of 1954), Cmd 9282 of 1954–55; ratified by the United Kingdom, 19 Feb. 1955, Cmnd 265 of 1956–57, Treaty series, 1957.

and are able to undertake its responsibilities'; to co-operate in promoting higher living standards, economic progress and social well-being in the region; and, under the South-East Asia Collective Defence Treaty, to prevent any attempts in the area to subvert freedom or destroy sovereignty or territorial integrity.[11]

The United States and Britain were the two main pillars of SEATO, but the negotiations for its formation underlined the growing division between the two allies. Britain's foreign secretary, Anthony Eden, hoped the Geneva conference would bring a lasting peace to Southeast Asia, based upon a compromise between all the parties involved, communist and non-communist. But Dulles had no confidence in the outcome of the conference, and in March 1954, even before it convened, he called for a joint Western stand to prevent the communists getting control in Indochina and for a formal collective security treaty, comprising the Western powers and Washington's Thai and Philippine allies. As Dulles declared publicly in March 1954:

> Under the conditions of today, the imposition on Southeast Asia of the political system of Communist Russia and its Chinese Communist ally, by whatever means, would be a grave threat to the whole free community. The United States feels that that possibility should not be passively accepted but should be met by united action.[12]

Eden refused to jeopardize the conference by opening negotiations for such a pact while the meeting was in session, and preferred a non-aggression Locarno-type arrangement which would include India and other Asian countries. Eventually, after the Geneva conference ended, a compromise was agreed in which Britain dropped the broad non-aggression concept and wider Asian membership, while the United States gave up the idea of a military alliance with a unified field command. It meant that from the beginning SEATO was flawed by dissension between the two main architects.

The Pacific Charter claimed to be 'inspired by the highest principles of justice and liberty', but SEATO roused intense suspicion among communist countries—particularly the People's Republic of China and Vietnam—which charged, with some justification, that the organization went much further than merely reinforcing the Geneva Agreement, as the United States and Britain claimed. In February 1955 Chinese premier Zhou Enlai alleged that the Manila Treaty was a charade and 'developments since signature of the Agreements have shown that the United States were using every method to wreck the Geneva settlements'.[13]

Even among the non-communist Southeast Asian countries, SEATO was seen as a foreign-dominated organization and 'regarded by some of its potential members as a more dangerous enemy than the enemy it is

[11] Pacific Charter, Manila, 8 Sept. 1954, Miscellaneous No. 32 (1954), Cmd 9299 of 1954.
[12] Department of State, *Bulletin*, XXX, no. 772 (12 Apr. 1954), 540, quoted in Charles O. Lerche, 'The United States, Great Britain and SEATO: a case study in the fait accompli', *Journal of Politics*, 18, 3 (1956) 459–78.
[13] Humphrey Trevelyan (British Chargé d'Affaires in Beijing) to Foreign Office, 26 Feb. 1955, FO 371/116921/1071/127.

supposed to guard against'.[14] But in view of recent Vietminh successes in Vietnam and the possibility of communist régimes in Cambodia and Laos, SEATO was welcomed by Phibun's Thailand when it established its headquarters in Bangkok, and the United States stepped up its economic and military aid to Thailand.

THE BANDUNG CONFERENCE AND THE NON-ALIGNED MOVEMENT

The polarization of international politics, with rival blocs and military alliances, in turn inspired the first Southeast Asian initiative for independent co-operation at Bandung in April 1955. The first Afro-Asian conference attracted representatives from twenty-nine countries, including all the independent states of Southeast Asia. It arose indirectly from the Colombo Plan, which by the end of 1954 had drawn in all the countries of Southeast Asia, apart from the Democratic Republic of Vietnam. While the Colombo Plan continued to concentrate on economic affairs, it strengthened contacts between the nations of South and Southeast Asia, and it was the 'Colombo powers' that sponsored the Bandung conference.

The conference did not result in the creation of a permanent organization for Asian co-operation, but it was the springboard for the non-aligned movement. As early as 1949 Pandit Nehru had said that India should adopt non-alignment as 'a positive and vital policy that flows from our struggle for freedom'. Non-alignment did not mean negative neutrality or pacifism but active independent participation in international relations. It was an expression of independence and separate identity, with peaceful co-existence as one of its central principles. This philosophy appealed to other nations newly emerging from the colonial experience and seeking a role for themselves in world politics divorced from any subservience to contending blocs.

Nehru and Zhou Enlai were the dominating characters at the Bandung conference, and Pancasila (Five Principles of Peaceful Co-Existence) became the stated instrument of Indian and Chinese foreign policy. But while China could claim to be a Third World country—and indeed Mao coined the term—its commitment to communism excluded it from the non-aligned movement which formally emerged in the early 1960s.

Up to this point India enjoyed a special place and prestige in Southeast Asian affairs, and it chaired the International Control Commission, comprising also Poland and Canada, which was appointed to oversee the implementation of the 1954 Geneva Agreement. But in the late 1950s India's prestige and influence waned for a variety of reasons, including the continuing dispute with Pakistan over Kashmir, the rift with China, and the declining powers of the ageing Nehru. Even at his peak, Nehru's approach to foreign policy tended to be simplistic and naive. His rather negative attitude towards the attempts at building up an independent

[14] Rupert Emerson, 'South and South-East Asia as a Political Region' in Saul Rose, ed., *Politics in Southern Asia*, London, 1963, 4 (being papers of a 1961 Oxford symposium).

non-communist government in South Vietnam in the early 1950s contrasted with the positive support which his government gave to the Indonesian republic in its fight against the Dutch in the late 1940s. While Nehru wanted to discourage the spread of communism in India itself, he misjudged Ho Chi Minh as a simple nationalist at heart rather than a hardline 'Kremlin communist'. And he failed to keep on good terms with China. China's brutal suppression of a rebellion in Tibet in 1959 sent refugees flooding into India and brought the two countries face to face across disputed boundaries, escalating into open war in 1962.

While Nehru gave birth to the idea of non-alignment, which the Bandung conference promoted, the decline of Indian influence, the exclusion of China and the admission of European and increasing numbers of African states to the non-aligned movement, shifted its focus away from Asia, and its relevance to Southeast Asian countries became vague.

REGIONAL TENSIONS AND PROBLEMS

Many tensions within the region acted as a brake on regional co-operation in the late 1950s: the continuing division of Vietnam and the Vietminh government's ambitions for hegemony in Indochina, set against internal subversion and instability in most Southeast Asian countries. Fears about the spread of communism were countered by allegations of neo-colonialism and Western imperialism. By the late 1950s most of the region was free from direct Western colonial rule, but all countries, whether independent or aspiring to early independence, still faced internal strains and external pressures. Inevitably the transfer of power disrupted administrative efficiency, sometimes to a major degree. Far from healing internal divisions, independence often exacerbated them, and all states faced the same continuing communist-led insurgencies as their colonial predecessors had done. Not all revolutionary leaders possessed the qualities needed to rule effectively in the more mundane post-independence climate. Some countries experienced disappointment when political independence did not bring immediate economic benefits, while in some cases the continued economic or military dependence on former colonial powers led to charges of neo-colonialism.

The Sino–Soviet split in 1960 created new problems for communists and their sympathizers in Southeast Asia. While President Sukarno had accepted a great deal of Russian equipment, after 1960 he and the Indonesian Communist Party leaned towards Beijing rather than Moscow. In Malaysia and the Philippines bitter feuds between rival pro-Russian and Maoist sects and sub-sects weakened the communist cause. Ho Chi Minh hoped for reconciliation between the two communist giants right up to the time of his death in 1969, and in the short term North Vietnam profited by keeping on good terms with both countries, which vied in giving Hanoi their support. Ho continued to emulate the Maoist Chinese model of development, which he considered more relevant to Vietnam. But it was the Soviet Union which supplied substantial economic aid for the Democratic

Republic's first five-year economic development plan (1961–5), and Hanoi turned increasingly to Moscow for vital military equipment and aid.

Meanwhile in Saigon the United States gave support to Ngo Dinh Diem, an ambitious Catholic politician, who became prime minister in 1954 and president of South Vietnam after a rigged election the following year. On the grounds that South Vietnam was not a party to the Geneva Agreement, Diem, with American backing, refused to hold the nation-wide elections laid down for July 1956, which would undoubtedly have resulted in a communist-dominated reunification. This refusal, and the excesses of Diem's régime, led to the creation in 1959 of a communist-led Vietminh-backed National Front for the Liberation of South Vietnam, known as the Vietcong. It formed a Provisional Revolutionary Government to work in the countryside in South Vietnam, setting up its own schools, seizing and redistributing land to peasants and encouraging them not to pay taxes to the Diem government.

By 1961 the Geneva settlement had completely broken down and Vietnam had reverted to all-out civil war. In October 1961 Diem declared a state of emergency and obtained full powers from the National Assembly. He arrested thousands of political opponents, appointed his own family and friends to high office, and his attacks on the Buddhist church brought opposition from the General Association of Vietnamese Buddhists, sparking off protests and public self-immolation by monks. While opposition mounted against Diem, the Vietcong attracted support not only from radicals but from anti-Diem patriots and peasants, who were disillusioned with only token land reforms. By the end of 1962 the Vietcong claimed to control two-thirds of the villages in the south.

For many years Washington saw Diem as a bulwark against communism and poured in resources to back him. In 1961 President John Kennedy sent the first American military advisers, thus taking the first major step leading to a dramatic escalation of American involvement. But while Diem was regarded in Saigon as an American puppet, in fact he refused to bend to Washington's will and became increasingly an embarrassment, until in 1963 the Americans allegedly connived at a plot by Vietnamese army officers to oust and kill Diem.

A Revolutionary Military Council took over after Diem's death, and the war intensified, leading to the build-up of conventional American forces during the presidency of Lyndon Johnson (1963–8). In 1965 the Johnson régime began the systematic heavy bombing of the north, and by 1967 the United States had more than half a million men under arms in support of the Saigon régime. Diem's successors proved more amenable puppet material, notably Major General Nguyen Van Thieu, who became president of South Vietnam in 1967 under a new American-style constitution and remained in power until the republic fell in 1975.

Although Laos was on the periphery of the Cold War, its proximity to Vietnam gave it strategic importance. Under the Geneva Agreement the Pathet Lao were permitted to occupy the two northern provinces 'temporarily' but this developed into a permanent occupation, leaving the royal government weak and vulnerable. The United States poured in aid and sent advisers to Vientiane in an endeavour to shore up the administration.

But Laos lacked the means effectively to channel foreign aid, which was of little help to the remote and poverty-stricken rural population. Consequently, over the years the communist Pathet Lao was able to consolidate its support among the peasantry.

In 1961 a second international conference was called at Geneva to try to resolve the problems of Laos and provide international guarantees for its neutralization. After fifteen months' debate the conference achieved a degree of accord, setting up a coalition régime under neutralist Prince Souvanna Phouma, with Pathet Lao participation. But the treaty arrangements soon broke down, and Laos degenerated into civil war. This intensified as the war escalated in neighbouring Vietnam, and the United States bombed North Vietnamese-held territory in Laos.

Cambodia seemed more settled. Guerrilla fighting ended after the Geneva Agreement was signed, with French and Vietminh troops withdrawing and the communist-led Khmer Issarak giving up the struggle. In January 1955 the country cut remaining economic and financial ties with the French Union and the other Associated States of Indochina to become fully independent. The following month Sihanouk abdicated as king in favour of his parents, but formed a People's Socialist Community party (*Sangkum Reastr Niyum*), which won every seat in the September 1955 national election and swept the polls again in elections held in 1958 and 1962. On his father's death in 1960, Sihanouk retained political power as chief of state without reverting to being king. He seemed firmly in control, supported by the Buddhist hierarchy, which helped his government to promote 'Buddhist Socialism'. Cambodia tried to conduct a neutral foreign policy and at that stage received aid from the West, the Soviet Union and China. But, wary of the dangers of becoming enmeshed in the Vietnam war, Sihanouk tried to keep on good terms with his communist neighbours, turning a blind eye to the Vietminh's use of Cambodian territory as part of the 'Ho Chi Minh trail', by which North Vietnam supplied the Vietcong. At the same time Sihanouk complained loudly about American violations of Cambodian territory, repudiated American aid in 1963, and broke off diplomatic relations with Washington two years later.

In Thailand, under pressure both within the country and from the West to liberalize the régime, Phibun legalized political parties, lifted press censorship and held general elections early in 1957, in which he managed to scrape only a bare majority in spite of blatant corruption. Later that year General Sarit Thanarat overthrew Phibun in a bloodless coup and arranged for fresh elections. But parliamentary government lasted only a few months and in October 1958 Sarit reimposed military rule. Sarit dealt firmly with the radical opposition, particularly the Communist Party of Thailand, while promoting economic development, education and social reform in order to dispel discontent. He also encouraged King Bhumibol to play a strong public role. But Sarit died suddenly in 1963.

Neighbouring Burma's elections in 1956 showed further decline in the ruling AFPFL's popularity, and U Nu retired into the background in order to reform the party and its policies. He returned to office in 1958, with a programme of conciliation involving concessions to the left wing and to the Shans, and an offer to consider setting up separate Mon and Arakan states. But these proposals roused much opposition in the AFPFL and the army. The AFPFL split into two factions, and, faced with the threat of chaos, in October 1958 U Nu invited General Ne Win to form a caretaker administration, which in the next eighteen months succeeded in restoring law and order, and curbing corruption and inflation.

New elections were held in February 1960, when U Nu's supporters were returned to power with a strong majority, but his liberal policies provoked great discord. In particular the adoption of Buddhism as the state religion, together with the concession of toleration to all religions, pleased neither Buddhists nor non-Buddhists. U Nu's announcement of his intention to resign as party leader that year, and as premier in two years' time, generated further uncertainty, and in March 1962 General Ne Win staged a coup. He suspended the constitution, imprisoned many politicians, and set up an army-led Revolutionary Council, with himself as chairman with full executive, legislative and judicial powers.

The 1962 coup was at first welcomed as only a temporary measure promising more orderly and efficient administration. But the Revolutionary Council ruled the country for the next twelve years. In July 1962 the council established its own political party, the Burma Socialist Programme Party, which became the sole legal party two years later.

A Revolutionary Council declaration in April 1962, entitled 'The Burmese Way to Socialism', aimed to complete the independence process by giving Burma control over its economy as well as its political system. It was an attempt to combine Theravāda Buddhism with Marxism-Leninism in a typically Burmese formula, by a pseudo-socialist economic system which it hoped would free the country from social evils and income inequalities. All foreign and most large domestic businesses, banks and trading houses were nationalized early in 1963; private trade was marginalized; and many thousands of Indians and Pakistanis were forced out of work and returned to their countries. Land was nationalized, land rents abolished, and the government took control of the rice trade. The aim was to do away with capitalism and entrepreneurial profit, but the economy remained stagnant; rice production dropped, with no surplus for export; and foreign earnings declined.

Immediately on seizing power, the Revolutionary Council confirmed its commitment to the principle of non-alignment, and Burma maintained good relations with both India and China, even when those countries went to war with each other. After 1962 Burma had even fewer contacts with international economic, educational and cultural bodies, refused to send students abroad and discouraged tourism. But Rangoon retained membership of the United Nations, the International Bank for Reconstruction and Development (the World Bank), the International Monetary Fund and the Asian Development Bank.

After the first national election held in 1955, the Indonesian parliamentary system soon disintegrated under the strains of the country's internal dissension and economic chaos. By that time the Indonesian Communist Party was recovering from the consequences of the abortive 1948 revolt, and Soviet President Khrushchev saw potential in Indonesia as part of his general policy of building up Russian influence in the Third World. In spite of its disasters of 1925 and 1948, the Indonesian Communist Party was still second only to the Chinese Communist Party in Asia. President Sukarno remained a revolutionary leader, eager to supplant Western orientation of the Indonesian economy, and he had personal ambitions to become a Third World leader of the movement against Western imperialism.

Sukarno's leanings towards the communists led Hatta to resign and displeased the army. Further resentment in the outer islands against increasing centralization by the Javanese sparked off revolts in late 1956 by army commanders who set up independent governments in Sumatra and Sulawesi. Martial law was declared throughout the archipelago in March 1957.

In mid-1959 President Sukarno formally abandoned the parliamentary constitution in favour of Guided Democracy under his personal rule, and the following year he formed a mass National Front organization, which stressed mutual co-operation between all elements of society. Although a brilliant revolutionary and a spell-binding orator with great charisma, Sukarno lacked statesmanlike qualities, and the six years of Guided Democracy (1959–65) brought economic chaos to Indonesia, with hyper-inflation, the collapse of its export trade, and shortages of food and other essential commodities.

The continuing campaign to suppress the rebels gave more power to the Indonesian army, who assumed control of much of the administration, including management of expropriated Dutch enterprises. As the army gained the upper hand over the rebels in the early 1960s, the dangers of a break-up of Indonesia receded and the rebellion formally ended in August 1962. Sukarno still needed army support but looked to the communists to counter domination by the military. He tried to run both the army and the left wing in tandem, playing one off against the other, yet turning increasingly to the communists, both at home and abroad.

In such areas as the build-up of the armed forces, President Sukarno bargained with the rival power blocs to secure advantageous terms. While the Russians were the ostensible winners, it was always on strictly commercial terms, and essential supplies dried up as Indonesia could no longer meet the Soviet bills. After the Sino–Soviet split, Sukarno threw in his lot with Beijing.

To divert attention from domestic ills, Sukarno embarked on foreign adventures, first claiming West Irian (Dutch New Guinea), which had been excluded from the territories transferred from the Netherlands under The Hague Agreement. Jakarta had abrogated the last links with the Netherlands Union in February 1956 and repudiated its debt to Holland six months later. When the West Irian claim was rejected by the United Nations Assembly in December 1957, Sukarno's government confiscated all Dutch property and enterprises and drove out Dutch nationals, including thousands of local-born Eurasians who had maintained Dutch citizenship. In 1960 Indonesia severed diplomatic relations with the Netherlands, and launched a further tirade against continuing Dutch rule in West Irian. The Netherlands put West Irian under United Nations administration in 1962 and the following year the territory was transferred to Indonesia.

Sukarno's next move was to denounce the formation of the Federation of Malaysia as a neo-colonialist plot.

MALAYSIA, BRUNEI AND CONFRONTATION

Proposals for a confederation of all British dependent territories in Southeast Asia were complicated from the mid-1950s by differences in political momentum in the various territories. Malaya gained independence in 1957, and progress towards self-government was speeded up in Singapore, but the Borneo territories remained political backwaters.

After the Alliance gained a sweeping victory at the first Malayan federal elections in 1955, the country moved rapidly to full independence two years later. The Alliance was a grouping of anti-communist communal parties, dedicated to preserving and expanding the export-oriented free economy of Malaya, and maintaining links with Britain and the Commonwealth, with its defence guaranteed under the Anglo-Malayan Defence Agreement.

With independence agreed, the Alliance offered an amnesty to the communist guerrillas, but this failed to end the Emergency which continued, officially, up to 1960. And the problem of reconciling economic divisions between the different racial groups—and notably between the Chinese and Malays—was further complicated by racial affinities either to communist China or to the concept of a Greater Indonesia.

Meanwhile the neighbouring colony of Singapore had embarked on cautious constitutional reform in 1948 when, for the first time, a small number of legislative councillors were elected by a restricted franchise. The pace of change quickened after a more liberal constitution was granted in 1955, and in 1959 Singapore attained internal autonomy with a People's Action Party (PAP) government, under Lee Kuan Yew, which was pledged to attain full independence by merger with the Federation of Malaya. Singapore's turbulent politics in the late 1950s and early 1960s, combined with the constant wariness of the island's Chinese majority and its commercial dominance, at first deterred Kuala Lumpur from any closer association. But by 1961 political unrest in Singapore reached a pitch where Lee Kuan Yew's government was in danger of falling to left-wing extremists, and the Malayan prime minister, Tunku Abdul Rahman, decided that merger with Singapore would be less dangerous than the risk of an independent 'second Cuba' on Malaya's doorstep.

To minimize the problem of absorbing Singapore, Tunku Abdul Rahman decided on a wider federation, which would also incorporate the three Borneo territories. This was welcomed by Britain as a means of providing a secure independence for these small, seemingly unviable states, and after protracted and at times acrimonious negotiations, the Federation of Malaysia was formed in 1963. The 1957 Anglo-Malayan Defence Agreement was extended to cover the whole of Malaysia, which incorporated Malaya, Singapore, Sarawak and British North Borneo (renamed Sabah).

The sultanate of Brunei opted out. London considered Brunei too small to stand on its own, but Sultan Omar preferred to seek internal autonomy, while retaining British protection. In 1959 a new but cautious constitution had been agreed, whereby Britain remained responsible for foreign affairs, defence and internal security, but Brunei acquired internal self-government. The sultan was to rule with the aid of executive, legislative and district councils, but only the latter were directly elective, and the sultan retained dominant power as chief executive.

Sultan Omar's wish to direct nationalism from above by means of paternal enlightened despotism brought him into conflict with the protagonists of democracy, led by Ahmad Azahari, whose left-wing Parti Rakyat Brunei (PRB) had links with radical peninsular Malays and with the Indonesian Communist Party. The PRB demanded immediate independence for Brunei, with full parliamentary democracy, as part of a federation of the three northern Borneo states. The party staged mass rallies and demonstrations, attracting considerable popular support. As a counterweight, Sultan Omar at first favoured joining the proposed Malaysia, as a means to acquire greater protection for Brunei from both external aggression and internal dissidence. But the PRB, fighting on an anti-Malaysia platform, swept the polls at the first district board elections held in August 1962. The following month Azahari formed an Anti-Malaysia Alliance with left-wing politicians in Sarawak and North Borneo, and rallied support in the Philippines.

Despite the strength of his constitutional position, in December 1962 Azahari needlessly resorted to armed force and declared himself prime minister of a unitary state of Kalimantan Utara (North Borneo). This alienated his more moderate supporters, and, with the intervention of British troops from Singapore, the sultan was able to crush the revolt within days. He proclaimed a state of emergency, proscribed the Parti Rakyat Brunei, imprisoned or drove its leaders into exile, and proceeded to rule by decree.

Initially the rebellion reinforced the sultan's enthusiasm to join Malaysia, but the final negotiations in June 1963 broke down, partly because of insensitivity on the part of peninsular Malays to the special nature of Brunei nationalism and the sultan's status in the proposed Council of Rulers, but mainly because of arguments about Brunei's oil revenues. In consequence, despite pressure from London and summit meetings between the sultan and prime minister Tunku Abdul Rahman, Brunei refused to join the federation.

The factors affecting Indonesia's opposition to Malaysia were complicated. There was an element of personal ambition in Sukarno's motives for promoting perpetual revolution and destabilizing the area. But there was also a measure of principle in his contention that colonial territories would achieve true independence only by cutting economic and defence ties—as well as political ties—with former colonial masters. Indonesia contrasted its own protracted fight for independence with the negotiated settlements achieved through constitutional means in Malaya and Singapore. Sukarno denounced as neo-colonialism the continuing links with Britain, and in particular the Anglo-Malaysian defence arrangement. Indonesia also felt some genuine fear that the far-flung Federation of Malaysia posed a physical threat. The proposed new grouping cut traditional links in the Malay world: the centuries-old contacts between Sumatra and the Malay peninsula; prewar Young Malay Union nationalism; the combination of Sumatra and the Malay peninsula into one administrative zone during the Japanese occupation; the aspirations of Ibrahim Yaacob's KRIS movement and the Malay Nationalist Party; the shadowy concept of an Indonesia Raya, which would embrace all Malay people. Malaysia was an artificial colonial creation, a consequence of British imperial rule. Sukarno's Indonesia itself was also an artificial relic of Dutch imperialism. But Indonesia gave support to Azahari's revolt in Brunei, and argued in the United Nations Assembly against the Malaysia proposal.

The Philippines also objected, and in 1962 officially laid claim to Sabah on the grounds that this came within the fief of the former sultanate of Sulu. In 1963 the Philippines convened meetings in Manila with representatives of the governments of Malaya and Indonesia to try to settle their differences, and the three countries tentatively agreed to a 'Maphilindo' (Malaya-Philippines-Indonesia) confederation. But this was unworkable. Sukarno launched a 'Crush Malaysia' campaign, leading to armed confrontation between the two states after the Malaysian federation was formed. This lasted for nearly three years and was marked by raids along the Sarawak–Kalimantan border and incursions into Singapore and the Malay peninsula. In January 1965 Indonesia left the United Nations in protest at the admission of Malaysia to the Security Council. While the Philippines did not join Indonesia in armed confrontation, it broke off diplomatic relations with Kuala Lumpur, and the Sabah claim was to be an irritant in Philippines–Malaysia relations for more than twenty years.

Confrontation was brought to an end only after a coup in Jakarta in September–October 1965 following an abortive attempt, which the army attributed to the Indonesian Communist Party, to eliminate the entire top military command. Hundreds of thousands of communist supporters were massacred over the ensuing months, and the party was outlawed in March 1966. In that same month General Suharto, the most senior surviving army officer, took over executive authority. Sukarno, who three years earlier had been made president for life, remained as nominal head of state for another eleven months, but finally surrendered all his powers to Suharto in February 1967. Suharto introduced a New Order to replace Guided Democracy. He called a halt to Sukarno's aggressive foreign policy, including confrontation with Malaysia, which formally came to an end in August 1966, and Indonesia rejoined the United Nations a month later.

THE REPUBLIC OF SINGAPORE

Meanwhile Singapore's incorporation into the Federation of Malaysia ended on a sour note in August 1965, when the island state became an independent republic. While merger with the federation and access to a Malayan Common Market had been central to PAP policy, the union was flawed by conflicting priorities, intolerance and distrust, aggravating communal tensions in peninsular Malaysia and sparking racial riots in Singapore. Secular urban Singapore did not lie easily with monarchist Muslim agrarian Malaysia. Arguments among leaders and resentment at interference in each other's affairs culminated in Singapore's attempt to mobilize the opposition parties in a cry for a 'Malaysian Malaysia', which by implication attacked the traditional role of the host Malays. Faced with the choice of separation or imposing direct rule on Singapore, the Kuala Lumpur government chose to let Singapore go.

This created new problems for the region. Singapore had long been regarded as an economic parasite, which produced nothing itself but battened on its neighbours' resources, conducting most of the area's rubber, tin and palm oil trade and prospering from smuggling into Indonesia. To complicate the issue, the republic was ill prepared for any form of separate existence, since no responsible Singapore politicians considered the island as viable if divorced from the rest of the Malay peninsula. To create a sense of nationhood and in an aggressive bid for survival, at first Singapore leaders adopted abrasive policies. As a cosmopolitan international trading city, Singapore needed to change its conception of itself from a largely immigrant Chinese colony to a multiracial society. To do this the republic stressed the rugged, energetic, competitive nature of its people as a whole, which often involved scathing comparison with its neighbours. This was particularly marked in regard to Malaysia, where initially prime minister Lee Kuan Yew promoted Singapore self-interest at the expense of future good relationships with Kuala Lumpur.

At the time of separation Singapore and Malaysia agreed to enter into a treaty for mutual assistance and external defence, but in the early years of independence Singapore continued to be dependent on the British military bases, both for a valuable (20 per cent) part of its economy and for military defence. At the same time the republic was keen to assert its independence and to avoid charges of neo-colonialism. To this end, in the immediate aftermath of independence, top ministers toured the world to explain Singapore's position vis-à-vis Commonwealth defence. The republic felt vulnerable, as a Chinese island in a predominantly Muslim sea. It therefore deflected resources it could ill afford into defence, both to deter aggression from unfriendly neighbours and to create a Singaporean identity by compulsory military service. But by using Israeli military advisers, it antagonized its Muslim neighbours.

In fact Singapore was no longer perceived as a threat to regional political stability. During the island's brief interlude as part of Malaysia, Kuala Lumpur had helped Lee Kuan Yew to neutralize local political extremists and in so doing had strengthened Lee's own position. The republic was a member of the United Nations and the Commonwealth, sheltered by the Anglo-Malaysian defence umbrella, firmly committed to developing its economy on free-market lines and to suppressing communism. And despite its precarious regional relationships, Singapore was eager to be a founder member of the Association of South-East Asian Nations.

THE FORMATION OF ASEAN

The Association of South-East Asian Nations was created by the governments of Indonesia, Malaysia, the Philippines, Singapore and Thailand through the Bangkok Declaration, which was signed by the deputy prime minister of Malaysia and the foreign ministers of the other four countries in August 1967.[15]

ASEAN replaced an earlier Association of Southeast Asia (ASA), comprising Thailand, the Philippines and Malaya, which had been created in 1961. Soon after Malaya became independent, Tunku Abdul Rahman mooted the idea of regional co-operation to combat communist subversion, and at talks with President Garcia of the Philippines in Manila in January 1959 agreed to a proposed Southeast Asian Friendship and Economic Treaty. Thailand's foreign minister, Thanat Khoman, was attracted to the idea of economic co-operation and tried to bring in all the other countries of the region, apart from North Vietnam. This failed, but in July 1961 the three governments agreed to set up an Association of Southeast Asia, as a loose association stressing economic co-operation.

From the start President Sukarno of Indonesia opposed ASA. While the association did not touch on security, its aims of economic development were designed to keep communism at bay, and the three signatories were aligned with the Western bloc for their defence: the Philippines and Thailand as allies of the United States and Malaya under the Anglo-Malayan Defence Treaty. Indonesian Foreign Minister Sumitro commented: 'The spirit behind the proposal is anyway anti-this and anti-that ... and Indonesia does not want any part in a negative policy in international affairs'.[16]

The proposal to form a Malaysian federation not only intensified Indonesian opposition but drove a wedge between the ASA partners themselves, when, in June 1962, the Philippines formally laid claim to Sabah. President Macapagal of the Philippines favoured the Greater Malay Confederation, or Maphilindo, as an alternative to Malaysia. It was stillborn.

ASA remained dormant throughout the period of confrontation between Indonesia and Malaysia, although Thanat Khoman did much to restore diplomatic ties between Malaysia and the Philippines. The association continued to exist in name until 1966, by which time the new régime in Indonesia was eager to bury the enmity of confrontation and seek regional collaboration. But Jakarta wanted no part of ASA, preferring to see the creation of a new organization, which would embrace the whole of Southeast Asia. While ASA failed to develop into an effective organization through lack of common ground between the partners, it was significant since it arose from local initiatives and referred specifically to Southeast

---

[15] ASEAN Declaration, in Association of South-East Asian Nations, *ASEAN Documents Series, 1967–1985*, ASEAN Secretariat, Jakarta, 1985, 8.
[16] Sumitro interview in *Far Eastern Economic Review*, 13 July 1961, quoted in Arnfill Jorgensen-Dahl, *Regional Organization and Order in South-East Asia*, London, 1982, 18.

Asian needs. Neither the New Delhi nor Bandung conferences had resulted in setting up any permanent organizations, and the Colombo Plan and SEATO were externally inspired.

While Burma and Cambodia refused to join ASEAN, the circumstances surrounding its birth were more auspicious than those of the early 1960s, which led to the rapid disintegration of ASA and Maphilindo. Adam Malik, who became Indonesian foreign minister in March 1966, was a statesman of high calibre and, while seeing the vital role of Indonesia as the largest country in Southeast Asia, was prepared to exercise restraint. Confrontation between Malaysia and Indonesia was over, and under General Suharto's New Order Jakarta was eager to restore harmonious relations with its neighbours. Ferdinand Marcos, who became president of the Philippines in January 1966, restored diplomatic relations with Malaysia five months later. As a newly independent republic, Singapore was still nervous about its prospects for survival. Moreover, these changes were set against the threatening background of escalating war in Vietnam. For the first time in the postwar era, there were genuine grounds for the non-communist powers to bury their differences and seek regional co-operation.

The first priority was conciliation: to heal the wounds arising from recent conflicts. From the start ASEAN saw itself as 'an Association for Regional Co-operation' but avoided any suggestion of forming a defensive alliance, relying rather on 'collective political defence'. This was a term coined by Thanat Khoman, who was largely responsible for reconciling the varied priorities and attitudes of the founding members of ASEAN. In theory security and stability took second place to the association's primary objective: 'to accelerate the economic growth, social progress and cultural development in the region'. But achieving peaceful accord would enable resources to be concentrated on fostering strong economies and social harmony, which were seen as essential to counter internal communist subversion and deter external interference. Apart from Indonesia, all the signatories depended upon the United States or Britain for their defence, but the Bangkok Declaration stated that foreign bases were temporary, maintained only with the express agreement of the country concerned, and not prejudicial to national development.

The Bangkok Declaration provided for collaboration in matters of common interest and maintaining close co-operation with existing international and regional organizations with similar aims. It was not meant to be exclusive: it held the door open for other Southeast Asian states to join, provided they subscribed to ASEAN's policies.

The highest policy-making body was the Meeting of Foreign Ministers, which convened annually in each ASEAN country in turn, and there were also regular meetings of ASEAN Economic Ministers and other subordinate committees.

The ASEAN countries were all anti-communist, bound together by fear of an aggressive North Vietnam and the perceived threat from communist China. Their governments tended towards authoritarianism, but with open economies. They were reliant on the market system of world trade dominated by the industrialized nations, committed to develop using foreign capital. They hoped to promote ASEAN commerce within and outside the region, to collaborate in practical matters such as transport and communications, to encourage tourism, and to foster cultural, scientific, educational and administrative exchanges.

But for many years ASEAN developed slowly. Its member states were a motley collection of diverse cultures and competing economies, paying only lip service to the association's ideals, and there were many points of friction. Tensions remained between Thailand and Malaysia in policing their common frontier: Malaysia was dubious about Bangkok's commitment to flushing out Malayan Communist Party remnants who had sought sanctuary over the border, while Bangkok was suspicious of Malaysian encouragement of the Muslim separatist movement in Thailand's southern provinces. Singapore's expulsion by Malaysia in 1965 embittered their relationship for many years, and the Philippines claim to Sabah continued to rankle. Singapore's insistence on executing Indonesian saboteurs in 1968, long after confrontation had ended, despite personal pleas for clemency by President Suharto, provoked violent demonstrations in Jakarta, during which the Singapore ambassador had to flee for his life.

By the late 1960s the polarization of the Cold War era was giving way to a more fluid and complicated situation, involving not only the United States and the Soviet Union but the People's Republic of China, the economic power of Japan and the growing cohesion of Europe through NATO and the European Economic Community (EEC). The most dramatic change arose from the total breakdown of Sino–Soviet relations, opening the way to eventual rapprochement between the United States and China. Consequently the measure of détente achieved in the Nixon era (1969–74) resulted in an ambivalent relationship between America and the communist world. These were unsettled times in which Southeast Asian nations had to adapt rapidly.

Meanwhile economic stringency forced the British to give up most of their defence commitments in the region. The cost of the Indonesia confrontation led to the British government's decision in 1966 to pull out its forces east of Suez by the mid-1970s—and two years later to accelerate this withdrawal date to 1971—leaving the United States with the prime responsibility for Western defence support for the region.

The Anglo-Malaysian Defence Agreement was replaced by a watered-down Commonwealth Five-Power Defence Arrangement (ANZUK), under which Britain, Australia and New Zealand kept small military contingents in Malaysia and Singapore with obligations to consult but not necessarily to act in the event of any external threat. Its effectiveness was never put to the test, and British, Australian and New Zealand involvement was whittled down in the ensuing years as Malaysia and Singapore built up their own military capability.

THE SECOND INDOCHINA WAR

The escalation of the Vietnam War from the mid-1960s drew Cambodia and Laos deeper into the conflict. While Sihanouk veered to the left in his foreign policy, at home he was authoritarian and anti-communist, combining traditional royal mystique with repression.

But criticism of Sihanouk was mounting by the late 1960s. The growing educated élite was against his idiosyncratic style of government, his frequent overseas travels and his intolerance of opposition. Peasant resentment of the heavy demands by the state and the Buddhist church was fertile ground for communism. The Cambodian Communist Party, or Khmer Rouge, had been in disarray since independence, but it began to revive from 1962 with the appointment of a French-educated schoolteacher, Saloth Sar, as secretary of the party's central committee; later, in 1976, he was to adopt the name Pol Pot. The Khmer Rouge supported a large-scale peasant revolt in the Samlaut region of northwest Cambodia in 1967, but this was put down with great brutality by Sihanouk, who continued to suppress left-wing activity, driving the Khmer Rouge leaders into hiding. Nor did the Khmer communists receive comfort from abroad. The Indonesian Communist Party was destroyed in 1965–6, and the North Vietnamese continued to foster their symbiotic relationship with Sihanouk. Hanoi's concern to safeguard the Ho Chi Minh trail and sanctuary areas in Cambodia outweighed any ideological considerations. Consequently the Khmer Rouge remained weak and divided, with Saloth Sar urging armed resistance to overthrow Sihanouk, while others preferred to lie low until a communist victory was achieved in Vietnam.

The most formidable opposition towards Sihanouk at this stage came from the right, notably among army officers who favoured a more pro-American policy, which would restore the benefits of foreign aid. While Sihanouk was away on one of his many overseas trips in March 1970, the National Assembly deposed him. The new régime, under General Lon Nol, tried to keep out of the Vietnam war, although in May 1970 the United States launched a month-long incursion into eastern Cambodia to attack the Ho Chi Minh trail. In October that year the country became the Khmer Republic, with aspirations towards parliamentary democracy, but the Lon Nol government became more repressive in the face of continuing resistance from Sihanouk's supporters and the Khmer Rouge.

In Vietnam, meanwhile, a surprise all-out offensive by Hanoi in the spring of 1968 (the Tet offensive) failed in its immediate military objective, but it helped to foster the growing disillusionment in the United States about the war and sapped the morale of its mainly conscript army. It led directly to President Johnson's decision not to stand for re-election in 1968, while Hanoi and Washington agreed to meet for peace talks in Paris later that year. Richard Nixon came to the presidency early in 1969 committed to ending American participation in the war, and in July that year he enunciated the Guam Doctrine, heralding the United States' military withdrawal from Vietnam.

This presaged a fundamental change in the international situation. The Eisenhower, Kennedy and Johnson administrations had seen South Vietnam as essential in stemming the tide of communist expansion, which the Americans believed would undermine the rest of Southeast Asia if the Saigon administration fell. A bi-partisan anti-communist policy in Washington had meant consistent antagonism to the People's Republic of China from its founding. Beijing reciprocated this hostility, but its break with the Soviet Union left China virtually isolated throughout the 1960s. Premier

Zhou Enlai realized that China could not confront both superpowers simultaneously, and overtures were made to Washington. Increasing opposition to the war at home, combined with a belated comprehension of the widening Sino–Soviet rift, led to changed perceptions of American interests overseas. The result was a dramatic rapprochement between China and the United States. In October 1971 the People's Republic replaced Taiwan as the Chinese representative in the United Nations and as permanent member of the Security Council, and in February 1972 President Nixon visited China.

The Sino–US accommodation appalled North Vietnam, which had regarded China as a staunch supporter for more than twenty years, during which time Beijing had given generous military and economic aid. China now urged North Vietnam to accede to American terms which would have meant the withdrawal of all foreign troops from South Vietnam. But Hanoi refused, and continued to fight with undiminished zeal. Under the peace terms finally agreed at Paris in January 1973, North Vietnam was allowed to keep its troops in the south after the American forces had withdrawn, while the participation of the Vietcong's 'provisional revolutionary government' in the peace negotiations implied its legitimacy. Although Washington continued to supply arms and equipment, the Thieu régime lacked any semblance of popular support and survived only on American economic and military aid. It was corrupt, it ignored the constitution, and it aroused opposition from a wide variety of people.

Similarly in Cambodia Lon Nol was largely dependent on United States support, while Sihanouk and the Khmer Rouge joined forces in an unlikely but effective united front. For several months in 1973 the Americans carried out heavy bombing of guerrilla positions in order to prop up the Lon Nol régime. But in December 1973 Congress ordered the bombing stopped, and by early 1975 the guerrillas controlled the countryside and were closing in on Phnom Penh.

THE ASEAN STATES

ASEAN was not yet sufficiently effective to take a common stance in face of the confusing and complicated changes brought about by Sino–American rapprochement, the entry of Communist China into the United Nations, and American disengagement from the Vietnam war. While for most ASEAN member states the traumas of the independence struggle were receding, in the late 1960s and early 1970s they were still largely absorbed with the tasks of nation-building and were unprepared for the dramatic transformation of the international political scene.

Malaysia survived the expulsion of Singapore without a major crisis, and after some initial friction Sarawak and Sabah gained materially from this wider association. But bitter communal riots in Kuala Lumpur and some other parts of peninsular Malaysia following elections in May 1969 were interpreted to mean that the policy of relying on a free-market economy to reduce racial inequalities was not working. Preferential opportunities made a minority of upper-class Malays richer, but left the mass of the Malay peasantry poor.

For a time parliament was suspended, and prime minister Tunku Abdul Rahman put administration in the hands of a National Operations Council under Tun Abdul Razak. Parliamentary government was restored in September 1970 and Abdul Razak became prime minister, putting renewed emphasis on consensus and unity. The new prime minister set out with considerable success to create a bigger Alliance by bringing most parties, including many from the opposition, under one National Front. A national ideology, the *Rukunegara*, demanded loyalty to the king, country and constitution, belief in God, and moral behaviour. Debate was banned on sensitive issues, notably the status of the Malays and the Rulers. And the government introduced a New Economic Policy, which was designed, through a series of development plans over a twenty-year period, to redress the economic imbalance between the different races. The policy did not aim to redistribute by large-scale transfers from one sector to another, but rather to give *bumiputra* (literally 'sons of the soil') a more equitable share in relation to foreigners and other Malaysians in an expanded economy.

While Malaysia continued to depend to a large extent on foreign investment and on world markets for selling its primary produce, Abdul Razak steered the country away from its traditional pro-Western stance towards the non-aligned movement and contacts with communist countries. At the non-aligned summit held in Lusaka in 1970 he put forward a proposal to make Southeast Asia a Zone of Peace, Friendship and Neutrality (ZOPFAN), guaranteed by the Great Powers. In 1974 Malaysia was the first ASEAN country to establish diplomatic relations with the People's Republic of China.

Singapore continued its policies of achieving national cohesion and rapid economic expansion. The 1968 announcement of the accelerated British military pull-out threatened the republic's economy as well as its security. Yet in practice the withdrawal proved beneficial, since the British handed over valuable defence installations and a trained workforce, together with a £50 million soft loan, just as Southeast Asia's boom in the search for offshore oil was starting. The crisis also enabled the government to instil new social discipline. The ruling People's Action Party swept the polls in 1968 and, from this position of power, the government took vigorous steps not only to build up its own armed forces, but also to accelerate industrialization and pass tough labour legislation. Political stability and economic drive enabled Singapore to reap the maximum benefit from the international boom of the late 1960s and early 1970s.

Of all the countries of Southeast Asia, Singapore was most dependent on world markets and the friendship of the Great Powers, yet it was determined to assert its sovereignty, control its own economy, and promote regional solidarity. As the immediate worries about survival faded, the infant republic's strident nationalism began to soften. From 1971 the government encouraged Singaporeans to invest in the Second Malaysian Plan, which was languishing for lack of public confidence following the May 1969 riots. Relations with Indonesia were repaired in an amicable exchange of visits between Lee Kuan Yew and President Suharto in 1973, with the Singapore prime minister putting flowers on the graves of the marine saboteurs his government had executed five years earlier. Some of these moves pre-dated the change in United States policy and were a positive regional initiative as distinct from a response to external activities.

Brunei's decision not to join Malaysia in 1963 soured its friendship with Kuala Lumpur, and allegations about Indonesia's involvement in the December 1962 revolt strained relations with Jakarta. The Brunei government officially revived a claim to the Limbang valley, which had become part of Sarawak under the Brookes in the late nineteenth century at the request of the local chiefs but without the then sultan's consent. Now Sultan Omar himself crossed into Limbang to drum up support. Brunei was isolated, more than ever dependent on Britain, while its autocratic government and semi-colonial dependent status laid it open to international censure. At a time when London was preparing to withdraw most of its forces from east of Suez, the Labour government in Britain was impatient at the slow progress of constitutional reform. To prepare for smooth constitutional change, Sultan Omar abdicated in 1967 in favour of his 21-year-old son, Hassanal Bolkiah, but for many years the ex-sultan remained the guiding power behind his son. A new treaty, signed with Britain in 1971, left the sultan in control of all internal matters and confined Britain to continuing responsibility for foreign affairs and defence. Brunei forged friendly ties with Singapore, after the island state was expelled from the Federation of Malaysia in 1965, but relations with Kuala Lumpur continued to be indifferent for many years.

In the late 1960s the internal stability of the Philippines was threatened by Muslim rebels in the south and by the communist New People's Army. The influx of Christian settlers from Luzon into predominantly Moro Mindanao compounded deep-seated Muslim hostility to Manila, leading in 1968 to the formation of the Moro National Liberation Front (MNLF). Pledged to fight for independence, the MNLF received material support from Sabah, whose ambitious chief minister, Tun Mustapha, was of Moro extraction. At the same time radical young communists revived the communist party, now renamed the Communist Party of the Philippines Marxist-Leninist, which created the New People's Army.

As President Ferdinand Marcos of the Philippines neared the end of his second term of office, which was the limit imposed by the constitution, he faced a challenge from the old traditional families, and notably from Benigno Aquino, who expected to be elected as the next president. In a bid to perpetuate his power, in September 1972 Marcos, warning of a communist takeover, suspended the constitution and proclaimed martial law.

The martial-law régime promised to build a New Society, based on stability, peace, substantial land reform and a more equitable distribution of wealth: 'constitutional authoritarianism' in place of the 'old order'. In the early years it seemed set to achieve its aims. A much-vaunted land-reform scheme was announced in 1973. The army was brought into mainstream Filipino politics for the first time since independence and strengthened to cope with the Muslim and communist insurgencies. Law and order were enforced in Manila by rigorous policing of crime combined with suppression of political dissidence. By 1976 resistance from both the New People's Army and the MNLF was broken. The top communist leaders were imprisoned, and a ceasefire was agreed with the MNLF, which lost its main outside support when Tun Mustapha was toppled in a 1976 Sabah election. Foreign investors regained confidence in the Philippines, and the economy boomed.

Marcos's New Society also aimed to win greater independence for the Philippines in foreign policy by drawing the country away from its close alignment with the United States. He put more stress on regionalism, strengthening ASEAN, and developing trade and diplomatic relations with communist countries, and identified the Philippines more closely with the Third World.

Whereas Malaysia, Singapore and the Philippines, while preserving links with the Western powers, simultaneously sought to gain control over their own economies and establish friendlier relations with non-Western countries in this period, Indonesia abandoned its left-wing orientation and looked more to the West.

The Suharto régime continued to consolidate its New Order under the slogan of 'national resilience'. Where Sukarno had championed anti-colonial revolution, Suharto stressed development and anti-communism. With an accent on stability, the army maintained its dominant position both in politics and the economy. Golkar, the government's party, comprising the military, bureaucrats and technocrats, won ever greater landslide victories at successive elections from 1971 onwards.

The aims of internal stability and economic growth also determined the New Order's foreign policy. Indonesia broke with the Soviet Union and China, holding the latter largely responsible for the activities of the Indonesian Communist Party and the attempted 1965 coup. While leading the way in encouraging the development of ASEAN, Indonesia refused to follow its allies in establishing diplomatic relations with China, and this suspicion of Beijing persisted into the late 1980s. Instead Suharto turned to the West and Japan for the aid, investment and technical expertise needed to revive the country's rundown economy. One of the New Order's early successes was to stabilize the rupiah and control inflation, and within a short time the economy was on the road to impressive growth. This underpinned the political stability of the early Suharto years.

The remaining ASEAN country, Thailand, under the rule of Sarit's chosen successor Marshal Thanom Kittikachorn, was increasingly affected by the escalation of the Vietnam war in the 1960s. Bangkok was anxious about Sihanouk's neutralism and displeased with the outcome of the 1961–2 conference, which set up a neutralist government in Laos. Thailand obtained guarantees of American support if it were seriously threatened and in exchange gave active help to the United States in the Vietnam war, providing troops and air bases.

Massive US financial aid helped to develop Thailand's communications and, in an attempt to deflect support from the communists, the Thanom government poured funds into social and economic development in the impoverished northeast. But by the late 1960s there was serious rural insurgency not only in the northeast but also in the extreme north and south, fomented largely by the Communist Party of Thailand, which by that time had lost its Chinese character and was predominantly ethnic Thai.

In 1969 elections were held to implement a new more liberal constitution, but Thanom reimposed military rule late in 1971 at a time when the first signs of American withdrawal from Vietnam caused Bangkok to fear the effects on Thailand. The clamp-down after this brief experience of more democratic government led to student unrest and violent mass demonstrations in Bangkok in October 1973. Thanom fled abroad and a civilian government took over.

Three years of uncertainty followed. This was a time of fluid volatile politics with coalition governments, first under Seni Pramoj, then under his brother, Kukrit, followed again by Seni. Groups of students, workers, professionals and intellectuals sought to take over from the military and bureaucrats who had dominated Thai politics since the 1932 revolution. The close alignment with the West also came under scrutiny. The turbulent period of civilian rule in Thailand from 1973 to 1976 occurred while there was radical change on the international scene: the 1973–4 world oil crisis, which halted economic growth; a slump in world commodity prices; and the communist victories in Indochina in 1975.

Meanwhile civil war continued in Burma, but over the years the government gained the upper hand. Beijing, during the early days of the Cultural Revolution in the late 1960s, denounced the Ne Win government as reactionary and gave help not only to the Burma Communist Party but also to the Kachin Independence Army. But Chinese aid to the insurgents dried up as relations with Rangoon improved from the early 1970s. By that time the Karen National Liberation Army was also in difficulties, and the government was able to exert its authority over much of the country. Twelve years of military rule came to an end in 1974 when a new constitution replaced the Revolutionary Council by a one-party state: the Socialist Republic of the Union of Burma. General Ne Win remained chairman of the Burma Socialist Programme Party, and elected People's Councils replaced the Security and Administration Committees in local government. But the government continued to endorse centralized economic development.

In Burma, Indonesia and the Philippines authoritarian régimes emerged partly in response to the need for security, and partly in the hope of achieving maximum efficiency in economic development and combating poverty.

As Cold War tensions eased and suspicions of ideological conspiracy faded, Southeast Asian nations responded in a variety of ways. Countries which had depended on an external defence umbrella had to rethink their defence strategy, building up their own defences, while working harder for regional security and co-operation. Partly because of the distancing by the Western powers, the non-communist countries of Southeast Asia came to review their own standing with their neighbours and the outside world. ASEAN countries responded less cautiously to overtures from the Soviet Union. They viewed Tun Abdul Razak's proposal for a Zone of Peace,

Friendship and Neutrality (ZOPFAN) with varying degrees of enthusiasm, and agreed to adopt it in November 1971 in modified form. Jakarta in particular was wary of Great Power policing for fear this might involve Beijing. The Indonesian foreign minister, Adam Malik, had long envisaged developing stability in Southeast Asia, so that its nations could preserve their own security without recourse to the support of outside powers. In consequence, the declaration by ASEAN establishing ZOPFAN was a vague document, aspiring to neutralization but providing no machinery or provision for Great Power involvement.

While the individual ASEAN countries gained in confidence and prosperity, ASEAN itself remained a relatively ineffective organization, and its members continued to confront each other on matters such as rights of navigation in the Straits of Melaka, establishing diplomatic relations with Beijing, and the nature of economic co-operation.

1975: THE COMMUNIST VICTORIES IN INDOCHINA

Paradoxically the consequences of the fall of Indochina to communist forces in 1975, long dreaded under the domino theory, were not realized. Instead the communists' triumph triggered off dissension and conflict within their own camp, which coincidentally set the stage for a move towards a measure of regional stability and cohesion in the rest of Southeast Asia. After thirty years in which nationalism and international alignments were strongly influenced by ideological reactions, from the 1970s the emphasis shifted to more conventional power politics. While external forces continued to be important in Southeast Asia, regional ties—notably ASEAN and the Vietnam-dominated bloc—assumed a more significant role in determining how those forces exerted their influence. Small nations found their bargaining position with great powers was often lost or reduced. Instead the Southeast Asian countries turned to closer co-operation with each other. Usually through self-interest, nations put behind them the disputes of earlier days and sank their differences to seek security through collaboration.

Nevertheless the speed and scale of the final communist victories in Indochina came as a shock. A triumphant Khmer Rouge proclaimed a revolutionary government in Phnom Penh in mid-April 1975. Saigon fell to North Vietnamese troops less than two weeks later, when Hanoi launched a final attack which ended in rout and the flight of Americans and their supporters by helicopter from the roof of the United States' Saigon embassy. In Laos the coalition government disintegrated over the next few months and the king abdicated, leaving the communist Pathet Lao as sole masters of a Lao People's Democratic Republic by November 1975. While these events had been foreseen, nevertheless they were recognized at the time as a dramatic turning-point for the region. The next few years were dominated by developments in Indochina and their effect on Southeast Asia.

While many of the dangers of the Cold War were receding, the communist domination of Indochina meant potential conflict within Southeast Asia itself, through a confrontation of two opposing blocs. Of the ASEAN states, Thailand and the Philippines had actively supported the United States' war in Vietnam and Cambodia, while the other three states had given moral backing and derived material benefits from supplying the American forces. Vietnam saw ASEAN as an anti-communist alliance, which could be used by the United States instead of SEATO to promote Western imperialism and neo-colonialism. ASEAN countries in turn feared the emergence of a militant communist Indochina Federation. With the largest battle-trained army outside the major powers, Hanoi had shown a taste for conquest. Residual worries about the domino theory still lingered, and ASEAN countries were alarmed lest Vietnam should sponsor communism throughout the region, either by direct military intervention or by encouraging or supplying local communist guerrilla movements from the stock of American military hardware left over from the war.

The situation remained confused for some months. While Vietnam, Cambodia and Laos declared 'militant solidarity', no Indochina Federation emerged.

In Vietnam the feared bloodbath of retribution did not take place, and a disciplined Hanoi leadership addressed itself to the task of reconstruction. In September 1975 the Vietnamese premier, Pham Van Dong, speaking on the thirtieth anniversary of the founding of the Democratic Republic of Vietnam, heralded a new period of peaceful reconstruction, in which Vietnam wished to strengthen existing friendships and build relations with the rest of Southeast Asia and all other countries on the principles of mutual respect, equality and non-interference in internal affairs. Vietnam at that time still hoped for normal relations with the United States and American aid on the basis of the 1973 Paris Agreement.

Vietnam proceeded with its prime object of reunification, and the two states were merged to form the Socialist Republic of Vietnam in July 1976. A five-year plan for 1976–80 concentrated on economic development and national unity. But, alongside repairing the ravages of war, the new republic aimed to promote socialist ideology and culture and to transform the economy from private ownership to socialism and state control within fifteen to twenty years. This demanded huge resources, and Vietnam was willing to accept aid from any quarter. It joined the World Bank, the International Monetary Fund and the Asian Development Bank, and forged trading links with Japan, India, Singapore, Australia, Sweden and western European countries. It was clear that a unified Vietnam must put greater priority on national rehabilitation than on continuing to spread international communism, at least in the short term.

In Laos initial hopes of peace and moderate reform turned sour in 1976 when the authorities began a programme of collectivization and the use of re-education camps. But over the years the régime stabilized, slowing the pace of collectivization, tolerating Buddhism, and accepting a fair amount of foreign aid from various sources. The leadership remained stable under prime minister Kaysone Phomvihane, secretary-general of the Lao People's Revolutionary Party, who continued to hold office into the 1990s. In foreign policy Laos stood firmly with Vietnam. Kaysone Phomvihane himself was half-Vietnamese, and senior members of his cabinet had close

Vietnamese connections. The republic made an agreement for co-operation with Hanoi in February 1976, but denied it was a Vietnamese satellite and insisted that the relationship was one of mutual friendship and respect.

The most dramatic change came in Cambodia, where the Khmer Rouge leaders, devoted to communist ideology but lacking practical experience of government, were determined to transform what they regarded as a stagnant and semi-feudal society as quickly as possible. On occupying Phnom Penh they ordered the immediate evacuation of all inhabitants from 'this wasteful consuming city' to labour in the countryside. A new constitution for a Democratic Kampuchea state of 'workers, peasants and other labourers' was proclaimed early in January 1976. Prince Sihanouk stepped down and, after some months under house arrest, went into exile in Beijing, while Pol Pot set out to eliminate the old régime, with mass killings of peasants as well as former leaders and intellectuals, and a ruthless purge of the communist party itself. Reportedly, more than one million Cambodians perished in the three years that followed, including five of Sihanouk's children and fifteen grandchildren. The entire population was drafted into restructuring society. Private property was nationalized, the Buddhist church was proscribed, the use of money was abolished, and people were forced into communal living.

Anxious to assert its independence, the Pol Pot régime preferred to rely on mobilizing Cambodia's own resources and regimenting the people rather than have recourse to general international aid. The Democratic Kampuchea constitution specified a policy of non-alignment, but, fearing a revival of traditional Vietnamese encroachment, which had been halted during the French colonial period, the Khmer Rouge leaders looked to China as a check against Hanoi's ambitions. In August 1975 Kampuchea signed an agreement for economic and cultural co-operation with Beijing.

ASEAN REACTIONS

Because of fears about Indochina, in May 1975 ASEAN foreign ministers met to try to work out a common policy, but member states were still divided in their attitudes towards Vietnam and the changed political climate. While Malaysia was willing to consider admitting the Indochina states into ASEAN, others were concerned that incompatible member states would undermine the character of the association.

Initially Malaysia, Indonesia and Singapore responded to the communist victories in Indochina by setting out to strengthen internal cohesion within their own frontiers: while stressing the need for enhanced economic development and social justice in order to maintain stability, the three governments also stepped up measures to counter communist subversion at home. Both Malaysia and Singapore took repressive measures against alleged communist subversives in the next eighteen months, while Indonesia increased its military capability with the help of American subsidies.

President Marcos of the Philippines and the Bangkok civilian government had already begun to draw away from their countries' military alignment with the United States. Marcos visited the Soviet Union and China, establishing diplomatic relations with both and with the new communist régimes in Vietnam and Cambodia. In 1976 the Philippines insisted on renegotiating its military agreements with the United States, agreeing to the continued presence of air and naval bases and US ground forces but at increased rents, for a limited period, and with a recognition of Filipino sovereignty over the bases.

As the only ASEAN country having common frontiers with Cambodia and Laos, Thailand was most directly affected by the communist victories: thousands of Indochinese refugees fled into Thai territory. Thailand was already engaged in combating serious insurgency on its borders with Indochina, and clashes with Lao communists on the Mekong River led Bangkok to close that frontier for a time in December 1975. But as early as January 1975 the North Vietnam government had put out feelers towards establishing friendly relations, and a Vietnamese delegation came to Bangkok immediately after Saigon fell. Hanoi's wish to see American bases and troops removed from Thailand and SEATO dismantled was in line with Thailand's current policy of distancing itself from the United States. This had started with the October 1973 civilian takeover in Bangkok in response to left-wing pressure, and the Kukrit government now ordered an American military pull-out, which was finally effected under the succeeding Seni government in July 1976. Thereafter full diplomatic relations were established with Hanoi, and Thailand then looked to the People's Republic of China as the best guarantee of containing any future Vietnamese ambitions. In 1976 Seni also compelled Malaysia to withdraw the police field force which it had maintained in southern Thailand under a 1964 Malaysia–Thai agreement facilitating hot pursuit of communist terrorists over their common border.

THE BALI SUMMIT

By the end of 1975 there was less Great Power involvement in Southeast Asia than at any point since the end of World War II. At the same time the non-communist states of the region had established some national cohesiveness and made big strides in establishing order and containing internal subversion. After the initial panic occasioned by the communist takeover of Indochina had died down, the other Southeast Asian states concluded that their best defence was to ensure internal stability and prosperity and seek a more effective regional consensus.

The ASEAN leaders assembled in Bali in February 1976 for the first summit meeting in the organization's nine-year history, which was preceded by a flurry of visits by leaders to each other's capitals. The occasion was clouded, a few weeks before it was due to meet, by the sudden death of Tun Abdul Razak, the chief advocate of the proposal for regional neutralization, but his hand-picked successor, Tun Hussein Onn, reaffirmed commitment to his predecessor's foreign policies. The Bali summit was a milestone, revealing a new atmosphere of confidence and a desire for effective co-operation. Two documents were issued: a Declaration of ASEAN Concord and a Treaty of Amity and Co-operation. A permanent ASEAN secretariat was also established in Jakarta, headed by a secretary-general to be chosen for a three-year term from each member state in turn.[17]

Invoking the United Nations Charter, the Ten Principles adopted by the Afro-Asian Bandung conference in April 1955 and the ASEAN Bangkok Declaration of August 1967, the Bali Declaration reaffirmed the goal of economic co-operation and the association's commitment to an early establishment of the Zone of Peace, Freedom and Neutrality agreed in 1971. It resolved to eliminate threats of subversion, but made no move to convert ASEAN into a military pact, its member states believing that such groupings tended to provoke hostile reaction without guaranteeing security.[18] The accompanying Treaty of Amity and Co-operation bound ASEAN leaders to rely exclusively on peaceful negotiations to settle intra-regional differences.

The Bali summit marked a progression from the aims of regional conciliation, which had been uppermost at the time of ASEAN's founding in 1967, to the goal of collective internal security, based upon promoting political stability and economic development within all member states. It followed the lead of President Suharto of Indonesia in seeing 'regional resilience' emerging from 'national resilience'.

When Vietnam was united in July 1976, Hanoi propounded a pragmatic policy of economic transformation, seeking trade and technical exchange with Southeast Asia, but Vietnamese statements about neutrality and co-operation were received suspiciously in ASEAN countries. At the non-aligned summit conference in Colombo in August 1976, Vietnam supported Laos in blocking the reaffirmation sought by Malaysia of its ZOPFAN declaration, which had been accepted at the last non-aligned conference in 1971. Instead Laos and Vietnam called for support for 'the struggle of the people of Southeast Asia against neo-colonialism', which brought shocked protest from Singapore and disappointment to the other ASEAN members, since it implied a challenge to their governments' legitimacy, and support for subversion.

Indochinese offers of friendship to individual ASEAN states did not extend to acceptance of ASEAN itself. While the Soviet Union and China spoke positively about the Bali summit, Vietnam vociferously criticized the organization as a substitute for SEATO, and Laotian prime minister Kaysone Phomvihane described ASEAN in 1976 as 'an organization set up by the US imperialists . . . to defend the interests of US neo-colonialism'. This feeling had probably intensifed as a result of President Gerald Ford's visit to Indonesia and the Philippines at the time of his China tour in late 1975, when he reaffirmed Nixon's Guam Doctrine and issued his own Pacific Doctrine, which drew a new American offshore defence line from Korea through to Japan, Guam, the Philippines and Indonesia.

[17] See A. Broinowski, *Understanding ASEAN*, London, 1982.
[18] A view propounded by Adam Malik at this time during a meeting at the ISEAS in Singapore.

Hanoi continued to call for the removal of foreign military bases, and urged developing countries dependent on commodity exports to co-operate in breaking the alleged Western imperialist hold on the world economic order.

Communist subversion was of greater concern to the ASEAN states than any fear of external aggression at this time. Establishing diplomatic relations with China did not bring relief from domestic communist insurgency, as Tun Abdul Razak had discovered. Indeed guerrilla activity increased in both rural and urban areas in Malaysia in the mid-1970s, following the Indochina takeover by the communists and continued moral support by the Chinese Communist Party (CCP) for its ideological comrades in Malaysia. Until the early 1980s the Chinese government adhered to its theory that friendly government-to-government relations were not incompatible with friendly party-to-party ties between the CCP and its counterparts in Southeast Asia, even if those parties were engaged in open revolt.

Singapore and Malaysia co-operated in clamping down on internal subversion, and in 1976 unmasked an international network of agents. This mainly comprised intellectuals and professionals, among them two prominent Malay editors and two Malay deputy ministers, showing that communism had penetrated even the United Malays National Organization.

In Thailand criticism of the inept Seni Pramoj government came to a head in October 1976 when the army intervened to suppress student riots at Thammasat University. General Kriangsak Chomanand, secretary-general of the National Reform Advisory Council, installed a new régime under prime minister Thanin Krivichien, who toured ASEAN capitals and found a ready response to his call for closer regional co-operation against communism. The Thanin government revived the border policing agreement with Malaysia which had run into trouble under the Seni administration. One year later, in October 1977, General Kriangsak took over the government himself, reaffirming Thailand's commitment to regional solidarity.

While the local Indonesian Communist Party remained shattered after the 1965 crackdown, the Suharto régime was concerned at the possible emergence of a left-wing state in East Timor. Following a revolution in Portugal in April 1974, Lisbon decided to abandon its imperial role and grant independence to its colonies. In January 1975 it pulled out of East Timor, leaving a weak coalition government comprising a right-wing Timorese Democratic Union and a militant Revolutionary Front for an Independent East Timor (Fretilin). Portugal's rapid disengagement caught Jakarta by surprise. While some Timorese favoured integration with the republic, Indonesia had never laid formal claim to East Timor, and indeed Adam Malik had earlier written unequivocally that the former Portuguese colony had a legitimate right to self-determination. The coalition government quickly broke down, plunging the territory into civil war, and in November 1975 Fretilin declared unilateral independence for a Democratic Republic of East Timor. Despite protests by the United Nations, Indonesia sent 'volunteers' to support the Timorese Democratic Union. The Fretilin leaders fled, and in July 1976 President Suharto accepted a petition from the pro-Jakarta government in East Timor to integrate the territory as the twenty-seventh province of Indonesia. Despite continuing Fretilin resistance and widespread international protest, the ASEAN countries overcame some initial hesitation to defend Indonesia's actions in the United Nations. International criticism died down, and Australia, New Zealand and the United States saw it in their own interests to accept the fait accompli, which averted the danger of East Timor's becoming a communist state.

While all ASEAN countries took measures to check subversion and strengthen security, they recognized that raising general living standards was the best answer to communism. As an outcome of the Bali ASEAN summit, a genuine attempt was made towards economic co-operation on programmes where each member was allocated a product to manufacture for tariff-free sale throughout ASEAN: diesel engines in Singapore; urea in Indonesia and Malaysia; soda ash in Thailand; and superphosphate in the Philippines. ASEAN ministers and officials met regularly to settle everyday problems: to co-ordinate policies on extradition treaties, sea pollution, anti-drug campaigns, and to work out a common stand on various international issues. But ASEAN was slow in breaking down tariff barriers, let alone establishing a free-trade zone. While developing friendly co-operation and combining effectively in economic negotiations with other countries, individual ASEAN countries were for the most part economic competitors.

They were even less prepared to sacrifice political nationalism, although they showed some solidarity in adopting a common voting pattern in the United Nations Assembly vis-à-vis the Soviet Union and Hanoi. But they did succeed in playing down traditional territorial and political disputes, notably the Philippines' claim to Sabah. At a second ASEAN summit meeting, held in Kuala Lumpur in August 1977 to celebrate the association's tenth anniversary, President Marcos indicated that the Philippines would take steps to waive the claim, although no formal action was taken to confirm this promise.

Despite a call by Singapore's prime minister for the Kuala Lumpur summit to give regional co-operation 'substance rather than form', the meeting did little in concrete terms to advance either economic or political co-operation. It was marked, however, by increasing international respect for the organization, notably by the participation of the prime ministers of Australia, New Zealand and Japan in post-summit discussions.

Most significant was the statement made in Manila by Japanese prime minister Takeo Fukuda at the end of a visit to Southeast Asian capitals. The Fukuda Doctrine of August 1977 committed Japan to the role of a peaceful economic power, working closely with ASEAN on terms of equal partnership, but acting as a 'bridge' to establish economic links between ASEAN and the rest of Southeast Asia. After the ASEAN summit Fukuda also visited Burma, where he offered similar grants, technical aid and trade facilities.

Japan had made spectacular progress in the third quarter of the century. The Korean War (1950–3) lifted the economy from its post-1945 trough, and the country prospered even more from the Vietnam War boom of the

1960s and early 1970s. Private Japanese investment in Southeast Asia increased from the late 1960s. Prime Minister Kakuei Tanaka visited ASEAN capitals in 1974 and after the end of the Vietnam War the Japanese government took steps to increase its influence in the region. In 1978, after six years of negotiations, Japan signed a Treaty of Peace and Amity with China and normalized its relations with Beijing.

As American interest in Southeast Asia waned, Japanese influence became more important. Some anti-Japanese feeling persisted; grim memories of the Japanese wartime occupation, coupled with resentment at perceived Japanese arrogance, sparked some hostile demonstrations against the Tanaka and Fukuda visits. Despite its disclaimer of political or military ambitions, Japan's economic strength provoked jealousy and suspicions of economic nationalism. Tokyo's main interests in Southeast Asia were its raw materials and its markets for Japanese manufactures, and the effects were to create uneven trade balances. Nevertheless, there was growing admiration for Japan's economic success, and many Southeast Asians looked to Japan and Japanese values as a role model for themselves. With its stress on economic development as the key to political stability, Japanese policy was in tune with ASEAN's aspirations. It was in Tokyo's interests to have peace, harmony and equilibrium in the region, to promote prosperity, to raise living standards, and to keep the Straits of Melaka open as an international waterway.

VIETNAM, CAMBODIA AND CHINA

Vietnam's relationship with China soured in reaction to Chinese détente with the United States in 1972, when Hanoi suspected that Beijing had abandoned Vietnam's cause in a deal with Washington over Indochina. This ended a friendship between the Chinese and Vietnamese Communist Parties which dated from the early Comintern days in the 1920s. The Chinese Communist Party had helped Ho Chi Minh to set up the forerunner of the Indochinese Communist Party, and the Democratic Republic of Vietnam remained closely aligned with Mao's China up to the death of Ho Chi Minh in 1969. While Beijing had given large-scale support to North Vietnam during its struggles against the French and the Americans, the People's Republic had no greater wish than the imperial China of the past to see a powerful united Vietnam on its southern frontier. Once the United States withdrew its forces from Vietnam, China gave no further encouragement for the unification of the country.

Beijing and Hanoi also quarrelled about claims to islands in the South China Sea and discrimination against ethnic Chinese in Vietnam. China occupied the Paracels in January 1974 and the Spratly Islands in the following year. Hanoi's nationalization of private trade in March 1978, as part of its economic restructuring, bore heavily on the Chinese community. Their dual citizenship was withdrawn and many fled as refugees to escape resettlement, starting the mass exodus of 'boat people' which was to become a major problem for the region.

But the Sino–Vietnamese conflict had wider implications because China resented Vietnam's growing dependence on Moscow. As friendship with China cooled, Vietnam drew closer to Eastern Europe and the Soviet Union, which supplied most of Hanoi's needs in the decisive last months of the Vietnam war. Russia was recovering from its disillusionment following its rebuff in Indonesia, where the Indonesian Communist Party had first turned away from Moscow to Beijing and had then been shattered. By 1968, as its rift with China deepened, the Soviet Union was contemplating setting up a collective security system for Asia, and building up Russian influence in Southeast Asia, particularly to safeguard its naval interests in the Indian Ocean and the Straits of Melaka. Soviet contacts with ASEAN countries in the early 1970s were increasingly cordial, but ASEAN's adoption of the ZOPFAN neutralization principle offered less scope for Russian ambitions than Indochina.

Accordingly Moscow invited the Vietnamese leader, Le Duan, to visit the Soviet Union in December 1975 and the following year signed agreements to give Hanoi immediate economic aid and long-term help in its five-year plan. In June 1978, one month before Beijing withdrew the last of its aid and technicians, Hanoi joined the Council for Mutual Economic Assistance (COMECON),[19] the Moscow-dominated communist trading bloc. Five months later Vietnam signed a 25-year friendship treaty with the Russians, and Beijing, fearing encirclement on the southern frontier, accused the Soviet Union of hegemony.

Beijing's worst fears seemed to be realized when, within a month of signing the Russian treaty, Vietnam invaded Kampuchea in December 1978 and established a client government in Phnom Penh. This removed the traditional buffer between Thailand and Vietnam and brought renewed Great Power conflict to Southeast Asia, dragging the region further into the ambit of Sino–Soviet rivalry and threatening to make Indochina the focus of a global war.

From early 1977 the Pol Pot régime had harassed the Vietnamese border; this escalated into fierce fighting, with the Vietnamese Communist Party giving support to a Kampuchean National United Front for National Salvation, led by Heng Samrin and Hun Sen, who had broken away from the Khmer Rouge in reaction to Pol Pot's reign of terror. When their forces backed by the Vietnamese seized Phnom Penh in January 1979, they established a People's Republic of Kampuchea with Heng Samrin as president and Hun Sen as prime minister. This pro-Hanoi government was to rule Cambodia for more than ten years, but thousands of Cambodian refugees settled along the Thai side of the border, and guerrilla bands continued to fight.

Hanoi's intervention brought a speedy reaction from China, which launched an incursion into the northern border zone of Vietnam in March 1979. The stated object of Beijing's attack was 'to teach Hanoi a lesson'. Although the conflict was bitter and costly to both sides, the Chinese

---

[19] The Council for Mutual Economic Assistance, formed about 1949 by the Soviet Union and East European countries to promote co-operation and socialist economic integration. By 1988 it comprised 21 members, plus observers who included Laos, but the organization was wound up in 1991.

withdrew within a few weeks without forcing any concessions from Vietnam. Beijing's brief expedition achieved little, except to make Vietnam even more dependent on the Soviet bloc, and the continued Vietnamese occupation of Cambodia remained the most vexing problem in Sino–Soviet relations for a decade.

The Sino–Soviet quarrel, Vietnam's invasion of Kampuchea and Beijing's retaliatory strike against Hanoi destroyed any concept of ideological solidarity, and marked yet another return to conventional power politics.

The Heng Samrin régime continued to be strongly supported by Vietnamese troops and advisers and kept a close relationship with Hanoi. Although foreign-backed, it was welcomed with some relief, since it put an end to the Pol Pot terror, tolerated the revival of Buddhism within limits, and modified the extreme socialism of the previous régime.

Although the People's Republic of Kampuchea had established fairly firm control over most of the country, the United Nations supported an ASEAN-sponsored resolution in November 1979 refusing to recognize it as the legitimate government. It was seen as in ASEAN's interests to achieve a comprehensive political settlement of the Kampuchea problem, and the association tried to promote a coalition of all opposition groups in Kampuchea, which would be more acceptable than the notorious Khmer Rouge. But the resistance was divided into three: Prince Sihanouk's monarchists; the non-communist Khmer People's National Liberation Front, under the leadership of former prime minister Son Sann; and the Khmer Rouge led by Khieu Samphan. For years the opposition factions bickered among themselves, and a United Nations conference on Kampuchea held in New York in July 1981 came to nothing. Eventually, in June 1982, the opposition groups sank their differences to form a coalition, which the United Nations recognized as the government-in-exile, with Prince Sihanouk as president, Khieu Samphan as deputy president and Son Sann as prime minister. But this was very much a marriage of inconvenience, and the Khmer Rouge remained the most effective force and the biggest threat to the Phnom Penh régime.

THE DEVELOPMENT OF ASEAN

The Vietnamese invasion and occupation of Kampuchea—the first sign of any substance to the domino theory—impelled the ASEAN countries for the first time to adopt a common stance in rejecting Hanoi's intervention as an affront to national sovereignty. Over the next ten years ASEAN was to lead the way in barring the Hanoi-backed régime's admission to the United Nations and supporting a government-in-exile. In so doing ASEAN acquired enhanced international respect as a body with political and diplomatic influence, promoting a policy in Indochina which found favour both in the United States and China.

Behind this public accord remained substantial differences in attitudes and interests among the ASEAN partners, ranging from frontline Thailand, who turned to China as a bulwark against its traditional Vietnamese rival, to the more remote Indonesia, which retained considerable respect for Vietnam's militant nationalist record and saw Beijing as a more ominous long-term threat. Most countries were concerned about increased Chinese involvement in the region, but all resisted becoming enmeshed in the Sino–Soviet dispute.

By the late 1980s most of the ASEAN countries had achieved fairly strong and secure governments through various forms of autocratic or quasi-autocratic régimes. In general, populations seemed content to sacrifice a degree of personal freedom in the interests of stability and strong government. The ruling parties of Malaysia and Indonesia drew different elements into their coalitions: the National Front and Golkar respectively. In Indonesia General Suharto was president, prime minister and minister of defence, with Golkar, the army's political wing, consistently winning overwhelming electoral victories. In Singapore, through successive elections, the ruling People's Action Party monopolized parliament for thirteen years from 1968 to 1981 and continued into the 1990s with only a minuscule opposition. Military rule persisted in Thailand until 1988 but was less autocratic than it had been in the days of Phibun, Sarit and Thanom. In July 1988 Thailand returned to civilian rule—as it turned out, for only eighteen months—under an elected prime minister, Chatichai Choonhavan. The Thai army remained in a strong position but, like its Indonesian counterpart, was committed to a 'war against poverty' in a nation where economic development was the first priority.

In 1984 ASEAN expanded its membership for the first time by admitting the newly independent state of Brunei, which had enjoyed observer status since 1981. This helped Brunei to re-establish harmonious relations with Malaysia and Indonesia and to gain a stake in the development of the region.

After the 1962 rebellion, Kuala Lumpur had given shelter to former PRB members and remained critical of Brunei's undemocratic system of government and continued dependence on Britain. In 1977 the United Nations adopted a Malaysia-sponsored resolution calling for the Brunei people to choose their own government, for the removal of the ban on political parties, and for the return of all political exiles to Brunei. But the sultan saw the tie with Britain as giving the greatest freedom for himself and his state, viewing the link as a protection against neighbouring governments, secessionists and political opponents within Brunei itself.

The sultanate was reluctant to revise the terms of its 1971 treaty with Britain until it received assurances that Malaysia and Indonesia would respect Brunei's independence, but in 1979 the sultan was compelled to sign an agreement under which Brunei was to become a sovereign independent state at the end of 1983. On the eve of independence, Brunei obtained a new defence agreement with the United Kingdom, whereby, at its own expense, it would continue to employ a battalion of British Gurkhas to protect the oilfields.

Unprecedented prosperity helped to preserve internal political calm in Brunei throughout these years, since, beginning in 1963, large offshore oil and natural-gas fields were discovered, and after the international oil crisis of 1973–4 export earnings from oil and gas soared, although Brunei itself was not a member of OPEC. This enabled wide-ranging welfare benefits to be given, which contributed to political contentment. Brunei became independent in January 1984, and the following year the sultan relaxed the ban on political parties. But the sultan and his brothers continued to head the top ministries in the cabinet, the emergency laws remained in force, and there was little popular demand for constitutional reform.

After independence Brunei became a member of the United Nations, the Commonwealth and the Organization of the Islamic Conference as well as ASEAN. In 1988 it offered to help finance economic development in the Philippines.

Brunei remained heavily reliant on Britain and Singapore for defence, but its major problems were its anachronistic political system and its almost total dependence on oil and gas, which were wasting assets. Beginning in 1953 five major National Development Plans stressed the need to diversify the economy, and in 1985 the Brunei government proposed a 20-year master plan to this end, but despite ample funds for development, by the late 1980s comparatively little had been accomplished within the state itself.

The offshore oil boom also helped Malaysia, Thailand, Singapore and Indonesia to achieve considerable economic growth and enhanced standards of living. Singapore joined the ranks of the newly industrialized countries and Thailand was well on the way to doing so by the late 1980s.

The odd one out was the Philippines, which faced economic chaos in the last years of the Marcos régime, because of its inefficient agrarian economy and large-scale corruption beyond the state's capacity to absorb. While Marcos staged a series of plebiscites which confirmed the continuation of martial law and his own tenure of power, by the 1980s there was mounting criticism of the flamboyant lifestyle of him and his wife, Imelda, and the corruption of influence peddling or 'crony capitalism'. Muslim insurgency flared up again in 1977 when the Moros were disappointed at the degree of autonomy accorded to them. And Marcos's repressive measures encouraged the rise of radical young Maoists, who won new converts as the peasants became disillusioned with the failure of land reform. The church and the middle classes became increasingly critical of the Marcos family's corruption and self-aggrandizement, and this opposition found a mouthpiece in Senator Benigno Aquino. The assassination of Aquino in August 1983, which was widely attributed to the Marcos clique, roused popular anger, and Aquino's widow challenged Marcos at a presidential election in February 1986, where emotions reached fever pitch. Marcos was proclaimed the victor although the elections were glaringly fraudulent, and this sparked mass demonstrations. Army leaders turned against Marcos, who fled abroad, and Corazon Aquino became president.

The collapse of Marcos's régime in face of 'People Power' brought in a more democratic but inherently unstable government. Corazon Aquino promulgated a new more liberal constitution and held elections in 1987 to confirm her presidency. But against a background of burgeoning population growth combined with rising expectations, and faced with crippling debts, she was hamstrung by the unsolved problem of the élite privileged class that had always bedevilled Filipino politics. Consequently, the Aquino régime battled with limited success to end the communist and Moro insurrections, to introduce land reform, and to overhaul the economy.

Over the years the reformists and experienced politicians of the original Aquino cabinet gave way to more conservative lawyers and businessmen. President Aquino's popularity waned amid renewed criticism of inefficiency, corruption and 'crony capitalism', and a series of military coups attempted to topple her. While these were unsuccessful, only American intervention saved the Aquino government in December 1989, when rebels held the commercial area in Manila for several days.

But there was no credible rival, with the exiled Marcos dying in Hawaii in September 1989, and little public support for Aquino's erstwhile colleagues: Senator Juan Ponce Enrile and vice-president Salvador Laurel. The defence secretary, Fidel Ramos, who had led the revolt against Marcos in 1986 and quashed attempts to overthrow President Aquino, commanded more popular support but he remained loyal to her. Internal instability continued to make the Philippines ASEAN's weak link, and a question mark hung over the future of the American military bases, whose lease was due to expire in 1991. While the bases were still very important for the republic's political and economic survival, they remained a badge of subservience.

The third ASEAN summit, marking the end of the association's second decade, met in Manila in December 1987. It was the first time the heads of state had assembled since the Kuala Lumpur gathering ten years before, despite calls to stage another summit which had been voiced from the early 1980s. The Philippines was next in line to host the conference, but this was delayed because of growing disapproval of the Marcos régime and because Malaysia's prime minister refused to visit Manila until the Sabah claim was formally laid to rest. Even at that late stage President Aquino's attempts to legislate finally to end this last remaining source of territorial dispute in ASEAN were qualified by the Philippines Congress. But the meeting, held at considerable personal risk to the leaders, was an expression of support for the precarious Aquino régime.

BURMA

Despite some signs of opening up to foreign investment and aid in the early 1980s, Burma still remained largely aloof, at the cost of stagnation of a once prosperous export economy and growing political unrest. Poverty, coupled with the alienation of educated youth, erupted in violence in 1988. General Ne Win stepped down from office in that year but continued to manipulate the government. He repressed the incipient opposition under the spirited leadership of Aung San's daughter, Aung San Suu Kyi, head of the National League for Democracy and the most effective spokeswoman for the pro-democracy opposition to Burma's military government. Aung San Suu Kyi was put under house arrest in July 1989, while many of her party members were jailed. The party swept the polls in a general election held in May 1990 but were not permitted to take up office, and in

July 1990 the ruling State Law and Order Restoration Council issued a decree confirming its retention of executive, legislative and judicial powers.

INTERNATIONAL COMMUNISM IN THE 1980s

While anti-imperialism had failed to unite Southeast Asia, concern about communist subversion and the Vietnamese threat became effective catalysts. But over the years the communist danger receded, both internally and externally.

This was partly because the People's Republic of China, in giving priority to good relations with the ASEAN countries in its own modernization drive, withdrew its moral support from communist parties in other countries during the 1980s. Local dissident movements became increasingly isolated and their activities were more a reaction to the shortcomings of national governments than part of a coherent international movement. The communists also lost ground on account of internal divisions, such as the splintering of the Malaysian communists into three rival factions, while subversion was effectively monitored and countered by the vigilance and co-operation of ASEAN governments. The most dramatic rift in the communist camp was Vietnam's invasion of Cambodia followed by China's retaliatory campaign.

Increasingly the Marxist-Leninist model for development in the region became discredited in face of the excesses of the Cultural Revolution in China, the brutality and degradation of the Pol Pot régime in Democratic Kampuchea and the floundering of Vietnam's economy, despite the massive Chinese and Soviet aid which had flowed into the country for more than twenty years. By the late 1980s Vietnam itself was torn between clinging to orthodox ideology and moving to a more open, less centralized economy.

A variety of factors contributed to dilute fears of communism: Vietnam's continuing confrontation of China and concern for economic revival; China's preoccupation in the 1980s with modernization; the stagnation of USSR and East European economies, with Poland and even the Soviet Union itself looking for Western aid by 1989; President Mikhail Gorbachev's new *glasnost* and *perestroika* policies in the Soviet Union and their dramatic impact in Eastern Europe; Russian withdrawal from Afghanistan and Moscow's disillusionment with the economic drain involved in supporting Vietnam. After some initial concern at the Soviet military presence in Cam Rahn Bay, ASEAN saw Vietnam as its own political master.

In 1975 Thailand and the Philippines followed Malaysia in establishing diplomatic ties with the People's Republic of China, and Singapore forged strong economic links with Beijing (although at the same time maintaining its ties with Taiwan). But in view of its predominantly Chinese population, Singapore deferred establishing formal diplomatic relations with the People's Republic until Indonesia did so in 1990.

Despite the general slackening of tension, these developments were not without problems. The modernization of China revived nagging fears that the Overseas Chinese could be used as a means to secure both investment and export markets, thereby becoming an 'economic fifth column'. The Vietnamese refugees also became an increasing burden. In the early days most were ethnic Chinese, fleeing from political persecution or relocation to rural areas, but increasingly the refugees were Vietnamese trying to escape from poverty, over-population, and the failures of the nation's economy. While their ultimate goal was to reach the developed countries of the West, notably the United States, they fled in the first place to Southeast Asia and Hong Kong.

There was also the doubt whether communist countries were abandoning the traditional goal of world revolution or merely seeking temporary accommodation with the West in order to build up their strength for renewed aggressive policies.[20] The Vietnamese constitution of 1980 provided for a proletarian dictatorship and talked of mobilizing the masses for revolution in production and opposing counter-revolutionaries. Hanoi's leaders took an even tougher line after the the suppression of the pro-democracy student movement in Beijing and the breakdown of communist solidarity in Eastern Europe in 1989.

In a comprehensive statement issued on National Day in September 1989, Vietnamese Communist Party secretary-general Nguyen Van Linh resolutely rejected any multi-party system or speeding up of democratic reform in Vietnam. Linh was an economic reformer, who in the past had promoted a certain measure of political liberalization, but he feared change might lead to similar disturbances in Vietnam itself.

The Indochina situation remained the most immediate threat to the peace and stability of Southeast Asia. The United Nations continued to reject the Heng Samrin régime as the legitimate government of Cambodia and to demand the withdrawal of the Vietnamese army. But Hanoi stood firm on its insistence that the Khmer Rouge should be excluded from any future government. In an attempt to break the deadlock, Sihanouk withdrew temporarily from leadership of the Democratic Kampuchea government-in-exile and in December 1987 began a series of informal talks with prime minister Hun Sen.

As economic difficulties mounted at home, Hanoi announced it would withdraw its troops unilaterally by September 1989. France called a high-powered conference of nineteen nations, co-chaired by Indonesia, in Paris for July–August 1989 in an attempt to reach a peaceful settlement for Cambodia. But the conference ended in failure, and Prince Sihanouk resigned once again, leaving the resistance in disarray. No agreement could be reached between Hun Sen and Sihanouk on quadri-partite power-sharing in the interim government prior to elections.

On the wider international level, the end of the Cold War offered better prospects for a Cambodian settlement. Soviet President Gorbachev's visit to Beijing in May 1989 was disrupted by anti-government student demonstrations, culminating in the Tiananmen Square incident. But the warming of Sino–Soviet relations promised to set a new scenario for Southeast Asia

<hr>

[20] Sinnathamby Rajaratnam (former Deputy Prime Minister of Singapore), 'Riding the Vietnamese Tiger', *Far Eastern Economic Review*, 4 May 1989.

and pave the way for restoring diplomatic ties between Beijing and Vietnam, which had been broken since 1978.

In September 1990 the four warring factions in Cambodia agreed to accept a United Nations role in an interim administration leading to free elections, and two months later the United Nations Security Council, including China and the Soviet Union, agreed on a draft peace plan to end the twelve-year war. This provided for a ceasefire and eventual elections, with an interim UN administration involving a Supreme National Council composed of representatives of the Hun Sen government and the three guerrilla groups. The agreement was finally signed in October 1991.

WESTERN INVOLVEMENT

Links with the West continued to weaken. SEATO, which was described at this time as 'a long moribund strategic basketcase',[21] was disbanded in June 1977. The weak presidency of Jimmy Carter (1976–80) combined with American negative reaction against involvement in the Vietnam War to compound Washington's neglect of mainland Southeast Asia.

The Colombo Plan was no longer a British nor even a Commonwealth-dominated organization, but had developed into a broader and more permanent international body. After being renewed for periods of five years, in 1980 the plan was extended indefinitely. By that time membership had expanded from the original seven Commonwealth nations to an international organization of twenty-six countries, including all the countries of Southeast Asia except Vietnam and Brunei. Its area was extended to cover Asia and the Pacific, with most aid coming from the six developed member countries, namely Australia, Canada, Japan, New Zealand, the United Kingdom and the United States. By 1988–9 Japan was the largest donor, supplying more than twice the amount of aid provided by the United States, which itself contributed more than the original four developed Commonwealth member countries combined.[22] In addition the Colombo Plan provided assistance, training and research, including technical co-operation among developing countries themselves. For example a Colombo Plan Staff College for Technician Education was established in Singapore in 1975 and transferred to the Philippines in 1987.[23]

In 1984 Britain and China issued a joint declaration arranging to hand Hong Kong back to China in 1997. Subsequently a similar document was signed between the Portuguese and Chinese to cover Macau, which would revert to the People's Republic in December 1999. These heralded the final disappearance of European political colonialism from the region by the end of the century.

As Anglo-American involvement declined, Japan became more important

---

[21] Justus M. Van der Kroef, *The Lives of SEATO*, Singapore: ISEAS, Occasional Paper no. 45, 1976, 1.

[22] *The Statesman's Year-Book, 1988–89.*

[23] *Colombo Plan Annual Reports* (HMSO, London, 1952–71); followed by *Colombo Plan Bureau* (Sri Lanka, 1971 onwards).

as mentor and model, achieving economic influence and material advantages beyond the dreams of the Greater East Asia Co-Prosperity Sphere of the militarist era. But Tokyo's impact was confined to the economic sphere.

NON-ALIGNMENT

Over the years ASEAN countries became disillusioned with the non-aligned movement, which was often out of step with their policies. At its first summit meeting at Belgrade in 1961, the so-called non-aligned movement had adopted an anti-colonial political stance. It grew more militant as membership expanded to incorporate newly independent nations, laying most ASEAN countries open to charges of neo-colonialism because of their continuing defence and economic ties with the West. The 1976 Colombo meeting, which was the first non-aligned summit to be held after the end of the Vietnam War, refused to re-endorse ASEAN's ZOPFAN proposal. It also issued a Declaration for a New Economic Order, calling for a restructuring of the world economy at the expense of the advanced nations. This attracted hostile comment from Singapore in particular, since it ran counter to co-operation with the West, an essential ingredient of ASEAN economies.

Burma withdrew from the movement at the Havana summit meeting in 1979 because other members, such as Cuba and the Philippines, were aligned to either communist or Western blocs. But by the late 1980s the non-aligned movement itself was changing: the Belgrade summit meeting in September 1989 agreed that it must adapt to the new situation of East–West détente by downplaying its traditional diatribes against colonialism and superpower domination in favour of concern over terrorism, human rights and protecting the environment. While some hardline African and Latin American states protested and insisted on including the customary references to the 'struggle against imperialism, colonialism, neo-colonialism, racism, apartheid and all forms of domination', Asian countries, and particularly Southeast Asia, were content to go along with the new realism.

By the end of the 1980s the countries of Southeast Asia seemed secure within their frontiers and were more concerned with economic prosperity than strident nationalism. Even Vietnam and Burma gave some priority to emerging from the economic stagnation to which their respective ideologies had brought them.

The search for security drew non-communist Southeast Asian countries into more urgent co-operation in ASEAN, yet it did not give ASEAN a military role. In principle member states still accepted the ideal of Southeast Asia as a zone of peace, freedom and neutrality, although they managed to attach a variety of meanings to this. But the prospects of Burma or the Indochina states joining ASEAN were still remote.

While only limited progress had been made in the economic, social and cultural fields, ASEAN was more successful in political and diplomatic co-operation, and by the late 1980s had achieved a major international standing. From the beginning ASEAN was important in providing a framework for co-operation and reconciliation in the post-colonial—and especially the post-confrontation—era, and from the early 1970s its members adopted some concrete measures of mutual help. But for many years the outside world had dismissed the association. Its value came to be recognized only after the Bali summit of 1976, when the ASEAN countries stood together in the face of the communist victories in Indochina and later when they maintained a common stance against the Vietnamese-backed Heng Samrin régime in Kampuchea throughout the 1980s. This showed what could be achieved by diplomatic and political pressure, without a parallel military pact. ASEAN's international prestige increased further over the years as it achieved dialogue with the advanced industrialized countries: the United States, the European Community, Australia, Canada, New Zealand and Japan.

While they remained committed to integration into the international economy, ASEAN countries tried to avoid dependence on, or the drain of profits to, their more powerful capitalist partners. Yet they relied to some extent on Great Powers—notably the United States and Japan—for the rapid economic development they saw as essential to political stability. Generous economic and military aid, technical help and development loans stimulated the economy of most Southeast Asian countries, but sometimes this benefited only a privileged few and fuelled further discontent. The new economic opportunities also encouraged corruption, particularly when most development funds were administered by the bureaucracy. The Pertamina scandal in Indonesia in 1976 highlighted bribery at the highest level of public life, while ten years later dishonesty in the Philippines reached such a scale that it jeopardized the economy and toppled the Marcos régime. The irregularities revealed in the running of Malaysia's Bank Bumiputra, linked to the Carrian group in Hong Kong, demonstrated how widespread the problem was and how the corruption network reached the highest level of government and permeated the region.

After a slow start ASEAN had succeeded in reducing political tension and eventually led to limited economic rationalization. While rural poverty, unequal development, and inequitable distribution of wealth were still serious problems in ASEAN countries, these were not so acute as in most other parts of the Third World. Its population was as large as the European Community, while its resources of primary produce made it one of the richest regions in the world. The Great Powers were beginning to see ASEAN as a political power bloc in its own right, and by the last decade of the century ASEAN was probably the most effective of Third World organizations.

The ASEAN countries had largely settled their traditional disputes and developed machinery for negotiating day-to-day problems. The initial objective of promoting regional security through reconciliation had largely been achieved, with an emphasis on consensus and not confrontation. Individual members generally remained unwilling to sacrifice political or economic nationalism to regionalism, but sought friendly co-operation.

The security of Singapore and Brunei within ASEAN showed that small states could not only survive but prosper in the late twentieth century, and the experience of both countries in relation to Malaysia indicated that it was not necessary or even desirable to seek a post-colonial future as part of a larger unit or federation. Tiny oil-rich Brunei enjoyed a high per capita income but one based almost entirely on two wasting assets. The feudalism of the sultanate, combined with its great wealth, posed the question whether this could ultimately create another Azahari-type problem that could split ASEAN.

Despite their common Marxist-Leninist ideology, the Indochina bloc was much less harmonious than ASEAN. While committed to rapid economic development through fundamental reconstruction, the socialist economic road they chose was a failure, despite massive aid from the Soviet Union and COMECON. Unlike ASEAN, the Indochina countries suffered from the revival of traditional rivalries such as those between Vietnam and Cambodia, and between Vietnam and China. At the same time the waning fear of communism opened the way for smoother relationships in the region, since communism was no longer seen as a monolithic movement which threatened internal stability or international peace. Outside the Philippines, communist insurgency ceased to be a danger, and in December 1989 the Communist Party of Malaya formally renounced its armed struggle. China continued to loom over the region, but as a large power rather than an ideological threat.

Thus as Southeast Asia reached the last decade of the most turbulent century in its history, it had come a fair way to determining the character of its nations and to establishing regional cohesion. As in the past, its strategic economic position at the cross-roads of international trade made it the continuing object of big-power interest, yet at the same time the small states of Southeast Asia were firmly established with sufficient regional co-operation to ensure at least some measure of control over their own destiny.

BIBLIOGRAPHICAL ESSAY

There is a wealth of literature on this topic, and most of the works mentioned in this brief note have detailed bibliographies.

Michael Leifer, *The Foreign Relations of the New States*, Melbourne, 1974, deals with Southeast Asia in the period from 1945 to the early 1970s. See also Evelyn Colbert, *Southeast Asia in International Politics, 1941–1956*, Ithaca, 1977; Russell H. Fifield, *The Diplomacy of Southeast Asia, 1945–1958*, New York, 1958; and Peter Lyon, *War and Peace in South-East Asia*, London, 1969.

Bernard K. Gordon, *The Dimensions of Conflict in Southeast Asia*, Englewood Cliffs, 1966, explores efforts at regional co-operation as well as conflict in the twenty years following World War II. Arnfinn Jorgensen-Dahl, *Regional Organisation and Order in South-East Asia*, London, 1982, deals with the development of regional organization from 1945 and particularly with ASEAN. Charles E. Morrison and Astri Suhrke, *Strategies of*

Survival: The Foreign Policy Dilemmas of Smaller Asian States, New York, 1978, includes Vietnam, all the founder ASEAN states and ASEAN itself. On ASEAN see the *ASEAN Documents Series, 1967–1988*, 3rd edn, Jakarta: ASEAN Secretariat, 1988; Alison Broinowski, ed., *Understanding ASEAN*, London, 1982; and Michael Leifer, *ASEAN and the Security of South-East Asia*, London, 1989.

Leszek Buszynski, *SEATO: Failure of an Alliance Strategy*, Singapore, 1983, deals in detail with the origins, development and winding up of SEATO. See also the organization's journal *Spectrum* and its annual reports.

Indonesian foreign policy from independence to the early 1980s is covered by Michael Leifer, *Indonesia's Foreign Policy*, London, 1983. Franklin B. Weinstein, *Indonesian Foreign Policy and the Dilemma of Dependence: From Sukarno to Suharto*, Ithaca, 1976, concentrates mainly on the 1960s and early 1970s. Jon M. Reinhardt, *Foreign Policy and National Integration: the case of Indonesia*, New Haven: Yale University Southeast Asian Studies, 1971, relates nation building to foreign policy up to the end of the 1960s. First-hand accounts are given by a variety of Indonesian diplomats and foreign ministers: Ide Anak Agung gde Agung, *Twenty Years Indonesian Foreign Policy 1945–1965*, The Hague and Paris, 1973, the detailed memoirs of a former Minister of Foreign Affairs, who was imprisoned by Sukarno; Ganis Harsono, *Recollections of an Indonesian Diplomat in the Sukarno Era*, edited by C. L. M. Penders and B. B. Hering, St Lucia, 1977, the memoirs of a pro-Sukarno minister who was imprisoned by Suharto; and Adam Malik, *In the Service of the Republic*, Singapore, 1980, covering the period from 1945 to 1980 including Malik's career as Foreign Minister.

For the Malaysia issue see Peter Boyce, *Malaysia and Singapore in International Diplomacy: Documents and Commentaries*, Sydney, 1968. J. A. C. Mackie, *Konfrontasi: the Indonesia-Malaysia Dispute 1963–1966*, Kuala Lumpur, 1974, is the most comprehensive study of confrontation. Chin Kin Wah, *The Defence of Malaysia and Singapore: The Transformation of a Security system, 1957–1971*, Cambridge, UK, 1983, covers the period of the Anglo-Malay(si)an Defence Agreement. For broader aspects of the relationship, see Stanley S. Bedlington, *Malaysia and Singapore: the Building of New States*, Ithaca, 1978.

Milton W. Meyer, *A Diplomatic History of the Philippine Republic*, Honolulu, 1965, covers the period from the formative years 1945–6 to the end of the Garcia administration in 1961. Michael Leifer, *The Philippine Claim to Sabah*, Zug, 1968, provides a concise historical background to this controversy, and Lela Garner Noble, *Philippine Policy towards Sabah: A Claim for Independence*, Tucson, 1977, deals in detail with the period from 1962 until Marcos abandoned pursuit of the claim in 1976.

On Indochina, the diplomatic background to the immediate postwar period is examined in R. E. M. Irving, *The First Indochina War: French and American Policy 1945–54*, London, 1975. The first two volumes of R. B. Smith's projected five-volume *An International History of the Vietnam War* cover the period 1955–65, I: *Revolution versus Containment, 1955–61*, London, 1983, and II: *The Struggle for South-East Asia, 1961–65*, London, 1985. William S. Turley, *The Second Indochina War*, Boulder, 1986, is a concise political and military account. Gene T. Hsiao, ed., *The Role of External Powers in the Indo-china Crisis*, Edwardsville, 1973, goes up to the 1973 Paris Peace Agreement.

The 1954 Geneva Conference and the events leading up to it are covered comprehensively. See Melvin Gurtov, *The First Vietnam Crisis: Chinese Communist Strategy and United States Involvement, 1953–54*, New York, 1967, and Robert F. Randle, *Geneva 1954: the Settlement of the Indochinese War*, Princeton, 1969. Kenneth T. Young, ed., *The 1954 Geneva Conference: Indo-China and Korea*, New York, 1968, is a collection of documents on the conference itself, and James Cable, *The Geneva Conference of 1954 on Indo-china*, London, 1986, is a lively eye-witness account.

Michael Leifer, *Cambodia: Search for Security*, London, 1967, deals with the post-1954 Geneva settlement years. Roger M. Smith, *Cambodia's Foreign Policy*, Ithaca, 1965, is a detailed study of the period from 1954 to the 1962 Laos settlement. On Laos, see MacAlister Brown and Joseph J. Zasloff, *Apprentice Revolutionaries: The Communist Movement in Laos, 1930–1985*, Stanford, 1986. Malcolm Caldwell and Lek Tan, *Cambodia in the Southeast Asian War*, New York, 1973, presents a radical left-wing analysis going back to French colonial days but concentrating mainly on the period from 1954 to the early 1970s. Donald Weatherbee, ed., *Southeast Asia Divided. The ASEAN-Indochina Crisis*, Boulder, 1985, includes 1979–84 documents.

William C. Johnstone, *Burma's Foreign Policy: A Study in Neutralism*, Cambridge, Mass., 1963, analyses Burma's policy in the 1948–62 period.

Much has been published about the role of the various external powers. Russell H. Fifield, *Americans in Southeast Asia: The Roots of Commitment*, New York, 1973, traces the US relationship from pre-war days to the aftermath of the 1954 Geneva Agreement. Andrew J. Rotter, *The Path to Vietnam: Origins of the American Commitment to Southeast Asia*, Ithaca, 1987, is a perceptive study of the late 1940s and early 1950s. See also R. Sean Randolph, *The United States and Thailand: Alliance Dynamics, 1950–1983*, Berkeley: Institute of East Asian Studies, University of California, 1986.

Charles B. McLane, *Soviet Strategies in Southeast Asia*, Princeton, 1966, explores Soviet policy from 1917 to the death of Stalin, with a useful final chapter on the 1948–54 period. Leszek Buszynski, *Soviet Foreign Policy and Southeast Asia*, London, 1986, is important for post-1969 policy and particularly developments following 1978. Douglas Pike, *Vietnam and the Soviet Union: Anatomy of an Alliance*, Boulder and London, 1987, traces the relationship from pre-Soviet contacts to the 1980s.

Phillip Darby, *British Defence Policy East of Suez*, London, 1973, deals with the postwar situation up to the changes of the late 1960s.

On China's involvement see David Mozingo, *Chinese Policy towards Indonesia 1949–1967*, Ithaca, 1976; Joyce K. Kallgren, Noordin Sopiee and Soedjati Djwandono, eds, *ASEAN and China: An Evolving Relationship*, Berkeley: Institute of East Asian Studies, University of California, 1988; and Leo Suryadinata, *China and the ASEAN States: The Ethnic Chinese Dimension*, Singapore, 1985.

On Australia, Alan Watt, *The Evolution of Australian Foreign Policy 1938–1965*, Cambridge, UK, 1967, has a chapter on relations in Asia 1945–65. A. W. Stargardt, *Australia's Asian Policies: The History of a Debate 1839–1972*,

Wiesbaden, 1977, deals extensively with the post-1945 period. J. A. C. Mackie, ed., *Australia in the New World Order: Foreign Policy in the 1970s*, Sydney, 1976, is largely concerned with the changed situation in Southeast Asia following Sino-American detente and the US withdrawal from Vietnam. Alan Watt, *Vietnam: An Australian Analysis*, Melbourne, 1968, gives a concise historical background, mainly of the post-1954 period.

From 1974 onwards *Southeast Asian Affairs*, an annual publication of the Institute of Southeast Asian Studies, Singapore, provides detailed reports and commentaries on domestic and international affairs throughout the region.

BIBLIOGRAPHIES

Besterman, Theodore (ed. J. D. Pearson). *A World Bibliography of Oriental Bibliographies*. Oxford: Basil Blackwell, 1975.
Bibliographic Index: A Cumulative Bibliography of Bibliographies. New York: H. W. Wilson, 1945– .
Brewer, Annie M., ed. *Indexes, Abstracts, and Digests: A Classified Bibliography Reproduced from Library of Congress Cards Arranged According to the Library of Congress Classification System*. Detroit: Gale Research Co., 1982.
Commonwealth National Bibliographies: An Annotated Directory. London: Commonwealth Secretariat, 1977.

ASIA

Asian Studies Indexed Journal Reference Guide. University of Pittsburgh, 1978.
[Association of Asian Studies]. *Cumulative Bibliography of Asian Studies 1941–1965*. Boston: G. K. Hall, 1969.
[Association of Asian Studies]. *Cumulative Bibliography of Asian Studies 1966–1970*. Boston: G. K. Hall, 1972.
Bibliography of Asian Studies. Ann Arbor: Association for Asian Studies, 1970– .
Birnbaum, Eleazar. *Books on Asia from the Near East to the Far East*. Toronto: University of Toronto Press, 1971.
Chen, Virginia. *The Economic Conditions of East and Southeast Asia: A Bibliography of English-Language Materials, 1965–1977*. Westport: Greenwood Press, 1978.
Embree, Ainslie T. *Asia: A Guide to Basic Books*. New York: Arno Press, 1976.
Goil, N. K. *Asian Social Science Bibliography with Annotations and Abstracts*. Delhi: Vikas Publications, 1970.
Hall, David E. *Union Catalogue of Asian Publications*. London: Mansell, 1971.
Kumar, Girja, et al. *Documentation on Asia*. New Delhi: Allied Publishers, 1963.
New York Public Library. Reference Department. *Dictionary Catalog of the Oriental Collection*. Boston: G. K. Hall, 1960.
Ng, Elizabeth W. *Directory of Current Hong Kong Research on Asian Topics*. Hong Kong: Centre of Asian Studies, University of Hong Kong, 1978.
Nunn, G. R. *Asia and Oceania: A Guide to Archival and Manuscript Sources in the United States*. London and New York: Mansell, 1985.
Nunn, G. R. *Asia: A Core Collection*. Ann Arbor: Xerox University Microfilms, 1973.

Nunn, G. R. *Asia: Reference Works—A Select Annotated Guide*. London: Mansell, 1980.

Orientalische Bibliographie. Berlin: H. Reuther's Verlagshuchhandlung, 1887– .

Pearson, J. D. *A Guide to Manuscripts and Documents in the British Isles relating to South and South-East Asia*. London and New York: Mansell, 1989.

Pearson, J. D. *Oriental and Asian Bibliography: An Introduction with Some Reference to Africa*. London: Crosby, Lockwood and Son, 1966.

Royal Commonwealth Society, Library. *The Manuscript Catalogue of the Library of the Royal Commonwealth Society*. London: Mansell, 1975.

Royal Empire Society. *Subject Catalogue of the Library of the Royal Empire Society*. London: Dawson of Pall Mall, 1967.

de Silva, Daya. *The Portuguese in Asia: An Annotated Bibliography of Studies on Portuguese Colonial History in Asia, 1498–c.1800*. Zug: Inter Documentation Co., 1987.

Toho Gakkai. *Books and Articles on Oriental Subjects Published in Japan*. Tokyo: Toho Gakkai [annual].

University of London. School of Oriental and African Studies. *Library Catalogue*. Boston: G. K. Hall, 1963.

Wainwright, M. D., and Matthews, Noel. *A Guide to Western Manuscripts and Documents in the British Isles Relating to South and South East Asia*. London: Oxford University Press, 1965.

SOUTHEAST ASIA

Senarai Bibliografi Mengenai Asia Tenggara Dalam Perpustakaan Universiti Kebangsaan Malaysia. Bangi: Perpustakaan Tun Seri Lanang, Universiti Kebangsaan Malaysia, 1981.

Arief, Sritua. *Southeast Asian Politics, 1967–1979: A Bibliography*. Kuala Lumpur: META, 1980.

Asian Studies Indexed Journal Reference Guide. University of Pittsburgh, 1978.

Attar Chand. *Southeast Asia and the Pacific 1947–1977*. New Delhi: Sterling Publishers, 1979.

Berton, Peter, and Rubinstein, Alvin Z. *Soviet Works on Southeast Asia: A Bibliography of Non-Periodical Literature, 1946–1965*. Los Angeles: University of Southern California Press, 1967.

Bibliografi Kaum Tani dan Pembangunan di Kawasan ASEAN. Bangi: Perpustakaan Universiti Kebangsaan Malaysia, 1980.

Bixler, Paul H. *Southeast Asia: Bibliographic Directions in a Complex Area*. Middletown, Conn.: Choice, 1974.

Carlson, Alvar W. *A Bibliography of the Geographical Literature on Southeast Asia, 1920–1972*. Monticello, Ill.: Council of Planning Librarians, 1974.

Chand, Attar. *Southeast Asia and the Pacific—A Select Bibliography: 1947–1977*. New Delhi: Sterling Publishers, 1979.

Chantornvong, Sombat, and Sonsri, Sida (Chety). *The ASEAN View: An Annotated Bibliography of ASEAN Theses and Dissertations on Southeast Asia from 1976 to 1984*. Bangkok: Foundation for the Studies of Democracy and Development, 1987.

Checklist of Southeast Asian Serials. Southeast Asia Collection, Yale University Library. Boston: G. K. Hall, 1968.

Chen, Virginia. *The Economic Conditions of East and Southeast Asia: A Bibliography of English-Language Materials, 1965–1977*. Westport: Greenwood Press, 1978.

Classified Catalogue of Books in Western Languages on South-East Asia in the Toyo Bunko (edited by the Seminar on South and South-East Asian History). Tokyo: Toyo Bunko (Oriental Library), 1978.

Clifton, Merritt et al., eds. *Those Who Were There: Eyewitness Accounts of the War in Southeast Asia, 1956–1975, and Aftermath.* Paradise, Calif.: Dustbooks, 1984.

Cordier, H. *Bibliotheca Indosinica.* New York: Burt Franklin, 1967 (1st edn, 1912). Vol. 1: *Burma, Assam, Siam, Laos.* Vol. 2: *Malay Peninsula.* Vol. 3: *French Indochina.* Vol. 4: *French Indochina.* Vol. 5: *Index.*

CORMOSEA (Committee on Research Materials on Southeast Asia). *Bulletin.* Ann Arbor: Association for Asian Studies.

Cornell University Libraries. Southeast Asia Program. *The John M. Echols Collection: Southeast Asia Catalog.* Boston: G. K. Hall, 1976 [Supplement Pertama, 1983].

Cornell University Libraries. *Accessions List: The John M. Echols Collection on Southeast Asia.*

Echols, John. 'Southeast Asia' in Howe, George F., *The American Historical Association's Guide to Historical Literature.* New York: Macmillan, 1961.

Embree, John F., and Lillian Ota Dotson. *Bibliography of the Peoples and Cultures of Mainland Southeast Asia.* New Haven: Yale University, Southeast Asian Studies, 1950.

Great Britain. Colonial Office. *An Annotated Bibliography on Land Tenure in the British and British Protected Territories in South East Asia and the Pacific.* London: HMSO, 1952.

Hay, Stephen N., and Case, Margaret H. *Southeast Asian History: Bibliographic Guide.* New York: Frederick A. Praeger, 1962.

Hobbs, Cecil. *Southeast Asia: A Bibliography of Writings, 1942–1978.* Carbondale: Center for Vietnamese Studies and Office of International Education, Southern Illinois University, 1980.

Hobbs, Cecil, *Southeast Asia: An Annotated Bibliography of Selected Reference Sources in Western Languages.* New York: Greenwood Press, 1968.

Hobbs, Cecil. *Southeast Asia Materials in the Australian National University Library: A Programme for Development and Use.* Canberra: Australian National University Library, 1975.

Huffman, Franklin E. *Bibliography and Index of Mainland Southeast Asian Languages and Linguistics.* New Haven and London: Yale University Press, 1986.

Ichikawa, Kenjiro, ed. *Southeast Asia Viewed from Japan: A Bibliography of Japanese Works on Southeast Asian Societies, 1940–1963.* Ithaca: Department of Asian Studies, Cornell University, 1965.

Insular Southeast Asia: A Bibliographic Survey, 1971. Washington, DC: Department of the Army, 1971.

Irikura, James K. *Southeast Asia: Selected Annotated Bibliography of Japanese Publications.* New Haven: Human Relations Area Files, 1956.

Iwasaki, Ikuro. *Japan and Southeast Asia: A Bibliography of Historical, Economic and Political Relations.* Tokyo: Library of the Institute of Developing Economies, 1983.

Johnson, Donald Clay. *A Guide to Reference Materials on Southeast Asia: Based on the Collections in the Yale and Cornell University Libraries.* New Haven: Yale University Press, 1970.

Johnson, Donald Clay. *Index to Southeast Asian Journals, 1975–1979: A Guide to Articles, Book Reviews, and Composite Works.* Boston: G. K. Hall, 1982.

Land Tenure Center, University of Wisconsin. *A Bibliography on Agrarian Economy in Southeast Asia* (1972).

Lim, Patricia, et al. *ASEAN: A Bibliography*. Singapore: ISEAS, 1984.

Lim Pui Huen, P. *Directory of Microfilm Facilities in Southeast Asia*. Singapore: ISEAS, 1973.

Lim Pui Huen, P. *News Resources on Southeast Asian Research*. Singapore: ISEAS, 1976.

List of Theses and Dissertations concerned with South East Asia 1965–1977. London: Centre of South East Asian Studies, School of Oriental and African Studies, University of London, 1977.

Loofs, H. H. E. *Elements of the Megalithic Complex in Southeast Asia: An Annotated Bibliography*. Canberra: Australian National University Press, 1967.

McVey, Ruth T. *Bibliography of Soviet Publications on Southeast Asia: As Listed in the Library of Congress Monthly Index of Russian Acquisitions*. Ithaca: Department of Far Eastern Studies, Cornell University, 1959.

Morrison, Gayle, and Hay, Stephen. *A Guide to Books on Southeast Asian History (1961–1966)*. Santa Barbara: ABC-Clio, 1969.

National Library of Australia. *Southeast Asian Periodicals and Official Publications*. (In 5 Parts.) Canberra: National Library of Australia, 1970.

Northern Illinois University. Library. *List of Recent Southeast Asia Acquisitions in the Swen Franklin Parson Library*. DeKalb: Northern Illinois University. 1970–

Northern Illinois University. Library. *Revised List of Southeast Asia Holdings in the Swen Franklin Parson Library, Northern Illinois University*. DeKalb: Northern Illinois University, 1968.

Pendakur, V. Setty. *Urban Transport in South and Southeast Asia: An Annotated Bibliography*. Singapore: ISEAS, 1984.

Oey, Giok Po. *Survey of Chinese-Language Materials on Southeast Asia in the Hoover Institute and Library*. Ithaca: Southeast Asia Program, Department of Far Eastern Studies, Cornell University, 1953.

Oey, Hong Lee. *Power Struggle in South-East Asia*. Zug: Inter Documentation Co., 1976.

Partaningrat, Winarti. *Masterlist of Southeast Asian Microforms*. Singapore: Singapore University Press, 1978.

Peninsular Southeast Asia: a Bibliographic Survey of Literature (Burma, Cambodia, Laos, Thailand). Washington, DC: Headquarters, Department of the Army, 1972.

Pryon, Robin J. *A Bibliography on Internal Migration in South East Asia*. Canberra: Department of Demography, Research School of Social Sciences, Australian National University, 1977.

Quah Swee Lan. *Oil Discovery and Technical Change in Southeast Asia: A Bibliography*. Singapore: ISEAS, 1973.

Rhodes House Library. *Manuscript Collections in Rhodes House Library*. Oxford: Bodleian Library, 1970.

Rhodes House Library. *Manuscript Collections in Rhodes House Library, Oxford (Supplementary Accessions to the End of 1977 and Cumulative Index)*.

Rony, A. Kohar. *Southeast Asia: Western-Language Periodicals in the Library of Congress*. Washington, DC: Library of Congress, 1979.

Scott, James C., et al. *A Bibliography on Land, Peasants and Politics for Malaysia, Indonesia and the Philippines*. Madison: Land Tenure Center Special Bibliography, 1972.

Senarai Bibliografi Mengenai Asia Tenggara dalam Perpustakaan Universiti Kebangsaan Malaysia. Bangi. Perpustakaan Tun Seri Lanang, 1981.

Smith, Myron J. Jr. *Air War Southeast Asia, 1961–1973*. Metuchen, NJ, and London: Scarecrow Press, 1979.

Sternstein, Larry, and Springer, Carl. *An Annotated Bibliography of Material Concerning Southeast Asia from Petermanns Geographische Mitteilungen, 1855–1966.* Bangkok: Siam Society, 1967.
Tregonning, K. G. *Southeast Asia: A Critical Bibliography.* Tucson: University of Arizona Press, 1969.
Union Catalogue of Documentary Materials on Southeast Asia (5 vols). Tokyo: Institute of Asian Economic Affairs, 1964.
United States of America. Library of Congress. Orientalia Division. *Southeast Asia Subject Catalog.* Boston: G. K. Hall, 1972.
University of Malaya, Library. *Literature, Drama and Dance in Southeast Asia.* Kuala Lumpur: Library, University of Malaya, 1976.
Van Niel, Robert, *A Survey of Historical Source Materials in Java and Manila.* Honolulu: University of Hawaii Press, 1970.
Willer, Thomas F., ed. *Southeast Asian References in the British Parliamentary Papers, 1801–1972/73: An Index.* Athens: Ohio University Center for International Studies, Southeast Asia Program, 1978.

MALAYSIA, SINGAPORE AND BRUNEI

Ding Choo Ming. *A Bibliography of Bibliographies on Malaysia.* Petaling Jaya, Selangor: Haxagon Elite Publications, 1981.

Arief, Melanie Sritua. *The Malaysian Economy and Politics, 1963–1983: A Bibliography.* East Balmain, NSW: Rosecons, 1984.
Aziz, Ungku A., and Yip Yat Hoon. *Projek-Projek Penyelidikan dan Penerbitan Universiti Malaya, 1959–1976.* Kuala Lumpur: University of Malaya, 1977.
Bibliografi Buku-Buku dalam Bahasa Malaysia, 1967–1970. Kuala Lumpur: Perpustakaan Negara Malaysia, 1981.
Bibliografi Buku-Buku Nadir dalam Perpustakaan Negara Malaysia. Kuala Lumpur: Perpustakaan Negara Malaysia, 1982.
Bibliografri Buku-Buku Nadir Malaysiana. Kuala Lumpur: Perpustakaan Negara Malaysia, 1982.
Bibliografi Negara Malaysia. Kuala Lumpur: Perpustakaan Negara Malaysia, Arkib Negara Malaysia, 1969–
Bibliografi Negeri Perak. Kuala Lumpur: Perpustakaan Negara Malaysia, 1983.
Bibliografi Negri Sabah. Kuala Lumpur: Perpustakaan Negara Malaysia, 1985.
Bibliografi Negri Trengganu. Kuala Lumpur: Perpustakaan Negara Malaysia, 1985.
Bibliografi Sejarah dan Politik. Kuala Lumpur: Perpustakaan Negara Malaysia, 1982.
Bibliografi UMNO dan Perjuangan Kebangsaan. Kuala Lumpur: Perpustakaan Negara Malaysia, 1985.
Bottoms, J. C. 'Some Malay Historical Sources: A Bibliographical Note', in Soedjatmoko et al., *An Introduction to Indonesian Historiography.* Ithaca: Cornell University Press, 1965.
Brown, Ian, and Ampalavanar, Rajeswary. *Malaysia.* Oxford, Santa Barbara, Denver: Clio Press, 1986.
Bryant, C. R. *Recent Bibliographical Activities in Malaysia and Singapore: A Brief Survey with a Selected, Annotated Bibliography.* New Haven: Yale University, 19– .

Challis, Joyce, ed. *Annotated Bibliography of Economic and Social Material in Sabah (North Borneo) and Sarawak*. Singapore: University of Singapore, 1969.
Challis, Joyce, ed. *Annotated Bibliography of Economic and Social Material in Singapore and West Malaysia: Governmental Publications*. Singapore: University of Singapore, 1969.
Challis, Joyce, ed. *Annotated Bibliography of Economic and Social Material in Singapore and West Malaya: Non-Governmental Publications*. Singapore: University of Singapore, 1969.
Cheang, Molly, Sng Yok Fong and Wee, Carolyn. *Index to Singapore/Malaysia Legal Periodicals, 1932–1984*. Singapore and Kuala Lumpur: Malayan Law Journal, 1986.
Cheesman, Harold. *Bibliography of Malaya: Being a Classified List of Books Wholly or Partly in English Relating to the Federation of Malaya and Singapore*. London: Longmans, 1959.
Chng, David K. Y. *A Select Bibliography of Chinese Sources for Nineteenth-Century Singapore*. Singapore: Singapore National Library, 1987.
Cotter, Conrad P. *Bibliography of English-Language Sources on Human Ecology, Eastern Malaysia and Brunei*. Honolulu: Department of Asian Studies, University of Hawaii, 1965.
Cotter, Conrad P. *Reading List of English-Language Materials in the Social Sciences on British Borneo*. Honolulu: Reference Bureau, University of Hawaii Library, 1960.
Drake, P. J. 'The Economic Development of British Malaya to 1914: An Essay in Historiography with some Questions for Historians', JSEAS, 10, 2 (Sept. 1979).
Habsah Hj. Ibrahim and Zainab Awang Ngah. *Bibliografi Aspek-Aspek Sosio-Budaya Penanaman dan Penggunaan Padi di Malaysia*. Kuala Lumpur: Perpustakaan Universiti Malaya, 1981.
Heussler, R. *British Malaya. A Bibliographical and Biographical Compendium*. New York: Garland Publishing, 1981.
Hill, Lewis. *A Checklist of English-Language Fiction Relating to Malaysia, Singapore and Brunei*. Hull: Centre for South-East Asian Studies, University of Hull, 1986.
Hill, R. D. 'Materials for Historical Geography and Economic History of Southeast Asia in Nineteenth-Century Malayan Newspapers', JMBRAS, 44, 2 (1971).
Index of Articles in the Journal of Southeast Asian History (1960–1969) and the Journal of Southeast Asian Studies (1970–1979).
Ismail Hussein. *Bibliografi Teks Cetakan Sastera Tradisi Melayu*. Kuala Lumpur: Jabatan Pengajian Melayu, Universiti Malaya, 1978.
Johore: A Bibliography. Kuala Lumpur: Perpustakaan Universiti Malaya, 1982.
Karni, R. S. *Bibliography of Malaysia and Singapore*. Kuala Lumpur: Penerbit Universiti Malaya, 1980.
Katalog Koleksi Melayu: Catalogue of the Malay Collection of the University of Malaya Library. Kuala Lumpur: Perpustakaan Universiti Malaya, 1980.
Khoo Kay Kim. 'Recent Malaysian Historiography', JSEAS, 10, 2 (Sept. 1979).
Krausse, Sylvia C. Engelen, and Krausse, Gerald H. *Brunei*. Oxford, Santa Barbara, Denver: Clio Press, 1988.
Kuah Sim Joo, Monica, and Che Puteh binti Ismail. *Prehistory and Archaeology of Malaysia and Brunei: A Bibliography*. Kuala Lumpur: Perpustakaan Universiti Malaya, 1982.
Leigh, Michael B. *Checklist of Holdings on Borneo in the Cornell University Libraries*. Ithaca: Southeast Asia Program, Department of Asian Studies, Cornell University, 1966.

Leong, Alice. *Select List of Singapore Parliamentary Papers, 1948–1976*. Singapore: Chopmen Enterprises, 1977.

Lent, John. *Malaysian Studies: Present Knowledge and Research Trends*. DeKalb: Center for Southeast Asian Studies, Northern Illinois University, 1979.

Lim, Beda. *Malaya: A Background Bibliography*. Kuala Lumpur: Malaysian Branch, Royal Asiatic Society, 1962.

Lim Huck Tee, Edward, and Wijasuriya, D. E. K. *Index Malaysiana: An Index to the Journal of the Straits Branch, Royal Asiatic Society, and the Journal of the Malayan Branch, Royal Asiatic Society, 1878–1963*. Kuala Lumpur: Malaysian Branch, Royal Asiatic Society, 1970. Supplement 1 (1964–1973), 1974; Supplement 2 (1974–1983), 1985.

Lim Pui Huen, Patricia, ed. *The Malay World of Southeast Asia, A Select Cultural Bibliography*. Singapore: ISEAS, 1984.

Lim Pui Huen, Patricia, ed. *Newspapers Published in the Malaysian Area, with a Union List of Local Holdings*. Singapore: ISEAS, 1970.

McIntyre, W. David. 'Malaya from the 1850's to the 1870's, and Its Historians, 1950–1970: From Strategy to Sociology' in C. D. Cowan and O. W. Wolters, eds, *Southeast Asian History and Historiography*. Ithaca: Cornell University Press, 1976.

Malaysian Historical Society. *An Index to 'Malaysia in History'*. Kuala Lumpur: Malaysian Historical Society, 1981.

Padma, Daniel. 'A Descriptive Catalogue of the Books Relating to Malaysia in the Raffles Museum and Library', JMBRAS, 19, 3, no. 141 (Dec. 1941).

Pelzer, Karl J. *Selected Bibliography on the Geography of Southeast Asia. Part 3. Malaya*. New Haven: Human Relations Area Files, 1956.

Pelzer, Karl. *West Malaysia and Singapore: A Selected Bibliography*. New Haven: Human Relations Area Files, 1971.

Quah, Stella R., and Quah, Jon S. T. *Singapore*. Oxford, Santa Barbara, Denver: Clio Press, 1988.

Roff, Margaret. *Official Publications of Malaysia, Singapore and Brunei in New York Public Libraries*. New York: Columbia University, 1971.

Roff, W. R. *Bibliography of Malay and Arabic Periodicals Published in the Straits Settlements and Peninsular Malay States 1876–1941*. London: Oxford University Press, 1972.

Roff, W. R. *Guide to Malay Periodicals, 1876–1941*. Singapore: Eastern Universities Press, 1961.

Roff, W. R. *Southeast Asian Research Tools: Malaysia, Singapore, Brunei*. Honolulu: Southeast Asian Studies, Asian Studies Program, University of Hawaii, 1979.

Saw Swee-Hock and Cheng Siok-Hwa. *A Bibliography of the Demography of Malaysia and Brunei*. Singapore: University Educational Press, 1975.

Saw Swee-Hock and Cheng Siok-Hwa. *A Bibliography of the Demography of Singapore*. Singapore: University Educational Press, 1975.

Shaika Zakaria, Datin, ed. *Poverty in Malaysia: A Bibliography*. Kuala Lumpur: Library, University of Malaya, 1986.

Singapore National Bibliography. Singapore: National Library, 1969– . Quarterly, with annual cumulations, 1977– .

Singapore National Library. *The Birth of a Nation—Singapore in the 1950s: A Select Bibliography*. Singapore: Singapore National Library, 1984.

Singapore, National Library. *Books About Singapore, 1970*. Singapore: National Library, 1970, 1975, 1979, 1982, 1984.

Soosai, J. S., and Kaw, H. W. *Fifty Years of Natural Rubber Research, 1926–1975: A Bibliography of Contributions from the Rubber Research Institute of Malaysia*.

Kuala Lumpur: Rubber Research Institute of Malaysia, 1975.

Stockwell, A. J. 'The Historiography of Malaysia: Recent Writings in English on the History of the Area since 1874', *Journal of Imperial and Commonwealth History*, 5, 1 (Oct. 1976).

Subbiah, Rama. *Tamil Malaysiana*. Kuala Lumpur: University of Malaya Library, 1969.

Tay Lian Soo. *Classified Bibliography of Chinese Historical Materials in Malaysia and Singapore*. Singapore: South Seas Society, 1984.

Tong Suit Chee. *Bibliography of Penang*. Pulau Pinang: Perpustakaan Universiti Sains Malaysia, 1974.

Tregonning, K. G. *Malaysian Historical Sources*. Singapore: History Department, University of Singapore, 1962.

Turnbull, C. M. 'Bibliography of Writings in English on British Malaya, 1786–1867'. Published as Appendix to Lennox A. Mills, *British Malaya, 1824–1867* (1966 edn). Kuala Lumpur: Oxford University Press, 1966.

Universiti Kebangsaan Malaysia. Perpustakaan. *Islam dalam Peradaban Melayu: Suata Bibliograpfi*. Kuala Lumpur: Universiti Kebangsaan Malaysia, 1976.

Universiti Malaya. Perpustakaan. *Koleksi Za'ba*. Kuala Lumpur: Perpustakaan University Malaya, 1976.

University of Singapore. Library. *Catalogue of the Singapore/Malaysia Collection*. Boston: G. K. Hall, 1968.

Wong Lin Ken. 'The Economic History of Malaysia: A Bibliographic Essay'. *Journal of Economic History*, 25, 2 (June 1965).

Wong Lin Ken, '20th Century Malayan Economic History: A Select Bibliographic Survey', JSEAS, 10, 1 (Mar. 1979).

Zainab Awang Ngah. *Kelantania di Perpustakaan Universiti Malaya*. Kuala Lumpur: Perpustakaan Universiti Malaya, 1979.

Manuscripts

Howard, Joseph H., ed. *Malay Manuscripts: A Bibliographical Guide*. Kuala Lumpur: University of Malaya Library, 1966.

Juynboll, H. H. *Catalogus van de Maleische en Sundaneesche Handschriften der Leidsche Universiteits Bibliotheek*. Leiden: E. J. Brill, 1899.

Manuskrip Melayu Warisan Budaya Negara. Kuala Lumpur: Perpustakaan Negara Malaysia, 1984.

THE PHILIPPINES

Bernardo, Gabriel., comp. [ed. by Natividad P. Verzosa]. *Bibliography of Philippine Bibliographies, 1593–1961*. Quezon City: Ateneo de Manila University Press, 1968.

Houston, Charles O. Jr. *Philippine Bibliography, I: An Annotated Preliminary Bibliography of Philippine Bibliographies (since 1900)*. Manila: University of Manila, 1960.

Hart, Donn V. *An Annotated Bibliography of Philippine Bibliographies: 1965–1974*. DeKalb: Center for Southeast Asian Studies, Northern Illinois University, 1974.

Saito, Shiro, *The Philippines. A Review of Bibliographies*. Honolulu: University of Hawaii, East-West Center Library, 1966.

Antonio, Celia M., and Tan, Allen L. *A Preliminary Bibliography of Philippine Cultural Minorities*. Quezon City: Commission on National Minorities, Republic of the Philippines, 1967.

Baradi, Edita R. *Southeast Asia Research Tools: The Philippines*. Honolulu: University of Hawaii, 1979.

Baylon, Concepcion S. *The National Library: guide to doctoral dissertations on microfilm (1937–68) in the Filipiniana Division*. Manila: National Library, 1971.

Bernardo, Gabriel A., and Vergosa, Natividad P., comps; Schumacher, John N., ed. *Philippine Retrospective National Bibliography: 1523–1699*. Manila: National Library of the Philippines and Ateneo de Manila University Press, 1974.

Bibliography of the Philippine Islands, Vol. 1: *A List of Books (with references to Periodicals) in the Library of Congress*. By A. P. C. Griffin. With Chronological List of Maps in the Library of Congress. By P. Lee Phillips. Vol. 2: *Biblioteca Filipina*. By T. H. Pardo de Tavera. Washington, DC: GPO, 1903.

Catalogue of Filipiniana Materials in the Lopez Memorial Museum (5 vols). Pasay City: Lopez Memorial Museum, 1962–71.

Conklin, Harold. *Ifugao Bibliography*. New Haven: Southeast Asian Studies Program, Yale University, 1968.

Doeppers, Daniel F. *Union Catalogue of Selected Bureau Reports and Other Official Serials of the Philippines, 1908–1941*. Madison: Center for Southeast Asian Studies, University of Wisconsin-Madison, 1980.

Eggan, Frederick Russell. *Selected Bibliography of the Philippines, topically arranged and annotated*. New Haven: Philippine Studies Program, University of Chicago, 1956.

Elaner, Emma Osterman. *Checklist of Publications of the Government of the Philippine Islands, September 1, 1900 to December 31, 1917*. Manila: Philippine Library and Museum, 1918.

Ferrer, Maxima Magsanoc. *Union Catalog of Philippine Materials* (2 vols). Quezon City: University of the Philippines Press, 1970.

Foronda, Marcelino A., and Cresencia R. *A Filipiniana Bibliography, 1743–1982 (A Classified Listing of Philippine Materials in the Marcelino A. and Crescencia R. Foronda Private Collection)*. Manila: Philippine National Historical Society, 1981.

Golay, Frank H., and Hauswedell, Marianne H. *An Annotated Guide to Philippine Serials*. Ithaca: Department of Asian Studies, Cornell University, 1976.

Griffin, Appleton Prentiss Clark. *List of Works Relating to the American Occupation of the Philippine Islands, 1898–1903*. Washington, DC: GPO, 1905.

Lietz, Paul S. *Calendar of Philippine Documents in the Ayer Collection of the Newberry Library*. Chicago: Newberry Library, 1956.

Medina, Jose Toribio. *La Imprenta en Manila desde sus origines hasta 1810*. Amsterdam: N. Israel, 1964.

Netzorg, Morton J. *The Philippines in World War II and to Independence (Dec. 8, 1941–July 4, 1946): An Annotated Bibliography*. Ithaca: Department of Asian Studies, Cornell University, 1977.

Palao, Trinidad E. *A Bibliography of Filipiniana Imprints: 1800–1850*. Manila: University of the Philippines, 1973.

Pardo de Tavera, Trinidad H. *Biblioteca filipina; o sea, Catalogo razonada de todos impresos tanto insulares como extranjeros, relativos a la historia, la etnografia, la linguistica, la botanica, la fauna, la flora, la geologia, la hidrografia, la geografia, la legislacion, etc. de las Islas Filipinas, de Jolo y Marianas*. Washington, DC: GPO, 1903.

Perez, Angel y Guemes, Ceciliio. *Adiciones y continuacion de 'La Imprenta en Manila' de D. J. T. Medina, O Rarezas y curiosidades bibliografico Filipinas de las bibliotecas de esta Capital*. Manila: Impr. de Santos y bernal, 1904.

Philippine Bibliography. Quezon City: Library, University of the Philippines, 1965–73.

Philippine National Bibliography. Manila: National Library of the Philippines, 1974.

Philippine Studies Program, University of Chicago. *Selected Bibliography of the Philippines*. Westport: Greenwood Press, 1973 (first published 1956).

Rebadavia, Consolacion B., comp.; Verzosa, Natividad P., and Austria, Pacifico M., eds. *Checklist of Philippine Government Documents, 1917–1949*. Quezon City: University of the Philippines Library, 1960.

Retana y Gamboa, Wenceslao Emilio. *Archivo del Bibliofilo Filipino. Recopilacion de Documentos Historicos, Cientificos, Literarios y Politicos y estudios Bibliograficos* (5 vols). Madrid, 1895.

Retana, W. E. *Aparato Bibliografico de la Historia General de Filipinas deducido de la Colleccion que Posee en Barcelona La Compania General de Tabacos de Dichas Islas* (3 vols). Madrid: Imprenta de la Sucesora de M. Minuesa de los Rios. Manila: Pedro B. Ayuda y Compania, 1964.

Richardson, Jim. *Philippines*. Oxford: Clio Press, 1989.

Robertson, James A., and Blair, Emma H. *The Philippine Islands, 1493–1898*, vol. 53: *Bibliography of the Philippines*. Mandaluyong, Rizal: Cachos Hermanos, 1973.

Robertson, James A. *Bibliography of the Philippine Islands*. New York: Kraus Reprint Co., 1970 (first published 1908).

Saito, Shiro. *Philippine Ethnography: A Critically Annotated and Selected Bibliography*. Honolulu: University Press of Hawaii, 1972.

Siega, Gorgonio D., et al. *A Classified Annotated Bibliography of Selected Filipiniana Materials at the Silliman University Library, Dumaguete City, Philippines*. Dumaguete City: Silliman University, 1977.

Tiamson, Alfredo T. *Mindanao–Sulu Bibliography*. Davao City: Ateneo de Davao, 1970.

Tubangui, Helen R. *A Catalog of Filipiniana at Valladolid*. Quezon City: Ateneo de Manila University Press, 1973.

University of the Philippines. Library. *Filipiniana 1968. A Classified Catalog of Filipiniana Books and Pamphlets in the University of the Philippines Library as of January 1, 1968*. Diliman, Quezon City: Library, University of the Philippines, 1969.

Welsh, Doris Varner. *A Catalogue of Printed Materials Relating to the Philippine Islands, 1519–1900 in the Newberry Library*. Chicago: Newberry Library, 1956.

INDONESIA

Tairas, J. N. B. *Indonesia: A Bibliography of Bibliographies*. New York: Oleander Press, 1975.

Anderson, Benedict R. *Bibliography of Indonesian Publications: Newspapers, Non-Government Periodicals and Bulletins, 1945–1958 at Cornell University*. Ithaca: Department of Far Eastern Studies, Cornell University, 1959.

Arief, Sritua, and Arief, Melanie Sritua. *The Indonesian Economy, 1967–1977: A Bibliography*. Jakarta: Sritua Arief Associates, 1978.

Australia. National Library. *Daftar Pengadaan Bahan Indonesia/Indonesian Acquisitions List*. Canberra: National Library of Australia.

Ave, Jan, King, Victor, and de Wit, Joke. *West Kalimantan: A Bibliography*. Dordrecht and Cinnaminson, NJ: Foris Publications, 1964.

Baal, Jan Van. *West Irian, a bibliography*. Dordrecht: Foris Publications, 1984.

Bhatta, J. N. *A Science Bibliography on Indonesia*. Djakarta: Departemen Angkatan Darat, 1965.

Bibliography of Indonesian Materials for the Humanities and Social Sciences (1960–1970). Djakarta: LIPI, 1972– .

Bibliografi Nasional Indonesia. Djakarta: Kantor Bibliografi Nasional, 1953– .

Boland, B. J. and Farjon, I. *Islam in Indonesia: A Bibliographic Survey, 1600–1942 with Post-1945 Addenda*. Dordrecht and Cinnaminson, NJ: Foris Publications, 1983.

Cense, A. A., and Uhlenbeck, E. M. *A Critical Survey of Studies on the Languages of Borneo*. s'-Gravenhage: Martinus Nijhoff, 1958.

Coolhaas, W. Ph. *A Critical Survey of Studies on Dutch Colonial History*. s'-Gravenhage: Martinus Nijhoff, 1960.

Damian, Eddy, et al. *Bibliografi Hukum Indonesia, 1945–1972*. Bandung: Lembaga Penelitian Hukum dan Kriminologi, Fakultas Hukum, Universitas Pengadjaran, 1974.

Dengel, Holk H. *Annotated Bibliography of New Indonesian Literature on the History of Indonesia*. Stuttgart: Franz Steiner Verlag Wiesbaden GMBH, 1987.

Excerpta Indonesica. Leiden: Centre for Documentation of Modern Indonesia, Royal Institute of Linguistics and Anthropology, 1971– .

Hicks, George L., and McNicoll, Geoffrey. *The Indonesian Economy, 1950–1965: A Bibliography*. New Haven: Yale University, Southeast Asian Studies Program, 1967.

Hicks, George L., and McNicoll, Geoffrey. *The Indonesian Economy, 1950–1965: A Bibliographic Supplement*. New Haven: Yale University, Southeast Asian Studies Program, 1967.

Hebig, Karl M. *Die Insel Borneo in Forschung und Schrifttum*. Sonderdruck aus den Mitteilungen der Geographischen Gesellschaft in Hamburg. Band 52. 1955.

Hooykaas, J. C. *Repertorium op de Koloniale Literatuur, of Systematische Inhoudsopgaaf van hetgeen voorkomt over de Koloniën, (beoosten de Kaap) in mengelwerken en tijdschriften, van 1595 tot 1865 uitgegeven in Nederland en zijne overzeesche besittingen*. Amsterdam: P. N. van Kampen & Zoon, 1877.

Indonesian Monographs: A Catalogue of Monograph Publications, 1945–1968. Zug: Inter Documentation Co., 1974.

Institute of Social Sciences, Waseda University. *The Nishijima Collection: Materials on the Japanese Military Occupation in Indonesia*. Tokyo: Waseda University, 1973.

Jang Aisjah Muttalib. *The History and Society of South Sumatra: Publications in New York Libraries*. New York: Columbia University Southern Asian Institute, 1971.

Joustra, M. *Overzicht van de Literatuur betreffende de Minangkabau*. Amsterdam: Minangkabau Instituut, 1924.

Karyeti, and Nurasin V. Suwahyono. *Daftar Koleksi Literatur tentang Nusa Tenggara Timur*. Jakarta: Pusat Dokumentasi Ilmiah Nasional, Lembaga Pengetahuan Indonesia, 1985.

Kennedy, R. *Bibliography of Indonesian Peoples and Cultures*. New Haven: Yale University Press, 1945.

Koentjaraningrat. *Anthropology in Indonesia: A Bibliographical Review*. 's-Gravenhage: Martinus Nijhoff, 1975.

Lan Hiang Char. *Southeast Asian Research Tools: Indonesia*. Honolulu: Southeast Asia Studies, Asian Studies Program, University of Hawaii, 1979.

Lev, Daniel S. *A Bibliography of Indonesian Government Documents and Selected Indonesian Writings on Government in the Cornell University Library*. Ithaca: Department of Far Eastern Studies, Cornell University, 1958.

Muljanto Sumardi. *Islamic Education in Indonesia: A Bibliography*. Singapore: ISEAS, 1983.

Nagelkerke, G. A. *Bibliografisch Overzicht uit Periodieken over Indonesië 1930–1945*. Leiden: Bibliotheek Koninklijk Instituut voor Taal-, Land- en Volkenkunde, 1974.

Nagelkerke, G. A. *A Selected Bibliography of the Chinese in Indonesia, 1740–1974*. London: Library of the Royal Institute of Linguistics and Anthropology, 1975.

Naim, Asma M., and Naim, Mochtar. *Bibliografi Minangkabau*. Singapore: Singapore University Press for ISEAS, 1975.

The Nishijima Collection: Materials on the Japanese Military Administration in Indonesia. Tokyo: Institute of Social Sciences, Waseda University, 1973.

Nolthenius, A. B. Tutein. *Overzicht van de literatuur betreffende de Molukken (exclusief Nieuw-Guinea)*, vol. 2 (1921–33). Amsterdam: Molukken-Instituut, 1935.

Ockeloen, G. *Catalogus van in Ned.-Indië verschenen Booken in de Jaren 1938–1941*. Batavia-Soerabaia: G. Kolff, 1942.

Ockeloen, G. *Catalogus van boeken en tijdschriften uitgegeven in Ned. Oost-Indië van 1870–1937*. Amsterdam: Swets and Zeitlinger, 1966.

Ockeloen, G. *Catalogus dari Boekoe-boekoe dan Madjallah-madjallah jang diterbitkan di Hindia Belanda dari tahoen 1870–1937*. Batavia-Amsterdam: G. Kolff, 1940.

Ockeloen, G. *Catalogus dari Buku-Buku jang diterbitkan di Indonesia*, Djilid 1: *1945–1949*. Djilid 2: *Buku dalam Bahasa Melaju, Djawa, D.L.L., 1937–1941*. Bandung: G. Kolff, 1950.

Ockeloen, G. *Catalogus dari Buku-Buku jang diterbitkan di Indonesia, 1950–51*. Bandung: G. Kolff, 1952.

Ockeloen, G. *Catalogus dari Buku-Buku jang diterbitkan di Indonesia, 1952–53*. Bandung: G. Kolff, 1954.

Ockeloen, G. *Catalogus dari Buku-Buku jang diterbitkan di Indonesia, 1954*. Bandung: G. Kolff, 1955.

Polman, Katrien. *The Central Moluccas: An Annotated Bibliography*. Dordrecht: Foris Publications, 1983.

Polman, Katrien. *The North Moluccas: An Annotated Bibliography*. The Hague: Martinus Nijhoff, 1981

Postma, Nel, Aeina Hadad, Sudarsono, B. *Bibliografi Wanita Indonesia*. Jakarta: Kantor Menteri Muda Urusan Peranan Wanita and Pusat Dokumentasi Ilmiah Nasional, Lembaga Limu Pengetahuan Indonesia, 1980 [with supplements in 1983 and 1985].

Rouffaer, G. P., and Muller, W. C. *Catalogus der Koloniale Bibliotheek van Het Koninklijk Instituut voor de Taal-, Land- en Volkenkunde van Ned.-Indië en het Indisch Genootschap*. 's-Gravenhage: Martinus Nijhoff, 1966.

Ruinen, W. *Overzicht van de Literatuur betreffende de Molukken*. Amsterdam: Molukken-Instituut, 1928.

Sherlock, Kevin. *A Bibliography of Timor, including East (formerly Portuguese) Timor, West (formerly Dutch) Timor and the Island of Roti*. Canberra: Research School of Pacific Studies, Australian National University, 1980.

Singarimbun, Masri. *The Population of Indonesia: A Bibliography.* Yogyakarta: Institute of Population Studies, Gadjah Mada University, 1974.

Soekanto, Soerjono. *Bibliografi Hukum Adat Indonesia: Akhir Abad XIX–1975.* Bandung: Alumni, 1976.

Stall, R. N. A. *A Bibliography of Indonesian Politics since 1966.* Bentley: Department of Library Studies and Department of Asian Studies, Western Australian Institute of Technology, 1979.

Stuart-Fox, David J. *Bibliography of Balinese Culture and Religion.* Jakarta: KITLV and LIPI, 1979.

Sukanda-Tessier, Viviane, with Sukanda Natasasmita, Haris. *Bibliographie d'une documentation Indonesienne Contemporaine, 1950–1970.* Paris: Ecole française d'extreme-orient, 1974.

Suzuki, P. *Critical Survey of Studies on the Anthropology of Nias, Matawi and Enggano.* 's-Gravenhage: Martinus Nijhoff, 1958.

Tan Sok Joo and Tan Hwee Kheng. *ASEAN: A Bibliography.* Singapore: ISEAS, 1976.

Teeuw, A., with Emanuels, H. W. *A Critical Survey of Studies on Malay and Bahasa Indonesia.* s'-Gravenhage: Martinus Nijhoff, 1961.

Telkamp, Gerard J. *Bouwstoffen voor de sociaal-economische geschiedenis van Indonesië van ca 1800 tot 1940; een beschrijvende bibliografie.* Amsterdam: Koninklijk Instituut voor de Tropen, 1977.

Thung, Yvonne, and Echols, John M., eds. *A Checklist of Indonesian Serials in the Cornell University Library, 1945–1970.* Ithaca: Southeast Asian Program, Cornell University, 1973.

Uhlenbeck, E. M. *A Critical Survey of Studies on the Languages of Java and Madura.* s'-Gravenhage: Martinus Nijhoff, 1964.

Van Baal, J., Galis, K. W., and Koentjaraningrat, R. M. *West Irian: A Bibliography.* Dordrecht and Cinnaminson, NJ: Foris Publications, 1984.

Van Delden, E. E. *Klein Repertorium. Index op tijdschriftartikelen met betrekking tot voormalig Nederlands-Indië.* Amsterdam: Koninklijk Instituut voor de Tropen, 1900.

Van Doorn, Marlene. *Bouwstoffen voor de sociaal-economische geschiedenis van Indonesië van ca 1800 tot 1940: een beschrijvende bibliografie.* Amsterdam: Koninklijk Instituut voor de Tropen, 1979.

Voorhoeve, P. *A Critical Survey of Studies on the Languages of Sumatra.* s'-Gravenhage: Martinus Nijhoff, 1955.

Wellen, J. W. J., and Helfrich, O. L. *Zuid-Sumatra. Overzicht van de Literatuur des Gewesten Bengkoelen, Djambi, de Lampongsche Districten en Palembang.* 's-Gravenhage: De Nederlandsche Boek- en Steendrukkerij, 1923.

Yayasan Idayu. *Bung Karno: Sebuah Bibliografi Memuat Daftar Karya oleh dan tentang Bung Karno.* Jakarta: Yayasan Idayu, 1981.

Manuscripts

Girardet, Nikolaus, et al. *Descriptive Catalogue of the Javanese Manuscripts and Printed Books in the Main Libraries of Surakarta and Yogyakarta.* Wiesbaden: Franz Steiner Verlag GMBH, 1983.

Juynboll, H. H. *Catalogus van de Maleische en Sundaneesche Handschriften der Leidsche Universiteits Bibliotheek.* Leiden: E. J. Brill, 1989.

Ricklefs, M. C., and Voorhoeve, P. *Indonesian Manuscripts in Great Britain.* Oxford University Press, 1977.

BURMA

Aung-Thwin, Michael. *Southeast Asia Research Tools: Burma*. Honolulu: University of Hawaii, 1979.
Barnett, L. D. *A Catalogue of the Burmese Books in the British Museum*. London: Longmans, 1913.
Bernot, D. *Bibliographie Birmanie (1950–1960)*. Paris: Editions du Centre National de la Recherche Scientifique, 1968.
Griffin, Andrew. *A Brief Guide to Sources for the Study of Burma in the India Office Records*. London: India Office Library and Records, 1979.
Morse, Ronald A., et al. *Burma: A Study Guide*. Washington, DC: Wilson Center Press, 1988.
Shulman, Frank Joseph. *Burma: An Annotated Guide to International Doctoral Dissertation Research, 1898–1985*. Lanhan, New York, London: University Press of America for the Wilson Center, 1986.
Tan Sok Joo. *Library Resources on Burma in Singapore*. Singapore: ISEAS, 1972.
Trager, Frank N. *Furnivall of Burma: An Annotated Bibliography of the Works of J. S. Furnivall*. New Haven: Southeast Asia Studies, Yale University, 1963.
Trager, Frank N. *Japanese and Chinese Language Sources on Burma: An Annotated Bibliography*. New Haven: Human Relations Area Files Press, 1957.
Whitbread, Kenneth. *Catalogue of Burmese Printed Books in the India Office Library*. London: HMSO, 1969.

THAILAND

Hart, D. V. *Thailand: An Annotated Bibliography of Bibliographies*. DeKalb: Northern Illinois University, Center for Southeast Asian Studies, 1977.

Amyot, Jacques, with Soontornpasuch, Suthep. *Changing Patterns of Social Structure in Thailand, 1851–1965: An Annotated Bibliography with Comments*. Delhi: UNESCO Research Centre, 1965.
Bernath, Frances A. *Catalogue of Thai Language Holdings in the Cornell University Libraries through 1964*. Ithaca: Department of Asian Studies, Cornell University, 1964.
Bibliography of Thammasat University Library. Bangkok: Thammasat University Library, 1979.
Bitz, Ira. *A Bibliography of English-Language Source Materials on Thailand in the Humanities, Social Sciences and Physical Sciences*. Washington, DC: Center for Research on Social Systems, The American University, 1968.
Chety, Sida. *Research on Thailand in the Philippines: An Annotated Bibliography of Theses, Dissertations, and Investigation Papers*. Ithaca: Southeast Asia Program, Cornell University, 1977.
Chulalongkorn University, Central Library. *Bibliography of Material about Thailand in Western Languages*. Bangkok: Chulalongkorn University, 1960.
Kawabe, Toshio. *Bibliography of Thai Studies*. Tokyo: Tokyo University of Foreign Studies, Institute of Foreign Affairs, 1957.
Keyes, C. F. *Southeast Asia Research Tools: Thailand*. Asian Studies Program, University of Hawaii, 1979.

Mabbett, Ian, ed. *Early Thai History: A Select Bibliography*. Clayton: Monash University, Centre of Southeast Asian Studies, [1978].

Mason, John Brown, and Parish, H. Carroll. *Thailand Bibliography*. Gainesville: Department of Reference and Bibliography, University of Florida Libraries, 1958.

National Library (Bangkok). *Periodicals and Newspapers Printed in Thailand between 1844–1934: A Bibliography*. Bangkok: National Library, 1970.

Raksasataya, Amara, with Veeravat Kanchanadul, Prachak Suthayakom, et al. *Thailand: Social Science Materials in Thai and Western Languages*. Bangkok: National Institute of Development Adminstration, 1966.

Saengthong, M. Ismail. *Library Resources on Thailand in Singapore*. Singapore: ISEAS, 1974.

Sangtada, Rattporn. *Isan (Northeast Thailand): A Select Bibliography*. Sydney: University of Sydney, 1986.

Sharp, Lauriston, et al. *Bibliography of Thailand*. Ithaca: Southeast Asia Program, Department of Far Eastern Studies, Cornell University, 1956.

Thrombley, W. G., et al. *Thai Government and Its Setting: A Selective, Annotated Bibliography in English and Thai*. Bangkok: National Institute of Development Administration, 1967.

Thrombley, W. G., and Siffin, W. J. *Thailand: Politics, Economy and Socio-Cultural Setting: A Selective Guide to the Literature*. Bloomington: Indiana University Press, 1972.

Watts, Michael. *Thailand*. Oxford, Santa Barbara, Denver: Clio Press, 1986.

Wyatt, David K. *Preliminary Thailand Bibliography*. Ithaca: Published privately by the author, 1971.

VIETNAM, CAMBODIA, LAOS

Auvade, Robert. *Bibliographie Critique des Oeuvres Parues sur l'Indochine Française*. Paris: G.-P. Maisonneuve & Larose, 1965.

Boudet, Paul, and Bourgeois, Remi. *Bibliographie de l'Indochine Française, 1913–1935*. Hanoi: Imprimerie d'Extreme-Orient, 1921–1943. 4 vols. Hanoi: IDEA, 1929–1932, 1943.

Burns, Richard D., and Leitenberg, Milton. *The Wars in Vietnam, Cambodia and Laos, 1945–1982: A Bibliographic Guide*. Santa Barbara: ABC-Clio Information Services, 1984.

Chen, John H. M. *Vietnam: A Comprehensive Bibliography*. Metuchen, NJ: Scarecrow Press, 1973.

Cotter, M. G. *Vietnam: A Guide to Reference Sources*. Boston: G. K. Hall, 1977.

Fisher, Mary L. *Cambodia: An Annotated Bibliography of Its History, Geography, Politics and Economy since 1954*. Cambridge, Mass: Center for International Studies, MIT, 1967.

Gaspardone, E. 'Bibliographie annamite', Hanoi: BEFEO, 1934.

Halpern, Joel, and Hafner, James A. *Bibliography of Miscellaneous Research Materials on Laos*. Bruxelles: Centre d'Etude du Sud-Est Asiatique et de l'Extreme Orient, 1971.

Halpern, Joel, and Hafner, James A. *A Bibliography of Miscellaneous Research Materials Pertaining to Laos, Cambodia, Vietnam and the Mekong River*. SEADAG (mimeo), n.d.

Hobbs, Cecil, et al. eds. *Indochina: A Bibliography of the Land and People*. New York: Greenwood Press, 1969 (first published in 1950).
'Indochine annamite', BEFEO, 21 (1921).
Jumper, Roy. *Bibliography on the Political and Administrative History of Vietnam, 1802–1962*. Saigon: Michigan State University Vietnam Advisory Group, 1962.
Keyes, C. F. *Southeast Asia Research Tools: Cambodia*. Honolulu: University of Hawaii, 1979.
Keyes, C. F. *Southeast Asia Research Tools: Laos*. Honolulu: University of Hawaii, 1979.
Keyes, Jane Godfrey. *A Bibliography of Vietnamese Publications in the Cornell University Library*. Ithaca: Department of Asian Studies, Cornell University, 1962.
Keyes, Jane Godfrey. *A Bibliography of Western-Language Publications Concerning North Vietnam in the Cornell University Library*. Ithaca: Southeast Asia Program, Department of Asian Studies, Cornell University, 1971.
Lafort, Pierre-Bernard. *Bibliographie du Laos* [Vol. 1: *1666–1961*; Vol. 2: *1962–1975*]. 2nd edn. Paris: EFEO, 1978.
List of Vietnam and Southeast Asia Holdings. Carbondale: Southern Illinois University, 1971.
Mekong Documentation Centre of the Committee for Coordination of Investigations of the Lower Mekong Basin. *Cambodia: A Select Bibliography*. Bangkok: Mekong Documentation Centre, 1967.
Mekong Documentation Centre of the Committee for Coordination of Investigations of the Lower Mekong Basin. *Viet-Nam: A Reading List*. Bangkok: Mekong Documentation Centre, 1967.
Ng Shui Meng. *Demographic Materials on the Khmer Republic, Laos and Vietnam*. Singapore: ISEAS, 1974.
Nguyen The-Anh. *Bibliographie Critique sur les Relations Entre Le Viet-Nam et L'Occident: Ouvrages et articles en langues occidentales*. Paris: G.-P. Maisonneuve & Larose, 1967.
Oey, Giok Po. *Checklist of the Vietnamese Holdings of the Wason Collection, Cornell University Libraries, as of June, 1971*. Ithaca: Southeast Asia Program, Department of Asian Studies, Cornell University, 1971.
Peake, Louis A. *The US in the Vietnam War, 1954: A Selected Annotated Bibliography*. New York and London: Garland Publishing, 1986.
Phan Thien Chau. *Vietnamese Communism: A Research Bibliography*. Westport: Greenwood Press, 1975.
Pretzell, Klause A., and Bode, Jutta. *Indochina: A Select Bibliography* [Vol. 1: *Indochina, Laos, Cambodia*; Vol. 2: *Vietnam*]. Hamburg: Institut fur Asienkunde, 1980.
Rony, A. Kohar. *Vietnamese Holdings in the Library of Congress: A Bibliography*. Washington, DC: Library of Congress, 1982.
Ross, Marion W. *Bibliography of Vietnamese Literature in the Wason Collection at Cornell University*. Ithaca: Southeast Asia Program, Department of Asian Studies, Cornell University, 1973.
Sage, William W., and Henchy, Judith A. N. *Laos: A Bibliography*. Singapore: ISEAS, 1986.
Sugnet, Christopher L., Hickey, John T., and Crispino, Robert. *Vietnam War Bibliography: Selected from Cornell University's Echols Collection*. Lexington, and Toronto: Lexington Books and D. C. Health, 1983.
Tanby, Zaleha. *Cambodia: A Bibliography*. Singapore: ISEAS, 1982.
Tran Thi Kim Sa. *Bibliography on Vietnam, 1954–1964*. Saigon: National Institute of Administration, 1966.

SPECIAL TOPICS

American Geographical Society. *Research Catalogue of the American Geographical Society*, Vol. 13: *Asia*. Boston: G. K. Hall, 1962.

American Geographical Society. Map Department. *Index to Maps in Books and Periodicals*. Boston: G. K. Hall, 1968.

Bartlett, H. H. *Fire in Relation to Primitive Agriculture and Grazing in the Tropics. Annotated Bibliography*. 1956.

Catalogue of the Colonial Office Library, London. Boston: G. K. Hall, 1964.

Catalogus der Koloniale Bibliotheek van het Koninklijk Instituut voor de Taal-, Land- en Volkenkunde van Ned. Indië en het Indisch Genootschap. The Hague: Martinus Nijhoff, 1980.

Conklin, Harold C. *The Study of Shifting Cultivation*. Washington, DC: Union Panamericana, 1963.

Coolhaas, Willem P. *A Critical Survey of Studies on Dutch Colonial History*. 's-Gravenhage: Martinus Nijhoff, 1960.

Cox, Edward Godfrey. *A Reference Guide to the Literature of Travel*. Seattle: University of Washington, 1935.

Ensor, A. G. S. *A Subject Bibliography of the Second World War: Books in English, 1939–1974*. London: André Deutsch, 1977.

Fan Kok Sim. *Women in Southeast Asia: A Bibliography*. Boston: G. K. Hall, 1982.

Farrington, Anthony. *The Records of the East India College, Haileybury, and Other Institutions*. London: HMSO, 1976.

Great Britain. Colonial Office. Library. *Catalogue of the Colonial Office Library*. London: G. K. Hall, 1964.

Great Britain. Colonial Office. *Reading List on Colonial Development and Welfare*. London, 1951.

Great Britain. Foreign and Commonwealth Office. *Accessions to the library, May 1971–June 1977*. Boston: G. K. Hall, 1979.

Halstead, John P., and Porcari, Serafino. *Modern European Imperialism: A Bibliography of Books and Articles, 1815–1972*, Vol. 1: *General and British Empire*; Vol. 2: *French and Other Empires; Regions*. Boston: G. K. Hall, 1974.

Hufner, Klaus, and Naumann, Jens. *The United Nations System—International Bibliography*. München: Verlag Dokumentation, 1976.

Nagelkerke, G. A. *A Selected Bibliography of the Chinese in Indonesia*. Leiden: Library of the Royal Institute of Linguistics and Anthropology, 1975.

National Maritime Museum. *Catalogue of the Library*. London: HMSO, 1968.

Nevadomsky, J.-j., and Li, A. *The Chinese in Southeast Asia: A Selected and Annotated Bibliography of Publications in Western Languages, 1960–1970*. Berkeley: University of California, Center for South and Southeast Asian Studies, 1973.

Postma, Nel, et al. *Bibliografi Wanita Indonesia*. Jakarta: Kantor Menmud UPW/LIPI, 1980.

Royal Empire Society. *Subject Catalogue of the Library of the Royal Empire Society*. London: Dawsons of Pall Mall for the Royal Commonwealth Society, 1967.

Tiele, P. A. *Mémoire bibliographique sur les Journaux des Navigateurs Neerlandais*. Amsterdam: N. Israel Publishing Dept, 1960.

UNESCO. *Bibliography of Publications Issued by UNESCO or under Its Auspices (The First Twenty-Five Years: 1946 to 1971)*. Paris: UNESCO, 1973.

United States of America. Library of Congress, Geography and Map Division. *The Bibliography of Cartography*. Boston: Micropublications, G. K. Hall, 1973. First supplement, 1980.

Winton, Harry N. M. *Publications of the United Nations System: A Reference Guide*. New York and London: R. R. Bowker and Unipub, 1972.

INDEX

comets, 221, 233–4, 236, 238
Comintern, *see* Russia
Common Alliance Society, *see* Tung
    Meng Hui
Commonwealth, 590, 595, 598, 614, 635,
    639
Commonwealth Five-Power Defence
    Arrangement, *see* ANZUK
communications revolution, 564
communism, 108, 168, 179, 241–317
    passim, 337–476 *passim*, 521–61
    passim, 586–642 *passim*;
    *see also specific countries, persons and
        political parties*
Communist Party of Kampuchea, *see*
    CPK
Communist Party of Thailand, 438,
    442–3, 608, 623
Communist Party of the Philippines
    Marxist-Leninist, 621
community:
challenges to, 509, 514–16, 525;
compromise between old and new,
    519;
'imagined community', 517;
popular culture and, 513–14, 519, 579;
traditional cultural values, 510,
    513–14, 517–18, 522, 577–8;
see also villages
computer industry, 484, 488;
see also electronics
concubinage, 178, 183;
see also sexual conduct
Confucianism, 58–155 *passim*, 202–4,
    216, 237, 243, 279, 515–16, 530, 536,
    540–4, 564, 575
Confucius, 575
Congress of Indonesian Mystics, *see*
    BKKI
Congress Party, 285, 302, 315–16
conservatism, 517
Constitutionalist Party, 317
Consultative Council of Indonesian
    Muslims, *see* Majlis Sjuru Muslimin
    Indonesia
consumerism, *see* economy
Consumers' Association of Penang, 432
Cooper, Duff, 355
copper, 482
coral reefs, 508
Coral Sea, Battle of the, 332
cordage fibre, 184
corn cultivation, 427
Cornwallis, Lord, 94
Corregidor, 331–2
Cotabato, 231
cottage industries, 193
cotton cultivation, 136, 467
Council for Mutual Economic
    Assistance, *see* COMECON
Council of Muslim parties, *see* MIAI
Cowie, W. C., 62
CPK, 401

Crawfurd, John, 36, 42–3, 46, 67
credit, 144, 146, 157, 160, 174–5, 190–1;
    see also banks and banking;
        moneylenders
creoles, 89
crime, 100, 191
Crosthwaite, Sir Charles, 40, 119–21,
    125
Cuba, 640
Cullinane, Michael, 96
Cuong De, 237
currency, *see* money
Curzon, Lord, 39
Cushman, Jennifer, 110
Czechoslovakia, 361, 441

Da Nang, 42–5, 220
Dahlan, Kijai Hadji Admad, 270
Dahm, Bernhard, 266
dakwah movements, 432, 562, 566, 573–4
Dalhousie, Lord, 37–8, 40
Dalrymple, Alexander, 8, 27, 62
Damrong, 121–2, 308
Danang, 505, 546
Danang Bay, 41
danhyang cult, 568
Dao Lanh sect, 221–2
DAP, 414–15, 429–30
d'Argenlieu, Admiral, 347, 359–60, 366
Darsano, 269
Darul Arqam, 573
Darul Islam, 363, 407–8, 520–1, 536,
    538, 547
Davao, 505
Davis, Vice-Admiral, 371
Davis, Sir John, 43
DDT, 484
De Gaulle, Charles, 342–3, 345–6
De Graaff, Simon, 107
De Graeff, A. C. D., 270
De Jonge, B. C. D., Jonkheer, 270, 273
De Latre de Tassigny, General, 369–70,
    376
death by burning, *see* self-immolation
debts, 144, 146, 161, 165, 173, 190, 232,
    234, 280, 416, 443
Declaration for a New Economic Order,
    640
Declaration of ASEAN Concord, 628
Decoux, —, 334
Defenders of the Fatherland, *see* PETA
deforestation, 181, 507–8, 533
Del Pilar, Gregorio, 259
Deli, 104
Deli Planters Association, 159
democracy, 250
Democrata group, 241
Democratic Action Party, *see* DAP
Democratic Party (Cambodia), 398–400
Dening, M. E., 355
Development Unity Party, *see* PPP
Dewan Da'wah Islamiyah Indonesia,
    574

1222888

education *contd:*
  elementary, 116–17, 124, 207–8, 223, 236, 301, 471, 495, 550–3;
  higher, 85, 90, 117, 124, 181, 267, 287–8, 295, 301, 495, 550–3, 573–4;
  investments, 186;
  languages of instruction, 90, 92, 116–17, 299, 312;
  medical, 181, 267;
  modern, 480, 514, 518, 532, 558, 560, 573, 577–8, 587, 593;
  private and boarding schools, 31, 90, 92, 116–17, 251, 534;
  religious schooling, 116, 124–5, 207–9, 219, 223, 236, 251, 271, 411, 534–74 *passim*, 577;
  women, 267, 502, 504, 515
EEC, 617
Egypt, 39, 593
Eisenhower, Dwight David, 371, 597–8, 618
Ekadasa Rudra ceremony, 563
electrical goods, 483
electricity, 492, 501
electronic media, 532, 571–2, 578;
  see also radio; television
electronics, 483
Elephant Mountain, 221–2
elephants, 240
Elysée agreement, 367
Emden, 253
Emerson, Rupert, 97–8, 113
Enche Mohamad, 75
England, *see* Britain
Enrile, Juan Ponce, 636
Entente Cordiale, 253
entertainment, 132, 191, 533;
  see also specific entertainments
entrepreneurship:
  banking, 157;
  British, 23, 25, 54;
  Chinese, 114, 139, 147, 152, 174, 413, 496–7;
  Chinese mestizos, 138, 159;
  European, 38;
  French, 39, 283;
  indigenous, 175, 186;
  investment field, 185;
  Italian, 39;
  land holdings, 146–7;
  Malay, 413;
  multinationals and, 477;
  rubber economy, 114;
  textile industry, 159;
  tin mining, 139, 147;
  see also trade and commerce
environment management, 159, 165, 193, 328, 507, 640;
  see also pollution
Erucakra, Sultan, *see* Dipanagara
ESCAP, 476

Eurasians, 83, 89, 106, 111, 115, 117, 275, 316, 610
Europe and Europeans:
  colonial policies advance and collapse in Southeast Asia, 3–383 *passim*, 639;
  colony restoration attempts, 341–83, 585–6;
  industrialization, 5, 11, 53–5;
  international relations and rivalry, 5–6, 9, 11–13, 39, 42, 50–1, 53–5, 71;
  world power distribution and, 380, 587–8
European Community, 480, 483, 641
European Defence Community, 370, 372, 389
European Economic Community, *see* EEC

Fabianism, 476
Falck, A. R., 18
family, 111, 113, 135, 189, 514, 519, 557;
  Chinese, 124, 148, 312
famines, 203, 212, 221, 467, 492
Far East, 353
fascism and anti-fascism, 274, 281, 337
Federated Malay States, *see* Malay States, Federated
Federated Shan states, 305;
  see also Shans
Federation of Buddhists, 518
Federation of Muslim Organizations, *see* Masjumi
Federation of Trade Organizations (Burma), 416
FELDA, 472
feminism, 516
Ferry, Jules, 39, 55
fertilizers, 186, 482, 488, 500, 508, 630;
  green revolution, 484, 490, 494, 534
festivals and feasts, 559, 574;
  see also entertainment
fibre, 185;
  see also cordage fibre
fishing, 189, 507–8
floods, 203, 238
Flores, 274
food:
  fish, 132–3, 488;
  meat, 133, 184;
  rice, 133, 184, 190;
  vegetables, 133, 189;
  wartime shortages, 335–6, 467, 491
Forbidden Mountain, 238
Ford, Gerald, 628
forest-dwelling peoples, 505, 508
Fort Dufferin, 219
Fort Marlborough, 13, 16
France:
  Britain and, 9, 11, 17, 26, 34–5, 38–46, 50–2, 253;

Greater Indonesia Party, *see* Parindra
Greece, 347, 361
green revolution, 484, 487–8, 491, 525, 531
Guam, 332
Guam Doctrine, 618, 628
Guardia de Honor, 235
Gunung Tidar, 567
Gurney, Henry, 376–7
gutta percha, 133, 140
Gutzlaff, Charles, 43, 47

Ha Tinh, 168, 280
Hadhramaut, Sayyid, 228
Hadiningrat, R. M. A. A., 267
Hague Agreement, The, 596, 610
Haiphong, 359–60
Haji Ahmad Shah, 430
Hall, Fielding, 75, 119–20
Ham Nghi, 67, 222, 237
Hamengku Buwono IX, 543
Hanoi, 169, 505, 564
Hanoi, battle for, 359–60, 365–6
Hanoi University, 107
Hardopusoro, 568
Hare–Hawes–Cutting Act, 263–4
Harrison, Francis Burton, 262, 304
Harrisons & Crosfield, 158
Hashim, Sultan of Brunei, 24–5, 61, 70
Hassan, Intje, 512
Hassanal Bolkiah, Sultan of Brunei, 621
Hassim, 61
Hastings, Warren, 94
Hatta, Mohammad:
    Japanese Occupation and, 335, 337;
    political work in Netherlands, 271, 274;
    politics and government, 266, 271, 273, 357, 361–2, 374, 406–7, 422, 540, 588, 596;
    resigns from vice-presidency, 424, 610;
    Sawito affair, 567
head-hunting, 85, 101
health and health services, *see* medical system
Heaven and Earth secret society, 242
Heng Samrin, 632–3, 638, 641
herbal medicine, *see* medical system
herbicides, 491, 508
hermits, *see* sage-hermits
Hevea brasiliensis, 148
hijacking of aircraft, 575
Hikayat Prang Sabil (Epic of the Holy War), 229
Hindu calendar, 563
Hindus and Hinduism, 529, 553–4, 557, 562–3, 576
Hirohito, Emperor, 333, 349, 356
Hitler, Adolf, 330, 332, 337
Hmong people, 119
Ho Chi Minh:
    death, 392, 606, 631;
    detention and exile, 253, 278, 280, 339, 346;

launches Vietminh, 338;
national leadership, 389–93, 395, 398;
political views, 278–9, 473, 588;
revolution and war, 338–9, 351, 358–60, 366, 373–4, 602, 606, 631;
underground communist activities, 279–81, 338
Ho Chi Minh City, 505, 564–5;
    see also Saigon
Ho Chi Minh trail, 608, 618;
    see also Cambodia
Hoa Binh, 370
Hoa Hao sect, 115, 243, 397, 516, 539–40, 545–6, 564
Hoang Hoa Tham, 67
Hoge Veluwe conference, 357
holidays, *see* festivals and feasts
Hong Kong, 43–4, 330, 486, 498, 638–9, 641
Hong River, 45–6
Hong River delta, 141, 221
hookworms, 181
Hoover, Herbert, 263
hospitals, 182, 574
Hou Yuon, 400
Hsinbyushin, 202
Hsipaw region, 219
Hué, 132, 169, 545–6
Hukbalahap, 339, 349, 375, 421–2, 426, 428, 523–4, 556, 592, 599–601
hulubalang/uleebalang, 228–9
human rights, 640
Hun Sen, 632, 638
Hunter, Robert, 47
hunting, 189
Hurgronje, Snouck C., 58, 60, 103, 224
Hussein Onn, Tun, 627
Huynh Phu So, 243
hydroelectricity, *see* electricity
hydrogen bomb, 367

IAIN, 553
Iban, 24, 57, 62, 71, 112, 412
Ibnu Sutowo, 511
Ibrahim, Anwar, 574
Ibrahim, Sultan of Aceh, 60
Ibrahim, Sultan of Johor, 31–2
Ibrahim, Temenggong of Johor, 57
Ibrahim Yaacob, 334, 338, 613
ICP, 242–3, 280–2, 339, 400, 631
Idris, 64
Iglesia Filipina Independiente, *see* Philippine Independent (Aglipayan) Church
Iglesia Ni Kristo, 232, 234, 516
Ilagas, 425
Ilanun people, 57
Ileto, Reynaldo C., 261
illiteracy, 172–3, 240;
    see also literacy
Ilmu Sejati, 568
Ilocos areas, 150, 419
Iloilo, 159–60, 173, 178, 232
IMF, 481, 609, 625
Imphal, 332

tobacco, 133, 136–8, 150, 159, 174, 185–6, 189, 263, 419
Tojo, General Hideki, 330, 333–4
Tokyo, 333
Ton Duc Thanh, 392
Tonkin, *see* Vietnam
Toraja, 579
tortoiseshell, 138, 140
Toungoo, 217
tourism and travel, 191, 252, 483–4, 488, 500, 532, 559, 577, 579–80
Toyota, 483
toys, 483
trade and commerce:
    China market, 132, 136, 140, 174, 292;
    Chinese retail stores, 174;
    galleon trade, 136;
    global interdependence, 532;
    India market, 136;
    international, 137–40, 180, 185, 192, 232, 292, 481–5;
    Japan challenges Western trade, 192;
    local trade, 132, 140, 174, 300;
    peddling trade, 174;
    smuggling trade, 486, 490, 501, 614;
    state-sponsored, 132, 140;
    trade boycotts, 312, 330, 443;
    see also entrepreneurship
trade exchange networks:
    barter system, 132–3, 136, 468;
    Bugis traders, 140;
    Chinese merchants, 133, 174;
    credit, 144, 146, 157, 160, 174–5, 190;
    Indian merchants, 175;
    indigenous traders, 175;
    monetarized transactions, 133;
    trade chain and mechanism, 174–5;
    trade routes, 133;
    Western and foreign merchants, 132–3, 135, 138, 140, 252
trade unions, 85, 173, 252, 264–5, 273, 442, 452, 468, 516, 523
trade wares:
    consumer goods, 173–5, 468;
    foodstuffs, 132–3, 140, 300;
    forest and marine products, 132–3, 138, 140, 413;
    local, 138, 140;
    luxury goods, 132, 136, 138, 140, 174, 468;
    minerals, 413, 482;
    tropical products, 482;
    see also specific products
Traiphum, 200
Tran van Huong, 394
Tran van Thanh, 221–2
transnational corporations, 162, 477, 482–3, 488, 497–8, 507, 523;
    see also specific corporations
Treaty of Amity and Co-operation, 628
Treaty of Paris, 260
Treaty of Peace and Amity, 631
Trincomalee, 14
Triton Bay, 28

Trotskyism, 281
trucks, 484
Truman, Harry, 361, 367, 370, 598
Truong Chinh, 391–3, 397–8
Truong Dinh, 220
tuberculosis, 180, 182
Tu-duc, 44, 76, 222
Tugeri tribes, 28
Tung Meng Hui, 312
tungsten, 482
Tunisia, 346
Turkey, 11, 48, 60;
    see also Ottoman empire
Tydings–McDuffie Act, 264, 346
typhoid fever, 180
typhoons, 203

U Ba Kin, 573
U Bos, 417
U Chit Hlaing, *see* Chit Hlaing, U
U Kelatha, *see* Kelatha, U
U Nu, *see* Nu, U
U Ottama, *see* Ottama, U
U Parama, *see* Parama, U
U Po Lu, *see* Po Lu, U
Ubon, 122
UMNO, 303, 354, 377–2, 410–11, 413–15, 451, 458, 602, 629
UMNO Baru, 458
UNCTAD, 482
unemployment, 172, 188–91, 280, 336, 442
UNESCO, 471
Ungku Sayyid Paloh, 231
Ungphakorn, Puey, 499
Unilever, 483
Union Buddha Sasana Council, 545
Union of Democratic Control, 595
Union of Myanmar, *see* Burma
Union of Peninsular Indonesians, *see* KRIS
Union Party (Burma), 417, 543
United Buddhist Association, 575
United Malays National Organization, *see* UMNO
United Nations:
    Brunei case, 634;
    Charter, 628;
    decolonization issue, 343–4, 595–6;
    East Timor issue, 629–30;
    forum, 382, 594–5, 630;
    founding of, 588;
    Indonesia's case, 358, 362, 364, 595–6, 610;
    Kampuchea problem, 633, 638–9;
    Malaysia issue, 613;
    membership, 343, 590–1, 593, 609, 613–14, 619, 635;
    Vietnam's case, 366
United Nations Conference on Trade and Development, *see* UNCTAD
United Nations Economic and Social Commission on Asia and the Pacific, *see* ESCAP